SEEKING OUR PAST

SEEKING OUR PAST

AN INTRODUCTION TO NORTH AMERICAN ARCHAEOLOGY

Sarah W. Neusius
Indiana University of Pennsylvania

G. Timothy Gross
Affinis Environmental Services

New York   Oxford
OXFORD UNIVERSITY PRESS
2007

Oxford University Press, Inc., publishes works that further Oxford University's
objective of excellence in research, scholarship, and education.

Oxford   New York
Auckland   Cape Town   Dar es Salaam   Hong Kong   Karachi
Kuala Lumpur   Madrid   Melbourne   Mexico City   Nairobi
New Delhi   Shanghai   Taipei   Toronto

With offices in
Argentina   Austria   Brazil   Chile   Czech Republic   France   Greece
Guatemala   Hungary   Italy   Japan   Poland   Portugal   Singapore
South Korea   Switzerland   Thailand   Turkey   Ukraine   Vietnam

Copyright © 2007 by Oxford University Press, Inc.

Published by Oxford University Press, Inc.
198 Madison Avenue, New York, New York 10016
http://www.oup.com

Oxford is a registered trademark of Oxford University Press

Library of Congress Cataloging-in-Publication Data

Neusius, Sarah Ware, 1951
    Seeking our past: an introduction to North American Archaeology/Sarah W. Neusius,
  G. Timothy Gross
        p.   cm.
    Includes bibliographical references and index.
    ISBN 13 978-0-19-517385-7 – ISBN 13 978-0-19-517384-0 (pbk.)
    ISBN 0-19-517385-6 – ISBN 0-19-517384-8 (pbk.)
        1. Indians of North America–Antiquities.   2.   North America–Antiquities.
  3. Archaeology–North America.   4. Archaeology–North Amercia–Case studies.   5. Indians
of North America–History.   6. North America–History, Local.   I. Gross, G. Timothy.   II. Title.

E77.9N47 2007
970.01–dc22

                                                                                    2006043796

Printing number: 9 8 7 6 5 4 3 2 1

Printed in the United States of America
on acid-free paper

CONTENTS

STUDENT CD CONTENTS xv
PREFACE xvii
CONTRIBUTORS xxv
CREDITS xxvii

PART 1: INTRODUCING NORTH AMERICAN ARCHAEOLOGY 1

Chapter 1: The Nature and Practice of North American Archaeology 3

The Scope of This Book 4
What Is North American Archaeology? 5

ISSUES AND DEBATES:
BOX 1.1 Who Were the Mound Builders? 8

The North American Archaeologist 13

FACES IN ARCHAEOLOGY:
PROFILE 1.1 W. James Judge, Professor and Director of the Chaco Project 14

FACES IN ARCHAEOLOGY:
PROFILE 1.2 Lynne Sebastian, Archaeologist and Historic Preservationist 18

ISSUES AND DEBATES:
BOX 1.2 Politics and Scholarship in the Investigation of New York City's African Burial Ground 22

An Overview of the Archaeological Process 25

Chapter Summary 30
Suggestions for Further Reading 31
Other Resources 32

Case Study   32
The Pueblo Grande Project: An Example of Multidisciplinary
Research in a Compliance Setting
Cory Dale Breternitz and Christine K. Robinson   33

Chapter 2: Culture and Environment in North
America's Past   43

North American Culture Areas   44

ISSUES AND DEBATES:
BOX 2.1   What Are You Called? Names and Politics   45

North American Environments   49

ISSUES AND DEBATES:
BOX 2.2   Is Environmental Reconstruction an Ancillary Study?   57

The Climate of North America   61
The Systematics of North American Culture History   67

FACES IN ARCHAEOLOGY:
PROFILE 2.1   Julie Stein, Archaeologist and Geoarchaeologist   68

FACES IN ARCHAEOLOGY:
PROFILE 2.2   Robert Kelly, Archaeologist and Professor   72

Themes in the Study of North America's Past   77
A Final Word About Dates and Dating   81

Chapter Summary   83
Suggestions for Further Reading   85
Other Resources   85

Case Study   86
It Takes a Team: Interdisciplinary Research at the Koster Site
Michael D. Wiant and Sarah W. Neusius   86

PART 2: THE NORTH AMERICAN PAST   95

Chapter 3: Peopling of the Americas   97

When Were the Americas Settled?   100
The Clovis-First Scenario   103

CLUES TO THE PAST:
EXHIBIT 3.1   Fluted Points: The Original American Invention?   104

Does the Clovis-First Scenario Account for All
the Evidence?   108
Key Puzzles in the Data on Early Settlement   112

ISSUES AND DEBATES:
BOX 3.1   Why Is the Kennewick Case So Significant?   123

Paleoindian Adaptations   127

Chapter Summary   133
Suggestions for Further Reading   134
Other Resources   134

Case Study
Sea Change: The Paleocoastal Occupations of Daisy Cave
Jon M. Erlandson   135

Chapter 4: Foragers of the North   144

Definition of the Area   145
The Environment   146
Early Cultures   149

CLUES TO THE PAST:
EXHIBIT 4.1   Microblades   151

Archaic   152
Arctic Small Tool Tradition   158
Later Cultures of the Arctic: Dorset, Norton, and Thule   163
Later Cultures of the Subarctic   173
Historic Period   174

ISSUES AND DEBATES:
BOX 4.1   How Far Did the Vikings Get?   175

Chapter Summary   179
Suggestions for Further Reading   180
Other Resources   181

Case Study
From Sites to Social Evolution: The Study of Emergent
Complexity in the Kodiak Archipelago, Alaska
Ben Fitzhugh   181

Chapter 5: Paths to Complexity on the Northwest Coast   192

Definition of the Area   194
The Environment   195

ISSUES AND DEBATES:
BOX 5.1   How Many Old Scarred Trees Do We Need?   198

Early Cultures   199
Archaic   200
Pacific Period   204

CLUES TO THE PAST:
EXHIBIT 5.1   Basketry and Cordage   212

Modern Period   219

Chapter Summary   221
Suggestions for Further Reading   222
Other Resources   223

Case Study   223
Archaeological/Anthropological–Native American
Coordination: An Example of Sharing the Research on the
Northwest Coast of North America
Rhonda Foster, Larry Ross, and Dale R. Croes   224

Chapter 6: Rivers, Roots, and Rabbits: The Plateau   233

Definition of the Area   234
The Environment   237
Early Cultures   239

ISSUES AND DEBATES:
BOX 6.1   Volcanoes and Human Settlement   240

Middle Period   245

CLUES TO THE PAST:
EXHIBIT 6.1   Pithouses   247

Late Period   249
Modern Period   253

Chapter Summary   **256**
Suggestions for Further Reading   257
Other Resources   258

Case Study   259
The Miller Site: Four Seasons of Backwards Archaeology
on Strawberry Island
G. Timothy Gross   260

Chapter 7: Diversity and Complexity in California   268

Definition of the Area   270
The Environment   270
Early Cultures   274
Foragers: The Archaic Pattern   277
Complexity: The Pacific Period   280

ISSUES AND DEBATES:
BOX 7.1   Chumash Complexity   282

Pacific Period Lifeways   288

CLUES TO THE PAST:
EXHIBIT 7.1   Bedrock Milling Features   288

Historic Period   292

Chapter Summary   299
Suggestions for Further Reading   300
Other Resources   301

Case Study   301
Cultures in Contact at Colony Ross
Kent G. Lightfoot, Sara Gonzalez, Darren Modzelewski, Lee Panich, Otis Parrish,
and Tsim Schneider   302

Chapter 8: Mobility, Flexibility, and Persistence in
the Great Basin   310

Definition of the Area   311
The Environment   312
Early Cultures: The Pre-Archaic   317
Archaic   318

ISSUES AND DEBATES:
BOX 8.1   Projectile Points and Time   326

CLUES TO THE PAST:
EXHIBIT 8.1   Rabbit Nets   329

The Fremont   330
Numic Peoples and Their Spread   335
Protohistoric and Historic Periods   337

Chapter Summary   340
Suggestions for Further Reading   342
Other Resources   342

Case Study   343
Deep-Site Excavation at Gatecliff Shelter, Nevada
David Hurst Thomas   343

Chapter 9: Foragers and Villagers of the Southwestern
Mountains, Mesas, and Deserts   355

Definition of the Area   356
The Environments of the Southwest   359
Hunters and Foragers   362
Farmers and Villagers   369

ISSUES AND DEBATES:
BOX 9.1 Interpreting the Chaco Phenomenon   376

CLUES TO THE PAST:
EXHIBIT 9.1   Fantasies on Clay: Mimbres Pottery   382

Reorganization, Aggregation, and Conflict in Late Prehistory   389
New Arrivals   391
Historic Period   393

Chapter Summary   395
Suggestions for Further Reading   396
Other Resources   397

Case Study   397
Casas Grandes at the Edge of the Southwestern and
Mesoamerican Worlds
Paul E. Minnis and Michael E. Whalen   398

Chapter 10: Bison Hunters and Horticulturists of the Great Plains   406

Definition of the Area   408
The Environment   408
Early Hunters of the Plains   412
Plains Archaic   416

CLUES TO THE PAST:
EXHIBIT 10.1   Hide Scrapers   421

The Woodland Period on the Great Plains   423
Plains Village Traditions   427
Late Prehistoric Bison Hunters of the Northern Plains   433

ISSUES AND DEBATES:
BOX 10.1   Historic Ethnicities and the Archaeological Record   434

Protohistoric and Historic Developments   436

Chapter Summary   440
Suggestions for Further Reading   441
Other Resources   442

Case Study   442
Investigations at Double Ditch Village, a Traditional Mandan
Earthlodge Settlement
Stanley A. Ahler and Phil R. Geib   442

Chapter 11: Tribes and Chiefdoms in the Southeast   452

Definition of the Area   453
The Environments of the Southeast   455
Hunter-Gatherers of the Distant Past   458

ISSUES AND DEBATES:
BOX 11.1   Ridges, Aisles, and the Map of Poverty Point   469

Woodland Peoples Across the Southeast 473
Mississippian and Other Societies of the Last
Thousand Years 482

CLUES TO THE PAST:
EXHIBIT 11.1 Design Motifs and Artifacts of the Southeastern Ceremonial
Complex 485

Protohistoric and Historic Times 491

Chapter Summary 495
Suggestions for Further Reading 497
Other Resources 497

Case Study 497
Mouse Creek Phase Households and Communities:
Mississippian Period Towns in Southeastern Tennessee
Lynne P. Sullivan 498

**Chapter 12: Foragers and Farmers of the Midwest
and Upper Great Lakes** 508

Definition of the Area 510
The Environments of the Midwest and Upper Great Lakes 510
Hunters and Foragers of the Distant Past 514
Woodland Farmers and Mound Builders 523

CLUES TO THE PAST:
EXHIBIT 12.1 Stone Platform Pipes 528

The Mississippians and Other Late Prehistoric Peoples 535

ISSUES AND DEBATES:
BOX 12.1 How Big and Powerful Was Cahokia After All? 536

The Protohistoric and Historic Periods 544

Chapter Summary 548
Suggestions for Further Reading 549
Other Resources 550

Case Study 550
The Hopeton Earthworks Project: Using New Technologies
to Answer Old Questions
Mark Lynott 550

**Chapter 13: Fishing, Foraging, and Farming in the
Northeast and Mid-Atlantic** 560

Definition of the Area 562
The Environments of the Northeast and the Mid-Atlantic 562
Hunters and Foragers of the Distant Past 567

Farming, Fishing, and Sedentism in the Early and
Middle Woodland   578
Late Woodland and Late Prehistoric Peoples   582

ISSUES AND DEBATES:
BOX 13.1   Iroquoian Origins   586

The Protohistoric and Historic Periods   589

CLUES TO THE PAST:
EXHIBIT 13.1   Iron Furnaces   595

Chapter Summary   597
Suggestions for Further Reading   599
Other Resources   599

Case Study   599
A New History of Maize-Bean-Squash Agriculture
in the Northeast
John P. Hart   600

PART 3: THE FUTURE OF NORTH AMERICAN ARCHAEOLOGY   609

Chapter 14: North American Archaeology for
the Twenty-first Century   611

A Perspective on North America's Past   612
Reconsidering the North American Archaeological Story   614

ISSUES AND DEBATES:
BOX 14.1   How Can We Stop Looting of Archaeological Sites?   615

The Changing Discipline   621

ISSUES AND DEBATES:
BOX 14.2   Displaying the Past at Dickson Mounds   626

Concluding Thoughts   628

ISSUES AND DEBATES:
BOX 14.3   Can Academia Train Archaeologists for the Twenty-first Century?   631

Chapter Summary   633
Suggestions for Further Reading   633
Other Resources   634

GLOSSARY   635
INDEX   680

STUDENT CD CONTENTS

Section A: A Brief History of North American Archaeology

Section B: Archaeological Fieldwork

Section C: Archaeological Laboratory Analysis

Section D: Bonus Case Studies

    D.1. Interpreting the Ripley Site: A Century of Investigations
Sarah W. Neusius

    D.2. Weaponry of Clovis Hunters at Blackwater Draw
Anthony T. Boldurian

    D.3. Eel Point and the Early Settlement of Coastal California: A Case Study in Contemporary Archaeological Research
L. Mark Raab and Andrew Yatsko

    D.4. The Dolores Archaeological Program: Documenting the Pithouse-to-Pueblo Transition
Sarah W. Neusius

    D.5. The Dust Cave Archaeological Project: Investigating Paleoindian and Archaic Lifeways in Southeastern North America
Renee B. Walker, Boyce N. Driskell, and Sarah C. Sherwood

    D.6. Ethnicity and Class in Colonial Foodways
Elizabeth M. Scott

Section E: Bonus Faces in Archaeology

    E.1. Arthur Parker, Archaeologist and Museologist

    E.2. Linda Mayro, Pima County Cultural Resources Manager

Section F: Bonus Issues and Debates

    F.1. What Do Professors and CRM Archaeologists Think of Each Other?

    F.2. The Curation Crisis

    F.3. A Local Reaction to NAGPRA: The Kumeyaay Cultural and Repatriation Committee

    F.4. Was There Cannibalism in the Prehistoric Southwest?

Section G: References

Section H: Exploring Further

    H.1. Recommended Websites

    H.2. Sites, Parks, and Museums to Visit

Section I: Student Study Guide

Section J: Glossary

PREFACE

This text developed out of classroom and archaeological field school experiences of one of us (S.W.N). Both my experiences in trying to teach these subjects and my students' experiences in trying to learn about the past of North America have been important because too often these experiences have been frustrating.

My sense has been that beginning students often assume that the past of North America, especially before the arrival of Europeans, was rather dull, peopled by simple hunter-gatherers who lived in harmony with nature but created very little of aesthetic, historical, economic, or other interest. What could this simple story have to do with the exciting field of archaeology that explores pyramids, palaces, and ancient mysteries? When teaching about North America's varied past or about the discipline that seeks to reveal it, I always have to combat the erroneous idea that there isn't much interesting to learn.

Whether instructor or student, you can see why I want an engaging and carefully written textbook and related resources—I need help in combating misconceptions. Unfortunately, there is little choice of texts and supplementary materials suitable for undergraduates. The resources available were pitched either too low or too high for college undergraduates or tended to be encyclopedic and bland. They also didn't incorporate materials about the realities of actual archaeological practice, which are important and interesting. I wanted to include a little about the development of cultural resource management (CRM), about current interactions with descendant populations, about the contributions of historical archaeology, about archaeological ethics, and about how new techniques were changing archaeology. Moreover, the texts available seldom included the pedagogical features such as chapter summaries, discussion questions, and web resources that today's instructors and undergraduates find useful.

Be careful what you complain about; someone will eventually persuade you to try to fix it. This is exactly what happened. After too many years of complaint, Jan Beatty, our editor, helped me decide to undertake writing this text by suggesting a workable structure. Fortunately, it was remarkably easy to persuade Tim Gross to get involved, relieving many concerns I had about my shallow knowledge of the archaeology in the westernmost parts of North America. Although a part-time university teacher, Tim also brings to this project a great deal of firsthand experience in cultural resource management, something I felt we needed to incorporate.

We believe that North America's past is fascinating and fun to learn about, and we think that it is scandalous that archaeological stories of this continent's past are not more widely known, especially by the people who live here. We also believe that these stories must be told in conjunction with information about the dynamic field of North American archaeology, in itself interesting and surprising to the uninitiated. It's important to understand the context of the stories told about the past, as there are multiple possible stories. We think that combining these topics is the most engaging and useful approach for both the casual student of North America's past and the future professional archaeologist. Above all, we are convinced that North American archaeology can be presented in an accessible and interesting way. With these beliefs in mind, our goal has been to create a resource for contemporary students and instructors, a truly twenty-first century North American archaeology text.

FEATURES AND ORGANIZATION

A number of organizational decisions and specific features set this text apart from existing texts and from the collections of articles sometimes adopted by instructors. The structure you see results from considerable thought about what makes a text useful to today's instructors and readable for today's students.

Basic Organization

As the table of contents indicates, this text is divided into three unequal parts. In Part 1 we introduce the discipline of North American archaeology in two chapters. The first chapter covers the scope of the field and what archaeologists actually do. Chapter 2 introduces North American environments and relevant anthropological themes as well as archaeological systematics. The case studies associated with these chapters introduce, respectively, a large CRM mitigation project and an interdisciplinary academic research project.

Part 2, which is the bulk of this text, covers the body of knowledge archaeologists have generated about the culture history and lifeways of the North American past. If you already are familiar with the contemporary practice of North American archaeology, you might begin with Part 2, since these topics are the meat of most courses in North American archaeology. This part of the text discusses the peopling of the continent (Chapter 3) and ten areas within it (Chapters 4–13). We combine the Arctic and the Subarctic culture areas, while we divide the Northeast culture area into two subareas: the Midwest and Upper Great Lakes and the Northeast and Mid-Atlantic, respectively. Each chapter ends with a case study about work done in that area. Topics covered by these case studies introduce the wide variety of research North American archaeologists do.

Part 3 is only one chapter long. Chapter 14 reconsiders what has been covered discussing the themes originally highlighted in Chapter 2. It also suggests what research topics promise to be important in the future and takes note of how the discipline and its techniques are changing. There is no case study in this chapter.

The Student CD includes bonus materials that instructors and students may find useful. Some of these materials, especially Sections D, E, and F, might be substituted for materials in the printed text. Each bonus feature further illustrates the archaeology discussed in one or more chapters. We also have included sections on the history of North American archaeology and on field and laboratory methods because some instructors may wish to emphasize the discipline's history or perhaps to assign sections on methods to students with less prior background than others. Students may want to read some of these on their own depending on their personal interests. For additional ideas about where these bonus sections might be incorporated, look for the CD symbol in the margin of the text.

We have provided an extensive glossary that includes both special archaeological terminology and culture history terms, such as names of phases and traditions used in the text. The complete list of references cited in the text is also on the CD. Our experience has been that students seldom need or consult these lists unless they have a research paper to write. Thus the Suggestions for Further Reading, near the end of each chapter, provide an introduction to the professional literature by listing some of the best places to start learning more about North American archaeology. However, instructors and serious students also will find a more thorough introduction to the literature on North American archaeology in the References section on the CD.

The CD also includes other resources that students may find useful. In Section H, "Exploring Further," we list links to websites concerning North American sites and archaeology and provide a partial list of places you might want to visit as you continue to learn about North American archaeology. You may be surprised by how much archaeology there is in your area. Additionally, Section I, "Student Study Guide," lists chapter learning objectives, suggests study questions, and provides self-quizzes. Although individual instructors may structure their courses in different ways, these study materials are good resources for students suddenly facing the large body of information contained in this text. Finally, for the convenience of the student, we have included a copy of the Glossary on the CD.

Balancing Explication, Summary, and Detail

Too much happened over the millions of square miles of this continent since humans first arrived here more than 12,000 years ago, and too much archaeology has been conducted, for us to write engagingly about all of it. Picking and choosing comes with the territory; but on the other hand, we want to make sure that we tell the story completely enough to be interesting. We think that neither dry detail nor summary pronouncements are very interesting in themselves. What is interesting is why archaeologists think what they think. We invite you to explore the past, working as archaeologists do from what may be the minutest pieces of evidence toward tentative conclusions. In effect we want to share with you the grand puzzle we are working out. We have found that our students like pondering the same things that puzzle us, and they often make us think further as well. We have tried to keep this philosophy in mind while writing this text, neither avoiding the evidence itself nor forgetting to stop and explain why it may mean what archaeologists claim it does.

A Culture Area Approach

In writing about North America's past, the two main options are the culture area approach and the thematic approach. We have chosen the former, not only because it is traditional and common but because we think it is the best way to provide novices with a context for further study. As flawed as the concept of culture areas is, especially when projected into the archaeological past, it still is how the discipline of North American archaeology organizes itself. Although professionals may seek comparative material when addressing broad themes like the origins of food production or the power of elites, individual archaeologists become specialists in one or more of these culture areas. Job announcements seek specializations by culture areas, and archaeologists self-identify in this manner. Finally, we also think that organization by culture area facilitates instructors elaborating on the archaeology of certain regions in which they have direct experience, something our students usually enjoy. We encourage instructors to plan their courses around their own experiences when possible, even if it means forgoing other portions of the text.

The culture area approach can create problems as well. These develop when the broad themes and linkages across culture areas are not noted, and when the boundaries of these areas are understood as rigid rather than permeable and shifting over time. In Chapter 2 we identify key themes, and we encourage readers to look for them throughout this text. There is much detail in this book, though our colleagues will miss details that we've chosen not to include. Try to use the details provided to think about broad themes and trends. Artifact names and types per se are not the point, nor are phase sequences, so try not to get hung up on these technicalities.

Case Studies

Possibly the most important feature of this text is the juxtaposition between culture area summaries and case studies written by researchers, with an undergraduate audience in mind. Case studies provide detail about a specific project or archaeological problem that should encourage discussion about archaeological conclusions. Each case study is tied to the culture area just summarized, though for each chapter there were multiple case study candidates. We believe that it is more important to sample what projects are really like than to include everything. However, we have provided additional case studies on the Student CD, noting the various places these might be used in the text. The case studies of Section D can be substituted or added depending on individual course constraints, instructor preference, and student interest. We assume instructors will also incorporate case studies from their own research as they are able. We hope instructors and students will spend time discussing as many of the case studies as possible so that such discussion becomes a routine part of classes that use this text. Treating the case studies as optional would alter this text's pedagogical vision.

Treatment of Both History and Prehistory

Although both of us have been involved in historical archaeology projects, we do not identify ourselves primarily as historical archaeologists. Nevertheless, we strongly believe that it is not intellectually valid to stop discussions of North American archaeology at European contact. Bridging the traditional gulf between Prehistoric and Historic archaeologists is essential. First of all, there is a historical story to be told about the Native past, and archaeology is one primary way to tell it. Second, there is simply no escaping the fact that separating the stories of the pre-Columbian past from those of the Historic past encourages the false belief that the Native people of North America are gone or have been assimilated into Euro-American culture. One of the things we want all our students to know is that Native Americans are very much still with us. Today Native people often have sincere interest in their cultural heritage, especially as it may help them maintain their unique identity in the modern world. As we discuss shortly, this has important ethical implications for contemporary archaeologists.

A third reason for not omitting historical archaeology is that in contemporary CRM, resources from all time periods must be documented, protected, and managed. Today's serious students are likely to do CRM at some point in their careers, and they should know something about both history and prehistory. We believe that CRM studies, undertaken to comply with relatively recent legislation have greatly added to understanding of the Historic past. For practical and scholarly reasons, we want our students to recognize the value in both Historic and pre-Columbian cultural resources.

Nevertheless, there aren't many models for a seamless treatment of the full past of North America, and there are real substantive differences between the methods of pre-Columbian and Historic archaeology. One of the most difficult aspects of writing this text has been including discussion of both the pre-Columbian and the Historic past in a balanced way. We hope that our readers will help us with constructive feedback.

Treatment of the Ethics and Nature of Contemporary Archaeological Practice

There is considerable discussion within North American archaeology about whether academia is properly training students to do archaeology in the twenty-first century. One of the most important points being made is that students of North American archaeology must be trained in the ethics of the discipline. We concur, and we incorporated ethical concerns and topics in our presentation of past culture history and lifeways. Moreover, we do not believe that the perspectives of archaeological science are the only valid perspectives. We are pleased to be able to include case studies about projects in which Native people have been involved. A number of our sidebars, including those on the Student CD, deal explicitly with issues of importance to archaeology's diverse constituencies, and we hope that our respect for Native viewpoints is evident. Topics related to archaeological stewardship collecting, looting, and curation, also are included often.

A second issue raised in the debates about teaching archaeology has been the apparent discrepancy between what is taught in classrooms and what most contemporary and future archaeologists actually do. Most university courses do not deal substantively with CRM, even though this is the context for the majority of North American archaeology done today. While we believe that this discrepancy between practice taught and work available may not be as great as has sometimes been suggested, the unfounded idea that CRM is second-class archaeology unquestionably persists. The truth is that there has been plenty of subpar archaeology in both academic and CRM contexts, while excellent, innovative research in both contexts has furthered the discipline, as well. In addition to directly addressing this issue in a text sidebar (Box 14.3), we include profiles of CRM and academic archaeologists, and CRM and academic archaeological case studies. We hope this encourages those who use this book to recognize the possibilities for exciting careers and the highest quality archaeology in all sectors of the archaeological world.

Sidebars

A quick look at the table of contents will show you there are three kinds of sidebars included in this text:

- The *Faces in Archaeology* sections profile particular archaeologists and are included in Part 1 as we introduce the nature of North American archaeology. We hope they help students understand the possibilities for careers in archaeology, though there are too few to be inclusive. Section E of the Student CD contains two more.

- The *Clues to the Past* sections discuss specific artifacts, features, or structures that are part of the material record that archaeology discovers and interprets. They are included in Part 2, which covers archaeological knowledge of North America's past. They are designed to clarify and illustrate aspects of how archaeologists work from the material record to interpret the past.

- *Issues and Debates* sections are found in all chapters of the text and in Section F of the Student CD. These sections treat both scholarly debates about the past and ethical and other issues related to doing archaeology today. We hope the controversies covered will be used in classroom discussions, raising student interest and helping to illustrate the true nature of North American archaeology.

These sidebars are intended to enrich our summaries of the North American past or of the nature of North American archaeology by adding relevant and interesting details. We believe they help make texts more readable and concepts more accessible to undergraduates. The topics of particular sidebars have been selected for a variety of reasons, but always because we believe they integrate well with the text. They are definitely not unrelated additions. We encourage instructors to assign them specifically and to incorporate them in class activities. Students should always read and think about them.

Pedagogical Aids

Because this text is designed to serve as a resource for teachers and students in courses that cover North American archaeology, we have incorporated a variety of pedagogical features besides those already mentioned. These include the following:

- an extensive glossary, which makes archaeological jargon and culture history designations more comprehensible,
- chapter openings that help students engage with the chapter materials while illustrating more about North American archaeology,
- chapter summaries that provide bulleted listings of key points from the chapters,
- lists of suggested further readings for each chapter,
- discussion questions at the end of each case study, to facilitate classroom discussion or possibly written assignments,

- Links to related websites and suggestions of archaeological sites, historic properties, and museums that can be visited (Section H of the Student CD),
- Chapter learning objectives, study questions, and self-quizzes for each chapter (Section I of the Student CD),
- an Instructor's Guide (available to instructors from OUP) that provides sample syllabi, chapter outlines, suggested class activities, test questions, a list of possible readings to be assigned along with this text, and PowerPoint images.

ACKNOWLEDGMENTS

The first people we thank are the case study contributors to this volume, an expert and impressive group. We were a little surprised as well as pleased at how enthusiastically these colleagues undertook to write about their work for undergraduates. We are most gratified, and not at all surprised, by the high quality of the case studies produced. We also were grateful for answers to specific questions concerning regional archaeology from several colleagues, although we are the only ones who should be held responsible for the non–case study sections. Without these people this text wouldn't be the resource it is.

We also thank the colleagues who agreed to be profiled for the *Faces in Archaeology* sections: James Judge, Robert Kelly, Linda Mayro, Lynne Sebastian, and Julie Stein. Each gracefully accepted our intrusion and commented helpfully on what we wrote. There also were several individuals who agreed to share their careers with us in the early stages of planning for this text, and we are grateful for their enthusiasm, though the final plans for this text excluded most of the *Faces* in the original outline.

This text certainly would not be a reality without the continual prodding of Jan Beatty. It was Beatty's suggestion of the case study format that as much as anything else finally spurred Neusius to stop talking and begin writing, and it has been a real pleasure to be able to benefit from her advice and editorial expertise throughout the project. The staff of talented people at Oxford, especially Christine D'Antonio, Marta Peimer, Jackie Ardam, Jason Przybylski, and Talia Krohn, has been invaluable to us, and the careful copyediting of Brenda Griffing much appreciated. Neusius would also be remiss if she did not thank Bob Gazdacko, who long ago, encouraged her to think she was up to this task.

A number of anonymous reviewers of our manuscript in various stages also have helped us improve the text. We have tried to listen carefully to all aspectsof what they had to say, and even though we have sometimes disagreed or not understood, we have been deeply grateful for their considerable effort in working through what we provided. More than a dozen colleagues shared information and advice: including Ken Ames, Eric Blinman, Bryan Byrd, Miriam Chaiken, Bev Chiarulli, Tom Conelly, Lynn Gamble, Bretton Giles, John Hildebrand, Terry Jones, Scott Moore, Phil Neusius, Ray Pettus, Mary Robbins-Wade, Glenn Russell, Joan Schneider, Rae Schwaderer, Lynne Sullivan, Claude Warren, and Michael Wiant. For help with illustrations we are grateful to helpful staff at the presses and institutions included in the illustration credits as well as to our case study authors. Others who gave illustration assistance included Stan Ahler, Ken Ames, Joyce Antorietto, James Bradley, Cory Breternitz, David Brose, David Carlson, Ray Carlson, Kurt Carr, Jim Cassidy, Joseph Chartkoff, Bev Chiarulli,

Deborah Confer, Linda Cordell, Alana K. Cordy-Collins, Dale Croes, Richard Daugherty, Penny Drooker, Don Dumond, Mary Etzkorn, Ken Farnsworth, Ellen Feeney, Linda Fisk, Bill Fitzhugh, Knut Fladmark, Mike Gramley, Bill Green, Brian Hayden, Ken Hedges, Adriel Heisey, Bill Iseminger, Dick Jefferies, Russ Kaldenberg, Bob Kelly, Kevin Kelly, Tristram Kidder, Erin King, Ruth Kirk, Greg Lattanzi, Steve Lekson, Linda Mayro, Robert McGhee, David Meltzer, John Montgomery, Martha Otto, Max Pavesic, Mike Rousseau, Mike Russo, Ken Sassaman, Louise Schmidlap, Lynne Sebastian, Sissel Schroedor, Cindy Stankowski, Julie Stein, Vin Steponaitis, Hilary Stewart, Bonnie Styles, Jason Titcomb, Sandy Tradlener, Frederick West, Rob Whitlam, Henry Wright, and Virgil Young. If we have missed anyone, please accept our apologizes; we have appreciated everyone's help.

We are grateful as well to our students who have helped us learn so much about teaching North American archaeology, and we especially appreciate the students in our spring 2004 (S.W.N.) and spring 2005 (G.T.G.) North American archaeology classes, who sometimes were guinea pigs for materials eventually incorporated in this text.

At Indiana University of Pennsylvania, several archaeology majors, student workers and archaeological technicians have assisted Neusius in producing her part of this text. These include Joe Bowman, Bill Caramana, Carin Gordon, Stefani Snowberger, Brandi Stewart, Anna Watson, and Brian Willis, as well as Ginny Neusius, who was a much needed assistant at many stages of this project. Linda Dreischalick, Department of Anthropology secretary, has done countless small things to help keep me sane during the juggling act this project required.

Gross thanks his colleagues at Affinis, especially CEO Mike Busdosh; his colleagues at San Diego State University and the University of San Diego, especially William Welsh; and the board of trustees, members, and staff of the San Diego Archaeological Center for encouragement and assistance throughout this process. Of course, his family's support and encouragement were immeasurably important.

Neusius also thanks her family for indulging her decision to undertake this project and accepting what it has meant for our lives. Ben, Ginny, and Phil Neusius all provided concrete pieces of help and steadfast encouragement and company as I tried to complete this task. Nothing I ever want to do, including this text, would seem as possible without Phil's counsel, support, and friendship.

"CONTACT US"

As we have indicated, our goal was to provide an engaging and useful introductory resource about North America's past as well as to North American archaeology. We are mostly happy with the product you are seeing. However, we are just vain enough to hope that future editions will be warranted and just humble enough to know that we haven't got it completely right yet. Ultimately you who use this book to teach and learn about North American archaeology will be the judges of our success. We look forward to your feedback, so please let us know what works and what needs to be changed or added.

Sarah W. Neusius, Indiana, Pennsylvania, sawn@iup.edu
Tim Gross, El Cajon, California, tigr@affinis.net

CONTRIBUTORS

STANLEY A. AHLER, Research Director, PaleoCultural Research Group

ANTHONY T. BOLDURIAN, Professor, Department of Anthropology, University of Pittsburgh at Greensburg

CORY DALE BRETERNITZ, President, Soil Systems, Inc.

DALE R. CROES, Professor, Department of Anthropology, South Puget Sound Community College and Adjunct Faculty, Department of Anthropology, Washington State University

BOYCE N. DRISKELL, Director, Archaeological Research Laboratory, University of Tennessee

JON M. ERLANDSON, Professor, Department of Anthropology, University of Oregon

BEN FITZHUGH, Associate Professor, Department of Anthropology, University of Washington

RHONDA FOSTER, Tribal Historic Preservation Officer, Cultural Resources Department, Squaxin Island Tribe

PHIL R. GEIB, Senior Supervisory Archaeologist, Navajo Nation Archaeology Department

SARA GONZALEZ, Department of Anthropology, University of California at Berkeley

G. TIMOTHY GROSS, Principal Archaeologist, Affinis Environmental Services, and Adjunct Professor, San Diego State University

JOHN P. HART, Director, Research and Collections Division, New York State Museum

KENT G. LIGHTFOOT, Professor, Department of Anthropology, University of California at Berkeley

MARK LYNOTT, Supervisory Archaeologist, Midwest Archaeological Center, National Park Service, U.S. Department of the Interior

PAUL E. MINNIS, Professor, Department of Anthropology, University of Oklahoma

DARREN MODZELEWSKI, Department of Anthropology, University of California at Berkeley

SARAH W. NEUSIUS, Professor, Department of Anthropology, Indiana University of Pennsylvania

LEE PANICH, Cultural Attaché, Phoebe Hearst Museum of Anthropology, University of California at Berkeley

OTIS PARRISH, Department of Anthropology, University of California at Berkeley

L. MARK RAAB, Adjunct Professor of History and Geosciences, University of Missouri-Kansas City

CHRISTINE K. ROBINSON, Vice President, Soil Systems, Inc.

LARRY ROSS, Cultural Resource Specialist, Cultural Resources Department, Squaxin Island Tribe

TSIM SCHNEIDER, Department of Anthropology, University of California at Berkeley

ELIZABETH M. SCOTT, Assistant Professor, Department of Sociology and Anthropology, Illinois State University

SARAH C. SHERWOOD, Research Assistant Professor, Archaeological Research Laboratory, University of Tennessee

LYNNE P. SULLIVAN, Curator of Archaeology, Frank H. McClung Museum, University of Tennessee

DAVID HURST THOMAS, Curator, American Museum of Natural History

RENEE B. WALKER, Assistant Professor, Department of Anthropology, State University of New York College at Oneonta

MICHAEL E. WHALEN, Professor, Department of Anthropology, University of Tulsa

MICHAEL D. WIANT, Director, Dickson Mounds Museum

ANDREW YATSKO, Cultural Resources Program Manager, Navy Region Southwest, San Diego

CREDITS

by Carol Steichen Dumond; 4.13 From McGhee 1978, Color Plate II, courtesy Robert McGhee; 4.14 From Dumond, 1987, line drawing by Carol Steichen Dumond after Knuth 1966/67; 4.15 From Maxwell, 1985, Figure 5.2, with permission from Elsevier; 4.16 From Dumond, 1987, Figures 57–61 photo by Don E. Dumond, objects in the collections of the Canadian Museum of Civilization; 4.17 From McGhee, 1978, Plate 10 courtesy Robert McGhee; 4.18a Floating or flying bear, ivory © Canadian Museum of Civilization, catalogue no. PgHb1:13692, photo Ross Taylor, image no. S90-2623; 4.18b Pair of swans, ivory © Canadian Museum of Civilization, catalogue no. JlGu-2:156, photo Ross Taylor, image no. S90-3058; 4.18c Miniature mask, antler © Canadian Museum of Civilization, catalogue no. PgHb-7:523, photo Ross Taylor, image no. S90-2633; 4.18d Shaman's teeth, ivory © Canadian Museum of Civilization, catalogue no. NhHd-1:1121, photo Ross Taylor, image no. S90-3192; 4.18e "Killed" human figure © Canadian Museum of Civilization, catalogue no. RaJu-1:109, photo by Ross Taylor, image no. S90-2944; 4.19 Douglas D. Anderson; 4.20 From Dumond 1987, photo by Don E. Dumond, items held by the University of Oregon Museum of Natural and Cultural History; 4.21 From Dumond, 1984a, Figure 8, by permission of the Oregon State Museum of Anthropology, and Colorado College; 4.22 From Dumond, Chapter 3 In Jennings, 1983, Figure 3.7; 4.23 adapted from Willey 1966 Figs 7.8 and 7.12; 4.24 From Arutinov and Fitzhugh, 1988, Figure 137 by permission of William Fithugh; 4.25 From Maxwell, 1985, Figure 8.3a © 1985, by permission of Eisevier; 4.26 From Dumond, 1987, Figure 90, by permission of the University of Alaska Museum of the North; 4.27 Ceramic pot © Canadian Museum of Civilization, catalogue no. EdKh.1, photo Jean-Luc Pilon, image no. S2000-5685; 4.28 Courtesy of Smithsonian National Museum of Natural History; 4.29 Courtesy of Smithsonian National Museum of Natural History; 4.30 "Bishop of Baffin," wooden carving © Canadian Museum of Civilization, catalogue no. KeDq-7:325, Image no. S94-6299; 4.32 Courtesy Ben Fitzhugh 4.34 Courtesy Ben Fitzhugh.

5.2 From Stewart 1977, courtesy Hilary Stewart; 5.3 Bob Whitlam, courtesy of the Washington State Department of Archaeology and Historic Preservation; 5.4 Photo by Ruth Kirk; 5.5 Frederick Hadleigh West; 5.6 courtesy Knut Fladmark; 5.7 Figure 18, p. 90, Ames and Maschner 1999; 5.8 Courtesy Kenneth M. Ames and Canadian Museum of Civilization;

5.9 Courtesy Kenneth M. Ames; 5.10 Photo by Ruth Kirk from Kirk and Daugherty 1978, p. 101 left side; 5.11 From MacDonald, George, 1983, *Prehistoric Art of the Northwest Coast*, Fig. 6.16, by permission of Archaeology Press, Simon Fraser University; 5.12 University of British Columbia Museum; 5.13 Courtesy of Dale R. Croes, illustration by Nancy Romaine, Royal British Columbia Museum; 5.14 From Hoff 1980, Figs 58, 59, 63 and 64; 5.15 Image OrHi 105047, Oregon Historical Society; 5.17 From Ayers 1980, Figure 49; 5.18 Photograph by Ruth Kirk, from Kirk and Daugherty 1978, p. 100; 5.19 From Suttles, 1990b, Fig. 1, by permission of the *Handbook of North American Indians*; 5.20 Figure 84, Ames and Maschner, 1999; 5.21 Photograph by Ruth Kirk from Kirk and Daugherty 1978, p. 104; 5.22 Photograph by Harvey S. Rice from Kirk and Daugherty 1978, p. 102; 5.23 Model of Kitwanga Fort © Canadian Museum of Civilization, CVH vol. 77, S24, Image no. D2006-05010; 5.24 Courtesy of the Qwu?gwes Cultural Studies Project; 5.25 Courtesy of the Qwu?gwes Cultural Studies Project; 5.26 Courtesy of the Qwu?gwes Cultural Studies Project; 5.27 Courtesy of the Qwu?gwes Cultural Studies Project.

6.2 Courtesy Mike Rousseau; 6.3 G. Timothy Gross; 6.4 Photo by R. M. Gramley, courtesy American Society for Amateur Archaeology; 6.5 Reproduced from Ames et al. 1998, figure 2, p. 105 (after Leonhardy and Rice, 1970) by permission of the *Handbook of North American Indians*; 6.6 After Butler, 1968, Fig. 13; 6.7 Courtesy Knut Fladmark and Canadian Museum of Civilization; 6.8 Courtesy of Max Pavesic; 6.9 Drawing by Roald Fryxell for Kirk and Daugherty; 6.10 From Osborne et al., 1961, Bureau of American Ethnology Bulletin 179; 6.11 Courtesy Knut Fladmark; 6.12 Courtesy Knut Fladmark; 6.13 Drawing by Chris Walsh Heady from Kirk and Daugherty 1978, p. 73; 6.14 Reproduced from Schalk 1983, Figure 6.6; 6.15 Reproduced from Osborne 1957, Fig. 2; 6.16 Reproduced by permission of the Society for American Archaeology from *American Antiquity* 62(1) 1997; 6.17 Photo by Brian Hayden; 6.18 From Osborne, 1957, Plates 29 and 30; 6.20 G. Timothy Gross; 6.22 From Schalk 1983, Figs 6.2 and 6.3.

7.2 G. Timothy Gross courtesy of the San Diego Museum of Man; 7.3 G. Timothy Gross; 7.4 G. Timothy Gross; 7.5 From Chartkoff and Chartkoff, 1984, Figure 30, courtesy Joseph Chartkoff; 7.6 From Chartkoff and Chartkoff, 1984, Figure 49, courtesy

Arizona Board of Regents, reprinted by permission of the University of Arizona Press; 9.22 Reprinted from *Archaeology of the Southwest* by Linda Cordell, p. 418, © 1997, with permission from Elsevier; 9.23 After Ortiz, 1979, p. *ix*, by permission of *Handbook of North American Indians*; 9.24 Adriel Heisey; 9.25 Courtesy Paul Minnis; 9.26 Adriel Heisey, 9.27 Courtesy Paul Minnis.

10.2 From *Archaeology of the Great Plains*, edited by the W. Raymond Wood, published by the University Press of Kansas © 1998, used by permission of the publisher, and reprinted from *Prehistoric Hunters of the High Plains* Second Edition by George C. Frison, p. 160, © 1991 with the permission from Elsevier; 10.3 Reprinted from *Prehistoric Hunters of the High Plains* by George C. Frison, p. 129, © 1991 with permission from Elsevier; 10.4 Reproduced from Dyck and Mooreland, 2001, Figs 2c, e, and g, p. 117 (after E. G. Walker 1992) by permission of *Handbook of North American Indians*; 10.5 Reprinted from *Prehistoric Hunters of the High Plains* Second Edition by George C. Frison, p. 133, © 1991 with the permission from Elsevier; 10.6 Reproduced by permission of the Society for American Archaeology from *American Antiquity* 56(2) 1991; 10.7 Reprinted from Reid 1983, p. 16 © 1983, with permission of Elsevier; 10.8 Courtesy Stan Ahler; 10.9 Denver Public Library, Western History Collection, photograph by Richard Throssel X31282; 10.10 Reprinted from the *Archaeology of Missouri, Volume II* by Carl. H. Chapman, by permission of the University of Missouri, © 1980 by the Curators of the University of Missouri; 10.11 Reprinted from *Prehistoric Hunters of the High Plains* Second Edition by George C. Frison, p. 106, © 1991 with the permission from Elsevier; 10.13 *Archaeology on the Great Plains* edited by W. Raymond Wood, published by the University of Kansas © 1998, used by the permission of the publisher; 10.14 Phillip D. Neusius; 10.15 Nebraska State Historical Society; 10.16 *Archaeology on the Great Plains* edited by W. Raymond Wood, published by the University of Kansas © 1998, used by the permission of the publisher; 10.17 Milwaukee Public Museum, Inc.; 10.18 Plate 2b, in Wood, 1971; 10.21 Photograph by Russ Hanson, courtesy of the U.S. National Park Service, used with the permission of the University of North Dakota; 10.22 Courtesy Stan Ahler.

11.2 Drawn by Simon S. S. Driver, from *Ancient North America: The Archaeology of a Continent*, by Brian Fagan, Thames and Hudson, London and New York;

11.3 Reproduced from Justice, Noel D. *Stone Age Spear and Arrow Points of the Midcontinental and Eastern United States* © 1987 Indiana University Press; 11.4 Reprinted from *The Prehistory of Missouri* by Michael J. O'Brien and W. Raymond Wood, by permission of the University of Missouri Press. © 1998 by the Curators of the University of Missouri; 11.5 Reproduced from Justice, Noel D. *Stone Age Spear and Arrow Points of the Midcontinental and Eastern United States* © 1987 Indiana University Press; 11.6 Courtesy Kenneth E. Sassaman; 11.7 Courtesy Kenneth E. Sassaman; 11.8 Courtesy Mike Russo; 11.9 Sarah W. Neusius; 11.10 Courtesy of Pictures of Record Inc.; 11.11 Reproduced by permission of the Society for American Archaeology from *American Antiquity* 67(1) 2002; 11.12 Reproduced by permission of the Society for American Archaeology from *American Antiquity* 67(1) 2002; 11.13 Reproduced by permission of the Society for American Archaeology from *American Antiquity* 67(1) 2002; 11.14 Reprinted from Bense, 1994, Figures 6.4, 6.5, 6.6, and 6.7 © 1994, with permission of Elsevier; 11.15 Reproduced from Justice, Noel D. *Stone Age Spear and Arrow Points of the Midcontinental and Eastern United States* © 1987 Indiana University Press; 11.16 After Gremillion 2002, p. 490, Permission granted by the University of Alabama Press; 11.17 Drawn based on Figure 5.15, Jennings, 1989; 11.18 Reproduced from Justice, Noel D. *Stone Age Spear and Arrow Points of the Midcontinental and Eastern United States* © 1987 Indiana University Press; 11.19 Reprinted from Bense, 1994, Figure 6.26, p. 179, with permission of Elsevier; 11.21 Courtesy of Pictures of Record Inc.; 11.22 Reprinted from the *Archaeology of the Central Mississippi Valley* by Dan F. and Phyllis A. Morse, p. © 1983, with permission of Elsevier; 11.23 After Waring and Holder 1945; 11.24 Woolaroc Museum, Bartlesville, Oklahoma; 11.25 After Lewis, Stout and Wesson 1998 Figure 1.2 by permission of he University of Alabama Press; 11.26 Courtesy National Museum of the American Indian (T18/9306). Photo by David Heald; 11.27 Sarah W. Neusius; 11.30 Reprinted by permission from *Southeastern Archaeology*, Volume 6(1); 11.31 Reprinted by permission from *Southeastern Archaeology*, Volume 6(1); 11.32 Courtesy Lynne P. Sullivan; 11.33 Courtesy Lynne P. Sullivan.

12.2 Reproduced from Justice, Noel D. *Stone Age Spear and Arrow Points of the Midcontinental and Eastern United States* © 1987 Indiana University Press and drawing by Henry T. Wright of specimens in

Credits xxxi

the collections of the Museum of Anthropology, University of Michigan; 12.3 Reproduced from Justice, Noel D. *Stone Age Spear and Arrow Points of the Midcontinental and Eastern United States* © 1987 Indiana University Press; 12.4 Courtesy Richard Jefferies; 12.5 Reprinted from Robertson et al. 1999, courtesy Michigan Department of Transportation, Michigan Department of History, Arts and Libraries and the Federal Highway Administration; 12.6 Plate 139, *The Carrier Mills Archaeological Project: Human Adaptation in the Saline Valley, Illinois,* edited by Richard W. Jefferies and Brian M. Butler, used with the permission of the Center for Archaeological Investigations, © 1992 by the Board of Trustees, Southern Illinois University; 12.7 Ceramic bowl from the Elizabeth site, Michael Brohm, photographer, by permission of the Illinois State Museum; 12.8 Reproduced from Justice, Noel D. *Stone Age Spear and Arrow Points of the Midcontinental and Eastern United States* © 1987 Indiana University Press; 12.9 Sarah W. Neusius; 12.10 Drawn based on Figure 5.6, Jennings, 1989; 12.11 Drawn based on Figure 5.12, Jennings, 1989; 12.12 Kenneth Farnsworth, Illinois Transportation Archaeological Research Program; 12.13 Kenneth Farnsworth, Illinois Transportation Archaeological Research Program; 12.14 Sarah W. Neusius; 12.15 Reprinted from *Late Woodland Societies: Tradition and Transformation Across the Midcontinent* edited by Thomas E. Emerson, Dale L. McElrath, and Andrew C. Fortier by permission of the University of Nebraska Press © 2000 by the Universiy of Nebraska Press; 12.16 Reproduced from Justice, Noel D. *Stone Age Spear and Arrow Points of the Midcontinental and Eastern United States* © 1987 Indiana University Press; 12.17 Wisconsin Historical Society, Image #5173; 12.18 Illustration by L. K. Townsend, by permission of the Cahokia Mounds State Historic Site; 12.19 Reprinted from *Cahokia: Domination and Ideology in the Mississippian World,* edited by Timothy R. Pauketat and Thomas E. Emerson by permission of the University of Nebraska Press, © 1997 by the University of Nebraska Press; 12.20 Sarah W. Neusius; 12.21 Courtesy National Museum of the American Indian, Smithsonian Institution (T23/0980) Photo by Carmelo Guadagno; 12.23 Sarah W. Neusius; 12.24 Reprinted from the *Archaeology of Missouri, Volume II* by Carl H. Chapman, by permission of the University of Missouri, © 1980 by the Curators of the University of Missouri; 12.25 Excavations at the Zimmerman site, Illinois State Museum 1947.56 by permission of the Illinois State Museum; 12.26 By permission of the Mariners' Museum, Newport News, VA; 12.27 Plate XVII in Squier and Davis, 1848; 12.28 Courtesy Mark Lynott; 12.29 Courtesy Mark Lynott; 12.30 Courtesy Mark Lynott.

13.3 Reprinted from *The Archaeology of New England* by Dean R. Snow, p. 123, © 1980 with permission of Elsevier; 13.4 From Petersen et al. in *Ice Age Peoples of Pennsylania,* edited by Kurt Carr and James Adovasio, p. 131, published by the Pennsylvania Historical and Museum Commission, 2002; 13.5 Reproduced from Figure 4.6, Cross, 1999 in *The Archaeological Northeast,* edited by Levine, Mary Ann, Kenneth E. Sassaman and Michael S. Nassaney, 1999 © 1999 Bergin and Garvey, Reproduced with permission of Greenwood and Garvey Publishing Group, Inc.; 13.6 Virginia W. Neusius; 13.7 Maritime Archaic artifacts from Cow Point © Canadian Museum of Civilization, photo by David Keenlyside, image no. D2006-11245; 13.8 Reprinted from Ritchie 1989, Bulletin 384, New York State Museum, printed by permission of the New York State Museum, Albany, NY; 13.9 Bureau of American Ethnology, Bulletin 60, Figure 104; 13.10 Reprinted from *The Archaeology of New England* by Dean R. Snow, p. 123, © 1980 with permission of Elsevier; 13.11 Reprinted from Ritchie 1989, Bulletin 384, New York State Museum, printed by permission of the New York State Museum, Albany, NY; 13.12 Reproduced by permission of the New Jersey State Museum; 13.13 Virginia W. Neusius; 13.14 Pottery vessel NYSM A-7491 © New York State Museum, Albany, NY; 13.15 After Trigger, 1978, p. ix, by permission of the *Handbook of North American Indians;* 13.16 Drawing by Ivan Kochsis, Courtesy of Museum of Ontario Archaeology, London; 13.17 Courtesy of James W. Bradley; 13.18 Sarah W. Neusius; 13.19 Phillip D. Neusius; 13.24 Courtesy John Hart.

14.1 Beverly A. Chiarulli; 14.2 Photo by Andy Gilletti, courtesy Affinis Environmental Services; 14.3 From Loubser, Johannes H. N. 2003 by permission of AltaMira Press; 14.4 Sarah W. Neusius; 14.5 Beverly A. Chiarulli; 14.6 Sarah W. Neusius; 14.7 Lobby Exhibit, Dickson Mounds Museum, by permission of the Illinois State Museum; 14.8 Sarah W. Neusius; 14.9 Beverly A. Chiarulli; 14.10 Courtesy New York State Museum, Albany, NY A1990.04 Photo 7:6; 14.11 Sarah W. Neusius.

A.1 Plate XIX in Squier and Davis, 1848; A.2 Harvard University, Peabody Museum Photo

2004.24.1365.1; A.3 National Anthropological Archives, Smithsonian Institution, Negative # 92-5784; A.5 Photo Courtesy of SIUC Media and Communications Resources; A.6 Courtesy Office of Public Affairs, Southern Methodist University; A.7 Courtesy New York State Museum, Albany, NY; A.8 Beverly A. Chiarulli.

B.1 Beverly A. Chiarulli; B.2 Beverly A. Chiarulli; B.3 Courtesy New York State Museum; B.4 Sarah W. Neusius; B.5 Sarah W. Neusius; B.6 G. Timothy Gross; B.7 Sarah W. Neusius; B.8 Sarah W. Neusius; B.9 Courtesy New York State Museum Albany, NY; B.10 Beverly A. Chiarulli, B.11 G. Timothy Gross.

C.1 Sarah W. Neusius; C.2 Redrawn based on student notebooks from excavations at the C.W. Harris site, San Diego County, CA; C.3 From Meltzer, 1993 courtesy David J. Meltzer; C.4 Reproduced from p. 6, Stokes and Smiley, 1968 by permission of the University of Chicago Press; C.5 Sarah W. Neusius; C.6 Virginia W. Neusius.

D1.2 Courtesy New York State Museum; D1.3 Courtesy New York State Museum; D1.4 Courtesy New York State Museum; D1.5 Courtesy New York State Museum; D2.2 Joanna Boldurian; D2.3 Figure 24, p. 57, Boldurian and Cotter, 1999 by permission of the University of Pennsylvania Museum of Archaeology and Anthropology; D2.4 Figure 25, p. 59, Figure 26b, p. 61 and Figure 33b, p. 71, Boldurian and Cotter, 1999 by permission of the University of Pennsylvania Museum of Archaeology and Anthropology; D2.5 Reprinted with permission from Lahren and Bonnichsen, *Science* 186:149 (1974) © 1974 AAAS; D2.6 Figure 46, p. 96, Boldurian and Cotter, 1999 by permission of the University of Pennsylvania

Museum of Archaeology and Anthropology; D2.7 Joanna Boldurian; D3.1 G. Timothy Gross; D3.2 Erin M. King; D3.3 Erin M. King; D3.4 Reproduced by permission of the Society for American Archaeology from American Antiquity 69(1), 2004; D4.1 Dolores Archaeological Program slide, curated at the Anasazi Heritage Center, Dolores, CO; D4.2 Dolores Archaeological Program slide, curated at the Anasazi Heritage Center, Dolores, CO; D4.3 Dolores Archaeological Program slide, curated at the Anasazi Heritage Center, Dolores, CO; D4.4 Figure 5.11, p. 405 in Kane, 1986a, image curated at the Anasazi Heritage Center, Dolores, CO; D4.5 Figure 5.13, p. 407 in Kane, 1986a, image curated at the Anasazi Heritage Center, Dolores, CO; D4.6 Figure 5.17, p. 413 in Kane, 1986a, image curated at the Anasazi Heritage Center, Dolores, CO; D5.1 Redrawn by permission from *Southeastern Archaeology*, Vol. 24(1); D5.2 Courtesy Renee B. Walker; D5.3 Reproduced from Walker et al. 2001 by permission of AltaMira Press; D5.4 Courtesy Renee B. Walker; D5.5 Courtesy Renee B. Walker; D5.6 Courtesy Renee B. Walker; D5.7 Illustration by Jennifer L. Kirkmeyer, courtesy Boyce N. Driskell; D5.8 Illustration by Jennifer L. Kirkmeyer, courtesy Boyce N. Driskell; D5.9 Courtesy Renee B. Walker; D5.10 Courtesy Renee B. Walker; D6.1 Donald P. Heldman, courtesy Elizabeth M. Scott; D6.2 Donald P. Heldman, courtesy Elizabeth M. Scott.

E1.1 Courtesy of the University of Rochester, Department of Rare Books and Special Collections; E2.1 Courtesy Linda Mayro.

F2.1 G. Timothy Gross, courtesy San Diego Archaeological Center.

Part 1

INTRODUCING NORTH AMERICAN ARCHAEOLOGY

CHAPTER 1

The Nature and Practice of North American Archaeology

Everybody has heard of Indiana Jones. This adventuresome Hollywood archaeologist is always getting himself into and out of scrapes in exotic locales while saving unique and mysterious artifacts from being put to evil uses. Indiana Jones is part of popular Western culture: he speaks to our yearning for the exotic and the mysterious, and he makes us laugh. Indiana Jones is immensely entertaining.

Of course, Indiana Jones is fictional. His adventures bear very little resemblance to actual archaeological work. Yet journalists often introduce stories about archaeology with references to Indiana Jones. The following headlines appeared as we wrote this book: "Robotic Indiana Jones to Penetrate Pyramid," "An Internet 'Indiana Jones' Receives AIA Award for Excellence in Undergraduate Teaching," and "University Archaeologist Brings Indiana Jones to Life." These are articles about serious archaeologists and archaeology in which the character created on film by Harrison Ford is merely a device to catch the interest of the reader. Then, having seduced people into reading further, the journalist begins the real story.

Admittedly Indiana Jones is a common point of reference and also great fun, but we think real archaeology is interesting in itself. It is unfortunate that archaeology is seldom taught in school and that only a few Americans have easy access to a public museum with archaeological exhibits. Books about archaeology rarely make the best-seller list, although mysteries with archaeologists as characters (see Chapter 10) seem to be quite common. Television, particularly the Discovery Channel and PBS, probably has raised archaeology's profile. However, little of this material focuses on the archaeology of the United States and Canada. Thus, perhaps unsurprisingly, even most Americans who have learned something about archaeology know nothing about North America's archaeological past. Indeed, one public opinion survey found most Americans unable to name important archaeological sites within the United States (Ramos and Duganne 2000, 16).

What we hope to do in this text is to provide you with many reference points for North American archaeology and to change and deepen your understanding of what archaeology is, erasing any perception that our continent's past is not as interesting as the past of other lands. To us, the past of North America is varied, fascinating, and even mysterious, and our discipline is dynamic and exciting. Most of all, we hope reading this book persuades you of the need to preserve America's archaeological past. Preserving our heritage is an important challenge for the increasingly multi-cultural societies of North America in the twenty-first century.

THE SCOPE OF THIS BOOK

FIGURE 1.1 One way in which archaeologists discover the traces of the past is through excavation, such as the test excavations being conducted at the Fleming site in Pennsylvania by students enrolled in field school at Indiana University of Pennsylvania.

You can easily find several different definitions of **archaeology** by consulting a dictionary or by finding the word in a textbook glossary. Most likely these definitions will have several common features. They will use words like "past," "ancient," and "prehistoric" because the word *archaeology* itself has as its root *archaeo*, which means old. Literally, archaeology is the study of the old. However, a good definition must include the idea that archaeologists use physical evidence to learn about the past. No one can study the past directly, but archaeologists can analyze the material traces of past people and places and consider what they can tell us. Archaeologists collect **artifacts**, objects made or modified by humans, and **ecofacts**, natural materials that have been used by humans, and record traces of past structures, fires, pits, and refuse dumps (Figure 1.1). We study these material remains, as well as the ways in which they are distributed in space and time; these are our clues to the past—our data. These data collectively are called the **archaeological record**. Thus, we say that archaeologists study the past through the examination of the archaeological record.

Such a general definition catches most of what all archaeologists have in common; but the definition is still not entirely satisfactory because it does not indicate what it is about the past that archaeologists are trying to find out. In fact, this is precisely what distinguishes different types of archaeologists, and it is the source of the variety of definitions for archaeology that you may encounter. Some archaeologists would stress that archaeologists study human lifeways, but other archaeologists might promote the idea that archaeology documents the history of material culture. The theoretical and methodological reasons for these various definitions are beyond the scope of this book. Our choice is to define archaeology as the study of past human behavior and culture through the analysis of material remains. Our definition is in keeping with an American tradition of archaeology because this is a book about the archaeology of North America.

Most of this book considers the body of knowledge archaeologists have generated concerning the past cultures of this continent. It introduces the variability in past ways of life and the record of culture change. We present consensus viewpoints on the past, illustrating the evidence for archaeologists' ideas through case studies of real archaeological projects. The fact is that there is too rich a literature about the North American past for an introductory text such as this one to be complete. Our goal was not to be an encyclopedia, but instead to make this body of knowledge comprehensible, whether a reader is satisfied with an introduction or intends to pursue the field further.

This text is primarily about what archaeologists think happened during the North American past, but it also introduces the practice of North American archaeology. This is because it is hard to understand the conclusions archaeologists have drawn, and impossible to evaluate them critically, without knowing how the data were derived. Thus, in this chapter and the next, we review how North American archaeologists do archaeology. This introduction also is not exhaustive, but we do introduce critical vocabulary and suggest the scientific context for studying this continent's past. The CD that accompanies the book offers more information about both the history of North American archaeology (Student CD, Section A) and the methods used by contemporary archaeologists (Student CD, Sections B and C). We encourage those who have little background in archaeology to explore these sections.

In addition, we have tried throughout this book to give a sense of what it is actually like to be an archaeologist today. You may be surprised to learn that North American archaeologists work in a variety of settings—in universities and museums but also in private businesses and government agencies. Moreover, since archaeologists are only one group of twenty-first-century stakeholders with an interest in North America's past, we must confront a number of public relations and ethical issues in our work. Finally, serious threats to the record of America's past exist in modern society. Not only can we destroy the evidence of the past as our cities grow and our use of the landscape changes, but some people are interested in artifacts largely for their market value. These contemporary realities affect the practice of North American archaeology in many ways. If you envision archaeologists as laboring primarily in the dusty reaches of museums and labs, you are likely to find these other aspects of contemporary archaeology particularly surprising.

One last note about scope is that when we say "North America," we are referring mainly to the continent north of central Mexico. In this book, we use the term **culture areas** (e.g., Kroeber 1963), geographical regions within which there is a general similarity of culture, to discuss the archaeology of North America. The areas that we treat usually are grouped in North America culturally, while the cultures of central and southern Mexico typically are placed in a unit known among anthropologists as Mesoamerica (Figure 1.2). This does not mean that there has been no contact between the cultures of Mexico and North America, but cultural contrasts, both ethnographic and archaeological, are clearly evident to anthropologists.

WHAT IS NORTH AMERICAN ARCHAEOLOGY?

In one sense, North American archaeology is simply the archaeology done within the culture areas of North America. However, most North American archaeologists also are guided by the principles of Americanist archaeology, an approach that developed largely in the United States but is practiced elsewhere as well. Three aspects of this approach are important to understanding it.

North American Archaeology Is Anthropology

At most North American universities and colleges, courses in North American archaeology are offered by an anthropology department. The American tradition is to see archaeology as a type of **anthropology**, the holistic study of the physical, cultural, and social aspects of humans in all times and places. The subfields of

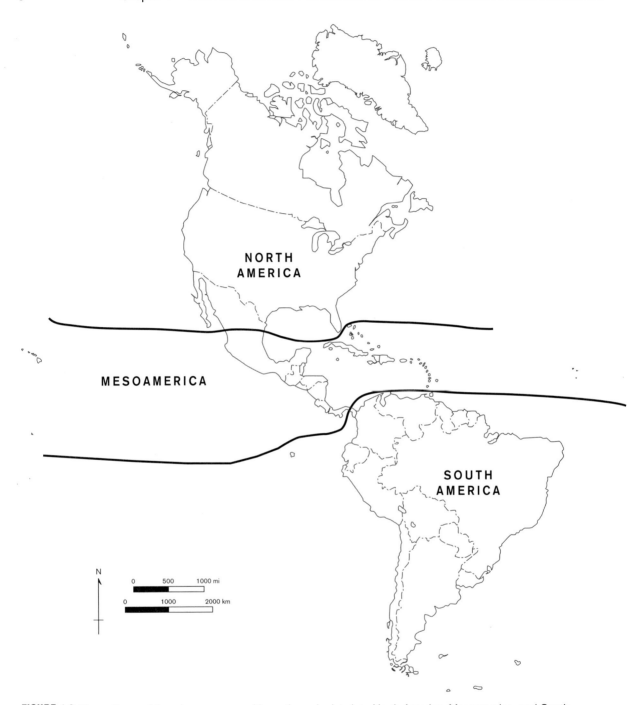

FIGURE 1.2 The cultures of America are grouped by anthropologists into North America, Mesoamerica, and South America with approximate boundaries as shown.

FIGURE 1.3 Archaeology is one of the four subdisciplines of anthropology.

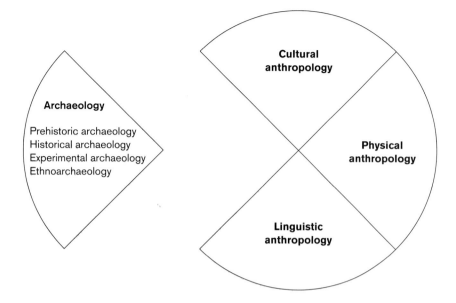

Archaeology

Prehistoric archaeology
Historical archaeology
Experimental archaeology
Ethnoarchaeology

Cultural anthropology

Physical anthropology

Linguistic anthropology

anthropology (Figure 1.3) are archaeology, **cultural anthropology**, which studies recent humans and their cultures through description of observed human behaviors, **linguistic anthropology**, which examines human language, and **biological anthropology**, which studies both human biological evolution and human biological diversity. Chances are that the department providing your course also offers courses in these other areas of anthropology. As the holistic and comparative study of humans, anthropology is concerned with humans in both the past and the present. As the social science that has most often studied non-Western societies, it is natural that anthropology incorporates the archaeological study of preliterate prehistoric people.

There also are historical reasons for the Americanist inclusion of archaeology within anthropology. Like other Western sciences, anthropology developed as Europeans encountered new areas, peoples, and cultures from the fifteenth century onward. Europeans needed to explain the newly apparent diversity among humans. In North America, anthropological scholarship naturally focused on American Indians. Thus as anthropologists tried to understand the diversity of native inhabitants, they framed many questions about the human settlement and history of this continent. To illustrate, one anthropologist might study contemporary Indian cultures that were assumed to be vanishing while at the same time exploring the artifacts and ruined structures of these Indians' ancestors. Yet the same anthropologist, in other contexts, might be interested in recording native language or in describing the physical appearance of people. In this way, archaeology became inextricably linked with other studies of Native Americans. The legacy of this approach is still felt by North American archaeologists. Indeed, most of us consider ourselves to be anthropologists. Graduate students in anthropology may focus on archaeology, but, with a few exceptions, they take their degrees in anthropology.

The historical inclusion of archaeology within anthropology leads to an important distinction between North American and European archaeology. In

Europe, archaeologists, who may be more likely to see archaeology as a type of history, have studied their own ancestors. In North America, interest in **historical archaeology**, which is the archaeological study of people who made written records, is considerable today, but this is a recent phenomenon (Deagan 1982). American archaeologists, who usually have been of European descent, most often have studied somebody else's ancestors. This is not a trivial matter. Among other things, it means that North American archaeology, like all anthropology, has its roots in the colonial encounter as well as in the ideologies of the dominant American culture. For example, the nineteenth-century concept of **manifest destiny**, which held that Americans were destined to displace North America's native inhabitants, also affected early anthropological ideas about American Indians. Fortunately, such viewpoints have become outdated, in part because the archaeological record has revealed the complexity of the past. The discussion in Box 1.1 gives some idea of how early misconceptions such as these were overturned as archaeological evidence mounted.

ISSUES AND DEBATES

BOX 1.1

Who Were the Mound Builders?

One of the great stories of the coming of age of North American archaeology is the Mound Builder debate that developed during the nineteenth century. This story illustrates both how preconceptions can influence scholarship and how careful data collection and analysis can lead scientists to discard erroneous ideas.

When the first American traders, surveyors, and speculators came over the Appalachian ridges into the Ohio country during the eighteenth century, they were amazed by what they found. **Mounds**, enclosures, and other earthworks dotted the landscape. As more and more land west of the mountains was explored and settled, it became obvious that these earthen constructions were not isolated phenomena. In all, hundreds of thousands of mounds and earthworks in many sizes and shapes once existed. The largest mound we know of, Monks Mound (Figure 1.4), located in the broad floodplain of the Mississippi River east of St. Louis, rises more than 98 feet (30 m) and covers nearly 14

FIGURE 1.4 The largest extant mound is Monks Mound, located at the Cahokia site, Collinsville, Illinois.

acres at its base (Milner 1998). However, Monks Mound was only one of at least a hundred mounds of various kinds at this site. The earthworks at Newark, Ohio, include octagonal, circular, and rectangular enclosures laid out with geometric precision. The Great Enclosure at

FIGURE 1.5 The Serpent Mound winds across a ridge top in Adams County, Ohio.

Newark has a diameter of 1200 feet (365 m) and encloses 30 acres (12 hectares) (Woodward and McDonald 2002, 189). The better-known stone circle at Stonehenge, with its diameter of 330 feet (100 m), would fit three times into this space with room to spare! There also are effigy mounds, constructed in the shape of animals, such as the Serpent Mound in Ohio (Figure 1.5). Even the earlier conical burial mounds can be quite impressive. For example, Grave Creek Mound, located on the floodplain of the Ohio River in Moundsville, West Virginia, is at least 62 feet (19 m) tall and contains an estimated 1.2 million cubic feet (34,000 m^3) of dirt (Hemmings 1984).

As the Ohio country was settled by European Americans, these constructions were sometimes ignored and obliterated, sometimes marveled at, and sometimes the stimulus for romanticism. Some of the earliest scholars such as Thomas Jefferson, whose many interests included archaeology, and Albert Gallatin, senator from Pennsylvania and secretary of the Treasury under Jefferson and Madison, concluded that the mounds must mean that American Indians once had been culturally sophisticated (Kennedy 1994). However, most European Americans believed that the tribal people they knew as fairly mobile, lacking in material possessions, and at least as dependent on wild food sources as on their garden products could not have had the knowledge to build these impressive earthworks. Instead, they credited a more sophisticated people with the constructions they were finding. Thus, by the early nineteenth century, the idea that a now extinct race of builders of mound once existed in the midcontinent made sense to most people. Even scholars often accepted the idea that the Mound Builders had been a different people from the Indian tribes in the area.

Speculations identified the Mound Builders as wandering Hindus, the lost tribe of Israel, or migrating Mexicans. In some versions, the Amerindians came later and annihilated the Mound Builders, while in others the Mound Builders abandoned North America and migrated to Mexico, where they built the great Mexican civilizations. Various hoaxes, such as stone tablets supposedly bearing alphabetic scripts, were also perpetrated in support of the "lost race" stories (Feder 2002). No matter the details, the idea of a lost race fed the romantic imagination of nineteenth-century Americans. Of course, stereotypes and racist assumptions also were at work. For example, some argued that Native Americans were too lazy and disorganized to have done the work required to build the mounds.

Fortunately, at the end of the nineteenth century, a resolution of the Mound Builder debate based on evidence became possible. In 1881 the federal government through the Bureau of American Ethnology of the Smithsonian Institution funded an expedition designed to determine who the Mound Builders had been. Hired to head this undertaking was a scientist named Cyrus Thomas. Before pursuing his interests in ethnology and archaeology, Thomas had been a lawyer, a Lutheran minister, and an entomologist. He had helped found the Illinois Natural History Society and was associated with John Wesley Powell in this endeavor. Powell is well known for his explorations of the Grand Canyon, but he is also notable for his directorship of the Bureau of American Ethnology. When Congress insisted that the then large sum of $5000 annually be spent on mound exploration, Powell turned to Thomas for help (Muller 1996).

What makes Thomas such a good example of a scientist, albeit a late nineteenth-century one, is that he let the empirical evidence guide his conclusions about the Mound Builders. By his own admission, he began his work believing that a distinct mound-building race had once existed. However, by the time he wrote his report (Thomas 1894), the overwhelming empirical evidence yielded by his investigations had changed his mind. Thomas made a systematic study of approximately 2000 mounds and earthworks in 21 states over a seven-year period. The linkages to American Indians were obvious, and Thomas concluded that the mounds were built either by the very Indians that Europeans first encountered or by their ancestors. He also found that there was no evidence that the Mound Builders had migrated from Mexico or elsewhere. Thomas's report not only settled the identity question to his own satisfaction, but it convinced the growing archaeological community. Archaeologists turned their attention to documenting the details of the mound-building past rather than to speculating about origins.

Today, most Americans know very little about these mounds (Figure 1.6), and ignorance fuels some present-day speculations and fantasies. Lacking knowledge of what Cyrus Thomas established more than a century ago, modern Americans might even be tempted to believe that aliens built the Serpent Mound, as some have claimed. Nevertheless, today's anti-

FIGURE 1.6 Saul's Mound, at Pinson Mounds in Pinson, Tennessee, is part of a large complex of earthworks and mounds that the public can visit.

dote to becoming mired in speculations is the same as Thomas's—look at the evidence and draw your conclusions accordingly. The Mound Builder controversy has long been settled, but its twofold lessons remain valid: that American Indians built the mounds and that our stereotypes can mislead us when we do not consider the evidence carefully.

For an example of current research on the Mound Builders see the case study by Mark Lynott, "The Hopeton Earthworks Project: Using New Technologies to Answer Old Questions," in Chapter 12.

Although more recent archaeologists have seen Native American culture as equal to European and other cultures, a focus on generalizing about cultures rather than on specific histories has resulted in some devaluing of native cultures (Trigger 1989, 315–316). Archaeologists also may have too easily accepted the idea that native culture vanished and was destroyed by the advancing dominant culture. An uncritical acceptance of this idea can lead to the dismissal of contemporary Native American culture as irrelevant as well as to the notion that the archaeologist is the only valid authority on past Native American culture. With such a mind-set, archaeologists can think of their work as a service to the descendants of early Americans and to society at large. While this idea of what archaeology is about may be well-meaning, it is more than a little patronizing.

In reality, there is both continuity and disjunction between contemporary Native American cultures and the diverse cultures of North America's past. There was not an abrupt break between the prehistoric and the historic periods. Instead, there have been a wide variety of cultural results spanning the centuries of interaction. This means that denying contemporary Native Americans direct input into the scientific story of their ancestors narrows our understanding of the past. It also serves to warn archaeologists not to ignore Native sensibilities about burials and artifacts. Unfortunately, Native Americans historically have had good reason to distrust archaeologists, and there has been considerable contention over the management of Indian **cultural resources** as native people have asserted their rights more forcefully in recent decades (Watkins 2003). Relationships between archaeologists and Native Americans still need improvement, but there is a much greater sensitivity to native concerns among today's archaeologists. What this will mean for the future of the discipline remains to be seen, but it is clear that new understanding does not involve a rejection of the anthropological character of North American archaeology. In fact, some have seen greater involvement with Native Americans as a rediscovery of archaeology's roots in a more holistic and culturally relative anthropology.

North American Archaeology Considers Itself a Science

A second point about North American archaeology is that, like other fields in anthropology, it is a social science. If the idea that archaeology is a science seems questionable, remember that the nature of science often is misunderstood. The most significant point to consider about science is that it is primarily a way of investigating our world. Individual sciences have very different methods, but they have in common a general way of proceeding (Thomas 1998, 44–47). You may have seen formulations of the **scientific method** when studying other sciences (Figure 1.7). In summary, this method provides a means of investigating interactions between things in the natural, observable world. It begins with examining and thinking about what has been observed and proceeds with the formulation of hypotheses about relationships between natural phenomena. Then, new observations of the natural world provide tests for hypotheses. New data are summarized and examined to see whether they are consistent with the ideas and assumptions originally held. They may cause a scientist to change his or her ideas or they may not. In the former case, we can say the hypothesis was disproved; in the latter, we can say it was confirmed. Findings may contribute to

FIGURE 1.7 Simplified representation of how the scientific method proceeds.

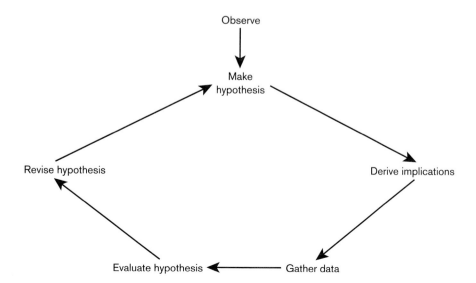

general theories, which, in turn, can lead to new hypotheses and further testing. Scientific investigation is considered fruitful if it causes new questions to be raised and new hypotheses to be formed.

Archaeology is a science because it follows these procedures. Archaeologists can explore ideas about the past by examining artifacts, fire pits, and house foundations. We cannot directly observe the past, but we can directly observe traces of what happened in the past. By checking and cross-checking our observations, drawing conclusions about what they mean, and then forming new hypotheses for further testing our ideas in new studies, we can build up an understanding of the past. Of course, we may draw incorrect conclusions; but because we are engaged in a process of hypothesis testing, new data should eventually lead to a revision of wrong ideas.

Archaeologists have long been concerned with being rigorous and scientific in their procedures, but it is true that ideas about what qualifies as "scientific" have varied among archaeologists in different times and places. There was a period during the 1960s and immediately thereafter when some archaeologists thought that using the scientific method, more or less rigidly defined as illustrated in Figure 1.7, was the only valid means of exploring the past. Such a method of study was supposed to lead archaeologists to the truth about the past, while earlier archaeological attempts to be scientific were understood as being limited to description or speculation. The position that there is one right way to do science—one rigid scientific method—is a form of **scientism**, a more general view that there is only one way to acquire valid knowledge about the natural universe. Most contemporary archaeologists are far more flexible, and today the viewpoints of some theorists of the 1960s seem overly simplistic.

Contemporary archaeologists are more aware that our individual perspectives and experiences as modern people affect both the questions we ask and the assumptions we make about meaning. We also recognize that nonarchaeologists also have ideas about the past that should not be ignored. There may be several viewpoints or stories to be told, resulting in a richer understanding overall. Some archaeologists explicitly try to include a humanistic approach in their investigations, seeking out more personal and individualistic assessments of the past, as well (e.g., Spector 1993). A few archaeologists even have argued that we cannot obtain an objective understanding of the past at all, though this view certainly is not held by all North American archaeologists. It also would be incorrect to say that the majority of North American archaeologists have given up the quest to be scientific or have abandoned the basic procedures of hypothesis testing outlined earlier. As with all anthropology, the goal remains increasing knowledge about people. Hypothesis testing still is a powerful means of working on this endeavor, even though archaeologists are learning to question their own biases and to incorporate a range of perspectives about the past.

North American Archaeology Contributes to History

The characterization of archaeology as anthropology and as a science may be new to you. You may have thought of archaeology as much more like history than anthropology. It certainly is true that archaeology can contribute to historical understanding. While there are some things that we cannot learn from artifacts and other material traces of humans, there also are ways in which archaeological studies can enhance a purely historical understanding of the past.

First, precisely because much of archaeology focuses on non-Western and preliterate peoples, it provides different perspectives on what happened in the past from those due to history. For example, Native Americans can be understood as "people without history" (Wolf 1982). This doesn't mean that Native Americans had no history before Europeans came to North America. Except where it specifically intersects with the story of literate Westerners, however, the story of the Native American past is not part of standard histories of humanity. Recognizing the limitations of the strictly historical perspective, archaeologists have sought to add to knowledge of human history by describing and explaining cultures not covered in the written records of the past. North American archaeologists have often felt strongly that the story of ancient Native America needed to be told so that it could be compared with the history of other places and more valid generalizations about the human past could be made.

Second, even in the case of historical archaeology, our discipline contributes in ways that history cannot. Many contemporary archaeologists primarily study the post-Columbian archaeological record of North America. Yet even when a great deal of historical study has been completed, the written records do not necessarily contain a complete picture of the past. As any historian knows, diaries, descriptions of events, and other documents are written from a particular point of view and can conceal nearly as much as they reveal. The artifacts and the remains of historic buildings explored by archaeologists provide different and sometimes startling information about the past. Archaeology can verify and amplify the story told in documents. It can piece together the details that chroniclers of earlier times neglected to mention. It can provide information about social classes or ethnic groups who have received scant attention in written documents. In this sense, as Charles Orser has written, "archaeology opens narrow thresholds to the past across which historians, relying on written words alone, typically cannot traverse" (Orser 1996, 11). Working together, archaeologists and historians can develop a richer understanding of the past.

You can gain more insight into the nature of North American archaeology from reading Section A of the Student CD. The historical context out of which this field developed contributes to an understanding of the Americanist approach just outlined, and it introduces the individuals who developed techniques and theories important in this field. The case study in Section D.1 of the Student CD illustrates the changing nature of archaeological practice during the twentieth century.

THE NORTH AMERICAN ARCHAEOLOGIST

Another way to understand the field of archaeology is to explore the biographies of some of its practitioners. Although questions about North America's peoples and their past began to be asked as soon as Europeans discovered the continent, it was not until the end of the eighteenth century and the beginning of the nineteenth century that anyone systematically investigated the antiquities of this continent. Even then, investigations such as Thomas Jefferson's into a Virginia mound were rare. Moreover, although careful description and cataloging became commonplace in the latter half of the nineteenth century, archaeology remained a hobby or sideline. Museum jobs for archaeologists began to be available after 1890, and the first graduate programs in archaeology and anthropology were established as American universities were developed in the early twentieth century. It was at this time that professional societies also began to form and new archaeological methods were developed that required training, while a growing body of data about our past also had to be mastered. Archaeology became an academic discipline within anthropology during these years. Arthur Parker (Student CD, Section E.1) stands as one example of an early twentieth-century archaeologist whose career spanned the development of the discipline of archaeology in North America.

Contemporary North American archaeologists still can be found working in museums, and many more are employed in universities. In fact, the university is the work setting for one of us (Neusius). Today, most archaeologists have careers that include several different work settings over their course. Profile 1.1 offers one example of an archaeological career centered in academic settings.

FACES IN ARCHAEOLOGY

PROFILE 1.1

W. James Judge, Professor and Director of the Chaco Project

Question: What do the central Rio Grande valley of New Mexico, Fort Lewis College in Durango, Colorado, and television's *Beavis and Butt-Head* have in common?
Answer: Jim Judge.

Jim Judge (Figure 1.8), who retired from teaching in 2001, began his professional career at the University of New Mexico. His doctoral research was on the early human occupations of the middle Rio Grande valley of New Mexico. That work, completed in 1970 and published in 1972, is still an important discussion of the nature of the earliest occupations of the Southwest. After completing his doctorate, Judge took a position at Colorado State University, later returning to the University of New Mexico as a professor.

Judge joined the Chaco Project, a cooperative effort between the National Park Service and the University of New Mexico, as a research archaeologist in 1974, after having designed and implemented a sample survey of the canyon as a contractor through the university. He served as director of the project from 1977 to 1985. As discussed in Chapter 9, Chaco Canyon was

a major regional exchange system between AD 900 and AD 1150. The Chaco Project set about the task of intensive study of the Chaco system. These investigators amassed an archive of previous published and unpublished work, conducted surveys, excavated key sites, and used

FIGURE 1.8 Archaeologist James Judge at Chaco Canyon.

remote sensing to study the area. The project also included studies of past environments in Chaco Canyon and the surrounding area. The Chaco Project was instrumental in increasing our understanding of the Chaco system and was important in focusing southwestern archaeologists on regional interaction systems. The project produced or contributed to many important reports and research papers. Judge coauthored the report on the survey of the canyon and coedited a volume comparing the **Hohokam** and Chaco regional systems.

After leaving the Chaco Project, Judge directed the Fort Burgwin Research Center, a research arm of Southern Methodist University located near Taos, New Mexico. In 1989 the center hosted the Society for American Archaeology's Taos Anti-looting Conference, bringing together over 70 participants to discuss methods of preventing **relic hunters** from destroying sites. Judge's participation in this conference is one reflection of his interest in preservation of the archaeological record.

In 1990 Judge moved to Fort Lewis College in Durango, Colorado, where he has held the position of professor emeritus since his retirement. Having taught field schools in his previous positions, he continued this interest at Fort Lewis, with investigations at two pueblos that made up part of the community surrounding the Lowry Ruin, a Chacoan outlier located near Cortez, Colorado. One of Judge's interests is electronic publication of archaeological results, and the report on one of these field school excavations, Puzzle House, is published on the Internet (http://anthro.fortlewis.edu/puzzlereport/default.asp).

Over the years, Judge has taught introductory courses in anthropology and archaeology, as well as courses in southwestern archaeology, field techniques, laboratory methods, and evolutionary archaeology. In addition to his Paleoindian

and Chacoan research, he had an interest in settlement patterns, predictive modeling, and remote sensing in archaeology. Judge has received awards for his teaching and his research and has published extensively. He is a member of the Preservation Technology and Training Board, a group of professionals who provide advice to the National Center for Preservation Technology. He is also on the board of directors for the Archaeological Conservancy and the steering committee for the Chaco Digital Initiative, the group responsible for the Chaco Portal (http://anthro.fortlewis.edu/ChacoPortal/index.htm), a web page bringing together information on Chacoan archaeology. Judge has also served on the Society for American Archaeology Governmental Affairs Committee and is an adviser for the GIS program at Fort Lewis College.

The career of Jim Judge illustrates a successful pursuit of research in a particular area carried out from different universities sequentially. It also demonstrates an interest in new and developing technologies like remote sensing and electronic publishing. Finally, Judge's time with the Chaco Project illustrates a fruitful collaboration between a government agency and an academic institution. Not only did that collaboration produce volumes of new information about the past in the Chaco region, information that continues to provide data for scholarly publications, but it also provided management information for the Park Service and information for the interpretation of the Chaco system to the public.

But where, you might be wondering, does *Beavis and Butt-Head* come into the picture? Well, in addition to the accomplishments just outlined, this archaeologist is the proud father of Mike Judge, creator of *Beavis and Butt-Head* and the hit series *King of the Hill.*

The varied work settings for today's archaeologist are attributable to the transformation of North American archaeology, beginning during the 1970s, by the development of **cultural resource management (CRM)**. CRM is an applied form of archaeology done in response to various laws that require archaeological investigations as part of federal and state programs. In the United States and in Canada, there is a history of government involvement with archaeological sites dating back to the nineteenth century, when the U.S. government sponsored investigations of mounds and explorations of the American West. Several large government-funded archaeological projects during the mid-twentieth century also established the government's role in archaeology within the United States (Neumann and Sanford 2001). The first piece of U.S. legislation involving archaeological sites was the Antiquities Act of 1906, which protected historic or prehistoric remains on federal lands and made it possible for the president to establish national monuments. Following this came a whole series of acts supporting the concept that archaeological sites, as well as historic buildings, are cultural resources for the public, and asserting that it is the responsibility of the government to protect them (Table 1.1). Cultural resources are sites, buildings, and artifacts that are significant to understanding of the past and thus are irreplaceable.

TABLE 1.1 Significant U.S. Federal Legislation Related to North American Cultural Resources	
Native American Graves Protection and Repatriation Act of 1990 (NAGPRA)	Protection of Native American graves and cultural materials uncovered on federal and tribal land; requires the inventory and, when requested, the return of skeletal, funerary, and other sacred items to federally recognized Native American tribes by any federal or federally funded institution
Abandoned Shipwreck Act of 1987	Allows for the protection and recovery of shipwrecks and underwater sites and encourages state management of underwater cultural resources
Archaeological Resources Protection Act of 1979	Stiffens penalties for looting or damaging of sites on federal and tribal lands; requires uniform regulations for treatment of archaeological resources on such lands with respect to permitting and penalties
Archaeological and Historic Preservation Act of 1974	Requires avoidance of the loss of archaeological data and allows agencies to spend a portion of their budgets to recover data being threatened
National Environmental Policy Act of 1969	Requires all federal agencies to specify the impact of their undertakings on cultural as well as natural resources
National Historic Preservation Act of 1966 (amended 1976 and 1980)	Protection of significant cultural resources through the National Register; provides a mechanism for integrating state agencies into the process through the Advisory Council on Historic Preservation and State Historic Preservation Offices; Sections 106 and 110 are particularly important in stipulating the assessment and management of cultural resources
Department of Transportation Act of 1966 Section 4(f) (amended 1968)	Requires any transportation project that will affect a National Register–eligible resource to avoid or minimize effects on that resource
Reservoir Salvage Act of 1960	National Park Service given the authority to administer the salvaging of archaeological resources threatened by the construction of dams and reservoirs (preceded by Smithsonian Institution River Basin Surveys and various Works Progress Administration programs)
Historic Sites Act of 1935	Provides for the designation of National Historic Landmarks; allows archaeological survey before site destruction
Antiquities Act of 1906	Protection for archaeological sites on federal land; penalties for looting

Today, anyone who plans to study North American archaeology must become familiar with an elaborate framework of laws affecting archaeological practice. In the United States, it is virtually impossible to move forward with any undertaking of the federal government or permitted or funded by it without considering whether the activity contemplated will affect important cultural resources.

Many state laws mirror federal legislation in protecting cultural resources potentially affected by state projects. For example, the **California Environmental Quality Act (CEQA)**, passed in 1970, was one of the first state laws calling for archaeological impact studies. Because of this long history, California has a large number of CRM firms, and state agencies like CALTRANS (California's Department of Transportation) and the various state parks have large CRM staffs, as well. CEQA compliance is administered at the local level. Many California jurisdictions require archaeologists to belong to the **Register of Professional Archaeologists (RPA)**, an organization of archaeologists dedicated to promoting standards and ethics among archaeologists. As a result, California has more members on the register than any other state. Recently, several other states have been adding the RPA requirement.

Both the number of jobs available to North American archaeologists overall and the percentage of these jobs found outside universities and museums have greatly increased as CRM has developed. One of us (Gross) has his primary employment in a private firm from which he does CRM archaeology. Neumann and Sanford (2001, 2) estimate that nearly 80 percent of archaeologists are employed in the private or government sectors. Zeder (1997), working with data drawn mainly from membership in the Society for American Archaeology (SAA), found this percentage to be approximately 50 percent. It is probable, however, that field technicians, who may not have a degree in anthropology but do most of the actual excavation and lab work in CRM firms, are not well represented in these estimates. CRM now plays an important role within the discipline and many academics are involved in one way or another in CRM-funded projects as well. These changes originally generated some mutual disdain between CRM and academic archaeologists, but we think the tensions may be mellowing as the field continues to develop. See Section F.1 on the Student CD for additional perspective on these two types of contemporary archaeology. You also can get an impression of what a career in CRM is like from Profile 1.2.

As Profile 1.2 indicates, Lynne Sebastian is a woman who has risen to the top of her profession. During the mid-twentieth century, despite the accomplishments of some renowned women archaeologists, there was a definite bias against women in the field. This began to change in the 1970s (Patterson 1995), and current data on gender distribution suggest that archaeology is no longer so heavily dominated by men. One recent survey (Zeder 1997) found that while under 40 percent of the professional archaeologists were female, a little more than 50 percent of the students were. Moreover, the highest proportions of females were in the younger cohorts, and the proportion of professional women tended to decrease as age increased. It is unclear whether these young women will remain in the profession, perhaps encountering a glass ceiling that keeps them from promotion, or whether they will choose other careers as they mature. A survey done in 2005 found that women were being paid less than men, but the causes of the apparent gender gap are unclear because the women surveyed generally were at earlier stages in their careers than the men (Association Research,

FACES IN ARCHAEOLOGY

PROFILE 1.2

Lynne Sebastian, Archaeologist and Historic Preservationist

Lynne Sebastian's career provides one example of a contemporary archaeologist who has chosen to work outside academia. As the president of the Society for American Archaeology from 2003 to 2005, Sebastian (Figure 1.9) can be seen as one of today's most prominent North American archaeologists. It is notable that she is only the fifth woman to become president of the SAA, but it is even more significant that she is the first president whose career has been spent solely in cultural resource management.

Sebastian did not pursue archaeology until she was in her thirties, after she had already earned a bachelor's degree in English and secondary education and a master's degree in English literature. When she was an undergraduate student, she was interested in classical archaeology and Egyptology, but her mother convinced her that it would be more practical to be a teacher. When Sebastian graduated from college trained to teach high school English, however, there was a teacher surplus. She took secretarial jobs and then found work as an editor of archaeological publications at the Museum of Anthropology of the University of Michigan. Eventually, she began doing copyediting for *American Antiquity*, the journal of the Society for American Archaeology, while she worked on her master's in English literature at the University of Utah. She credits the professors with whom she came in contact at that time with opening up the world of anthropology and archaeology for her. Upon coming to see that archaeology provides a way to understand human culture and behavior, she decided to pursue archaeology rather than literary criticism.

After taking some anthropology and archaeology classes at the University of Utah and getting some field training, Sebastian worked for the Dolores Archaeological Program (see Student CD, Section D.4). Sebastian entered graduate school at the University of New Mexico in 1980 and became interested in the archaeology of Chaco Canyon in northwestern New Mexico, which was then being studied for the National Park Service (NPS) by New Mexico professor Jim Judge, whose career was highlighted in Profile 1.1. Although she did not work on the NPS Chaco Project, Sebastian explored political leadership in the Chaco system for her doctoral dissertation. While obtaining her doctorate, Sebastian worked for the University of New Mexico's Office of Contract Archaeology, a CRM unit based at the university. Through this latter job, Sebastian gained practical background in excavation, analysis, and report writing. She feels fortunate to have had the chance to work on several large contract projects

FIGURE 1.9 Lynne Sebastian at Chaco Canyon.

during those years. Because these were full-time projects, several times she took a term off from graduate school, but the fieldwork was interesting and challenging. In fact, she loved this work so much that she discarded any notion of pursuing a career in academia.

Sebastian's career took another turn in 1987 when she began a job as Deputy State Historic Preservation Officer for New Mexico. Part of this job's attraction was that it provided benefits, unlike the CRM project work that both she and her husband, another archaeologist, had been doing. Although she missed archaeological fieldwork and analysis at first, once again a new world was opened to her. This time it was the world of historic preservation, which involves far more than review of archaeological contract reports. She also found herself consulting with Native American tribes and government agencies, educating the public, and working to lessen threats to the archaeological record. She was good at putting people together to solve preservation problems, and this important work was satisfying. Although she began her employment with the state with the idea that the job would be temporary, she stayed 12 years. From her original position, she was named State Archaeologist and then promoted to **State Historic Preservation Officer (SHPO)**, which meant that she had responsibility for all facets of New Mexico's historic preservation program. She became a voice for archaeology in the National Conference of State Historic Preservation Officers (NCSHPO) and also grew active in the Society for American Archaeology, serving on the Public Education Committee and as secretary of the organization.

By the mid-1990s, Sebastian expected that she had made her last career move. In 1999, however, caught in political cross fire, she abruptly lost her job. Despite an outcry from the preservation community, there was no going back. Sebastian's career had taken another turn, and she landed in the private sector working for Statistical Research, Inc. (SRI). This company provides services in CRM and historic preservation in the Southwest and along the West Coast. Unlike most CRM firms, SRI has a division devoted to public outreach, and it was interested in developing professional education programs. Sebastian began holding seminars for cultural resource managers and others who needed to know about CRM law and techniques. Soon the decision was made to separate these activities from the profit-making ones, and a not-for-profit foundation, SRI Foundation, was established. Although this foundation has only a small staff, Sebastian is enthusiastic about being involved in professional development programs and about providing technical assistance concerning archaeological practice to government agencies. Once again, she is finding many new uses for her various skills.

The career of this committed CRM professional suggests that being an archaeologist can lead to rewarding work in government and private companies as well as in universities and museums. Clearly, there is an important place for archaeologists in broader fields such as historic preservation. Indeed, accomplishments like Sebastian's earn as much professional respect as more traditional archaeological pursuits. See the Student CD, Section E.2, for another example of a career in CRM archaeology.

Inc. 2005). Certainly the number of women in the field has been growing, but, only more assessment over the next few decades will establish whether gender equality is increasing within archaeology.

Advances made by women in the field of archaeology not withstanding, recent surveys show that there is very little ethnic diversity among Americanist archaeologists. Zeder (1997) found that 89 percent of the respondents to her survey, were of European American ancestry. This number does not include Canadians, who objected to being classified as European American. Zeder estimates that only about 2 percent of American archaeologists have a non–European American ancestry. This is a startling figure, especially since the populations most North American archaeologists study are not European American, and scholars today agree that individuals' personal social experience cannot help but affect their understanding of the past. No wonder that professional organizations like the SAA are actively trying to expose students of other ethnicities to archaeology.

Avocational Archaeology

Avocational archaeologists are people who lack formal education in anthropology and archaeology and are not paid for work that they do in the field. Indeed, some avocational archaeologists pay for the opportunity to work on archaeological projects. Avocational archaeologists can work alone, through avocational societies like the Mid-Columbia Archaeological Society in Washington State, or through organizations like Crow Canyon School (Figure 1.10) and Earth Watch, which take paying participants on archaeological projects. Avocational archaeologists vary in the diligence with which they report their work, but many are very conscientious. In fact, we know about the location of many sites across the country thanks to the work of avocationals. There are even avocational societies with journals, like the *Pacific Coast Archaeological Society Quarterly*, that not only report the projects conducted by the society but also include papers by professional archaeologists. Others, like the Society for Pennsylvania Archaeology, which publishes the *Pennsylvania Archaeologist*, include both amateurs and professionals as members.

It is important to make the distinction between legitimate avocational archaeologists and relic hunters or **pothunters**, however. Avocational archaeologists observe good archaeological procedure and are careful to keep records of

FIGURE 1.10 Volunteers from Crow Canyon Archaeological Center excavating an Ancestral Pueblo site.

where materials are found. Many work closely with professionals. Some avocational societies have developed certification programs, often in association with colleges or museums. Ethical avocational archaeologists do not do archaeology primarily to add to their personal collections; rather, they are interested in learning about the past and its people. They make sure that the artifacts and records of their work are properly maintained. Relic hunters, on the other hand, generally dig sites for the artifacts, paying little attention to the locations of finds. They heedlessly destroy the archaeological record to get a few more items for their trophy cases or for the black market in antiquities. You can read more about the destructive nature of such activities in the opening sections of Chapters 6 and 12. In Chapter 14 we discuss efforts to deter destructive behaviors especially in Box 14.1.

Native Americans and Other Descendant Populations

As touched on earlier in this chapter, an important aspect of the contemporary archaeological scene in North America is the growing involvement of Native Americans, whether as collaborators and informants in archaeological projects or as full partners in investigations (e.g., Dongoske et al. 2000). A number of tribes have developed cultural heritage programs that involve archaeological investigations. An **indigenous archaeology** in which native people themselves control the course of archaeological studies is developing (Watkins 2003). Progress has been slow, however: many Indians still distrust archaeologists and many archaeologists are still resistant to the loss of control that full collaboration entails.

However, besides the growing political savvy and power of Native Americans, two circumstances help ensure that indigenous involvement is a real trend, likely to change archaeological practice and enrich archaeological understanding of the past. First, today's North American archaeologist is aware that archaeology does not hold the only viable view of the past. The **postmodernist** critique of science has made archaeologists reluctant to cloak ourselves in science and more concerned with how experience and social context influence people's ideas of the past. Within North American archaeology, these ideas have been expressed especially in what is known as **postprocessualism** (see Student CD, Section A, for discussion of this theoretical approach and its significance).

Second, laws now bind archaeologists to respect the concerns of descendant populations. For example, the Native American Graves Protection and Repatriation Act of 1990 (**NAGPRA**) stipulates consultation with descendants in the event of the discovery of new skeletal material. This law also requires the notification of descendants and possible return of human skeletal remains and grave goods held in museums. Recent changes in regulations about the implementation of **Section 106** of the **National Historic Preservation Act** require consultation with Native Americans and other descendants in a wide variety of CRM projects in the United States. Moreover, it is now possible for tribes to conduct their own CRM studies on tribal lands, which means that today some archaeologists actually work for Native American tribes.

Archaeological collaboration with Native Americans is evident in several places in this text. See the case study by Rhonda Foster, Larry Ross, and Dale Croes, "Archaeological/Anthropological Native American Coordination: An Example of Sharing the Research on the Northwest Coast of North America," in Chapter 5, and "Cultures in Contact at Colony Ross," by Kent Lightfoot et al., the case study in Chapter 7, for examples of archaeological projects that have involved direct native input. The discussion in Section F.3 of the Student CD is also relevant.

Of course, other descendant populations may be affected by archaeology. The same aspects of contemporary archaeology that have been promoting cooperation with Native Americans also have led to involvement with other ethnic groups. One example of the complexities involved in such interactions is provided in Box 1.2.

ISSUES AND DEBATES

BOX 1.2

Politics and Scholarship in the Investigation of New York City's African Burial Ground

The middle of Manhattan seems an unlikely place for a major archaeological discovery. It's not that there hasn't been a long history of human habitation, or even that the majority of that history already has been documented by written records (Cantwell and Wall 2001). Rather, it seems logical to assume that construction and development in Manhattan as the city grew have obliterated most of the earlier uses of this land. Realistically, how likely is it that intact cultural remains lie beneath the streets and tall buildings with their subbasements that now cover the island? In 1989, when the General Services Administration (GSA) announced plans to build a large federal office complex in lower Manhattan, few people anticipated the discovery of any significant remains. Nevertheless, following the procedures set out by various CRM laws, the project had to begin with research on the history of the site, including a determination of what if any archaeological materials might be preserved beneath the ground.

The initial researchers found that the lots on which the federal building was to be constructed included the city's dedicated African Burial Ground. Although most people think of slavery as part of the history of the Southeast, the Dutch began to bring African slaves to

New Amsterdam in 1626, and it is believed that just before they left the colony, 40 percent of the population consisted of enslaved Africans. The British continued to practice slavery, primarily because they needed the labor provided by slaves to run the thriving port and city. Thus, at the time of the American Revolution, New York had the second highest number of enslaved Africans of any colonial city (Harrington 1996). Beginning in 1697, applicable law forbade the burial of Africans in the New York's churchyards, and a spot then located away from the populated area was designated for the burial of Africans. Until 1790, when the expanding city grew into and over the area, thousands of free and enslaved Africans as well as some poor white people and possibly prisoners of war captured by the British during the American Revolution were buried there (Cantwell and Wall 2001, 281).

However interesting and historically significant the proposed construction site was, it seemed unlikely that two centuries of development and construction in lower Manhattan had left any of the original burials intact. Still, a careful record search suggested that if remains had been left undisturbed, they would be beneath a small alley that had been laid out in the 1790s. Thus, test excavations in this area were recommended, and they were begun in 1991, even as the larger project got under way. Everyone was in for a surprise, including the archaeologists. Not only were intact burials found beneath the alley, but it became clear that a deep layer of landfill had been dumped over the burying ground at the beginning of the nineteenth century so that, in fact, a good deal of it lay undisturbed, well beneath the probing of nineteenth- and twentieth-century construction projects. Eventually, over 400 human burials were uncovered at the site. What to do with this find and the excavated human remains was not settled without major controversy.

Historians, archaeologists, and preservationists knew that a tremendous amount of information about the lives of colonial period Africans could be gained from the recovery of the newly discovered graves and their contents. Research into the origins of the African slaves, their state of health, their retention of African culture, the work they did, and a host of other anthropological and biological matters could be explored. Yet retrieving this kind of information would mean very slow and painstaking work in the midst of a major construction site, and years of careful, detailed laboratory analysis of the finds. It would mean the expenditure of a large sum of money and the loss of millions more due to construction delays. Perhaps unsurprisingly, the GSA wanted to find the simplest and quickest way to remain in compliance with the law and get on with the construction of the office complex. The pressure on the archaeologists and the forensic anthropological team they had brought in to speed up their excavation, even to cut corners, was enormous. They were working 12-hour days, seven days a week, trying to maintain careful procedures but still satisfy their client, the GSA. This project had turned into a nightmare, but what they were discovering was terribly important!

Yet, neither the GSA nor, initially, the archaeologists had reckoned with another aspect of the significance of the African Burial Ground: its importance to African Americans interested in their slave heritage. Many African Americans saw the cemetery, remote and rude as it had been, as having belonged to their ancestors; it was one place Africans could congregate, and certainly, it had been a place of ritual significance as well. Moreover, its discovery afforded an opportunity to tell the story of the people as well as to honor their memory.

Predictably, conflict and misunderstanding erupted. Led by New York City's first African American mayor, David Dinkins, the African American community became increasingly assertive. They insisted that their ancestors buried at this spot had been discriminated against during their lives, and now, the GSA and the archaeologists were going to discriminate against them after death by not developing a new and thorough research design, by not exercising enough respect and care in their work, and by not properly curating and studying the recovered remains. Dinkins and others wanted African American archaeologists and scholars to be in charge so that the sacred and social significance of the site would not be overlooked, and they wanted a memorial to their ancestors. It became a classic American media circus. The GSA tried to stand firm; politicians up to the congressional level got involved; and prominent African American scholars inserted themselves into the situation. The original archaeological firm resigned.

Eventually, out of this chaos, people arrived at solutions that were largely beneficial to everyone. The GSA agreed to build only the office tower originally contemplated, not an adjacent four-story structure. Here, excavation was stopped and an estimated 200 burials left intact in the ground. A new, larger archaeological firm with experience in the excavation of African burials completed the excavation of exposed materials, and then the excavation was stopped. African American biological anthropologists and other scholars from Howard University in Washington, D.C., one of America's top historically black universities, took over the analysis of the human remains and graves. As a result, we have learned a tremendous amount, especially about the health and living conditions of these early African Americans; in addition, the history of Northern slavery during the colonial period has been illuminated. Finally, an on-site memorial was eventually built and the site became a National Monument in February 2006. In the fall of 2003, after years of careful study at Howard University, the skeletal materials were reinterred with the pomp and circumstance befitting the people on whose backs, both in life and in death, the great city of New York was built.

Looking back, we might express regret —that politics and the media exacerbated a difficult situation—or we might say that it simply takes clout to achieve the preservation of cultural resources in our society today. We might consider it unfortunate that activist ethnic communities can determine the course of scientific projects, or we might consider involvement and respect for descendant communities to be the only ethical course. We might say that it was unfair that the hard work of the original archaeologists was not deemed adequate, or we might say that this story proves the need for minority scholars. We might bemoan the information lost to construction or even in leaving some skeletons undisturbed, or we might celebrate the information eventually gained (Blakey and Hill 2004; Medford 2004). There are many possible perspectives. Nevertheless, it is clear that modern archaeological research does not take place in a social vacuum, nor is it so esoteric that only archaeologists care. It also should be clear that great archaeological finds can still be made, even in unlikely places. We all stand to learn about our past provided we can sort out the complexities of the modern contexts within which archaeology is done.

Other Stakeholders

A wide variety of people who are not archaeologists or scholars in allied fields like history interact with archaeologists in a diverse way. We shall consider two groups: educators and private collectors.

As archaeologists have become more involved in managing cultural resources, they have naturally become more focused on interpreting these resources for the public (Jameson 1997). In fact, a public education component may be required in CRM contracts. Museum and university archaeologists often have interest in public education as well. Today's archaeologists give public talks about their work but also develop curricula for schoolchildren, plan museum exhibits, hold teachers' workshops, and organize volunteer programs. In this work, they collaborate with museum educators, teachers, historic preservationists, and a host of other specialists involved in education and cultural tourism. Most states also have annual archaeology months, and many offer special programs to schoolchildren such as essay contests or volunteer digs. As a result, a growing number of educators and other specialists have become knowledgeable about archaeology, and some are involved with archaeological organizations like the Society for American Archaeology or state avocational groups. Today's archaeologists must not overlook the expertise of these individuals in communicating with students and the rest of the public.

The potential contribution of private **collectors**, those who accumulate artifacts and art for personal enjoyment and financial gain, is harder to determine. There is some disagreement among archaeologists today about the private collection of artifacts. Many archaeologists believe that even legal artifact collecting only fuels the looting of sites and the dispersion of artifacts that together might be informative. Some private collectors have come into possession of very important artifacts and are willing to share information about these artifacts with archaeologists. These individuals may maintain that their activities actually protect artifacts from languishing unseen and unused in museums, universities, and other repositories. Archaeologists generally do not believe these are valid arguments, but some are more willing than others to use private collections in the pursuit of what happened in the past.

One controversial collector is Forest Fenn, who has acquired some important Paleoindian material. He also owns property in New Mexico on which he has been excavating a pueblo site. Fenn offered local archaeologists an opportunity to document what he was recovering. Some archaeologists believed it was important to record the material for science, even if it was going into a private collection or might be sold to support further excavation. Other archaeologists thought it better to let the material go unrecorded than to have anything to do with a collector who would sell artifacts. Fenn was also the principal organizer of the Clovis and Beyond conference in Santa Fe in 1999. A great deal of important information about the first settlers of the New World (see Chapter 3) was exchanged at this conference. Even though the Museum of New Mexico and two departments of the Smithsonian Institution also were sponsors, other archaeologists felt that attending the conference wrongly legitimized Fenn. This example illustrates the complexity of ethical dilemmas involving private collectors.

AN OVERVIEW OF THE ARCHAEOLOGICAL PROCESS

Professional archaeologists make their living by studying what others might call trash. It is from the things that people left behind that we learn what happened in the past—how people made their living, how they arranged themselves and their settlements on the landscape, how they governed themselves, how they interacted with one another, how they died, and how their loved ones treated them after they passed away. Archaeologists study artifacts, ecofacts, features, and their patterned relationships in the ground or on the ground surface, to make inferences about past lifeways. This is true for all archaeologists, but the goals and sources of funding for research investigations conducted by academics and for cultural resource management studies are somewhat different.

Projects conducted by colleges, universities, and museums look at the past for answers to specific research questions. Although some colleges and universities have conducted projects as "classroom" exercises with the primary goal of training students, most archaeologists work within the framework of **conservation archaeology** and regard archaeological sites as irreplaceable resources that should be preserved, as opposed to excavated if at all possible. As a result, archaeological sites are considered too important to be sacrificed to student training alone, and field school excavations (Figure 1.11) also are directed at answering important research questions about the past. Academic research projects are generally funded by grants, although student fees and the institution's budget may also make contributions to the costs of the research. Grants are made by federal agencies such as the National Science Foundation or the National Park Service and by private foundations like the National Geographic Society and the Wenner-Gren Foundation. Numerous small grants are made by states and other organizations as well. The granting process generally requires a detailed proposal that explains the **research design** or what the project intends to find out and the justification for the work proposed. Specific research questions are stated, and the plan for gathering the necessary data is presented.

FIGURE 1.11 Field school students at the Mary Rinn site learning to set up excavation units. They learned excavation techniques as part of research concerning the Late Prehistoric period in western Pennsylvania.

As indicated earlier, government agencies like the U.S. Forest Service and the Army Corps of Engineers as well as consulting firms under contract to agencies or private clients, also perform archaeological studies. These studies are done as part of the environmental permitting process, often in conjunction with **Environmental Impact Statements (EISs)**, which assess the environmental impacts of a proposed undertaking. These documents are required by laws designed to ensure that before issuing permits for land-altering activities, governments have considered archaeological sites, historical structures, and **traditional cultural properties (TCPs)**, places that have a special meaning to members of an ethnic group or community. Federal agencies are also required to inventory and manage the archaeological sites and historical properties on lands they own.

Cultural resource management studies are funded either by the governmental agency doing the land-modifying project or by the entity requesting the federal permit. These latter entities may be private companies proposing projects like new gas pipelines, or they may be state or local governments proposing new roads or urban renewal projects. In fact, local laws relating to historic properties may be just as important to the protection of archaeological sites as federal legislation, especially in densely populated areas coping with urban sprawl.

Although governmental agencies perform archaeological studies for their projects, private companies or university research divisions conduct much of the cultural resource management archaeology done today. These companies contract with the agency doing the work or with the private company seeking the permit. Contracts are often awarded through a competitive bid process with cost to the client most often (but not always) the major factor in the award decision. This chapter's case study, "The Pueblo Grande Project: An Example of Multidisciplinary Research in a Compliance Setting," by Cory Breternitz and Christine Robinson, illustrates the nature of a large CRM project.

Archaeological investigations involve both fieldwork and laboratory analyses. Fieldwork may start with searching records about known site locations followed by finding new **archaeological sites**. An archaeological site is any location at which there are material remains of the human past. Sometimes this discovery is fortuitous, but often sites are found as part of an **archaeological site survey**, a field program that systematically locates, identifies, and records sites (Figure 1.12). Such surveys often are required in CRM investigations. The various techniques that can be employed in finding sites systematically are described in the Student CD, Section B. During the survey, artifacts are often collected from the surface of the sites or are picked up as **isolated artifacts**, items not found on archaeological sites.

When sites are thought to contain information relevant to research questions or when they are likely to be destroyed by anticipated activities, they are excavated. Testing may be used to determine if sites are worthy of extensive excavation, and **geophysical prospecting** may be conducted. Geophysical prospecting is the use of such special techniques as **ground-penetrating radar (GPR)**, which provide subsurface information without excavation. These techniques allow archaeologists to target their excavations more precisely, and they reduce both the labor expended in excavation and the destruction of sites. Nevertheless, full-scale excavations still are required, particularly when site destruction by development is inevitable. During excavation, artifacts and other remains are collected, their positions in the site soils are recorded, features are explored, and the site is documented. The Student CD, Section B, provides more description of the specific techniques used in excavation.

FIGURE 1.12 Field crew surveying in parallel transects on Otay Mesa near the Mexican border in California.

FIGURE 1.13 A lithic analyst records information about the attributes of projectile points.

Excavation is not the end of the process, however; it is actually the beginning. Following fieldwork, the finds are cleaned and **cataloged**, that is, inventoried and assigned unique numbers that associate each item with the location at which it was found. Only then can materials be analyzed. Analysis involves the study of the recovered artifacts and ecofacts (Figure 1.13) according to archaeological

typologies, which are archaeological systems of classification or, when appropriate, in accordance with biological systems of classification. Analysis also involves the dating of objects, the determination of how they were used, and in some instances sourcing, which involves determining where an item originated. Studies of the spatial distribution of sites, artifacts, ecofacts, and features also may make use of **Geographical Information Systems (GIS)**, which retrieve, store, and manipulate geographic data. In archaeology, GIS can be used to compare site distributions against environmental information and also to analyze the location of features and artifacts at a site. Section C of the Student CD provides more information about analytical procedures commonly used by archaeologists.

The final step in the laboratory phase of archaeological investigations is packaging artifacts and ecofacts for **curation**. Curating archaeological materials is more than just storing them. In proper curation facilities (Figure 1.14), artifacts and other archaeological materials are stored under conditions that keep them from deteriorating, but they are also available for use in public education and for future study by archaeologists as new techniques are developed. It is important to realize that archaeologists cannot study every possible aspect of the materials they recover, nor can they anticipate every new analytic technique that may be developed. For these reasons, the long-term curation of collections, which may allow later reanalysis even after a site is destroyed, is particularly important. At least three of our case studies illustrate the use of collections. These are "Weaponry of Clovis Hunters at Blackwater Draw," by Anthony Boldurian (Student CD, Section D.2), "Mouse Creek Phase Households and Communities: Mississippian Period Towns in Southeastern Tennessee," by Lynne Sullivan (Chapter 11), and "A New History of Maize-Bean-Squash Agriculture in the Northeast," by John Hart (Chapter 13), all of which utilized existing collections to conduct significant research.

Are all collections properly cared for? Unfortunately, the answer is no. Some older collections have never been properly cataloged while the large size of CRM collections has sometimes proved overwhelming. As explained in "The Curation Crisis" (Student CD, Section F.2), today, there are more collections than there are places, space, and funding to care for them. There is a growing awareness of this problem within the archaeological community, and innovative solutions have sometimes been developed, but none is a cure-all.

When research is completed, archaeologists are obligated to share the information they have acquired with other archaeologists, agency managers, their clients, and the public. This is done in a variety of ways. Granting organizations require reports from research archaeologists at the end of the project and may require progress reports throughout the course of the work. The results of the investigations may be published in monographs or articles in scholarly journals. Cultural resource management contracts also result in reports to the funding or permitting agencies. The reports are reviewed by specialists at the agencies as well as by the state historic preservations officer (SHPO). Sometimes the results of cultural resource management reports are published, but most often they languish in the storehouses of agencies and state clearinghouses as part of the vast, unpublished **gray literature**. Despite attempts to create report repositories, researchers often have a hard time finding copies of gray-literature reports, making use of the information difficult. Some large cultural resource management

FIGURE 1.14 Artifacts at the Hopewell Culture National Historical Park in Ohio are carefully stored so that they can be studied by researchers or used in exhibits.

projects have produced a full series of reports, and some private companies do in-house publishing of at least some of their reports. Other firms have made arrangements with publishers and make some of their reports available through this mechanism. Nevertheless, the problem of how to provide access to the information in the gray literature remains a great concern to North American archaeologists. Finally, archaeologists increasingly recognize an obligation to share their findings with the public, and popular articles, public talks, web presentations, and even videos aimed at the public rather than the scholarly community are becoming more common.

Other Ways to Learn About the Past

Fieldwork and laboratory analysis are not the only ways archaeologists learn about the past. When available and relevant, historical records are consulted. **Ethnohistory** is a field allied to archaeology. It is the use of historical documents, ethnographic accounts, linguistic data, ecology, and archaeology to provide insight into recent cultures. Although ethnohistory has a long tradition in American scholarship, it has become popular recently both with Native American tribes, which are developing cultural centers, and in the environmental review process. This multidisciplinary approach is often used to document sacred sites and traditional cultural properties for consideration in the planning of development projects.

Ethnoarchaeology also helps archaeologists build understanding of the patterns discernible in the archaeological record. In ethnoarchaeology, the researcher observes living people to see how their behavior creates the archaeological record. Questions like "Do living flintknappers leave their **debitage** where it falls, or do they clean up after themselves?" and "Where are waste bones discarded after meals?" provide a basis for making inferences about past behaviors when similar patterns are found in the archaeological record. As one example, ethnoarchaeologists have done important work with the breakage rates of pots and the numbers and kinds of pots households use. Such quantitative information can provide a basis for estimating the length of occupation of a site and the number of households that lived there.

You may look at illustrations in this book and wonder, "How was that stone tool made?" or "How much effort did it take to build a mound like that?" Answers to questions like this are the realm of **experimental archaeology** and replicative studies. Here, researchers try to duplicate features of the archaeological record to better our understanding of that record (Figure 1.15). Experimental archaeologists have built pithouses to see how well our notions about the structures work, and then burned them down to find out how charred beams, artifacts stored in and on the roofs, and the remains of the roof covering are distributed in the pit after the fire. Both ethnoarchaeology and experimental archaeology contribute to the development of **middle-range theory**—theory that is aimed at understanding the meaning of patterning in the archaeological record. Experimental archaeology is part of two case studies in this text: "Weaponry of Clovis Hunters at Blackwater Draw," by Anthony Boldurian (Student CD, Section D.2), and "A New History of Maize-Bean-Squash Agriculture in the Northeast," by John Hart (Chapter 13).

FIGURE 1.15
Archaeologists built this reconstruction of the framework supporting a Late Prehistoric Monongahela house in conjunction with Pennsylvania Archaeology Month public programs, but they also clarified their understanding of such structures and their construction in the process.

CHAPTER SUMMARY

In this chapter we have introduced the nature of North American archaeology and its contemporary practice. The following points have been made:

- Archaeology is the study of past human behavior and culture through the study of material remains.

- This text introduces the body of knowledge that archaeologists working in North America north of central Mexico have developed through their studies, but it also familiarizes readers with the nature of archaeological practice among contemporary archaeologists.

- North American archaeology is a type of anthropology, the holistic study of the physical, cultural, and social aspects of humans in all times and places. It originated in the study of the native peoples of North America following settlement by people of European descent.

- North American archaeology is a form of social science because it proceeds by making observations in the natural world, forming hypotheses based on these observations, and testing the hypotheses against other natural evidence.

- North American archaeological research contributes to scholarly understanding of the past, but it differs from historical research because it interprets material remains rather than written records.

- The field of North American archaeology did not develop as a profession until the early twentieth century, when universities began to offer anthropology programs with archaeological training as a component.
- North American archaeologists traditionally have worked in museum or university settings. Today, however, many are employed in cultural resource management positions either in the government or in the private sector, where they manage archaeological resources or conduct investigations as part of federal, state, or local undertakings.
- Avocational archaeologists can be distinguished from pothunters and relic hunters because they follow archaeological procedures, particularly those of recording information, work closely with professionals, and do not buy and sell artifacts for personal gain.
- Native Americans as well as other descendant populations have begun to assert control over their own cultural heritage, changing the practice of North American archaeology to a more collaborative, though sometimes also more complicated, undertaking.
- Relic hunters and collectors and educators and their students play various roles in the contemporary archaeological scene, and professionals must take each of these groups into account as they work to understand our past.
- Archaeological investigations in both academic and CRM settings may involve archaeological surveys, excavations, laboratory analyses, cataloging of collections, curation of collections, and report writing.
- Archaeologists also use the methods of ethnohistorical research, ethnoarchaeological investigation, and experimental archaeology to understand the past of North America.

We hope that this chapter has begun to convey an understanding of the nature and methods of North American archaeology. Because the text focuses mostly on what archaeologists have learned about North America's past, Chapter 2 will provide an introduction to North American cultures and environments as well as discuss some broad themes in North America's past.

SUGGESTIONS FOR FURTHER READING

For more information on the nature of archaeology and its methods:

Thomas, David Hurst, and Robert L. Kelly. 2006. *Archaeology*, 4th ed. Belmont, CA: Thomson/Wadsworth.

For a classic source on the history of American archaeology:

Willey, Gordon R., and Jeremy A. Sabloff. 1993. *A History of American Archaeology*, 3rd ed. San Francisco: W. H. Freeman.

For more information on specific archaeological field methods:

Hester, Thomas R., Harry J. Schafer, and Kenneth L. Feder. 1997. *Field Methods in Archaeology*, 7th ed. Mountain View, CA: Mayfield.

Stewart, R. Michael. 2002. *Archaeology: Basic Field Methods*. Dubuque, IA: Kendall/Hunt.

For more information on specific methods of archaeological laboratory analysis:

Sutton, Mark Q., and Brooke S. Arkush. 2002. *Archaeological Laboratory Methods: An Introduction,* 3rd ed. Dubuque, IA: Kendall/Hunt.

For more on CRM archaeology:

King, Thomas F. 1998. *Cultural Resource Laws and Practice: An Introductory Guide.* Walnut Creek, CA: AltaMira Press.
Neumann, Thomas W., and Robert M. Sanford. 2001. *Cultural Resources Archaeology: An Introduction.* Walnut Creek, CA: AltaMira Press.

For more on archaeological curation:

Sullivan, Lynne P., and S. Terry Childs. 2003. *Archaeologist's Toolkit,* Vol. 6, *Curating Archaeological Collections: From the Field to the Repository.* Walnut Creek, CA: AltaMira Press.

OTHER RESOURCES

Sections H and I of the Student CD supply web links, places to visit, additional discussion questions, and other study aids. The Student CD also contains a variety of additional resources, including a complete list of references (Section G) for this chapter as cited in the text. See, in particular, "A Brief History of North American Archaeology" (Section A), "Archaeological Fieldwork" (Section B), "Archaeological Laboratory Analysis" (Section C), "Investigating the Ripley Site: A Century of Investigations," by Sarah Neusius (Section D.1), "Arthur Parker, Archaeologist and Museologist" (Section E.1), "Linda Mayro, Pima County Cultural Resources Manager" (Section E.2), "What Do Professors and CRM Archaeologists Think of Each Other?" (Section F.1), and "The Curation Crisis" (Section F.2).

CASE STUDY

A great deal of contemporary North American archaeology is done in the context of cultural resource management as **compliance archaeology**—archaeological investigations performed to meet the requirements of laws and regulations rather than as basic research. Although this means that location and scope are dictated by the parameters of the overall project, it also means that archaeological investigations are conducted in places such as growing urban areas that otherwise might not be excavated. In this case study, the construction of an expressway in Phoenix required testing of the highway right-of-way. The project area went through a portion of Pueblo Grande, a large **Hohokam** village ruin that the City of Phoenix maintains as a cultural park. As you will learn in Chapter 9, *Hohokam* is the name archaeologists have given to the major cultural tradition that developed in southern

Arizona well over a thousand years ago. Testing of the right-of-way revealed an unexpected number of features including human burials dating to the Hohokam Classic period. These burials had to be removed and then rapidly returned to Native descendants. Although some of the original topics of interest could not be explored, multidisciplinary analyses have yielded important insights into the health of Classic period Hohokam people and into the environment in the Phoenix Basin just prior to the disappearance of this culture from southern Arizona around 600 years ago. As you read this case study, pay particular attention to the steps in the CRM process and to the surprises the archaeologists received as the project unfolded. Ask yourself, as well, if we would know what we now do about the Hohokam and their demise if CRM investigations had not been required.

THE PUEBLO GRANDE PROJECT
An Example of Multidisciplinary Research in a Compliance Setting

Cory Dale Breternitz and Christine K. Robinson

PUEBLO GRANDE IN A MODERN CONTEXT

In 2004 Phoenix, Arizona, surpassed Philadelphia as the fifth largest city in the United States. Rapid growth in the city and in the greater metropolitan area has been occurring for the past two decades. The increase in population has led to a building boom that includes housing, commercial development, and the necessary infrastructure to support greater numbers of people. As a result of federal, state, and other publicly funded projects, southern Arizona in general and the Phoenix metropolitan area in particular support some of the largest and oldest private CRM consulting firms in the country. Major freeway construction projects in the 1980s in the Phoenix metropolitan area provided the start-up opportunities for many private archaeology consulting firms, such as Soil Systems, Inc. (SSI), that assist state and federal agencies in reaching compliance with state and federal historic preservation legislation (Roberts et al. 2004). The number of CRM companies registered to do business in Arizona reflects the number of compliance-based projects that are being undertaken every year in one of the fastest growing states in the country.

The Phoenix Basin is defined geographically by linear mountain ranges typical of the Basin and Range Province, which includes all of southern Arizona, Nevada, southern Oregon, and southeastern California. The three largest rivers in southern Arizona all converge in the western Phoenix Basin. The Santa Cruz River flows into the Gila River just south of the basin, and the Salt River joins the Gila River in the western margins of the Phoenix Basin. Prior to the construction of dams in the early twentieth century, the Gila and Salt rivers provided the Arizona Sonoran Desert with a year-round water supply (Figure 1.16). Ironically, the historic occupation of the Phoenix Basin and the founding of the largest cities in Arizona did not become possible until dams had been built to control the Gila and Salt rivers. For over a millennium, control and management of the available water supply in the Sonoran Desert has been the key

element to survival in this harsh and fragile landscape. A reliable water supply continues to be most important in accommodating future growth and in maintaining a sustainable population.

Visitors to the Phoenix metropolitan area today see an urban oasis supporting over 1.5 million people surrounded by an arid, seemingly inhospitable desert landscape. Yet, Phoenix has thousands of acres of green grass, palm trees, parks, lakes, and canals. One-third of Arizona's population resides in Maricopa County. Yet strikingly, other than the artificial lakes and canals, there is no apparent natural water source. The contrast between the artificial urban oasis and the surrounding desert gives the impression that day-to-day survival could not have been possible without modern amenities. Visitors and long-time residents alike are amazed to learn that the Phoenix Basin and the Salt and Gila River valleys supported one of the most successful and technologically advanced prehistoric societies in pre-Columbian North America.

The Hohokam culture thrived in southern Arizona for over a thousand years and included large villages with thousands of permanent residents. The Hohokam built public architecture, including large artificial **platform mounds**, **ball courts**, and multi-storied **great houses**, and controlled an extensive trade network for the exchange of exotic and utilitarian goods. This society owed its existence to over a thousand miles of well-engineered irrigation canals that harnessed, controlled, and distributed the most highly valued commodity—water. The sophisticated network of canals invented and engineered by the Hohokam distributed domestic and agricultural water to thousands of prehistoric residents in the Phoenix Basin and irrigated tens of thousands of hectares of agricultural land between 1500 and 600 years ago (AD 500–1400). Today, urban sprawl and agricultural fields largely cover evidence of the Hohokam. To the untrained eye there is little visible evidence for the Hohokam remaining in southern Arizona, yet the Sonoran Desert is dotted with thousands of archaeological sites consisting of adobe compounds, platform and trash mounds, ball courts, and over a dozen great houses.

FIGURE 1.16 Locations of Pueblo Grande and other major Hohokam sites in central Arizona.

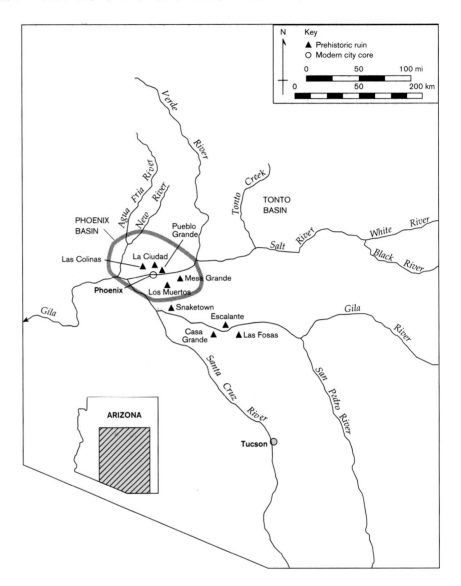

The most famous Hohokam site is Casa Grande National Monument in Coolidge, Arizona, on the Gila River 40 miles (65 km) south of Phoenix. Casa Grande was the first archaeological monument to be designated by Congress and is protected by the National Park Service. Unlike the more famous Ancestral Pueblo culture in the Four-Corners and Colorado Plateau region of northern Arizona, represented by dozens of archaeological sites in the National Park System, the Hohokam culture is underrepresented by parks and monuments and is largely unknown to the general public.

At the headgates of the largest canal system in the Phoenix Basin, Canal System 2, was Pueblo Grande, or Big Town, one of the largest and longest-lived Hohokam village sites (Figure 1.17). Pueblo Grande was occupied for nearly 800 years. At its greatest extent, the village covered nearly one square mile (2.59 km²) and had over a thousand permanent residents. Prominent southwestern archaeologists

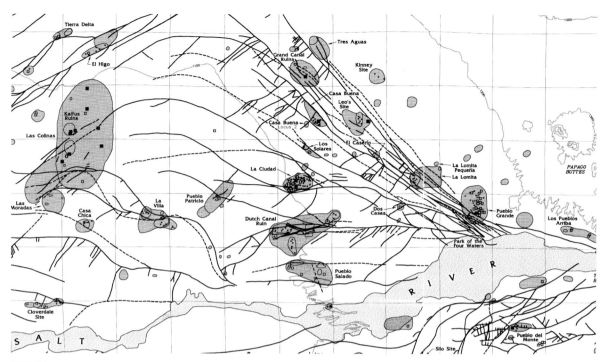

FIGURE 1.17 Canal system 2 with Pueblo Grande at its head is just part of the extensive system of canals built by the Hohokam in the Phoenix Basin.

have studied Pueblo Grande for more than a century. The first archaeological work at Pueblo Grande occurred in the late 1800s, when Adolph Bandelier visited the site and Frank Hamilton Cushing conducted the first excavations. Early scholars observed the site before the expansion of agriculture, industry, and urbanization in later decades destroyed most of the surface features. Pueblo Grande was then described as an extensive area of small mounds and ruins on the north side of the Salt River, dominated by a large platform mound and a multistory adobe tower, the Great House (see Downum and Bostwick 1993). The Pueblo Grande mound is one of the largest monumental mounds in the western United States, and the Great House was one of a handful of similar Hohokam structures, of which only the one at Casa Grande National Monument remains today.

Omar Turney and Frank Midvale, who mapped the extensive Hohokam canal systems throughout the Phoenix Basin in the 1920s through 1940s, recognized the prominence of Pueblo Grande. It is primarily

through the efforts of Turney and Midvale that we know the extent of the Hohokam irrigation system and the many sites along these miles of canals that now lie buried beneath metropolitan Phoenix. By the 1920s, the Great House at Pueblo Grande had been destroyed, but the City of Phoenix succeeded in preserving the mound by establishing a cultural park that eventually grew to include over 100 acres (40 hectares) in the southern part of the site. The foresight on the part of the city has preserved the most visible features of the site. The rest of Pueblo Grande has remained in private hands and been subjected to urban development.

Between the 1920s and mid-1980s, excavations at Pueblo Grande were carried out by several researchers, mostly in and around the platform mound and the area to the west of the mound. Although these efforts were conducted for a variety of purposes and were not part of an integrated research plan, they resulted in the excavation and study of at least 400 houses and burials, a ball court, several trash mounds, and irrigation features. These efforts also resulted in a basic understanding of the construction and use history of the mound and helped establish that the southern part of the site was occupied from before 1200 **BP** (see Chapter 2 for discussion of dating conventions in archaeology). The mound itself belongs to a later part of the sequence (for summaries, see Bostwick and Downum 1994; Downum and Bostwick 1993).

Today, Pueblo Grande is at the intersection of major transportation corridors, which include freeway interchanges, important surface transportation arteries, a transcontinental railroad, and the sixth busiest passenger and freight airport in the country. This location has placed Pueblo Grande at the center of commercial development and has had major impacts on this significant cultural resource. Ironically, it is this concept of a central place that created Pueblo Grande originally. Pueblo Grande's location at the head of the largest prehistoric canal system, which provided domestic and irrigation water to numerous large villages and thousands of prehistoric residents downstream, allowed Pueblo Grande to become prominent in the Hohokam settlement and social systems.

In the early 1980s, planners in Phoenix realized that an urban freeway system was needed to accommodate increasing population growth. The Arizona Department of Transportation (ADOT) was the state agency responsible for constructing the freeway system throughout the Phoenix Basin. The aptly named Hohokam Expressway was designed to connect urban freeway corridors to Sky Harbor International Airport, which is less than a mile from Pueblo Grande. As a state agency, ADOT must comply with the Arizona Antiquities Act and is required to evaluate and mitigate any impacts to cultural resources that might result from any construction project. The Hohokam Expressway was to be constructed through a portion of Pueblo Grande adjacent to the city-owned park. The preferred alignment would cut a north-to-south swath through the site and destroy approximately 20 percent of the eastern edge of Pueblo Grande.

ADOT asked for proposals for the **mitigation** of the information loss that would be incurred at Pueblo Grande when the freeway was constructed. Qualified archaeological firms including our company, Soil Systems, Inc., prepared technical proposals for a **data recovery program** that was to be reviewed and approved by ADOT, the State Historic Preservation Officer, and the City of Phoenix. A research design

that posed questions to be addressed with the data and artifacts recovered by the excavations was required. SSI's data recovery plan also had a public education and outreach component, outlined the field and laboratory methods to be used, discussed the company's qualifications to undertake the job, and named the key personnel who would be part of the research team. The results of the project had to be published, and all artifacts and data recovered during the excavations and subsequent analysis, including all photographs, maps, field notes, and analytical data, were to be permanently taken care of at the Pueblo Grande Museum.

IMPLEMENTING A RESEARCH DESIGN AND WORK PLAN IN AN URBAN ENVIRONMENT

SSI was awarded the contract for the archaeological data recovery at Pueblo Grande in 1987. Since only a few sherds were visible on the modern ground surface, and it was unclear if there were any subsurface deposits, the first stage of the fieldwork was to conduct systematic testing of the entire project area. Testing began with the excavation of 398 systematic backhoe trenches, each 10 meters (33 ft) long throughout the entire freeway corridor, supplemented by 206 judgmental trenches. Systematic trenches were placed at set intervals, while judgmental trenches were placed where project archaeologists suspected important remains might be found. This allowed us to quantify the types and condition or degree of disturbance (**integrity**) of the prehistoric deposits in the project area. One of the initial questions centered on the preservation of any houses, burials, or pits (features). What, if anything, was left in the project area, and what was the condition of any found items? Were there any data to recover, or had the buildings and feedlots that covered the freeway corridor destroyed everything? Many, including ADOT, suspected that most of the prehistoric features in the project area had been destroyed. The results of the backhoe trenching showed numerous prehistoric features, including hundreds of human burials. Another surprise was that the features that were present dated almost exclusively to the Classic period (800–550 BP).

Despite extensive excavations at other Hohokam sites in the Phoenix area, largely associated with other ADOT freeway projects, very few features dating to this part of the Hohokam sequence had been investigated. Because the Classic is the last major period of the Hohokam occupation, Classic period remains at any Hohokam site tend to be the closest to the modern ground surface. Consequently, these remains are usually the first to be destroyed by modern development. Because the Hohokam Expressway project area contained prehistoric features that dated almost exclusively to the Classic period, and because there were so many burials, a major shift in the data recovery field strategy was required. Very little was known about the Classic period in the Phoenix Basin. Besides, the burials had to be recovered, which meant sampling was replaced by nearly 100 percent recovery of remains.

At the conclusion of the testing phase, SSI had a good understanding of what types of prehistoric features were present and their distribution across the project area. Nevertheless, the excavation phase of the Pueblo Grande Project required innovation because so many features were distributed over such a large area. A stripping bucket was specially developed that consisted of a toothless backhoe bucket nearly 4 feet wide (1.22 m), attached to the arm of a backhoe. This allowed the backhoe operator to remove a 4-foot-wide swath of overburden in a highly controlled manner, sometimes only a few inches at a time. An archaeologist monitored all stripping of the

overburden, and when nearly 80 acres had been stripped, the tops of buried features lay exposed, increasing excavation and mapping efficiency. Areas that contained stratified deposits were stripped multiple times. Once all the exposed features had been excavated and recorded, they were stripped away to expose any underlying features.

This methodology revealed clusters of habitation architecture, including pithouses and aboveground adobe structures surrounded by encircling adobe walls (Figure 1.18). These clusters of habitation structures, referred to as compounds by students of the Hohokam, were called habitation areas. Clusters of inhumation and cremation burials were found adjacent to each habitation area. These burial clusters were referred to as burial groups. Fourteen habitation areas and 17 burial groups were identified in the Hohokam Expressway project area. Scattered throughout the project area and associated with the habitation areas and burial groups were hundreds of undifferentiated pit features, **borrow pits**, roasting pits, and trash deposits (Figure 1.19).

The Pueblo Grande Project research design initially developed by SSI (Foster 1994) addressed site structure, socioeconomic organization, and interaction patterns by emphasizing **households**—archaeological remains reflecting family units that had lived together and cooperated economically. Other research goals

FIGURE 1.18 Overview of Pueblo Grande during the Hohokam Expressway Project, showing work on architecture.

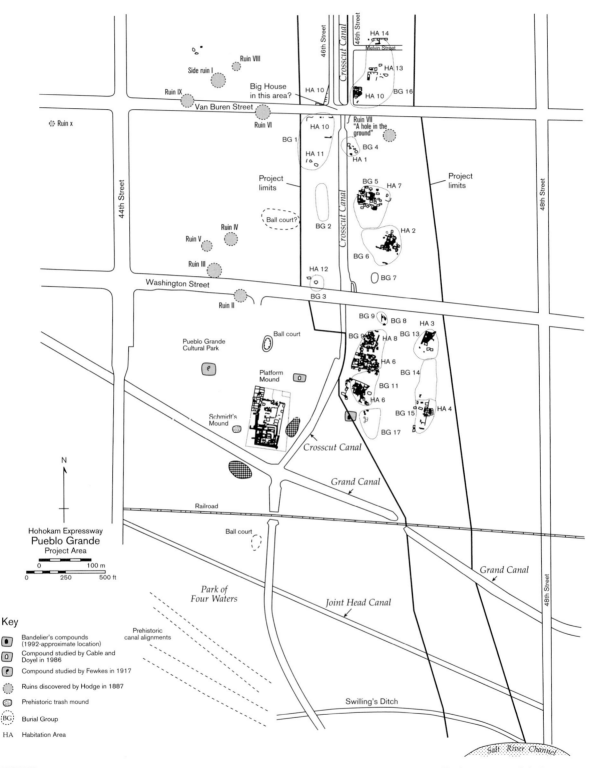

FIGURE 1.19 Distribution of habitation areas and burial groups in the Hohokam Expressway Project area and their relation to known features at Pueblo Grande. (Data from Soil Systems, Inc. Computer cartography by GEO-MAP, Inc., 1982.)

included paleoenvironmental reconstruction, the examination of mortuary patterns, and **bioarchaeological** or skeletal analyses. In many respects, the research goals were successfully met. The excavations demonstrated that the site underwent a dramatic expansion after 850 BP (AD 1100), during the Classic period.

However, we had mixed success obtaining data to address some questions. Most significantly, households proved to be largely unworkable as units of analysis. The long, continuous site occupation, which included ongoing use, remodeling, and modification, left relatively few unmixed and undisturbed contexts other than burials. Enormous quantities of discarded artifacts accumulated over the centuries left large amounts of temporally mixed deposits and a low proportion of nonburial features that had temporally recognizable contents reflecting specific behaviors. Very few houses with intact, associated artifact **assemblages** were encountered, probably because houses were routinely cleaned out before being abandoned, so that the bulk of artifact assemblages from houses consisted of refuse that washed into the empty structures. Nonetheless, some observations about changes in site structure over time were possible. We were able to identify groupings of houses or habitation areas and associated burial groups that reflected social entities larger than households, and these socially related groups could be compared across a large part of the site.

Another set of unforeseen problems related to burials. We didn't anticipate the poor condition of the human remains, and osteological analysis was conducted only after the remains were removed to the laboratory. As a result, the collection of measurements and observations of some types was limited because the bone further deteriorated after it was removed from the ground. Because of an accelerated schedule of **repatriation**, or return of remains to the Native American descendants, the remains were reburied before we could conduct dental analyses that would have assessed the cultural affiliation of the burial population. On the other hand, the bioarchaeological research team did complete some analyses on the human remains and so was able to make observations about aspects of nutrition and health.

To successfully accomplish an urban archaeological project of the magnitude of the Pueblo Grande Project, SSI enlisted the assistance of many outside consultants and experts. We established a peer review team consisting of experts in Hohokam research to review all aspects of the fieldwork, analysis, and interpretation. SSI also hired several experts for the analysis and interpretation of specific artifact classes such as shell artifacts, **obsidian** sourcing, argillite sourcing, analysis of faunal (animal) bone, turquoise sourcing, pollen analysis, human osteology, and mortuary patterns. Throughout the course of the five-year project, SSI met with the multidisciplinary research team members in the field and at our office to discuss the results. This allowed all project team members to interact and to question, debate, and discuss analytical results. Thus, each analyst was able to become familiar with the results of the other analysts. Everyone kept in touch with the big picture that was developing and provided input into the overall research. By maintaining a flexible research strategy, we were able to refocus the research goals of the project to accommodate the data that were being recovered. As the project developed, the concepts of environmental degradation, poor health, and nutritional stress of the Classic period Hohokam population at Pueblo Grande became the focus of our research.

PUEBLO GRANDE DURING THE CLASSIC PERIOD

The Pueblo Grande Project resulted in the complete excavation of over 40 acres of the site, including 807 burials, over 300 houses, and more than 1600 other prehistoric features, the vast majority of which dated to the Classic period. Project results were reported in a multivolume report series (Breternitz 1994), an edited synthetic volume (Abbott 2003), an award-winning doctoral dissertation (Abbott 2000), peer-reviewed articles, and numerous topic-specific technical reports, conference papers, and master's theses. The project cost over $4.5 million and was the largest, single study of a major Hohokam village to date. It also revolutionized our understanding of the Hohokam Classic period.

We now know that the Classic period was a time of many changes for the Hohokam (Abbott 2003). These changes were manifested in architecture, ceramics, trade and exchange, burial practices, and sociopolitical organization. At Pueblo Grande there was as much change during the 250-year Classic period, as in the previous 400-year transition from Sedentary to Classic. During the Classic period at

Pueblo Grande, we defined the Soho phase as lasting between 800 BP and 650 BP (AD 1150–1300), and the Civano phase, which lasted a relatively short period of time, no longer than 100 years between 650 BP and 550 BP (AD 1300–1400). A Polvorón phase (600+ to 525 or 500 BP/AD 1350+ to 1425 or 1450) is also identifiable at Pueblo Grande.

During the Soho phase, population at Pueblo Grande increased over that of the preceding Sacaton phase (Abbott 2003). We have attributed this increase to the immigration into Pueblo Grande of peoples living elsewhere in the Phoenix Basin (Van Gerven and Sheridan 1994). During this period of aggregation and population increase, health, subsistence, and the availability of natural resources appear to have been in decline in comparison to the previous periods (Kwiatkowski 1994; Van Gerven and Sheridan 1994). The aggregation of population at Pueblo Grande during the Soho phase related in part to a general degradation of the local environment brought about by 600 years of intensive use of the Phoenix Basin by the Hohokam (Kwiatkowski 1994). Things began to go badly for the Hohokam living at Pueblo Grande during the Soho phase. During the Civano phase, things got worse.

We noted the appearance of compound architecture and changes in exchange networks, artifact assemblages, and burial practices occurred during the Civano phase. Pithouses arranged around courtyard groups gave way to the construction of compounds—aboveground adobe structures surrounded by enclosing walls. Platform mounds and ball courts were abandoned, and great houses appeared at some of the larger primary Hohokam centers in the Salt and Gila River valleys. The Pueblo Grande data suggest that the appearance of compounds of pithouses and surface structures enclosed by adobe walls during the Civano phase coincided with a population decline both in actual numbers of people living at the site and in their general health. Compound architecture may have been an attempt by the Hohokam to establish physical boundaries between their closest neighbors because resources had become so scarce.

To reconstruct the Classic period environment surrounding Pueblo Grande, our research team used contemporary and historical information to approximate the prehistoric plant communities within a 5-kilometer radius (3.1 mi) of Pueblo Grande during the Classic period. This **carrying-capacity** model was

developed independently of the human remains and architectural data to arrive at estimates of the population that could be supported by historically important native plant resources. Our results suggested that the peak population at Pueblo Grande would have been closer to thousands of people than to tens or hundreds of thousands (Kwiatkowski 1994). Population estimates generated from architectural and human remains data supported the notion that the maximum population at Pueblo Grande during the Classic period did not exceed 1000 to 1500 people (Mitchell 1994a,b).

The residents of Pueblo Grande probably lived through a number of droughts and floods, including flooding events in the late part of the sixth century BP (late AD 1300s). If the stream flow model developed by researchers at the University of Arizona (Nials et al. 1989) is correct, during this century the Hohokam of the Salt River valley experienced both droughts and floods of a magnitude greater than at any other period in the past 1200 years. These major droughts and floods would have had a disastrous effect on the canal system. Floods and droughts also would have affected the natural resources along the riverbanks and floodplain, which would have served as potential backup resources for crop failures.

Our carrying-capacity study indicates that during the Classic period, the residents of Pueblo Grande may have been living with little or no buffer against natural disasters such as floods and droughts. These catastrophes would have been most detrimental to the success and surpluses of both cultivated and natural resources. Years of exploitation by sedentary populations of the natural resources for food, fuel, and shelter, as well as heavy use of the land available for irrigated agriculture during the Classic period, eventually began to erode any buffers that may have existed during earlier periods. Combined with population aggregation into fewer and larger settlements, such as Pueblo Grande, these factors produced serious problems.

Faunal remains recovered from Pueblo Grande included aquatic species including muskrat, beaver, and fish (James 1994). The presence of these animals is significant because, until recently, few prehistoric specimens of muskrat, beaver, or fish had been identified from any Hohokam sites. The quantity of muskrat at Pueblo Grande represents the largest number of specimens recovered to date from a single Hohokam site (James 1994). The muskrat remains showed signs of charring, and they occurred in contexts that indicated that the animals were being consumed as food. Muskrat is considered a starvation food, and the increased use of muskrat as a food source between the early and the late Classic suggests growing subsistence stress among the inhabitants (James 1994).

Fish remains accounted for over 25 percent of the total faunal assemblage. In fact, fish was second in importance only to rabbit as a food resource at Pueblo Grande. The size of the fish represented in the collections decreased markedly from the Early to Late Classic, suggesting that by the Late Classic period at Pueblo Grande, only relatively small fish were available. Possible explanations for this decrease include overexploitation in the vicinity of the site (James 1994), degradation of the local riverine microenvironment, or a combination of both.

Deer remains from Pueblo Grande are few and are represented by finished artifacts, such as awls and hairpins. This suggests that during the Classic period, deer bone was brought into the site as finished artifacts rather than as a source of edible animal protein. The deer bone recovered from Classic period contexts does not appear to have been acquired by hunting, and the lack of deer remains also probably results from environmental degradation and overexploitation by the Hohokam of that time (James 1994; Kwiatkowski 1994). Based on the animal remains from Pueblo Grande, animal protein available to the Classic period Hohokam consisted almost exclusively of meat from rabbits, fish, and rodents.

Pollen and **flotation** samples from Pueblo Grande, which provide information on plant materials in the deposits, indicate that maize was an important food source (Miller 1994). Trace-element analysis of the human remains indicates that maize may have played a greater role in the diet of Late Classic inhabitants than that of Early Classic inhabitants and that protein was less available during the Late Classic period (Jones and Sheridan 1994). The proportion of corn to wild plant remains increases during the Late Classic. That is, native plant remains were less abundant in the Late Classic pollen and flotation samples, which further supports the notion of a general deterioration of the environment surrounding Pueblo Grande and a decrease in native plants. During the Late Classic, the Hohokam may have become more dependent on corn as a primary subsistence resource because native plant resources were in decline and of

limited availability. Animal protein was limited to rabbits, fish of decreasing size, and aquatic rodents. Corn was becoming the primary source of nutrition, so that *any* impact on the successful corn crop yield, such as droughts, floods, or malfunction of the canal system, or failure to maintain it, would have had a disastrous effect on an already precarious food supply, which provided only limited protein.

The analysis of over 800 inhumations and cremations recovered from Pueblo Grande provided an unprecedented glimpse into the lives of the Classic period Hohokam. We were not limited to architectural and material culture data; we had access to the stories of the people who actually lived and died at Pueblo Grande. Despite the many accomplishments of the Hohokam, analyses of the health and nutrition of the Classic period Pueblo Grande population paint a bleak picture and support many of the conclusions arrived at independently by the paleoenvironmental and subsistence studies.

The rate of mortality among the Pueblo Grande Hohokam was high. The mean life expectancy of a newborn was only slightly more than 15 years, and the modal age at death was birth (Van Gerven and Sheridan 1994). This means that although the most frequent age at death was 15, half the children born at Pueblo Grande did not survive to see their first birthday. The data indicate that 66 people per 1000 died each year. Simply to maintain the population with so many deaths would have required a comparable birthrate, which would be higher than any birthrate observed in the world today. It appears, then, that the Pueblo Grande Hohokam population was either in decline or dependent on immigration to maintain its numbers (Van Gerven and Sheridan 1994). Immigration to Pueblo Grande during the Early Classic period probably maintained a relatively stable population. During the Late Classic, however, immigration was probably not a significant factor, and the population at Pueblo Grande began a steady decline. Adding to the difficulty of everyday survival, the demographic data indicate that relative to producers, there would have been a large number of consumers under 15 years of age, and a handful over 50. This situation would have placed a heavy burden on the young adult population.

During the Late Classic period, severe conditions appear to have affected almost everyone. Infant mortality remained stable, but for individuals beyond age 10, there was an 8 percent reduction in mean life expectancy during the Late Classic (Van Gerven and Sheridan 1994).

Ninety-nine percent of the Pueblo Grande burials that could be studied had been nutritionally stressed over the course of their lives (Van Gerven and Sheridan 1994). The average Pueblo Grande child experienced nutritional stress for 33 months during its first 84 months (7 years) of life. Iron deficiency anemia is the most common nutritional deficiency in the world today. Among Pueblo Grande individuals, extensive iron deficiency anemia was observed in both sexes and across all ages, and an 18 percent increase in iron deficiency anemia was observed between the Early and Late Classic periods (Van Gerven and Sheridan 1994).

Analyses also showed differences between males and females at Pueblo Grande. Females were consuming more plant resources, whereas males had greater access to animal protein, such as it was. The lack of animal protein, combined with high reproductive demands, would have aggravated female dietary stress and increased the likelihood of death for females during the reproductive years. Between the Early and Late Classic periods, there was a general decrease in the amount of animal protein consumption, combined with an increased reliance on corn as opposed to native plant resources (Jones and Sheridan 1994). All the lines of evidence lead to the conclusion that the people of Pueblo Grande experienced dietary stress that worsened over time.

The Hohokam maintained a stable and impressive culture in the Sonoran Desert for over a thousand years. However, the human remains, paleoenvironmental reconstructions, and subsistence data collected by the Pueblo Grande Project indicate that by the late Classic period, the Pueblo Grande Hohokam were experiencing dire problems: nutritional and reproductive stresses that severely diminished their numbers. By the end of the Late Classic period, the struggle was lost and the Hohokam all but disappeared from the archaeological record. Although there is now some evidence that the Salt River valley may never have been completely abandoned, the essence of the Hohokam culture disappeared. Thus the Late Classic period marks the physical, social, and economic decline of these people and perhaps the physical environment they had once so successfully exploited.

The Pueblo Grande Project was sponsored by the Arizona Department of Transportation, contract 87-53.

DISCUSSION QUESTIONS

1. What is Pueblo Grande, and why is it a significant cultural resource? What can archaeologists infer from the site's location and from the presence of great houses, ball courts, and platform mounds?

2. Why were the excavations and analyses described here conducted? Did the project's origins affect what archaeology was done?

3. Why weren't the archaeologists very successful in using the household as the basic unit of analysis? Does this deviation from the original research design mean that the information obtained was not useful?

4. What kinds of evidence for environmental deterioration and nutritional stress during the Hohokam Classic period were recovered from the Pueblo Grande Project? Why do archaeologists pursue multiple lines of evidence through multidisciplinary research like that described here?

CHAPTER 2

Culture and Environment in North America's Past

> "In a hole in the ground there lived a hobbit. Not a nasty, dirty, wet hole, filled with the ends of worms and an oozy smell, nor yet a dry, bare, sandy hole with nothing in it to sit down on or to eat: it was a hobbit-hole, and that means comfort."
>
> (Tolkien 1966, 9)

With these words, J. R. R. Tolkien begins his well-known book *The Hobbit*, drawing us into the Shire of the hobbits and the fantastic world of which it is a part. Fantasy writers like Tolkien create imaginary places and creatures with their prose. Tolkien's vivid accounts of hobbit holes, the Shire, and the Misty Mountains enable us to picture these places and their inhabitants, and the *Lord of the Rings* movies reinforce what we have imagined about the land of the hobbits and their friends.

The world of North America's past also is a place we must imagine and in a sense recreate through archaeology. To understand North American archaeology, one needs to cultivate a perspective on this world both culturally and environmentally. In the archaeologist's mind's eye, the land of the past spreads out peopled with cultural groups, and telling of long-ago events and perhaps forgotten places that are fascinating, if not in the same way as Tolkien's Middle Earth. The past of North America that archaeologists seek is elusive because the archaeological record is incomplete, but it still can capture our curiosity. Unlike the world Tolkien describes, North America's past stretches over thousands of years during which landscapes and characters have changed again and again. Discovery of the evidence for even one small portion of this past can draw people into an endlessly intriguing intellectual exploration.

While we cannot claim Tolkien's gift for engaging description, this text provides archaeological glimpses of America's past. This chapter, as the second of our background chapters, provides specific information that will promote a better understanding of this continent's past. We have discussed some highlights of the nature and practice of North American archaeology; we now turn to what archaeologists and other scientists understand about the geography of the past, to archaeological conventions for talking about the past, and to the broad themes of North American archaeological research. Thus, we begin with a discussion of the culture area concept that we use to structure the rest of this text, followed by a brief outline of North American environments and climate. Next, we explain some key terms and frameworks that archaeologists use to talk about North America's cultural past, and we introduce several themes in the archaeological study of this continent. Finally, we comment on dating North America's past. This material is designed to help readers keep their bearings in the remaining chapters of this text.

NORTH AMERICAN CULTURE AREAS

As noted in Chapter 1, a culture area is a geographic area within which ethnic groups tend to have similar cultural traits. It has long been assumed that such areas result primarily from adaptation to similar environmental circumstances. Thus, culture areas tend to be closely related to physiographic regions within North America. For example, the Great Plains roughly corresponds to the Plains culture area recognized by anthropologists.

The concept of culture areas developed among North American anthropologists at the end of the nineteenth century as a means of organizing the large quantity of American Indian data that was being generated. Instead of arranging museum collections by the type of article being displayed, anthropologists wanted to use cultural information in grouping cultures together. Because it was then believed that American Indians did not have long histories, cultural areas originally were conceptualized in geographic terms (Holmes 1914). Clark Wissler (1926) and Alfred Kroeber (1963) expanded on the concept by identifying centers from which cultural traits spread outward. Kroeber attempted to systematically define culture areas by using trait lists and statistical techniques designed to show similarity between groups of traits. Although originally ethnographic in nature, these areas have long been used by archaeologists for studying the past as well.

Thinking about Native Americans, whether past or present, in terms of culture areas has become convention because it is useful in describing diverse Indian cultures. We use it in this book for convenience in grouping the data we are presenting. The boundaries of culture areas are not rigidly fixed, however, and throughout history there have been contacts and influences across the boundaries between areas. Moreover, despite considerable similarity in cultural traits, the human groups located within a given culture area have differed, as well. The European populations who immigrated to the Americas at various times, representing other cultural traditions not included in this formulation, illustrate clearly that cultural entities are not fixed in time and space.

It is apparent by now that we use the terms "Indian" and "Native American" interchangeably. We also will use an array of tribal and archaeological culture names. Which terms are correct? Why are there multiple terms? Box 2.1 addresses these issues.

ISSUES AND DEBATES

BOX 2.1

What Are You Called? Names and Politics

The name *Indian* comes from Columbus's search for a route to the Indies and his assumption that the people he encountered were "Indians." Many descendants of the people who were living in the Americas when Columbus bumped into the West Indies resent being called Indian. Some prefer to be designated Amerind, Native American, or First Nation (common in Canada). Others, however, find nothing offensive in the term "Indian." An elder from a southern California tribe expressed this when addressing the San Diego Archaeological Center Board. Paraphrasing, she said: "I've been an Indian for all of my 65 years. My father was an Indian and his father was an Indian. I don't know where you get off changing what we are called." Because there is no clear consensus, we shall generally use Native American, First Nation, or Indian.

Many living tribes have been called by names other than their own name for themselves. Explorers often assigned names to one tribe based on what other tribes called them rather than what they called themselves. The Spanish called the people living near the present town of Yuma, on the Colorado River, Yumans, apparently based on the name used by the Tohono O'odham. The "Yumans" called themselves Quechan and prefer to be called that today. The Tohono O'odham were called Papago for many years, based on the name the Spanish gave them. In Chapter 4, "Eskimo" is used sparingly because the people in Canada find that term offensive and prefer to be called Inuit. However, "Inuit" is not appropriate for all those formerly designated Eskimo, especially peoples of Alaska like the Yup'ik, who don't seem to be uncomfortable with the more general name.

Not all tribes have reasserted their names for themselves, however. For example, the Navajo call themselves Diné, and many tribal offices use that name, but the official term is "the Navajo Nation."

In addition, some Native American groups express discomfort with what archaeologists call the archaeological groups they discuss. To be able to communicate with one another and with the public about what they are learning, archaeologists have had to devise names for ancient cultural traditions. For example, in the Southwest, we do not know what the people who built Cliff Palace at Mesa Verde, or Snaketown, in present-day Arizona, called themselves. As you will learn in Chapter 9, we commonly recognize four general, geographically distinct traditions—the Mogollon, the Patayan, the Hohokam, and the Anasazi. The name **Mogollon** comes from the Mogollon Mountains in New Mexico, and the mountains were named for a Spanish governor of the Province of New Mexico. **Patayan** comes from a Walapai word meaning "old people." "Hohokam," which comes from the Pima language is said to refer to people who have disappeared or vanished. Emil Haury (1976, 5) says his Pima workers explained to him that *hohokam* actually means "all used up." **Anasazi** is derived from a Navajo term that, like Hohokam and Patayan, was thought to mean old people or ancestors. Often "Anasazi" is translated as "enemy ancestors," an appellation some modern Pueblo people find offensive. **Ancestral Pueblo** has been offered as an alternative name, but this is not altogether satisfactory because the Mogollon also are almost certainly ancestral to at least some of the modern Pueblos. Since, however, most of the published literature still uses "Anasazi," we use the term sparingly, alongside "Ancestral Pueblo."

Throughout North America, there is an abundance of names and terms for the diverse peoples of the past as well as for their present-day descendants discussed in this text. To learn about archaeology is to become familiar with many of these terms, and to develop sensitivity to the wishes of the descendants.

What Culture Areas Are Commonly Recognized?

Although various researchers have recognized slightly different culture areas for North America, today anthropologists commonly recognize ten areas (Figure 2.1). With a few exceptions, the chapters in this text correspond to these culture areas.

We combine discussion of two culture areas, the **Arctic** and **Subarctic culture areas**, including most of Canada and Alaska as well as Greenland, in Chapter 4. The division between these areas is essentially defined by the northerly extent of forests. These two culture areas encompass a very large region in which a variety of Eskimo and American Indian cultures were found at European contact. Traditionally, these people have supported themselves through hunting and collecting wild marine, riverine, and terrestrial resources. Arctic and Subarctic people were first contacted by the Norse about 1000 years ago, while the French, the British, and eventually Russians and Americans began arriving about 500 years ago. Especially in the interior and extreme north, traditional lifeways persisted into the twentieth century.

A third culture area, the **Northwest Coast**, is introduced in Chapter 5. This narrow culture area is located along the Pacific coast of North America from northern California to southern Alaska. Native peoples in this area long relied on the sea and on fish such as salmon that spawn in the area's rivers. They developed cultures that were complex economically, socially, and politically. Russian, Spanish, and British traders began to enter this culture area during the eighteenth century, and Americans followed in the nineteenth. These Europeans brought disease and considerable social disruption to the native inhabitants. Historically, lumbering and fishing were important pursuits.

Inland from the Northwest Coast in both Canada and the United States, anthropologists have defined the **Plateau culture area**, which we discuss in Chapter 6. As in the culture areas mentioned already, people living here were hunter-gatherers who used a variety of resources including salmon, land mammals such as bison and elk, and roots. They developed a number of different cultural patterns, each of which shows the influence of an adjacent culture area. Plateau cultural groups were not contacted until Lewis and Clark passed through the region in 1805, but European diseases preceded actual European Americans by at least 25 years. British and a few American traders established themselves on the plateau as the nineteenth century progressed, and native groups eventually lost most of their land base.

Diversity in human adaptation was well developed in the **California culture area**, which includes a little of the northern part of Baja California as well as most of the present state of California. We discuss this area in Chapter 7, noting that while some people were organized into small groups of hunter-gatherers, fairly

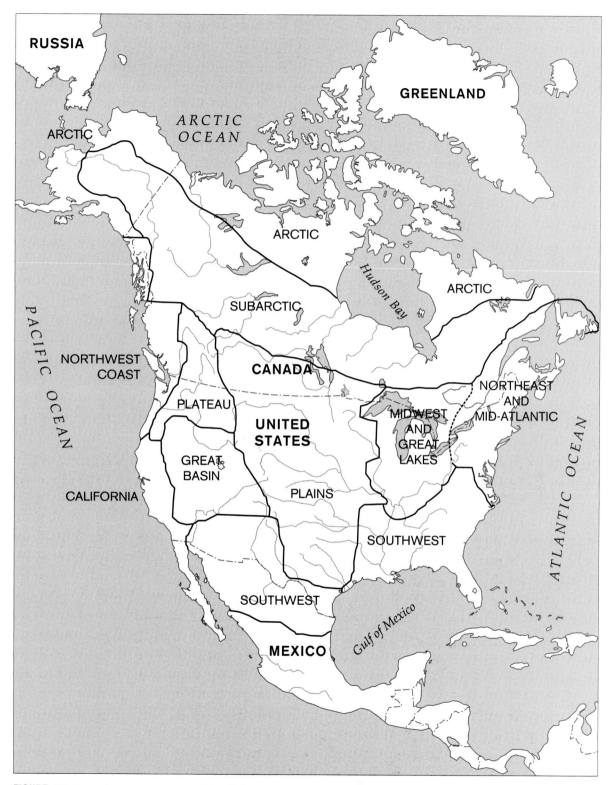

FIGURE 2.1 Ten culture areas have traditionally been recognized for North America. In this text, we have subdivided the traditional Northeast culture area as shown, into a Midwest and Great Lakes section and a Northeast and Mid-Atlantic section.

complex sociopolitical groups did develop, and some small-scale experimentation with agriculture occurred as well. Native Californians were first contacted by the Spanish in the sixteenth century, but the Spanish missions were not established until the eighteenth century. California was a province of Mexico for a short time during the nineteenth century and became part of the United States in 1848, when the famous gold rush developed. Russians also established trading posts in California. Each incoming group brought disease and serious cultural disruption to native populations. Particularly during the American period, native populations were annihilated and lifeways destroyed as miners and other settlers entered the area.

In Chapters 8 and 9, we discuss the two culture areas of the desert West. The first of these is the **Great Basin culture area**, which corresponds to the large area between the Sierra Nevada in eastern California and the Rocky Mountains. Environmentally, this area includes large deserts that are in some places interspersed with forested mountain ranges and lakes. The Great Basin's inhabitants were hunter-gatherers, although some groups experimented with agriculture. Most of these cultural groups were not affected by European Americans until the middle of the nineteenth century, although trappers and traders had entered the area earlier. After this, fencing by ranchers as well as the construction of dams disrupted native subsistence practices significantly.

The second desert culture area is the **Southwest**, introduced in Chapter 9. Although deserts do occur here, the mountainous areas of the Southwest are relatively well watered and heavily forested. Many southwestern peoples developed agriculture, although most supplemented their subsistence with hunting and gathering. By the early sixteenth century, hunter-gatherers including ancestral Navajo and Apache had entered the northern Southwest area. Shortly thereafter, in the mid-sixteenth century, Spanish explorers arrived from Mexico and began establishing towns, forts, and missions. Although the Spanish were ousted in the 1680s by a native revolt, they returned before the end of the seventeenth century. During the nineteenth century, Mexico and then the United States took control. Historic settlers were ranchers, farmers, and miners.

Chapter 10 introduces the **Plains culture area**, which extends through the midsection of North America from southern Canada all the way to central Texas. This vast area is grassland, although the topography and elevation, the amount of water, the types of grasses, and the animal resources available vary considerably. This area was home both to nomadic bison hunters and to more settled horticultural groups, who may have hunted bison seasonally or not at all. Spanish explorers first entered the southern Plains during the sixteenth century, while British fur traders came into the northern Plains. The biggest impact on Plains Indian lifestyles came from the reintroduction of the horse after European contact. Although horses had existed in North America, they became extinct by the end of the Pleistocene. Another important development was the spread of smallpox by the early 1800s, decimating Plains Native populations, especially the less nomadic villagers of the river valleys. As American farmers and ranchers settled on the Plains, military conflicts developed between native populations and the settlers.

The ninth commonly identified culture area is the **Southeast**, which we discuss in Chapter 11. Although hunter-gatherer as well as horticultural adaptations characterized residents of this region of rivers and forests, many of the people were sedentary, and complex chiefdoms with well-developed social hierarchies existed here prior to the arrival of Europeans. The de Soto expedition in the 1540s affected the balance of power among these groups and spread disease that decimated several formerly large Indian chiefdoms. The Indians of the Southeast were also subject to forced removal in the 1830s, although some escaped into isolated areas. Europeans and Americans utilized the land of the Southeast to produce agricultural commodities for cash and export. Of course, this system was supported by a massive influx of African slaves. Even after the Civil War, much of this culture area remained agrarian.

Convention defines the **Northeast culture area** as extending from approximately the Mississippi River to the Atlantic coast and from Kentucky and Virginia to north of the Great Lakes into southern Canada. We have divided the Northeast culture area into two sections because of the native cultural diversity as well as differing traditions of archaeological study. Our divisions are the Midwest and the Upper Great Lakes subarea, discussed in Chapter 12, and the Northeast and Mid-Atlantic subarea, discussed in Chapter 13. Here mixed fishing, hunting, and gathering, and in some areas horticulture, usually formed the subsistence base. In some instances, sedentism, social ranking, and organization into chiefdoms developed. European fishermen were exploiting the waters off the Northeast coast even before 1500, but the natives of this culture area began to be affected by French, British, and Dutch arrivals during the sixteenth century. As Europeans and eventually Americans settled further and further west, many native populations migrated, resettled, or were exterminated in wars and other conflicts. Some entire tribes moved to the Indian Territory (Oklahoma) after the passage of the **Indian Removal Act** of 1830. Nevertheless, native populations also remained on reservations within this area or assimilated into the general population of farmers and tradespeople, so that even here there is cultural continuity with the past. Eventually, the Northeast became the center for much of the early industrial development in the United States.

NORTH AMERICAN ENVIRONMENTS

Biomes and Habitats

The concept of culture area subsumes both environmental and cultural attributes of geographic areas. Thus, before discussing archaeological concepts about culture, we must survey the diversity of North American environments. Kroeber (1963, 13) argued that vegetation patterns provide the most useful basis for further understanding the environmental features of North American culture areas. We prefer a more ecological approach that focuses on interactions between physiography, vegetation, and animals. North America includes many diverse **habitats**. In the language of ecologists, a habitat is an area of land with physical characteristics that affect and are modified by living organisms such as plants and animals. **Communities** of interrelating plants and animals develop in habitats, and at the largest scale we call these aggregations of organisms **biomes**. Humans are both part of these biomes and users of the resources available in them. **Ecotones** are communities that are transitional between biomes or among their biotic communities. Archaeologists have been particularly interested in human association with ecotone communities, sometimes arguing that it is the high resource density and diversity of these regions that attract people to them.

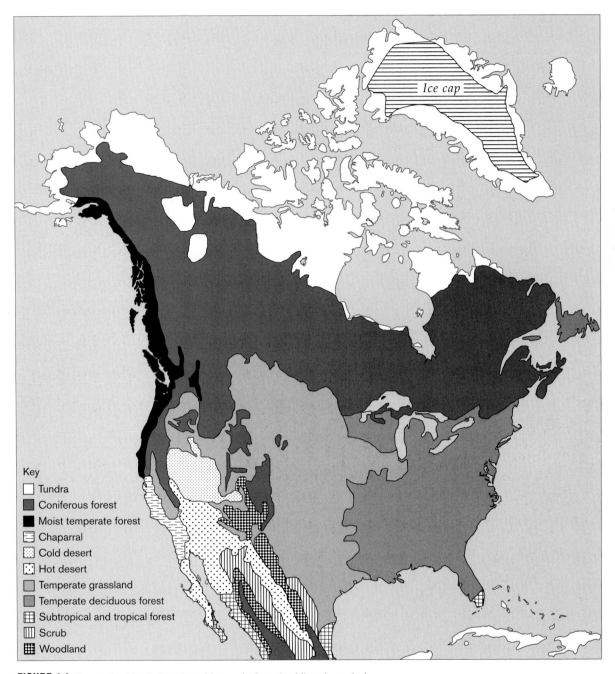

FIGURE 2.2 The major North American biomes before the Historic period.

Key
- Tundra
- Coniferous forest
- Moist temperate forest
- Chaparral
- Cold desert
- Hot desert
- Temperate grassland
- Temperate deciduous forest
- Subtropical and tropical forest
- Scrub
- Woodland

Figure 2.2 shows the general location of the major North American biomes before historic times. This map assumes that it is possible to generalize about communities that develop when areas are left undisturbed for long periods of time. However, within these biomes, there always has been much local variation.

FIGURE 2.3 Arctic tundra on Baffin Island. House remains are visible on the far side of the stream.

These biomes also have been dramatically modified over the last two centuries as human settlements grew in size and number. Of course, even pre-Columbian North Americans had a dynamic relationship with their environment.

The **tundra** is the treeless biome of the North American and European Arctic (Figure 2.3). In North America, tundra is found at latitudes 57° or more north, although it also is found in the northern Rocky Mountains above the **tree–line**. Shelford (1963, 182) notes that the southern margins of the tundra are defined by mean January temperatures between –20 and –26°F. There are many lakes and ponds in tundra areas, but another important feature of the tundra biome is the relative lack of precipitation, which ranges from 12 to 20 inches (30.5–50.8 cm) annually. Most of this precipitation falls as snow. In tundra areas, the ground (except for a surface layer) never thaws but remains frozen year round. This feature, called **permafrost**, prevents the growth of trees whose root systems cannot develop adequately. Plants commonly growing in this biome include reindeer moss, which is a kind of lichen, dwarf huckleberries, bilberries, and, in the many poorly drained areas, sedges. Dwarf birches and willows also are found in brushy tundra areas. The caribou was the dominant animal species before modern times. Other large game animals include musk ox, tundra wolf, and polar bear, while many smaller mammals and birds also are found in tundra areas (Shelford 1963, 182–210).

FIGURE 2.4 Coniferous forest covers vast portions of Canada and North America's mountains.

FIGURE 2.5 The temperate forest that covers much of the eastern part of North America contains many distinct forest communities. The pre-European climax forest in Pennsylvania would have had less brushy undergrowth than appears in this modern area of regrowth.

Coniferous forest (Figure 2.4) is a second biome of great areal extent in North America, stretching across Canada and extending southward into the United States in the continent's mountain chains. Within this biome, precipitation varies between averages of 10 to 20 inches (25.4–50.8 cm) in the west and 20 to 50 inches (50.8–127 cm) in the east, while mean January temperatures are between −14 and −20°F in the west and −4 and 14°F in the east. Evergreens in this biome include species of pine, spruce, fir, and hemlock, but tamarack, willow, birch, alder, and poplar are often found. Common mammals and birds include moose, woodland caribou, wolf, bear, wolverine, lynx, red squirrel, snowshoe hare, grouse, woodpeckers, jays, and a variety of small birds. White-tailed deer feed on shrubs in the more open areas in this forest (Shelford 1963, 120–181).

The **moist temperate forest biome** of the northern Pacific Coast also is dominated by coniferous trees, but ecologists consider this to be a separate, third biome. This biome is located at lower elevations than mountain coniferous forest and is adjacent to the Pacific coast extending from central California northward to southern Alaska. The annual precipitation here is between 50 and 100 inches (127–254 cm), with most of the precipitation being winter rainfall. Mean annual temperatures vary between 56°F in the south and 40°F in the north. Important trees in this biome are hemlock, western red cedar, spruce, and in some areas redwood and Douglas fir. The canopy of this forest in its mature state is so dense that shrubs and other low plants are greatly inhibited. Animals of importance in this biome are elk, mule deer, mountain lion, black bear, and blue grouse (Shelford 1963, 211–237).

The **temperate deciduous forest biome** (Figure 2.5) is found south of the coniferous forest in most of the eastern part of the continent from the Great Lakes area to the Gulf of Mexico, including the northern two-thirds of the Florida

Peninsula. It also extends from the Atlantic Ocean westward to the Mississippi River in the north and to the south, across it into the Ozark Mountains. Rainfall in this forest ranges between 28 and 60 inches (71.1–152.4 cm), and precipitation is not seasonally concentrated. The northern boundary of this biome has a mean January temperature of 14°F.

There are important ecological distinctions within this broad region. In the northern and upland forests, beech and sugar maple are the original tree dominants and elk and deer are important animal species. The southern and lowland portions of this forest biome are dominated by either oak and hickory or, along the southern coast, by magnolia. Coniferous tree species intermix with the deciduous trees in this biome, and where fire or other conditions result in drier than normal habitats, pine trees may be common. The riverine forests along the many rivers and streams also are distinct ecological communities. In addition, openings in this forest occur both naturally and as the result of human activities. Throughout this biome, white-tailed deer, wolf, mountain lion, black bear, raccoon, bobcat, and gray squirrel can be found, with elk and gray wolf characterizing the northern parts of the forest and the red wolf being found in the southern deciduous forest. The turkey is the most important bird, but many other bird species are present. Major waterfowl flyways, in the Mississippi valley and along the east coast, are traveled by large numbers of birds annually (Shelford 1963, 17–88).

In northern Baja California, southern California, and north into central Oregon, biotic communities adapted to arid conditions are grouped into the **chaparral biome** (Figure 2.6). Both sclerophyll vegetation with thick, water-retaining leaves and woodland with grassy ground cover typify this biome. Although the annual amount of rainfall is adequate, the summer months see very little precipitation—in some areas less than 1 inch (2.54 cm). The Christmasberry, various species

FIGURE 2.6 Chaparral covers these slopes, with riparian vegetation in the valley bottom and some pine trees in the distance.

FIGURE 2.7 The desert biomes of the American West include (a) the cold desert biome and (b) the hot desert biome.

a

b

of live oak, other oaks, mountain lilac, manzanita, mountain mahogany, and sagebrush are common, along with many other shrubby species. Mule deer, mountain lion, bobcat, wolf, coyote, skunk, ground squirrel, kangaroo rat, pocket gopher, cottontail, and many other mammals can be found here. Many birds, including hawks, owls, the kingbird, the mourning dove, the California quail, and the roadrunner, also are part of this biome (Shelford 1963, 238–259).

The biotic communities of the Great Basin in western Utah, most of Nevada, south central Oregon, southwestern Wyoming, and some of eastern California can be grouped together as the **cold desert biome** (Figure 2.7a). This area is a desert because much of the ground surface is bare, but it becomes cold in the winter, with mean January temperatures ranging between 29 and 39°F. The western portions of this area have very low annual rainfall, less than 6 inches (15.2 cm) annually, while to the east this amount is somewhat higher and more variable, averaging around 10 inches (25.4 cm) per year. Since the Great Basin drains internally rather than into the ocean, salt tends to build up in soils, a factor as important in the area's biotic character as its general aridity. Shadscale and sagebrush are the dominant plant species, but saltbush, antelope brush, ricegrass, and other grasses also are part of biotic communities. Piñon-juniper woodland occurs at higher elevations, where there is just a little more water. Ecologists note an association between shadscale and the kangaroo rat and between sagebrush and rabbits. Other mammals include the pocket mouse, grasshopper mouse, antelope ground squirrel, badger, kit fox, coyote, and pronghorn antelope. Some mule deer are present during the winter. Birds like owls, falcons, hawks, and the bald eagle, as well as many smaller species also are found here (Shelford 1963, 260–281).

The hot desert areas of North America are confined to the Southwest, California, and the states of northern Mexico (Figure 2.7b). These deserts have very hot summer temperatures, and rainfall ranges between 3.5 and 13 inches (8.9–33 cm) annually. Plants in this desert area rarely touch each other so that their roots do not compete for scarce water. Ecologists recognize a western portion of the hot desert centering on the lower Colorado River in California, Arizona, and the Mexican states of Baja California and Sonora. They differentiate this desert from a more easterly desert centered on the Rio Grande and the Rio Conchas in New Mexico, Texas, and the Mexican states of Chihuahua, Coahuila, Durango, Zacatecas, and San Luis Potosí. The creosote bush is the dominant plant species throughout both deserts, and it is associated with the white bur sage in the west and the tar bush in the east. Merriam's kangaroo rat is found in all parts of the hot desert, along with the desert pocket mouse. There is both seasonal and areal difference at a number of scales within these deserts, so that at some times of the year, depending on when the rains tend to come, there are many flowering plants. Although there are numerous animals in the desert, large ones like deer and even good sized carnivores are rare. Instead, mice, ground squirrels, jackrabbits, some birds, and snakes and lizards are well represented in the **hot desert biome** (Shelford 1963, 373–394).

A variety of woodland and bushland communities also are found as important ecotones in the western part of North America, especially in the foothills of the southern Rocky Mountains and the mountains of northern Mexico. These areas are designated Woodlands in Figure 2.2. They contain low, short-trunked trees including pine, oak, and juniper, and a variety of shrubs. The mule deer is often the dominant animal species, but jackrabbits, cottontail rabbits, rock squirrels, chipmunks, mice, other mammals, and many species of birds also are found in these areas.

Grasslands occur in North America at high elevations as alpine meadows above timberline, and they also occur as openings in the temperate deciduous forest. However, the greatest extent of grasslands on this continent is the **temperate grassland biome** that stretches from Alberta southward into northern Mexico and from the margins of the forest on the east all the way to the Rocky Mountains with other areas of grassland occurring west of the Rockies stretching to the coastal ranges in California. Rainfall varies considerably within these grasslands, from about 40 inches (101.6 cm) annually in areas on the east to about 12 inches (30.5 cm) annually in the western regions. Importantly, except in the eastern portions, more precipitation evaporates annually than is acquired in rainfall. Temperature extremes also vary considerably within this vast grassland: only a few months of the year are frost free in the north, whereas there is no frost at all in the south.

We can divide this grassland into four subareas. These are (1) the tall grass and mixed grassland from approximately longitude 100° west-east to the margins

FIGURE 2.8 An important subdivision within North America's grasslands is between the (a) tall-grass prairie, found east of the 100th meridian, and (b) the short-grass areas that characterize the western Great Plains.

a

b

of the temperate deciduous forest, (2) the short-grass grassland west from approximately the same longitude to the foot of the Rocky Mountains, (3) a bunch grass region that is found between the Rocky Mountains and the coastal mountain ranges, and (4) a desert or mesquite grassland found in the highlands of southern Arizona, southern New Mexico, southwestern Texas, and portions of northern Mexico. Shelford (1963, 356–372) considers this last a separate biome, where communities contain short grasses and mesquite. Although some species of grasses, including June grass, blue grama, side-oats grama, hairy grama, needle-and-thread, green needlegrass, sheep fescue, little bluestem, and buffalo grass, are found throughout this biome, the average height of grasses varies among the subareas mentioned previously (Figure 2.8). Grasses in the tall-grass prairie average about 20 to 60 inches (50.8–152.4 cm) tall, while grasses in the mixed grass areas are of two types, 12 to 24 inches (30.5–61 cm) and 8 to 20 inches (20.3–50.8 cm). In the short-grass areas, grass species heights range between about 2 and 16 inches (5.1–40.6 cm). In the bunch grass prairie, there are both tall and short grasses, even though bunch grasses themselves range from about 24 to 40 inches (61–101.6 cm) in height (Shelford 1963, 332). Dominant animals in this grassland biome are bison, pronghorn, badger, and jackrabbit, but many other mammals and birds are found as well (Shelford 1963, 328–372).

Other biomes and communities also occur in North America. These include a southern coniferous forest in the high mountains of northern Mexico, which is dominated by species of pine, and the subtropical and tropical forests in southern Florida. Communities representative of the latter biomes are found in areas that are close to sea level, receive at least 50 inches (127 cm) of rain annually, and very rarely experience frost.

This brief description of North American biomes provides an introduction to the continent's ecological diversity. Archaeologists are interested in this environmental information because it helps them understand human adaptations over time and across space. Contemporary archaeologists use a variety of interdisciplinary methods to reconstruct past environments as discussed in Box 2.2.

ISSUES AND DEBATES

BOX 2.2

Is Environmental Reconstruction an Ancillary Study?

Most people think the central activities of archaeology are the excavation of sites and the interpretation of their artifacts; the reconstruction of hunting and butchering practices or the delineation of past environments is seldom seen as central to archaeology. This chapter's description of North American environmental features and climatic change may seem somewhat beside the point. As anthropologists, however, archaeologists today have a holistic interest in culture and behavior. Information about site distributions and material culture, is necessary to document the **culture history** of an area. In addition, however, we hope to reconstruct how people lived and why their behavior changed. Understanding the environmental context in which behavior occurred doesn't explain everything about culture change, but it does provide one important perspective on human behavior.

Thus, archaeological interest in human subsistence and in human interactions with plants, animals, and landscapes has developed directly out of the desire to know how people actually lived in the past. Mid-twentieth-century developments in anthropological theory, especially in **cultural ecology**, the study of interactions between human societies and ecosystems, also have been influential. The result is that contemporary archaeology is hardly ever just about sites, features, and artifacts. Ecofacts are just as important. The analysis of subsistence remains is a normal part of excavation projects, as is the delineation of the geological setting of sites and local environmental features. Today's archaeological undertaking is likely to be highly interdisciplinary, involving specialists with expertise in geology, botany, zoology, and other sciences. Some of these specialists have their primary training in archaeology, while others have specialized in a related science such as geology.

The various interdisciplinary subfields are covered in courses in archaeological methods. We mention a few subfields here. First, **palynology** is important to reconstructing past environments. Palynologists study fossil pollen extracted from soil samples collected at archaeological sites or at other locations where sediments are known to be old. Ideally, they sample locations in which pollen has been deposited year after year for long periods of time and for which the **stratigraphy** can be interpreted in terms of time. On the basis of counts of pollen grains of various types, palynologists reconstruct the plant life of a region at a given time in the past. Since the distance that pollen grains are likely to travel and the amount of pollen produced vary among plants, interpretation can be a complicated matter.

Geoarchaeologists also can contribute to the reconstruction of environment. These archaeologists reconstruct the depositional characteristics of sites and identify the natural processes involved in site formation by evaluating sediments and stratigraphy. This kind of research cannot help but aid in the reconstruction of past environments. For example, simply knowing whether sediments were deposited by wind or by water provides important information about an area's environmental history. Julie Stein shortly highlighted in Profile 2.1, is a geoarchaeologist, and geoarchaeology was important in the Koster site research discussed in this chapter's case study.

Ethnobotanists, who study plant remains from archaeological sites, and **zooarchaeologists** (Figure 2.9), who study animal remains from archaeological sites (see Student CD, Section D.6), are concerned both with reconstructing human subsistence and diet and with interpreting past environmental conditions. Because the plant and animal parts recovered from excavations represent species with habitat preferences, their presence in a collection can be considered evidence of those habitats in the vicinity of a site. For example, the presence of hickory nut shells and wild turkey bones in an archaeological site most likely indicates that mixed deciduous forests were present nearby. It is also true, of course, that some plants and animals are traded into an area, and in any given area, humans select only some of the species for use.

A wide variety of other indicators also can provide environmental clues. For example,

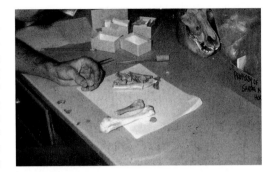

FIGURE 2.9 A zooarchaeologist compares a turkey bone fragment with a comparative specimen that is complete, while other fragments of bone from the same provenience wait to be identified.

the varying widths of tree rings indicate changes in moisture and temperature, and **packrat middens**, the accumulations left where packrats have hoarded food, provide a partial list of plant species in the immediate area. In addition, tiny land snails in sediment columns, which are very sensitive to microenvironmental factors like vegetation and moisture, can be important. Archaeologists also can reconstruct vegetation by studying hard, nearly indestructible silica particles found in plant cells. These particles, called **opal phytoliths**, have distinctive shapes, which can, in many cases, be used to identify the plant from which they came. Unfortunately, this kind of study is complicated because a single plant species can produce phytoliths of different kinds in different parts of its structure.

All these interdisciplinary methods make important contributions to contemporary North American archaeology. Although they are sometimes called "ancillary studies," with the implication that they are supplementary to the main archaeological analyses, it is difficult to imagine modern archaeologists being able to investigate the myriad subjects that interest them without data from such research. Arguably, the palynologist, geoarchaeologist, ethnobotanist, or zooarchaeologist is as important to archaeological research today as the lithic or ceramic analyst. Together, teams of archaeologists build a more complete understanding of the past than would be possible for any researcher alone.

Rivers, Coasts, and Nonterrestrial Resources

Our focus on terrestrial biomes should not imply that past inhabitants of America did not use aquatic resources. River systems are a major environmental feature on this continent. Figure 2.10 shows the major river drainages and lakes of North America. Keep in mind that plant and animal communities at the margins of rivers and streams often are distinct. These are ecological edges in which plants and animals from several habitats are found. Much the same can be said concerning lakes and their margins. In North America, there are countless small lakes besides the large ones such as the Great Lakes and the Great Salt Lake, which can be seen on continental maps. These rivers, streams, and lakes themselves are home to a wide variety of fish and invertebrates such as freshwater mussels, while waterfowl, aquatic mammals, some reptiles, and amphibians cluster near water as well. On both the east and west coasts, **anadromous fish**, which seasonally spawn in fresh water but spend much of their lives in the ocean, were important additions to the available resource base. Examples of such fish are salmon, alewife, and smelt.

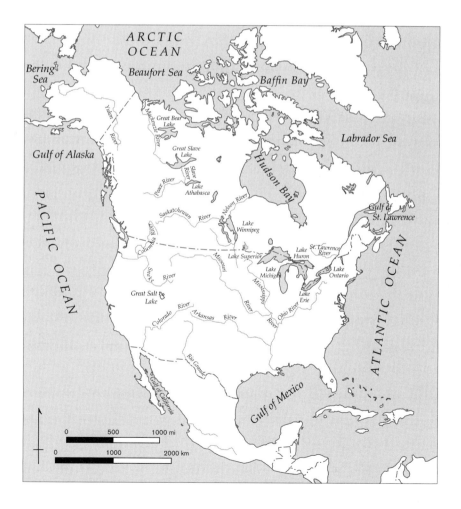

FIGURE 2.10 The many lakes, rivers, and other bodies of water as well as their shorelines of North America have always been important features of the resource base.

Of course, resources of the ocean are important environmental features of coastal environments. Marine mammals, ocean fish, clams, crustaceans, and seaweed are just a few examples of useful resources found in the ocean near the coast. Many birds nest here, and a variety of other species make their homes in coastal areas. As in lake margins and river floodplains, a number of habitats may be found close together, adjacent to the ocean, giving the coast the high diversity and density of plants and animals that is found in ecological edges.

Finally, waterfowl migrations are an important seasonal feature in a number of areas of North America. We can recognize several major migratory flyways that bring birds south across much of North America in the winter and north again during the summer months. There is an east coast flyway, a Mississippi River flyway, a central flyway on the Plains, and a Pacific flyway that includes some parts of the Rocky Mountains. The numbers of birds that migrate through these pathways are monumental today and may have been greater in the past.

Human Impact on North American Habitats and Landscapes

It is very common to think of North America prior to the arrival of Europeans as unspoiled, natural land. In this view, Euro-American culture is blamed for spoiling the vast wilderness of this continent. The biomes we have just discussed, which Shelford argued were essentially pre-European, have undergone gradual environmental degradation culminating in the industrial period with massive pollution. However, the idea of a pristine pre-Columbian wilderness is not strictly accurate.

First, ecosystems are dynamic and changing by their nature: plants and animals in biotic communities influence one another and can modify the characteristics of the community as a whole. As discussed in the next section, climatic change can affect environmental characteristics dramatically, but subtler interactions between species always are taking place. It is simply naive to think that the environment was static in the past.

Second, Native Americans should be seen not as passive constituents of the environment but as dynamic actors in past ecosystems. Archaeologists are increasingly aware of this latter point, but descriptions of native manipulation of plants, animals, and landscape are not commonly available outside anthropology and geography. Nonindustrial people can modify their environments by clearing land for houses and villages, burning vegetation to promote the growth of seed plants or to promote suitable browse for large mammals, and overhunting certain species of game, causing their disappearance. Gradual deforestation of land as wood for fuel is acquired, terracing of fields to promote water retention, and irrigating of land to improve the water supply to cultivated crops are other practices that alter the habitat. The North American ethnographic and archaeological records document the existence of these and other practices among Native Americans (Doolittle 2000; Minnis and Elisens 2000).

Moreover, Native Americans should not be understood too simplistically as people who lived in harmony with their environment. This is a modern myth, which serves us in critiquing the dominant American society; it is a contemporary version of the "noble savage" image (Krech 1999). The truth is that Native Americans interacted with their environments in a number of complicated ways, reflecting a variety of cultural traditions. Some stressed balance in their interactions with the environment, but others seem to have been less concerned with this issue. Where human populations grew large, it was possible for the Indians to deplete their environs of wood, water, and other resources, just as they encouraged and sustained key resources in other settings.

Nevertheless, pre-Columbian modifications of the landscape were very different from those that occurred after European contact. As ecological historians (e.g., Cronon 1983; Crosby 1994; Silver 1990) remind us, the ecological consequences of European arrival were complex. Europeans did not simply deforest the land or deplete populations of beaver; they brought different systems of living on the land, which changed habitat distributions subtly at first, and later dramatically. Whereas Indians affected the landscape in ways that promoted certain species of animals and plants and indeed certain habitat types, like old field habitats left by shifting cultivators, some European settlers, from their first arrival, looked at North America in terms of the commodities it provided rather than as a place to subsist. The establishment of the fur trade, the concept of permanent rather than shifting cultivation of fields, and the relatively rapid depopulation of Native settlements were among the many factors that worked together to transform the aboriginal landscape in colonial times. Eventually, of course, the shift from an agrarian to an industrial economy, accompanied by major increases in human population size, had dramatic impacts on North American habitats. Lumbering, the growth of a variety of industries, the impoundment of rivers, the growth of cities, and many other factors must be considered in any environmental history of this continent.

THE CLIMATE OF NORTH AMERICA

Climatologists also have developed a series of classifications for the North American continent. They base these on empirical data concerning temperature and precipitation. The classifications recognize a number of climatic zones, including a polar zone far to the north, a boreal zone stretching across Canada and generally corresponding to the coniferous forest biome, a variety of temperate and dry zones in what today is the continental United States, as well as a subtropical humid zone in the Southeast.

Various airflows control North American climatic regimes (Lydolph 1985, 203–209). An arctic airstream originates in the polar area and moves south into interior North America. A tropical airstream flows north into the United States. Meanwhile, the Pacific maritime airstream is characterized by a northern flow out of Asia and, south of this, an airflow from the subtropical eastern Pacific. The relative positions of these airstreams are responsible for climatic fluctuations on a seasonal and annual basis, although there also are upper airflows that affect North American weather (Figure 2.11).

The Rocky Mountain chain forms a more or less continuous north–south obstacle for air masses and is a dominant feature in North American climate. East of the Rockies, air masses are not blocked by topography, and the climatic regime, based on seasonal variation in air mass dominance, is relatively simple (Bryson and Hare 1974). The amount of moisture generally decreases from the Atlantic Coast westward to the western portion of the Great Plains, which lie in the **rain shadow** of the Rocky Mountains. A boundary between humid and dry climates, mirrored in the distribution of tall-grass as opposed to short-grass prairies, can be recognized at approximately the 100th meridian. North of southern

FIGURE 2.11 North America's climate is controlled largely by the airflows shown, which originate in polar regions, flow out of the tropics, or develop over the Pacific Ocean.

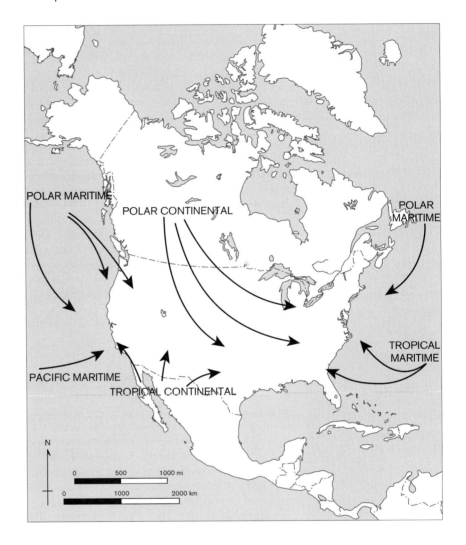

Saskatchewan and Alberta, where the grassland stops and coniferous forests begin, this distinction is not clear because of the cooler overall temperatures.

It is much more difficult to generalize about the climate of North America from the Rocky Mountains westward, as the various mountain ranges and the basins between them disrupt and affect air masses in complex ways. However, temperature and moisture are still largely affected by flows of cold air from the north and by warmer, westerly airflows that drive out the cold air. The tropical airflow from the Gulf of Mexico tends to invade only the southern portions of the West in the summer months, when it brings much needed rainfall.

The west coast itself has a relatively mild, temperate climate even into southern British Columbia, where average January temperatures may be above freezing. More importantly, seasonal changes in temperature are less pronounced than in the rest of the continent because of the effects of ocean currents. However, there is a moisture gradient such that southern California is dry year round and northern British Columbia and southern Alaska are wet year round. In between, northern California is wet only in the winter, while Washington State and southern British Columbia are dry only in the summer (Bryson and Hare 1974, 7–8).

Paleoclimatic Change

Because cultural change may result from environmental change, archaeologists must consider the role of climatic change in the composition of North American habitats. The most significant climatic change with continent-wide effects was the **Pleistocene** or Ice Age. In popular movies, the Ice Age is depicted with vast expanses of ice and snow, large and fearsome animals like mammoths and saber-toothed cats, and humans who huddle under skins in caves and rockshelters sometimes venturing out at great risk to hunt mighty beasts. The reality was that the environment was highly variable during the Pleistocene, as were human adaptations to it. Many parts of North America were not glaciated at all; but, nonetheless, the Pleistocene biotic communities may have been quite different from those we can observe today. A good understanding of North America's Ice Age environments is important to archaeologists because this is when humans first entered the continent. The Pleistocene usually is dated from 1.8 million until approximately 10,000 years ago, but human entry into the Americas does not seem to have occurred until the end of this epoch, within the last 25,000 years or less.

During the Pleistocene epoch, large, thick glaciers expanded southward over much of the Northern Hemisphere. However, within the Pleistocene, there were major fluctuations in climate. Parts of the Pleistocene that were colder are called **glacials** and parts that were warmer are called **interglacials**. Periods of glaciation within the Pleistocene are given different names in Europe and in the United States. In North America, the last period of glaciation is called the **Wisconsin glaciation**. It is believed to have begun before 100,000 years ago and to have ended around 10,000 years ago. However, the exact timing is complicated to reconstruct, and understanding remains incomplete (Pielou 1991). The climatic and geologic epoch following the Pleistocene, which began 10,000 years ago and continues in the present, is called the **Holocene**. Many scientists have made the point that the Holocene is not much different in warmth, or so far in length, from one of the interglacials that have occurred at other points in the Pleistocene. This means that, hard as it is to imagine, the Ice Age probably is not over at all!

During the cold peaks of the Ice Age, the outline of the North American continent was different. The massive glaciers that formed during the Ice Age captured enough of the earth's water to lower the level of the oceans, exposing areas of land, now under water (Figure 2.12). Normally, rain and snow that is absorbed into rivers and lakes eventually returns to the oceans, but during the Pleistocene this water remained trapped in the ice of glaciers, changing the ratio between two forms, or isotopes, of the oxygen in the oceans' waters. Thus in comparison to the atmosphere, seawater contains proportionately more of the heavier isotope, ^{18}O, than of the more common form of oxygen, ^{16}O. The capture of rain and snow in glaciers prevents the oxygen contained in these waters from returning to the oceans and rebalancing the isotopic. This means that an indirect measure of the degree of glaciation is the ratio between the isotopes ^{18}O and ^{16}O found in the contents of ocean sediments (Bennett and Glasser 1996, 13–14).

FIGURE 2.12 During the Pleistocene, massive ice sheets covered much of North America. This map shows the continent as the Cordilleran and Laurentian ice sheets began to part. Now-submerged areas of Beringia and the coastlines were exposed at this time (after Meltzer 1993, p. 13).

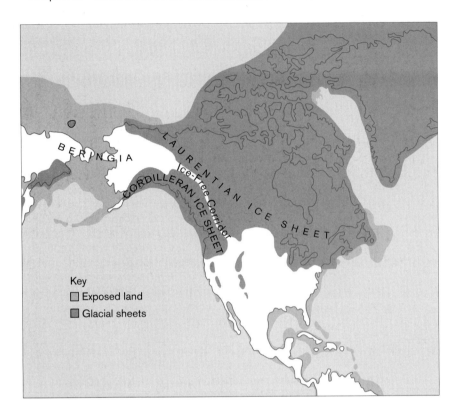

Beringia, the large area of dry land that connected Siberia and Alaska during the Ice Age, was exposed as a result of the glaciation just described. At times during the Pleistocene, North America and Eurasia were a single continent—one continuous landmass over which animal populations, including humans, roamed freely. Coastlines also changed, as shown in Figure 2.12. It is not just that more land was exposed and biotic communities shifted. Rather, different land configurations affected ocean currents and the gradients of rivers, resulting in habitat change.

You may be surprised to learn that much of Alaska was not glaciated during the Ice Age. Warm ocean currents from the south kept coastal and interior Beringia free of ice. Instead, Beringia was an expanse of tundra where low, cold-tolerant grasses also grew. Herds of animals frequented these areas, and human hunters were attracted there because of these herds. Although there is some debate among paleoecologists over how resource rich Beringia actually was during the Pleistocene (Pielou 1991, 147–155), at the peak of the glaciation, massive ice sheets would have blocked animals and humans present there from moving southward into the interior of Canada.

Actually, there were two North American ice sheets during the Wisconsin glaciation (Figure 2.12). One of these, the **Cordilleran ice sheet**, expanded over the northern Rocky Mountains, while the second, the **Laurentian ice sheet**, formed to the east over Hudson Bay and eastern Canada. As temperatures fluctuated during the Wisconsin glaciation, these ice sheets sometimes touched and, when the glaciers shrank, sometimes were separated. At the peak of the Wisconsin glaciation, nearly 20,000 years ago, the combined ice sheets were much greater in extent than those in Europe, covering an area about the size of Antarctica. When the ice sheets did not touch, the unglaciated land between them is thought to have formed an ice-free corridor down which animals and their human hunters could have traveled. Some scientists question what sorts of biotic communities could have existed in this corridor unless it was very wide. In this view, the corridor is an unlikely route south. Refugia, where animals and plants adapted to nonglacial climates may have been able to survive, also probably existed along both coasts throughout the Wisconsin glaciation. The location of refugia along the Pacific Coast may have made it possible for humans to come south from Beringia via a coastal route (see Chapter 3).

The Wisconsin ice sheets were not inert masses of ice. They formed when the snow that fell during the winter failed to melt away during the summer, and as this happened year after year, the snow was compacted into ice. However, over time ice domes built up at the center of the ice sheet and squeezed the underlying ice outward, causing growth in the ice sheet's areal extent. If the sheet reached a region in which summers were warm enough to melt the ice at the glacial margins, the spread of the glacier stopped. Thus, as climate fluctuated during the Wisconsin glaciation, the edge of the ice sheets advanced and retreated.

During the Ice Age the biomes of North America generally were shifted southward. However, because of the complexity of temperature fluctuations and of ice sheet advances and retreats, there is room for debate about what vegetation looked like on a local level. As the ice sheet advanced during periods of cooling, the plants originally growing ahead of the ice would be replaced by species that could tolerate the cold. Much of the area immediately in front of the ice must have been characterized by permafrost and tundra vegetation. However, evidence suggests that in some places coniferous forest also existed (Pielou 1991, 84). Different biotic communities probably filled adjacent areas in a kind of patchwork. Dryness most likely prevented the development of forests in most areas of the western part of North America, except for a narrow area just south of the ice. Mammoths, mastodons, dire wolves, and saber-toothed cats were only some of the now extinct Ice Age mammals that roamed North America. As today, the biotic communities of the Pleistocene were so diverse, and interrelated in such complex ways, that they are best discussed at the local level.

Archaeologists have been very interested in what happened environmentally as the ice began to shrink. The Pleistocene–Holocene boundary at around 10,000 years ago had been preceded by several millennia of warming during which there were glacial retreats and advances. As the ice melted, sea levels rose; but at first the great ice sheets decreased in thickness rather than extent. This meant that for a time, as coastlines were drowned, the area of ice-free land in North America actually got smaller (Pielou 1991, 167). Other processes besides global warming aided the reduction of ice. At the margins of the sea, icebergs often calved off and eventually melted, cooling ocean temperatures. Fresh meltwater from the glaciers also was flowing into the sea. This fresh water was less dense than the salt water and thus remained at the surface of the ocean, where it readily froze in the winter. The result of these processes was less evaporation of water vapor from the ocean surface and less snowfall. Less snowfall meant, in turn, that the glaciers no longer could grow. As climate continued to warm, glaciers wasted away, back from the coasts. This helped the ocean warm and brought warm onshore winds, promoting the establishment of new biotic communities.

Another aspect of postglacial change was that as the thickness of the ice decreased, the earth's crust that had warped under the weight of massive layers of ice began to rebound. This resulted in an **isostatic** change in which the land rose in relation to the sea. Since, however, this process of rebounding took some time, when the ice first melted, the exposed land surface was actually lower than sea level in some places. Thus, the ocean flooded these areas, forming large inland seas in the valley of the St. Lawrence River and in the vicinity of Hudson Bay. Although these seas eventually shrunk away, the process of isostatic rebound is still going on.

The Beringian land bridge was progressively submerged as the ice melted. This process continued, with the Bering Strait widening over time. As this happened, the climate of the land on either side became moister and milder, and the vegetation changed from arctic herbs and low grasses to a more shrubby tundra dominated by dwarf and shrub birches. The largest animals, such as the mammoths and bison of Ice Age Beringia, were reduced in numbers, but elk and other species that could adapt their diets to eating the shrubs flourished. Along the coast, sea mammals migrated northward, and conditions improved for humans (Pielou 1991, 208–210).

Large proglacial lakes also formed in the middle of the North American continent as the Cordilleran and Laurentian ice sheets receded. For example, the Laurentian ice sheet shrank toward the east northeast, but the elevation of the Great Plains rose toward the west, as it still does today. This pattern of shrinkage and elevation meant that the large volume of water melting off the glacier sometimes became trapped between the ice edge and the rising land. In other areas, meltwaters cut massive river channels for the drainage of the proglacial lakes. Scientists have been able to trace the formation and drainage history of a series of lakes between about 15,000 and 8000 years ago.

Another topic of great interest to archaeologists is the nature of animal and plant migrations into formerly glaciated lands. We can expect that as soon as land was ice free, the strong winds along the ice front brought soil and seeds to exposed areas. The biotic communities that first developed no doubt varied and formed a patchwork, just as in communities south of the ice during the Pleistocene. Forests probably were quite open at first, filling in only over time. Bogs were particularly common on the Great Plains after proglacial lakes drained. Overall, the transformation as climate warmed was more complicated than just a northward shifting of biomes. Forest composition as well as location changed after the Pleistocene; in fact, in some places several communities developed in succession (Pielou 1991, 229–232). Animals, of course, also migrated as the ice shrunk, finding suitable habitats in places other than those of the Wisconsin glaciation.

If you live in a part of North America that was glaciated, you probably know that many glacial features are still present on the landscape. These features affect the modern environment in many ways. For example, in much of the Upper Midwest, there are numerous **kettle holes** or lakes, where stagnant ice blocks were left isolated, eventually becoming overlain and surrounded by glacial deposits of various sorts. When the ice finally melted, a depression was formed that has filled with water. These kettle lakes often are associated with **glacial kames**, which are mounds and ridges that represent deposition of outwash from melting glaciers. This topography influences the biotic communities that develop. For example, landscapes dotted with small lakes and kames have a great deal of ecological diversity.

During the Holocene, climate has not remained constant either. A particularly important climatic interval during the mid-Holocene is called the **Hypsithermal**, or sometimes the **Altithermal**. This was a period of warmer and, in some places, drier climate than we have today. The Hypsithermal lasted at least 3000 years, and in the center of North America it peaked about 7000 years ago. In general, biotic communities shifted northward or upward in elevation during the Hypsithermal. However, there is some variation in the timing of the Hypsithermal, and not surprisingly there also are regional differences in the precise effects. In the Arctic Ocean, the Hypsithermal probably caused melting of large areas of ice (Pielou 1991, 277). Archaeologists have attributed some cultural developments to the onset, peak, or end of this climatic period, and we will be referring to it on occasion in the following chapters.

A second climatic episode that has interested North American archaeologists is the **Little Ice Age**. Climate began to deteriorate after 650 years ago, but the coldest period from 400 to 100 years ago (AD 1550–1850) profoundly affected cultural events in Europe (see Fagan 1999). North American archaeologists also have sought connections among changing human settlement patterns, subsistence practices, and the Little Ice Age. In reality, small oscillations in climate have been occurring throughout the Holocene. Just prior to the Little Ice Age, there was a warm period, sometimes called the Medieval Warm period because it stretched between AD 900 and 1300. Although not as profound as the Hypsithermal, its changes certainly did affect North American environments.

Events like El Niño and La Niña are alterations in climate on an even smaller scale. El Niño and La Niña (more formally, the El Niño Southern Oscillation, or ENSO) are an interannual oscillation in which the atmosphere and the ocean of the tropical Pacific interact and affect the climate of large portions of the globe including North America. During El Niño years, conditions in the southern United States are wetter than normal, but conditions in western Canada and the northwest and north central United States are drier. In La Niña years, the reverse conditions prevail, so that the southern United States is dry and the northwest and north central parts of the continent are wet (D'Aleo 2002). A weaker North Atlantic Oscillation may affect the northeastern parts of North America (Fagan 1999).

There is much to consider about past environments, but this brief introduction may help explain the fascination some archaeologists have with the environmental context for the sites they study. As introduced earlier, one of the interdisciplinary fields that contributes to this understanding is geoarchaeology. In Profile 2.1, we describe a career in this type of archaeology.

THE SYSTEMATICS OF NORTH AMERICAN CULTURE HISTORY

Now that you know something about North American environment and climate, we can discuss systematics, that is, the classificatory schemes and conceptual units that archaeologists use to study past cultures. Thus far we have introduced only one concept that is in wide use—the concept of culture areas. This concept,

FACES IN ARCHAEOLOGY

PROFILE 2.1

Julie Stein, Archaeologist and Geoarchaeologist

Julie Stein (Figure 2.13) is an archaeologist whose interests in the context of archaeological remains have led her into the interdisciplinary field of geoarchaeology. Convinced even as an undergraduate that archaeologists needed to better understand sediments and stratigraphy, Stein has done much to make geoarchaeology more widely appreciated. She is a professor of anthropology at the University of Washington in Seattle. Although her career has included stints as curator of archaeology at the Burke Museum and as divisional dean of research for the College of Arts and Sciences, she remains most interested in North American geoarchaeology. She received the Rapp Award from the Geological Society of America (GSA) in 1999 for her contributions to the field of geoarchaeology.

As an undergraduate at Western Michigan University, Stein pursued anthropology because

FIGURE 2.13 Julie Stein doing fieldwork at an archaeological site.

she had found the paleoanthropological finds of Louis and Mary Leakey in Africa exciting. Taking her first archaeological field school in 1972, she discovered her passion when she realized how the beach deposits and glacial tills containing the site being excavated fascinated her. She knew that many archaeologists were relatively uninterested in learning more about the deposits they excavated, but after discussions with her introductory geology professor, she began to identify a contribution she could make to archaeology by combining her interests. Eventually, Stein majored in both geology and archaeology. As she tells it, it was her undergraduate professors' insistence that she attend the meetings of the GSA that really helped her define professional goals. In the 1970s, the connections between geology and archaeology were just beginning to be appreciated, but at the GSA Stein discovered she wasn't the only one to see the potential of combining these fields. By attending GSA symposia at this time, she was able to meet many of the small group of geologists and archaeologists developing the field of geoarchaeology. Eventually, Stein was offered a three-year fellowship in an interdisciplinary graduate program at the University of Minnesota.

Although her master's thesis was a geoarchaeological study at a Bronze Age site in Greece, Stein really was most interested in North American archaeology. Thus, as she began to work on her doctorate, she became involved with the Shell Mound Archaeological Project (SMAP), which was then exploring shell mounds located along the Green River in Kentucky. Shell mounds have fascinating and complex histories of cultural and noncultural accumulation. Stein may be best known for her work on **shell middens** in Kentucky and, later, along the

Northwest Coast and the Hudson River in New York. *Deciphering a Shell Midden* (Stein 1992) is a basic reference for archaeologists working in this kind of context.

Stein received her doctorate in 1980 and began an appointment as an assistant professor of anthropology at the University of Washington. As a woman geoarchaeologist, she was something of a pioneer. At a time when geoarchaeology was marginal, Stein persuaded faculty at the University of Washington that her geoarchaeological expertise would be an asset to the school's program in anthropology and archaeology. Since then, geoarchaeology has become more mainstream within archaeology, and both women and men are entering this specialty more frequently.

Throughout more than 20 years at the University of Washington, Stein has remained an advocate for the importance of geoarchaeology. She has been active in professional societies in both archaeology and geology, and she helped found the Geoarchaeology Interest Group of the Society for American Archaeology. Included in her list of research consultations is work in Peru, Belize, Mexico, and the Marianas, but most of her research has been in North America. Besides continuing work on shell mounds in various locations, Stein has consulted with both historic and prehistoric archaeologists working at Monticello in Virginia, at Cape Addington in Alaska, and at Fort Jefferson, Wickliffe Mounds, and Big Bend in Kentucky; she has even helped look for Lewis and Clark's privies in Oregon.

Closer to home, she has developed expertise in Northwest Coast archaeology through directing a series of excavations in the San Juan Islands. Among these, her Vashon Island Project was noteworthy for its involvement of the public. Recently, she was asked to analyze the sediments adhering to the Kennewick skeletal remains, which are among the oldest human remains in North America (see Chapter 3: Box 3.1, "Why Is the Kennewick Case So Significant?").

As a university professor, Stein has put much energy into teaching and mentoring students, but she also has been a curator of archaeology at the University of Washington's Burke Museum. This work got her deeply involved in the proper curation of the museum's archaeological collections, including many collections the museum was maintaining for the National Park Service. In addition, Stein has been a dean for research at the University of Washington, facilitating the research endeavors of about 900 faculty colleagues from diverse disciplines in the College of Arts and Sciences. She believes that the skills she developed as an interdisciplinary archaeologist have paid off for her as an administrator. Nevertheless, she is happiest as a geoarchaeologist.

Recently, Stein has become the Director of the Burke Museum of Natural History and Culture at the University of Washington. Without a doubt she will continue to promote geoarchaeology, while also meeting the challenges of directing one of the Northwest's most significant natural history museums.

however, does not incorporate information about temporal change. Cultural change is a topic of great interest to archaeologists. This has been true especially since the early part of the twentieth century, when a culture history paradigm developed in archaeology (see Student CD, Section A). Culture history is the ordering of artifacts and other cultural phenomena into a sequence of events over time and in space. However, it is more than a simple chronology. Culture history offers an account of how cultural phenomena have changed. Prior to the early twentieth century, North American archaeologists did not articulate this goal very clearly because they assumed that there was little time depth to human occupation of this continent. However, as more was learned, delineating culture history became an important focus of archaeological work. Although in the latter part of the twentieth century, archaeologists rejected the notion that cultural historical formulation was the ultimate goal of archaeology, many still understand an area's culture history as the baseline from which other questions about the past can be addressed.

To construct culture histories, archaeologists need units of analysis with which to order cultural items. For example, archaeologists group the artifacts they find into types based on a set of attributes that they consider important (see Student CD, Section B). These attributes may be stylistic/morphological, functional, or technological. For the construction of culture history, archaeologists construct **temporal types** that are believed to have temporal significance. In a sense, these types are like **index fossils** in paleontology. Their presence is indicative of a particular time frame during which they are known to have been made by a particular cultural group. The temporal meaning of these types is determined through stratigraphic analysis, direct dating, and comparison with other sites of known age. For example, imagine future archaeologists finding iPods at several sites. Once they had determined that this item of material culture wasn't associated with contexts that predate the twenty-first century, they would be able to use the presence of iPods as an indicator of when sites were inhabited.

After types having temporal significance have been identified, patterning and clustering of types is examined. In this work, archaeologists try to separate sites into **components** by using **stratification** or other indicators. A component is a culturally unique part of a particular site, often thought to represent a single occupation by a group of people or at least repeated occupations by the same social group. Some sites have only one component; others have many. The assemblage of artifacts from each component can then be assumed to represent a distinct community's activities at a particular point in time.

Comparisons of assemblages provide an understanding of patterning in space and time, allowing for a regional perspective on culture history. A **phase** is a grouping of similar components at multiple sites in a region. Types of artifacts, features, the spatial plan, and other attributes of these components are similar. Yet they also are distinct from the characteristics of other components elsewhere. The relationships between phases, sites, and components are illustrated in Figure 2.14. The phase is the basic unit of regional archaeological analysis, corresponding loosely to a culture. Archaeologists try to assign assemblages from various sites to one phase or another, and thus place them in regional cultural history.

Sometimes archaeologists also want to link phases or types that seem to be related. American archaeologists use two terms, **horizon** and **tradition**, to make such linkages. As initially defined, the horizon marks traits and assemblages whose distribution in space suggests a rapid spread over a broad area (Willey and Phillips 1958, 33). In contrast, traditions have to do primarily with temporal continuity in technology or material culture (Willey and Phillips 1958, 37).

These units of classification allow archaeologists to construct regional culture histories. But what about broader, continent-wide patterns in North America's past? Similarities in traditions and horizons may indicate some pre-Columbian evolutionary stages (Willey and Phillips 1948). A **culture stage** is a general level of cultural development as defined by formal attributes. The focus in stage definition has been on technological and economic aspects of cultural development. Traditionally, for all of the Americas, five basic stages have been suggested for

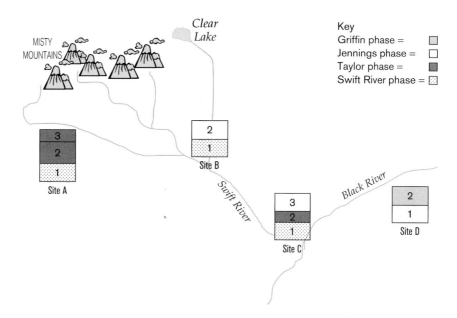

FIGURE 2.14 Hypothetical map illustrating the relationships between components and phases for four excavated sites with various components numbered 1, 2, or 3 at each site and shaded to indicate the regional phase (Griffin, Jennings, Taylor, or Swift River) to which each component has been assigned.

pre-Columbian times. These were the Lithic stage, for which stone tools were the main evidence; the preceramic hunting and gathering Archaic stage; the Formative stage, in which agriculture and social ranking first appeared; the Classic stage, when the first American civilizations appeared, and the post-Classic stage after the collapse of these first civilizations. Only the first three stages have been considered evident in North America, while the Classic and post-Classic have been applied to civilizations that developed in Mesoamerica and South America.

Archaeologists still use these designations to refer to North American culture history to some extent. However, the existence of stages in American cultural evolution is less clear than we once thought. There is now so much variation evident in the cultural sequence across the North American continent that most archaeologists prefer to use periods of time rather than developmental stages. A brief discussion of period designations commonly in use will introduce the broad outlines of the pre-Columbian past in North America.

Instead of the Lithic stage, archaeologists now more commonly recognize a **Paleoindian period** in which the first human cultures developed and flourished in North America. There is no question that these first inhabitants of North America were hunter-gatherers who used stone and bone tools to acquire and process the wild resources available throughout the continent. Arguing against a continent-wide stage, however, there may have been great variation in how mobile people were, in the types of wild resource they utilized, and even in their social organization. This period begins when humans first settled in North America and extends to approximately 10,000 years ago. As we will discuss in Chapter 3, when the Americas were settled and by whom is a matter of great debate. In addition, the end of this period varies a little among culture areas. Some archaeologists, like Bob Kelly (highlighted in Profile 2.2), are particularly interested in Paleoindians, and throughout the continent fascinating new data are emerging.

FACES IN ARCHAEOLOGY

PROFILE 2.2

Robert Kelly, Archaeologist and Professor

Like many archaeologists, Bob Kelly (Figure 2.15) is fascinated by hunter-gatherers. He has studied archaeologically known **foragers** and conducted ethnoarchaeological research among living foragers. Today, Kelly's research interests center on the classic North American foragers, the Paleoindians.

Bob Kelly has been interested in archaeology for as long as he can remember. As a child growing up in New England, he loved Sir Leonard Wooley's book *The Young Archaeologist*. He also loved the outdoors, and during his many hours enjoying nature, he imagined a kinship with those who lived off the land. In the 1960s, the early days of the environmental movement, the stereotype of the American Indian as having lived in harmony with the environment was widely promoted. These images encouraged

FIGURE 2.15 Bob Kelly doing archaeological fieldwork.

Kelly's interest in the past people of North America, so that when he learned of a scholarship to participate in an archaeological excavation, he jumped at the chance to apply. He got the scholarship, and that summer, at 16, he participated in his first excavation at Gatecliff Shelter (see the case study by David Hurst Thomas, "Deep-Site Excavation at Gatecliff Shelter, Nevada" in Chapter 8). After the initial summer he returned several times to the Gatecliff excavation, and his pursuit of archaeology as a career was determined.

Kelly entered Cornell University after only three years in high school, knowing that he would study anthropology and archaeology. While in college he continued to work in the Great Basin, now serving as a field supervisor on various projects. He also got a chance to do some archaeology in Chile on Inca sites and on St. Catherine's Island, Georgia, at shell middens and burial mounds. After graduating from Cornell in 1978, Kelly went to the University of New Mexico for his master's degree and then in 1980 to the University of Michigan for his doctorate, which he earned in 1985. Throughout his graduate work, he continued to focus mainly on Great Basin archaeology, specifically on the cultural ecology of the hunter-gatherers who had lived there. His dissertation research, funded mainly by the American Museum of Natural History, involved survey and test excavation in the vicinity of the Carson Sink and the Stillwater Mountains in Nevada. This research was designed to explore the subsistence and settlement patterns of past foragers in this part of the Great Basin.

Since graduate school, Kelly's career has taken a traditional academic track. He taught briefly at Colby College in Maine before accepting a position at the University of Louisville in Kentucky, where he taught between 1986 and 1997. At Louisville, he had a heavy academic load, teaching classes on archaeological methods, North American archaeology, Native Americans, hunter-gatherer ecology, and both cultural and physical anthropology as well as archaeological field school. Kelly also shouldered major administrative responsibilities, serving his department first as coordinator of the archaeology program and then, for five years, as chair. He chaired the College of Arts and Sciences Social Science Division for his last two years at Louisville, as well.

The many teaching and administrative responsibilities at Louisville made Kelly's fieldwork in the Great Basin difficult, although he did continue his research there as much as possible. During 1988 and 1989, he had a research fellowship at the School of American Research in Santa Fe, New Mexico, which allowed him to further explore the diversity of hunter-gatherer lifeways. Out of this research came his book *The Foraging Spectrum* (1995), which explores both anthropological theory about foragers and the diversity of hunter-gatherer behavior, exploding many stereotypes in the process.

Having read extensively about foragers and having studied them archaeologically, Kelly wanted to conduct ethnoarchaeological research among foragers. He and his wife, cultural anthropologist Lin Poyer, also were looking for an opportunity to do fieldwork together. This opportunity came during the summers of 1993, 1994, and 1995, when Kelly did ethnoarchaeological work among the Mikea in Madagascar. These people were reported to be foragers but they were barely known ethnographically. In fact, they actually only forage seasonally, depending on maize horticulture as well. Although Kelly has not returned to this fieldwork since 1995, he helped set up Bram Tucker, then a graduate student from the University of North Carolina and now a professor at Ohio State University, to continue the work with the Mikea.

A move to the University of Wyoming in 1997 gave Kelly more opportunity to pursue his archaeological interests. His teaching load was reduced, although he still teaches many of the same courses topically, and he no longer fills administrative positions. Moreover, the proximity to the Great Basin and other parts of the West makes the logistics of family and teaching easier to coordinate with fieldwork. On the other hand, between 2000 and 2003, much of Kelly's time was taken up as president-elect and then president of the Society for American Archaeology. As mentioned earlier in connection with Lynne Sebastian (Profile 1.2), this professional service position is a sign of high professional stature but demands much time and energy. Here he experienced new aspects of archaeology, working on a controversial court case concerning Paleoindian skeletal remains, the effect of the World Trade Center disaster on archaeology (there were large collections in one of the subbasements, and the SAA offered its help in the recovery of human remains), and the effect of the war in Iraq on antiquities. Though he enjoyed this work, he was glad to return to his research and teaching.

Currently, Kelly is concentrating on Paleoindian foragers at the Pleistocene–Holocene boundary. He has reinvestigated the Pine Springs site, where archaeological work in the 1960s had suggested that there were Paleoindian materials in association with extinct fauna. He is now focusing on the intriguing fact that the fluted points associated with earlier Paleoindians (see Chapter 3) have rarely been found in North American rockshelters. Kelly wants to explore the question of why this is the case by looking more closely at a number of such sites in the Big Horn Mountains of Wyoming.

Bob Kelly's successful balancing act incorporating teaching, research, and service exemplifies the academic path in archaeology. His consistent fascination with hunter-gatherers, in both the past and present, also illustrates that archaeologists are anthropologists. In both ways, his career provides an important perspective on contemporary North American archaeologists.

FIGURE 2.16 Artist's conception of life during the Middle Archaic at the Black Earth site in southern Illinois, showing the broad range of food items (deer, turtle, fish, crayfish, nuts, and water lily roots) utilized by Archaic people.

An Archaic stage may be recognized by archaeologists, but many also have ceased to treat this as a formal stage. Like Paleoindians, Archaic cultures had hunter-gatherer economies, although these postglacial ones may have been more centered on the use of a broad variety of resources in a local area (Figure 2.16). Originally, the Archaic was distinguished from the later Formative by what was missing from the Archaic. Cultural traits that were absent were agriculture, settled villages, burial mounds or earthworks, and pottery, all of which were associated with Formative cultures. However, we now know that each of these traits was not entirely absent among people considered Archaic. In addition, in some parts of North America, people never developed agriculture but did become sedentary villagers, with social and economic differentiation. On the other hand, in the Great Basin and in many parts of the Subarctic, where people almost always lived in small foraging bands, the entire cultural sequence after Paleoindians can be considered Archaic. These exceptions make it difficult to talk about a continent-wide Archaic stage. The now more commonly designated **Archaic period** follows the Paleoindian, beginning about 10,000 years ago and extending until between 3000 and 2000 years ago. You will see some variation in this date range as we discuss each culture area, and along the Pacific Coast, the term Archaic often is not used at all.

North American archaeologists generally do not use the concept of a Formative stage. West of the Rockies, except in the Southwest culture area among people like the Hohokam discussed in Chapter 1's case study, agriculture did not play a major economic role. However, settled life and the development of social hierarchies often did. Along the Pacific Coast, **complex hunter-gatherers**, who developed social ranking, had hereditary chiefs, and lived in large, settled communities, are found in the later pre-Columbian times. Here archaeologists are far more likely to simply designate Early, Middle, and Late periods, abandoning the traditional terminology altogether. East of the Rocky Mountains, there are many cultures that fit the Formative definition, although the term Woodland is applied instead. Archaeologists generally designate a **Woodland period** beginning between 3000 and 2000 years ago and characterized by all four of the Formative characteristics. Woodland variants have been recognized in the Plains, Midwest, Great Lakes, Northeast, Mid-Atlantic, and Southeast culture areas.

Still more recent settled agriculturalists, including the Mississippians of the Midwest and the Southeast, the Iroquoians of the Northeast, and the Plains Village groups of the Missouri River valley, also could be considered Formative. These people were agriculturalists who lived in settled villages, although their sociopolitical organization varied. Convention is to separate these cultural phenomena from Woodland complexes. The later groups are sometimes called **Late Prehistoric**, but generally they are simply referred to by their culture name directly.

Of course, European exploration and settlement marks the beginning of an **Historic period**, for which there are written records and many complex cultural changes. This period cannot be seen as part of the stage sequence proposed by earlier archaeologists but has often been understood to have truncated the evolutionary development of North America before phenomena called Classic appeared.

Other Important Concepts

Archaeologists also use many general anthropological concepts. One very commonly employed set of terms concerning human sociopolitical organization consists of Elman Service's (1962) concepts of the band, the tribe, the chiefdom, and the state. This simple classification scheme helps us examine the various ways interrelationships among groups within a society are managed and controlled in the process of making a living.

A **band** is the simplest form of sociopolitical organization; it refers to small, mobile groups of related people among whom there is little differentiation in power and wealth. People with this form of organization are hunter-gatherers who subsist on wild resources. Band composition itself is fairly fluid so that people can adjust their position on the landscape based on the availability of resources. People in bands tend to have little personal property, and economic exchange is based primarily on **reciprocity**, or the sharing of food, tools, and labor among social equals. Leaders in bands have no real authority; rather, they try to achieve consensus. This type of sociopolitical organization certainly can be applied to some past Native American groups.

A **tribe** is a larger group of people, often living in villages without well-developed governmental structures. People in tribes usually are divided into kinship groups such as **clans**, which may collectively own the land on which crops are grown. It is kinship relationships that dictate social interaction in tribes. Herders often are tribal, but this type of subsistence pattern did not occur in North America prior to European settlement. In the classic formulation, tribal people are food producers. However, some pre-Columbian North American groups that depended on hunting and gathering or had mixed economies had a tribal sociopolitical organization. Economic exchange continues to be largely reciprocal, and there are very few differences among individuals and their families in terms of wealth and power. Although there are a number of leadership structures in tribes, authority is limited and permanent positions of leadership are rare. However, **big men**, individuals who enjoy higher status and power owing to their entrepreneurship and their skillful use of social obligation, may exist within tribes, but most North American tribal cultures do not seem to have produced such leaders. Tribal sociopolitical structures were very common among the native peoples of North America.

A **chiefdom** is a type of organization intermediate between the tribe and complex state systems. Kinship is an important organizing feature, but families and lineages as well as individuals have differential access to resources and labor, as well as variable amounts of power and prestige. In other words, there is social ranking, but true classes are lacking. The key to the chiefdom system is the production of some surplus, which is redistributed by those in power. Permanent positions of leadership such as chief exist in this type of society, but the amount of authority and power chiefs actually have can vary. Chiefdoms typically have an agricultural basis. However, in North America a number of native hunter-gatherer societies with access to marine resources or fish also can be classified as chiefdoms.

A **state** is a large, autonomous political unit having a centralized government and containing many communities. Don't confuse this concept with the states of the United States such as Pennsylvania or California. In anthropology, the concept refers to a type of sociopolitical organization, which could take the form of a monarchy or a democracy. People in states are divided into social classes based on differences in wealth and power. The government of a state, often staffed by a large bureaucracy, has considerable power and authority. The various offices in government have a permanent reality apart from the individual incumbents. The state did not develop among the native peoples of North America. Of course, once Europeans came to North America, states become a part of the sociopolitical landscape.

Another way to talk about variability in sociopolitical organization is to group societies as **egalitarian**, **ranked**, or **stratified**. Egalitarian societies are ones in which status distinctions are based largely on age, gender, and individual talents and accomplishments. Generally, hunting-gathering bands and some tribes fit into this type, but of course many Pacific Coast hunter-gatherers in North America were not simply egalitarian. These societies are more appropriately called ranked, which means that social position can be inherited; alternatively, ranking of citizens often is based on genealogical nearness to a chief. The important point is that in such societies there is uneven distribution not only of goods and services but also of power and prestige. Obviously a ranked society is closely related to the chiefdoms recognized by Service, and it is often, but not always, associated with agricultural production. Stratified societies are those in which there are sharp class distinctions in wealth, prestige, and power. Stratification usually is associated with the state and may not have characterized any pre-Columbian North American culture. However, some of these societies exhibited internal differences in power, prestige, and wealth, and many North American archaeologists are interested in exploring these topics.

Typologies of sociopolitical organization assume an evolutionary relationship, but as is often the case with cultural phenomena, a neat progression is not really evident in the cultural history of North America. In fact, it is important to remember that although all the typologies mentioned here provide archaeologists with useful terminology, the concepts are abstractions, and exceptions will always be found. Sometimes it is variation rather than types that is most useful in trying to understand and explain change. Types are tremendously useful when we try to answer the questions of what, when, and where; but clues to how and why are more likely to come from looking at cases that don't easily fit into types or even culture areas. Archaeologists use types to communicate effectively but are fascinated by broader questions, such as why agricultural strategies were or weren't adopted or why social hierarchies developed. As you read the following chapters, be alert to questions about the processes of culture change, especially those suggested by the next section.

THEMES IN THE STUDY OF NORTH AMERICA'S PAST

So much happened in North America's past and so many fascinating cultures and places catch our interest, that it is very easy to lose sight of the big picture. Yet, particularly in an introductory text, the ways in which the North American archaeological record can inform the study of broad anthropological questions are important. Introducing developments in the various culture areas is only one goal. Any meaningful understanding of North American archaeology also must involve some sense of what the study of North America's past can contribute to understanding of the nature and history of humans as a whole.

In this text, we suggest that most North American archaeological research can be seen as contributing to the study of seven questions about North America's past. Each of these in turn relates to broad research questions archaeologists and anthropologists have about the nature and history of humans. These thematic questions are listed in Table 2.1 and discussed briefly here; each is addressed by the information provided in Part 2, and we will return to them in Chapter 14.

First, one of the most fascinating things about humans is that we can be found so widely around the globe, while many other species are much more restricted in their distribution. Although it is clear that modern humans evolved from tropical African primates and colonized areas outside Africa only after several million years of evolution, modern humans eventually settled all the continents except Antarctica. The settlement of North America is part of the history of this

---

TABLE 2.1 Thematic Research Questions in North American Archaeology

1. How and when did the original settlement of North America occur?
2. How have humans adapted to the diverse environments of North America and to climatic change over time?
3. How, when, and where did food production develop in North America?
4. How, when, and where did sociopolitically complex, internally differentiated cultural systems develop in North America?
5. What ethnic identities can be identified and historically traced in North America's past?
6. How did settlement by Europeans and culture contact between Native Americans and Europeans transform North American cultural and natural landscapes?
7. How did the United States and Canada develop into global and industrial powers?

dispersion. Most scholars agree that the settlement of the Americas occurred relatively late in this story, no earlier than 25,000 years ago. A variety of questions concerning the nature of human migratory behavior and the timing of key cultural developments, such as the hunting of large game animals and boat building, as well as historical questions about past population composition and movements, can be addressed by using North American evidence. We examine these issues in more depth in Chapter 3 as the second part of this book begins, but some information also is considered in each of the culture area chapters that follow when we discuss the first occupants of particular areas. Besides Jon Erlandson's case study, "Sea Change: The Paleocoastal Occupations of Daisy Cave" (in Chapter 3), "Eel Point and the Early Settlement of Coastal California: A Case Study in Contemporary Archaeological Research" by L. Mark Raab and Andrew Yatsko (Student CD, Section D.3) is particularly relevant to these issues.

Second, the main reason that humans have been so successful in global colonization is that we are a highly adaptable species that uses culture to adjust to the varying circumstances encountered during migration and settlement. Thus we are able to live in environments that would be uninhabitable were we dependent on biology alone. Given the diverse natural environments of North America and what the continent's archaeological record tells us about changes in climate since humans arrived here, there is a tremendous amount of evidence about how people have used culture to adapt in North America. Human adaptations to local environments will be particularly evident when we discuss the ways in which hunter-gatherer populations settled into local environments during the Archaic period after initial colonization of each culture area. At least two general types of hunter-gatherer strategy have been recognized by archaeologists. The distinction between foragers and collectors is that **foragers** move residentially as a group when resources are depleted, while **collectors** move less frequently, establishing longer-term camps and sending out foraging parties to acquire resources and bring them back to the main camp for the everyone's use (Binford 1980). This distinction is thought to relate to the evolution of sedentism, or more permanent village sites among hunter-gatherers. Two case studies in this text are most closely related to this theme: "It Takes a Team: Interdisciplinary Research at the Koster Site," by Michael Wiant and Sarah Neusius (in this chapter), and "The Dust Cave Archaeological Project: Investigating Paleoindian and Archaic Lifeways in Southeastern North America" by Renée Walker et al. (Student CD, Section D.5). However, human adaptation is one important theme throughout this book, and it is discussed in connection with other populations as well.

A third significant question in anthropology is when, how, and why humans stopped being hunter-gatherers and shifted to the production of their own food. This transition is widely recognized as one of the most important points in human cultural evolution: it not only changed how people acquired food and what they ate, it had social consequences of great importance. Although stereotypical views of Native North Americans may suggest otherwise, experiments with farming occurred in southern California and the Great Basin, and the majority of populations inhabiting the Southwest, the Plains, and the Eastern Woodlands became farmers.

In fact, one of the important archaeological discoveries since flotation (see Student CD, Section C) became routine in archaeology is that groups in the interior parts of the Eastern Woodlands domesticated a variety of native plants as long ago as the Archaic period. This development provides an important example of the independent shift to food production in a temperate forest region. In addition, throughout the culture areas noted previously, later adoption of tropical cultigens, notably maize and beans, has provided insights into the diffusion of farming across diverse environments. Material relevant to the shift to food production can be found primarily in discussions of later pre-Columbian groups contained in Chapters 9 to 13. Chapter 13's case study by John Hart, "A New History of Maize-Bean-Squash Agriculture in the Northeast," describes recent archaeological findings about how and when agricultural systems centered on the cultivation of maize, beans, and squash came into existence in the Northeast. Food production should not be seen as an inevitable development in human culture, however, and Native Americans who lived in very rich environments, like those of the West Coast, but did not develop food-producing strategies provide important comparative cases.

A fourth overarching research question addressed by anthropologists is when, where, and how complex sociopolitical systems developed among humans. In other words, how did chiefdoms (ranked) and states (stratified) come into being? As used by anthropologists, "complexity" refers to the existence of social hierarchies and/or various mechanisms for integrating large groups of people. Even though North American states did not develop, this might have happened if Europeans had not arrived when they did. Moreover, there were a variety of pre-Columbian groups organized as chiefdoms, and the archaeological record (Figure 2.17) contains considerable evidence concerning the early stages of sociopolitical complexity. These developments occur in coastal areas among hunter-gatherers as well as among agriculturalists. Anthropologists have found that sociopolitical complexity is much more common among food-producers than

FIGURE 2.17 The main plaza at Moundville in Alabama. Like many others considered Mississippian by archaeologists, this large site, includes a large open plaza with regularly spaced, flat-topped mounds indicating community planning, labor mobilization, and perhaps ritual activity on a scale usually associated with chiefdoms.

among foragers, but this only makes the North American cases of complex hunter-gatherers all the more fascinating and important. In addition, very interesting nonhierarchical forms of complexity, or **heterarchy**, may also have existed in some Native American societies. The topic of developing complexity is addressed in each of our culture area chapters because some degree of complexity was introduced in later pre-Columbian times throughout most of the continent. Sociopolitical complexity also is addressed directly in the case study by Ben Fitzhugh, "From Sites to Social Evolution: The Study of Emergent Complexity in the Kodiak Archipelago, Alaska" (Chapter 4), and later in "Chumash Complexity" (Box 7.1). Several other case studies describe investigations of either foragers or farmers whose cultures archaeologists consider sociopolitically complex.

Fifth, anthropologists are fascinated with human cultures and the groups that share them, and North American archaeology has much to contribute in this respect. Unfortunately, it is not necessarily a simple matter to recognize ethnic groups in the past. **Ethnicity** is based on identification with an ethnic group and is an elusive, dynamic, and nonmaterial property. Of course, there are material expressions of the sense of belonging to a particular group. People of different ethnicities may dress differently, cook differently, and use different tools, among other things. Ideally, archaeologists identify these material correlates of ethnicity in the archaeological record. Patterning in the archaeological record, however, does not have to be related solely to ethnic identity; instead, it might indicate differences in activities among closely related people. The systematic concepts introduced in the preceding section of this chapter are intended to help archaeologists identify patterning in a consistent way, but as Section A of the Student CD explains, perceptions about what archaeological units mean have changed over the last century. Archaeologists have moved from a fascination with ordering these units in culture histories to a focus on behavior, activities, and the processes of culture change and, now, to suggesting the possibility of multiple potential histories of North America's past based on gender, various ethnic traditions, and differences in power, wealth, and prestige.

Regardless, the problem of identifying ethnic or cultural groups in the past, and telling something about their lifestyle, remains an important theme in North American archaeology. Today's recognition that one of archaeology's contributions is helping marginalized groups recapture their history has actually made ethnic identification more important. NAGPRA also has made identification of ethnicity a requirement in the disposition of human remains. Unfortunately identification of ethnicity over many generations can be challenging. Archaeologists have been most successful in identifying specific ethnicities in the very late pre-Columbian, Protohistoric, and Historic periods. Later, in Box 10.1, "Historic Ethnicities and the Archaeological Record," we shall look directly at this topic, and "Ethnicity and Class in Colonial Foodways," by Elizabeth Scott (Student CD, Section D.6), shows how food remains can be evidence of ethnicity.

A sixth closely related topic, the topic of culture contact, also interests anthropologists. Of course, native North American cultures were coming into contact and affecting each other for millennia before Europeans arrived, and archaeologists have contributed to our understanding of these dynamics, as shown in several instances in the chapters that follow. However, one of the greatest historical stories of culture contact has to do with the Columbian encounter. North American archaeology has a great deal to contribute to understanding of this dynamic period. Historical records recount events and developments from the perspective of European settlers, but the archaeological record helps show that what actually happened was much more complex. At the very least, there are alternative perspectives on the encounter that make clear the active role of natives in structuring contact and its aftermath. In the fifteenth century, future European dominance was hardly a given, and the common perception that replacement of native populations was inevitable should be questioned. As we mentioned in Chapter 1, it is also true that many native ethnicities have survived into the present, greatly transformed but nevertheless testaments to the persistence of early cultural traditions. While we cannot trace the history of all native peoples, the nature and complexity of the Protohistoric and early Historic contacts are raised in each culture area chapter as we begin discussion of the Historic era. The case study in Chapter 7, "Cultures in Contact at Colony Ross," by Kent Lightfoot et al., also provides insight into a little-known colonial encounter on the Pacific Coast.

Finally, from an anthropological perspective, another great transition in the human story is the relatively recent development of global capitalism and the industrial state. This transformation in human culture also involves much more than a technological change and has had important economic, demographic, social, and political consequences. Moreover, this transformation is ongoing in many parts of the globe today. The stories of European colonization, the slave trade, nation building, immigration, and industrial development in the United States and Canada during the Historic period are directly associated with this transition. At the very least, historical archaeology can enrich understanding of these processes. However, because of its focus on the material record, archaeology also is particularly well suited to other tasks: the exploration of the lives of those about whom there is little written record, and the investigation of topics like the impact of mass production and the development of industrial technology. Each of our chapters looks at this range of topics in its section on the Historic period. In addition, Exhibit 13.1, "Iron Furnaces," directly addresses one part of the early industrial record.

Much of the excitement of North American archaeology comes from the different examples it provides about the questions listed in Table 2.1. What makes a piece of archaeological evidence most interesting may be what it contributes to discourse about one of them. Keep these themes in mind as you read about the North American culture areas in the rest of this text.

A FINAL WORD ABOUT DATES AND DATING

As discussed in Section C of the Student CD, archaeologists use several dating techniques. The two most important methods of **absolute dating** used in North America are **radiocarbon dating**, based on measurements of carbon isotopes in organic materials, and **dendrochronology**, based on analysis of tree rings. In addition to learning about these techniques, however, it is necessary to understand the variety of conventions for reporting dates, which can be confusing to beginning students.

First of all, saying that something happened 1000 years ago would seem to be a straightforward statement, but precisely what "1000 years ago" means in calendar years will be different in the year of publication of this text and 50 years later. This may not be a great problem when the span of years is large or when the author is not far removed in time from the reader, but it obviously makes a difference for the scientist wishing to be precise. Reporting radiocarbon dates relative to the year AD 1950, the approximate year of the invention of this technique, is the archaeological convention for resolving this problem. Thus, when you see a date of 1000 BP for before present, it will always mean AD 950 no matter when you are reading the date.

Second, it might seem most sensible to report dates in BC/AD (before Christ/in the year of the Lord) as is common in the calendar used popularly today. However, those who object to the religious connotations of BC/AD propose the designations BCE/CE, for before the common era/of the common era. Archaeologists often have preferred to bypass the issue entirely by sticking to BP dates.

Unfortunately, this also is not necessarily simple when it comes to specific dates. A date obtained from a particular radiocarbon sample would be reported as a date range by giving the date as 1000 ±100 BP to indicate that the true date most likely falls between 1100 BP and 900 BP (AD 850–1050). This means that dates like 1000 BP are obvious simplifications of complex data. Moreover, since radiocarbon years must be adjusted or calibrated based on what we know about the fluctuation in the atmosphere of carbon-14 (^{14}C), there is not a direct correspondence between a radiocarbon year and a calendar year. Especially for longer time spans, the discrepancy may be significant. For this reason, archaeologists always mark dates as calibrated by using "cal BP" (or even "cal BC/AD") when they have adjusted them. For example, 930 cal BP is roughly equivalent to an uncorrected date of 1000 BP, and 13,990 cal BP is roughly equivalent to 12,000 BP (Table 2.2). (Another suggestion is that BP be used for calibrated and bp for uncalibrated dates.) However, radiocarbon dates can be calibrated in several ways by using tree-ring or other date estimates, and calibration curves almost certainly will continue to be adjusted as we learn more about these fluctuations and refine other dating techniques. Thus, scholarly journals often ask that dates simply be reported in uncalibrated radiocarbon years, to ensure that they are comparable.

Finally, in some instances BC/AD dates may be most appropriate. In areas of North America such as the Southwest, for which dendrochronology is well established, calendar years based on tree rings rather than radiocarbon years often are obtained. Here archaeologists are most likely to use the BC/AD convention for reporting dates because the correspondence is straightforward. A second instance in which AD dates commonly are used is in writing about historical archaeology, where calendar dates may actually appear in written records.

All of this is more than bewildering to novices; it presents a problem for authors of books like this one who wish to provide understandable and comparable dates throughout many chapters. We considered several possible ways of resolving the problem and found none of them to be perfect. In the end, we have used BP dates except for the Historic period. In Chapter 9 on the Southwest culture area and in a few other places where they may be helpful, we provide BC/AD dates in parentheses. We also provide approximate calibrated dates as well as BP dates in the timelines provided for Chapters 3 to 13. Our goal has been to make the dates we use clear and comparable.

TABLE 2.2 Comparison of Uncalibrated and Calibrated Radiocarbon Dates

Uncalibrated Years BP	Calibrated Years BP	Calibrated Years
500	520	AD 1,430
1,000	930	AD 1,020
1,500	1,350	AD 600
2,000	1,940	AD 10
2,500	2,610	660 BC
3,000	3,190	1,240 BC
3,500	3,770	1,820 BC
4,000	4,440	2,490 BC
4,500	5,150	3,200 BC
5,000	5,730	3,780 BC
5,500	6,300	4,340 BC
6,000	6,840	4,880 BC
6,500	7,380	5,440 BC
7,000	7,790	5,840 BC
7,500	8,270	6,320 BC
8,000	8,860	6,910 BC
8,500	9,500	7,550 BC
9,000	9,980	8,030 BC
9,500	10,510	8,560 BC
10,000	11,160	9,210 BC
10,500	12,420	10,470 BC
11,000	12,920	10,970 BC
11,500	13,420	11,470 BC
12,000	13,990	12,040 BC

Adapted from Gibbon (1998, Table 1).

CHAPTER SUMMARY

This chapter has introduced background information about North American environments and cultures that will be helpful in understanding what archaeologists have learned about the human past in this part of the world. The following points were made:

- A culture area is a geographic area within which ethnic groups tend to have similar cultural traits.
- The ten culture areas commonly recognized for North America are the Arctic, the Subarctic, the Northwest Coast, the Plateau, California, the Great Basin, the Southwest, the Plains, the Southeast, and the Northeast.
- North American environments can be divided into several macroscale biomes including tundra, coniferous forest, moist temperate forest, temperate deciduous forest, chaparral, cold desert, hot desert, and temperate grassland. In southern Florida, semitropical and tropical communities also exist, as do southern coniferous forest communities in some mountain areas of northern Mexico.

- Besides these terrestrial biomes, riverine and coastal habitats are important aspects of the North American environment.

- Humans were an important factor in North American ecosystems even in pre-Columbian times, when the various activities of people depleted or favored certain resources at the expense of others. European settlement changed the nature and extent of human impact on the environment but did not begin it.

- North American climate is largely controlled by the interaction of arctic, tropical, and Pacific airstreams, but mountain ranges disrupt and affect these airstreams, particularly from the Rocky Mountains westward.

- Many environmental changes of significance to the human past of North America were associated with the last glaciation of the Pleistocene epoch, which is called the Wisconsin glaciation. At the peak of this glaciation, much of northern North America was covered by two massive ice sheets, the Cordilleran and the Laurentian. Sea level also was lowered so that a large area known as Beringia connected North America and Eurasia and areas along the coasts that now lie underwater were exposed.

- Complex changes took place as the Wisconsin glaciation waned and the Holocene began: the drowning of land areas, the isostatic rebound of the earth's crust, many changes in the lakes, rivers, and runoff regimes of the continent, and the colonization of newly deglaciated land by plant and animal species.

- During the Holocene, possibly significant climatic changes are associated with the Hypsithermal or Altithermal warm–dry period of the mid-Holocene, the Medieval Warm period (AD 900–1300), and the Little Ice Age (AD 1300–1850). Smaller-scale climatic phenomena, the El Niño Southern Oscillation and the weaker North Atlantic Oscillation, may also have affected human adaptations.

- Conceptual units important to the archaeological construction of culture histories are temporal types, components, phases, horizons, and traditions.

- Possible stages in the development of North American cultures have been proposed and are sometimes used. In general, however, contemporary North American archaeologists utilize periods that do not imply a progression of cultural developments to discuss the past. Common periods are the Paleoindian, the Archaic, the Woodland, the Late Prehistoric, and the Historic in the eastern two-thirds of the continent, while west coast archaeologists may simply refer to Early, Middle, and Late periods preceding Historic times.

- North American archaeologists often refer to sociopolitical characteristics by utilizing Elman Service's typology for bands, tribes, chiefdoms, and states or by designating egalitarian, ranked or stratified societies.

- Key research questions relate the study of North America's past to broader themes in the anthropological study of humans. These involve human migration, human adaptation to diverse environments, the development of food production, the development of sociopolitical complexity, the identification of ethnicity, culture contact, and the development of globalization and industrialization.

- Archaeologists follow various conventions for dating North America's past, but in this text, for consistency, we refer primarily to uncalibrated BP dates prior to the Historic period.

This chapter concludes our introduction to the study of North America's past. In the next chapter we begin to look at what archaeologists have concluded about the culture history and past lifeways of this continent. The first consideration—how and when this continent was settled by humans—is the focus of Chapter 3.

SUGGESTIONS FOR FURTHER READING

For a classic description on the culture areas of North America:

Kroeber, Alfred L. 1963. *Cultural and Natural Areas of Native North America*, 4th printing. Berkeley: University of California Press.

For a classic on North American environmental characteristics:

Shelford, Victor E. 1963. *The Ecology of North America*. Urbana: University of Illinois Press.

For more on the various interdisciplinary methods used by archaeologists:

Pearsall, Deborah M. 2000. *Paleoethnobotany: A Handbook of Procedures*. New York: Academic Press.

Reitz, Elizabeth, and Elizabeth Wing. 1999. *Zooarchaeology*. Cambridge: Cambridge University Press.

Sobolik, Kristin D. 2003. *The Archaeologist's, Toolkit*, Vol. 5, *Archaeobiology*. Walnut Creek, CA: AltaMira Press.

Stein, Julie, and William Farrand, eds. 1999. *Sediments in Archaeological Context*. Salt Lake City: University of Utah Press.

For a readable account of environmental change associated with the end of the Wisconsin glaciation:

Pielou, E. C. 1991. *After the Ice Age: The Return of Life to Glaciated North America*. Chicago: University of Chicago Press.

For information on the impact of native North Americans on their environment:

Minnis, Paul E., and Wayne J. Elisens. 2000. *Biodiversity and Native America*. Norman: University of Oklahoma Press.

For other views on the North American past:

Gibbon, Guy. 1998. *Archaeology of Prehistoric Native America: An Encyclopedia*. New York: Garland.

Pauketat, Timothy R., and Diana Di Paolo Loren, eds. 2005. *North American Archaeology*. Malden, MA: Blackwell.

For greater understanding of how North America's past fits into broader anthropological and archaeological themes:

Scarre, Chris, ed. 2005. *The Human Past: World Prehistory and the Development of Human Societies*. London: Thames and Hudson.

For more on archaeological dating:

Nash, Stephen E. 2000. *It's About Time: A History of Archaeological Dating in North America*. Salt Lake City: University of Utah Press.

OTHER RESOURCES

Sections H and I of the Student CD supply web links, places to visit, additional discussion questions, and other study aids. The Student CD also contains a variety of additional resources, including a complete list of the references cited in this chapter. Particularly relevant resources include "A Brief History of North American Archaeology" (Section A) and "Archaeological Laboratory Analysis" (Section C). "The Dust Cave Archaeological Project: Investigating Paleoindian and Archaic Lifeways in Southeastern North America" (Section D.5) nicely illustrates interdisciplinary investigations of human adaptations, and "Ethnicity and Class in Colonial Foodways" (Section D.6) is an example of zooarchaeological analysis.

CASE STUDY

This chapter has introduced several aspects of North American environment, climate, and culture history. In Box 2.2, we offered perspective on the importance of interdisciplinary research in contemporary archaeology. The complex questions archaeologists address often require the integration of many lines of investigation. This chapter's case study is about a large interdisciplinary research project at the Koster site, an Archaic period site located in west-central Illinois. Specifically, this research focused on changes in the environment and in human strategies during the Hypsithermal interval, a warm–dry mid-Holocene period mentioned briefly in the chapter. The Koster case highlights the need for

scholarly teamwork in addressing complex archaeological problems and reviews the development of a project-related archaeological research center that was opened to the public. Although the work described here took place in the 1970s, the story of the Koster Project exemplifies the complexity of archaeological research problems and illustrates one way in which archaeologists and other scientists can work as a team. As you read this case study, pay attention to the many different kinds of data generated. Could human cultural ecology have been explored as effectively without the contributions of all the researchers involved?

IT TAKES A TEAM

Interdisciplinary Research at the Koster Site

Michael D. Wiant and Sarah W. Neusius

PROLOGUE: KOSTER SITE EXCAVATION, KOSTER FARM, GREENE COUNTY, ILLINOIS, 1975

We finally had reached Horizon 11, the remains of an Early Archaic settlement more than eight millennia old, at the depth of 29 feet (9 m) below the present-day ground surface. This deposit had been our objective since it was discovered in 1970 at the bottom of a 6-by-6-foot (1.8 × 1.8 m) shaft. In that test pit, an excavator had unearthed the remains of an ancient campfire with red-orange sediment, ash, and fragments of wood charcoal so well preserved that the fire appeared just extinguished, rather than 8500 years ago (Figure 2.18). For six summers, we had used shovels to excavate an immense hole in Theodore and Mary

Koster's 3-acre cornfield, removing vast amounts of sediment while uncovering the remains left by those who had repeatedly occupied this spot over the millennia. The hole measured 40,000 square feet (3715 m^2) at the surface. For safety, we had terraced the walls, installed pumps around the perimeter of the excavation to lower the water table, and placed pumps in the excavation area to remove rainwater.

Now, with these precautions in place, we kept digging. In a 1512-square-foot (140 m^2) area at the bottom of the hole, we explored the remains of another ancient settlement. Setting aside our shovels, we excavated with trowels, brushes, and bamboo picks to expose each and every artifact larger than an inch (2.54 cm) and map its location. In many areas, we mapped the location of every artifact bigger than a quarter-inch (0.64 cm) and placed it in a coin

FIGURE 2.18 An excavator uncovers evidence of a hearth in one of the original Koster test pits in 1970. Note flecks of black charcoal, gray areas of ash, and white speckles of mussel shell. The sediments themselves have been reddened as a result of the fires in this ancient hearth.

envelope marked with the depth and horizontal position of the specimen. From this level the terraced walls of the excavation rose skyward, and when we raised the tarps protecting them, we could see a layer cake of what remained of camps and villages occupied between 8500 and 4000 years ago.

While a crew of 40 Northwestern University Archaeological Field School students continued the excavation at the Koster farm, others worked in Kampsville, a small town on the bank of the Illinois River, 9 miles (15 km) and a ferry ride from the Koster site. Structures that were once homes, a hardware store, a funeral parlor, and a post office now served as a paleoethnobotany laboratory, an archaeozoology laboratory, a central data processing and flotation laboratory, and a lithic artifact analysis laboratory. Within, a variety of scientists and students studied the objects we'd unearthed days before. At night, professors and students alike came together to discuss what Archaic period life had been like in the Illinois River valley.

During the past century, there have been many noteworthy multidisciplinary archaeological expeditions, but the Koster Project conducted during the 1970s remains an extraordinary example of the potential of coordinated archaeological research. We were fortunate to have been part of the team that excavated and interpreted the Koster site. In this case study, we introduce the many facets of this project, which was only one of the projects undertaken through the Kampsville research facility.

ORGANIZING ARCHAEOLOGICAL RESEARCH: STUART STRUEVER'S VISION

The Koster Project began with the vision of Stuart Struever, which transformed the practice of archaeology in the lower reaches of the Illinois River valley. Raised along the Illinois River, Struever had discovered prehistory as a young man in the farm fields around Peru, Illinois, where he collected artifacts and organized them into a museum display in his grandparents' home. Later, while a graduate student at Northwestern University, Struever became intrigued with the concept of a long-term, multidisciplinary archaeological program that could focus on complex problems like the reconstruction of regional subsistence and settlement systems. He saw the typical organization of North American archaeological projects at that time as limited by a failure to incorporate multiple researchers with distinct specialties. His ideas began to crystallize while he was working on his dissertation on Woodland subsistence-settlement systems, using the lower Illinois River valley as his research universe.

In 1963 Struever began to "conceptualize the idea of building an independent archaeological research center with a staff, facilities, and budgets necessary to sustain a long-term, regional scale, multidisciplinary research program" (Struever, personal communication, September 16, 2003). Five years later, he published a paper arguing that although advances in anthropological theory had fostered new and exciting problems for archaeology, solutions to these new problems required tools not then available. He concluded that archaeology lacked the institutional framework necessary for archaeologists, natural scientists, and technicians to work together on a problem. Both facilities and funding were inadequate for the kind of long-term cooperation necessary (Struever 1968a, 150). With the discovery and subsequent excavation of the Koster site, Struever would have the opportunity to apply these ideas.

DISCOVERY OF THE KOSTER SITE: AN EXCEPTIONAL RESEARCH OPPORTUNITY

In 1961, following his excavations at the Koster Mound Group, Gregory Perino of the Gilcrease Institute in

Tulsa, Oklahoma, had excavated a single test pit in a cornfield behind the Koster farmhouse. He discovered Early Woodland and Late Archaic artifacts and mentioned the finds to Struever. In 1969 Struever and his field school students, who were then excavating at a nearby Middle/Late Woodland site (see Chapter 12), decided to do some work at Koster. They were studying the rise of a local culture called White Hall. Encouraged by a local farmer who had discovered White Hall pottery at the Koster site, Struever and his field school arrived at the site late that summer to excavate a series of test pits.

Before long, the team discovered a stratified, multicomponent site in which prehistoric occupations could be clearly delineated. In each of the six Archaic period (10,000–3000 BP) cultural horizons identified that season, they found well-preserved plant and animal remains, large quantities of debris such as limestone and chipped stone debitage, and a variety of chipped stone, ground stone, and bone tools (Houart 1971). Here was an opportunity to explore a relatively unknown period of prehistory. The Koster site soon became the focus of the lower Illinois River valley archaeological program, and this program grew into the multidisciplinary research center, then known as the Foundation for Illinois Archaeology, of which Struever had been dreaming.

The Koster site excavation provided the chance to develop an institutional framework. A cadre of natural scientists, archaeologists, and students was drawn by the opportunity to explore an exceptional archaeological site (Struever and Holton 1979). Kampsville, an old riverboat town struggling in the new era of trucking, had numerous empty houses and storefronts to house the facilities of Struever's archaeological enterprise. Not surprisingly, fund-raising proved to be the most challenging endeavor, but with the guidance of Chicago businesspeople, Struever publicized the Koster Project throughout the United States. American archaeological sites long in the shadow of those in distant lands were illuminated by this exposure, and private funding followed.

By the mid-1970s, more than 200 students, staff, and faculty, including Struever's Northwestern University colleagues Jim Brown, Jane Buikstra, and Bob Vierra, were assembling each summer to work and study in a grassroots archaeological institute headquartered in Kampsville. The excavation of the Koster site proceeded in full view of an unprecedented audience frequently numbering more than 1000 visitors

each week, many of whom had read national news stories about the site. The visitors peered over the rim of the excavation and watched four dozen students reveal the past, while guides provided information on what had been found. Many visitors would then drive the 9 miles to the Kampsville Archeology Museum to see ancient artifacts in interpreted museum exhibits.

Struever seized the opportunity to transform Kampsville by establishing a dispersed campus of laboratories, offices, dormitories, a library, museum, collection repository, and lecture hall, all nestled among the homes and businesses of the community. The Koster site was the centerpiece of archaeological research for a decade; but at the same time, archaeologists explored Archaic and Woodland period habitation and mortuary sites elsewhere in the region. We transported artifacts and a variety of samples back to the laboratory complex in Kampsville, where they were analyzed, often quickly enough to inform those in the field, who, in turn, could adjust excavation strategies if necessary. The flotation laboratory alone processed hundreds of half-bushels of sediment per day and sent samples of carbonized plant remains and small animal bones to the paleoethnobotany and archaeozoology laboratories, respectively. Archaeologists, botanists, geologists, **malacologists**, palynologists, zoologists, and many others worked together to uncover part of the past and develop an understanding of the natural and human history of the region.

The integration of the enterprise was articulated in Archaeology and the Natural Sciences, a field school course in which students, staff, and faculty had the opportunity to hear firsthand from those exploring the information potential of bits and pieces of the past. Guest lectures by leading archaeologists and scientists provided a unique vista of contemporary thought and research as well as constructive criticism.

All this, and more, created an unparalleled learning environment that fueled conversation and study well into many nights. Struever's experiment in the organization of archaeological research created an extraordinary milieu of discovery, expertise, information, and opportunity. Not only was it a heady time, but a surprising number of today's archaeologists passed through Kampsville in those years, going on to incorporate parts of Struever's vision in their own understanding of how to do archaeology. We were fortunate to be two of these young scholars.

EXPLORING THE ARCHAIC PERIOD: THE KOSTER PROJECT RESEARCH DESIGN

In the midcontinent, investigations of shell mounds in Kentucky during the 1930s and 1940s provided the first substantial inventory of preceramic material culture and evidence of cultural sequences. A decade later, the excavation and analysis of the Modoc Rock Shelter at the edge of the Mississippi River valley in southwestern Illinois signaled a major paradigm shift in the study of the Archaic period (Fowler 1959). At Modoc, researchers departed from the then prevalent classificatory approach by interpreting the sequence of occupations in terms of ecological adaptations. These were thought to have evolved from generalized foraging (10,000–8000 BP) to more localized adaptations (6000–4000 BP). Stratified deposits elsewhere further refined our understanding of Archaic period cultural ecology. The Koster site provided another, and in some ways a better, opportunity to explore the Archaic period.

The Koster site is located in Greene County, in west-central Illinois, in the lower reach of the Illinois River valley (Figure 2.19). In this stretch of its course, the Illinois River is deeply entrenched in a bedrock valley. Precipitous limestone cliffs mark the edge of the valley, some rising more than 200 feet (60 m) above the valley floor. **Loess**, a windblown sediment deposited near the end of the Pleistocene epoch,

mantles the bedrock and forms the upland surface. The wall of limestone is broken only where tributary streams enter the valley and by steep ravines that channel precipitation runoff from small drainage networks reaching onto the upland surface. In many instances, sediment eroded from the upland surface has accumulated, creating landforms known as **colluvial** or **alluvial fans**, depending on the process by which sediment was deposited.

One such fan may be found on land formerly farmed by Theodore Koster. Here an intermittent stream, Koster Creek, which is rarely more than a few feet wide when flooded, reaches from the upland surface to the Illinois River floodplain. Historically, at least, Koster Creek emptied into the now-drained Calamus Lake, one of many large, shallow backwater lakes in the area. As the stream's drainage network expanded, sediment eroded from its tributary headwalls and valley flanks accumulated where the creek enters the Illinois River valley, creating what is now known as the Koster fan. People lived on the surface of the Koster fan and abandoned it many times during the Archaic, so that the remains of their settlements have been buried and preserved in its body.

Unlike stratified deposits in many rockshelters, which often consist of thin, laminated beds of artifact-bearing sediment, the Koster fan consisted of artifact-bearing strata separated by relatively thick deposits almost entirely devoid of artifacts. Furthermore, Koster's inhabitants were not limited by the walls of a rockshelter, and their settlement could have been larger and longer term, while evidence of a wide range of activities might be preserved there. Finally, the long sequence of occupations at Koster provided a view of culture over a long span of time at a single site. What an opportunity to consider the complex Archaic period dynamic between environment and culture!

At the outset, Koster site research addressed two concerns: (1) a cultural chronology for the Archaic period in the lower Illinois River valley and (2) cultural development during the Middle to Late Archaic periods. The former required careful excavation of the stratified deposits at Koster and recovery of charcoal in sufficient quantities to assay its age. The latter required information on the environment around each settlement, the activities undertaken during each occupation, and comparisons between the settlements at different times.

Archaeologists have long been interested in how human societies adapted to environmental change,

FIGURE 2.19 The location of the Koster site and the town of Kampsville in the lower Illinois River valley (after Cook 1976, Figure 1).

and those who study the Archaic period in the Midwest are particularly concerned with how the region's hunter-gatherers coped with environmental change during the Hypsithermal interval (Phillips and Brown 1983). The Hypsithermal interval, which occurred between 10,000 BP and 4000 BP, is the warmest postglacial interval to date. During the Hypsithermal, mean surface temperatures may have been as much as 3.6°F (15.8°C) above those recorded today. At the same time, an influx of dry Pacific air created more arid conditions. As a consequence, there was a significant change in vegetation and other aspects of the environment. In the American Midwest, for example, prairie expanded at the expense of forest, changing the distribution and abundance of a variety of plants and animals and, presumably, the way people lived. Koster provided an opportunity to search for evidence of climate change and how it may have influenced human history.

As excavation and analysis proceeded, a revised research design emerged that addressed four problems:

1. Refining the Archaic period cultural chronology for the central Mississippi drainage based on Koster site's clear, layered stratigraphic record

2. Using the large excavation exposures to delineate what people were actually doing (their activities) during each occupation

3. Reconstructing selected aspects of the regional and local paleoenvironment from the diverse but complementary indicators preserved in the deposits

4. Formulating and testing models of cultural–ecological adaptation in the lower Illinois River valley area for both Archaic and Woodland occupations

Undertaking an ambitious research agenda such as this was beyond the means of a single scholar. The complexity of these problems required the skills of a variety of scholars; it took a team.

Some regional-scale studies had already provided a foundation for Koster site research. Of particular note is a study on the early vegetation of the lower Illinois River valley (Zawacki and Hausfater 1969), which drew on U.S. government land survey notes and plat maps as well as other sources. In addition, Meyers (1970) explored the distribution and abun-

dance of chert resources used in making stone tools, and Parmalee et al. (1972) provided information on the Prehistoric animals in the region.

The significance of flotation to Koster site research also cannot be overstated. The recovery of small-scale plant and animal remains in large quantities through flotation was particularly important in addressing the paleoenvironmental and ecological questions raised in the Koster research design. Archaeologists had long sieved or screened excavated sediment, collecting objects that did not pass through and casting off the sieved sediment. However, as archaeologists developed a greater interest in subsistence and settlement during the mid-twentieth century, they began to realize that their samples were biased against small items. Struever was among those who recognized the presence of a variety of small-scale objects such as carbonized plant remains and animal bones in screened sediment. He developed "tub flotation" (Figure 2.20), a means to process large quantities of sediment and recover small-scale items (Struever 1968b). Larry Noble, a Northwestern University geologist, assisted with the development of a second step, chemical flotation, by which carbonized plant remains were readily separated from the remainder of the sample. In the end, the Kampsville Flotation Laboratory processed more than 10,000 flotation samples from Koster and provided unprecedented amounts of plant and animal remains to the

FIGURE 2.20 Tub flotation in the Illinois River: as a sediment sample is poured by one person, the washtub is rotated back and forth, keeping light materials from dropping to the mesh bottom of the washtub as the sediment disperses. This floating material will be skimmed from the surface of the water.

botany and zoology laboratories. It is fair to say that the data generated revolutionized how we see the past.

THE ARCHAIC PERIOD AS SEEN FROM KOSTER: THE PATH TO SEDENTARY LIFE

We have a more sharply focused view of Archaic period environment and culture thanks to information from Koster and related sites studied by Kampsville archaeologists. A brief recapitulation of our present understanding illustrates the value of interdisciplinary research undertaken at a regional scale.

Using geological studies, analysis of artifacts, and abundant and well-preserved plant remains, Koster Project scientists developed a fine-grained chronology of geological events and Archaic period occupation. They documented the timing of episodes of deposition and erosion of fan deposits and determined that 19 distinct cultural components dating between roughly 9000–3000 BP could be recognized (Figure 2.21).

Studies of the geology and geomorphology of the Koster site, the Illinois River valley, and a variety of other archaeological sites chronicle landscape history and the forces that shaped it. Of particular interest was the depositional history of the Koster fan (Butzer 1978; Hajic 1990). Hajic's research drew on the analysis of stratigraphic exposures in the excava-

FIGURE 2.21 The north wall of the main excavation block at the Koster site, with tarps rolled back to reveal the layered strata within which Koster researchers identified 19 distinct cultural components.

tion area, continuous sediment/soil cores taken from the Koster fan, mechanical analysis of sediment, and a study of regional surficial geomorphology. Hajic (1990, 69) concluded that regional paleoenvironmental changes, such as those associated with the Hypsithermal, correlated closely with the sequence of fan formation and stability at Koster. Comparison between the Koster fan and a similar deposit at the Napoleon Hollow site, some 40 miles (65 km) upstream, suggested that both sequences reflected these adjustments. Furthermore, because the depositional history of these fans is patterned, it is possible to predict where one might encounter similar deposits (Wiant et al. 1983). One of the most important conclusions to be drawn from these findings is that a substantial proportion of the Archaic period landscape is buried, especially in floodplain and valley margin settings. In other words, the archaeological record for such early times is incomplete because of the natural burial of landforms. This means that when one considers where people lived during the Archaic, as well as how they acquired food and other resources, this partial exposure of sites must be taken into account. Other sites and the information they contain may still remain buried.

Evidence for the impact of the warmer and drier Hypsithermal interval on vegetation and fauna in the Illinois River valley remains equivocal. A single sequence of pollen samples from Koster suggests a relatively dry, open forest that persisted through the Middle Archaic, giving way to wetter woodlands later. Analysis of the land snails found at Koster generally supports the palynological study. Dry and open conditions persisted through the late Middle Archaic, until about 5700 BP, after which moister conditions prevailed.

Drawing on a variety of research, but especially plant remains, Asch et al. (1972) suggested that local rather than climatic factors are more important with respect to the distribution of forest and prairie in the Illinois River valley. In their view, the rugged valley margin landscape provided shelter for trees and seedlings, and forest has persisted here throughout most of the Holocene. Evidence for vegetation in the Illinois River floodplain itself remains sketchy. Butzer (1977, 1978) suggested expansion of bottomland prairie at the expense of forest at the outset of the Hypsithermal. Most researchers, however, have envisioned the persistence of forested areas within the relatively well-watered floodplain even if prairie was expanding in the uplands. Further work is required to determine which viewpoint is the more valid.

The faunal database indicates that between the early Middle Archaic and the late Middle Archaic at Koster, people increased their reliance on white-tailed deer as opposed to a variety of smaller animal resources. This might be due to the opening of the forest because deer prefer the forest edge. However, it might also be attributable to changing settlement dynamics among human hunters, as suggested later in our discussion (Neusius 1986a).

The depositional history of the Illinois River floodplain has also been the subject of numerous studies by geoarchaeologists (e.g., Butzer 1977; Hajic 1990). In this case, the conclusions about environmental change drawn from the various databases have been similar. Of particular note with respect to hunter-gatherer subsistence potential, the Illinois River approached its modern-day stand at nearly 7000 BP. As a result, soon thereafter resource-rich backwater lake habitats were established. Lakes of this type are formed when spring floodwaters recede, leaving water and fish in low-lying floodplain areas such as the meander scars left by the former path of the river. Analysis of animal remains from Middle Archaic settlements at Koster demonstrates that an increase in the use of freshwater mussels and fish corresponds with the evolution of backwater lakes, underscoring the importance of this development for Koster's residents (Neusius 1986b; Styles 1986).

In addition to aiding paleoenvironmental research, Koster site data have been used to pursue several lines of inquiry concerning Archaic period cultural development. This work has allowed us to understand how the site was used and what specific activities people engaged in while living there. We also have been able to formulate and test models of cultural–ecological adaptation for the area by studying chipped and ground stone technology, subsistence and settlement organization, and sedentism. Much of this research concerns factors affecting foraging strategies and the development of sedentary, year-round communities. Archaeologists have become increasingly interested in how sedentism developed during the latter part of the Archaic, and the Koster site has taught us much about the first steps in this direction in the lower Illinois River valley.

These various types of research helped us develop a coherent picture of changing adaptation at Koster. It seems probable that increased reliance on abundant and storable resources promotes occupa-

tions of longer duration (Brown and Vierra 1983, 186). In the lower Illinois River valley, we think that longer occupations, or base camps, have been characterized by more permanent structures, more dependence on aquatic resources, food storage, and expanded use of processed foods. Duration of occupation may also have affected how people used stone. Chipped stone technology may have become less expedient when people stayed for longer periods at Koster. The idea is that as local lithic resources were more heavily exploited, people had to be more careful with how they used stone (Lurie 1982).

The combined Koster research suggests that Early Archaic and early Middle Archaic people lived in residential camps, defined as briefly occupied, generally unstructured settlements. Base camps, defined as long-term structured settlements, appear next, and people lived in increasingly organized settlements as the Middle Archaic continued. Studies of the spatial patterning of artifacts, ecofacts, and features support this assertion (Carlson 1979).

Subsistence data also may support this idea. Animal usage during the Early and early Middle Archaic was generalized, which means that a wide variety of mammals, fish, and other animals were being utilized by people camped at the Koster site. However, beginning at 7500 BP, there is evidence of specialized nut harvesting and selective use of backwater habitats. By 6500 BP, Koster had become a large base camp positioned with access to a variety of habitats, and residents substantially increased their use of backwater lakes. Fish, mussels, and waterfowl contributed significantly to people's diet, and for the first time there is evidence that people collected small-scale seeds. Deer also were being taken in larger numbers by Koster's residents. This more focused use of deer may represent the need at Koster to feed larger numbers of people, who were living for longer periods at Koster.

Thus, we can conclude that during the Middle Archaic period people made the transition from highly mobile residential foragers to more sedentary collectors. This change may be attributable to the increased attractiveness of floodplain as opposed to upland settings, particularly during the warmest and driest parts of the Hypsithermal, as well as to the arrival of the floodplain at its modern gradient. On the other hand, these changes also could have been part of the development of integrated group decision making and task organization by people experiencing population growth and social change (Neusius

1986b). We do not fully understand the interplay of these different variables.

CONCLUSIONS

The Koster site provides important information on Archaic period paleoenvironment and changing human strategies in the lower Illinois River valley. Perhaps most significantly from an anthropological perspective, the development of sedentary life in this area has been documented. In essence, Koster taught archaeologists more about what happened than about why; but in our interpretations are many hypotheses that can be tested elsewhere: ideas about the development of sedentism, the role of environmental change, and human adaptation during the Archaic.

The Koster Project is but one example of a large-scale interdisciplinary archaeological investigation—one that illustrates the necessity of drawing on the expertise of a variety of scientists to address the problems of modern archaeology. It took a team, but it also took a leader to coordinate the research effort. In this regard, Koster exemplifies the realization of a challenging vision. The value of long-term, coordinated, regional research is clear, despite the complexity of developing a center to accommodate such research. Faced with increasingly complicated archaeological problems, archaeologists have developed innovative means of addressing them, and we will continue to do so. In the old river town of Kampsville, Struever's vision lives on today, though reduced in size and changed in scope, in the field schools and public programs conducted by the Center for American Archaeology. Most importantly, what we learned at Koster informs continuing research on the Archaic period.

EPILOGUE: KOSTER FARM, 1978

For a decade we spent 12 weeks each summer in Theodore Koster's former cornfield. By the end of the 1978 field season, we had reached a settlement occupied 8700 years ago, but the effort had called for an increasing struggle to control the flow of groundwater and precipitation into the excavation (Figure 2.22). Now, we found we had no more reason to continue this struggle. Data from a few test pits and coring showed no evidence of more deeply buried artifact-bearing deposits. The decision was made to backfill the excavation.

FIGURE 2.22 The bottom of the Koster site excavation just before closing. Hoses indicate where pumps were placed in the block excavation; tarps held down by tires and, in the deepest test pit, plywood supports were used to help keep the sediments in place.

The crews and visitors were gone as we removed the 500 tires that secured the wall tarps. We pulled these off and exposed the layer-cake record for a last time. The excavation was over, but the collection of artifacts, notes, and photographs remained, and they would continue to provide information for years to come. Meanwhile, we'd heard about the discovery of another site on a colluvial fan at Napoleon Hollow, 40 miles upriver. This time the excavation was to be funded through a contract to evaluate the highway corridor for a major new highway and bridge in the planning stages. Perhaps it would shed light on those parts of the Archaic period that Koster did not illuminate.

DISCUSSION QUESTIONS

1. Where and what is the Koster site? Can you think of several reasons for its status as an important site?

2. What was Stuart Struever's vision? Why was facilitating interdisciplinary research so important to the success of the Koster research?

3. The Koster site was buried in the layers of an alluvial/colluvial fan deposit. Why is it important to understand this context when looking for other Middle Archaic sites with which to compare Koster?

4. What is the Hypsithermal interval? Why was it relevant to understanding cultural change at the Koster site? Do you think it caused the cultural changes in the Koster record, or could there have been other factors? Explain.

Part 2

THE NORTH AMERICAN PAST

CHAPTER 3

Peopling of the Americas

E very American schoolchild learns that when Christopher Columbus and his expedition arrived in the Caribbean in October 1492, Columbus assumed that he had found some outer islands of the Asian mainland and, thus, a route around the world. It is clear from the journal of Columbus's first voyage that he was searching for Asian commodities and people. Finding these would have confirmed his belief that the West Indies were part of Asia. However, America was not Asia, and once this was realized, it raised the question of who the people living in America actually were. Thus opened a chapter in both human mythmaking and scientific debate that remains unfinished today.

Tales and ideas about where Indians came from are plentiful. One idea was that the New World was first settled by merchants from Carthage, an ancient city in North Africa established by the great seafaring traders, the Phoenicians. According to Aristotle, Carthaginian merchants sailed out into the Atlantic and found an uninhabited island, but explorations ceased when the Carthaginian Senate banned all travel to the island (Huddleston 1967, 17). Another idea, which was suggested very early by Europeans, is that Native Americans originally were the inhabitants of the lost continent of Atlantis. In this tale, as Atlantis sank, the Atlanteans escaped to the previously uninhabited American continents, diversifying into many tribes and nations. Of course, the story of Atlantis itself is a parable told by Plato in relating a discussion between Socrates and his students concerning the perfect society (Feder 2002, 178–188). You may also have heard of various ideas that American Indians are the descendants of the lost tribes of Israel or of other peoples mentioned in the Bible. For example, there is a biblical reference to King Solomon's navy visiting a place called Ophir, which either was already inhabited or then was settled by some of the men in Solomon's navy (Huddleston 1967, 33–47). Of course, the Book of Mormon, based on golden tablets Joseph Smith said he found in New York State, also links the American Indians to biblical lands. It details a history of several migrations from Palestine to America before the time of Jesus, and identifies the American Indians as Lamanites, who defeated related mound-building emigrants, called the Nephites (Williams 1991, 159–167).

These tales reflect efforts to make sense of New World peoples previously unknown to Europeans. Many early scholars thought the original settlers must have been forgotten by their homeland contemporaries, but could be accounted for in European religious or classical writings. The earliest explanations represent efforts to integrate the Americas and their inhabitants into European cosmological assumptions. In the prescientific sixteenth-century world of Europeans, the presence of people in the Americas had to be reconcilable in this way. As for the Book of Mormon, its story of the Lamanites fits quite well with nineteenth-century myths about the Mound Builders (see Box 1.1). Modern culture has produced attempts at explanation such as Goodman's (1982) claim that the Garden of Eden was in California and that all human life originated there, or the various claims of von Däniken (e.g., 1970) for alien rather than Native American origins for some of the more spectacular traces of the past. Each of these efforts probably tells us more about the writer's worldview than about the settlement and origin questions that interest archaeologists.

Like all people, Native Americans themselves also have origin stories. These stories are significant in many ways, and anyone who plans to pursue North American archaeology is encouraged to explore them for cultural insights. Like Judeo-Christian creation accounts, Indian stories are meant to explain the place of humans in the universe and to provide lessons concerning right behavior. Sometimes they contain information useful to tracking the history of the people who tell them, some people take them quite literally; but they are sacred stories, not scientific accounts of the past.

Another tradition of explanation by Europeans also began during the sixteenth century, soon after Columbus's voyages. In this tradition, scholars used their experience of American Indians and their observations of Indian artifacts, physical characteristics, and behaviors to answer origin questions. Early scholars noticed the physical similarities between American Indians and Asians and concluded that the Indians' ancestors had migrated from Asia. Even before the Bering Strait was found, some (e.g., Acosta 1604) suggested that America was connected to Asia in the unexplored far north. Subsequently, as Western science matured and stressed empirical data, a scientific approach to the problem was developed.

North American archaeology, of course, belongs to this latter tradition. Through the discovery and excavation of sites, through the material remains we recover, and through interdisciplinary studies of past environments, archaeologists have tried to address the settlement of the Americas. Our research has been formulated to address the how, when, and where of migration. Using many kinds of evidence, archaeologists have constructed various scenarios. The state of archaeological knowledge on the settlement of the Americas is the topic of this chapter. Reading and studying this chapter should provide a general orientation to archaeological viewpoints. You may also want to explore Native American origin stories, beginning with those indicated in this chapter's Suggestions for Further Reading.

Archaeologists have identified a large number of early North American sites that provide information about the settlement of this continent (Figure 3.1). Nevertheless, there is still debate about how, when, and from where human entry into the Americas occurred, not to mention interest in the adaptive strategies of these first Americans.

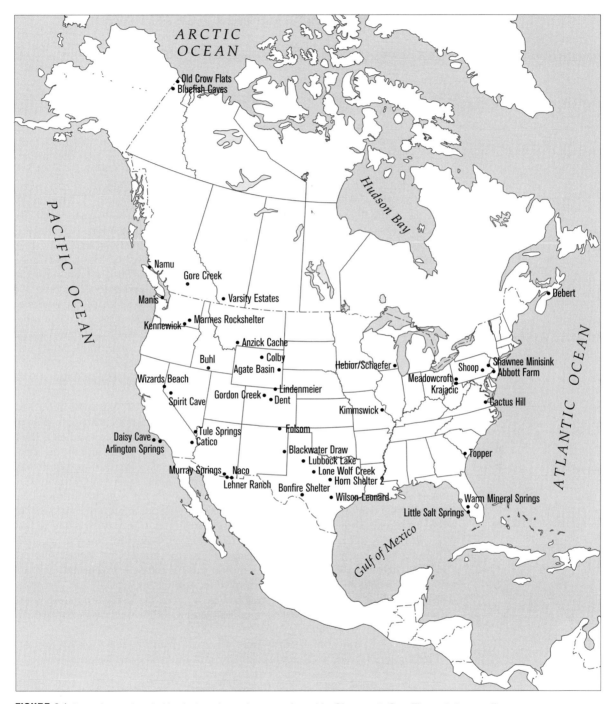

FIGURE 3.1 Locations of early North American sites mentioned in Chapter 3. See Figure 3.8 as well.

WHEN WERE THE AMERICAS SETTLED?

Early North American anthropologists took an essentially "flat view" of the Native American past. Generally, they did not believe a great deal of time could have passed since people arrived on this continent. The idea of an ancient human past anywhere in the world did not develop until after 1859, when the coexistence of humans with the fossil remains of extinct animals in Europe was established (Grayson 1983). The **Paleolithic** period, stretching back long before biblical times into the Ice Age, became increasingly well documented in Europe. In North America, however, there was certainly no consensus that the Indians had been here more than three or four thousand years.

Some scientists sought evidence for an American Paleolithic extending back into the Ice Ages. During the latter half of the nineteenth century, many people claimed to have evidence supporting this view. For example, in the 1870s, Dr. Charles Abbott, a physician whose farm was near Trenton, New Jersey, was convinced that crude artifacts he had recovered came from Ice Age gravel deposits. Abbott interested scholars in his finds and published his claim widely. The similarity of Abbott's "**paleoliths**" to European Paleolithic artifacts was the primary support for assigning them to an early human presence. For a time, the Trenton gravels and the tools found there were thought to be legitimate evidence of the Ice Age presence of humans in North America. Also during the late nineteenth century, other, far less plausible evidence such as the fraudulent Lenape stone, which some believed was an Indian drawing of a mammoth hunt, was considered possible evidence for Ice Age humans (Williams 1991, 116–129). The fledgling discipline of North American archaeology initially accepted the idea of an American Paleolithic (Meltzer 1991b, 15).

However, the evidence for an early human presence in North America had not been critically evaluated. This bothered some influential anthropologists, in part because an early presence for humans in the Americas contradicted their own ideas about historical linkages between contemporary tribes and the archaeological past. William Henry Holmes of the Smithsonian Institution established that similarities in form to Paleolithic tools from Europe were not sufficient by themselves to document human presence during the Ice Age. In addition, the stratigraphic context of an artifact would have to be unambiguously glacial. In case after case, Holmes found that the deposits did not date to the Ice Age or that the artifacts could be considered more recent ones that had intruded into glacial deposits by other means. In the case of the Trenton gravels, he argued that the artifacts actually were more recent Indian quarry refuse—**preforms** for more sophisticated tools—that had been moved by rodents or erosion and incorporated into older deposits. By the first few decades of the twentieth century, the archaeological consensus concerning possible Paleolithic tools was with Holmes (Adovasio and Page 2002).

A second Smithsonian anthropologist, Aleš Hrdlička, also took up the role of debunker. Trained as a medical doctor and interested in skeletal pathology, Hrdlička often was consulted on discoveries of possible human bones in glacial context. He consistently argued that these bones could not represent Paleolithic or glacial man because they did not resemble **Neanderthal** remains found in Europe. He also insisted that stratigraphic evidence concerning skeletal and other finds be carefully documented.

FIGURE 3.2 Spear point found in clear association with the ribs of an extinct bison at the Folsom site in New Mexico left no doubt that humans had been in North America before the close of the Pleistocene.

Both Holmes and Hrdlička were imposing and impressive individuals, who were vehement in their rejection of poor evidence and not afraid to intimidate less established scientists. In the end, their position was proved wrong, but not because they were wrong to reject the specific claims they reviewed. Holmes and Hrdlička established the rules of evidence archaeologists still use. To prove the early existence of humans in the Americas, we need objects that are unquestionably artifacts or human bones, as well as a context for these objects that clearly establishes the early date and the undisturbed nature of the deposits (Adovasio and Page 2002, 99). For one reason or another, these criteria were not met prior to the late 1920s.

What changed the consensus was the discovery, near Folsom, New Mexico, of a stone spear point in clear association with the rib cage of an extinct species of bison (Figure 3.2). The Folsom site was discovered in 1908 by George McJunkin, an African American ranch foreman for the Crowfoot Ranch. Following a particularly heavy rainstorm that had resulted in flash floods, McJunkin was checking fencelines when he found that a newly cut gully had left a large gap beneath one section of fence, exposing several large bones. McJunkin was an amateur naturalist, and he saw that although the bones resembled modern bison bones, they were much larger. Over the years, McJunkin continued to remove bones from this bone bed, and he also made many unsuccessful efforts to interest others in what he was certain was an important fossil find.

However, shortly after McJunkin died in 1922, two men he had tried to interest in his find finally visited the spot, recovering a bag of bones. Both the men, Carl Schwacheim and Fred Howarth, were known locally for their interest in fossils. However, it was not until Howarth purchased an automobile in 1922 that the trip from their homes in Raton became an afternoon outing as opposed to a two-day trip (Preston 2002, 16). Although quickly convinced that the bones they recovered came from an extinct animal, the two amateurs weren't positive whether it was an elk or a bison. It was not until 1926, however, that they traveled to Denver to bring some bones to Jesse D. Figgins, director of the Colorado Museum of Natural History (now known as the Denver Museum of Nature and Science). Figgins already had been involved in a dispute about early Americans at the Lone Wolf Creek site in Texas. Figgins had championed this find, while Hrdlička and others had rejected it because of the circumstances of the site's excavation (Meltzer 1991b, 31–32).

Figgins was immediately interested in the Folsom finds. Excavations at the Folsom site began in the summer of 1926, and in July workers uncovered well-made spear points of the type archaeologists now call Folsom points in association with the bison bones. Unlike the "paleoliths" of Abbott and his contemporaries, these artifacts were far from crude and represented very sophisticated flaking techniques. Figgins wrote up the results of this excavation, claiming that the artifacts proved that the bison at Wild Horse Arroyo had been killed by humans. He even visited Hrdlička in Washington with his finds. Hrdlička remained skeptical and urged Figgins to leave any future finds in situ until other scientists could review the context.

Renewing excavations at Folsom in the summer of 1927, Figgins's excavators found another spear point embedded in the sediments surrounding an articulated bison rib cage. This time Figgins directed them to leave the point in place until other scientists could confirm its location. Meanwhile, Figgins telegraphed Hrdlička and others inviting them to come see the discovery. Hrdlička himself could not make the trip, but three other experts soon arrived: Hrdlička's colleague Frank Roberts, who was already in the Southwest; Alfred Kidder, who was working at Pecos Pueblo in New Mexico; and Barnum Brown, a paleontologist from the American Museum of Natural History in New York who had found the first *Tyrannasaurus rex* skeleton. Under the leadership of Brown, the excavation uncovered 17 other spear points in association with the extinct bison remains, making it possible for each wave of scientists who visited to see Folsom points in direct association with bison bones as the excavation progressed (Meltzer 1991b, 33). In 1928 the Pleistocene age of the sediments was established by the geologist Kirk Bryan of the U.S. Geological Survey, and from that time on there could be no doubt that humans were indeed associated with Ice Age fauna. Hrdlička's admonition to let the experts establish the validity of any potential early man finds had paid off, ironically refuting his own views on the subject.

After the Folsom finds had been recognized as clearly dating to the Ice Age, there was renewed searching for other early sites. Other bison-hunting groups were suggested by points of different types found at other sites (Fagan 1987, 52), and before long, even older cultural assemblages were documented. Once again it wasn't a scientist who first suspected the significance of finds, this time in the vicinity of Clovis, New Mexico, far to the south of Folsom. Here, in blowouts created by the winds of the Dust Bowl, a young Native American cowboy, James Ridgely Whiteman, found what he called "warheads" along with mammoth and bison bones. In 1929 Whiteman contacted the Smithsonian Institution about his finds but was rebuffed when a Smithsonian paleontologist pronounced these sites unlikely to produce significant archaeological finds.

Edgar Billings Howard saw Whiteman's finds quite differently. Since 1929, Howard had been leading a "Southwest Early Man Project" funded by the University of Pennsylvania Museum of Archaeology and Anthropology and the Philadelphia Academy of Sciences. In the Guadalupe Mountains of New Mexico, he had found and excavated some dry cave deposits that contained well-preserved **Basketmaker** materials and hints of Folsom-like materials also in association with the bones of Pleistocene animals like musk ox, horse, and bison. Howard already was hoping to find the actual bones of "Folsom man," as well as other evidence for Folsom people in his excavations. Whiteman took Howard to a place called Blackwater Draw near Clovis in 1932, and the academic investigator immediately determined to excavate there the following summer.

From 1933 to 1937, Howard's project shifted focus to Blackwater Draw. Here, another point type, originally called "generalized Folsom point" and now called the Clovis point, was first documented. In addition, Howard's work established that the hunters who made the Clovis points and associated tools hunted mammoths as well as other now extinct animals. Using an interdisciplinary approach that drew on geology and paleontology as well as archaeology, Howard was eventually able to demonstrate that Clovis points were located stratigraphically beneath Folsom points and that early mammoth hunting had been followed by focus on bison during Folsom times. See the case study in Section D.2 of the Student CD for a discussion of recent reanalysis of the lithic artifacts collected by Howard's team, and Exhibit 3.1 for information on the distinctive Paleoindian points.

Absolute dating methods such as radiocarbon had not been developed when the Folsom and Clovis discoveries were made. Thus, archaeologists did not know when these cultures had existed in terms of dates. Nevertheless, they thought the Ice Age had ended about 10,000 years ago and that at this time various types of large game animals had become extinct. On this basis, they soon designated Clovis and Folsom people as Paleoindians, Ice Age inhabitants of the Americas. We will discuss Paleoindian culture at the end of this chapter, after considering the complicated problem of how and when first settlement of the Americas actually occurred.

THE CLOVIS-FIRST SCENARIO

Following the recognition of Folsom and Clovis, many more sites were found to contain evidence of associations between these or similar point types and large game. In addition, similar points were found throughout much of North America, and sequences of point styles were established in some regions. After radiocarbon dating had been invented, in the late 1940s, archaeologists were able to confirm that many of these contexts did date to the end of the Ice Age or the beginning of the Holocene. Clovis sites were shown to date to a very short period of time, from 11,500 BP to 10,800 BP. Despite claims for older sites and deposits,

CLUES TO THE PAST

EXHIBIT 3.1

Fluted Points: The Original American Invention?

Fluted projectile points are a classic example of a **diagnostic artifact**. Such archaeological artifacts are considered markers of particular cultural entities restricted in space and time. Thus, when such a diagnostic is found, it conveys temporal, spatial, and cultural meaning to archaeologists. In the case of fluted points, a Paleoindian presence and a terminal Pleistocene time frame are indicated. There are more than 11,000 documented fluted points from the continental United States alone. Not surprisingly, the distribution of these points is not even, and specific varieties of fluted points are still more restricted in spatial extent (Anderson and Faught 1998).

The Clovis point is the best known of the fluted point varieties, and it represents the earliest fluted point tradition. This point has a lanceolate form with a narrow blade, a concave base, and at least one major flute or flake taken from a prepared **platform** at the base up the center of the point. Fluting generally has taken place as the final step in the production of the point. Grinding on the base of the point also is common. Within the general Clovis designation, there is variation as shown in Figure 3.3 (bottom row). Some Clovis points exhibit **overshot flaking**, with thinning flake scars traversing the entire facial surface; flake scars may instead meet at the middle, however. The sides of the point may be straight, slightly convex, slightly concave, or strongly concave and waisted. The degree of basal concavity also varies.

Folsom points (Figure 3.3, top row), which are found stratigraphically above Clovis at a number of Paleoindian sites on the Great Plains and in the Southwest, also are well known. Folsom points represent a very refined technology in which the basal striking platform for fluting has been carefully prepared. As a result, fluting

FIGURE 3.3 Fluted points exhibit considerable variability in size and morphology: bottom row, Clovis points; upper row, Folsom points.

leaves a broad channel, well up into the point. In addition, the point often is broadest above the middle of the blade so that the tip looks a little "snub nosed," and the basal concavity may be deep enough to create straight ears at the sides of the base.

However, there is considerable spatial and temporal variability in fluted points. On the Great Plains, archaeologists have recognized a sequence of Paleoindian points that begins with Clovis and is followed by Folsom and later by unfluted, but still lanceolate varieties of points grouped together as the **Plano complex** (see Chapter 10). More recently, points identified as Goshen points have been suggested as possible intermediaries between Clovis and Folsom on the Plains because they exhibit flaking techniques reminiscent of Folsom and have been found in contexts suggesting pre-Folsom activities (Frison 1991a). Further west, fluted points, sometimes called **Western Clovis**, have been found in western Washington, southern British Columbia, the Columbia and Snake River basins, California, the Great Basin, and the Basin and Range country of the Southwest (Willig 1991). Most of these western fluted points are surface finds, but some occurring in stratigraphic contexts have been dated between 10,500 BP and 7500 BP and thus postdate Clovis on the Great Plains. Besides this, these Western Clovis points either co-occur or precede points usually assigned to the **Western Stemmed point tradition**, 11,000 BP to 7000 BP (Dixon 1999).

As mentioned elsewhere in this chapter, the earliest fluted points in Alaska are younger or contemporaneous with fluted points south of the ice sheets. Most of these Alaskan points exhibit multiple flutes or basal thinning flakes and have been dated to no earlier than 10,500 BP. Fluted points also have been found in Alberta, but again the dates are after 10,500 BP. Triangular, basally thinned points found in this area also may be associated with fluting (Carlson 1991b).

Interestingly, given the traditional focus on Paleoindian kill sites from the Great Plains and the Southwest, the majority of fluted points come from the east, where large numbers have been found in the major river valleys and on either side of the Appalachian Mountains. Many of these points also are surface finds, but some have been found in datable stratigraphic contexts, and a number of varieties are recognized. This fact has allowed archaeologists to develop sequences of fluted point types that subdivide the Paleoindian period (see Chapters 11–13).

Archaeologists are particularly interested in exploring the question of how fluting of points developed. Because fluted points are not found outside North and Central America and seem to be later in the north than in the south, we might argue that they are an American invention. Fluted projectile points probably began to be made as terminal Pleistocene hunters with a **blade** and **biface** technology adapted to changing postglacial environments, but under what specific circumstances? Several have proposed that the density and diversity of point types in the Southeast means fluting began there (Bryan 1991; Mason 1962; Stanford 1991).

Although fluted points have been studied since the late 1920s, archaeologists still have a great deal to learn about their diagnostic significance. Besides this, the technological variation among fluted points remains important to investigate.

the professional consensus came to be that the **Clovis culture** represented the first human occupation of the Americas. This was because in the majority of proposed **Pre-Clovis** cases, further analyses showed either the dating, the stratigraphy, or the human origin could not be verified. A few examples will help define both kinds of claims and explain why they were rejected.

The Calico site in California's Mohave Desert briefly enjoyed fame because Louis Leakey, renowned for his early hominid finds in Africa, supported its authenticity. Located above what once was the Pleistocene Lake Manix near Yermo, California, Calico was investigated by archaeologist Ruth "Dee" Simpson from the San Bernardino County Museum. In 1963, while Leakey was in the area on a lecture tour, Simpson took him to the areas where her archaeological survey was finding what seemed to be primitive stone tools. On Leakey's advice, Simpson dug at the Calico site. This site was situated in a geologic feature known as the Yermo fan, then estimated to be between 50,000 and 100,000 years old, may be as old as 200,000 years (Mueller 2005). During return visits, Leakey identified a small number of artifacts among the many broken pieces of stone recovered. He also designated a particular concentration of rocks as a possible hearth. Based on Leakey's assertions, the National Geographic Society funded further excavation, requiring specific evaluation of both the artifacts and their geologic context.

Vance Haynes, a geologist from the University of Arizona, who eventually examined many of the Pre-Clovis sites, was among those who studied the Calico site and found its evidence for human antiquity wanting. Haynes pointed out that an interglacial alluvial fan like the Yermo fan is not a good source of materials on which to base a claim for ancient humans. Such fans consist of deposits of sand, gravel, and mud laid down by the action of water. They often contain naturally broken rocks, some of which may superficially resemble crude human artifacts. At Calico, a small number of simple "artifacts" had been picked out of a mass of obviously naturally occurring rocks. Moreover, when careful comparisons were made between these "flaked" stones and unquestionable artifacts, the Calico site items appeared even less like artifacts. It also became clear that the supposed hearth actually was a natural cluster of rocks that appeared hearthlike only after partial excavation of the area. For all these reasons, Haynes concluded that Calico was not a valid Pre-Clovis site, and most archaeologists today concur with him (Adovasio and Page 2002, 38–141; Meltzer 1993, 63–65).

Other eventually rejected Pre-Clovis claims include those for the Tule Springs site near Las Vegas, Nevada, and Old Crow Flats in the Yukon Territory close to the Alaskan border. At Tule Springs, artifacts as well as the bones of large, extinct animals had been found. Moreover, a radiocarbon date of 28,000 BP had been obtained. This seemed to be the kind of evidence archaeologists were seeking. Later, however, blackened "hearth" deposits at the site were shown to be decayed plant remains rather than evidence of ancient fires. Reexamination of the context of the artifacts showed that they came from younger deposits and had been redeposited where they were found. As a result, archaeologists had to change their ideas about Tule Springs (Meltzer 1993, 59).

The Old Crow area is a glacial lake basin with a complex depositional history that has resulted in the exposure of many vertebrate fossils dating to the Pleistocene. Among these fossils were large numbers of apparently modified bones, which unfortunately had been redeposited out of their original contexts. The most famous Old Crow artifact is a caribou tibia that had been worked into a flesher similar to bone tools used for processing hides by more recent Indians in the area (Figure 3.4) (Fagan 1987, 125). This tibia, which most certainly is an artifact, was originally dated to 27,000 BP, a finding that placed humans in northern North America well before Clovis times. However, the tool was found in redeposited sediments, and eventual redating by means of **AMS dating** techniques indicated that it actually was only about 1350 years old.

The numerous other bones from Old Crow, which look as if they might have been flaked, scratched, and otherwise altered, also are problematic. This is not only because of their questionable context, but also because it is unclear whether humans actually modified them. In fact, the Old Crow case has fueled the investigation of how to identify modified bones reliably (e.g., Irving et al. 1989; Morlan 1984, 1986). It has been reported (e.g., Cinq-Mars and Morlan 1999) that new AMS dating of some of the possibly flaked mammoth bones from Old Crow places them between 40,000 BP and 25,000 BP. However, most archaeologists simply agree that the Old Crow case is not strong enough to provide evidence for a Pre-Clovis human occupation.

FIGURE 3.4 The tibia flesher from Old Crow.

These few cases are by no means an exhaustive list of sites and artifactual finds that have been considered and then rejected as Pre-Clovis in origin since the 1930s. There are simply too many instances for us to discuss them all here. Solid evidence for a Pre-Clovis human occupation in the Americas is hard to come by, but just as clearly, there has been no shortage of such claims. Solid evidence after all must include evidence for humans that cannot be refuted, such as artifacts or human skeletons. These artifacts or skeletons must be in an undisturbed context, and unambiguous dating of the evidence must be available. These criteria only make sense, but they have been hard to satisfy.

Until recently, many archaeologists simply concluded that Pre-Clovis settlement did not happen. As a result, they developed a model of the human settlement of the Americas that revolved around Clovis being the first American culture. The **Clovis-First** scenario can be stated in four central propositions as follows:

1. Humans did not enter the Americas until the very end of the Wisconsin glaciation and did not settle south of the ice sheets until about 12,000 BP, approximately the time we first find Clovis sites.

2. These first Americans were big-game hunters who followed large herd animals such as mammoths from Siberia into an unglaciated and productive Alaskan landscape before the Beringian land bridge (see Figure 2.12) was drowned.

3. Eventually, during the waxing and waning of the ice sheets associated with the end of the Wisconsin glaciation, the first Americans followed their prey down an **ice-free corridor** between the Cordilleran and Laurentian ice sheets into North and South America.

4. Once south of the ice, the big-game hunters were able to exploit a pristine niche without competition from other human residents, which allowed them to multiply rapidly and spread widely, as indicated by the wide distribution of Clovis and other Paleoindian sites.

The Clovis-First scenario also became associated with a proposal by Paul Martin (1973) that early Americans were such efficient hunters of mammoths, horses, giant bison, and other **megafauna** that they figured in the extinction of these animals at the end of the Pleistocene. The question of why so many species of game became extinct at the end of the Pleistocene has been variously investigated and explained (Martin and Klein 1984). Martin's ideas are a version of the explanation that human predation reduced these species' populations so greatly that they could no longer survive. However, Martin was quite specific about the timing of this human predation, suggesting that the first settlers of the Americas were highly specialized big-game hunters who arrived in eastern Beringia about 13,000 years ago and followed megafaunal herds down the ice-free corridor in western Canada as it opened, arriving in the Edmonton area about 12,000 years ago. From there they rapidly pushed south, exterminating herds until they reached Tierra del Fuego about 11,000 years ago (Figure 3.5). Mosimann and Martin (1975) also published a statistical simulation showing how hunter-gatherers could have moved so far, so rapidly.

Although Martin's explanation for Pleistocene extinctions is not widely accepted because of the obvious significance of environmental change at the end of the Ice Age, the Clovis-First scenario benefited from his formulation in at least two ways. First, it cemented the notion that the first Americans were specialized

FIGURE 3.5 Martin's model of how, once an ice-free corridor had opened up, Paleoindians who were big-game hunters could have moved rapidly through North America, pushing their prey to extinction while quickly populating the continent.

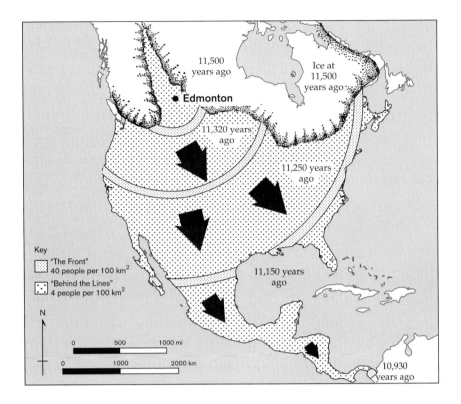

big-game hunters, an assumption that subsequent data may call into question. Second, Martin showed how very rapid settlement by mobile, highly specialized hunter-gatherers might have been possible. Settlement within a little over a thousand years is required because South America appears to have been settled widely by 11,000 years ago. Thus, although not strictly dependent on Martin's ideas, many elements of the Clovis-First scenario were bolstered by the incorporation of elements of the Pleistocene overkill model.

DOES THE CLOVIS-FIRST SCENARIO ACCOUNT FOR ALL THE EVIDENCE?

For a long time, the Clovis-First scenario represented the archaeological consensus about the settlement of the Americas. Today, many archaeologists question aspects of the Clovis-First scenario and are actively exploring alternative formulations. Others believe that most aspects of the Clovis-First scenario are correct. Nearly all would recognize that a more complicated story of first settlement has been emerging, and the Clovis-First scenario is not sufficient to explain it fully.

The main reason for the current lack of consensus is the probable existence of Pre-Clovis sites. As we have noted, many proposed candidates for Pre-Clovis sites have been rejected upon further investigation. Nevertheless, some sites now seem to have withstood archaeological scrutiny, and two stand out as most important in shifting perspectives.

FIGURE 3.6 The interior of Meadowcroft Rockshelter; depositional strata are marked by white tags. The excavation has been covered by a wooden superstructure to protect the exposed deposits, and electric lighting has been installed.

0 1 2 3 4 5 cm

0 1 2 in

FIGURE 3.7 The Miller lanceolate specimen type from Meadowcroft Rockshelter.

The first of these is Meadowcroft Rockshelter, located in the Cross Creek drainage of extreme southwestern Pennsylvania near the small town of Avella. Meadowcroft Rockshelter is a stratified, multicomponent site with a long record of human use (Figure 3.6). Because of its careful excavation under the direction of James Adovasio, as well as the suite of radiocarbon dates obtained, Meadowcroft provides archaeological information of regional significance throughout the Holocene. However, the greatest significance of this site stems from the deposits in Stratum IIa that have early radiocarbon dates. If a conservative approach is taken and the various radiocarbon dates obtained from this stratum are averaged, the deepest cultural evidence dates to approximately 14,500 BP. These deposits were found beneath a major rockfall from the roof of the shelter. They contain a distinctive stone tool assemblage called the Miller complex, which is distinguished by small, **prismatic blades** that have been detached from small cores. Figure 3.7 shows the unfluted projectile point that is the **type specimen** for Miller lanceolate projectile points. Although not stratigraphically dated, the Krajacic site, also in the Cross Creek drainage, has yielded similar stone tools (Adovasio et al. 1999).

There have been two main criticisms of the Meadowcroft data. First, the small assemblages of plant and animal remains from Stratum IIa, which indicate the presence of a mixed coniferous/hardwood forest, are said to be inconsistent with a Pleistocene date. Critics have argued that this kind of environmental setting was not likely even at the end of the Wisconsin glaciation. However, given that these ecofactual assemblages are very small samples, that the actual glacier probably was at least 100 miles (160 km) north of Meadowcroft during this early occupation, and that our understanding of the mosaic of habitats at the end of the Pleistocene is poor, Adovasio and others do not believe the critics' points are sufficient grounds for rejection of the radiocarbon dates.

The second criticism has centered on whether the dating sequence is valid. Some archaeologists maintain that the dates have been contaminated by the presence in the deposits of either coal or fossilized wood fragments called vitrite. Again, Adovasio believes that he has answered his critics on this score, noting that the upper part of the Meadowcroft sequence has never been questioned, nor has the reliability of his stratigraphic sequence. Redating by different radiocarbon labs has produced consistent results as well. Careful searches not withstanding, no radiocarbon lab has noted evidence of contaminants, and analyses of sediment have produced no evidence of contamination from groundwater (Goldberg and Arpin 1999). In short, despite its critics Meadowcroft Rockshelter remains a possible—perhaps even probable—Pre-Clovis site. This does not, however, set back the time of first human entry by many millennia, nor is the Miller complex of tools drastically out of line with what might be expected.

A second site is even more significant to the Pre-Clovis case, though it is not in North America. Monte Verde is located on Chinchihuapi Creek, a tributary of the Maullin River, in south central Chile, approximately 500 miles (800 km) south of Santiago. It has been painstakingly investigated by an international research team headed by Tom Dillehay, who was teaching at the Southern University of Chile in 1976 when materials from the site were brought to him. At Monte Verde, an ancient campsite was buried in terrace deposits and covered by a layer of peat 6 to 12 inches (15–30 cm) thick. Since the peat inhibited decay, preservation of normally perishable artifacts and ecofacts is outstanding. Excavators have recovered stone, bone, and wood artifacts as well as cordage fragments, mastodon bones, hide fragments, pieces of mastodon tissue, and a wide variety of plant remains. The remains of hearth features have also been found, along with a structure 22 yards (20 m) long apparently made of wood and animal hides. A second wishbone-shaped structure is believed to have been used to process mastodon carcasses. In addition, a human footprint from a child or teenager has been preserved in clay apparently brought in to line the hearths. Whatever its dates, Monte Verde is an unusual and important site because of its preservation and because it seems to have been more than a temporary encampment.

There are two possible use surfaces in Stratum MV-7 at Monte Verde beneath the layer of peat. The older of these has not been extensively exposed but has yielded a date of 33,000 BP. Because it has not been thoroughly investigated, the researchers do not make claims for Pre-Clovis use of Monte Verde on this basis. Instead, they focus on the younger use surface, designated MV-II, which contains the bulk of the materials, including the structural remains. This use surface has been dated to between 12,700 BP and 12,300 BP. Although these dates are only slightly more than a millennium older than those for the Clovis sites in North America, Monte Verde is much further south. Assuming that humans entered the Americas via Beringia, they must have begun their migration long before its occupation, and much more than a millennium before Clovis.

Of course, Monte Verde also has had its critics. Both the dating and the artifact analysis have been questioned. Yet the validity of the dating just cited (12,700–12,300 BP) was settled to most archaeologists' satisfaction in 1997 after a site visit by a panel of experts. Among those examining the site were skeptics like Vance Haynes and Dena Dincauze, who has worked on Paleoindian sites in New England, and Pre-Clovis proponents like Jim Adovasio. Although a much heralded consensus from this visit was that the upper cultural surface at Monte Verde was indeed more than 12,000 years old and did break the Clovis barrier, subsequent criticism of the Monte Verde research has led to some backtracking by some Clovis-First proponents. Much was made of supposedly muddled procedures in excavation and analysis (Fiedel 1999), but most archaeologists do not accept the conclusion that the Monte Verde evidence has been invalidated.

In fact, there is other evidence from South America that corresponds well with the Monte Verde findings. A wide human distribution in South America by 11,000 years ago is indicated. The diversity of early locations and subsistence evidence suggest that big-game hunting was not the sole means of subsistence. This might indicate that humans had a long time to settle into South American environments or that there were multiple migration waves from the north. There also have been claims for much earlier human occupation in South and Central America. These sites either have been rejected by most archaeologists as invalid or have not yet been investigated thoroughly. For example, a rockshelter called Pedra Furada located in northeastern Brazil has yielded dates as old as 46,000 BP. This site, however, is not widely believed to meet all the criteria for a truly Pre-Clovis site. Investigating South American data remains of central importance to solving the puzzle of the human settlement of the Americas (Kelly 2003).

There are other possible Pre-Clovis sites in North America as well. Few are as satisfactory candidates as Meadowcroft and Monte Verde, but some of them may yet meet challenges to their authenticity. Among these are the following sites:

1. The Bluefish Caves, located southwest of the Old Crow Basin in the Yukon, where possible bone tools have been suggested to mark Pre-Clovis human entry. The stone tools from these caves appear to be similar to assemblages at other early Alaskan sites but are not firmly dated. The AMS technique has been used to date a split caribou tibia that may be a fleshing tool at 24,800 BP and a mammoth bone flake and its parent core 23,500 BP (Cinq-Mars and Morlan 1999).

2. The Topper site, located on the Savannah River in South Carolina, where microblades, flakes, **burins**, and small cores, but no bifaces, have been found in a distinct stratum beneath a layer containing Clovis artifacts. This Pre-Clovis stratum was dated to 16,000 to 15,000 years ago by **optically stimulated luminescence (OSL)** (Adovasio and Page 2002). Older radiocarbon dates (ca. 50,000 BP) from still deeper levels of this site were reported in the fall of 2004, but the tools associated with that period are not believed to be truly artifacts by some authorities (Powell 2004).

3. The Cactus Hill site, located in a sand dune on the Nottaway River in Virginia, where two different archaeological teams have found a distinct stratum beneath deposits containing Clovis artifacts. In this lower stratum, investigators have found stone tools and a charcoal concentration, as well as a hearth. Radiocarbon dates on the charcoal concentration and on the hearth, respectively, are 16,670 ±730 BP and 15,070 ±70 BP (McAvoy and McAvoy 1997). The artifacts include small blades and lanceolate, unfluted points or knives that may have affinities to the assemblage from Stratum IIA at Meadowcroft Rockshelter (Adovasio and Page 2002, 267).

4. The Shaefer and Hebior sites, located in southeastern Wisconsin. Mammoth bones at these sites exhibit evidence of human butchering. Bone collagen subjected to AMS testing has yielded a date of 12,310 ± 60 BP for Shaefer and dates of 12,480 ±60 BP and 12,520 ±50 BP for Hebior (Overstreet and Stafford 1997).

5. The Little Salt Spring site, located near Charlotte Harbor in southwestern Florida, which is a freshwater *cenote*, or limestone solution pit. The shell of an extinct tortoise impaled with a sharpened wooden stake was found on a ledge within the *cenote*. A bone from the tortoise dated to 13,450 ±190 BP and the stake itself dated to 12,030 ±200 BP (Clausen et al. 1979).

6. The Manis site, located on Washington State's Olympic Peninsula. Here the tip of a bone projectile point was found embedded in the rib of a mastodon. Two dates from this site place it at 12,000 ±310 BP and 11,850 ±60 BP (Gustafson et al. 1979).

Given these indications, Clovis may not have been first, though claims of human presence in the Americas much before 16,000 BP remain more unlikely. Archaeologists need much more evidence to be able to reliably sort out what most probably did happen, and it is certainly premature to propose a new scenario that will account for all the data. Instead of a new consensus, archaeologists and other scientists are exploring many new questions about first settlement.

KEY PUZZLES IN THE DATA ON EARLY SETTLEMENT

There are three particularly important research areas on which interdisciplinary research is now focusing: (1) the archaeology of Beringia, (2) the route of human entry, and (3) biological affinities of founding populations. Each of these is intriguing, and the data being collected are likely to greatly increase our understanding of when and how the Americas were settled.

What Can Be Learned from the Beringian Archaeological Record?

It is most probable that humans first entered the Americas via the region of the Bering Strait (Figure 3.8). Moreover, such entry almost certainly took place at the end of the Ice Age, when Siberia and Alaska were connected and also effectively isolated from areas further south, both in Eurasia and in North America. This means that the archaeology of the area known as Beringia is likely to provide important information relevant to human settlement of the Americas. Until recently, however, a number of factors have combined to make investigating the archaeology of Beringia extremely difficult. These factors include the vastness and inaccessibility of the region, the harshness of the climate and conditions, the political and language boundaries that divide Beringia, and the condition of large portions of the Late Pleistocene surfaces in this region: either buried under deep deposits of windblown sediments or inundated by Holocene rises in sea level. Nevertheless, researchers have steadily been learning more about Beringia, which is now the site of much exciting research.

First, although it was once argued that human entry into the Americas had to be relatively recent because humans had not developed the ability to penetrate the cold lands of Siberia and Beringia until the very end of the Pleistocene, there is now evidence that humans were in eastern Siberia and perhaps western Beringia by 35,000 BP. For example, a recent report of a 30,000-year-old site on the Yana River north of the Arctic Circle (Stone 2004) further confirms the

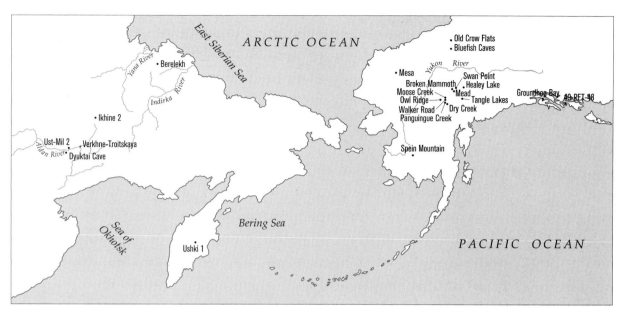

FIGURE 3.8 Beringia, showing the location of Beringian sites mentioned in Chapter 3.

presence of humans in the far north during the Ice Age. The most important Siberian sites are those found in the valley of the Aldan River in northeast Siberia. Dyuktai Cave, located along the Dyuktai River, a tributary of the Aldan in the Sakha Republic, is the most often cited of these sites. It is the **type site** for the **Dyuktai tradition** of northeast Siberia, dated between 35,000 BP and 10,500 BP by Siberian archaeologists. The three cultural horizons recognized at Dyuktai Cave itself all have been dated to the end of this tradition (Horizon A, 13,000–12,000 BP, Horizon B, 15,000–13,000 BP, Horizon C, 16,000–15,000 BP) (Mochanov and Fedoseeva 1996a). Other stratified sites in the Aldan River valley, including Ust-Mil 2, Verkhne–Troitskaya, and Ikhine 2, have produced radiocarbon dates defining the greater time range (Table 3.1).

Further north and east in the Sakha Republic and in Kamchatka and Chukotka, areas we might properly call western Beringia, the oldest known sites are younger. The Berelekh site, located along a tributary of the Indigirka River, which drains into the East Siberian Sea in the northern part of the Sakha Republic, is the northernmost occurrence of the Dyuktai tradition. The site has been long known as a mammoth cemetery of paleontological significance; the archaeological component, which is spatially distinct from the mammoth bone accumulations, was first recognized in the 1970s. The archaeological component has been dated to around 13,000 BP (Mochanov and Fedoseeva 1996b). Another important site is one of four sites located along the shore of Ushki Lake in the Kamchatka River valley, Kamchatka. Known as Ushki 1, this site has been thoroughly investigated. Besides an important dated artifact assemblage, the remains of numerous structures have been found here. The lower cultural layer at Ushki 1, Cultural Layer VII, has been radiocarbon dated at 13,980 ±146 BP, while the stratigraphically separated Cultural Layer VI above it has been dated at 10,643 ±68BP (Dikov 1996).

TABLE 3.1 Some Dated Beringian Sites Important to the Settlement of the Americas

Site Name	Location	Dating of Early Components	Key Artifacts
SIBERIA			
Dyuktai Cave	Aldan River Basin	16,000–12,000 BP	Wedge-shaped and prismatic blade cores, burins, blades, bifaces, microblades, scrapers, worked bone
Ust-Mil 2	Aldan River Basin	35,000–30,000 BP	Blade fragments, pebble core, wedge-shaped cores, bifacial knives, burins, worked bone
Verkhne–Troitskaya	Aldan River Basin	23,000–18,000 BP	Wedge-shaped cores, blades, knives and end scrapers on blades, blade insets, burins, worked bone
Ikhine 2	Aldan River Basin	35,000–25,000 BP	Wedge-shaped cores, pebble cores, blades, knife on a blade, scrapers, worked bone
Berelekh	Indigirka River Basin	13,500–10,000 BP	Blades, microblade core made on flake, fragments of bifaces, stone pendants, worked bone
Ushki 1	Ushki Lake, Kamchatka River valley	14,500–13,350 BP	Blades made on subprismatic cores, burins, stemmed, leaf-shaped, and teardrop-shaped points, scrapers, stone beads and pendants
ALASKA			
Dry Creek	Nenana River valley	10,700–9300 BP	Upper level—microblades, wedge-shaped cores, blade cores, blades, tools on blades, burins, bifaces, scrapers
		11,100 BP	Lower level—blade cores, blades, tools on blades, bifaces, triangular and lanceolate points, scrapers
Walker Road	Nenana River valley	11,300–11,000 BP	Blade cores, blades, tools on blades, burins, bifaces, scrapers, drills or gravers
Moose Creek	Nenana River valley	11,200 BP	Bifaces, Chindadn, triangular and lanceolate points, scrapers
Panguingue Creek	Nenana River valley	8600–7000 BP	Wedge-shaped cores, microblades, blade cores, blades, tools made on blades, burins, bifaces, lanceolate points, scrapers
		10,000–9500 BP	Blade cores, burins, bifaces, lanceolate points, scrapers
Owl Ridge	Nenana River valley	8500–7500 BP	Bifaces, blade fragment
		11,300 BP	Blades, bladelike tools, bifaces
Broken Mammoth	Tanana River valley	11,800–10,300 BP	Bifaces, triangular points, concave base points, scrapers, worked bone

TABLE 3.1 (continued)

Site Name	Location	Dating of Early Components	Key Artifacts
Swan Point	Tanana River valley	10,200 BP	Microblades, blades, tools on blades, burins, bifaces, convex, straight and concave base points, worked bone
		11,600 BP	Microblades, blades, tools on blades, burins, bifaces
Mead	Tanana River valley	10,400 BP	Flakes
		11,600 BP	Bifaces, scrapers, worked bone
Healey Lake	Tanana River tributary valley	11,500–10,000 BP	Microblade cores, microblades, blades, tools on blades, bifaces, burins, Chindadn, triangular and lanceolate points, scrapers
Tangle Lakes	Alaska Range	10,000–8200 BP	Wedge-shaped and other microblade cores, microblades, blade cores, blades, tools on blades, burins, bifaces, lanceolate points, other points, scrapers
Mesa	Iteriak valley	11,700–9700 BP	Tools on blades, bifaces, lanceolate points with concave bases (fluted?), scrapers, drills or gravers
Spein Mountain	Kisaralik River valley	10,000 BP	Pentagonal leaf-shaped and lanceolate points (fluted?), bifaces, gravers, scrapers

Data from Goebel and Slobodin (1999), Hamilton and Goebel (1999), and West (1996).

In Beringian cultural assemblages, there are stone tools and also some worked bone tools. Two different ways of making stone tools are represented (Table 3.1; Figure 3.9). First, people flaked or chipped cores of rock into bifacial points, as well as other bifacial tools and blades that could be made and used in various ways. Second, archaeologists believe that **microblades**, made from small cores of rock, were then set into slits cut into bone or antler spears. Microblades have been made from flakes or from pebbles or cobbles, resulting in a **wedge-shaped core**. Interestingly, microblade technology was not part of the Clovis and other Paleoindian manufacture of stone tools in most of North America.

In eastern Siberia and western Beringia, the Dyuktai tradition stone tool technology is characterized by bifacially worked tools, including projectile points and knives, as well as wedge-shaped cores, microblades, and burins. These tools have been found in association with remains of mammoths and other large Pleistocene game. Some of the mammoth bone and ivory has also been worked into tools. The stone tools from the earliest levels at Ushki 1, dated at more than 14,000 BP, diverge from this pattern because they include stemmed bifaces. In the overlying cultural stratum, however, the assemblage is reminiscent of the Dyuktai assemblages elsewhere.

FIGURE 3.9 Examples of tools found in Dyuktai Cave: (a) wedged-shaped microblade core, (b) microblades, (c) base of bifacial knife, (d) bifacial knife, (e) biface, and (f) side scraper. (Adapted from Mochanov and Fedoseeva 1996a, Figures 3.5 and 3.6.)

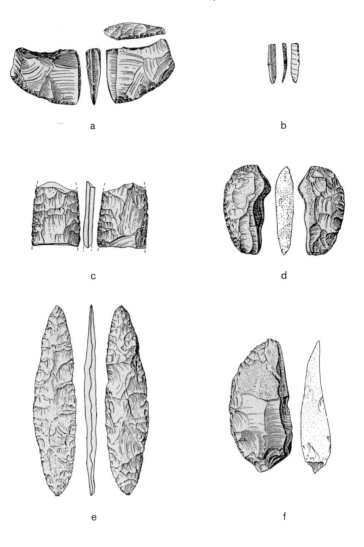

The oldest sites in eastern Beringia, or Alaska, are more or less contemporaneous with Clovis sites further south. Among these, several central Alaskan sites located along the Tanana River have yielded reliable radiocarbon dates. The Broken Mammoth site has been shown to have four cultural zones with the stratigraphically lowest of these called Cultural Zone IV having a date range of 11,800 BP to 11,200 BP. Cultural Zone III at Broken Mammoth dates to approximately 10,300 BP. Swan Point, also in the Tanana River valley, is multicomponent, with the oldest materials at the site having been dated to 11,660 BP and slightly younger deposits dated at 10,230 ±80 BP. Other important sites have been found in the Nenana River valley, a major tributary of the Tanana River that originates in the Alaska Range. The most important of these is Dry Creek, a deeply stratified site for which the stratigraphy has been well dated by a series of radiocarbon samples. Here the oldest component (Component I) has a radiocarbon date of 11,120 ±85 BP, while the overlying Component II is dated at 10,690 ±250 BP

FIGURE 3.10 Nenana
(a–i) and Denali complex
(j–o) artifacts: (a, b) bifaces,
(c, d) blades, (e–g) end
scrapers, (h, i) perforators,
(j, k) bifaces, (l) burin,
(m) microblade core, and
(n, o) microblades.

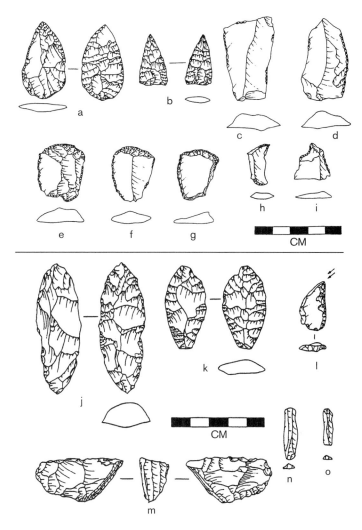

(Hamilton and Goebel 1999; West ed. 1996). Table 3.1 provides information on the dating for some of the early Alaskan sites.

Archaeologists recognize two early tool traditions in these central Alaskan sites (Figure 3.10). The first, known as the **Nenana complex**, is a blade and biface industry that lacks microblades and is believed to date between 12,000 and 11,000 BP. The complex contains Chindadn points or knives which are thin, teardrop-shaped bifaces. The younger **Denali complex**, beginning at approximately 10,600 BP, has obvious similarities to the Dyuktai tradition in Siberia and western Beringia. This assemblage includes wedge-shaped cores, microblades, and burins. Similar tool assemblages have been found in Alaska well into the Holocene (see Chapter 4). These data suggest that tool traditions in which wedge-shaped cores, microblades, and burins figure prominently were preceded in Alaska by an older blade and biface industry. However, closer consideration of the site assemblages may suggest an even more complicated and regionally variable sequence (Hamilton and Goebel 1999).

Other sites that seem to be quite early are Spein Mountain, which is located in the Kuskokwim River drainage of southwestern Alaska, and the Mesa site, located on the northern side of the Brooks Range in Arctic Alaska. The Spein Mountain site has only one AMS radiocarbon date ($10,050 \pm 90$ BP) obtained from charcoal found in a soil sample, but it is an important site because of the lanceolate projectile points recovered there are reminiscent of Paleoindian point styles found further south (Ackerman 1996c). The Mesa site appears to have been a hunting station where hunters made and resharpened their stone tools while watching game movements below the mesa on which the site is located. A series of AMS radiocarbon dates from hearth features found at this site range between 11,700 BP and 9700 BP, with the majority of dates postdating 10,500 BP. Tools found at the Mesa site, which include fluted points, also appear to be similar to Paleoindian tools found further south (Kunz and Reanier 1996).

It appears that fluted points were not made in Alaska before they were made to the south and that some technological differences distinguish Alaskan fluted points and those found further south (Clark 1991). Fluting and perhaps other technological traits traditionally associated with Paleoindians may have first developed south of the ice sheets in North America, and then, been brought northward. These data continue to perplex archaeologists, and they are stimulating a good deal of research in Beringia.

How Did Humans Come South from Beringia into North and South America?

Two potential routes of entry have been most favored by archaeologists (Figure 3.11). As noted already, the Clovis-First scenario assumes that the First Americans moved south into North America through an ice-free corridor that opened between the two North American ice sheets in Canada. This open corridor would have stretched south from the Yukon through portions of the Northwest Territories, Alberta, and southern Saskatchewan. However, for most of the Ice Age this route would have been blocked by glaciers. Only during interglacials and as glaciation came to an end would the Cordilleran and Laurentian ice sheets have retreated away from each other, opening unglaciated areas. The gap between glaciers would have had to be large for vegetation, large herbivores, and human hunters to enter the corridor. There has been considerable geologic and climatological investigation of when an ice-free corridor traversable by human hunters and their prey might have existed. The current viewpoint is that this corridor was not truly open between about 22,000 BP, as the last glacial advance developed, and about 14,000 BP. Certainly, a corridor would have been open to hunters around 11,500 BP if entry did not occur until then, but it would also have been a possible route south before 22,000 BP if humans arrived that early.

Although there have been a number of proposed Pre-Clovis sites in western Canada, these sites have eventually been rejected for one reason or another. For example, at Varsity Estates, near the city of Calgary, Alberta, possible artifacts such as choppers, cores, scrapers, and **gravers** have been reported from glacial till deposits believed to be more than 21,000 years old. However, most archaeologists suspect a natural origin for these objects. Bluefish Caves in the Yukon may mark the northern end of the corridor and, as noted earlier, may provide evidence of human presence in Pre-Clovis times. However, sites in the corridor to the south have provided no indication of pre-12,000 BP occupation (Wilson and

FIGURE 3.11 Possible routes of human entry into North America: (1) traditionally accepted ice-free corridor route, (2) coastal route along the West coast, and (3) recently proposed route across the northern Atlantic.

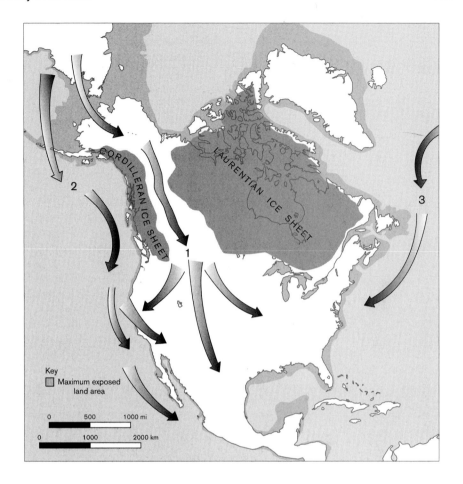

Bums 1999). We don't know whether earlier sites have been deeply buried, were destroyed by subsequent glacial advances or retreats, or never existed in the first place. Only much more serious deep-testing programs can hope to improve understanding of these issues.

A second route along the west coast of North America has also received considerable attention, particularly recently. In this view, the first settlers followed the South Alaskan coast and then the Pacific Coast of North America and eventually Central and South America. These people would have been coastally adapted hunter-gatherers with boats who did not penetrate the interior of the continent until they were south of the ice. Some proponents of this route have argued for very early entry—even during the Middle Pleistocene—reasoning that once the last glacial maximum had begun, the southern coast of Alaska would have been blocked by massive glaciers (Gruhn 1994). Others favor a much more recent use of this route, perhaps 14,000 years ago, as warming began (Dixon 1999). If, as Fladmark (1979, 1983) has maintained, there were small, ice-free pockets along the Pacific Coast that could have served as refuges for humans, then a coastal migration seems more plausible.

Until recently, most archaeologists have not taken this idea seriously, offering several reasons. First, for a long time, it was thought that early peoples could not have had boats and other technology sufficiently advanced to permit travel through northern coastal areas. However, it is now clear that at least by 50,000 BP, people were able to cross to Australia by boat. In addition, evidence of coastal adaptations by generalized foragers in several places during the last 40,000 years increases the plausibility of the argument for settlement of the Americas in this manner. Second, as long as archaeologists assumed that the first migrants were terrestrially focused big-game hunters, a coastal route seemed highly unlikely, but if other adaptive strategies existed, movement along the coasts is more reasonable. Third, some scholars maintain that the idea of intrepid big-game hunters migrating through a windswept, ice-free corridor simply captured American archaeologists' imagination, resonating with the notion that the United States is a nation of immigrants (Mandryk 2004).

The coastal route theory was also questioned because of the lack of evidence for early sites in this region. However plausible, there was simply no evidence from the Alaskan or Canadian coast of sites prior to about 9000 years ago. An early date of 10,180 ±800 BP has been obtained from the Ground Hog Bay site located near Juneau, Alaska, but this date, which does not conform to other radiocarbon dates obtained from the site, may not be reliable (Ackerman 1996b). The basic problem is that most of the Pleistocene age coastline was drowned as sea level rose owing to the melting of the ice sheets. It is highly unlikely that we will find sites representing Late Pleistocene occupation of the continental shelf, although we might find sites slightly inland or perhaps on coastal islands.

Certain early sites along the Pacific Coast of the United States provide evidence for generalized coastal foragers. The most important cluster is in southern California, where several sites on the Channel Islands are more than 10,000 years old (see Jon Erlandson's case study, "Sea Change: The Paleocoastal Occupations of Daisy Cave," in this chapter). Lowered sea level during the Ice Age meant that what today are separate islands were a single, exposed landmass. The remains of pygmy mammoths have been recovered here, and some researchers have suggested an association with stone tools and hearths. However, careful sediment and other analyses have not supported this contention. Occupation of the Channel Islands that is contemporaneous with Folsom beginning about 10,500 BP is apparent at sites like Daisy Cave. Carbon isotopic studies of human remains from 49-PET-408, a site on Prince of Wales Island in Alaska, also suggest a largely marine diet at 9200 BP (Dixon 1999). These data indicate that coastal adaptations developed early and that at least some Paleoindians were not terrestrial big-game hunters but generalized foragers.

As long as the consensus was that the Clovis-First scenario was basically correct, it was not necessary to consider this alternative route very seriously. Now that there is increasing acceptance of Pre-Clovis occupation of the Americas, the coastal route is being reexamined. Dixon (1999) has proposed that a revised coastal model provides the best fit for the data. Specifically, he proposes that the initial human colonization of the Americas began about 13,500 BP, when generalized foragers used boats to travel along the southern coast of Beringia and then southward into the Americas. Making use of a coastal–intertidal biome found along the entire Pacific Coast, these people moved rapidly southward before the glaciers of the continental interior had melted. Dixon proposes that interior areas were inhabited more gradually over the next few thousand years, and that coastal foragers also rounded the tip of South America and came north again before the midcontinents were settled. In Dixon's model, Clovis comes at the end of the migratory sequence after about 11,500 BP. Although this entry model is entirely speculative, some archaeologists think it fits the data we now have better than the formerly popular idea of an ice-free corridor route.

One final idea about routes of entry must be mentioned. In 1999 Dennis Stanford and Bruce Bradley reminded archaeologists of early observations (e.g., Renaud 1931) that beautifully made fluted points of Clovis and other Paleoindians resemble artifacts made in Europe during the Upper Paleolithic (Hall and Wisner 2000). Specifically, the leaf-shaped, sometimes stemmed projectile points of the **Solutrean culture** (22,000–18,000 BP) found in France, Portugal, and Spain seem similar technologically to Paleoindian points. These points exhibit retouch and parallel flaking across the surface of the point similar to the same properties in Clovis points. In the spirit of "thinking outside the box" of the Clovis-First scenario, these archaeologists have suggested that we rethink a route of entry westward from Europe across the Atlantic. Why couldn't the first migrants have come westward by boat, skirting the margins of the North Atlantic ice? This route of entry might explain the presence of some indications for Pre-Clovis occupation in eastern North America as well as why fluted points may have appeared later in the far north than south of the ice sheets. This proposal of a **"Solutrean connection"** also remains primarily speculative at this time. Most archaeologists have not accepted it as a serious possibility, arguing that the Solutrean is too early and totally terrestrial in its focus and that the technological similarities cited may be superficial rather than indicative of common cultural heritage (Straus 1998). In addition, as discussed in the following section, biological and linguistic evidence tends to support an Asian origin for those who first colonized the Americas.

What Can Be Determined About the Biological Affinities of the First Americans?

Cultural remains are not the only materials that provide scholars with an understanding of the settlement of the Americas. Human remains are also important sources. Not surprisingly, there have been some claims of Pre-Clovis human remains from North America, but AMS dating has established that they probably all date after 11,000 BP (Taylor et al. 1985). Examples include the Taber child, a human infant whose skeleton was recovered from the Stalker site in southern Alberta, and a variety of skeletal finds from California.

In fact, a number of other human skeletal remains have been reliably dated between 11,000 and 8000 years ago (Table 3.2). Although this database is small and some of the material is fragmentary, it does allow preliminary investigation of the biological features of the earliest Americans. Comparison of the characteristics of these skeletons with the skeletons of present-day Native Americans and also with the characteristics of Asian and other populations may shed light both on where migrants came from and on their route of entry. In fact, such comparisons are fascinating and puzzling. This is because the dimensions of the face and cranium of at least some of these earliest Americans differ in significant ways from those of modern-day Native Americans (Steele and Powell 1994). The **Kennewick skeleton** (see Box 3.1) is one of the examples, but there are others. As a group, the crania older than 8500 BP are less like modern northern Asians and modern Native Americans in certain characteristics than we might expect.

TABLE 3.2 Partial List of Early North American Skeletal Remains

Site Name	Location	Skeletal Materials	Dating
49-PET-408	Prince of Wales Island, Alaska	Lower jaw, teeth, vertebra, rib and pelvic fragments from one individual	9200 BP
Namu	Coastal British Columbia, Canada	Tooth crowns with sinodont pattern	9000–8000 BP
Gore Creek	Kamloops, British Columbia	Postcranial skeleton of a male	8250 BP
Marmes Rockshelter	Southeast Washington	Cranial and tooth fragments from four individuals and fragmentary remains of at least six individuals from crematory hearths	10,000–8000 BP
Gordon Creek	Northern Colorado	Partial female skeleton	9700 ±250 BP
Kennewick	Kennewick, Washington	Nearly complete skeleton of a male with Cascade point embedded in hip	8410 ±60 BP calibrated to 9300 BP
Buhl	Snake River in southern Idaho	Adult female skeleton, nearly complete	10,675 ±95 BP
Arlington Springs	Santa Rosa Island, southern California	Two femora, a humerus, and an unidentified bone now believed to be from a female	ca. 11,000 BP
Spirit Cave	Nevada	Adult female wrapped in a mat above adult male wrapped in rabbit skin blanket and mat with human hair preserved	9300 ±70 BP for female, 9414 ±25 BP for male
Burial B, Wizards Beach	Pyramid Lake, Nevada	Male skeleton missing vertebrae, pelvis, and some limb bones	9500–9100 BP
Wilson–Leonard site	Central Texas	Crushed, nearly complete skeleton of female	10,000–9600 BP
Horn Shelter 2	Brazos River near Waco, Texas	Double burial of adult male and adult female	ca. 9650 BP
Warm Mineral Springs	Sarasota County, Florida	Three individuals from Zone 3 and cranium with intact brain tissue, recovered by amateurs	Deposits in Zone 3 appear to be 10,500–10,000 BP

Adapted from Dixon (1999).

Specifically, the braincase is narrower and longer than that generally found among modern North Asians and Native Americans. However, it is wider and shorter than the norm for modern South Asians and Europeans. These earliest Americans also seem to have had faces that were intermediate between the two later groups in terms of the width of the face and of the nasal aperture.

As indicated in Box 3.1 on the Kennewick skeleton and case, millennia-old human remains cannot easily be classified as belonging to some non-Asian race. Rather, our modern racial groupings have even less meaning in considerations of the Late Pleistocene and Early Holocene remains than they do today. We might consider Paleoindians to predate modern racial groupings. This is supported by

ISSUES AND DEBATES

BOX 3.1

Why Is the Kennewick Case So Significant?

In 1996 many human bones, including a skull, were found washing out of the bank of the Columbia River near Kennewick, Washington. The county coroner consulted James Chatters, an archaeologist/physical anthropologist who often consults on forensic cases involving skeletal materials in the area. Chatters took the usual measurements, made the usual observations, and concluded that these skeletal materials were those of a male Caucasoid who had died between the ages of 40 and 55. He also noticed that this man had had a rough life. For example, a large object had penetrated his right hip, and the bone had healed over the wound site. Chatters first presumed that the wound had been caused by a bullet or a piece of shrapnel, but an x-ray image showed that the object wasn't metal. Then a CT scan revealed a stone spear point with a distinctive leaf shape! The man whose bones had been found had been injured by a point, made by hunters living on the Columbia Plateau between 9000 and 4500 years ago! Chatters was intrigued. Could a white settler have been injured with a stone point that was thousands of years old? Was this a bizarre recent murder? On the other hand, if this was a white person, why did the teeth show the heavy wear and lack of cavities typical of Native American hunter-gatherers because of their high-grit, low-carbohydrate diet? At this point, Chatters took a small scrap of bone from the skeleton to the University of California–Riverside Radiocarbon Laboratory. When the bone sample was dated as between 9200 and 9500 years old, a major controversy was ignited.

As indicated earlier, human skeletal material of this age is rare. A skeleton as complete as the Kennewick specimen is even rarer. Moreover,

the features of the skeleton are different from those of contemporary Native Americans, which is why Chatters originally thought he was looking at the bones of a white settler or even a modern Washingtonian. These skeletal materials can be grouped with other early skeletons that have crania narrower and longer than is typical of Indian populations found today in the Americas. Detailed knowledge of the features of the Kennewick cranium—features that most closely resemble Polynesians, southern Asians, and the Ainu of Japan—could provide important clues to the source of early migrations into the Americas (Figure 3.12). As older consensus positions on early settlement seem to be unraveling in the face of new data, a skeleton like Kennewick is a scientific prize. You might expect that it would be the focus of careful study.

However, the story is not that simple. The Kennewick bones were recovered on land retained for flood control purposes by the U.S. Army Corps of Engineers. This meant that all federal laws and regulations about the handling of skeletal materials had to be considered. Notably, the Native American Grave Protection and Repatriation Act of 1990 (NAGPRA) appeared to apply. Among other things, this law states that when Native American skeletal remains are recovered on federal property, possibly affiliated tribes must be contacted and the remains offered to them for reburial. Study of the remains beyond determination of affiliation is not allowed unless granted by the tribes. Once the early date for the Kennewick bones had been obtained, it seemed reasonable to consider the Kennewick skeleton Native American. Five days after the radiocarbon results were made public, the Corps announced its intent to repatriate the

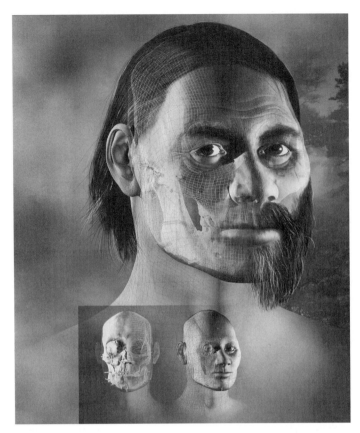

FIGURE 3.12 Possible reconstruction of the Kennewick man's facial features.

remains to an alliance of Northwest Indian tribes, the Umatilla, the Yakima, the Nez Perce, the Wanapum, and the Colville. The Umatilla, taking the lead, insisted that Chatters turn over the bones and stop immediately any further study, including scheduled DNA testing and examination by Smithsonian Institution staff. To the tribes, this was a matter of sovereign rights and respect for the dead. Over some protest that the remains were not really Native American, the Corps took possession of the bones and proceeded with plans to turn them over to the tribes.

Before the tribes had received the remains, however, eight prominent physical anthropologists and archaeologists sued the federal government, stopping the NAGPRA process. At issue was whether the government had violated NAGPRA by ignoring evidence that the skeleton might not be affiliated with the tribes, thus nulli-

fying any tribe's right to prevent scientific study of the materials. Also at issue was whether the Corps burial of the discovery site along the Columbia River without allowing further scientific excavation and study violated the National Historic Preservation Act (NHPA), which requires the federal government to prevent destruction of cultural resources in its undertakings. Since its inception, this complicated case has had many twists and turns.

Before ruling on the matter, the judge ordered the government to carefully reconsider all the issues especially those of affiliation. Biological and cultural studies done at this time reestablished that physically the Kennewick individual did not closely resemble modern Native Americans, although Polynesian and South Asian affiliations rather than European were suggested. Archaeological studies indicated connections between the tribes and people in the area as long ago as 5000 BC, while linguistic evidence indicated that the tribes' ancestors had been present in the region for at least 2000 years. Indian oral traditions that they had always been in the area also were considered.

In early 2000 the government agencies reaffirmed the position that the Kennewick bones were Native American based on their age and on tribal oral traditions, and in September 2000 the agencies indicated that they still believed NAGPRA required them to repatriate the remains to the tribal coalition. Many physical anthropologists and archaeologists questioned the validity of this decision, which did not take into account all the evidence the government itself had gathered. The court also found much fault with the government's reasoning, ruling that NAGPRA did not apply because the skeleton was not Native American and that the scientists who brought suit could study the remains. The court also determined that burial of the discovery site had violated NHPA.

This opinion was issued at the end of August 2002, but before the required protocols for study of the remains could be approved and investigations could begin, the government appealed the decision. This stopped study once again. Then in February 2004, the Ninth Circuit Court of Appeals upheld the original court's decision. This decision was not appealed, but changes in the statute itself are now being sought. Meanwhile, this skeleton is finally being studied.

There is no single position about the Kennewick case held by all archaeologists or among all Indians. Indeed, the case is significant precisely because it encapsulates many policy issues that students of North American archaeology need to consider. In the court case itself, the issue was not whether scientific and scholarly interests outweigh descendant's rights or about respecting nonscientific as well as scientific ideas concerning the past. The question was whether the government followed NAGPRA appropriately. With respect to human remains, NAGPRA establishes what most archaeologists believe—when direct descent is evident, the descendants should have the primary say with respect to dis-

position. Many archaeologists see the NAGPRA process as a way to balance possibly competing interests in human skeletal material.

The Kennewick case also is muddled by facile references to modern racial types such as Indian, white, and Asian. Most anthropologists question whether biological races are meaningful ways to explore human variation, noting that there is relatively little covariation among traits and, thus, more variation within racial categories than between. In forensic cases, scientists can assess certain cranial characters with a view to making a guess about the population from which an individual came. Yet in the Kennewick case, we don't know enough about the configurations and distributions of human populations 10,000 to 12,000 years ago to make much sense out of a racial type. This is why scientists want to study the skeleton in the first place!

Ultimately, this case may help all concerned parties to sort out difficult issues, but the court decisions so far have only muddied the waters. Indians may feel that progress in recognizing their rights has been lost. Government officials may remain confused about how to apply NAGPRA. Moreover, some archaeologists are concerned about the implications of the court's classification of the remains as non–Native American. They would prefer a category designated "unaffiliated Native American remains," and NAGPRA in fact acknowledges that procedures for such a category should be developed. The important questions here are very hard to answer. Should Native Americans have sovereign rights over all pre-Columbian human and cultural materials or just some? How are we to determine the descendants for people who inhabited North America many millennia ago? What is to be done if affiliation cannot be established? Also, what was the intent of NAGPRA, and how should it be applied by government agencies? The Kennewick case should remind us of the continuing need for fair and balanced policy and procedures. Many of the issues we must confront with respect to human skeletal remains have not been resolved. Hopefully, as the Kennewick case and reactions to it continue to unfold, we will both develop better policy and learn more about the complex peopling of the Americas.

craniofacial similarities between Paleoindians and the Jomon people, who were early inhabitants of Japan, and also by similarities with some early *Homo sapiens sapiens* skeletons from the Upper Cave at Zhoukoudian, China.

There is another way to use biological characteristics to draw conclusions about the settlement of the Americas. Scientists have studied contemporary populations in terms of biological similarities and differences and used their results to suggest how migration took place. The general idea is that Native Americans should be more like other modern populations also descended from the source population for the first American migrants. A variety of biological characters have been explored in this way. Sometimes these characters can also be studied in archaeological specimens. Most important among these studies has been investigation of dental and mitochondrial DNA (**mtDNA**) characteristics.

Dental characteristics have been carefully evaluated by comparing both modern and prehistoric Native American specimens with the teeth of other human populations. A large number of tooth crown and root traits have been shown to vary in consistent ways between populations. For example, both **shovel-shaped incisors** and three-rooted first lower molars are rare among Europeans but commonly found among Asians and Native Americans. In contrast, **Carabelli's cusp**, an extra reduced cusp or tubercle sometimes found on the upper molars, is much more common among people of European descent than among other populations (Figure 3.13) (Turner 1983).

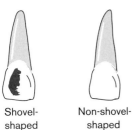

Shovel-shaped incisor   Non-shovel-shaped incisor

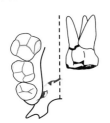

Carabelli's cusp on an upper first molar

Three-rooted lower first molar   Two-rooted lower first molar

FIGURE 3.13 Dental characteristics that occur in differing frequencies in populations of Asian and Native American as opposed to European descent.

Christy Turner's evaluation of dental data indicates little dental variation among Native American populations, although the greatest variability characterizes northern populations, as would be expected if settlement of the Americas occurred recently and proceeded north to south. In addition, all Native American populations appear to be more closely related to Asian populations than to those from Europe or Africa. These data also led Turner to argue that Native Americans result from three separate migrations out of northern Asia. Turner believed these to be (1) a Paleoindian migration that, based on dental traits, originated in North Asia and was responsible for most American Indian populations, (2) a later Aleut-Eskimo migration also starting in North Asia, and (3) a third migration of the ancestor of Na-Dene-speaking groups of western North America.

Turner identifies the dental pattern found among Native Americans and North Asians as **Sinodont** and contrasts it with a South Asian pattern he calls **Sundadont**. Thus, Turner argues strongly for a single ancestral population that was located in North Asia, perhaps in eastern Siberia. Turner tends to accept the Clovis-First scenario, arguing that Native American Sinodonts have been diverging from North Asian Sinodonts since approximately Clovis times (Greenberg et al. 1986; Turner 1983, 1994).

Turner's interpretation is supported by some linguistic analyses, notably those of Joseph Greenberg (Greenberg et al. 1986, 1987), who has proposed that all Native American languages cluster into three groups: a large Amerind group, an Aleut-Eskimo group, and a Na-Dene group. Obviously these fit perfectly with Turner's idea of three waves of migration into North America. Greenberg has accumulated a vast amount of data on Native American languages; however, his methods are somewhat controversial. Other linguists (e.g., Goddard and Campbell 1994) believe that there are many more linguistic groupings among Native American languages and argue for more detailed linguistic analyses.

Recent mtDNA studies also have been brought to bear on the question of the origins of Native American populations. According to Schurr et al. (1990), mtDNA from Native Americans suggests four common founding lineages, which are identified as **haplogroups** A, B, C, and D. Approximately 97 percent of Native Americans can be placed in one of these four lineages based on mtDNA. A fifth but minor lineage, called **haplogroup X**, has received a great deal of attention because it is extremely rare among East Asian populations, but more common among Southwest Asians and Europeans. Among Native Americans, haplogroup X has been identified in the mtDNA of the Ojibwa, the Nuu-Chah-Nulth, the Sioux, the Yakima, and the Navajo (Brown et al. 1998; Scozzari et al. 1998). Although haplogroup X might indicate recent admixture with modern European Americans, differences between European and Native American haplogroup X characteristics argue against this interpretation.

Originally, there were no known Asian populations with haplogroup X, but in 2001 it was reported that this haplogroup had been identified in the mtDNA of Altaians, a group native to southern Siberia. In addition, the Altaian haplogroup X appears to be intermediate in character between European haplogroup X and American Indian haplogroup X (Derenko et al. 2001). Altaians also have haplogroups A–D in their mtDNA at fairly high frequencies (57.2 percent) that exceed the frequencies among Mongolians, Chinese, and Tibetans. In addition, recent Y-chromosome analyses indicate that the Altaians, as well as other groups in Siberia, could be closely related to Native Americans (Karafet et al. 1999).

Genetic and other studies of biological distance among Native Americans are proliferating. Though not a panacea, they promise to help us sort out the origins of native populations. As with other puzzling areas, the data we now have raise as many questions as they answer. More direct studies of early American human skeletal remains should also continue when possible. All these studies seem to be indicating that multiple human migrations were responsible for the settlement of the Americas. Some researchers have suggested that we call the first settlers **Paleoamericans** rather than Paleoindians, to emphasize the current perspective that there may not be biological and cultural continuity between the first wave of migration and modern American Indians (Bonnichsen and Turnmire 1999). We use the more traditional term in this text because the new distinction is not yet widely used.

PALEOINDIAN ADAPTATIONS

The preceding discussion has focused on when, where, and how the Americas were first settled by humans. Archaeologists interested in the earliest Americans have also expended much effort investigating the cultural nature of these people. While possible Pre-Clovis adaptations are poorly understood, a great deal has been learned about Clovis and other Paleoindian lifestyles. A brief review of archaeological thinking on the nature of Paleoindian culture is in order here. More discussion of Paleoindian lifeways can be found in the culture area chapters that follow.

The first Paleoindian discoveries, reviewed at the beginning of this chapter, have strongly conditioned archaeological understanding of the nature of Clovis and Folsom adaptations. The association of stone tools and extinct fauna not only established the greater time depth of humans in the Americas, but suggested that the First Americans were hunters of large game such as mammoth and bison. As more kill sites were discovered on the Plains and in the Southwest, the concept

of Paleoindians as big-game hunters became established in archaeological thinking. The close similarity among Clovis points from all parts of the continent reinforced the idea that the Clovis culture was a single, continent-wide adaptation.
Moreover, the Pleistocene overkill model seemed to explain how specialized big-
game hunters could have rapidly colonized the entire continent. As a result, the
traditional viewpoint has been that cultural differentiation among Paleoindians
was largely a temporal phenomenon.

In this view, Paleoindians were specialized terrestrial hunters who focused
on large herd animals. The Clovis people were mammoth hunters, reminiscent of
Upper Paleolithic mammoth hunters from eastern Europe. While plant resources
certainly were used by Paleoindians, they were not emphasized in the diet. As
the Ice Age ended and environments changed, mammoths became scarcer and
eventually extinct, with overhunting by Clovis people possibly contributing to
their demise. Successor Paleoindian groups including Folsom had to rely on
other game but remained focused on large herd animals for several millennia,
especially on the Great Plains, as represented by the various Plano complexes
(Chapter 11). Other aspects of these Paleoindian adaptations included short-term
use of camps and high mobility, small group size, the use of high-quality raw
materials, often obtained at a distance, and sophisticated stone-working techniques.

Archaeological evidence supports this traditional reconstruction for
Paleoindians in many instances. Mammoth remains have been found at a number of dramatic Clovis kill sites (Figure 3.14). For example, at Blackwater Draw
(see Student CD, Section D.2), there are remains from six mammoths apparently
killed when they came to the spring for water. At the Dent site in Colorado,
eleven mammoth cows and one mammoth bull, possibly driven over a bluff and

FIGURE 3.14 Excavations
at the Naco site in Arizona
where a Clovis mammoth
kill site was uncovered.

later dispatched, have been found in association with Clovis points. Other sites, including Naco, Murray Springs, and Lehner Ranch in southern Arizona and the Colby site in northern Wyoming, also contain mammoth bones in association with Clovis points. Many of the known Folsom sites were kill sites as well. Examples include the Folsom-type site, Lindenmeier in northern Colorado (Wilmsen 1973), the Folsom level at the Agate Basin site in Wyoming, and many others. Similarly, many Plano tradition sites on the Great Plains are kill sites. On the other hand, recent reanalysis using GIS and zooarchaeological techniques at Bonfire Shelter in Texas has suggested that it was merely a processing site, not a bison jump or kill site per se (Byerly et al. 2005).

The idea that Paleoindians were highly mobile hunter-gatherers who lived in small social groups is supported by a variety of lines of evidence. Although there are far more Clovis and later Paleoindian sites than possible Pre-Clovis sites, the former sites still are fairly widely dispersed, and they seldom contain evidence of **midden** deposits or permanent structures. Consider, for example, the Shoop site in Pennsylvania, where concentrations of lithic debris are dispersed in clusters about 33 feet (10 m) in diameter along a ridge from which game movements may have been visible (Figure 3.15) (Witthoft 1952). Similarly the Debert site in Nova Scotia has been interpreted as the locus of short-term encampments used to monitor the movements of game (MacDonald 1968).

FIGURE 3.15 Artist's conception of Paleoindians hunting caribou.

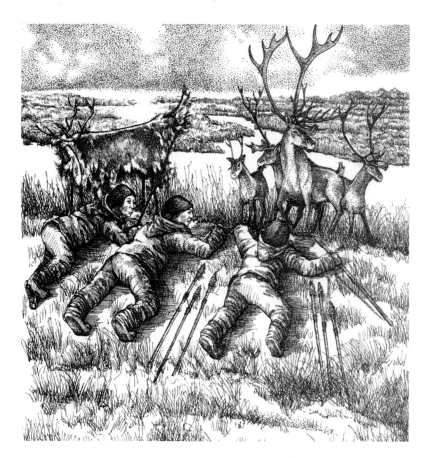

Paleoindian tools found together in the same site often are made from a variety of raw materials, some of which have been transported long distances from their sources. Although exchange between different groups of Paleoindians has been proposed as one mechanism for the movement of lithic materials to sites far from natural outcroppings (Hayden 1982), most archaeologists believe Paleoindian hunters procured the raw material themselves, often initially making it into large bifaces, which were kept for later use (Meltzer 1984–1985). The role of bifaces in Paleoindian technology has been explored by several researchers (Boldurian 1991; Kelly 1988).

The selection and transport of high-quality raw materials is one aspect of the evidence that Paleoindians were master flintknappers as well. They clearly knew what stone was good to flake and went to some lengths to obtain it. The skill of Paleoindian flintknappers also is obvious to anyone who studies Paleoindian lithic assemblages. The Clovis toolkit included fluted points, bone **shaft wrenches**, bone points with beveled ends, bone and ivory foreshafts for spears, large bifaces, large, prismatic blades, blade cores, end and **side scrapers**, gravers, and more expedient flake tools (Figure 3.16).

A number of spectacular artifact caches of Clovis origin also have been found. These caches are concentrations of artifacts including well-made Clovis points, blades, and other bone and stone artifacts. One idea about these caches is that they were burial offerings, as suggested by the Anzick cache, near Wilsall, Montana: over 100 artifacts were covered with red ocher, a pigment tradition- ally associated with the mortuary practices of Native Americans. Another idea is that mobile Paleoindian hunters were simply storing valuable, but heavy raw materials at these locations. In any case, these caches have allowed archaeologists

FIGURE 3.16 Clovis toolkit showing large biface, two Clovis points, a stone blade, a bone shaft wrench probably used for straightening spear shafts, a bone foreshaft, a wedge, a scraper, and other stone artifacts.

to closely study Clovis technology. Some archaeologists maintain that Clovis flintknappers often deliberately used the difficult bifacial thinning technique of overshot flaking (see Frison and Bradley 1999). Folsom and later Paleoindians also made a wide variety of tools and display considerable craftsmanship in the manufacture of stone tools.

It has been proposed that Paleoindians were not like any ethnographically known recent hunter-gatherers because they were not "place oriented." Instead of foraging within a known territory, they focused on terrestrial fauna, some of which was on the move, often in unknown terrain. This meant that they relied on their knowledge of animal behavior as well as their hunting technology, that they did not store resources, and that they moved often in response to seasonal and year-to-year fluctuations in resource availability. These attributes of the earliest Americans would have changed over time as the resource structure altered, human population levels grew, and territoriality developed (Kelly and Todd 1988). More recent modeling builds on these ideas, similarly noting the unusual nature of the colonizers of the Americas and the need for better controlled data to test competing models (e.g., Meltzer 2004; see also Barton et al. 2004).

However well these ideas explain some of the Paleoindian evidence, it also is true that they do not explain all the evidence adequately. For example, large-game kill sites are almost completely restricted to the Great Plains and the Southwest. The Kimmswick site located in eastern Missouri, where Clovis is associated with mastodon remains, is atypical for eastern Paleoindian sites (Graham et al. 1981). Although perhaps archaeologists have simply failed to find existing buried kill sites in other parts of the country, evidence of Clovis and other Paleoindian use of the rest of the continent is plentiful, as is paleontological evidence of extinct fauna not associated with humans (Meltzer 1993). Thus it is less likely that kill sites of large game exist but haven't been found.

Much Paleoindian evidence from the Eastern Woodlands is from surface finds of fluted points (Brennan 1982; Meltzer 1988) or from quarry sites (Lepper and Meltzer 1991), but where sites have been found and efforts made to collect a full range of subsistence remains, the results do not suggest specialization on big game (see Levine 1997). For example, the Shawnee Minisink, a stratified site near the Delaware Water Gap, occupied nearly 11,000 years ago, provides a different picture of Paleoindian adaptations for the Delaware River valley. Although apparently occupied only briefly, the first Paleoindian encampment seems to represent late summer or early fall harvesting of fish, berries, and other fruits, as well as tool production and maintenance activities (Dent 2002). One consideration of Paleoindian presence in the Maritime Provinces of Canada suggests that Late Paleoindians on what now is Prince Edward Island were beginning to exploit various coastal and marine resources (Keenlyside 1991). In New England, Paleoindians may have been attracted to proglacial lakes and rivers from which waterfowl and other resources rather than megafauna might have been obtained (Dincauze and Jacobson 2001).

West of the Great Plains, evidence for a big-game hunting focus also is lacking in Paleoindian sites (Dixon 1999). Because the largest concentrations of fluted points are along the shorelines of former lakes that dried up after the Pleistocene, some have proposed that Paleoindians in the Far West exploited a variety of fish and waterfowl resources as well as small and large game. Along the California coast, early people certainly used coastal resources beginning about 10,500 years ago. (See the case study at the end of this chapter and the Student CD, Section D.3.) Even at Lubbock Lake, a Clovis site in Texas where mammoth, horse, camel, and bison appear to have been exploited, many smaller mammals were also utilized. These include jackrabbit, muskrat, and wild turkey, as well as ducks, geese, and turtles (Johnson 1977).

Reexamination of old data as well as new reports from Paleoindian sites has convinced most archaeologists that many Paleoindians were not specialized big-game hunters at all but were instead generalized foragers who exploited big game at times. Thus, regional variation in subsistence seems probable, suggesting that the traditional viewpoint, postulating a single Clovis or Paleoindian adaptation, is wrong. Researchers studying the lithic technology also now believe that a variety of fluted point traditions developed during Paleoindian times, and they propose a number of other traditions that may have been coeval with Clovis and other fluted point traditions. For example, in the Northwest, the **Windust phase** may overlap with Clovis and continue beyond it (Bonnichsen and Turnmire 1999), and a Western Stemmed Point tradition may coexist with Clovis in the Great Basin and Snake River plain (Bryan and Tuohy 1999).

New approaches to the interdisciplinary study of Paleoindian adaptations (see recent articles in Barton et al. 2004) are actively being developed (Figure 3.17). Traditionally, very little attention has been paid to possible social interactions among Paleoindian groups or to the role of women in these early societies. Undoubtedly, women contributed both to the subsistence and to the social fabric of Paleoindian society, but one result of the focus on big-game hunting in Paleoindian studies has been a dearth of information on women's activities. Searching for women in the Paleoindian record as well as recognizing a broader range of economic and other activities could lead to new understandings of early lifestyles (Chilton 2004).

FIGURE 3.17 Excavation of the Gault site in Texas. This is one of the sites now providing new insights about the variability in Clovis adaptations.

CHAPTER SUMMARY

This chapter has introduced archaeological views about the early settlement of North America as well as many of the questions that remain for archaeologists. It also has sketched in the lifestyles of the people who first settled the Americas. The following points have been made:

- Early scholars did not believe that humans had been in the Americas for more than a few thousand years; this view hardened when early claims of an American Paleolithic could not be substantiated. However, in 1927, discovery of a fluted projectile point embedded in the rib cage of an extinct bison at the Folsom site in northeastern New Mexico established that humans had been in the Americas during the Ice Age.

- Following the Folsom discovery, an earlier culture was recognized, first at Blackwater Draw near Clovis, New Mexico, and then at many sites. Other styles and forms of fluted and unfluted early projectile points also were recognized by archaeologists, and Clovis components were eventually found to date between 11,500 BP and 10,800 BP.

- Many claims for Pre-Clovis materials, some as old as 50,000 BP, have been made, but few have been verified. This preponderance of invalid claims led to the consensus known as the Clovis-First scenario. The central proposition in this scenario is that humans did not settle the North American continent until after 12,000 BP, at the time of Clovis. These first Americans are understood as big-game hunters who followed herds of large game south through the ice-free corridor that opened between the glaciers at the end of the Ice Age, spreading rapidly across the continent thereafter.

- However, the evidence for Pre-Clovis at Meadowcroft Rockshelter in Pennsylvania and at Monte Verde in Chile has not been easily refuted. It appears that Meadowcroft was used at approximately 14,500 BP, while far to the south humans lived at Monte Verde between about 12,700 BP and 12,300 BP. These sites, as well as other data suggestive of a human presence a few millennia before Clovis, have led to active reevaluation of the Clovis-First scenario. However, there is no new consensus about when and how humans first entered this continent, only a great deal of interesting research on the topic.

- Exciting research is taking place on the archaeology of Beringia. Sites in eastern Beringia are not much earlier than Paleoindian sites further south. Moreover, they do not show antecedent fluted point technology as might be expected. Instead, either a blade and biface technology or a microblade industry is found in early Beringian sites. It even appears that fluted point technology could have spread northward after being developed south of the ice sheets.

- Recent attention has focused away from the idea that the initial settlement of the Americas occurred through the ice-free corridor as big-game hunters followed their prey. Instead, much attention has been given to the evidence for early coastal adaptations and the possibility of a coastal entry route.

- Human skeletal and biological indicators are being brought to bear on the puzzle of the settlement of the Americas. Evidence includes morphological differences between some early Paleoindian skeletons and the skeletons of contemporary Native Americans. These data combined with the results of mtDNA and dental analyses strongly suggest that multiple migrations, most likely from Asia, were responsible for the Native populations of North America. However, there still is a great deal to be learned about possible biological relationships.

- Paleoindians have been characterized as unique among known hunter-gatherers in that they were not strongly territorial or place oriented. This model explains much of what we have learned about Paleoindians, including the wide distribution of fluted points, the ephemeral nature of sites other than kill sites, and the people's lithic use patterns including caches. However, this model does not explain the evidence for generalized foraging by Paleoindians in the Eastern Woodlands or the early coastal foraging now known to have occurred.

SUGGESTIONS FOR FURTHER READING

For a good start in gaining familiarity with Native American origin and other stories:

Erdoes, Richard and Alfonso Ortiz. 1997. *American Indian Myths and Legends.* London: Pimlico Press.

For thoughtful and readable summaries of the topics covered in this chapter:

Dixon, E. James. 1999. *Bones, Boats and Bison: Archaeology of the First Colonization of Western North America.* Albuquerque: University of New Mexico Press.

Meltzer, David. 1993. *Search for the First Americans.* Montreal and New York: St. Remy Press and Smithsonian Institution.

For an accessible summary of the implications of South American evidence on the settlement of the Americas:

Dillehay, Thomas D. 2000. *The Settlement of the Americas: A New Prehistory.* New York: Basic Books.

For a highly individualistic account of the search for the First Americans emphasizing the Meadowcroft Rockshelter case:

Adovasio, James M., with Jake Page. 2002. *The First Americans: In Pursuit of Archaeology's Greatest Mystery.* New York: Random House.

For more on the Clovis era:

Haynes, Gary. 2002. *The Early Settlement of North America: The Clovis Era.* Cambridge: Cambridge University Press.

For a collection of some of the classic articles about Paleoindian archaeology:

Huckell, Bruce B., and J. David Kilby (compilers). 2004. *Readings in Late Pleistocene North America and Early Paleoindians: Selections from American Antiquity.* Washington, DC: Society for American Archaeology.

OTHER RESOURCES

The Student CD (Sections H and I) gives weblinks, additional discussion questions, and other study aids. The Student CD also contains a variety of additional resources, including a complete list of the references cited in this chapter. Particularly relevant resources include case studies by Anthony Boldurian, "Weaponry of Clovis Hunters at Blackwater Draw" (Section D.2), and by L. Mark Raab and Andrew Yatsko, "Eel Point and the Early Settlement of Coastal California: A Case Study in Contemporary Archaeological Research" (Section D.3).

CASE STUDY

As has been discussed, the nature of Paleoindian adaptations is a topic of considerable debate among archaeologists. Traditional models of Paleoindians as hunters of terrestrial big game have been questioned as archaeologists have found that sites other than the kill sites of the Great Plains and Southwest often present a different picture of subsistence and lifestyle. One reason for the debate is that archaeologists now know that around the world human use of coastal environments has a much longer history than formerly thought. Some Paleoindians appear to have used coastal resources, and the possibility of a coastal route of entry into the Americas is being reconsidered. The term **Paleocoastal people** is sometimes preferred to Paleoindians in discussions of these coastal settlers. This case study introduces one of the key sites supporting early use of the west coast: Daisy Cave, located on San Miguel Island off California. Although a Pre-Clovis case cannot be made based on current data from this site, it is clear that humans were using the island in Folsom times. As you read this case study, think about the implications of the site for routes of human entry into the Americas, for the antiquity of maritime adaptations, and for arguments concerning more variable early subsistence strategies.

SEA CHANGE

The Paleocoastal Occupations of Daisy Cave

Jon M. Erlandson

On windswept San Miguel Island, located 44 kilometers (27 mi) off the coast of California, excavations at a small cave have helped change our views about the colonization of the Americas, the antiquity of maritime adaptations, and the nature of the earliest peoples of the Pacific Coast. For decades, the peopling of the Americas was seen as a wholly terrestrial enterprise, in which groups of hunters trekked across the frigid plains of Beringia, through the fabled ice-free corridor, and into the heartland of North America. In this scenario, the first Americans arrived in the "New World" about 13,000 years ago and spread rapidly through uninhabited interior regions, leaving scattered Clovis points, kill sites, and campsites to mark their passage. According to this story, American coastlines were not systematically settled until at least 4000 to 5000 years later, as large game were hunted out of interior regions and people were forced to adapt to the supposedly less productive habitats and resources (shellfish, etc.) of coastal zones. Thus, coastlines were largely irrelevant to questions related to the initial colonization of the New World and the early stages of human cultural development in North America. This story fit comfortably in a larger body of anthropological theory according to which seafaring, coastal foraging, and maritime adaptations were relatively late developments in human history (Erlandson 2001, 2002).

Recent data from Africa and the Pacific Rim challenge these models, however, showing that early anatomically modern humans (*Homo sapiens sapiens*) had settled some South and East African coastlines at least 125,000 years ago, had reached Australia by boat 50,000 to 60,000 years ago, and had colonized several island archipelagoes of the eastern Pacific between about 40,000 and 15,000 years ago. Such discoveries, along with new doubts about the availability of the ice-free corridor route at key times, have pushed a coastal migration theory to the forefront of the debate about how and when the Americas were first colonized. The coastal migration theory has also gained credibility in recent years, however, because of new evidence from early sites along the Pacific Coast of North and South America, some of which have been dated to roughly the same time period as the Paleoindian Clovis and Folsom sites of interior regions (see Keefer et al. 1998; Sandweiss et al. 1998).

In North America, these early coastal sites include Daisy Cave (aka CA-SMI-261) on San Miguel Island and the Arlington Springs site (CA-SRI-173) on nearby Santa Rosa Island (Erlandson et al. 1996; Johnson et al. 2000; Rick et al. 2001). As described next, Daisy Cave has produced evidence for multiple occupations by Paleocoastal peoples between about 11,500 cal BP and 8500 cal BP. Although terminal Pleistocene occupation of the cave was relatively ephemeral, the excellent preservation of archaeological materials in the Early Holocene strata provides a wealth of information about early maritime peoples along the Pacific Coast, including evidence for the use of seaworthy boats and shellfish by Paleoindian peoples, what appear to be the oldest fishhooks in the New World, and the earliest basketry from the Pacific Coast of North America. In this case study, I present some of the highlights of our findings from Daisy Cave. First, however, to provide a context for understanding the results of our recent work at Daisy Cave, I describe briefly the geographic setting of the site and summarize the history of the investigations.

ENVIRONMENTAL SETTING

Located between about 20 and 42 kilometers (12–26 mi) off the coast of California, the Northern Channel Islands have been separated from the mainland for millions of years. During the last glacial, however, the Northern Channel Islands of San Miguel, Santa Rosa, Santa Cruz, and Anacapa were joined together as a single island known as **Santarosae**. Twenty thousand years ago, with sea levels about 125 meters (410 ft) lower than today, the east end of Santarosae was only about 6 to 8 kilometers (4–7 mi) from the mainland. Pygmy mammoths (*Mammuthus exilis*) roamed the island at the time, and the cooler and moister climate supported extensive conifer forests. As sea levels rose rapidly after the end of the last glacial, roughly 70 percent of Santarosae was flooded, becoming a series of islands and islets; extensive

coniferous forests shrunk to tiny relict communities, and the diminutive mammoths disappeared forever.

San Miguel, the westernmost of the Northern Channel Islands, is a maximum of about 13 kilometers long and 7 kilometers wide (4 × 8 mi), with a land area of about 37 square kilometers (14 mi²). With two hills rising to maximum elevations of 253 and 229 meters (830 and 750 ft) above sea level, the island has literally been sculpted by the sea, with a series of ancient marine terraces forming extensive central tablelands separated from the coast by steep escarpments. Other than the pygmy mammoths (if any still survived), the giant mouse, and the vampire bat, the first humans who landed on San Miguel Island probably found no terrestrial mammals endemic to the island. Historic accounts describe much of the island as a relatively barren landscape of shifting sand dunes and blowing sand. Since the 1850s, when Americans introduced sheep and other livestock, the island has been sparsely vegetated and poorly watered. Under the management of the National Park Service, however, the sheep and other introduced animals have been removed and the vegetation and hydrology of the island have begun to recover.

Today, the coastline of San Miguel Island is a mix of rocky shores and sandy beaches, but rocky coast was probably more abundant prior to historical overgrazing and severe erosion of the island's dune fields. In contrast to the depauperate terrestrial flora and fauna, the ocean surrounding San Miguel is extremely productive. The island lies at the boundary of two major marine biogeographic provinces (the Oregonian and the Panamanian), and the upwelling of nutrient-laden deep-ocean waters supports a wealth of marine life. Primary and secondary productivity are very high, driven by plankton production in continental shelf waters and kelp forest communities near shore. This productivity is passed up the food web, with abundant and diverse marine shellfish (abalone, mussel, urchin, etc.), fish (rockfish, clupeids, shark, etc.), mammal (cetaceans, pinnipeds, etc.), and seabird populations. Extensive kelp forests provide a three-dimensional habitat for a diverse array of marine fish. More than 100,000 seals and sea lions haul out on island beaches each year, and whales, dolphins, and porpoises are also common in Santa Barbara Channel waters. Sea otters (*Enhydra lutris*) were common until their local eradication in the 1800s by commercial hunters engaged in the Euro-American fur trade.

CULTURAL BACKGROUND

For at least 11,000 years prior to European contact, San Miguel was home to the island **Chumash** people and their predecessors. Occupying coastlines from Malibu to the San Luis Obispo area, the coastal Chumash are well known for their high population densities, sociopolitical complexity, and elaborate maritime technology—including the *tomol*, or plank canoe. It now seems likely that the development of the sophisticated culture of the Chumash was the product of over 10,000 years of cultural evolution in the Santa Barbara Channel area. A deep connection to the island and the sea is supported by Chumash creation stories, which state that the first Chumash came from the islands, crossing to the mainland via a rainbow bridge. Archaeological data also suggest a long and deep connection of the Chumash to the sea, showing that Paleoindian peoples first explored the landscapes and seascapes of the Channel Islands by boat at least 12,000 years ago.

Over the years, scholarly views about when the Channel Islands were first settled have been fraught with controversy and debate. Some early archaeologists believed the islands were colonized relatively recently, in part because one of the earliest well-documented archaeological cultures of the adjacent mainland, the Millingstone tradition, is not found on the islands. In the 1950s and 1960s, Phil Orr (1968) of the Santa Barbara Museum of Natural History argued that humans first settled the Channel Islands more than 40,000 years ago, that they hunted mammoths there for tens of thousands of years, and that they left several Pleistocene shell middens as further proof of their presence. Even now, no clear association of human artifacts with mammoth remains has been found, and most archaeologists have rejected the claims of Orr and his colleagues for a Pre-Clovis occupation of the islands.

In the 1990s, I systematically relocated and dated the "Pleistocene" shell middens described by Orr, showing that all were less than 9400 years old (Erlandson 1994; Erlandson and Morris 1993; Erlandson et al. 1999). One of Orr's early sites has withstood the test of time, however: the Arlington Springs site, where a few bones of "Arlington Man" were found eroding from a canyon wall over 11 meters (37 ft) below the surface. Orr (1962, 1968) dated charcoal associated with these bones to about 10,000 radiocarbon years, an age equal to about 12,000 calendar years after calibration. Subsequent studies have shown that "Arlington Man" was actually a woman, and extensive AMS carbon-14 dating—including small samples of the skeleton itself—suggests that she died on Santa Rosa Island between about 11,000 and 10,000 BP, or about 13,000 to 12,000 calendar years ago (Johnson et al. 2000). These dates demonstrate that Paleoindian peoples had used boats to reach the Northern Channel Islands by the time that Clovis or Folsom hunters roamed the Great Plains.

DAISY CAVE

Further evidence for a Pleistocene colonization of the Northern Channel Islands comes from Daisy Cave, located on the northeast coast of San Miguel Island (Figure 3.18). Daisy Cave is situated along a rough and rugged stretch of rocky coast. The site consists of a narrow fissurelike cave—almost certainly an ancient sea cave—about 11 meters (36 ft) long and 1 to 2 meters (3.2–6.5 ft) wide, with three small chambers, a small rockshelter about 4 by 5 meters (13 × 26 ft) wide located just outside the cave mouth, and a dense shell midden deposited on the slope in front of the cave and rockshelter. Today, the cave is located about a kilometer from the nearest fresh water, but there may have been closer springs or seeps during the terminal Pleistocene or early Holocene. The cave provides a rare opportunity for shelter from the strong northwesterly winds that buffet San Miguel Island for much of the year. The rocky shoreline in the site vicinity provides an excellent source of shellfish, and

FIGURE 3.18 Location of Daisy Cave on San Miguel Island in the Northern Channel Islands off California.

nearshore waters contain a mosaic of kelp forest, rocky reef, and sandy bottom habitats that support a diverse array of fish, sea mammals, and seabirds. Because offshore waters drop off relatively steeply, the cave remained relatively close to these coastal habitats throughout the Holocene. The unique combination of shelter and proximity to the riches of the sea attracted people to Daisy Cave for more than 11,000 years. Coastal erosion is gradually destroying the site, however, leading the National Park Service, the National Science Foundation, and the University of Oregon to support limited archaeological explorations of the cave.

History of Investigation

The materials the Chumash and their predecessors left at Daisy Cave have attracted relic hunters and scientists for more than a century. The first excavations of the cave were by amateurs and antiquarians. The diary of a rancher's wife describes an 1888 outing in which a human skull was dug from a cave at "Eagle's Cliff" (Daly 1990), a historical place name for the Daisy Cave area. Heye (1921) depicted a locality excavated by Ralph Glidden at or near Daisy Cave, one of 23 cemeteries plundered during a poorly documented 1919 expedition sponsored by Heye. These excavations appear to have been focused primarily on the fissurelike cave, which was used by the Chumash to bury their dead.

In 1967 and 1968 the first systematic excavation of Daisy Cave was directed by Charles Rozaire of the Los Angeles County Museum of Natural History (LACMNH). Rozaire's team excavated about 20 percent of the site, which once covered an area of about 200 square meters (2150 ft²). They excavated with methods typical of California archaeology at the time: test pits measuring 5 by 5 feet (1.52 × 1.52 m), arbitrary 6-inch (15.2 cm) horizontal levels, and mostly quarter-inch (6 mm) dry screening. Rozaire (1978) recovered a large assemblage of artifacts, including cordage and basketry, chipped stone, ground stone, bone, and shell objects. No radiocarbon dates were obtained at the time, but comparative analysis of the artifacts suggested that the deposits dated to the last 3000 to 4000 years (Rozaire 1978). Rozaire's team excavated primarily in Late and Middle Holocene deposits, but we now know that the investigators also encountered early Holocene and terminal Pleistocene sediments in several test units just outside the rockshelter. Unfortunately, many of the arbitrary horizontal levels excavated appear to have crosscut the finely stratified cave sediments, especially in the deeper deposits in front of the rockshelter, where the strata slope down to the east and north. Consequently, many of the artifacts now housed at the LACMNH cannot be confidently attributed to specific components.

In 1985 and 1986 Pandora Snethkamp (University of California, Santa Barbara), Daniel Guthrie (Claremont Colleges), and Don Morris (National Park Service) returned to Daisy Cave, collecting materials from the site surface and stratigraphic profiles, clearing and redocumenting portions of Rozaire's trench walls, excavating two small test pits inside the cave, and collecting two small column samples from the walls of Rozaire's test units in front of the rockshelter. The column samples were carefully excavated in natural stratigraphic levels, and Guthrie, a biologist and paleontologist, recognized the bones of an extinct giant mouse species in the lower archaeological layers in the cave. Suspecting that the cave was first occupied earlier than previously believed, Guthrie and Snethkamp obtained the first radiocarbon dates for the site, including uncorrected dates of 10,700 ±90, 8730 ±120, 8700 ±120, and 8460 ±100 BP for marine shells from the lower layers. The three early Holocene dates were associated with a wide variety of tools and ornaments, but no unequivocal artifacts were found in the small samples excavated in the terminal Pleistocene strata.

A few years later, in response to erosion of the site deposits, the National Park Service asked me to conduct further excavations at Daisy Cave. From 1992 to 1998, I directed meticulous small-scale excavations designed to collect additional archaeological and paleontological materials, recover a sample of unique woven artifacts identified in the early Holocene levels at the site (see Connolly et al. 1995), and explore the evidence for a terminal Pleistocene occupation of the cave. We excavated several test units measuring 50 by 100 cm (20 × 40 in.) in the midden deposits outside the rockshelter and reopened Rozaire's test pit inside the cave. At the time, I was actively studying the behavior of a variety of animals (otters, eagles, seagulls, etc.) known to deposit marine shells and animal bones in caves and other archaeological sites (see Erlandson and Moss 2001), and I was skeptical about the human origin of the terminal Pleistocene "shell midden" identified by Snethkamp, Guthrie, and Morris.

Stratigraphy, Site Structure, and Chronology

With a chronology anchored by over 40 radiocarbon dates, we now know that Daisy Cave was occupied numerous times, beginning with a brief occupation about 11,500 cal BP. A series of more substantial occupations took place between about 10,000 and 8600 years ago, followed by additional episodes about 6600, 4400, 3300, 1400, and 700 years ago (see Erlandson et al. 1996, Table 1). Remarkably, for several periods when Daisy Cave does not appear to have been occupied, nearby Cave of the Chimneys (CA-SMI-603) often was. Current evidence suggests that Cave of the Chimneys was occupied from about 8500 to 7500 years ago, 4400 to 4000 years ago, and about 2450 years ago (Vellanoweth et al. 2000, 2003). Between the two sites, we have compiled a record of human occupation and interaction with marine environments that spans much of the past 11,500 years.

At Daisy Cave, the best dated sequence comes from stratified shell midden deposits located along the drip line in front of the rockshelter. The deposits here were once well over a meter thick, but the upper layers were lost to erosion during the late 1980s. Snethkamp, Guthrie, and Morris designated archaeological strata A, C, E, F, and G in this area (Figure 3.19), separated by essentially sterile (noncultural) Strata B and D, which appeared to represent occupational hiatuses of 2000 to 3000 years. Extensive radiocarbon

dating of paired samples of marine shell and burned twigs has demonstrated that the earliest cultural layers were deposited about 11,500 years ago (Stratum G), 9000 to 10,000 years ago (Stratum F), and 8600 to 9000 years ago (Stratum E). Remnants of these early layers have been identified inside Daisy Cave itself, but they appear to have been heavily disturbed by burials placed in the cave by the Chumash and by the early looters and archaeologists who unceremoniously dug them up. On the slope below the cave and rockshelter, Strata E, F, and G merge into one well-developed paleosol studded with stone tools, marine shells, animal bones, and other debris left behind by the Paleocoastal occupants of the cave. In excavations on this slope and in collections made from the eroding sea cliff profile, it was difficult to differentiate between materials left behind during various early occupations.

Along the drip line just outside the rockshelter, the structure of the earliest layers is very different. Here, sheltered from the rains and runoff that wash the slope annually, midden debris from numerous discrete occupations is stacked like a layer cake, interspersed with windblown sand, silt, and organic debris, as well as small pebbles derived from the weathering of the conglomerate cave walls. Also mixed with the archaeological materials along the drip line is the debris left behind by a variety of animals that have used the cave area over the millennia, including dense accumulations of rodent bones probably left by

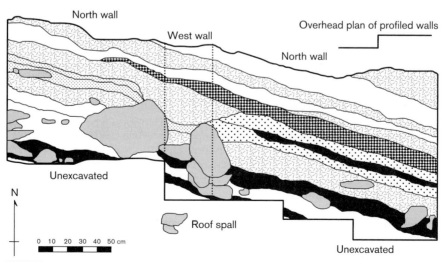

FIGURE 3.19 Stratigraphic profile at Daisy Cave.

barn owls nearly 10,000 years ago, and bird guano that may have been deposited by cormorants and other seabird species that still nest and roost at the site. Concentrations of cormorant bones identified in Rozaire's collections were interpreted as evidence for Chumash hunting of seabirds, but in 1992 we found the site littered with the nests and carcasses of over 20 cormorants that probably starved because of El Niño conditions. Fortuitously, however, the accumulation of salty seabird guano inside the drip line of the rockshelter also pickled the archaeological materials deposited there, leading to the extraordinary preservation of a variety of materials. Testing of the site sediments has shown that the soil pH ranges from neutral to mildly alkaline, ideal conditions for the preservation of bone, shells, and other animal remains. The seabird guano also led to the preservation of over 1600 unique artifacts (cordage, etc.) made from sea grass (*Phyllospadix* sp.) in the Early Holocene strata (see later discussion). Analysis of pollen grains found in the cave strata, including a number of discrete soils found below the shell midden, also showed that the site vicinity had been covered with coniferous forest until about 13,000 years ago (Erlandson et al. 1996), after which island pines retreated into small relict communities still found on Santa Rosa and Santa Cruz islands. By about 10,000 years ago, local vegetation communities appear to have taken on an essentially modern character, similar to the historic island vegetation before it was devastated by overgrazing and the introduction of numerous exotic species.

Terminal Pleistocene Occupation: A Postcard from the Past

Along with substantial evidence for multiple occupations between about 10,000 and 8600 years ago, Daisy Cave has produced tantalizing evidence for human occupation by maritime Paleoindian peoples during the terminal Pleistocene. In a sounding excavated inside Daisy Cave, we found two small stone flakes and a poorly preserved bone bead buried well below a shell midden layer dated to about 9800 years ago. Surprisingly, a carbonized twig from this deeply buried, artifact-bearing layer was dated to almost 17,000 years ago. While it is conceivable that the bead and flakes from this layer are this old—something only further excavation could prove—it seems more likely that they are associated with an 11,500-year-old occupation of the rockshelter. It is possible that the

bone bead and stone flakes were deposited on an older surface or trampled into an older stratum by people crawling in and out of the cave.

The terminal Pleistocene occupation is better defined in our excavations in the rockshelter area. Here, beneath nearly a meter of younger cultural deposits, we recovered a few stone artifacts associated with a sparse scatter of charcoal and marine shellfish in a thin dark soil designated as Stratum G. Radiocarbon dates for well-preserved marine shells and a burned twig from Stratum G suggest that this brief occupation took place between about 10,700 and 10,400 BP, or about 11,500 years ago. Despite my initial skepticism about the cultural origin of the Stratum G shells, our discovery of definitive siliceous shale and Monterey chert artifacts in Stratum G, along with the lack of a mechanism that could have moved the flakes downward from the overlying Early Holocene strata without also moving the much more abundant shells and bones, convinced me that the shells had been deposited by humans. Because of the relatively ephemeral nature of the terminal Pleistocene occupation, however, our sample from Stratum G represents little more than a postcard from the Pleistocene, announcing that people were there but telling us little about their lives. Aside from a few nondescript stone tools and a few pieces of debris from toolmaking, the archaeological remains recovered consist almost entirely of marine shells. Thus we know that Paleoindian peoples staying at Daisy Cave were foraging for abalone, mussel, turban snail, and crab in the intertidal zone of nearby rocky shorelines. A comparison of sea-level curves with the bathymetry of the Daisy Cave area suggests that the coastline was hundreds of meters from the cave at this time, which may help explain the limited nature of the occupation. It appears that a small group of people camped at the cave roughly 11,500 years ago, probably attracted by a commanding view of the coast and the opportunity to escape the wind or weather. While they were there, they shucked the shellfish they carried to the cave, cooked meals over an open fire, made and repaired stone tools, and lost or discarded a few artifacts. Despite the limited nature of the occupation, these materials tell us that Paleoindian peoples were building and using seaworthy boats, living along the coast, exploring offshore islands, and relying on sea foods at a date much earlier than most archaeologists would have believed possible 20 years ago.

Paleocoastal Occupations and Adaptations

We have a much clearer idea of what people were doing at Daisy Cave between about 10,000 and 8600 years ago because they visited the site repeatedly and left behind a much broader range of materials with which to reconstruct aspects of their lives. Overlying Stratum G along the drip line of the rockshelter, Strata E and F contain a finely stratified and extremely well-preserved series of occupational layers. By far the most extensive of the archaeological deposits at Daisy Cave, these Early Holocene strata have produced a wide variety of artifacts and faunal remains associated with early maritime peoples of the Channel Islands. Stone, bone, shell, and other diverse artifacts were recovered from the Early Holocene strata, along with thousands of animal bones and shells.

Several thousand chipped stone artifacts were recovered, for instance, including cores, expedient flake tools, a few bifaces or projectile point fragments, and abundant toolmaking debris. The chipped stone tools are made primarily from Monterey cherts and siliceous shales of varying quality, rock types probably brought to San Miguel Island from the mainland in cobble form. Most of the chipped stone implements are expedient or informal types, simple tools made on flakes or chunks that were only minimally retouched or utilized. A few projectile points or bifaces, mostly leaf-shaped specimens, were found, suggesting that hunting was not a major activity of the early site occupants. One of the most unusual of the chipped stone artifacts was a notched "eccentric crescent" (Figure 3.20a), a bifacial tool similar to examples found in other early sites of the California coast. Although their function probably varied, such crescents are often interpreted as transverse projectile points used to hunt aquatic birds.

Numerous shell beads were also recovered from the Early Holocene strata, all of them consisting of whole olive snail (*Olivella biplicata*) shells with their

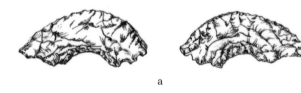

a

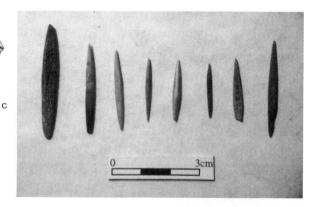

c

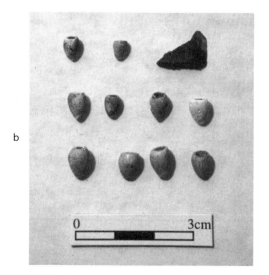

b

d

FIGURE 3.20 Artifacts from Daisy Cave: (a) notched "eccentric crescent" tool; (b) shell beads (whole olive scale), ready for stringing; (c) assorted bone bipoints, or fish gorges; and (d) twined sea grass bundles (fragments of basketry).

tops (spires) removed to facilitate stringing (Figure 3.20b). Similar *Olivella* beads have been found in other early sites along the California coast, as well as early interior sites, where they indicate long-distance trade with coastal peoples. The earliest specimens from Daisy Cave are among the oldest shell beads found in North America.

Another extraordinary aspect of the Daisy Cave assemblage is found in a series of small bipoints or fish gorges made from bird, sea mammal, and land mammal bone (Figure 3.20c). These bone gorges—the oldest known fishhooks in the Americas—were used to catch a variety of fish in rocky reef or kelp forest habitats. Unlike most barbed hooks, which catch fish by piercing their mouth or lip, bone gorges, with a line tied around them just off center and wrapped with bait, were designed to be swallowed by a fish. The gorge toggled as the line was jerked, becoming caught in the throat of the fish. Associated with the gorges in the early levels at Daisy Cave were other bone artifacts that are almost certainly the debris from manufacturing bone gorges. These suggest that Paleocoastal peoples sometimes used a "saw-and-snap" technique to cut bird and other bone fragments into the general shape desired; then these "blanks" were carefully ground into finished and highly symmetrical shapes.

Perhaps most extraordinary of all were the more than 1600 woven sea grass artifacts recovered from the Early Holocene strata. Between about 10,000 and 8600 years old, the vast majority of these botanical artifacts were pieces of cordage, but a few woven items and several bundles or clumps of unwoven sea grass were also found. The two most complete basketry fragments are pieces of twined sea grass bundles (Figure 3.20d) that retain several finished edges. The function of these objects is not clear, but they may be sandal fragments—possibly toe flaps that would have covered the top of the foot (Connolly et al. 1995). If so, the **provenience** and width of the most complete specimen suggest that it was probably worn by a child about 8600 years ago. Over 1500 pieces of cordage include several different types and many knotted specimens. In the field, cordage was found in discrete concentrations that we hoped might be fragments of nets or other woven structures. As a result, we excavated these concentrations extremely carefully, using a straw to blow away the surrounding sediment and small paintbrushes and tweezers to help expose and collect the fragments. Despite the

excellent preservation of the cordage, none of the pieces were connected. Instead, we found hundreds of small pieces of cordage that appear to represent the debris and "cutoffs" left over from the manufacture of cordage, maintenance of fishing nets, and similar activities.

Strata E and F were also extremely rich in faunal remains, especially those of marine shellfish and fish, but also the bones of sea otter, pinnipeds, and seabirds. The shellfish were dominated by California mussel, black abalone, turban snail, and other species from rocky intertidal habitats. Over 27,000 fish bones from at least 18 types of fish were also found in the Early Holocene levels. The fish are dominated by surfperch (Embiotocidae), rockfish (*Sebastes* spp.), cabezon (*Scorpaenichthys marmoratus*), and California sheephead (*Semicossyphus pulcher*), all relatively small fish found near the shore in rocky coast and kelp forest habitats. Although the ratios vary for individual strata, our dietary reconstructions for the Early Holocene strata as a whole suggest that shellfish and fish made up roughly equal amounts of the edible meat consumed by the site occupants, with marine mammals and birds being supplemental resources (Rick et al. 2001). Nonetheless, the remains of seal, sea otter, and seabird all suggest that the Paleocoastal peoples at Daisy Cave were capable of taking a full range of marine resources and that their economy was fully maritime by as much as 10,000 years ago.

The faunal remains from Daisy Cave also raise fundamental questions about a common assumption of archaeologists applying optimal foraging theory to coastal peoples. In modeling or interpreting the behavior of hunter-gatherers, archaeologists often assume that it is more productive for humans to pursue large animals than small game and that evidence for the exploitation of smaller animal and plant resources signals an intensification of human subsistence. At Daisy Cave and other early shell middens of the Santa Barbara Channel region, however, faunal and technological evidence suggests that the subsistence economies of some of the earliest maritime peoples were focused not on large animals (deer, elk, seal, etc.) but on small types of shellfish and fish. This is particularly evident in the Early Holocene levels at Daisy Cave, where small turban snails (*Tegula funebralis*) and mussels (*Mytilus californianus*) dominate the shellfish assemblage at a time when human populations almost certainly would have been too small to have seriously depleted the larger animals available in the area. Instead, we believe mussels, turbans, other shellfish, and small nearshore fish—all of which can be easily caught or collected in large quantities—were the most productive resources for early San Miguel Island peoples to pursue. In this view, the diverse and highly productive habitats of the Channel Islands and southern California coast have attracted Paleoindian and other peoples for more than 12,000 years.

SUMMARY AND CONCLUSIONS

The submergence of coastlines around the world by rising postglacial sea levels makes early coastal sites particularly difficult to find. Along the Pacific Coast, however, early sites have been found in formerly glaciated areas where isostatic rebound has preserved ancient shorelines, where steep bathymetry has limited lateral movements of postglacial shorelines, and where springs or other natural features pulled people inland from shorelines now long submerged. On San Miguel and Santa Rosa islands, where the latter two conditions apply, more than 25 sites occupied between about 13,000 and 8500 years ago have now been identified. The earliest of these sites show that the Channel Islands were settled by Paleoindian peoples at about the same time as the earliest well-documented sites found in interior regions of North America. Along with evidence for Pleistocene seafaring in Australia, western Melanesia, and islands in Japan, evidence from California's Channel Islands has helped force a reevaluation of traditional terrestrial models for the Pleistocene colonization of the Americas and has transformed the Pacific Coast from an area peripheral to Paleoindian studies to one central to current theories and debate about the peopling of the New World. Although we still don't know when and how the Americas were first settled, recent evidence suggests that the peopling of the New World was a complex process that involved multiple migrations, quite possibly both by land and by sea.

At Daisy Cave, the small assemblage of shells and stone artifacts from Stratum G currently represents the oldest coastal shell midden in North America

and, along with the remains of Arlington Woman, the earliest evidence for the use of boats in the Americas. These findings add to the diversity of Paleoindian adaptations in the Americas and further erode the notion that Paleoindian economies were focused primarily on large game animals. The Early Holocene strata have produced the earliest fishhooks known in the New World, the earliest basketry from the Pacific Coast of North America, some of the earliest shell beads from the Americas, and an extraordinary wealth of information about the early cultures and environments of San Miguel Island and the California coast. Because of the amazing antiquity, preservation, and diversity of Daisy Cave's archaeological and paleontological contents, and the importance of the site to living Chumash descendants, the National Park Service has recognized the extraordinary significance of the site to the long cultural and natural history of California and the United States. Already on the National Register of Historic Places, the site is now being nominated as a National Historic Landmark. It has been a rare honor and privilege to have been allowed to work there.

DISCUSSION QUESTIONS

1. Where is Daisy Cave, and what has been found at this site? Why is this site important? List several reasons.

2. What does Daisy Cave's "postcard from the Pleistocene" tell us about early boat-building and seafaring skills, as well as diet? What are the ramifications for generalizations about Paleoindian adaptations?

3. The brief description of the assemblages recovered at Daisy Cave suggests that items of several types may have been manufactured or repaired there. What are these items, and what is the significance of each for understanding the lifestyle of early coastal people?

4. Having read about Daisy Cave, do you think archaeologists need to modify their traditional optimization arguments, namely, that it is more productive for hunter-gatherers to pursue large game and that the use of shellfish and fish signals subsistence intensification? Why or why not?

CHAPTER 4

Foragers of the North

An archaeologist, wearing a jacket and rubber boots, kneels next to a marine biologist on the shoreline of a small inlet. They are tabulating data on oil coverage and damage in a sampling area they have set up. As they work away, the biologist from another team is frantically trying to get their attention, for she has seen something alarming—a huge Alaskan brown bear, running across the beach right at her two colleagues. The archaeologist hears his name being called and looks back up the beach. He stands, sees the bear closing in, and taps the biologist on the shoulder. They both know these bears can be dangerous, but neither has had the bear training session promised when they took the job. They try to control the sense of panic that threatens to overwhelm them as they decide whether to run or take some other course of action. The bear, which actually had been chasing salmon down the creek that flowed next to them and had not noticed the people, suddenly sees them. It stops, puzzled for a second at these tall creatures standing out on the treeless shore, and after taking a few halting steps toward the humans, turns instead to wander back to the other side of the low beach ridge to fish in a small pool.

Breathing a sigh of relief, the experts return to examining the oil-soaked shoreline. For the rest of the morning the humans and the bear cautiously check each other out, while tending to their own business. Later the scientists and the bear leave, having done what they set out to do. But why is the archaeologist looking for damaged archaeological sites along the Alaskan shore? His team is part of the massive response to the 1989 Exxon *Valdez* oil spill.

Archaeologists were very much a part of the activity after the Exxon *Valdez* disaster, one of the worst oil spills in U.S. history. Twenty-four archaeologists were employed as part of the cleanup team. They cooperated with state and federal officials, as well as Native corporations that had cultural resource responsibilities, and they developed a program to identify archaeological sites on the shoreline that were either soaked with oil or threatened with damage as a result of the cleanup. The program proved to be a big success.

One heartening result of this work was the finding that the oil did little damage to materials in the archaeological sites, because the portions of sites affected were subject to wave erosion, and the fragile materials from these parts of the sites had already been destroyed by wave action. Because of the cultural resource identification program and a coordinated program of sensitizing cleanup workers to the value of cultural resources (as well as the legal protections that apply to the sites and artifacts), damage from cleanup was also minimal. There was some disturbance to a few shoreline deposits and, unfortunately, there were two documented acts of vandalism to sites, but given the large area involved, the track record is not bad at all.

As damaging to other aspects of the environment as the oil spill was, ironically the site identification program enhanced our knowledge of area archaeology. In the process of assessing the archaeological sites, many previously unrecorded sites were added to the archaeological site inventories. Synthesis of the data has contributed important new information to our understanding of this part of the Arctic and Subarctic (Wooley and Haggarty 1995).

This is not the first time oil has played a role in the development of northern archaeology. The construction of the Trans-Alaska Pipeline from the North Slope oil fields to the port of Valdez required archaeological study to clear the right-of-way. Surveys were conducted by the University of Alaska and Alaska Methodist University in the late 1960s and early 1970s. Archaeologists had to work in very remote places to conduct the first really large-scale cultural resource management project required by federal law. Over 330 sites were recorded and $2.2 million was spent on a project that provided important information on this 800-mile (1290 km) transect across Alaska.

These oil-related projects have revealed that there are many cultural resources within the vast Arctic and Subarctic culture areas covered in this chapter. Because of the remoteness as well as the low density of human populations, many of these sites are unrecorded. Thus large oil-related CRM projects like those mentioned here have been a boon to the archaeological study of the area.

DEFINITION OF THE AREA

This chapter discusses the archaeology of the North, including most of Alaska and the northern part of Canada. This broad area encompasses both the Arctic and the Subarctic culture areas, but there are some good reasons to discuss these areas together (Figure 4.1).

The Arctic extends from Alaska's Yakutat Bay along the Alaska coast to the Bering Sea, taking in the Aleutian Islands and those in the Bering Sea. As the land turns east, the Arctic includes the coast and adjacent tundra of the Yukon and the Northwest Territories, the northern islands, most of **Nunavut**, parts of northern Quebec, the Labrador coast, and Greenland. The Subarctic lies inland from the Arctic, including interior Alaska and Canada below the Arctic from the Alaska border through the Yukon Territory, the Northwest Territories, and part of northern Alberta, Saskatchewan, and Manitoba, as well as the areas north of the St. Lawrence River and the Great Lakes, with the exception of southern Ontario and southern Quebec.

The physiographic boundary between the Arctic and the Subarctic is essentially the tree–line—the area where the tundra gives way to coniferous forest

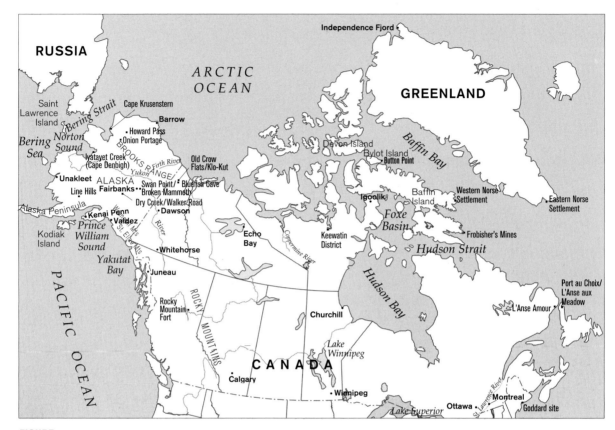

FIGURE 4.1 The Arctic and Subarctic culture areas showing the locations of sites mentioned in Chapter 4.

to the south. The July 50°F (10°C) isotherm, a line indicating areas of similar temperature, and the southern extent of permafrost, the condition of the ground being frozen at depth all year long, also form reasonable boundaries for the Arctic. From a cultural point of view, the line separating the Inuit and Eskimo from other Indian or First Nation groups defines the boundary between the Arctic and the Subarctic. To the south, the Arctic borders the Northwest Coast at Yakutat Bay in Alaska. The Subarctic borders the Plateau, the Plains, the Midwest and Upper Great Lakes, and the Northeast (Helm 1981; Stager and McSkimming 1984, 27; Willey 1966, 410–411). The cultural chronologies for the Arctic and the Subarctic are outlined in Table 4.1.

THE ENVIRONMENT

Arctic

The Arctic is a land of harsh cold, with little diversity in plant and animal species. There is little soil, and the growing season is short. Precipitation is slight, and high winds help shape a plant life that is low growing, hugging the ground. The

TABLE 4.1 Introduction to Arctic and Subarctic Culture History

Uncalibrated Years BP	Pacific Alaska	North/Central Alaska	Central/Eastern/High Arctic	West Greenland	Subarctic		Calibrated Years
				Thule			AD 1,800
500			Thule	Norse		Selkirk tradition	AD 1,430
1,000		Thule tradition			Taltheilei Shale tradition	Blackduck tradition	AD 1,020
1,500			Dorset tradition	Dorset tradition	Central Subarctic Woodland tradition		AD 600
2,000	Kodiak tradition	Norton tradition					AD 10
2,500	Aleutian tradition						660 BC
3,000			Pre-Dorset Independence	Sarqaq			1,240 BC
3,500		Arctic Small Tool tradition					1,820 BC
4,000							2,490 BC
4,500		Northern Archaic tradition			Shield Archaic tradition		3,200 BC
5,000						Maritime Archaic tradition	3,780 BC
5,500	Ocean Bay tradition						4,340 BC
6,000							4,880 BC
6,500							5,440 BC
7,000							5,840 BC
7,500							6,320 BC
8,000							6,910 BC
8,500		Paleoarctic tradition					7,550 BC
9,000							8,030 BC
9,500							8,560 BC
10,000							9,210 BC
10,500		Denali complex					10,470 BC
11,000							10,970 BC
11,500 and Prior		?Nenana complex?					11,470 BC and Prior

terrain varies from west to east, with Alaska having rugged mountains in the south and a tundra plain in the north. Included in the highlands are volcanic mountains that have been active within the last 200 years. Across Canada the tundra continues, with ample signs that the area was covered by glacial ice in the past. These signs include eskers, winding ridges of sand and gravel that were streambeds on or in the glaciers, and drumlins, clumps of elongated hills resulting from glacial action. Although precipitation is low in this area, it is poorly drained, so boggy conditions prevail in many areas. In Greenland, the coastal strip that concerns us here is generally steep, sloping from the sea to the ice-capped mountains (Dumond 1987).

Sea ice is a prominent feature of the Arctic environment. During the winter months, sea ice reaches land throughout most of the Arctic, and in the summer, the pack ice in the northern parts of the Arctic can reach land at times. Ice can persist in sheltered bays into the summer, and the northern Arctic islands are usually surrounded (Stager and McSkimming 1984).

The sea in the Arctic provided marine mammals—whales, seals, and walruses—all of which were hunted. Fish like Pacific salmon or the arctic char were important anadromous fish that were taken where they were available. Land animals available included caribou, polar bear, musk ox, fox, and arctic hare.

Subarctic

The Subarctic is divided into four physiographic zones: the Canadian Shield, the Cordillera, the Yukon-Kuskokwim-Tanana plateaus, and the Alaska and Coast Ranges. The Canadian Shield is a vast area where bedrock hills are spread among valleys and bogs. Thin soils lie over crystalline bedrock. The Cordillera, which includes the northern end of the Rocky Mountains, is an area of mountains and valleys that separate the shield from the Yukon Plateau. This is a region of rugged relief, and its vegetation zones vary with altitude on the mountain ranges. The Yukon, Kuskokwim, and Tanana plateaus are a complex of hills, low mountain ranges, valleys, and plateaus that make up the central part of Alaska and parts of the adjoining Yukon Territory and British Columbia. The Yukon and Kuskokwim rivers are prominent features of this area, which, unlike the Canadian Shield, was little affected by the glaciers. Beyond the plateaus of central Alaska are found high, glaciated mountains including the Wrangell, Alaska, Kenai, Saint Elias, Chugach, and Aleutian ranges. Generally, the mountains slope steeply into the sea (Gardner 1981).

Forest characterizes the Subarctic, although the area also includes transition to the tundra of the Arctic. Coniferous trees like white spruce, black spruce, and tamarack are major elements in the forest, and balsam fir and jackpine are also important. Much less common, but important to the inhabitants of the area, are broadleaf trees like poplar, aspen, and birch (Gardner 1981, 12–13). The birch was important as a source of bark for making canoes and containers.

Animals are much more diverse and abundant in the Subarctic than in the neighboring Arctic. Large game like caribou and moose were most important to people living here, but mountain goat, Dall sheep, elk, bison, musk ox, and deer also were present. Small mammals included snowshoe hare, beaver, woodchuck, hoary marmot, muskrat, porcupine, and arctic ground squirrel. Birds of economic importance in the past were species of grouse, goose, and duck, while salmon and many other fish were available in the rivers (Gillespie 1981).

Climatic Change

The most important climatic changes in the harsh environments of the North certainly have been those associated with glaciation, as discussed in Chapters 2 and 3. During the peak of the last or Wisconsin glaciation, two massive glaciers, the Cordilleran and the Laurentian, covered the Canadian Subarctic (see Figure 2.12), but the Arctic was not uniformly covered with ice. Most significantly, much of Alaska was ice free, although the Cordilleran glacier did cover the mountainous southern areas extending to the coastline. A small glacier also existed in the Brooks Range in north central Alaska, and most of the eastern portions of the North American Arctic were glaciated. As explained in Chapter 2, the sea level had been lowered significantly, reconfiguring the coastline, and a broad landmass known as Beringia linked the continents of Asia and North America. As we touched upon in Chapters 2 and 3, there is considerable debate about the precise environmental characteristics of Beringia during the Pleistocene.

Later environmental changes certainly also affected the Arctic and Subarctic, although these modifications have received somewhat less attention from archaeologists. The Medieval Warm period (ca. 1050–650 BP) was a time of warmer climate when sea ice appears to have been reduced. This would have allowed greater sea travel and better whaling conditions, as bowhead whales changed their migration routes. The Little Ice Age (ca. 400–100 BP) may well have affected Arctic populations in a variety of ways. Many scholars believe this episode was responsible for the demise of the Norse settlement in Greenland, and increases in the amount of sea ice probably impeded the migration of bowhead whales in Arctic Canada. This, in turn, almost certainly had an effect on the native communities that depended on whale hunters for much of their subsistence.

EARLY CULTURES

As we showed in Chapter 3, the Arctic and Subarctic are critical areas for understanding the early cultures of the New World. We might have expected the earliest evidence for people crossing the land bridge into the Americas to have been found at the eastern edge of Beringia. Since, however, there are no clear antecedents for fluted point technology in Siberia at the appropriate time, and since Clovis appears fully developed in the areas south of the continental glaciers, it is also reasonable to seek antecedents for the Clovis technology in the western Arctic and Subarctic.

We discussed early sites in Alaska and northwestern Canada at some length in the preceding chapter and will only review this material here. First, unambiguous evidence for Pre-Clovis humans has not been found in the Far North. Claims for great antiquity of bone artifacts at Old Crow Flats either have not been supported upon redating by means of the AMS technique or are based on materials not universally accepted as bone artifacts. Possible bone artifacts from Bluefish Caves in the Yukon also have yielded Pre-Clovis dates (24,800 BP).

Fluted points have been found in Alaska and western Canada, but they are generally surface finds or have come from contexts in which there is not a clear association of the points with datable material (Dumond 1987; Loy and Dixon 1998, 21). The Mesa site in northern Alaska has yielded dates between 11,700 BP and 9700 BP for a fluted biface. Although fluted points have not been found associated with bone, **blood residue analysis** indicates some of them were used to kill or butcher large mammals, including mammoths (Loy and Dixon 1998, 21). However, it is unclear how these points relate to the Clovis and Folsom material found further south. Some researchers believe that these points indicate cultures in the north that began developing fluted point technology and were ancestral to the Clovis and Folsom. An alternative interpretation is that the Arctic and Subarctic fluted points represent movement to the north of fluted point technology that had developed in the south.

The earliest well-dated materials from eastern Beringia are the Nenana and Denali complexes discussed in Chapter 3 (Figure 3.10). The Nenana complex is considered to be Paleoindian and is found at the Walker Road and Broken Mammoth sites. The complex dates to before 11,000 BP, based on radiocarbon dates from these two sites, and has both core-and-blade and core-and-flake technologies. However microblades, an artifact type important in other early complexes, are absent (Goebel et al. 1996; Holmes 1996; Matson and Coupland 1995, 57). Artifacts include teardrop-shaped Chindadn points, scrapers of various types, and perforators. Technological analyses on material from Dry Creek and Walker Road suggest similarities to Clovis technology as seen at Murray Spring in Arizona and Blackwater Draw in New Mexico, and the material from these two Alaskan sites seems to have been quite different from that found in the Denali complex (Goebel et al. 1991).

The Denali complex, believed to date between 11,000 and 8000 BP, is part of the larger **Paleoarctic tradition** (or American Paleoarctic tradition). Characteristic of these sites are numbers of microblades and wedge-shaped microblade cores (see Exhibit 4.1) as well as bifacial tools and burins (Dumond 1984b; West 1996a, 546–547). The Bluefish Caves in the Yukon have Denali complex microblades and cores dating to 12,000 BP, and perhaps a little earlier (Ackerman ed. 1996). Microblades have also been found in the Swan Point site in strata dating to 11,660 BP, along with worked fragments of mammoth tusk (Holmes et al. 1996). People of the American Paleoarctic tradition appear to have been primarily inland hunters (West 1996a, 549).

As discussed in Chapter 3, there are similarities between the American Paleoarctic tradition and assemblages found in the interior of Siberia. The Dyuktai material (Mochanov and Fedoseeva 1996a) is particularly close to the American Paleoarctic tradition, and it is clear that the Denali complex and other related microblade technologies are derived from Asia (West 1996a). The similarity between American Paleoarctic tradition artifact technology and that of Siberia led Dumond (1987) to offer "Siberian–American Paleoarctic tradition" as perhaps a more appropriate term.

The Western Subarctic

The earliest occupations of the western Subarctic include both material apparently related to the Nenana complex of interior Alaska, which lacks microblades but includes leaf-shaped points and prismatic blades, and assemblages that do include microblades. The materials possibly related to the Nenana complex are sometimes referred to as the **Northern Cordilleran complex** (10,000–7000 BP). Microblades appear in the area later in time, coming from the west. These have been assigned to the **Northwest Microblade tradition**, but some authorities would subsume sites once assigned to this complex in other traditions such as the Paleoarctic and **Northern Archaic traditions** (Clark 1998). The question of whether

CLUES TO THE PAST

EXHIBIT 4.1

Microblades

Archaeologists define blades as flakes that are at least twice as long as they are wide. Generally, they are also parallel sided, and they are produced in small numbers during flaking activities like biface manufacture. When larger numbers of blades are found, it is usually concluded that they were struck from specialized cores. Blades are part of the Clovis toolkit, for example.

As the name indicates, a microblade is a small blade, generally less than 20 mm ($\frac{3}{4}$ in.) long and 5 mm ($\frac{13}{64}$ in.) wide. In addition to parallel sides, a microblade generally has one or more ridges (edges of the scars from the removal of previous flakes) on the **dorsal surfaces**. Microblade cores were made on flakes or bifaces that were set up to allow a number of microblades to be struck from them, usually from a single platform. Such cores were normally about the size of a book of matches and could yield several dozen small, sharp microblades. This technology is a good way to get the largest possible cutting edge out of a small piece of quality raw material. But what good is a cutting edge if the blade is too small for a person to hold?

Actually, the small, sharp blades were very useful. Prehistoric toolmakers fitted microblades into slots cut into bone or wood and glued them in side by side so that the length of the razor-sharp edge of the finished implement was not limited by the size of the individual blades (Figure 4.2). These composite tools included knives and projectiles, and although slotted bone shafts have been recovered in places like Lime Hills, Cave 1 (Ackerman 1996a, 471; Fig. 10-7), they have more often weathered away, leaving only the tiny slivers of sharp stone behind.

Although they appear in several areas of North America, including at the Poverty Point site in Louisiana (Chapter 11), in many Middle Woodland sites in eastern North America, and along the California coast, microblades are particularly important in the Arctic and Subarctic, as well as in the northern parts of the adjoining Northwest Coast and Plateau. Furthermore, microblade technology provides a tangible link between North American cultures and those of Asia, where the technology appeared earlier. Microblades are found in sites from the Ural Mountains, which divide Europe and Asia, into central British Columbia (Goebel et al. 2000).

The cores of microblade technology are wedge shaped and distinctive. Other characteristic by-products of blade manufacture include **crested blades** (*lames à crêtes* is the name given them in the French literature on lithic technology), blades removed from the face of the core that remove a ridge created by flaking (West 1996b, 305), and **core tablets** removed from the top of the core to form or rejuvenate a platform. Microblades appear to have been made by pressure rather than by freehand percussion

FIGURE 4.2 Composite tool made by using microblades.

or indirect percussion from a punch rested on the platform and struck by the hammer (West 1996b, 305).

Microblades appear first in the western part of their range, in the Transbaikal area of Asia, and dates become more recent as they moved east. At the Studenoe-2 site in the Transbaikal area, they are dated to between 18,000 BP and 17,000 BP, and at the Bering Strait they date to about 10,000 BP (Goebel et al. 2000). They also are found in early sites from the western Subarctic. Microblades and wedge-shaped cores are linked to early migrants in the Arctic, although these people may have been preceded by others who did not make microblades (see Chapter 3).

microblades were moved by diffusion of ideas or by actual people bringing the technology with them is still open. Furthermore, there is a real possibility that microblade-using peoples created sites where microblades were not used. If microblades are one of the defining characteristics of the tradition, such sites would not be recognized as part of Northwest Microblade tradition. The question of the relationship of the nonmicroblade and microblade sites is, then, a difficult one (Wright 2001).

ARCHAIC

By 8000 BP archaeologists see the beginnings of the Archaic period, but its manifestations vary considerably from place to place within the Arctic and Subarctic. In the interior, the **Northern Archaic tradition** developed, and on the Pacific Coast, the first maritime cultures, the **Ocean Bay**, **Kodiak**, and **Aleutian traditions**, appear. In the eastern Subarctic, the **Shield Archaic** and the **Maritime Archaic** are commonly recognized traditions.

The Northern Archaic

The Northern Archaic tradition includes a variety of assemblages that have been found in sites from the interior of Alaska and west of the MacKenzie River in northwestern Canada. This tradition is distinguished largely on the basis of side-notched projectile points and the absence of microblades and microblade cores, but other bifacial stone tools, various scrapers, and other implements also are associated with it. The Northern Archaic tradition was originally based on material from the site of Onion Portage in Alaska, where two different complexes, the Pallisades and the Portage, were recognized. The **Pallisades complex** originally was described at Cape Krusenstern, where several sites have been found on a series of beach ridges. These people left behind convex based side-notched points, unifacial knives, and **end scrapers** (Figure 4.3), and these are joined later in the period (ca. 6000–4500 BP) by notched pebbles that may have been hafted for use as axes. Leaf-shaped points mark the change from the Pallisades to the **Portage complex** at 4500 BP, and by 4400 BP the Northern Archaic tradition occupation of Onion Portage ends (Anderson 1968; Dumond 1987). Apparently, Northern Archaic spread south and eastward over time (Workman 1998).

There is very little subsistence and settlement data for the Northern Archaic people, but they are believed to have been generalized foragers who at least

FIGURE 4.3 Artifacts from the Portage and Pallisades complexes: (a) knife, (b) projectile point, (c) end blade, (d) beaked tool, and (e) adze blade.

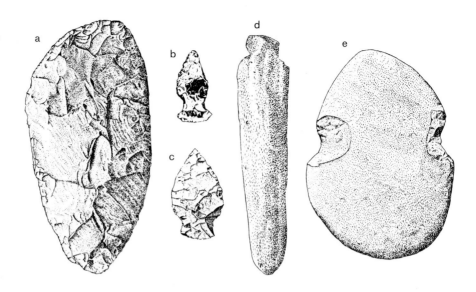

utilized caribou, moose, mountain sheep, hare, beaver, and muskrat. Bison was hunted in the southern Yukon as well (Workman 1998, 568). The Northern Archaic is thought to be a result of influences from the northern Plains. This tradition, which persisted for millennia, is ultimately seen as being ancestral to that of the Na-Dene or Athapaskan speakers evident by 2000 BP to 1500 BP (Pilon 1996, 516; Wright 2001).

The Shield Archaic

After the glaciers retreated from the Canadian Shield, people from the northern Plains moved into this area. This movement started about 8000 BP and is marked by finds of Agate Basin points at sites that include camps in the Keewatin District. The occurrence of these camps at known caribou crossings (places where caribou were concentrated while crossing rivers) suggests that the abundant herd animals may have been what attracted people to move here. Archaeologists believe the Shield Archaic developed out of the Agate Basin (Wright 1981, 87–88). As the glaciers continued to shrink northeastward, Shield Archaic groups expanded eastward all the way to the coast of Labrador, reaching there by about 2950 BP (Wright 1998). Thus, eventually, this cultural expression characterized a vast area in the boreal forest of Canada.

Scrapers, bifaces, and knives are characteristic of Shield Archaic assemblages (Figure 4.4). Early in the Shield Archaic, points tend to be lanceolate, but side-notched points become the most common at the end of the period. Millingstones are almost completely absent (Wright 1981, 88–89). Unfortunately, the generally acidic soils of this region have destroyed most perishable artifacts and ecofacts. The resources of the northern boreal forests are dispersed. As a result, Shield Archaic groups were highly mobile, probably dividing into small family groups over the winter, and living in somewhat larger summer camps from which a variety of resources could be procured.

The Shield Archaic groups almost certainly represent the ancestors of the Algonquian-speaking peoples of the area in Historic times. The emphasis on

FIGURE 4.4 Artifacts of the Shield Archaic, including bifaces, scrapers, and projectile points.

FIGURE 4.5 Ground and flaked tools of the Ocean Bay tradition: (a–c) flaked projectile points, (d) harpoon head, (e) flaked point, (f) knife or blade, (g) blade, (h) ground slate projectile point or blade, (i) ground slate blade.

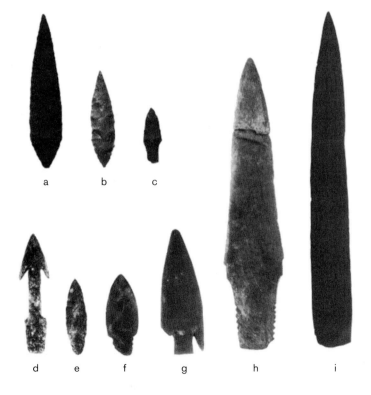

hunting and fishing seen in Shield Archaic sites continued with the Innu or Algonquians, as did the organization into small bands (Wright 1981, 96).

Ocean Bay, Kodiak, and Aleutian Traditions

The Ocean Bay tradition (7000–4500 BP) is found on Kodiak Island, although similar material is found on the adjacent Alaska Peninsula and much of Pacific Alaska, and may be related to material from Anangula in the Aleutians. This tradition is significant for at least two reasons. First, Ocean Bay sites represent the earliest known maritime adaptations in the Pacific area of Alaska. Focus on the sea would persist here for many millennia, leading to a degree of sociocultural complexity uncommon among hunter-gatherers. These developments are discussed in this chapter's case study by Ben Fitzhugh, "From Sites to Social Evolution: The Study of Emergent Complexity in the Kodiak Archipelago, Alaska." Second, tools made of ground slate, a raw material of great importance in several parts of the Arctic and Subarctic, appear in this early tradition. These tools contrast with the chipped stone tools we have been discussing thus far.

The Ocean Bay tradition began about 7000 BP, with the introduction of ground slate tools to an inventory still dominated by flaked stone (Figure 4.5). The flaked stone includes percussion-flaked, leaf-shaped knives or projectile points; long, narrow, weakly stemmed percussion-flaked knives or projectile points; and scrapers. Although not common, bone harpoon heads (Figure 4.6) are found. These have grooves in their tips where a stone point or end blade could be fitted (Dumond 1987).

Based on the little bone that has been found and on the presence of the harpoon heads, archaeologists have deduced that the Ocean Bay people made their living by hunting sea otter, seal, sea lion, porpoise, and whale. Site locations are consistent with this way of life, but at least one site, located on the Afognak River, is so situated that salmon might have been taken during the summer migration.

The Ocean Bay tradition appears to have developed into two different traditions, the Kodiak and the Aleutian. The Kodiak tradition, which begins about 4500 BP, is found in the area around Kodiak Island. The hallmark of the Kodiak tradition is the extensive use of ground slate for tools. There are two stages in the Kodiak tradition, the earliest, the **Takli stage**, has been variously labeled the Takli Birch phase, Ocean Bay II, and Chirikof Island's Old Islander phase. Characteristic of this stage are slate lance or dart points, the oil lamp, and chipped stone that resembles that of the Ocean Bay tradition. Although ground slate is important in Takli stage assemblages, the transverse knife called the *ulu* was not part of the toolkit (Dumond 1987).

The oil lamp (Figure 4.7) bears a little further discussion. Open bowls were used to hold oil rendered from the fat of sea mammals; a wick of moss placed in the oil was lit to provide both light and heat in Arctic dwellings. Although a bowl that may have served as an oil lamp was recovered from an Ocean Bay tradition context, oil lamps are more clearly a part of the Kodiak tradition.

Dwellings are indicated by patterns of postholes and what appears to be the depressed floor of a tent. Sea mammal hunting was important in the Takli stage, and bone harpoon heads continue to be found. Fishing probably also continued to be important, but evidence also exists for land mammal hunting in the form of broken bits of land mammal bone. Sites of this stage are found in locations appropriate for each of these activities (Dumond 1987).

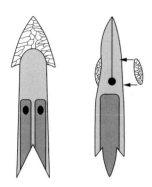

FIGURE 4.6 Schematic representations of the use of end blades and side blades in harpoon heads.

FIGURE 4.7 Kodiak tradition oil lamp from a site on the upper Naknek drainage of the Alaska Peninsula.

FIGURE 4.8 Implements of the Kachemak stage: (a) flaked slate blade, (b), ulu blade, (c) spear side-prong, (d) sawn bone tube, (e) bipointed bone (possibly a gorge), (f) fishhook shank, (g) fishhook barb, (h–i) flaked stone points, (j) bone arrowhead with slits for blades, (k) barbed dart, (l) toggle harpoon head, (m) carved bone, perhaps representing a seal, (n) notched ulu, (o) jet labret, (p) flaked stone drill, (q) chert wedge, (r) U-notched scraper.

Following the Takli stage is the **Kachemak stage**, dated from 3500 BP to 1000 BP. Ground slate implements continue to occur in a variety of forms. However, the beginning of the process of making these tools differs from that in the preceding stage. In the Takli stage, ground slate tools were first shaped by sawing, while in the Kachemak stage chipping was the first step in ground slate tool production. One of the forms of ground slate included in the Kachemak stage is the *ulu*. This tool is a transverse knife with a curved blade and its handle mounted parallel to and opposite from the cutting edge. In Inuit and Eskimo culture these were "women's knives" used for a variety of cutting tasks, especially butchering animals taken in the hunt. Other forms of ground slate tool include knives and weapon blades (Figure 4.8).

Oil lamps are common in Kachemak sites, and some are highly decorated, especially toward the end of the stage. A variety of bone tools, including barbed harpoon heads, also occur. In addition to these harpoons, which are secured in the flesh of the wounded prey animal by barbs carved into the heads, the bone tool assemblage includes **toggling harpoon** heads (Dumond 1987). Toggling harpoons have heads that detach from the shaft and turn sideways in the prey animal. A line connected to the harpoon head allows the hunter to stay tethered to the prey (Figure 4.9). This is a critical development in sea mammal hunting technology because it improved the hunting success.

Labrets of stone and bone are also found in Kachemak sites. Similar to those worn by people who practice body piercing today, these prehistoric labrets are plugs that are inserted into the lip or cheek. Kachemak is followed by the Kodiak Island **Koniag tradition** of later prehistory. For more on the prehistory of the Kodiak Archipelago, including discussion of the rise in social complexity there, refer to this chapter's case study.

The Aleutian tradition, which is found to the west of the Kodiak tradition and begins about 5000 BP, also developed out of the Ocean Bay tradition. This tradition is distinguished from the Kodiak tradition by the absence of ground slate tools until very late. Flaked tools are common, and among these are stemmed

FIGURE 4.9 Action of barbed harpoon heads (left) and toggling harpoon heads (right).

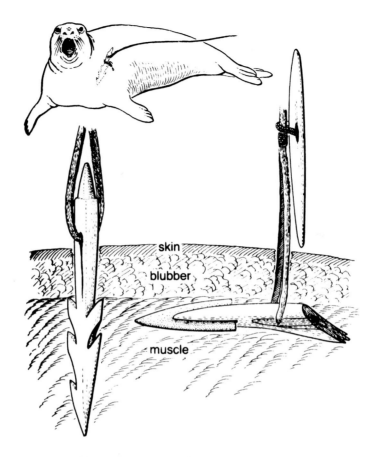

points and knives (Figure 4.10). As in the Kodiak tradition, oil lamps are found, and the bone tools of the Aleutian tradition are similar to those of the Kodiak tradition.

Sea mammal bones are a common element in Aleutian tradition middens, but marine invertebrates like the sea urchin are also common in some sites. Marine fish like cod, halibut, sculpin, and greenling were important, as were both migratory and resident birds. Land mammals taken include foxes in the western Aleutians, and caribou and bear in the east. Sites of this tradition can be large coastal middens that people seem to have inhabited on a semipermanent basis. This emphasis on marine resources probably was possible because sea level stabilized around 5000 BP, creating improved habitat for shellfish and fish along the shorelines (McCartney 1998).

About 500 BP ground slate *ulus* begin to make an appearance in the Aleutians. Some other traits appear to have spread into the area with the *ulu*, but most of the material culture remained the same. The Aleutian tradition people appear to have been the ancestors of the modern Aleuts.

Maritime Archaic

Use of sea resources also characterizes Archaic people located on the far northeast coast of North America. Here groups have been considered part of a Maritime

FIGURE 4.10 Artifacts of the Aleutian Tradition: (a–b) large flaked bifaces, (c–f) flaked projectile or lance points.

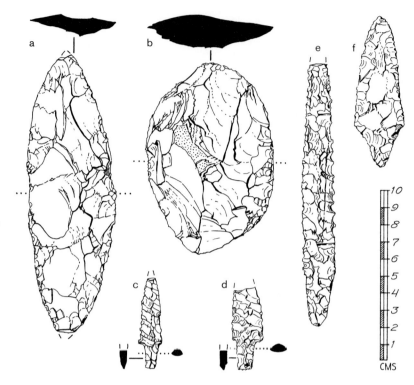

Archaic tradition, which dates from about 7500 BP to 3000 BP. This tradition was first recognized based on a cemetery at the site of Port aux Choix in northwestern Newfoundland, and the Maritime Archaic is one of several Middle–Late Archaic traditions of importance in the archaeology of the Northeast culture area (see Chapter 13). However, subsequent work has indicated that by 6000 BP, a northern branch of this tradition had spread from the Strait of Belle Isle north of Newfoundland, along the Labrador coast past the treeline (Tuck 1998).

Artifacts associated with this tradition include ground slate points and *ulus*, bone, shell and tooth pendants, ground slate bayonets, and many tools or ritual objects made of bone, antler, and ivory. Maritime Archaic people were marine hunters, as evidenced by the recovery of toggling harpoons made from antler or bone, fish bones, and walrus tusks. The site of L'Anse Amour in Labrador is the best-known northern Maritime Archaic site. Eventually, around 3000 BP, the Maritime Archaic in Labrador disappears and people called **Paleoeskimos** by many archaeologists are in evidence. The Paleoeskimos can be related to a new cultural tradition that first develops far to the west, the **Arctic Small Tool tradition**.

ARCTIC SMALL TOOL TRADITION

Denbigh Flint

Between 4000 BP and 3900 BP, a new archaeological manifestation appears in northern Alaska, characterized by tools that are generally smaller than those of the preceding archaeological cultures. Originally called the **Denbigh Flint**

FIGURE 4.11 Artifacts of the Arctic Small Tool tradition: (a) microblade, (b) burin, (c–e) projectile points, (f) side blade, (g) scraper, and (h) adze blade with the bit polished.

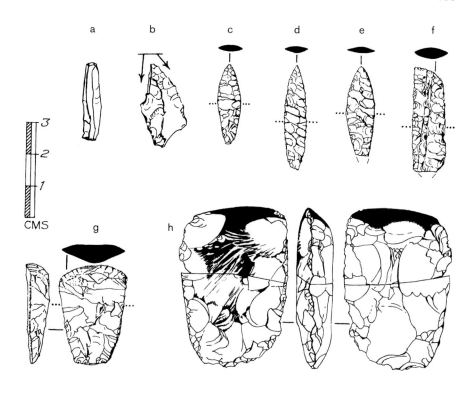

complex from the discovery of such artifacts in a site at Iyatayet Creek on Cape Denbigh on the shore of Norton Sound, Alaska (Giddings 1964), it was renamed the Arctic Small Tool tradition after similar artifacts were found over a much greater area, eventually including the High Arctic from Alaska to Greenland. The originators of this tradition were the first people to colonize the Arctic Ocean coast.

The Arctic Small Tool tradition assemblages contain small, finely worked end blades and side blades that probably were mounted in bone projectiles (Figure 4.11). Microblades are also part of the assemblage, as are burins made on small bifaces. **Burin spalls** sometimes show evidence of use as engraving tools. Arctic Small Tool tradition assemblages may include **adzes** with polished bits and an interesting burinlike tool, with the bit created by grinding the area that would normally be the burin spall scar (the scar of the long flake that creates the burin tip on standard burins). Oil lamps are not present at the beginning of the tradition but are incorporated into it by the end. Bone needles, bone or antler foreshafts for projectiles (probably arrows, indicating use of the bow and arrow), and small bone harpoon heads round out the kinds of artifact found at Arctic Small Tool tradition sites, although these organic items are known only from the eastern part of the range of the tradition. This pattern is attributed to poor preservation of organic materials in the Alaskan sites explored so far (Dumond 1984b, 74; 1987).

The Arctic Small Tool tradition may have developed from the Paleoarctic tradition, but if this in fact happened, it appears to have occurred in Siberia rather than Alaska. The separation of the Paleoarctic materials from the Arctic Small Tool

FIGURE 4.12 Plan of an
Arctic Small Tool tradition
house from the Brooks
River, Alaska.

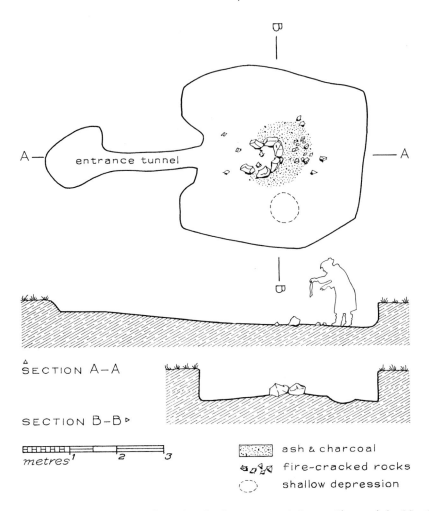

FIGURE 4.12 Plan of an Arctic Small Tool tradition house from the Brooks River, Alaska.

tradition occupations at key sites by layers containing artifacts of the Northern Archaic indicates that the development did not occur in Alaska but most likely resulted from a migration out of Siberia. The Arctic Small Tool tradition is found in eastern Siberia and could easily have developed out of the Paleoarctic tradition there. There is an absence of Arctic Small Tool material from the Aleutians, and, as indicated earlier, the Aleutian tradition is thought to have continued until historic times. The evidence clearly suggests two different migrations of people into the Americas (Dumond 1984b, 74–75).

Houses have been reported from a number of the Alaskan sites, including Onion Portage and Howard Pass, and at Brooks River in the upper Naknek drainage. Fourteen houses have been at least partially excavated at Brooks River, and all appear to be roughly square and about 4 meters (13 ft) across (Figure 4.12). They were partially dug into the prehistoric ground surface, and a sloping entry ramp led into the house from the side. A fire area, sometimes ringed with rock, occupied the center of the house floor. In one case there appears to be four post-holes around the hearth that may have served as roof supports. Rectangular slab structures in some of the houses are associated with fire-altered rock and may have been used for **stone boiling**. The fill of some of the structures indicates that the roofs were probably sod. Though hunting caribou seems to have been the primary occupation at many of the Arctic Small Tool sites, at least a few on the Alaska Peninsula appear to be situated in such a way as to have taken advantage of summer salmon runs.

Independence and Pre-Dorset

The Arctic Small Tool tradition spread out of Alaska throughout the High Arctic all the way to Greenland. In the eastern part of the Arctic there are two phases recognized—**Independence** and **Pre-Dorset**. The Independence sites are the earliest sites in the extreme northern Arctic, with occupation at Independence Fjord in the far north of Greenland occurring between 4000 BP and 3700 BP. The Independence artifacts are similar to those found in the Alaskan sites of the Arctic Small Tool tradition, with microblades, small burins, small side and end blades, and end scrapers. As in the west, the eastern sites lack stone lamps. Implements are, overall, slightly larger in the eastern sites, and tapering stems are found on many of the end blades (Figure 4.13). The edges of flaked tools are often serrated (Dumond 1987).

FIGURE 4.13 Artifacts of the Independence culture.

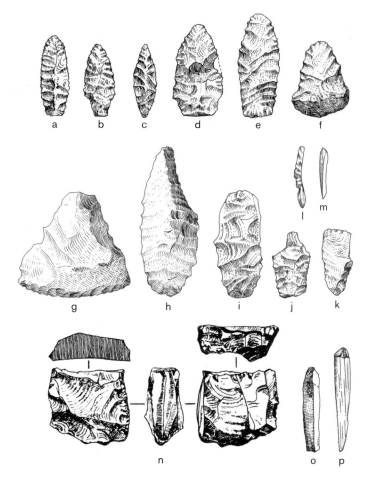

FIGURE 4.14
Independence house
illustrating the midpassage
(viewed from above).

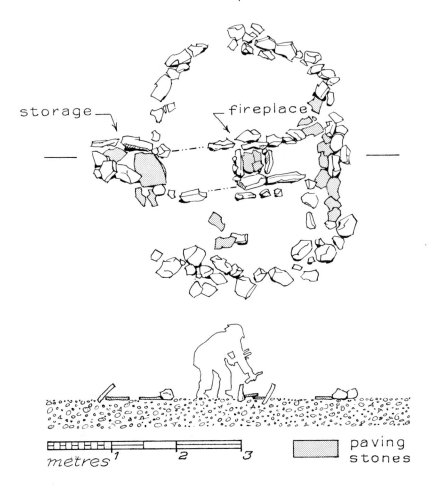

Unlike most of the Alaskan sites, preservation of organic materials is good on many of the Independence sites. Bone arrowhead fragments and barbed, non-toggling harpoons have been recovered. The harpoons come from Devon Island in the Arctic Archipelago. They are not found in Greenland sites, where faunal remains indicate an emphasis on hunting musk ox. At Independence sites, people also made needles, suggesting the manufacture of tailored clothing.

The Greenland sites appear to represent both summer and winter habitations. Sites inferred to have been summer residences have areas paved with flagstone that would have provided outside work areas. Sites thought to be winter camps have pits for caching food. Houses tend to be elliptical rings of rock with parallel lines of vertical rock slabs defining the **midpassage**, an area that cuts the house in half (Figure 4.14). In the center of the midpassage is usually a square, slab-lined hearth. Because there is no evidence of roofing material like sod, these structures appear to represent the remains of tents, probably of musk ox hide. We know that the houses were not built of snow, like later Inuit houses, because the open indoor fires would have given off significantly more heat than the flames of small oil lamps. Whatever the construction of the superstructure, these houses must

FIGURE 4.15 Pre-Dorset harpoon heads.

have been substantial enough to shelter people during the long winters of the north. The northern Greenland winter is marked by $2\frac{1}{2}$ months of total darkness (Dumond 1987; McGhee 1996, 50). The Independence sites are farther north than those in Alaska. Some of the Greenland sites are within 700 kilometers (435 mi) of the North Pole (Dumond 1987).

Postdating the Independence material, although sometimes treated at a regional variant, is the material known as Pre-Dorset. This material is found in northeast Canada north of Hudson Bay, in the Hudson Straits, and in the Foxe Basin, as well as in parts of Greenland south of where the Independence materials are found. In Greenland, it is known as the **Sarqaq culture** (Saqqaq) (Dumond 1987).

The tools from Pre-Dorset sites differ from those found in Independence sites. Burins and scrapers included in these assemblages indicate the working of bone, antler, and ivory. Burins have ground tips, and burinlike tools with ground rather than flaked faces are found. End blades that are bipointed, thin, and slender were made for use on arrows, and bows appear to have been similar to the small and recurved type the Eskimo used in historic times. People used harpoon heads with open sockets for hunting seal and walrus, while beluga and narwhal may have been hunted, as well (Figure 4.15). Lance heads of antler were also open socketed and had grooves for both side and end blades. Dogs apparently helped in the hunt, as their remains are found in the Pre-Dorset levels at Igloolik (Maxwell 1984, 361).

The artifacts of the Sarqaq sites are predominantly stone tools, since organic materials are not preserved at most of the sites. Stemmed and bipointed end blades for arrows are common, and many of these have serrated edges. Some of the arrow points have partially ground faces. End and side blades for larger lances are also found, but harpoon end blades are not recovered. Perhaps self-tipped harpoons of bone or antler were used. Spalled burins with ground tips occur, along with scrapers of various types. Large knives with pointed or rounded tips and triangular transverse knives were used for cutting. Soapstone lamps provided light and heat during Sarqaq times. Microblades are part of the Sarqaq collections, but they are relatively rare (Fitzhugh 1984, 536). The Sarqaq assemblages resemble those of Alaska at the same time period, but they differ from other eastern Arctic assemblages. The Sarqaq materials tend to be somewhat larger than the Alaskan artifacts, however (Dumond 1987).

LATER CULTURES OF THE ARCTIC: DORSET, NORTON, AND THULE

Dorset (2500–800 BP)

Certainly derived from the Arctic Small Tool tradition, and often considered part of it, is the **Dorset tradition**. This tradition developed in the eastern Arctic and is marked by the disappearance of both the bow and arrow and stone drills (McGhee 1996, 142–144), and by the rarity of dog remains (Dumond 1987). Harpoon heads with closed sockets (until late in the Dorset tradition, when open sockets reappear), rectangular soapstone lamps, side-notched end blades, slate knives, and polished burinlike tools (Figure 4.16) are characteristic of the Dorset tradition (Dumond 1987; McGhee 1996, 131).

FIGURE 4.16 Dorset artifacts: (left) lance blade, (center) harpoon head with chipped stone end blade, (upper right and right center) harpoon heads, (bottom) ice creeper.

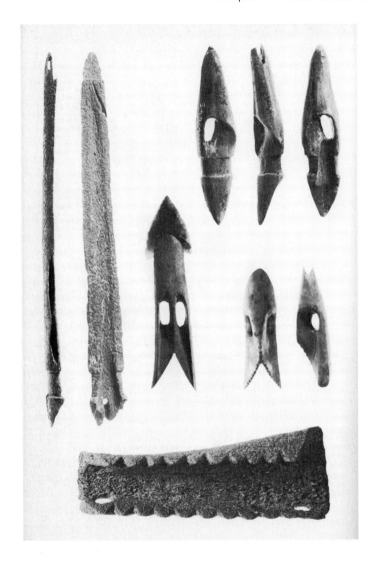

The preservation of organic material is excellent in many Dorset sites, so we have insights into the perishable culture of these people. In addition to closed-socket harpoon heads, archaeologists have found other bone, ivory, antler, and horn artifacts, including broad bone knives that are called snow knives. These knives resemble tools used by more recent Inuit people to cut snow into the blocks from which their domed snow houses are constructed. Bone artifacts identified as sled shoes indicate the presence of sleds, an important means of transport for the Inuit. Since, however, there are no dog remains and no artifacts resembling Inuit dog harness hardware, it is likely that humans powered the sleds. Another type of Dorset perishable artifact identified by comparison to Inuit objects is the **ice creeper**, a flat bone or ivory item having pointed projections carved into one side. The Inuit strapped similar gear to the bottoms of their feet to give them traction on the ice. Needles of bone and ivory bear witness to the continued presence of tailored clothing. In some Dorset sites the needles even are accompanied by actual fragments of hide clothing (Dumond 1987; McGhee 1996, 144–145).

Dorset people appear to have occupied sites for longer periods of time than their predecessors. Greater accumulations of the bones of their prey suggest these longer stays. The makeup of the bone refuse indicates that sea mammals, especially seals, were playing a larger role than caribou in the diet (Dumond 1987). At winter Dorset settlements people built substantial houses with sod coverings. These houses were rectangular, 4 to 5 meters (13–16 ft) across, excavated up to half a meter (1.6 ft) deep, and they had midpassages. The midpassages in these houses lacked charcoal in the central box, as stone lamps provided light and warmth. The occurrence of snow knives suggests the presence of snow houses, and clearly demarcated deposits of artifacts and bone, as would be left when such houses melted, support this inference (Dumond 1987; McGhee 1996, 131). Tent rings (rock circles), also sometimes occur in association with midpassage houses; probably the tents were summer homes.

Toward the end of the Dorset tradition a new type of structure—the **longhouse**—was built (Figure 4.17). These structures, which were 6 to 7 meters (20–23 ft) wide and from 10 to 40 meters (33–131 ft) long, were outlined either with vertically set slabs of rock or with large boulders. The outlining walls are up to a meter (3 ft) high. Since no roofing materials have been found in these structures, they probably were not roofed. It also is hard to imagine roofing such a large structure with the meager building materials available in the Dorset environment. There is little habitation debris near these structures, and there is no evidence of fires having been built in most of them, although they usually have a

FIGURE 4.17 The remains of a Dorset longhouse.

SITE OdPc·5 PLAN of STRUCTURE

line of hearths outside the structure. The longhouses may not have served as dwellings; instead, they may have been enclosures in which related groups built their shelters at times when people came together in larger groups, perhaps for social or ceremonial activities (McGhee 1996, 207).

One striking thing about the Dorset culture is its portable art (Figure 4.18). Although art is not common in comparison to utilitarian items from Dorset sites, the organic preservation at Dorset sites has led to the recovery of carvings in wood, ivory, antler, and bone. Human beings were the most common subject of Dorset carvings, followed by sea mammals, bears, birds, caribou, fish, weasels, and a few other creatures. Sea mammals, of course, represented food, but bear figures appear to have been part of a ceremonial aspect of Dorset life. Some bear figurines have been found that appear to have been amulets buried with an individual (Dumond 1987). Bears are often depicted as if they were flying or floating, and are also often embellished with straight lines that suggest the animal's skeleton. Among the human depictions are miniature masks, again hinting at ceremonial activity. The site of Button Point on Bylot Island, north of Baffinland, yielded two life-size masks. Button Point also had human and animal figures

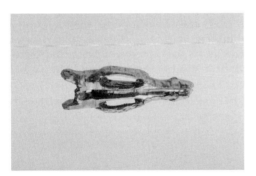

FIGURE 4.18 Dorset portable art.

carved in wood; splinters of wood had been inserted in small slits carved in the objects.

The masks, the bears, and the wooden figures with slits and splinters suggest the presence of shamanism, which is highly developed in Inuit and Eskimo culture. Many of the carvings suggest spirit animals or transformation, a theme also indicated by an interesting type of artifact—"**shaman's teeth**." These are depictions of mouths with teeth (Figure 4.18, lower left), including exaggerated canines, carved in bone, some of which have the marks of the human teeth that once clasped them (Dumond 1987; Maxwell 1984, 366–367; Taylor and Swinton 1967).

There is a correlation in Dorset toolkits between raw materials for stone tools and the function of the tool. Toolmakers usually chose quartz crystal for making microblades, colored cherts for making scrapers and harpoon end blades, jade for polished chisel-like tools for carving bone and ivory, and slate for other ground tools. Trade moved materials throughout the Dorset world, allowing people to make their tools from the appropriate material even if it did not occur in their local territory. Traded materials included stone for tools, especially jade and the related materials **nephrite** and jadeite, but also copper from the Coppermine River valley and iron from meteorites found in northwestern Greenland. The iron was used in some end blades for harpoons and to make other tools (McGhee 1996, 139–140).

Dorset sites are restricted to the central and eastern Arctic, getting as far east as Greenland. Warming conditions beginning around a thousand years ago appear to have disrupted the Dorset way of life, but what became of the people is unclear. McGhee (1996, 211–212) suggests they may represent the Tunit, who according to Inuit legend lived in Inuit territory, not always peacefully. In the legends, the Inuit eventually displaced the Tunit. The Tunit are portrayed as having prepared the land for humans by locating productive hunting spots and building the lines of cairns that directed caribou to the waiting hunters.

Norton Tradition (3000–1200 BP)

While the Dorset people were occupying the central and eastern Arctic, and even a little before the Dorset, the Norton tradition developed in the western Arctic. The **Norton tradition** is a series of three recognized cultures, the **Choris**, **Norton**, and **Ipiutak** (Table 4.1). The tool assemblage of the Norton tradition is similar to that of the preceding Arctic Small Tool tradition, especially the Denbigh Flint material, but also included ceramics and oil lamps, at least among the Choris and the Norton peoples.

The Choris culture (3000–2500 BP), the earliest of the Norton tradition, is found in northern Alaska north of the Bering Strait. Choris flaked stone tools are very similar to Denbigh materials from the Arctic Small Tool tradition, both in form and in execution. Points, knives, and side blades, as well as chipped and ground burins, and flake knives, all show continuity with earlier forms. As the Choris complex developed, however, people began making new point styles, chipped adze blades, and burin spalls struck from irregular flake cores. At about the same time, **feather-tempered pottery** appears. The surface of the pottery may be **cord-marked**, bearing impressions left from the use of a cord-wrapped paddle, or stamped or incised with linear designs (Douglas D. Anderson 1984, 85–86). The pottery is well made and appears to have come to Alaska as part of a developed

FIGURE 4.19 Choris lanceolate points.

FIGURE 4.20 Fragment of Norton pottery.

technology rather than having been locally invented. Asia is the most likely source for the ceramic industry (Anderson 1968). Among the Choris artifacts are lanceolate points (Figure 4.19) that resemble Scottsbluff and Angostura points, Paleoindian points of the Plains. These points date much earlier than do the Choris materials, and the relationship, if any, is still unclear (Anderson 1968; 1984, 87).

Oval Choris houses have been found measuring about 13 by 7 meters (42 × 24 ft). The details of construction of the houses are not clear from the sediment stains and postholes. At Onion Portage an interesting arrangement of structures, perhaps tents, was found surrounding and connected through passageways to a central oval structure that was dug into the ground. A stone hearth was found in the central structure and stone-lined hearths warmed the surrounding structures. The artifacts in the central structure differed from those found in the structures located around it. The round structures had evidence of food preparation and the working of hides, whereas the central structure had evidence of the manufacture of hunting implements and wood carving. These differences may suggest a division of labor similar to that of the modern Eskimo, with the central structure activities being like those of Eskimo men and the other activities such as food preparation and hide working being like the activities of Eskimo women (Anderson 1984, 86–87).

The Norton complex, apparently derived from the Choris, appears about 2500 BP and occurs from the Alaska Peninsula to the Firth River in northwestern Canada (near the Alaska–Canada border) (Dumond 1987, 106). The use of checked stamped designs on pottery, a surface treatment that began late in Choris times, suggests continuity with Choris (Figure 4.20). The use of ceramic and stone lamps is also carried over from Choris. Stone tools include end and side blades, knives, ground burinlike tools, scrapers, and notched net sinkers. Ground slate knives were also part of the Norton toolkit (Figure 4.21). Caribou hunting, sealing, and net fishing for salmon was done at least at the southern end of the Norton range. Whaling is also indicated (Douglas D. Anderson 1984, 87–88; Dumond 1987).

Dwellings for the Norton people were generally square, dug into the ground about 0.5 meter (1.6 ft), and had short entryways, although there is considerable variability in the Norton structures. One structure excavated at Unakleet is 8 by 12 meters (26 × 39 ft) and appears to have been essentially a men's house similar to the Eskimo *kazigi*. The fact that this structure is larger than others and had predominantly artifacts like projectile points, which are associated with men in Eskimo culture, support this identification (Dumond 1987).

About 2000 BP the Ipiutak complex can be defined. It shares a number of traits with the Choris and Norton complexes but lacks both lamps and pottery. In addition, houses with entry ramps, ground slate tools, and evidence of the pursuit of whales in Ipiutak. The Ipiutak complex is especially well known for its art, much of which comes from burials. People made elaborate carvings of animal and human figures, as well as linked chains and pretzel-like objects (Figure 4.22). Utilitarian objects like harpoon socket pieces and snow goggles are also elaborated with incised geometric designs. The style of the art is reminiscent of Scytho-Siberian art found to the west (Anderson 1984, 88–89).

Thule (2000 BP to Modern Times)

The **Thule tradition** developed out of the Norton tradition in the islands of the Bering Strait beginning about 2000 BP. Perhaps people or influences from Asia

FIGURE 4.21 Artifacts of the Norton complex: (a–n) side blades and end blades, (o), polished adze blade (p–r) harpoon heads, (s) check-stamped pot.

also were responsible for this tradition. The hallmark of this culture is a new technology for hunting sea mammals, particularly whales, in open water, and it produced a successful occupation that ultimately spread from Alaska through the eastern Arctic all the way to Greenland. The Thule people are the direct ancestors of the Inuit; their culture also diffused southward into the area of Pacific Eskimos.

FIGURE 4.22 Ipiutak art.

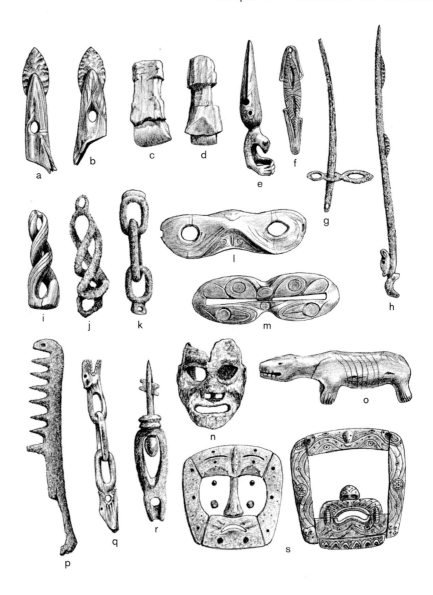

The **Old Bering Sea** and **Okvik** cultures are the earliest expression of the Thule tradition. These people lived on Saint Lawrence and adjacent islands, as well as on the Asian coast. The tools of these two groups are quite similar, and the distinction between them is based on decorative art styles. Although some archaeologists have suggested that the Okvik style is older than the Old Bering Sea, Dumond (1987) treats them as contemporary cultures that developed at about the same time that Ipiutak sites were being created on the Alaskan mainland (also Ackerman 1984, 108). The styles are characterized by differences in the design elements used (Figure 4.23). Okvik articles are decorated with spurred lines, Y patterns, circles, and ladder elements. Old Bering Sea decorations, on the other hand, use flowing, curvilinear designs (Collins 1937).

FIGURE 4.23 Okvik (a) and Old Bering Sea (b) style artifacts. The Okvik piece is a decorated ivory object and the Old Bering Sea item is a "winged object." Note the differences in the style of decoration (adapted from Willey 1966: Figures 7.8 and 7.12).

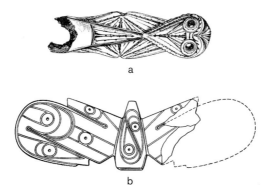

During the Okvik/Old Bering Sea times (2200–1250 BP), ground stone artifacts, particularly polished slate, were common. These included projectile points, adzes, *ulus*, and lanceolate ("men's") knife blades. Chipped stone was present in the form of end blades, side blades, knives, and drills, while bone, antler, and ivory artifacts took a number of forms. Drills, needles, awls, needle cases, hide scrapers, picks, mattocks, harpoon heads (Figure 4.24), foreshafts, sockets, counterweights (called "winged objects" based on their appearance), and harpoon butt ice picks are all part of the bone/antler/ivory part of the toolkit. Cooking pots and lamps were made of pottery that was marked with linear or check designs imposed by application of a carved paddle to the moist clay. The earliest pottery of this period was tempered with fiber, but a shift occurs to gravel temper later in Okvik/Old Bering Sea times (Ackerman 1984, 108; Dumond 1987).

The Okvik/Old Bering Sea people made their living hunting sea mammals. They were hunted from the ice edge, but the presence of mouthpieces and plugs of the type used by modern Eskimos for floats to be attached to harpoon lines indicates hunting on open water with this new technology. The large open boat called an **umiak** was introduced at this time. Harpoon shaft ice picks suggest the practice of winter hunting for seals at their breathing holes. This practice, documented in historic times, involved patient waiting at a breathing hole for the seal to appear, harpooning the seal, and using the ice pick to enlarge the hole in the ice to allow removal of the animal. People also hunted on land with the bow and arrow. Fish were caught by hooks or were speared. Humans powered sleds that were used to transport materials, and from kayak parts and models of kayaks we know that closed boats were in use (Ackerman 1984, 108; Dumond 1987).

The **Birnik culture** (2200–1250 BP) developed on the northern Alaska coast, but some sites are found in Siberia, as well. These people hunted sea mammals (possibly including whales) in open water from kayaks and umiaks. A distinctive flat toggling harpoon head, usually made of antler, characterizes the culture.

FIGURE 4.24 Schematic of a harpoon.

Sleds were improved, though the lack of harness parts suggests that dogs were still not being used to pull them. Pottery lamps and other items were marked with circles and spirals impressed into its surface (Dumond 1987).

Birnik people made houses that were square and measured 10 to 13 feet (3–4 ms) across. The houses had driftwood or whalebone superstructures and were entered through a passageway. Floors were lined with planks, and a sleeping platform was constructed along the rear wall. The entire affair was covered with sod for insulation (Dumond 1987).

It is from the Birnik that the **Thule culture** (1050–400/250 BP) itself developed. The Thule culture is indicated by a complex range of specialized tools seen in the historic Eskimo and Inuit. These included hunting gear such as arrows, spears, and harpoon heads (both toggling and barbed) made of bone, antler, or ivory, and stone implements, as well as mouthpieces for floats. The proportion of ground stone in the artifact assemblage rose to approximately 50 percent of the stone tools (Dumond 1987, 136), and these included end blades, double-edged knives, and *ulus*, as well as labrets. People made gravel-tempered as opposed to fiber-tempered ceramics, and their pots were shaped like flowerpots rather than in the globular forms of the early Thule.

The Thule expanded quite rapidly from northern Alaska through the eastern Arctic. As mentioned earlier, the Dorset people inhabiting this area were displaced by the Thule. A climatic change (the Medieval Warm period), resulting in warmer conditions, probably allowed the expansion of the Thule culture. The umiaks, capable of carrying a large number of people, their gear, and even their dogs, allowed for rapid movement. The ability to go into the open ocean to hunt whales, including the largest Arctic whale, the bowhead, meant that large stores of food could be amassed for getting the village through the winter, and winter villages of subterranean pithouses are present at a number of locations dating to Thule times. Dogsleds first appear during this time, as indicated by specialized harness hardware including swivels and buckles and the remains of ladderlike sleds (Dumond 1987; McGhee 1984). Snowshoes have also been found in Thule culture sites (Dumond 1984a, 101). Pauketat and Loren (2005: 20) point out that the differing social histories of the Dorset and Thule peoples also help explain the Thule expansion. Following Whitridge (1999), they suggest that gender divisions and the nature of the cultural experience, as well as the nature of corporate groups, are important in understanding the replacement of the Dorset by the Thule people.

The Thule culture spread all the way to Greenland, probably following their principal prey, bowhead whales. The distribution of a particular type of hunting artifact, the **Sicco-type harpoon head** (Figure 4.25), is a marker for this early expansion. Sicco-type harpoon heads are found from Point Barrow, Alaska, through the islands of the High Arctic to Thule, the place in northwestern Greenland after which the culture was named. As the Thule adapted to the Canadian Arctic, they left small winter villages of pithouses, but also used domed snow houses. Typical houses were similar to the Birnik houses, but they were round or oval and were lined with boulders. Because driftwood was scarce in the Canadian Arctic, people made the superstructure of whale bones, instead. Stones lined the floor rather than planks, and stone was used to pave the sleeping platform at the rear of the house (McGhee 1984, 369–372).

Between 800 BP and 700 BP, the Thule began to expand into the southern Arctic Archipelago, and further to the Hudson Bay and mainland coast. Some-

FIGURE 4.25 Sicco-type harpoon head.

FIGURE 4.26 Thule fishing gear: (left) fishhook, (center) ivory fishline weight, (right) fishhook.

what later they moved down into the coast of Labrador. As they moved into the areas away from the bowhead whale migration routes to places where these large creatures were not available, they began to emphasize other foods. Caribou, fish, and ring seal became the staples. Following this broadening of the food spectrum, people of the Thule culture were able to move further south yet, into the Barren Grounds, where caribou hunting and fishing sustained them (McGhee 1984, 373–375).

A number of foods were pursued in addition to the whales. Along with small whales, for example, seals and walrus were hunted from kayaks, using the **atlatl** and barbed darts. Birds were hunted in the same way, but multipronged darts were used. Winter ice hunting of seals continued, as well. Land animals were hunted using the recurved bow and arrow. Arrowheads were of antler. Prey species included caribou, musk ox, bear, and smaller mammals. Bolas were used, probably to hunt birds, and fish were speared using leisters (fish spears with three prongs) or were caught on lines equipped with composite fishhooks or gorges (Figure 4.26) (McGhee 1984, 370–371).

The Thule were certainly the ancestors of the historic Inuit, and the continuity in material culture is striking. This is seen particularly in the bone, antler, wood, and ivory material—material that is preserved in the dry and frozen Arctic. Organic material usually disintegrates in archaeological soils because of the action of bacteria. To survive, bacteria need moisture, warmth, and oxygen. Oxygen is in good supply in the Arctic, but moisture and warmth are seriously lacking. We shall see in later chapters how other conditions such as intense dryness or oxygen deprivation in waterlogged sites can preserve perishable artifacts. Much of the material made and used by Prehistoric people was perishable, however, and is found in archaeological sites only under unusual circumstances.

LATER CULTURES OF THE SUBARCTIC

Although the people of the Subarctic seem to have persisted in essentially Archaic lifeways until the Contact period, archaeological work in this area has defined a number of archaeological complexes besides the Archaic ones noted earlier in this chapter. Most of these refer to Late Prehistoric developments after approximately 1000 BP, but after about 2100 BP, a **Central Subarctic Woodland culture**, possibly associated with a new emphasis on wild rice gathering, appeared. This cultural development is coincident with the appearance of **Laurel culture** ceramics in the central Subarctic of northern Ontario, Manitoba, and eastern Saskatchewan. These ceramics, which are characterized by coarsely tempered conoidal pots (Figure 4.27), are also found to the south, where burial mounds and other characteristics suggest they have affinities with Middle Woodland developments in the Midwest and Upper Great Lakes (see Chapter 12). This first Subarctic pottery does not appear until between 2150 BP and 2050 BP. Other than the pottery, however, subsistence and settlement practices generally resembled those of the Shield Archaic (Pilon 1996, 1998).

Late Prehistoric, or Terminal, Woodland complexes also have been defined for the interior Subarctic. The **Blackduck culture**, found in the boreal forests from the north shore of Lake Superior west into Manitoba, north to the lowlands around Hudson Bay, and as far east as western Quebec, is a ceramic complex that first appears around 1450 BP. Blackduck also has some Plains affinities and is still

FIGURE 4.27 Central Subarctic Woodland pottery.

evident in Historic times. Archaeologists believe that this culture is the ancestral culture for many of the Ojibwa bands in this area historically. A related, somewhat later culture recognized by archaeologists, the **Selkirk culture**, is evident beginning about 1050 BP. Selkirk is believed to be ancestral to the historic Cree.

The later prehistory of the northwestern Canada is called the **Taltheilei tradition** (Gordon 1998), within which a series of projectile points can be defined beginning about 2600 BP and continuing to Contact times. These people apparently were caribou-hunting ancestors of the historic Dene. Athapaskan archaeology in the Subarctic is particularly well represented at the Klo-kut site in the Middle Porcupine drainage of the Yukon. This site, which has deposits dating back to about 1200 BP, reflects continuity in occupation from these earliest deposits to the historically known Athapaskan-speaking Kutchin. Subsistence at this site seems to have been constant through time; the people hunted caribou herds, intercepting them as they migrated north in the late spring and early summer. While there is some change through time in stone tools, the quality of bone and antler tools, and the use of birch bark, the basic pattern can still be traced into the Historic period (Morlan 1973).

HISTORIC PERIOD

The earliest contact between indigenous people of the Arctic and Europeans came with Norse voyages into the area starting in about AD 1000. Dumond (1987) equates the **Skraelings** of Norse sagas with the Dorset peoples. By AD 1200, items manufactured by the Norse had found their way into Eskimo settlements in northwest Greenland, providing evidence of both contact and trade (Dumond 1987). Norse colonies in Greenland, the Eastern and Western Settlements, were established on the southwest coast. Although these colonies are believed to have persisted until approximately 1450 (Arneborg and Seaver 2000), Norse penetration beyond Greenland is a subject of debate, as discussed in Box 4.1.

In 1576 British mariner Martin Frobisher began exploration of the Arctic. On behalf of Queen Elizabeth I, he was searching for the fabled Northwest Passage, a hoped-for water route from the Atlantic to the Pacific. He encountered natives of the area, as did later explorers like Henry Hudson (Dumond 1987). Frobisher returned to the Arctic in 1577 and again in 1578, this time in search of gold. On the third voyage he and his men built a house, established seven mines, and cached supplies when they left. Crews from Parks Canada have located and excavated three of the mines and excavated the house; they also tested the cache, finding, among other things, thousands of shriveled peas and 400-year-old bread (Berkowitz 1997). Although there were many such explorations and many encounters over the next few centuries, the events did little but introduce a few European trade items into the area's sites. Native lifeways continued essentially unabated, and through the nineteenth century some native groups of the Arctic had yet to encounter Europeans.

At European contact there was a distinction between the peoples of the Arctic and those of the Subarctic. The Arctic people were the Inuit or Eskimo, and the Aleut; they spoke separate but related languages that can be grouped into the Eskimo–Aleut linguistic family (Woodbury 1984). The peoples of the Subarctic were Indian people who were distinct from the Inuit and Eskimo. They spoke two kinds of languages, the Athapaskan in the west and the Algonquian in the

ISSUES AND DEBATES

BOX 4.1

How Far Did the Vikings Get?

The Vikings, legendary warriors and voyagers of the North, are well known and a source of pride among people of Scandinavian descent. The Viking is an icon in American culture, as exemplified in football mascots, comic books, and movies (Ward 2000). There is a long history of tales about early Viking settlement of the Americas as well. The term "Norse," which refers to the Nordic peoples who settled the Faeroe Islands, Iceland, and Greenland during medieval times, might be preferable for these early explorers of the North America. Whether we call the people Vikings or Norse, the extent of their travels in North America is still being investigated.

Many finds claim to provide evidence of a Viking presence in areas as far inland as Minnesota. An example nearer the coast, the Newport Tower in Rhode Island, has been considered a Norse religious structure. This stone building has a round second story supported on round pillars. The tower's supposed Viking origin and that of the Fall River skeleton, a human skeleton found buried with copper sheeting in Massachusetts, were immortalized in Longfellow's poem *The Skeleton in Armor*. Longfellow tells a romantic tale of a Viking and his love who settle in America to be together. The Viking builds the Newport Tower over his wife's grave, and when he dies, he is buried in his Viking armor, later to be known as the Fall River skeleton. It's a wonderful story poem; but the tower is a seventeenth-century windmill, and the skeleton represents an Indian burial from the early Historic period (Hertz 2000).

The most famous example of Viking claims that cannot be substantiated is the **Kensington stone** (Figure 4.28), found buried on a farm in Minnesota in 1898. This relic bears a runic

inscription that tells of Goths and Norwegians exploring westward from Vinland in 1362. The inscription evokes the tale of a medieval missionary expedition to Greenland, which some claim continued into the interior of North America via Hudson Bay, Lake Winnipeg, and the Red River. The Kensington stone created an immediate sensation even though most serious scholars considered it a fraud from the beginning. Among other factors tending to negate its authenticity, the runes used are more recent than the fourteenth century. Zealous amateur historians and politicians were able to persuade the Smithsonian Institution to display the Kensington stone for a time. Nevertheless, the weight of evidence is that it is not an authentic artifact, and the Smithsonian no longer even hints that it is valid (Wallace and Fitzhugh 2000).

There is, however, some truth to tales of Viking settlement of North America. Greenland was colonized by the Norse under the leadership of Erik the Red a little more than a thousand years ago. Norse sagas known as the *Greenlander's Saga* and *Erik the Red's Saga*, long part of the Viking oral tradition, were written down in the thirteenth century. The sagas tell of Viking voyages in the North Atlantic, and specifically of journeys to North America by Leif Eriksson, son of Erik the Red, and Thorfinn Karlsefni around 950 BP (AD 1000). The sagas identify three lands, Helluland, Markland, and Vinland. Helluland (the name refers to the area's rocky nature) is believed to have been Baffin Island, while "Markland," named for the fine forests it supported, is thought to refer to southern Labrador. The location of Vinland, perhaps named for the grapevines that grew there, has been much more disputed. The sagas indicate

FIGURE 4.28 The Kensington stone.

that a settlement was established briefly in Vinland but abandoned in the face of menacing local native groups. Recent finds lead most archaeologists to believe that Newfoundland is Vinland, but because grapes do not grow this far north, the New England coast could also be Vinland. Some archaeologists note that the word *vin* may refer to pasture land, which was abundant in Newfoundland, rather than to vines or grapes (Ingstad and Ingstad 2001, 103–109).

Archaeological evidence of Norse settlement was not found until excavations were done between 1961–1962 at L'Anse aux Meadows (Figure 4.29) at the tip of Newfoundland's north-

FIGURE 4.29 L'Anse aux Meadows.

ern peninsula. These established without a doubt that there were ruins of a Norse settlement here (Wallace 2000). Three multiroom halls, each flanked by at least one single-room building, are spaced along a terrace overlooking Epaves Bay, and an eighth structure interpreted as an iron furnace hut, sits apart from these. About 50 radiocarbon dates indicate that the Norse settlement was used during the eleventh century. There is a record of Native use of this site at other times, as well.

The Norse settlement at L'Anse aux Meadows is the only one known in North America outside Greenland, but besides this settlement, there also is good evidence of contact between Norse and native people in the eastern Subarctic and Arctic. First, the sagas refer to Native people, calling them *skraeling*, a term used for aboriginal people in Greenland as well. Second, Native art sometimes seems to depict Norsemen (Figure 4.30). Third, European metal and other objects indicate that Norsemen continued to sail to the continent until the Greenland settlements failed during the fifteenth century. Such objects are found in Dorset sites and later in Thule sites, though they remain rare. It is not clear whether the European artifacts that have been found represent direct contact or trade. They might represent scavenging after hostile encounters or shipwrecks. A Norse penny from the eleventh century AD found in the Goddard site in Maine is the most southerly find of an authentic Norse artifact (Cox 2000). This penny, which is the only Norse artifact at this site, probably was traded southward rather than brought directly by Norsemen.

How far into North America did the Vikings get? We still have more to learn, but most Norse contact and exploration seems to have been

FIGURE 4.30 Wooden image called the Bishop of Baffin, believed to represent a Norseman.

in the eastern Arctic and Subarctic. L'Anse aux Meadows probably was the most southerly base for the Norse, although they certainly explored south of that location. Isolated finds are insufficient evidence of settlement. Native trade networks can explain such finds, while only substantial remains like those at L'Anse aux Meadows will establish a true Viking presence in an area.

east. The Athapaskan languages were related to the Navajo and Apache languages of the Southwest, as well as to languages in the Plateau, the Northwest Coast, and California. Athapaskans such as the Kutchin, Tanana, Ahtena, and Ingalik of today occupied the interior of Alaska, while the Canadian Athapaskans included the ancestors of the Tutchone, Slavey, Dogrib, Chipewyan, Beaver, and Carier (Krauss and Golla 1981). The Algonquian speakers included groups ancestral to the Cree, Montagnais, and Naskapi in the north and the Ojibwa in the south. The Ojibwa, clustered around the Great Lakes, and thus, extended southward into the Northeast culture area (Rhodes and Todd 1981).

The story of European exploration in the Arctic and Subarctic is a fascinating tale of adventure and hardship, though beyond the scope of this chapter. Besides seeking the Northwest Passage, Europeans saw this vast region primarily in terms of what could be extracted from it: furs, whale oil, fish like cod, and even minerals. They were not interested in settlement per se, although many European powers did establish settlements along the coasts, and between the late seventeenth and the early nineteenth centuries, traders penetrated deep into the interior. Archaeological excavations can reveal much about these early settlements and outposts.

In the east Danes recolonized Greenland in 1721, while the French and the British entered the eastern Subarctic and then the interior as they developed the fur trade. Trading posts of the Hudson Bay Company and the Northwest Company were widely dispersed through the Subarctic by the early nineteenth century, and their excavation can be revealing. For example, a zooarchaeological study at Rocky Mountain Fort on the upper Peace River (Hamilton 1996) reminds us that fur traders themselves had to be provisioned, and as the fur trade grew and established semipermanent settlements, demand for food as well as furs could have an environmental impact. In 1870, however, Canada was established, and after that many treaties were made with First Nation peoples of the Subarctic. Even so, the way of life of the interior tended to persist, with only incremental change. A distinctive native ethnic group, the **Métis**, resulted from the intermarriage of Indian women and British and French traders.

In the western Arctic, Russian exploration of Alaska and the Bering Strait began in the mid-eighteenth century, leading to development of fur trading there. The Russians established settlements on Kodiak Island, on the Alaska Peninsula, on the Kenai Peninsula, and in the Prince William Sound area. Russian Orthodox missionaries followed the explorers and traders, but their effect was felt mainly in southern Alaska. Today archaeological explorations of these Historic sites are being conducted in cooperation with various Alaskan Native corporations.

Commercial whaling and fishing began in the nineteenth century. By the mid-1800s, ships began overwintering in the Arctic, a practice that allowed for more sustained contact between Europeans and Inuits. This led to increased trade and, ultimately, to dependence of the Inuit and some interior groups on trading furs for European goods. Mining has been another extractive enterprise that has developed in the Historic period.

There is a continuity between the Historic and Prehistoric archaeology of the Far North that is not found in other North American culture areas. Historic events did not alter the native way of life as greatly as elsewhere, and this is one reason lifeways can be so vividly reconstructed for this area. However, it is important to recognize that trade modified native economies; natives were attracted to the opportunities afforded by trade, and they changed their lifestyles to facilitate it. Ethnographic accounts written after the fur trade developed may not correlate as well as with prehistoric patterns as has often been assumed.

CHAPTER SUMMARY

This chapter discussed what we have learned about the archaeology of the Arctic and Subarctic culture areas. The treatment should open the way to a more detailed exploration of these fascinating areas. Points of particular importance are as follows:

- The tundra plain is the major physiographic unit of the Arctic, although mountains meet the coast in parts of Alaska, and the Greenland coast is very steep. Sea ice also is a prominent feature of the Arctic landscape, with ice persisting into the summer in sheltered bays and surrounding some of the northern islands the year around. The Subarctic is dominated by the crystalline bedrock of the Canadian Shield, although the northern end of the Rocky Mountains (the Cordillera), the mountains of southern Alaska, and the Yukon-Kuskokwim-Tanana plateaus are all included within the area.

- At the height of glaciation, the Canadian Subarctic was completely covered with ice, and glaciation has significantly marked the landscape there. Parts of the Arctic, on the other hand, remained ice free, including much of Alaska. Both the Medieval Warm period and the Little Ice Age had important effects in the Arctic.

- Unambiguous evidence for Pre-Clovis humans has not been found in the Far North, although both Old Crow Flats and Bluefish Caves have been offered as candidates. Fluted points, including some with blood residues indicating the hunting of large game such as mammoths, have been found, but no true Clovis material has been recovered from the Arctic or Subarctic.

- The Nenana and Denali complexes are the source of the earliest generally accepted remains from the Arctic. Dating to before 11,000 BP, the Nenana complex has both core-and-blade and core-and-flake technologies, but it lacks microblades and microblade cores. The Denali complex (12,000–8000 BP) is part of the larger American Paleoarctic tradition and includes microblades and wedge-shaped microblade cores, as well as bifacial tools and burins.

- The earliest occupations of the western Subarctic include Northern Cordilleran complex (10,000–7000 BP), which, like the Nenana complex, lacks microblades, and Northwest Microblade tradition sites, which are characterized by microblades.

- The Archaic period begins by 8000 BP, and its manifestations vary considerably within the Arctic and Subarctic. On the Pacific Coast we see the Ocean Bay, Kodiak, and Aleutian traditions and the beginnings of the exploitation of sea resources, as well as the early use of ground slate implements. In the western Subarctic the Northern Archaic tradition appears to represent generalized foragers who made side-notched points but no microblades. In the eastern Subarctic, the Shield Archaic and the Maritime Archaic are commonly recognized traditions.

- Between 4000 BP and 3900 BP, the Arctic Small Tool tradition, characterized by finely worked end blades and side blades, microblades, adzes with polished bits, and burinlike tools, developed in the western Arctic, probably in Siberia. The Arctic Small Tool tradition spread east from Alaska through the Canadian Arctic all the way to Greenland, where there are two phases: Independence and later, Pre-Dorset.

- Derived from the Arctic Small Tool tradition, the Dorset tradition (2500–800 BP) developed in the eastern Arctic. Dorset sites lack evidence of the bow and arrow and of the stone drill, but bone is well preserved in these sites, revealing a rich bone tool industry and striking bone carvings. The Dorset disappeared around 800 BP, probably replaced quickly by Thule people, who were spreading east out of Alaska during the Medieval Warm period.

- The Norton tradition, including the Choris, Norton and Iputiak cultures, signals the beginnings of material culture much like that used by the historic Eskimo and Inuit, with ceramics and specialized hunting equipment appearing. About 2000 BP, the Thule tradition developed out of the Norton and spread eastward. Hunting of sea mammals, particularly the bowhead whale, was very important, and the specialized boats of the Historic period, the umiak and the kayak, are both present, as is the dogsled. Ultimately the Thule expanded in the southern Arctic, reaching all the way to Hudson Bay.

- Several late cultures have been defined for the Subarctic, including the Central Woodland culture (after ca. 1000 BP), marked by Laurel ceramics, and the Blackduck and Selkirk cultures, which are thought to have developed into the historic Ojibwa and Cree, respectively. In northwest Canada, the Taltheilei tradition associated with Athapaskans has been defined.

- The Historic period starts with contacts between the Norse and the peoples of the Arctic. After the Norse, in the 1570s, other explorers began visiting the area, but the early exploration had little affect on the native people. Indeed, the harsh conditions of the Arctic and Subarctic allow people to retain their aboriginal lifestyles relatively intact until quite recently despite whaling expeditions, trading posts connected to the fur trade, and mining activities.

SUGGESTIONS FOR FURTHER READING

For a classic treatment of the archaeology of the Arctic:
Dumond, Don E. 1987. *The Eskimos and Aleuts*, 2nd ed. London: Thames and Hudson.

For an account of Arctic archaeology written for the general public and emphasizing the Dorset way of life:
McGhee, Robert. 1996. *Ancient People of the Arctic*. Vancouver, BC: University of British Columbia Press.

For two volumes that cover the prehistory of the Canadian Arctic and Subarctic up to 1450 BP:
Wright, James V. 1995. *A History of the Native Peoples of Canada*, Vol. I. Mercury Series, Paper 152, Archaeological Survey of Canada. Canadian Museum of Civilization, Ottawa.
——. 1999. *A History of the Native Peoples of Canada*, Vol. II. Mercury Series, Paper 152, Archaeological Survey of Canada. Canadian Museum of Civilization, Ottawa.

For a series of papers on sites in Beringia—both the Alaskan and Siberian portions:
West, Frederick H., ed. 1996. *American Beginnings: The Prehistory and Palaeoecology of Beringia*. Chicago: University of Chicago Press.

For additional resources on Vikings in North America:
Fitzhugh, William W., and Elisabeth I. Ward. 2000. *Vikings: The North Atlantic Saga*. Washington, DC: Smithsonian Institution Press.

Ingstad, Helge, and Anne Stine Ingstad. 2001. *The Viking Discovery of America: The Excavation of a Norse Settlement in L'Anse aux Meadows, Newfoundland.* New York: Checkmark Books.

OTHER RESOURCES

Sections H and I of the Student CD give web links, additional discussion questions, and other study aids. The CD contains a variety of additional resources including a complete list of the references cited in this chapter and the case study that follows it.

CASE STUDY

Although they were consistently hunter-gatherers, the peoples of the Arctic and Subarctic varied considerably in their cultural adaptations. This isn't surprising, given the vast region encompassed and the many environmental circumstances within these culture areas. As this chapter has demonstrated, time adds another dimension to this variability over which archaeologists have traced many changes. Along the Pacific Coast of Alaska, hunter-gatherer societies with a maritime subsistence base eventually developed aspects of sociocultural complexity usually associated with agriculturalists. These include sedentism, social ranking, chiefs, endemic warfare, and differential accumulation of wealth and prestige. Contemporary Native Alaskans have become increasingly interested in reclaiming this heritage, and they often have asked archaeologists to help them document it. This case study shows how changing site characteristics and distributions discovered through archaeological survey and some excavation on Kodiak Island were used to evaluate a model of growth in social complexity among hunter-gatherers. This work provides a good example of how archaeologists can use information on settlement to test their ideas about what happened in the past. As you read this case study, pay attention to the research process, noting how the data were generated and how they were related to the expectations derived from the model.

FROM SITES TO SOCIAL EVOLUTION

The Study of Emergent Complexity in the Kodiak Archipelago, Alaska

Ben Fitzhugh

Mention Alaska, and most Americans who have not been there are likely to conjure up images of ice and snow, polar bears and walruses, and Eskimos in igloos. Alaska has its share of these (with the exception of igloos, or snow houses, which were primarily a winter dwelling of the Canadian Arctic Inuit cultures), but Alaska is much more varied and diverse than its stereotypes. From the frozen and tundra-covered north country along the Arctic Ocean and interior north of the Arctic Circle, to the vast boreal forests of the central interior and southeastern coasts, to the treeless Alaska Peninsula and volcanic islands of the Aleutians, Alaska presents a complex landscape full of challenges and opportunities that have helped shape unique cultural adaptations and social traditions throughout the Holocene.

Alaska has a 12,000-year legacy of hunting, fishing, and gathering cultures. The earliest known archaeological evidence is found in the interior mountain regions and dates to the terminal Pleistocene, when people in the area were perhaps still hunting megafauna like mammoths, as well as smaller game, fish, and birds. The oldest coastal occupations date between 9000 and 10,000 years ago and are found around the North Pacific Rim of southern and south-eastern Alaska. By contrast, the colder coastal plains and ice-bound coastlines of the Bering Sea and Arctic Ocean were not occupied until 4500 years ago. The variation in colonization histories of the different Alaskan landscapes (coastal and interior, forested and tundra, mountains and plains) and the cultural trajectories that unfolded on them make this region one of the most intriguing for studying hunter-gatherer adaptation and social evolution.

While in graduate school, as I began looking for a place to begin my research career, I focused on Alaska's legacy of hunter-gatherer adaptation and evolution for two reasons. First, I was fascinated by maritime hunter-gatherer culture and its development, and Alaska was a great place to study that. Second, the development of relatively complex hunter-gatherer groups around much of Alaska's coasts, in the absence of agriculture, provided an interesting context for the study of emergent complexity. For decades, anthropological archaeologists had assumed that agriculture was a necessary and sufficient stimulus for cultural complexity—ranked and stratified societies with socioeconomic classes, economic specialization, monumental architecture, organized military, and so on. In common models of social evolution, hunter-gatherers were the baseline, the evolutionary origins *away from which* more complex cultures evolved! Accordingly, existing hunter-gatherers were viewed as marginal populations living where agriculture could not flourish, and surviving, perhaps easily, perhaps desperately (depending on the model), in a constant state of dependency on nature. By contrast, the coasts of Alaska, especially its Pacific coasts, from the Aleutian Islands to the Southeast Panhandle, saw the development of cultural groups with a suite of relatively complex characteristics such as social ranking with powerful chiefs, endemic warfare, slavery, wealth accumulation, competitions for prestige, and at least in Southeast Alaska, monumental houses and totem poles (part of the broader Northwest Coast cultural tradition). These characteristics are well established in the ethnohistoric and ethnographic literature of the region (Townsend 1980). Something about adapting to the coastal environments seemed to encourage the development of the kind of complexity seen in southern Alaska. I wanted to understand this. While several anthropologists had approached this kind of question from the perspective of comparative ethnography, few had used archaeological evidence

to document actual trajectories of hunter-gatherer social evolution over the long term. That became the goal of my first major research project.

GETTING STARTED

Research questions are important, but they don't do much good without a place to study them. Finding a place to conduct research is particularly challenging at the beginning of one's career, without a solid basis on which to select a research area. I was fortunate to spend three summers working on field projects in different parts of Alaska as an undergraduate and early graduate student. The first of these projects, in 1987, was on a fabulous **wet site** in the Kodiak Archipelago (Figure 4.31; Jordan and Knecht 1988). On that project I gained familiarity with the generous archaeological

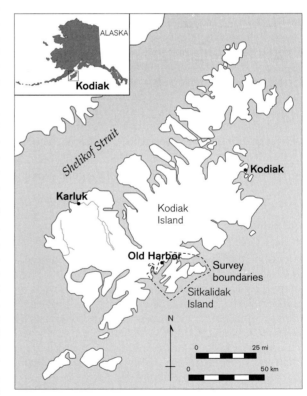

FIGURE 4.31 The Kodiak Archipelago, showing the location of Sitkalidak Island.

record of the region and the growing enthusiasm of the local people to learn more about their archaeological heritage. In the summer of 1992 I returned to Kodiak to make contacts and explore possible research locations for my Ph.D. dissertation. I soon learned that the village of Old Harbor, in southeast Kodiak, was interested in having someone inventory the archaeological resources of their region. I jumped at the chance.

It is helpful to consider the historical context of this opportunity and why the residents of a small Alaskan village were eager to support my archaeological research. To do this, we need to take a brief detour to explore the history of Native–white interactions over the past 200 years. Of course, Native Alaskans had controlled their own fate for millennia prior to Russian contact in the mid-eighteenth century. From contact until 1867, when the territory was sold to the United States for pennies an acre, Russia controlled the southern Shelikof Strait and Alaskan territories—including Kodiak, which had been the location of the first Russian settlement and colonial headquarters. Russians had been mainly interested in sea otter pelts, and the occupation was primarily entrepreneurial in spirit. Native Alaskans in the Aleutians and around the Gulf of Alaska were drawn into this enterprise both willingly and unwillingly as hunters and support personnel for the Russian colonists. Over the decades, disease ravaged the area, killing 75 percent or more of the Native population during the Russian occupation. Orthodox missionaries came in after initial contact and defended Native rights to humane treatment and wages. They brought Orthodox Christianity to southern Alaska, where it remains a staple of Native belief today. And ultimately Native Alaskans were recognized by the Russian Empire as citizens.

With the transfer of possession, the U.S. government took a markedly different approach. Following policies established to "manage" Native Americans elsewhere in the country, the federal government treated the Alaskans as conquered subjects, not making them citizens until 1924 when all aboriginal descendants in the United States were granted U.S. citizenship. As lucrative natural resources were discovered in the territory, Native use of the land came increasingly into conflict with resource extraction by outsiders. The lack of a legal basis for the dispossession of Native Alaskans of their land became critical with the discovery of oil fields in North Alaska and

the birth of a plan to build a pipeline south to Prince William Sound. To settle the legal issues once and for all, in 1971 the United States formally acknowledged Native Alaskan land rights with the passage of the **Alaska Native Claims Settlement Act (ANCSA)**. This historic legislation awarded large tracts of ancestral lands across Alaska to regional and village Native corporations established to manage them (Mitchell 2001).

While not without its own problems, ANCSA signaled a turning point for Alaska Natives. The law came after more than a century of institutionalized cultural suppression born of racism, a rush by outsiders to exploit the "natural" wealth of Alaska (furs, gold, fish, oil, etc.), and assimilation policies that collectively discouraged Native language, culture, and identity. Social, economic, and educational policies of the early twentieth century left many Native communities physically, psychologically, and spiritually depressed (Pullar 1992). High rates of alcoholism and suicide were symptomatic of a broader loss of control over subsistence resources, limited access to newly introduced market economies, and a social environment that privileged Euro-American values and history. In this context, Native heritage was suppressed and devalued. Many identified more with Russian than indigenous ancestry. The passage of ANCSA, and the change in political climate it signaled, finally gave Native Alaskans a basis on which to reclaim their heritage and assert positive cultural identities as Native Alaskans. In an effort to reconnect with their precolonial past and heal the social and psychological damage of the preceding century, many Native groups began to develop cultural heritage programs that sought to document their past through study of archaeology, oral history, language, and traditional knowledge.

Archaeological research in the 1970s and 1980s was one of several sources of data used to establish ANCSA land claims, and on Kodiak, this research raised awareness among Native and non-Native alike of the rich Alutiiq past. In the 1980s, excavations at the phenomenal Karluk wet site produced amazing examples of the perishable art, tools, and textiles. With these discoveries, the Alutiiq Cultural Center (later the Alutiiq Museum and Archaeological Repository) was formed to foster exploration of the archaeological history and cultural heritage of the Alutiiq people. The study of archaeological sites and artifacts became a focal point for cultural revival.

In this context, different village corporations on Kodiak were interested in gaining archaeological databases of their own and promoting archaeological investigations in their respective regions. The Old Harbor Native Corporation (OHNC) had sponsored previous archaeological work at the location of the event, in 1784, that had initiated the Russian conquest of Alaska: the attack on Kodiak Island. Two years later, OHNC approved my offer to conduct an archaeological survey of their ANCSA land (primarily Sitkalidak Island: see Figure 4.31), throwing in unsolicited funding to assist in the effort. I also received financial support from the National Science Foundation, the Wenner-Gren Foundation, and the University of Michigan, where I attended graduate school at the time. The Alutiiq Culture Center in the town of Kodiak was instrumental with logistical support. I began fieldwork in June 1993 with a crew of three, a small motorboat ("skiff" in Alaskan terminology), and assorted camping and archaeological gear. The project lasted three summers.

WHAT DID THE SITKALIDAK ARCHAEOLOGICAL SURVEY PROJECT DO?

In a general sense all archaeological surveys are variations on a common theme. Archaeologists look at maps, select areas to investigate—often through some more or less formal strategy—and then go looking around, trying to find the remnants of human activities, sometimes soliciting help from locals with intimate knowledge of the area. When **archaeological deposits** (sites) are identified, they must be located on maps so they can be found again. And in most surveys, some attempt is made to discern cultural material that will provide clues to the age and kinds of activities performed at a given location. Sometimes surface site maps are drawn and small excavations are made to better understand the history of site occupation.

Some surveys are geared to finding "good sites" or "significant sites" to excavate or protect from destruction, and no explicit effort is made to use the data generated to answer regional-scale questions. Other surveys have more analytical and synthetic goals, seeking information on the distribution of sites across a landscape and, from that, occupation history at a regional scale. Site testing and excavation can then be used to add clarity and detail to the regional

picture. While less detailed information about any single site can be gleaned from a survey analysis, the results give us a more comprehensive understanding of changes in settlement and land use patterns. Eventually, survey and excavation data become complementary, allowing archaeologists to synthesize the regional patterns and local details into a more representative model of past cultural systems and their change.

While the Old Harbor Native Corporation's primary goal was to protect sites by listing them and noting their distributions on a map, my research interests compelled me to make the survey more synthetic (hence more comprehensive). Kodiak has long been rich in sea life such as fish, sea mammals, seabirds, and shellfish and relatively poor in terrestrial resources. The primary terrestrial game, grizzly bear, fox, land otter, and weasel, were hunted for furs and occasionally for food, but were relatively unimportant. This explains the observation that most archaeological deposits around Kodiak are close to shore. Within the study area shown in Figure 4.31, therefore, I decided to survey most intensively around the coasts, where marine-oriented hunter-gatherers would have conducted most of their land-based activities. We also surveyed all rivers large enough to support salmon runs, but looked less intensively at steep slopes and mountaintops in this relatively rugged region.

The survey took three summers of roughly three months each. In the first season and continuing through the project, the primary goal was **reconnaissance**—searching for sites, describing them, mapping their location, and sketching their size and appearance. Finding the sites involved a combination of looking for house depressions, lush vegetation, and eroding shell midden and using soil probes and **shovel test pits** to dig for archaeological evidence. Once a site was discovered, we also dug small test pits or cleaned off eroding bluffs to describe the stratigraphy and to collect representative artifacts, faunal samples, and charcoal for radiocarbon dating. In the second summer, we also opened up larger test excavations at two sites to improve our understanding of poorly known time periods (Figure 4.32). The final season was spent excavating a third site with students from the Old Harbor School and wrapping up the reconnaissance in areas that had not yet been visited.

Upon completion of the fieldwork, we had documented 150 archaeological sites distributed in age from 7500 to 50 years ago. These sites ranged from

FIGURE 4.32 Test excavations conducted by the Sitkalidak Archaeological Survey.

small, short-lived campsites and activity areas to large sod house villages. Prior to our work, fewer than 40 sites had been recorded for this area and most were relatively recent—and conspicuous—such as large village sites. As a result, this project added considerably to what was known about the variety of past settlement types and land uses in the region. Using this new information to understand the evolution of Kodiak societies and emergent complexity required countless hours of analysis back in the lab. Before discussing the results of these analyses, we must consider the theoretical model that was developed to guide research and analysis.

FRAMING THE RESEARCH QUESTIONS

Philosophers of science have long noted that the development of scientific knowledge involves both the generation of ideas and the evaluation of ideas with evidence. This leads to a bit of a chicken-and-egg problem—do you start by generating ideas or by collecting information? Science is an ongoing process that tacks back and forth between these two activities. And one of the hardest parts of becoming a scientist is deciding where to jump into the cycle. It is generally accepted that in formal research, the articulation of a set of research questions and ideas about their possible solution usually precedes the collection of data. And that's how I got started.

As already noted, my big research questions related to the evolution of "complex hunter-gatherers" or the relatively more coordinated and ranked or even hierarchical hunter-gatherers seen around the North Pacific. This topic was too general to guide specific research, and it was necessary to develop a series of more focused questions and hypotheses relating to expected sequences of events. I did this by constructing a model or scenario outlining what I thought might have been the processes guiding Kodiak social evolution. To do this, I used two sources of information: a half-century of prior archaeological research in the area, which provided a reasonable culture history for the region, and a rich history of anthropological theory.

Culture History

The culture history was worked out for Kodiak in a series of projects beginning in the 1930s. Since the late 1960s, we have understood Kodiak archaeology in a series of four periods (Ocean Bay, Kachemak, Koniag, and Historic; Clark 1984). The Ocean Bay period began sometime before 7000 years ago (calibrated to calendar years) and lasted for about 3500 years. This period is defined by chipped stone tools (including core-and-microblade technology in the first 2000 years), yielding gradually to ground slate tools late in the period (Clark 1979, 1982; Steffian et al. 2002). Slate is a common raw material in the Kodiak Archipelago, and grinding slate into projectile points and knives may have been an adaptation to the abundant local material and/or an innovation that improved the success of sea mammal hunting. Slate tools tend to shatter upon entry into prey and would have been effective in disabling swimming animals. Limited evidence of organic tools and fauna suggests that people were active maritime foragers from the beginning of the period. They used bone hooks to catch fish and barbed bone harpoon points to hunt sea mammals, most likely from boats, though we have no direct evidence of the kinds of boats used. The Ocean Bay period is also notable for the predominance of floors coated in **red ocher**, an iron pigment. Small pithouses make their appearance in the late Ocean Bay period. These were constructed of sod walls and floors sunk partially into the ground. From the earliest times, small pecked and ground stone lamps were used with sea mammal oil, presumably to light dark quarters during the long winter nights.

The Kachemak period, beginning around 3500 years ago, is defined primarily by the addition of new tool types and the loss of core-and-blade technologies. Continuities in technology suggest that this was a local development, not a population replacement (Clark 1996). Among the new tools were toggling harpoon heads, ground slate ulus or semicircular knives, and plummet-shaped sinker stones. Notched stone sinkers, made for holding down nets, had been used in the late Ocean Bay period but became much more prevalent in the Kachemak. The first aggregations into villages are observed during the Kachemak period. Late in the period, after about 500 BC, we also see increased use of bodily ornamentation with labrets and other jewelry (Steffian and Saltonstall 2001), the decoration of large lamps with relief carvings of human, animal, and abstract figures, and the development of a mortuary tradition that appears to relate to mummification and ancestor worship (Simon and Steffian 1994).

The Koniag period also appears to represent continuity with previous occupations, though this conclusion remains somewhat controversial (see Fitzhugh 2003, 53–54). The period witnesses the expansion of houses from small single-roomed dwellings to multifamily units with a large main room surrounded by smaller side chambers (Figure 4.33). Excavations of Koniag period houses at the New Karluk wet site uncovered elaborate objects indicative of status competition, warfare, ceremonialism, gambling, and shamanism (Jordan and Knecht 1988). Large multiroomed houses were packed close together in this large village, with clear evidence of permanent occupation over 600 years. These finds and other evidence from Koniag period archaeological sites support ethnohistoric accounts made in the early years of the Russian occupation on Kodiak: These accounts suggest that village chiefs and "rich men" controlled resources, became powerful through trade and warfare, owned war-captive slaves, and threw potlatch feasts to honor their houses, villages, and guests. As noted earlier, the political domination of Russians and later Euro-Americans after 1784 changed Alutiiq society dramatically.

Kachemak houses   Koniag houses

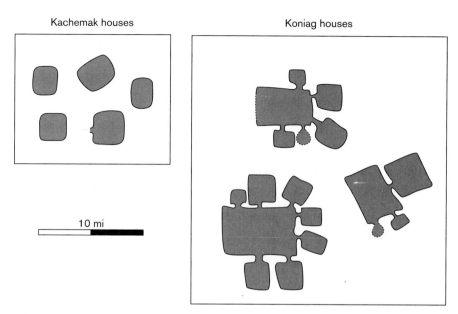

10 mi

FIGURE 4.33 Kachemak and Koniag houses.

The Model

The culture history revealed through archaeological study around Kodiak suggests a number of changes in the organization of hunter-gatherer societies through this 7500-year sequence, ending with the relatively complex social, political, and economic organization of the Late Koniag. Some of the more significant changes included increased residential permanence or sedentism, economic intensification and increased emphasis on seasonal food storage, and the development of a competitive social structure that encouraged status competition, trade in prestige valuables, and endemic warfare. These are some of the same developments that have been implicated in the emergence of social hierarchy in agricultural societies. My goal was to account for how and why these changes occurred on Kodiak, and to do that, I needed a model (Fitzhugh 2003, 101–132). Here are some of the core features.

Drawing primarily on ideas from ecological anthropology, I suggested that the Kodiak sequence could be understood as a series of behavioral and organizational changes generated by people trying to adapt to their dynamic and changing physical and social environment. Early on, the Kodiak region was largely empty of people, and immigrants would have benefited from residential flexibility. They should have targeted the most profitable game, which would have included the sea mammals and large fish that give more calories for the effort and also generate secondary products such as skins and bone for tools. To facilitate residential flexibility, tools and facilities should have been portable. As population began to grow, small groups would have broken off, occupying new territories around the archipelago. This should have led to a gradual increase in the concentration of people around the islands and eventually to a restriction on mobility. At the same time, hunting and fishing by an increasingly dense population should have eventually caused a decline in the success rates as certain slowly reproducing species became over-harvested. This is more likely for sea mammals and really large fish like halibut than it is for schooling fish like salmon and herring, and shellfish.

As more people put pressure on the available resources, technologies should be developed to try to counter the declining success in hunting and fishing. The more successful innovations would be those that reduced the costs of catching and processing smaller species, which come in denser concentrations and are rapid reproducers. Schooling fish would have been among the most attractive targets for these intensified technologies. Nets that could capture large numbers of fish and processing tools and techniques that could increase the rate of cleaning them would allow people to raise their overall return rates. With higher overall return, it would be possible to store the spring, summer, and fall catch of schooling fish for use in the lean, cold, and dark winter months.

With the successful innovation of intensive foraging/processing technologies, like nets and ulus, people could afford to aggregate during winter months, eating stored foods and socializing. Winter villages should form and become more permanent, and overall population densities should continue to increase. But again, with higher population densities, people also lose some ability to move around freely. The emphasis on storage for lean periods would reduce the incentive to share stores, increasing the importance of the concept of private property, which typically is alien to small and mobile hunter-gatherer groups. And the higher population densities would also increase levels of competition over the most stable and productive resource patches. With more sedentary residence, people could also claim ownership of particular resource patches, and defend them.

Ethnographic research has shown that people in all human societies, even the most egalitarian, engage in political competition to one degree or another. Where people tend to depend more or less equally on one another for survival, this competition is minimized in favor of cooperative adaptive strategies. And when interdependence becomes less equal, competitive strategies become more pronounced. This is the situation expected when people become more densely packed onto a landscape, and when their vital resources are excludable and vary in reliability. Then some people are better off than others. Those lucky or shrewd enough to control the better hunting and fishing locations need to work hard to defend their privileged access. They can do this by establishing alliances with other elites and attracting subordinates to help control the resource. Allies and subordinates are also potential challengers, and so effort must be expended on appeasing these populations. Feasts and food giveaways are a common way of solidifying alliances and attracting subordinates. The ability to give away food and other goods sends a message of affluence and strength to recipients and

bystanders. Symbols of power in the form of exotic and nonutilitarian products and labor-intensive crafts and monuments (all part of a new prestige economy) emerges to signal elite access to alliances and subordinate labor. Warfare, from local skirmishes to organized long-distance raids, provides a context for warriors to gain status and for kin groups or villages to demonstrate their strength to allies and competitors. Slaves captured in raids raise the labor potential of successful warriors and chiefs and increase their ability to compete for prestige in feasts and giveaways.

At this point the model brings us to a state reminiscent of social organization and interaction at European contact throughout the North Pacific from northern California to the Aleutian Islands. Ecological characteristics prevented elites from expanding control beyond the areas of one or a few villages, and yet some commanded sizable local populations. Wealthy and powerful chiefs and rich men (and women) sat at the top of a social system in which individuals were ranked both through inheritance and through achievements in life. Others measured their status by their genealogical proximity to elites and/or through their participation in the household activities of more or less powerful families. Slaves occupied the lowest category, though they could be freed or marry into free families, and earn higher status in time.

RESULTS OF THE SITKALIDAK ARCHAEOLOGICAL SURVEY

It is important to remember that models are plausible accounts, not actual descriptions of events. Models are useful to the extent that they make sense of existing observations and simultaneously call our attention to new observations that can be made to support or contradict aspects of the model's account. Thus to turn a model into a scientific tool, we must draw from it archaeological predictions that do not simply refer to the information we used to create the model in the first place, which would create a logically circular argument.

The model I developed included a series of archaeological predictions for the Ocean Bay, Kachemak, and Koniag time periods. Some of these predictions could be evaluated with data from the Sitkalidak Archaeological Survey, and others could not. The model generated expectations about the nature of site size, permanence, location, and density

FIGURE 4.34 Red ocher floor (marked by string), indicating the previous location of an Ocean Bay tent site.

on the landscape, as well as differences in habitation structures, artifacts, and faunal remains. I shall discuss a few broad lines of evidence.

As expected, Ocean Bay sites in the Sitkalidak survey were universally small, most with thin deposits and little apparent investment in fixed structures. Extended excavations at one of these sites suggests that red ocher floors are the remnants of aboveground tent facilities, perhaps with earth holding down the tent edges (Figure 4.34). This general observation, supported by other early Ocean Bay excavations around Kodiak, is significant because tents are portable structures in which the investment made in construction is not lost when the group moves to a new area—a sign of residential flexibility. A different kind of flexibility is indicated by the location of Ocean Bay sites, themselves. All ten Ocean Bay sites located on the coast were sited in strategic locations halfway between exposed outer-coast and protected inner-bay locations. This allowed residents the daily choice of foraging near home or traveling to the outer coast or inner bays, depending on the weather and expectation of resource availability. Thus, Ocean Bay peoples appeared to select camps that gave them the greatest number of options, and they were prepared to move those camps when local resources flagged. Artifacts from the Ocean Bay sites suggested a focus on hunting and processing.

By contrast, the Kachemak settlement pattern suggested a significant change in the nature and intensity of site occupations. Kachemak sites were found both in the midbay locations and in the inner-bay and river areas. This shift is consistent with the development of a more intensive summer salmon fishery. Recall that net sinkers and *ulu* processing knives become abundant in this time period. The largest salmon streams discharge into the inner-bay zones, making these prime locations for salmon fishing in summer. By this time, semisubterranean sod houses, first built in the late Ocean Bay period, were well established. This signals increased investment, at the expense of portability. Sod houses take considerable labor to construct and are not designed to be moved, suggesting more permanent occupation of territories and the anticipation of continued future use of constructions. Also as seen in other archaeological studies around Kodiak, significant village aggregations are first seen in the Kachemak period. Villages occur in midbay locations, suggesting a continued interest in maintaining foraging flexibility when the people were not targeting fish in rivers. These sites are more heavily developed, with thicker deposits, clay-lined storage pits, and other features. In many of the early Kachemak sites, recent excavations by other archaeologists have also shown massive fish processing and smoking facilities, indicative of the new focus on food storage. The early part of the Kachemak period was also a time of increased cold and wet climate (Mann et al. 1998). Low winter temperatures would have lasted longer, and increased storminess would have hampered maritime foraging in winter, increasing the importance of storage.

Indications of social competition are seen in the Sitkalidak settlement patterns starting in the late Kachemak period, around 1200 years ago. Small defensive sites made up of single house features on top of defendable promontories and small islands begin to appear at this time. The ones we found were inside Sitkalidak Strait and suggest localized skirmishes between competing families. Later, during the Koniag period, defensive sites grew to include as many as 50 house pits, situated strategically around the outsides of Sitkalidak Island and along the strait, apparently for defense against nonlocal marauders. Artifacts from the Kachemak sites show a general decline in emphasis on hunting and an increase in fishing and processing tools. Ornaments such as labrets and other decorative pieces also increase in importance, suggesting greater attention to social display and competition. These new emphases become most important in the following Koniag period.

The end of the Kachemak and Koniag periods witnesses another significant expansion of the settlement system. Village sites grow larger and are primarily located in an area previously unsettled: the outer-coast zone. This shift appears to relate to the expansion of both whale hunting in open water and political competition. Locating villages in exposed coasts allowed villagers access to whale migration routes and, significantly, greater visibility of whales and approaching enemies. The largest villages were often located adjacent to large defensive sites. As mentioned previously, house size expanded in this period to include multiple side rooms and large central rooms. Measurements of house areas from Kachemak and Koniag sites around Sitkalidak also showed an increase in the variability of house areas in Koniag times. This development, which is expected when some families become larger and more powerful than others, provides our first indication of significant social differentiation. Larger houses supported larger extended families, more slaves, and more storage of food and other goods. Larger central rooms enabled wealthy families to host neighbors and allies in gift-giving potlatch feasts. Interestingly,

while hunting tools decline in proportion to other tool types on average in the Koniag period, they are strongly represented on defensive sites.

These findings were generally supportive of the model. While the Sitkalidak survey was unable to recover preserved faunal material from sites older than Koniag, additional support comes from a study of faunal remains from sites around the Kodiak Archipelago. In his dissertation research on faunal collections from other areas around Kodiak, Robert Kopperl (2003) showed that sea mammals and codfish were under increased pressure toward the end of the Ocean Bay period just prior to the shift to intensive net fishing, processing, and storage. Other results of the Sitkalidak survey and more recent research suggest revisions of the model.

One of the biggest mysteries at the present time is an apparent drop in human population (number of sites and site sizes) during the late Ocean Bay and early Kachemak. The model had anticipated population increase with the ability to feed more people as more efficient fishing and processing technologies were developed. One possible explanation is that the colder climate imposed such harsh conditions that even with the more effective fishing technologies, populations suffered for centuries. A more likely explanation is that the archaeological evidence for the early Kachemak period is poorly represented and people were actually doing well, but living in areas that have been less thoroughly investigated. Recent research suggests that people might have moved onto the larger rivers elsewhere in the archipelago. Sea-level fluctuations might also have obliterated some coastal sites from this time.

CONCLUSION

The Sitkalidak Archaeological Survey contributed new information to help us understand how maritime hunter-gatherers on Kodiak become more economically, socially, and politically complex. Many questions remain. For example, we still don't understand why political competition and emergent inequalities took more than 2000 years to develop after the shift to intensive fishing practices. Perhaps it just took that long for conditions to grow so crowded that some people could not survive the bad resource years without assistance from those controlling the more productive commodities.

It is also important to recognize that the complexity that occurred around Kodiak was much less pronounced than that seen in some other areas, such as Mesoamerica, the southeastern United States, and the Andes. Indeed, some archaeologists question the use of the term at all for these hunter-gatherer groups. What the Sitkalidak Archaeological Survey project succeeded in showing is that social evolution occurs in hunter-gatherer history, just as it does among food producers. There probably are limits to the degree of hierarchy and political centralization that hunter-gatherer elites can accomplish. Because of their greater productivities and shelf-lives, agricultural resources are often significantly more alienable from producers. This allows agricultural elites to manipulate food surpluses to a greater extent than is possible for hunter-gatherer elites. This also means that hunter-gatherer commoners often retain relatively more autonomy than peasants in some agricultural economies. It would, however, be a grievous mistake to assume that all hunter-gatherer societies were necessarily egalitarian. This research adds to a growing number of studies that show the error of such thinking.

To the Alutiiq students and Old Harbor community, this research has helped to flesh out a more detailed picture of the archaeological heritage of their region. The project itself included students from the Old Harbor School. After each season of fieldwork, the broader community turned out for exhibitions of artifacts and discussions of project results. And the Old Harbor Native Corporation is now actively protecting the archaeological sites on its land with the help of maps and inventories produced by the project. As the twenty-first century begins, the Alutiiq people of Kodiak have their eyes set firmly on the future. The archaeological past provides a benchmark, a historical record of some 7500 years, that dwarfs the most recent and often tragic 200 years since Russian contact.

DISCUSSION QUESTIONS

1. Why was archaeological work done on Sitkalidak Island in the first place? How well did Fitzhugh's research interests and goals fit with the OHNC's interest in documenting its heritage?

2. In the model outlined in this case study, what role do population growth and pressure have? What other factors help explain the changes expected?

3. How well do the data about site size, location, and density, as well as about structures, storage pits, and artifacts, fit expectations of the model? What do you think should be investigated further?

4. Do you think that agriculture is a necessary precursor to any significantly greater complexity than that observed in the ethnographic and late archaeological record for Kodiak? Why or why not? Is increasing cultural complexity inevitable or beneficial to members of a society? Be prepared to justify your opinion.

CHAPTER 5

Paths to Complexity on the Northwest Coast

Imagine walking through the Makah Cultural and Research Center (MCRC) galleries past baskets, whaling gear, house planks, fishing tackle, and dugout canoes. A wooden ramp leads into a plank house built inside the gallery. Walking up the ramp, you pass whale bones that have been carefully aligned. Inside the plank house, you immediately notice the aromas: cedar and dried fish. As your eyes adjust to the light, you begin to see, arrayed around the edges of the house, the living areas of several families. The items each family used are there sitting as if just abandoned: baskets, bentwood boxes, fishhooks of wood, clubs, and harpoons with blades ground out of thick mussel shell. The fish smell comes from dried and smoked salmon stored in the rafters for safekeeping.

The house in the museum is a replica of a house at Ozette, an extraordinary archaeological site on Washington's Olympic Peninsula not far from Neah Bay, the home of the MCRC. Ozette is extraordinary in several ways. First, it is a village site where mudslides buried houses under layers of mud. The site stayed wet over the centuries, excluding the oxygen needed by the organisms that destroy perishable archaeological materials. As a consequence, items of wood and fiber, seldom found in dry sites, were preserved. Second, the excavation techniques were very different from the shovel, trowel, brush, and screen methods one generally associates with archaeology. At Ozette, as at most wet sites, excavation was carried out by using water hoses, ranging from fire hoses to remove overburden (the sediments and soils that lie on top of the archaeological deposits) to garden hoses fitted with nozzles that gave a fine and delicate spray. Finally, Ozette was excavated at a time when relations between archaeologists and Indians in most parts of the country were at best strained, with some research undertakings marred by almost violent confrontations between Native Americans and archaeological field crews. In this turbulent time, Ozette was excavated by archaeologists at the invitation of the Makah Tribal Council and with full cooperation of the tribe (Erikson et al. 2002; Kirk and Daugherty 1978). Tribal members participated in all stages of the project, from excavation to conservation (a special problem for the water-saturated artifacts from the site) to curation of the collections, ultimately at the Makah Cultural and Research Center.

The artifacts in the museum's plank house are replicas made by Makah artisans: the actual artifacts from Ozette are in the galleries, too, displayed in cases that help keep them well preserved. Modern Makah also built the plank house. They split the planks and assembled the house outside to allow the boards to weather appropriately. They held a number of social events and salmon bakes in the building before disassembling it and rebuilding it in the Cultural Center as part of the displays. The dugout canoes are also replicas, made by Makah carvers directed by elders who had memories of canoe making. The reawakening of traditional art forms like carving and basket making, required to make the replicas of the Ozette artifacts, is just one way in which this site and its excavation touched the members of the Makah tribe.

In 1970, when storm waves cut into the terrace at Ozette and spilled planks and artifacts from the original house out onto the beach, it was the Makah who contacted Richard D. Daugherty of Washington State University. The site had been tested years earlier, but the threat of destruction of this part of the site prompted the excavations, which lasted until 1981. Not only did the Makah Tribe request the excavations, but they were partners in the process all the way along. As the excavations began to yield artifacts, the elders identified them and explained how they were used and what they meant to Makah life.

The organization of both the exhibits and the archaeological collections further reflects the success of the Makah Tribe in taking possession of its heritage. In the galleries of the MCRC are many displays with labels in Makah and English. Photos of Makah people are seen throughout the hall, and their voices are heard. Makah people staff the museum, give the tours, and run the educational programs, which include programs in language preservation that date back to the 1960s. The artifacts from Ozette and nearby Hoko River are stored in the collections management portion of the MCRC, not according to archaeological classifications, but by Makah linguistic classes. Further, because Makah society was based strongly on gender divisions, there are classes of items that were strictly men's items, others that were strictly women's, and a class that was appropriate for either gender. Cultural rules prohibited members of one gender from handling some items associated with the other gender, and thus the Makah have developed curation rules that specify which items may be handled by male staff, which can be handled by female staff, and which can be handled by either. Clearly Makah cultural traditions permeate the MCRC in many ways, both in the public areas and behind the scenes.

The Ozette excavations were truly a remarkable collaboration between archaeologists and Indian people. The archaeologists understood the material they were excavating better than would have been possible without the Makah elders there to identify and explain the artifacts. The Makah found a new enthusiasm for their old material culture and validation for many of their beliefs about the past. The MCRC continues to be a thriving museum and a central part of Makah life, and archaeologists continue to learn from the Ozette artifacts. Ozette is just one of many places in the Northwest Coast where such collaboration can be fruitful for all parties.

DEFINITION OF THE AREA

The Northwest Coast archaeological area is defined on the basis of the Northwest Coast culture area and encompasses a strip of land running from Yakutat Bay in Alaska on the north, down along the coasts of British Columbia, Washington State, and Oregon, to end in northern California at Cape Mendocino (Ames and Maschner 1999, 17; Matson and Coupland 1995, 19–20; Suttles 1990a, 1). The crest of the coastal mountains and Cascade Range defines the eastern edge of the area, so the area encompasses the Puget Lowlands and its Oregon expression, the Willamette Valley (Figure 5.1).

The Arctic borders the Northwest Coast on the north, and there was some influence from that area. The Plateau lies to the east of the southern portion of the Northwest Coast, and there was certainly considerable interaction between these areas. Indeed, the two are often considered together in general discussions. California is the southern neighbor of this area, while the Subarctic borders it along the northeast. Anthropologists and archaeologists have developed several different schemes for dividing the Northwest Coast into subareas. There are considerable differences as one proceeds from north to south, and for this discussion we will use a simple scheme of Northern subarea, Central subarea, and Southern subarea, following Ames and Maschner (1999, 19).

A number of different chronological sequences have been developed for different regions of the Northwest Coast. We use the general chronology (Table 5.1) presented by Ames and Maschner (1999, Fig. 7) to organize our discussions.

THE ENVIRONMENT

The landscape of the Northwest Coast consists of elements arranged generally in north-to-south strips of territory—the continental shelf, the Outer Mountains, the coastal lowlands, and the Inner Mountains (Ames and Maschner 1999, 44). The continental shelf is the broad area of relatively shallow water between the coast and the deeper water to the west. In some areas, such as the coasts of Washington and Oregon, the shelf is exposed and forms a broad coastal plain. The Outer Mountains rise abruptly to the east of the continental shelf/coastal plain and include the mountains of Alaska's Alexander Archipelago, the coastal mountains of British Columbia's islands, the Olympic Mountains of the Olympic Peninsula, Washington's Willapa Hills, and the Coast Ranges of Oregon and California. In some areas the Outer Mountains form the coastline and there is no coastal plain. In these areas the shore rises steeply and is not particularly hospitable. The coastal lowlands are partially submerged by Puget Sound, and in the south they form the Puget–Willamette Lowland, including the Willamette Valley. To the east of the coastal lowlands are the Inner Mountains, primarily the Cascade Range.

The coastline is variable, with the central coast presenting a jumble of islands and inlets, many stretching island for quite a distance. This has the effect of increasing the amount of coastline for this stretch of coast. Both to the north and the south of the island and inlet areas are stretches of relatively straight coast, broken only by a few bays and estuaries (Suttles 1990a, 16).

The major rivers in the Northwest Coast, which run east–west, include the Columbia and the Fraser rivers, each draining substantial areas and extending east out of the Northwest Coast. Many of the rivers, especially those along the

FIGURE 5.1 The Northwest Coast culture area, showing the location of sites mentioned in Chapter 5.

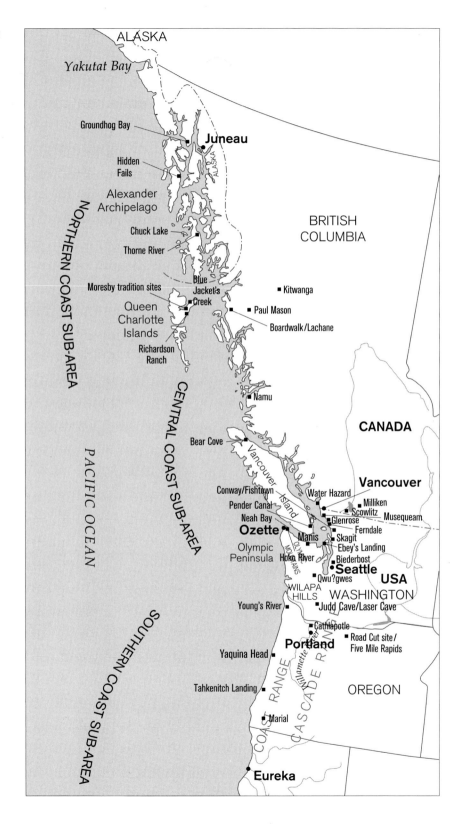

TABLE 5.1   Introduction to Northwest Coast Culture History

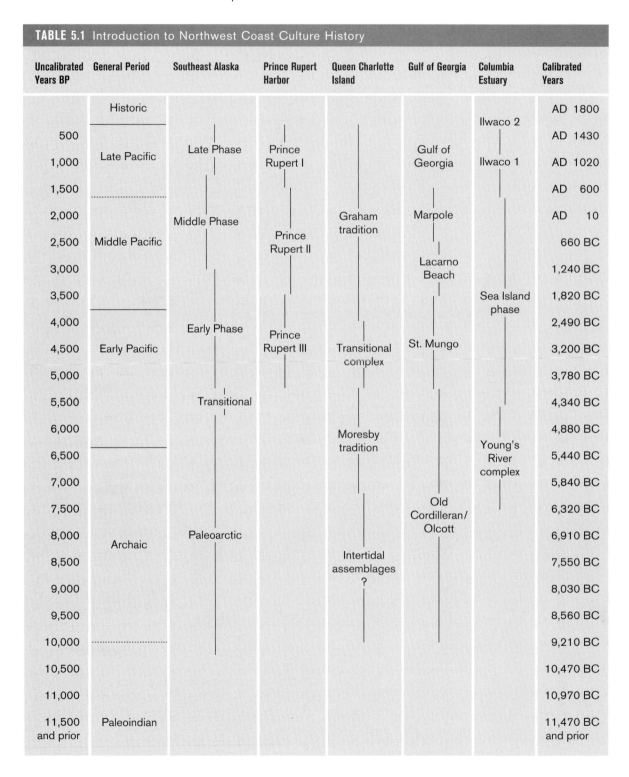

Uncalibrated Years BP	General Period	Southeast Alaska	Prince Rupert Harbor	Queen Charlotte Island	Gulf of Georgia	Columbia Estuary	Calibrated Years
	Historic						AD 1800
500		Late Phase	Prince Rupert I		Gulf of Georgia	Ilwaco 2	AD 1430
1,000	Late Pacific					Ilwaco 1	AD 1020
1,500							AD 600
2,000		Middle Phase		Graham tradition	Marpole		AD 10
2,500	Middle Pacific		Prince Rupert II				660 BC
3,000					Lacarno Beach		1,240 BC
3,500						Sea Island phase	1,820 BC
4,000		Early Phase					2,490 BC
4,500	Early Pacific		Prince Rupert III	Transitional complex	St. Mungo		3,200 BC
5,000							3,780 BC
5,500		Transitional					4,340 BC
6,000				Moresby tradition			4,880 BC
6,500						Young's River complex	5,440 BC
7,000							5,840 BC
7,500					Old Cordilleran/ Olcott		6,320 BC
8,000	Archaic	Paleoarctic					6,910 BC
8,500				Intertidal assemblages ?			7,550 BC
9,000							8,030 BC
9,500							8,560 BC
10,000							9,210 BC
10,500							10,470 BC
11,000							10,970 BC
11,500 and prior	Paleoindian						11,470 BC and prior

FIGURE 5.2 Eulachon on a drying rack.

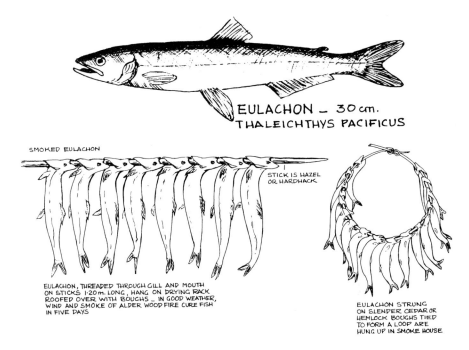

EULACHON – 30 cm.
THALEICHTHYS PACIFICUS

SMOKED EULACHON

STICK IS HAZEL
OR HARDHACK

EULACHON, THREADED THROUGH GILL AND MOUTH
ON STICKS 1·20 m. LONG, HANG ON DRYING RACK
ROOFED OVER WITH BOUGHS – IN GOOD WEATHER,
WIND AND SMOKE OF ALDER WOOD FIRE CURE FISH
IN FIVE DAYS

EULACHON STRUNG
ON SLENDER CEDAR OR
HEMLOCK BOUGHS TIED
TO FORM A LOOP ARE
HUNG UP IN SMOKE HOUSE

Oregon coast and the Olympic Peninsula, have relatively small drainage areas. A major exception is the Willamette River, which flows north through Oregon in the lowland between the coastal mountains and the Cascade Range and empties into the Columbia River. These rivers and their tributaries have important runs of anadromous fish, including steelhead and varieties of salmon that were very important in the development of the distinctive Northwest Coast way of life, at least in some areas. Eulachon, or candlefish (Figure 5.2), is a small anadromous fish that has high oil content and was also a major element of the Northwest Coast pattern. Anadromous fish were important because they entered the rivers and streams in great numbers at predictable times during the year and could be harvested in a number of ways.

The ocean also provided important resources. The nearshore waters and wetlands along the coast were very productive. Shellfish were collected from the shores and estuaries, and coastal wetlands provided plant foods, waterfowl, and terrestrial animals that live along the wetlands. Fish were also taken in the nearshore waters and in estuaries. Puget Sound is a particularly rich shallow-water environment (Ames and Maschner 1999, 44–45). Sea mammals, including otters, seals, and sea lions, could also be taken along the coast. Some Northwest Coast peoples like the Makah practiced whaling, hunting gray whales from large dugout canoes. The recent reinstatement of traditional whaling in Makah culture has been very controversial among environmentalists (Dark 1999).

The Northwest Coast is essentially a rain forest, but a temperate one. Dominant trees include western hemlock, Sitka spruce, and Douglas fir. One forest tree, western red cedar, provides a critical construction material for items as diverse as dugout canoes, houses, bentwood boxes, and baskets (see Box 5.1). Although the forests dominated the landscape, there were also prairies or open grasslands in parts of the Puget Lowlands and the Willamette Valley. The forests

ISSUES AND DEBATES

BOX 5.1

How Many Old Scarred Trees Do We Need?

The Indian and First Nation peoples of the Northwest Coast used forest products heavily for everything from dugout canoes to planks for house construction to bark for making basketry and cordage. Often these products were harvested from living trees, leaving visible scars. It is these trees, trees with evidence of use by native people in the past, that are called **culturally modified trees** or CMTs (Figure 5.3). The trees can be living or they can be standing deadwood, but they have value both to the native people and to archaeologists. If you don't know what to look for, however, you can walk right past them without even noticing.

Culturally modified trees can often be dated by using dendrochronology. Their distribution, dating, and the type of modification (e.g., house

plank harvest, bark stripping) provide the archaeologist with intimate knowledge of how people used the land in the past. One study for the Gifford Pinchot National Forest in Washington State found correlations between CMTs and trails, camps, huckleberry patches, and huckleberry processing sites, and it provided information on huckleberry patch management and continuity of culture in the area (Eldridge 1997, 3–4). For First Nation and Native Americans, these trees are both tangible remains of their heritage and proof that their ancestors made use of particular areas. In an age of reawakening of old ways, the trees show where materials once were gathered and provide silent testimony to past technologies.

CMTs receive some protection by governments in Canada and the United States; for example, they are routinely recorded on cultural resource surveys. In addition, there have been attempts to inventory some large areas outside the development process. In British Columbia, a province that has a very large number of CMTs, the Heritage Conservation Act protects those modified before 1846 (Eldridge 1997, 5). Other protections are available for trees modified after 1846, and many First Nation people are of the opinion that all CMTs should be preserved: these organic artifacts demonstrate use of specific areas of land and can be seen as support in land claim cases.

The controversy surrounding CMTs basically entails the questions of how many should be preserved in any area and whether preservation efforts should be allowed to impact local logging and development. The debate is ongoing, with litigation and legislation changing the playing field (Keith Clark 2004). Preservation of every CMT would preclude much development

FIGURE 5.3 Culturally modified tree.

and certain economically important pursuits such as logging. Should we preserve all the CMTs? And if not, which ones and how many should we preserve? In any event, trees die (and many CMTs are already dead), and they decay. Thus from the long-term viewpoint any preservation is only temporary. This is a hard issue, and one that will take some time to resolve.

Modified trees are present in many forms. In areas that were logged in the late nineteenth and early twentieth centuries, stumps with the notches cut for springboards (boards the loggers stood on to saw through the tree with crosscut saws), survive, sometimes in large numbers. In the Rocky Mountains and Sierra Nevadas, where aspen trees grow, Hispanic and Basque sheepherders in the same time span left what

is referred to as "aspen art" or **arborglyphs** (Thurman 2001). These range from simple signatures or initials to elaborate depictions of camp scenes or people. In other areas, unmodified trees can be historic, spurring preservation battles. In California, where eucalyptus trees were imported in the 1800s and planted on farms and ranches, there is often debate about preserving the groves of trees as part of the historic cultural landscape, if not the last remnant.

From a strictly archaeological point of view, these tree resources can be documented and will provide information about the past. The real question is one of heritage value. Should we preserve these bits of the past, or is it too costly to do so? The debate continues, and the ultimate answers will depend on how we value the past.

provided plant foods like berries, and corms or bulbs were also collected. The productivity of the forests decreases from south to north; thus, plant foods were generally more important in the southern Northwest Coast (Ames and Maschner 1999, 46). Deer, wapiti or elk, mountain sheep, and mountain goats were hunted on the land.

Climatic Change

Pleistocene glaciers covered large areas in the Northwest Coast, particularly the northern and central portions. Land immediately adjacent to the Pacific Ocean in Washington, Oregon, and northern California was not glaciated, however. The glaciers started melting between 14,000 and 15,000 years ago, and by 12,000 years ago the entire coast was ice free (Ames and Maschner 1999, 48–49; Carlson 1990, 60). In Chapter 2, our discussion of the process of deglaciation and its effects pointed out not only that sea level rose as water from melting glaciers returned to the sea, but that isostatic changes cause the land, which had been deformed by the weight of the great ice sheets, to spring back. In the Northwest Coast, this meant the flooding of areas of the continental shelf that had been exposed during the height of the glacial periods. Because of isostatic rebound, some areas that are under water today were actually exposed for a time after glaciation as the land rose faster than the sea level. Other areas that are currently dry also were dry land during the glaciation but flooded as the glaciers melted because the land did not rebound as fast as sea levels rose. The story of sea level rise, isostatic rebound, and coastal flooding during the first several millennia of the Holocene is a complicated one (Ames and Maschner 1999, 50–51).

EARLY CULTURES

Recall from Chapter 3 that the earliest people in the New World may well have traveled down the coast from the Bering Strait. There is currently no direct

FIGURE 5.4 Archaeologist working on mastodon bone at the Manis site, in Sequim, Washington. Note the use of a water hose in the excavation.

evidence for such a migration in the Northwest Coast area, although that is not surprising, given that the critical coastal areas where the camps of such people are expected to have been are now under water on the submerged continental shelf. The earliest site in the Northwest Coast is the Manis site, at Sequim, Washington. At the Manis site (Figure 5.4), the owners encountered mastodon tusks in the course of digging a pond. Investigation by Carl Gustafson and other archaeologists from Washington State University uncovered the remains of a mastodon radiocarbon dated to about 12,000 BP. One of the ribs of the mastodon had a fragment of bone stuck into it. From x-ray images of the rib, it was apparent that the intruding bone was a point and that the rib had grown new bone around the wound, indicating the mastodon had lived for a while after receiving the injury. Disarticulation of parts of the skeleton suggested that later, the animal may have been butchered. The absence of unequivocal artifacts in association with the mastodon bones has made acceptance of this site difficult for at least some archaeologists, however.

Some Clovis points have been found in the Northwest Coast, but they are restricted to surface finds. A cache of Clovis points, the Richey–Roberts Clovis cache, from just over the Cascade Range in the Plateau (see Chapter 6) is the closest Clovis site to the Northwest Coast.

ARCHAIC

Microblade Tradition

The oldest well-documented materials in the area consist of the two contrasting patterns, a northern one focused on microblades and a southern one with connections to the adjacent Plateau. The **Microblade tradition** is sometimes called the Paleoarctic tradition to emphasize the connections with the north. Found from the Alaska Panhandle to the area south of Vancouver Island in British Columbia, it is characterized by sites that produce microblades, as well as the

FIGURE 5.5 Artifacts for Groundhog Bay site 2: (a–d, f–h) wedge-shaped microblade cores, (e) burin, (i) microblade with a graverlike tip, (j–m) biface fragments, and (n, o) side scrapers.

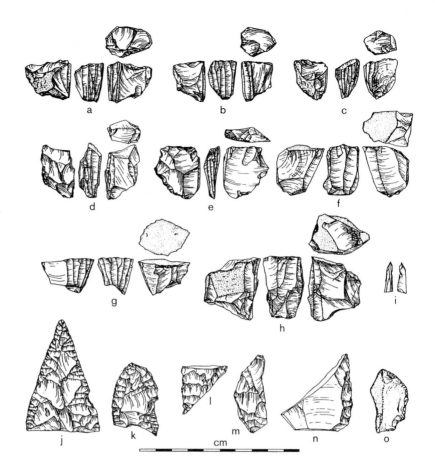

cores from which they were struck, pebble tools, and flakes. Bifaces are very rare in these sites.

Ground Hog Bay 2, located on Alaska's Chilkat Peninsula, is the earliest generally agreed upon site on the Northwest Coast, with dates ranging from around 9200 BP to 4200 BP for the earliest strata. Wedge-shaped microblade cores, microblades, scrapers, cobble choppers, blade cores, and flake cores are all found in these strata (Figure 5.5). This site is also one of the few to have bifaces associated with microblades (Ackerman 1996b, 426–429).

Other sites with microblade assemblages include Hidden Falls in southeast Alaska (dated to about 9000 BP: [Davis 1996, 421]), Thorne River (ca. 9000 BP), and Chuck Lake (ca. 8200 BP). Of these, Chuck Lake is particularly important for the animal remains found there, which include shellfish, fish, and land mammals (Ames and Maschner 1999, 68).

Among the numerous sites in British Columbia that have produced microblades are those of the **Moresby tradition** on the Queen Charlotte Islands (7500–5000 BP), the Paul Mason site on the Skeena River (5000–4300 BP), and the stratified site of Namu in Fitzhugh Sound. Roy Carlson (1991a) dates the microblade assemblage at Namu to between 8000 BP and about 5200 BP. This southern microblade site also has evidence of bifaces, suggesting some influence

FIGURE 5.6 Old Cordilleran artifacts from various sites in British Columbia: (top row, from left) three leaf-shaped bifaces, a flaked scraper, two microblade cores; (center row) snubnose scraper, four microblades; (bottom row) two pebble tools (the one on the right came from an intertidal site, as indicated by the barnacle near the flaked edge). The pebble tool with the barnacle is 4.4 inches (11.4 cm) wide.

from the south. Similarly, Laser Cave and Judd Cave in the Cascades on the southern slopes of Mount St. Helens yielded collections with both microblades and stemmed bifaces reminiscent of points from the Plateau (see Chapter 6). These deposits date to between 7700 BP and 5850 BP.

Because of the nature of the microblade cores found at the sites, Ackerman (1996, 429) suggests that Ground Hog Bay 2 and Hidden Falls represent the spread of microblade technology from interior Alaska, with roots in the Denali complex (see Chapter 4). He attributes the other microblade sites to a spread of this technology from the south.

One of the most interesting aspects of the archaeology of the Northwest Coast is the presence of saturated archaeological sites in which normally perishable artifacts of wood and fiber are preserved. The earliest basketry from a Northwest Coast site is from waterlogged deposits at the Silver Hole site on Prince of Wales Island in Alaska. Radiocarbon dated to 5945 BP, this basket exhibits characteristics similar to those found in Historic Tlingit–Haida basketry, suggesting to Dale Croes (1997) a degree of cultural continuity from the Microblade tradition into modern times.

Old Cordilleran Tradition

The other major Archaic tradition on the Northwest Coast is characterized by stemmed leaf-shaped points and pebble tools and is called **Old Cordilleran** or sometimes the **Pebble Tool tradition**. The Northern Cordilleran tradition, located further north (see Chapter 4), probably is related. First described for the Plateau (Chapter 6), Old Cordilleran (Figure 5.6) material occurs on the central and southern portions of the Northwest Coast as well. Matson (1976) attributes artifacts from the oldest strata at the Glenrose Cannery site, located on the Fraser River, to the Old Cordilleran. These deposits dated between about 8500 BP and

5500 BP and produced 11 antler wedges, an antler punch, and a barbed bone point, as well as numerous cobble tools. Only a few leaf-shaped points and knives were recovered (Matson and Coupland 1995, 70–72).

Other sites with similar assemblages and dates include the Milliken site (Borden 1961), about 80 miles (130 km) up the Fraser from Glenrose, and Bear Cove (Carlson 1979) on the northern end of Vancouver Island (Matson and Coupland 1995, 78). The Milliken site dates to about 9000 BP, and Bear Cove to about 8000 BP. In Washington, sites grouped under the term **Olcott** produced material considered to be part of the Old Cordilleran, primarily from surface contexts. The Ferndale site on the Nooksack River is the only dated site with Olcott material, and the date of 4180 ±20 BP is a minimum date for the end of the occupation there (Matson and Coupland 1995, 78). Olcott material is generally assigned dates between 5000 and 9000 BP. Much of the material from these sites is heavily patinated and includes leaf-shaped points (Cascade points), knives, and pebble tools (Matson and Coupland 1995, 78; http://www.washington.edu/burkemuseum/apop/research/html).

One of the most important Old Cordilleran sites is the Dalles Roadcut site at Five Mile Rapids on the Columbia River, on the border between the Northwest Coast and the Plateau. Excavated in 1953 by Luther Cressman (Cressman et al. 1960), this site yielded the expected leaf-shaped points and pebble tools, but burins, bola stones, and edge-ground cobbles were also recovered in sediments that date to approximately 9000 BP to 7500 BP. Large quantities of salmon bone were recovered from these levels, as well, and the bone of birds such as cormorants, bald eagles, and condors, were also found. Recent work by Virginia Butler at the site confirms that humans butchered the fish. Five Mile Rapids was an historically known fishing spot for Indians along the Columbia River, and the site deposits indicate considerable time depth for fishing in the area. The Young's River site at the mouth of the Columbia River is an unexcavated site that appears, based on surface collections, to be Old Cordilleran, as well. The assignment is based on the presence of leaf-shaped points and knives, bola stones, and what are described as net sinkers of baked clay. The Tahkenitch Landing and Marial sites extend the range of the Old Cordilleran south. Tahkenitch Landing, dated to between 8000 and 3000 BP, is located near Coos Bay. The artifacts recovered from the oldest layers at the site are sparse and do not indicate a particular cultural affiliation. The faunal assemblage is rich, however, with remains of mammals, birds, and fish. Although most of the fish could have been collected from estuaries, the Pacific hake would most likely have been collected from offshore. The Marial site, on the Rogue River, is located 80 miles (130 km) from the coast. Radiocarbon dates for the portions of the site that produced leaf-shaped points and cobble tools of the kind associated with the Old Cordilleran ranged from 8560 BP to 5850 BP (Matson and Coupland 1995, 79–80).

Summary

Archaic sites in the Northwest Coast are generally hard to find, but those that have been investigated suggest that there was greater cultural diversity on the coast at this time than at any time afterward. The evidence suggests small, mobile populations exploiting large territories and moving frequently, never staying in one place too long. Subsistence remains are sparse at most sites, but there are indications of the use of terrestrial and marine foods. These early northwesterners

FIGURE 5.7 Early Pacific period bone and antler tools from the St. Mungo site: (a) wedges and points and (b) points, a needle, and other tools.

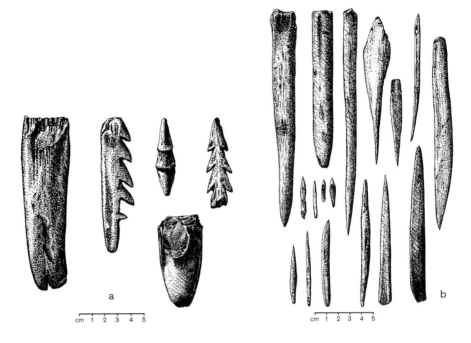

harvested shellfish, fish, and sea mammals from the ocean. There is also evidence that they hunted large mammals, especially at inland sites. Salmon, a mainstay of later diets, was exploited during this period, as indicated by the quantities of salmon bone from The Dalles Roadcut site at Five Mile Rapids.

In the northern part of the area, these early populations made microblades and did not, for the most part, use bifaces. In the south, bifaces were more common, accompanying cobble tools. The microblade assemblages are likely related to complexes in central Alaska, while the Old Cordilleran assemblages have affiliations with similar materials found in the Plateau to the east, as well as to material from the Great Basin, California, and the Southwest. Sites like Namu in British Columbia and Judd and Laser caves in Washington have both bifaces and microblades, showing an apparent fusion of the two traditions.

PACIFIC PERIOD

Ames and Maschner adopt the name **Pacific period** for the period after the Archaic on the Northwest Coast. Chartkoff and Chartkoff (1984) first described this period in California to recognize the development of complexity in that area's prehistory (see Chapter 7). Ames and Maschner (1999, 87) see general similarities between developments in California and the Northwest Coast. During the Pacific period, which Ames and Maschner (1999, Fig. 7) divide into Early, Middle, and Late subperiods, the traits that set the Northwest Coast apart as a culture area developed. Populations grew, becoming sedentary with the cyclical occupation of permanent village sites. Pithouses appeared first, but ultimately the cedar plank house became the preferred dwelling style. The economy began to be focused on acquatic resources. In many areas this meant salmon, but shellfish, sea mammals, and fish of other types were also important. Storage of fish and other resources became important, and population densities increased to levels unparalleled in most other parts of North America. Woodworking, a necessary technology for house construction, became a major industry, and the people produced cedar canoes, storage boxes, clubs, and art. Indeed, the distinctive Northwest Coast art style developed during this period, as well. Evidence from burials, village organization, and house size indicate an increasing complexity in social organization, with the development of both an elite class of nobles and a class of slaves.

Early Pacific Period

The Early Pacific period, which extends from 6400 BP to 3800 BP, saw the disappearance of microblade cores and the introduction of a variety of bone and antler tools. Microliths were made, but a **bipolar technology** now allowed use of small nodules of stone; other types of flaked stone, including projectile points and cobble tools, also are found. The bone tools included unilaterally and bilaterally barbed harpoons, bone points, awls, and punches, and antler wedges (Figure 5.7) became more common than they were in the Archaic. One reason for the greater abundance of bone and antler tools in the Early Pacific period is that many of the sites are **shell middens**, an excellent environment for the preservation of bone. These middens and their extent are also new in the Pacific period, contrasting with the more sparse shell deposits at those Archaic sites that produced shell. Examples of shell middens of this time period are the Namu, Glenrose Cannery, and Yaquina Head sites.

At Namu this period starts with a diverse economy, but in Namu 3 (6000–5000 BP), considerable amounts of shell accumulated, indicating an increase in the people's use of shellfish. Salmon were also more heavily used than in the prior levels. In Namu 4 (5000–4000 BP), subsistence remains indicate a diversification in resource use, although fishing also increased a bit. Herring was used heavily during the entire period. Hunters and fishers took sea mammals (seal and sea otter), rockfish, and cod (Ames and Maschner 1999, 137–138). Throughout the coast, people seemed to have had a diversified economy, but seafoods played an important part. **Isotopic analysis** of bone from 90 Early Pacific and early Middle Pacific period burials indicates that 90 to 100 percent of the protein the individuals consumed was from the ocean (Ames and Maschner 1999, 138).

Ground stone tools also began to replace chipped stone in many areas. Ground slate points were probably used as tips for harpoons but also could have been used on spears or as knives (Figure 5.8). **Celts** are another type of ground stone found during this period. Associated with woodworking, these artifacts probably served as the blades for adzes. Ground stone mauls, used for driving the bone and antler wedges in splitting wood, are also part of some Early Pacific period assemblages.

Burials are common during this period, and they provide considerable important information. In addition to the isotopic analyses mentioned earlier, grave goods and the patterning of burials provide information on the relative status of the people who were buried in the middens. Burials occur as early as 5400 BP at Namu, and by 4500 BP, cemeteries were also in use on the Queen Charlotte Islands (Blue Jacket's Creek) and in the Gulf of Georgia (Pender Canal). A small portion of the individuals in cemeteries of this period had distinctive

FIGURE 5.8 Early Pacific period ground and flaked points, celt (inset), and mauls (bottom row). The scale for the celt is unspecified, and the mauls are not to scale.

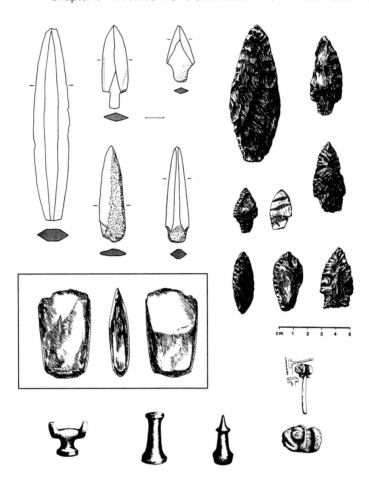

wear on their teeth, as well as patterns of tooth loss that the wearing of labrets caused. Labrets are seen in later periods as symbols of status, and the distribution of labret wear, as well as the circumstances of some of the burials, suggests that it was an indicator of status in the Early Pacific period, as well. Because labret wear was restricted to adults and was split equally between men and women, it may well have been a mark of **achieved status**, which results from an individual's accomplishments, rather than **ascribed status**, which is based on the circumstances of an individual's birth.

Graves also provide evidence about violence experienced by individuals during their lives. Skeletons with evidence of trauma have been found in a number of sites. The types of trauma include depressed skull fractures of the sort clubs would cause, injuries to the face and front teeth, and breaks in the forearm that are called parrying fractures because they tend to be incurred when a person uses the arms to fend off an attacker who is armed with a club. Decapitated skeletons are also found in some sites of this period. These data suggest conflict between groups, a conclusion that is further supported by sites in southeast Alaska built around 4200 BP on bluff tops, which would have been defensible locations.

0   in.   1

0   1   2   3
cm

FIGURE 5.9 A girdled
stone (top) and a
perforated stone. Such
artifacts, believed to have
been used as net weights,
are found in sites of the
Middle Pacific period
and later.

FIGURE 5.10 Bentwood
box recovered from the
Late Pacific period at
Ozette. These wooden
artifacts are first found in
Middle Pacific contexts
but many were found on
the floors of Ozette's
houses buried by the
mud that demolished the
houses.

Many of the patterns found in the ethnographic cultures of the Northwest Coast are foreshadowed in the Early Pacific period. Although the subsistence base is broad, there are signs of developing emphasis on coastal and riverine resources. Bone and antler implements became more common, though this may be due in part to better preservation, and ground stone became important. It is in the Middle Pacific period that the patterns really begin to resemble the ethnographically recorded lifestyle of the Northwest Coast.

Middle Pacific Period

The Middle Pacific period, in which sea level generally was stabilized, is dated between 3800 BP and 1800/1500 BP. In parts of the Pacific Northwest, however, tectonic adjustments of the land after the glacial ice had melted caused the coast to sink relative to the land, flooding areas of the coast. This process stopped around 2000 BP.

The food quest is marked at this time by intensification of certain activities, especially fishing. New methods of obtaining fish appear in the archaeological record. These include extensive use of nets, as evidenced by the common occurrence of net sinkers (Figure 5.9), an artifact type that was rare before the beginning of the Middle Pacific period. Large fish weirs appear in southeast Alaska, and there is evidence for them further south (see this chapter's case study by Rhonda Foster, Larry Ross, and Dale R. Croes, "Archaeological/Anthropological–Native American Coordination: An Example of Sharing the Research on the Northwest Coast of North America," for a discussion of a more recent fish trap). Fish weirs consist of stakes driven into the mud of the intertidal zone to direct fish, and ultimately, to catch them.

Another important development in this period is the development of storage boxes. These bentwood boxes (Figure 5.10) are made from a plank of cedar that has been scored and bent into a rectangle. A wooden bottom is sewn on, and a lid is fitted to the box. Seams are waterproofed. In ethnographic times these were the primary storage devices, although items were also stored in baskets and allowed to hang in the house rafters. The boxes first appear in the archaeological record as coffins, but it is inferred that they were being used for storage at the same time. Storage is a critical aspect of the Northwest Coast pattern, with the large population densities dependent on stored foods.

It appears that populations grew substantially during this period. Ames and Maschner (1999, 55, Fig. 4) indicate that populations on the southern Northwest Coast grew rapidly between 4500 BP and 3200 BP, peaking at 3000 BP. In the north there was a period of growth before the Middle Pacific period, but another period of rapid growth occurred at 3200 BP, with the highest populations levels attained at 3000 BP. This assessment of population growth is based on numbers of radiocarbon dated sites as indicators of population. Modeling of population on the Northwest Coast by Dale Croes and Steven Hackenberger (1988) supports this general trend.

Rectangular houses make their appearance during this period. These are probably the earliest plank houses, made by securing planks split from cedar logs to posts sunk in the ground. The planks could be removed and set up on another framework at another site, facilitating some residential mobility. At the Paul Mason site, rectangular houses are present between 3450 BP and 2950 BP, and they are arranged in two rows just as they were in villages known ethnographically.

FIGURE 5.11 Bone clubs recovered from Prince Rupert Harbor. Specimen on the left dates to circa 2500 BP, while the others are more recent.

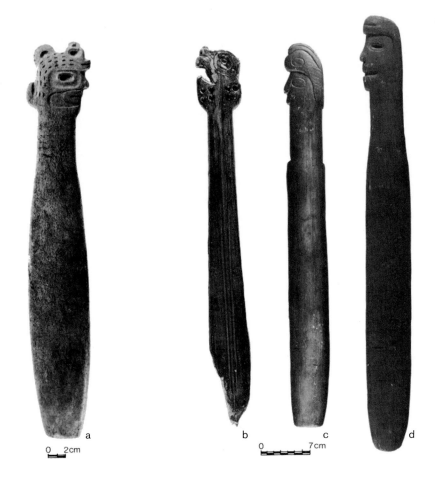

Another early site with houses arranged in rows was the Boardwalk site at Prince Rupert Harbor. Located on the lower Fraser River, the Katz site has a two-row arrangement, but the structures are pit houses.

The northern part of the Northwest Coast experienced an increase in violence. Prince Rupert Harbor provides the best evidence of this, with a high proportion of the burials from this time period showing signs of violence ("parry" fractures and depressed skull fractures), primarily to males (Cybulski 1992; Matson and Coupland 1995, 233–234). Weapons (Figure 5.11) are also present in the Prince Rupert Harbor sites, including stone and bone clubs, ground slate daggers, and bipointed ground stone artifacts (Fladmark et al. 1990, 234). Evidence of trauma and violence is much less common on the southern coast.

Social ranking developed during this period, with strong evidence by 1500 BP (500 BC). There is evidence that both individuals and villages were ranked. Individual differences in status are indicated by cranial deformation in the south and by the wearing of labrets in the north. Labret wear in the Middle Pacific period is restricted almost solely to males, and the labrets were larger than before. Burial patterns are also important indicators of status. Grave goods are found in relatively few burials, with exotic items, rare items, and the apparent

FIGURE 5.12 Three views of the Skagit atlatl, dating to about 1700 BP, show the complex design of the carving.

FIGURE 5.13 This mat creaser, recovered from the Hoko River wet site, is the oldest example of carving from the area.

work of specialized artists such as copper artifacts particularly concentrated in a few burials. Young individuals are among those with grave goods, indicating that status now was ascribed rather than achieved. There are also possible indications of the practice of slavery during this period. An anomalously low ratio of women in the burial population at the Prince Rupert Harbor sites and the presence of beheaded burials, burials in positions that differed from the norm, and burials with evidence of scalping have been pointed to as evidence of slavery, although the case is far from strong. Another line of evidence perhaps suggesting status differentiation is the knob-topped hats from Hoko River, discussed shortly.

Art objects from the Middle Pacific period are few, and most of them have been found in the Gulf of Georgia region. These include carved clubs, carved stone bowls, and a carved wood atlatl fragment. Known as the Skagit atlatl because it was found near the mouth of the Skagit River, the fragment is carved of yew wood in an elaborate representation of a creature poised above a human face (Figure 5.12). The oldest carved wood from the Northwest Coast, based on analogy with ethnographic artifacts, is a carved mat creaser from the Hoko River site that has stylized birds forming its handle (Figure 5.13). The beginnings of the elaborate Northwest Coast art style are foreshadowed in the small sample of pieces from this period.

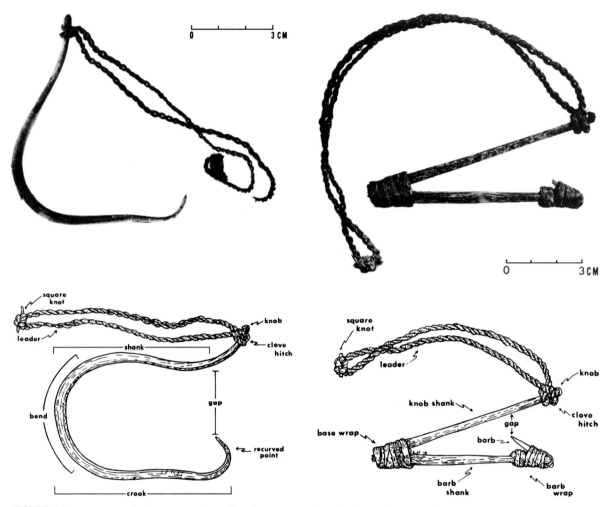

FIGURE 5.14 Bentwood (left) and composite (right) fishhooks from the Hoko River wet site.

Wet sites provide a glimpse at perishable artifacts during the Middle Pacific period. In the Prince Rupert Harbor area, the Lachane site has saturated deposits that date to between 2500 BP and 1600 BP (Matson and Coupland 1995, 231). Artifacts include wood boxes and bowls, wedges, chisel and adze handles, and canoe paddles, as well as basketry and cordage. Croes (1997) sees continuity between the basketry styles at the site and Historic Tsimshian basketry.

Hoko River (Croes 1995) is a wet site located on the Strait of Juan de Fuca on Washington's Olympic Peninsula. The site complex includes saturated deposits, an adjacent dry site, and a rockshelter. The wet site and its adjacent dry occupation date to between 3000 BP and 2500 BP. The artifacts accumulated on a growing river bar, with the wet components remaining saturated. The mat creaser shown in Figure 5.13 was one of these artifacts. Other perishable items recovered include both bentwood fishhooks and **composite fishhooks** made of several pieces (Figure 5.14). A wide variety of baskets were also found, including

large open-weave pack baskets, small fine-weave baskets, flat bags, and medium to large baskets interpreted as storage baskets. Basketry hats, tule mats, cordage, wooden wedges, a variety of pointed wooden items (including barbed projectile points), wooden floats for fishing line, the base to a fire drill, and a wooden comb were also found, along with the debris from woodworking, including split wood and wood chips. A fragment of split western red cedar may be a piece of a small bentwood box, but this is far from certain. Unmodified stones were found with lines attached in various ways. These are interpreted as net anchor stones, but they differ from stone anchors recognized at other Northwest Coast sites in that the stones themselves have not been modified. Artifacts identified as anchors at sites without the level of preservation found at Hoko River generally either have grooves ground or pecked into them or have biconical holes drilled in them. Croes (1995, 177–180) says that the Hoko anchor stones would not be recognized as artifacts if they were found without the lines attached to them.

The hats from the site are of particular interest. They are conical and have knobs on the top (Figure 5.15). This style of hat was an indicator of high status in the ethnographic period, and the finding of such headgear in the Hoko River wet deposits offers tantalizing evidence for the possible presence of status differentiation during the Middle Pacific period. Exhibit 5.1 discusses some of the other kinds of information archaeologists get from normally perishable artifacts.

Microliths, primarily of quartz, were found both in the wet site and in the dry deposits. In the wet site many of the microliths were found in cedar handles

CLUES TO THE PAST

EXHIBIT 5.1

Basketry and Cordage

Perishable materials are preserved in archaeological sites only in rare instances. In the Arctic the cold arid conditions sometimes preserve wood, bone, antler, ivory, hide, and fiber, including basketry and cordage. In the Northwest Coast area, perishable items are most often preserved in wet sites, where the saturated conditions deprive destructive organisms of oxygen they need to live. In the Great Basin and the Southwest, perishable items are preserved in arid settings in dry caves. These settings provide a glimpse at items not normally preserved for archaeologists to study. Basketry and cordage have proved to be particularly interesting artifact types.

Basketry can be made by a number of different techniques, but **twining**, **plaiting**, and **coiling** are the most common (Figure 5.16). Twined and plaited baskets have two kinds of elements—**warp** and **weft**. The warp elements run lengthwise in the basket, and weft elements run perpendicular to the warp. In twined baskets the weft elements are crossed over between the warp elements, and in plaiting the warp and weft are simply interwoven. In coiling, a foundation of material is coiled, and each coil is sewn to the adjacent coils to hold the basket together. For cordage the fibers can be twisted up to the right (**Z-twist**) or up to the left (**S-twist**). In addition, the twisted strands can be combined into cordage of two, three, or more plies by braiding or by twisting, again using the Z- or S-twist.

There are, then, a number of alternative methods of achieving the finished basketry or cordage product, be it a storage basket or twine for tying things together. In addition to the different techniques, there is also considerable variability in raw materials that can be used. The choices of a basket or cordage maker in producing the finished product are conditioned to a large part by the way the person learned the craft, generally from relatives. For that reason, there tend to be general similarities within groups, and the products of a particular set of craftspeople can be contrasted with the work of others. In short, basketry and cordage styles carry information about the group that made the artifacts, and, because methods of manufacture (the choices made in producing the basket or cordage) change through time, the products can be used as time markers, as well.

In the Northwest Coast, with the extraordinary number of wet sites with good preservation, basketry has been used to explore the development of ethnicity through time. Croes (1995, 116–132) used attributes such as basket base construction technique, hat construction techniques, ways in which handles were attached, and **selvage** or edge-finishing type to compare basketry from wet sites along the Northwest Coast. He found that the perceived division between northern and southern areas has considerable time depth (Croes 1997). He also concluded that the distinct regions of the Northwest Coast have differed from one another for at least 3000 years, and that there is considerable continuity in ethnic groups and their territories over that time (see this chapter's case study). Interestingly, the preserved basketry suggests ethnic differences in areas that had been lumped into a single archaeological unit based on stone, bone, and shell artifacts (Croes 1995, 132).

Basketry construction techniques are important in other areas, as well, as we explain in connection with the Great Basin (Chapter 8) and the Southwest (Chapter 9). One of the

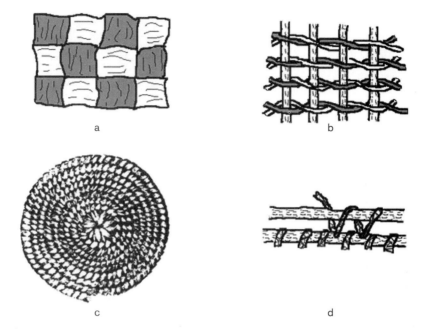

FIGURE 5.16 Techniques of basketry construction: (a) plaiting, (b) twining, (c) coiling, plan view, and (d) coiling, detail of stitching.

hallmarks of the **Fremont culture** in the Great Basin is a distinctive type of coiled basket, and the types of basket made help to define the cultural periods in the Southwest. Indeed, the spread of **Numic speakers** in the Great Basin has been investigated by examining the distribution of basketry (Adovasio and Pedler 1994).

Likewise, cordage studied by Croes (1995, 148–151) shows patterns similar to the Northwest Coast baskets, indicating ethnic continuity over time. Cordage is seen as an ethnic marker in other areas, as well, including the Northeast (Maslowski 1996; Petersen 1996). As one might suspect, though, considerable research remains to be done on this topic.

(Figure 5.17). Although some were found hafted at the end of the handle, most were inserted in the side to provide a cutting edge (Croes 1995, 180). Most of the microliths were of bipolar spalls off quartz pebbles collected near the site. Jeff Flenniken (1981) replicated the manufacture and hafting of these tools and demonstrated they could be used efficiently as knives for cleaning fish. A few true microblades of crystal quartz, two of which were hafted on the ends of cedar handles, were recovered as well.

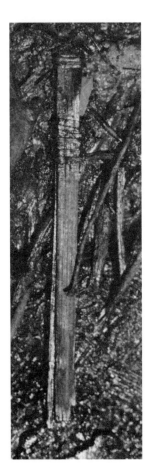

FIGURE 5.17 Hafted microlith in place in the deposits at the Hoko River wet site.

Replication has been an important part of the Hoko River project, and important information has come from replicating fishhooks and using them. Ricky Hoff (1980) replicated hooks and fishing tackle and conducted fishing experiments in consultation with Makah elders. Experiments both in the open sea and at the Seattle Aquarium provided data on the kinds of fish that could be taken with hooks of different kinds. The bentwood hooks appear to have been used for taking Pacific cod. This conclusion is supported by the fishbone from Hoko River. The composite hooks, on the other hand, were probably used on bottom fish like flounder and sculpin (Croes 1995, 99–104).

Late Pacific Period

The Late Pacific period begins after the Middle Pacific period at 1800 BP to 1500 BP and continues until exploration of the Northwest began in AD 1775 (175 BP). Between 800 BP and 650 BP (AD 1150–1300), the climate was warm and dry, while the cooling of the Little Ice Age between 600 BP and 100 BP (AD 1350–1860) variously affected the Northwest Coast. It is during this period that the patterns of the ethnographic period really became evident in Northwest Coast sites.

A major change in technology occurred during this period, namely the replacement of flaked stone tools by bone, antler, and ground stone tools. The tools in use during the Late Pacific period are very much like those of the Historic period. This change is most marked on the south and central coast; flaked tools were not particularly important in the north coast during the entire Pacific period.

Subsistence activities appear to have intensified during the Late Pacific. Salmon are important in many areas, but other resources were locally important, in some cases almost replacing salmon in the local menus. Storage, however, was a critical aspect of the economy throughout the area. One aspect of subsistence intensification is the greater use of nearshore and offshore organisms. Halibut was an important fish in some areas where salmon were not present in sufficient numbers to be a staple. Schooling fish such as cod and herring were caught in quantity, and smelt were also important. Eulachon, a type of smelt, produced rendered oil that was prized and traded widely. Whaling was practiced in areas of exposed coast, and other sea mammals, especially fur seals, were also taken (Ames and Maschner 1999, 145). Fishing was accomplished in a number of ways, including the use of a wide variety of nets, weirs and traps, and fishing tackle with hooks, weights, and lines. Toggling harpoons were used in whaling and in hunting seals.

Bent wooden boxes continued to be made and used for storage. These boxes were watertight and could be used for boiling food, as well as for storing it. As documented at Ozette, storage was also done in baskets.

Population in the Northwest reached a peak during the Late Pacific period. At around 900 BP to 1000 BP, populations reached higher levels than any previous time. Following this peak there was a decline in populations, with Modern period populations being somewhat smaller.

Remains of houses are more common in Late Pacific period sites, especially those dating after 500 BP. As discussed in the opening section of this chapter, whole houses were preserved at Ozette. The site shed light on the methods of construction and repair of plank houses, and it provided insight into the organization of material inside the house. The lessons from Ozette are discussed at the end of this section. Other houses from this period include those from the Meier

FIGURE 5.18 Quileute Chief Charlie Howeattle uses his hand adze while preparing to add a piece to the dugout canoe he has fashioned from a red cedar log.

site near Portland, Oregon. Based on excavation of over a third of the houses, this village appears to have been occupied for about 400 years, from AD 1400 to 1830, indicating considerable continuity in house use. Village arrangement in rows was well established at this time, and in many villages some houses were noticeably larger than the others, suggesting ranking of households. There is also evidence for pithouses at some sites during this period.

People continued to make many woodworking tools. These included wedges for splitting planks, as well as adzes of various sizes for hewing the timbers. Chisels are also found on sites and were used in wood carving. Adze blades were commonly made from ground stone, but ground shell blades were also made. The blades were fitted into wooden handles. These woodworking tools were used to make houses, but were also used in the manufacture and decoration of bentwood boxes and canoes. Carved wood dugout canoes (Figure 5.18) were critical in fishing, whaling, and in transportation of people and goods. Movement of house planks was made possible by the use of large cargo canoes. New tools (Figure 5.19) were added to the toolkit during this period, including pile drivers for placing wooden posts.

The evidence for social ranking changes in the Late Pacific period, when midden burial ceases all along the coast. Apparently historic practices of placing

FIGURE 5.19 Late Pacific period woodworking tools.

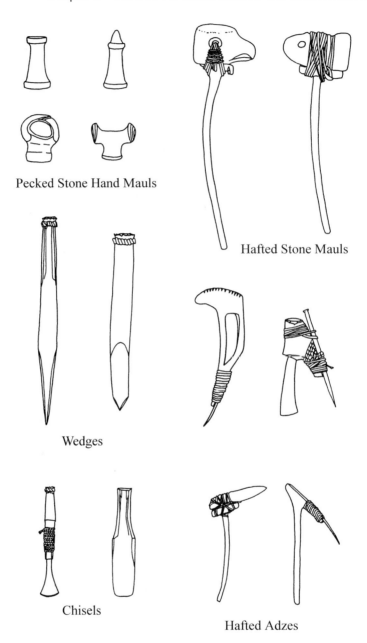

Pecked Stone Hand Mauls

Hafted Stone Mauls

Wedges

Chisels

Hafted Adzes

the dead in areas away from the village, often leaving the body exposed on a platform or in a tree, had been established. In the Fraser River area and in the Willamette Valley, some burials were made in specially constructed mounds. Significant effort went into the construction of the Scowlitz mounds on the Fraser River, and the presence of quantities of grave goods in one mound suggests that some individuals controlled considerable wealth and labor. The distribution of mounds, with some villages having associated mound complexes and others not having them, suggests that villages may have been ranked relative to one another, complementing the ranking of individuals (Ames and Maschner 1999, 190–194).

Evidence of warfare increased during the Late Pacific period. Burials provide indications of increased violence and the spread of high levels of conflict throughout the Northwest Coast. Some villages are clearly built in defensive locations such as at the top of bluffs, and refuges with temporary shelters built inside fortifications (walls and ditches) were located near some villages in southern British Columbia and northern Washington. Fortified villages were found on the northern Northwest coast, as well. Maschner (1997) suggests that the rise of defensive locations and fortifications is a result of the replacement of hand-to-hand confrontations in combat with a new technology: the bow and arrow.

The distinctive Northwest Coast art pattern (Figure 5.20) was fully developed in the Late Pacific period, although there are generally fewer art objects in many areas because the practice of burying the dead in middens ceased. Fewer burials mean fewer grave goods, and consequently fewer art objects for some parts of the coast. Carved bone, stone, and antler items are recovered from several sites. Carved stone bowls have come from sites along the lower Columbia. Figurines

FIGURE 5.20 Stone bowls from the Gulf of Georgia area.

FIGURE 5.21 Hardwood bowl carved in the form of a man replete with a braid of human hair.

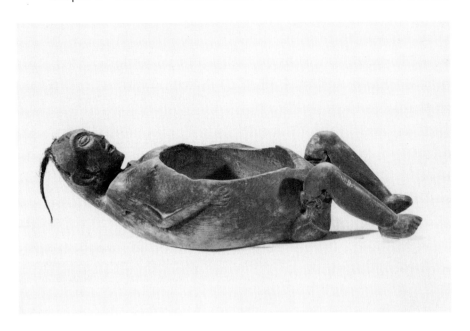

FIGURE 5.22 A whale fin effigy carved of red cedar and inlaid with 700 sea otter teeth.

of clay also are found in the lower Columbia area, the only ceramic artifacts in the Northwest Coast area. There are numerous examples of wooden art from Ozette.

Ozette provides many lessons about aspects of Northwest Coast culture. One of the most sobering aspects of the excavations for archaeologists is that over 90 percent of the artifacts recovered from the house excavations were perishable and would not have survived at a normal site. The houses were shed roof plank houses that range from 69 by 36 feet to 56 by 33 feet (21 × 11 m to 17 × 10 m). Each house had from six to ten hearth areas that probably indicate the locations of specific families in the house, though the entire population of the house may have used some of the hearths. The spatial arrangements of artifacts reflected ethnographic patterns and indicated where high-status occupants lived, as shown by ceremonial paraphernalia and whaling equipment (Kirk and Daugherty 1978, 94). Differences in size and distribution are clues to status differences between the houses, as well as within them (Matson and Coupland 1995, 266–267). A study of shellfish use at the Ozette houses examined the distribution of different species. Patterning indicated that different houses were acquiring shellfish from different portions of the coast, suggesting household ownership of resources (Huelsbeck 1989). Knob-topped hats of the type discussed earlier for Hoko River were also found at Ozette.

A number of the items from the Ozette houses were decorated. Two house planks carved with whale designs, for example, apparently were parts of decorative screens. The handles of wood-carving tools were themselves carved into designs that included human and animal heads. A bowl (Figure 5.21) was carved in human form with the legs at one end and the head, complete with a braid of human hair attached, at the other. One of the most spectacular objects was a carving of a whale fin that was decorated with over 700 inlaid sea otter teeth (Figure 5.22).

Summary

The major trends in the development of Northwest Coast culture during the Pacific period are population growth and grouping into large households, the intensification of the use of the ocean's resources, and development of ranking of individuals, households, and perhaps even villages. There is regional variation in such details of culture as basketry and art styles, and in the emphasis in food-getting activities, but many strong similarities unite the area. There have been many attempts to link the archaeological cultures of the area to the First Nation peoples who inhabit it today, people whose ancestors were present when the explorers arrived. Evidence of relationships stretching back into the Archaic period demonstrates considerable continuity in the locations of groups over time.

MODERN PERIOD

The **Modern period** on the Northwest Coast is marked by voyages of exploration. These journeys began in AD 1741 with Vitus Bering's Russian expedition, which reached southern Alaska. The discovery of sea otters was the impetus for the Russian exploitation of the area from the north. In 1774 and 1775 Spanish sailors explored the coast north of their foothold in California. Another notable voyage was that of James Cook, who sailed north to the Gulf of Alaska. These voyages paved the way for the period of fur trade expeditions (Suttles 1990c).

When the Modern period began, this region was home to the Tlingit, Tsimshian, Wakashan (e.g., Haida, Heiltsuk or Bella Bella, Nuu-chah-nulth or Nootka, and Makah), Salishan (e.g., Nuxalk or Bella Coola, Squamish, Samish, Lummi, Clallam, and Lushootseed), and Penutian (e.g., Chinook, Multnomah, Yaquina, Kallapuya, and Lower Umpqua) peoples, as well as some Athapaskan peoples like the Klatskanie, Upper Umpqua, and the Tolowa (Thompson and Kinkade 1990). Ames and Maschner (1999, 13) describe these people as "the most socially complex hunting and gathering societies known on earth." These societies had rigid, ranked social classes, usually composed of a small group of nobles, a larger group of commoners, and, at the bottom of the social heap, slaves, who were essentially property. The peoples of the Northwest Coast also achieved some of the highest population densities anywhere in North America outside central Mexico and California (see Chapter 7).

The period of fur trading lasted until about 1850, and there was considerable interaction between Indians and Europeans during this time. Beginning in 1799, permanent trading posts were established. The Russians were first, with a post among the Tlingit, and Americans established a post on the lower Columbia in 1811. The Hudson's Bay Company established a number of posts and became a dominant force in the central part of the coast (Cole and Darling 1990).

The Modern period is well represented in the archaeological record of the Pacific Northwest. Many sites have components dating to this time, often indicated by the presence of goods received by the villagers as part of the fur trade. Excavations have tended to focus on the nature of changes brought about by contact. Examples include Fladmark's (1973) excavation of an early Modern period house at the Richardson Ranch site in the Queen Charlotte Islands. He found that the house differed from the houses described for the historic Haida of the area. He was also able to show that argillite was being carved prior to the

Historic period, refuting the notion that Haida carvings of this soft black stone started after the Europeans arrived. The village of Cathlapotle, located in the Wapato Valley along the Columbia River not far from Portland, Oregon, was excavated under the direction of Ken Ames in the early 1990s; the work was sponsored by the U.S. Fish and Wildlife Service, the Chinook Tribe, and Portland State University. The village had been visited by the Lewis and Clark expedition on March 29, 1806, and there are descriptions of the village from that encounter. The excavation exposed plank houses that range in size from 200 by 45 feet to 60 by 30 feet (61 × 14 m to 18 × 9 m). Glass trade beads serve as a marker of deposits from the Modern period, and the excavations document the replacement of bone tools with metal tools after contact. The data from the excavation are serving as the basis for the reconstruction of a Chinook plank house at an interpretive center being built near the site (Ames and Maschner 1999, 12; U.S. Fish and Wildlife Service 2003).

The excavation of a fortified site on the middle Skeena River in British Columbia is another example of investigation of Modern period deposits. Kitwanga Fort (Figure 5.23), excavated in 1979 by George MacDonald, provides information about conflict after the commencement of the fur trade. Although established before European contact, the fort was occupied throughout the eighteenth century. The site was associated with the trade trail system along the Skeena River that moved eulachon oil from the coast to the interior. Excavation provided details about the construction of the site, revealing, for example, that houses had large storage pits and escape hatches. The fort has been rebuilt and is now a Canadian National Historic Site (Ames and Maschner 1999, 215; MacDonald 1989).

Archaeological work has also been done at some of the trading posts established for the fur trade. Fort Langley, in British Columbia, has seen some excavation, as has Fort Vancouver in Washington. Starting with excavations by Luis Caywood in 1947, Fort Vancouver has been a site of archaeological work for over 50 years. Early work focused on architectural features, but by the 1960s there

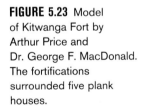

FIGURE 5.23 Model of Kitwanga Fort by Arthur Price and Dr. George F. MacDonald. The fortifications surrounded five plank houses.

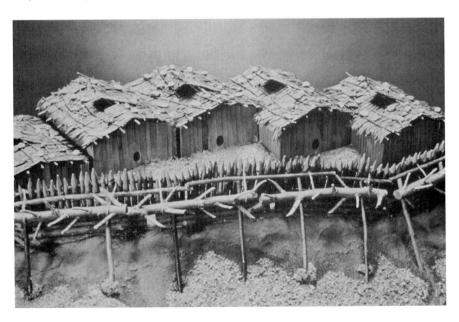

was serious investigation into the nature of relations between the various ethnic groups inhabiting the fort and its vicinity: Native Americans, Native Hawaiians, Europeans, and others. Subsequent excavation has included more work on structures. Collections from the excavations are housed at the fort, which is now a U.S. National Historic Site (U.S. National Park Service 2004).

The settlement in the Northwest Coast during the nineteenth century included diverse economic pursuits such as ports for shipping, agriculture, commercial fishing, logging, and mining. Because relations between the settlers and the Indians were often hostile, many communities built blockhouses, or wooden refuges in case of attack. Whidbey Island in Puget Sound has several of these preserved. In addition Ebey's Landing National Historic Reserve, an innovative preserve made up mostly of private land, maintains the rural agricultural landscape.

Logging, very much in evidence in the Northwest Coast today, has a long history. Many areas still have evidence of some of the earliest logging. Such evidence includes stumps with the notches for springboards (see Box 5.1, earlier), the roadbeds of logging railroads, and skid roads where logs were dragged from the cutting site to some sort of transportation. Such remains are often encountered on archaeological surveys, and some effort is being made to preserve at least part of this heritage. This leads both to arguments about just how many old notched stumps we need to preserve and to innovative approaches to preservation such as converting out-of-service railroad beds to riding and hiking trails.

CHAPTER SUMMARY

In this chapter we have summarized the development of the distinctive cultures of the Northwest Coast, which prehistorically was one of the most densely populated and socially complex areas of North America. The following points are particularly important:

- Much of the Northwest Coast area is covered by dense forests, although areas of open prairie also occur. The oceans in this area are very productive. Large portions of this area were covered by Pleistocene glaciers, though by 12,000 BP the entire coast was ice free. Adjustments due to rebounding of the earth's crust upon release of the weight of ice continued in some areas for millennia.

- The oldest site in the area is the Manis site, where archaeologists found a partially disarticulated mastodon skeleton with a bone point stuck in one of the ribs. Not all archaeologists accept the Manis site, however, and a handful of Clovis points are the only other remains of very early occupations.

- Two contrasting patterns form the earliest well-documented material of the Archaic period: the Microblade tradition and the Old Cordilleran tradition. The Microblade tradition is found in the northern part of the Northwest Coast from southern Alaska to Vancouver Island in British Columbia. Sites of this tradition have, in addition to microblades and microblade cores, pebble tools and flakes. The Old Cordilleran is found in the southern part of the area, as well as in the Plateau, and is marked by leaf-shaped bifaces (including Cascade points) and cobble tools. There appears to be an area of overlap in southern British Columbia and Washington State, where sites have produced both bifaces and microblades.

- The Pacific period (6400–175 BP) was a time of developing sociocultural complexity, significant population growth, the establishment of permanent villages with houses (first pithouses and then cedar plank houses). The economy became increasingly focused on aquatic resources, and woodworking became very important. The Pacific period had been divided into three parts: Early, Middle, and Late.

- The Early Pacific period (6400–3800 BP) is marked by the disappearance of microblade cores and the introduction of a variety of bone and antler tools. Ground tools also became important at this time. Although subsistence was broad, the beginning of the focus on marine and riverine resources is seen, and many of the sites from this period are extensive shell middens. There is also evidence of warfare.

- While many of the traits characteristic of Historic cultures in the Northwest Coast are foreshadowed in the Early Pacific period, it is during the Middle Pacific period (between 3800 BP and 1800/1500 BP) that they begin to be evident. Food storage, particularly in large bentwood boxes, along with plank houses and social ranking (both of individual and, perhaps, of villages) all develop in this time frame. Wet sites such as Hoko River, the Lachane site, and Qwu?gwes provide insights into the very important part of the archaeological record that does not survive under normal circumstances.

- It was in the Late Pacific period (1800/1500 to 175 BP) that the elements of the ethnographic pattern came together and human population was at its greatest. Ground stone, bone, antler, and ivory technology replaced flaked stone, and subsistence became more intensely focused on marine and riverine resources; storage of food was very important. The historic village pattern of plank houses arranged in rows is well established in the Late Pacific period, and some sites were fortified, adding to other evidence of an increase in warfare. There is ample evidence of social ranking at this time. Ozette and other wet sites provide glimpses of the more perishable aspects of material culture.

- In the Modern period the Northwest Coast was home to a variety of tribal groups. These peoples had rigid, ranked social classes ranging from nobles at the top through commoners to slaves. They had some of the highest population densities anywhere in North America except central Mexico and California (see Chapter 7). Many groups appear to have been in essentially the same location since the Archaic.

- In addition, Euro-American settlement brought diverse economic ventures to the area. At first, the most important was the fur trade, but logging, shipping, agriculture, commercial fishing, and mining developed over time.

SUGGESTIONS FOR FURTHER READING

For an excellent discussion of the archaeology of the Northwest Coast area:

Ames, Kenneth M., and Herbert D. G. Maschner. 1999. *Peoples of the Northwest Coast: Their Archeology and Prehistory.* London: Thames and Hudson.

Matson, R. G., and Gary Coupland. 1995. *The Prehistory of the Northwest Coast.* San Diego: Academic Press.

For a frank and moving museum ethnography of the Makah Cultural and Research Center:

Erikson, Patricia Pierce, Helma Ward, and Kirk Wachendorf. 2002. *Voices of a Thousand People: The Makah Cultural and Research Center.* Lincoln: University of Nebraska Press.

For a collection of recent papers on aspects of Northwest Coast prehistory:

Matson, R. G., Quentin Mackie, and Gary Coupland, eds. 2003. *Emerging from the Mist: Studies in Northwest Coast Culture History.* Vancouver: University of British Columbia Press.

For a popular treatment of the archaeology of the state, including the Northwest Coast and the Plateau areas:

Kirk, Ruth, and Richard D. Daugherty. 1978. *Exploring Washington Archaeology.* Seattle: University of Washington Press.

For good discussions of the prehistory of the area, as well as ethnographic and historic information on the Northwest Coast:

Suttles, Wayne, ed. 1990. *Handbook of North American Indians,* Vol. 7, *Northwest Coast.* Series editor William C. Sturtevant. Washington, DC: Smithsonian Institution.

For a collection of papers addressing the archaeology of the north coast of British Columbia with reference to native collaboration:

Cybulski, Jerome S. 2001. *Perspectives on Northern Northwest Coast Prehistory.* Archaeological Survey of Canada Paper 160, Mercury Series, Canadian Museum of Civilization, Ottawa.

OTHER RESOURCES

The Student CD, Sections H and I, gives web links, additional discussion questions, and other study aids. The Student CD also contains additional resources, including a complete list of the references cited in this chapter and in the case study that follows it. Early coastal occupations that may provide some perspective on the maritime cultures of the Northwest Coast and comparisons with the inhabitants of Qwu?gwes described in the this chapter's case study are discussed in the case study by L. Mark Raab and Andrew Yatsko, "Eel Point and the Early Settlement of Coastal California: A Case Study in Contemporary Archaeological Research" (Section D.3).

CASE STUDY

As we have made clear in a number of places, North American archaeologists increasingly work directly with Native Americans when sites and artifacts are discovered and investigated. The relationship has not always been easy, but with experience, cooperative efforts are increasingly productive. Along the Northwest Coast, the presence of wet sites with truly remarkable preservation provides archaeologists with a chance to study artifacts such as nets, baskets, and wooden implements that seldom are preserved. These sites also can give tribes a greater sense of their links with the past and become a focus of tribal heritage preservation efforts. Today many tribes have their own cultural resource management programs, staffed by archaeologists who conduct comprehensive CRM, and skilled tribal craftsmen often can recognize recovered artifacts and share insights into their use that enrich everyone's understanding of past practices. In this case study, a cultural resources director who also holds an appointment as **Tribal Historic Preservation Officer (THPO)**, the tribe's CR specialist (archaeologist), and a college professor describe their collaboration. Based on a formal cooperative agreement between the tribe as a government and the college as a state entity, the authors have cooperated in the uncovering of a remarkable wet site and nearby fish trap. Each party gives us unique insights about the finds themselves and about the value of their collaboration. In order to keep different perspectives clear, personal narratives are italicized in this case study while coauthored sections are in roman type. As you read about what these researchers have found, pay attention to the contrasting perspectives each author brings to the investigations. What are the elements that have made this collaboration so successful?

ARCHAEOLOGICAL/ANTHROPOLOGICAL–NATIVE AMERICAN COORDINATION
An Example of Sharing the Research on the Northwest Coast of North America

Rhonda Foster, Larry Ross, and Dale R. Croes

The conflict, over who "owns" the past—scientists or tribes—does not need to happen. Both groups have equal legal and other claims to be involved. If scientific technical skills and tribal cultural expertise are shared, an equal partnership can be forged that produces the best all-around results. This case study, which exemplifies how the formalized, 50/50 sharing of the research has expanded both the scientific and cultural outcomes in the Pacific Northwest, is from both tribal and scientific archaeological points of view. We describe how the Squaxin Island Tribe and South Puget Sound Community College arrived at a formal cooperative agreement that helped set the stage for developing (1) a tribal cultural resources department, (2) the first full-scale investigation in the region of a site that contains a wet (waterlogged) component, (3) outreach CRM training through online classes at the community college, and (4) interpretation of the site for the public at the tribe's new museum. Working together, respecting each other's needs, archaeologists and tribes can create the scientific and cultural results they both require.

(Cultural Resources Department-CRD) *More than a decade ago, the Elders of Squaxin Island Tribe determined the importance of protecting our cultural resources and recording our history so that we could both teach our history to our people and correct the inaccuracies that were written about us by scientific professionals. The outcome was to create a cultural resources department that would allow us to manage our cultural sites within our traditional area and to build a tribal museum. The main goal of the tribe was for staff in the Cultural Resources Department (CRD) to obtain the skills necessary to manage cultural sites. Not only did we learn the skills required in archaeology, we were gifted with an archaeologist with whom we could build a trust relationship. Later we hired our own archaeologist. In the tribe's opinion this was rare.*

What we came to realize while learning archaeology is that large portions of our culture were not being addressed by any professional archaeologist. It always amazed the tribe that the outside world viewed our past as dead and long gone, and ignored our traditional cultural properties. Archaeologists have often ignored tribes during their quest to make a "big find," and when they did, they portrayed themselves to the public as the experts about the cultures of the peoples who inhabited those sites. In Native societies this is extremely rude and unimaginable. You must understand that there is very little trust by tribes of professional anthropologists and archaeologists who do not have the skills to work with tribes to conduct comprehensive cultural resource management. In addition, it is important for the tribe to manage their cultural resources themselves, as this strengthens the connection between us and our ancient past and our ancestors, and helps us to continue our culture into the future with our children.

(Dale Croes) *As a wet site archaeologist on the Northwest Coast of North America, I typically have worked in partnership on projects with Native Americans. Initially, I worked with the Makah Tribe as a graduate student at the Ozette Village wet site, and later I directed the Hoko River wet site (Croes 1995, 1999). However, no formal cooperative agreement was signed between Washington State University, where I went to graduate school, and the Makah government for those projects. The formal cooperative agreement [with the Squaxin Island Tribe] creates the foundation for the relationship between tribes and archaeologists on two main levels. First, it sets an immediate foundation for trust that rapidly promotes the sharing of scientific technical training and cultural expertise of the tribe—expertise that is particularly important for well-preserved wet site work. Second, with the president of my state institution and the chairman of the tribe's government signing, we can point to the agreement to justify taking the time needed (as part of our regular duties) to work together as a 50/50 team on important projects. In this case, our agreement led to the discovery of the wet site on Mud Bay and to the follow-up scientific and cultural interpretation of the ancient nets, baskets, fish traps, and woodworking tools found there (see full agreement published in Foster and Croes 2002).*

We worked together to initiate the first ever field course in archaeology (Anthropology 280) at South Puget Sound Community College. A local property owner, long-time Washington secretary of state Ralph Munro, had urged Croes to visit his beach on the southern tip of Puget Sound near Olympia, to look at a shell midden site and see what it might represent. A record search at the State Historic Preservation Office revealed that this site had never been recorded. The decision was made to conduct a summer field class at the site as a training tool for students. Normally, the tribe neither condones nor encourages excavations, and it was never the tribe's intent to be involved with one. However, shortly after the start of the summer testing program we found something that led the tribe to reconsider its position about excavating at that location. The find was a twisted cedar bough rope fragment, discovered in a wet portion of the site. The students had been using a screw auger (3 in., 7.6 cm), driven to a depth of 20 cm (7.87 in.), every 5 meters (15 ft) across a 5 by 5 meter gridded site area.

A test square measuring 1 by 1 meter (3.3 × 3.3 ft) was dug in 5 cm (2.5 in.) increment levels in this area

to explore the deposits. The water table was reached at a depth of 50 cm. While using a fine stream of water to uncover delicate wood and fiber, Croes noticed that a small section of two-strand cedar bark string was being exposed. He called to Foster, who was screening, that a string was being found, and he privately hoped more would be there. The string quickly turned into a large section of preserved gill net. Croes knew it was certainly a wet archaeological site, and Foster knew it was a gift from the ancestors! As the cedar bark gill net was discovered (Figure 5.24), the tribe, recognizing that this gift could be lost forever if not protected, decided to support the decision to excavate.

(CRD): *Guided by the Creator and through our ancient ancestors, we were gifted with irreplaceable artifacts used hundreds of years ago. Our link, our culture, and our future were all incorporated at this site we now called Qwu?gwes (Quot-Qwass), which means "a place to come together, share, and gather" in Lushootseed, our traditional Salish language.*

We began co-managing the investigations of this ancient but unrecorded Squaxin Island Tribe shell midden and possible village on Mud Bay. The testing demonstrated that the site complex was much larger than anticipated. It was a shell midden 100 meters (330 ft) long, and it included a possible living area where plank longhouses may have stood, a freshwater spring, an activity/food-processing area next to the

a   b

FIGURE 5.24 (a) Cedar bark gill net as first exposed in midden. (b) Section of the net after cleaning in the lab for preservation.

housing, and a waterlogged, buried, intertidal shell midden area in front of the freshwater spring.

(Croes): *Almost anyone could recognize that we had found a fiber net, but through the cultural expertise of the tribal members, we learned what the net was made of, how it had been made, and how it had operated as a salmon gill net. We also learned how and why it probably had come to be located in this intertidal area—through the ambition of an overenthused youth.*

With careful hydraulic excavation—using water and fine-adjust hose nozzles—we were able to recover approximately 18 square meters (60 ft²) of cedar bark gill net, which was placed in a polyethylene glycol preservation solution and taken to the lab at the college for conservation.

The need for our team to become officially organized for this and other efforts to preserve cultural material, protect cultural sites, and train cultural resource technicians rapidly expanded. Under the guidance of the CRD, we formulated our cooperative agreement so that we had a formal understanding between our governments, signed by the heads of each entity, which clarified our responsibilities to each other's programs. Therefore, our state community college institution of higher education, our state archaeological regulatory institution (the Office of Archaeology and Historic Preservation), and the Tribal Council were brought together to sign the agreement on May 31, 2000 (Foster and Croes 2002). The State Historic Preservation Officer, the president of South Puget Sound Community College, and the chairman of the Squaxin Island Tribe gave speeches on forming the team and looking forward to a partnership that allowed for true comprehensive cultural resource management well beyond Mud Bay, to cover the tribe's entire traditional area. Then these leaders signed the cooperative agreement clearly outlining our responsibilities as tribal and state representatives. We believe this is the first such formal agreement in the country, and that it could serve as a model for others (Foster and Croes 2002). Now, whenever we have a need to cooperate on a project, we can point to this agreement to justify our working together, and the regulatory agency, the State Historic Preservation Officer, has a commitment to come to our aid if needed. Our agreement does not guarantee smooth coordination, but it does provide a formal commitment to be available to work together on mutually beneficial projects.

EXAMPLES OF SCIENTIFIC AND CULTURAL APPROACHES AT THE QWU?GWES WET SITE

To demonstrate the results of sharing the research between the college and the tribe, as well as the value in general of wet site explorations on the Northwest Coast to the tribes of the region we will present the scientific approach to the analysis of fiber and wood artifacts from the site complex followed by the CRD's cultural approach to the analysis of the same artifacts. This shows the contrast and benefit of an equal partnership and ownership of research. This arrangement is particularly beneficial for studying waterlogged areas at shell midden sites, which contain the 90 to 95 percent of the ancient Northwest Coast material culture lacking in other sites (see also Foster and Croes 2004). We will briefly discuss the cedar bark gill net, the upbay fish trap area, and the woven basketry.

The Gill Net

(Croes): *Once we began finding the fiber net, we were faced with the task of archaeologically recovering and preserving a sizable section of it. The tribal weavers immediately recognized the fiber to be from the inner bark of the western red cedar (*Thuja plicata*), and Foster, as a fisherperson, observed the web size and identified the probable function as a gill net for small salmon species (see her discussion below).*

I will follow through a common scientific descriptive and comparative analysis of the Qwu?gwes net. The identification of [the artifact] as a net was primarily through visual inspection, where a series of knots was established to create a web with consistent sized openings. Like all other reported Northwest Coast wet site ancient nets, the Qwu?gwes net is made of string gauge cordage tied into a net with square knots (sometimes called reef knots and/or, if collapsed, lark's head knots; Figure 5.24). The square knot is a no-slip knot, and therefore very practical for nets. Also, square knots in western nets are typically said to be tied by hand, without using a netting needle (Ashley 1944, 64–65). The cordage was twisted using two strands, and most of the cordage's single elements were twisted to the left (L, or clockwise) and plied together with a right-directed twist (R, or counterclockwise). This forms a Z lay. Z lay is also the main type recorded for twisted 2+-strand cordage at most other Northwest Coast wet sites.

Nets have been found at many other presently reported Northwest Coast wet sites. The oldest net so far dates to approximately 5000 years old (^{14}C dating) from the Lanaak wet site (49 XPA 78) on southern Baranof Island, southeastern Alaska (Bernick 1999). Therefore, netting is a very ancient technology along the Northwest Coast.

All ancient Northwest Coast wet site nets are of string gauge cordage and tied with square knots. Other characteristics vary widely, from materials used to number of elements used in making the net strings to size of mesh. The uses also vary from smaller mesh dip nets to larger web gill nets.

(CRD): The net was made from cedar bark and measured as a 5-inch (13 cm) stretch mesh, which was measured in three separate locations the day of the discovery while it was still wet. In our traditional area this type of gill net was used to fish for the smaller species such as coho, blueback, and steelhead. It is important to have a gill net in addition to a fish trap, as gill nets allow a fisherman to go where the salmon are. There are several ways to fish using this gill net including using it with a landline, drifting, and to round-house or beach-seine a school of salmon.

When we started removing the gill net in layers, it was immediately evident to me that there was something out of the ordinary. Hundreds of salmon jaws were still in the net. No fisherperson in their right mind would leave salmon in a gill net, even today. For one person to hand-make a cedar gill net would take over 8 months. Salmon left in the net would rot the net out very rapidly. Something had happened that was not usual. The possibilities are:

1. *A major disaster took place which covered up the gill net or caused our ancestors to leave in a hurry*

2. *The net was being used and got caught on a snag underwater, which would require the fisherman to cut the net, leaving a portion of the net underwater and unreachable*

3. *It is normal for a young person to ask an elder if there is any abandoned gill net nobody wants that they could use for practice. Some young person, although he or she had participated in many fishings, might have been overwhelmed by catching more salmon than anticipated, and lost or broken the net. Most fishermen could read a run, determine the amount of net to let out, and harvest only what the family could process, but I have witnessed teenagers get in over their heads, sink a boat, sink a net, and lose a lot of equipment.*

The Fish Trap

(Croes): On the other side of the point from the Qwu?gwes site at the mouth of a stream is a well- preserved, waterlogged, cedar stake, intertidal fish trap. To properly record this large structure, which consisted of over 440 stakes crossing in two perpendicular directions across the cove, we needed to do extensive mapping. We all agreed that we needed a detailed map of each stake's location and elevation before we sampled any stakes. To do this, I made arrangements for the college survey class to map the entire area, including the possible ancient village and shell midden/waterlogged site areas, and the fish trap. For this complex mapping task, the students used Professor Michael Martin's CADD/Survey program and the Hewlett Packard 48 Total Station, with a programmed Survey GX Card. The objective was to compile a complete set of generated maps that chart, categorize, classify, and visually document the entire area (Figure 5.25).

The resulting fish trap maps show the contour of the inlet, the shoreline, and the position of each of the visible fish trap stakes. Fish trap A contains the positions of 108 visible stakes, and fish trap B contains the positions of 332 visible stakes across the channel of the inlet.

With these maps completed, we decided that students would remove a fish trap stake every 5 meters and replace that stake with a visibly mapped and labeled modern stake. These sampled stakes would be placed in conservation. The recovered stakes were photographed (with stake map number) before excavation, excavated and cleaned, photographed in position, removed, measured, and photographed on all sides before being taken to the lab. Now stabilized, they are displayed in the new Squaxin museum.

Removal of the stakes allowed us to see how the stakes were manufactured. Each stake is a split cedar post approximately 10 × 10 cm (4 × 4 in.) in cross section, and the bases are sharpened for placement. Some of the stakes' points were cut with a metal axe, as seen through the sharp angled cuts. These are thought to be possibly later, post-Contact period, replacement stakes. In the central "door" area, where there are double rows of stakes and the remnants of split plank that slid between these rows, we found stakes that appeared to be adze cut—less sharp angled, followed by splitting off sections of wood (Figure 5.25). To determine whether this was an ancient structure, we submitted a sample from the outer ring of an adzed stake for radiocarbon dating. This sample returned a calibrated date of 470 years

a   b

FIGURE 5.25 (a) Mapping in the fishtrap stakes. (b) Students remove a mapped stake and point to adze cut area at bottom—this stake was found by radiocarbon dating to be 470 years old.

old, removing any doubt that the fish trap was con-structed pre-Contact (Figure 5.25).

(CRD): *Herding schools of salmon takes talent, so the fish traps were used in conjunction with one another. The side trap was used first, as it is very similar to a natural back eddy, whose slower water the salmon love to rest and pool up together in. The trap's door would be opened to catch as many chum and/or chinook salmon as needed or was possible. Once the side trap was full, or held the amount of salmon needed, the door to the side trap would be shut. Then the door to the main fish trap would be opened to allow the remainder of the school to go upstream or be caught.*

Numerous stone choppers have been found at these traps. They are perfect to use on chum salmon, which to the Squaxin people are the strongest spirited salmon, as they are determined, independent, and they will not give up. Therefore, the nets for catching chum have to be replaced much sooner than any other gear. The cedar posts used to make the fish trap would last much longer than a net, and would be the ideal way to catch a chum. When the salmon are caught in the trap, the whole village would be excited. To the Squaxin Island people, this is the best time of year.

THE BASKETRY

(Croes): *So far, three main types of basketry have been found at the Qwu?gwes site: (1) cedar bark checker-weave matting, (2) open-twined, small to large "pack" baskets of cedar splints, and (3) fine twill and checker-plaited ornamental basketry.*

(CRD): *Cedar splints open-weave baskets: When the tribe realized a portion of basket was exposed, and knew a basket would be excavated the following day, invitations were sent to "The People." In addition, other tribal groups were encouraged to be a part of bringing out the baskets. Tribal basket weavers were present to identify, interpret, and teach about the designs, materials, and weaving tech-niques (Figure 5.26). To not be allowed to participate while so-called experts were studying and interpreting your cul-ture would have been a violation to all humankind. This would have been disrespectful, and it was something to shy away from. Distrust prevents positive communication, and without communication how can anyone present a com-prehensive theory, interpretation, or view of any culture?*

The two baskets excavated that day were made of cedar splints (from roots or boughs). The design, although

a   b

FIGURE 5.26 (a) Sumiko Yashado helping to recover pack baskets with water excavation. (b) Tribal basket weavers Rhonda Foster (left), Lynn Foster (center), and Barbara Henry (right) discuss the composition of an ancient Squaxin basket.

not complete, is a statement by the weaver, and sometimes explains which family is represented. These types of baskets are utilitarian, made to haul heavy items. We call them pack baskets. The handles were woven in a special way to handle heavy loads, and a strap could be used to tie to the handles if using it as a burden basket (Figure 5.27). Most clam baskets were built to hold at least 50 pounds [23 kg]. They needed handles such as the ones on these baskets, because the basket was lifted and moved many short distances while collecting oysters or clams.

Cedar bark checker and fine twill basketry: Cedar was the main wood and fiber used to make tools, clothing, containers, etc. for "The People." The fragmented cedar bark weave could have once been either a mat or basket bottom. Whatever was made of the cedar bark strips, the process to thin and cut these small identical pieces took skill.

(Croes): With this growing basketry database, I conducted an initial and preliminary basketry attribute presence/absence comparative analysis with other ancient basketry collections from Northwest Coast wet sites to begin to see what degrees of similarity to them might be demonstrated by this new southern Puget Sound wet site. These "pack" baskets are distinctive because of the way they were constructed, with the distinct open twining, the looped

rim, and especially the double-looped opposing two-strand cordage handles and elaborate topstitching (Figure 5.27). Qwu?gwes clustered with two other recent (within last 1000 years) Lushootseed language area wet sites, Fishtown and Conway; however these Lushootseed area sites are about 150 miles [240 km] north of Qwu?gwes on the Skagit River Delta. Though baskets do not speak, I am sure the weavers of these baskets shared an ancient tradition of Coast Salish Lushootseed teachings and learning in terms of basketry traditions.

In comparison to the typical Northwest Coast stone and bone artifacts, wet site basketry is a better signal of lines of ethnicity. They indicate who the people were who carefully passed on the complex family basketry traditions from generation to generation. We have seen these styles change, but still statistically relate in style through thousands of years in different major linguistic regions established along the Northwest Coast (Croes 1995). This signaling of ethnicity follows a process called phylogenesis, demonstrating an ethnic identity style passed exclusively through a cultural group from one generation of family to the next. In our traditionally Coast Salishan region, we have documented at least 3000 years of Salishan basketry phylogenesis different from other areas and demonstrating

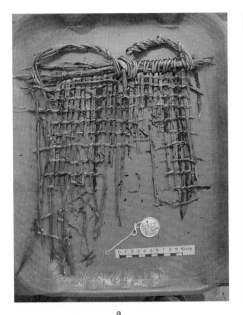 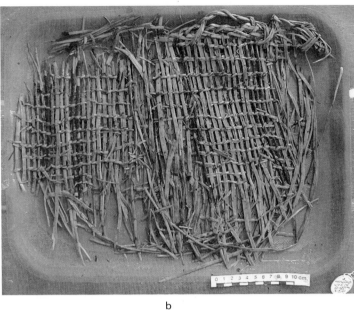

a   b

FIGURE 5.27 Two open-twined cedar pack baskets found one on top of the other. Note double loop handles and decoration applied by leaving bark on certain warp elements. The basket on the right is in full round.

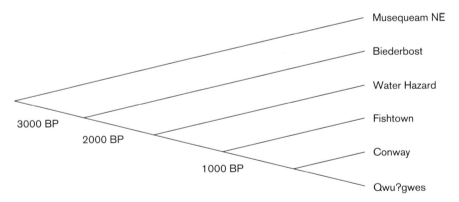

Musequeam NE

Biederbost

Water Hazard

Fishtown

Conway

Qwu?gwes

3000 BP

2000 BP

1000 BP

FIGURE 5.28 Slanted cladogram derived from Gulf of Georgia–Puget Sound wet site basketry attributes (modes) creating a phylogenesis tree of Coast Salish basketry styles and proposed ethnic linguistic interconnections for 3000 years (based on PAUP software) (see also Croes et al. 2005).

part of their deep-rooted heritage. Figure 5.28 is a phylogenetic branching chart through time, representing ancient Coast Salish wet sites including Qwu?gwes. Few of us can point to specific evidence of at least 3000 years of our cultural identity. Now, with well-preserved wet site archaeology, several major Northwest Coast ethnic groups, including the Squaxin Island Tribe, whose oral history documents this, can point to scientific proof of at least 3000 years of their identity through basketry styles.

REVIEW OF QWU?GWES SITE EXPLORATIONS

(Croes): We have provided a preliminary summary of three categories of wood and fiber artifacts from the Qwu?gwes wet site. I have considered these items from a "scientific" analysis approach and the tribe has provided the cultural knowledge passed down by multiple generations of its people. These approaches have proven to be complementary,

and have provided everyone a much better understanding of the more complete material culture common to water-logged sites.

(CRD): *All cultural sites are important to the Tribe. We now categorize them as archaeological or traditional cultural properties that include spiritual, burial, sacred, and gathering sites. It is important to stress that the tribe looks to these sites as a connection to our ancestors, who have instilled in us values that are different from modern societies. Very few people understand that the Native People who embrace the Earth, Creator, and all living things, are also the first natural scientists of the land, always striving to work with our surroundings, being a part of, not conqueror of, the things we hold as sacred and give "continuous thanks" for. The Squaxin Island Tribe embraces science (archaeology) as a base platform to build on, but recognizes the importance of including the people and their knowledge of their culture. When this happens, it is what the Cultural Resources Department calls comprehensive cultural resource management, which is much richer and more comprehensive than just basic archaeology.*

(Croes): *Wet sites are important to archaeological analysis, since they contain the vast majority of items once deposited in any Northwest Coast or other site. They also have been found dating to some of the earliest time periods known on the Northwest Coast—recent discoveries of ancient cordage, possible basketry and wooden wedges on the southern Queen Charlotte Islands, British Columbia, Canada, date to over 9400 years old.*

For some time we have investigated Northwest Coast wet sites, but they have yet to be a central focus of Northwest Coast archaeology. More and more tribes have encouraged archaeologists to start moving their focus in this direction to best understand the rich heritage of this region. Possibly it will be the tribes' interests in the preservation of their material culture that will require archaeologists to shift their training into working with the native peoples to locate and properly investigate wet sites in any part of the Americas.

ADDITIONAL TRIBE–COLLEGE COOPERATIVE EFFORT FOCUSES

Several other equally important outcomes have resulted from the cooperative agreement. For a full detailing of these efforts, see Foster and Croes (2002, 2004). Such actions, which will contribute to the future of archaeology and comprehensive cultural resource management in our region and all of North America, include the following:

- The Squaxin Island Tribe Cultural Resources Department, established to co-manage all the cultural resources of interest to the tribe within the 2.5 million acres of the tribe's traditional area.

- College-based and accredited outreach training programs, developed and conducted online with tribes and agencies. Information about cultural resource technician training is available online at this website: http://www.library.spscc.ctc.edu/crm/crm.htm.

- Ongoing archaeological field school training at South Puget Sound Community College (Anthropology 280, 12 credits) and research at the Qwu?gwes cultural site complex (2000–2004).

- Opportunities for students from the community college to work with CRD, the Squaxin Island Museum Library and Research Center, and tribal members on various cultural resource management activities, giving students personal experience in working with a tribe and a better understanding from tribal members about their culture.

- Coordination with the new Squaxin Island Museum Library and Research Center (see http://www.squaxinisland.org/) in developing public outreach and exhibits.

Larry Ross, former civil engineer and environmental specialist with the state Department of Transportation and a former student of anthropology at South Puget Sound Community College and anthropology graduate of Washington State University, now works full-time as the cultural resource specialist for the CRD. He has participated in all aspects of the cooperative agreement and adds his personal perspective of his work with the Squaxin Island Tribe:

(Larry Ross): *During my time as a student at South Puget Sound Community College and later as an employee of the tribe, I have seen what an effective tool the cooperative agreement has been to provide a framework for cooperation. As a student, I got to know and work with tribal members during the summer field school I attended at Qwu?gwes. Tribal members and students learned archaeological skills, got to know each other, and shared the experience of discovery. We students were exposed to the culture we were studying through interaction with people from that culture. For example, as basketry and cordage fragments were found, tribal weavers who were there could identify the materials used, why those materials were chosen, how the item had been made, and its use. In some cases, such as with cedar bark cordage, they would demonstrate how to make it.*

The cooperative agreement continues to provide opportunities for tribal members to connect with their culture and to teach others about it. It also provides training that will help them and the tribe to more directly co-manage the cultural resources within their traditional area for the future. Students have opportunities to work with the CRD doing research, conducting field surveys, and hopefully, gaining a personal connection with tribes that will influence their later careers to be more than just about science.

CONCLUSION

We believe we have shown not only an example of how a tribe and a scientific anthropology unit can work in sharing research, but also a general direction in which American archaeology and anthropology is headed. With tribes participating in the responsibilities of managing the cultural resources in their traditional areas, anthropologists and archaeologists will more and more have to work directly with Native peoples in pursuing their own research interests. If the desire of each party is to protect the cultural resources and share the research, an effective way to formalize that goal together is to establish a formal cooperative agreement that is signed by the heads of each of the entities (not by the cultural resource man-

ager of the tribe or an anthropologist at the college, but by their respective institutional heads). An agreement signed at that level can provide the best validation, authorization, justification, and foundation of trust to pursue these important cultural resource management goals as a formal team.

Our third cooperative agreement, extending our formal relationship, is expected to be signed in May 2006. For a full discussion of these efforts and a copy of the agreement, see Foster and Croes (2002).

DISCUSSION QUESTIONS

1. Who is sharing the research in the collaboration described here? What knowledge and skills do each of the parties bring to their work together?

2. The authors argue that having a formal agreement between the tribe and the college as a representative of the state has been important to the successful collaboration. Do you agree that a less formal agreement between Foster and Croes as individuals would have been less effective? Why or why not?

3. Why are archaeologists so interested in wet sites like Qwu?gwes, and why is it important that they seek the cultural expertise of tribal members? Why would tribes want to participate in excavations at such sites?

4. What was learned by comparing attributes in the Qwu?gwes basketry with those in basketry from other sites along the Northwest Coast? What makes this information significant to archaeologists and also to the tribe?

CHAPTER 6

Rivers, Roots, and Rabbits: The Plateau

Members of an archaeological field crew once knocked on the door of a house overlooking the Snake River in Washington. They were arriving at a party hosted by a man who had showed up at their field camp a few days before, proclaiming himself the "local archaeologist." Although the guests had been told a bit about what to expect, they were not prepared for what they would see in the basement recreation room. The walls were covered with frames full of arrowheads, knives, and spear points neatly mounted on black velvet backgrounds. Some were arranged in artful patterns. Other frames held beads of several types of marine shells traded from the Pacific Coast. On the mantle over the fireplace were two human skulls, stained green by the copper ornaments that had been included in their graves. Another skull, flanked by the host's favorite stone tools and bits of green, corroded copper, looked up from inside the glass-topped coffee table in front of the large, comfortable sofa. The host seemed proudest of a work in progress in the recreation room, for he visibly enjoyed showing everyone where he was covering his air conditioner ducting with notched cobble net weights.

Unfortunately, collections like this are all too common on the Plateau, particularly along the Columbia and Lower Snake rivers. There is a long tradition of looting sites for the artifacts they contain. Many of the large village sites yield spectacular numbers of arrowheads and fancy ground stone objects like the clubs called "slave killers," which are often carved in animal shapes. In the past there was a lucrative market in material from these sites, and a simple search of the World Wide Web will show that such items still bring a good price. Indeed, the host of the party offers material for sale on the web, still proclaiming himself an archaeologist. He says on his website that all the artifacts he has for sale are authentic and come from private land, making them legal.

Stories about the relic hunters abound. A book on Columbia River archaeology published in 1959 describes this type of collecting and illustrates something of the lore of the old-time relic hunters (Strong 1959, 149–152). The author reports that collectors working a site on the Deschutes River could expect to find a thousand points in a week and that one individual had collected 600 points from a 3 square foot (0.28 m^2) area of the site. Indeed, a collector with fewer than 5000 arrowheads was considered "just a dabbler" (Strong 1959, 150). Collecting points replaced the sale of fruit for at least one orchard owner living along the Columbia during the Depression. The book also introduces a character known as Arrowhead Charley, a legendary collector who worked the river banks for 35 years. He is said to have found over 150,000 points during his career, and he kept the very best ones for sale in case of emergency, thinking of them as his bank account.

There are also stories about relic hunters dynamiting sections of the river bank at old Indian villages and washing the sediment through sluice boxes, following the earlier practice of hydraulic gold miners. The wooden troughs had slats nailed across the bottom so that the sands and silts washed through and the heavier items like stone tools were caught by the bars and could be picked out. Another story comes from the town of Umatilla, Oregon. When John Day dam was being built, the town was in the path of the floodwaters. Between 1965 and 1966 the Corps of Engineers actually jacked up a number of the buildings and moved the town to higher ground (Umatilla Chamber of Congress 2004). A large village had once been located on the original site of Umatilla, and once the buildings had been moved, relic hunters started digging in the old town. Rangers were sent to patrol the site to prevent vandalism, but, so the story goes, the relic hunters were not easily dissuaded. They avoided the daytime patrols simply by coming at night, using the old foundations as access points from which to tunnel into the site like miners. They worked by lantern light and put tarps up over the tops of the foundations to keep their activities from being detected.

With almost industrial relic hunting going on, it is not surprising that vandalism has destroyed many important parts of the area's archeological record. This type of relic hunting, which destroys so much information about the past, is not, after all, archaeology. Not everyone with an interest in artifacts in the area is a collector, however. Groups like the Mid-Columbia Archaeological Society have come together to help preserve the past. Members are supposed to sign a code of ethics that prohibits relic hunting, and when they conduct excavations it is with the proper permits and under the supervision of trained archaeologists. One marvelous example of their work is Bateman Island near Richland, Washington. This island was a major pithouse village and was described in the journals of the Lewis and Clark expedition. By the 1960s the site had been heavily picked over by collectors, and unfilled pits were everywhere. There appeared to be no undisturbed portion of the site left to excavate scientifically. The Mid-Columbia Archaeological Society arranged to have the asphalt road that ran across the site taken up, revealing an undisturbed swath across some important deposits on the site. These avocational workers excavated the roadbed and their work that is the only record we will ever have of undisturbed deposits at this important site. Through the cooperation of amateurs and professionals, we can still learn important things about the Plateau culture area's past.

DEFINITION OF THE AREA

The Plateau (Figure 6.1) is an in-between culture area: it lies between the Cascade and British Columbia Coast Ranges on the west and the Rocky Mountains on the east. Culturally it is in between the Northwest Coast on the west and the Plains

FIGURE 6.1 The Plateau culture area, showing the location of sites mentioned in Chapter 6.

TABLE 6.1 Introduction to Plateau Culture History

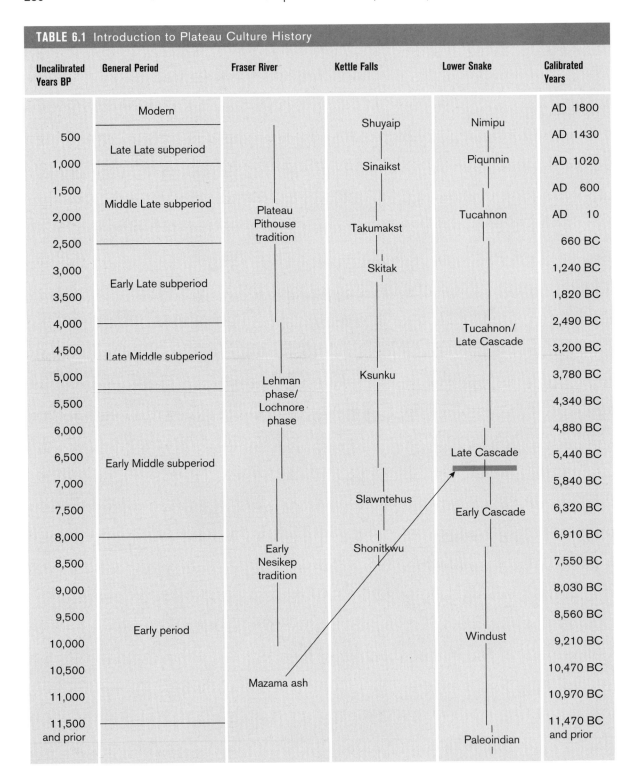

Uncalibrated Years BP	General Period	Fraser River	Kettle Falls	Lower Snake	Calibrated Years
	Modern			Nimipu	AD 1800
500	Late Late subperiod		Shuyaip		AD 1430
1,000			Sinaikst	Piqunnin	AD 1020
1,500	Middle Late subperiod				AD 600
2,000		Plateau Pithouse tradition	Takumakst	Tucahnon	AD 10
2,500					660 BC
3,000	Early Late subperiod		Skitak		1,240 BC
3,500					1,820 BC
4,000				Tucahnon/ Late Cascade	2,490 BC
4,500	Late Middle subperiod				3,200 BC
5,000		Lehman phase/ Lochnore phase	Ksunku		3,780 BC
5,500					4,340 BC
6,000					4,880 BC
6,500	Early Middle subperiod			Late Cascade	5,440 BC
7,000					5,840 BC
7,500			Slawntehus	Early Cascade	6,320 BC
8,000		Early Nesikep tradition	Shonitkwu		6,910 BC
8,500					7,550 BC
9,000					8,030 BC
9,500	Early period				8,560 BC
10,000				Windust	9,210 BC
10,500					10,470 BC
11,000		Mazama ash			10,970 BC
11,500 and prior				Paleoindian	11,470 BC and prior

on the east, and between the Great Basin (and a small portion of California) on the south and the Subarctic on the north. It is defined as most of the area drained by the Fraser River in the north and the Columbia River in the south, although part of the Snake River, a tributary of the Columbia, is included in the Great Basin (Deward Walker 1998b, 1; Willey 1966, 396). The coastal portions of both rivers are included in the Northwest Coast. The modern states and provinces covered by the Plateau include the interior of southern British Columbia, eastern Washington, northern Idaho, western Montana, northeastern Oregon, and a band that extends from central Oregon a short way into California. Although there are a number of traits that came to the Plateau from elsewhere during the ethnographic period, there is good archaeological and historical evidence that the cultures of the Plateau are, indeed, an independent development (Willey 1966, 396). Prior to the 1960s one of the main archaeological research topics in the Plateau was establishing the timing and history of the initiation of the Plateau pattern, as seen in the ethnography of the area. The chronology that has been developed is outlined in Table 6.1.

THE ENVIRONMENT

The terrain of the Plateau is quite varied, ranging from the mountains that form its eastern and western borders to the flats of the Columbia Basin and the Fraser and Thompson plateaus. The Fraser Plateau is the lowland around the upper Fraser River and varies from flat to rolling topography. South of it, along the Thompson River, is the Thompson Plateau, which is actually a series of low ridges and the valleys in between, except where streams have cut deep valleys. The relief in this area has been affected by glaciation, with the ridges becoming rounded and the valleys filling up with glacial till (Chatters 1998).

The Okanagan Highland, which straddles the border between British Columbia and Washington, is also a series of ridges, again sculpted by glacial ice into a terrain of rolling north–south hills and small plateaus, although some peaks in the area reach heights of 5000 feet (1500 m). The Columbia Basin covers much of central and eastern Washington, with fingers extending into Oregon along the Deschutes River and into Idaho between the Spokane and Snake rivers. Made up primarily of horizontal layers of basalt that escaped from ancient volcanic vents, the basin has a topography of flat to rolling hills, although the Yakima Folds form a series of low ridges on the west side. Loess, or windblown silt, covers much of the Columbia Basin, and one area of it has been cut by a number of old drainage features resulting from periodic floods caused when glacial Lake Missoula drained catastrophically. This region of the basin has been given the graphic name the Channeled Scablands (Chatters 1998).

In Oregon south of the Columbia are the High Lava Plains, a relatively flat volcanic landscape with lava tubes, old volcanic craters, and cinder cones (Sanders 1999). The plains are nearly a mile above sea level, and only the westernmost portion of this physiographic region is in the Plateau culture area. South of that is a section of the Basin and Range province, discussed further in Chapter 8. This western portion of the Basin and Range province in Oregon and further south in northern California is the home of the Klamath and the Modoc. Culturally this area is part of the Plateau. Finally, in the northeast corner of Oregon is a series of mountain ranges called the Blue Mountains. These are ranges of folded rock with valleys like the Grand Ronde and the Wallowa Valley in between. The Snake River has cut a deep gorge through the eastern part of this area called Hells Canyon (Chatters 1998).

The Cascade and Coast ranges receive a good deal of rain, as do the higher peaks of the Rocky Mountains. The Blue Mountains also receive more rainfall than the areas around them, owing to their elevation. The Plateau is considerably drier than the surrounding highlands, however, because the western mountains create a rain shadow throughout most of it. The major water sources are the rivers that flow through the Plateau. The Fraser and Columbia rivers and their tributaries, like the Thompson and the Snake, drain most of the Plateau. The Klamath River system, which includes Upper and Lower Klamath Lakes, is the major river for the southernmost Plateau. The Columbia Basin has almost no surface water away from the rivers (Chatters 1998).

Not only do the rivers provide water, they also provided one of the critical subsistence resources—anadromous fish. Plateau species include chinook, coho, sockeye, chum, and pink salmon, steelhead trout, and Pacific lamprey. The fish runs varied in the abundance of fish, the size of particular runs, and the particular species that were available from place to place (Schalk 1978), but the timing of the runs was predictable enough to permit people who were prepared for the return of the fish to harvest sizable catches, at least in the good years. Of these, chinook salmon, sockeye salmon, and steelhead trout were the most important species prehistorically on the Plateau. Large waterfalls serve as obstacles in the migration of the fish, and they prevent anadromous fish from reaching much of the eastern Plateau. The catches of fish were generally much larger on the downstream portions of the rivers, decreasing with distance upstream (Chatters 1998). In addition to fish, the rivers provided freshwater shellfish. The freshwater pearl mussel, the western ridge mussel, and several species of the floater, or *Anodonta*, have been recovered from archaeological sites in the Plateau (Lyman 1980).

A wide range of vegetation types is found in the Plateau, ranging from shrub steppe and grassland steppe in the lower-lying areas to forests and alpine meadows in the mountains. Xeric (dry) montane forest and mesic (moderately moist) montane forest, with fir trees, cedar, hemlock, and pine, are more common in the northern portions of the Plateau and in the mountains. Grassland steppe is found on the Fraser Plateau and, along with shrub steppe, dominates the Columbia Basin. Some areas of woodland transition association, an open forest of pine with some oaks, occur around the Columbia Basin, and juniper is added to this association in the Lava Highlands and in the Klamath/Modoc area of the far southern Plateau (Chatters 1998).

Many mammals were available in the various habitats of the Plateau, including elk, moose, caribou, deer, bison, mountain sheep, mountain goat, and pronghorn. Moose and caribou are common only in the north, although moose are found in the Rocky Mountains and the northern Cascade Mountains. Bison historically ranged into some of the mountain valleys in the eastern Plateau, but they are found in archaeological sites in the Columbia Basin (Schroedl 1973). Mountain goats are restricted to the mountains and generally are found above tree line. Deer (both white-tailed and mule deer) are found throughout the area in suitable habitats, as are mountain sheep. Elk occur in the mountains and in adjacent grasslands, while pronghorn are restricted to the driest portions of the Plateau. Rabbits are another significant resource, with both jackrabbits and cottontails being important (Chatters 1998).

Climatic Change

Glaciers covered much of the northern Plateau and capped the mountain ranges in the Pleistocene. By 11,000 BP, the ice was gone. Chatters (1998, 42–46) describes climate change through five broad periods. The trend in climate is one of post-glacial aridity from 11,000 BP to 9500 BP, followed between 9500 BP and 6400 BP by moister conditions in the northern Plateau but greater aridity in the Columbia Basin. Between 6400 BP and 4500 BP there was a period of cooling across the Plateau. The cooling culminated in the period between 4500 BP and 2800 BP, with wetter conditions occurring in this time range, as well. The period from 2800 BP to the present has been one of warming.

FIGURE 6.2 Volcanic ash strata at the Gore Creek site in the South Thompson River valley, British Columbia, showing two white bands of volcanic ash. The lower thin band is Mount Mazama ash (7000–6700 BP) while the upper thicker band dates to the eruption of Mount St. Helens that occurred about 3200 BP.

One geological aspect of the region that may have affected resources was the heavy volcanic activity of the region. The area is part of the volcanically active area that rings the northern Pacific, and the major eruption of Mount St. Helens in 1980 is but one in a long string of events. The eruption of **Mount Mazama**, the name given to the volcano that stood where Crater Lake is today, spread volcanic ash over a wide area of the Plateau. Often visible as a separate stratum in Plateau archaeological sites (Figure 6.2), this layer of ash provides a time marker in the stratigraphic sequence—strata above the ash postdate the eruption and those below the ash predate it. The explosion of Mount Mazama, and, therefore, the age of the ash layers found in archaeological sites, is dated to somewhere between 7000 BP and 6700 BP. The ash layer is thickest close to Crater Lake and gets thinner with increasing distance, but it is a handy reference strata through-out much of the Plateau. Other volcanic ashes, which can be distinguished from one another on the basis of chemical and optical characteristics, occur in more limited ranges and are generally thinner than Mazama ash. Where they are available and have been independently dated, however, they too can be used as time markers. In addition to the use of volcanic ash as a chronological marker, there is debate in the archaeological literature about the effect the ash fall may have had on populations living in the area about 7000 years ago (see Box 6.1).

A general series of periods has been developed for the entire Plateau, although its subregions may have patterns that vary from the periods in this scheme. The sequence starts with the **Early period**, from 11,500 BP to 8000 BP. This is followed by the **Middle period**, from 8000 BP to 4000 BP, which is divided into the Early Middle period (8000–5300 BP) and the Late Middle period (5300–4000 BP). The **Late period** then extends from 4000 BP to AD 1720, with three subdivisions—the Early Late period (4000–2500 BP), the Middle Late period (2500–1500/1000 BP), and the Late Late period (1500/1000 BP to AD 1720) (Chatters and Pokotylo 1998). These periods are shown in Table 6.1.

EARLY CULTURES

First Settlement: The Early Period (11,500–8000 BP)

Pre-Clovis evidence is lacking from the Plateau, and even evidence of Clovis age occupation is relatively scarce. The Richey–Roberts Clovis cache (also called the East Wenatchee Clovis cache) was mentioned in Chapter 5. It is the only site in the Plateau with Clovis materials in place in archaeological deposits. All other Clovis finds are scattered surface artifacts, and these are scarce. The Richey–Roberts Clovis cache was discovered in an orchard near Wenatchee, Washington,

BOX 6.1

Volcanoes and Human Settlement

May 18, 1980. I (Gross) am lying in a sleeping bag camped in west central Idaho at the Washington State University Anthropology Department Pig Roast. It's 8:20 in the morning when my wife, my dog, and I are awakened by what sounds like two sonic booms. We scratch our heads because we can't recall the last time we heard a sonic boom in this area, but don't think too much more about it as we get up, socialize a bit, and then pack to return to Pullman, Washington. We get home in the early afternoon and find ourselves standing on the front lawn of our little rental house with our neighbors (flintknapper Jeff Flenniken and his wife and son), watching an ominous line of dark clouds roll toward us from the west. My wife says, "If I didn't know better, I'd think we were watching a Texas squall line and I'd be looking for a tornado shelter." Young Josh Flenniken says, "Maybe it's something from the volcano." We pat Josh on the head and say "Sure" as we wander back into the house. Though we had been following the news of the rumblings and spewings foreshadowing an eruption of Mount St. Helens, none of us had listened to the news that day. If we had, we would have realized the sonic booms we heard all the way over in Idaho were the sounds of the eruption and that the roiling black clouds were volcanic ash that was to float down on Pullman later that afternoon, covering everything with a concretelike grayish-white powder. It got so dark that the birds began to sing, as they do at dusk.

None of us knew what effect the ash would have on us, but soon everyone in Pullman and most of the rest of eastern Washington was wearing a painter's mask around town. We avoided driving because we feared the fine glass shards of the ash would destroy car engines. School was closed the next day; the stores quickly sold out of painter's masks, and people generally stayed inside. Many worried that supply trucks would not be driving the ash-strewn roads, and the stores sold out of beer!

Volcanism is nothing new in the Northwest. As we discuss in this chapter, volcanic ash layers are often encountered in archaeological and geological profiles. Ash layers from Mount Mazama are used as stratigraphic markers throughout the Plateau, as well as in the northern Great Basin (see David Hurst Thomas's case study in Chapter 8, "Deep-Site Excavation at Gatecliff Shelter, Nevada"). Other volcanoes also have distinctive ashes that can be identified; Glacier Peak ash has been cataloged, as has ash from earlier eruptions of Mount St. Helens. Knowing that the Plateau has been covered in ash a number of times in the past, a natural question is: "What effect did the ash fall have on the people living there?"

The area around Fort Rock Cave in the part of Oregon included in the Northern Great Basin was abandoned after the Mazama eruption. Fort Rock Cave is closer to Mount Mazama than are most parts of the Plateau, and its eruption in the seventh millennium BP coincided with the beginning of a long dry period that might well have led to depopulation of the area even without the volcanic ash. On the other hand, in the Southwest (Chapter 9), the dark-colored, coarse ash or cinders from the eruption that created Sunset Crater are seen as increasing agricultural productivity by holding solar heat and providing mulch.

In the Plateau, an extreme view is that widespread volcanic ash would have made the area uninhabitable. The argument is that the rain of ash would have killed off fish, especially the all-important salmon. It then would have taken a long time for the runs to recover to a point that salmon could again be a mainstay of the diet. It also has been argued that the ash might have hurt plant foods, not only affecting people directly but exerting the indirect effect of reducing the animal populations that fed on the plants—animals like deer, pronghorn, and rabbit. According to an alternative view, recovery from the ash fall would have been rapid, with little effect on prehistoric populations.

The Mount St. Helens eruption provided a test for the arguments in this debate, as scientists had the chance to monitor recovery from the event. Although the area around the volcano itself initially was devastated, plant life returned relatively quickly. Further away, there was little effect on vegetation or wildlife, and fish runs recovered much more quickly than many had expected (Figure 6.3).

Mount St. Helens is rumbling again, sending up small (actually tiny in comparison to the

FIGURE 6.3 Recovery of vegetation 14 years after the 1980 Mount St. Helens eruption.

1980 eruption) bursts of steam and ash almost daily. We may have a chance to see the effects of ash fall firsthand again in the near future, or the mountain may simply blow off a little more steam and then get quiet again for a while. While it rumbles, we are reminded that volcanism may have shaped some of the past events in the areas covered in this chapter.

in 1987. Peter J. Mehringer, Jr., of Washington State University conducted brief excavations in 1988, and Michael Gramly of the Buffalo Museum of Science in Buffalo, New York, conducted a second excavation.

A large number of Clovis points have been found at this site, along with other flaked bifacial and unifacial stone tools and bone rods, all of which appear to have been in a cache. Blood residue studies of points and knives from the cache suggest that some specimens bear traces of blood from bison, deer, members of the rabbit family, and humans. Finding human blood does not necessarily indicate violence, however, as flintknappers often cut themselves in the process of making stone tools, and the users of tools may accidentally cut themselves, as well. Another aspect of the cache that is remarkable is that the Clovis points are large, including some of the largest ever found (Figure 6.4). Gramley suggests that bone rods may have been used as the runners of sleds, but Bruce Bradley refutes that suggestion and posits a ceremonial use for the rods, which he believes were lashed together end to end to form staffs or scepters (Bradley 1995). The intentional burial of the material, along with the unusual size of the points, suggests a ceremonial connection for the site (Ames et al. 1998, 103). Regardless of the nature of the site, the artifacts it contains demonstrate the presence of Clovis people in the Plateau.

Following whatever Clovis occupation there was in the Plateau, the area appears to have been inhabited by small groups of mobile hunter-gatherers who

FIGURE 6.4 Clovis points exposed in excavation at the Richey–Roberts site. Note the size of the points in relation to the person. Copper cutouts under the excavator's arm mark the location of artifacts removed earlier.

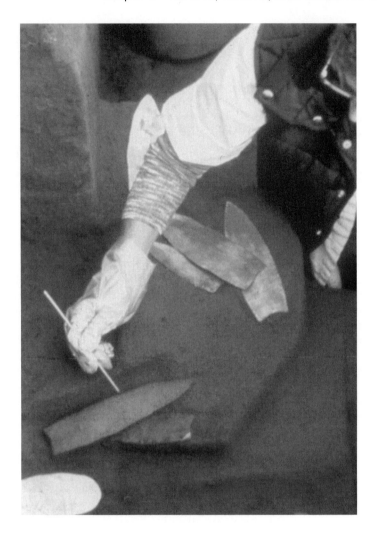

exploited a wide range of subsistence resources. Throughout most of the Plateau the first real evidence of occupation comes at this time. The Old Cordilleran tradition, discussed in Chapter 5, was defined based on material from the southern Plateau.

Also discussed in Chapter 5 was the Dalles Roadcut site at Five Mile Rapids on the Columbia, at the boundary with the Northwest Coast. This is a very important site for its time because it demonstrates that fishing was important in the early prehistory of the region. Fish bone, as well as leaf-shaped points, pebble tools, burins, bola stones, and edge-ground cobbles were recovered there from strata that are 7500 to 9000 old. Bird bone, including elements identified as cormorant, bald eagle, and condor, were also recovered. Historically the Five Mile Rapids was an important Native American fishing spot.

Faunal remains such as those found at the Dalles Roadcut site are not common because most of the sites from this period are open sites. Among sites with

bone preservation, some sites like Marmes Rockshelter and Lind Coulee are
dominated by large game, including bison, along with elk, deer, and pronghorn,
but many sites have evidence of the use of rabbits, large rodents, and birds. Fish
remains are also common, with some sites dominated by salmon and others
by sucker and minnow. Harpoons and net weights may be found in sites of this
age (Ames et al. 1998, 103–104). Interestingly, in the Fraser River Basin of the
Northern Plateau, isotopic analysis of bone from the Gore Creek burial (dated
to 8300 ±115 BP) indicates that only 8 percent of the protein consumed by the
individual in his lifetime was from a marine source, most probably salmon. The
Drynoch Slide site in the Thompson River valley, with a radiocarbon date of
7580 ±270 BP, has yielded bones of fish along with those of deer and elk. It is
clear, then, that people of this time period on the Plateau used a wide range of
resources.

Projectile points are common elements for this period, and they vary temporally and spatially. Early in the period, before 9000 BP, Windust and related
points are found (Figure 6.5). These are lanceolate points that were shouldered
and stemmed or unstemmed, often with indentations or notches in the base.
Leaf-shaped Cascade points are the points found almost exclusively between
9000 BP and 7800 BP, after which they are found alongside large side-notched
points called Northern Side Notched and corner-notched points called Bitterroot.
A Cascade point was reported to be embedded in the hip of the Kennewick
skeleton (see Chapter 3). These point types are important in distinguishing the
cultural phases for the Lower Snake River developed by Frank Leonhardy and
David Rice (Leonhardy and Rice 1970). In their scheme, the Windust points were

characteristic of the Windust phase and the Cascade points of the **Cascade phase**. The Cascade phase could be divided into an early part with only Cascade points and a late part when the notched points are found, as well. Leonhardy and Rice's phases have been very important in the development of the archaeology of the Lower Snake River and the Mid-Columbia region.

Other artifacts commonly found during this time are cobble tools, bifaces, scrapers, gravers, burins, and bola stones. Some sites have also yielded bone points, needles, bone awls, edge-ground cobbles, beads, and antler wedges. Milling stones are found at a few sites, as are anvil stones, abraders, and antler flakers (Ames et al. 1998, 103).

Marmes Rockshelter, located on the Lower Snake River, is a very important site for this period and for subsequent periods in the prehistory of the Columbia Basin. The site was excavated beginning in 1962 as part of the cultural resource management efforts for Lower Monumental Reservoir. Three years later, work was assumed to be finished, but Roald Fryxell, geologist for the Washington State University team that excavated the site, had a geological test trench cut in the floodplain in front of the shelter. The discovery of burned bone at 14 feet (4 m) below the ground surface led to continued excavation that lasted until the area was flooded by the reservoir in 1969. Efforts had been made to buy additional time by constructing a coffer dam to keep water away from the site, but this measure ultimately proved to be ineffective.

The site created quite a stir at the time of its investigation, and preliminary reports indicated that the site contained much information. Unfortunately, only preliminary reports and some specialized studies were published. Lack of a solid report on the site was a serious problem and an embarrassment for the archaeological community until 2004, when the final report for the project was published (Hicks 2004). The initiative for completing the report came from the Confederated Tribes of the Colville Reservation, and contracts were let to perform studies on the materials and to bring together the notes. Ultimately the remains of five individuals were discovered in what had been a single cremation, dated to about 11,500 BP. An additional five burials were found, and these included grave goods like *Olivella* beads, points, and bifaces (Ames et al. 1998, 105; Ames and Maschner 1999, 125; Kirk and Daugherty 1978, 36–38).

There is regional variation in the material recovered at Plateau sites from the Early period. The few sites from Northern Plateau generally have small assemblages with microblades and flake tools. As noted earlier, microblades occur in the northern Northwest Coast in early sites, as well as in the Arctic and Subarctic (Chatters and Pokotylo 1998, 74). In the Southern Plateau, most sites of the Early period appear to be short-term habitation sites marked by small, low-density artifact deposits lacking microblades. In the Wells Reservoir and at Kettle Falls there is evidence of surface structures built on the ground surface with floor areas of 118 to 162 square feet (11–15 m^2). At Wells Reservoir, hearths were found outside the structures but not inside, suggesting that these areas were primarily for sleeping (Ames et al. 1998, 106; Chatters and Pokotoylo 1998, 74). Evidence of another structure was found at the Paulina Lake site in southern Oregon. This structure had pine support posts, and rocks outlined a cleared area with a hearth in the center. Radiocarbon dates on the posts average 9490 BP. The floor space inside the structure is estimated to have been about 13 by 16 feet (4 × 5 m) (Tveskov and Connley 1997). There is a tendency for assemblages to contain more expedient tools toward the end of the period.

MIDDLE PERIOD

Early Middle Subperiod (8000–5300 BP)

Continuity with the Early period marks the Early Middle subperiod, as many elements carry forward. In the Northern Plateau the **Nesikep tradition** represents people who used a foraging strategy to hunt deer and elk (Chatters and Pokotylo 1998, 74). In the Nesikep tradition microblades and wedge-shaped cores are found, along with corner-notched points, scrapers, antler wedges, bone points and needles, and red ocher. Animal remains from Nesikep tradition sites include deer, elk, salmon, steelhead trout, and birds, as well as freshwater mussels (Pokotylo and Mitchell 1998, 83–84). Pithouses are absent (Stryd 1998). The **Lochnore phase**, apparently representing the replacement of local populations by Salishan speakers from the coast, follows in the Northern Plateau. This migration is attributed to the coastal people following salmon up the river as the salmon runs became more developed after the melting of the glacial ice. Lochnore sites date to the same period as some of the later Nesikep tradition sites (Lehman phase), suggesting a period of coexistence, if the linguistic interpretations are correct (Chatters and Pokotylo 1998, 74; Pokotylo and Mitchell 1998, 83–84).

In the Southern Plateau there is a simplification of technology at this time, although microblades are found in much of the upper middle Columbia, suggesting influences from the north. Tools generally became more expedient during this time, and some items, like needles, apparently were no longer made. Animal remains vary and appear to reflect the most abundant resource or the resource that gave the greatest yield for the effort required to get it. In some areas deer were the dominant resource, but fish, rabbit, and shellfish dominate at other sites. The use of roots as food appears to have increased throughout the period, and the **hopper mortar** and pestle were introduced (Figure 6.6), replacing millingstones and edge-ground cobbles. On the eastern edge of the Plateau, large concentrations of fire-altered rock mark the location of earth ovens (Figure 6.7) beginning around 6400 BP, and there is direct evidence of camas use by 5500 BP.

In the Early Middle subperiod, a burial pattern known as the **Western Idaho burial complex** is recognized. Defined by Pavesic (1985) based on material from collectors and museums and data from limited professional excavation, the Western Idaho burial complex is an elaborate set of burials made away from habitation sites. The burials consist of the interment of multiple individuals in **flexed** or semiflexed positions, sometimes accompanied by what may be cremated remains. Grave goods include large, distinctive leaf-shaped bifaces called **turkey tail points**; the name comes from notches at one end (Figure 6.8) (see later, Figure 12.5, as well). Also accompanying the burials are large unnotched bifaces, caches of obsidian blanks and preforms, and large side-notched points. The use of red ocher is common, and *Olivella* shells, crystals of a mineral called specular hematite, and pipes are also found. Pavesic suggests that many of the items found in graves of this complex were made especially for burial ceremonies because they are larger than their presumed function requires and show almost no wear on the biface edges. The presence of shell from the Pacific coast indicates long-distance trade (Pavesic 1985). The burial pattern is dated to between 6000 BP and 4000 BP (Roll and Hackenberger 1998, 129).

FIGURE 6.6 Drawing of a hopper mortar in use.

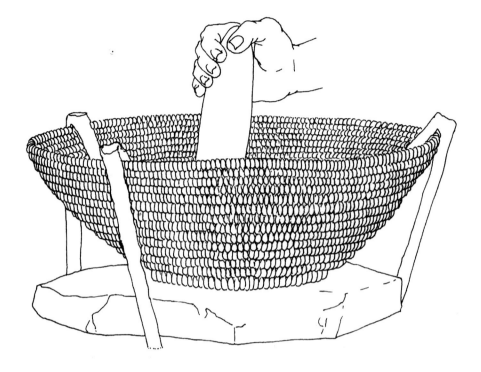

FIGURE 6.7 Earth oven from the Thompson River area. Such ovens were used in processing roots.

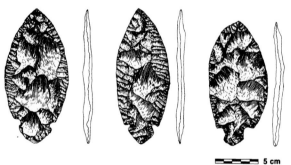

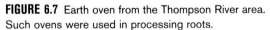

5 cm

FIGURE 6.8 Turkey-tail bifaces from the Western Idaho burial complex.

Late Middle Subperiod (5300–4000 BP)

During the Late Middle period people began to settle down in some of the best locations, places that were close to resources that could be collected during all seasons of the year. This is indicated by the appearance of sites with at least one **pithouse** (see Exhibit 6.1), generally close to the steppe–forest margins. Indeed,

CLUES TO THE PAST

EXHIBIT 6.1

Pithouses

One of the distinctive characteristics of the Plateau is the occurrence of large villages of pithouses. Pithouses are not, however, restricted to the Plateau. They provided winter homes in the Arctic (Chapter 4), and on the Northwest Coast they precede the plank houses (Chapter 5). Pithouses also occurred in many of the other areas discussed in this text, and they are especially important in California and in the Southwest. Just exactly what is a pithouse?

As the name implies, pithouses are houses built in pits. Generally, a pit the size of the desired house floor is excavated, and then a framework is built and covered to roof the structure. The pits can be shallow, perhaps only a few centimeters, or as deep as several meters. The walls of the pit often serve as at least part of the walls of the houses, although some houses are built within the pit rather than incorporating the pit into their structure. Where wood is scarce, builders used other material, such as whalebone in the Arctic and on California's Channel Islands.

Some pithouses have substantial roofs, often supported by large posts inside the house. These houses were usually entered through a hole in the roof that also served as a chimney, letting the smoke from the hearth escape. Pithouses with roofs that were not substantial enough to support a person's weight were generally entered from the side. In areas of extreme cold in the Arctic, people used tunnels for entry and these tunnels often sloped to below the floor level to make a sink for cold air and keep the heated air of the house inside.

The superstructures of pithouses can be conical, as in Figure 6.9 or domed; in the case of very deep pithouses, the roof can be flat and flush with the ground surface. Internal features

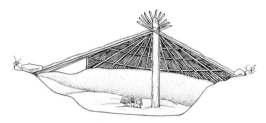

FIGURE 6.9 Harder phase pithouse reconstruction. (After Leonhardy and Rice 1970.)

like benches, platforms, and storage pits are found on the floors of some pithouses. In the Southwest (Chapter 9), early pithouses have antechambers attached to them by tunnels; later in time, a **ventilator** shaft, which is connected to the main chamber of the house by a much smaller tunnel, replaces the antechamber.

The earliest evidence of pithouses in western North America comes from southwestern and south central Wyoming (Ames 2000), where Larson (1997) has discussed 45 structures from 28 sites, with the oldest dating to between 8400 BP and 7700 BP. The oldest dates for pithouses in the Plateau come from a period between 7500 BP and 4600 BP at the Johnson Creek, Hatwai, and Givens Springs sites (Ames 2000).

Pithouses probably were built for a number of reasons, but heat conservation is certainly one possibility. Pithouses, especially the deeper ones, use the insulating properties of the soil to retain warmth. Many have evidence of earth or sod coverings over the roofs that would further have served to keep heat in. Indeed, development of pithouses is generally seen as a signal in the archaeological record of a decrease in a group's mobility. This is because the effort in constructing a pithouse–digging the pit, obtaining the wood or other material for the roof structure, and covering the framework with some material like hides, tule mats, thatch, earth, or sod–represents a substantial investment in labor and materials. A study by Patricia Gilman (1987, 541–542), which looked at ethnographic evidence of pithouse use around the world, concluded that most people who have used pithouses in recent times have done so primarily in the winter. However, there is evidence that specific pithouses were used at other times. For example, Larson (1997) suggests that the Wyoming pithouses in her study were used residentially in the summer and then as storage during the rest of the year (Ames 2000).

Although pithouses may seem unusual to our modern sensibilities, they were efficient, functional homes for many North Americans of the past.

this change in mobility was the major difference between the Early and Late Middle subperiods, as artifact technologies continue relatively unchanged. Houses at these sites are variable in size, both within and between regions. For example, houses along the South Thompson River range from 10 to 15 feet (3–4.5 m) in diameter, while on the Lower Snake River they were between 23 and 30 feet (7– 9 m), and in southwestern Idaho they were between 13 and 20 feet (4–6 m). Round, oval, and rectangular forms are known.

During the Late Middle subperiod, the diversity of animal bone in the sites is the greatest of any time in Plateau prehistory. Resources varied from place to place, however. In areas like the Lower Snake River, people ate deer and roots, primarily, while large mammals and freshwater mussels were important in the upper reaches of the Middle Columbia River. Salmon may have been more important in the north (Chatters and Pokotylo 1998, 75–76).

Salmon storage is suggested, at least at one site in the Northern Plateau called the Baker site. At this site archaeologists found small, circular pits inside three excavated pithouses (Stryd and Rousseau 1996, 196). Isotopic analysis of human bone from the Northern Plateau indicates that diets consisted of almost 49 percent marine foods (Chatters and Pokotylo 1998, 76). Stryd and Rousseau see the Late Middle subperiod as marking the beginning of the **Plateau Pithouse tradition**, a pattern understood to be very similar to the ethnographic pattern for the area. Further, they see the period as a time of logistic mobility in which people brought resources in to the residential site rather than moving themselves to the resources (Stryd and Rousseau 1996, 198). The same kind of evidence for salmon storage is not found in the Southern Plateau, however, suggesting that populations there did move to resources, but less frequently than in earlier periods.

Shell artifacts and obsidian are more common than in earlier times at some sites during the Late Middle period. This suggests the possibility that people increased trade as a means of buffering the natural fluctuation in availability of resources. Desirable trade goods could have been acquired during times when resources were relatively more abundant and traded away in exchange for food at times of relative local food scarcity. Such a buffering mechanism could have been important in allowing the reduced mobility apparent at this time (Chatters and Pokotylo 1998, 76).

Pithouse settlements suggesting sedentism become rare after 4500 BP, and there appears to have been a major population reduction in the Southern Plateau (Chatters and Pokotylo 1998, 76). Archaeologists assume that areas like the

Eastern Plateau saw relatively high mobility throughout the Middle period. Thus the end of the sedentary pithouse sites probably marked a return to a more mobile lifestyle throughout the Plateau. Although most of the settlement in the Middle period was in low-elevation settings, at the end of the period (ca. 4500 BP) there is some evidence in the Eastern Plateau of the use of high elevations for limited collecting, probably of pine nuts (Chatters and Pokotylo 1998, 76).

LATE PERIOD

It was during the Late period (4000 BP to AD 1720) that the ethnographic pattern of the area really took form. This period is divided into three subperiods, while the coming of the horse to the Plateau, which brought many changes to Plateau societies, marks the end of the period.

Early Late Subperiod (4000–2500 BP)

FIGURE 6.10 Notched cobble net weights.

The general trend in the Early Late subperiod throughout most of the Plateau is toward storage-based economies and toward a collector strategy (Binford 1980). This means the establishment of long-term base camps, intensive use of key resources such as salmon, and storage.

In the Eastern Plateau, although use of roots intensified, mobile hunting appears to continue. Based on radiocarbon dating of features thought to be camas ovens, Thoms (1989, 444) sees the time between 3500 BP and 2500 BP as having heavy root use, with a fall-off in use after this time, followed by increases in the next subperiod. Fish may have become more important in the Eastern Plateau at this time, as well, because notched pebbles thought to be net sinkers (Figure 6.10) become common on some sites there (Chatters and Pokotylo 1998, 76–77).

Elsewhere on the Plateau a shift toward the collector strategy is more apparent. Sites with clusters of pithouses become common again after a 500-year period when they were scarce. Storage pits are often associated with these pithouses; pithouses tend to be deeper and larger than before, and earth ovens also are frequently found at pithouse sites. Reuse of pithouse depressions (see this chapter's case study by G. Timothy Gross, "The Miller Site: Four Seasons of Backwards Archaeology on Strawberry Island"), and increases in the density of the associated artifacts suggests greater settlement permanence. In addition to the pithouse sites, specialized resource extraction camps appear in the archaeological record, supporting the inference that people were practicing a collector strategy. Fish, roots, game, and freshwater mussels were obtained at such camps (Chatters and Pokotylo 1998, 76–77).

Salmon appears to have become more readily available at this time because of cooler and moister climatic conditions. Large game animals, on the other hand, probably were less available because forest cover increased. Increases in salmon use are indicated on the Columbia, Fraser, and Thompson rivers, both by high densities of salmon bone in sites and by isotopic analysis of human skeletons from this subperiod, which indicate that more than half the protein in the diets came from marine sources (Chatters and Pokotylo 1998, 76–77). Along the Lower Snake River an increase in net weights and **harpoon valves** (Figure 6.11) in artifact inventories indicates fishing, although fish bone is only the third most common type of bone in the faunal assemblages from sites of this time, and deer

FIGURE 6.11 Harpoon valves and reconstructions of their use.

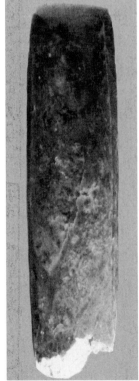

FIGURE 6.12 Nephrite adze.

dominate these collections. Deer clearly was important, but artifact assemblages do not contain large quantities of projectile points; instead they have large numbers of cobble tools, fishing-related artifacts, and milling equipment (hopper mortar bases and pestles) (Ames et al. 1998, 112).

Trade items are less common in this subperiod, and stone tools are generally made of locally available materials, often of low quality. Regional styles of projectile points develop. A notable exception to the lack of trade items is the recovery of **steatite** beads and nephrite adzes (Figure 6.12) in the Upper and Middle Columbia River areas. These artifacts originated in the Fraser River area (Chatters and Pokotylo 1998, 76–77; Hayden and Schulting 1997).

Middle Late Subperiod (2500–1000 BP)

The Middle Late subperiod saw expansion of territories and coalescence of populations into large pithouse villages, especially in the lower reaches of the larger rivers. There is also growing evidence for social inequality and for intergroup violence. Trade increases again, possibly fed by a need for prestige items to reinforce the social hierarchy.

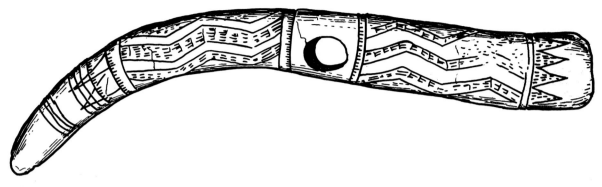

FIGURE 6.13 Antler digging stick handle.

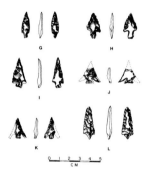

FIGURE 6.14 Arrowpoints from the Miller site.

Although most Plateau people continue to focus on salmon fishing, root crops became more important at this time. In the north, large earth ovens in highland sites indicate an increase in the use of roots. In the valleys of the Columbia and Snake rivers, people ventured out into uplands and into the arid Columbia Basin. During this time the Columbia Basin saw a boom in bison population, which may have attracted people to these arid lands, as indicated by mass bison kill sites (Schroedl 1973). Highland camps often have hopper mortar bases, suggesting processing of roots. Antler digging stick handles (Figure 6.13) are first found in the Plateau at this time. Camas roasting in the Eastern Plateau declined during the Middle Late period, however, perhaps because of drying of the meadows where the roots are found (Chatters and Pokotylo 1998, 77–78; Roll and Hackenberger 1998, 132). The bow and arrow was adopted at this time, becoming established in the south between 2400 BP and 2100 BP, but not until 1500 BP in the north (Chatters and Pokotylo 1998, 78). This is marked by the appearance of smaller points (arrowheads) in the archaeological record of the area (Figure 6.14).

Large pithouse villages, with the individual houses generally smaller than in preceding periods, were built in the lower reaches of the major rivers. Over 100 pithouses were built at some of these sites (Figure 6.15). Pithouse settlements are found in the Middle Columbia and in Hells Canyon along the Snake River by the end of this period. Chance and Chance (1985) note an increase in salmon fishing at Kettle Falls at this time.

An increase in the territory traveled by people in the course of their expeditions to resource camps may have contributed to an increase in both the quality and the diversity of tool raw materials. Either people extracted raw materials from new geological sources while traveling, or they increased the frequency of contact and trade with other groups. Trade goods increase at sites during this period, especially at the large population centers. Carved steatite, antler, and whalebone, as well as **dentalium shells** (sometimes incised), shell disk beads, pipes, stone clubs, whalebone clubs (Figure 6.16), and exotic materials like nephrite and obsidian were important in this trade (Chatters and Pokotylo 1998, 78; Hayden and Schulting 1997). Many of the elaborately carved items display art styles similar to those of the Northwest Coast, and raw materials also show similarities. Some sites, such as Wakemap Mound on the Columbia and the village sites of the Middle Fraser River valley, were located at important points

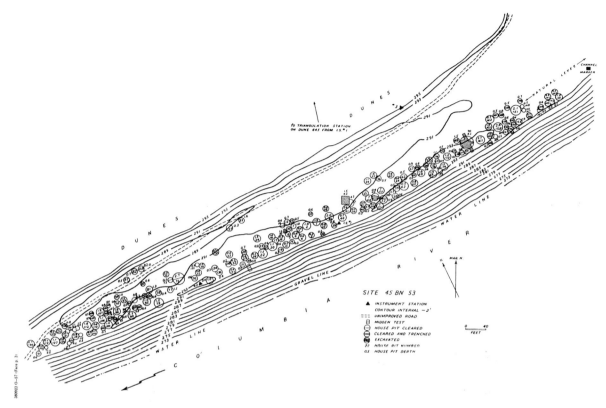

FIGURE 6.15 Map of site 45 BN 53, a Late period pithouse village site near Umatilla, Washington; circles represent former pithouse locations; 40 feet (scale) = 130 meters.

on trade routes, and their inhabitants may have been trade specialists (Chatters and Pokotylo 1998, 78).

It appears that social inequality fueled the expansion of trade, with elite members of society reinforcing their positions through the display of luxury items. Toward the end of the Middle Late subperiod, some sites have a few houses that are larger than the majority, suggesting the presence of elite households. Elaboration of some burials also occurs, and there are concentrations in the occurrence of exotic trade items, again suggesting the presence of elite individuals. Violence also is evident in this period. The occurrence of projectile points embedded in human bone indicates conflict, as do fortified sites and the location of sites on islands, which are hard to attack. People built storage facilities in caves, also suggesting a defensive strategy relating to the critical stored resources. People may have marked their territories both with the distinctive rock art and with the large cemeteries that appear in this subperiod.

Late Late Subperiod (1000 BP to AD 1720)

The Late Late subperiod represents continuity with the Middle Late subperiod, but there are a few important changes. There appears to have been a decline in

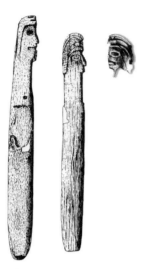

FIGURE 6.16 Whalebone clubs recovered from Plateau sites: left and center artifacts, from the Kamloops area of British Columbia; artifact on the right was recovered from The Dalles.

FIGURE 6.17 Keatley Creek circular, a pithouse village along the Fraser River; depressions mark former pithouse locations.

population at the beginning of this subperiod. Village size decreased, and the differences among individuals in burial treatment disappeared, for the most part. Hayden and Ryder (1991) note that the decline in the villages along the Fraser River in the Lillooet area may have been due to a natural disaster—a landslide on the Fraser that prevented the normal running of salmon. Among the Lillooet area villages is Keatley Creek (Figure 6.17). Population size appears to have increased in the Upper Columbia River area. The Arrow Lakes–Slocan Valley area, which had been abandoned during the preceding subperiod, had village sites again. Camas-roasting features increased in the Calispell Valley in the Eastern Plateau at this time, as well (Chatters and Pokotylo 1998, 79).

As in most areas, the history of the ethnographic pattern of people on the landscape has been an important research topic. Movements of people during the Late Late subperiod established Historic period territories and ethnic configurations, although the earlier **Lochnore phase** apparently represented a movement of Salish people from the coast into the Plateau. The Athapaskans appear to have moved into the Chilcotin Plateau after 600 BP, as indicated by changes in house form, settlement pattern, and artifacts. Numic speakers probably entered the Southern Plateau around 1000 BP. Later, in Historic times, plank houses in the area of The Dalles indicate an expansion there of the Chinook.

MODERN PERIOD

The Protohistoric or Modern period begins with the introduction of non-Indian influences on the peoples of the Plateau. Although the end of the Late period is set at AD 1720, non-Indian influences really start to have an effect between the years 1600 and 1750. These influences included epidemic diseases, trade goods, the coming of missionaries, and the coming of the horse. Most of the Indians living in the Plateau in Historic times spoke languages of one of two families. Speakers of Interior Salish, a close linguistic relative of Coast Salish on the Northwest Coast were found in the Northern Plateau. The Salish speakers include the Shuswap, Lillooet, Thompson, Okanagan, Colville, Sanoil-Nespelem, Kalispel, and Coeur d'Alene. The Southern Plateau was home to Sahaptins, including the Nez Perce, Yakima, and Umatilla. At the western edge of the area along the Columbia River there was a small area of Chinookan language groups such as the Wasco and Wishram. In southern Oregon and into northern California the Klamath and Modoc spoke closely related Klamath languages. In the north are Athapaskans like the Kootenai. Finally, the Cayuse and the Molala spoke language isolates without known affinities (Kinkade et al. 1998; Willey 1966, 397).

Epidemic diseases were devastating to Plateau populations. The epidemics may have started as early as the 1500s, based on discontinuities in the archaeological record at some sites. The first epidemics probably came from the coast as sailors brought communicable diseases to the people of the Northwest Coast, who passed them along to the interior peoples. Smallpox was one of these diseases, and it hit the Plateau a number of times, the final epidemic occurring in 1853. The mobility of the Plateau peoples and their extensive kin and trade ties encouraged the spread of epidemics throughout the region. The widespread fatalities due to the epidemics led to changes in burial patterns, with some elaboration of grave goods. New styles of interment included canoe burials, burials in cedar cists, burials in fenced enclosures, and burials in log enclosures. Cremation also became more common, and in some cases, a horse was sacrificed at an individual's grave site!

European and Asian trade goods (Figure 6.18), observed among Plateau groups by the Lewis and Clark expedition in 1805, are found in late archaeological sites in the region. These include artifacts like blue glass beads, Spanish coins, and copper kettles. These items became important commodities in Plateau trade. Trade centers on the Plateau were sites of trade fairs that brought people from distant places. The major trading locations, like The Dalles and Kettle Falls, had been important in trade prehistorically, as well. In Historic times, Plateau people traded well outside the Plateau, participating in trade with Spanish settlements in New Mexico, for example, and with trade centers on the Upper Missouri River. There are even documented expeditions of Walla Walla, Cayuse, and Yakima to the Central Valley of California, where they obtained slaves, beads, metal goods, and bows in exchange for horses, buffalo robes, dried salmon, and dentalium shells.

One factor that contributed to the long-range trade in this period and had a major effect on lifestyles in parts of the Plateau was the introduction of the horse. Horses descended from stock originally brought to the Spanish settlements in New Mexico moved north along existing trade routes and arrived in the Southern Plateau in the 1700s. The Plateau people, especially the Cayuse, Nez Perce, Palouse, and some Yakima, adopted the horse readily, increasing their mobility considerably. Lewis and Clark reported huge herds of horses owned by Plateau groups, and historic reports attribute approximately 200,000 horses to the Cayuse, Umatilla, and Walla Walla tribes in the mid-nineteenth century.

Not only did the horse provide greater mobility, it also allowed heavier loads to be transported. This led to an increase in warfare, as mounted combatants had

FIGURE 6.18 Historic trade items from the Plateau.

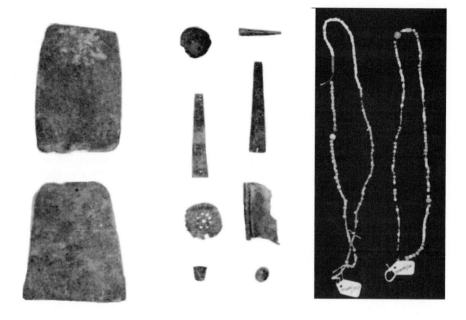

a strong advantage over people on foot, and raiders on horseback could strike over longer distances. As raiding from the Plains became more common, warfare developed along the lines of the Plains tribes, with war chiefs and warrior societies. Although tribes of the eastern periphery of the Plateau had occasionally traveled over the mountains to hunt buffalo before the horse, the horse allowed such trips to become more common and more productive (Walker and Sprague 1998).

Archaeology of European Americans

Missionaries began to contact Plateau peoples in the early nineteenth century. Catholic missionaries covered most of the Plateau, but Protestants like Marcus and Narcissa Whitman, who established a mission at Waiilatpu in Cayuse Territory, were also represented. The Whitmans not only preached Christianity, but also attempted to persuade the Cayuse to become farmers rather than mobile hunter-gatherers. This activism, combined with the problems created by the coming of white people journeying along the Oregon Trail, led to a retaliation against the Whitman Mission in which the Cayuse killed the missionaries and took hostages, who were later ransomed. Archaeological excavations were conducted at the Whitman Mission site, now a national park, in 1948 (Garth 1948). These excavations provided important information about the nature of the buildings and about the artifacts in use at the site.

The European exploration period is marked by the Lewis and Clark expedition. Although there have been excavations at some sites associated with the expedition, most camps were for stays of a single night and are expected to be quite ephemeral archaeologically. The longer winter camps, such as Fort Clatsop, near Astoria, Oregon, are outside the Plateau. The fur trade was also important on the Plateau, beginning around 1811 to 1812. Trading posts were a major site type established at this time. Forts such as Fort Walla Walla, Spokane House, and Fort Colville were built as well. Several of these have been excavated, providing information on their construction, the lives of their inhabitants, and the nature of interaction between the traders and the Indians.

Eventually, the Oregon Trail, in all its variations, was important for settling the area. Although the trail is mostly preserved as a series of cultural landscapes, artifacts are recovered from along the route that, combined with documentary records, provide insight into the movement of people westward. Some of the most important historical archaeology was done for the clearance of reservoir pool areas in the Plateau. Work at historic towns like Silcott, Washington, has provided archaeologists with a glimpse of trade and interaction in the Plateau in historic times, in this case from about 1880 to 1930.

One of the more interesting historic "excavations" in the Plateau occurred at Washington State University, where a field class used the joists of the roof in a dorm that was to be demolished as collection units and collected material that had been discarded by the dorm's residents. The Ferry Hall archaeological project demonstrated something of what student life was like at the beginning of the twentieth century in rural Washington (Riordan 1977).

CHAPTER SUMMARY

In this chapter we have introduced the Prehistoric and Historic archaeology of the Plateau. The archaeology of the Plateau received much attention lately as a result of the discovery of the Kennewick skeleton in 1996 and the ensuing legal battles over its ultimate disposition. The following points about the Plateau are important:

- The Plateau is located between the Northwest Coast and the Plains on west and east, and between the Subarctic on the north and California and the Great Basin on the south. All these areas influenced development of cultures in the Plateau, especially the Northwest Coast and the Plains, while the Plateau, in turn, influenced the developments in the other areas.

- Surrounded by mountains (the Cascades on the west and the Rocky Mountains on the east) the Plateau is dominated by the Columbia and Fraser rivers and their tributaries. The topography consists of the Columbia Basin and various plateaus and highland areas surrounding it. The highlands can receive considerable rainfall, but much of the Plateau is in the rain shadow of the Cascades and is arid away from the rivers.

- The postglacial climate has been one of periods of aridity followed by moister times, and periods of warming alternating with cooling trends. Beside climate change, volcanoes were important in shaping the environments of the area. The eruption of Mount Mazama, creating Crater Lake (7000–6700 BP), spread a blanket of volcanic ash throughout the Plateau. This would have affected growing conditions, but it also left a stratigraphic marker in archaeological sites.

- People have found only a scatter of fluted points on the ground surface in the Plateau, but the area also is home to a buried Clovis site, the Richey–Roberts Clovis cache near Wenatchee, Washington. Some of the largest Clovis points ever found come from this cache, as well as bifaces, unifacial tools, and bone rods.

- The Old Cordilleran tradition (9000–7500 BP) was characterized by leaf-shaped bifaces, cobble tools, burins, and bola stones. Large quantities of fish bone at the Roadcut site on the Columbia indicate that fishing was well established at this time. Some Early period sites in the northern Plateau have produced microblades.

- The Middle period (8000–4000 BP) continues trends established in the Early period and is typically divided into an Early Middle period and a Late Middle period. One basic distinction is that Late Middle period groups seem to have been more sedentary, relying more heavily on salmon. After 4500 BP there was a decrease in population, and the remaining people seem to have been more mobile again.

- The Late period extends from 4000 BP to AD 1720 and is the period in which Historic patterns are fully developed. The Late period is usually divided into Early, Middle, and Late subperiods. During the Early Late period, clusters of pithouses again become common, and there is evidence for an increase in the permanence of settlements as well as a collector strategy. In the Middle Late period populations came together in large pithouse villages (some with over 100 pithouses), and group territories expanded, especially in the lower reaches of the major rivers. The evidence suggests that social ranking and intergroup conflict occurred at this time, and trade increased. Patterns established in the preceding period continue in the Late Late period (1000 BP to AD 1720), although populations declined and villages became smaller over much of the area.

- The Modern period is marked by the coming to the Plateau of non-Indian influences. These include epidemic disease, the horse, Euro-American trade goods, and missionaries. All these factors had important effects on the people of the Plateau, but the horse became particularly important, allowing increases in mobility, and some of the Plateau people moved seasonally to the Plains to hunt bison.

- European exploration led to the establishment of forts such as Fort Walla Walla and Spokane House. Some of these sites have been explored archaeologically, as have portions of the Oregon Trail, the route by which so many settlers entered the area. There are a variety of topics for historical archaeologists to explore on the Plateau.

SUGGESTIONS FOR FURTHER READING

For an introduction that includes much useful information about Plateau archaeology:

Aikens, C. M. 1993. *Archaeology of Oregon.* U.S. Department of the Interior, Bureau of Land Management, Oregon State Office, Portland.

For a far-ranging book that also covers areas outside the Plateau but treats Plateau archaeology in a straightforward way:

Cressman, Luther S. 1977. *Prehistory of the Far West: Homes of Vanished Peoples*. Salt Lake City: University of Utah Press.

For excellent summaries of the prehistory of the various regions of the Plateau:

Walker, Deward E., Jr., ed. 1998. *Handbook of North American Indians*, Vol. 12, *Plateau*. Washington, DC: Smithsonian Institution.

For a recent collection of articles on Plateau prehistory that discusses complexity and new chronological information:

Prentiss, William C., and Ian Kuijt, eds. 2004. *Complex Hunter-Gatherers: Evolution and Organization of Prehistoric Communities on the Plateau of Northwestern North America*. Salt Lake City: University of Utah Press.

For the long-awaited report on the excavations at a very important Plateau site:

Hicks, Brent A., ed. 2004. *Marmes Rockshelter: A Final Report on 11,000 Years of Cultural Use*. Pullman: Washington State University Press.

For an accessible description of a large pithouse village and the issue of emerging sociocultural complexity:

Hayden, Brian. 1997. *The Pithouses of Keatley Creek: Complex Hunter-Gatherers on the Northwest Plateau*. Fort Worth, TX: Harcourt Brace College Publishers.

For important discussion of the Plateau and other portions of British Columbia:

Carlson, Roy L., and Luke Dalla Bona, eds. 1996. *Early Human Occupations in British Columbia*. Vancouver: University of British Columbia Press.

OTHER RESOURCES

The Student CD, Sections H and I, supplies web links, additional discussion questions, and other study aids. The Student CD also contains additional resources, including a complete list of the references cited in this chapter and in the case study that follows it. Pithouses, emphasized in Exhibit 6.1 and in the following case study, "The Miller Site: Four Seasons of Backwards Archaeology on Strawberry Island," were also used by the earliest inhabitants of the Dolores River valley in southwestern Colorado, as described in Section D.4, "The Dolores Archaeological Program: Documenting the Pithouse-to-Pueblo Transition."

CASE STUDY

As indicated in this chapter, the people of the Plateau often lived in villages consisting largely of a series of pithouses, and sites containing multiple telltale depressions from these structures are common. Since differences among pithouses and their contents both between and within sites can have chronological, social, or ethnic significance, the careful study of houses and house contents is warranted. The following case study describes how the erosion of several pithouses located on an island in the Snake River in Washington State brought archaeologists to a large pithouse village. Initially investigations were limited to documenting the contents and nature of the pithouses actually being eroded by river waters. Over the course of several field seasons, however, the focus of research changed to investigating the nature of the whole site. The increase in scope has allowed the U.S. Army Corps of Engineers to better manage this important archaeological resource.

It also has shown that there were several occupations of this site, as well as greater variability within pithouse villages than archaeologists once thought. Experimental archaeology has shown as well how people at this site processed antelope for marrow, providing insights into Plateau adaptations in general. As you read this case study, pay particular attention to the three different occupations. How and why are they different?

THE MILLER SITE

Four Seasons of Backwards Archaeology on Strawberry Island

G. Timothy Gross

A barge loaded with wheat lumbers down the Snake River, powered by the pushboat behind it. The barge rides low in the water, and the two craft send a V-shaped wave or wake out through the channel of the river, now a reservoir backed up behind McNary Dam. The spreading wave hits the cobble apron that surrounds the upstream end of Strawberry Island and climbs the short distance to the sand and silt bank that sits atop the apron. Next the wave hits the soft sediments of the bank, ripping a little more away from the already undercut base, and a piece of the bank crashes down on the cobbles below. The lapping of the reservoir waters against this block of sediment slowly removes the sands and silts, leaving behind rocks and bits of broken bone. Some of the rocks are blocky, jagged, and blackened from heat; others are flakes; one or two are cobble choppers. The bone is mostly pronghorn, but a few fish vertebrae may be seen, as well. In the newly exposed section of bank there is visible a gently curving band of charcoal, making a thin black smile in the tan sands and silts. This band marks the floor of a pithouse.

When a survey team from Washington State University (WSU) visited Strawberry Island in 1975, they found the beaches of the upper end of the island littered with artifacts and the sand and silt banks showing stratified deposits. They noted the presence of over 100 depressions thought to represent the former sites of pithouses. They also noted that, in addition to damage from barge wakes, the island had been vandalized by relic hunters. They recommended that measures be taken to protect the banks from erosion and noted that a mapping and testing project was slated for 1976 (Cleveland et al. 1977, 34–36). That project was the beginning of the four field seasons that I will discuss in this case study. I joined the project in 1977 as a crew chief and was the field director for the last two seasons (Schalk 1983, v).

Strawberry Island is located in the Snake River about 5 miles (8 km) upstream from the confluence of the Snake and the Columbia, not far from Columbia Park, where Kennewick Man was found (see Box 3.1 in Chapter 3). This area in general is known as the Pasco Basin and is one of the driest parts of the Plateau. The river is no longer free-flowing in this stretch, as the construction of McNary Dam on the Columbia River created Lake Wallula, which includes this portion of the Snake. A channel that is flooded most of the time by reservoir waters, but was dry except during floods before the dam was built, bisects the island. Strawberry Island Village, also known as the Miller site, occupies the portion of the island that is upstream from this channel. The site was first recorded as part of the Smithsonian River Basin Survey in 1948, and excavations were conducted in 1951 (Osborne and Crabtree 1961) as part of the salvage work connected with the construction of McNary Dam.

The 1951 project on Strawberry Island recorded 131 depressions on the surface of the Island that were thought to represent house pits. Seven were excavated in some fashion. A square measuring 5 by 5 feet (1.5 × 1.5 m) was excavated in four of the depressions, two adjacent depressions were excavated with a trench that intersected both, and one additional depression was excavated intensively with a block of 19 of the 5 by 5 foot squares.

BACKWARDS ARCHAEOLOGY

When I talk about the excavations at Strawberry Island, I often joke that we excavated the site backwards. By that I mean that we started by taking a very fine look at small parts of the site and extended operations each field season, putting the previous season's work into a little broader context each year, until in the last year we sampled space across the island to see how the areas we had been excavating fit in. This was not a result of backwards thinking by the archaeologists; instead, it reflected the evolution of the attitude of the project sponsors, the U.S. Army Corps of Engineers, toward archaeology and toward their legal responsibilities. This evolution mirrors changes that took place across the country, signaling the change from a **salvage approach** to federal agency archaeology to one that focuses on managing the resources. That is, rather than doing no more than what was needed to save any resources that were threatened by projects or their long-term effects, the agencies began to develop understandings of sites and their contexts, trying to preserve those that were truly important.

The initial WSU project in 1976, directed by Greg Cleveland with Richard D. Daugherty serving as principal investigator, created a map of the site showing all the visible depressions. The map was made by a combination of aerial photography and land surveying. White crosses were placed in each depression that could be recognized and aerial photographs were taken. A transit survey was also undertaken, not only to locate the depressions but also to set up **datum points** for the construction of a grid system. The detailed map that resulted showed the location of 133 depressions (Figure 6.19). Each of the depressions was assigned a number, though it was later discovered that the WSU numbering system differed from that used by Osborne and Crabtree (1961).

Excavation during the first field season was confined to trenches in three contiguous depressions on the southeast side of the island (also referred to as the left bank, in keeping with the convention of referring to the banks as if the viewer was looking downstream). Items within the trenches were point plotted (mapped in three dimensions) in the hope that the vertical distributions would indicate the location of house floors both in the field maps and in computer mapping that followed the field season. This was deemed appropriate excavation strategy because floors were very hard to define in the sandy sediments of the island. Plotting each individual item encountered was a time-consuming process, but it resulted in detailed information about sections of house pits. Provisions in the contract restricted excavation to areas that were being lost to erosion. The Corps of Engineers saw their responsibility as limited to saving what was being destroyed (Cleveland et al. 1977; Cleveland 1978a).

The 1977 the excavation was again restricted to areas being eroded. Again under Cleveland's supervision, excavation continued in two of the house pits investigated in 1976 (**piece plotting** artifacts in the third had been completed in 1976), and excavations were begun in a depression on the right bank of the island (Figure 6.20). Excavation in some open areas between depressions was also begun in 1977. The trenches that allowed examination of stratification were excavated with a backhoe, which had been

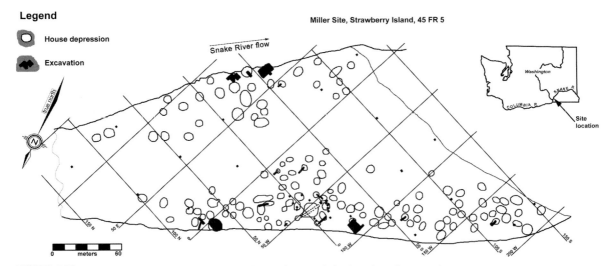

FIGURE 6.19 Map of the Miller site showing the depressions and the location of excavations.

FIGURE 6.20 Excavation in progress on Strawberry Island pithouses.

transported in a surplus military landing craft, and passed through the boat lock in Ice Harbor Dam, located just upstream from Strawberry Island.

In 1978 Randall Schalk took over as project director. He negotiated with the Corps of Engineers and got permission to excavate in areas of the island beyond those that were eroding. Excavation that year continued in the open areas, and a new sample of depressions was designed. Upon evaluating the variability in the kinds of depression seen on Strawberry Island, Schalk noted first of all that there were two clusters of depressions, one on the right bank and one on the left. Further, the depressions varied both in size and in shape. Some of the depressions were round, while others were elliptical. Creating a chart of the possible attributes, Schalk noted which combinations on the chart had already been examined by the WSU program. He then went to Osborne and Crabtree's report and noted the types they had examined. With WSU and the Smithsonian's River Basin excavations considered, it was easy to tell from the chart which combinations of attributes had not been sampled. All the possibilities for the unsampled combinations were listed, and examples were chosen with the aid of a table of random numbers until at least one of each combination had been picked for further work. For each depression chosen in this way, a trench was laid out from the rim of the depression on the north side to the center of the depression. Depending on the size of the depression, these trenches were 5 to 7 meters (16 to 23 ft) long. Each

trench was excavated using standard 10 cm (4 in.) levels. This exercise allowed us to explore the range of variation in depression types.

By the 1979 field season, in which Schalk assumed the role of principal investigator as well as project director, we had some idea of the range in variation in depressions and had detailed data on the contents of some depressions, including piece-plotted provenience on material in several pithouses. We also had some information on the space between houses on the site from the two area excavations that had been conducted. We knew as well that depressions in the right-bank cluster exhibited some structure in their distribution, with groups of depressions appearing to be clustered together, perhaps forming compounds. In the final year of the project, again being allowed to dig outside the areas immediately threatened with erosion, we designed one last sample so that we could put the existing data into a larger context. In this sample, excavations were laid out on a grid at 25 meters (82 ft) intervals on the north–south axis and 50 meters (164 ft) on the east–west axis. Each excavation on the grid was a 1 by 1 meter (3 by 3 ft) test unit excavated to the sterile cobble basement stratum of the island. In the 1979 excavation we also examined spatial variability by selecting one of the pithouse clusters and excavating 29 small 1 by 1 meter units in it. The final task was carrying one of the open area excavations begun in 1978 down to the cobble layer.

Thus what we did was the reverse of what is often done. Generally, the first stage of an excavation is designed to provide information about the structure of the entire site, and subsequent areas for detailed excavation are selected based on the results of the initial sampling. In the Strawberry Island case, owing to the Corp of Engineer's interpretation of their responsibilities, we were restricted at first to detailed excavation; only at the end of the project could we do the sampling across the site that allowed us to establish a context into which to fit our detailed information. This sequence of events reflects changes that were happening nationwide in cultural resource management. In the early days of federal archaeology, with the notable exception of some projects run by the National Park Service, most federal archaeology was considered to be salvage work, aimed at rescuing some data from sites that were disappearing, owing to such federal actions as dam building. Ultimately federal archaeology in many agencies took on an active role in managing the resources under government jurisdiction, a task that called for information beyond the identification of what was being destroyed. The responsibility of federal agencies to manage their resources, rather than merely reacting to proposed impacts, is now part of the law: a 1980 amendment to the **National Historic Preservation Act (NHPA)** outlines these responsibilities in **Section 110**.

Beginning with the initial excavations in 1976, the Strawberry Island project was funded on a year-to-year basis. Accordingly, a report was supposed to be prepared after each field season. The 1976 and 1977 field reports (Cleveland et al. 1977, 1978a) were prepared, but the Corps of Engineers ruled that a spate of high-priority contracts from the federal agency to Washington State University took precedence over the preparation of reports for the 1978 and 1979 field seasons. As Schalk began working on the combined report on the last two field seasons (Schalk 1983), it became apparent that there were more data than could be adequately reported with the available budget and that additional analyses were needed to make the existing data fully useful. Although a request was made to the Corps of Engineers for the additional funding to carry out a full reporting of the excavation, no such monies could be obtained. The final report on the 1978 and 1979 seasons (Schalk 1983) summarizes what was done and provides some analysis and synthesis, but there are no detailed discussions of individual excavation units or areas, and little tabular presentation of data by excavation area. Nonetheless, the project has contributed considerably to the understanding of Lower Snake–Mid-Columbia archaeology, as we shall see.

WHAT WE LEARNED

Three occupations have been documented, although the earliest is represented by material from the bottom of only one trench, at the meeting of the sands and silts and the cobble base of the island. Items found at the contact include a few fire-altered rocks, cobble tools, three projectile points, siliceous flakes, shell fragments, and a sliver of bone (Mierendorf 1983, 47). This contact, is dated in a different part of the site at 2472 ±110 BP.

The first major occupation of the Miller site is in the group of house pits on the right bank of the island. Most of the pithouses in this large cluster appear to have been built over a very short time. These pithouses, with a single date of 1395 ±80 BP, were deep, and steep pit walls were indicated by truncation of the bedded natural sands and silts of the island (Figure 6.21).

The final village occupation was a series of saucer-shaped pithouses that were built on both banks of the island. A number of radiocarbon dates indicate that this occupation started about 600 BP and ended around 200 BP. This later date is reinforced by the complete absence of Historic trade goods, which are so common on Contact period sites in the area.

One of the important aspects of the analysis carried out for this project is the use of replication. Jeff Flenniken (1977, 1978) studied the lithic material from the site and described four main modes of flaked stone tool production. The first system he describes, based on experimental manufacture of artifacts and comparison of the resulting artifacts and debitage to those found in the excavation, is the production of

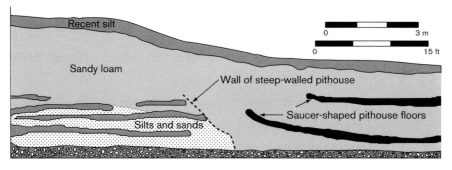

FIGURE 6.21 Schematic profile of a depression on the Miller site showing the difference between saucer-shaped and steep-walled pithouses.

flaked tools by means of a biface reduction technique. Raw materials for this system were generally cherty materials and obsidian, and they were often collected as cobbles. Flakes were heat-treated prior to further reduction. The second system was the reduction of pebbles or large flakes through bipolar reduction into flat flakes that were either used as produced or worked into arrow points. The raw materials were essentially the same for this system, but the cores may have been heat-treated prior to flake removal. The third system is the production of oval flake tools from basalt, quartzite, and granite cobbles, probably picked up along the cobble beaches of the island. The flakes (Figure 6.22a, b), which were excellent knives without any further modification, were produced by a block-on-block technique in which a thin, oval cobble was held between the thumb and fingers and struck on the edge against a stationary anvil stone. Generally a single oval flake would result. The final system was the production of cobble choppers. This was accomplished by freehand percussion on basalt cobbles. Relatively thin cobbles were selected, and a few flakes were removed unifacially from one end to produce a steep working edge. Such tools are common on sites in the area (Figure 6.22c, d).

Many of the cobble choppers recovered in excavation were bifacial, and they show varying signs of wear, from unused edges to edges that are a band of crushed and pockmarked stone with the remnants of flake scars behind them (Figure 6.22e, f). This kind of wear indicates considerable battering and may have resulted from the use of an anvil stone to process materials. The crushing would be a result of contact between the chopper and the anvil. Flenniken believes that the bifacial cobble choppers started out as unifacial tools and that the flake scars on the other face were acquired during use, as the tools accidentally struck the anvil with enough force to detach a flake. Although these choppers were almost certainly multipurpose tools, one activity represented in the archaeological record at Strawberry Island Village was the processing of long bones from large mammals like pronghorn for the marrow they contain. That is one of the activities that Cleveland (1977) and Flenniken (1977) explored in greater detail through replication.

To test whether marrow extraction was a reasonable explanation for the cobble choppers, often heavily worn, the anvil stones with their pockmarked surfaces, and the quantities of splintered long bones,

Cleveland contacted Fish and Game departments throughout the Northwest. The Department of Fish and Game in Wyoming was able to provide two dead pronghorns, which were shipped to Pullman for experimental purposes. Cleveland's goals were to understand the food value of marrow and meat from pronghorns, to see whether marrow extraction produced the kinds of splintered bone found at the site, and to see whether the process of butchering and marrow extraction produced the same kinds of wear patterns seen in the archaeological record on replicated ovate flake knives and the cobble choppers. The meat and marrow weight yields were used to estimate the nutritional yield of pronghorns.

Flenniken (1977, 100–101) summarizes the observations made on the use of the cobble choppers. He notes that unmodified cobbles were unsuitable for marrow extraction. The rounded surfaces slipped off the greasy bone, and if enough force was used to break the bone with the cobble, the bone shattered, driving tiny bone splinters into the marrow. Removal of a flake or two from the edge of the cobble provided the edge necessary to fracture the bone without shattering it, leaving the marrow tube to be picked out, relatively bone free. The edges of the choppers incurred pockmark wear from hitting the anvil stone as well as the bone, which damaged the tool edge and the anvil surface. Sometimes, when contact was made with the anvil, flakes were driven off the chopper. These could be distinctive, having pockmarked platforms. In the experiments, cobble choppers that started out as unifaces became bifacial through the process of contact flake removal. With sufficient use, pockmarks obliterated the flaked edge of the tool. The ovate flake knives made by Flenniken's third technological system were used in the butchering process. The wear patterns on the cobble tools and on the ovate knives used in the experiment matched those on the archaeological specimens.

The bone from the site did, indeed, match the bone from the experiments well enough to support the inference that people had been able to collect marrow by breaking bones. The ends of bones and portions of bone, like the scapula, were also used to provide marrow. In many cases these bones were broken to expose the spongy bone (cancellous tissue), and this was probably boiled to provide a rich broth. Evidence of both kinds of marrow extraction was found in houses at the Strawberry Island village.

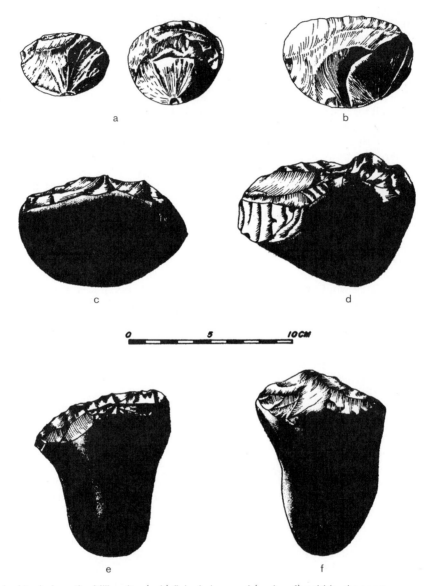

FIGURE 6.22 Flaked tools from the Miller site: (a, b) flake knives and (c, d, e, f) cobble choppers.

What were the houses like at Strawberry Island? The earlier houses were deep pithouses (20–28 in., or 30–50 cm deep) with abrupt sides. They tended to be smaller than the later houses, but had sizable postholes. Beyond the postholes there is no evidence of the nature of the superstructure. Later houses were shallower and had saucer-shaped floors that lacked postholes. Again, the nature of the superstructure is unknown. There is a patterning in the distribution of artifacts around and within the structures. Around the structures immediately outside the house is a ring of debris that appears to be trash associated with the occupation of the house. Often called the **midden ring**, this area contains discards that are assumed to be contemporaneous with the living floors. The use zone within the house is another matter. In the earlier, steep-walled houses, the floors are ephemeral, and little debris is associated with them. Relatively thick and dark deposits suggesting a greater intensity of use, on the other hand, mark the saucer-shaped floors. Interestingly, however, no traceable compact floors can be found in Strawberry Island's pithouses, since the sediments in which they were made were so sandy.

The identification of animal remains from the site provided the material for Deborah Olson's master's thesis (Olson 1983) and yielded some important information. Three classes of animals—rabbit, pronghorn, and salmon and related fish (salmonids)—dominated the bone collections from the site. The rabbit class of bones includes both jackrabbit and cottontail, though jackrabbits are by far the more common. Deer and elk bones are found in the collections, but both are much less common than pronghorn. The salmonids are difficult to identify more specifically from the parts that were preserved at the Miller site, but the species represented probably include chinook salmon, which appears to be the most common type, as well as sockeye salmon, coho salmon, and steelhead trout. Bones from fish of the sucker family were also recovered. Other animals noted in smaller numbers are ground squirrel, mouse, beaver, dog, coyote, black bear, weasel, and river otter, along with unspecified reptiles, birds, and snakes. Interestingly, no bison bones were identified in all the collections, though cow/bison-sized bone fragments were recovered from the beach and from the surface of the island. These are most likely modern cow, however, unrelated to the prehistoric occupation of the site.

Faunal remains were compared across the island, and an important pattern emerged—a strong association between types of faunal remains and types of houses. Steep-walled houses are associated with faunal assemblages that have salmonids as the most common element. The houses with saucer-shaped floors, on the other hand, are dominated either by pronghorn or by rabbit. Schalk and Olson conclude a discussion of the faunal remains by saying:

> To our knowledge, this is the first demonstration in the Plateau of a recurrent association between architectural forms and faunal assemblages. It is also the first reported occurrence on the Columbia Plateau of a Late Prehistoric residential site in which pronghorn is the dominant ungulate in the faunal assemblage. (Schalk and Olson 1983, 107)

Cleveland (1978b, 37–40) reviewed the evidence for pronghorn hunting and concluded that the pronghorn found at the Miller site probably were caught in large communal game drives. This conclusion was based on the age structure of the pronghorn in the assemblage. The presence of individuals that were six to eight months old at the time of death (based on the characteristics of their mandibles) both reinforces this conclusion and points to late fall or winter as a time for the hunts. The distribution of faunal remains suggests that whole animals were distributed to the individual houses, a pattern consistent with communal hunting (Schalk and Olson 1983, 103–104). If individual hunters had procured individual animals, it is expected, based on ethnographic meat-sharing patterns, that portions of animals would have been distributed rather than whole animals.

Schalk reconstructs the occupation of the island and examines the differences between the two major periods of use. The first occupation was that of the right bank, where deep, steep-sided pithouses were built, probably around 1400 BP. The number of depressions on the right bank suggests that the population of that early occupation would have been large, "possibly numbering in the hundreds" (Schalk 1983, 139). Most of these features do not show signs of reuse, although a few contained multiple floors. Schalk suggests that there was an occupational hiatus, perhaps caused by unfavorable climatic conditions, although there is some evidence for reuse of some of the right-bank pithouses by a smaller group of people after the initial building of the pithouses.

The second major occupation, from 600 BP to 200 BP, was the one associated with the saucer-shaped floors, and it occupied both the right and left banks. Stratigraphic evidence, both in the fill of the depressions and in the open areas, indicates some accumulation of natural sediment between the two occupations. These houses were larger and tended to occur along the river's edge, contrasting with the earlier occupation, which spread into the center of the island. Schalk also notes that the houses of the earlier occupation of the right bank form groups or clusters, while the later houses are more scattered. The occurrence of clusters of houses into compounds suggests the existence of some sort of group organization at a level higher than the individual household in the earlier pithouse occupation. This tantalizing suggestion is just one of the many avenues for further research that can be pursued with data from this project.

The patterning in faunal remains has already been mentioned, with the early, steep-walled houses having faunal assemblages dominated by salmonids and the later occupation having either rabbit or pronghorn as the dominant animal. Schalk does not think that fish use decreased, however; instead, he suggests that it actually increased in the later occupation. It is the nature of the use that is seen to have changed, with a greater reliance on stored salmon—fish that were caught and dried at a location away from the village—leading to the lower relative numbers of fish bones.

Schalk explains the changes as resulting from an imbalance between population and resources. Basically, arid conditions that set in after the right-bank occupation ended caused a scarcity of terrestrial resources. As noted at the beginning of this case study, the Pasco Basin is one of the most arid parts of the Plateau, so drying would have been particularly severe there. Since similar droughts had occurred prehistorically without leading to similar changes, Schalk suggests that the number of people had grown during relatively good times and that the region was so heavily populated that prior solutions to environmental stress, involving increased movement of groups of people over larger territories, were not feasible. With the larger populations restricting the ranges over which people could hunt and gather food, the alternative was to intensify efforts to collect a specific resource. Migrating fish populations were the resource for which increased effort would have paid off. Such a "quantum increase" in fishing, Schalk suggests (1983, 146), led to longer stays in residential bases, and the period of use of the later pithouses on the island was longer, explaining the greater quantities of artifacts associated with these house floors.

Two trends are seen in the artifact assemblages that support the foregoing explanation of change. First, the bipolar reduction system is more common in the later pithouses, indicating a more frugal use of the raw material, since this technique provides more cutting edge per unit of rock than freehand percussion. This scenario is consistent with a reduction in mobility and territory size, accompanied by fewer opportunities to collect raw materials, since previous sources now lay beyond the boundaries of the smaller home range. Both projectile points and ovate

flake knives are also more common in the later occupation. This is consistent with a greater emphasis on hunting pronghorn and rabbit to supplement the diet of stored fish that probably formed the staple for the occupation of Strawberry Island Village.

IMPACTS OF THE PROJECT

Although the level of reporting for the Strawberry Island Project is not as thorough as we would like, the work at the Miller site has made some substantial contributions to Plateau prehistory. The site is used as evidence for the formation of large pithouse villages in the Southern Plateau (e.g., Ames 2000; Ames et al. 1998). It also marks a change in the way Plateau prehistory was addressed. Prior to the Strawberry Island Project, Plateau developments were seen as primarily additions to a static cultural base. New artifact types appeared in the record and projectile points changed through time, but the adaptation was seen as relatively constant. The Miller site, which allowed comparisons between occupations that were about 800 years apart, showed that there were also changes in the relative proportions of materials in assemblages, and that there was important, previously unexplored variability. Adaptations were not static but changed in response to such factors as increased aridity and population growth.

Strawberry Island illustrates another point, as well. The collections from the Strawberry Island Project still exist at Washington State University. Clearly, there is a great potential for further study of those collections to address important questions raised in the original analyses and questions that have arisen as our understandings of regional prehistory have grown. Further, the ready availability today of techniques like AMS dating means that samples that could not be dated back in 1979 can be dated today. This should allow testing the reconstruction of two occupations and refined dating of the early occupation at the contact between the cobbles and the sands on the island. The site has been protected since the end of the excavations. Riprap has been placed around the banks of the island to shield them from further damage. Productive new research that adds substantially to the study of Plateau prehistory can be accomplished with the existing collections, and the site remains for further research when questions requiring new excavation arise.

DISCUSSION QUESTIONS

1. Why was the Miller site excavated backwards? How and why did the excavation strategy change over the course of the project? What's the difference between salvaging and managing archaeological resources?

2. When was the Miller site inhabited, and what periods in Plateau culture history does it represent? What was the basis for concluding that there were three distinct occupations of the site?

3. What evidence leads to the conclusion that the inhabitants of this site were extracting marrow from pronghorn bones? How did people apparently obtain the marrow?

4. Contrast the evidence for subsistence practices in the two pithouse occupations. Can you think of other ways to interpret the lack of fish in the later pithouses? How might you test Schalk's ideas about what was happening?

CHAPTER 7

Diversity and Complexity in California

"I can get better stuff than this down the street at the antique store!"

That sentiment was expressed in 1993 by a member of the City Council of El Cajon, California. A local archaeologist had just shown the council a sample of artifacts he had collected during an excavation in the city's redevelopment area, and the council was concerned about the cost of the project. To qualify for federal funds in its planned redevelopment, the city was obliged to pay for excavation of the Corona del El Cajon Hotel site, a late-nineteenth-century hotel that had burned in 1920. Shops had been built over the burned basement and abandoned yard of the hotel, and most people forgot the hotel was ever there. Archaeologists not only uncovered the basement essentially intact, but also found trash pits and privies associated with the hotel.

The council member, however, saw the price tag for a project that seemed to have merely produced a collection of dirty and broken bits of pottery, glass, rusty metal, animal bone, and similar items as exorbitant. The nearby antique store had whole dishes, complete jars, unrusted metal tools, and usable tableware that looked better and would cost less than the archaeological artifacts the consultant had exhibited.

The council member's view is, unfortunately, a common one. Many members of the public view archaeology as an Easter egg hunt in which the object is to find the best goodies from the past. Archaeologists certainly enjoy finding spectacular objects, but that is not the goal of their research. The archaeologist seeks information about human life in the past. Sometimes, as in the case of the Corona del El Cajon Hotel excavations, it is the relatively recent past that is the topic of concern; but the more distant past, measured in centuries or millennia rather than in decades or years, also piques the archaeologist's intellectual curiosity.

Objects play a part in the process of learning about past human life, but only a part. Even more important than the artifacts are the circumstances under which they are found—their **context**. Context includes the location in space and the associations with other artifacts. A bottle base, for example, can provide information about when the item was made and what it may have contained. It might be determined that a certain bottle base is from a liquor bottle made in the first decade of the twentieth century. If it was found in a privy pit along with a number of other pieces of liquor bottles, we can gain insight into the liquor consumption in historic El Cajon. The occurrence of a quantity of liquor bottles in the privies and trash pits associated with the hotel is particularly interesting. Records indicate that when the privy was in use, El Cajon was a dry town—one in which liquor was illegal. The artifacts from the hotel excavation demonstrate the actual behavior of people who worked at or patronized the hotel rather than the behavior prescribed by the laws of the city.

The complete assemblage of bottle fragments from the layer in the privy was used to calculate an index of bottled product use that was then compared with lists from other sites to see where rural El Cajon fit. When the entire assemblage was considered, including the animal bone, ceramic sherds, and the glass, a picture of a rather elegant hotel emerged. The consultant noted that the hotel had what was, for the time, an upscale menu featuring high-quality cuts of meat, but the food apparently was served on plain ceramics. The hotel created an elegant ambiance through the use of pressed glass tableware and decorated toilet seats in the guest rooms. Layers of refuse that dated later in time document the change in the nature of the hotel from a resort to a boarding house. All this was inferred from the nature of the remains and their distribution in the ground.

Archaeological approaches to trash pits and privies stand in stark contrast to those of relic hunters and bottle collectors. Archaeologists excavate slowly, exposing and recording artifacts as they go. Records of artifact location are critical because the scientists are interested in the context of each find. For the archaeologist, a broken bottle base tells as detailed a story as the whole bottle, and even small fragments of ceramics and bits of bone are collected and recorded. Bottle hunters also excavate old trash pits and privies, often illegally. Their focus is on the whole bottles and adding new specimens to their collections. Although there are a few exceptions, bottle hunters generally dig quickly, without regard to associations of materials. They do not record the location of their finds, sometimes not even noting the site from which objects were obtained. In the process of their digging for pretty specimens—the kind the city council member perhaps had expected to see—they destroy any patterning in the deposits.

To bring to a close the story of the archaeological consultant and the city council, we note that about a year later, the consultant presented his report on the excavation project. The lengthy document detailed the research goals, the historical background, the methods used, the artifacts found, and their associations, as well as the conclusions drawn from the research. A picture of life at the Corona del El Cajon Hotel was sketched that would not have been possible without the excavation. The same city council member who had talked about the antique stores earlier complimented the consultant on the high quality of his work.

Investigations like those at Corona del El Cajon Hotel, which occur all over North America, are particularly common in California where development is proceeding rapidly, and the rich archaeological heritage is threatened. In this chapter we examine this heritage.

DEFINITION OF THE AREA

The California archaeological culture area (Figure 7.1) does not exactly match the modern political boundaries of the state, although it includes most of California's territory. Portions of the northwest corner of the state were considered in Chapter 5 on the Northwest Coast area, and parts of northeastern California were covered in Chapter 6 on the Plateau area. The arid Mojave Desert and the areas east of the mountains of the Sierra Nevada are part of the Great Basin area presented in Chapter 8. Further, the California archaeological area extends down into Mexico to below Ensenada in Baja California, although this area and the adjacent parts of southern California could be considered with the southwest (Chapter 9) because ceramics and rudimentary stone architecture, both southwestern traits, are found there. However, the area has sufficient Californian traits to legitimately be included in the California culture area, as we have done in this chapter.

Researchers have proposed often-contradictory time schemes for various regions of California, and, because of the regional diversity, there have been few attempts to discuss chronological periods for the area as a whole. In their 1984 synthesis of California archaeology, Joseph L. and Kerry Kona Chartkoff (1984, 15–16) discuss the area's archaeology in terms of four major periods: Paleoindian, Archaic, Pacific, and Historic. All these terms are used in other areas and have essentially the same meaning in California as elsewhere. The Pacific period was defined to reflect the level of complexity attained by cultures in the late Prehistoric and ethnographic periods: it was akin to that of the agricultural Pueblo or Woodland and Mississippian people elsewhere, but it was based on a hunting and gathering economy (Chartkoff and Chartkoff 1984, 16). As we saw in Chapter 6, some archaeologists working along the Northwest Coast also recognized the Pacific period as being useful. This scheme, along with those for subregions in California, is presented in Table 7.1.

THE ENVIRONMENT

Both the state of California and the archaeological culture area are characterized by environmental diversity, with differing environments often being found in relatively close proximity. In the San Diego area, for instance, it is possible to start at the beach or San Diego Bay and drive east through the coastal plain, the chaparral-covered foothills that grade into oak forests in the mountains, and finally into very arid desert, all in less than 2 hours or 60 miles (100 km). Although diversity is the key, the environment can be broken down into three major regions: the coast, the Central Valley, and the Sierra Nevada.

One of California's most striking features is its long coast, with its sandy beaches, rocky cliffs, bays, lagoons, and estuaries. Traveling inland from the coast, one finds either the mountains of the Coast Ranges or coastal plains of varying widths. The Coastal Ranges parallel the coast from Point Conception north and are divided into the North Coast Ranges and the South Coast Ranges by San Francisco Bay. At Point Conception the Transverse Ranges reach the coast. Their offshore extension is seen in the Northern Channel Islands (Santa Cruz, Santa Rosa, San Miguel, and Anacapa). South of the Transverse Ranges is the broad Los Angeles Basin, and the Peninsular Range. Sandy beaches are found

FIGURE 7.1 The California culture area, showing the location of sites mentioned in Chapter 7.

TABLE 7.1 Introduction to California Culture History

Uncalibrated Years BP	General Period	Central California	Chumash Area	San Diego	Calibrated Years
	Historic				AD 1550
500			Late		AD 1430
1,000	Late Pacific	Augustine	Transitional	Late Prehistoric	AD 1020
1,500					AD 600
2,000	Middle Pacific	Berkeley	Middle		AD 10
2,500					660 BC
3,000		Windmiller			1,240 BC
3,500	Early Pacific				1,820 BC
4,000					2,490 BC
4,500			Early		3,200 BC
5,000	Late Archaic			La Jolla/Pauma	3,780 BC
5,500					4,340 BC
6,000		Unknown			4,880 BC
6,500					5,440 BC
7,000	Middle Archaic				5,840 BC
7,500					6,320 BC
8,000			Early Holocene		6,910 BC
8,500					7,550 BC
9,000				San Dieguito	8,030 BC
9,500	Early Archaic	Buena Vista Lake, Tulare Lakes (Western Pluvial Lakes)			8,560 BC
10,000					9,210 BC
10,500			Paleoindian?		10,470 BC
11,000				Paleoindian	10,970 BC
11,500 and prior	Paleoindian				11,470 BC and prior

primarily in the south, although cliffs occur all along the coast. Bays, estuaries, and lagoons provided salt marsh vegetation, while the coastal plain and the Coast Ranges had coastal sage scrub, chaparral, and oak woodlands, as well as some native grasslands. From Monterey north, coastal redwood forests are found. Shellfish and ocean fish, as well as sea mammals in some places, were important foods.

East of the Coast Ranges lies the long, broad, fertile Central Valley. This relatively flat valley is a sediment-filled basin that runs 400 miles (645 km) north–south, and is as wide as 95 miles (155 km) in places. Major rivers drain the Central Valley, the Sacramento on the north and the San Joaquin on the south. These rivers and their tributaries host major runs of anadromous fish. Vegetation in the Central Valley includes marshes, grasslands, oak parkland where oaks are found on grassy hills, and oak woodlands.

The foothills of the Sierra Nevada ranges mark the eastern edge of the Central Valley. The mountains of the Sierra Nevada rise relatively gently, but their eastern side is quite steep. This is because they are fault-block mountains. Mount Whitney, in the Sierra Nevada, is the highest point in the United States south of Alaska, at 14,497 feet (4419 m). Oak woodlands, pine forests, and areas of alpine meadow are all found in the Sierra Nevada, as are isolated groves of giant sequoias.

Climate and Climatic Change

California's climate, like its topography, is variable. The south is sunny much of the time, but fog is common along the coast and in the Central Valley. Rainfall is heavier in the north than in the south, and periods of extended drought are not uncommon in southern California. Air temperatures along the coast are affected by the ocean, which serves to stabilize temperatures, lessening the extremes recorded inland.

Past climates in California have exerted important influences on the archaeological inhabitants of the state, although the effects of some climatic events are the center of heated debate among archaeologists. The most important changes were associated with the end of the Pleistocene. As mentioned in Chapter 2, a warming trend was accompanied by a rise in sea level, which had the effect of drowning large areas of the coastal plain, including the areas where early camps would have been if people had migrated down the coast. At low sea level, about 12,000 BP, the four Northern Channel Islands were connected to form the paleoisland of Santarosae. Because a 9-mile (15 km) strip adjacent to the coastline was exposed, Santarosae was effectively closer to the mainland than any of the Channel Islands are today (Porcasi et al. 1999).

This rising sea level flooded river valleys on the mainland, in many areas creating lagoons that were very productive environments for early Archaic peoples. As sea level stabilized, the lagoons began to accumulate silt, which eventually choked them, leaving mudflats rather than open water. Where the rising sea met highlands, sea cliffs were cut. Old middens preserved in some coastal areas have strata that slant shoreward, stopping abruptly at an eroded cliff face. This indicates that in the past, shell mounds extended well out beyond the current cliff level. Thus considerable archaeological evidence has been lost to sea cliff erosion. Changes in the coastline must be taken into account, then, in reconstructing the lifeways of ancient coastal inhabitants.

EARLY CULTURES

In Chapter 3 we discussed some of the claims for very early occupations of California based on the Calico site. California has had more than its share of such claims. Another example is the Texas Street site in the San Diego area. Discovered in the mid-twentieth century, this site yielded quartzite cobbles (Figure 7.2) thought to be large blade cores and large, thick blades, along with segments of cobbles that resembled Siberian cleaving tools called *skreblos*. The resemblances are superficial, however, and few archaeologists accept these items as tools. In the 1970s, a number of localities with broken quartzite items were suggested to represent what George Carter (1978) called the American Lower Paleolithic.

Another development that drove the interest in the possibility of very early occupations in California was the application to some previously excavated human bone of the new technique of **aspartic acid (amino acid) racemization dating**. Burials from La Jolla and Del Mar produced remains that were, respectively, dated to 28,000 and between 41,000 and 48,000 years old (Bada et al. 1974). A caliche-coated bone from a cairn burial in the Yuha Desert area east of San Diego was radiocarbon dated to 21,500 BP, as well (Childers 1974). More recent dating of these remains by accelerator mass spectrometry (Taylor et al. 1985) has shown that errors were made in all dates for these sites, and most archaeologists no longer believe that valid Pre-Clovis evidence has not been found in California.

FIGURE 7.2 Material from Texas Street considered by George Carter to be artifacts.

Clovis and Folsom

The first evidence most archaeologists accept is a scattering of fluted points that generally are Clovis-like. These points have been found primarily as surface artifacts. Concentrations have been found at Tulare Lake and at Borax Lake. At Tulare Lake in the southern Central Valley, numerous fluted points have been recovered, along with the remains of extinct Pleistocene animals. Based on similarities to Clovis material, dates earlier than 11,000 BP seem appropriate. Recent investigations by Gerrit Fenenga have provided uranium series dates for mineralized bones of extinct animals at Tulare Lake that range between 17,745 BP and 10,788 BP. Mineralized human bone from the area produced dates of 15,800 BP and 11,380 BP. Because the bones of dated animals are surface finds, they cannot be associated with any great confidence with the artifacts, but the dates on mineralized human bone strongly suggests a human presence by Clovis times (Stepp 1997).

At Borax Lake, in the North Coast Range, fluted points of obsidian have been found and appear to be of Clovis age (12,000–11,000 BP). Fredrickson (1973) has defined the **Post pattern** to include these fluted points along with single-shouldered points, and crescents. The age is supported by obsidian hydration readings on artifacts, including Clovis points. It is thought that Post pattern people were generalized foragers rather than specialized big-game hunters (Chartkoff and Chartkoff 1984).

The evidence from the fluted points in California is tantalizing. The scatter of surface finds indicates a human presence at Clovis times, but the scarcity of sites with subsurface material is frustrating. Information from the adjacent Great Basin, where fluted points are found around dry lakes, often associated on the surface with bones of extinct animals, provides evidence that users of fluted points lived just east of the California archaeological area.

San Dieguito

Southern California is home to the C. W. Harris site, the site where the **San Dieguito complex** is best represented. Located on the San Dieguito River near San Diego, C. W. Harris is one of the few well-stratified sites in the San Diego region. At this site the San Dieguito material lies at the bottom of up to 6 feet (2 m) of deposits, separated from the overlying Archaic material by river deposits that lack artifacts. The Harris site is in an area where a number of other San Dieguito sites have been recorded, primarily as surface sites. Leaf-shaped points and knives (including Lake Mohave and Silver Lake points), a variety of scrapers made on large flakes, and unusually shaped artifacts called eccentric crescentics (Figure 7.3) characterize the San Dieguito complex. Though occasionally found with San Dieguito artifacts at surface sites or in mixed contexts, millingstones have not been definitively linked to the San Dieguito. Given both the lack of millingstones and the nature of the artifacts found at San Dieguito sites, the people who left these remains are thought to have been hunters of large game. Radiocarbon dates indicate that San Dieguito people lived in southern California in at least 9000 BP and perhaps as early as 10,000 BP, with their occupation ending around 8500 BP.

As we stated in Chapters 5 and 6, similarities to San Dieguito are noted for appropriately early archaeological materials on the Northwest Coast and in the

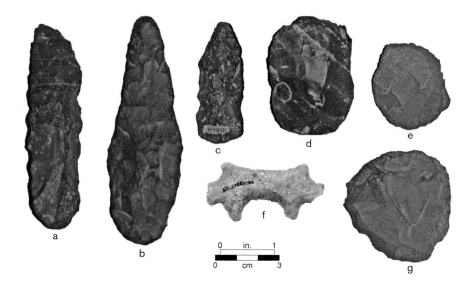

FIGURE 7.3 San Dieguito artifacts from western San Diego County: (a) biface or knife, (b) reworked stemmed point, (c) smaller point, (d, e, g) unifaces or scrapers, (f) crescentic.

Plateau. Other assemblages in California have also been suggested to resemble the San Dieguito. These include Borax Lake and Buena Vista Lake. The San Dieguito is seen as a coastal representative of the Western Pluvial Lakes tradition, to be discussed more in the next chapter. This is the name given to a pattern of settlement around lakes or wetlands throughout the arid west and into coastal California. The San Dieguito material qualifies for membership in the Western Pluvial Lakes tradition because of its association with coastal rivers (e.g., at the Harris site), and with lagoons, as well as the inclusion of leaf-shaped points, scrapers, bifacial knives, and crescents in the artifact assemblages. Some researchers believe that the Western Pluvial Lakes tradition developed out of the Fluted Point tradition.

Early Coastal Sites

Of growing interest is a series of sites that indicate a possible early maritime adaptation separate from the Fluted Point tradition, as discussed in Chapter 3. Sites like Daisy Cave on San Miguel Island (see Chapter 3's case study by Erlandson "Sea Change: The Paleocoastal Occupations of Daisy Cave") and Eel Point on San Clemente Island, discussed in Section D.4 of the Student CD, point to an early adaptation to seafaring (Cassidy et al. 2004).

The Arlington Springs site on Santa Rosa Island is another early coastal site of importance. Human bones were recovered at this site in 1959. Recent reexcavation of the site and dating of animal bone and charcoal associated with the stratum in which the human bones were found has produced dates calibrated to 13,000 BP. Other evidence indicates that the Arlington Springs human bone is contemporaneous with pygmy mammoth fossils found on the island (Agenbroad et al. 2003), although definite stratigraphic association between human occupation and the mammoths has yet to be demonstrated (see Chapter 3). Because Daisy Cave, Eel Point, and Arlington Springs occur on islands, watercraft must have been used to gain access to them. In the case of San Clemente Island, the trip from the mainland was a long one (Cassidy et al. 2004)—over 50 miles (80 km). These sites also are significant because of their age and because fluted points and bifaces like those of the Western Pluvial Lakes tradition are not found in them.

On the mainland, the Cross Creek site in San Luis Obispo County has a discrete shell midden component dated to between 9900 BP and 9340 BP. This site is clearly representative of what elsewhere in southern California is the Archaic period **Millingstone horizon**, but it dates earlier than previously known Millingstone horizon sites. Because the site has an assemblage that is nothing like the Fluted Point tradition or the Western Pluvial Lake assemblages, the researchers (Jones et al. 2002) working with the Cross Creek material see it as potential support for a coastal migration.

FORAGERS: THE ARCHAIC PATTERN

With the changes at the end of the Pleistocene (ca. 10,000 BP), people began to adapt to warmer and drier conditions and the loss of many of the resources that originally attracted people to the area. This is when the Archaic pattern developed. As in other areas of the North America, the California Archaic has been understood as a reaction to changing resources in which people broadened their food base, incorporating hard seeds that could not be processed without specialized grinding equipment. It is because these grinding implements are such a hallmark of the Archaic in California that the period in southern California is often referred to as the Millingstone horizon (William J. Wallace 1955).

Coastal

Along the California coast from San Luis Obispo south into Baja California are found sites assigned to the Millingstone horizon, the Archaic expression along the southern California coast. Although Cross Creek might indicate that this way of life dates back to 9900 BP, the Archaic is generally thought to have started about 8500 BP or later. Since sea level rose after the disappearance of the continental glaciers at the end of the Pleistocene, many of the sites of the early Archaic peoples are underwater today or have been eroded away by wave action. Only the tantalizing remnants at Cross Creek and on the Channel Islands provide glimpses of what the earliest Archaic adaptation was like. Sites increase in number as time goes on, and a picture of Archaic development emerges.

The **La Jolla complex** (8500–2000 BP), known from sites in southern California and northern Baja California, is an example of the Millingstone horizon. The La Jolla complex, originally called the Shell Midden people by Malcolm J. Rogers, is marked by sites along the coast containing considerable amounts of shell, along with relatively simple flake and cobble tools, as well as **manos** and **metates**. Manos are handheld grinding stones, and metates are the bases on which manos were used to grind seeds or other material. Some sites have yielded flexed burials, and cemeteries have been found at some of the larger sites. Inland Archaic sites in the San Diego area have some characteristics in common with the La Jollan sites, but have a greater range of flaked stone tools, many not made from cobbles. They also lack shell. These sites, which have been given the name

Pauma complex in the northern part of San Diego County, are not common, although in many cases inland Archaic occupations may go unnoticed because of mixing with later components. In southern San Diego County and northern Baja California, sites with general similarities are known but have not been assigned to a named archaeological complex.

On the Santa Barbara coast and the adjacent Channel Islands, various observers have defined a number of phases, but a simple scheme of Early, Middle, and Late periods commonly is used today. Chester King's (1990) chronological studies of beads provide a large part of the basis for these periods. The Early period is equivalent to the Archaic and part or all of the Early Pacific period. This time frame encompasses what earlier archaeologists in the Santa Barbara Coast called the **Oak Grove** and **Hunting phases**. Oak Grove material is much like the La Jolla, but with **extended burials** with red ocher. In contrast to the La Jolla, some pithouses have been found in Oak Grove sites. The Hunting people used mortars and pestles and had relatively fewer millingstones or metates. Projectile points were also more common on Hunting than on Oak Grove sites. Hunting sites were closer to the ocean and had flexed burials.

Central California

In the San Francisco Bay area and in the Central Valley, the earliest Archaic times are poorly represented in the archaeological record. This probably is because San Francisco Bay did not exist as a body of water at the end of the Pleistocene. Rising seas of the early Holocene began to flood the lowlands behind the Coast Ranges, forming an ever-growing bay fringed by productive marshlands. Many of the earliest sites in the Bay area may be underwater today. In the Central Valley there has been very active deposition of sediments in the floodplains of the Sacramento and San Joaquin rivers, also probably burying most Archaic sites. Deposits at the Grayson site in Merced County include small mortars, pestles, millingstones, and simple shell beads and are thought to date to between 5250 BP and 4550 BP (Moratto 1984, 191). Sites at Buena Vista Lake (Ker-39 and Ker-60) also have some material that may be germane to this time. The lower levels of these two sites produced millingstones and manos, and extended burials were found at one of them. The Skyrocket site, excavated in the 1990s as data recovery associated with mining operations, is a stratified site on the eastern edge of the southern Central Valley that provides a long record of human occupation in the area. The final report on this site is not yet available, but the literature that exists about it indicates that millingstones found there may date back to 9200 BP (Fagan 2003, 86–88). At the very end of the Archaic and the beginning of the Pacific period the **Windmiller pattern**, which will be discussed further shortly, developed.

Northern Coast

On the northern California coast from San Francisco Bay to the Klamath River a Middle to Late Archaic occupation known as the **Borax Lake tradition** is found. The hallmark for this tradition is the Borax Lake point, a distinctive projectile point with a square stem (Figure 7.4). Little excavation has been conducted at Borax Lake tradition sites, and the original work at Borax Lake is the best known. Recent excavation at the Nursery site in Humboldt County documents the pres-

FIGURE 7.4 Borax Lake points.

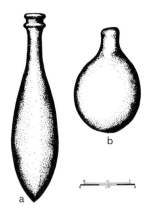

FIGURE 7.5 Borax Lake charmstones: (a) plummet-shaped and (b) bulb-shaped.

ence of the Borax Lake tradition on the coast (Humboldt State University 2004). This tradition is represented in the archaeological record by manos and metates, scrapers, scraper planes, knives, and bifaces of other kinds (Chartkoff and Chartkoff 1984, 111–113). Mortars and pestles are found in the later part of the pattern, and a few polished stone items known as **charmstones** (Figure 7.5) have also been recovered from Borax Lake tradition sites (Bennyhoff and Fredrickson 1994, 24).

Settlement Pattern

Archaic settlement patterns have been best delineated for southern California. Millingstone horizon sites are found along the coast and are usually situated on high ground such as bluffs and marine terraces (Erlandson 1994, 258). The choice of high ground for sites may represent a real trend in occupation, or it may be that the sites on high ground are the only ones readily available to archaeologists. Sites at lower elevations may have been flooded, eroded by the sea, or buried under alluvial fill. People of the Millingstone horizon preferred to settle near the lagoons and estuaries that formed as the rising sea flooded river and stream mouths at the beginning of the Holocene, and many coastal lagoons are ringed with a large number of Millingstone horizon sites. The productivity of these lagoons would have been considerable first as open-water systems with lush salt marshes around the shores and schools of fish and open-water shellfish (like scallops). These marshes would have attracted seasonal flights of birds migrating along the coast, as well. Over time, the streams, whose mouths were flooded to form the lagoons, carried sediment from the uplands they drained and began to fill these bodies of water. As mudflats formed, these also became productive habitats, being colonized by clams that burrow into the soft mud.

Ultimately, though, many small bays and estuaries were closed off from the open ocean or were filled with silt and ceased to be useful as resource areas for humans. Later Archaic populations adjusted to this change by moving to the open coast or to permanent bays and wetlands like San Diego Bay. The larger coastal sites probably served as seasonal base camps, with inland sites being occupied at least part of the year. In the southern part of the California coast, Jon Erlandson (1994, 258–259) sees a highly mobile existence for the early Archaic populations, with relatively small groups occupying the sites. In the Santa Barbara and San Luis Obispo areas, on the other hand, he believes people at this time were semisedentary, moving from large coastal sites to a variety of seasonal camps.

Subsistence

The Early Archaic people probably had a very diverse diet, gathering from a wide variety of environments. Along the coast, shellfish were very important, supplemented by seeds and land animals. Interestingly, the remains from early sites indicate that fish were not favored resources. The presence of millingstones, which begin to be found in sites dated to between 8000 BP and 9000 BP, is evidence of the importance of seeds. Seeds and shellfish complemented each other in the diets of coastal people, with shellfish being high in protein and low in calories, while seeds provided the carbohydrates and calories needed for good health (Erlandson 1991). In inland areas such as northwestern California, hunting of large game was important early, combined with collection of hard seeds.

In the Middle Archaic there is considerable evidence of a rise in importance of hunting throughout California, and on the Channel Islands there is an increase in fishing activity (Hildebrant and McGuire 2002). Indeed, this was the period of time of the Hunting phase on the Santa Barbara Coast.

Acorns, which are so important to the later people of California, were probably first used in the early Archaic. Evidence from the Skyrocket site in the foothills of the Sierra Nevada suggests that acorns may have been a supplementary food as early as 8500 BP, but mortars and pestles used to process them in quantity are not common until between 6000 BP and 5000 BP (Erlandson 1994, 262; Fagan 2000, 209).

Population Density

Populations at the beginning of the Archaic appear to have been small: few sites have been found, and their size generally was small. Population grew throughout the Archaic, with the pace of growth increasing significantly with time. Erlandson (1994, 258) notes that population increased considerably in the Early and Middle Archaic (9500–6000 BP)—perhaps as much as ten times. Late Archaic populations continued to grow.

COMPLEXITY: THE PACIFIC PERIOD

Nature of Complexity

The Pacific period marks the transition from the Archaic to more complex lifeways. As noted earlier, this California post-Archaic pattern is seen by many archaeologists as equivalent to post-Archaic developments elsewhere in North America. Developments during this period ultimately led to the historic populations of Native Americans encountered by the explorers and colonists. The post-Archaic people of California achieved a farminglike level of complexity, not by adopting agriculture but by adopting a few stable foods and focusing their economic activities on them (Chartkoff and Chartkoff 1984, 147). These strategies led to higher population levels in some parts of California than were reached on the Northwest Coast—indeed, the highest population densities recorded in North America north of Mexico. The large populations were organized by settlement with hereditary leaders. Trade was important and extensive, and helped support the leaders. The appearance of luxury items, along with the development of notions of ownership of property, led to inequality, with some families and individuals having more access to resources than others. These changes were almost certainly a reaction to imbalances between growing populations and the available resources, and these imbalances, in turn, were often caused by changes in climatic conditions. The specific nature of the climatic changes is one of the hotly debated topics in California archaeology.

Coastal

In coastal southern and central California the beginning of the Pacific period is called the Middle period or the **Campbell tradition**. The Middle period is based

FIGURE 7.6 Canaliño artifacts: (top row) projectile points; (middle row) whole *Olivella* shell bead, *Olivella* barrel bead, split and punched *Olivella* bead, fishhook; (bottom row) various disk and tube beads.

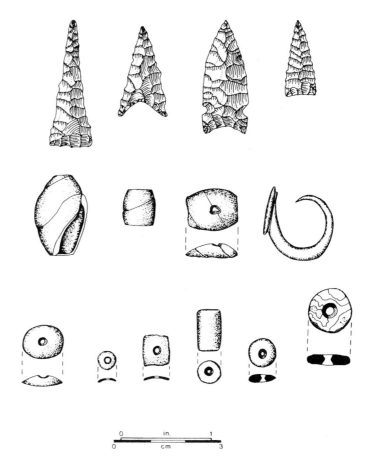

FIGURE 7.7 Carved and inlaid artifacts: (top) flanged stone pestles; (bottom) sandstone bowl with appliqué of beads in asphalt.

primarily on changes in bead and ornament styles. The Campbell tradition has its roots in the late Archaic, but sites of this tradition show a more focused economy. In the Santa Barbara region the emphasis was on hunting land animals and procuring marine mammals, while farther south acorns and other hard seeds were the focus. Shellfish remained important along the coast, and fishing increased. In the San Diego area the Campbell tradition was originally thought to be represented by a few intrusive sites or components at sites. However, the nature of the Campbell occupation of that area is being reconsidered today because it appears to have been more widespread than previously believed. Campbell tradition sites are marked by the presence of mortars and pestles, as well as an increase in projectile points over earlier occupations (Warren 1968). Trade goods become more important in Campbell tradition sites than in earlier sites. Traded material includes shell, steatite, and obsidian (Chartkoff and Chartkoff 1984, 165–166).

The Middle period was followed by the development of Late period cultures. In the Santa Barbara region the Late Prehistoric occupation is the **Canaliño**, which is marked by the occurrence of small arrowheads, the mortar and pestle, and a wealth of ground stone artifacts (Figure 7.6). There is an elaboration of artifacts of many types, and shell inlay was applied to bowls, pipes, and pestles (Figure 7.7). Engraving was used to enhance the appearance of stone items. There also is clear evidence of extensive use of marine resources, including fish and sea mammals.

The Canaliño people made the *tomol*, or plank canoe, that was so important to the Chumash, although there is a suggestion that boat manufacture may date back much further in the Channel Islands area (see Section D.3 on the Student CD). The use of the plank canoe, which could navigate in ocean waters, made the development of interdependent economic systems on the islands and the mainland possible. The nature of the rise and maintenance of complexity among the Chumash is currently a topic of debate, as discussed in Box 7.1.

ISSUES AND DEBATES

BOX 7.1

Chumash Complexity

When the Spanish explorers and missionaries first encountered the people of the Santa Barbara Channel, they found one of the most populous areas in North America. As many as a thousand people lived in villages, each one composed of groups of houses, the largest being reserved for the head chief or *wot*; there were sweathouses dug partially into the ground, as well as an enclosed ceremonial area, a gaming area, storehouses, and a cemetery (Grant 1978, 510). The Chumash sailed the waters of the channel in unique canoes made by splitting planks from driftwood logs, shaping them, sewing them together, and using natural asphalt caulking to seal the seams (Gamble 2002). The people used these *tomols* for fishing, for hunting sea mammals, and for traveling to the Channel Islands. The islands were linked to the mainland communities through intricate webs of trade and marriage relationships. Villages on Santa Cruz Island specialized in the manufacture of beads from California purple olive shell (*Olivella biplicata*). Villages on the island controlled the quarries where chert was mined to produce thin bladelets used in drilling the beads, as well as the production of those drills (Arnold 1992). Shell beads served as a kind of money

throughout southern and central California (Grant 1978, 516).

The Chumash also made trade items, including stone bowls and tubular pipes. They excelled in basketry, producing water bottles, trays, storage baskets, and other forms. Stone mortars and pestles were finely made, and prestige items such as raptor talon pendants, bone rings and tubes, and shell beads of many kinds were produced for the upper crust of Chumash society.

The ethnographic record provides evidence of both elite families and commoners, and the archaeological record reinforces this social ranking. Early work in the Chumash area focused on cemeteries because of the plentiful, and often spectacular, grave goods. More recent analysis of patterning within cemeteries indicates both differential distributions of prestige items among burials and spatial segregation of high-status burials within the cemeteries. These findings point to differences in access to status items, and, therefore, differences in social class. The discovery that very young individuals were buried with elaborate grave goods indicates that status was inherited, since the children had not lived long enough to have distinguished themselves (Gamble et al. 2001).

Archaeologists working in the Chumash area liken the social organization of the area to that of a simple chiefdom, and there is evidence that some *wots*, or chiefs, presided over regions containing multiple villages. Some villages had subchiefs, as well. The *wot* inherited his or her position and was responsible for administering resource areas controlled by the village, for accumulating and distributing surplus food and other material, for organizing ceremonies and feasts, and for warfare. The chiefs were drawn from a larger elite or noble class in Chumash society (Erlandson and Rick 2002).

Not only were resource areas controlled by the *wots*, but members of the noble class also owned the *tomols*, which were so important in fishing and trade. Since tomols represented a substantial investment in time and materials, only wealthy members of the upper class could afford to commission their construction. Arnold (1992, 71) has estimated that the construction of a tomol required between 180 and 540 person-days. Members of the Brotherhood of the Tomol owned and manufactured these plank canoes, and membership in the group crosscut localized villages (Gamble 2002, 312).

It is clear, then, that the Chumash were complex hunter-gatherers. They epitomize trends we see in California for hereditary leadership, ownership of resources, development of social classes, and large, semisedentary to sedentary populations. Just when this complex organization developed and why are subjects of considerable debate among archaeologists.

Chester King (1990), in a seminal study of beads and other materials associated with burials, developed a sequence of bead types that is widely used in southern California. He also suggested that the Chumash developed steadily for over 7000 years, with the hallmarks of complexity developing by the end of the Early period, around 2550 BP. Arnold and O'Shea (1993) criticized King's work for the assumption that the meaning of artifacts, particularly shell ornaments, could be projected 7000 years into the past. Arnold (1992) instead believes that the development of chiefdoms was a relatively late phenomenon, occurring between 800 BP and 650 BP. She sees this development as a result of individuals exploiting economic hard times brought on by the elevated sea surface temperatures that reduced the productivity of the ocean in the Santa Barbara Channel. Individuals would have stepped in to organize labor in the production of shell beads, as well as the quarrying and manufacture of the microlithic chert drills necessary to manufacture the beads. The beads, manufactured almost exclusively on the islands, could have been traded to the mainland for food. On the mainland they became currency that was intricately woven into the complex exchange relationships developing there (King 1976).

Two important studies by Lynn Gamble (Gamble et al. 2001; 2002) support King's position, to a degree. Gamble (2002) looked at the development of the tomol and its antiquity, concluding that the plank canoe technology was at least 1300 years old in the Santa Barbara Channel area. To the extent that canoes were owned, this dating bolsters King's position of early development of social hierarchies. In another study with Phillip Walker and Glenn Russell (Gamble et al. 2001), patterns at the Historic and Prehistoric cemeteries at Malibu were interpreted as suggesting the presence of ascribed status in the Middle period, again supporting King's conclusions.

Although agreeing with Arnold on the timing of changes, Raab and Larson (1997) argue that the period of higher sea surface temperatures noted by Arnold was not a time of reduced marine productivity, but rather a relatively bountiful time. They find evidence for extended and severe droughts during this period, however. These authors argue that the droughts, associated with the Medieval climatic anomaly, caused populations to concentrate at areas with reliable water. The concentration of population led to the development of fixed territories, increases in intergroup conflict, and ultimately to the development of the leadership hierarchy, in their view.

Using oxygen isotope measurements with fine resolution, combined with archaeological data, Kennet and Kennet (2000) reexamined the relationship between climate and culture change in the Northern Channel Islands. They conclude that there is a relationship between the development of complexity and climatic change. Their data indicates change beginning at 1650 BP and accelerating after 650 BP. They agree with Raab and Larson that marine productivity at this time was high and that drought was a problem. They also note that fluctuations in land resources would have been quite unpredictable.

Finally, in a recent treatment of the problem, Erlandson and Rick (2002) note the difficulty in identifying specific indicators of a chiefdom level of complexity in the archaeological record. Instead of looking for hallmarks of complexity, they focused on the development of specific traits known in historical Chumash society. These traits include elaboration of material culture, development of village layout, and specific architectural forms and burial practices. They conclude that Chumash development was both gradual and punctuated by sudden bursts of change. They note a key transition at about 3450 BP and another between 1450 BP and 550 BP. They also highlight the variability within the Chumash adaptation.

The timing and explanation of the development of complexity among the Chumash is important not only for California studies, but also for the general understanding of complex hunter-gatherers. Thus, Chumash complexity will continue to be a topic of considerable debate contributing to the larger anthropological dialog for some time.

There also is considerable evidence for the development of status differentiation or social ranking among the people of the Late period. As discussed in Box 7.1, much of the evidence comes from cemeteries and the differential distribution of rare items in cemeteries.

Farther south on the coast and in the adjacent foothills and mountains archaeologists have defined the **Cuyamaca** and **San Luis Rey complexes** for the Late period. These are seen as the ancestors of the modern Kumeyaay and the Luiseño, respectively. Sites of these complexes have brownware ceramics (Figure 7.8), as well as triangular and side-notched arrowheads. Mortars are common, as are metates and manos for processing hard seeds. Ceramics seem to have a longer history with the Cuyamaca complex, given the wider variety of forms, including not only **ollas** and bowls, but also trays, pipes, rattles, pottery anvils (used in shaping the paddle-and-anvil pottery), and effigies of various kinds. Both complexes cremated their dead, in contrast to the earlier Archaic practice of

FIGURE 7.8 Southern California ceramic vessels.

flexed burial. Cremation and ceramics probably originated to the east and were adopted first by the Cuyamaca complex peoples and then by those of the San Luis Rey complex. Similarities in ceramics, cremation practices, projectile points, and effigies between the Cuyamaca complex and the Hohokam of Arizona (see Chapter 9) suggest interaction between these groups. Findings in coastal sites of scattered but sparse Hohokam artifacts such as shell beads, sherds, and ground axes reinforce this inference of contact.

Central Valley

The Windmiller pattern in the Central Valley, especially the Sacramento Delta area, straddles the boundary between the Archaic and the Pacific periods. It also marks the earliest well-known occupation of the area. The Windmiller pattern is known mostly from excavation of cemeteries on clay knolls that rise above the floodplain of the delta. Windmiller burial patterns were quite elaborate, with graves including red ocher. Burial goods or offerings were present with most burials, and they include mortars, shell beads and ornaments, and ground charmstones (Figure 7.9). Most burials are extended and were placed in the grave on their backs, although occasional flexed burials and even cremations are found. Windmiller sites include large numbers of baked **clay cooking balls**, which are thought to have substituted for rock in stone boiling, since the delta lacked ready supplies of rock for this purpose. Bone remains indicate that people hunted deer, elk, pronghorn, rabbit, and water birds, and the large number of projectile points

FIGURE 7.9 Windmiller pattern artifacts: (a–f) projectile points, (g) millingstone, (h) mano, (i) mortar, (j) pestle, (k) ground stone pipe bowl, (l) charmstone, (m–s) shell ornaments, and (t–x) bone implements.

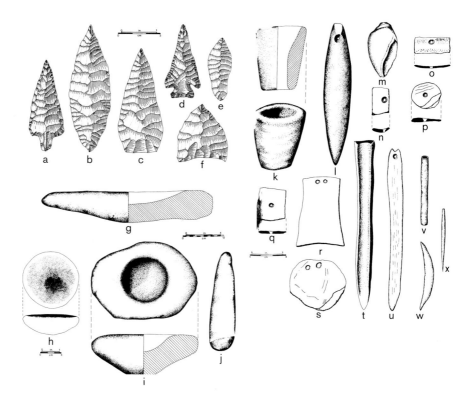

FIGURE 7.10 Berkeley pattern artifacts from the Napa District; scales variable.

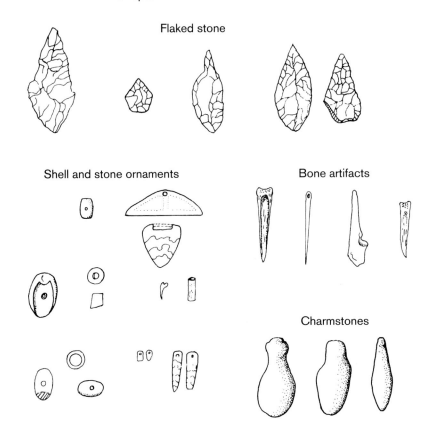

Flaked stone

Shell and stone ornaments

Bone artifacts

Charmstones

from Windmiller sites underscores the importance of this hunting. Salmon and other fish were taken with fish spears or hooks. Ornaments are well developed, and throughout the Central Valley, periods are defined in part on the basis of differences in shell and stone beads, pendants, and jewelry of other types. One interesting use of shell was an appliqué effect created by affixing shell beads to objects with **asphaltum**. Obsidian, shell, quartz crystals, alabaster, asphaltum, and other exotic materials indicate that the people who occupied the Windmiller sites participated in well-developed trade networks (Moratto 1984, 201–207).

Berkeley pattern sites, which follow Windmiller, have more mortars and pestles; bone artifacts are more common and are found in greater variety; and there are large projectile points that exhibit diagonal flaking, as well as specific forms of beads and ornaments. Manos and metates, on the other hand, are rare. Burials are flexed and are generally accompanied by fewer artifacts. The Berkeley pattern (Figure 7.10) was defined in the San Francisco Bay area at the West Berkeley site, and it appeared in that area about 4000 BP. It spread into the Delta region by about 2500 BP (Moratto 1984, 209–211, 278). A decrease in projectile points relative to millingstones, suggests that the collecting and processing of plants was becoming more important in the economy (Bennyhoff and Fredrickson 1994, 23).

The final pattern in the Delta area, the **Augustine pattern**, is characterized by the presence of well-shaped mortars and pestles, small projectile points,

FIGURE 7.11 Augustine pattern artifacts from the Napa District; scales variable.

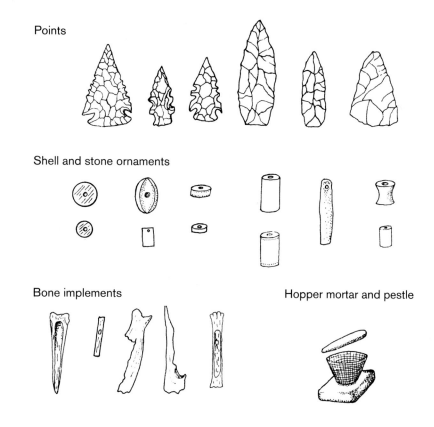

Points

Shell and stone ornaments

Bone implements

Hopper mortar and pestle

numerous shell artifacts, worked bone (including awls for coiled basket making), charmstones, and polished stone pipes (Figure 7.11). Fishing equipment is more abundant than in earlier contexts, but it is not common. New to the fishing gear is the harpoon. Burial practices change in the Augustine pattern. Flexed burials occur, but cremation is also found. Grave pits as well as grave artifacts were often burned. Fishing increased during Augustine times, but acorns were still the staple (Bennyhoff and Fredrikson 1994, 23).

The Augustine pattern is seen as being influenced by the movement of peoples in the more northerly regions of the Delta. It is suggested that the Wintuan peoples moved into the Sacramento Valley at about the time the Augustine pattern developed, and that Gunther barbed points, grave burning, the harpoon, and certain types of pipe can be attributed to this source (Moratto 1984, 211). The Blodget site, an important Augustine pattern and Historic Miwok site, has produced evidence of a well-developed pottery-making industry.

North Coast

On the North Coast there are similarities to the Delta sequence. In the Eel River region, for instance, materials known as the **Shasta aspect** of the Augustine pattern are found. Artifacts from this time include Gunther barbed points, hopper mortars, manos and metates, bifaces of chert, charmstones, and spire-lopped *Olivella* beads. The Shasta pattern shares elements with both the adjoining

Northwest Coast and the northern Central Valley. Semisedentary winter villages were located in lowland settings, and camps occupied by portions of the village population in other seasons have been found in the uplands (Fredrickson 1984).

PACIFIC PERIOD LIFEWAYS

Settlement Pattern

A variety of site types characterizing the Pacific period are found in the archaeological record. These include permanent villages, seasonal camps, and specialized resource extraction sites (quarries for acquiring materials for stone tools, weirs in rivers to help with catching fish, etc.), and rock art sites. Trading sites also developed that facilitated the exchange of goods and were important parts of the networks that connected various populations in Prehistoric California. Specialized sites replaced the more generalized camp sites of the Archaic period. In some areas, such as the Santa Barbara Channel and the Central Valley, populations became sedentary, occupying the same spot for generations, while elsewhere people became semisedentary, splitting their time between permanent village sites and seasonal camps of various kinds. The increase in the permanence of villages led to the formation of defined cemeteries in many areas (Chartkoff and Chartkoff 1984, 205–218). Many sites of this period also are marked by the presence of **bedrock milling features** (see Exhibit 7.1).

CLUES TO THE PAST

EXHIBIT 7.1

Bedrock Milling Features

If you ever hike in California's mountains you will be likely to turn a corner and come upon a boulder covered with holes. These are bedrock milling features, which Indians used for grinding seeds or other material. Bedrock milling features come in several different forms, ranging from conical holes called mortars to oval basins. Some boulders have rather amorphous areas where the rock has been worn smooth in an irregular fashion, creating neither holes nor basins. These are called "slicks," and their use is uncertain. Mortars, on the other hand, are associated with the processing of large seeds such as hulled acorns, which can be pulverized into flour by pounding with a cylin-

drical pestle. The basins are essentially metates worn into bedrock and would have been used with a mano to grind smaller hard seeds (Figure 7.12).

Bedrock milling features are found in many parts of North America where suitably hard rock crops out at the surface. They are particularly common in California and adjoining states, as well as in the Southwest. West Texas has a number of recorded bedrock milling sites as well. Ethnographically, they are primarily known from California, Oregon, and the Southwest.

Mortars were used in the processing of acorns to make them edible, and ethnographic descriptions for Sierra Nevada groups identify

FIGURE 7.12 Bedrock milling features (mortars and grinding basins) on a granite boulder near Lakeside, San Diego County, California.

shallow mortars as "starter mortars" in which initial pounding was done, with deeper mortars used to finish the processing (McCarthy et al. 1985). Following the grinding, the flour had to be treated to remove the bitter-tasting tannic acid (the same chemical used to tan leather). This was usually done by placing the meal in a shallow basket set over a bed of sand. Water was poured through the meal to dissolve the acid and carry it away. The flour was deemed ready when it no longer tasted bitter.

The acorn meal could be cooked as a gruel, left to set up as a gelatinous cake (like grits left to cool in the pan), made into a bread, or added to stews as a thickener. Because the acorn stored so well, it was a staple food, and

the mortar was important in its efficient use. The earliest mortars were shallow depressions in rocks. These depressions were not deep enough to contain the acorns during pulverization, so basketry hoppers (conical baskets without bottoms) were glued to the mortars edges to keep the acorns under control. Archaeological evidence for this practice has been found in the form of mastic (usually asphaltum) adhering to shallow mortars.

Bedrock mortars are generally found where suitable bedrock occurs in areas that have oak trees. They are often near water. In California they are concentrated in the Sierra Nevada but are also common in northeastern California, in the Monterey area, and in the mountains and foothills of southern California. Some bedrock milling is even reported from the Channel Islands (Meighan 2000, 63). Granite is the most common bedrock used for milling, but mortars, basins, and slicks are found on just about any type of hard rock outcrop including schist, limestone, volcanic rock, and hard sandstone. The largest concentration of bedrock mortars in North America is preserved in the Sierra Nevada northeast of Stockton in Chaw'se Indian Grinding Rock State Historic Park. There, in an area of grasslands and oak forest, are found 1185 bedrock mortars on marbleized limestone. Wherever these humble bedrock milling features occur, they can tell archaeologists important things about the lifestyles of the past.

Subsistence and Social Organization

The key to the economies of the Pacific period was the intensified pursuit of specific resources: what has been called a focal economy. Acorns were the staple plant food almost everywhere in California, but other important foods included hard seeds, especially of large-seeded grasses, anadromous fish, and marine resources such as fish and sea mammals. Focusing on these resources allowed populations to grow, but whether and to what extent most of these foods were used depended on the people's ability to store them.

Acorns are abundant when they ripen, and because of the oils they contain, they store very well. A prominent feature of most villages in California in the Pacific period would have been acorn granaries, structures designed for storing large quantities of nuts. These were often large basketlike constructions coiled out of willow or other brush and set on posts (Figure 7.13). They were furnished with lids, and each granary would hold many bushels of acorns. In the desert areas of the South Coast, where mesquite and screwbean took the place of acorns, such granaries were used to store these staples, as well. In the far south of the state, large ceramic vessels were also made to store seeds. Anadromous fish were dried and stored just as on the Plateau (Chapter 6) and Northwest Coast (Chapter 5).

The increase in population led to the development of hereditary leadership. Such systems most likely evolved as individuals demonstrated their abilities to lead and to acquire surpluses, as well as to be successful at trading with other groups for goods not available in the home territories. Before long, however, talented leaders developed systems under which they could pass their positions of primacy on to family members. Unsurprisingly, the families that controlled the leadership also had greater access to material goods. Luxury goods such as shell beads (Figure 7.14) became symbols of wealth, and these served as money in the Santa Barbara Channel and in the San Francisco Bay area and Central Valley. On Santa Cruz Island, the production of shell beads, along with the control of the chert needed to make the drills used in their manufacture, formed the basis for a complex chiefdom.

Trade became critically important during this period. Large networks developed to move shell beads, obsidian for toolmaking, asphaltum, and steatite, as well as food items. These networks served to bolster the leadership hierarchies, and they provided critical raw materials; but they also served as a hedge against hard times, as luxury goods could be traded for food when local harvests were sparse.

FIGURE 7.13 Large basketry granary.

FIGURE 7.14 Late period shell beads.

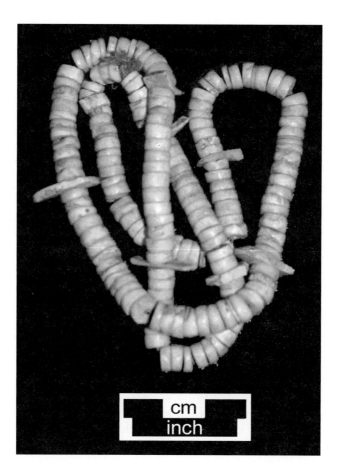

The leadership structure and the trade networks also served to control violence, to a degree. Early in the Pacific period, roughly between 1950 BP and 1050 BP, many of the cemeteries investigated contain individuals who bear signs of violence, including broken bones and arrowheads embedded in the bone. Resource shortages probably caused by droughts may have led to widespread fighting among groups over productive areas. Later in the Pacific period, there are fewer signs of trauma in burials (Fagan 2003, 32–33).

Population Density

Populations grew dramatically during the Pacific period. Not only are more sites of this period found, but many of the sites are very large. Villages in the Santa Barbara Channel area, as well as those in the San Francisco Bay area, which produced massive shell mounds on the shore, and in the Central Valley, grew to considerable size, with accessory sites used seasonally and for special resource procurement. As noted earlier, at the time of European exploration, California had the highest population densities of any area of North America north of Mexico.

Prehistoric Archaeology in California Today

We have already discussed NAGPRA and how it permeates the practice of American archaeology today. California archaeologists had a history of resolving burial issues with Native Americans before NAGPRA became law, however, and California Indians are very active in the repatriation process. For example, the **California Native American Burial Act**, passed in 1982, requires involvement of the Native American community in determining the fate of human remains discovered in the state by archaeologists or by anyone else.

Several California reservations have responded to the pace of development and to the demands of NAGPRA by hiring archaeologists or, as in the case of the Pechanga Band in southern California, establishing a cultural resource department. The Barona Reservation led the way in the establishment of the Kumeyaay Cultural and Repatriation Committee (see Student CD, Section F.3).

HISTORIC PERIOD

Exploration Period (1542–1769)

Despite earlier exploration of Baja California and present-day Arizona by the Spanish, the exploration period in California really starts with the voyage of Portuguese-born João Rodrigues Cabrilho (known often as Juan Cabrillo). In 1542 Cabrilho led the first European expedition to see San Diego Bay, sailed through the Channel Islands, and reached at least as far north as Cape Mendocino (Chartkoff and Chartkoff 1984, 252–253). Succumbing to injuries sustained in a skirmish with the Indians on San Miguel Island, Cabrilho died and was buried on the Island. His explorations and those to follow brought knowledge of California to European attention, and left a few trade goods among the Native Americans encountered, but had little effect that can be seen in the archaeological record.

British privateer Sir Frances Drake, who sailed the California coast as part of his circumnavigation of the globe in 1579, stopped in a convenient bay to repair his ships. This bay was probably Drake's Bay, north of San Francisco. A brass plaque found in the area in 1934 bore an inscription claiming the land for Britain. Drake's records mention such a plaque, but the authenticity of this find is questionable. European goods have been recovered from archaeological middens in the Drake's Bay area, and they may be items obtained by the local Miwok during Drake's stay. Other European and Asian artifacts from Marin County middens are probably from wrecks of the Spanish galleons in the late sixteenth century.

When Europeans began to arrive, California had the highest population densities of any North American area (Moratto 1984, 2). It also had the greatest linguistic diversity (Figure 7.15). Two language stocks, the Penutian and the Hokan, dominated the state, but a number of other language stocks were represented, as well. Penutian was found throughout much of the central part of the area, both in the Central Valley and along the central California coast. The Miwok, Yokut, Wintun, Coastanoan, and Maidu all spoke Penutian languages. The Hokan stock included groups scattered around the margin of the Penutians, such as the Kumeyaay and Chumash of southern California, the Shasta, Yana, Yahi, and Pomo of northern California, and the Esselen and Salinan of the central California

FIGURE 7.15 Language stocks and language families of the California area.

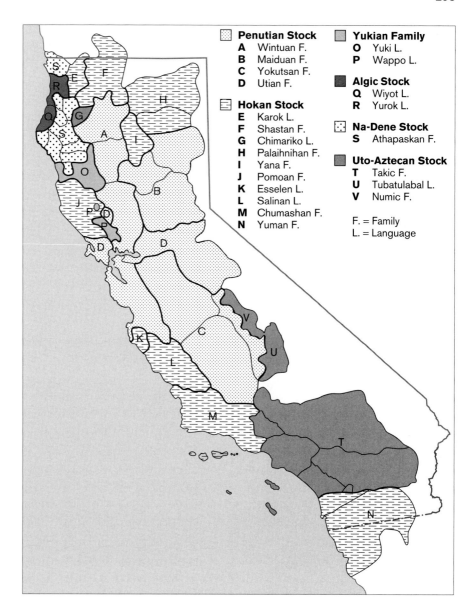

	Penutian Stock		Yukian Family
	A Wintuan F.	**O**	Yuki L.
	B Maiduan F.	**P**	Wappo L.
	C Yokutsan F.		
	D Utian F.		**Algic Stock**
		Q	Wiyot L.
	Hokan Stock	**R**	Yurok L.
	E Karok L.		
	F Shastan F.		**Na-Dene Stock**
	G Chimariko L.	**S**	Athapaskan F.
	H Palaihnihan F.		
	I Yana F.		**Uto-Aztecan Stock**
	J Pomoan F.	**T**	Takic F.
	K Esselen L.	**U**	Tubatulabal L.
	L Salinan L.	**V**	Numic F.
	M Chumashan F.		
	N Yuman F.	F. = Family	
		L. = Language	

coast. The Yukian language was made up of two languages, Yuki and Wappo, which were found north of San Francisco Bay. The Wailaki and Kato in northwestern California represented the Athapascan family of the Na-Dene stock, related to languages in Canada and in the Southwest. Finally, the Luiseño, Cahuilla, Tongva, and Cupeño of southern California were representatives of the Uto-Aztecan family. All of these people were seriously disrupted by European colonization.

Contact with Europeans not only brought exotic goods like glass beads, china, and iron, but also diseases. Indeed, epidemic diseases from Europe for which the Indians had no natural immunity spread well ahead of the European explorers, so that smallpox and other illnesses probably reduced the population of California substantially prior to the first encounter of many Native Americans with the explorers and missionaries. One estimate is that disease had reduced California's Native American population by two-thirds prior to the arrival of the Spanish missionaries. Since this loss of population must have had a substantial effect on the social organization and the subsistence activities of the Indians, the cultures described by the explorers may not closely resemble those that existed only a century before their coming.

Hispanic Period (1769–1821)

The Hispanic period began in California in 1769, when a land expedition from Baja California reached San Diego and established a fort, or presidio, and a mission. The goal of Spanish settlement was to protect Spain's interest in the Crown's claim to the land, given both Russian and English forays into the area. In addition, the Catholic Church sent missionaries to convert the Indians to Christianity and to get them settled at the missions. Generally three kinds of establishment were founded in the Hispanic period—**presidios**, missions, and **pueblos** (Figure 7.16).

Presidios are fortified military housing for garrisons of soldiers. The Spanish built four presidios in California—at San Diego, Santa Barbara, Monterey, and San Francisco. All of these have seen some archaeological excavation. The San Diego Presidio excavations, largely unreported, have been conducted in the chapel area, in the area of the gateway, and in the soldiers' quarters along the northern wall of the fort. In Santa Barbara (Figure 7.17) and San Francisco, ongoing excavation programs are exposing and interpreting the remains of presidios. These presidio excavation programs have provided important information on the interaction between the Indian populations and the Spanish, as well as presidio lifestyles and the role of imported goods in the Spanish settlement of California.

Franciscan missionaries established 21 missions in what is now the state of California. These missions were established in places that had large Native American populations and where water and fertile land were available. They were designed to bring the local Indians in as residents of self-sufficient mission communities. Impressive adobe brick chapels anchored compounds of adobe buildings (Figure 7.18) built with Native American labor. In the southern part of California, where water always has been a problem, the missionaries had the Indian laborers build extensive irrigation systems at several of the missions, generally of *ladrillos* (fired tiles). Jim Deetz conducted a classic excavation in the Indian barracks at La Purísima Mission (Deetz 1963). Deetz was able to examine the differential effects of missionization on male and female Native Americans. He concluded that traditional male activities were replaced by Spanish-derived pursuits, while female activities continued relatively unchanged. There was a lack of traditional male artifacts and an abundance of milling tools and stone bowls, items associated with traditional female activities. Archaeological projects are being conducted at several of the missions today. One example is the ongoing field school at Mission San Antonio de Padua, which has run for nearly three decades.

The Hispanic period also saw the founding of two pueblos or towns—San Jose and Los Angeles (Chartkoff and Chartkoff 1984, 259). In addition, during the Spanish period, Russia claimed land in California, establishing a colony at Fort

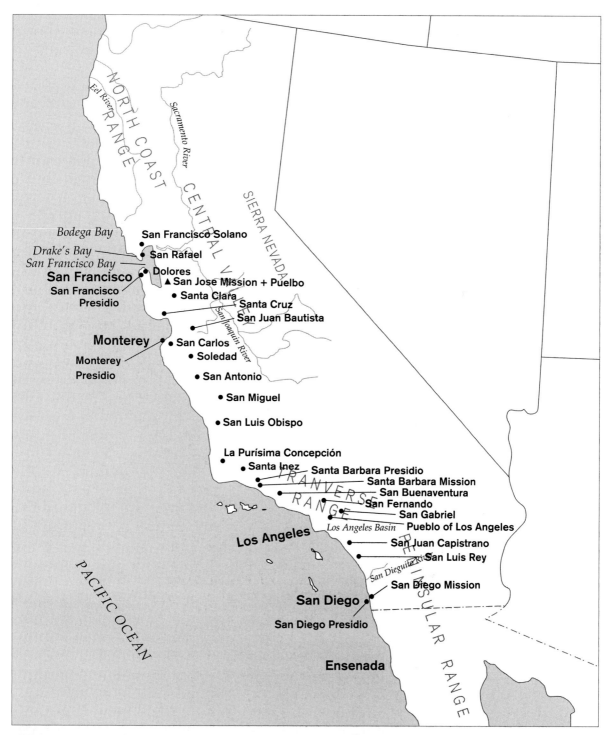

FIGURE 7.16 Location of Spanish missions, presidios, and pueblos in California.

FIGURE 7.17
Reconstruction of the chapel and surrounding buildings of the Santa Barbara Presidio, based in large part on the results of archaeological excavations. The site had been built over as Santa Barbara developed, and buildings had to be removed to allow excavation and reconstruction.

Ross, north of San Francisco, in 1812. The archaeology of this colony is discussed in this chapter's case study by Lightfoot et al. ("Cultures in Contact at Colony Ross").

Mexican Period (1821–1846)

The Hispanic period drew to a close when Mexico gained independence from Spain in 1821. The Mexican period saw the continuation of patterns begun in the Hispanic period, but with the emphasis shifting from the church to private hands. In 1834 the Mexican government secularized the missions. This process basically stripped the missions of their lands. Much of the land in California was divided up into ranchos, great estates that give rise to the mythical and romantic notions about the bucolic early days of the state. Ranchos are the most commonly investigated site from this period, but pueblos also grew, and new ones were established.

The adobe haciendas of the ranchos have attracted considerable archaeological attention over the years. Excavators of the adobes who have researched the architecture not only have learned how it changed over time, they have also discerned economic patterns at the ranchos. At the Sepulveda adobe, near Newport Bay, archaeologists found little evidence in the archaeological record for Indians known to have lived and worked on the rancho, other than utilitarian Tizon brownware pottery. Made primarily in the San Diego region and in the Mohave Desert prior to the mission period, this pottery was adopted as a utility ware in Hispanic and Mexican stage sites. Analysis of other ceramics at the site demonstrates the dependence of the ranchos on international trade, with English ceramics dominating the collection. Excavations at the Petaluma adobe, on the other hand, have focused on finding the workers' dormitory at this site, located in the San Francisco Bay area. Abundant evidence of the presence of Native American laborers was found at this site (Silliman 1998).

FIGURE 7.18 Mission La Purísima Concepción, now a California state park.

Anglo-American Period (1846–present)

The Anglo-American period was ushered in by the Mexican War and followed by the California gold rush. The war left some battlefields and monuments, but archaeologists have not systematically explored these. The gold rush of 1849 and subsequent mining booms in the state, on the other hand, resulted in a number of sites that archaeologists have explored. These sites include remains of old mines, the boomtowns that grew up with the mines, the infrastructure that serviced the mines, and the trails and camps of the immigrants who flocked to the gold fields. Gold was originally found at a mill site owned by John Sutter, whose settlement on the Sacramento River was called Sutter's Fort. Today this fort, built in 1839 under Mexican rule, is a California state historic park. Excavation at the site, provided evidence of architectural details for the reconstruction of the fort and provided grounds for understanding the history of the early American period.

Another theme of the Anglo-American period is the development of towns into cities. Archaeologists are examining the archaeology of these developing cities, looking at their growth, ethnic makeup, and the economics of urbanization. In the Hotel del Corona example at the beginning of this chapter, urban archaeologists demonstrated the use of alcoholic beverages at the hotel even though El Cajon, the location of the site, was incorporated as a dry town.

Another development of early cities was the establishment of ethnic enclaves. The Chinese were often forced to live in restricted areas or Chinatowns in the late nineteenth and early twentieth centuries. Several of these Chinatowns have been excavated, including ones in San Diego (Figure 7.19) and Riverside. The Woolen Mills Chinatown in San Jose was excavated as part of a parkway development project in the late 1990s. The excavations helped demonstrate the connection of the Chinatown residents to their homeland, as indicated by the Chinese ceramics, opium tins, coins, buttons, and evidence that a great deal of fish had been imported from China. Although a wide variety of goods were recovered during the project, the items were generally inexpensive, consistent with the low wages of the laborers who were the primary residents of the Woolen Mills neighborhood (Allen and Hylkema 2000).

Utopian communities developed as a reaction to the commercialism of the late nineteenth and early twentieth centuries. These communities set themselves apart from the mainstream commercial society and tried to establish what they saw as a better way of life. The ornate buildings of one such communal group, the Theosophical Society of San Diego's Point Loma, are now part of Point Loma Nazarene University, but the group's trash dump is located on City of San Diego park land. When a sewer line was planned to cross the dump, test excavations were conducted. Although local bottle hunters had been digging in the dump for decades, the archaeologists found a large number of bottle fragments and other material not taken by the relic hunters, and these artifacts provided considerable information about life in the Theosophists' community.

For example, the Theosophical Society had a boarding school, as reflected in the archaeological record by bone toothbrush handles and children's toys (doll parts, miniature dishes, marbles, and animal figurines) (Figure 7.20). Albumenized meat, a processed meat product, was a common offering at the Theosophist tables, as indicated by fragments of the brown jars the meat was packed in. The consumption of fresh meat does not appear to have been common, however.

FIGURE 7.19 Artifacts from excavations in San Diego's Chinatown: (a) beads, (b) jade bracelet fragment, (c) glass bracelet fragment, (d) Chinese button, (e) cabinet key, (f) chain links, and (g) coins.

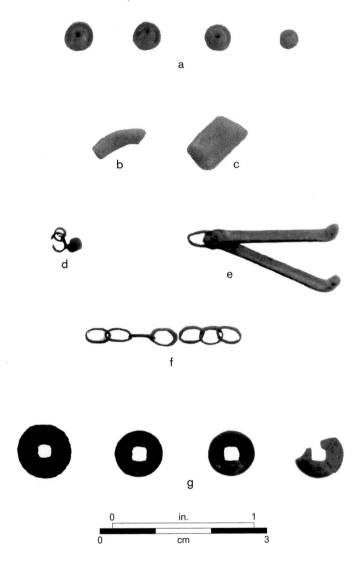

Beverage bottles, which include liquor bottles, made up only 6 percent of the bottled products at the Theosophical Society dump, while at the San Diego city dump from the same time period, 40 percent of the bottles had contained alcoholic beverages. Finally, numerous distinctive medicine vials indicate that the Theosophists practiced homeopathic medicine (Van Wormer and Gross 2006).

The movie industry is probably one of the first things people think of when California is mentioned, but few are aware that Hollywood has created an archaeological record. One archaeological project set out to examine part of that record. In 1923 Cecil B. DeMille filmed the silent epic *The Ten Commandments* in the Nipomo Dunes north of Santa Barbara. As part of this production, the filmmaker had an Egyptian city built. At the completion of the film the city was quietly dismantled and buried in a secret location in the dunes. In 1983 the site of the burial was located and an archaeological project was mounted to excavate

FIGURE 7.20 Artifacts from the Theosophical Society dump: (a) bone toothbrush handle, (b–d) china doll parts, (e–g) toy dishes, (h, i) ceramic animals, and (j–l) marbles.

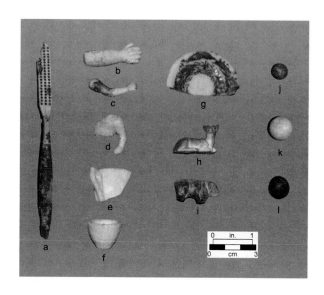

the site. The project is ongoing, but many pieces of the set have been discovered, and these artifacts are helping to build understandings of how the early movies were filmed.

CHAPTER SUMMARY

Like the environment of the state, the archaeology of the California archaeological area is diverse. The following points summarize the prehistory of the area as presented in this chapter:

- The California culture area does not exactly match the boundaries of the state of California: extreme northwestern California is part of the Northwest Coast, part of northern California lies in the Plateau, and the Mohave Desert and the areas east of the Sierra Nevada are in the Great Basin.

- Three general environmental units are discussed: the coast, the Central Valley, and the Sierra Nevada. The coast of California is one of its most prominent features and includes sandy beaches, bays and lagoons, and rugged sea cliffs. The Coast Ranges run along much of the coast from Point Conception northward. The Central Valley is the name given to the long, broad valleys of the Sacramento River in the north and the San Joaquin River in the south. The mountains of the Sierra Nevada mark the eastern edge of the California archaeological area and include Mount Whitney, the highest point in the United States south of Alaska.

- Climate change is very important in California archaeology. One of the most important changes is the rising of sea levels after the end of the Pleistocene, which led to the flooding of coastal areas that may have been occupied by early people. The Medieval drought is another important event, though the particular effects of this climatic anomaly on people in California are hotly debated.

- The C. W. Harris site in southern California is the best representative of the San Dieguito complex. Some archaeologists see the San Dieguito complex as a coastal expression of the Western Pluvial Lakes tradition. Meanwhile, several important sites, including Daisy Cave, Arlington Springs, Eel Point, and Cross Creek, with assemblages that either include evidence of early fishing or are distinctly not San Dieguito–like, suggest an early population of the area that might be evidence for a coastal migration of people into North America.

- As in other areas, the Archaic in California represents an adaptation to diverse resources. In southern California the Archaic is often collectively called the Millingstone horizon, as exemplified by the La Jolla complex (8500–2000 BP) in the San Diego area. In the Santa Barbara region the Archaic is encompassed in the Early period or the Oak Grove and Hunting peoples. In central California, materials from Buena Vista Lake and the Skyrocket site represent the Archaic. The Borax Lake tradition, with distinctive Borax Lake points, along with millingstones, is an Archaic expression in northern California.

- The Pacific period was defined to recognize the complexity of the late Prehistoric peoples of California—a level of complexity normally associated with the production of crops rather than with hunter-gatherers. Regardless of area in California, the Pacific period is marked by population growth, the establishment of permanent settlements, extensive trade, social ranking, and ownership of productive resources. The Chumash culture epitomizes this in the Santa Barbara area. The Windmiller, Berkeley, and Augustine patterns, and related manifestations, represent this period in the San Francisco Bay area.

- The European exploration of California began in 1542 but did not leave an extensive archaeological record. Settlement by Europeans began in 1769 with the establishment of the mission system. The Spanish also built presidios and founded towns or pueblos at this time, and most of these have seen archaeological investigations to varying degrees, as have ranchos of the Mexican period (1821–1846) that followed.

- The Mexican War and the California gold rush mark the end of the Mexican period. Archaeologists have excavated mining sites and the institutions that supported them. Urbanization was an important theme at the end of the nineteenth century, and the ethnicity of the citizens is often reflected in the archaeological record.

- California's Native American population is diverse, and Indians have interacted vigorously with archaeologists. California had laws protecting Native American burials dating back to 1982 before the passage of NAGPRA. Many Indian reservations and nonreservation bands play a key role in monitoring archaeological excavations and exercise their rights to be consulted under the laws.

SUGGESTIONS FOR FURTHER READING

For a summary of California archaeology written primarily for the nonarchaeologist:

Chartkoff, Joseph L., and Kerry Kona Chartkoff. 1984. *The Archaeology of California.* Stanford, CA: Stanford University Press.

For the most recent summary treatment of California archaeology, written in a lively style for a nonarchaeologist audience:

Fagan, Brian. 2003. *Before California: An Archaeologist Looks at Our Earliest Inhabitants.* Lanham, MD: Rowman & Littlefield.

For the classic text on California archaeology:

Moratto, Michael J. 1984. *California Archaeology.* Orlando, FL: Academic Press. Reprinted in 2004 by Coyote Press, Salinas, CA.

For a case study written for undergraduate students of archaeology:

Glassow, Michael A. 1996. *Purismeño Chumash Prehistory: Maritime Adaptations Along the Southern California Coast.* Fort Worth, TX: Harcourt Brace College Publishers.

For a three-volume series on the archaeology of the California Coast:

Erlandson, Jon M., and Roger H. Colton, eds. 1991. *Perspectives on California Archaeology,* Vol. 1, *Hunter-Gatherers of Early Holocene Coastal California.* Los Angeles: Institute of Archaeology, University of California.

———, and Michael A. Glassow, eds. 1997. *Perspectives on California Archaeology,* Vol. 4, *Archaeology of the California Coast during the Middle Holocene.* Los Angeles: Institute of Archaeology, University of California.

———, and Terry L. Jones, eds. 2002. *Perspectives on California Archaeology,* Vol. 6, *Catalysts to Complexity: Late Holocene Societies of the California Coast.* Los Angeles: Cotsen Institute of Archaeology, University of California.

OTHER RESOURCES

The Student CD, Sections H and I, supplies web links, additional discussion questions, and other study aids. The Student CD also contains additional resources including a complete list of the references cited in this chapter and the case study that follows it. Early coastal occupations in California are discussed in "Eel Point and the Early Settlement of Coastal California: A Case Study in Contemporary Archaeological Research" (Section D.3). Section F.3, *"A Local Reaction to NAGPRA: The Kumeyaay Cultural and Repatriation Committee,"* is particularly relevant to this chapter as well.

CASE STUDY

When thinking about the European colonization of California it is easy to forget that Russia as well as Spain was a colonial power along this part of the Pacific Coast. Yet Russians competed for trade well south of Alaska, establishing a colony, called Colony Ross, north of what today is San Francisco. Here the Russian-American Company rather than the Spanish had considerable effect on Native people, as detailed in this case study about the Fort Ross Archaeological Project. The fort community was multiethnic, including Alaskan Natives, Coast Miwok and Kashaya Pomo Indians, and Russians. This case study describes a collaborative program between the Fort Ross State Historic Park, the Kashaya Pomo Tribe, California State Parks, and the University of California at Berkeley that focuses on the impact of Russian colonialism on the Native peoples of this area. Because of their collaboration with Kashaya Pomo elders, the archaeologists were able to develop low-impact strategies for gathering data primarily by using geophysical testing as well as traditional excavation. They also are major contributors to changes in the interpretive program at Fort Ross through their work on a Kashaya Pomo interpretive trail and a digital website that will make the native story at Colony Ross more widely accessible. As you read this case study, reflect on the example it provides of how archaeologists now try to incorporate diverse stakeholders in their work. How does this context change the story that gets told?

CULTURES IN CONTACT AT COLONY ROSS

Kent G. Lightfoot, Sara Gonzalez, Darren Modzelewski, Lee Panich, Otis Parrish, and Tsim Schneider

For thousands of years before the coming of Europeans, Kashaya Pomo and Coast Miwok peoples inhabited the coastal lands north of San Francisco Bay. Like many other California Indians, they were hunter-gatherers who harvested wild plants and animals from the sea and land for food, medicine, clothing, housing material, and ceremonial regalia. Villages nestled along protected coastal embayments and ridge tops of the Northern Coast Ranges mountains contained tule-thatched or redwood bark houses, ceremonial structures (round houses), sweat houses, dance enclosures, and extramural cooking and work areas. Large villages served as the political centers for broader communities of dispersed family groups who would come together for periodic dances, ceremonies, initiation rites, and feasts.

With the founding of Colony Ross in 1812 by the Russian-American Company (RAC), a mercantile enterprise licensed by the tsar of Russia, life would change forever for the Kashaya Pomo and the Coast Miwok. The Russian merchants placed the primary administrative center of the colony, which they called the Ross settlement, in the heart of Kashaya Pomo territory, and they chose Bodega Harbor in Coast Miwok country to be the principal port facility (Port Rumiantsev) (Figure 7.21). The Russian-American Company came to California to profit from the exploitation of the region's natural bounty. The mercantile enterprise harvested sea mammals, primarily sea otters and fur seals, to fuel the lucrative maritime fur trade that supplied sea mammal pelts to China, Europe, and the United States, primarily for use as robes, fur trim, and other clothing accessories. The Russian merchants attempted to grow wheat, barley, and other crops, and to raise livestock at Colony Ross to feed other RAC colonies in the North Pacific (Aleutian Islands, Kodiak Island, Prince William Sound, etc.), which experienced periodic food shortages. The Ross settlement also served as a manufacturing center for the production of goods (timber, bricks, metal utensils, and tools) that were shipped to the other North Pacific colonies and also traded to the Franciscan missionaries in **Alta California** for foodstuffs grown in the extensive mission complexes.

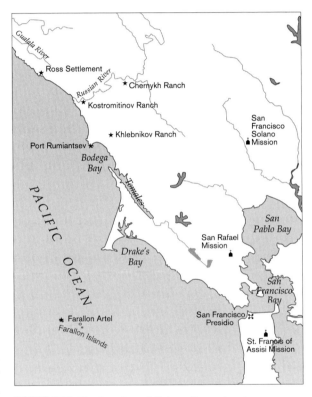

FIGURE 7.21 The location of Colony Ross showing Russian settlements and ranches.

FORT ROSS ARCHAEOLOGICAL PROJECT

Today the historic Ross settlement and its nearby environs comprise the Fort Ross State Historic Park. The Fort Ross Archaeological Project is examining the culture history of the Kashaya Pomo people and the long-term implications of their encounters with the first mercantile colony in California. Members of the collaborative research team include archaeologists and rangers from California State Parks, faculty and students from the University of California at Berkeley, and elders and tribal scholars from the Kashaya Pomo Tribe. The collaborative team is investigating how the Kashaya Pomo negotiated the mercantile colonial program introduced by the Russian-American Company that exposed local hunter-gatherers to a pluralistic, international workforce and to a market economy.

Company managers recruited eastern Europeans, Native Siberians, Creoles (people of mixed Russian and native ancestry), and Native Alaskans—primarily from Kodiak Island and Prince William Sound—to live and work at Colony Ross. The Native Alaskans brought their sophisticated maritime technology (*baidarkas*, or skin kayaks, carved harpoon points, compound fish hooks, etc.) to Colony Ross to harvest commercially sea otters and fur seals by the thousands, and to hunt other sea mammals, seabirds, and fish for food. The managers also recruited nearby Kashaya Pomo and Coast Miwok Indians to work as seasonal laborers in shipbuilding, brick making, and agriculture. The Indians were hired for specific tasks (e.g., harvesting wheat, tending livestock), with compensation negotiated on a case-by-case basis; the merchants paid the Native people "in kind" for their services, usually with food, tobacco, beads, and clothing.

RESEARCH QUESTIONS

The historical circumstances surrounding Colony Ross help to shape the questions asked by the Fort Ross Archaeological Project. Our current focus is to understand better the cultural practices and social interactions of the Kashaya Pomo and Coast Miwok people who lived and worked in a mercantile social setting and to compare their experiences to other Native Californians who were incorporated into European (as well as Mexican and American) colonial institutions of other kinds (e.g., missions, presidios, pueblos, ranchos). Some aspects of the history of the Russian colony are well known because RAC employees and other European visitors kept detailed records and personal journals. From these historical documents, archaeologists are able to learn important details about how life at Colony Ross was organized. Yet historical documents often only give one side of the story, leaving out others. In the case of Colony Ross, most documents describe the colonial situation from a European point of view. Because of our interest in the Kashaya Pomo and Coast Miwok who lived and worked at Colony Ross, we used careful

and critical readings of these documents, alongside inferences drawn from the archaeological record of the colony, to generate conclusions about how Colony Ross differed from other colonial endeavors in California. Documents and archaeology are also employed to examine how Native American groups negotiated the constraints that the Russian colony imposed on their traditional lifeways.

One of the interesting things we learned from the history of Colony Ross is that it differed significantly from contemporaneous European colonies. During the period in which the Russian-American Company operated its mercantile outpost in northern California, the coastal regions to the south were being actively colonized by Spain (Figure 7.21). Although Spain had ruled parts of Central and South America for centuries, the first Spanish colonists did not arrive in Alta California until 1769 (Costello and Hornbeck 1989). In much of the New World, Spain's colonial empire was based on three interrelated institutions: presidios, pueblos, and missions. In other words, the Spanish relied upon soldiers, civilian colonists, and missionaries to maintain control of their colonies. In Alta California, Spain's main colonizing agents were Franciscan missionaries. Although the missionaries themselves worked to convert Native peoples to Christianity, both the archaeological and historical records suggest that their role in the larger colonial framework was much broader.

In Alta California, the mission period lasted from roughly 1770 through the 1830s. The Franciscan padres, under the leadership of Junípero Serra, founded a chain of 21 missions that ran along the Pacific coast as far north as San Francisco Bay. The Spanish brought local Native people to the missions, and additionally forced groups from outlying areas to relocate to mission sites. At the missions, tightly controlled social practices were intended to "civilize" Native Californians by converting them to both Christianity and European lifestyles. Native Californians who lived at the missions were also forced to grow crops and raise livestock for trade and to supply other parts of Spanish California. Poor living conditions at the missions exacerbated the spread of disease, and several devastating epidemics struck the Native populations of the California missions. Within the framework of Spanish colonialism, the missions provided the colonies with cheap labor and cleared the territory of an uncontrolled indigenous population (Jackson and Castillo 1995; Milliken 1995).

From historical sources and from the archaeological record, we know that at Colony Ross, the relationships between the Russian-American Company and Native Alaskans and Native Californians were structured very differently. Colony Ross was a multicultural community in which certain ethnicities held greater and lesser status, but no real attempt was made on the part of the Russians to eradicate Native cultural practices. Russian colonialism, however, was driven by profit, and this is manifested in the Russians' dealings with Native groups (Dmytryshyn et al. 1989; Tikmenev 1978). In the eighteenth century, Russian traders moved across Siberia and Alaska, physically coercing Native peoples into the colonial workforce in relentless pursuit of furs and skins. In Alaska, the Russian traders treated the local indigenous populations so poorly that eventually the tsar was forced to intervene on their behalf. But by the time the RAC founded its colony in California, the company's policies toward Native groups had softened, and its leaders even signed treaties with some of the Native Californians. The land incorporated into the Ross Colony was territory already claimed by Spain, and these treaties served to legitimize the Russian claim to what is now the Sonoma County coast. For the Coast Miwok and Kashaya Pomo groups who lived in the area, the Russians represented the lesser of two colonial evils, and the treaties were likely signed in the hope that a Russian presence in the area might prevent the expansion of the Spanish mission system into their homelands.

During the early years of the colony, relations between the Russians and their indigenous neighbors were relatively benign. Allied against the Spanish, the RAC and local Native groups coexisted without much conflict; indeed, the area around the colony became a refuge for Indians fleeing the Spanish missions further south. Yet as the Native Alaskan hunters rapidly decimated the otter population, the Russian colony intensified its agricultural and manufacturing programs. These undertakings required a large amount of labor, and often Native Californians who were prisoners of the Russians were forced to work for the colony. In the early 1820s the Russians, like the Spanish, began to mount armed raids into the countryside to capture Native Californians to be used as laborers. Demand for labor increased again in the 1830s with the establishment of three outlying ranches that were designed to increase the agricultural output of the colony, and relations with local Native groups deteriorated (Lightfoot et al. 1991).

Unlike the Spanish, who hoped to assimilate Native peoples into new societies based on a European ideal, the Russian managers of Colony Ross simply wanted to turn a profit. Although certain individuals within the RAC advocated for the fair treatment of Native Californians, the company's policies toward Native groups were driven by economic, rather than religious or governmental concerns. The contrasting aims of the Spanish and Russian colonies are clearly demonstrated in California, both historically and archaeologically. These differences are also reflected in the histories and experiences of the various indigenous groups whose members were forced to negotiate the complex colonial worlds of the late eighteenth and early nineteenth centuries.

COLLABORATION WITH NATIVE AMERICANS

In addition to historical documents and the archaeological record, a third crucial source of information on the history of the Colony Ross region derives from the descendants of the Kashaya Pomo people on whose land the Russians established the Ross settlement. The once extensive tribal territory of the Kashaya, which included the Gualala River to the north and extended south of the Russian River, has shrunk to the 40-acre Stewarts Point Reservation located about 15 miles (24 km) north of the Fort Ross State Historic Park. About 600 Kashaya Pomo live in northern California today, and while many work in nearby cities and towns, they return to the reservation for the seasonal cycle of dances, feasts, and ceremonies. Consultation with Kashaya Pomo elders provides an avenue for incorporating their oral traditions into the research and interpretation program of the Fort Ross Archaeological Project (Figure 7.22). The development of our collaborative partnership with the Kashaya Pomo has benefited from the hindsight of decades of encounters between archaeologists and Native people—relationships that have witnessed dramatic changes over the past 35 years in North America (Downer 1997).

In the 1960s and 1970s, during the height of **processualism** in North American archaeology, collaborative research with Native Americans was more the exception than the rule. Most archaeologists either

FIGURE 7.22 Consultation between archaeologists and Kashaya Pomo elders at the Fort Ross State Historic Park, June 2004.

ignored or passively listened to the concerns of native people with respect to the protection of ancestral sites. The civil rights movement of the 1960s, however, gave Native Americans a platform to assert their inherent rights as sovereign tribes and to find ways to more readily protect and manage their cultural property and resources.

Native advocacy led to the passage of several laws either directly or indirectly calling for archaeologists and other officials wishing to conduct research on federal or Indian land to *consult* with tribal people about proposed research. Some of these laws are the Native American Graves Protection and Repatriation Act of 1990 (NAGPRA), **The Archaeological Resources Protection Act of 1979** (**ARPA**), and the National Historic Preservation Act of 1966 (NHPA). Additionally, most states including California have their own versions of these federal laws. For example, the **California Environmental Quality Act** (1970) requires consultation with affected tribes before and during archaeology done on state land. As a consequence of these legislative actions, laws now exist that protect sacred sites by mandating consultation before any archaeological research can be conducted.

These and several other federal and state laws have affected archaeological practice on both federal and nonfederal land. Furthermore, in concert with federal and state laws requiring consultation, many Native Californian groups have developed procedures for the management, protection, and preservation of

sites and ancestral territories, as well as guidelines for recording and studying archaeological sites. Many of these practices are being incorporated into the method and theory of North American archaeology. In 1994 members of the Society for American Archaeology met to discuss moral and ethical issues surrounding the archaeology of Native people in America. This resulted in the adoption of a code of ethics that acknowledges the rights and beliefs of Native people (Lynott and Wylie 1995). The overall consequences are significant; archaeologists are developing more innovative ways in which to gather data, to analyze and curate archaeological materials, and to interact and work with stakeholders and descendant communities. While these indigenous archaeologies are still developing in the context of North American archaeology (Watkins 2000), projects such as the one at Colony Ross, illustrate that consultation and collaboration with local Native people can lead to meaningful, insightful, and exciting conclusions.

The Fort Ross Archaeological Project has benefited from consultation with the Kashaya Pomo in two significant ways. One is in the incorporation of Native oral histories and oral traditions that inform us about the culture history, cultural practices, and worldviews of the Kashaya Pomo people. By incorporating indigenous voices into archaeological projects, we can gain a better understanding of the experiences of the ancestral communities that created and lived at many of the archaeological sites of the region (Echo-Hawk 1997). Stories and memories handed down from one generation to another provide a window into the past for examining traditional technology and lifeways (e.g., hunting and gathering practices, ceremonies, village organization) and for obtaining insights into their entanglements with foreign colonists. Native consultation also provides important insights into contemporary Kashaya perspectives on colonialism and the maintenance of native cultural practices and language retention. The Fort Ross Archaeological Project incorporates native narratives in the study of pre-Contact archaeological remains, as well as historic sites that witnessed encounters between Kashaya and Native Alaskans, Creoles, Russians, and others.

It is the judicious use of Native oral histories and oral traditions, in combination with archival documents and archaeology, that provides the most powerful approach, outside a time machine, for investigating the past. The integration of multiple lines of evidence from documentary, oral, and archaeological sources, which comprises the holistic study of historical anthropology, provides a more balanced and inclusive view of history. Each source can contribute a somewhat distinctive historical perspective from the vantage of people of varied cultural backgrounds and homelands. This kind of multisourcing approach is critical in the study of pluralistic social contexts such as Colony Ross. Specifically, we employ Native oral traditions, ethnohistoric records from European visitors to the northern California coast, ethnographic information about the Kashaya Pomo, maps of the region, and archived photographs of cultural landscapes and family members, all of which present unique lines of evidence on the history of the Kashaya coast.

The second significant contribution of native participation in the Fort Ross Archaeological Project is in the theory and method of our archaeological practice. Collaboration with Kashaya elders has emphasized the need to protect and preserve ancestral archaeological remains. This has led to a concerted effort to develop low-impact or less intrusive methods of investigating archaeological places in the Fort Ross State Historic Park. Archaeological methods are employed to limit the amount of excavation, especially in the initial "testing" phases. Excavation by nature is a destructive activity; but it provides necessary information on site stratigraphy and the context of artifactual remains.

Our field program attempts to maximize information about the spatial organization of sites based on surface and near-surface investigations before subsurface testing takes place. We attempt to develop an increasingly detailed picture of the site structure before any significant excavation work is begun. As the site structure comes into focus, and potential house structures, midden areas, and workplaces take shape, we work with Kashaya participants to develop plans for "surgical strikes" where limited excavation may take place that will be most useful for evaluating our research questions and understanding site histories. This field program also tells Kashaya elders what they need to know about archaeological procedures to make informed decisions about where investigations should be prohibited for spiritual or other reasons.

We employ a multiphased field program that begins with the least intrusive methods. Surface pedestrian survey is undertaken in areas with limited ground cover to detect archaeological sites and to define site boundaries. Detailed topographic maps of the site surface are then produced, followed by geophysical survey, and the systematic surface collection of artifacts. We use geophysical survey methods to search for anomalies belowground that may be produced by cultural features or artifacts. Magnetometers measure sub- and near-surface magnetic anomalies, while other instruments measure the electrical conductivity or resistance subsurface deposits. Cultural features that retain moisture or alter the flow of electricity through the subsurface matrix may be detected by means of these low-impact methods, thus providing a tentative picture of site structure prior to subsurface investigation (A. J. Clark 1990).

The low-impact approach was recently employed in the study of the Metini Village, a Kashaya village that dates to the Russian and post-Russian occupation of the region and may also predate Colony Ross (Lightfoot et al. 2001). Kashaya Pomo oral tradition emphasizes the sacredness of this place; the center of the site is dominated by a large surface depression that is the remains of a round house used for ceremonies and religious practices. Following a "ritual blueprint" for the investigation of the Metini Village Project, archaeological crews adhered to specific Kashaya cultural practices (Parrish et al. 2000). For example, women field workers were not allowed to work within the sacred village area during their menstrual periods, nor could they cook or do any kitchen chores at camp. We defined the boundaries of the village through surface pedestrian survey, mapped the topographic features of the site, employed a Geometrics G-858 cesium gradiometer and a Geonics EM-38 electromagnetic conductivity instrument to search for subsurface anomalies, and completed a systematic collection of surface materials from 4 percent of the site's surface. The completion of this multiphased surface investigation resulted in a series of overlay maps that showed the topography, subsurface anomalies, and artifact distributions across Metini Village—spatial information that was used by archaeologists and Kashaya elders to place several excavation units measuring 1 meter by 1 meter (3.281 ft × 3.281 ft) in strategic places across the site.

The benefits of the low-impact approach extend beyond site investigation, accountability to various stakeholding communities, and publication of a site report. Research designs with limited but strategically placed excavation units have implications for the collection and curation of archaeological materials. The smaller assemblages of artifacts produced from low-impact studies takes pressure off crowded curation facilities and artifact repositories. Furthermore, the recovery of fewer materials addresses the unease of many Indian communities about the curation of ancestral remains in museums and curation facilities. Finally, the use of low-impact field methods and limited collection of archaeological materials leaves sites in condition for any future excavations that may be desirable when improved technologies become available.

PUBLIC OUTREACH AND EDUCATION

Collaboration with Kashaya Pomo elders and tribal scholars has also led to renewed emphasis on public outreach programs that highlight Kashaya culture history and the people's encounters with foreign colonists. In the past decade the importance of public outreach and education in archaeology has developed into a dynamic and emerging enterprise. Whereas 20 years ago outreach typically meant posted signs on trails in state or national parks indicating the precious nature of the archaeological record, today the presentation and representation of cultural heritage occupies a significant portion of archaeological research programs. This growth is witnessed in the creation of countless interpretive centers, in public archaeology days held during a field season and, importantly, in the various educational outreach programs run by local, state, and national society organizations, government offices, academic departments, and even research teams themselves (Stone and Planel 1999). The importance of outreach is further enshrined in the Society for American Archaeology's Principles of Archaeological Ethics document that consistently stresses the importance of accountability to the public through eight ethical principles concerning stewardship, accountability, commercialization, public outreach and education, intellectual property, public reporting and publication, records and preservation, and training and resources (Lynott and Wylie 1995). And as training programs begin to offer more courses in ethics and to instruct their students in education and outreach, archaeological interpretive programs and outreach efforts will likely become mandatory components of research projects.

Considering archaeology's accountability to its multiple publics, the Fort Ross Archaeological Project, in collaboration with the Kashaya Pomo Tribe and California State Parks, will embark on the creation of the Kashaya Pomo Interpretive Trail at Fort Ross State Historic Park. Currently, the park consists of an interpretive center and at its core, a dominating reconstruction of the Russian stockade and enclosed buildings (Figure 7.23). Although the park has a well-developed interpretive program run by California State Parks and the Fort Ross Interpretive Association, the pure physicality of the stockade and the less developed interpretive plan for cultural sites outside the stockade emphasizes the park's elite Russian past (Parkman 1996/1997). This is a framework that minimizes the role of the Kashaya, as well as those of Native Alaskan, Coast Miwok, and Creole descent, in the creation of the park as a heritage site.

Every interpretive program must decide to tell its audience a finite number of stories, or narratives, and this interpretive trail is no different. To represent the full scope of Colony Ross's past, the interpretive trail must focus on representing the diversity and complexity of the park's multiple histories and find a way for people to literally step outside the stockade and experience different aspects of the region's cultural heritage. The role of collaboration has been especially important in this process, and the Kashaya people's modern connection to the site was instrumental in selecting specific narratives for the trail and in conceiving of the appropriate methods and means of representation. Thus the trail will not focus solely on the Russian period of occupation. Instead, it will lead visitors physically and mentally away from the imposing stockade and allow them to consider the Kashaya heritage and the multiethnic community that once defined Ross.

With the trail, we have the opportunity to tell a complicated and intriguing history that features the Kashayas' deep past at the park (ca. 6000–8000 years ago), the foundation of a multiethnic colony oriented around fur hunting and agricultural production, and the region's subsequent occupation by Mexican and American ranchers. Segmenting these stories in coherent trail segments will take planning and coordination. Thus the trail itself comprises two loops, each of which will feature a different aspect of the park's history. The West Loop will wind itself along the coast and through the Kashayas' Prehistoric past, featuring the oldest sites in the park, and will cover

FIGURE 7.23 Fort Ross: the proposed interpretive trail will take park visitors outside the reconstructed Ross stockade complex into the nearby landscape.

a wide range of topics such as views of the landscape, folklore, and subsistence practices. In contrast, the East Loop will provide a tour through the fort that accentuates the history of colonial encounters between the Kashaya and Colony Ross's multiethnic colonists, exposing the public to the entirety of the historic Ross settlement. Each trail stop incorporates archaeology, Native oral traditions, European firsthand accounts, historic photographs and illustrations, site maps, and other forms of documentation to provide comprehensive overviews of the natural and cultural heritage of the region. Archaeological sites such as lithic scatters, cupule rocks, which bear small pecked concavities, and shell middens may be used in on-site interpretation. The critical combination and presentation of diverse lines of evidence offers a unique context within which to construct and present indigenous perspectives on the archaeological record to the public.

It is the overall intention of the Kashaya Pomo Interpretive Trail to create interpretations that reflect the multiethnic heritage of Fort Ross as well as Native perspectives on this heritage. Extensive collaboration between Kashaya Pomo and archaeologists contribute to Native perspectives in all aspects of archaeological research and resulting interpretations (Dowdall and Parrish 2003). In the interpretive project, the incorporation of Native oral traditions, Kashaya participation in the interpretive process, historic photographs and documents, and Kashaya interpretations of artifacts and the landscape will complement archaeological evidence and will be used to construct Native-infused perspectives on the archaeological record at Ross. This critical combination of diverse lines of evidence is viewed as an essential part of the process of creating multivocal and Native-inspired interpretation of Ross's heritage (Lightfoot et al. 1998).

Unfortunately, the degree to which any interpretive trail can convey its messages is constrained by the medium of trail signposts and accompanying materials: they are costly and nondurable, and the format prohibits the imparting of extensive interpretation. Therefore, in addition to the signposts and panels, brochures, guided tours, public lectures, and "archaeology days" will supplement the proposed interpretive program, providing additional outlets

FIGURE 7.24 Guided tour for park visitors of the proposed Kashaya Pomo Interpretive Trail during the initial phase of testing possible interpretive scenarios, June 2004.

for interaction between project staff, local communities, and park visitors (Figure 7.24).

The impact of the trail upon people's understandings of Ross also is limited by the ability of various publics to visit the park in its isolated location, or physically walk the trail. Development of a digital website as an extension to the current interpretive trail program both overcomes these limitations and provides an opportunity to reach out to and interact with a wider audience. Digital interpretive environments combine the ability to use multiple media to construct interpretations within a format of increased accessibility, interactivity, and reflexivity between multiple audiences—real and virtual. Although access to the technology poses certain ethical problems, a digital Kashaya Pomo Interpretive Trail can serve as an alternative point of access for audiences otherwise unable to visit the park in person, as well as an enhanced educational tool for teachers, students, and others interested in the park. As archaeologists attempt to grapple with issues of accountability, education, outreach, and collaboration, the use of digital interpretive environments for archaeological interpretation has great potential for satisfying these ethical and moral requirements.

CONCLUSION

The Fort Ross Archaeological Project exemplifies a collaborative research program that is holistic, broadly comparative, and focused on change over time. We draw inferences from a number of different sources, including native oral traditions, historical records, and archaeological research. The knowledge gained from these investigations is used to achieve a better understanding of the social contexts of the pluralistic mercantile endeavor of Colony Ross, and to examine the experiences of Native Californians who lived there against the backdrop of other indigenous peoples who witnessed colonialism firsthand elsewhere in the world. The daily practices and social relations of the Kashaya Pomo and Coast Miwok people who lived and worked at Colony Ross are additionally examined diachronically, that is, through prehistory to the present. In close collaboration with members of the Kashaya Pomo Tribe and the California State Parks, the Fort Ross Archaeological Project strives to practice archaeology that meets the demands and expectations of a diverse array of stakeholders including native peoples, academics, archaeologists, and the general public.

DISCUSSION QUESTIONS

1. Who were the native people affected by the Russians at Colony Ross? How did the colonization efforts of the Russians differ from those of the Spanish? How do you suppose these differences ultimately affected natives?

2. How has consultation with the Kashaya Pomo changed the program of archaeological work at Fort Ross? What advantages and disadvantages do you see?

3. Why should archaeologists be concerned with the nature of public outreach at Fort Ross? Do you agree that the new interpretive trail should focus on representing "the diversity and complexity of the park's multiple histories"? Explain.

4. Compare and contrast this case study with the one in Chapter 5. How do the archaeologists and native people in these case studies illustrate new trends in the practice of archaeology?

CHAPTER 8

Mobility, Flexibility, and Persistence in the Great Basin

It's a hot summer evening in the mid-1940s at the Wendover Air Base gunnery school. The airmen, tired from a hard day's training for World War II combat duty, are casting about for something to fill the time until lights out in this remote part of the Great Salt Desert of western Utah. Some of them wander to the new base club, built in a cave in the side of a mountain. Base personnel have leveled the floor, poured a concrete dance floor, installed a jukebox, and put in a full bar. Here the airmen drink and dance and laugh, most of them not noticing the dim figures of mounted people painted on to the walls. It is quite likely that none of them suspect what lies beneath their feet, for excavations of the cave (named Jukebox Cave by its excavator) later yielded preserved basketry and other artifacts from a long human occupation. The airmen were literally dancing on the past without knowing it.

Archaeological sites are not always evident to the general public without the help of trained interpreters. It is not uncommon, for instance, for a consulting archaeologist to visit a property with an owner who plans to develop it but has learned that an archaeological survey is first required. "I've lived on this property for 30 years," the owner often says, "and I never found any Indian stuff." In some cases the archaeologist can actually bend over and pick up a flake or sherd for the inspection of an owner who had not recognized an artifact in plain sight. In other cases, the sites are found during survey. As we have seen, however, it is quite possible for people to walk (or dance) over archaeological sites without knowing it. That is one reason for the loss, each year, of many archaeological sites—they are bulldozed into oblivion simply because people did not know they were there. Another reason is deliberate destruction on the part of a developer who does not want to pay for archaeological studies or to have a project delayed if important finds are made.

Caves like Jukebox Cave are emblematic of Great Basin archaeology. In the course of their everyday lives, people who took refuge from the region's heat in caves and rockshelters left behind artifacts, and deposits grew both through natural processes and because quantities of material had been brought to the caves. Since many of the caves are dry, items left in them remained dry, as well. As we have already discussed, the organisms that destroy organic material need both moisture and oxygen to survive. In the case of Jukebox Cave and other dry caves, the lack of moisture prevents the decay of wood, fiber, hide, and other natural materials not usually found in archaeological sites.

Dry cave sites have produced a wealth of material that allows insight into past lifeways. Duck decoys fashioned out of tule stalks, hint at hunting practices on the ancient lakes that filled the desert basins at times in the past. Atlatl throwing boards, darts, and foreshafts show the articulation of pieces not obvious when only stone hooks, points, and throwing board weights are recovered. Flaked knives hafted into handles provide insight into the use of these tools. **Coprolites**, which are preserved feces, even tell us about the contents of specific prehistoric meals, and some caves contained many, many coprolites. Feather and rabbit skin blankets, leather pouches with their contents still together, snares, and rabbit nets all would have disappeared from open sites. Another interesting class of artifacts found in dry caves are **quids**. These are masses of chewed fiber, often of yucca, that were spit out in the caves and still often preserve the tooth marks of the person who had chewed them. Whether they were chewed for their nutritional value, as part of fiber extraction, or as a precursor to chewing gum is not known. Preserved textiles also are particularly important. As we saw in Chapter 5 (Exhibit 5.1), manufacturing techniques can provide evidence of cultural contact and affiliation. For this reason much attention has been paid to basketry and cordage in the Great Basin as well.

The excavation of dry caves has made critical contributions to the understanding of the past in the Great Basin. Indeed, Danger Cave, located in the vicinity of Jukebox Cave and excavated at the same time by Jesse D. Jennings (1957) of the University of Utah, provided the basis for the definition of the **Desert culture**, one of the main interpretive frameworks for Basin prehistory for many years, and one that had far-reaching implications for the study of the archaeology of the entire West. It's a good bet that those airmen at Jukebox Cave had no idea what marvelous information lay in the dust beneath their feet, but it's also obvious that archaeology can benefit from sites not generally recognizable as significant.

DEFINITION OF THE AREA

The Great Basin occupies the area between the Sierra Nevada and the Rocky Mountains (Figure 8.1). The heart of this area is the hydrographic Great Basin, which is an area of internal drainage where all streams and rivers end in lakes or playas within the basin itself. This area covers most of the states of Utah and Nevada. The cultural Great Basin encompasses a larger area, including parts of Oregon and Idaho, eastern California, western Colorado, and western Wyoming that drain into rivers that ultimately reach the sea (D'Azevedo 1986, 1; Jennings 1986, 114). Culturally the area is bounded by the Plateau on the north, California on the west, the Southwest on the south, and the Plains on the east. Contact with these regions and influences from them occur with varying degrees of intensity throughout the prehistory of the area.

There are a number of regional chronologies, and these often fail to match. In Table 8.1 we present regional timelines, along with a basinwide set of periods offered by Jesse Jennings, albeit reluctantly, knowing, as he did, the level of

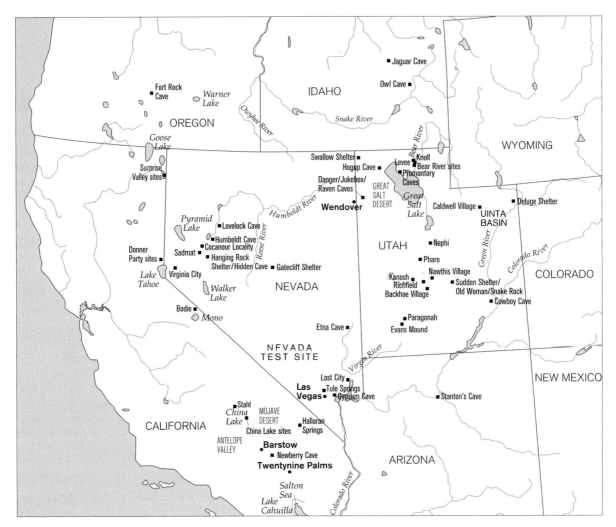

FIGURE 8.1 The Great Basin culture area showing the location of sites mentioned in Chapter 8.

variability present both in the record and in archaeologists' interpretation of that record. In this chapter we will use very broad periods to organize the discussions. Since except for the agricultural adaptation of the Fremont **culture**, the Great Basin exemplifies what archaeologists once called the Archaic stage (see Chapter 2) from nearly the beginning of human occupation, we shall focus on the Archaic.

THE ENVIRONMENT

The Great Basin is a region of great variation in landform and climate. High mountains overlook deep valleys, often with broad, arid floors. As noted earlier, the heart of the region is the vast area of internal drainage—an area where rivers

TABLE 8.1 Introduction to Great Basin Culture History

Uncalibrated Years BP	General Periods	Northern	Eastern	Areas Southwestern	Western	Calibrated Years
					Yankee Blade	AD 1800
500	Late Archaic	Ethnographic peoples/Shoshonean Period				AD 1430
1,000					Underdown	AD 1020
1,500				Anasazi		AD 600
			Fremont			
2,000		Fort Rock V				AD 10
2,500	Middle Archaic			Gypsum	Reveille	660 BC
3,000						1,240 BC
3,500		Fort Rock IV	Black Rock			1,820 BC
4,000					Devils Gate	2,490 BC
4,500						3,200 BC
5,000				Pinto		3,780 BC
5,500		Hiatus ?			Clipper Gap	4,340 BC
6,000	Early Archaic	Mazarna ash				4,880 BC
6,500						5,440 BC
7,000		Fort Rock III				5,840 BC
7,500			Wendover			6,320 BC
8,000					Grass Valley	6,910 BC
8,500		Fort Rock II		Lake Mohave		7,550 BC
9,000						8,030 BC
9,500			Bonneville			8,560 BC
10,000						9,210 BC
10,500	Pre-Archaic		Clovis ?			10,470 BC
11,000		Fort Rock I				10,970 BC
11,500 and prior				Clovis ?		11,470 BC and prior

FIGURE 8.2 Pluvial lakes of the Great Basin.

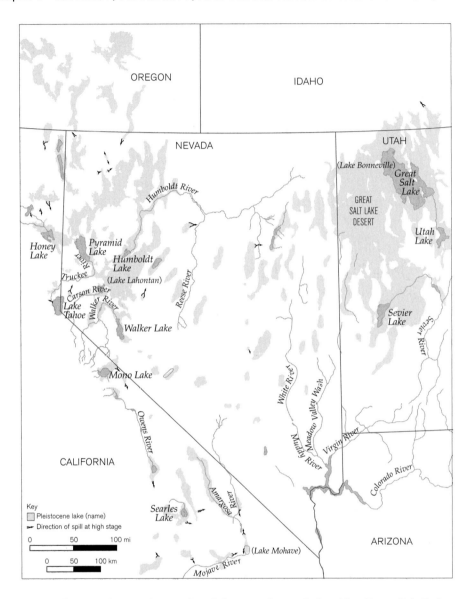

do not flow to the sea but end in lakes or playas. Lakes like Great Salt Lake, Pyramid Lake, Humboldt Lake, Mono Lake, and Walker Lake result from this pattern of internal drainage, and they are mere remnants of huge lakes that filled large parts of the basin at the end of the Pleistocene (as well as other, even earlier times). Among these large bodies of water called **pluvial lakes** (Figure 8.2) were Lake Bonneville, a lake that included much of northwestern Utah, and Lake Lahontan in western Nevada. To the south in the Mojave Desert portion of the region, Lake Mohave filled playas along the Mojave River.

Like the ethnographic Great Basin, the archaeological Great Basin extends beyond the boundaries of the hydrographic Great Basin, into areas drained by the Snake River, the Pitt River, and the Colorado River. Uniting the area, however, is

FIGURE 8.3 Vegetation of the Northern Great Basin, northern Utah.

the general topography of mountain ranges and intervening basins (the Basin and Range province).

The occurrence of mountain ranges and adjacent valleys leads to increased environmental diversity, for there is variability within each valley based on elevation, as well as variation among valleys. Within a valley the contrast between the often-dry valley floor and the mountain slopes is great, with the mountains being relatively more moist, sometimes supporting forests and subalpine meadows. The local and regional variability leads to patterns of associations between landforms, plants, and animal populations that are relatively predictable; and the ethnographic and archaeological records suggest that the inhabitants of the Basin understood these patterns well.

Vegetation is also variable. In the north the valleys are covered with cold desert vegetation (Figure 8.3) characterized by saltbush and sagebrush; in the south (Figure 8.4), warm desert vegetation is dominated by creosote. Grasslands are found in the north on the Snake River Plain, and combinations of sagebrush and grassland cover foothills. Mountain range vegetation is zoned by elevation, with piñon–juniper forests on the lower slopes, followed by the scrub oak zone, the ponderosa pine forest, the aspen forest, the spruce and fir forest, and the alpine herb zone above the tree line in the southern mountains. Northern ranges go from sagebrush to piñon–juniper, to sagebrush again, and then to open conifer forests; the alpine herb zone is less common in the north (Harper 1986).

Water is, of course, a critical resource in the deserts of the Great Basin. Water is found in the lakes mentioned earlier and the rivers that feed them, but significant areas of marsh in the basins today were lakes in the Pleistocene. Although such marshlands were limited in distribution, they were very productive areas, yielding rushes, grasses, and succulent plants that provided important food resources (Harper 1986).

FIGURE 8.4 Vegetation of the Southern Great Basin.

Lake Cahuilla, located in the California culture area west of the Colorado River, is a lake with a particularly interesting history that contrasts with climatically controlled lakes of the Great Basin. The Pleistocene lakes of the Great Basin were controlled by climate, with higher rainfall or cooler temperatures resulting in an accumulation in the basins of more water than had evaporated. In contrast, Lake Cahuilla appeared and disappeared over the millennia as a result of slight changes in the Colorado River levees and in the course of the river, which sent the water into the Imperial Valley and ultimately into the Salton Trough, landforms that are below sea level. When the river again changed course, returning to the channel that took it to the Sea of Cortez, the water supply for Lake Cahuilla was cut off, and the lake began to shrink through evaporation, ultimately disappearing (Mehringer 1986, 36–37; Wilke 1978). Today, southern California's Salton Trough is home to the Salton Sea, a lake that appeared in the early twentieth century as a result of levee failure during railroad construction along the Colorado River.

Animal populations vary with the vegetation, and the aridity often leads to low population densities. Small mammals, jackrabbit, deer, elk, pronghorn, and mountain sheep can be found in various Great Basin environments, while bison once ranged into its northeastern part (Harper 1986). Fish and clams were available in rivers and some lakes, and ducks and other waterfowl were also found in the lake and marsh environments. Some reptiles, such as the desert tortoise and the chuckwalla, a large lizard, were sizable enough to have been important foods. Additionally, insects, such as caterpillars of the Pandora moth, crickets, and grasshoppers, were abundant enough to be collected as food. The larvae and pupae of a brine fly were abundant in some lakes in the west central Great Basin, and they were also collected (Fowler 1986).

Climatic Change

Changes in environment have long been a research topic in the Great Basin, where the Altithermal has often been used to explain gaps in the archaeological record. Climatic studies have been part of major excavations, particularly in recent years, and a wealth of climatic data abounds, ranging from preserved plant material in fossil packrat middens to fossil pollen in lakes and marshes to tree rings of bristlecone pine in the White Mountains, which provide a long and detailed record of precipitation and temperature. Humans, by leaving debris in the dry caves, also contributed to the environmental record, and the study of plant parts, pollen, and bone from these sites has made significant contributions to our understanding of how past environments in the Great Basin changed over time.

The classic three-part scheme of Ernst Antevs (1948) divided postglacial time into **Anathermal**, Altithermal (also called the Hypsithermal in the east) and **Medithermal** intervals. During the Anathermal, which lasted from 9000 BP to 7000 BP, temperatures were cooler and more moist than at present. The Altithermal was seen as a long drought, lasting from 7000 BP to 4500 BP. It is portrayed as a time of hotter temperatures and much less moisture. It was during the present interval, the Medithermal, which began at the end of the Altithermal that current climatic conditions were attained. Although sometimes applied simplistically and regionally variable, this scheme still provides a broad, general outline useful to understanding climatic change in the Great Basin.

However, in a review of past environments in the Great Basin, Mehringer (1986) notes that the greatest environmental change faced by people in the Great

Basin was the end of the Pleistocene, marked as it was by the drying or shrinking of lakes and streams and the disappearance of the megafauna. He goes on to point out that within a single year, the inhabitants of the Great Basin would have encountered great ecological variation even without climatic change. Although there obviously were periods in the past when regional climatic change would have been significant, local variation due to the availability of water or to volcanic and tectonic activity usually would have been more important to humans (Mehringer 1986, 50).

One recent change in vegetation also is particularly interesting. This is the relatively rapid change in the character of the vegetation of the valleys and foothills. At contact with European Americans, these areas had more grasses and much less brush than they do now, and this change began within a few decades of the newcomers' arrival. It turns out that this change is due to suppression of fires that once periodically swept portions of the Great Basin. Many of these fires had been set by the Indians to keep the land open (Harper 1986, 52–53). This example of the intimate environmental knowledge acquired by the original residents of the Great Basin also demonstrates that even hunter-gatherers can alter habitats, albeit on a smaller scale than is seen in the changes wrought by more recent industrialized societies.

EARLY CULTURES: THE PRE-ARCHAIC

Like the surrounding culture areas, there is sparse, scattered evidence for the earliest occupation of the Great Basin, primarily in the form of isolated fluted points. Many areas have also yielded the bones of extinct animals, but there are almost no provable associations between these fossils and human artifacts. The China Lake region, investigated by E. L. Davis (1978) and her colleagues, is a case in point. Meticulous field work there documented the presence of fluted points, other artifacts, and fossil bone, but always in surface situations, where there can be some doubt about the actual association (Moratto 1984, 70).

Tule Springs is an important early site located on Las Vegas Wash near the city of Las Vegas, Nevada. Originally a paleontology site excavated by Mark Harrington in 1934 and 1955–1956, Tule Springs yielded the remains of extinct Pleistocene animals, material that appeared to be charcoal, and some artifacts found in association with some bone. An early radiocarbon date on the charcoal from the site was over 28,000 BP (26,000 BC) (Fowler 1986, 18; Harrington and Simpson 1961). In the early 1960s a team of archaeologists, geologists, paleontologists, and paleobotanists descended on the site and, through extensive study, determined that the material originally dated was not charcoal and that there was no clear association of tools with the extinct animals. The project results indicate the earliest occupation occurred between 11,000 BP and 10,000 BP (Wormington and Ellis 1967).

Gypsum Cave is another site once thought to demonstrate the association of humans and extinct animals, specifically the ground sloth, in the Great Basin. Subsequent dating of the artifacts at the site indicate that they are later (2900–2400 BP) than the dated sloth dung (radiocarbon-dated to 11,700–8500 BP). In southern Idaho, Owl Cave has produced the remains of elephants, bison, and camels in association with stone tools, four of which were parts of Folsom points dated to about 11,000 BP. In later deposits in the cave, the remains of extinct bison are found associated with Plano points dating to approximately 8000 BP. Jaguar Cave, also in southern Idaho, has produced the remains of mountain sheep that were larger than the modern species, along with the bones of domestic dogs. This cave dates between 11,600 BP and 10,300 BP, contemporaneous with the Clovis points, some of which have been found on the surface in the general vicinity. This suggests that people have hunted sheep from the first occupations of the Great Basin. A recent study of lithic sourcing for stone tools made by some of the first inhabitants of the central Great Basin suggests that mobility patterns and foraging territories were established even at this early date, though they changed as resource distributions also were altered over time (G. Jones et al. 2003).

ARCHAIC

Danger Cave Sequence and the Concept of the Desert Culture

When the University of Utah Summer Archaeological Field Schools resumed in 1949 after a hiatus during World War II, a young archaeologist named Jesse Jennings took his students to the Wendover area along the Utah–Nevada border. He excavated Jukebox Cave, discussed in the opening to this chapter, as well as Raven Cave and Danger Cave. This excavation and the subsequent analysis and reporting of the project in 1957, especially the material from Danger Cave, would have a long and important role in the study of Great Basin archaeology and would help shape understanding of the prehistory of the entire West.

Located on a shore of ancient Lake Bonneville on the western edge of the Great Salt Desert, Danger Cave represented occupations ranging back to 11,000 BP (9000 BC). The cave had a wide mouth, but the entrance had been choked with more than 14 feet (4 m) of deposits so that it appeared to be only a shallow rockshelter. Jennings recognized five periods of occupations in the strata that had artifacts (Figure 8.5). Unlike caves excavated earlier, like Lovelock Cave with its cache of duck decoys (see later: Figure 8.10), Danger Cave was a site where

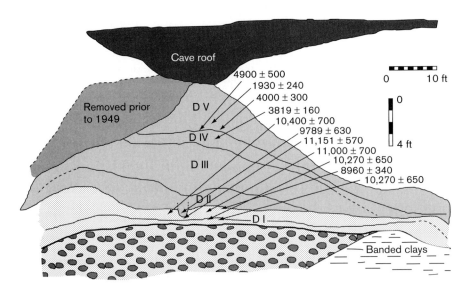

FIGURE 8.5 Stratigraphy of Danger Cave with the location of radiocarbon dates (years BP). Note the difference in the vertical and horizontal scales.

people lived, not just a place where they cached things. Indeed, much of the cultural fill of the cave was chaff from pickleweed, a plant that was gathered for its edible seeds. Because people lived in Danger Cave, it provided evidence for a much greater range of activities and a more detailed picture of the inhabitants' lifeways than did caves used primarily for storage.

The earliest human use of the cave came from sands that overlay gravels from Lake Bonneville. These sands had hearths, millingstones, a lanceolate point, and cordage. The artifact inventory became richer in subsequent levels, yielding over a thousand whole and broken millingstones, numerous manos and flaked tools, bone, basketry, cordage, bone tools, food bones, and plant material. From the assemblage at the Wendover cave sites, Jennings developed the concept of the Desert culture.

Looking at the artifacts and their distributions in Danger Cave and, at the same time looking at Julian Steward's (1938) ethnographic work with Numic speakers of the Basin, Jennings saw continuity in adaptation. He noted changes in the artifacts over time in the Danger Cave deposits, to be sure, but he felt the basic cultural adaptation, the Desert Culture, remained the same. From this base, which he saw going back in time 11,000 years, he postulated a widespread basic Archaic stage hunting and gathering culture not only in the Great Basin, but throughout the West. He saw connections with the **Cochise tradition** of the Southwest (see Chapter 9), materials from the Plateau, and even the San Dieguito material of California (Jennings 1964, 166–169).

The Desert culture was a focal point of much subsequent research, and it became the primary lens through which the prehistory of the Great Basin was viewed. Objections began to be raised, however, as people found exceptions to the patterns suggested by the Desert culture model, and as archaeologists began to better appreciate both the spatial and temporal diversity of the Great Basin's past. Eventually even Jennings (1973), in an article titled "The Short Useful Life of a Simple Hypothesis," abandoned the idea, although Great Basin archaeologists still refer to a **Desert Archaic**.

Hogup Cave, also in the Great Salt Desert of Utah, had deposits that were even deeper than those at Danger Cave. Pickleweed was a major food at Hogup Cave between 8400 BP and 3200 BP, too, and although large game animals like bison, pronghorn, desert sheep, and deer were all represented in the bones found at the site, rabbits and rodents made a much greater contribution to the diet. Marshes near the site provided not only habitat for pickleweed, but also attracted waterfowl that were hunted by the inhabitants of the cave. After 3200 BP, hunting larger game became more important as rising lake levels flooded the marsh environments near the cave. Hogup Cave contains a record that continues to the Historic period and figures heavily in understanding Great Basin prehistory, but the picture provided by Hogup Cave, Danger Cave, and the other important cave sites shows only part of the Great Basin's past.

Current Trends: Beyond the Desert Culture Concept

Archaeologists now believe that cave sites, though providing important glimpses of the Great Basin's past, do not tell the whole story of the Desert Archaic. Large-area surveys were initiated to examine the inventory of site types within defined regions, often valleys. For example, surveys of Surprise Valley in northeastern California documented a range of site types over a period of 6000 years

(O'Connell 1975). The earliest occupation, the **Menlo phase** (6500–4500 BP), produced evidence of semisubterranean pithouses in valley sites, suggesting substantial base camps. From lakeshores to the mountains, temporary camps that could have been used by groups moving out from the base camps were found in a variety of settings. Artifacts from Menlo sites include millingstones and distinctive projectile points (Northern Side Notched and others), mortars with conical depressions and pointed pestles for use in them, and stone pendants. Bone indicates that large mammals—sheep, antelope, deer, and even bison—were hunted. These findings contrasted with the picture of Great Basin life based on cave excavations.

Other important regional surveys have included work in Nevada by David Hurst Thomas. His investigations in the Monitor Valley and the Reese River valley have provided insights into changes in settlement pattern and in subsistence over time (Thomas 1988; Thomas and Bettinger 1976). Thomas discusses the project in the Monitor Valley and the role of the excavations at Gatecliff Shelter in this chapter's case study, "Deep-Site Excavation at Gatecliff Shelter, Nevada."

Cultural resource management studies also have required study of areas outside the cave sites favored by archaeologists of the mid-twentieth century. Surveys for the potential deployment of the MX missile system in the 1970s covered some large areas of Nevada and Utah. Cultural resource inventories for military bases like the Nevada Test Site, Fort Irwin, the Naval Weapons Center at China Lake, and the Marine Corps base at Twentynine Palms also added to the knowledge of the Great Basin's archaeology. Further, large surveys and management plans for desert lands conducted by the U.S. Bureau of Land Management (BLM) included both surveys and the production of overviews that have synthesized the archaeology of regions within the Great Basin (e.g., Warren et al. 1980). Considered together, this newer body of work provides some understanding of variability within the Desert Archaic.

Western Basin and Adjacent California

Following the poorly represented Fluted Point tradition occurrences, and in some cases overlapping with them, Stephen Bedwell (1973) has included a widespread number of complexes in the Western Pluvial Lakes tradition. This concept, based on Bedwell's work in the Fort Rock Valley, includes the San Dieguito complex discussed in Chapter 7, the **Lake Mohave complex**, **Death Valley I**, and similar materials like the Sadmat site in Nevada and the Haskett locality in Idaho. It is dated to a period from 12,000 BP to 7000 BP. Sites and artifacts from the various complexes are generally found around the margins of pluvial lakes like Lake Mohave or Lake Lahonton, although the distribution of points associated with this tradition indicates their use in other environments, as well.

Artifacts associated with the Western Pluvial Lakes tradition include stemmed points like the Lake Mohave, Silver Lake, and Haskett types (Figure 8.6), leaf-shaped bifaces, a variety of scrapers, and at some sites, milling equipment. At Fort Rock Cave a distinctive kind of sagebrush sandal, one of which was dated to 10,200 BP (8200 BC ±250), is found with material assigned to the Western Pluvial Lake tradition. Crescentics are also associated with this period. These are generally lunate or crescent-shaped, bifacially flaked artifacts (Figure 8.7). Although they have been suggested to be transverse-mounted arrow points used

FIGURE 8.6 Great Basin projectile points and their distribution in time: (1) Desert Side Notched series, (2) Cottonwood Triangular, (3) Bull Creek Concave Base, (4) Parowan Basal Notched, (5) Nawthis Side Notched, (6) Rose Springs–Eastgate series, (7) Martis series, (8) Gypsum Cave, (9) McKean Lanceolate, (10) Elko series, (11) Pinto series, (12) Humboldt series, (13) large Side Notched, (14) Cascade, (15) large unnamed stemmed, (16) large stemmed, (17) Haskett, (18) Scottsbluff, (19) Folsom, and (20) Clovis.

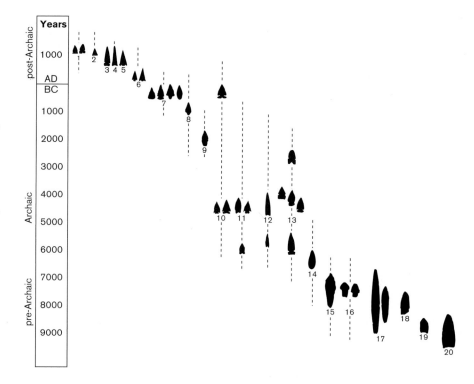

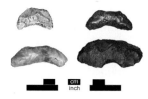

FIGURE 8.7 Lunate crescents from the Mojave Desert.

to stun small game like birds, they have not been found hafted in any of the dry cave sites and have not even been found with any sign of hafting mastic like pine pitch. Other suggested uses have included amulets or tools for ritual scarring (Rogers 1939).

Bedwell (1973) believed the Western Pluvial Lakes tradition to represent the remains of adaptations focused on lake side or river resources generally associated with the Pleistocene lakes, but others see this adaptation as a generalized one focusing on hunting (Warren and Crabtree 1986, 184). Some archaeologists consider the Western Pluvial Lakes tradition to be Paleoindian, based on the assumed hunting emphasis. Others, pointing to both the dates and the presence of milling equipment in at least some sites, consider it to be Early Archaic. Generally, however, the Early Archaic in the Great Basin is assigned to the time after the drying of the lakes.

The **Pinto period** represents the Early Archaic in the southwestern Great Basin and is dated from 7000 BP to 4000 BP. This period occurred just after the great pluvial lakes in the Great Basin dried up. Pinto period sites contain assemblages that include Pinto points (Figure 8.6), leaf-shaped bifaces, and scraper forms that resemble those of the earlier Western Pluvial Lakes tradition, which is generally seen as being ancestral to the Pinto period complexes. Some Pinto period sites have produced a few Lake Mohave and Silver Lake points, reinforcing the perceived continuity. Drills and gravers are added to the assemblage, along with manos and shallow basin metates at some sites. At the Stahl site in California's Owens Valley, excavators found a deep midden and postholes in patterns that suggest houses. Basin metates were common at the Stahl site.

In the Lahonton Basin a number of Early Archaic sites are found. The Cocanour locality on the Humboldt Sink is a site where the evidence of two structures were found. The remains of these structures are shallow circular depressions having diameters between 8 and 11 feet (2.4–3.4 m). Pinto points, millingstones, bifaces, scrapers, and choppers were found associated with the houses (Stanley et al. 1970). This was a residential site, based on the houses (Elston 1986). Lovelock Cave, Hanging Rock Cave, Hidden Cave, and many other cave sites of the area, were used during this period sporadically, when water was available in the lake basin (as it was at various periods); they seldom were residential sites, but rather served as burial and cache sites (Elston 1986, 140).

Hidden Cave provides an excellent example of a cache cave site, though its most recent investigator, David Hurst Thomas, makes a point of doing away with the notion of a "typical site" because of the variation inherent in Great Basin prehistory (Thomas n.d.). The site produced evidence of tool caches, food caches, and a huge number of human coprolites. The tool caches held tools that were used in seasonal activities near the shelter, eliminating the need to cart the items around during moves to various other resource locations. Food caches helped even out the availability of food. Most plant foods and some animal foods are available only at certain times, but when they are available, they may be abundant. Other parts of the year can be lean, so collecting storable food beyond immediate needs and caching it makes sense. Evidence for caching was actually found in the coprolites, some of which had remains of foods that are available either at different times of the year or at different locations, indicating transport and storage. The quantity of coprolites found in the cave suggested the practice documented among the historic Indians of Baja California called the "second harvest." Since seeds can pass through the human digestive system undigested, human coprolites can be a reserve of seeds, assuming they can be found. By intentionally depositing feces in the cave or by collecting and storing fecal material in the dry environment of the cave, the people at Hidden Cave (and elsewhere) may have maintained an emergency food reserve in the seeds contained in coprolites (Thomas n.d., 1985). The coprolites from Hidden Cave provided an important glimpse into the diet in the region. The coprolites contained evidence of people having eaten fish, birds, cattail seeds and shoots, piñon nuts, and bulrush seeds (Elston 1986, 141; Thomas n.d.).

The Middle Archaic is dated to between 4000 BP and 1500 BP. In the Mojave Desert and the southwestern Great Basin, this is called the **Gypsum period**. The beginning of the Middle Archaic was also the beginning of the **Little Pluvial**, a moist period that filled some desert basins with lakes, but the end of the period was more arid. The Gypsum period was a time of intensive occupation in the Mojave Desert, and subsistence activities became more diverse. Millingstones became more common, and the mortar and pestle also appear during the Gypsum period. Points (Figure 8.6) during this time include the Elko Eared, Elko Corner Notched, Gypsum Cave, and Humboldt Concave Base points (Warren and Crabtree 1986).

Newberry Cave, located east of Barstow in the Mojave Desert, has important deposits that bear on this period. The site produced radiocarbon dates on artifacts ranging from 3765 ±100 BP to 2970 ±250 BP. Excavations at the site produced Elko, Gypsum Cave, and other points, many of them hafted in dart foreshafts. Also found in the cave were rocks with colored powder adhering to them; probably these had been used to grind and mix pigment derived from red and green

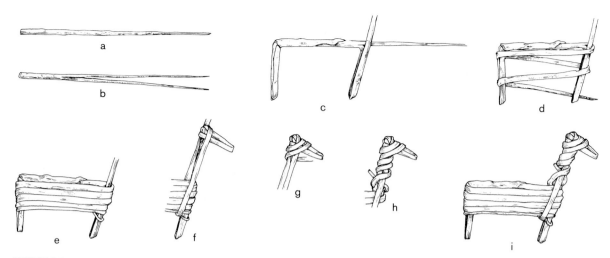

FIGURE 8.8 Split-twig figurine construction steps, based on examples from Etna Cave.

stones found in the deposits. Crystals of quartz and calcite, fire drills, sandals, cordage, leather, and sinew were also recovered. Both feathers and sheep dung were found wrapped in sinew. **Split-twig figurines** were also found at the site, and pictographs decorate the walls of the cave with design elements primarily representing quadrupeds. Based on the preponderance of hunting gear combined with these other indicators, investigators conclude that the site was used in hunting ritual (Davis and Smith 1981).

The split-twig figurines (Figure 8.8) are found in a much wider area than just Newberry Cave. They have been recovered from at least 16 sites in northern Arizona, Nevada, Utah, and California. The oldest are about 4000 years old and come from Stanton Cave in the Grand Canyon. At Newberry Cave they dated to about 3000 BP, and in Cowboy Cave, Utah, they date to about 500 BP (AD 455). The figurines were made by splitting a twig and forming the resulting pieces into the stylized image of a quadruped. Sometimes the figurines have a stick piercing them that may have been intended to represent a spear, reinforcing the notion they were used in hunting ritual. Rock art depicting quadrupeds, particularly mountain sheep, is common over much of the same region, with California's Coso Range having a particularly rich set of panels (Figure 8.9). Much of this rock art was made at the same time as the figurines. It has been suggested that there was a connection between the two. Because of their wide distribution, it may be that these figurines spread as part of a shamanistic ritual even across cultural lines. The rock art may be a related aspect of the same ritual system (Warren 1984, 417–419).

Elsewhere in the western Basin, hunters of the Middle Archaic stashed duck decoys in Lovelock Cave (Figure 8.10). In the Lahontan Basin a distinctive kind of basketry called Lovelock wickerware first appears. Lovelock wickerware baskets were most often conical burden baskets used to carry quantities of material, and they often had places for **tumplines** to be attached (Adovasio 1986, 197). The burden baskets were important in gathering piñon and in transporting materials over long distances. There is evidence that people in some parts of the western Great Basin decreased their range of mobility at this time (Elston 1986, 142–143).

FIGURE 8.9 Sheep depicted in rock art from the Coso area, California.

FIGURE 8.10 Lovelock Cave cache that contained 11 duck decoys.

In the Fort Rock region, for example, the Middle Archaic saw a dramatic increase in the use of local obsidian over obsidian brought in from a distance, suggesting that people were spending more time in the area (Jenkins et al. 1999).

The Late Archaic, which some researchers would call the Late Prehistoric, spans the time from the end of the Middle Archaic (about 1500 BP) to European contact. In the southwestern Great Basin this encompasses the **Saratoga Springs period** (1500–800 BP) and the **Shoshonean period** (800 BP to contact). The Saratoga Springs assemblages resemble those of the preceding Gypsum period, but the projectile points become smaller at about this time. This most likely reflects use of the bow and arrow instead of the atlatl. Rose Springs and Cottonwood Triangular points are the most common. Millingstones also continued to be important.

Different regions of the southwestern Great Basin exhibit influences from their neighbors. Influence from Southwestern groups of the lower Colorado River region is seen in the areas of the Mojave Desert south of the Mojave River. North of the Mojave River and in southern Nevada, **Virgin Branch Anasazi** interaction is evident. As we will discuss in Chapter 9, Ancestral Pueblo or Anasazi people

FIGURE 8.11 Turquoise mines at Halloran Springs, California.

were agriculturalists of the northern Southwest. They occupied parts of the Great Basin at some points in time as shown by sites like Lost City in Nevada. In the Mojave Desert the Anasazi influence is seen in pottery sherds found in sites and in their presence at the turquoise mines at Halloran Springs (Figure 8.11) between 1300 BP and 1100 BP. Following the Anasazi use of the mines, other Southwesterners, the **Hakataya**, controlled them from 1100 BP to 700 or 800 BP until the Southern Paiutes used them (Warren and Crabtree 1986, 191).

Desert Side Notched points and brownware pottery mark the Shoshonean period. In southern Nevada this period follows the Virgin Branch Anasazi occupations of the area. Assemblages in the northern Mojave Desert include large triangular knives, millingstones with unshaped manos, mortars and pestles, incised stones, slate pendants, and shell beads. Trade with the Pacific Coast is apparent, and large village sites in the Antelope Valley and along the upper Mojave River appear to owe their existence to their position on trade routes (Sutton 1980; Warren and Crabtree 1986, 191–192). This period marks the spread of Numic speakers into this part of the Great Basin. The descendants of these people were the main occupants of the entire Great Basin at contact with people of European descent. Eerkens (2004) has argued that there was a linkage between the simultaneous appearance of pottery and the intensification of seed use by individuals in the western Great Basin. He points out that pots not only can be used to efficiently process seeds, but they facilitate use of seeds by individuals, in contrast to other resources that had to be procured communally.

In the northwestern Great Basin the Late Archaic is marked by Rose Springs and Eastgate points, again indicating the replacement of the atlatl by the bow and arrow. Subsistence became more diverse, with more types of resource being used and more ecological zones being exploited. Rabbit and other small game, along with plant food, became more important in the diet than larger animals.

A change in lithic technology accompanied the change in projectile points, with the emphasis shifting from biface reduction and quarried raw materials to one that focused on expedient production of flakes and simple flake tools from locally available raw materials. Lovelock wickerware became less popular during this period.

Interpretation of the numerous styles of projectile points recovered from sites is an important issue in the archaeology of the western Great Basin. Box 8.1 discusses the use of points as time markers and explains why some have urged caution in the application of this practice.

ISSUES AND DEBATES

BOX 8.1

Projectile Points and Time

Our discussion of the Archaic cultures of the Western Great Basin, has necessarily referred to projectile points of many types. These artifacts are important to archaeologists because they are believed to be diagnostic of different periods in the past. However, there is controversy about whether projectile points really can be used as time markers. The crux of this debate concerns contentions by master flintknapper and replicator Jeff Flenniken and his associates that the use life of various Great Basin projectile points could include breakage and repair. They maintain that this scenario makes possible the transformation of a point from one of the temporally sensitive types to another. In use experiments conducted by Flenniken (Flenniken and Raymond 1986; Flenniken and Wilke 1989), flintknappers made various common types of Great Basin projectile points, used them and broke them, and then repaired them, noting their morphological trajectories. These authors concluded that it was quite possible for a point to start out as one type and become transformed into another type through breakage and repair. For example, the Elko point, generally seen as a hallmark of the Middle Archaic, can be reworked

into a Pinto point, which is generally assigned to the Early Archaic (Figure 8.12). Knowing this, it is easy to anticipate problems with chronologies inferred on the basis of projectile points alone.

Nevertheless, as the Gatecliff Shelter case study in this chapter makes clear, Thomas is a proponent of projectile point chronologies. Indeed, one of the reasons he sought out a site like Gatecliff Shelter was to establish chronological control for the surface sites he had been finding on survey. Thomas (1986a) wrote a reply to Flenniken, and others have also defended the use of points as time markers (Bettinger et al. 1991). They argue that although it is possible to transform one point type into another through breakage and repair, the temporal value of points has been demonstrated time and time again at stratified Great Basin sites like Gatecliff Shelter, Danger Cave, and Hogup Cave.

The debate has focused attention on **artifact use lives** and has led archaeologists to look for signs of reworking. Many points that might have been considered atypical can now be placed at the end of a breakage and repair trajectory. The debate has also led archaeologists to examine the criteria used in defining

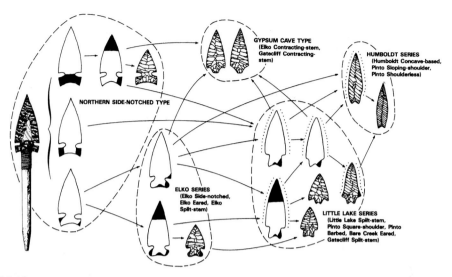

FIGURE 8.12 The Flenniken hypothesis: a model of the transformation of points from one type to another through breakage and repair.

various projectile point types (e.g., Basgall and Hall 2000; Vaughn and Warren 1987; Warren 2002) with an eye toward making those definitions more secure.

The debate may be far from over, as replicative experiments continue, but the bottom line is that most Great Basin archaeologists continue to find projectile points useful in dating sites and components in sites. Indeed, Justice (2002) has published a large volume on projectile points of California and the Great Basin, including discussions of chronology.

Eastern Great Basin

The prehistory of the eastern Great Basin has been divided into five periods. The **Bonneville**, **Wendover**, and **Black Rock periods** all come before 1500 BP, when the Fremont culture, which is discussed shortly, spreads over the area. The final period is the Shoshonean, which follows the Fremont in the eastern Great Basin. Cave sites like Danger Cave (Figure 8.13), Hogup Cave, Sudden Shelter, and Deluge Shelter contribute greatly to our knowledge of the prehistory of the area.

The Bonneville period (11,000–9500 BP) is represented by remains at only a few sites. The lowest levels of Danger Cave, for instance, are assigned to this period. Although the artifacts associated with this period are sparse owing to the small sample, some affinities are noted to the Western Pluvial Lakes tradition based on the occurrence of stemmed points resembling Lake Mohave points in deposits dated between 10,000 BP and 11,000 BP. It has been suggested that the Bonneville period may represent a transition between the big-game hunting of the Paleoindian period and the plant-oriented subsistence of the Desert Archaic in the area (Aikens and Madsen 1986, 154).

The Wendover period (9500–6000 BP) is better known than the Bonneville, being represented at more sites. Sites from this period occur over a wide range of

FIGURE 8.13 Members of an archaeology class exiting Danger Cave, Utah.

environmental zones, and a mobile existence at sites that change with the season is inferred. Plant foods were important in the diet, as seen both in the plant remains preserved in dry caves (the layers of pickleweed chaff found in Danger and Hogup Caves) and in the presence of seeds and pollen in coprolites (Aikens and Madsen 1986,155; Fry 1976; Kelso 1970). Plant-processing equipment includes manos and metates, and basketry for transport and storage is quite common in the dry cave sites (Aikens and Madsen 1986, 154–155).

A wide range of animals were taken, including deer, pronghorn, mountain sheep, elk, and bison, as well as birds and small mammals. The atlatl was used to bring down large game, and whole and fragmentary specimens of these weapons have been recovered from the dry cave sites. Projectile points from this period include Pinto, Humboldt, Northern Side Notched, and Elko types (Aikens and Madsen 1986, 155–156). During the Wendover period in Hogup Cave there was a strong correlation between cordage, netting, and the bones of rabbits and hares, suggesting that the practice of using nets in rabbit drives was an old one in the Great Basin (Aikens and Madsen 1986, 155). Incised and painted stones are found in some sites, and there is also jewelry made from Pacific Coast shells. Exhibit 8.1 introduces an important perishable artifact type often preserved in the dry caves of the eastern Great Basin.

During the Black Rock period (6000–1500 BP), Danger Cave apparently continued to be occupied, but many new sites were being established, as well, and often in upland areas that previously had been used infrequently (Aikens and Madsen 1986, 157–158). Changes in the degree to which plant and small-animal resources were used at different places in the region also have been noted. The period begins with a trend toward drying of the environment, but later more moist conditions prevailed. Adjustments to these changing conditions in site location and in activities at sites probably explain the new patterning in site distributions.

CLUES TO THE PAST

EXHIBIT 8.1

Rabbit Nets

The principle behind the fishing nets of the Pacific Northwest is not hard to grasp, but how would you catch rabbits in a net? In the fall, when jackrabbits were especially abundant and fat from their summer feeding, Indians of the Great Basin, such as the Washo, used to take long nets and stretch then across flats (Downs 1966, 27). We know this because archaeologists have used ethnographic information to reconstruct how the nets recovered from sites like Hogup Cave were used.

A rabbit net, which was made from string about the thickness of kitchen twine (Figure 8.14), was long and about as tall as a tennis net is high. The net was staked to the ground, the top edge held up with stakes or bushes, and it was often deployed in a **V**. Half the people would stand at the end of the flat or valley opposite the net and start moving toward the net, where the other half was waiting. As the people moved toward the net, they made noise and beat the brush, scaring the rabbits so that the animals ran away from the noise and toward the net. Inevitably, many rabbits became entangled

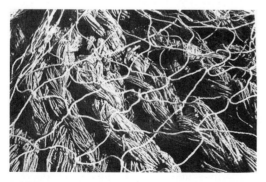

FIGURE 8.14 Paiute rabbit net spread over net coiled for storage.

in the net, and some of the waiting people would kill them with clubs (Downs 1966, 27; Wheat 1967, 59).

Although the making of a net was a very time-consuming activity, the drive technique could be used to harvest a large number of rabbits in a short time. The rabbits would then be cleaned and generally split in half to be dried and stored. Rabbits were also cooked up for immediate feasting. Large numbers of people gathered for rabbit hunts, and the feasting could go on for days, until the population of rabbits was depleted. These large drives, at least among the Washo, were organized by a hereditary leader called the "rabbit boss" (Downs 1966, 27).

Rabbit nets were very finely made. First, string was made, often from Indian hemp (Wheat 1967, 59), although the Washo used cord made from sage (Downs 1966, 27). Hemp can be found in areas with moist soils such as stream banks. Hemp stalks were harvested, and the straightest and longest were selected for string. First the Washo used a knife, often a flake of obsidian, to remove the reddish skin that covers the stalks. Then the stalks were split, and the pith was removed, leaving the fibers, which were separated from one another by gentle rubbing. When a sufficient supply of fiber had been processed, the task of making string began. A few fibers were rolled together on the maker's thigh with the palm of the hand. When about 2 feet (0.6 m) of twisted fiber had been produced, the maker would start a second ply in the same way. The final string would consist of these two plies, twisted together (Wheat 1967, 55–59).

String was next knotted into a net, designed so that the openings were just large enough for a rabbit's head to fit through—the rabbit's ears usually prevented the creature from backing out. Kroeber (1925, 572) describes the Washo rabbit nets as having a 3-inch (8 cm) mesh and being approximately 1.5 to 2 feet (ca. 0.5 m) high. An historic net owned by Captain Wasson of the Walker Lake Paiutes was over 300 feet (100 m) long, although it was cut in half at his death and divided between his two daughters (Wheat 1967, 59).

Besides food, the rabbits caught in nets provided another important commodity—their skins. These were cut into strips while fresh, and the strips curled as they dried, producing a fur-covered cord that was woven into blankets.

The archaeological record of the Great Basin indicates that such nets have a long history. Fragments of netting are found in many of the dry cave sites, and a whole specimen was found by early guano hunters in Lovelock Cave. Thus we can surmise that rabbits were hunted in a similar manner for many millennia. The recovery of these artifacts reminds us again how much we may be missing in archaeological sites at which good preservation is lacking.

Points from the Black Rock period are Elko and Gypsum Cave types. By the end of the period, Rose Springs and Eastgate points replace the larger types, signaling the appearance of the bow and arrow. Following the Black Rock period, the area was occupied by the Fremont.

THE FREMONT

FIGURE 8.15 One-rod-and-bundle basketry technique.

FIGURE 8.16 Utah metate from a San Rafael Fremont site.

Fremont is the name given to a set of archaeological phenomena that occur relatively late in the prehistory of the eastern Great Basin and disappear before the coming of European Americans. The Fremont sites, which exhibit a great deal of regional diversity, occur in a 900-year span between 1600 BP and 700 BP (AD 400–1300) (Marwitt 1986, 161), although most of the sites found are between 1300 BP and 800 BP (AD 700–1200) (Barlow 2002, 65). Sites attributed to one or another of the Fremont variants are found from southern Idaho in the north as far south as the Colorado River, and from northwestern Colorado across the Colorado Plateau and into the Great Basin to eastern Nevada (Barlow 2002, 65).

A number of characteristics set the Fremont apart from earlier and later cultures of the area, and to some extent from their neighbors. The Fremont grew maize to varying degrees, and a particular type of maize, **Fremont dent corn**, occurs on Fremont sites. The maize cobs are often found with sticks inserted into the stem end of the cob. Plain gray ceramics are also characteristic of the Fremont, although some of the vessels are decorated with appliqué designs. Painted ceramics are also found. Projectile points of the Fremont are small and vary from region to region. Basketry has been recovered from Fremont sites, and a technique of coiling called **one-rod-and-bundle coiling** (Figure 8.15) is associated with the Fremont. There is a distinctive kind of metate called the **Utah metate** (Figure 8.16) that has a trough grinding surface and a flat shelf at one end. An art style that depicts broad-shouldered anthropomorphic figures with elements of clothing and adornment such as headdresses, necklaces, and earrings is also associated with the Fremont. These humanlike figures are found as clay figurines and as rock art (Figure 8.17). Finally, moccasins made in a distinctive style are found at Fremont sites. Made from skin from the forelegs of deer or antelope, these moccasins (Figure 8.18) are cut in such a way that the **dew claws** of the animal are on the sole of the moccasin (Barlow 2002, 65–66; Marwitt 1986, 161).

FIGURE 8.17 Fremont anthropomorphs as depicted in petroglyphs (top) and figurines from the Old Woman site in Utah (bottom).

FIGURE 8.18 Fremont moccasins.

Hamlets with pithouses and aboveground architecture, often of adobe, are part of the Fremont settlement pattern (Figure 8.19), although caves were also used both for habitation and for storage. Some Fremont sites have storage pits, and multiroom surface structures have been found. There is considerable variability in site size, with the largest sites having multiple pithouses or numbers of surface rooms. Other sites may consist only of storage structures, artifact scatters, or the distinctive rock art.

FIGURE 8.19 Snake Rock site, Utah: beneath a plan of the site are profiles of the relative vertical positions of the features in Strata 1 and 2.

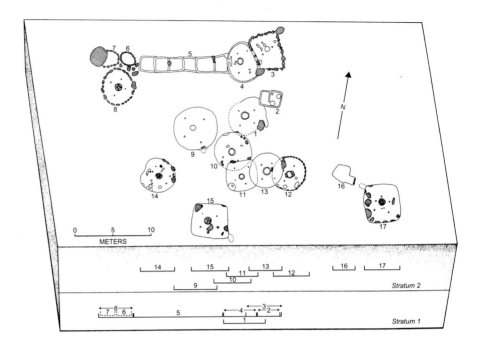

Although maize is present at Fremont sites, in some areas it appears to have made only a minor contribution to the diet, whereas in other areas it was a staple. The evidence for focus on maize includes the presence of irrigation ditches for fields near some sites, the common occurrence of maize cobs in the middens of sites, and the presence of Utah metates, which are often associated with very well worn manos. In addition, isotopic analysis indicates large quantities of maize in the diet. The analysis of human skeletal material from Backhoe Village, Evans Mound, and Caldwell Village suggests maize in the diet at levels similar to those found in the remains of the Anasazi to the south (Barlow 2002, 67–68). However, in other Fremont sites hunting or gathering of plant foods appears to have been more important than maize cultivation.

Regional Variation

Differences in the importance of maize are just one way in which variation is evident among Fremont sites. There is some temporal change within Fremont, consisting of the appearance of decorated and corrugated ceramics, a shift in pithouse form from round to rectangular, and the appearance of surface structures, all trends seen in the Southwest, as well. However, the major variability in Fremont sites is regional (Barlow 2002, 69). Five regional variants are recognized: **Uinta, San Rafael, Parowan, Sevier,** and **Great Salt Lake** (Figure 8.20). Some researchers reserve the term "Fremont" for the first two, which occur on the Colorado Plateau east of the Wasatch Range, referring to the other three—all found west of the Wasatch in the eastern Great Basin—as Sevier (Marwitt 1986, 163). Choosing to emphasize the similarities and relationships, we shall refer to all these groups as Fremont.

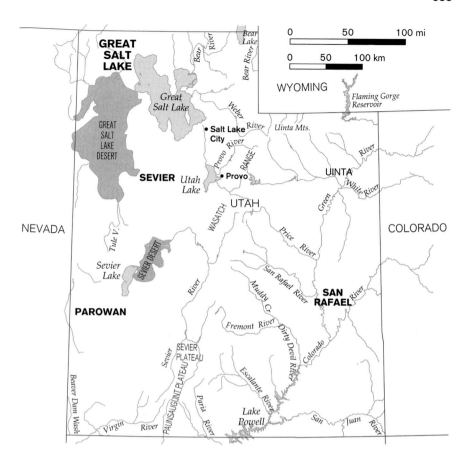

FIGURE 8.20 Location of Fremont variants.

The Uinta Fremont occupied the Uinta Basin of northeastern Utah for a short period of time between about 1350 BP and 1050 BP (AD 650–950). Population density seems to have been low, and most of the sites are small, comprising a few shallow circular pithouses. Aboveground structures are not found accompanying the pithouses, but isolated storage rooms were built on rock ledges. The pithouse sites, which tended to be on knolls, buttes, or the slopes above creeks, often had storage pits (Marwitt 1986, 196).

The food quest apparently focused on gathering plants and hunting deer, antelope, and small game. Maize appears to have been less important in the diet. Both the Utah metate and the distinctive anthropomorphic art are missing in the Uinta area (Marwitt 1986, 196).

South of the Uinta, sites are attributed to the San Rafael Fremont. Sites in this area tend to be small as well, but surface storage structures are associated with the pithouses. Masonry surface structures with multiple rooms are also found at some sites, and stone masonry is common. The San Rafael Fremont used small caves and rockshelters for storage and sometimes for house sites. The San Rafael diet probably included maize as a staple, although wild foods were also important. The San Rafael area demonstrates one of the traits of Fremont regions—borders are poorly defined. The various regions tend to grade into one another, and in the San Rafael case the southern boundary with the **Kayenta Branch**

Anasazi (see Chapter 9) is very indistinct. Some sites share Kayenta and San Rafael traits to such an extent that they can be classified as either (Marwitt 1986, 170).

Like the Uinta, the Parowan Fremont were influenced by the Kayenta Anasazi. The Parowan region is located in southwestern Utah. Some of the earliest excavation of Fremont sites was in this region, including work at Paragonah and Kanosh. Evans Mound is also a Parowan site. In the Parowan area the Fremont built relatively large settlements consisting of pithouses and surface adobe storage rooms. When artifact assemblages are considered, projectile point style and distinctive bone artifacts help set off the Parowan area from other Fremont groups.

Growing maize appears to have been central to the Parowan way of life, but hunting and wild plant gathering were also important in some parts of the Parowan area. Sites were usually located on the valley floors, where water was available for irrigation of crops (Marwitt 1986, 185).

The Sevier Fremont area is just north of the Parowan in central western Utah and adjacent parts of Nevada. Important sites of this variant include Backhoe Village, Nephi, and Pharo. As in other areas, the boundaries are not at all clear, and there is disagreement among archaeologists about how to designate some sites. Sites are generally small, having a few pithouses accompanied by adobe surface rooms; but a few sites, like the Richfield site and Nawthis Village, are much larger. Both architecture and artifact assemblages are quite variable within this variant. A particular type of gray pottery known as Sevier gray was locally made and serves to tie the otherwise diverse artifact assemblages together.

The Sevier Fremont built permanent settlements on the eastern edge of the area, with sites in the west being mostly seasonal sites or camps. Permanent sites tended to be located near marshes; indeed, in at least some Sevier sites marsh products may have been more important than maize and may have been critical in making sedentism possible.

The fifth variant, the Great Salt Lake variant, is found around that body of water and extending into southern Idaho. This variant lacked masonry for the most part and emphasized wild crops and hunting for subsistence. Major sites of this variant include the Bear River sites, the Levee site and the Knoll site. Many of the sites are seasonal, and caves such as Hogup Cave, Swallow Shelter, and the Promontory caves were used as camps. At Hogup Cave the Fremont materials are found in sediments that cover the entire range of Fremont occupation in the Basin, from 1600 BP to 700 BP (AD 400–1350). The use of the cave by the Fremont was apparently seasonal, and the fall harvest of the small seeds of the pickleweed, a salt flat plant, seems to have been the major activity (Marwitt 1986, 167–169).

The assemblage at Great Salt Lake Fremont sites has several artifact types not found in other Fremont areas, including side-notched points, cylindrical pestles, slate knives, and etched stone tablets. These items appear in the Hogup Cave assemblages prior to the Fremont strata and continue through Fremont. Other unique Great Salt Lake artifact types include saws made from deer and mountain sheep scapulas, bird-bone whistles, and harpoon heads.

Both the origins and the ultimate fate of the Fremont are enigmatic. The occurrence of maize, ceramics, and architecture led some early archaeologists to consider the Fremont as simply an extension of the Southwest. Dates for the beginning of the Fremont vary, ranging from near 1600 BP (AD 400) in the north to around 1200 BP (AD 800) in the south. The early dates in the north are early enough to preclude Anasazi influence as a possible explanation. Maize cultivation and pottery among these groups must have had another origin.

Most archaeologists today see the continuity of many elements between the Archaic and the Fremont, as well as important differences between the Anasazi and the Fremont (e.g., in the nature of the ceramics), as evidence of a Great Basin origin for the Fremont. Influences probably came from both the Southwest and from the Plains. Marwitt (1986, 163) notes that distinctive Fremont traits, including the one-rod-and-bundle coiled basketry, Fremont hide moccasins, anthropomorphic figurines, and incised stones all predate the appearance of the full constellation of Fremont material culture, in a few cases by several millennia. In Hogup Cave, for example, Fremont is recognized at after 1550 BP, when maize, pottery, and other Fremont items are found added to the existing Archaic inventory (Marwitt 1986, 162–163).

Aikens (1966) proposed a Plains origin for the Fremont, seeing them as Athapaskan people who moved into northern Utah and, through influences from the Southwest, developed the Fremont pattern. Madsen (1979), on the other hand, believes that the Fremont may represent regional developments of different groups of Archaic Basin people who wound up sharing the Fremont traits through trade and contact or through the spread of a religious cult that encompassed the area. Madsen (1979, 721) views the shared elements in the larger Fremont area as "superficial" and would divide this set of sites into a Sevier culture, a Fremont culture, and perhaps, a third as yet unnamed culture in the north.

Although the Fremont are closest to the Anasazi, and clearly interacted with them, there also are some affinities with the Mogollon, another cultural tradition from the Southwest (see Chapter 9). Among these is the similarity between the Utah metate of the Fremont and Mogollon metates. Perhaps Mogollon rather than Anasazi was the inspiration for the development of Fremont (Marwitt 1968, 161).

What became of the Fremont also is a puzzle. Although some archaeologists have argued that the Fremont gave rise to the Numic speakers of the Great Basin, there is evidence that contradicts this suggestion. There is a distinct discontinuity in both basketry styles (one-rod-and-bundle basketry disappears with the Fremont) and in ceramics between the Fremont and the later Numic populations (Adovasio 1986, 204; Madsen 1986, 208). These data suggest replacement of people rather than development of the Fremont into the Numic peoples. Thus what became of the Fremont is unknown, though some archaeologists suggest that they moved onto the Great Plains.

NUMIC PEOPLES AND THEIR SPREAD

As indicated earlier, post-Fremont times in the eastern Great Basin are assigned to the Shoshonean period because of the dominance of groups ancestral to Shoshone as well as the linguistically related Paiute and Ute. The Shoshonean period is also recognized as the end of the Late Archaic or Late Prehistoric in the western Great Basin. Distinctive brownware pottery is associated with Shoshoneans. These people utilized a wide variety of wild seeds in their subsistence.

Ethnographers and archaeologists have been able to document a number of practices of the Shoshoneans that resulted in human modification of the environment. For example, Phil Wilke and his associates have documented bow stave trees—generally juniper trees that were scored to provide straight blanks for fashioning into bows (Figure 8.21). Scars from the removal of staves remain as testimony to this practice (Wilke 1988). We also know that controlled burning

FIGURE 8.21 Living tree from which a bow stave was removed.

promoted the seed plants that were so important to these groups, and that other land management practices were important as well (Fowler 1986).

These Shoshonean or Numic-speaking groups occupied nearly the entire Great Basin when Europeans began to arrive. Since there seems to be a cultural discontinuity between these groups and archaeologically known groups in many areas, one long-standing problem confronting Great Basin archaeology has been explaining this **Numic spread**. Questions still debated include where Numic speakers came from, when they came, and why they dispersed.

Most archaeologists believe that the Numic speakers expanded recently and rapidly, having originated at the southwestern margins of the Great Basin beginning about 950 BP, but reaching the height of the expansion in the eastern Great Basin only after the disappearance of Fremont cultures. One of the primary pieces of evidence for this conclusion has been the fanlike distribution of Numic language branches in the Great Basin, with each branch forming a wedge that was

FIGURE 8.22 Distribution of Numic speakers.

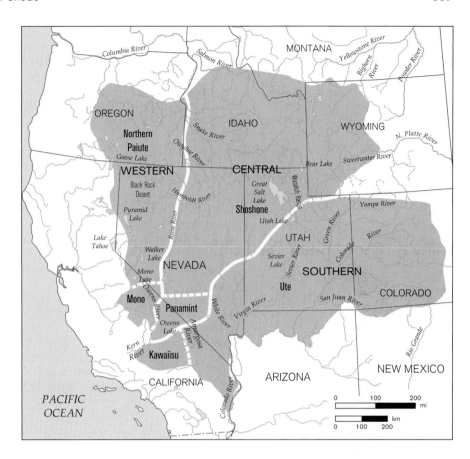

narrowest in southeastern California (Figure 8.22). If longer periods of time had passed since the dispersal, or if another origin for these groups were correct, this distribution should not be so clear. However, explaining why and how the dispersal happened has been difficult. Bettinger and Baumhoff (1982) suggested that Numic speakers had a highly successful subsistence strategy based on resource generalization, and that they essentially outcompeted earlier Archaic peoples. However, both the Numic spread itself and the distinctive nature of Numic adaptive strategies have been difficult to demonstrate archaeologically (Bettinger 1998). Some researchers (e.g., Grayson 1994) consider the beginnings of the Numic spread to be the result of earlier environmental changes at the end of the Altithermal; others attribute it to warlike traits among Numic speakers (Sutton 1986). Resolving the nature, timing, and reasons for the Numic spread remains an important research topic.

PROTOHISTORIC AND HISTORIC PERIODS

The Great Basin was one of the last areas of the United States to be fully explored, and the post-Contact population has always been relatively light, making it possible for the Native Americans to continue their original lifeways later than was possible in most other parts of North America. Nearly all these peoples spoke Numic languages, as we have just discussed (Wick R. Miller 1986, 98). The lone exception was the Washo, who spoke a language probably of the Hokan family found in California. The Washo apparently had been in contact with their Numic neighbors long enough to have accepted a number of loan words and also to have adopted some structural characteristics of the Numic languages (Jacobsen 1986, 108–109). The Numic speakers included the Northern, Southern, and Owens Valley Paiute, the Northern Shoshone, the Eastern and Western Shoshone, the Mono, and the Kawaiisu.

The Washo were centered on Lake Tahoe in California and Nevada. The Northern Paiute occupied a strip along the western edge of the Great Basin, primarily in Nevada and southern Oregon. Southern Idaho was home to the Northern Shoshone and Bannock, while the Eastern Shoshone occupied the western edge of Montana. The Utes covered central and eastern Utah and the adjacent part of western Colorado. Southern Nevada, southern Utah, part of northern Arizona, and part of eastern southern California were home to the Southern Paiute. The Kawaiisu lived in California's Mojave Desert, while to the north, the Owens Valley Paiute occupied the Owens Valley and surrounding territory, including a small area of Nevada. The Western Shoshone took up the middle of the distribution, living in eastern California, central and northeastern Nevada, and northwestern Utah.

The coming of Europeans brought about changes to the cultures of the area, perhaps even prior to actual encounters with the outsiders. Three Historic subperiods can be recognized: a Spanish period from late seventeenth to early nineteenth centuries, a Mexican period from 1821 to 1847, and an American period thereafter.

Contact between Europeans and Native Americans was minimal during the Spanish period, being largely restricted to some explorations into portions of the Great Basin by Franciscan priests searching for routes to Alta California and to illegal trade (e.g., trafficking in human slaves) with Spanish colonists to the south. The most significant changes during the Spanish period came from the introduction of the horse. By the time exploring parties reached the area in the 1770s, the people of the Basin had already been exposed to some European influences indirectly through contact with their neighbors. From the Plains, especially, the people of the Basin had encountered the horse. While some groups in areas where the environment was suitable for keeping horses took to these animals as transportation in much the same way as the people of the Plains, others saw the horse in a different light. People who lived in areas where the vegetation was too sparse to graze horses saw the animals not as transportation, but as food. These different reactions to the horse changed the power dynamics in the Great Basin, with tribes adopting the horse benefiting while others were weakened (Malouf and Findlay 1986).

During the Mexican period, trade to the south continued in a similar way, with some increase in the trafficking for slaves. However, contact with other Europeans increased as British and American traders entered the Great Basin from other directions seeking furs. More and more people traversed the region traveling on overland trails to California, as well. Conflicts between Native inhabitants and these newcomers were sometimes hostile, but far more serious were the impacts of the fur trade on fragile but productive habitats and on the ability of Native people to persist in traditional subsistence practices.

However, it was not until the American period, which began after the Treaty of Guadalupe Hidalgo in 1848, that great change began in the Great Basin. The Mormon migration into the region beginning in 1847 brought the first real settlers, and the archaeology of early Mormon settlement can be significant (e.g., Ferg and Wilhelm 2005). The Mormons made serious attempts to get along with the people already living in the Great Basin, but as the number of church members grew, they could not help but affect the human and environmental balance of the area. Shortly non-Mormons also came in large numbers, either heading to California or establishing cattle ranches in the Basin.

Mining

Mining had been an important activity in the Great Basin even before the Historic period, as the turquoise mines of the Mojave Desert attest. However, the California gold rush of 1849 and the discovery of the Comstock lode in Nevada in 1859 brought hordes of people seeking their fortune, many of whom passed through the Great Basin on the way to the California gold fields. The Oregon Trail is well preserved in parts of Nevada, especially where there is actually an accumulation of tracks rather than a single trail. This dispersed trail (Figure 8.23), which can cover large areas, can create headaches for land managers who have to decide which tracks are important and what uses are conducive to the preservation of the important remnants of the trail.

Even before the discovery of gold, however, people were attracted to California, including a group of unlucky immigrants who left Springfield, Illinois, in 1846 and became trapped by winter snows in the Sierra Nevada. This was the Donner party, who were stranded for months in makeshift camps and some hastily constructed cabins. Archaeological research has located remnants of the camps and has and continues to shed light on the ordeal of the Donner party, whose survivors are said to have resorted to cannibalism, eating parts of their fellow campmates who died. Advanced techniques such as DNA analysis and study of indicators of nutritional stress in bones will provide considerable information about what really happened in those snowbound camps. While no direct evidence of cannibalism has been found, some bone fragments that could

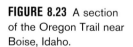

FIGURE 8.23 A section of the Oregon Trail near Boise, Idaho.

be human will be assayed to see whether the remnant DNA indicates human origin. The excavations already have cleared up some misconceptions about where the encampments were, and many more important contributions are expected (Hardesty 1997).

Related directly to mining are the many ghost towns, as well as many towns that are still occupied. The historic town of Bodie in eastern California is a state park that preserves an abandoned mining town. Virginia City, in Nevada, made famous by the television series *Bonanza*, is another such town, although it has had a second life as a tourist destination. Recent archaeological work in Virginia City, which grew to exploit the riches of the Comstock lode, has revealed remains of the Boston Saloon, an establishment that served the African American members of this bustling community between 1864 and 1875. The excavations have changed stereotypical views of the western mining camp, which had been seen as primarily inhabited by white males. The discovery of 21 fragments of glass that, when reassembled, turned out to be the oldest known Tabasco® bottle, suggest that African Americans on the frontier were in the forefront of experimentation with cuisines. Chemical testing of food residues confirms that ingredients consistent with the use of the commercial hot sauce were present. DNA analysis of material from a clay smoking pipe indicates use by a woman, suggesting that the view of mining camp saloons as exclusively male preserves may not be completely accurate. This ongoing project is expected to continue to add to our appreciation of the world of the western mining camp and to our understandings of the African American experience on the frontier (State of Nevada Department of Cultural Affairs 2003).

Other Historic Archaeology

Historical archaeology of the American period can contribute significantly to many other stories. One theme in the arid west is water, and there is important archaeology to be done in connection with federal water reclamation projects begun in the early twentieth century (Hardesty 1991). Another theme is the federal usage of the Great Basin, for example, at and around the Nevada test site, where the United States tested its nuclear weapons from 1951 until 1992. In addition to documenting pre-Columbian sites, archaeologists have been documenting the archaeology of the nuclear weapons program. From standing structures used in the testing and weapons research to Camp Peace, a spot across the highway from the boundary of the test site where protesters camped and demonstrated, archaeologists recorded the artifacts and features associated with the program. For example, one site is a furnished bomb shelter that looked like something out of a 1950s TV show, complete with a stocked kitchen and a television set. This work provides insights on the Cold War period, a time in world history during which the possibility of nuclear war seemed quite real (Trivedi 2002).

CHAPTER SUMMARY

This chapter has introduced the archaeology of the Great Basin. Although hunting and gathering adaptations persisted through the millennia with only a short interruption from the Fremont, there still was important cultural variation in this area's past. This introduction provides background for further exploration. The main points made in this chapter are as follows:

- Great Basin environments vary from forested high mountains to broad, arid valleys, and a wide variety of plants and animals inhabit this mix of environments. Most of the area is drained internally in lake basins, and the resources of lakes and their margins have always been important to human survival in the area.

- During the Pleistocene, massive lakes filled much of the Great Basin. Since the end of the Ice Age, the cool, moist Anathermal period, followed by the warm dry Altithermal and then by the present Medithermal, which began in about 4500 BP, have affected resource distributions. However, environmental change important to humans also occurred within shorter time frames, and seasonal change always was significant.

- The earliest people in the Great Basin appear to have been contemporaneous with fluted point makers on the Great Plains and in the Southwest, as evidenced by sites dated to the twelfth millennium BP.

- The Desert Archaic is a name frequently applied to the hunter-gatherers of the Great Basin whose lifeways persisted with relatively minor changes over millennia. However differences between the western and eastern Great Basin cultural sequence are notable, and a uniform Desert Culture spanning the period of human occupation is no longer envisioned by archaeologists.

- The Western Pluvial Lake tradition, which includes both stemmed-point types and leaf-shaped bifaces and milling equipment, marks the Paleoindian–Archaic transition in the western Great Basin. The Early Archaic Pinto period follows (7000–4000 BP), succeeded by the Middle Archaic Gypsum period (4000–1500 BP) and then the Late Archaic or Late Prehistoric. All the cultures of these periods were based on hunting and gathering, but interesting differences in the material culture help archaeologists define the subperiods.

- In the eastern Great Basin the Bonneville period from 11,000 BP to 9500 BP is evident at a few sites like Danger Cave. Much more evidence is available for the Wendover period (9500–6000 BP), when the preservation of normally perishable items is excellent. Finally the Black Rock period (6000–1500 BP) is notable because of the appearance of the bow and arrow. Again these are mobile hunting and gathering societies, distinguishable largely on the basis of artifacts.

- The Fremont culture of the eastern Great Basin (1600–700 BP) represents people who experimented with growing maize, built pithouses and aboveground storage rooms, made plain gray pottery, and used the one-rod-and-bundle coiling technique to create basketry. Regional variants within Fremont reflect differences in the level of dependence on maize as well as contrasts in material culture. Both the origins and the disappearance of Fremont are poorly understood.

- Numic-speaking or Shoshonean people inhabited most of the Great Basin in the Late Prehistoric and were present everywhere except around Lake Tahoe, where the Washo lived when Europeans began to arrive. The reasons for and mechanisms of the spread of these people throughout the Great Basin have been much debated but remain poorly understood.

- The Great Basin was one of the last areas explored by Europeans, but the Spanish were marginally evident beginning in the late seventeenth century. The horse was adopted by some Great Basin tribes but not by others, and this led to disparate fortunes for the Native people of the Great Basin. During the Mexican period (1821–1847), fur traders and others began to traverse the Great Basin in greater numbers. In the American period settlement, first by Mormons and then by others, brought major change to the Great Basin for the first time. Historical archaeology has much to contribute to our understanding of the recent past in the Great Basin.

SUGGESTIONS FOR FURTHER READING

For discussions of the archaeology as well as material on the environment, history, and ethnographic peoples of the Great Basin:

D'Azevedo, Warren L. 1986. *Handbook of North American Indians*, Vol. 11, *Great Basin*. Washington, DC: Smithsonian Institution.

For treatment of both the environmental and cultural history of the Great Basin:

Grayson, Donald K. 1993. *The Desert's Past: A Natural Prehistory of the Great Basin*. Washington, DC: Smithsonian Books.

For an account of what archaeology tells us about the experience of the ill-fated Donner party:

Hardesty, Donald. 1997. *The Archaeology of the Donner Party*. Reno: University of Nevada Press.

The classic paper by Julian Steward that provided the ethnographic model for the Desert culture concept is still in press:

Steward, Julian. 1938. *Basin-Plateau Aboriginal Sociopolitical Groups*. Bureau of American Ethnology Bulletin 120. Washington, DC. (Reprinted by the University of Utah Press, Salt Lake City.)

This collection of papers contains recent thought on Great Basin prehistory:

Beck, Charlotte, ed. 1999. *Models for the Millennium: Great Basin Anthropology Today*. Salt Lake City: University of Utah Press.

For discussions of adaptations to the Great Basin's wetlands:

Hemphill, Brian E., and Clark Spencer Larsen, eds. 2000. *Prehistoric Lifeways in the Great Basin Wetlands: Bioarchaeological Reconstruction and Interpretation*. Salt Lake City: University of Utah Press.

For a classic paper on the eastern Great Basin by one of the founders of Great Basin archaeology:

Jennings, Jesse D. 1978. *Prehistory of Utah and the Eastern Great Basin*. Anthropological Paper 98, University of Utah.

OTHER RESOURCES

Sections H and I of the Student CD provide web links, additional discussion questions, and other study aids. Section G contains additional resources including a complete list of the references cited in this chapter and in its case study. It is particularly interesting to compare Gatecliff Shelter, the subject of this chapter's case study, with an early cave site in a very different setting, described in the case study in Section D.5 of the Student CD.

CASE STUDY

Caves and rockshelters have long been important in Great Basin archaeology because when deeply stratified, these sites contain a long record of use by various hunting and gathering groups. In addition, the arid climate of the high desert sometimes preserves usually perishable artifacts, providing archaeologists with unusual information unavailable elsewhere. Thus, caves and rockshelters in the Great Basin have the potential for preserving a record of environmental change that can parallel the cultural sequence. Such places are "dream sites" for the committed archaeologist. Gatecliff Shelter, located in Monitor Valley of Nevada, is a well-known site in the central Great Basin that has provided important information on chronology and projectile point change as well as lifeways in the ancient Desert West. This site, which has been used as an example in other textbooks (e.g., Thomas 1998), provides insights into the nature of the archaeological record in this part of North America. This case study also illustrates how archaeologists find and excavate sites, and more than a little about why they choose the strategies they do. As you read this case study, think about what it took to find and excavate Gatecliff. Would you have the persistence to conduct this kind of research?

DEEP-SITE EXCAVATION AT GATECLIFF SHELTER, NEVADA

David Hurst Thomas

My interest in Gatecliff Shelter arose from a much broader project examining prehistoric land-use patterns in the central Great Basin (Nevada). Based on a close reading of the available ethnohistory, we conducted two large-scale regional surveys (in the Reese River and Monitor valleys), each of which relied entirely on surface remains—picking up artifacts and plotting their distribution (Thomas 1983a, 1983b, 1988; Thomas and Bettinger 1976). While these surveys provided valuable insights into ancient mobility and subsistence patterns, surface archaeology requires key assumptions about cultural chronology and about paleoenvironmental conditions. This is why we were seeking a site with deeply stratified deposits: to provide independent verification of our chronological and paleoenvironmental assumptions.

In this brief discussion, I will focus on how we found Gatecliff Shelter, how we excavated the site, how we defined the stratigraphy, how we defined the time markers contained there, and how we reconstructed the human activities that played out inside Gatecliff Shelter during the last 6000 years.

GOOD OLD GUMSHOE SURVEY

We found Gatecliff through a fortunate combination of happenstance, hard work, and trial and error.

James O'Connell calls the process "gumshoe survey," probably because such rudimentary archaeological reconnaissance closely resembles detective work: set out a problem, get some leads, track them down, and, if you're fortunate, you crack the case. In archaeology, "cracking the case" can mean turning up just the right site to answer a question that's bothering you. This is precisely how we found Gatecliff Shelter.

At the time, I was a graduate student at the Davis campus of the University of California, supporting my doctoral fieldwork by conducting archaeological field schools. We offered green, untrained students the chance to join our fieldwork in the Reese River valley of central Nevada. The students paid for the summer's research through their enrollment fees, and they also supplied the physical labor. In return, I taught them what I could about archaeological fieldwork. The trade seemed fair enough. I progressed in my doctoral research, and they acquired training and credits toward graduation.

The summer was taken up doing "systematic archaeological survey"—basically mapping and collecting the archaeological stuff that we could find on the ground surface in the Reese River valley. While the so-called surface survey was going well, we badly needed to check our findings against the kind of data you get only from excavating buried sites, such as caves or deep trash deposits. Although we looked everywhere, we never could seem to find the right place to dig. It was frustrating.

As it turned out, we eventually found the very deep cave site we were seeking—a place with great stratigraphy and plenty of archaeological stuff buried inside. While I'd like to be able to tell you about the sophisticated research strategy we designed to find Gatecliff Shelter, the truth is that we just lucked into it. But it's worth telling that story, I think, because it illustrates how great archaeological sites are found—as windfalls for those fortunate enough to be in just the right place at the proper time. It also helps to know what you're looking for. So here's how we found Gatecliff Shelter.

At the end of our first field session in Reese River, we assembled the crew for steak dinners in the nearby town of Austin, Nevada. In the high desert, "nearby" meant a dusty ride of an hour or more, but the push seemed worth it. We relaxed, gnawed T-bones, and spun rattlesnake and stuck-truck stories into the morning hours. Austin is a pocket-sized Nevada mining town with fewer than 250 citizens, a picturesque little desert dive, which has attracted its share of attention. In his epic journey across back-roads America, *Blue Highways* author William Least Heat Moon wrote, "Austin . . . a living ghost town: 40 percent living, 50 percent ghost and 10 percent not yet decided" (1984, 200).

But above all, Austin is small-town America, and when two dozen grubby archaeologists show up for steaks and beverages, word soon gets around. When our waitress politely inquired who was in charge and somebody pointed to me, she told me about her husband, a mining geologist who had prospected the western mountains for 40 years. There are few places Gale Peer had not been. So when we met, I asked him about any archaeological sites he might have seen. We were hoping to find a local cave or rockshelter with some stratified cultural deposits to check our Reese River findings.

Mr. Peer indeed knew of such a cave—over in Monitor Valley, a dozen miles east of Austin. He had not been there in years, but the details were fresh in his mind. "You take the main dirt road south in Monitor Valley, then turn west, up one of the side canyons. I don't remember which one. As you drive along, oh, let's see, maybe ten or fifteen miles, there's a large black chert cliff. It goes straight up. A thousand feet or so. At the bottom of the cliff is a cave. Some time, a long time ago, the Indians painted the inside

of the cave. There are pictures of people and animals, plus a lot of writing I don't understand. Top of the shelter's caved in. Maybe in an earthquake. There's not much of the cave left. Drive out there when you get a chance. I'd like to know what's in that cave." He sketched a map on his business card. He remembered exactly where the cave was relative to the canyon, but he was not sure exactly which canyon. I stashed the card in my shirt, and thanked him for the tip.

This is the essence of gumshoe survey—hanging out in bars, gas stations, and grocery stores, listening to those who know more about the landscape than you do. I hoped that Mr. Peer's advice was as good as his memory seemed to be. Maybe this was the deep cave site I'd been looking for. But of course I had heard of a dozen similar caves, all of which proved uninteresting when investigated.

The season ended, the students went their various ways, and I resumed my graduate studies. But throughout that academic year I kept remembering Mr. Peer's cave. At times I felt like dropping everything, hopping into a pickup truck, and taking off for Monitor Valley. But the classroom sometimes seems to get in the way of an archaeological education, and my graduate student commitments kept me from breaking away, even for a weekend. Besides, I consoled myself, the mountains of Monitor Valley reach 11,000 feet (3350 m), and the October snowfall can last until late spring. Even if I knew where it was, the cave would probably be snowed in until May. So I plugged along, working on the summer's artifacts, every now and again reflecting on a make-believe cave somewhere in the Nevada backwoods.

Summer finally arrived, and once again I rounded up undergraduates to help out at Reese River. With the necessary state and federal excavation permits in hand, we drove to central Nevada, scouting out new campsites and hoping to find the cave that Mr. Peer had spoken of nearly a year before. The rockshelter had to be in a canyon—but which one? We had 15 canyons to choose from.

Beginning at the southern end of Monitor Valley, we drove up and down each side canyon, working our way slowly northward. The roads were rough, and the weather was no ally. We were snowed into one campsite for 3 days—and it was June! When the sun appeared, it melted the snow, washing out the only road. At times it took all our concentration to remember why we were there.

Still, there was this cave. . . . Mr. Peer seemed too astute a geologist and observer of nature simply to have imagined a rockshelter covered with prehistoric paintings, and we kept looking. Each canyon had potential. We would see something, stop the truck, skitter up the hillside. But each time, it turned out to be a shadow, an abandoned mine shaft, or just a jumble of boulders. The cave with its rock art eluded us.

After a week of this we came to Mill Canyon, just the next one on the list, with no greater potential than the 10 canyons we had already combed. The road was a little worse than most, and we had to inch down a steep ridge into the rocky canyon. Even in four-wheel drive, our truck lurched downslope, on a path so steep it seemed barely glued to the mountainside. Finally, as we started up the flat canyon bottom, a brooding black cliff loomed ahead. The scarp was riddled with small caves and rockshelters.

And sure enough, the caves were empty, unless you counted the occasional coyote scat, owl pellet, or packrat midden. The cliff face was nearly a half-mile long, and we became more and more discouraged as we moved up canyon, scanning each small alcove for pictographs. Finally, only one section remained to be inspected, where the black cherty formation was swallowed up beneath the alluvial Mill Canyon bottomland. We saw a dim shadow near the bottom, but a dozen similar shadows had been just that—shadows.

The paintings were not visible until we crawled into the mouth of the cave. There they were, just as Mr. Peer had said a year before: small human figures, painted in red and yellow pigments. On the other wall were cryptic motifs in white and black. And, yes, the roof had caved in years before. Half the floor was buried beneath tons of chert. One boulder would have dwarfed the pickup we had left in the canyon.

I scoured the shelter floor, looking for artifacts, animal bones, pieces of basketry. Anything. But no matter how hard I looked, there was nothing remotely suggesting that people had lived here. We had the rock art, of course, but pictograph caves sometimes have no habitation debris at all.

Retrieving some digging gear from the truck, we carefully excavated a small test pit in the floor of the cave. Old World archaeologists sometimes call these exploratory excavations *sondages*. I always like the ring of that word—what class. In Nevada, we just call them test pits. Anyway, we set out a small square, 50 centimeters (20 in.) on a side, and I scraped away the rocks and rat dung with my favorite Marshalltown trowel.

An old-time archaeologist once told me about digging in a cave just like this. "It smelled brown," he recalled.

We dug through the afternoon, taking notes and measuring artifacts. We finally stopped, armpit deep, when I could no longer reach the bottom of the test pit. It was a pretty meager haul: several pieces of broken bone, a few of them charred, and a dozen stone flakes, probably debris from resharpening stone knives or projectile points. Not exactly treasure, but we knew that at least one flintknapper had paused here to ply his craft. Still we were disappointed. The rock art already spoke of the occasional prehistoric visitor. We were looking for something more.

Across the sagebrush campfire that night our small crew assayed the finds. The rock art was neat; only two similar sites were known in the central Great Basin. The stones and bones were suggestive enough, but the shelter seemed hardly the deep site we had hoped for all year. The deposits were maybe 2 or 3 feet deep, and the strata probably jumbled. People had most likely dug storage pits, cleared bedding areas, and scooped out fire hearths in there for centuries. It probably had stratigraphy like most desert caves, which are so jumbled that they look as though they have been rototilled. At best, our test pit results were borderline.

As it turned out, we were wrong about this site, which we eventually called Gatecliff Shelter (after a local geological formation). The site came to dominate my archaeological life for more than a decade. The prehistoric deposits were not a few feet deep, as I had initially thought. Gatecliff turned out to be 40 feet (12 m), deep, apparently the deepest rockshelter in the Americas. The strata were also not mixed, as I had first feared. Over the millennia, the shelter had been inundated again and again by flash floods. The surging waters laid down thick layers of mud, forming an impenetrable cap of rock-hard silt. This flooding occurred at least a dozen times, stratifying the deposits into horizontal "floors."

Gatecliff had what textbooks (including my own) describe as "layer-cake stratigraphy." The shelter had been occupied for much longer than the past few centuries, as I had thought at first. Gatecliff was old, at least 7000 years old, as radiocarbon dating would later establish. The sediments also contained ample evidence about the past environments of Monitor Valley.

After finishing graduate school, I took a job at the American Museum of Natural History in New

York City, where I convinced the museum to dispatch five major field expeditions to Gatecliff Shelter. More than 200 people helped excavate the site over the years. The National Geographic Society supported part of the fieldwork and prepared an educational film about the site. The society also wrote a book about our excavations at Gatecliff. *The New York Times* and *The New Yorker* magazine published stories about Gatecliff. There was coverage on television and radio. A U.S. congressman even became involved in the struggle to preserve the site. Gatecliff Shelter was decidedly on the map.

A VERTICAL EXCAVATION STRATEGY

It's electrifying to find a site like Gatecliff, but the "discovery" was only the beginning. Our excavation strategy and tactics evolved dramatically as we learned more about the site and its potential.

We began with two simple test pits dug the same year we found the site. From day one, we wanted to learn two things: how long people had used Gatecliff Shelter, and whether the buried deposits could tell us about the human chronology of the region. These two questions were clear-cut, and so was our fieldwork. Our earliest excavation strategy was vertical, designed to supply, as expediently as possible, a stratified sequence of artifacts and ecofacts associated with other potentially datable materials.

Like most archaeologists, I dig "metrically" in typically 1-meter squares. There is, of course, a minimum size in such exploratory soundings: squares much smaller than 1 by 1 meter (3.28 by 3.28 ft) would squeeze out the archaeologists, and larger units are overly destructive (and too time-consuming).

Test pits tend to be quick and dirty, particularly because they must be excavated "blind," without knowing what stratigraphy lies below. Nevertheless, even in test pits, archaeologists must maintain three-dimensional control of the finds: the x axis (front to back), the y axis (side to side), and the z axis (top to bottom). This is why archaeologists dig square holes. Provided the sidewalls are kept sufficiently straight and perpendicular, excavators can use the dirt itself to maintain horizontal control on the x and y axes by measuring directly from the sidewalls. As test pits deepen, however, the sidewalls may start sloping inward, cramping the digger and biasing the mea-

surements. Field archaeologists call these sloppy pits "bathtubs"—decidedly bad form.

What about vertical control? At Gatecliff, we dug test pits in arbitrarily imposed 10-centimeter (3.9 in.) levels. Everything of interest—artifacts, ecofacts, soil samples, and so forth—was kept in separate level bags; we had one bag for each 10-centimeter level. The z dimension for each level was usually designated according to distance below the ground surface: level 1 (surface to 10 cm below), level 2 (10–20 cms below), and so forth.

Excavation procedures vary widely, depending on the stage of excavation, the nature of the deposit, and the impulse of the archaeologist in charge (remember, digging is perhaps still as much craft as science). Because they are so small, test pits are often dug by trowel (rather than by shovel), maintaining a horizontal working surface. Dirt is scooped into a dustpan, dumped into a bucket, then carried off-site for a closer look.

The test pits told us that Gatecliff Shelter warranted a closer look, and we returned the next year for just that reason. The site was divided into a 1-meter grid system, oriented along the long axis of the shelter. We assigned consecutive letters to each north–south division and numbered the east–west division. By this method, each excavation square could be designated by a unique alphanumeric name (just like Bingo—A-7, B-5, and the ever-popular K-9). The east wall of the "7-trench," so named because it contained units B-7 through I-7, defined a major stratigraphic profile, a vertical section against which all artifacts, features, soil and pollen samples, and radiocarbon dates were correlated.

A vertical datum was established at the rear of the shelter. For all on-site operations, this single datum point was arbitrarily designated as zero. All site elevations from this point on were plotted as "x centimeters below datum." Then, using an **altimeter** and a U.S. Geological Survey topographic map, we determined the elevation of this datum point to be 2319 meters (7607 ft) above sea level; today we might use satellite-driven technology to provide such controls.

All archaeological features—fire hearths, artifact concentrations, sleeping areas, and the like—were plotted on a master site map, and individual artifacts found in situ were plotted in three dimensions. All fill was first carefully troweled, then passed outside the cave for screening; artifacts and ecofacts found in the screen were bagged by stratigraphic or arbitrary level. Field notes at this stage were kept by individual excavators in bound, graph paper notebooks. Good field notes record everything, whether or not it seems important at the time. Depending on the nature of the site (and the stage of excavation), field notes can either be taken "formless" or recorded on specific unit-level forms, with precise categories defined for each kind of necessary information.

At this stage, we were looking primarily for change through time. At Gatecliff, this meant looking for key time-sensitive artifacts to be grouped into temporal types, which would enable us to place previously undated archaeological contexts into a meaningful sequence as we excavated. Laboratory work subsequently tested these preliminary field hypotheses, what geologists call their "horseback correlations."

The vertical excavation strategy is a deliberately simplified scheme designed to clarify chronology. Although this strategy blurs much of the complexity in the archaeological record, it can be justified for these initial temporal aims.

UNLOCKING THE STRATIGRAPHY AT GATECLIFF SHELTER

By the end of our fourth field season, our major strata-trench had reached a depth of 9 meters (30 ft) below the ground surface, generating a stratigraphic profile that illustrates some of the quandaries involved in the workaday archaeological situation.

During our first three seasons at Gatecliff, I recorded and interpreted the Gatecliff stratigraphy myself. Drawing upon my somewhat limited classroom training in geology, soil science, and microstratigraphy, I drew and described the gross stratigraphy. This master profile served as the major descriptive device throughout the excavations.

As the field season wound down, it became clear that Gatecliff was too complex for me to continue the geological interpretation. This is not unusual in archaeology. On small-scale digs, archaeologists must often cover all the bases, from stratigrapher to photographer, from engineer to camp cook. But as the operation expands, specialists must be recruited to take over selected aspects. The trick is for an archaeologist to recognize the critical line separating flexibility from irresponsibility.

At Gatecliff, I was in danger of crossing that fine line, so we soon arranged for four experienced Great Basin geologists to join the team. Although all had somewhat different ideas—and some rather heated debates took place—the diversity fostered a better overall interpretation of the stratigraphic column.

In the course of a decade, we had exposed a remarkably well-stratified profile, more than 40 feet (12 m) deep, spanning the last 7000 years. The Gatecliff profile resulted from a complex interplay of natural and cultural factors. The master stratigraphy demonstrates how deposits of two very different kinds resulted from each set of processes. The thin dark levels (such as those numbered 9, 11, and 13) are living surfaces, or cultural horizons. Each dark horizontal band represents a single campsite. The 16 cultural horizons occurred as the result of human habitation, and these surfaces contain the fire hearths, broken stone tools, grinding slabs, flakes, food remains, and occasional fragments of basketry and cordage. This stratigraphy allowed us to analyze material culture on a horizon-to-horizon basis at Gatecliff, allowing us to define "time markers" that are invaluable for dating other sites (especially surface sites). We were also able to record patterning of these artifacts on each floor, which allowed us to reconstruct the activities that had occurred on each living surface.

But what makes Gatecliff so unusual is that living surfaces were capped by sterile, noncultural layers of purely geological origin. After the excavation was finished, we divided up the Gatecliff profile into a sequence of 56 geological strata: layers of more or less homogeneous or gradational sedimentary material, visually separated from adjacent layers by a distinct change in the character of the material deposited.

Some strata, such as 2, resulted from small ponds that occasionally formed at the rear of Gatecliff Shelter (Figure 8.24). The pond water acted as a sink for windblown dust particles, which settled out as finely laminated silts. Other strata, such as 8, consist of coarser sediments grading from gravels at the bottom to fine sand silts at the top. Apparently, the ephemeral stream flowing in front of Gatecliff Shelter occasionally flooded and coursed through the shelter. The water of such flash floods would first deposit coarse sediments such as pea-sized gravels. As the water's velocity diminished, its carrying capacity decreased, and the particles deposited were smaller. Finally, when the water slowed, the tiniest silt particles would cap the stream deposits. Such floods occurred several times throughout the 7000 years of deposition at Gatecliff, and each time the previous occupation

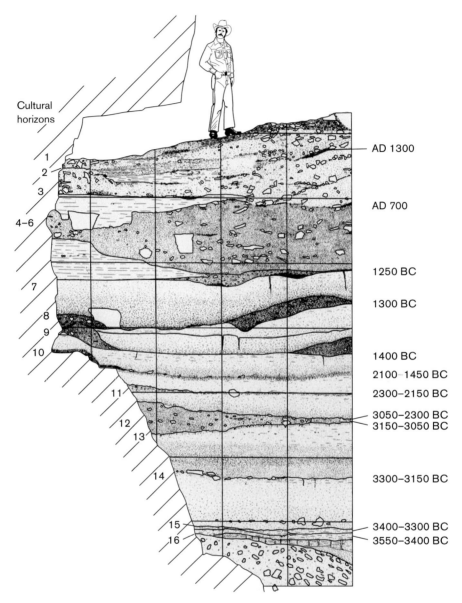

Cultural
horizons

1
2
3
4–6
7
8
9
10
11
12
13
14
15
16

AD 1300

AD 700

1250 BC

1300 BC

1400 BC
2100–1450 BC
2300–2150 BC
3050–2300 BC
3150–3050 BC

3300–3150 BC

3400–3300 BC
3550–3400 BC

FIGURE 8.24 Stratigraphy in Gatecliff Shelter. In this scale, the standing figure is exactly 6 feet (1.83 m) tall, and each grid square is 1 meter across.

surface was immediately buried. When the inhabitants returned to Gatecliff, they thus lived on a new campsite, separated from the previous one by as much as 2 feet of sterile alluvial sediments.

Fifty-six such depositional strata were stacked up inside Gatecliff. Here is how we described one stratum at Gatecliff (evident at the bottom of the master stratigraphy):

Stratum 22, Rubble: Angular limestone clasts, charcoal firepit, and baked area at top, somewhat churned into the underlying silty top of Stratum 23. Maximum thickness 50 cm on the southwest pile and formed continuous layer up to 15 cm thick in eastern parts of excavation, but was discontinuous elsewhere. Almost as voluminous as Stratum 17, the top was about {min}4.85 m on the southwestern pile and ranged from {min}5.50 to {min}5.30 m elsewhere, and its bottom was about {min}5.30 m in the southwest corner, {min}5.35 m in the Master Profile, and {min}5.32 m in the present excavation. . . . Stratum 22 was deposited by gradual accumulation of roof fall and talus tumbling over the shelter lip between 5250 and 5100 years ago. Stratum 22 was called GU 6R-74 in the field and contained cultural Horizon 14.

Several important points can be made about Stratum 22 at Gatecliff. Note, for instance, the detail of description. Exact depths are given relative to a central-site datum point, arbitrarily assigned a zero value of 0.0 meter. (Actually, as noted earlier, the Gatecliff datum is 2319 meters [7606 ft] above sea level.) When paired with our horizontal grid system, these arbitrary elevations document the exact configuration of each geological stratum.

Each geological term is sufficiently well defined to permit geologists who have never visited Gatecliff to understand what Stratum 22 looked like. Note also how we separate such descriptions from our interpretation. This way, others can use our data to make their own assessments (disagreeing with us, if they wish). Geoarchaeologists sometimes use the term "stratification" to refer to the physical layers in a site, reserving "stratigraphy" for the geoarchaeological interpretation of the temporal and depositional evidence.

Forty-seven radiocarbon dates were processed on materials from Gatecliff (Table 8.2), and four of these dates were available from Stratum 22. This information, combined with the added radiocarbon evidence from adjacent strata, allowed us to estimate that stratum 22 was laid down between about 5250 and 5100 years ago.

Other strata at Gatecliff provided different clues to help date the site. Stratum 55, near the very bottom of the site, contained an inch-thick lens of sand-sized volcanic ash (**tephra**), fragments of crystal, glass, and rock once ejected into the air by a volcanic eruption. Not discovered until the last week of the last field season, the tephra was indistinct, mixed with the cobbles and rubble of Stratum 55. In the laboratory, the late Jonathan O. Davis, one of our geologists and a leading expert on the volcanic ashes of the American West, confirmed that this ashy deposit was Mount Mazama ash. When this mountain in the Oregon Cascades blew up 6900 years ago, it spewed out 11 cubic miles of pumice and related materials; the caldera formed by the Mazama explosion now contains Crater Lake. The Mount St. Helens eruption in 1980 was a cherry bomb in comparison. The prevailing winds, coupled with the force of the explosion itself, carried Mazama ash across the western

TABLE 8.2 Physical Stratigraphy of Gatecliff Shelter

Stratum	Soil	Nature of Deposit	Field Designation	Cultural Association	Radiocarbon Dating (years)	
					Age	Date
1	S-1	Rubble	GU 14	Horizons 1–3	0–1250 BP	AD 700–present
2		Sand and silt	Upper GU 13		1250 BP	AD 700
3	S-2	Rubble	Part of GU 12	Part of Horizon 4	1250–1350 BP	AD 600–700
4		Sand and silt	GU 13 and GU 12 silt		1350 BP	AD 600
5	S-3	Rubble	Part of GU 12	Parts of Horizons 4–6	1350–3200 BP	600
6		Sand and silt	GU 11		3200 BP	1250 BC
7		Rubble	GU 11 and GU 10R	Horizon 7	3250–3200 BP	1300–1250 BC
8		Sand and silt	GU 10		3250 BP	1300 BC
9		Rubble	GU 9R	Horizon 8	3300–3250 BP	1350–1300 BC
10		Sand and silt	GU 8 A and B		3300 BP	1350 BC
11		Rubble	GU 7R	Horizon 9	3400–3300 BP	1450–1350 BC
12		Sand and silt	GU 7		3400 BP	1450 BC
13		Rubble	6 Living Floor	Horizon 10	4050–3400 BP	2100–1450 BC
14		Sand and silt	GU 5 Silt		4050 BP	2100 BC
15		Rubble	Part of GU 5		4100–4050 BP	2150–2100 BC

TABLE 8.2 Physical Stratigraphy of Gatecliff Shelter (continued)

Stratum	Soil	Nature of Deposit	Field Designation	Cultural Association	Radiocarbon Dating (years)	
					Age	Date
16		Sand and silt	Part of GU 5		4100 BP	2150 BC
17		Rubble	GU 4	Horizon 11	4250–4100 BP	2300–2150 BC
18		Silty sand	GU 3		4250 BP	2300 BC
19		Sand and rubble	GU 2	Horizon 12	5000–4250 BP	3050–2300 BC
20	S-4	Silt and clay	GU 1A	Horizon 13	5100–5000 BP	3150–3050 BC
21		Sand and silt	GU 1 and GU 7-74		5100 BP	3150 BC
22		Rubble	GU 6R-74	Horizon 14	5250–5100 BP	3300–3150 BC
23		Silt	GU 6-74 and GU 5-74		5250 BP	3300 BC
24		Rubble	GU 4R-74	Horizon 15	5350–5250 BP	3400–3300 BC
25		Silt	GU 4-74		5350 BP	3400 BC
26		Rubble	GU 3R-74	Horizon 16	5500–5350 BP	3550–3400 BC
27–29		Silts	GU 3A-74		5500 BP	3550 BC
30		Sand	GU 3B-74		5500 BP	3550 BC
31		Rubble	GU 2R-74		5700–5500 BP	3750–3550 BC
32		Fine sand and silt	GU 2-74			
33		Fine sand and silt	GU 12-76, GU 1–78, and GU 1-74			
34		Sand	GU 2-78			
35		Rubble	GU 3R-78			
36		Silty medium sand	GU 3-78			
37		Sand and silt	GU 4-78 and GU 11-76			
38		Silt and fine sand	GU 5-78			
39		Rubble	GU 6R-78 and GU 10-76			
40		Sand	GU 6-78 and GU 9-76			
41		Sand	GU 7-78			
42		Sand and silt	GU 8-78 and lower GU 9-76			
43		Rubble	GU 9R-78 and GU 8-76		6250–5700 BP	4300–3750 BC
44		Sand	GU 9-78			
45		Sand	GU 10-78			
46		Rubble	GU 11R-78			
47		Sand and silt	GU 11-78			
48		Rubble	GU 12R-78			
49		Sand and silt	GU 12-78			
50		Silt	GU 13-78			
51		Sand and silt	GU 14-78			
52		Rubble	GU 15-78			
53		Sand	GU 16-78			
54		Rubble	Basal Rubble 1 [BR 1]		6900–6250 BP	4950–4300 BC
55		Rubble and tephra	Basal Rubble 2 [BR 2]		6900 BP	4950 BC
56		Rubble	Basal Rubble 3 [BR 3]		7100–6900 BP	5150–4950 BC

Adapted from Thomas (1988, Table 3).

United States. Wherever the ash settled out, it created a "marker bed." **Tephrochronology** has become a valuable tool for dating sites in volcanically active areas. When Davis identified the Mazama ash at the bottom of Gatecliff, we had a critical, independent check on the largely radiocarbon-derived chronology at Gatecliff, and so we knew that Stratum 55 must be 6900 years old.

In truth, I am not certain whether I would have recognized the volcanic ash at the bottom of Gatecliff. At Mummy Cave (Wyoming), near Yellowstone National Park, the excavators confused the thin layers of Mazama ash with wood ash; the important tephra lens was later recognized under the microscope. Fortunately, the Mazama tephra at Gatecliff was instantly recognized by Jonathan Davis. Both cases highlight the importance of having specialists work on-site, during excavation.

GATECLIFF PROJECTILE POINTS AS TIME MARKERS

Geologists proposed the **law of superposition** rather early in the game, in 1669! But fossils did not become a worthwhile tool for geological correlation until much later, during the early nineteenth century. Whereas eighteenth-century archaeologists commonly applied the principles of superposition to their excavations, we had to wait nearly two centuries to learn—once again from geologists—how the index fossil concept might make human artifacts useful tools in dating archaeological sites.

As noted earlier, the stratigraphy of Gatecliff Shelter looks like a huge layer cake stacked 40 feet high. Geology's law of superposition tells us that, all else being equal, the oldest artifacts will lie at the bottom, with later artifacts showing up progressively higher in the stratigraphic column. The Gatecliff deposits thus provide extraordinary temporal control over the past 7000 years. We can plot the vertical distribution of the more than 400 classifiable projectile points from Gatecliff Shelter (note that additional types were required to classify the entire Gatecliff collection).

Look at the sharp stratigraphic differences evident on Figure 8.25. All the Desert Side Notched and Cottonwood Triangular points occurred in the uppermost part of Gatecliff Shelter. The Rosegate series points were found in slightly older strata; Elko points are older than this, and Gatecliff points older still.

Because 47 radiocarbon dates were available to date the geological sequence at Gatecliff, it was possible to assign the following time ranges to each category:

> Desert Side Notched: post-AD 1300
> Cottonwood Triangular: post-AD 1300
> Rosegate series: AD 500–1300
> Elko Corner Notched: 1500 BC–AD 500
> Gatecliff Contracting Stem: 2500–1500 BC

Each time similar points are found in undated contexts, we receive a clue (a hypothesis, really) to their time of manufacture.

A related issue emerges here about the nature of archaeological data. Keep in mind that data are not objects. Data are observations made on objects, and the point typology from Gatecliff illustrates this principle. Using a series of formal attributes (weight, distal shoulder angle, and so forth), we grouped the individual Gatecliff artifacts into morphological types, each a hypothesis to be tested against independent temporal data. But our "independent" data—the datable context of each point inside Gatecliff Shelter—were merely other observations made on the same objects from which we had derived the initial hypothesis. Because formal attributes are autonomous relative to context, the criterion of independence holds, and so the test is valid.

This principle is critical to archaeology. Hypotheses (even simple ones like time markers) need continual testing. We should never become too comfortable with our "verified" hypotheses. Even without lifting a shovel, we can refine the Gatecliff chronology in several ways. Why not measure the microscopic **hydration rim** on each obsidian projectile point? This would give us an independent age estimate. Some points still have hafting sinew adhering to the base. Why not use the new accelerator technology to radiocarbon-date these fibers? Here would be another independent estimate of age. Both tests elicit more data without requiring more objects. This is one reason for the importance of well-curated museum collections as research tools, enabling scientists of the future to generate new data from old objects.

Although critical to archaeology, time markers have distinct limitations. Archaeology can proceed with its initial objective—establishing cultural chronologies—only by making simplifying assumptions, and this is what we did with the projectile point chronology defined for Gatecliff Shelter. Never mind (for now) what the artifacts mean—we care only

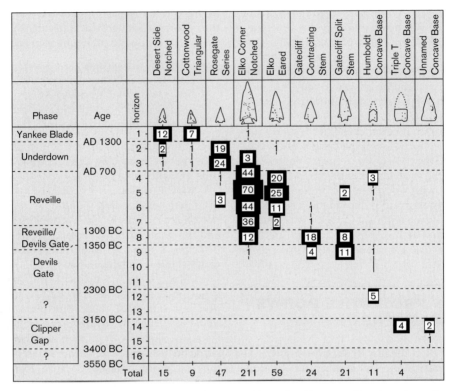

FIGURE 8.25 Projectile point distribution by depth. The horizontal dimension (frequency) is plotted on a logarithmic scale, which dampens the effect of differential sample size.

whether they change through time. As a result, some first-rate time markers were discovered at Gatecliff.

We have paid a price to find our time markers. Although we now know that Desert Side Notched and Cottonwood Triangular points postdate AD 1300, much ignorance remains. Why should two morphological types exist simultaneously? Are two social groups living at Gatecliff in the post-1300 time period? Are Desert Side Notched points designed for hunting bighorn, whereas Cottonwood points are for rabbits? Are Cottonwood points really for "war arrows," left unnotched so that they cannot be pulled out once lodged in an enemy's flesh? Or perhaps the difference is technological: could the Cottonwood Triangular points be unfinished, intended to be later notched (and thereby becoming Desert Side Notched points)? These guesses are hypotheses at present untested.

The master stratigraphic sequence (and the dozens of radiocarbon dates available from that column), allowed us to successfully define the cultural sequence of Gatecliff Shelter. But our vertical excavation strategy had also left us with a series of extremely

steep and hazardous sidewalls. Even though the excavation was stairstepped downward to minimize these sidewalls, the sheer verticality of the site made it dangerous. Change was clearly in order, both conceptually and logistically.

A HORIZONTAL EXCAVATION STRATEGY

Gatecliff Shelter held potential far beyond mere chronology. Establishing cultural chronology is only archaeology's first objective; our early excavations amply demonstrated that Gatecliff could make useful contributions to paleoethnographic objectives as well. Several stratigraphic units contained short-term, intact occupational surfaces, and the remaining excavations at Gatecliff concentrated on the spatial distributions within these key stratigraphic units.

As we transcended our chronological objectives, we also shifted our digging strategy. We began looking beyond the modal aspects of culture to view things as part of the overall cultural matrix. In other words, the focus moved from the when and where to the more elusive what. Viewed in this manner, digging mine shafts becomes inappropriate. Culture in the broader sense embraces the structural elements basic to adaptive and ideational aspects, rather than merely aggregates of functional traits that happen to be shared. The paleoethnographic approach requires looking at the interrelationships among artifacts, waste debris, cultural features, and cave walls. We must understand what activities took place, not just which artifacts were deposited.

The tactics required to pursue paleoethnography likewise change, sometimes radically. With the stratigraphy suitably defined, extensive vertical sections were no longer necessary, and we concentrated on opening entire living surfaces simultaneously. The cultural lenses at Gatecliff were slowly excavated by hand, with thicker stratigraphic units removed in arbitrary 10-centimeter levels. Exposing the living floors proceeded more slowly than had the previous vertical excavations, and excavators were instructed to recover and map all artifacts in situ. Features were screened separately, and flotation samples were retained for laboratory processing. Significant debitage scatters were plotted, as were concentrations of bone and other artifacts. The excavated deposits were then placed in buckets and carried to the screening

area (Figure 8.26), where they were passed through one-eighth-inch screens, and as before, artifacts missed by the excavators were saved, along with all fragments of chippage and bone.

The horizontal strategy required significantly more control within contemporary stratigraphic units. A single crew chief took excavation notes for the entire site at this point (rather than having individual excavators do it, as before). Three-dimensional data were transferred to site notebooks, and living floor maps were plotted for each surface at the time of the excavation. A single excavator was assigned to each 2-square-meter unit, and all artifacts, features, and large ecofacts were plotted onto the large-scale living floor maps. Since then, sophisticated computer-driven systems have been developed to assist in piece-plotting objects on living surfaces.

The intrasite patterning of artifacts and ecofacts at Gatecliff is heavily size sorted. Smaller, lighter items tend to be fumbled or otherwise discarded in a "drop zone," whereas larger, heavier items are commonly "tossed" outside the central zone of the campsite. This means that, all else being equal, debris will tend to accumulate in concentric zones, centering in the central hearth area. On most of the horizons at Gatecliff Shelter, the smallest debris was found in a distinct drop zone at the rear of the shelter. Larger debris was discarded in a "toss zone" near the mouth of the shelter.

FIGURE 8.26 Gatecliff Shelter during excavation.

The Horizon 2 pattern is unique at Gatecliff Shelter because the central garbage heap took up most of the enclosed area, leaving virtually no room to construct hearths, create sleeping areas, or establish a specialized area of manufacture and tool repair, as we observed on most of the Gatecliff horizons.

We could plot three dozen fire hearths on the various living surfaces at Gatecliff Shelter. Although most horizons are spatially independent from the others, the hearths were built in a distinctive "hearthline," approximately 13 feet (4 m) from the rear wall. Even though the shape of Gatecliff Shelter changed markedly throughout its occupation period, this hearthline–rear wall distance remained virtually constant, as did intrasite zonation. In other words, as Gatecliff Shelter became larger, the hearths move farther inside the site in a predictable, linear fashion. So positioned, these small hearths offered several advantages: a distinct work zone was defined between the hearthline and the rear wall. Such placement, somewhat inside the drip line, protects the fires from precipitation and windy gusts, the smoke venting outside. In effect, each hearth created a relatively warm and smoke-free "rear room," a heated work and sleep area of nearly constant size between 160–215 ft^2 (15 and 20 square meters). The rear wall effectively functioned as a heat sink, warming the inner part of the shelter with only a small fire.

The exception was Horizon 2 (occupied about AD 1300), which showed an almost total reverse of the drop zone/toss zone pattern. For one thing, horizon 2 lacks a definable hearthline; in fact, Horizon 2 lacks hearths of any kind. And rather than having debris increasing in size toward the drip line, in Horizon 2 the debris accumulated in the middle of the site. This central dump zone contained the partially articulated, field-butchered carcasses of about two dozen bighorn sheep; assorted butchering implements were discarded near the edges of the bone mass.

Overall, we think that Gatecliff Shelter functioned mostly as a short-term field camp, visited by all-male task groups who were exploiting a logistic radius too far to allow them to return at night to their base camp.

EVALUATING THE RESULTS

Gatecliff was like a giant birthday cake. The sterile strata are the layers, and the cultural horizons are the icing capping each layer. The more than 10 meters of stratified deposits contained datable artifacts and ecofacts that could be used to reconstruct the human events and environmental background. In this brief presentation, we have emphasized the so-called Monitor Valley cultural chronology, grounded in the 47 radiocarbon dates processed at Gatecliff Shelter. Although this chronology has been refined somewhat based on more recent excavations, it remains the primary chronological device for ordering the archaeology of the central Great Basin.

The paleoenvironmental record was reconstructed from geomorphological, palynological, paleontological, and macrobotanical analysis. We know that prior to (and shortly after) the eruption of Mount Mazama (about 6900 years ago), the Gatecliff Shelter area was a sagebrush-dominated steppe. The single most striking paleoenvironmental event after this time was an invasion of the piñon–juniper woodland about 6000 years ago, likely facilitated by an increase in summer precipitation. The dramatic entrance of *Ephedra* (Mormon tea) into the paleobotanical record at Gatecliff Shelter (about 2800 years ago) may have been conditioned by generally cooler temperatures.

The important point is that such artifact and environmental indicators would have been relatively meaningless to archaeologists, were it not for the stratigraphically controlled contexts in which they were recovered.

DISCUSSION QUESTIONS

1. Why was Thomas so interested in finding a site like Gatecliff? Explain why a site like Gatecliff is worth looking for when one is doing regional surveys.

2. Describe the vertical strategy employed at Gatecliff. What were the goals of this phase of excavation? Why was a horizontal strategy eventually employed, and how did it help meet other goals?

3. Explain why the Gatecliff projectile points make good time markers for this part of the Great Basin. How else might these projectile points be understood by archaeologists?

4. Does determination of chronology logically precede paleoethnography, as Thomas suggests? Can it be argued that either the chronological goals or the paleoethnographic goals mentioned are more important in archaeology?

CHAPTER 9

Foragers and Villagers of the Southwestern Mountains, Mesas, and Deserts

On a moonlit night a lone hiker makes her way up a winding sandstone canyon, miles from the nearest road. She stops to look at petroglyphs in the dim light, and then pushes on to her goal, a set of ruins in an alcove in the canyon. After making camp, Dr. Eleanor Friedman-Bernal struggles up a talus slope and takes a trail to one of the ruins, only to find that pothunters, thieves of time, had been digging at this isolated ruin, leaving the ground scattered with human bone. Dr. Friedman-Bernal makes her way to a small pool below the ruin and is surprised to find frogs tethered to pegs around the edge of the water. She is also surprised to hear the strains of a flute playing a Beatles tune, "Hey Jude," out in the desolate canyon country where she had expected to find no one.

This is the way Tony Hillerman (1988, pp. 1–10) opens his Navajo detective novel, *A Thief of Time*. Dr. Friedman-Bernal has made the trek to this ruin to look for a particular kind of pottery with a distinctive design that she is certain will validate her reconstruction of population movement after the collapse of the Chaco system. She expects this find to make her reputation as an archaeologist. When her associates at Chaco Canyon become worried because she has not returned, Hillerman's heroes, Lieutenant Joe Leaphorn and Officer Jim Chee, become involved in the case. The unfolding mystery takes Leaphorn and Chee through more vandalized ruins and the black market in Anasazi pottery, and through the Chaco Canyon Cultural Center. The two Navajo policemen encounter another archaeologist and a physical anthropologist along the way.

The canyons of the American Southwest, with their spectacular ruins, are popular settings for works of fiction, and archaeology is woven into these tales to varying degrees. Besides mysteries, some novels try to portray life in the ruined towns that we see on the ground today. Archaeology and archaeologists are included in these books, but with varying degrees of accuracy. When archaeologists are portrayed, most often they are depicted as lone researchers working on a big career-making or career-saving discovery. Like Dr. Friedman-Bernal, they search for a big find to prove a pet theory, to prove themselves right, and often to justify themselves and their unorthodox ideas. Generally, in fiction, the archaeologist seeks a specific significant artifact and knows when she or he has found it. There is the sense that these fictional archaeologists can go on to great fame as a result of their discoveries, and there is also a sense that the press will be drawn to report the great discoveries without much work on the part of the archaeologist.

No archaeologist would discount the role of discoveries in enhancing our knowledge of the past, but such discoveries are only one aspect of archaeological research. In reality, today's archaeology is quite different from the solo endeavor suggested by fictional accounts. It usually is a team effort involving many individuals, whether conducted as part of the CRM process or as academic research. Also, finding the sites, deciding which ones have important information to yield, and getting the artifacts out of the ground comprise only the beginning of the process. Cleaning, **cataloging**, and analysis are critical, as well. Curation of the resulting collections usually isn't mentioned at all in popular books; yet the ability to return to old, curated collections with new questions is vital for the effort to expand knowledge about the past. Archaeologists write descriptive reports and prepare research articles to disseminate the results of their work, but they seldom become famous, and only occasionally do their finds attract the popular press.

Of course, fictional accounts do not set out to educate the public about archaeology; they use archaeology as an element of plot and setting designed to tell an interesting story and keep readers involved. While the details of the depictions of archaeologists may not be completely accurate, the inclusion of archaeologists as characters certainly is. One idea that Hillerman and other novelists communicate well is that there is a lot of anthropology and archaeology to be done in the Southwest. This is a region rich in far more than breathtaking, arid landscapes. A variety of contemporary Indian, Hispanic, and Anglo cultures and a rich and visible archaeological heritage also attract scholars. Anthropologists and archaeologists have been studying this area since the nineteenth century and have learned much about its past. This chapter introduces what has been learned.

DEFINITION OF THE AREA

Anthropologists define the Southwest culture area to include the entire state of Arizona, the western portions of New Mexico, southwestern Colorado, the southern portions of Utah and Nevada, and the Mexican states of Sonora, Chihuahua, and Durango. Indeed, the Southwest is often described as stretching from Durango, Mexico, north to Durango, Colorado, and from Las Vegas, Nevada, on the west to Las Vegas, New Mexico, on the east (Figure 9.1). This is an area where agriculture often was practiced prehistorically, in contrast to the areas surrounding it on the west, north, and east. Architecture of stone or adobe masonry is also found throughout the pre-Columbian Southwest, as is the production of pottery. Some anthropologists have included Eastern Utah and adjacent Colorado, home of the Fremont culture in the Southwest, but in this text we treat these areas as part of the Great Basin (Chapter 8).

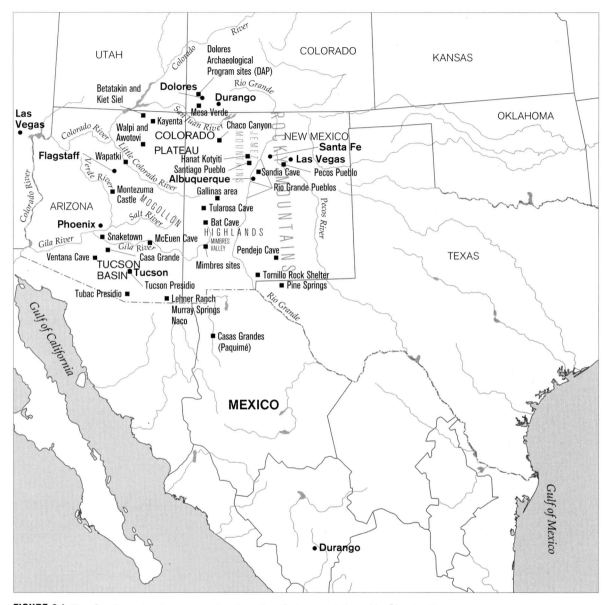

FIGURE 9.1 The Southwest culture area, showing sites that are mentioned in Chapter 9.

The Southwest culture area has a rich and varied archaeological past that can be broken down into periods of varying length for convenience in discussion (Table 9.1). The descendants of the various aboriginal groups evident in the archaeological record populate the Southwest today, some of them living in pueblos that have been occupied for centuries. The Native peoples of the Southwest are the subjects of an extensive body of scholarly works describing their culture, their social organization, their arts and crafts, and their diverse

TABLE 9.1 Introduction to Southwest Culture History

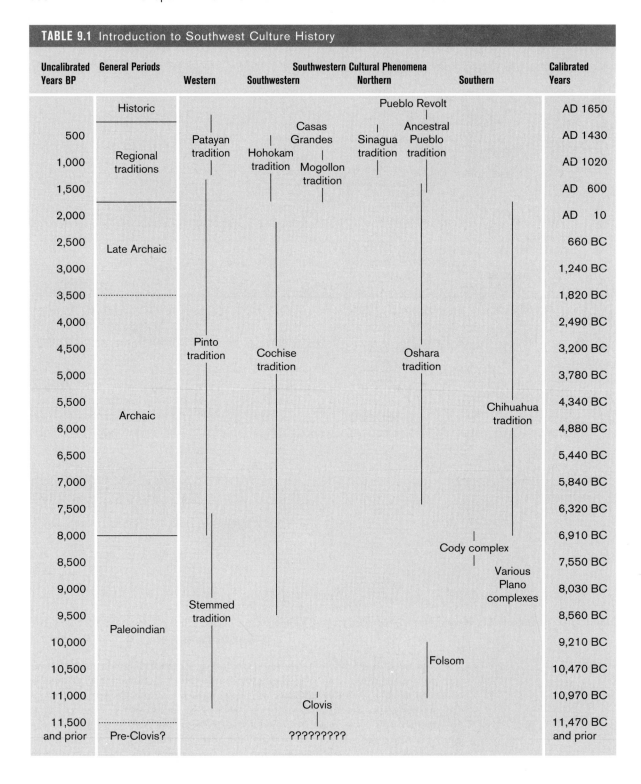

Uncalibrated Years BP	General Periods	Southwestern Cultural Phenomena					Calibrated Years
		Western	Southwestern	Northern		Southern	
	Historic			Pueblo Revolt			AD 1650
500		Patayan tradition	Casas Grandes	Sinagua tradition	Ancestral Pueblo tradition		AD 1430
1,000	Regional traditions		Hohokam tradition				AD 1020
1,500				Mogollon tradition			AD 600
2,000							AD 10
2,500	Late Archaic						660 BC
3,000							1,240 BC
3,500							1,820 BC
4,000							2,490 BC
4,500		Pinto tradition	Cochise tradition	Oshara tradition			3,200 BC
5,000							3,780 BC
5,500						Chihuahua tradition	4,340 BC
6,000	Archaic						4,880 BC
6,500							5,440 BC
7,000							5,840 BC
7,500							6,320 BC
8,000					Cody complex		6,910 BC
8,500							7,550 BC
9,000		Stemmed tradition				Various Plano complexes	8,030 BC
9,500							8,560 BC
10,000	Paleoindian						9,210 BC
10,500					Folsom		10,470 BC
11,000			Clovis				10,970 BC
11,500 and prior	Pre-Clovis?		?????????				11,470 BC and prior

ways of life, as well as the mechanisms they have developed to deal with the presence of the European Americans among them (Ortiz 1979). It is important for Southwestern archaeologists to keep in mind the linkages between these ethnographically known groups and the peoples of the distant past.

THE ENVIRONMENTS OF THE SOUTHWEST

When you think of the Southwest, you may envision landscapes resembling those in Figure 9.2. In fact the region contains a diversity of environments and habitats to which humans have always had to adjust. Formally, this culture area includes portions of three major physiographic regions. These are the Basin and Range province in the west, the Colorado Plateau in the north, and the southern Rocky Mountains in the east. In addition, at various times in the past, southwesterners also inhabited the western margin of a fourth physiographic province, the Great Plains. Elevational variation within the Southwest is extreme. In the basins of the western Southwest, elevations may be close to sea level, while the highest peaks of the southern Rocky Mountains can reach over 13,000 feet (3965 m). Much of the Southwest is a rugged land, but there are also broad valleys and flat mesa tops.

The overriding environmental feature for humans living in the Southwest is the arid climate. Availability of water always has been of central importance to southwesterners. The amount of rainfall varies, and several major river systems are important environmental features as well, but in general, the western and southern portions of the Southwest are drier than the northern and eastern portions. Average annual precipitation can be as low as 5 inches (127 mm) in the western Basin and Range province but three times as high in the southern Rocky Mountains.

FIGURE 9.2 Canyon country of the Southwest: Arches National Park, Utah.

Average precipitation estimates are misleading, however, because the cyclonic storms that bring much of the Southwest's moisture vary in pattern. In some areas, winter precipitation that is not lost to runoff is more important than rainfall from short summer thunderstorms. In other areas, most of the rainfall is attributable to summer thunderstorms, which sometimes are violent and localized. Both the positioning of the jet stream from year to year and longer-term shifts in rainfall regimes could have greatly affected regional adaptations in the past (Cordell 1997). In addition, the mountains of the Southwest receive the precipitation that results when air masses carrying moisture are uplifted in their journey over the peaks. Mountain slopes on the windward side receive a great deal of moisture, while the slopes on the other side are in a **rain shadow**. Potential changes in prevailing wind patterns—bringing moisture from either the Gulf of California or the Gulf of Mexico—must also be considered in reconstructing past climate.

Rivers and streams cannot be discounted as important sources of water in the Southwest. In the driest areas to the west and south, the Colorado, Gila, and Salt river drainages have always been major sources of water for survival and, once agriculture became important, river water was essential for irrigation. Similarly, farmers have long used water from the Rio Grande, the east, for irrigation. However, historically the Rio Grande also has flooded, destroying crops and damaging towns, and presumably it had this potential throughout the past as well. In much of the Colorado Plateau, the rivers and streams have cut deeply into their beds, greatly diminishing their usefulness for irrigation. Not surprisingly, people in this part of the region often have acquired water from springs and seeps and have collected rainfall to assist them in farming, rather than being tethered to rivers and streams.

Perhaps counterintuitively, the dry climate does not mean that the area is uniformly hot; in fact, temperature is variable over the Southwest. Elevation has a great deal to do with this, with cooler temperatures being characteristic at higher elevations, especially at night and during the winter. Once again, this is a complicated matter. For example, in the steep-sided canyons and narrow valleys, the phenomenon called **cold-air drainage** results in the trapping of cold air at the bottom of the canyon, so that it actually is warmer higher up the canyon sides than at the bottom. Especially once Southwesterners began to rely on agriculture, they had to be particularly attuned to microenvironmental factors affecting both temperature and precipitation. A period of cooler climate could seriously alter the distribution of arable environments on a local or even regional scale (see the case study in Section D.4 of the Student CD).

Plant and animal life is highly variable in the Southwest as well, though the resources nearly always are sparsely distributed. Deserts cover much of the Southwest, but along some of the larger rivers a riparian forest with cottonwood, willow, and cattail can be found. In mountainous areas (Figure 9.3) vegetation is broadly zoned by elevation, with grasses and brushy species mixing with scrub oak, piñon, and juniper at the lower elevations, and species such as ponderosa pine, Douglas fir, and aspen being found somewhat higher. In the southern Rocky Mountains, subalpine forests are dominated by Engelmann spruce and subalpine fir, while at the highest elevations, treeless meadows occur. The Colorado Plateau also supports zonation by elevation. Although piñon–juniper woodland is the most common type of vegetation, there are many areas of bare rock, and low elevations support sagebrush and grasslands; the highest elevations usually have conifers of various types.

FIGURE 9.3 Typical forest vegetation of the southern Rocky Mountains.

Animal species density reflects these vegetational differences. Many Southwestern animals combine a nonselective diet with movement between multiple vegetational and physiographic zones. In general, large- and medium-sized animals are rarest in low-elevation, more desertic areas, while small animals, including a wide variety of rodents, are highly diverse in the same areas. Similarly, larger-bodied animals show much more diversity in the higher elevations of the Southwest. This generalization should not obscure the presence of a great variety of birds throughout the Southwest, especially in the better-watered and agricultural areas. Migratory waterfowl fly across the region annually, though not in the numbers found in other parts of the United States. Aquatic mammals like muskrats and beavers, as well as turtles and fish, can occur in significant numbers where water habitats are present, and snakes and lizards also are widely distributed.

In reviewing resources, it should not be forgotten that today the Southwest is known as a region rich in minerals, including copper, lead, coal, and uranium. The extraction of these minerals, along with timber and other resources, has been an important factor in the history of this culture area at least since the beginning of the American period. Furthermore, the mountains of the Southwest contained fine-grained chert, turquoise, and obsidian outcrops that are known to have been important even outside the Southwest during pre-Columbian times.

Climatic Change

Although the various factors that structure the region's environment can be outlined, a changing environment has been a constant in the Southwest. The bedrock geology and the generally arid conditions of this area haven't changed greatly during the time of human habitation, but climate has experienced both long- and short-term variation. Major climatic changes such as those associated with the Pleistocene and the beginning of the Holocene affected the precipitation regimes of the Southwest in complex and fascinating ways. In addition, seasonal and annual changes in factors such as precipitation and temperature, as well as erosional and depositional events, have affected Southwestern environments greatly over time. Human modifications to the environment have been important as well—at least since Southwestern peoples became farmers and began to live in significant population concentrations. For example, the processes of clearing land for fields and acquiring wood for fuel probably significantly altered fragile Southwestern environments on a local scale during pre-Columbian times. For all these reasons, archaeologists have given particular attention to the task of paleo-environment reconstruction in the Southwest.

HUNTERS AND FORAGERS

Paleoindian

As in other culture areas, the earliest archaeological remains in the Southwest are from the Paleoindian period. At this time small groups of mobile hunter-gatherers roamed throughout the area. A number of important Paleoindian sites have been found, but despite the discovery of more reliable Pre-Clovis sites elsewhere, no Southwestern sites provide unassailable evidence of a Pre-Clovis human presence. Sandia Cave, located north of Albuquerque, New Mexico, produced distinctive, single-shouldered projectile points (Figure 9.4a, b), in addition to other material long held to be the earliest remains in the Southwest. However, reinvestigation of the site indicates problems with the excavation and with the integrity of the early strata. Although there have been a number of radiocarbon dates processed from Sandia Cave, ranging from 35,000 BP to 17,000 BP, the true age of this material is not known (Haynes and Agogino 1986). Excavations in the early 1990s at Pendejo Cave in southeastern New Mexico produced claims of occupations up to 40,000 years old, predating the Clovis occupation of the site. The site is said to be well stratified, and it has produced a number of radiocarbon dates. The evidence for Pre-Clovis occupation includes impressions of dermal ridges (fingerprints) in clay and hair identified as human. Both the stratigraphic integrity of the site and the contention that the dermal ridges belonged to humans have been questioned, however (Cordell 1997, 78–79).

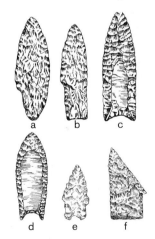

FIGURE 9.4 Early Southwestern points and a knife: (a, b) Sandia point, (c) Clovis point, (d) Folsom point, (e) Pinto point, and (f) Cody knife.

Occupation of the Southwest by Clovis hunters is widely accepted. Lehner Ranch, Naco, and Murray Springs, three important sites in the San Pedro Valley of southeastern Arizona, demonstrate Clovis mammoth hunting (Cordell 1997, 79–82). Lehner Ranch is a kill and butchering site where Clovis points (Figure 9.4c), scrapers, knives, and a chopper were found associated with mammoth bones in stratified deposits. At Naco (see Figure 3.14) the remains of a mammoth were found with eight complete Clovis points. This find has been interpreted as evidence for an unsuccessful mammoth hunt because it is difficult to imagine why, if the hunt had been successful, so many usable points would not have been recovered in the butchering process and taken from the site by the Clovis hunters. Murray Springs is a campsite with associated mammoth and bison kills. Piles of disarticulated bones may be the remains of meat caches left for later use. Lehner and Murray Springs have both provided stratigraphically secure radiocarbon dates for Clovis. Dates from Lehner average 10,930 ±40 BP, while those from Murray Springs average 10,900 ±50 BP (Haynes 1993). Surface finds of Clovis points occur sporadically throughout the Southwest.

The end of the Clovis period in the Southwest may be associated with environmental change or with the final extinction of the mammoth, but in any case, it is clear that after Clovis, Paleoindian settlement of the Southwest can be divided into western and eastern strategies. East of the border between Arizona and New Mexico distinctive Folsom points (Figure 9.4d), apparently dating to the eleventh millennium BP, have been found over a wide area stretching onto the Southern Plains. Now extinct forms of bison were the most important resource for these Folsom hunters. However, hunters also took elk, mountain sheep, and small game, and most likely exploited various plant foods as well. Folsom sites have been documented in the central Rio Grande valley, in the San Juan Basin of northwestern New Mexico, as well as in other parts of western New Mexico.

Materials of the later Paleoindian complexes that follow Folsom elsewhere are sparse in the Southwest. The best represented may be the **Cody complex**, dating to between approximately 8500 BP and 8000 BP, which has been recognized in the central Rio Grande valley and in the San Juan Basin. Cody material, including the distinctive asymmetrical Cody knife (Figure 9.4f), is more common on the Great Plains to the north and east of the Southwest, perhaps because bison populations were denser there (Cordell 1997, 85–86). There are also Late Paleoindian sites in the foothill and mountain areas of the eastern Southwest that generally lack diagnostic projectile points. Subsistence in the foothills and mountains of the eastern Southwest probably included hunting diverse game and gathering.

Folsom materials have not been found in the western part of the Southwest. In fact, although the Late Paleoindian remains from this area appear to be distinct from those in the eastern Southwest in that big-game hunting is not indicated, post-Clovis Paleoindian remains have not been easy to recognize. The San Dieguito complex, discussed in Chapters 7 and 8, has been found in western Arizona as well as in southern California, but it is known almost exclusively from surface remains. The **Ventana complex** (Figure 9.5) from Ventana Cave has been associated with both San Dieguito and Folsom but is not considered to represent either (Haury 1950). Recently reported dates from Ventana Cave suggest that this material is early Holocene rather than Paleoindian (Huckell 1998). This redating is consistent with findings, in the western Southwest, of San Dieguito materials associated with the beginnings of the second period of foraging, the Archaic.

FIGURE 9.5 Ventana
complex materials from
Ventana Cave, Arizona:
(a, b) projectile points,
(c, d) flake knives,
(e) curved knife, and
(f, g) discoidal scrapers.

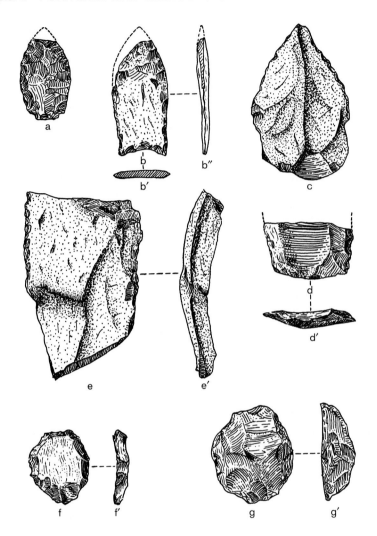

FIGURE 9.5 Ventana complex materials from Ventana Cave, Arizona: (a, b) projectile points, (c, d) flake knives, (e) curved knife, and (f, g) discoidal scrapers.

Archaic

The Archaic peoples of the Southwest practiced more generalized—or at least more diverse—ways of making their livings than did the Paleoindians. While the Paleoindian period was typified by uniformity in the artifact assemblages of the recognized groups over vast areas, regional variation in the Southwest is apparent during the Archaic. In this book, we consider the Southwestern Archaic period to have lasted from about 8000 BP to 1750 BP. Less distinction can be made between the early, middle, and late parts of the Archaic than in some of the other North American culture areas. The early part of the Archaic corresponds to a climatic interval usually called the Altithermal (ca. 7000–4500 BP) in the Southwest (Antevs 1948, 1955). During this time, unusually warm conditions prevailed. There is debate over whether this interval was warm and moist or warm and arid, and there is considerable evidence of local variation in moisture during the Altithermal. Nevertheless this warm period, combined with the disappearance of the Pleistocene large game animals, may have had much to do with shaping the Southwestern Archaic adaptation. In any case, the Late Archaic (after about 3500 BP) was a time of significant adaptive change that may correspond to the onset of more nearly modern, moister climate conditions. At this time, the larger numbers and sizes of sites suggests an increase in human population levels. This is also the period when Southwestern hunter-gatherers incorporated the cultivation of crops into their subsistence, and some researchers (e.g., Huckell 1995) have proposed the use of the term **Early Agricultural period** instead of Late Archaic.

Many of the attributes that archaeologists can use to clearly distinguish the Archaic from the preceding Paleoindian period are technological. In the first place, ground stone implements occur in much higher frequencies after the Paleoindian. These include millingstones, which were used to process the seeds that became of greater significance in the diet. Second, there were changes in the types of chipped stone implements being made. Projectile points from the Archaic tend to be smaller than those produced earlier, in the Paleoindian period. In addition, the side- and corner-notched morphology of the Archaic points reflects newer hafting techniques not used by Paleoindians, who made fluted or stemmed points. Alongside the projectile points was an array of other flaked stone tools, including scrapers, choppers, and knives of various kinds (Figure 9.6).

FIGURE 9.6 Early Oshara tradition artifacts from the Jay phase: (a) bifacial knife, (b) projectile point, (c–e) scrapers and the Bajada phase: (a) projectile points and (b, c) scrapers.

Jay Phase

Bajada Phase

There seems to have been considerable regional variation within the Southwestern Archaic. This regionalization is consistent with archaeological observations from other culture areas within North America, as well. Archaeologists have generally recognized three or four regional traditions, named **Pinto**, **Oshara**, **Cochise**, and **Chihuahua**.

The Pinto tradition, found in the western portions of the Southwest, was originally described in the Pinto Basin of California. It is found primarily at surface sites in western and southern Arizona (including Ventana Cave), southern Nevada, and into southern California. Pinto points (Figure 9.4e) are the hallmark of this tradition. Other artifacts include milling equipment (generally cobble manos and basin metates), scraper planes, flake scrapers, and choppers. Based on the location of sites in dry lake basins and along drainages, it appears that the Pinto adaptation included a broad-based foraging strategy. As mentioned in Chapter 8, posthole patterns at the Late Pinto Stahl site, near Little Lake in southern California, are thought to represent houses. Dating for the Pinto tradition is difficult because most of the sites are restricted to the surface. Based on the few available radiocarbon dates, an age of 8000 BP to 1450 BP has been assigned to the tradition (Irwin-Williams 1979, 38). Note that the Pinto period in the Great Basin ends before the Pinto tradition in the Southwest (see Chapter 8).

The Oshara tradition (7450–1550 BP) is a long Archaic sequence defined for the northern Southwest. Five phases are described for this tradition as shown in Table 9.2. The Jay phase can be considered to be late Paleoindian because the Jay projectile point resembles Late Paleoindian points from the Great Plains. On the other hand, such aspects of the flaked stone assemblage as leaf-shaped knives have resemblances to San Dieguito material. There has been disagreement over whether Jay represents continuity with Paleoindian occupation of the northern Southwest or in-migration of a population from further west. The Bajada phase clearly develops out of the Jay phase, however. Grinding slabs and cobble manos are introduced in the San Jose phase, suggesting an intensification of seed processing. The Armijo phase marks the appearance of maize, based on pollen evidence; milling equipment also increased proportionately. What appear to be seasonal camps occur for the first time in this phase. Between 30 and 50 people appear to have used these seasonal camps in the fall or winter, depending on the greater availability of food in the fall and on small agricultural surpluses. In the En Medio phase agriculture continued to be practiced. Storage pits appeared and population grew.

The Cochise tradition is the Archaic in the southwestern Southwest. Three phases are generally recognized for the Cochise (see Table 9.3), although the

TABLE 9.2 Oshara Tradition Phases in the Northern Southwest	
Phase	**Dates (BP)**
En Medio	2750–1550
Armijo	3750–2750
San Jose	5150–3750
Bajada	6750–5150
Jay	7500–6750

TABLE 9.3 Cochise Tradition Phases in the Southern Southwest	
Phase	**Dates (BP)**
San Pedro	3450–2150
Chiricahua	5450–3450
Sulphur Springs	9450–5450

chronology of the phases is debated (Cordell 1997, 109–111). A phase called Cazador was at first thought to come between Sulphur Springs and Chiricahua, but subsequent research indicates the material so designated does not represent a separate phase. Indeed, there is considerable debate over the utility of the entire Cochise concept, which originally was broadly applied in the Southwest. Grinding stones are particularly common in Sulphur Springs sites, with flaked stone scrapers, scraper planes, and occasional points. Changes through time include the introduction of new projectile point types, deepening of the grinding basins in metates, and the introduction of mortars and pestles. Maize and other cultigens are found in late Cochise contexts, as are simple houses.

The southeastern portion of the Southwest has been seen as home to the Chihuahua tradition (Beckett and MacNeish 1994). This tradition is not well understood, because it shares similarities with both the Oshara and Pinto traditions, and yet has distinctive elements as well, particularly among the projectile points. A date range of 7950 BP to 1700 BP has been assigned to the tradition, based on numerous radiocarbon dates. Milling equipment occurs throughout the sequence in the Chihuahua tradition sites.

As with the Archaic elsewhere in the United States, the subsistence adaptation of Southwestern Archaic groups regardless of regional tradition can be referred to as a "broad-spectrum" adaptation. This term captures the notion that a very wide variety of plant and animal foods was consumed (Vierra 1994). Hunting of large game was an important part of the Archaic lifestyle, but added to this base were the trapping of small game and the gathering of wild seeds. Actually, the character of Archaic hunting and foraging probably was more complicated than this brief introduction allows. For example, researchers working with materials from Ventana Cave in southern Arizona have shown that the exploitation of small, locally available animals like the rabbit was highest prior to the middle of the Archaic and that selective hunting of larger game like deer began to increase in importance at this time (Szuter and Bayham 1989). Similar trends toward selectivity have been suggested for the use of plants in the San Juan Basin of the northern Southwest (Cordell 1997, 120–121). In any case, ethnobotanical analysis at a variety of Archaic sites has resulted in the recovery of a wide variety of plant remains from Archaic contexts. These include ricegrass, dropseed, goosefoot, pigweed, hackberry, walnut, prickly pear, and other species. Storage of seeds to meet needs in winter is indicated by the presence of storage pits, especially in the northern part of the Southwest.

By the Late Archaic, plant cultivation had been adopted by the Archaic peoples of the Southwest. Plant cultivation spread to the Southwest from Mesoamerica, but the specific timing for the adoption of individual cultigens seems to have varied, and Archaic peoples failed to adopt some of the plants used later in the

Southwest, such as cotton. Maize was first planted in the Southwest between about 4000 BP and 3500 BP, and early maize dates continue to accumulate as more research is conducted. Early dates have come from sites in the Mogollon Highlands of west central New Mexico and adjacent Arizona at sites such as Bat Cave and Tularosa Cave, and from southern New Mexico at Tornillo Rockshelter. McEuen Cave in the Gila Mountains of southeastern Arizona has maize remains that date at or near 4000 BP. In the Tucson Basin, maize is found associated with early pithouses at 3250 BP (Reid and Whittlesey 1997). Early irrigation features have also been found near Zuni Pueblo in west central New Mexico (Damp et al. 2002).

Along with maize, squash has been found in early contexts. Between 2500 BP and 2200 BP, other important cultigens including the common bean and the bottle gourd seem to have been cultivated, although not in the northern Southwest (Ford 1981). Human manipulation of native plants for seeds and fibers may also have begun during the Archaic. Much later, additional plants, including cotton, were domesticated by Southwesterners in the Hohokam area, but the evidence for Late Archaic adoption of agriculture is significant because it happened among foragers, who did not immediately abandon their mobile lifestyles.

Although a variety of explanations have been proposed for the incorporation of plant cultivation into Southwestern Archaic adaptations, one scenario might be as follows. The practice of casual planting of crops, casually tended, could easily be incorporated into a mobile, broad-spectrum adaptation. A successful crop would be harvested and stored like other seed, but an unsuccessful crop represented little lost effort. Whereas population levels were generally low prior to the adoption of maize agriculture, as agriculture was successfully incorporated into the subsistence strategies of the Late Archaic peoples, population grew dramatically. The decision to put more effort into tending crops probably resulted from an imbalance between population and food resources. Unlike the case of gathered or hunted resources, additional effort put into tending crops can result in increased yields. At some point, restricting mobility to tend crops and to keep an eye on the stored agricultural products made sense. Agriculture also allows, and may actually encourage, people to have more children. Nursing youngsters are harder to transport than older children, and prolonged nursing depresses female fertility. Agriculture, particularly when it involves grains like maize, which can be ground to make gruels, provides more suitable early weaning foods than do hunter-gatherer diets. Earlier weaning increases female fertility, and not having to transport nursing infants as often made it easier for a woman to have more children. By watching fields and helping with chores such as weeding, children can make an economic contribution to sedentary farm families, further encouraging population growth.

In their settlement patterns, Archaic hunter-gatherers were still organized in small, mobile groups, following the blooming and ripening of plant resources. Groups in the northern part of the Southwest were probably more mobile than those in the south, where people would have been drawn to the valleys of the permanent rivers. Caves and rockshelters were frequently used as campsites, and many of these have remained dry since their occupation, preserving organic remains such as basketry, wood, and sandals (Figure 9.7). On the whole, Archaic sites tend to be fairly ephemeral because they were used only for short periods by a few people. However, simple houses are first seen in the Southwest in about 5150 BP. These houses are small, shallow pithouses, circular to oval in shape.

FIGURE 9.7 Yucca
wickerwork sandals
from Tularosa Cave,
New Mexico.

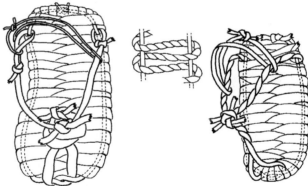

Such structures may indicate that some people achieved a measure of sedentism, especially as plant cultivation was added to the subsistence base. In any event, more dramatic changes did eventually take place as commitment to a farming lifestyle increased, and the later, more familiar Southwestern cultures developed.

FARMERS AND VILLAGERS

The best-known archaeological cultures of the Southwest, those whose ruins are tourist destinations like Mesa Verde, Chaco Canyon, and Casa Grande, intrigue us in part because their mere presence seems counterintuitive to modern people. Given the environmental constraints discussed earlier in this chapter, settled communities of any size would not necessarily be expected in these areas. However, after its introduction in the Archaic period, agriculture was widely adopted, and people eventually committed to the process of settling down. To varying degrees, subsistence for these late Southwestern peoples depended on growing crops, especially the agricultural big three; maize, beans, and squash. Maize and beans are particularly important because beans contain the amino acid lysine, which helps humans digest the protein available in corn. Moreover, while corn depletes the nitrogen in the soil in which it is grown, legumes like beans return nitrogen to the ground. Thus, these crops complement each other nicely, and it is no surprise that Native American farmers often grew them together.

Other cultigens were eventually grown in southern areas, where extensive canal systems were constructed for irrigation purposes (see Figure 1.17). Between 1650 BP and 1450 BP, these new crops, including cotton, sieva beans, jack beans, and cushaw squash, were adopted from Mexico. These cultigens can tolerate the high desert temperatures as long as they have enough water, and this was provided through irrigation. Other cultigens used in the area may have been locally domesticated because they are native southwestern plants: agave, which was used for its fibers as well as for food, amaranth, and little barley grass, for example.

Even as reliance on cultivated plants increased, hunting continued, as did the gathering of wild plant foods. Farming actually opened up some new possibilities for both hunting and gathering, as crops attracted game animals that could be hunted in the gardens, and the cultivated fields were colonized by wild plants known as **ruderals**, which thrive in disturbed soils. Greens, roots, shoots, and seeds from ruderal plants were collected and possibly even nominally tended by Southwestern farmers. Hunting game attracted to the fields not only added to the meat portion of the diet, but also protected the crops by reducing the pests (Neusius 1996b). The only domesticated animals in the Southwest are the dog and the turkey. Turkeys were kept in pens at some sites and may have been raised more as a source of feathers than as food. In some places people also kept macaws and parrots imported from Mexico. These birds provided a source of colorful feathers for decorative and ceremonial uses.

Eventually farming and more sedentary lifestyles were associated with increased aggregation into larger settlements throughout the Southwest. This was not necessarily a slow and gradual process, because settlements grew both through births and by in-migration of people from other areas. The climate of the Southwest, which often changed in ways that made areas more or less suitable for farming, sometimes led to abandonment of areas and migrations to more favorable locations.

A related trend is the elaboration of architectural features that served to unite or integrate members of the community. With the development of very large villages came a need to knit together the disparate households that made up the settlement into a cohesive unit. The increasingly larger multifamily dwelling structures called pueblos that become common in the various parts of the Southwest can be understood as evidence of increased community integration. Archaeologists also have reasoned that large structures, accommodating activities that involved the whole community, such as dances, elaborate ceremonies, or ball games, helped foster common interests among the members of the various families or households.

The story of these changes is fascinatingly variable from region to region throughout the Southwest. However, archaeologists generally group the settled village dwellers of the Southwest in terms of four regional traditions: the Anasazi,

FIGURE 9.8 Anasazi grayware vessels from northern Arizona: (left) neck banded and (right) corrugated.

FIGURE 9.9 Spruce tree house at Mesa Verde in winter.

the Hohokam, the Mogollon, and the Patayan. A fifth grouping, the **Sinagua**, has been variously considered part of each of these other traditions, and its affiliations remain poorly understood.

Anasazi (Ancestral Pueblo)

Archaeologists recognized the culture known as the Anasazi, or Ancestral Pueblo, before they could distinguish the other cultural traditions of the area (Use of the terms Ancestral Pueblo and Anasazi was discussed in Chapter 2, see Box 2.1). The Ancestral Pueblo inhabited the Plateau country of the northern Southwest. They used the **coil-and-scrape technique** to make gray as well as black-painted white and red ceramics, scraping away surface imperfections and thinning the walls as a vessel was constructed. Geometric and other designs were applied with black paint. Some gray pots had neck bands or were corrugated (Figure 9.8). Much Anasazi farming was dry farming, dependent on rainfall for the moisture needed for successful germination and maturation of crops, though features that diverted the rainwater to fields were sometimes built. Housing consisted of pithouses and masonry surface rooms of various kinds. In the later phases, the Ancestral Pueblo built the large pueblos and cliff dwellings for which the Southwest is so well known (Figure 9.9).

The **Pecos classification**, one of the first archaeological attempts at regional synthesis, as discussed in Section A of the Student CD (see especially Table A.1), was developed based on Anasazi sites, and a modified version is still used to order Ancestral Pueblo archaeology. Today this sequence starts with Basketmaker II around 1550 BP and ends with **Pueblo** V in the Historic period. Basketmaker II is preceramic and really marks the end of the Archaic. Many subregional phase schemes—**Mesa Verde**, **Chaco**, Kayenta, Virgin, and **Rio Grande branches**—have been developed to account for the specifics of cultural development in particular areas (Table 9.4). Archaeologists often prefer to use these schemes, which are too many and varied to present here, except for general references to the Pecos classification. Many of the Ancestral Pueblo areas were abandoned in Pueblo III times, but there is clearly continuity between the Ancestral and the contemporary Pueblo peoples of Arizona and New Mexico (Cordell 1997).

TABLE 9.4 Phase Sequences for Selected Anasazi Branches

Date				
BP	AD	Mesa Verde	Chaco Canyon	Kayenta
550	1400			
600	1350			
650	1300		Mesa Verde	Tsegi
700	1250			
750	1200	Mesa Verde	Late Bonito	
800	1150			Toreva
850	1100	McElmo	Classic Bonito (Pueblo II)	
900	1050			Lamoki
950	1000	Mancos		Wepo
1000	950	Ackmen	Bonito	
1050	900			Dinnebito
1100	850			
1150	800	Piedra	Pueblo I	Tallahogan
1200	750			
1250	700			
1300	650			Dot Klish
1350	600	Lino	Basketmaker III	
1400	550			
1450	500			

Adapted from Cordell 1997 Table 7.1.

Both water and length of growing season were important considerations for Anasazi farmers. In many parts of the Plateau, the agricultural cycle depended on sufficient soil moisture remaining after the snow melt to allow germination of the crops. Summer monsoonal rainfall would water these fields later in the growing season. In areas where rainfall was marginal for crop growth, **check dams** and water diversion structures were used to take advantage of runoff. Toward the end of the Ancestral Pueblo sequence, some rudimentary canal irrigation may have been practiced, especially in the Rio Grande valley. The case study in Section D.4 of the Student CD provides an example of a setting in which Anasazi had to cope with complex environmental factors or abandon their homes.

Maize, beans, and squash were the primary crops. These were supplemented by wild plants and by the shoots, leaves, and seeds of ruderal plants that grew in the agricultural fields. Animals were hunted, as well, including deer, elk, and small mammals, especially jackrabbits and cottontail rabbits. Some hunting may have been done in the fields, taking deer, rabbits, or other animals that were attracted by the crops. Because of the limited growing season and the dramatic seasonal changes in the northern Southwest, storage of agricultural products was very important to the Anasazi. We know that some features were used for storage because burning at some sites has left charred remains of stored maize and other foods; other structures have been found in dry caves, where the maize cobs (with the kernels long ago gnawed off by rodents) are still preserved.

The development of Anasazi architecture has provided one of the key elements used in defining the Pecos periods and regional phases for the Southwest. There was regional variation in the timing of changes, but the same trends are evident throughout the Ancestral Pueblo area. As just mentioned, the earliest Anasazi structures are various storage pits. Both bell-shaped pits and slab-lined pits served as storage features for maize and other materials. Early Ancestral Pueblo houses were pithouses with jacal or cribbed log superstructures. In the Basketmaker III period, pithouses (Figure 9.10) were developed into relatively standardized structures with antechambers connected to the main chamber by a short passageway. Roofs were supported by posts. Fire pits are found in the center of the structures, and **wing walls** divide the main chamber. Deflectors, sandstone slabs set on edge, were placed between the opening of the passageway and the fire, presumably to divert air currents that came in through the passageway. Accompanying the pithouses are generally round, slab-lined surface rooms with **jacal** superstructures. These were presumably used for storage.

Pit structures underwent several important changes over time. Although the wing walls and deflector continued to be present, the antechamber and passageway gave way to a vertical **ventilator** connected to the pithouse by a horizontal, floor-level shaft. Eventually, pithouses became **kivas**, structures that are assumed to be integrative facilities, based on analogy with modern Pueblos. The kivas lack wing walls, are circular, and are often lined with masonry. Roofs were cribbed, and masonry support structures, called pilasters, occurred regularly around the perimeter of the kiva on a raised bench. A small hole north of the fire pit is analogous to the ceremonial hole that in modern kivas represents the entrance into the Lower World. This hole is called a **sipapu** and is found in earlier pithouses as well as in kivas.

Surface rooms also changed through time. The earliest round jacal rooms usually occurred in groups, but they stood as independent units. Surface structures changed from round to rectangular early in the sequence, and the squared-off units were built adjacent to one another. Construction went from slab-lined to jacal walls, with vertical sandstone slabs incorporated into the bottom of the walls to masonry. As rectangular rooms began to be built, a standard pattern began to emerge. This pattern was one of suites of three rooms: two small storage rooms in the back fronted by a surface habitation room. Suites of rooms were built side

FIGURE 9.10 The changing plans of Anasazi pit structures from Basketmaker III pithouse to Pueblo V kiva: H, hearth; S, sipapu.

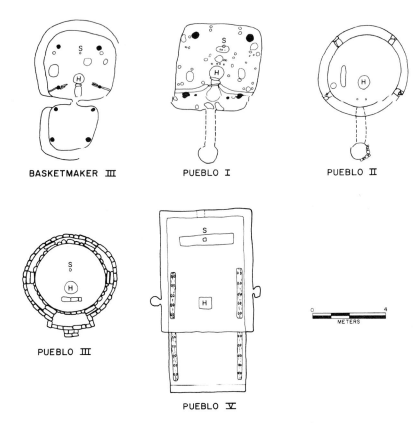

BASKETMAKER III

PUEBLO I

PUEBLO II

PUEBLO III

PUEBLO V

by side to form arcs of rooms archaeologists call room blocks. As masonry rooms became the norm, more compact room blocks began to be built.

During what archaeologists call the **Pithouse-to-Pueblo transition**, village layout generally changed from small groups of pithouses and storage rooms to arcs of room blocks with one or more pithouses located to the south. South of the pithouse was the midden, or trash disposal area. Larger villages were formed by adding groups of three-room suites and pithouses to the room blocks or by adding additional room blocks and pithouses. Along with the transition of pithouses into kivas, room blocks began to change, as well. Kivas were incorporated into the room blocks or were located in plazas surrounded by surface rooms. Room blocks became compact rectangular structures or were built in rockshelters with rooms laid out as the space in the shelter allowed. Eventually, multistory structures were built both in shelters and in the open.

Archaeologists think of kivas as integrative structures that functioned to bring together people from different households or segments of a community. We also think pithouses probably served this function among the Anasazi before the people began to build kivas. Large pit structures are found at early sites, and oversize semisubterranean structures called **great kivas** are found in later sites. Oversized pit structures and great kivas (Figure 9.11) have been interpreted as indicative of integration on a community-wide scale. Masonry towers were also built. Some of these, referred to as tower kivas, may have served the function

FIGURE 9.11 The great kiva at Chetro Ketl in Chaco Canyon, New Mexico.

of a kiva. Others probably functioned as lookout structures. Thus, the complex changes in settlement pattern and architecture that have been documented for the Ancestral Pueblo sequence are presumed to relate to the aggregation of human populations and to their political and social integration over time (Cordell 1997).

Perhaps the most dramatic Anasazi developments were centered on Chaco Canyon in northwestern New Mexico. Here a regional system, sometimes called the **Chaco Phenomenon**, developed by about 900 BP and persisted until approximately 650 BP (Judge 1991). The Chacoan system dominated much of the northern Southwest during these times, as shown by the roads and outlying settlements or **great houses** associated with it (see Box 9.1). However, not all of the Ancestral Pueblo world was incorporated into the Chacoan system. Elsewhere large aggregated settlements also are found. These include the well-known ones from Mesa Verde and others among the Kayenta Anasazi (e.g., Betatakin and Kiet Siel). Both the Mesa Verde and Kayenta settlements are later than the Chaco system. Although not regionally integrated, such large settlements do suggest a degree of community organization beyond the household. Ancestral Pueblo settlements in the Rio Grande valley remained small and dispersed until after AD 1300, but this area of the Southwest is one that received large numbers of people during the fourteenth century. This in-migration led to new patterns of aggregation and new social hierarchies. Other Anasazi contributed to similar fourteenth-century population increases elsewhere in the Southwest, as well.

Hohokam

The Hohokam occupied the low desert regions of Arizona. Archaeologists recognize red pottery or buff pottery decorated with red paint and manufactured using the paddle-and-anvil method as distinguishing characteristics of the Hohokam. Designs on the pottery include human and animal forms, as well as

ISSUES AND DEBATES

BOX 9.1

Interpreting the Chaco Phenomenon

Chaco Canyon always has been a place of great mystery to Americans. Here in the midst of the desolate country of northwestern New Mexico a small stream, the Chaco Wash, flows through a canyon lined by sandstone bluffs. It is a place not unlike other spots on the Colorado Plateau; yet in this canyon large multistory great houses line the north bluff base or are situated on the bluff tops, while numerous small unit pueblos and associated kivas are scattered elsewhere. These structures stand as testaments to earlier use of the canyon at a surprising scale. As discussed in Section A of the Student CD, at the turn of the twentieth century Richard Wetherill was attracted to this spot, and he was joined in excavating and exploring Chaco's ruins by several notable archaeologists of his day. Archaeological interest in Chaco has continued for a century, and the public also has been drawn to the site. Today many people visit the Chaco Culture National Historic Park maintained by the National Park Service, even though it requires a drive of many miles off Highway 44, New Mexico's principal highway between Farmington and Albuquerque. All those who visit wonder and try to understand how a place so empty and desolate today could have been the location for such significant constructions.

Of course, archaeologists have wondered more than most, and the investigations they have undertaken allow us to describe what is found at Chaco in considerable detail if not to fully explain what happened there. The dating of Chaco's many sites is now reasonably well established. There are Archaic and Basketmaker II (prior to 1550 BP) sites in the canyon, as well as many sites with structural remains dating to

Basketmaker III and Pueblo I times (ca. 1550–1050 BP), but the small, one-story unit pueblos and the multistory great houses that have attracted so much attention at Chaco are Pueblo II and early Pueblo III structures, built between approximately 1050 BP and 800 BP. After this period of building, Chaco was in decline until the general abandonment of the northern Southwest around 650 BP (Sebastian 1992; Vivian 1990). Thus, the greatest cultural florescence at Chaco Canyon dates to a relatively short period of two and a half centuries.

Of the great houses, Pueblo Bonito (Figure 9.12), with its D-shaped block of nearly 800 rooms, is the best known, but at least 10 other great houses also were built during this period: planned, multistoried masonry constructions containing enclosed plazas, many small kivas, and at least one great kiva as well. Some, including Pueblo Bonito, were expansions of earlier pueblos; but the rooms in the great houses also are larger than those found in smaller sites of the same period. In addition, features such as hearths, associated with domestic activities, are

FIGURE 9.12 Pueblo Bonito, Chaco Canyon's best known great house.

lacking in many parts of the great houses, suggesting that they weren't actually habitations, but public buildings perhaps used periodically. The numerous smaller pueblos dating to the period of greatest growth do appear to be habitations. These are single-story constructions with an average of 16 rooms, each of which is relatively small and has a low ceiling. They have unenclosed plazas and small kivas, although several of the sites may be associated with an isolated great kiva at Casa Rinconada on the south side of Chaco Wash. Chacoans also constructed water control and collection features such as diversion dams, canals, and headgates to catch rainfall runoff as it came down the side canyons.

Rare cylindrical vases, copper bells imported from Mexico, macaw skeletons, turquoise, mica, marine shells, human effigy vases, painted tablets, and other exotic items have been found at Chaco. These items indicate a remarkable accumulation of trade items for the time period. Some of the material (e.g., turquoise) appears to have been manufactured locally into beads and pendants; but because much of this material was recovered in a small number of burials as well as in kiva offerings, the ritual significance of such items also should not be overlooked (Mathien 2001). Pottery, which may have been periodically dumped in great house refuse mounds in association with periodic gatherings, also occurs in Chaco's sites in unusually large amounts (Toll 2001).

One of the most intriguing aspects of the Chaco Phenomenon is the evidence for linkages between the sites in the canyon itself and the rest of the region. Not only did Chaco's inhabitants build roads within and around the canyon, but these roads extend for great distances within the region. In some instances, roads were actually cut into the sediments and bedrock or lined with boulders; other roads are simply slight swales marked by the removal of vegetation (Figure 9.13). Nevertheless, they are amazingly straight paths with uniform widths of about 30 feet (9 m) for major roads and about 15 feet (4.5 m) for secondary routes (Cordell 1997, 320). These roads also are associated with signaling stations located on high points visible from the canyon's great houses. Moreover, the

FIGURE 9.13 Chaco road segment.

roads often lead to outlying great houses and communities located elsewhere in the San Juan Basin and beyond. Such outliers, even those found as far away as southeastern Utah, eastern Arizona, and southwestern New Mexico, also were planned communities with layouts similar to those found in Chaco Canyon itself. Recognition of the recurring pattern has fueled speculation concerning the nature of the regional system indicated by these arrangements.

In fact, the proper interpretation of the Chaco system is debated among archaeologists. Some of the oldest explanations noted the items of Mexican origin and attributed Chaco's development to trade with the Mexican civilizations far to the south. Since the 1960s and 1970s, archaeologists have attempted to understand Chaco as a local development by reference to ecological and evolutionary models. Despite differences in the particulars, most often these models have viewed Chaco as the center of a chiefdom supported in part by a system of agricultural redistribution that arose in response to the stresses of population aggregation in such a harsh environment. In such models, great houses, whether at Chaco or at outlying locations, were first understood largely as storage facilities and the road system as the means of moving food and other goods about. The obvious emphasis on ritual at Chaco was viewed as a formal means of maintaining Chaco's control of the system, which broke down when extended drought, beginning about 820 BP, made it impossible to maintain adequate resources to redistribute. When new data indicated that the deposits at various great houses such as Pueblo Alto had been made periodically, it was proposed that Chaco had been the venue for pilgrimage festivals through which the distribution of goods and services was regulated by Chacoans.

More recent debate concerning how to understand the Chaco Phenomenon expresses problems with applying models of redistributive chiefdoms to the data on this regional system. Since the system's florescence actually is associated with a period of better climate, it is difficult to understand it as a response to environmental stress, and thus other models of political evolution are being explored. These tend to place more emphasis on the use of ritual and surplus to alter power relationships within human societies (e.g., Sebastian 1992). There is debate about how hierarchical the Chaco system actually was; there are differing viewpoints, as well, about how economic production was organized within it (see Cameron and Toll 2001). Some archaeologists have argued that Chaco lacked individual elites, illustrating, instead, a form of communalism in which labor and production were collectively managed. Other researchers (e.g., Lekson 1999) believe that archaeologists need to pay more attention to astronomically related aspects of ritual and cosmology in the Chacoan and subsequent systems of the Southwest like the Paquimé system highlighted in this chapter's case study by Paul E. Minnis and Michael E. Whalen, "Casas Grandes at the Edge of the Southwestern and Mesoamerican Worlds."

Chaco and the Chaco Phenomenon remain mysteries despite great improvements in the quality of the archaeological data and increased sophistication of scholarly debate. Archaeologists and lay people alike agree that Chaco was special. Its buildings amaze us; its artifacts excite us, and its ancient roads and water features astound us. As we ponder these phenomena, we are drawn into debate and further research. What **was** the Chaco system, and what does it tell us about the past?

geometric patterns (Figure 9.14). Hohokam farmers used irrigation canals along the rivers, but they also planted **akchin** fields, which were watered by the floodwaters at the mouth of arroyos. Houses were jacal constructions in pits, and some massive adobe structures were built (Cordell 1997). Hohokam artisans made a wide variety of jewelry, including shell jewelry made from materials obtained primarily from the Gulf of California.

The Hohokam sequence in the Arizona desert has been divided into four subperiods: **Pioneer, Colonial, Sedentary**, and **Classic** (Table 9.5). Phase systems have been developed for the Gila and Salt River valleys around Phoenix, the Tucson Basin, and the intervening desert, reflecting differences in the paths of development in these areas. There has been considerable debate about the chronology of the Hohokam, with some researchers suggesting a beginning for the sequence as early as 2250 BP and others placing it as late as 1450 BP. The general consensus today is that a beginning in the early centuries of the Common era is most likely (Gumerman 1991). The end of the sequence is not clear. One school of thought holds that the Pima and Tohono O'odam are descendants of the Hohokam, while another holds that there is a hiatus between the latest Hohokam occupation of the area and the historic inhabitants (Cordell 1997).

Cultural resource management studies have been especially important in developing our understanding of the Hohokam. With few exceptions, excavations prior to the advent of CRM focused on large site with impressive features such as Snaketown, with its platform mounds, or Casa Grande with its great house. Cultural resource management required investigation of sites without the impressive features and helped flesh out the nature and range of variation in

FIGURE 9.14 Hohokam red-on-buff ceramics: (a–c) jars and (d) cauldron.

a

b

c

d

TABLE 9.5 Hohokam Periods and Dates		
	Dates	
Period	**BP**	**AD**
Classic	800–550	1150–1400
Sedentary	975–800	975–1150
Colonial	1175–975	775–975
Pioneer	1750–1175	200–775

the Hohokam pattern. The case study by Cory Dale Breternitz and Christine K. Robinson, "The Pueblo Grande Project: An Example of Multidisciplinary Research in a Compliance Setting," in Chapter 1, provides a good example of a CRM contribution to Hohokam archaeology.

In the arid southern Southwest, the Hohokam were limited in their farming by the availability of water for their crops. In the valleys of the major rivers such as the Gila and the Salt, this problem was solved by drawing water from the flowing rivers and distributing it to fields on the river terraces through an elaborate system of canals. Some of these canal systems were several kilometers long. The canals had headgates and brush structures that allowed the water to be directed to specific fields. Because the major rivers in the Hohokam area experienced two periods of peak flow (late spring and late summer) during the yearly cycle, it was sometimes possible to grow two crops in one year. Many of the historic canals in the Phoenix area follow in the paths of Hohokam canals (see Figure 1.18). In areas away from the rivers, the Hohokam planted akchin fields that took advantage of runoff. Elaborate clusters of rock piles have also been recorded, and it has been suggested that these were used to retain moisture for the cultivation of agave (Masse 1991, 210–211).

FIGURE 9.15 Hohokam representations of water-loving animals. (a) turtles, (b) pelican, (c) fish, (d) pelican effigy in shell, (e) frog effigy carved from whole shells.

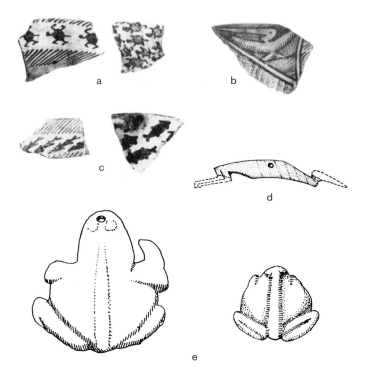

Water was, indeed, critical to the Hohokam survival. This was reflected in their art (Haury 1976). Depictions of water-loving creatures are found in ceramic decoration, in carved stone, and in shell jewelry (Figure 9.15). Frogs and pelicans are particularly frequent subjects of the Hohokam artisans.

As suggested by their impressive irrigation works, the Hohokam were highly successful farmers, who cultivated maize and five species of beans, as well as squash, bottle gourds, cotton, and several native plants such as little barley grass and amaranth. As noted previously, some of these cultigens required irrigation and were not adopted from Mexico until the period from 1650 BP to 1450 BP. The Hohokam also let chenopodium, tansy mustard, and maygrass grow in their fields, and they harvested these and other ruderal plants for their food value as well. Success in farming in the desert does not, however, mean that the Hohokam abandoned hunting and gathering. Like other Southwestern groups, the Hohokam supplemented their agricultural products with wild foods in season. Mesquite pods and cactus fruit, including that of the giant saguaro cactus, were particularly important. In addition, fish and shellfish were collected from the rivers and from the canals to supplement the diet. Hunting continued to be practiced, as well. Small mammals such as jackrabbit, cottontail, and squirrel were most important, but bighorn sheep and deer were also killed.

The earliest Hohokam settlements are clusters of pithouses, generally occurring in household groups. More accurately, the dwellings would be called houses built in pits: the walls of the house were separate from the walls of the pit (Figure 9.16). Later villages consist of groups of clusters. Integrative facilities at these sites include ball courts, plazas around which structures occur, and mounds

of trash capped with soil. Ball courts are particularly interesting and are derived from farther south in Mexico. The structures, which today are marked by two long mounds defining an oval space with its floor lower than the surrounding desert, are believed to have been used in a ceremonial ball game. Ball courts appear to have served the same kind of integrative function in Hohokam society as great kivas did for the Anasazi and Mogollon.

Some very large villages such as Snaketown are found along the rivers. This site, located south of Phoenix, Arizona, was occupied from the Pioneer through the Classic periods (1650–550 BP) and had hundreds of pithouses, as well as trash mounds, formal platform mounds, and ball courts. Snaketown was situated on a canal system that stretched over 10 miles (16 km). Excavations at this site in 1934, followed by excavations in 1964, provided much of the basis for our early understanding of the Hohokam (Haury 1976).

The Classic Hohokam is characterized by walled compounds of adobe surface rooms. The adobe structures were not made of bricks as later adobes were; rather, they were built up by adding basketsful of mud to the growing walls. Multistory great houses of adobe were built at some sites. One Arizona site, Casa Grande, was four stories in height. Classic Hohokam sites also feature formal **platform mounds**, level rectangular mounds that were purposefully constructed of adobe and refuse. The platform mounds tended to be remodeled through time and often had structures built on their tops. These mounds were surrounded by walls that restricted access, and the recovery of ritual items in mound contexts may indicate a ceremonial function. Another possible interpretation is that these represent compounds for the elite to which commoners had only restricted access (Neitzel 1991, 216). Some archaeologists have assumed that platform mounds and the structures associated with them mark a shift in the power relationships within Hohokam societies. Hegmon (2005) notes that in contrast to earlier

Hohokam sites with **ball courts** to which everyone had access, access to these compounds was restricted to elites. Perhaps this indicates that elites were now in control of ritual aspects of Hohokam society. It should be noted, however, that not all archaeologists accept the existence of elites (Crown and Judge 1991, 303).

In fact, just as a regional system developed in Chaco Canyon, a high degree of regional integration developed among the Sedentary and Classic period Hohokam. This system centered in the Gila and Salt River basins near Phoenix but is thought to have extended over a much wider area. Comparisons between the Hohokam and Chacoan regional systems are of great interest to archaeologists (Crown and Judge 1991). In both cases the theme of sociopolitical complexity can be profitably explored. The lack of hierarchy evident in the archaeological record for these systems suggests that we have much to learn about the development of inequality and integration in human societies.

Mogollon

Archaeological sites recognized as Mogollon are found across southern New Mexico and west to the Verde River in Arizona, as well as in the Mexican states of Sonora and Chihuahua. The considerable variability in this large area is relatively poorly understood, although the **Jornada Mogollon** of the extreme southeastern Southwest can be distinguished from those in the Mogollon Highlands of Arizona and New Mexico. Mogollon ceramics, at the beginning of the sequence, are red- and brownwares made by the coil-and-scrape technology. Red-on-white and black-on-white pots were added to the ceramic repertoire with time. **Mimbres** pottery, with its highly stylized depictions of animals and humans, occurs at the end of the Mogollon sequence (see Exhibit 9.1). Pithouses are the primary form of architecture, but surface pueblos occur at the end of the Mogollon occupation of the area. Dry farming was practiced by the Mogollon, but hunting was also very important to these mountain-dwelling people (Cordell 1997; Reid and Whittlesey 1997).

CLUES TO THE PAST

EXHIBIT 9.1

Fantasies on Clay: Mimbres Pottery

Between 950 BP and 820 BP (AD 1000–1130), potters in the Mimbres Valley of New Mexico, part of the Mogollon region, produced a distinctive black-on-white pottery. This Classic Mimbres pottery includes spectacular painted bowls with geometric and pictorial designs that are visually very appealing (Figure 9.17). The

bowls have frequently been found in burials, often covering the head of the interred individual, and burials most often occur under the floors of rooms in the Mimbres pueblos. This association has led to massive destruction of Mimbres sites by relic hunters, sometimes using earthmoving equipment to explore for graves containing the

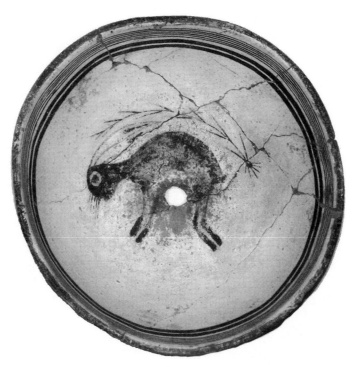

FIGURE 9.17 Mimbres depiction of a rabbit. Note the hole in the center of the bowl and the intricate geometric border.

precious pottery, which can command very high prices from international art collectors. Much of our ability to understand this fascinating pottery has been lost because of wanton destruction of the sites that held not only the pottery but also the keys to its role in Mimbres life.

Some have inferred that because Classic Mimbres pottery is black on white and bears some resemblance to Anasazi ceramics, the Mimbres were actually Anasazi who had occupied the Mogollon area. Mimbres Classic pottery differs from Anasazi pottery in some significant details, however, suggesting that it is a development from preceding Mogollon ceramic traditions. Most notably, Anasazi pottery uses gray clay, whereas Mimbres pottery continues to use the brown clay that characterizes earlier Mogollon pottery. The black-on-white effect was achieved by applying black paint to a white **slip** that coated the brown clay.

Brody (1977) made an extensive study of designs on Mimbres pottery. He reported that

while geometric forms are found on jars, ladles, and other household items, as well as on bowls, pictorial designs are limited to bowls. A number of different kinds of animal are depicted on these representational bowls, including antelope and bear, bats, birds of various kinds (including macaws and perhaps parrots), fish (some clearly representing species from the Pacific Ocean), and insects (see Figure 9.18). Humans are also depicted, as are unidentifiable creatures that probably represent mythical figures. Included among these possible mythical figures are depictions that appear to represent the horned serpent, a theme found throughout the pre-Columbian Southwest, which is probably derived from Mesoamerica. Most of the bowls depict a single animal or human, but multiple figures were also painted on some bowls, and occasionally the depiction represents actions like hunting or dancing.

Although whole bowls are most often found with burials, there are strong indications that

FIGURE 9.18 Mimbres depiction of a fish.

the ceramics were in daily use and were not specifically made as grave offerings. Sherds of Classic Mimbres pottery are found in household refuse, indicating everyday use. Further, the whole vessels found with burials often have wear marks from dippers that were used to serve from the bowls.

Interestingly, the bowls found with burials almost always have a hole in them. These holes, generally punched from the outside of the vessel, are almost certainly part of the burial ritual.

Sourcing studies indicate that Mimbres pottery was made at numerous locations in the Mimbres area and that there was no particular craft specialization involved in its manufacture.

Based on the nature of the activities depicted and on the observation that men are portrayed more often than women (though it is impossible to determine the gender of many of the human figures), it is suggested that men were important in painting the designs on the pottery, if not in the entire manufacturing process.

The beauty of Mimbres Classic pottery still speaks to us today, but it is perhaps unfortunate that it is so hauntingly beautiful. The price that such pots bring on the art market has led to destruction of the sites that could answer the myriad of questions about the role of this art in the lives of the Mimbres people and, perhaps, about the meaning of these enigmatic designs.

TABLE 9.6 Mogollon Phases and Dates		
	Dates	
Phase	**BP**	**AD**
Mimbres	950–820	1000–1130
Three-Circle	1050–950	900–1000
San Francisco	1250–1050	700–900
Georgetown	1450–1250	500–700
Pine Lawn	1750–1450	200–500

A number of phase schemes have been proposed for the Mogollon, reflecting the regional variation in the tradition. Dating of the phases is controversial, but a starting date of AD 200 seems reasonable on the basis of available evidence. Five phases as shown in Table 9.6 are used in the discussion that follows. After this sequence, the Mogollon area shows Pueblo traits, suggesting strong influence from the Colorado Plateau. Aggregation into large communities, including displaced Ancestral Pueblo populations, seems to have occurred in late pre-Columbian times, and people from this area probably contributed to the populations of Hopi, Zuni, and Acoma pueblos.

Agriculture among the Mogollon involved the cultivation of maize, squash, beans, and cotton. Some check dams and other water control features have been noted, and there is a suggestion of ditch or stream-fed irrigation as well. Mogollon subsistence depended more on hunting than appears to have been the case among either the Anasazi or the Hohokam. Deer, rabbits, rodents, and birds were all hunted. Piñon and acorns were among the collected foods. Based on evidence from cave sites like Tularosa Cave, the relative dependence on cultivated food and gathered food fluctuated with time.

Pithouses of various designs are characteristic of the Mogollon for most of their occupation of the area (Figure 9.19). The earliest pithouses, those of the Pine Lawn and Georgetown phases, are D-shaped or round, generally have ramp entries on one side, and vary in size, in orientation with regard to cardinal points, and in type and arrangement of internal features. Roofs of these early pithouses were usually supported by a central post, and additional posts ringed the edge of the structure. Through time the pithouses became rectangular, with roofs supported by four posts. Between AD 850 and 1000 there was a tendency for pithouses to be lined with masonry. Ramp entries continue, but some pithouses had ventilator systems and roof entries like Ancestral Pueblo pithouses. Generally, Mogollon built their houses and great kivas oriented to the east, southeast, and south, although there is variability in this trait (Riggs 2005). After 950 BP (AD 1000), surface pueblos resembling those of the Ancestral Pueblo were built.

Settlements tended to be small, consisting of a few pithouses arranged in no particular pattern. Early settlements tended to be on hilltops or mesas, and were walled, suggesting that defense was an important consideration. Site location shifted to river terraces in the Georgetown phase, and sites tended to have fewer pithouses. Population, as indicated by site size, increased considerably during the San Francisco phase, and sites continued to occupy river terraces. Site size

FIGURE 9.19 Suggested reconstructions of the superstructures of Mogollon pithouses: (a) Georgetown phase, (b) San Francisco phase, and (c) Three-Circle phase.

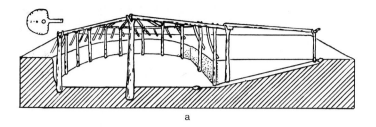

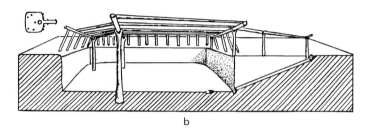

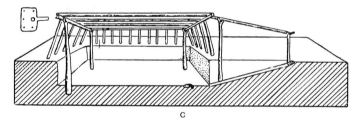

continued to increase in the Three-Circle phase, suggesting an increase in the population occupying the sites. The surface pueblos built after 950 BP vary in size, and some very large sites, as large as 200 rooms, have been found.

Community structures are found on Mogollon sites, as well. The oversized structures referred to as great kivas are found from the earliest occupations. The first great kivas are round or bean shaped, with D-shaped great kivas being introduced between 1300–1100 BP (the San Francisco phase). In the Three-Circle phase these structures become rectangular. Great kivas continue into the period after AD 1000 and are accompanied by small, rectangular kivas similar in other respects to those of the Anasazi. While these large sites contain evidence of community integration, it does not appear that regional systems developed here. Instead, communities merely aggregated, particularly among the Classic Mimbres between 950 BP and 800 BP (AD 1000–1150), and developed local hierarchies and mechanisms for social integration (Cordell 1997). These processes of aggregation continued in late prehistory, when pueblos with 500 to 1000 rooms were built (Riggs 2005).

Patayan

The western Southwest is the home of the Patayan tradition, a diverse group of archaeological complexes found in the Colorado River valley and in the adjacent

FIGURE 9.20 Patayan ceramic jars: (a) vessel 12.6 inches (32 cm) tall and (b) vessel 13.2 inches (33.5 cm) tall.

a   b

lands to the east and west. The Patayan tradition is less well known than the other Southwestern traditions. Most of the area of the Patayan tradition sites was occupied by Yuman speakers in the Historic period. There is a distinction made between the lowland Patayan, who lived along the Colorado River, and the upland Patayan. The upland Patayan includes considerable variability, though three general groups are recognized within this division: the **Cerbat** and **Cohonina** in northwestern Arizona, and the **Prescott** in west central Arizona.

One of the principal uniting themes of the diverse archaeological complexes considered under the name Patayan is pottery thinned by the **paddle-and-anvil technique**, in which the pottery finishing involves beating or pressing the coils used in construction until they are smoothed. In the lowland areas of the Arizona and California deserts, as well as the Colorado River valley, the pottery is primarily a buff ware (Figure 9.20), sometimes decorated with red paint. In the upland areas on both sides of the Colorado, brown pottery is found. Decoration of this pottery is generally confined to incised designs, and these are rare. Rock features are another hallmark of the Patayan. Such features include dry-laid masonry walls, earth ovens with considerable burned stone fill, and rock piles, often called trail shrines, along trails (McGuire and Schiffer 1982).

Little is known about Patayan settlement, at least along the Colorado River, because of the setting in which that settlement occurred. Settlements were apparently along the river during the growing season, and the areas where they were to be found have since been altered by flooding and by modern agriculture. Based on the Quechan and Mohave patterns historically, villages were probably scattered arrangements of jacal structures strung along the river terraces. These structures were generally rectangular, and both surface structures and pithouses occurred in the historic villages.

In the upland areas of the Cerbat, domed brush structures were built for houses, although rockshelters were frequently used, as well. The Cohonina built a variety of structures in small settlements. Houses included pit structures and surface rooms that were constructed partly of rock.

Much less is known about Patayan subsistence than about that of the other southwestern traditions. The paucity of excavated sites makes reconstruction difficult. The historic pattern observed among the Quechan and the Mojave of the lower Colorado River appears to have some time depth and is the basis for present ideas about Patayan subsistence, at least along the river. Ethnographically, agriculture along the lower Colorado River was flood agriculture akin to that practiced by the ancient Egyptians along the Nile. Each spring the Colorado would overflow its banks, fed by snow melt from the Rocky Mountains. This flooding deposited a layer of rich topsoil onto the floodplain. The residual moisture allowed people to plant and raise crops in this soil. Away from the Colorado, rainfall farming was practiced, but in many areas hunting and gathering remained very important (Cordell 1997).

Sinagua

The Sinagua, who were located in Arizona in the vicinity of Flagstaff and southward toward Phoenix, are an enigmatic cultural group about whom we understand surprisingly little. The people were farmers who built pueblo-style communities and made plain red- or brownware ceramics that were distinctive for being tempered with cinders or crushed volcanic rock. The **paddle-and-anvil technique** was used in making these ceramics. Sinagua sites date from approximately 1250 BP in the Flagstaff area, but they also have been found to the south in the Verde River valley (Reid and Whittlesey 1997). The mix of Sinagua traits has led archaeologists to consider these people closely related to the other southwestern traditions, especially the Anasazi and the Patayan, yet today there is a tendency to agree that whatever Sinagua represents, it is best treated as a unique cultural tradition.

The most important event in Sinagua history was the eruption of the volcano at Sunset Crater, which occurred in 866 BP (AD 1064), followed by additional eruptions over the next several hundred years. Although the first eruption buried many settlements in volcanic ash layers, the absence of human remains encased in this ash suggests that people had sufficient time to abandon their homes and flee.

In addition, although you might think this eruption would devastate farming in this area, there is considerable evidence that after the eruption people from many southwestern regions were actually attracted to the Flagstaff area. One theory is that the blanket of cinders worked as a sort of mulch, making the land more productive (Kamp 1998); but it is possible that supernatural powers were attributed to the volcano, and this drew people as well. Another possibility is that trade with other people simply increased at this time. In any case, after the eruption that created Sunset Crater, the Sinagua were influenced by the influx of ideas. Ceramics from several other areas, ball courts, and pithouses that seem to be a mix of Hohokam and Anasazi building styles all suggest this change. Several large sites date after the eruption, including the well-known Wupatki National Monument and cliff dwellings at Walnut Canyon National Monument, both of which can be visited today. Large and spectacular sites dating toward the end of the Sinagua sequence are found as well in the Verde Valley, with the best known being the impressive five-story cliff dwelling called Montezuma's Castle. Most of the northern part of the Sinagua area was abandoned after about 650 BP, at about the same time the Anasazi left the Colorado Plateau. Thus, just like the people of the other major Southwestern traditions, the Sinagua were part of the population movements and reorganizations that took place after this time throughout the Southwest.

REORGANIZATION, AGGREGATION, AND CONFLICT IN LATE PREHISTORY

Economic and sociopolitical organization at a regional level first developed among the Late Sedentary and Classic period Hohokam (ca. 950–700 BP) and among the Anasazi at Chaco Canyon (ca. 1050–800 BP). In both cases, the regional systems have important implications for understanding possible interrelationships between developing social hierarchy, exchange, and political power. However, developments after 800 BP reflect new reasons for aggregation and aggregated villages characterized many areas of the Southwest after about a thousand years ago.

First of all, by 650 BP, a widespread abandonment of the northern Southwest had taken place. The abandonment of some areas began as early as 800 years BP, as is reflected in the decline of Chaco. Southwesterners had, of course, abandoned individual sites and even local areas before. One example is given in the case study in Section D.4 of the Student CD. Nevertheless, in this case the dislocation of human populations was particularly widespread. The Virgin Anasazi area of southeastern Arizona, the Kayenta Anasazi of northern Arizona, the Mesa Verde region of southwestern Colorado, the San Juan Basin of northwestern New Mexico, most of the Sinagua homeland, and some parts of the Mogollon Highlands were literally vacated by human populations around 650 BP. This widespread abandonment has long been billed as one of the great mysteries of Southwestern archaeology, and archaeologists are still trying to understand what happened.

What is just as interesting about this period is that populations relocated and reorganized in several distinct areas that were important in late Southwestern prehistory and into the Historic period. One such area is the Rio Grande valley and areas near it in eastern New Mexico. Here pithouse villages and small pueblos characterize the archaeological record until after 650 BP, when a number of very large aggregated communities appeared. Some of the sites built during the Late Prehistoric received attention by early archaeologists developing culture history methods in the first few decades of the twentieth century, but more recent excavations also have been conducted (Cordell 1997, 404). Both the San Juan Basin and the Mesa Verde region have been considered source areas for the populations that moved into this area at this time.

Several other areas also seem to have received populations. The Western Pueblo areas of west central New Mexico and eastern Arizona experienced an influx of population. Sites in this area change from small pueblos to large aggregated communities beginning about 750 BP. These seem to suggest movement of populations from further north and west out of the Virgin and Kayenta Anasazi areas into new areas. Settlement aggregation also characterizes the occupation of Hohokam heartland after about 600 BP, as already mentioned. Developments associated with distinctive Gila and Tonto polychrome pottery (Figure 9.21) and the appearance of adobe compounds have been called **Salado** by some archaeologists (Crown 1994; Dean 2000; see also Reid and Whittlesey 1997, 230–258). Salado has been variously interpreted, and it is not clear that it should be considered representative of a distinct cultural group separate from Classic period Hohokam, but one view is that it represents the influx of newcomers into the Hohokam area. Sites like Casa Grande in Arizona seem to be associated with Salado, but these phenomena are evident outside the Hohokam area as well. It may be best to understand Salado as another example of the complicated

FIGURE 9.21 Gila polychrome sherds, sometimes referred to as Salado pottery.

population movements and amalgamations that is dated between about 750 BP and 500 BP. In any case, the central Hohokam area itself experienced abandonment after 500 BP.

Perhaps the most significant development in the late prehistory of the Southwest occurred at Casas Grandes, or Paquimé, in northern Chihuahua, Mexico, where some affinities with the Mogollon tradition have been recognized and a population influx may have occurred after 650 BP. This chapter's case study is about recent work at Paquimé and associated sites. Now known to principally date to the period after 750 BP and to have been at its height more recently still, Paquimé has been interpreted as the center of its own regional system (e.g., Lekson 1999). Distinctive polychrome pottery may be diagnostic of this system. However, there is little agreement on the size and importance of the Paquimé polity, which is one reason it is necessary to establish the context for this large and impressive site, as described in the case study. Once thought to have Mesoamerican origins, Paquimé is interpreted by some contemporary researchers as linked to post-Chacoan developments in the Puebloan world (e.g., Lekson 2005).

The causes of the abandonments, reorganizations, and large aggregations of late Southwestern prehistory are not fully understood. Environmental factors may well have played a role in the abandonment of the northern Southwest. The villagers of this area may not have been able to survive droughts thought to have occurred here between approximately 674 BP and 651 BP (Varien et al. 1996), just as drought may have affected the Chacoan system earlier. Areas settled after the drought of the mid-seventh century BP may have had more favorable precipitation regimes. Perhaps the areas to the south and east into which populations moved were generally less risky because the summer rainfall was simply more reliable. However, some studies have indicated that the northern Southwest as a region probably could have supported a sizable population during these droughts even though local areas might have had to be abandoned (Van West 1996).

Moreover, the aggregated settlements that resulted elsewhere are not as easily explained by reference to the environment alone. One argument has been that warfare between towns and villages encouraged aggregation into defensive positions. Possibly scarcity of resources contributed to such conflict. Although there has been a tendency to see the peoples of the Southwest as peaceful, there always have been some Southwestern archaeologists who have attributed cultural historical changes to warfare. Recent discussions have recognized that there is evidence for intercommunity violence in the Southwestern record (e.g., Haas and Creamer 1993; LeBlanc 1999). There is little question that at least some violence, possibly even cannibalism (Turner and Turner 1999; White 1992), occurred in the late prehistory of the Southwest. See "Was There Cannibalism in the Prehistoric Southwest?" (Section F.4 of the Student CD). For example, in the Gallinas area of New Mexico's Jemez Mountains, sites dated 750 BP to 650 BP include mass burials of skeletons with arrow tips embedded in the bones, a high percentage of burned habitation sites, and a large number of skeletons found unburied on the floors of burned structures (Cordell 1997, 378). Even though it is not completely clear what role warfare might have played in the abandonments and aggregation of late prehistory, renewed interest and investigation of this topic promise that new insights will be forthcoming.

Finally, it should be noted that besides aggregation into very large sites, the end of the pre-Columbian period in the Southwest may also have been marked by new pan-regional mechanisms of integration. Casas Grandes has been interpreted as a center for religious pilgrimage (Fish and Fish 1999), and shamanic images on its pottery have been cited by some to suggest the presence of priest-shamans at the site (Van Pool 2003). One interpretation of Gila polychrome or Salado pottery is that it represents a religious ideology associated with fertility and water control. Crown (1994), who identifies images of parrots, snakes, horned serpents, eyes, the sun, and stars (Figure 9.22) as central symbols of this **Southwest Regional cult**, notes such images on polychrome pottery and in rock art from Mimbres times into the Late Prehistoric. Studies of decorative styles and imagery may ultimately help archaeologists understand the late developments we have mentioned. Imagery of religious significance associated with the later development of the **Katchina cult** found among modern Pueblos has also been explored by archaeologists (Adams 1991).

FIGURE 9.22 Design motifs of the Southwestern Regional cult.

Studies of late pre-Columbian and Protohistoric Pueblo societies have contributed to debate about hierarchy and inequality in significant ways. For example, it has been argued that Rio Grande pueblos at this time represent confederacies, in which relatively equal villages were allied, rather than chiefdoms. Another idea that might apply is that of heterarchy (Crumley 1995), in which relative equality is maintained by different villages based on power or superiority in different aspects of culture (e.g., military, vs economic, vs spiritual). Thus, the classic models of tribe versus chiefdom or egalitarian versus ranked, briefly introduced in Chapter 2, may not be easily applied to larger and more complex Southwestern societies after all.

NEW ARRIVALS

Much of the northern Southwest had been abandoned by AD 1300, and an early explanation for the evacuation of this large area was the arrival of the Navajo, the

Apache, and the Utes. It is clear today that the entrance of these peoples into the Southwest postdates the great abandonment, but authorities disagree about the timing and direction of the Navajo and Apache in-migration. One position holds that the earliest evidence for these tribes is in the **Dinétah phase** in the upper San Juan drainage that has been dated about 500 BP (e.g., Winter and Hogan 1992). Other archaeologists argue that these people first entered the Southwest from the Great Plains in the Historic period after the Pueblo Revolt of 1680 (e.g., Schaafsma 1996). Navajo and Apache entered the Southwest as hunter-gatherers and developed territories north of and between the territories of the Pueblos of the time. These people continued to hunt and gather, but also began raiding the Pueblos for food. Archaeological sites indicate some experimentation, with settlement into pueblolike villages, and some agriculture was incorporated into the subsistence system (Towner 1996). The Utes also entered the northern Southwest about the same time as the Apache and Navajo, though most of their territory was in the Great Basin (see Chapter 8). Sites attributed by some to the Navajo and the Apache may in fact be Ute in origin. Because the Utes were highly mobile foragers, early Ute sites are difficult to detect in a landscape dominated by large and impressive Ancestral Pueblo ruins.

The other recent inhabitants of the Southwest all can be related to pre-Columbian peoples in the Southwest (Figure 9.23). The Pima and Tohono O'odham

FIGURE 9.23 Historic groupings of Native people in the Southwest.

(formerly called Papago) of the Sonoran Desert occupy the territory where Hohokam sites are found, and they may be descended from the Hohokam. Close study of traditional Native histories can help archaeologists sort out whether there was a hiatus after Hohokam (Teague 1993). These people speak languages from the Uto-Aztecan family and, in the Historic period, lived in **rancherias**, or settlements of dispersed houses, practicing a combination of farming and gathering. The Pueblo people of Arizona and New Mexico are clearly the descendants of the Ancestral Pueblo, although the Mogollon almost certainly made contributions to recent Puebloan populations, as well. The Pueblos speak a diversity of languages, including languages of the Uto-Aztecan, Kiowa-Tanoan, and Keresen families, as well as Zuni, which is a language without close relatives. The Pueblos live in compact villages and practice irrigated and rainfall farming today, as they have in the historic past. The Mohave, Quechan, Cocopa, Maricopa, and various Pai groups (Yavapai, Walapai, Havasupai, Paipai) living along the lower Colorado River, Gila River, and adjacent upland areas, are the successors to the Patayan. These people speak Yuman languages of the Hokan family. In the Historic period they made their living as floodwater agriculturalists along the Colorado River and its major tributaries, or practiced rainfall farming in the uplands. Together, all of these people had to deal with the next newcomers: the Europeans.

HISTORIC PERIOD

The Historic period begins in the Southwest with Spanish exploration around AD 1540. An archaeological site adjacent to Santiago Pueblo in New Mexico is thought to represent a campsite of the Coronado expedition during the winter of 1540–1541. Metal artifacts, one found in the chest of an individual, are thought to be bolt heads of Spanish crossbows (Espinoza-Ar 2005). Early explorations were followed by Spanish colonization of the area. By 1598 towns were established, generally in the major river valleys, and Santa Fe was founded in 1610. Along with towns, the Spanish built presidios and missions, just as in California (Chapter 7). Presidios were established either where there were populations to be protected or where other Spanish interests that needed looking after. Missions, established to introduce Christianity to Native Americans, were built near populated areas (Cordell 1997). The archaeology of the encounter between the Spanish and Southwesterners is the subject of much fascinating contemporary research (Thomas 1989).

In 1680 the Pueblos, frustrated by the injustice of the tax and labor demands of the Spanish, as well as by the deliberate repression of Pueblo religion, revolted and drove the Spanish from their land. The Spanish were unable to reestablish their presence until 1692. The revolt is most visible archaeologically in refuge sites, where Pueblo people relocated in defensive positions. Important excavations have been carried out at the mission of San Bernardo de Aguatubi, at the Hopi village Awotovi (Montgomery et al. 1949), and at the presidios of Tucson and Tubac. Excavations at the Hopi town of Walpi illustrate the influence of the Spanish on the Hopi. The excavations at Walpi demonstrate that although the Hopi rejected the religion and governmental institutions the Spanish had sought to impose, they adopted useful items of material culture such as metal plows and hoes and crops like apples, peaches, and apricots. European ceramic elements

such as ring bases on vessels and certain design motifs, which had become established in Hopi pottery making prior to the revolt, were conspicuously absent at
Walpi, which was founded in 1690, 10 years after the Pueblo Revolt (Adams
1981). In the Cochiti area, Hanat Kotyiti, a mesa-top pueblo established just after
the revolt, has also been excavated. Preucel (2000) sees evidence of revitalization
of Pueblo culture at the site. Both traditional foods and ritual activities appear
to have been reestablished at Hanat Kotyiti, but elements of Spanish material
culture were retained, as well, including religious gear.

Interactions between the Pueblos of the Southwest and the Plains during
the Historic period also can be documented. For instance, Pecos Pueblo in New
Mexico became the locus of trade fairs at which people traded corn, obsidian, and
turquoise for meat and hides (Speilmann 1998). Archaeology can fruitfully explore
this little-understood exchange.

In 1821 the Republic of Mexico won independence from Spain and began to
control the lands formerly occupied by the Spanish in the Southwest. The Spanish
towns continued to be occupied, as did some of the presidios; but large, fertile
tracts of land suitable for farming and livestock raising were granted to Mexican
citizens. Many prominent Hispanic ranch families in the Southwest are descended
from the recipients of these land grants. Adobe haciendas were features of many
ranchos, and excavations have been carried out at a number of old adobes.

The Mexican period ended with the Mexican War in 1848, and the **Gadsden
Purchase** of 1854 officially added much of the Southwest to the United States.
In this period more ranches and farms were established, and the mineral wealth
of the area was exploited on a large scale. Boom towns grew up around the
mines but often were short-lived; the ghost towns that dot the Southwest are
settlements that were abandoned when the mineral deposits played out. Archaeological excavation of homesteads, ranches, mines, and ghost towns provides
important information on the economics and lifestyles of the Southwest after the
mid-nineteenth century. Unfortunately, such sites often have been damaged by
vandals and scavengers who steal any usable fixtures they can carry away.

An interesting example of archaeological investigations for the American
period is recent work at the Pine Springs **Buffalo Soldiers** camp located in the
Guadalupe Mountains National Park, east of El Paso. "Buffalo Soldiers" is the
name given to two regiments of African American cavalry established in 1866
and posted to various spots on the western frontier to build forts, and roads,
and to protect railroads, stage coaches, and settlers. The Apache were often the
soldiers' adversaries in the West Texas area near the Pine Springs encampment.
Survey and limited testing at Pine Springs by African American students from
Howard University and by Mescalero Apache high school students reveals that
the Apache used this site when the soldiers were not in residence. This project is
an example of cooperation between Native Americans and African Americans in
the search for the history of both groups (Davis 2005).

The early part of the twentieth century saw the beginning of the growth
of the major cities of the Southwest. Cities like Phoenix, Tucson, Flagstaff,
Albuquerque, and Santa Fe began to take on something of their modern forms.
Areas were subdivided, neighborhoods grew, industrial areas were developed,
and often the growth impacted archaeological sites. Redevelopment has led to
the construction of new buildings and neighborhoods, which replace older
houses. Archaeology is often done as part of redevelopment projects, exposing
the earlier historic remains and the prehistoric sites.

CHAPTER SUMMARY

This chapter has introduced the archaeological story of the Southwest culture area. We hope it has given a working perspective on the cultural context in which the well-known spectacular cliff dwellings of Mesa Verde developed, as well as on related aspects of the region's past. The main points made in this chapter are as follows:

- There is a great deal of environmental variability within the Southwest based on elevation and precipitation regimes, and both moisture and the length of the growing season were limiting factors for farming peoples of the Southwest. In addition, both short- and long-term environmental changes had roles in determining the habitability of local areas in the Southwest at different times in the past.

- Pre-Clovis evidence from the Southwest is lacking, although claims have been made for several sites. On the other hand, Paleoindian use of the Southwest is clear: several Clovis mammoth kill sites in southeastern Arizona are well known to archaeologists, and Folsom sites are well documented from various areas in New Mexico. Late Paleoindian artifacts in the northern and eastern Southwest may be related to developments on the Great Plains, while in the western Southwest the Late Paleoindian and Early Archaic periods may be represented by the San Dieguito and Ventana complexes. This evidence suggests that big-game hunting did not characterize the post-Clovis Paleoindians of the western Southwest.

- The generalized foragers of the Southwestern Archaic, indicated in part by the appearance of side- and corner-notched points, also produced assemblages with large numbers of millingstones. These are believed to be associated with the processing of wild seeds. Four regional traditions have been recognized for the Southwestern Archaic: Pinto, Oshara, Cochise, and Chihuahua, though archaeological understanding of these different traditions remains limited.

- Plant cultivation began in the Late Archaic, with the oldest dates for maize being between 4000 BP and 3500 BP. Squash also has been found in early contexts, and common bean and bottle gourd were certainly cultivated by sometime between 2500 BP and 2200 BP. Manipulation of native plants is also probable during the Late Archaic. Despite this experimentation with food production, Late Archaic Southwesterners continued their mobile ways.

- After approximately 1550 BP the settled villagers of the northern Southwest were part of the Anasazi or Ancestral Pueblo tradition. These people were dry farmers, growing maize, beans, and squash and developing mixed economies that incorporated ruderals, wild plants, garden animals, and large game. A transition from settlements of dispersed pithouses and surface storage rooms to unit pueblos and kivas is an important part of the Ancestral Pueblo record, which culminates in populations aggregated into towns and regional systems such as those represented by the Chaco Phenomenon and other regional centers.

- The Hohokam tradition developed in the deserts of the southern Southwest, especially along the Gila and Salt rivers. Although they supplemented their diet with wild foods, the people were farmers who depended on irrigation;

they grew maize, beans, and squash, cultivated cotton, and harvested several native plants. Hohokam settlements often include ball courts and plazas, features that suggest community integration, but Classic period Hohokam sites also are known for their multistory great houses, platform mounds, and walled compounds. These features suggest increased social inequality and elite control of ritual in the Classic period, though this point is subject to debate.

- The Mogollon tradition of southern New Mexico, eastern Arizona, and northern Mexico is another tradition that extended from approximately 1750 BP to 950 BP, after which the people seem to have been incorporated into the Ancestral Pueblo tradition. The Mogollon were farmers who constructed check dams and other water control features, built pithouses and some large integrative structures such as great kivas, and made ceramics, including the well-known, highly stylized Mimbres pottery.

- The fourth and fifth Southwestern cultural traditions are less well understood Patayan and Sinagua traditions. Patayan represents a number of distinct cultures including lowland groups along the Colorado River, and the Cerbat, Cohonina, and Prescott of northwest and central Arizona. The Sinagua tradition encompasses farming peoples who built pueblo-style communities near Flagstaff, Arizona.

- The northern Southwest had been largely abandoned by 650 BP. At the same time, population growth and aggregated settlements developed in places like the Rio Grande valley of New Mexico and portions of west central New Mexico and eastern Arizona. Aggregation of population also characterizes the end of the Hohokam sequence, while after 500 BP the central Hohokam area itself seems to have been abandoned. The growth of the regional system at Casas Grandes in northern Mexico also occurred at this time. These Late Prehistoric population movements and aggregations seem to be associated with intercommunity violence and pan-regional religious and/or economic integration, but the extent to which these societies were hierarchically ranked is not clear.

- The Navajo and Apache were late entrants into the Southwest, although the precise timing and origins of these ethnicities are unclear and are complicated by Ute presence in the northern Southwest. However, beginning in AD 1540, the Spanish entered the Southwest, and although the Pueblo staged a successful revolt in 1680, the Spanish returned before the end of the century. Transformations in southwestern societies during the Spanish period, which continued until Mexican independence in 1821, were many and complicated, although many Southwestern tribes remained intact. This area became part of the United States in 1854 after the Gadsen Purchase. Archaeology continues to document important aspects of Native American, colonial, Mexican, and American history in the Southwest.

SUGGESTIONS FOR FURTHER READING

For a thorough introduction to the archaeology of the Southwest:
Cordell, Linda. 1997. *Archaeology of the Southwest*, 2nd ed. San Diego: Academic Press.

For a more detailed account of Mimbres pottery and the culture it represents:

Le Blanc, Steven A. 1983. *The Mimbres People: Ancient Pueblo Potters of the American Southwest.* London: Thames and Hudson.

For an excellent summary of a long-term archaeological research project in the northern Southwest:

Powell, Shirley, and Francis E. Smiley. 2002. *Prehistoric Culture Change on the Colorado Plateau: Ten Thousand Years on Black Mesa.* Tucson: University of Arizona Press.

For a highly readable case study on a Sinagua site intended for undergraduates:

Kamp, Kathryn. 1998. *Life in the Pueblo: Understanding the Past Through Archaeology.* Prospect Heights, IL: Waveland Press.

For comparisons between the Chaco phenomenon and the Hohokam:

Crown, Patricia L., and W. James Judge, eds. 1991. *Chaco and Hohokam: Prehistoric Regional Systems in the American Southwest.* Santa Fe: School of American Research.

For more detail on the research at Casas Grandes highlighted in the chapter's case study:

Whalen, Michael E., and Paul E. Minnis. 2001. *Casas Grandes and Its Hinterland: Prehistoric Regional Organization in Northwest Mexico.* Tucson: University of Arizona Press.

For insight into the topic of regional interaction currently important in southwestern archaeology:

Hegmon, Michelle, ed. 2000. *The Archaeology of Regional Interaction: Religion, Warfare and Exchange Across the American Southwest and Beyond: Proceedings of the 1996 Southwest Symposium.* Boulder: University Press of Colorado.

For discussion of the Hohokam at Pueblo Grande (see Chapter 1's case study):

Abbott, David R., ed. 2003. *Centuries of Decline: The Hohokam Classic Period at Pueblo Grande.* Tucson: University of Arizona Press.

OTHER RESOURCES

Sections H and I of the Student CD supply web links, additional discussion questions, and other study aids. The Student CD also contains additional resources, including a complete list of the references cited in this chapter and the case study that follows. Particularly relevant to this chapter are "The Dolores Archaeological Program: Documenting the Pithouse-to-Pueblo Transition" (Section D.4) and "Was There Cannibalism in the Prehistoric Southwest?" (Section F.4).

CASE STUDY

The pre-Columbian Southwest was the location of several large, aggregated Late Prehistoric sites. Understanding the nature and structure of the societies these sites represent is a major topic of research for Southwestern archaeologists. This case study describes investigations of the sociopolitical system centered in northern Mexico at the site of Casas Grandes, or Paquimé. Casas Grandes has been interpreted as a trading center that gained power from control of trade between the Mexican civilizations and Southwestern centers to the north. More recent interpretations have viewed this site as the powerful center of a Late Prehistoric regional system in the southern Southwest. Yet, as this case study indicates, until recently little research has been done to place this large site in the context of other sites in northern Mexico. Thus, we have known very little about the internal functioning of the Casas Grandes system. In some ways the work described here is quite basic because it is being done in an area about which so little is known. As you read this case study, think about how the kinds of information collected through survey and excavations at other related sites allow archaeologists to better understand Casas Grandes itself. What does this tell you about the nature of archaeology and about what makes a site important to archaeologists?

CASAS GRANDES AT THE EDGE OF THE SOUTHWESTERN AND MESOAMERICAN WORLDS

Paul E. Minnis and Michael E. Whalen

One of the major transformations among human groups was the development of complex societies. Such polities vary, but they are often characterized by the presence of cities, complicated economies in which individuals and families specialize in the production of specific goods, bureaucracies, monumental architecture, and rulers. The best-known examples of complex societies are the ancient states of the Near East, Mesoamerica, Asia, Africa, and South America. Yet, examples of complex societies are found throughout the world, including North America. Many factors must be examined in considering how such societies developed, as the matter is far from simple. For example, the rulers of early complex societies often exerted substantial influence over the local economy through tradition and taxation. At the same time, elites usually participated in a special economy involving the manufacture, distribution, and use of rare and exotic goods. Commonly, these goods were traded over long distances. Thus it is reasonable to ask how local and long-distance economies were related to the development of complexity.

The remains of one complex polity in North America were first visited by outsiders nearly four centuries ago. After an exhausting trek through what is now northern Mexico, an area that was thought to be a desolate hinterland, a small group of Spanish explorers lead by Francisco de Ibarra entered an unusually lush valley in present-day Chihuahua, Mexico. Here they encountered the ruins of a spectacular town, Casas Grandes, or Paquimé (Figure 9.24), probably deserted not much more than a century before the Spanish explorers set foot there. The expedition's chronicler, Baltzar de Obregón, described in 1584 what the Europeans saw:

> There are many houses of great size, strength, and height. They are of six and seven stories, with towers and walls like fortresses for protection and defense against the enemies who undoubtedly used to make war on the inhabitants. The houses contained large and magnificent patios paved with enormous and beautiful stones resembling jasper. There are knife-shaped stones which supported the wonderful and big pillars of heavy timber brought

FIGURE 9.24 Aerial view of Casas Grandes, or Paquimé, in Chihuahua, Mexico. (Photo by Adriel Heisey.)

> from far away. The walls of the houses were whitewashed and painted in many colors and shades with pictures of the buildings. The structures had a kind of adobe wall. However, it was mixed and interspersed with stone and wood, this combination being stronger and more durable than boards. (translated by Hammond and Rey 1928)

Although Paquimé had been known as an unusually important site since Obregón's time, it was not until three and one-half centuries later that its grandeur revealed, during three years of excavation by the Joint Casas Grandes Project, a collaborative effort between the Amerind Foundation, a private research organization in Arizona, and Mexico's National Institute of Anthropology and History. This massive project mapped the site and excavated hundreds of domestic rooms, ritual features, and other contexts. Our work as well as other projects around Casas Grandes have added to and revised the pioneering research of the Joint Casas Grandes Project, especially of its director, Charles C. Di Peso.

Any research is influenced by its historical context, and our work is no exception. Far northwestern Mexico is a poorly known area between two of the world's most intensively studied regions. Hundreds of archaeologists have studied thousands of archaeological sites for over a century to the north of Casas Grandes in the southwestern United States, where massive archaeological projects have been undertaken recently in compliance with cultural resource management statutes. To the south in Mesoamerica are the spectacular ruins of central Mexico, like the enormous ancient city of Teotihuacán and the Aztec capital of Tenochtitlán, as well as Mayan ruins still farther south. Relatively few Mexican archaeologists have devoted their lives to studying the less monumental remains in northern Mexico, and few North American archaeologists have crossed the border to work in a country with a different culture, language, and laws, as well as with fewer opportunities for research funding. Consequently, the prehistory of northwestern Mexico is not as well known as that of adjacent regions, and this affects the research questions one can ask.

WHAT WAS KNOWN

Because of the Joint Casas Grandes Project, we know a great deal about this one site, an unusual situation in northwestern Mexico. Casas Grandes reached its height during the **Medio** (Spanish for "Middle") **period**, from approximately 750 BP to 500 BP (AD 1200–1450), when it was one of the largest, if not the largest, community in northern Mexico and the southwestern United States, with 2000 rooms and a population of 2000 to 5000 inhabitants. Not only large, this site was very influential, the center of a regional society bound together by a web of social, religious, cultural, and economic relationships.

Casas Grandes is at the far southern end of the Puebloan world, a large area centered on what is now New Mexico and Arizona. Modern Puebloan groups, such as the Hopi, the Zuni, and the pueblos around the Rio Grande in New Mexico, are the descendants of those who built many ancient communities. Like today's Puebloan peoples, their ancestors were not all exactly alike, and Casas Grandes is but one variation of a general Puebloan way of life. The site's overall appearance is more Puebloan than Mesoamerican in its unplanned layout. The domestic architecture of Casas Grandes consists of suites of contiguous aboveground rooms arranged in room blocks. Yet, Casas Grandes is different in other ways; the rooms are unusually large, sometimes in eccentric shapes, with very thick adobe walls, and some room blocks were more than two stories tall. Even the Mesoamerican-inspired ceremonial architecture, like ball courts and platform mounds, are not arranged in as orderly a manner as they are at Mesoamerican centers.

Compared with other communities in the area, Casas Grandes has a far greater number of features suitable for ceremonies that would bring people together in shared rituals. Four types of ritual architecture are known: ball courts, platform mounds, feasting ovens, and ceremonial rooms. Ball courts usually have a flat I-shaped center, sometimes with embankments on either side. It is thought that ball courts in the Casas Grandes area and other parts of the southwestern United States, such as among the Hohokam to the northwest, were used to play a ball game with strong religious elements, as in Mesoamerica. Platform mounds probably hosted or marked important ceremonies, and enormous amounts of food to accompany public events were prepared in feasting ovens, some quite large (Figure 9.25). Various rooms throughout the site had unusual artifact assemblages, leading Di Peso to interpret them as ceremonial rooms.

No doubt very important ceremonies took place at Casas Grandes, and Paul Fish and Suzanne Fish (1999) suggest that Paquimé may have been a pilgrimage destination for people outside the immediate area. A recent analysis of symbols on painted pottery from the Casas Grandes region suggested to Christine Van Pool (2003) that the leaders of Casas Grandes may have been shaman-priests whose sacred knowledge was a major source of their power.

In addition to being a religious center, Casas Grandes was also an economic powerhouse. While so much attention has been focused on exotic and rare

FIGURE 9.25 Student standing inside excavated feasting oven at site 204.

goods, farming was its economic mainstay. Ever since Obregón's time, visitors have recognized that the river valley next to Casas Grandes was especially well suited for agriculture, with an unusually wide, fertile, and well-watered floodplain. This allowed the town to support a large population that ultimately grew to around ten times larger than the next largest communities. The farming productivity also facilitated surplus production, some of which may have been used by elites to help build their power and authority through giving feasts and other gifts.

Long-distance trade was important to Casas Grandes. Parrots, shell, and copper moved north, whereas turquoise was traded south. Parrots are especially significant. It appears that Casas Grandes learned how to raise scarlet macaws, a parrot native to the tropic forests of Latin America but not the high desert of Chihuahua. Most likely, Paquimé controlled if not monopolized trade in these parrots, whose feathers were prized by the ancient people of the North American Southwest. Both copper and shell artifacts ultimately came from west Mexico to the southwest. Charles Di Peso believed that Casas Grandes was founded by long-distance traders, known in Mesoamerica as *pochteca*, to coordinate trade between the North American Southwest and Mesoamerica.

Regardless of how the Casas Grandes economy was specifically organized, much surplus flowed in, probably creating one of the wealthiest communities in the ancient North American Southwest. As you might expect, wealth was not distributed equally; some families or groups had access to more wealth than others. This is most clearly seen in several locations at Casas Grandes. Excavation crews located several rooms that must have been warehouses, each packed with special goods, such as raw minerals, magnificent painted pottery vessels, and especially shell, over a ton of it. Whether these caches were hoards of devotional offerings made by pilgrims or part of a more secular economy is not yet known, but the concentration of such goods is evidence of differential access to wealth at Casas Grandes.

Wealth accumulation probably was reserved for elites, small groups of people with greater power or prestige than others. Perhaps the term "rulers" overemphasizes the power they were able to exert over their fellow citizens. There are no obvious palaces or especially fancy housing, so the best evidence for social hierarchy comes from burials. John Ravesloot (1988) analyzed the 576 human burials recovered by the Joint Casas Grandes Project. While some individuals were interred with more grave goods than others, the most obvious characteristic indicating elites was burial location. Most people were buried in simple pits with a few grave goods. However, two burial clusters were uniquely placed. The most unusual was a group of three people buried in large ceramic vessels in tombs within a platform mound. No one else in Casas Grandes was accorded such a burial. Most likely these were very special people during their lives.

One could devote much effort to describing the spectacular site of Casas Grandes; Di Peso and his colleagues did . . . in eight dense volumes. The remarkable site has been designated as a **World Heritage Site** by UNESCO. The uniqueness of Casas Grandes extends beyond its fancy trade goods, abundant ritual architecture, and monumental apartment buildings. One example of what would seem to be of mundane interest should suffice to illustrate this point. This site probably has the most complicated intrasite water distribution system of any community in pre-Columbian North America. Water was drawn from a spring 6 kilometers (3.7 mi) from the community and sent via a master canal to a collection reservoir, complete with a settling basin, which then fed water through a series of smaller sinuous canals that snaked through the room blocks. A second set of canals drained water away from the building, an important detail, since adobe walls are very vulnerable to water damage.

WHAT WE WANTED TO KNOW

For all the questions that remain about Casas Grandes—about its origin, dynamic history, social and political structure, and finally its demise—we now have a much better understanding than we did several generations ago. We know that for up to 250 years, it was one of the largest and most influential towns in the Puebloan world. Its leaders oversaw a thriving community of farmers with many artisans; it was a town that undoubtedly awed its neighbors. Fortunately, the careful work and detailed publications from the Joint Casas Grandes Project laid a strong foundation for future work.

But what should the future work be? That was the question facing us in the middle 1980s. As tempting as the prospect might be, expending more major efforts on Casas Grandes did not seem like a good idea. After some reflection, it became clear that while we knew much about Casas Grandes itself, little was known about its regional context. How did Casas Grandes relate to the hundreds of Medio period villages and hamlets scattered about the International Four Corners, where Arizona, New Mexico, Chihuahua, and Sonora join? How could we understand the role of long-distance relationships, such as those with Mesoamerica, if at the same time we didn't understand the local relationships? Therefore, we began a long-term, multiphase project to address these concerns.

The results, however, are not just of interest for understanding Casas Grandes. This site represents but one example of the beginnings of complexity, a problem that is being studied by archaeologists worldwide. Examining Casas Grandes can, therefore, help build a comparative base to address this issue. For example, a number of scholars have begun to suggest that the simplest, complex polities control an area smaller than previously thought. That is, power in such societies was weaker and spottier than anticipated. Was this the situation between 750 BP and 500 BP in what is now northwestern Chihuahua?

WHAT WE ARE DOING

With these thoughts in mind, we began our field research in the summer of 1989. We hope the results of our research will be a systematic body of data allowing us to interpret the local setting of Casas Grandes. The work should also be useful for future generations of archaeologists, even if they use the data to disagree with our conclusions, just as we have used Di Peso's data to disagree with his interpretations.

Reconnaissance and Systematic Survey

The logical first research step was to conduct a reconnaissance survey in the region, a location that had not had a wide-ranging archaeological survey since the 1930s. In 1989 we conducted a short two-tiered field season. First, we visited archaeological sites in northwestern Chihuahua that were known, either from the early surveys or to local residents with whom we spoke. Needless to say, we could not record all the sites; rather we concentrated in four areas of varying distances from Casas Grandes. The idea was that Paquimé's power and influence may have varied with different distances from the center. We chose four areas, from directly around Casas Grandes up to more than 60 kilometers (37 mi) away. Reconnaissance surveys like this one are an excellent way to acquire quickly and cheaply a basic understanding of the archaeological landscape. However, such quick surveys usually produce biased data; large, highly visible, and unusual sites are more likely to be recorded. To enable us to better judge the representativeness of our reconnaissance survey data, it was necessary to fit in some systematic surveying. Thus we chose two areas west of Casas Grandes at the foothills of the massive Sierra Madre Occidental to be surveyed systematically.

Unlike reconnaissance survey, during systematic survey crew members walk parallel lines covering all terrain in the survey unit. This type of survey is an excellent data-gathering technique in semiarid environments, where crews can easily see artifacts and remnants of structures on the surface because trees are few and groundcover sparse. In this setting, shovel testing, to remove the surface vegetation that commonly occurs in locations like eastern North America, can be dispensed with.

We do have to face one unfortunate problem: massive looting of sites. Because of the demand for prehistoric relics, almost all Medio period sites have been looted by hand digging to recover ceramic vessels originally left as grave offerings. Most pots then end up north of the border in the United States. Much irreplaceable information is lost forever, but we collect what data we can.

During our first field season, we visited nearly a hundred sites, filling out site forms, making systematic collections of surface artifacts, taking photographs, and preparing maps. As is common with many countries having a rich archaeological record and a history of many important artifacts leaving the country, Mexico prohibits removal of artifacts, so archaeologists must do basic artifact analyses in the field.

We were pleased that our first efforts in 1989 seemed to reveal some basic patterns. It seemed that sites within about a day's walk of Casas Grandes, an area we termed the core, were different from those farther away. For example, features such as ball courts and feasting ovens, of special importance for integrating the society, are far more abundant in the core than outside. Doughnut-shaped stones used as entrances to macaw pens, likewise, were far more common in the core area. We suspected that these patterns reflect tight control by Casas Grandes of communities within the core, whereas those more than a day's walk away (over 30 km, or a bit less than 20 mi), were relatively more independent. Despite the size and grandeur of Casas Grandes, its hegemony seemed to have been less extensive than anticipated.

The initial reconnaissance survey provided tantalizing patterns, but these were based on very small data sets. Fortunately, the National Science Foundation funded a large grant for a multiyear systematic survey. Our objective was to acquire a database large enough to support a proper evaluation of the hypotheses derived from the reconnaissance survey.

Despite the larger budget, we couldn't cover all of northwestern Chihuahua, so we needed to devise a research protocol to match our budget and research questions. Therefore, we worked in two major zones: the core zone within about 30 kilometers of Casas Grandes and what we termed the middle zone, centered on the San Pedro River about 60 kilometers north of Casas Grandes. The environments are not uniform within each study area, so from each zone we selected several similar survey areas, such as river valley and foothill settings, to help investigate the distribution of remains across the landscape.

Survey crews spent two long summer field seasons carefully and systematically walking over the survey locations, recording all archaeological remains encountered. By the end of this process, we had systematically covered over 200 square kilometers (80 mi^2) and recorded about 450 sites, of which the majority dated to the Medio period. As with our initial survey, we mapped and photographed each site, filled out a form, and collected surface artifacts, mostly chipped

stone and ceramics, but occasionally shell, turquoise, and other uncommon artifacts.

In general, we found that the patterns noted during the initial survey were replicated during systematic survey. Of course, the quality and variety of data were vastly better, and we continue to analyze these data. In addition, we now had data for the pre-Medio time periods, information we believe will be useful in research examining the origins of Casas Grandes. We published a number of articles about our results, but a book, *Casas Grandes and Its Hinterland: Prehistoric Regional Organization in Northwest Mexico* (Whalen and Minnis 2001b), was the major result of the systematic survey.

EXCAVATION

Excavation can provide information to answer questions that can't be adequately addressed with survey data alone. But which sites should we study? The most efficient approach for our research since 1996, given our time and funding limits, was to excavate ancient communities that probably played different roles in the regional system. Of course, much was already known about the center, Casas Grandes. We first decided to study the most common types of sites, hamlets where small groups lived in unremarkable communities. We chose two such sites having slightly different surface ceramic collections, which might indicate that they dated to slightly different times within the Medio period. Site 317, was small, and we excavated seven rooms and a small oven. Site 231 was a little larger, and here we had time to excavate about five rooms.

The next site studied, number 242, drew our attention when we first recorded it on reconnaissance survey. It had one of the largest and most elaborate ball courts outside of Casas Grandes itself (Figure 9.26). More importantly, it had the *only* platform mound we know of from a site other than Casas Grandes, which had about 18 platform mounds. The domestic mound also appeared different. On the basis of these characteristics, site 242 appeared to be an excellent candidate for study.

Unfortunately, we only had six weeks to test the site, and most of our efforts concentrated on the unusual domestic mound. As we suspected, excavation of a portion of the domestic mound revealed unusual architecture. Unlike the two villages we

FIGURE 9.27 Excavation of the floor of a room at site 204, La Tinaja.

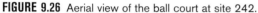

FIGURE 9.26 Aerial view of the ball court at site 242.

tested, which had small rooms and thin walls, the rooms at 242 were large and often more than simple rectangles. One room had 14 walls. Furthermore, the room walls were unusually thick. The domestic architecture of site 242, then, was more like Casas Grandes, 30 kilometers away, than like its neighbors. We have called the building form an "architecture of power" (Whalen and Minnis 2001a), and its presence, combined with the presence of the ball court and platform mound, suggests to us that this site was a secondary center within the Casas Grandes–dominated polity. Here agents or relatives of elites lived and held important ceremonies to help build and maintain the loyalty of outlying groups.

The three sites we tested through excavation are quite small, but there are larger sites in the Casas Grandes area. While much smaller than Casas Grandes (200 rooms vs 2000), they are still large by regional standards. The basic question for this phase of research regarded the role of large sites. Were they simply large communities, aggregations of families little different from the smaller villages, or were they structurally distinct, perhaps functioning like Casas Grandes?

Of two possible large sites to excavate, we chose the one that was more protected from looting. We had recently completed a three-season project at this site, number 204, or La Tinaja. A total of about 35 rooms from several different parts of the site were excavated, as were two feasting ovens, trash deposits, and the ball court (Figure 9.27). We are finishing up

our analysis, but it appears that there was a pre-Medio occupation and that the Tinaja site was most heavily occupied during the early part of the Medio period. This might suggest that the explosive growth of Casas Grandes occurred as it absorbed people from hinterland sites like La Tinaja. Our preliminary interpretation is that the Tinaja site was not a peer of Casas Grandes in the breadth and depth of its ritual importance.

Early during the excavation phase, we conducted a small study of prehistoric agricultural fields around Casas Grandes. Because of the low groundcover and the lack of historic farming that might have obliterated the remains of prehistoric fields, ancient rock walls (*trincheras*) built to retain soil and moisture, small canals, and rock pile fields can be seen on the surface. We had undertaken this study in anticipation of a future, larger-scale study of agriculture, but the results of our farming study helped interpret some of our excavation data. For example, the secondary center, site 242, is located next to a field system of nearly 100,000 square meters (25 acres), while the next largest field system was 8000 square meters (1.98 acres), with the average being about 2000 square meters (.5 acre). It appears that the elites at 242 were controlling some basic food production, but for what? An analysis of ceramics from this site showed an unusually high frequency of large pottery jars with interior pitting. It is quite likely that this pitting is due to acids from the fermentation of corn beer, which probably was consumed during important festivals held at 242. This example simply demonstrates how important it is in archaeology to draw together data from multiple sources to construct as complete as possible an interpretation of the past.

WHAT STILL NEEDS TO BE DONE

In an area where little archaeological research has been conducted, there are so many questions to answer and topics to address. Our work focused on the landscape of power: how extensive was Casas Grandes' power and influence? We have argued that Casas Grandes exerted its strongest control within an unexpectedly small region, on the order of 30 kilometers. Beyond this core area, the influence of Casas Grandes was felt to lesser degree and in differing ways. Not unexpectedly, not everyone agrees with our interpretations. Some other scholars argue that Casas Grandes exerted more powerful and wide-ranging control (see various articles in Newell and Gallaga 2003; Schaafsma and Riley 1999).

How power is distributed across the landscape, our research focus, does not tell what the power was like. Power and control can come in many forms: economic, political, social, and religious. Much more research is needed to understand the exact nature of power in middle-scale polities. Van Pool's recent argument that the elites of Casas Grandes derived (some) power through manipulation of sacred knowledge is important. Does this suggestion conflict with ideas that emphasized the economic aspects of power, or are the two types of power complementary, and if so, were they both important in the development of Casas Grandes?

We must also consider what the Casas Grandes area was like before the Medio period. Both Di Peso and some more recent scholars believe that the Casas Grandes region was a sleepy backwater in the Puebloan world, and that Casas Grandes had few cultural antecedents in the area. We believe that our survey and excavation at the Tinaja site demonstrate that there was a larger pre-Medio population than previously thought and that there are clear connections between pre-Medio and Medio peoples. Unfortunately, the only excavation of pre-Medio sites in the area around Casas Grandes was conducted nearly a half-century ago. More needs to be done.

Until recently, Casas Grandes was discussed only in relation to the question of Mesoamerican–

Southwest relationships. While our work emphasizes the local context of Casas Grandes, this region is still pivotal in addressing the issue of long-distance relationships. How were Mesoamerican symbols and religious structures used at Casas Grandes? How significant was trade between Casas Grandes and west Mexico? After all, Casas Grandes has more Mesoamerican goods and Mesoamerican-inspired symbols than any other site in the North American Southwest. Briefly, we think that Mesoamerican items, ideas, and icons were used by the local elites to help capture the loyalty of others and to help maintain their tenuous hold on power. Aspiring leaders used symbols and exotica known to have come from the great and powerful city to the south in an attempt to enhance their status among people in the region (Whalen and Minnis 2003). And it seems to have worked, but for only two centuries. Furthermore, understanding local and distant relationships in this case contributes to our understanding of the beginnings of civilization worldwide. The lesson, of course, is that we need to investigate our ancient past from many different approaches.

It is a cliché that research opens up as many questions as it answers, and our archaeological research in northern Mexico is no exception. New research not only provides fresh data but also directs us in more specific and productive ways of thinking about the distant past and about ourselves.

ACKNOWLEDGMENTS

Archaeological research is collaborative, involving many individuals and institutions. We have received funds from the National Science Foundation, the National Geographic Society, and the J. M. Kaplan Fund, as well as support from our home institutions, the University of Oklahoma and the University of Tulsa. Mexico's Instituto Nacional de Antropología e Historia, especially the Consejo de Arqueologia and the Centro Chihuahua, courteously provided oversight and advice. Project crew members, most of whom were students from many different states and five different countries, are responsible for the quantity and high quality of our data. Finally, the people of northwestern Chihuahua—landowners, colleagues, officials, and friends—all contributed to our ability to conduct research for the past 14 years.

DISCUSSION QUESTIONS

1. What and where is Casas Grandes, or Paquimé? Why is this site important to archaeologists?

2. Why is relatively little known about the regional archaeology around Casas Grandes, even though this site has long been of interest? How does the approach taken by the authors help remedy this situation?

3. What indications are there of the complexity and power of the Casas Grandes system? Compare these patterns with what you have learned about the Chacoan system.

4. At the end of this case study the authors suggest some of the areas in which further research is needed. Which of these would you choose to investigate first, and how would you structure your research?

CHAPTER 10

Bison Hunters and Horticulturists of the Great Plains

Like several other areas near western cities, Larimer County, Colorado, has a growing population. During the past decade, communities like Fort Collins, Loveland, and Windsor, with close access to Interstate 25, and thus the Denver metropolitan area, have been experiencing a major housing boom. The dry rangeland surrounding these communities is being transformed into suburban residential developments. In 1997 construction teams building one such development, River West in Windsor, made an unusual find. While grading for home sites and roads, they cut into a hillside and nicked the top of a large bed of bones about 18 feet (5.5 m) below the surface. Not that this interested the workers much; they had a job to do and their work continued. Then someone who happened to volunteer at the Denver Museum of Nature and Science stumbled upon the exposed bones, which were mainly from bison. As their existence and possible significance became known, archaeologists at Colorado State University (CSU) were contacted to take a look (Dold 2003).

It turned out that this deeply buried, well-preserved bone bed is the result of a bison kill dating to about 2700 years ago. Despite later disturbance by scavengers and by runoff from thunderstorms, this is one of the largest kill site accumulations ever found. Although there may be as many as 300 bison represented here, the kill site apparently was used only once, when Plains Archaic hunters drove a herd of bison into a steep-sided arroyo and trapped them so that others could spear them from above. Given the age data from tooth eruption in bison calves studied so far, this kill appears to have taken place in the late summer or the early fall, when archaeologists speculate people were seeking meat to dry and store for the winter. Interestingly, large amounts of available meat may never have been processed at all, perhaps because so many animals were trapped. Also, there are two different projectile point styles, believed to be diagnostic of both local and nonlocal ethnic groups during the Late Archaic. This raises questions about whether people were cooperating in dispatching the bison or competing for the meat made available by the kill.

Learning about this find, now called the Kaplan–Hoover site, has not been a simple matter. Excavation and analysis by CSU archaeologists led by Dr. Larry Todd (Todd et al. 2001) has been a major undertaking. The first problem, of course, was getting permission to excavate. Because the site was on private land, not to mention in the middle of a large construction site, archaeologists had no automatic right to work here. The property owner could proceed with development as he saw fit. Thus, an agreement had to be reached with the property owner that would not affect the construction plans. Fortunately, this was possible, and the site name honors the landowner and the owner of the cooperating construction company.

The physical excavation of the site was complicated by the nature of the deposits as well as by their location. While the excavation was under way a plastic shelter was erected over the site and heated in colder weather with portable propane heaters. Construction continued around the bone bed as the excavation took place. The site literally was a mass of bones, and there often was nowhere to stand or sit. Archaeologists ended up laying boards over the bone bed and working while lying prone on the boards, hanging over the bones. Just imagine how soon that must have become uncomfortable! Because bones cannot be excavated with the same tools that are suitable for more durable objects, recovery is a slow, painstaking process of brushing and picking with small bamboo sticks. To develop a detailed picture of what happened, archaeologists also needed to record very detailed information about the position, orientation, and associations of each bone. This meant careful measuring and recording of data points that could later be analyzed. Once in the lab, bone reconstruction also required a long and careful process. The upshot of all these requirements was that the entire Kaplan–Hoover site could not be excavated. An area having a cross-sectional width of only 3 feet (ca. 1 m) has been excavated; but this small sample has yielded at least 10,000 bones and artifacts for study (Dold 2003).

The Kaplan–Hoover excavation was a very public undertaking. In part this was the result of its location and the circumstances of its discovery, but the archaeologists working there viewed it as an educational resource for the community as well as a research opportunity. Thus, they opened their excavation to the public. Schoolchildren, teachers, and many others saw the site under excavation and learned about archaeology and bison hunters in the process. The local chapter of the Colorado Archaeological Society, an organization through which amateurs can become involved in archaeology, developed a public outreach program that sought to present both archaeological and Native American perspectives on bison hunting, eventually creating a traveling exhibit about the site. The Kaplan–Hoover site was placed on the **National Register of Historic Places**, which lists and protects sites and buildings of significance in the United States. Once National Register designation was obtained, funding for its purchase and preservation became possible. This funding was obtained from the Colorado State Historical Fund, which receives monies from gambling tax revenues. Thus, although most of the site has been reburied, its long-term management is now assured. Cooperation among the homeowners' association for River West, the Town of Windsor, and archaeologists has been critical in the preservation plan for the site.

The story of Kaplan–Hoover illustrates the unfolding of one contemporary archaeological project. Through the cooperation of many people and the application of preservation laws, an important site that was threatened is being studied and preserved rather than destroyed. This story also introduces a type of site that has been found many times on the western Great Plains, although few known examples are as large as Kaplan–Hoover. On the Plains, bison hunting was an ancient and persistent way of life, and bison kill sites are a colorful aspect of its cultural remains. Indeed, the Historic period version of this pattern, involving equestrian pursuit of bison herds, often is taken as culturally emblematic of the Plains. Nevertheless, there is much more to the story of the human past on the Great Plains, as we shall see in this chapter.

DEFINITION OF THE AREA

The Plains culture area incorporates the people and places of both the tall-grass prairie and the short-grass high plains that stretch from the Saskatchewan River to the Rio Grande and east from the foothills of the Rocky Mountains to the upper Mississippi River valley (Figure 10.1). The area comprises southern Alberta, Saskatchewan, and southwestern Manitoba, the eastern portions of Montana, Wyoming, and Colorado, all of North Dakota, South Dakota, Nebraska, and Kansas, and major portions of Texas and Oklahoma, as well as small parts of eastern New Mexico, northwestern Missouri, and western Iowa, and most of Minnesota. This huge area excludes the Prairie Peninsula discussed in Chapter 12, as well as the intermontane grasslands found further west, but otherwise corresponds roughly to the northern temperate grassland biome. The Plains culture area is routinely subdivided into five subunits: the Southern Plains, the Central Plains, the Northeastern Plains, the Middle Missouri, and the Northwestern Plains. These subareas are labeled in Figure 10.1, but boundaries for them are imprecise and are not drawn. In fact, as with all the culture areas we use in this text, the Plains culture area has been defined largely on the basis of historically known peoples. Since the nature and distribution of ethnic entities changed dramatically during the Historic period, it is important to remember that the boundaries of the whole culture area also are somewhat arbitrarily defined. Table 10.1 provides an outline of Plains culture history.

THE ENVIRONMENT

Most people think of the Great Plains as uniformly flat grasslands, but in fact, the area exhibits considerable internal environmental variability. For instance, climate varies tremendously within the Plains. Near the eastern margins annual rainfall is over 39 inches (99 cm), while in eastern Colorado it is less than 14 inches (35.6 cm), and in some areas it is even lower. Much of the western Plains lies in the rain shadow of the Rockies, but at higher elevations, as in the Black Hills of South Dakota, there is more rainfall (Wedel and Frison 2001). Because most of the rainfall comes in the winter, seasonal variation also is the rule. Particularly on the western Plains, droughts are frequent results of even slight changes in the controlling air mass flow. From north to south there also is great difference in the length of the growing season. While killing frosts are almost totally lacking in Texas, on the Canadian Plains the growing season is only three months long.

The topography of the Plains also is not uniform, though overall there is a gentle drop in elevation from west to east. The land surface is a product of sediment-laden streams flowing out of the Rocky Mountains in **Tertiary** times

FIGURE 10.1 The Great Plains culture area, showing sites that are mentioned in Chapter 10.

TABLE 10.1 Introduction to Great Plains Culture History

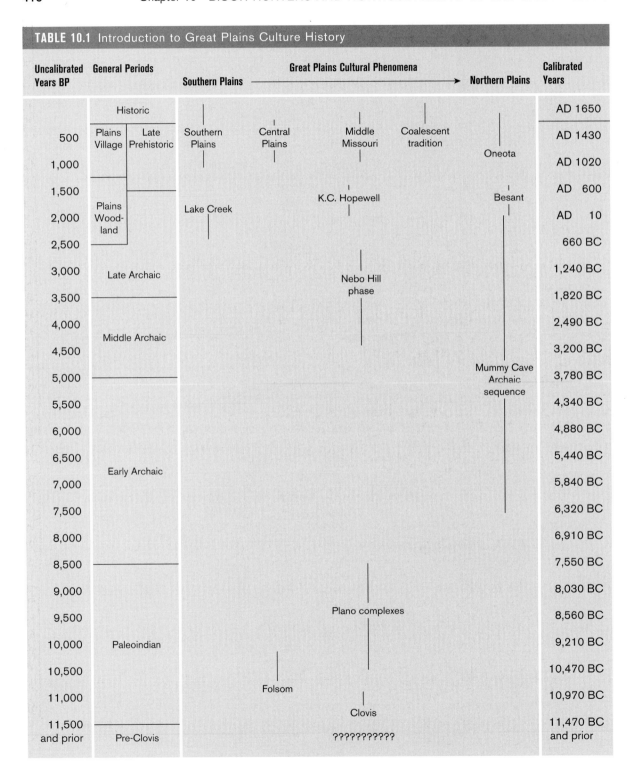

Uncalibrated Years BP	General Periods	Great Plains Cultural Phenomena						Calibrated Years
		Southern Plains →					Northern Plains	
	Historic							AD 1650
500	Plains Village / Late Prehistoric	Southern Plains	Central Plains	Middle Missouri	Coalescent tradition		Oneota	AD 1430
1,000								AD 1020
1,500	Plains Wood-land			K.C. Hopewell			Besant	AD 600
2,000		Lake Creek						AD 10
2,500								660 BC
3,000	Late Archaic			Nebo Hill phase				1,240 BC
3,500								1,820 BC
4,000	Middle Archaic							2,490 BC
4,500								3,200 BC
5,000						Mummy Cave Archaic sequence		3,780 BC
5,500								4,340 BC
6,000								4,880 BC
6,500	Early Archaic							5,440 BC
7,000								5,840 BC
7,500								6,320 BC
8,000								6,910 BC
8,500								7,550 BC
9,000								8,030 BC
9,500				Plano complexes				8,560 BC
10,000	Paleoindian							9,210 BC
10,500								10,470 BC
11,000		Folsom						10,970 BC
11,500 and prior	Pre-Clovis			Clovis				11,470 BC and prior
				???????????				

and depositing outwash across a wide area. This outwash has been variously eroded and dissected over time, as well as modified by glaciers in the northern sections. A mantle of **loess**, fine windblown sediment derived from glacial outwash, blankets many areas as well. These deposits, which can be several feet thick, are thought to have been created when wind picked up and redistributed fine sediments left by glaciers.

Two main physiographic provinces have been identified (Fenneman 1931, 1938): the Central Lowlands province on the east and the Great Plains province to the west. In the Central Lowlands province, a northern area that extends south to Iowa and includes the parts of the Plains in Minnesota and the eastern Dakotas, was glaciated recently. South of this, the Central Lowlands include the Dissected Till Plains, which contain older glacial deposits that have begun to erode, and further south still the Osage Plains, an unglaciated area of low relief with east-facing escarpments. The Great Plains physiographic province is also quite variable. Only the northernmost parts like the Alberta Plains and the Missouri Plateau north of the Missouri River Trench actually were glaciated (see Figure 2.12). The Unglaciated Missouri Plateau has at its center the Black Hills of Wyoming and South Dakota, which are underlain by older Precambrian rocks. Other parts of the Great Plains province are the High Plains, which are particularly featureless areas, the Plains Border in Oklahoma and Nebraska, and the Edwards Plateau in Texas.

There is one major distinction in Plains vegetation, the division between the tall-grass prairies to the east and the short-grass plains to the west at approximately the 100th meridian. At present, most areas west of the 100th meridian do not receive more than 20 inches (50.8 cm) of rain annually, and this dryness helps determine what grass species can grow there. The boundary, however, has undoubtedly shifted in the past just like the prairie–forest ecotone boundary on the east. Plains rivers incised into the landscape allow fingers of forest biomes to snake westward as well. Even further west, canyons containing watercourses support species that require more moisture. These valleys are ecotones with relatively high species diversity.

It also is true that distinct vegetation communities characterize particular locations within the Great Plains, such as the Sand Hills of western Nebraska. The Sand Hills cover about 20,000 square miles (51,800 km^2) and represent a stabilized dune field that formed during postglacial times in episodes of aridity (Koch and Bozell 2003). Upland areas within the Plains (e.g., the Black Hills in South Dakota) also provide variation in plants and animals. The margin with the Rockies also is not abrupt, particularly in the Northwestern Plains, where mountains and their foothills interfinger with plains across a broad area.

Climatic Change

The most significant environmental changes that have affected the human settlement of the Great Plains are those associated with the waning of the Wisconsin glaciation after its maximum at approximately 18,000 BP. As we showed in Figure 2.12, at its greatest extent the Laurentian glacier extended southward across the Canadian Plains and into the northern portion of Montana as well as through most of North Dakota into South Dakota, and via a separate lobe through Minnesota into central Iowa. In Alberta and northern Montana the two ice sheets parted at times as the glacier waxed and waned. This area is where the ice-free corridor (see Chapter 3) would have ended. Portions of southeastern Minnesota and northeastern Iowa were not glaciated during the Wisconsin, however.

The cooler climate of the Late Pleistocene meant less evaporation of moisture on the Great Plains as well as less seasonal variation in temperature. A spruce forest is believed to have spread from Iowa across northeastern Kansas, Nebraska, and the Dakotas, where it met a western coniferous forest from the Rockies (Kay 1998b). This forest may have been more open than dense boreal forests today. Grasslands probably characterized southeastern Montana and northeastern Wyoming, and there is growing evidence that a sagebrush grassland covered the southern High Plains (Hall and Valastro 1995). It is important to remember that the plant and animal communities of this period do not have modern analogues; rather, they comprised mixes of species not usually found together today.

As the Laurentian glacier shrank, complex and fundamental changes took place rapidly. Coniferous forest retreated northward along with the glaciers. At least on the eastern margins of the Plains, it first was replaced by deciduous forest, but by 10,000 BP grasslands were established in the majority of the Great Plains as the climate became drier and more seasonal. As more drought-tolerant grasses became dominant, large herbivorous species including mammoths were not able to survive. It is likely that reduction in habitat diversity and loss of more nutritious plant foods at the end of the Pleistocene were the critical factors in the demise of megafauna.

Another aspect of the northeastward retreat of the Laurentian glacier is the formation of large proglacial lakes. The most famous of these lakes is glacial **Lake Agassiz**, a giant lake that at one point or another, until it disappeared about 7500 years ago, inundated most of the area between the Rocky Mountains and the Lake Superior Basin and between South Dakota and Hudson Bay. The history of this large lake is important to local archaeological sequences in these parts of the Great Plains (Teller and Clayton 1983). As the ice sheet retreated toward Hudson Bay, drainage was blocked in every direction but south, trapping water between the rising land to the west and the glacier. Drainage first became possible through the Great Lakes, and finally the waters drained into the Tyrell Sea, which preceded Hudson Bay. As with all of North America's formerly glaciated areas, the landscapes of the northern parts of the Great Plains retain many glacial features including the pothole lakes that dot the northeastern prairies.

We also know that the Great Plains climate continued to warm in the early through mid-Holocene. The mid-Holocene warm, dry period called the Altithermal (ca. 7000–4000 BP) was especially important on the Great Plains. On the east, the extent of the grasslands increased and prairie vegetation extended well into the Midwest. Prairie also expanded in Manitoba. In the western High Plains it became appreciably drier and warmer than it is today. Sometime between 4500 and 4000 years ago—sooner in some areas, later in others—essentially modern conditions began to develop on the Plains (Kay 1998b). This does not mean that no climatic fluctuations occurred after this date; these lesser fluctuations, however, have had more localized effects. Of course drought continues to be a significant factor for the inhabitants of the Great Plains.

EARLY HUNTERS OF THE PLAINS

The earliest hunters on the Great Plains may have lived there during Pre-Clovis times. However, evidence for this occupation is as scarce and ambiguous here as in other parts of North America. Sites containing mammoth and other extinct fauna have been found in a number of places, but in contrast to the Kaplan–Hoover site described in this chapter's opening, the human association of these materials remains less clear. Several sites have provided possible evidence of this kind: Selby, Dutton, and Lamb Spring in eastern Colorado, Burnham and Cooperton in Oklahoma, as well as La Sena and Shaffert in Nebraska. In these sites, the fracture patterns of the megafaunal bones and their spatial distributions suggest humans, but stone tools have either been absent, not clearly tools, or rare enough to be considered intrusive. Pre-Clovis dating has not always been reliable, in any event (Hofman and Graham 1998; Stanford 1999).

The case of La Sena and Shaffert in the Medicine Creek valley of Nebraska is an example. Dates on the mammoth bones from these sites are, respectively, 19,000 BP to 18,000 BP and 15,600 BP. Although there are no stone tools in association with these bones, their fracturing is similar to fracture patterns noted in later Clovis sites, while the deep burial of this material away from a water hole setting argues against trampling by other animals as the fracturing agent (Holen and May 2002). At the Burnham site the skull of an extinct species of bison was recovered in apparent association with a cobble, a possible biface fragment, and flakes within deposits believed to be 26,000 years old. These tools, however, may be intrusive from younger deposits (Wyckoff 1999). Thus, a Pre-Clovis presence is not established on the Great Plains.

Clovis and Later Paleoindians on the Plains

The Plains are the part of North America in which archaeologists first found Paleoindian evidence. Both the Folsom and Blackwater Draw sites (see Chapter 3 and "Weaponry of Clovis Hunters at Blackwater Draw," in Section D.2 of the Student CD) are located in the Southern Plains. Clovis points actually were first discovered at the Dent site in eastern Colorado in 1932, but they were not recognized as a separate type of fluted point until after they also had been found at Blackwater Draw. Today, the evidence for Clovis and later Paleoindians is pervasive on the Plains, and a significant number of buried and stratified kill sites are known.

Archaeologists identify a series of Paleoindian projectile points assumed to relate to temporally, and to a lesser extent spatially, distinct groups of people living on the Great Plains (Figure 10.2). The deeply buried, stratified sites of the Great Plains have allowed archaeologists to construct a detailed sequence of projectile point types. Clovis represents the oldest well-documented Paleoindian complex. Dates from Plains Clovis sites are tightly clustered between 11,500 BP and 10,900 BP (Stanford 1999). Folsom points, with their lengthier flutes, follow Clovis points in many stratified sites, including Blackwater Draw. This complex is generally considered to date between 10,900 BP and 10,200 BP. A point type called Midland, after a site in Texas, may be an unfluted Folsom variant, although its interpretation is debated (Amick 1995). In the northern Plains the unfluted Goshen point, dating to approximately 10,900 BP or 10,800 BP, may be intermediate between Clovis and Folsom. Goshen is also similar technologically to the Plainview point of the Southern Plains, which has been found in deposits dating throughout the Paleoindian sequence. The sequences for these point types are still being refined.

In Plains Paleoindian sequences, younger unfluted lanceolate, stemmed, and unstemmed projectile points collectively called Plano points also are prevalent.

FIGURE 10.2 In the Great Plains archaeological record, fluted points are followed by a series of unfluted lanceolate points.

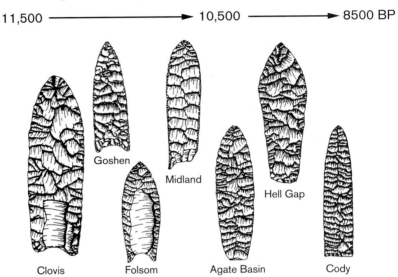

Plains Paleoindian Points

11,500 ————————————→ 10,500 ————————→ 8500 BP

Goshen

Midland

Hell Gap

Clovis   Folsom   Agate Basin   Cody

These are the Late Paleoindian points of the Great Plains. The first of these is the unstemmed Agate Basin point, which was made on the High Plains between approximately 10,500 BP and 10,250 BP. It occurred above the Folsom levels at the Agate Basin and Hell Gap sites in eastern Wyoming. Agate Basin–like points have been found in the eastern Rocky Mountains, in northern Canada, and along the Plains–Prairie margin. In the latter case, at sites like Cherokee Sewer in Iowa and Packard in northeastern Oklahoma, they have been called the **Packard complex** with dates between 9400 BP and 8500 BP—much later than Agate Basin on the High Plains. Stanford (1999) suggests that Agate Basin technology originated further west in the Plateau or Great Basin, while others propose a derivation from Folsom (Hofman and Graham 1998). The Hell Gap point, a second variety of lanceolate point, is a little younger than Agate Basin on the High Plains (ca. 10,000 BP). These stemmed points have been found at a variety of kill sites such as the Casper site in Wyoming, where 100 or more bison were trapped in a parabolic sand dune (Frison 1974). They also have been found in sites of other types, such as the quarry-related Seminoe Beach site in Wyoming, where quartzite cobbles from the bed of the North Platte River were used to make these points. The Cody complex subsumes a variety of stemmed Plano points with square bases and shoulders (e.g., Scottsbluff, Alberta Cody). Cody complex points are found in association with a distinctive knife form known as the Cody knife (Figure 10.3). Defined in this way, the Cody complex is the most widespread of the Plains Plano complexes. It dates between 10,000 BP and 8000 BP. Between 9000 BP and 8500 BP a variety of lanceolate point types including Allen, Frederick, Lusk, and Angostura points have been found on the Plains. Certainly, they denote the transition to the Archaic, which might be called the Terminal Late Paleoindian.

Although projectile point typologies are important, Paleoindians did make other tools. For example, Clovis lithic assemblages include large stone bifaces,

FIGURE 10.3 The Cody knife.

blades, blade cores, gravers, burins, and many cutting and scraping tools (Stanford 1999). Clovis contexts also have yielded bone foreshafts and projectile points, ivory billets, and flaked mammoth bones (see Figure 3.16). Engraved cobbles have been found at the Gault site in Texas (see Figure 3.17). Similarly, Folsom stone tool assemblages commonly include unifacial and bifacial knives, end scrapers, drills, burins, and wedges; the same people are known to have made eyed bone needles, projectile points, fleshers, and more ornamental objects such as bone beads and incised disks. The complete toolkits of Paleoindians are consistent with the presumed emphasis on hunting, and the common use of high-quality raw materials provides the general impression that quality and reliability were important to these early people.

Biface and blade cache sites also are important indicators of the high value placed on lithics. At the Anzick cache site in Montana, the Clovis artifacts were covered with red ocher, a substance often reserved for ritual use, and human remains recovered here indicate that this was a burial site. Other caches such as Clovis blade caches from Blackwater Draw did not appear to be associated with burials. At the Drake cache in northeastern Colorado, 13 new or resharpened projectile points and a hammerstone were recovered (Stanford and Jodry 1988). Caches are not just from Clovis hunters. At the Ryan site near Lubbock, Texas, 13 Plainview points, 50 blanks or preforms and, unifacial tools mostly of chert that outcrops 125 miles (200 km) away were recovered (Litwinionek et al. 2003).

Because Plains Paleoindian sites so often have been kill sites, the association of Paleoindians with the hunting of large game is clear. Clovis is associated with mammoth hunting, although the remains of other animals, such as camels, horses, and bison that left traces of their blood on Clovis points have been found in Clovis sites (e.g., Kooyman et al. 2001). In addition, other subsistence remains are known from Clovis sites. At the Lewisville site in Texas, the bases of several hearth features have produced the remains of small mammals, amphibians, reptiles, reptile eggs, baked mud-dauber larvae, and hackberry seeds (Stanford 1999). Of course, the mere presence of other species at Clovis sites does not tell us that they were important dietary items (Waguespack and Surovell 2003).

Folsom and later Paleoindians were the originators of the bison hunting way of life that persisted in one form or another on the Great Plains into the Historic period. There is some evidence that Folsom corresponds to a relatively wet period when the grassland environment that favored the bison became stabilized in the southern part of the Plains. Bison population numbers must have increased dramatically, both because the grassland was expanding and because herbivorous competitors had become extinct. Many sites provide examples of how bison were hunted by Folsom and later Paleoindians. In Folsom times ambushing bison at springs and playa lakes seems to have been the most common strategy. Reliance on simple ambushing, usually as an isolated event, could explain the generally small number of bison found in Folsom sites (Stanford 1999). For example, at the Lubbock Lake site in Texas only a few individuals have been found in the Folsom levels.

Later Paleoindians sites often contain a hundred or more bison, and more than one episode of hunting may be represented at a single site. Archaeologists have found drives, traps, and jumps. For example, at the Jones–Miller site in eastern Colorado, an impoundment was built at the head of an arroyo by Hell Gap hunters. Based on the age profiles of more than 150 bison, there were at least two episodes of hunting, one in the late fall and one in the early spring (Stanford

1999). At the Olsen–Chubbock site in eastern Colorado, 200 bison were killed and systematically butchered (Wheat 1972).

It also is clear that Folsom and later Paleoindians exploited other animals besides bison. Diverse faunal assemblages were recovered from these levels at Lubbock Lake in Texas (Eileen Johnson 1987). Approximately 50 kinds of animals were recovered from the Allen site, a Paleoindian site containing Agate Basin and Hell Gap points in Nebraska. Included in the faunal assemblage were bison, deer, antelope, jackrabbit, cottontail, prairie dog, and small amounts of freshwater mussel, catfish, birds, bear, and wolf (Bamforth 2002).

The Paleoindian archaeological record from the Great Plains suggests strongly that these hunters were highly mobile and lived in small bands. The same bands probably ranged between the mountains and the High Plains, while bands located toward the east may well have ranged into the woodlands. However, as mentioned in Chapter 3, there is a significant amount of debate about the character of Paleoindian lifestyles. Archaeological interpretations have been hampered by the relative lack of non-kill sites. Other special-purpose sites like quarry-related sites (e.g., Hell Gap) add less detail to the picture than we would like to have. Only a few sites provide a more complete picture of Paleoindian lifestyles. One of the most famous is the Lindenmeier site, which is located in the same Colorado county as the Kaplan–Hoover bone bed but was excavated back in the 1930s. Folsom hunting bands used this campsite repeatedly, as attested by the variety of activities represented in the tool assemblages and the size of the site (Wilmsen 1974). The Allen site in Nebraska may have been a similar sort of site (Bamforth 2002).

Archaeologists disagree over whether Paleoindians on the Great Plains were specialized or generalized hunter-gatherers. Kelly and Todd's (1988) highly influential model, which viewed Paleoindians as unlike any known hunter-gatherers, suggested that these people were specialized hunters, highly mobile and "technology oriented." However, many researchers believe that even on the Plains, Paleoindians were opportunistic hunters with a more generalized subsistence base (Eileen Johnson 1991), and some have argued that local records indicate repeated reuse of sites and movement within more localized territories (Bamforth 2002). In reality, much more data on Paleoindians must be obtained before archaeologists can reliably assess subsistence and settlement patterns.

PLAINS ARCHAIC

Paleoindian lifeways persisted on the Great Plains even after they had disappeared in other parts of North America. In fact, because subsistence and settlement do not seem to have abruptly changed, archaeologists have had difficulty defining the beginning of the Archaic except by using changes in projectile point morphology. On this basis, the Paleoindian period can be considered to end and the Archaic to begin at approximately 8500 BP when lanceolate projectile points were replaced across the Plains by a variety of notched forms.

There are several schemes for subdividing the millennia that follow this change, for although a hunting and gathering way of life persisted in many parts of the Plains throughout Columbian past, a horticultural lifeway did develop along the river valleys and in the prairies after approximately 2500 BP. This second type of lifestyle can be considered Woodland, and is usually so designated;

FIGURE 10.4 Side-notched and corner-notched projectile points mark the beginning of the Archaic period on the Great Plains.

FIGURE 10.5 Late Archaic tanged knives; the specimens at the top have been worn and resharpened.

but calling everything after 2500 BP "Woodland" seems to deny the continuation of ancient patterns of hunting and gathering. The problem is one encountered in many parts of North America after discovery of much greater diversity in human adaptations than had been envisioned in the traditional concepts of stages. In this chapter, we approach this problem by designating periods, while recognizing considerable variation from one part of the Plains to another (Table 10.1). This means that although we end the Archaic period at approximately 2500 BP and follow it with **Plains Woodland** and later periods, we emphasize the arbitrariness of this ending. The dashed line at 2500 BP in Table 10.1 indicates that the end of the Archaic is difficult to fix precisely. Within the Archaic, we refer to the three traditional subperiods: Early Archaic (ca. 8500–5000 BP), Middle Archaic (ca. 5000–3500 BP), and Late Archaic (ca. 3500–2500/1500 BP), but we consider these designations largely arbitrary. Our approach doesn't completely resolve the difficulty just described, but we hope it simplifies variable adaptations in a way that is sensible for the novice student. If you pursue the archaeology of the Plains, expect to encounter different terminology and schemes (e.g., Vehik 2001).

The change to notched projectile points that marks the beginning of the Archaic has sometimes been interpreted as indicative of hunters adopting the atlatl, which is thought to require smaller darts and points than the thrusting spears of the Paleoindians (Frison 1998, 151). A variety of projectile point forms have been recovered from stratified deposits, which allows archaeologists to date them (Figure 10.4). For example, the sequence of points at Mummy Cave in northwestern Wyoming has been useful in developing northern Plains sequences. Here the Archaic strata, which are preceded by Paleoindian strata, have been dated from 7630 BP to 2050 BP (Frison 1991b, Table 2.6). The majority of Plains Archaic points are believed to have been dart points, but some Late Archaic points may be small enough to have served as arrow points. Distinctive notched or tanged knife forms also have been recognized in the Archaic (Figure 10.5). These knives have a beveled edge and initially were made with side notches. During the Late Archaic, knife notches were placed at the corner opposite from the knife edge to create a tang, and the bevel was emphasized by resharpening along one edge from one side so that the knives became increasingly asymmetrical (Frison 1991b, 132).

Archaic sites also contain more grinding implements than are found in Paleoindian sites. Grinding tools are considered evidence of increased emphasis on plant foods, notably seeds that must be ground to be digestible. In addition to these sorts of implements, rock-filled pits, slab-lined hearths, and other fire pit features believed to have been used to cook vegetables and other foods are common Archaic period features. The stones in such pits are thought to have been heated on a bed of coals, with food to be cooked placed on top, perhaps in a green hide, and covered with earth or mulch to enable it to cook slowly. Processing of vegetable foods is inferred from the frequent association of grinding implements with these features, which nevertheless also sometimes contain mussel shell and small-animal remains. For example, at the Gore Pit site in southwestern Oklahoma, dated between 7000 BP and 6000 BP, several large circular basins containing burned rock, mussel shell, and some animal bone apparently were earth ovens. Late Archaic rock middens in central Texas are believed to have been used in processing desert plants like sotol and yucca (Vehik 2001, 150).

There also is some indication of structure types during the Archaic. Pithouses dating as early as the end of the Early Archaic have been found on the

Northwestern Plains. Fire pits and storage pits often are present, and the structures most frequently seem to have been circular, with a single central post supporting a conical roof. For example, a well-preserved pithouse dated to 5300 BP to 3100 BP was found at the Medicine House site on the North Platte River in south central Wyoming. Pithouses, which continue to be found in Middle Archaic sites from this area, are thought to have been winter houses. In other Plains contexts, postholes that have been found suggest houses of other types. Stone circles presumed to have been tipi rings also occur, but because these circles often have very little artifactual debris, they are difficult to date (Frison 2001). In the Northwestern Plains of Wyoming, Montana, Alberta, and Saskatchewan, **medicine wheels**, or circular stone alignments with central cairns and radiating spokes, also are enigmatic. These apparently ritual or sacred constructions have captured the popular imagination, but they are not well understood. At least some of these constructions date to the Archaic, but they continue into the Late Prehistoric as well.

The subsistence constant for the Archaic on the Plains was, of course, the buffalo or bison. The modern species of bison, *Bison bison*, evolved from larger Pleistocene bison species, *Bison antiquus* and *Bison occidentalis*, that have sometimes been found in Paleoindian sites. Bison provided meat, hides, and bones for tools and other purposes. Bison kills in late summer to fall would have provided animals with the most meat and fat, since at this time of year the animals themselves were preparing for the onslaught of winter by fattening up. Archaeologists believe that Plains Archaic people cached surpluses of meat for their own use in winter. Bison were hunted both by individuals or small groups and communally by large numbers of people. The communal hunts have captured our imagination, but smaller kills probably also were frequent. We know that Archaic hunters drove bison into arroyo traps, parabolic sand dune traps, and artificial corrals, as well as off steep bluffs.

Many Archaic period sites help archaeologists understand the ways in which bison were hunted. The Hawken site in the Black Hills of Wyoming represents an arroyo trap bison kill site used for several bison drives during the Early Archaic around 6400 BP. Nearly 300 projectile points have been recovered from this site. At the Middle Archaic Scoggin site in south central Wyoming, a corral was built to contain bison at the base of a steep talus slope. Archaeologists believe that hunters drove the bison down the slope and then, standing on the top, were able to pick off the bison before the animals could escape by charging back up the slope. Stone boiling pits outside the corral area probably were used to process the animals (Frison 1991b, 193). Partially butchered bison have also been found on the eastern margins of the Great Plains at sites like Cherokee Sewer in Iowa (Duane C. Anderson et al. 1980). Of course, the Kaplan–Hoover site from the chapter opening also is a Late Archaic site.

These dramatic bison kill and butchering sites captured the American imagination and led to stereotypes about Plains bison hunters. Like all stereotypes, there is some truth in such a characterization, but anachronistic artistic representations of these events abound: contrary to many depictions, the horse was not present until Protohistoric times; bison hunting thus was done on foot, and dogs were the only pack animals as hunters journeyed to and from the kill sites. Moreover, bison was not the only resource utilized by the Archaic hunter-gatherers of the Great Plains. Other animal resources like deer, antelope, rabbit, prairie dog, birds, and even fish and freshwater mussels are known. Plant remains found in Archaic sites include acorns, various native seeds, fruits, and in some areas xerophytic edible plants like yucca and sotol. For example, at the Coffey site, north of Manhattan, Kansas, faunal remains from a series of encampments dating to 5270 to 5055 years ago include much bison but also deer, other mammals, fish, and migratory waterfowl, while archaeologists also have recovered plant remains from lamb's quarter, hackberry, bulrushes, grape, knotweed, and Solomon's seal. Shell midden sites and rock midden sites where plants may have been roasted are common in the Southern Plains.

In fact, archaeologists have just begun to understand the great variability in Archaic adaptations across the Plains. Part of this variability is related to climatic and other environmental change during the Archaic. The Early Archaic roughly corresponds to the mid-Holocene warm, dry period called either the Hypsithermal or Altithermal. While on the eastern and northern margins of the Plains this led to an expansion of grasslands, in the short-grass areas of the western Plains it may have meant conditions dry enough to reduce the amount of forage for bison and prevent the survival of other resources. Earlier archaeologists proposed that the western Plains were mostly abandoned during the Altithermal, but today we know that some people did continue to live on the Plains, perhaps exploiting mountain habitats at certain times of the year (Vehik 2001). Archaeological work at the High Plains Mustang Springs site, near Midland, Texas, revealed that foragers dug wells to obtain water during the Altithermal (Figure 10.6) (Meltzer 1991a). In better times, this site was at the location of a spring-fed pond, but after 6800 BP the spring failed, and humans who came there dug over 60 wells into the dry lake bed. Similar wells have been found at other Southern Plains sites including Blackwater Draw.

Although we can expect considerable variability, the Archaic hunter-gatherers of the Plains were mobile hunter-gatherers. In the Southern Plains, particularly in drier periods, these people may have camped near water sources, making forays into the surrounding region to obtain meat. Elsewhere a more cyclical pattern of nomadism probably obtained, with small bands having an approximate seasonal round that could be adjusted to seasonal and annual conditions. Group structure would have been flexible, so that at some seasons and in some places aggregations of bands took place, perhaps to cooperate in bison hunting and/or to find mates, share information, and exchange raw materials (Hofman 1989). Sites like Spring Creek in southwestern Nebraska apparently represent base camps in such a system. Here one finds widely spaced hearths, bone piles, storage pits, **postmolds**, and a variety of subsistence remains including bison, deer, antelope, beaver, and migratory waterfowl, as well as chipped and ground stone tools of many types, all indicative of a multipurpose site (Kay 1998a).

Late Archaic Developments

The lifestyles of most Plains people during the Archaic represent broadly similar generalized foraging adaptations to local resource availability and distribution. This way of life persisted for millennia. On the Canadian and Northwestern Plains, the Archaic can be considered to continue for another millennium after 2500 BP and to directly precede the Late Prehistoric beginning about 1500 BP (Frison 2001).

In contrast, some Middle to Late Archaic complexes in the Central Plains already foreshadowed later Plains Woodland developments. A distinctive Nebo

FIGURE 10.6 Wells dug during the Altithermal by Archaic period foragers at the Mustang Springs site near Midland, Texas.

Hill lanceolate point (Figure 10.7) has been known for some time by archaeologists working along the Kansas–Missouri border in an area centering on Kansas City. Although once thought to be a Paleoindian or Early Archaic point type because of its form, this point has been radiocarbon dated to between 4500 BP and 2600 BP, spanning the Middle to Late Archaic of the area (Reid 1984). Other artifacts associated with this phase are bifacial hoes, bifacial gouges, rectangular and ovate manos, rectangular celts, and three-quarter-grooved axes (O'Brien and Wood 1998). Besides lithic artifacts, **fiber-tempered pottery**, untempered pottery, and ceramic human effigy fragments have been recognized in sites of this phase. Pottery with shredded fibers mixed through the clay (Kay 1998a, 180) is the oldest pottery in the Plains culture area and older than any midwestern pottery, as well.

Large sites of the **Nebo Hill phase** are found in the uplands bordering the Missouri River, while smaller encampments have been found in the valleys of the

FIGURE 10.7 Nebo Hill lanceolate points.

5 cm

Missouri's tributaries. Upland biface caches and burial mounds also are known. The chert in Nebo Hill burial mounds appears to be exotic, having come from central Missouri or further away. In addition, one rolled copper bead and a lump of **galena** indicate some long-distance interaction. Subsistence information suggests that Nebo Hill people exploited deer, squirrel, bird, turtle, fish, nuts, and seeds, including chenopodium, but no obvious cultigens have been found.

CLUES TO THE PAST

EXHIBIT 10.1

Hide Scrapers

The scraper, a tool with a steep working edge used to scrape hides or wood, was made and used so often by the inhabitants of the Great Plains that it deserves further discussion. For

example, at the Lashley Vore site in Oklahoma, which may have been the Wichita site visited by the French trader Jean Baptiste Bénard de la Harpe in 1719, Odell found that 30 percent of

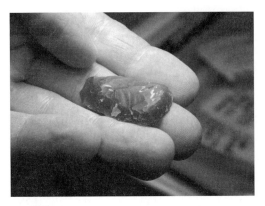

FIGURE 10.8 Plains end scraper.

the tools were scrapers (Odell 2002). It is not unusual in Great Plains sites for scrapers to outnumber projectile points.

An important tool type throughout the post, scrapers usually were made from flakes or cores by further chipping or retouching to create the necessary steep edge. A scraper made from a flake required chipping on one face only. Such unifacial scrapers were made with the scraping edge on one side (side scrapers), on the end (end scrapers), or even on both the sides and the ends (**distolateral scrapers**). Unifacial end scrapers made from flakes are the most frequent type found on the Great Plains (Figure 10.8). They have one face that is relatively flat. The other face is convex in cross section because of the steep retouch, which was done with percussion flaking or, in small specimens, with pressure flaking. Such a unifacial implement is called a plano-convex end scraper. The snub-nosed end scraper, another form, is triangular in outline, with the scraping edge made on the broader end (Lehmer 1971, 75). Bone also was used as the scraper bit and, starting in the Protohistoric, metal; but until then, stone scrapers were most common.

Plains end scrapers may have been held in the hand, particularly if they were large, but smaller ones probably were most often hafted to a wooden or bone shaft. Sinew was used to fix the stone to the shaft. Several haft styles would have been possible, but unfortunately the handles and the sinew have not been preserved often enough to allow an assessment of any variability.

An antler scraper handle was found at the Kruse site in Kansas (Rohn and Emerson 1984).

Archaeologists can assess the function of scrapers by examining edge wear and breakage microscopically, but this has been done infrequently. At Lashley Vore, Odell found that hide scraping was the most frequent single type of wear on the stone tools (Odell 2002, 252). Most archaeologists have simply assumed that scrapers were used to work the many hides obtained from bison and other animals. Hides were processed prior to use so that they did not rot and were pliable enough to be worked into clothing and other items. Most of us today do not know how to tan a hide, but there are many accounts of how Plains and other people processed hides. Once removed from the carcass, a hide must be scraped to clean off hair on the outer surface and any fatty tissue adhering to the inner surface. Hides probably were pegged on the ground or stretched on a frame before scraping (Figure 10.9). Tanning, which today may be done with chemicals, was first accomplished by mashing animal brains to release tannic acid and conditioners, and rubbing the paste into the hides. After tanning has rendered the hide soft and supple, it is soaked in water. Additional scraping and buffing of the hide and smoking it over a fire sealed the leather from moisture and made it usable.

Plains people used hides for clothing, for skin bags and other containers, and for tipi covers. Native Americans in the Middle Missouri

FIGURE 10.9 Scraping of a hide staked to the ground in one traditional Native American method of preparation.

area also made a kind of skin boat known as a **bullboat** (Ahler et al. 1991). After Europeans arrived in North America, natives processed hides for trade as well as domestic uses. The trade in hides probably is related to the manufacture of larger numbers of scrapers, although this connection has been better documented in the Southeast (Cobb 2000) than on the Plains. Calculations of the ratio of scrapers to projectile points would be one simple measure archaeologists could employ to test this idea.

Just as hide processing was a universal activity, the presence of scraping tools in the Great Plains is ubiquitous. However, there is some variability in the types, the sizes, and the numbers of scrapers found across the Great Plains, and these differences have sometimes been helpful in distinguishing cultural complexes. In general, variability in scrapers has not been explored to the degree reached for projectile points or pottery vessels. In fact, consistent morphological categories for scrapers have not been employed. In contrast to projectile points, which were implements of the hunt and warfare, hide scrapers might be considered women's tools because ethnohistorically the processing of hides was a female activity. Women may have manufactured scrapers as well as used them. These gender implications have not been explored. Clearly, new areas of research concerning the apparently humble and domestic scraper may yet be possible.

THE WOODLAND PERIOD ON THE GREAT PLAINS

Despite the persistence of many aspects of the foraging way of life, archaeologists recognize a Woodland period on the Great Plains that begins when pottery, burial mounds, and sometimes horticulture began to be adopted by many Plains groups. Corner-notched projectile points may be another diagnostic for the Plains Woodland (Ann Mary Johnson and Alfred E. Johnson 1998). Given earlier developments like the Nebo Hill phase, it isn't surprising that the first Woodland complexes are found in the Central Plains and the Northeastern Plains at approximately 2500 BP. In the Kansas City area, specimens of thick, stone-tempered pottery with geometric designs incised on the rim has been found in several sites that have been radiocarbon dated as early as 2495 BP. In northwestern Iowa, the first ceramics are dated to 2345 BP. In southwestern Minnesota, ceramics were made as early as 2150 BP (Alfred E. Johnson 2001).

Such early developments are not found elsewhere on the Plains; but pottery, mounds, and sometimes horticulture in many areas of the Plains have been dated after approximately 2000 BP. Some authorities call the period after 2000 BP the **Ceramic period** (e.g., Adair 1988). One of the best-known Woodland complexes is **Kansas City Hopewell**, which after approximately 2000 BP produced pottery with cord-wrapped stick impressions, dentate stamping, and eventually punctated, crosshatched, or plain rims suggestive of Hopewell ceramics found in the Illinois River valley in the Midwest (Figure 10.10). Large villages located on the stream bluffs as well as smaller camps occupied for shorter periods and burial mounds have been assigned to Kansas City Hopewell. These mounds, located on the bluff tops near villages, have central stone tombs and also contain cremations, as well as **secondary** and **primary burials**. Horticulture was present, and maize, squash, and marsh elder have been recovered, but hunting and gathering were still important subsistence pursuits. Deer, fish, turkey, nuts, and wild seeds all were utilized.

FIGURE 10.10 Examples of Kansas City Hopewell pottery.

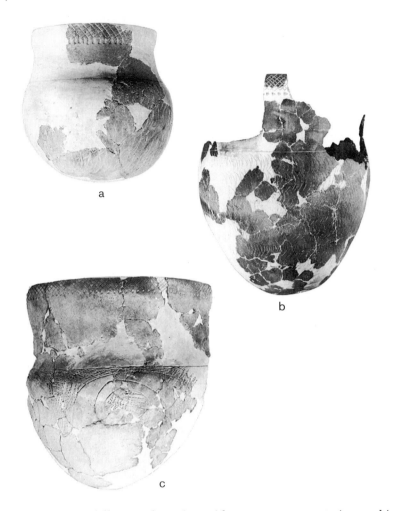

a

b

c

A very different adaptation with an economy centering on bison hunting rather than horticulture is associated with the **Besant phase** of the Northwestern Plains beginning about 1850 BP. Often designated as Late Plains Archaic because of their proficiency in bison hunting (e.g., Frison 1998), Besant people made grit-tempered, cord-roughened, undecorated ceramics, and they also constructed burial mounds, at least in the Dakotas along the Missouri River bluffs, where archaeologists have designated a **Sonota Burial complex** (A. M. Johnson and A. E. Johnson 1998). The large and broad, corner-notched Besant point (Figure 10.11), as well as Besant ceramics, are found widely in the Northwestern Plains, and the dilemma of determining whether such artifacts are Archaic or Woodland illustrates the problems associated with generalizing about these patterns on the Great Plains.

An example of Middle Woodland developments on the Southern Plains is the **Lake Creek focus** in the Texas and Oklahoma panhandles and adjacent areas in which ceramics and corner-notched points have been found along with quartz and limestone-tempered ceramics, as well as some brownware similar to Jornada

FIGURE 10.11 Examples of the Besant projectile point.

Mogollon pottery in the Southwest. People's lifeways were very similar to those of the generalized hunter-gatherers of the Archaic period in this area, with the addition of ceramics and arrow points (Hofman and Brooks 1989).

Many Late Woodland complexes also have been defined based on ceramic attributes as well as the widespread presence of arrow as opposed to dart points. Arrow points, recognized by their small size, may occur in earlier Woodland and even Late Archaic complexes, but they are more common after 1500 BP. For example, the **Keith complex**, which is found in sites extending from the prairies into western Kansas and Nebraska between the Platte and the Arkansas rivers, is an example of the Late Woodland in the Central Plains. Cord-roughened pottery tempered with calcite and small expanding stemmed or corner-notched points, often called Scallorn points, indicate this complex (O'Brien 1994). Keith complex subsistence was based on a variety of wild plants and animals and apparently did not include horticulture.

The **Avonlea phase** (ca. 1500–950 BP), characterized by small, very finely made side-notched arrow points and **fabric-impressed ceramics**, represents a widespread, nomadic Late Woodland manifestation on the Northwestern Plains. Bison hunting was central to Avonlea subsistence, and many pound and jump sites are assigned to it. One of the best known is located in Alberta and has a colorful name, Head-Smashed-In. This jump site actually was used many times during the Archaic as well as the Late Prehistoric. It has been suggested that Avonlea represents Athapaskan migration into the area, but others think it developed more locally.

It is impossible to mention all the human groups or archaeological cultures that make up Plains Woodland. The pot shown in Figure 10.12 is representative of the type of ceramics Plains Woodland people made. Other artifacts also tell us important things about the lifeways. Sometimes these indicate exchange or other interactions with people elsewhere. For example, at the Trowbridge site, a Kansas City Hopewell site, small Middle Woodland blades were made of exotic cherts from central Missouri almost as often as from more local varieties. On the other hand, people usually made figurines and pipes of local clays, and copper is rare in Kansas City Hopewell sites (Adair 1988). Thus, we cannot envision exchange at the scale found among Middle Woodland groups in the Southeast and Midwest (see Chapters 11 and 12).

The variability of findings from the Great Plains during the Woodland period is not unexpected, given the environmental diversity. Nevertheless, we can note four significant developments that should be kept in mind: the introduction of pottery, the widespread adoption of the bow and arrow, the introduction of horticulture into some people's economies, and the development of mound building or other group mortuary rituals. All these cultural developments were even more significant further east, as Chapters 11 to 13 will make clear. Thus it seems most probable that such developments happened largely because of contact with people from the Eastern Woodlands. In addition, with the exception of the bow-and-arrow technology, each development is most common on the eastern margins of the Great Plains and in wooded river valleys that are most ecologically similar to areas to the east. In the Southern Plains, Southwestern influences also are sometimes clear. Plains Woodland nevertheless has Plains roots and many aspects of more ancient hunting and gathering lifeways persisted throughout the Woodland. There have been proposals of the actual migration of Midwestern

FIGURE 10.12 Typical Plains Woodland pot.

Middle Woodland groups up the Missouri River and into the Plains (e.g., Chapman 1980), but the diffusion of ideas usually provides a better explanation for Plains Woodland developments.

The development of pottery clearly represented a new and revolutionary way to carry, store, and cook foodstuffs. One factor in adopting pottery may well have been increased sedentism, and this is probably why pottery was adopted later outside the valleys of the eastern prairies. These valleys were places where a living could be made without a great deal of mobility. After all, for nomadic peoples, heavy and breakable pots are not as efficient as skin bags. Pottery also represents changes in how food was cooked. The rock-filled pits, slab-lined hearths, and similar features of the Archaic were methods of indirect heating and cooking. Baskets covered with pitch could also be used to stone-boil food, but receptacles woven of organic materials are less likely to be preserved than ceramic pots. One of the advantages of pottery certainly was the ability to cook directly over a fire, and the sooted bottoms of pottery specimens indicate that cooking was done in this fashion. Careful studies of pottery technology over time show that potters gradually adjusted the thickness of pot walls and the size and character of the temper particles to cope with the thermal stresses of firing and cooking, while improving the thermal conductivity of the vessels (O'Brien and Wood 1998).

The adoption of the bow and arrow, which was widespread by the Late Woodland, but certainly began before this among some Great Plains people, also was significant. You already may think of the bow and arrow as superior for hunting in comparison to the atlatl and dart. One advantage may be deeper penetration into the prey (Odell and Cowan 1986). Another could be that arrow points can be more easily hafted than dart points. Regardless, it has been argued that the adoption of the bow and arrow is correlated with more efficient hunting of game from bison to deer. Moreover, evidence from the Eastern Woodlands showing a high incidence of human skeletons with small points embedded in them suggests a possible correlation with increases in intergroup conflict beginning in the Late Woodland (O'Brien and Wood 1998, 232).

Changes in subsistence during Woodland times also may have been significant. It is important to note that for most people living on the Great Plains, the Woodland did not bring profound economic changes. In the river valleys and prairies of the eastern Plains, however, horticulture not only was possible, but would eventually lead to population growth, aggregation in large villages, and other sociocultural developments. The first reliable indication of domesticated plants on the Great Plains is from the Middle Woodland in the Central Plains. We have mentioned that Kansas City Hopewell people cultivated corn, squash, and marsh elder, all of which have been recovered from the Trowbridge site. Adair (1988) argues that on the Great Plains the process of adopting agriculture was gradual and variable, but involved a response to high population levels within key areas. When local wild resources were insufficient for more sedentary existence in the river valleys, people naturally took steps to increase the yield of plants they were already exploiting. Over time, this led to the **domestication** of native seed plants like marsh elder and the adoption of tropical cultigens. These simple steps also had longer-term effects, not only on subsistence but on village aggregation and structure, technology, and the organization of labor.

The appearance of burial mounds and, in some areas of the Great Plains, **ossuaries** also must be considered an important Woodland development.

Archaeologists generally assume that such formal disposal areas for the dead as mounds, cemeteries, and ossuaries are indicative of social groups with some measure of sedentism, or at least a territory of normal group use (e.g., Charles and Buikstra 1983). Mounds and other features provide reliable information on group membership because only those who belonged to a given group were buried in its dedicated mortuary places. These public monuments also symbolically mark the group's territory by their placement. Thus the appearance of burial mounds on the Plains during Middle Woodland times could mean both that people were tied to particular territories if not sites and that their social relationships were formalized, most likely through such kinship structures as lineages. Some archaeologists also have argued that the mounds represent opportunities for public manipulation of labor and wealth to gain prestige and status.

PLAINS VILLAGE TRADITIONS

Beginning about 1150 BP, societies began to appear in the river valleys of the Great Plains that were semisedentary and had mixed economies in which both farming in the river bottomlands and seasonal bison hunting were important. These societies are named **Plains Village** by archaeologists because of the small and large village sites that are found after this time. Despite general similarities, some distinctions can be drawn between Plains Village adaptations in various parts of the Plains. Older lifeways, which did not include horticulture, also persisted where either aridity or a short growing season made it difficult to grow crops. Nevertheless, it is clear that in the Central Plains, the Middle Missouri, and some parts of the Southern Plains, the combination of horticulture and seasonal bison hunting led to a material richness and security that allowed larger and more permanent aggregations of people. Marked status differentiation did not develop, and a tribal social organization was maintained. Archaeologists have defined many variants and phases for Plains Village (Table 10.2) based on pottery, house form, and other characteristics.

The **Central Plains tradition** includes Plains Village adaptations in the Central Plains between about 1000 and 500 BP (AD 800–1500). People archaeologists assign to this tradition generally made grit-tempered, cord-roughened, or smoothed surface vessels with vertical, flared, or collared rims, as well as plain, incised, or cord-impressed decorations. Their small arrow points were either unnotched, side notched, or notched at both the side and the base (Wedel 2001, Table 1). Other characteristic artifacts include stone end and side scrapers, hoes made out of bison scapulae, split bone awls and other bone tools (Figure 10.13), as well as a variety of ground stone items such as millingstones, abraders, and celts. The square to rectangular Central Plains Village houses, often built below the ground surface, had rounded corners and covered entranceways. Usually the people were maize-bean-squash horticulturists. Bison hunting, other hunting, gathering, and fishing all were economic components as well. Central Plains tradition villages usually were small, unfortified, and most often seem unplanned in arrangement. However, sites commonly have a number of large storage pits, including bell-shaped pits, which expanded outward beneath the surface.

One example of the Central Plains tradition is found in sites that have been assigned to the **Upper Republican phase** located in the Republican River valley of southern Nebraska. Along the stream terraces and hillslopes, are small

TABLE 10.2 Well-Known Plains Village Variants and Phases

Tradition	Variant	Phase	Dates (BP)	Location
Central Plains tradition		Steed–Kisker	1000–650	Missouri River upstream from Kansas City
		Smoky Hill	950–600	Eastern and north central Kansas
		Upper Republican including Solomon River	830–600	Western Kansas and Nebraska
		Loup River/Itskari	850–600	Nebraska
		Nebraska	850–500	Missouri River in northeastern Kansas, eastern Nebraska and western Iowa
		St. Helena	600–500	Missouri River in northeastern Nebraska
Middle Missouri tradition	Initial, Eastern	Great Oasis	1050–750	Northwestern Iowa, eastern South Dakota, southern Minnesota, northeastern Nebraska
		Mill Creek, Over, Cambria	1050–500	
	Initial, Western	Anderson	950–600	Missouri River in south central South Dakota
		Grand Detour		
	Extended	Nailati	750–550	Missouri River in South Dakota and North Dakota
		Clark's Creek		
		Fort Yates		
	Terminal	Thomas Riggs	550–400	Missouri River in North Dakota (Cannonball/Heart River area)
		Huff		
Coalescent tradition	Initial		650–350	Missouri River in South Dakota (mouth of White River to mouth of Bad River)
	Extended		500–300	Missouri River in South Dakota and North Dakota
Southern Plains tradition	Redbed Plains	Custer/Paoli	1150–700	Western Oklahoma
		Turkey Creek/ Washita River	to 700–500	Western and southern Central Oklahoma
	Upper Canark	Antelope Creek	750–450	Texas and Oklahoma Pandhandles
		Apishapa	950–500	Southeastern Colorado, northeastern New Mexico
		Buried City complex	800–620	Western Oklahoma
		Zimms complex	685–525	Southern Kansas
		Bluff Creek complex	900	South central and west central Kansas
		Pratt complex	500–400?	Upper Red and Brazos rivers
		Henrietta complex	700–500?	

communities consisting of scattered houses or clusters of houses, with storage pits both within and outside the dwellings. The excavation of a house structure at the Mowry Bluff site, just downstream from the Medicine Creek Dam (Wood 1969), provided some systematically recovered subsistence data for Upper Republican, and additional excavations have added more data on subsistence and settlement. These data indicate that people had a diverse subsistence base in which maize contributed approximately 30 percent of the diet, while bison contributed about 10 percent and deer and antelope together contributed another 10 percent. The other half of the diet came from other cultigens including sunflower, beans,

FIGURE 10.13 Bone artifacts of the Central Plains Village tradition.

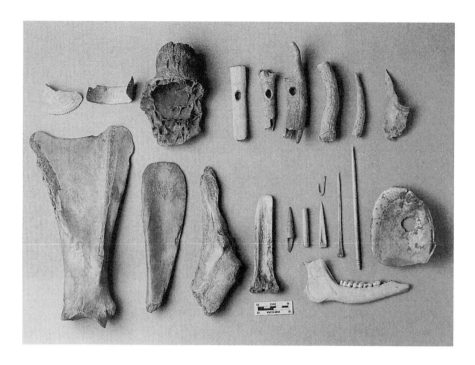

and squash, as well as small game, birds, and fish, wild greens, seeds, nuts, and fruits (Nepstad-Thornberry et al. 2002).

The **Steed–Kisker phase** (ca. 1000–650 BP), located along the Missouri River north of Kansas City, is noteworthy because of its **shell-tempered ceramics**, which have incised designs that resemble **Mississippian tradition** pottery from Cahokia, near St. Louis (see Chapter 12). This phase has been interpreted as the result of Mississippian immigration up the Missouri River (e.g., O'Brien 1978). Instead, however, it may simply represent Mississippian contact and influence on populations native to the Kansas City area. The members of this society were buried with exotic trade goods in low hilltop mounds or in cemeteries. Like other Central Plains tradition groups, Steed–Kisker groups practiced horticulture, hunted bison, fished, and gathered other resources.

The **Middle Missouri tradition** is a second Plains Village tradition that archaeologists date between about 1050 BP and 400 BP (AD 900–1550). It is found initially in the tall-prairie region of northwestern Iowa, southwestern Minnesota, and southern South Dakota, as well as along the Missouri River and its tributaries in North and South Dakota. Archaeologists recognize a number of variants and phases within this tradition. Globular, grit-tempered pottery vessels were made by modeling and shaping with a paddle and anvil. People made triangular arrow points that were unnotched or side notched. Other tools included end scrapers, drills, bifaces, a variety of ground stone items, bison or elk scapula hoes, bone and horn scoops, bone arrowshaft wrenches, and many other bone tools. Mussel shell beads, pipes of various types, and items made of exotic materials like copper from the Great Lakes, shell from the Gulf or Atlantic coast, as well as steatite from northern Wyoming and obsidian from the area of Yellowstone Park, also are found in sites of the Middle Missouri tradition.

FIGURE 10.14
Reconstructed earthlodges located at On-A-Slant Village in North Dakota.

People built rectangular structures including both houses and larger community buildings, and some of them may have been true **earthlodges**, covered with a layer of earth (Figure 10.14). These structures were placed in rows in villages that had been fortified by ditches and palisades. Sites are found near areas with wide bottomlands, where horticulture was undertaken; the sites themselves, however, usually are on bluffs or high terraces overlooking the bottomlands. People grew maize, beans, squash, and sunflower and also apparently cultivated marsh elder, goosefoot, and other native seed plants (Wood 2001, 188). Bison was the most important animal resource, but people also hunted other animals and collected many wild plants. Tobacco seeds have been recovered from the Mitchell site in southeastern South Dakota (Winham and Calabrese 1998).

The Terminal variant of the Middle Missouri tradition is dated between approximately 550 BP and 400 BP (AD 1400–1550) and marks dramatic changes. Environmental changes beginning in the thirteenth century may be partially responsible for a northward shift in Middle Missouri settlements; or, this shift may have resulted from the intrusion into central South Dakota of people related to Central Plains tradition or to Oneota groups living to the east. At this time, Middle Missouri groups withdrew into large, fortified communities near the mouth of the Heart and Cannonball rivers in North Dakota. They also began to construct circular earthlodges with a four-post support structure. The Shermer and Huff sites of North Dakota are examples of Terminal Middle Missouri tradition sites. Both were fortified villages with 80 to 100 dwellings.

The **Coalescent tradition** represents a third Plains Village tradition that is understood to represent a blending of the Central Plains and Middle Missouri traditions. Earlier Coalescent groups can best be understood as immigrants from the Central Plains into South Dakota, perhaps in response to drier climatic conditions (Krause 2001). The Coalescent tradition begins at approximately 650 BP and continues into the Historic period. It is first evident in sites along the Missouri

River in South Dakota between the mouths of the White and Bad rivers, but after about 500 BP (AD 1450), Coalescent people utilized a larger area, including locations outside the Missouri Valley itself. Pottery was made with cord-roughened, simple stamped, or smoothed exteriors. Bone and lithic tools are similar to those found in other Plains Village sites, again suggesting affinities with both Central Plains and Middle Missouri tools. Included are bison scapula hoes, bison skull scoops, split bone awls, snub-nosed end scrapers, diamond-shaped knives with beveled edges, and small triangular notched and unnotched projectile points. Like other Plains Village people, Coalescent groups were horticulturists and bison hunters who supplemented their subsistence with hunting and plant gathering.

People in the Coalescent tradition initially constructed square or rectangular earthlodges, but after 500 BP houses became more circular, and the term Extended variant is used to identify them. At first villages were fortified like Middle Missouri villages, but the placement of houses seems unplanned and discontinuous, as in the dispersed Central Plains village communities. For example, at the Arzberger site near Pierre, South Dakota, 44 square earthlodges were enclosed by a palisade and ditch with earthen bastions a mile and a half (2.5 km) long. The earthlodges, however, were strung out around the inner side of the palisade in no particular pattern. Sites of the Extended variant after 500 BP are not always fortified except at the northern and southern frontiers, and the population appears to have been dispersed. Coalescent tradition villagers however, did have hostile relationships with their neighbors, as indicated by the Crow Creek site in South Dakota (Figure 10.15). Here at least 486 skeletons, including remains of many partially dismembered and scalped individuals, were found in the fortification ditch (Willey 1990); the perpetrators of the massacre are not known with certainty. Ultimately Coalescent people became the historically known Mandan and Hidatsa tribes. This chapter's case study by Stanley A. Ahler and Phil R. Geib, "Investigations at Double Ditch Village, a Traditional Mandan Earthlodge Settlement," is about a Coalescent site that spans pre-Contact through early Historic times.

Plains Village societies also developed on the Southern Plains beginning around 1150 BP. The **Southern Plains tradition** way of life resulted from the addition of horticulture to the Woodland hunting and gathering lifestyle of this area. Plain and cord-marked pottery was made, as well as stone arrow points of various types and bone tools including bison scapula hoes, bone digging sticks, and awls. Maize and beans have been documented in Southern Plains Village sites, but initially maize may have been the main tropical cultigen, supplemented by collection of native seed plants (Bell and Brooks 2001, 208). It is assumed that squash, tobacco, and other crops were part of the farming complex as well as a wide variety of wild plant foods, including various types of nut. Bison bone dominates the faunal assemblages that have been recovered, emphasizing the significance of bison hunting to Southern Plains Village people. Deer and small game were exploited too, and both fishing and harvesting of shellfish were minor parts of the economies (Brooks 1989). Sites are generally found along major stream drainages where there were floodplain expanses suitable for gardening.

Archaeologists have defined a wide variety of phases, variants, and complexes within the Southern Plains Village tradition. One of the earliest Southern Plains Village phases is the **Custer phase**, located in western Oklahoma along the drainages of the Washita and Canadian rivers. This phase is dated between 1150 BP and 700 BP. Cord-marked pottery wares predominated, although some

FIGURE 10.15 Plan of the Crow Creek site showing earthlodge depressions, the fortification ditch, and the location of the bone bed containing the remains of nearly 500 people.

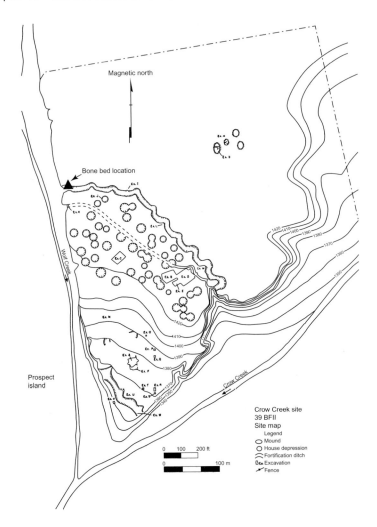

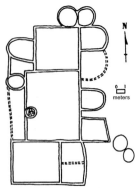

FIGURE 10.16 Plan of multiroom Antelope Creek phase structure showing Southwestern influence.

plain wares also were made. Clay figurines and perforated sherd disks have been recovered. People made small arrow points including triangular, side-notched, and corner-notched forms. Houses of this phase are square to rectangular wattle-and-daub structures, but they have not been as well documented as other Plains Village structures. Maize horticulture, wild plant gathering, and bison hunting were important subsistence pursuits. Very little evidence for trade with other groups has been found, but there is stone from the Alibates quarries near Amarillo, Texas, and granite from the Wichita Mountains to the south.

Other Southern Plains Village phases, like the **Antelope Creek phase** of the Texas panhandle, are distinctive because of the use of large stone slabs in house construction. There is considerable variability in the structures, and multiroom single-story pueblos were built at some sites (Figure 10.16). This phase probably represents the influence on local Southern Plains people of Puebloan groups in the Southwest, although some researchers have argued for actual migration onto the Plains by Southwesterners or for southerly migration by Upper Republican groups (Drass 1998).

Plains Village lifeways also are reflected to some extent in the adaptations of the **Oneota tradition** of the Prairie Peninsula (see Chapter 12). Interactions between Plains Village and Oneota groups also probably occurred (Henning 2005). Henning (1998) suggests that this archaeological culture should be viewed as a "bridging culture" that develops around 950 BP, linking the Plains and the Eastern Woodlands. Oneota sites are found from northwestern Iowa to the shores of Lake Michigan in Wisconsin and northeastern Illinois. Like Plains Village adaptations, Oneota economies were based on a mixture of hunting, gathering, and horticulture, with bison hunting and maize agriculture being particularly important. Bison scapula hoes and many other items of Oneota material culture remind us of Plains Village artifacts, but the shell-tempered pottery made by Oneota people is more like Mississippian pottery found in the Midwest and Southeast (see Chapters 11 and 12). Sites are seldom fortified, but enclosures and mounds are often found. The Oneota built longhouse-style structures rather than earthlodges. In the Red Wing region of Minnesota during the Oneota **Silvernale phase** (850–650 BP), the construction of pyramidal mounds, village fortifications, and some of the pottery designs may indicate direct linkages to Midwestern Mississippians.

LATE PREHISTORIC BISON HUNTERS OF THE NORTHERN PLAINS

In the Northwestern and Northeastern Plains, hunting and gathering persisted without horticulture throughout the Plains Village period. Beginning with the widespread adoption of the bow and arrow, bison hunting could be conducted even more easily. At this time, which most archaeologists begin at approximately 1500 BP and call the Late Prehistoric, communal hunting reached its peak efficiency (Figure 10.17). All these northern adaptations are characterized by

FIGURE 10.17 Artist's conception of Late Prehistoric Plains bison hunters running bison into a chute and corral in which the animals can be more easily shot.

dependence on bison hunting, pottery making, and use of the bow and arrow. For example, many bison hunting camps and kill sites after 1150 BP are considered part of the **Old Women's phase**, which may represent the ancestors of the North Piegan, Blood, and Gros Ventre Indians. Other, more forest oriented hunter-gatherers seem to have been located on the northeastern margins of the Great Plains. The Blackduck Culture (see Chapter 4) refers to people living in southwestern Manitoba who exploited fish and small game and may have collected wild rice, but also took bison by constructing buffalo pounds (Dyck and Morlan 2001). These are only a few of the archaeological entities recognized for the Late Prehistoric in the northern parts of the Plains.

Linkages with historically known tribes on Great Plains can often be surmised from the archaeological record of these Late Prehistoric and Plains Village groups (Hanson 1998; Schlesier 1994). Sometimes we can be fairly certain of this kind of connection, but as discussed in Box 10.1, this is not always the case.

ISSUES AND DEBATES

BOX 10.1

Historic Ethnicities and the Archaeological Record

Early ethnographies as well as the long and excellent ethnohistorical record from the Great Plains make the identification of linkages between archaeological sites and complexes and historically known ethnicities desirable. Establishing such anthropological linkages also can put more interesting detail into the bare bones and stones of archaeology. However, this task is not as simple as you might imagine.

Sometimes archaeological sites can be directly linked to ethnohistorical accounts. This is often true for the villages along the Missouri River in the northern Plains. Double Ditch Village, described in this chapter's case study, is one such place, having been inhabited by the Mandan Indians and recorded by Lewis and Clark in 1804. At the Knife River Indian Villages National Historic Site in North Dakota, Hidatsa Indian villages are documented as well (Ahler et al. 1991). Other more tenuous but widely accepted ethnic assignments include the correspondence of Apachean groups with the

Protohistoric **Dismal River phase** of western Nebraska and western Kansas (Hofman 1989). In this case, however, precisely which Apache bands or subtribes might be responsible is a matter of dispute, as is the correspondence of Apachean people with other archaeological complexes (Hanson 1998). In still other cases, particularly among nomadic tribes that did not leave an extensive material record, archaeological sites have not been identified at all (Hanson 1998, 461).

Despite its thematic importance within North American archaeology (see Chapter 2), the ethnic identity of the inhabitants of archaeological sites is quite difficult to establish. There are several reasons for this. First, the correspondence between ethnicity and archaeological cultures always is problematic. Ethnicity is an ideological and political matter of identity, while archaeological phases are constructed from similarities in material culture. Certainly people use items of material culture to symbolize their ethnic affiliation; but archaeological categories do not necessarily correspond to what people themselves might have perceived and wished to convey.

Second, even a passing acquaintance with the history of the Great Plains points to tremendous change in the distribution and character of ethnic identities during the Protohistoric and early Historic periods. As a result, the tribes located in various areas in approximately 1800 were not necessarily those found in the same area throughout the pre-Columbian past. The arrival of the horse greatly affected both distributions and lifestyles, and cultural character changed dramatically within some ethnicities as well.

Third, although historic accounts are tremendously useful in understanding what happened as Europeans arrived on the Plains, they are fallible and incomplete. Names and designations for groups often are confusing because they fail to recognize ethnic differences perceived by Native peoples or neglect ethnic connections the people considered important (Syms 1985). This means that we cannot use the written record uncritically; careful scholarship is essential.

Fourth, other types of evidence of ethnic affiliation must be approached with a healthy skepticism as well. Historical linguistics, though very important to the problem of identifying ethnicities, is an area in which methodological concerns are much debated. **Glottochronology** has been of great interest to archaeologists because it provides an apparently objective and quantitative way to explore language differences, but it is less popular among linguists themselves. Also a number of researchers have attempted to use biological characters such as cranial morphology to distinguish ethnicity (e.g., William F. Bass 1964; Ossenberg 1974). Once again the movement and mixing of populations add greatly to the complexity of such tasks. Moreover, ethnic groups are not necessarily biologically distinct, although there are usually some genetic and linguistic continuities within them.

In sum, the assignment of historic ethnicities to archaeologically evident populations is a highly complex research problem. It involves study of historical, archaeological, linguistic, and osteological data, and is therefore a holistic anthropological undertaking (Syms 1985). Nevertheless, when we can make accurate links, the results are rewarding. For example, it is possible to associate the Historic period Pawnee with archaeological sites located on the Republican River in Nebraska and Kansas (Wedel 1986). The Pawnee were one of the most populous historic groups in Nebraska during the nineteenth century, and we have available a good deal of observational material about their lifestyle. They were a loose confederacy of four subtribes, and the Kitkahahki, or Republican, band of Pawnee were located on the river of the same name. The Hill site, the Kansas Monument site, and site 14GE1 are documented in the early historical record, and Wedel has been able to draw a vivid picture of life in these villages from historic accounts and descriptions of the Pawnee (Wedel 1986, 152–185).

It is always essential to examine the basis for identifications between ethnic groups and archaeological sites carefully. Extension of connections backward for many centuries or even for millennia (e.g., Schlesier 1994) is most problematic, but even during the Protohistoric and Historic periods it is not always reliable. Because we do know that archaeological populations generally represent the ancestors of historically known tribes, pursuit of possible direct linkages is a worthy undertaking if only because it underscores the more basic point that the Native past is not completely disconnected from people in the present. Contemporary tribes and Native individuals have a real interest in identifications of these kinds, and when we can link to known tribes, we can enrich everyone's appreciation of the true history of cultures and interactions. Perhaps this is why an increasing number of archaeological accounts have been exploring such linkages (e.g., Spector 1993; Odell 2002).

PROTOHISTORIC AND HISTORIC DEVELOPMENTS

Europeans arrived on the Plains from three directions. They came through New Mexico and Texas into the Southern Plains, through the drainages of the Mississippi River to the east, or across the Canadian prairies. The first contacts were in the Southern and Central Plains during the sixteenth century. Best known is the expedition of Coronado, who after wintering at the pueblos along the Rio Grande in New Mexico, struck out to the east and north in 1541. Ultimately this expedition arrived at the settlement of Quivira in central Kansas, which probably was a Pawnee settlement (Wedel 1986). Further north contact was made with the Santee Sioux by the middle of the seventeenth century, and French traders reached the Pawnee from the east by 1700 (Swagerty 2001). These Europeans were followed by many more although, of course, settlement of the Plains by people of European descent did not begin in earnest for several centuries.

The Europeans encountered a dynamic cultural landscape with many ethnicities and languages in which alliances changed and populations moved. The Historic period Plains tribes included farmers like the Mandan, Hidatsa, and Arikara in the Dakotas, and the Omahas, Iowas, Missouris, and Osages in Nebraska and Kansas. Other historically known tribes emphasized bison hunting and were more mobile. These included the Comanche, Wichita, and Kiowa in Oklahoma, Colorado, and Texas, and the Arapaho, Pawnee, Dakota, Cheyenne, Crow, and Gros Ventre further north. Canadian Plains tribes were the Blackfeet, Assiniboin, Plains Cree, and Plains Ojibwa. However, abandonments, relocations, and in-migration from the Woodlands were an important feature of the Protohistoric and Historic periods, and these groups had not necessarily inhabited the Plains for centuries. Groups originally located further east were the Arikara, the Wichita, the Pawnee, the Cheyenne, the Crow, the Lakota and Dakota, the Assiniboin, the Cree, and the Ojibwa. In each case a complicated story of movement has been reconstructed.

A glance at what is known of Cheyenne relocations during Historic times will quickly give a sense of how complicated the cultural geography could be. At the end of the seventeenth century the Cheyenne apparently lived in eastern Minnesota, but Sioux expansions during the early eighteenth century led to their relocation along the Sheyenne River. In their new territory, they established the fortified earthlodge village archaeologists call the Biesterfeldt site (Figure 10.18) and adopted an essentially Plains Village lifeway (Wood 1971). Yet by the middle of the eighteenth century they had moved further west again, edged out by the Plains Cree, the Plains Ojibwa, and the Assiniboin. This time they established themselves in the area of the Black Hills and became nomadic hunters. In this incarnation they are mentioned by Lewis and Clark in 1805. Thereafter the Cheyenne moved once again, being pushed west and south by the Teton Lakota (Swagerty 2001, 256). The Cheyenne are just one tribe of many, and certainly all tribes did not undertake so many moves and transformations. However, the Cheyenne case does suggest the fluidity of Great Plains cultural geography during Protohistoric and Historic times.

Besides these kinds of relocations, three factors contributed profoundly to the cultural character of the Great Plains beginning in the Protohistoric. The first of these was the introduction of the horse by Europeans. Although there once were native horses in North America, the American horse was extinct by the end of the Pleistocene. The pack animal of the pre-Columbian Plains Indians was the

FIGURE 10.18 Aerial shot of the Biesterfeldt site in southeastern North Dakota, looking southwest. Note circular earthlodge depressions and fortification.

FIGURE 10.19 Dogs outfitted with travois were the primary pack animals of the pre-Columbian Great Plains.

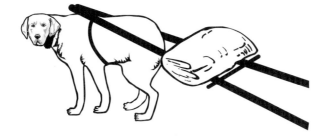

dog (Figure 10.19), which served secondarily as a food source when meat was scarce. Even in the early nineteenth century, Arikara families are reported to have had 30 to 40 dogs (Swagerty 2001, 258). On the other hand, the introduction of the European horse, preadapted to the grasslands of the Plains and the long-distance movements of the tribes that lived there, brought a sort of revolution to the Plains. Horses impacted trade, mobility, the economy, intergroup relations, and internal social structures. Although the early explorers like Coronado had brought horses with them, there is no record of what happened to any horses still living when the expeditions left North America. By the mid-seventeenth century the Apaches may have been trading some horses on the Plains, but it was not until the successful Pueblo Revolt in 1680–1692 that several thousand horses were confiscated by Native Americans. Most of these horses probably were traded onto the Great Plains. By the late eighteenth century a complex trade in horses was established. The extent to which various tribes could control or manipulate this trade affected both their economic and military fortunes.

Trade in European goods also transformed the Great Plains. The most important item of trade was the gun, since the tribes possessing firearms could dominate militarily. Thus guns affected alliances and political relationships among the tribes. In the mid-eighteenth century, guns were traded in the Plains for furs and hides. For trading partners the tribes had the British of the Hudson's Bay Company, working from Hudson Bay to the north, and French traders, traveling out from New France, or Louisiana. The Spanish were reluctant to allow trade in guns, which meant that New Mexico was not an early source of guns on the Great Plains (Binnema 2001). However, by the late eighteenth century multiethnic **Comancheros** dealt in arms, ammunition, and Indian captives on the Southern Plains. In the Southern Plains the horse generally was adopted before the gun, while further north the gun often came first.

Finally, as in so many areas of North America, contact with Europeans meant the spread of devastating diseases. Disease may well have traveled with trade items ahead of actual Europeans, and eventually depopulation was a major disrupting factor among the societies of the Great Plains. A number of epidemics occurred. The first well-documented case probably was a smallpox epidemic from 1687 to 1691 on the Southern Plains. By the early eighteenth century, the Arikara on the Missouri River may have been infected with measles, smallpox, and tuberculosis. A series of epidemics between 1734 and 1800 resulted in a major population decline across the Plains. Perhaps the worst epidemic was the smallpox epidemic of 1837–1838. The Mandan lost 95 percent of their already reduced population in that single year, and mortality was significant in many other tribes. Diseases continued to be devastating until the 1850s; they brought great suffering, but they also were the cause of migrations and changes in settlement patterns, as well as political breakdown and amalgamation (Swagerty 2001). This chapter's case study offers additional perspectives.

The Fur Trade

The story of Native Americans' culture change is only part of the story of the centuries of exploration and commercialization after Europeans arrived on the Plains. The trade for furs and hides was the focus of the first Europeans on the Great Plains, as well as the focus of tribes that served as middlemen in indirect trade with other Native societies. In the northern part of the Plains much of the trade was with the Hudson's Bay Company, which controlled most of the trade in areas draining into Hudson Bay. This vast area includes the Canadian portion of the Northern Plains, considered part of **Rupert's Land** until 1869, as well as some of North Dakota and Minnesota. The French, however, also traded on the Plains; they came up the tributaries of the Mississippi or west from the Great Lakes, establishing trading posts along the rivers, their main routes of access. For example, Jean Baptiste Bénard de la Harpe had a trading post on the Red River in Texas, but in 1719 participated in a trade fair with the Wichita on the Arkansas near Tulsa, Oklahoma (Odell 2002).

In what is now Canada, a new ethnic group developed when the British and French traders married Native women, establishing alliances that favored both the traders and the Natives. The offspring of these unions formed an ethnicity that still exists in Canada today: the *Métis*, who added to the mix of people involved in the trade on the Canadian Plains (Jennifer S. H. Brown 2001). Of course, the Spanish traded for hides from the Southern Plains, but most of this trade seems to have been accomplished indirectly. After peace was made between the Spanish and the Comanche in 1786, a mix of *mestizos*, Pueblo Indians, and some Hispanics began to bring back hides and dried meat, bypassing Indian middlemen.

The American and Canadian Periods

With the Louisiana Purchase in 1803, the United States gained control of the Great Plains except for Texas and the Canadian portion of the Plains. Lewis and Clark's famous expedition extended from 1804 to 1806. The recent bicentennial of this expedition stimulated archaeological investigations of sites associated with it. One site investigated was the campsite at the lower portage of the Great Falls of the Missouri in Montana (Saraceni 1998).

After Lewis and Clark, Americans began to establish their own trading houses on the Great Plains. These enterprises were called factories and were supported by military forts. One example was Fort Union, established in 1828 at the confluence of the Yellowstone and the Missouri rivers by the American Fur Company. Fort Union was an important center of the Northern Plains fur trade until it was sold to the U.S. Army and razed in 1867. Extensive archaeological excavations at this site yielded large quantities of artifacts for future study and were helpful in the reconstruction of this fort, which can be visited by the public.

Canada was not established until 1867, although the 49th parallel was set as the northern boundary of the United States in 1818. Canada acquired Rupert's Land and the Northwest Territory in 1869 and established the various provinces in the 1870s, but Saskatchewan and Alberta were not established until 1905. The transfer to Canadian control did not happen completely peacefully. The Métis feared losing their lands and livelihood and established their own provisional government under Louis Riel, but the Canadians rapidly crushed this rebellion. Batoche, a Métis settlement where the last battle of the rebellion occurred, has been excavated in association with Parks Canada's interpretation of this part of Canadian history (Lee 1983, 1984).

In both countries, there is a long and complicated story of trade and settlement, conflicts between Indians and white, treaties, and the eventual movement of Native peoples to reservations. There also is the story of the settlers, ranchers, and homesteaders who moved into the Great Plains as permanent residents. Histories are available that give much detail about the experiences of each of these groups, but archaeology can add new information and provide new insights. For example, archaeology done at the site of Custer's famous "last stand" has provided fresh perspective on exactly what happened in this battle. By plotting the locations of spent bullets, weaponry, other equipment, and skeletal remains, as well as by excavations, archaeologists have added to our understanding of how the combatants positioned themselves, bringing into new focus various accounts by Indians and others of how the battle actually proceeded (Scott et al. 2000).

Unfortunately, historical archaeology, other than attempts to project backward from Plains tribes into the pre-Columbian past, is a very recent endeavor on the Great Plains. Military forts and trading posts have been the sites most frequently investigated. Of course, there are significant stories of the past to be told from archaeological work at sites of these two kinds, but other aspects of Plains history could also be aided by archaeology. One example is recent excavation in Deadwoode South Dakota's Chinatown, which is revealing a little known chapter in the Chinese presence in the West. Archaeological study of homesteads and ranches, of early mining towns and labor history (e.g., Saitta 2005), of the railroad and industrial developments, as well as of urban areas, also could be significant. The advent of CRM has been extremely fortunate for historical archaeology on the Great Plains because it has meant that more archaeological sites of these other types are being excavated (Scott 1998).

CHAPTER SUMMARY

This chapter has introduced the archaeological past on the Great Plains, demonstrating among other things, that popular depictions of mobile bison hunters with horses do not apply to most of the past peoples of the Great Plains. The main points made in this chapter are as follows:

- The climate and the topography of the Great Plains are variable, and although trees are largely restricted to the river valleys, the grasslands of the Great Plains can be subdivided into short- and tall-grass sections, with the 100th meridian as the approximate dividing line. Major portions of the northern Great Plains were glaciated during the Ice Age, leaving many topographic traces.

- Although there is a large and well-documented Paleoindian record from the Great Plains, a Pre-Clovis presence has not been established for this culture area. The Paleoindian sequence on the Plains begins with Clovis mammoth hunting groups and later bison hunters, notably those who made Folsom points. Younger unfluted, lanceolate point styles have been grouped in the Plano complex, which also can be associated with bison hunting owing to the large number of kill sites.

- Bison hunting continued to be central to Great Plains adaptations throughout the Archaic period (ca. 8500–2500 BP), which is first indicated by the appearance of notched projectile point styles. Although numerous kill sites have helped archaeologists understand how bison were hunted by Plains Archaic peoples, the mobile foragers of this time used other plant and animal resources as well.

- In the Central Plains, several Middle and Late Archaic phenomena seem to foreshadow the Woodland. Notably, the first Plains ceramics and burial mounds appear in the Nebo Hill phase along the Missouri River.

- The first Plains Woodland complexes are found in the Central Plains at approximately 2500 BP, and pottery, mounds, and sometimes horticulture dated after 2000 BP occur more widely. Late Woodland complexes dated after approximately 1500 BP also show that the bow and arrow became prevalent at this time. Thus, Woodland innovations on the Great Plains were in the areas of pottery manufacture, the construction of mounds in burial rituals, the addition of horticultural products to the diet, and the widespread adoption of the bow and arrow.

- Beginning around 1150 BP, semisedentary societies with mixed economies, called Plains Village by archaeologists, are evident on the Great Plains. Four broad Plains Village traditions, each with many variants and phases, have been recognized by archaeologists. These are the Central Plains tradition, the Middle Missouri tradition, the Coalescent tradition, and the Southern Plains tradition. Plains Village societies persisted into Historic times and can sometimes be linked to ethnohistorically known ethnic groups.

- Besides Plains Village, other ethnicities were part of the cultural mix of the late pre-Columbian period. These include the bison hunting societies of the Northeastern and Northwestern Plains as well as the Oneota, who spread into the area from the margins of the Plains and Woodlands. The Oneota were farmers possibly affiliated with the Mississippian societies of the Eastern Woodlands, but they hunted bison seasonally.

- The Protohistoric and early Historic periods on the Great Plains were particularly dynamic culturally, with some tribes reinventing themselves as they changed locations dramatically. In addition to the reintroduction of horses, the gun trade and the spread of devastating diseases like smallpox exerted transforming influences on Great Plains cultures during these periods.

- The archaeology of the Historic era is of growing importance on the Great Plains. The history of the fur trade and of military forts and battles has been of interest to archaeologists for some time, but many other topics related to the settlement and development of the Great Plains since European arrival also can be profitably investigated.

SUGGESTIONS FOR FURTHER READING

For excellent summaries of Great Plains archaeology and ethnohistory:

De Mallie, Raymond J. 2001. *Handbook of North American Indians*, Vol. 13 *Plains* (Part One). Washington, DC: Smithsonian Institution.

Wood, W. Raymond, ed. 1998. *Archaeology of the Great Plains*. Lawrence: University Press of Kansas.

For an excellent review of the Plains bison hunting lifestyle and the evidence for it:

Frison, George C. 1991. *Prehistoric Hunters of the High Plains*, 2nd ed. San Diego: Academic Press.

For a well-illustrated and accessible review of what has been learned about the Hidatsa from archaeological work along the Knife River in North Dakota:

Ahler, Stanley A., Thomas D. Thiessen, and Michael K. Trimble. 1991. *People of the Willows: The Prehistory and Early History of the Hidatsa Indians*. Grand Forks: University of North Dakota Press.

For an archaeologist's attempt to involve Native descendants and envision the women who used the artifacts being excavated:

Spector, Janet D. 1993. *What This Awl Means: Feminist Archaeology at a Wahpeton Dakota Village*. St Paul: Minnesota Historical Society Press.

For a fascinating account of the exploration of a fur trade site in the Southern Plains:

Odell, George. 2002. *La Harpe's Post: A Tale of French–Wichita Contact on the Eastern Plains*. Tuscaloosa: University of Alabama Press.

For the story of how archaeology has changed ideas about Custer's last stand:

Scott, Douglas D., Richard A. Fox, Melissa A. Connor, and Dick Harmon. 2000. *Archaeological Perspectives on the Battle of the Little Bighorn*. Norman: University of Oklahoma Press.

OTHER RESOURCES

Sections H and I of the Student CD provide web links, additional discussion questions, and study aids. The Student CD also contains a variety of additional resources, including the complete list of references as cited in this chapter and the following case study. "Weaponry of Clovis Hunters at Blackwater Draw" (Section D.2) is particularly relevant to this chapter because it discusses the reanalysis of archaeological collections from the Clovis-type site in the Southern Plains.

CASE STUDY

Although the Indians of the Great Plains are most often associated with bison hunting, high mobility, and teepees, this chapter has shown that many inhabitants resided in villages in the river valleys for much of the year, relying on both horticulture and seasonal bison hunting for survival. In Historic times, Arikara, Hidatsa, and Mandan Indians were aggregated into fortified settlements in the Missouri River trench. This case study describes the archaeological investigation of a village that was utilized by Mandan Indians and their ancestors. The investigations at Double Ditch Village were conducted both for research reasons and to provide information that could be used in the public interpretation of the site. They involved the collaboration of archaeologists and other specialists from a variety of institutions, incorporating geophysical techniques as well as excavation. For these reasons this case study provides a good example of the complexity of many contemporary archaeological projects. In addition, the research reveals that Double Ditch's inhabitants reconfigured the settlement several times, building four rather than two defensive ditches, mounding earth and planing off the village ground surface at various times. These findings raise new questions about how these transformations reflect changing social dynamics among the Mandan and other tribes. As you read this case study, ask yourself what the history of Double Ditch Village indicates about how people adjusted to the population relocations, outbreaks of intersocietal aggression, and epidemics of the Late Prehistoric, Protohistoric, and Historic eras on the Great Plains.

INVESTIGATIONS AT DOUBLE DITCH VILLAGE, A TRADITIONAL MANDAN EARTHLODGE SETTLEMENT

Stanley A. Ahler and Phil R. Geib

On the upper Missouri River, early summer days are 17 hours long, allowing much time for experimental field archaeology. On such a day in June 2003, when the prairie glowed orange in the hour before sunset, the silence was broken by the drone of a powered parachute crisscrossing high above Double Ditch Village. Two archaeologists in the steel cage hanging beneath the nylon canopy shot thermal infrared still and video images of the uneven, shadowed surface below them, recording patterns created by the remnant heat of the day. At the dawn of the twenty-first century, this ancient village was largely quiet except for occasional visitors who walked its surface and a small crew of archaeologists that briefly probed its secrets. Had aerial cameras been available 450 years ago, they would have recorded 1500 people living in a closely packed, heavily fortified settlement with adjoining gardens stretching far up and down the Missouri River floodplain. Over a few years, such cameras would have recorded many events that defined and reshaped the lives of the village residents, the ancestral Mandans. Corn planting and harvesting, bison hunting, feasting, and celebrations occurred in scheduled annual cycles. Less predictable but more momentous were influxes of foreign peoples to the ancestral Mandan homeland, episodes of intense warfare, and onslaughts by new, savage diseases such as smallpox that took one of every two lives on each appearance at the village.

By 750 BP, the ancestors of the historic Mandans occupied nearly the entire valley of the Missouri River in what is now South and North Dakota. Their lifeway, which archaeologists call the Plains Village tradition, centered on intensive hunting of the bison combined with cultivation of the tropical cultigens maize, beans, and squash; the people lived in villages composed of large bark- or earth-covered timber houses. By 550 BP, the ancestral Mandans had vacated the Missouri Valley in South Dakota, coalescing in a smaller number of much larger, fortified settlements in North Dakota where the Cannonball and Heart rivers join the Missouri. By fifty years later, the ancestral Mandans were concentrated in a few large settlements near Heart River and Square Butte. Their village neighbors included ancestors of the Hidatsas upstream to the north and of the Arikaras downstream to the south. Several settlements near the Heart River were occupied without interruption until the late eighteenth century, when smallpox and warfare with the encroaching nomadic Sioux and Assiniboins drove the villagers farther upstream, where they emerged in written history as the Mandan tribe. Several sites are known as the traditional villages of the Mandans, and Double Ditch Village is one of at least seven such locations (Figure 10.20). In 1804–1805, several of the abandoned Mandan villages were observed by Meriwether Lewis and William Clark. On their expedition map they recorded Double Ditch as an "Old Indian Village Killed by The Sioux" (Moulton 1983, Map 28). Ethnographic information recorded early in the twentieth century indicates that Double Ditch was known to the Mandans as Yellow Earth Village (Bowers 1950, 217, footnote 9) or Yellow Bank Village (Thiessen et al. 1979). The state of North Dakota purchased the site in 1936 for purposes of preservation and interpretation.

Double Ditch Village is today one of the most spectacular archaeological sites extant in North America. This is due to its large size (more than 20 acres), its commanding view of the Missouri Valley both upstream and downstream, and its many internal surface features (Figure 10.21). Readily visible are a relatively complete inner fortification ditch and a portion of a concentric outer ditch (hence, the site name). The inner ditch has several small bastions, or outward projections along the fortification line.

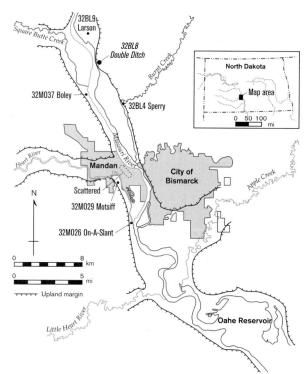

FIGURE 10.20 Double Ditch Village site location map showing traditional Mandan villages near the mouth of the Heart River, North Dakota.

FIGURE 10.21 Aerial photograph of Double Ditch Village, June 3, 1988.

Within the area defined by this ditch are depressions in the ground that mark locations of about 33 circular earthlodges, 10 to 11 meters (33–36 ft) in diameter, much like those built by the historic Mandans. The visible outer ditch lies about 60 to 70 meters (197–230 ft) beyond the inner ditch. The surface in that area is irregular, and there are several basins, the largest of which are possibly borrow areas or plazas devoid of houses, and for these reasons, observers disagree on the number of lodge depressions between inner and outer ditches. A striking feature of the village is the more than three dozen earthen mounds, some of them huge, that lie at the perimeter of the settlement. Some mounds are just inside the second ditch; many more are outside it. Early archaeologists recorded the largest mounds as 3 meters (almost 10 ft) high; today they are still at least 2 meters (6.6 ft) high and no less impressive. Altogether, these mounds contain an estimated 6000 cubic meters (7850 yd^3) of fill. Based on test excavations in the mounds, this amount of fill also includes an estimated 1.6 million stone tools and tool fragments (arrow points, scrapers, used flakes, cores, etc.), more than 30,000 broken pottery vessels, and 142 metric tons (313,000 lbs) of animal bone.

PREPARING FOR FIELDWORK AT DOUBLE DITCH

One hundred years ago, Double Ditch Village was a large and impressive archaeological site, but not necessarily unique regarding its appearance and internal features. Today, however, a site in this condition is rare on the Upper Missouri. Among the seven abandoned Mandan villages recorded by Lewis and Clark near the Heart River, Double Ditch is unusually well preserved. Two of the other six were obliterated before they could be accurately located; one has been incrementally and nearly completely destroyed; and three are now severely circumscribed and altered by cultivation, uncontrolled digging, and modern construction. Until the recent work at Double Ditch, not one of these sites had been extensively studied, and only one had been sampled using modern archaeological methods. Further underscoring the importance of Double Ditch Village, five man-made reservoirs have drowned 80 percent of the Missouri Valley in the Dakotas (Lehmer 1971) and most of the hundreds of Plains Village sites contained therein. The region around Heart River was spared from flooding, but since the Heart region was bypassed by the salvage archaeology programs driven by reservoir construction, it has remained one of the least studied and least understood (Thiessen 1999). Thus, Double Ditch Village holds a key position. It lies at the heart of a

little understood archaeological region that can document much of the prehistory and history of Plains Village peoples, and it is one of only a few large settlements sufficiently preserved for study in its spatial entirety.

In addition to the site's unusual size and condition, several other factors prompted recent investigations at Double Ditch Village. The village is a centerpiece among several archaeological sites preserved and managed by the state of North Dakota that range in age from Late Woodland to Historic. These sites are open to public visitation, and in the 1990s the State Historical Society of North Dakota (SHSND) began a systematic program of upgrading the interpretive and educational information available for these sites. For Double Ditch, existing information was meager, dating from excavations carried out in 1905 by two undergraduate students at Harvard University (Will and Spinden 1906). While their work was remarkable for its time—the first professional study of a Plains Village site in the Dakotas—the questions posed by the young archaeologists in 1905 were far different from those of today. In addition, the Lewis and Clark Bicentennial Celebration of 2004–2006 was expected to bring countless new visitors to the Missouri Valley and North Dakota. Many visitors would be eager to learn about prominent sites such as Double Ditch, first recorded by Lewis and Clark and figuring clearly in the history of the Native peoples impacted by the Corps of Discovery and the events it foretold.

Sound interpretations and educational information are based on sound research, and the state of North Dakota provided special appropriations for new research at Double Ditch Village. New information has reached the public in several ways. Each major archaeological field season in 2002, 2003, and 2004 included an on-site interpretation program. Scheduled tour groups and drop-in visitors alike were met by interpreters who guided them through the site and explained the excavations in progress. The site is open to visitors throughout the year, and several movable interpretive displays allow self-guided tours. New information from current research is systematically input into updated versions of these displays. Results of research are summarized in technical reports that appear each year (e.g., Ahler, ed. 2004; Kvamme 2004). During the final two years of the project, new information will also be published in outlets for both public and scholarly audiences. In future years, project findings will be presented in museum exhibits at the

North Dakota Heritage Center in Bismarck and in digital formats accessible via the Internet.

Like many modern archaeological endeavors, the Double Ditch program is a collaborative effort involving several partners. While much of the direct funding for the project has come from the state of North Dakota, many other entities have also provided support and have made "in-kind" contributions. Most of the archaeological staff members at the SHSND have been directly involved in the fieldwork. At the core of excavation programs in 2002 and 2003 were archaeological field schools involving 27 students from the University of Missouri—Columbia and the University of Kansas—Lawrence directed by W. Raymond Wood. The University of Missouri also supported a soil-coring program at the site directed toward graduate thesis research. Each summer from 2001 to 2004 experts in **remote sensing** led by Kenneth L. Kvamme at the University of Arkansas have conducted geophysical survey. At the request of the SHSND, the PaleoCultural Research Group (PCRG) has coordinated all research on the project. A non-profit research and education organization with public membership, PCRG has drawn heavily on its members for volunteer field efforts and analytic studies. Twenty-six persons, including 16 PCRG members, have donated effort to the field program. For lab work conducted at its headquarters in Flagstaff, Arizona, PCRG has involved students majoring in anthropology at nearby Northern Arizona University, with some of the funding for student assistance provided through an arrangement with the university. Detailed studies of pottery, stone artifacts, faunal remains, botanical remains, radiocarbon samples, and trade artifacts are undertaken at the Flagstaff lab and at distant locations.

What are the specific research objectives at Double Ditch Village, and what are the methods for achieving these goals? Given the site size and visible features at Double Ditch, our broadest research objectives have been as follows:

1. To understand the chronology of the site

2. To document in detail the structure of the site (positions of fortifications, earthlodges, basins, mounds, plazas, etc., as well as smaller features)

3. To reconstruct and explain changes in the community structure, or how and why the relationships of internal features and settlement size changed through time

Another goal has been to learn about the social dynamics of the region during the history of the site, or how the early Mandan inhabitants of the village were affected by and interacted with people moving into the region and living in nearby areas. Social interactions at Double Ditch were complex and involved residents of other Mandan settlements at Heart River, eastern Hidatsa peoples migrating into the Missouri Valley during the seventeenth century AD or perhaps earlier, several eastern groups such as the Sioux, who were pushing westward into Mandan territory to become nomadic bison hunters on the Great Plains, and European Americans moving westward who spread before them manufactured artifacts and deadly diseases previously unknown in North America. There are few precedents from modern Plains Village archaeology regarding "whole-village" investigations of sites as huge and complex as Double Ditch Village. One important model for Double Ditch research has been the study of large Hidatsa villages at the mouth of the Knife River (Ahler et al. 1991; Thiessen 1993). At Knife River, research was guided by detailed contour maps and by some of the first remote-sensing data from magnetic instrumentation to be applied on a whole-site scale.

At the start of the project, we held several assumptions regarding physical remains at Double Ditch Village. We assumed that the earthen mounds that ringed the village were heaps of refuse, and from the size of the mounds, we expected the village to have been lived in for two centuries or longer (established perhaps around 400 BP or AD 1550). Some evidence on the surface indicated that the inner ditch cut through existing features and was therefore the youngest fortification system in the site. From this we expected that the site had contracted in size through time, probably owing to depopulation due to disease, with the center of the village having been used the longest. The second, outer ditch would be the older one, defending a larger community, and the inner ditch more recent. Based on data from Hidatsa sites at Knife River, we expected refuse within the center of the village, beneath and around houses, to be 1 to 2 meters or more in thickness, owing to the long history of occupation and the effects of building repeatedly on the same location.

State-of-the-art remote-sensing technology played a major role in Double Ditch investigations. Since 1998 Kenneth Kvamme has had great success in applying a suite of methods including magnetic gradiometry, electrical resistivity, and ground-penetrating radar at village sites in the Dakotas (Kvamme 2003). Magnetic survey has proven the most useful remote-sensing method at many village sites where buried features lie near the ground surface. To collect magnetic data, a person carries a very sensitive magnetic gradiometer across the site along transects in measured spatial units, collecting 6400 or more readings from a survey block measuring 20 by 20 meters (22 × 22 yd). Resulting data are displayed as patterns in gray-scale or as colors representing variations in magnetic intensity. From many previous applications at villages in the Dakotas, we knew that magnetic survey could pinpoint the locations of hidden features such as underground storage pits subsequently filled with refuse, hearths and central fire pits within lodges, localized concentrations of refuse rich in rocks or organic matter, burned house floors and roof falls, and linear arrangements of sod and topsoil stacked along fortification ditches, as well as the ditches themselves (Kvamme 2003). We expected to document many if not all of these kinds of features at Double Ditch, and over the course of several years, we planned for remote sensing to map out details of the entire community not visible at the ground surface. The remote-sensing data would in turn be a tremendous boon to planning excavations.

A STAGED, MULTIYEAR PROGRAM

The approach to fieldwork and addressing the research goals has been staged, with the strategy for each new cycle of study adjusted according to results from recently completed work. This is a logical approach for complex archaeological sites, and a natural process for studies occurring over several years. Remote-sensing work was conducted over a four-year period from 2001 through 2004, with about 20 percent of the site surveyed during each of the first three seasons and the remaining 40 percent surveyed during 2004. Only a small hand-coring program, involving no excavation and focused on ground-truthing some of the first data from geophysical survey, was conducted in 2001. Progressively larger excavation programs involving field schools were conducted in 2002 (three weeks) and 2003 (five weeks), and a final five-week excavation and interpretive mapping program took place in 2004 involving a smaller field crew. In 2004, as this case study account was being drafted,

the fieldwork of 2004 had just been completed, but much of the laboratory work was ongoing. In the two-year period after the 2004 field season, analytic studies were to be completed and all summary reports and publications for the project developed.

Remote sensing identified many unexpected features that proved important in all later work phases during the first field season (2001). Both magnetic and electrical resistance surveys revealed two large basins to be free of any detectable subsurface features. Follow-up coring with a simple tool called the Oakfield probe indicated that these basins were likely borrow locations from which large amounts of sediment, including all topsoil, had been removed. Several unexplainable linear anomalies, or patterns, were documented beneath the featureless surface near the village margin. Magnetic data and coring also documented large numbers of deep storage pits along the village margin where no indications of houses could be seen. Apparent rectangular houses (a form that predates the circular earthlodge) were documented near the village center. The greatest surprise came from coring these houses: artifact-bearing deposits within and around the houses were quite shallow, a half-meter (20 in.) or less in depth. This was quite contrary to the 2-meter-thick layer of debris found at other Late Plains Village sites, and it indicated *removal* of earth and refuse from the center part of the village.

With these 2001 findings, our attention was more focused during the next cycle of fieldwork. Coring studies in both the basins and residential areas indicated that the villagers had conducted large-scale earthmoving, and a new goal was to confirm and explain such activity. Because the core of the village appeared to lack deep stratified deposits, we shifted excavation focus to other locations that could provide long stratigraphic records. Unusual features had been discovered on the periphery of the village, in areas we had previously considered to lie beyond the limits of the settlement. Where was the village margin, and what was the purpose of the pits and linear features at what appeared to be the edge of the settlement?

The second round of remote-sensing fieldwork in summer 2002 yielded amazing discoveries. Late in the evening of the next-to-last day of geophysical survey, Ken and Jo Ann Kvamme asked the staff to assemble and prepare for a celebratory toast as they displayed the most recent composite magnetic map of the village. In the area mapped just that day along the village margin, well outside the ring of mounds, two remarkably regular, long curving lines marked the indisputable existence of two unsuspected fortification systems that lay well outside the outer visible ditch. The third ditch system appeared to connect several of the larger and outermost earthen mounds at the site, and the revealed portions of the outermost or fourth ditch system lay entirely beyond the mounds. The outermost ditch clearly included several large, squarish bastions that projected outward. The unexplained linear features on the village margin mapped the year before were now understood! The survey maps showed other unusual patterns, as well, including, in the nearly flat areas between the mounds and well outside the residential core of the settlement, large zones containing many pit features but no houses. A new series of presumed house depressions with rectangular form could also be seen in the north central part of the village.

A completely new picture of Double Ditch Village had suddenly appeared. The size of the fortified area in the settlement had mushroomed from 11 acres to more than 20 acres. Given the density of apparent houses within the inner ditch, a fortified area this large could have contained an estimated 190 earthlodges. Based on historic accounts of the number of people occupying a single lodge, this would imply a population of nearly 2000 people! The purpose of the large earthen mounds was suddenly of major interest. They no longer seemed to be merely trash heaps placed just outside the living area, but they appeared to bear some relation to placement of the fortifications. Perhaps they were intentionally constructed defensive features, closely integrated with ditches and palisades. And why were there no apparent houses outside the visible outer ditch? Had the village really consisted of 190 houses, or were the outer defenses designed to encircle pit storage zones or perhaps cemeteries? The bastioned fortifications appeared similar to systems at some villages dating 500 to 600 years ago, when rectangular houses were the norm. Was Double Ditch Village established at this time? If so, it would contain an unbroken three-century-plus record of Mandan cultural development.

The three-week round of excavation in 2002, following directly on the heels of the Kvammes' discoveries, could not begin to address all these questions. Paramount was developing a chronology for the site grounded in radiocarbon dating. The 1905 excavations had shown one of the largest mounds

(Mound B) to be horizontally stratified, meaning that it had been built laterally, or outward from the village, in an accretional fashion. On the assumption that the mound was composed of trash built up over a few hundred years, the part of the mound laid down first could contain some of the oldest deposits in the site. In 1905 the Harvard students had dug a massive trench through this feature. We decided to use machinery to remove fill from their trench and efficiently sample mound contents along one wall (Figure 10.22). In addition, we needed to understand the two outermost, newly discovered fortification systems. What was their form, why did they have no surface expression, when were they constructed, and when were they abandoned and filled? Would the village contraction model hold up, with the outermost ditch being the oldest and the ditches to the interior being successively younger in age, until the site was abandoned around AD 1785? To answer these questions, we cut three sections across various parts of the outermost ditches, documenting them in profile and sampling their contents for artifacts and material that was datable by radiocarbon assay. In addition, we excavated parts of three isolated pits near the site periphery, wishing to learn the source of their fill, their purpose, and their age. Placement of the ditch and pit excavations was guided precisely by the magnetic survey maps.

Archaeological excavation is a destructive process. To minimize the loss of information, field workers not only record pages of information about what they see in the ground, they also apply artifact recovery methods that return even the smallest items of potential value to the lab. In the case of Double Ditch Village and many other Plains Village studies conducted since 1969, field recovery has involved water screening of nearly all excavated sediments over fine mesh (16-per-inch) window screen. This screening system assures recovery of not only large artifacts such as pottery and bison bones, but also thousands of small yet important items such as tiny stone flakes, bones of micromammals and fish, charred seeds, and tiny glass trade beads and small fragments of iron and copper that document the beginnings of contact and trade between Natives and European Americans.

The 2002 excavations provided their own surprises. As expected, Mound B proved to be stratified from one side to the other, but it was composed of not so much individual loads of trash as a homogenized mixture of earth and artifacts laid down in massive

FIGURE 10.22 Excavation in progress during 2002 in the reopened Will and Spinden trench through Mound B. Diagram represents the Harvard students' cross section through Mound B: 5-foot increments on the scales represent about 1.5 meters; letters designate the strata recognized in the profile. (After Will and Spinden 1906, Plate XXX.)

layers. Trade artifacts occurred throughout the mound, and pottery in the mound showed no measurable change from one side of the mound to the other. Together, this information indicated that Mound B was intentionally constructed from dirt hauled from elsewhere in the village (it was not a refuse heap, per se). Moreover, Mound B was built during a very short period of time, being constructed late in the history of the village, well after when trade artifacts first reached the region about 450 BP. The cleared-out trench also showed that those who had built the mound had borrowed away the ground beneath before the mound was constructed, and that the outer visible ditch (Ditch 2) was dug at precisely the time Mound B was completed. The cross sections through the outer two fortification systems, Ditches 3 and 4, revealed them to be deep, narrow trenches, having sharp edges and no spoil dirt on either side. This was unusual for fortification ditches, which usually have

rounded margins and spoil dirt thrown to the inside. Artifacts in Ditches 3 and 4 were clearly older than those in Mound B. Check-stamped pottery, a variety normally found only in sites dating 650–450 BP, was found in one storage pit near the village margin. This was another clue, in addition to apparent rectangular house depressions and bastioned fortifications, that the village may have been founded between 550 BP and 450 BP.

The 2003 and 2004 field seasons saw continuing and concluding geophysical surveys and a greater emphasis on excavation. These studies revealed much about the layout and dynamics of the community (Figure 10.23) and went a long way toward fulfilling several of our broader research goals. Remote sensing showed the outermost fortification system, now called Ditch 4, to include at least 10 large bastion loops. Ditch 4 generally lay well outside most of the earthen mounds, but it intersected four of the smallest

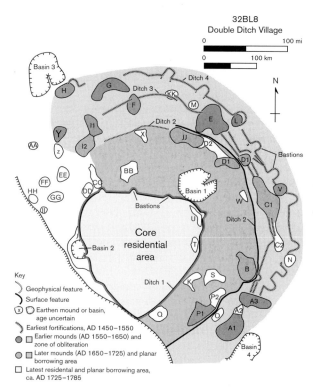

FIGURE 10.23 Double Ditch Village plan showing major features and change through time. Letters and Letter/Number combinations are used to label the mounds.

the village chronology, we sampled what appeared on the surface to be a rectangular house depression, one of several such features in the north central part of the site, and several pit features near the village margin, outside Ditch 2. We designed the outer ditch studies to clarify details of construction and chronology, building on the 2002 excavation data. A number of test pits targeted magnetic signals for storage pits inside houses in the core of the village, inside Ditch 1. Here our goals were to sample the latest period of site occupation and to learn more about house-building and earthmoving activities near the village center.

The mound tests revealed more than we had expected. At four locations the tests exposed parts of open ditches directly beneath the mounds, clearly indicating that in many cases the ditches did not connect the mounds but, rather, the mounds had been built on top of fortification ditches no longer used for defense. But this relationship was not a simple one of mounds replacing ditches: it became clear that both ditches and mounds continued to be built late in the history of the settlement. At several mounds, stratigraphy showed that the surface *around* the mounds had been artificially lowered in some manner. The search for a rectangular house was unsuccessful. The rectangular depression between Ditches 1 and 2, thought to be a house location, proved to be a large, elongated borrow pit. The inhabitants had artificially truncated the entire area inside and around by digging out the earth and taking it away. Perhaps the depression marked a former rectangular house obliterated by borrowing.

Excavations within houses inside Ditch 1 and near the village core confirmed that this entire area had been planed off and borrowed away, as was the case at the location of the supposed rectangular house between Ditches 1 and 2. Floors of earthlodges in the village core lay only 20 cm (8 in.) below the present ground surface, and they rested directly on sterile sediment. The entire area within Ditch 2 had been subjected to what we call *planar borrowing*, or horizontally continuous earth removal over a large area, after which the dirt and artifacts were transported to the mounds or elsewhere. The villagers had removed the shallow parts of all except the latest earthlodges inside Ditches 1 and 2.

Excavations outside Ditch 2 and across Ditches 3 and 4 revealed that all traces of dwellings along with the upper parts of pit features and the ditch systems

of these features. Ditch 3, the next toward the interior, contained only three visible bastion elements and consisted, in places, of two closely spaced parallel ditch lines. Ditch 3 also appeared to be more intimately linked to some of the largest mounds on the village margin, with six or seven large earthen mounds lying along the line of Ditch 3. A portion of Ditch 2, the outer originally known ditch, was visible in magnetic data even where no evidence was visible on the surface.

Excavations in 2003 and 2004 focused on the mounds, a potential rectangular house, the outermost fortification ditch, and many pit features. We dug 15 deep test pits in 13 mounds. We wished to date each mound and learn whether it had been constructed rapidly from earth hauled over a short period of time, like Mound B, or in some other manner. Ultimately, we wished to know the chronological and functional relationships between the mounds and fortification systems. Seeking hard data about the earliest end of had been completely obliterated in that area. Only the lower parts of deeper features remained, with these overlain by a homogenized sediment layer containing small artifacts. This obliteration of the outer parts of the original settlement documents a severe, localized environmental impact resulting from activities of the villagers that continued after the dwelling area shrank and the outer part of the community was abandoned. It was only beneath mounds placed outside Ditch 2 that the old ground surface on which the village was settled was still preserved.

SUMMARY OF FINDINGS

Radiocarbon dating and artifact studies are ongoing as this is written, but several results bear mention. The earliest dates produced so far fall between 550 BP and 450 BP, and more dates from deepest and earliest contexts are expected to confirm that the community was founded around 500 BP (AD 1450). This founding date is consistent with the nature of the bastioned fortification system, the presence of check-stamped pottery, and many suggestions that rectangular houses once existed there. The three-century-long period of continuous occupation at Double Ditch makes the site a remarkable laboratory of continuing study of cultural change.

Stone artifacts from the excavations indicate a shift in geographic and presumed social connections outside the village during the history of the site. Early on, the villagers used Tongue River silicified sediment, a stone from near-local sources south of the village, and connections by travel or trade brought in quartzite and dendritic chert from distant sources far to the southwest, near the Black Hills in South Dakota and Wyoming. Later in time, the southern and southwestern connections faded, and people made heavier use of stone sources for Knife River flint and porcellanite to the west and northwest. This change in stone raw material use may reflect the influx of the nomadic Sioux into areas south and southwest of Double Ditch, as well as village alliances that shifted through time from the Arikaras who lived south of Double Ditch to the Hidatsas who lived to the north. We can easily organize pottery from the excavations into an "early" group and a "late" group. The contrast between groups is strong and suggests the sudden addition to the village pottery assemblage of ceramic products from one or two new social groups,

a change occurring about 300 BP (AD 1650). This may imply a sudden increase in exchange with new, nearby peoples, or perhaps incorporation of foreign potters directly into the settlement. The cause underlying this abrupt change in pottery is a significant question for future research.

Figure 10.23 summarizes current knowledge regarding the internal dynamics of the settlement. The model of village contraction over time has been supported. Ditches 3 and 4 are clearly the oldest, with Ditch 4 likely dating between 550 BP and 450 BP (to be confirmed by more radiocarbon assays). Most if not all of the outer mounds are more recent than these two fortification systems, however, and it is clear that by perhaps 350 BP ditch systems 3 and 4 had been abandoned and several mounds had been built over them. Not all the mounds were constructed as rapidly as Mound B, but it is likely that several mounds were intentionally constructed as "strong points" or parts of village defenses. Based on historical data, wooden palisades or pickets consisting of closely spaced vertical posts were undoubtedly part of the village fortifications, but our excavations poorly documented the palisades. Several palisades may have linked to the large mounds or perhaps skirted around them, to complete the fortification system used after Ditches 3 and 4 were abandoned and some of the mounds were built.

After the outer mounds had been built, the village contracted to an area roughly demarcated by Ditch 2, and the process of obliteration of the older, abandoned, outer parts of the settlement began to occur. Degradation of the older perimeter of the original settlement continued until around 1785, when the village was abandoned. This "impact zone" around the settlement was probably devoid of vegetation and subject to erosion, and people may have located their garden plots and hobbled their horses there late in the history of the village. Planar borrowing and removal of earth for placement in mounds occurred throughout most of the area inside Ditch 2 and Ditch 1, and it may also have extended into the areas around some of the mounds. Based on the long period of mound construction beginning between 450 BP and 350 BP, several cycles of extensive earth removal may have occurred, continuing up until the time the village was abandoned. Such borrowing is a very unusual, labor-intensive activity, not well documented at any other Plains Village site. While one purpose of planar borrowing may have been to create mounds as elements in village defenses, this process of earth and artifact removal may also have functioned as a village-wide cleansing and renewal mechanism triggered by repeated and horrendous smallpox epidemics. One inescapable theme in the history of the site is that its population became continuously smaller over time. When the village residents threw up the palisade and dry moat that proved to be their last line of defense (Ditch 1), it protected a population that was only 20 percent the size of the village at its peak. The last ditch and palisade could not defend against the spotted demon that struck again in AD 1781–1782, nor against the Sioux who followed closely on the heels of the disease.

The Double Ditch Village Project is a testament to successful collaboration among several interested and dedicated parties. As with most archaeological studies, we have learned much more than we sought and many things we did not expect. Fortuitous discoveries are some of the finest rewards from planned and focused investigations. New investigative tools, such as closely coordinated remote-sensing and excavation studies, played a central role in the project. Without new methods to guide and direct the more conventional and indispensable forms of archaeological investigation, such as hand excavation, radiocarbon dating, and artifact studies, the cost of meeting the goals set for this project would have been prohibitive. While Double Ditch Village is practically unique from the perspective of its preservation and complexity, the lessons we are learning there about how to approach Plains Village archaeology and how to interpret Mandan prehistory will be applied several times over at many other sites during the coming decades. The people of North Dakota are to be commended for supporting this exciting and informative study in archaeology.

DISCUSSION QUESTIONS

1. Why was the research described here undertaken? What were its goals? Who was involved?

2. Could as much have been learned about Double Ditch Village if the investigators hadn't done the geophysical studies they describe? Contrast the advantages and disadvantages of these techniques with those of traditional hand excavation.

3. Explain why these investigators came to believe that the mounds at Double Ditch Village were intentionally constructed rather than simply accumulations of refuse. What are the implications of this finding for what was happening at the village?

4. What might explain the changes in the raw materials used for making stone tools and in the types of pottery being made between the early and late parts of the occupation at Double Ditch Village? How would you investigate further?

CHAPTER 11

Tribes and Chiefdoms in the Southeast

One famous event of the American Civil War is the first submarine attack in history: the "South's secret weapon," a small submersible watercraft, the *H. L. Hunley*, set out to attack the U.S.S. *Housatonic*, a Union sloop-of-war that was blockading Charleston, South Carolina. No more than 40 feet long (12.2 m), less than 4 feet (1.2 m) wide at her widest, and about 4 feet high, the *Hunley* truly was a tiny vessel for her intended crew: eight men to turn the cranks that powered her, and a ninth to steer. She was made from a modified iron boiler and was lowered and raised by filling or evacuating ballast tanks at either end.

On February 17, 1864, the *Hunley* rammed the *Housatonic* with a long iron rod extending from her bow. At the end of the rod was a torpedo packed with explosives. Then the submarine backed up, playing out a rope attached to the torpedo. When a *Hunley* crewman pulled the rope, the torpedo detonated and within a few minutes the *Housatonic* sank. It was not until World War I that another successful submarine attack took place, but the potential of submarine warfare certainly had been shown by the *Hunley*'s attack. Inexplicably, although she signaled her success to Confederates waiting anxiously on nearby Sullivan's Island, the *Hunley* never made it to shore, sinking at an unknown spot for unknown reasons.

The fate of the *Hunley* remained a mystery for over 130 years. Then in May 1995 a team from the National Underwater Marine Agency (N.U.M.A.), a private not-for-profit organization funded by best-selling author Clive Cussler, found her buried in sediment. She was lying on her starboard side only about 4 miles (6.5 km) from Sullivan's Island, still pointed home. Many people had searched for the *Hunley*; P. T. Barnum even offered a $100,000 reward. N.U.M.A. itself had looked for the *Hunley* for nearly 15 years, finding the wreckage only while investigating the results of a systematic **magnetometer survey** of the bay. The good news was that the *Hunley* apparently had been rapidly buried and thus, sealed as a true time capsule very much intact. It also meant that great care had to be taken to recover materials that likely included the remains of individuals and perhaps information about why the boat sank.

Once she was found, the real work began. Three options for dealing with the wreck were considered: (1) leaving the *Hunley* in a protected grave site, (2) excavation in place through **underwater archaeology** followed by reburial, and (3) raising the *Hunley* for thorough study and conservation. The visibility at the site was less than 2 feet (0.6 m), the currents were strong, and swarms of stinging jellyfish plagued divers. Moreover, tests suggested that the *Hunley* still retained considerable structural integrity. Thus, the third option was selected, a difficult and delicate process that required the collaboration of many government and private agencies and work by engineers, divers, and underwater archaeologists. After the *Hunley* had been cradled in an elaborate truss fitted with a padded sling, the vessel was raised in the same position in which it was lying; this prevented the shifting of the sediments inside, so that other parts of the hull were not overstressed. Since the *Hunley* was raised, years of careful excavation, conservation of the sub itself as well as its contents, and study have been required. The wreck of the *Housatonic* also was investigated, though it remains buried in place (Lenihan 2002).

The *Hunley* now is yielding its secrets (Swan 2000). For one thing, it was not clear whether eight or nine crewmen were aboard when the attack took place and the *Hunley* disappeared. Excavation produced the remains of eight crewmen. DNA and other studies have identified some of these crewmen, which was something historians hadn't been able to ascertain. Among these men were Frank Collins, James Wicks, and Joseph Ridgaway. Specific remains also have been recognized for Lieutenant George E. Dixon, who was known to have been piloting the boat that night. Facial reconstructions now have given faces to these heroes of the Confederacy. Eventually, in April 2004, all the remains were reburied in a public ceremony at Charleston's Magnolia Cemetery.

Much about the construction of this sub also has been learned, and specific artifacts help dramatize the story of the *Hunley*'s crew. For example, it was long said that Lt. Dixon always carried a $20 gold piece given to him by a sweetheart. At the battle of Shiloh, Dixon was shot in the leg, but supposedly the gold coin deflected the bullet and saved his life. Imagine how amazing it was for archaeologists to find a bent gold piece that had been sanded and inscribed as follows: "Shiloh April 6, 1862 My life Preserver G.E.D." Some old tales actually turn out to be true!

The story of the *Hunley* has excited students of the Confederacy for generations. It is a true southern icon (Steven D. Smith 2000), but its discovery, raising, and excavation have introduced countless people to underwater archaeology as well. This type of archaeology is very colorful and apparently full of adventure. It certainly takes unique skills, and it can be dangerous. However, underwater archaeology also has much in common with terrestrial archaeology. Though sometimes mistaken for treasure hunting, both pursuits are conducted to help us learn about the past. Both are painstaking processes, every step of which must be carefully recorded. As we begin this chapter on the Southeast, it is appropriate to keep in mind that stories of the Civil War are an important part of what Southeastern archaeologists can help us understand.

DEFINITION OF THE AREA

Chapters 11 through 13 cover the Eastern Woodlands of North America, which stretch from the margins of the Plains to the Atlantic Ocean across nearly a

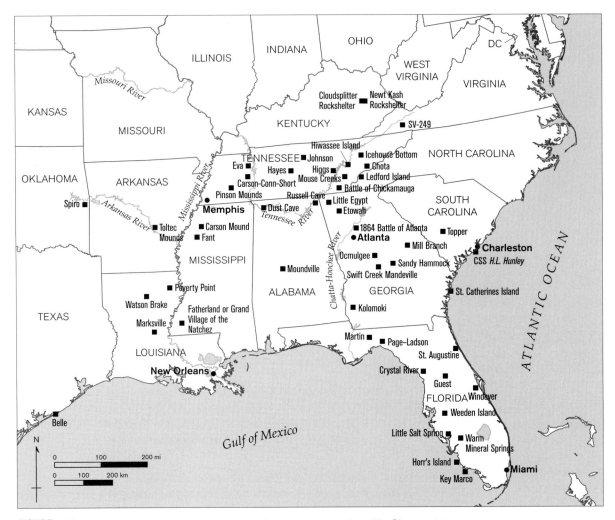

FIGURE 11.1 The Southeast culture area showing sites that are mentioned in Chapter 11.

quarter of the continent. The subject of this chapter, the Southeast culture area, extends from eastern Texas, including some of the Gulf Coast, and southeastern Oklahoma east and north to Lousiana, eastern Arkansas, southeastern Missouri, Mississippi, Alabama, Tennessee, southern Kentucky, southeastern West Virginia, western Virginia, all of North Carolina except the northeastern corner, South Carolina, Georgia, and Florida (Figure 11.1). Although this is a traditionally recognized culture area for North America, its boundaries are particularly arbitrary.

In the first place, for much of the pre-Columbian past, people living in the Ozarks of northwestern Arkansas and southwestern Missouri were much more similar to Southeastern people than to Plains cultures, but during the Historic period tribes like the Osage adopted a Plains lifestyle. This was part of the complicated movement of people and cultural transformation throughout the Plains during the Protohistoric and Historic periods discussed in Chapter 10. Thus the boundary between the Southern Plains and the Southeast was anything but fixed.

Second, it can be argued that the entire Eastern Woodlands should be treated as one cultural area because of the general environmental and cultural similarities among the areas treated in this chapter and in Chapters 12 and 13. Archaeologists working throughout the Eastern Woodlands use similar broad sequences recognizing Paleoindian, Archaic, Woodland, and Mississippian or Late Prehistoric periods (e.g., Table 11.1), and they often make comparisons across the culture areas we recognize. As you read these three chapters you will find many similarities.

Nevertheless, discussions that treat the Eastern Woodlands as a single unit obscure the cultural variability that formerly existed in this vast part of North America. Specifically, the emphasis in such summaries necessarily becomes the story of the relatively spectacular developments of the interior Southeast and Midwest heartland, where farming, mound building, and powerful chiefdoms were found in later pre-Columbian times. This is an important story, but the other peoples of the East, such as those of the Plains–Woodland margin, the Great Lakes, New England, the Atlantic Coast, and Florida, have significance, too. The pre-Columbian archaeology of these other areas is also rich and important, and somewhat distinctive traditions of study tend to mirror the tripartite division we use in this text. Certainly we also can draw historical contrasts among the three areas. Starting with the Southeast culture area as we do in this chapter seems to us to be most helpful in understanding both the similarities and the differences within the eastern culture areas.

In focusing on the Southeast, remember that culture area designations are arbitrary devices that help us organize materials about the past and only generally correspond to past environmental and cultural differences. Any boundaries drawn should be regarded as quite diffuse and temporally variable, and it is wise to make a practice of thinking about similarities among areas, particularly within the Eastern Woodlands.

THE ENVIRONMENTS OF THE SOUTHEAST

Most of the Southeast has a humid subtropical climate with mild winters and hot and muggy summers punctuated by frequent thunderstorms. There are distinct seasons, but snow and persistent freezing temperatures are rare. The southern tip of Florida has a more tropical climate, with temperatures seldom dropping below 65°F and little seasonal variation in temperature. From February through October, however, typical rainfall exceeds 50 inches (127 cm).

Physiographically, the Southeast has two main units: the Appalachian Mountain system and the Coastal Plain. The Appalachian system trends from the northeastern margins in West Virginia toward the southwest into northeastern Alabama and northwestern Georgia. Within the Appalachian mountain system there are a number of distinct provinces, which include from west to east the Appalachian Plateau, the Ridge and Valley province, the Blue Ridge Mountains, and the Piedmont, an older plateau that has been heavily eroded. The boundary between the Appalachian system and the Coastal Plain is called the **Fall Line**, in reference to the waterfalls that form as rivers flow over this often steep feature. Swamps and offshore islands characterize much of the actual coast, and southern

TABLE 11.1 Introduction to Southeast Culture History

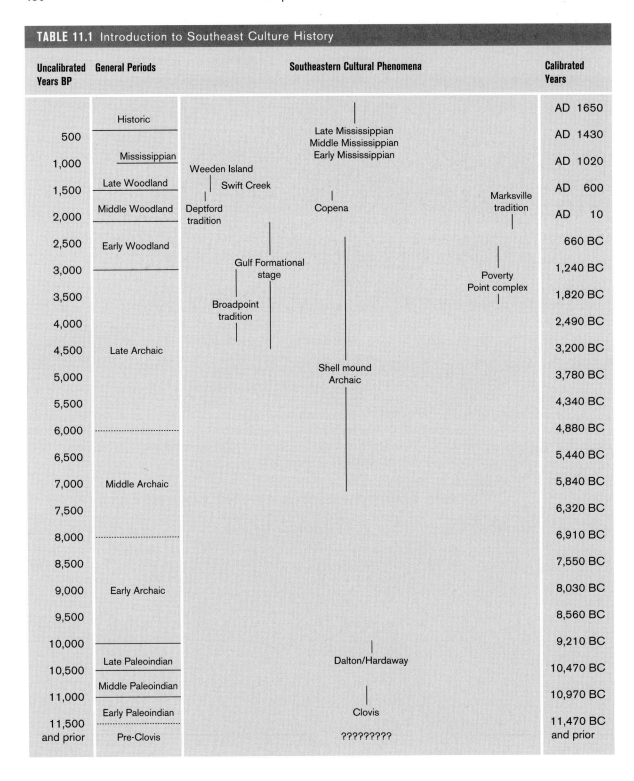

Uncalibrated Years BP	General Periods	Southeastern Cultural Phenomena	Calibrated Years
	Historic		AD 1650
500		Late Mississippian	AD 1430
	Mississippian	Middle Mississippian	
1,000		Early Mississippian	AD 1020
1,500	Late Woodland	Weeden Island	AD 600
		Swift Creek	
2,000	Middle Woodland	Deptford tradition — Copena — Marksville tradition	AD 10
2,500	Early Woodland		660 BC
3,000		Gulf Formational stage	1,240 BC
3,500			Poverty Point complex 1,820 BC
4,000		Broadpoint tradition	2,490 BC
4,500	Late Archaic		3,200 BC
5,000		Shell mound Archaic	3,780 BC
5,500			4,340 BC
6,000			4,880 BC
6,500			5,440 BC
7,000	Middle Archaic		5,840 BC
7,500			6,320 BC
8,000			6,910 BC
8,500			7,550 BC
9,000	Early Archaic		8,030 BC
9,500			8,560 BC
10,000			9,210 BC
10,500	Late Paleoindian	Dalton/Hardaway	10,470 BC
11,000	Middle Paleoindian		10,970 BC
	Early Paleoindian	Clovis	
11,500 and prior	Pre-Clovis	?????????	11,470 BC and prior

Florida is so low lying that most of it is swamp. The sediments of the Coastal Plain often are sandy and gravelly, reflecting deposition as the ocean moved back and forth across this extension of the continental shelf.

West of the Appalachian Mountain system and north of the Coastal Plain in Tennessee and Kentucky is the Low Interior Plateau, where the underlying rocks dip gently northwestward into the Midwest. The valley of the Mississippi River is very extensive, containing terraces and old channels as well as erosional remnants such as Crowley's Ridge and the Macon Ridge, both of which are situated in the center of the floodplain. The Ozark and Ouachita mountains are areas of greater relief, to the northwest at the margins of this culture area (Fenneman 1938).

This Southeastern landscape naturally supports a variety of forest types although agricultural activities have reduced the extent of forest in many areas, and burning and cutting has altered the forest composition. In southern Florida the forest contains many tropical hardwood and animal species. The rest of the Southeast is part of the temperate deciduous forest biome. The forests of the southern Coastal Plain are dominated by evergreen trees, although deciduous species are present. Long-leaf pines, loblolly pines, slash pines, live oak, and magnolia may be important trees depending on soils, elevation, and moisture. North of these evergreen forests is a broad ecotone with the forests of the interior Southeast in which oak becomes more common. The forests of the Appalachian Mountain system, the Interior Low Plateau, and the Ozarks are complex deciduous forests with a mix of trees and a wide variety of plant and animal resources (e.g., E. Lucy Braun 1967; Shelford 1963). The character of the forest varies at higher elevations and also toward the west and north, where it is somewhat less rich, while riverine forests are distinct, highly productive habitat types throughout the Southeast.

Climatic Change

You might think that the Ice Age was relatively unimportant in the Southeast because glaciers never were a factor, but significant environmental changes have occurred in this area since the Wisconsin maximum. During the Wisconsin glaciation, seasonal variation probably was less pronounced than it is today (Bense 1994, 18), and this lack of seasonality affected vegetation significantly. At the height of the Wisconsin the main vegetation types in the Southeast most likely were a spruce and jack pine forest in the northern Southeast and an oak–hickory–southern pine forest to the south. Along the crest of the Appalachians tundra was found. Southern Florida was very dry and seems to have supported only oak scrub and grassland vegetation (Delcourt and Delcourt 1981). Ecological communities were unlike any we know today, with very high diversity and mixes of species currently found in widely separated environments (Graham and Mead 1987).

Lowering sea levels by more than 300 feet (90 m) also meant that at the maximum Wisconsin glaciation, much more of the continental shelf was exposed than is today. Another glance at Figure 2.12 will serve as a reminder of how different the coastal configuration was at the height of the Wisconsin glaciation. Given this more extensive Coastal Plain, rivers had to travel greater distances and fall to lower depths. Particularly the Mississippi and rivers that traversed the Atlantic Coastal Plain are thought to have cut deeply into their beds, scouring out tons of deposits before reaching the sea. The rivers of the Gulf Coastal Plain do not appear to have cut down as much during the Pleistocene (Bloom 1983).

Environmental changes in the Southeast must have been truly complex throughout the end of the Pleistocene and the beginning of the Holocene. There most likely was a mosaic of vegetation change rather than a simple zonal northward shifting of vegetation types. Also as water levels rose, the coast underwent a complex process of drowning. The interaction of rising sea level, isostatic rebound, drainage patterns, and local topography in various parts of the Southeast is a fascinating story that is still being explored.

During the Holocene, the Hypsithermal (ca. 9000–2500 BP) warm period meant changes in forest cover. Dry conditions around 7000 BP are particularly noteworthy. The most significant change in the Southeast was the disappearance of hardwood trees as dominants from the forests of the Coastal Plain, except in the river valleys and swamps. At this time various pine species became the dominants in these forests. Major change in river regimes and coastlines also occurred during the Mid-Holocene. At the beginning of this period braided streams gave way to lower-energy rivers. Eventually meander belts and aquatic habitats similar to those of the recent past developed. Along the coast estuaries and barrier islands formed as sea levels stabilized.

Human populations also were responsible for altering habitats long into the past. We usually think of this happening when Southeasterners shifted to fully agricultural economies within the last thousand years. This process, however, likely began on a small, but perhaps locally significant scale, well before the eleventh century AD. For example, in the Little Tennessee River valley, the record of pollen and plant remains suggests that human impact on the environment increased as soon as squash, gourd, and seed plants began to be cultivated, approximately 4000 BP. After this time, land clearing and other disturbances only increased (Delcourt et al. 1986). Of course, following European settlement Southeastern landscapes were even more significantly modified by human activities.

HUNTER-GATHERERS OF THE DISTANT PAST

Paleoindians in the Southeast

Unequivocal documentation of Pre-Clovis settlement has not been found in the Southeast, but several sites may provide Pre-Clovis evidence. First, there is the Topper site, mentioned in Chapter 3 (Rose 1999). This site, located in South Carolina along the Savannah River, has a layer below the Clovis level containing possible tools such as chisels and scrapers, and even deeper layers in the site have been reported to contain artifacts as well. While it has been estimated by optical luminescence that the layer immediately below the Clovis level could be 16,000 years old (Wilford 2004), radiocarbon dates first reported in late 2004 indicate that some of the lower strata with possible artifacts are more than 50,000 years old. However, the validity of the radiocarbon dates must be evaluated by the scientific community, and there is no broad agreement that the stone objects recovered from Topper really are Pre-Clovis tools.

Other possibly Pre-Clovis finds are from the Saltville Valley in southwestern Virginia. Three levels at site SV-2 have been dated between approximately 14,150 ±80 BP and 13,000 BP. They contain mastodon remains in configurations

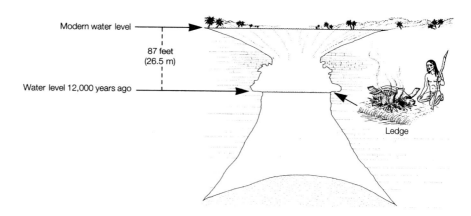

FIGURE 11.2 Artist's conception of the sinkhole at Little Salt Spring in which a speared tortoise shell was found on a submerged ledge. Sinkholes and other wet sites in Florida provide important information about early lifestyles.

Modern water level

87 feet (26.5 m)

Water level 12,000 years ago

Ledge

suggestive of human activities, chert flakes, possible tools made of bone and ivory, and fire-cracked rock (McDonald 2000). Like Topper, SV-2 is not accepted by all archaeologists as evidence for Pre-Clovis occupation.

Perhaps the most famous potentially Pre-Clovis site from the Southeast is Little Salt Spring, a wet site located in Sarasota County, Florida. Here a giant land tortoise apparently was killed by driving a pointed wooden stake through it. The wooden stake or spear was dated to 12,030 ±200 BP, and the bones of the now extinct tortoise to approximately 13,450 BP (Clausen et al. 1979). This site is one of many **sinkhole** sites in Florida, some of which have Paleoindian materials (Figure 11.2). In fact, Paleoindian materials from Florida have been found in regions in which sinkholes are common, in riverine sites, as well as in once exposed areas now underneath the waters of the Gulf of Mexico. Fortunately for archaeologists, these underwater sites can yield extremely well-preserved artifactual and ecofactual materials, which can be directly dated. So far, most of this material appears to be from the Clovis era or more recent times (Milanich 1994).

Conventionally, Southeastern archaeologists recognize three Paleoindian subperiods from Clovis times onward. These are Early Paleoindian or Clovis (11,500–11,000 BP), Middle Paleoindian (11,000–10,500 BP), and Late Paleoindian or Dalton (10,500–10,000 BP). Well-dated Paleoindian contexts in the Southeast as a whole are fairly rare. In the Cumberland River valley in Tennessee, the Johnson site has yielded three dates, 11,700 ±980 BP, 12,660 ±970 BP, and 11,980 ±110 BP, and fluted point preforms as well as features (Goodyear 1999). However, the standard deviations for the first two dates are quite large. Radiocarbon dates from the Page–Ladson site, an underwater stratified site located on the Aucilla River in northern Florida, range from 13,130 BP to 9540 BP. Dates from the Warm Mineral Springs, also in Florida, range from 9880 BP to 10,630 BP representing Late Paleoindian use.

Southeastern Paleoindian projectile point types are shown in Figure 11.3. These forms are similar to Paleoindian point forms found elsewhere in the Eastern Woodlands (Chapters 12 and 13). True Clovis points have been found in the Southeast, particularly in Virginia and in northern Alabama, Tennessee, and Kentucky, but they are not common in the Gulf and South Atlantic Coastal Plains (Goodyear 1999). Similarly, Clovis points are less common than other fluted point types in Florida (Milanich 1994). Middle Paleoindian projectile point types may be smaller, waisted, and even unfluted. Bases often are concave. They

FIGURE 11.3 Fluted and unfluted Paleoindian point forms found in the Southeast.

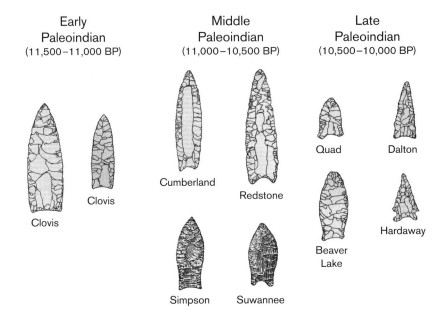

Early
Paleoindian
(11,500–11,000 BP)

Middle
Paleoindian
(11,000–10,500 BP)

Late
Paleoindian
(10,500–10,000 BP)

Clovis

Clovis

Cumberland

Redstone

Simpson

Suwannee

Quad

Dalton

Beaver
Lake

Hardaway

include the Cumberland point, which is primarily found in the Midsouth, and the Simpson and Suwannee points of Florida and the Coastal Plain. Thus there may be some regional cultural variation beginning in Middle Paleoindian times. Some lanceolate Plains forms are found on the western margins of the Southeast as well. Beaver Lake, Quad, and Redstone point types often occur at the beginning of the Late Paleoindian in the Midsouth, but Late Paleoindian projectile points typically are Dalton and Hardaway points.

Items other than projectile points and preforms characterize the Paleoindian toolkit as well. End scrapers for working hides and wedges for splitting bones, as well as a variety of bone tools, are common, particularly in Early Paleoindian assemblages. Wet sites in Florida have yielded various bone and antler tools, including double-ended bone points, ivory foreshafts for hafting projectile points to spears, bola stones, and weights for spear throwers, along with wooden items. In Dalton assemblages the Dalton adze (Figure 11.4), a heavy, triangular biface, is as distinctive as the Dalton point. It generally is the first woodworking tool in Southeastern assemblages.

The exploitation of Pleistocene megafaunal and other species by Paleoindians is assumed for much of the Southeast. However, outside Florida's wet sites, there is little actual evidence of cultural remains in association with extinct fauna. Examples from Florida include the giant tortoise at Salt Spring already mentioned, a possible mammoth kill site at the Guest site near Ocala (Goodyear 1999), and from the Wacissa River, the skull of a now-extinct bison, in which a broken projectile point was embedded (S. David Webb et al. 1984). From northern Florida, there are numerous remains of mammoths, mastodons, and other Pleistocene fauna and a significant number of Floridian Paleoindian tools manufactured from the bones and tusks of megafauna (Dunbar and Webb 1996).

These associations don't necessarily indicate that Paleoindian subsistence focused on megafauna. In fact, the excellent preservation in Florida underwater

FIGURE 11.4 Dalton adzes, believed to have been some of the first woodworking tools used by Southeasterners.

sites has proved by that Paleoindians during the Early and Middle Paleoindian subperiods exploited a broad range of both extinct and modern animals. Among them are sloth, tapir, horse, deer, panther, raccoon, opossum, rabbit, muskrat, wood ibis, box turtle, and gopher tortoise; frogs, fish, and shellfish are present, as well. Thus, most scholars assume that Early and Middle Paleoindians in the Southeast were generalized foragers. By Late Paleoindian times, there is little question that generalized foraging characterized the subsistence strategy (e.g., McGahey 1996; Walker 2000). For example, both botanical remains (nuts, fruit seeds, chenopodium) and animal remains (waterfowl, muskrat, swamp rabbit, turtle, some deer) are documented for the Late Paleoindian at Dust Cave, Alabama. (See "The Dust Cave Archaeological Project: Investigating Paleoindian and Archaic Lifeways in Southeastern North America," Section D.5 of the Student CD.)

Of course what fascinates archaeologists about the evidence for Paleoindians in the Southeast is how it may fit into broad pattern of early material across the continent. We cannot fully discuss the many interpretations that have been made in this brief introduction, but two models illustrate the issues often considered.

First, Anderson (1990, 1996) suggests that very high densities of Early Paleoindian projectile points in the Ohio, Tennessee, and Cumberland river valleys indicate that Paleoindians entered the Southeast via these valleys and then explored outward, eventually establishing new staging areas and populating the entire Southeast. In this way, distinctive regional traditions began to develop as early as the Middle Paleoindian period. Sites like the Carson–Conn–Short site in Tennessee, which has 60 clusters of heat-treated chert from a locally exposed alluvial fan, along with Clovis and Cumberland points and other Paleoindian artifacts, can be seen as staging areas (Broster and Norton 1996). Anderson's model obviously assumes that Paleoindians arrived in the Southeast from west and north.

Second, for the Eastern Woodlands as a whole, David Meltzer (Meltzer 1988; Meltzer and Smith 1986) has proposed that two subsistence–settlement patterns developed among the earlier makers of fluted points. He argues that in the Southeast, which was never glaciated and throughout the Pleistocene supported complex forests with a mix of deciduous and coniferous trees and both boreal and temperate zone resources, specialized hunting of large game would not have made ecological sense. Instead, generalized foraging by small residential groups should be expected. In contrast, deglaciated regions to the north, where tundra and spruce parkland predominated at the end of the Pleistocene and beginning of the Holocene, specialized hunting from large base camps may have been a reasonable strategy. Table 11.2 lists the proposed characteristics of these two different strategies.

Although archaeological knowledge of the Paleoindian period in the Southeast remains limited, there is tantalizing evidence to consider. The evidence for particular subareas of the Southeast is better than others. In Florida, where lowered sea level and climatic alterations meant great dryness during the Pleistocene, well-preserved Paleoindian sites have been found, mainly in regions where sinkholes and other limestone-related features are common. Here an oasis model proposes that Paleoindians clustered close to water sources (Milanich 1994). The wealth of Dalton sites in the central Mississippi River valley also has allowed construction of detailed subsistence and settlement models for the Late Paleoindian groups (Morse and Morse 1983; Schiffer 1975).

TABLE 11.2 Possible Contrasts in Paleoindian Subsistence and Settlement Strategies

Environmental Location	Subsistence	Mobility Patterns	Site Characteristics	Lithic Procurement[1]
Recently glaciated, periglacial tundra and spruce parkland	Some focus on caribou hunting, but also collecting of plants and small animals	Highly mobile	Some large sites, sites associated with glacial features	High frequencies of exotic chert in at least some sites
Never glaciated areas, forested	Generalized foraging for mammals, birds, fish, and plant foods	Mobile, tethered to quarries	Small sites, but quarry-related base camps, sites in floodplains	Mainly local chert use

[1] Exotic chert: sources over 40 kilometers (25 mi) away; local chert: sources 40 kilometers away or nearer.

Adapted from Adovasio and Carr (2002) and Meltzer (1988).

Archaic Foragers of the Southeast

Originally defined as a stage of cultural development during which people were nomadic, egalitarian hunter-gatherers who did not make pottery, the Eastern Archaic is more often treated today simply as a period in time. In many parts of the Eastern Woodlands, but particularly in the Southeast, there is ample evidence that generalized foraging characterized Paleoindian as well as Archaic adaptations. On the other hand, even before 3000 BP, Archaic populations in some areas, such as the river valleys of interior Southeast and the Midwest, had developed many of the characteristics of the Woodland: settled villages, pottery making, horticulture, mound building and mortuary ceremonialism, and social hierarchy.

In many ways, the growing body of data on the Archaic period in the Southeast and in the rest of the Eastern Woodlands is fascinating because of its lack of uniformity. Where and when did cultural change occur during the Archaic? Where did patterns of adaptation fail to change much at all? Why did change occur in the first place? The questions that interest Archaic period researchers throughout the Eastern Woodlands have to do primarily with the adoption of more sedentary lifestyles, shifts in the types of resource exploited, experimentation with the cultivation of plants, and the development of mechanisms of social differentiation associated with production and trade in prestige items, mound building, and mortuary ceremonialism. In reading this section on the Archaic period in the Southeast, and the material in the next two chapters about the same period in other parts of the Eastern Woodlands, look for data relevant to these topics.

The Archaic period in the Southeast spans 7000 years, from approximately 10,000 BP to 3000 BP. As is the case throughout the Eastern Woodlands, three Archaic subperiods typically are designated: Early Archaic (10,000–8000 BP), Middle Archaic (8000–6000 BP), and Late Archaic (6000–3000 BP). Some archaeologists have argued for a **Gulf Formational stage** between approximately 4500 BP and 2100 BP in the Gulf Coastal Plain of the Southeast (e.g., Walthall 1980). This would encompass the period of fiber-tempered pottery making as well as the **Poverty Point complex** of the lower Mississippi valley. A Late Archaic **Broadpoint tradition** marked by broad-bladed stemmed points also may be recognized,

TABLE 11.3 Lithic Traits Associated with the Paleoindian-to-Archaic Transition in the Eastern Woodlands

1 Presence of notched and stemmed projectile points
2 Use of a wider range of lithic raw materials, including some that are harder to flake (e.g., quartzite, argillite, slate)
3 Predominant use of locally available stone, including cobbles from streambeds as opposed to exotic stone transported some distance
4 Less resharpening and other maintenance of chipped stone tools and more use of expedient stone tools, which are discarded after minimal use
5 Increase in ground and polished stone items, especially those associated with plant processing, woodworking, and fishing

especially on the Atlantic Coastal Plain and in the Piedmont, as well as in areas discussed in Chapters 12 and 13.

A variety of lithic traits mark the Archaic as opposed to the Paleoindian period throughout the Eastern Woodlands. These are shown in Table 11.3. Greater quantities of bone tools may also mark the Archaic.

Because Southeastern archaeologists had the opportunity to excavate deeply stratified sites, they were among the pioneers in developing Eastern Woodlands Archaic chronologies based on technological change. The first efforts to develop an Archaic sequence of projectile points used sites in North Carolina's Piedmont (Coe 1964). A series of deep excavations in the Little Tennessee River valley, which were conducted in advance of the TVA's flooding of the Tellico Reservoir, further clarified this sequence (Chapman 1975, 1977, 1985). Figure 11.5 illustrates some of the projectile point types that have been found in Archaic sequences in the Southeast. Notice that side-notched forms such as the Big Sandy point generally are followed by corner-notched forms such as the Kirk Corner Notched and

FIGURE 11.5 Archaic period projectile point forms found in the Southeast.

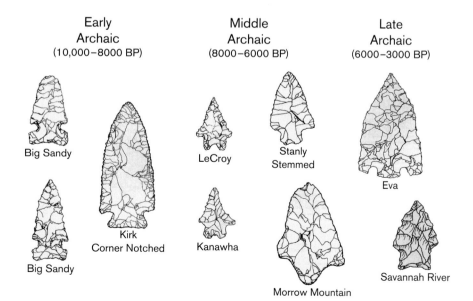

Early Archaic (10,000–8000 BP)

Middle Archaic (8000–6000 BP)

Late Archaic (6000–3000 BP)

Big Sandy

Big Sandy

Kirk Corner Notched

LeCroy

Kanawha

Stanly Stemmed

Morrow Mountain

Eva

Savannah River

0   1   2 in.
0 1 2 3 4 5 cm

FIGURE 11.6 Bannerstones have central holes and come in a variety of shapes and raw materials; these specimens are presumed to have been atlatl weights.

then by bifurcate forms such as the LeCroy and Kanawha points. The later Middle Archaic is marked by the appearance of stemmed forms like Stanly Stemmed and Morrow Mountain. Late Archaic forms often are stemmed as well, although some notched forms occur. Broad blade forms also are important in the Late Archaic, as represented by the Savannah River point from the Atlantic Coastal Plain.

Other Archaic traits are also evident in Southeastern lithic assemblages from this period. While Early Archaic stone tools are often described as formal and highly **curated**, like those of the Paleoindian period, archaeologists have noted that Middle Archaic lithics are more expedient. Moreover, fewer nonlocal raw materials are evident by Middle Archaic times (Amick and Carr 1996). Ground stone tools also increase in frequency and diversity during the Archaic as opposed to Paleoindian times. Finely made **bannerstones** presumed to have been used as atlatl weights are one example of Archaic tools made in this way (Figure 11.6).

Thanks to wet sites in Florida, we have some idea of more perishable Archaic implements as well. For example, Windover is an Early Archaic mortuary pond located in east central Florida. Among the grave goods found at Windover were various antler and bone tools and ornaments, turtle shell containers, seed necklaces, shark's teeth used as drills and scrapers, wooden stakes and tools, and various textiles showing several different types of twining (Doran 2002). Early Archaic clay hearths in Tennessee have produced fabric or basketry impressions as well (Chapman 1985).

Other items of material culture are associated with the Late Archaic, and artifacts that represent the use of different methods of indirect cooking are particularly interesting. Two such items are clay cooking balls, which are found on the Atlantic Coastal Plain and in the lower Mississippi Valley, and perforated steatite slabs, which are widely distributed during the Southeastern Late Archaic. The clay cooking balls, amorphous or shaped in a variety of forms, appear to have been heated in a fire and placed in pits or earth ovens to supply heat for the slow cooking of food. While people elsewhere used stones for indirect cooking, the inhabitants of the Coastal Plain and lower Mississippi valley had little stone to use in this manner. Steatite slabs, which archaeologists originally thought were net sinkers, most likely were used in stone boiling. Sassaman (1993) argues that the slabs would have been more thermally effective in cooking liquids than clay balls.

During the Late Archaic, Southeasterners began to manufacture flat-bottomed stone bowls of steatite and sandstone, particularly in northern Alabama, Georgia, and the Carolinas, where steatite can be quarried. It is most likely that the first steatite vessels were receptacles for indirect cooking, rather than for use directly over fires. Although archaeologists long assumed that stone vessels represented experimentation with new types of containers and thus, preceded the development of pottery, it has now been shown that this technology does not appear before 3650 BP in the Southeast. Thus, while in some areas steatite bowls precede pottery, in others pottery appears first. Regardless, the appearance of stone bowls is associated with what has been called the **container revolution** (Bruce D. Smith 1986). Some scholars have argued that changes in subsistence practices as discussed shortly required new food preparation techniques using bowls. Others have pointed out that the choice of soapstone or pottery could be indicative of ethnicity (Sassaman 1993, 1997).

The first pottery in the Eastern Woodlands began to be manufactured during the Late Archaic in the Southeast (Figure 11.7). This fiber-tempered pottery is found along the Atlantic Coastal Plain in Georgia and South Carolina beginning

FIGURE 11.7 Centers of the earliest pottery manufacture during the Late Archaic in the Southeast.

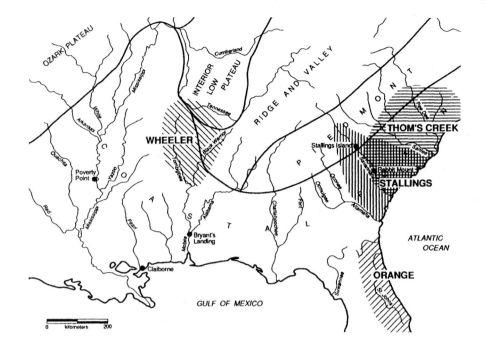

about 4500 BP where Stallings and St. Simons series are recognized. Besides being fiber tempered, this pottery has either plain, punctuated, or incised surfaces and is usually in bowl or open basin form. One early type, Stallings ware, is best known for its distinctive "drag and jab" punctuate designs, although the first vessels were plain (Sassaman 2002). Fiber-tempered pottery was made in several parts of Florida by 4000 BP (Milanich 1994), but the Orange series pottery of the St. Johns River valley is best known. Another early center of fiber-tempered pottery production lies along the middle Tennessee River in northern Alabama, where it is called Wheeler and dated after 3500 BP (Sassaman 1993). Both pottery and soapstone vessels may have been used in exchange networks and alliances as symbols of ethnic identity.

Archaeologists also have learned much about subsistence and settlement change during the Archaic. During the Early Archaic and Middle Archaic people apparently subsisted on a variety of resources and moved in small groups from campsite to campsite. Although local variations in diet occurred, the primary plant food for the interior Southeast was nuts, including hickory nuts, acorns, walnuts, and to a lesser extent hazelnuts, chestnuts, butternuts, and beechnuts. Seeds seem to have been less important in the diet at this time than later, although people did eat fleshy fruits and greens when available (Gremillion 1996, 2004). In contrast, the data from Windover in Florida, with its distinctive habitat types, suggest primary usage of edible fruits including grape, elderberry, persimmon, prickly pear, and passion flower. A crushed bottle gourd found in association with one of the burials at Windover has been AMS dated to 7290 ±120 BP, making it the oldest known example of bottle gourd in eastern North America (Newsom 2002). See the case study by John P. Hart, "A New History of Maize-Bean-Squash Agriculture in the Northeast," in Chapter 13 for more detail on early cultivation of gourds and other squashes.

There also is faunal evidence for the Early and Middle Archaic in the interior Southeast (Styles and Klippel 1996). Diverse faunal assemblages of fish, birds, and mammals, in which small mammals, most notably squirrel, are surprisingly important, characterize the Early Archaic. For example, at Russell Cave in northeastern Alabama, squirrel is more abundant than deer in the Early Archaic faunal assemblages. These distributions clearly are consistent with generalized foraging. In the Middle Archaic, a narrowing of the faunal species being exploited indicates that people began to focus on procuring deer and fish. The Hayes site in central Tennessee provides a particularly interesting Middle Archaic faunal assemblage. Deer, primarily procured in the fall, dominates the assemblage, with fish and aquatic turtles also being represented; the site, however, is a shell midden made up primarily of gastropods or snails. The researchers at this site believe the gastropods were collected as a food resource (Klippel and Morey 1986). Changes in animal prey may be attributable to warmer and drier climatic conditions associated with the opening of the forest canopy, which would have favored edge-loving species like deer. Subsistence change also may be associated with more logistical hunting and gathering as population levels increased.

Beginning in the Middle Archaic and continuing in the Late Archaic, greater usage of freshwater mussels and marine shellfish is reflected in the wide variety of shell mounds and rings dating to this period. Such sites also are common elsewhere in the Eastern Woodlands, particularly in the Midwest and along the coasts. In the Southeast they cluster on Tennessee River in Tennessee and Alabama, in the Nashville Basin, on the Atlantic Coastal Plain in Georgia and South Carolina, and along the St. Johns River in Florida. The term **Shell Mound Archaic** has been applied to these Southeastern sites, as it has to Midwestern shell mounds of the period, but it applies best to interior rather than coastal sites. Dating on these sites extends from 7180 BP to 2400 BP.

The increase in shellfishing during the Middle and Late Archaic most likely is attributable to environmental changes that brought sea level and river morphology to essentially modern conditions. Due to these changes, shellfishing became a productive part of the seasonal round of hunting and gathering during the summer months (Steponaitis 1986). However, other researchers (e.g., Claassen 1996) believe that that environmental change alone is an insufficient explanation. Rather than being simple midden features, some shell mounds and the shell rings on the coast may have been constructed features placed over cemeteries. Oftentimes these features do contain burials. Russo (1994) has argued that the Horr's Island shell mound in Florida accumulated as the result of on-mound rituals. Here a large horseshoe-shaped shell midden is associated with four mounds, the largest of which contains layers of shell midden interspersed with sand layers and no occupational debris or features (Figure 11.8). Most likely, many shell features are primarily midden deposits into which burials have been placed, but in some cases ceremonial construction seems more probable.

Perhaps the most important finding about Archaic Period subsistence has to do with the development of plant domestication, a topic that has international significance in the field of anthropology, as noted in Chapter 2. Paleoethnobotanical studies have established that the cultivation of domesticated plants began among the foragers of the Eastern Woodlands during the Archaic. This was not the cultivation of maize, beans, and squash that was so important to many Native Americans at European contact, but the cultivation of gourds and several weedy seed plants sometimes called the **Eastern Agricultural complex**. It has been

FIGURE 11.8 Mound D at Horr's Island.

proposed that the process of control and manipulation of these seed plants began in the Middle Archaic as the river valleys of the midcontinent were transformed into resource rich locales (Bruce D. Smith 1992b). In upland areas, opening the forest canopy to promote nut production might also have favored the disturbed environment in which weedy seed plants thrive (Paul Gardner 1997). It is likely that the first steps toward food production came about in different ways in different regions (Gremillion 1996).

By the end of the Archaic, between 5000 BP and 3000 BP, Archaic foragers had domesticated several of the weedy plants that naturally colonize disturbed environments. The first domesticates were sumpweed or marsh elder, native species and subspecies of gourds, goosefoot or chenopodium, and sunflower. A variety of additional weedy seed plants including maygrass, little barley, and erect knotweed also probably were cultivated, but not truly domesticated during the Late Archaic. The seeds of these native plants provided starches and oils in amounts that could have had dietary significance. These seeds may have been cooked in gruels or porridges in the pots and bowls people were beginning to make by the end of the Archaic.

The process of domestication probably took place primarily in the Midwest and Midsouth. Domesticated sunflower seeds AMS dated to 4265 ±60 BP have been recovered from the Hayes site in central Tennessee (Crites 1993). Sunflowers also have been found, and dated to about 2850 BP, at the Higgs site in eastern Tennessee (Bruce D. Smith et al. 1992). Domesticated chenopodium or goosefoot has been dated to 3400 BP at the Newt Kash and Cloudsplitter rockshelters on the Cumberland Plateau in eastern Kentucky at the northeastern edge of the Southeast. This plant also has been AMS dated to 2340 BP at Russell Cave in northern Alabama. Participation in this developing pre-maize Eastern Agricultural complex does not characterize the Piedmont and Coastal Plains of the Southeast, where farming was not adopted until Late Prehistoric times (Fritz 1990). Even where Archaic peoples did adopt farming, hunting, fishing, and collecting of wild plants remained significant economic activities. True food-producing economies did not develop for another millennium (Fritz 1990; Bruce D. Smith 1992).

Another topic of great interest to Southeastern archaeologists has been the development of sedentism. It is generally believed that Early and Middle Archaic foragers were organized into bands of closely related people that seasonally coalesced into **macrobands**. People who were part of a single macroband are thought to have foraged within a territory, such as a segment of a river valley. Beginning in the Middle Archaic, in areas where resources were abundant, this pattern of residential mobility may have given way to a strategy of logistical foraging from a base camp. Multiseasonal villages may have been established, allowing collecting parties to go out to acquire specific resources, like deer.

Some early shell mound sites like the Eva site in Tennessee (Lewis and Lewis 1961) often are cited as longer-term settlements. Structures, sometimes with clay-lined floors, appear in the Southeastern archaeological record beginning in the Middle Archaic and Late Archaic. Possible Late Archaic pithouses also have been recorded. For example, at the Mill Branch site in Georgia, a large midden-filled pit overlaid a flat-bottomed feature that was 4 by 5 meters (13.1 × 16.4 ft) in plan and contained a deeper pit with a hearth. Postmolds surrounded the large feature edge, and the accumulation of large amounts of debris (over 7000 artifacts) has been assumed to indicate long or repeated occupation (Sassaman and Ledbetter 1996, 87–90).

Finally, there is a growing body of evidence for Archaic period mounds in the Southeast. In addition to the shell mounds and rings already mentioned (Russo 1996), evidence for mound building comes from the lower Mississippi valley in Louisiana, where a number of mounds and mound complexes have been assigned to the Middle Archaic. For example, in northeast Louisiana the site of Watson Brake on the Ouachita River is quite early (Joe W. Saunders et al. 1994, 2005). Here 11 mounds encircle a central area more than 300 meters (330 yd) wide. A low ridge of alternating midden and mound fill connects the mounds, the largest of which, Mound A, is over 7 meters (23 ft) tall (Figure 11.9). Radiocarbon dates from this site indicate that people built these mounds between 5450 BP and 4850 BP. Clay cooking objects in various shapes, fire-cracked rock, and other artifactual debris suggest that people lived on these mounds, but the lack of debris in the center may mean that the area served as ritual space.

The Poverty Point site, located on Macon Ridge in northwest Louisiana, is a much better known, and somewhat later, example of early earthwork and mound building. Here large, concentric, C-shaped earthen ridges were built, separated from each other by ditches and in association with several mounds (see Box 11.1). Even today, after plowing has seriously reduced the ridges in height, the size of Poverty Point impresses the visitor (Gibson 2000, 219). The people of the Poverty Point complex built earthworks and mounds while supporting themselves by hunting, fishing, and gathering. Many sites are attributed to them, with dates spanning the Late Archaic to the Early Woodland (ca. 3700–2500 BP).

As significant as Poverty Point complex earthen constructions are, the artifact inventories and indications of exchange also are impressive. Thousands of tiny, highly polished stone beads, pendants, plummets, and effigies have been found, as well as a variety of stoneworking tools (Figure 11.10). Because local

FIGURE 11.9 Students from Indiana University of Pennsylvania walking down from Mound A at Watson Brake along the earthen ridge that connects the mounds at this site.

FIGURE 11.10 Distinctive carved stone items and lapidary raw materials from the Poverty Point site.

ISSUES AND DEBATES

BOX 11.1

Ridges, Aisles, and the Map of Poverty Point

Poverty Point is one of the best-known archaeological sites in eastern North America. Dated to the Late Archaic, the earthworks at this site are not North America's oldest, but they dwarf any other construction until Middle Woodland times. Archaeologists have variously interpreted this site as a vacant ceremonial center, as a great town at the center of a ranked polity, as the location of regional trade fairs, and as a more modest community inhabited by impressively talented stoneworkers. Whatever the correct interpretation, this site's plan, with its six open, concentric rings and large irregular Mound A to the west, is instantly recognizable to most North American archaeologists (Figure 11.11). Yet an understanding of the site plan at Poverty

Point has been less straightforward than this statement might suggest, and small but possibly significant modifications from the most widely known map may be warranted (Kidder 2002a).

On one foray in his boat *Gopher*, C. B. Moore, who was an early explorer of earthworks, visited Poverty Point. During the winter of 1911–1912, Moore did not notice the rings, but he thought there were six mounds at the site arranged in the shape of a "rude circle" (Moore 1913, 67). In fact, the concentric ridges or rings were not noticed until the 1950s, when archaeologist James Ford noticed them in aerial photographs. Ford believed that Moore and others had missed the rings because they covered so much area. This is a believable explanation to

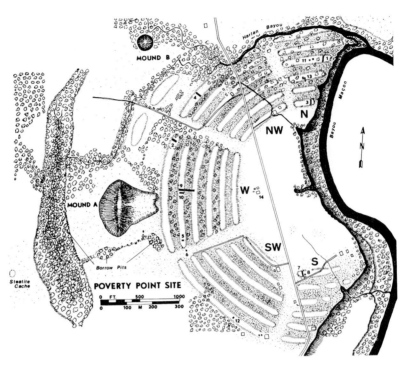

FIGURE 11.11 The familiar site plan of Poverty Point based on tracings of aerial photographs.

anyone who has visited Poverty Point. Without the park's aid in marking the ridges, their low height would make them hard to see as they stretch out across an area more than three-quarters of a mile in diameter!

The well-known plan of Poverty Point comes mainly from the map Ford drew by tracing features on an enlarged aerial photograph. Since trees covered parts of the rings in the photograph, we know some estimation was involved. Ford's map was published in 1954 (Ford 1954) and revised slightly two years later (Ford and Webb 1956). A still later version (Webb 1977), that is shown in Figure 11.11, has become the most familiar. These maps all showed six highly symmetrical, concentric rings that faced east, with the large Mound A to their west and the smaller Mound B toward the northwest, though the ring configuration evolved from subtly octagonal to circular. The rings were nearly identical in size and were divided into five sectors by radiating breaks or aisles. The sectors, labeled North, Northwest, West, Southwest,

and South, have been used to sort materials recovered. Some have proposed significant differences between site activities or possibly kin groups based on these sectors.

Maps of this site have emphasized symmetry, regularity, and planning of the aisles and ridges. These characteristics fit well with the idea that Poverty Point was a planned community built more or less at once. Excavations show that people lived at the site before the rings were built and that they lived on the rings themselves. Nevertheless, the regularity of the site plan also has been thought by many to have a symbolic significance. For example, Gibson (2000) suggests that the rings were built to follow a cosmological blueprint for which 6 is a sacred number. Another popular idea is that alignments in the site plan can be associated with astronomical events (e.g., Brecher and Haag 1980).

Yet by the 1980s, archaeologists working at the site suspected that the standard site plan maps ought to be revised. Work at this time resulted in several additions to the site plan but

FIGURE 11.12 Updated basic plan of Poverty Point.

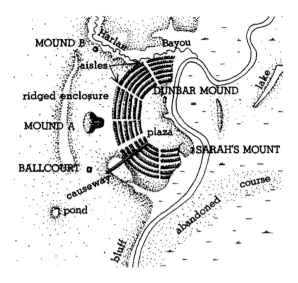

little change in its overall symmetry and regularity (Gibson 1984). Three additional mounds were recognized, and the Motley Mound to the north was perceived as part of the site. Note Dunbar's Mound, Sarah's Mount, and the Ballcourt Mound on Figure 11.12, as well as a fifth aisle bisecting the West section of rings. The eastern edge of the site also was found to be much more irregular than is indicated on earlier maps, and one section that has a gentle, stepped slope down to the bayou is apparently not natural, but the result of prehistoric earth-moving. Finally, the existence of a causeway traversing the Southwest ring segment and a depression between the rings and the Ballcourt Mound was also noted. Amazingly enough, given the site's importance, a detailed topographic map of the entire Poverty Point site was not attempted until 1999–2000 (Kidder 2002a). The sheer size of the site as well as limited resources had kept completion of this task out of reach. However, Total Data Station mapping equipment, which records point coordinates directly into a computer file and is now standard in cartography, has made the process more efficient. The topographic map of Poverty Point generated in this manner is based on 10,385 data points (Figure 11.13).

Review of the new map tends to confirm the additions made to the site plan in the 1980s but raises several questions. Both Ring 2 and the south segment are not evident topographically, while other segments vary in their visibility. These deviations from the traditional plan probably are due to repeated plowing. On the other hand, the aisle usually shown between the Northwest and North ridge segments does not appear. This absence is not easy to explain unless such an aisle never existed. More importantly, this topographic map argues against the kind of symmetry and regularity suggested in earlier maps. Indeed, Figure 11.13 may appear confusing in comparison to the neat drawings of Figures 11.11 and 11.12.

Clearly the mapping of Poverty Point is a work in progress. It is important to realize that topographic survey gives us one type of data that must be interpreted and then tested against other sources of information. Many questions remain about the plan of Poverty Point. Should the standard site plan be modified to drop the northern aisle? Should the plan show less symmetry and regularity? If the plan were considered to be less symmetrical, what would be the significance for propositions about cosmology and astronomy? Ultimately, what does the site plan tell us about the organization of the community and the reasons for earthwork construction? With this amazing site as in all good research, the more we learn, the more questions we have.

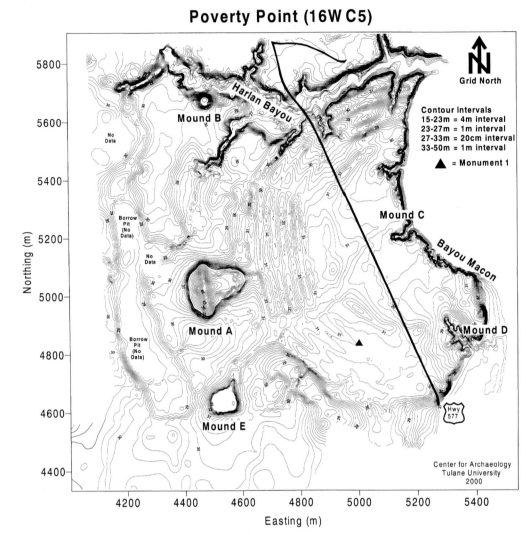

FIGURE 11.13 Contour map of the Poverty Point site based on topographic data gathered between 1999 and 2000.

stone was lacking, Poverty Point people imported argillite, chert, slate, copper, galena, jasper, quartzite, sandstone, hematite, and steatite from the Appalachian Mountains, the Piedmont, the Rocky Mountains, the Ouachita Mountains, and the Great Lakes. Although it is not clear what was traded in return—perhaps perishable items—tons of rock seem to have been imported. Some of the rock was preliminarily shaped into bifaces or other standardized forms before importation, while steatite seems to have arrived already in bowl form. Besides this lapidary work in creating ornaments, microliths made from prepared pebble cores are commonly found, as are the ubiquitous clay cooking balls called Poverty Point objects (PPOs), which can be grouped into several types based on their morphology and possible functions.

Thus, the 7000 years of the Archaic were a significant part of the Southeastern past. There was great diversity in human culture and adaptation. Moreover, developments once thought to have been associated with Woodland societies, such as pottery, settled villages, farming, and mound building, all first occurred during the Archaic. To understand the origins of such phenomena, archaeologists must look to Archaic sites that may be buried, smaller, or otherwise less obvious than later sites. Fortunately, the modern CRM mandate has encouraged more attention to sites of all types.

WOODLAND PEOPLES ACROSS THE SOUTHEAST

In introducing the term "Woodland" in Chapter 10, we noted that Woodland developments on the Plains may represent contact with the peoples of the Eastern Woodlands whose lifestyles were characterized by farming and pottery making as well as by the construction of permanent settlements and burial mounds. As with the Archaic, the Woodland is now treated as a period of time beginning everywhere in the Eastern Woodlands around 3000 BP.

Although the characteristics that once were understood to distinguish the Woodland from the preceding Archaic have been shown to occur in some Eastern Woodland locations before the Woodland, this is the period in which all of these become widespread. At this time the peoples of the Eastern Woodlands were generally living in at least seasonally settled camps or villages and often grew some crops, but they engaged in hunting, fishing, and gathering as well. They had some interaction with cultural groups elsewhere through trade in raw materials and finished items, and mortuary ceremonialism often was associated with mound building. Archaeologists once assumed that various Woodland mound-building groups were organized as simple chiefdoms with hierarchical social structures, but at present a model of tribal organization in which membership in kin groups such as clans and lineages was of importance seems more likely. Nevertheless, there is some distinction in burial contexts suggesting variation in status. Thus, sedentary life, horticulture, manufacture and use of ceramics, exchange and interaction, mound building and mortuary ceremonialism, as well as other indications of social differentiation are the main characteristics of the Woodland that interest archaeologists.

The Woodland is typically divided into Early Woodland, Middle Woodland, and Late Woodland subperiods throughout the Eastern Woodlands. Specific mound-building cultures including the Early Woodland **Adena** of the upper Ohio River valley and the Middle Woodland **Hopewell** of Ohio and Illinois are the best-known Woodland cultures (see Chapter 12). However, Adena mounds do occur in portions of northeastern Kentucky and West Virginia that we include in the Southeast, and a number of the Middle Woodland cultures of the Southeast often are considered Hopewell variants. These complexes, which were characterized by a sophisticated and elaborate material culture, complex earthworks and mortuary ceremonialism, and long-distance trade, have understandably received a great deal of attention in summaries of the Eastern Woodland's past.

However, Woodland cultural variability throughout the East, and especially the Southeast, cannot be subsumed under these two cultures alone.

As you learn about the Woodland in the Southeast, consider where Southeastern Woodland peoples might have been drawn into some interaction with Midwestern Woodland groups. If such interaction did not happen, how are we to understand the distinctive Woodland developments that did occur? If it did happen, was participation primarily economic, religious, or political? As you read about the evidence for Woodland period societies, think about the general theme of developing sociocultural complexity. Where and when can we see evidence for more complex societies? What types of evidence exist?

The Woodland period in the Southeast can be dated from approximately 3000 BP to 950 BP. Note that the Poverty Point complex is usually considered Late Archaic but spans the Archaic/Woodland temporal boundary. In this text, we date the Early Woodland from approximately 3000 BP to 2200 BP and the Middle Woodland from approximately 2200 BP to 1450 BP (Table 11.1). During these periods, in addition to the wide acceptance of ceramic technology, horticulture may grow in importance, and mortuary ceremonialism and interaction networks may link some parts of the Southeast to Midwestern Woodland developments. We also date the Late Woodland between 1450 BP and 950 BP. In some parts of the Southeast, researchers (e.g., Morse and Morse 1983) also recognize the Late Woodland as ending about 1150 BP, when an **Emergent Mississippian** period begins. This was an important time. Late Woodland change foreshadows the agricultural intensification, settlement in town centers, and development of social hierarchies associated with the Mississippian (Anderson and Mainfort 2002). However, in some areas of Florida and close to the Mid-Atlantic area, Mississippian developments have not been recognized at all, and the Woodland period continues until Contact.

Early and Middle Woodland Material Culture

The pottery that becomes widespread in the Southeast as the Woodland period begins was constructed by coiling, and it was variously decorated and tempered. At first, vessel forms are tall jars or beakers with conoidal bases, with a trend toward thinner vessel walls over time. Such vessels are efficient containers for direct heating and cooking (Sassaman 2002). Perhaps their appearance coincided with the development of new cooking techniques for native seeds.

Archaeologists have recognized four broad geographically overlapping traditions of Woodland pottery in the Southeast (Figure 11.14). Complicated incising, pinching, punctuating, brushing, and stamping characterize the surface treatments of the **Gulf Coastal tradition**. Some vessels have additional support from pods projecting below the base. Middle Woodland Marksville pottery in this region had stamping, curvilinear designs, and bird motifs suggestive of Midwestern Hopewell motifs incised into its surface (Kidder 2002b). Dentate and rocker-stamped decorations, some of them very complicated, were applied with carved paddles to pottery of the **South Appalachian tradition**. Again, vessels with pods also were made. Surface treatments in the **Northern Pottery tradition** were characterized by cord marking similar to that found in Woodland pottery from other parts of the Eastern Woodlands. Early Woodland vessels in this tradition are tempered with steatite, coarse sand, shell, and grit. Fabric-impressed surfaces characterized the **Middle Eastern tradition** vessels, which were tempered with

FIGURE 11.14 Examples of the decoration styles for the four commonly recognized Southeastern pottery traditions.

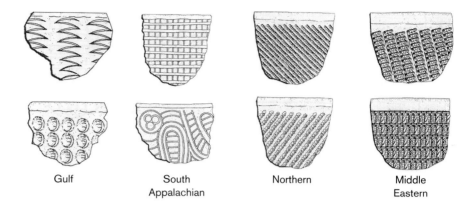

Gulf   South Appalachian   Northern   Middle Eastern

sand, grit, quartz, and limestone. Brushing was added as a surface treatment to the Middle Eastern and Northern pottery traditions during the Middle Woodland (Bense 1994).

A few generalizations about projectile points can be made for the Early and Middle Woodland (Figure 11.15). Stemmed points characterize the Early Woodland, but they tend to be smaller than those dating to the Late Archaic. Motley points may have first appeared in the Late Archaic, but this point type was still made in the Early Woodland in the Mississippi River valley. Contracting stemmed points with triangular blades called Gary Contracting Stemmed also span the Late Archaic and the Early Woodland in the western portions of the Southeast (Justice 1987). Adena points, a type associated with the Adena of the upper Ohio valley, have been found as far south as northern Florida, but usually are not found in the lower Mississippi valley. Other points may have square

FIGURE 11.15 Early and Middle Woodland projectile point forms from the Southeast.

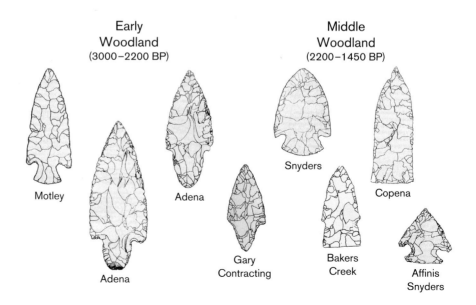

Early Woodland (3000–2200 BP)

Middle Woodland (2200–1450 BP)

Motley

Adena

Adena

Gary Contracting

Snyders

Bakers Creek

Copena

Affinis Snyders

or expanded stems. Large triangular points like Badin points are known from the Carolina Piedmont and Tennessee, where they may be intrusive from the Northeast (Oliver 1985). Middle Woodland point forms vary considerably. They include trianguloid forms, expanded-stemmed lanceolate points, small thick points called spikes, and in the central Mississippi valley, the distinctive, broad-bladed Snyders point.

Other aspects of lithic assemblages may be important indicators of Middle Woodland. Both the presence of blades and high proportions of nonlocal stone are common on sites whose residents may have participated in exchange with Hopewell people from the Midwest. For example, at the Fant site, a **Marksville phase** site in the Yazoo Basin of northern Mississippi, more than 50 percent of the stone was nonlocal. Included were cherts from west central and southern Illinois, novaculite and quartz from the Ouachita Mountains of central and southern Arkansas, as well as a biface possibly made from Knife River flint from the Dakotas. Over 200 blades recovered from this site were made out of nonlocal Illinois cherts (Jay K. Johnson and Hayes 1995). The Marksville tradition often is considered a southern variant of Hopewell as discussed shortly.

Subsistence and Settlement in the Early and Middle Woodland

Southeastern adaptations during the Early Woodland have sometimes been characterized as Archaic adaptations with pottery. People continued their hunting, gathering, and fishing ways of life, moving between base camps and special-purpose camps from which particular resources were extracted or certain activities performed. Terrestrial fauna of importance include white-tailed deer, rabbit, raccoon, squirrel, and wild turkey, while fish and other aquatic fauna were more important in some locales such as South Florida. Although shellfishing has been associated primarily with Middle and Late Archaic populations, both freshwater mussels and marine mollusks remain important parts of the diet during the Woodland (Peacock 2002). Exploitation of wild plants, including nuts, greens, and fruits, continued as well.

Within this general pattern, however, there were local differences in strategies. Some were subtle and some more major. For example, the adaptations in South Florida, where people focused on the sea, the estuaries, and the swamps, were very distinct. Relative commitment to the cultivation of plants also varied. Maize is sometimes found in Middle Woodland floral assemblages, such as in the Middle Woodland at Icehouse Bottom in east Tennessee (Chapman and Crites 1987). Regardless, the amount of maize represented in Southeastern assemblages before the Late Woodland is very minor.

Native seed plants are known from a number of sites in the Southeast as well. Major caches of seeds have been found in rockshelters in the Ozarks of northwestern Arkansas and in eastern Kentucky (Fritz 1993). Still, the existence of pre-maize farming similar to that which developed in the Midwest during the Early and Middle Woodland (see Chapter 12) can be documented only in the northern and western Southeast. South and east of the Fall Line, pre-maize farming apparently did not develop (Figure 11.16). Some archaeologists have questioned the source of this patterning. Gremillion (2002) favors explanations that attribute the lack of pre-maize farming to the success of existing hunting, gathering, and fishing economies, while others (Bruce D. Smith 1992a) suggest that environmental variables precluded the cultivation of native seed plants.

FIGURE 11.16 Patterning in the development of pre-maize farming in the Southeast.

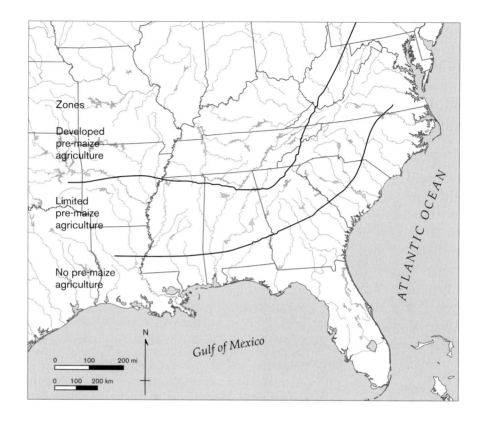

Settlement variability also is evident. While most Early and Middle Woodland people may have persisted in millennia-old lifeways, living in small, seasonally mobile, egalitarian groups, large communities and centers developed in some areas, and in these places the roots of social differentiation that became important later may be discerned. Shell midden and mound sites of Georgia, Alabama, and northern Florida are potential examples of the latter. For example, Sandy Hammock on the Ocmulgee River is a large circular **Deptford tradition** shell midden site, where the shell ring has a diameter of approximately 300 meters (Stephenson et al. 2002). Nevertheless, mound building provides the best evidence for social integration and differentiation.

Early and Middle Woodland Mound Building, Ceremonial Life, and Interaction

The construction of mounds and earthworks is an important pan-Eastern cultural phenomenon from the end of the Archaic until the time of European contact. However, a large proportion of the known constructions can be dated to the Early Woodland and Middle Woodland. Much of this activity obviously had to do with burial of the dead, but since mounds and earthworks do not always contain burials, it is also obvious that earthen constructions had other purposes and significance. It seems clear that these constructions of earth were means of marking group identity, if only to establish where certain social groups, like clans or lineages, buried their dead. However, the elaborate layout of many mound and earthwork complexes, some of which seem to correlate with astronomical phenomena, lend themselves to speculation about religious or ceremonial activities as well. In some cases, the apparent absence of habitation debris suggests that people did not necessarily live within or near the earthworks they built. Both mortuary rituals and feasting (Knight 2001) seem to have been associated with the construction of mounds and earthworks. Understandably, archaeologists have many unanswered questions about the mound-building tradition of the Eastern Woodlands, and the Southeast culture area is an important place to explore them.

Participation in Early and Middle Woodland periods interregional exchange and interaction is suggested by many mound and earthwork complexes in the Southeast. Of course, the Adena heartland in the upper Ohio valley is on the north and east margins of the Southeast, and some Adena mounds are found in the eastern portions of Kentucky and West Virginia within areas covered in this chapter. However, most of the Southeast does not appear to have participated in Adena ceremonialism. This does not mean that Early Woodland people in the Southeast did not have their own mound-building and mortuary customs, only that Adena artifacts, other than the Adena point itself, are not often found in Southeastern burials and sites. Archaeologists have in fact identified Early Woodland mound-building complexes of note. For example, in the **Tchula phase** of the lower Mississippi valley small conical burial mounds were constructed in single episodes. Flexed or bundle burials in these mounds are thought to represent communal interments. On St. Catherines Island, Deptford tradition low sand mounds containing both extended and **bundle burials** with a small number of grave goods have been found (Thomas and Larsen 1979). Nevertheless, most Early Woodland burials seem to occur within villages and to consist of tightly flexed individuals placed in oval or circular burial pits along with a few grave goods.

The Middle Woodland begins when mound construction and participation in a Hopewell-like burial ceremonialism (see Chapter 12) and exchange are evident. Although most Middle Woodland societies in the Southeast participated in these phenomena only in the most peripheral way, there are a number of mound and earthwork complexes suggesting significant ceremonialism and possible interaction with Midwest Hopewell people. Here are some of the examples:

1. Late Deptford mounds (after ca. 2100 BP) in the eastern part of northwest Florida are associated with a ceremonial complex called **Yent**. The largest site is the multimound complex at the Crystal River site, but smaller sites also are known. There seems to be a dichotomy in these sites between mounds and domestic contexts, with the mounds containing copper panpipes, copper **earspools**, shell **gorgets**, shell cups, pottery made in exotic shapes, plummets, and secondary bundle burials (Stephenson et al. 2002).

2. The **Copena Mortuary Complex** of the Tennessee River valley in northern Alabama includes about 50 burial mounds constructed over subsoil burial pits, but containing secondary burials in their fill as well. Copena burial caves also are known (Crothers et al. 2002). Some burial pits are lined with clay brought from another source; others have log and bark troughs in which the bodies were placed on bark matting. These burials have produced copper reel-shaped gorgets, earspools, bracelets, celts, and beads; marine shell cups and beads; greenstone celts, ground galena nodules, and steatite elbow pipes (Walthall 1979).

3. The Pinson Mounds site south of Jackson, Tennessee, is the largest Middle Woodland site in the Southeast: its 12 mounds, geometric enclosure, and other areas of use cover approximately 400 acres (160 hectares). Construction of the mounds has been radiocarbon dated to between 2100 BP and 1600 BP. There are at least five rectangular platform mounds at this site, and Saul's Mound, the tallest mound in the complex, is 72 feet (22 m) tall (see Figure 1.6). A pair of intersecting conical mounds, the Twin Mounds, contained undisturbed burials in log and/or fabric covered tombs. *Marginella* **beads** made from marine snail shells, fiber headdresses with copper ornaments, freshwater pearl necklaces, and other exotic and finely made grave goods were also recovered (Mainfort 1996).

4. In the lower Mississippi valley, the long-standing local mound-building tradition continues between approximately 2150 BP and 1450 BP. Connections with Hopewell ceremonialism are obvious for the first half of this period, the Marksville phase, when mound building is most frequent. The Marksville site in Louisiana has a large C-shaped, segmented enclosure surrounding several platform and conical mounds and fronting on the bluff edge. This enclosure has a diameter of roughly 520 meters (570 yd), but it is only one of several enclosures of mounds at the site. Mound 4 at Marksville had a mortuary platform with a central roofed vault, lined with matting and containing the remains of several individuals. Marksville ceramics (Figure 11.17) have iconography such as raptorial bird motifs, curvilinear designs, stamping and U-shaped incisions that are like Hopewellian motifs from the Midwest. Blade tools, greenstone celts, boatstones, mica, galena, copper earspools, and plummets also are found in Marksville burials. After approximately 1750 BP, still in the Marksville Middle Woodland period, mound building becomes less frequent, ceramics are more often plain, and Hopewell exchange items disappear. This **Issaquena phase** seems to last until Late Woodland times (ca. 1450 BP), but it is less obviously Hopewellian (Kidder 2002b).

5. **Swift Creek tradition** sites, which follow Deptford sites in southern and central Georgia, have multiple mounds and are interpreted as ceremonial centers. The Kolomoki site is one example. Swift Creek designs are curvilinear motifs applied with carved paddles over the entire surface of the decorated vessel. They have been found on ceramics over a wide area of the East—in Indiana, Tennessee (at Pinson Mounds), and Ohio. Compositional analyses of sherds with these patterns generally have suggested that the ceramics were locally made, using paddles with distinctive Swift Creek designs that most likely had been acquired through trade. At the Swift Creek Mandeville site, located on the Chattahootchee River in Georgia, burial pits containing copper panpipes and earspools, clay platform pipes, prismatic blades, ceramic figurines, and mica and greenstone celts suggest Hopewell ceremonialism.

a b

FIGURE 11.17 Marksville ceramics displaying (a) curvilinear design and (b) incised bird motif.

Although Hopewell people in Ohio and Illinois were influencing Southeastern people, at least in the lower Mississippi valley and the South Appalachia area, Middle Woodland phenomena arose as well from local roots. Archaeologists believe that local social imperatives were being met through trade and ritual; it does not seem likely that belief systems simply were being exported from the Midwestern heartlands.

Late Woodland in the Southeast

The Late Woodland in the Southeast is dated from approximately 1450 BP to 950 BP (AD 500–1000). It is generally recognized that many Mississippian phenomena first developed at the end of the Late Woodland after around 1150 BP (AD 800). We have followed the preference of most Southeastern archaeologists by including these phenomena in the Late Woodland rather than designating an Emergent Mississippian, as is often done in the Midwest. Traditionally, archaeologists have understood the Late Woodland period as the time of the "**good gray cultures**" (Williams 1963). This designation reflects the idea that sandwiched between dramatic Hopewell and Mississippian developments between approximately 1500 BP and 1100 BP (AD 450–850), the Late Woodland was a drab period of decline. During the past few decades, thanks in part to CRM-generated data, archaeologists have been rediscovering the Late Woodland as a period of variability and change. Out of this variability major transformations began to take place that foreshadow the Mississippian.

Three generalizations can be made about the Late Woodland in the Southeast. First, about 1250 BP (AD 700) as in other parts of the Eastern Woodlands, there was a widespread adoption of the bow and arrow. Because of its presumed efficiency as a hunting implement and as a weapon, the bow and arrow's introduction seems significant to archaeologists. Earlier arrow points are known, but the small triangular points, small corner-notched and small stemmed, triangular-bladed points of the Late Woodland and Mississippian periods suggest that people were making mostly arrow points. Several Southeastern varieties of these arrow points are shown in Figure 11.18. There is debate about the possible association of this change with an intensification of deer hunting and with increases in intergroup conflict and warfare (e.g., Blitz 1988; Nassaney and Pyle 1999).

Second, both greater numbers of sites and larger site areas have been noted for the Late Woodland. However, settlement pattern change was sometimes toward nucleation and at other times toward dispersal; no single pattern seems to have developed (Nassaney and Cobb 1991). Some archaeologists suggest that higher population levels caused resource stress and the adoption of second line resources like small mammals and shellfish (Jackson and Scott 2002; Peacock 2002). Intensification in the use of native seed plants also might have been a response to stress.

Indeed, agricultural production intensifies, but not uniformly. Native seeds and eventually maize became important to subsistence first in the northern Southeast. During the Late Woodland, people in the interior Southeast grew several kinds of native seed plant as well as sunflower, squash/gourd, bottle gourd, and tobacco (Johannessen 1993). In the southern Southeast, foraging and fishing persisted until the development of Mississippian economies.

Because Southeastern Late Woodland cultural phenomena defy generalization, archaeologists now concentrate on local cultural sequences rather than broad evolutionary trajectories. The cessation of possible Hopewellian interactions normally preceded the end of the Middle Woodland, dating closer to 1750 BP than 1450 BP. Thus, phases that span the traditional temporal periods for Middle and Late Woodland are common.

One example that illustrates how the Mississippian transformation began comes from the central Mississippi River valley. Here the Late Woodland is considered to begin with the **Baytown period** (1650/1550–1250 BP), while the

Sequoyah   Alba   Scallorn

Madison   Hamilton

FIGURE 11.18
Southeastern projectile point types dating after 1250 BP usually considered to be arrow points rather than to spear points.

Terminal Late Woodland is called **Plum Bayou period** (1250–950 BP) (Rolingson and Mainfort 2002). Baytown ceramics were clay tempered and have either cord-marked or plain surface treatments, while people made several small notched, stemmed arrow points (Nassaney and Pyle 1999). Nuts and a small amount of native seeds have been found in botanical assemblages, and white-tailed deer and fish, smaller mammals, and reptiles make up faunal assemblages.

In the later Plum Bayou sites, **grog-tempered ceramics** were the most common, but bone- and shell-tempered wares also were made. Surfaces are usually plain, but people used a red slip, incised, and punctated pottery as well. Obvious arrow points including triangular Madison points were being made. Maize was a minor cultigen, while native seeds as well as nuts appear to have been significant plant foods. The diet was dominated by deer meat, but small mammals, turkey, the now-extinct **passenger pigeon**, fish, and turtles also were taken. Large towns suggestive of later Mississippian ones developed as well as mound centers. Toltec Mounds on the Arkansas River covers about 100 acres and has 18 mounds surrounded by an embankment and a ditch (Figure 11.19). Astronomical alignments apparently exist at this site. The largest mound at Toltec is about 50 feet (15 m) in height, but lower platform and burial mounds also were built there. Archaeologists recognize a hierarchy of site types for Plum Bayou including single household, multiple household, multiple household with a single mound, and centers consisting of multiple mounds (Rolingson 2002). Fragments of copper and conch shell indicating long-distance exchange have been found in Plum Bayou sites. Although there is little evidence for powerful elites, many of

FIGURE 11.19 Plan of the Toltec Mounds in Arkansas; note the embankment enclosing the mounds, which are indicated by letters and arranged in regular fashion around plazas.

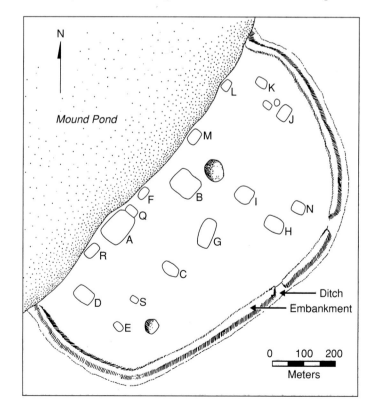

the foregoing characteristics are similar to Emergent Mississippian traits to the north as well as to those of emerging polities in the lower Mississippi valley (Nassaney 1991).

Weeden Island developments (1750/1650–950 BP) provide a second example of Late Woodland transformations in the Southeast. Weeden Island is named after a site at Tampa Bay, but similar ceramics are found in sites that extend northward along the Florida coast into Alabama as well as into Georgia. Weeden Island I (before 1200 BP) ceramics had complicated stamped designs reminiscent of Swift Creek, or other highly stylized motifs and effigy forms. In Weeden Island II (after 1200 BP), new pottery types called Wakulla Check Stamped were common. In some areas, Weeden Island obviously precedes Mississippian developments, while in other sequences Late Woodland phenomena follow it (Kohler 1991; Milanich 2002). The subsistence focus for early Weeden Island I was on fish, shellfish, and other aquatic resources. Burial mounds were common and may have been the centers of lineage-based mortuary rituals. They may contain charnel houses for the processing of the dead before interment as bundle burials. It is also believed that some villages were more important than others.

In Weeden Island II, the **Wakulla culture** is recognized in northwest Florida. There are a greater number of sites; more of them are in upland areas, and settlement is less nucleated. Archaeologists have proposed that this change marks the introduction of slash-and-burn agriculture, causing frequent relocation to be close to fields. Ceramics made especially for ritual use disappear, and it has been argued that this was because corporate rituals were less frequent. People were still buried in mounds, but sometimes earlier mounds were simply reused. Over time Weeden Island II people made an increasing commitment to agriculture and eventually developed the Mississippian expression called **Fort Walton** by archaeologists (Scarry 1990).

The Late Woodland period may best be understood as one in which shifts in the centers of exchange and power took place (Anderson 1998). Exchange networks as well as mound centers do not completely disappear in the Late Woodland, though the quantity of goods moving about certainly was reduced, and Hopewell objects were no longer traded (Nassaney and Cobb 1991). At the very least the Late Woodland sets the stage for the Mississippian emergence.

MISSISSIPPIAN AND OTHER SOCIETIES OF THE LAST THOUSAND YEARS

Between 1150 BP and 950 BP, cultures archaeologists call Mississippian began to develop in the major river valleys of the Southeast and Midwest. Mississippians were maize-bean-squash agriculturalists who also exploited fish, waterfowl, and wild plants. They were the first easterners to settle large permanent towns containing central plazas, public buildings, platform mounds, and encircling stockades. These towns, some of which were very large, apparently were centers for outlying agricultural hamlets and homesteads. Mississippians developed social hierarchies and chiefly political control, while maintaining large-scale production and long-distance exchange of raw materials and craft items. The quality of Mississippian craftsmanship is unparalleled north of Mexico. A major thematic issue in Mississippian archaeology is the nature and development of sociocultural complexity.

FIGURE 11.20 Cultural regions within the Mississippian tradition in the Southeast.

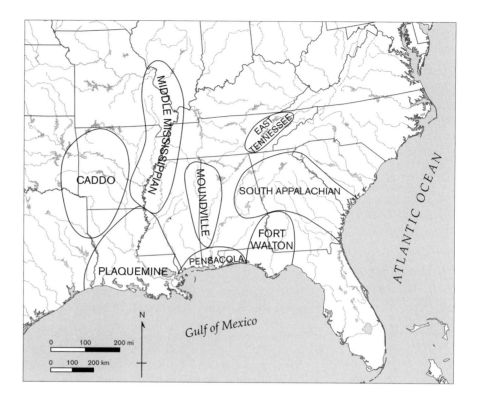

Figure 11.20 presents the locations of some of the Mississippian regions archaeologists recognize. This cultural tradition crosscuts the culture areas we use in this text, and examples of Mississippian societies will also be discussed in Chapter 12. In addition, although the period from 950 BP to 400 BP often is referred to as "the Mississippian period" in both the Southeast and the Midwest, other societies that more properly are considered Late Woodland or Late Prehistoric also existed in coastal and northern portions of the East at this time.

As we have discussed, the emergence of Mississippian phenomena prior to 950 BP is an aspect of the terminal Late Woodland by most Southeastern archaeologists. Following this, Mississippian is divided into an Early Mississippian from 950 BP to 750 BP (AD 1000–1200), Middle Mississippian from 750 BP to 550 BP (AD 1200–1400), and Late Mississippian from 550 BP to 400 BP (AD 1400–1550). The initial spread of maize agriculture and shell-tempered pottery occurred during the Early Mississippian, while complex chiefdoms linked by a shared ceremonial complex developed in several river valleys of the Southeast during the Middle Mississippian. Emphasis on public ritual and mound building declined in Late Mississippian time, while warfare and political turmoil increased.

Mississippian Material Culture

The traditional ceramic marker of the Mississippian is shell-tempered pottery, but this type of temper wasn't used universally. In Early Mississippian times shell-tempered ceramics are most common in the central Mississippi valley and in the river valleys of the interior and northern Southeast (e.g., the Cumberland,

FIGURE 11.21 Finely made painted Mississippian bottle with a spiral motif.

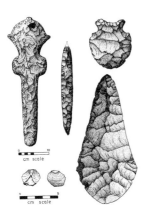

FIGURE 11.22 Artifacts of Mill Creek chert from the central Mississippi Valley: object on upper left is a mace; also shown are a stone sword, hoes of two varieties and at lower left two hoe chips.

Tennessee, and upper Tombigbee). Elsewhere sand- and grog-tempered ceramics were predominant. By the Middle Mississippian shell tempering was common in most of the Southeast except for the eastern part of the Coastal Plain. However, during the Late Mississippian period shell tempering once again was most common in the central Mississippi and other river valleys, while grit- and sand-tempered vessels were being made in the eastern Southeast and clay-tempered ceramics were made in some parts of the lower Mississippi Valley.

Other aspects of the ceramic technology may be just as noteworthy. People made a wide variety of vessel forms at this time: jars, bowls, pans, bottles, beakers. Human and animal effigy vessels also became common in some areas, especially during the Late Mississippian. There also was an expansion in decorative techniques such as slipping and painting of vessels. Many Mississippian period ceramics were very finely made (Figure 11.21), but more utilitarian wares with coarser shell tempering are found as well. Traditionally, Southeastern archaeologists have spent a great deal of effort studying variations in these ceramics.

Mississippian projectile points are usually small triangular varieties, but small stemmed and side-notched points also were made, as was shown in Figure 11.18. Large hoes for cultivation purposes also were made by Mississippians, and raw materials used in their production were exchanged over some distance. For example, the Mill Creek chert of southern Illinois was used to make hoes and a variety of other items throughout the Mississippi River valley (Figure 11.22). Otherwise, stone tools were mainly perforators and knives made from flakes. Nevertheless, there was a certain amount of standardization in the production of these flake tools. For example, Jay K. Johnson (1987) found that core technologies nearly identical to those identified at Cahokia in Illinois were in use at the Carson Mound site, a site in northwestern Mississippi dating from Middle to Late Mississippian.

Of course more perishable items also were made by Mississippians. Some idea of their fabrics can be discerned from impressions in ceramics. For example, pans believed to have been used in salt reduction often have fabric-impressed surfaces (e.g., Kuttruff and Kuttruff 1996). Sometimes actual fabric is unearthed: in one burial context at Etowah in Georgia, pieces of fabric were recovered, having been preserved due to their association with copper. This fabric, which incorporated feathers, hair, yarn, and other fibers, might have been part of a garment of ceremonial significance (Sibley et al. 1996). Utilitarian bone tools such as awls and needles, as well as bone and shell ornaments, also are common.

One aspect of Mississippian material culture that should not be overlooked is the elaborate artifactual material often found in Mississippian mortuary contexts. These include finely executed pottery, copper and shell ornaments, stone figurines, rattles, fans, and headdresses, as well as items with particular designs, as discussed in Exhibit 11.1. Such artifacts were symbols of prestige and wealth found in elite burial and ritual contexts. Besides being beautiful, they are strong evidence that Mississippian societies were hierarchical, and the iconography they exhibit provides important clues to beliefs.

Households and Communities

Part of what distinguishes Mississippians from earlier peoples of the Southeast is their settlement in towns. Southeasterners did not establish plaza-centered residential communities with both mounds and domestic structures until the

CLUES TO THE PAST

EXHIBIT 11.1

Design Motifs and Artifacts of the Southeastern Ceremonial Complex

Examination of design motifs on artifacts and also of key artifact types from Mississippian sites in the Southeast, particularly Etowah in Georgia, . Moundville in Alabama, and Spiro in Oklahoma, led archaeologists over 60 years ago to propose the **Southeastern Ceremonial complex** (Waring and Holder 1945). This complex, which is also called the **Southern Cult**, can be abbreviated as SECC.

The original definition of the SECC carried the claim that during the latter part of prehistory, very similar design motifs and objects were found over a wide area in association with platform mounds and, presumably, agriculturally based economies. It was also suggested that this complex of designs and artifacts contrasted with the earlier complex of designs and artifacts associated with the Hopewell. The proportions of each type of motif or artifact were known to vary from site to site, but far-flung similarities were stressed.

Design motifs identified included the cross, the sun circle, the bilobed arrow, the forked eye, the open eye, the barred oval, the hand and eye, and various death motifs. These designs were also found in association with various "god-animal beings" including birds, the rattlesnake, wild cats, and humans. As the examples of the design types associated with the SECC shown in Figure 11.23 indicate, the design elements often are combined. For example, the cross often is placed within a sun circle. Some animal figures may be more correctly considered monsters, as they combine the features of several animals (e.g., birds and serpents with antlers). In addition, artifacts assumed to have ceremonial functions because of the contexts in which they were found were used to identify the SECC. These were gorgets of shell and copper (Figure 11.24), mask gorgets, pendants of *Columnella* shell,

embossed copper plates, copper badges and hair ornaments, earspools, celts, batons, **monolithic axes** made from a single piece of stone, effigy pipes, stone disks, discoidal stones, shell cups and bowls, as well as some forms of pottery jars and large chipped stone bifaces. These artifacts are the prestige goods found in Mississippian elite burials and associated contexts.

The SECC has received much archaeological attention, but it is not well understood; nor is there agreement about its existence, its chronology, or its significance. The study of SECC designs and the objects has been approached in a wide variety of ways (see Galloway 1989). The designation has been broadly applied so that it subsumes many design motifs with a longer history in the Eastern Woodlands, as well as objects found in only restricted parts of the Southeast. This practice leads to confusion and makes drawing any conclusions difficult. More careful examinations have suggested that unless we mean this term to refer to Southeastern art or religion in a more general sense, a restricted set of motifs and objects should represent the SECC. The SECC also was most important during a short time frame from about 800 BP to 600 BP (AD 1150–1350). This was the period in which the production and exchange of ceremonial objects and finished goods bearing SECC motifs peaked (e.g., Muller 1989). Even then, regional variation in the evidence for the SECC can be noted.

Since archaeologists originally conceived of the SECC as related to religious belief, they expected to find linkages with the mythology and cosmology of Southeastern Indian tribes as documented ethnographically. SECC designs certainly evoke issues related to ancestor worship, fertility, and warfare that are explored in the

Cross   Sun circle   Bi lobed arrow   Forked eye

Open eye   Barred oval   Hand and eye   Death motif

Animal figures

FIGURE 11.23 Common motifs of the Southeastern Ceremonial complex.

art of many agricultural peoples. Connections with the art and religion of ethnographically known Native farmers probably can be made (e.g., Hall 1989).

However, can the SECC be explained solely as a pan-Eastern Mississippian religious system? SECC phenomena may be much more complicated in their origin and function. They are associated with the trade and exchange of raw materials and finished items, as well as with the manipulation of symbols to attain political power and elite identity. Stylistic analyses have been useful in helping archaeologists explore the production and distribution of objects of some specific kinds. Engraved designs on shell have been the most intensively studied (e.g., Brown 1989; Phillips and Brown 1978, 1984). A number of styles of shell gorgets have been identified and their distributions studied (Muller 1997, 370–378).

A second issue often raised in discussions of the SECC has been the apparent similarities in the symbolism with Mesoamerican design motifs and themes. Themes such as fire, the sun, or human sacrifice have been used as examples of possible connections. However, there also

FIGURE 11.24 Engraved shell gorget showing multiple SECC design motifs.

are similarities with earlier designs and symbols from the Eastern Woodlands. Moreover, SECC motifs do not appear abruptly, nor are they fixed in form. Most archaeologists do not believe that the SECC can be attributed to sudden Mesoamerican immigration or to long-distance trade with Mesoamerican polities even if some contacts did occur occasionally. Instead, the SECC and Mississippian systems in general must be understood as separate developments that at best paralleled cultural trajectories in Mesoamerica (Webb 1989).

There is a great deal to be learned about the meaning of SECC symbolism, about the various SECC art styles, about the context in which SECC items were produced, and about their distribution both within sites and across the Southeast. Nevertheless, even beginning students can learn to recognize some of the design motifs and artifact types that may have had special significance in Mississippian society. At a minimum, these artifacts testify to the quality of Mississippian craftsmanship as well as to the complexity of Mississippian societies.

Mississippian. Both the plazas aligned with and bounded by mounds and the platform mounds themselves are important aspects of these planned communities (Lewis et al. 1998). Although platform mounds were built during the Middle Woodland in the Southeast (Jefferies 1994), they have long been associated with Mississippians because so many more of them were built after 950 BP. Mississippian platform mounds usually served as substructures for the houses of the elite, charnel houses, public buildings, or religious structures, while Woodland platforms were centers of activities but most lacked substantial structures. Mississippian towns or at least their cores also often were bounded by stockades, palisades, and/or ditches. Compare the idealized Mississippian town

FIGURE 11.25 Idealized
Mississippian town plan
featuring platform mounds
arranged around plazas
and enclosure encircling
houses.

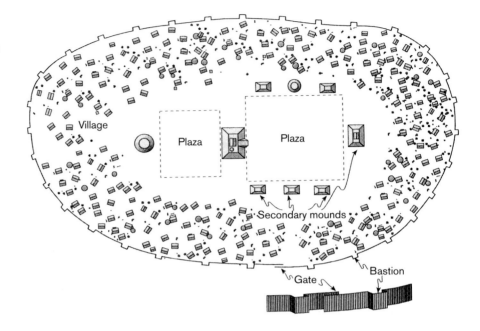

plan in Figure 11.25 with the plan of the Hopeton earthworks at Newark, Ohio,
shown later (see Figure 12.27, in the case study by Mark Lynott). The issue of
town plan is an important subject, as exemplified by this chapter's case study
by Lynne P. Sullivan, "Mouse Creek Phase Households and Communities:
Mississippian Period Towns in Southeastern Tennessee." Consult Section H of
the Student CD for some of the Mississippian towns you can visit in person or on
the web today.

One feature of importance in defining the Mississippian is the rectangular or
square wall-trench house. It was a structure made by excavating narrow trenches
and placing posts in these so-called wall trenches. Structures of other types also
have been identified on Mississippian sites; some were made by placing the posts
in individually dug holes. House floors quite often were dug slightly into the
ground, and the dirt from the excavation was mounded up along the sides of the
walls. Earthlodges, known from sites in Georgia and eastern Tennessee, were circular structures that apparently were sod or earth covered. Larson (1994) questions
whether these buildings were indeed covered with earth, though the existence of
relatively circular structures in this part of the Mississippian Southeast is clear.

The notion of a hierarchy of settlement types also has long been important
to students of the Mississippian. The minimal unit of Mississippian society seems
to have been the farmstead. In Early and Middle Mississippian times, farmsteads
often were dispersed in floodplains around towns, which in turn sometimes
related to regional centers. In Late Mississippian times settlements may have
been more aggregated, in response to intergroup conflict. Depending on the size
and complexity of the chiefdom, archaeologists recognize between two and four
levels of settlement hierarchy. Important research now focuses on the relationships between political or ceremonial centers and outlying districts. Some of the
largest Mississippian settlements certainly were important ceremonial and political

venues. At Moundville in Alabama, one of the biggest known Mississippian sites in the Southeast, there is a large central plaza surrounded by platform and conical mounds (see Figure 2.17). Knight (1998) has argued that the plan of this site may represent a model of the social order of the chiefdom, with pairs of mounds representing different kin groups and their placement symbolizing the relative ranking of these kin groups within the polity. That is, elite kin groups might have located and constructed the monuments and burial mounds to reinforce their power and prestige.

Mississippian Subsistence and Economics

Bruce D. Smith (1978) has characterized Mississippians as adapted to a specific niche in the floodplains of the interior river valleys of the Eastern Woodlands, but more recent investigators (e.g., Schoeninger and Schurr 1998) believe that Mississippian adaptations were more varied, both geographically and temporally. Mississippians grew maize, beans, and squash, as well as native seed plants. At some sites, like Ocmulgee in Georgia, ridges and furrows in Mississippian fields have been found (Riley 1994). Mississippians also exploited the abundant wild resources available in the floodplains and adjacent uplands. These wild resources included wild varieties of native seed plants, nuts, greens, deer, raccoon, turkey, migratory waterfowl, and fish. Coastal resources including shellfish were of obvious importance to people living immediately along the coasts, such as some Fort Walton Mississippians. The common thread in Mississippian subsistence was reliance on maize, beans, and squash cultivated in fields.

There is considerable debate about how Mississippian economies worked. Analyses of the paramount chiefdom centered at Moundville have suggested that Moundville residents were provisioned with foodstuffs from people living at smaller sites outside Moundville. Studies indicate that choice, meaty parts of deer were sent to Moundville from its outlying districts. There also seems to be evidence that craft items, often made of nonlocal raw materials, moved from Moundville to smaller settlements. For example, an area of manufacture for greenstone celts has been found at Moundville, and it is believed that these largely utilitarian items were passed out to people in outlying districts. Moundville also participated in exchange with other Southeasterners. The data show that nonlocal commodities including copper, greenstone, mica, graphite, and conch shell came from many places to Moundville. Prestige items may have been manufactured from imported materials at Moundville, or they may have arrived in completed form. Circular stone paint palettes, red slate pendants, and pottery probably were manufactured there and traded from Moundville to people outside this chiefdom (Welch 1991). It may be that neither the provisioning of elite subsistence nor elite control of the production and exchange of prestige items suggested by this example applies elsewhere. Others have suggested that Mississippian craft production and exchange were much more decentralized (e.g., Muller 1997).

Recent studies have been exploring possible differences in the diets of elites and commoners in various Mississippian polities (e.g., Jackson and Scott 2003). The social context of food consumption also is important, and we may learn a great deal about Mississippian societies from the analysis of the remains of feasts as well as from domestic middens. Feasting and associated ceremonies could have been as important in the social order as burial ceremonialism.

FIGURE 11.26 Red cedar mask, from the Spiro site in Oklahoma, incorporating deer antlers and shell insets.

Ranking and Mississippian Polities

Besides architectural evidence in mounds and site plans, burial contexts and skeletal populations provide archaeologists with indicators of social differentiation among Mississippians. In mortuary rituals, burials containing copper headdresses and other artifacts, ceremonial weapons, quantities of shell beads, other ornaments, and finely made pottery were commonly placed near or in mounds and public structures. The richness of some mound burials is amazing, as suggested in the high-status burials from the Craig Mound at the Spiro site in eastern Oklahoma. This mound, a large saddle-shaped earthwork consisting of conjoined mounds, was partially destroyed by a famous episode of commercial looting in the 1930s. The "Great Mortuary" at the center of this mound contained a large collective burial with deposits of spectacular artifacts including copper axes, copper-covered reed baskets, ceremonial maces, large quantities of shell beads, many conch shell cups, and the wooden headdress shown in Figure 11.26 (James A. Brown 1996).

Skeletal analyses have shown differences in health and diet between Mississippian elites and commoners. In eastern Tennessee elite males, who may have had greater access to meat, seem to have been taller than male commoners and may have experienced less stress as children (Steponaitis 1986). Studies at Moundville and comparisons with several other Mississippian burial populations do not, however, indicate great differences in general health between elites and commoners (Mary Lucas Powell 1992, 1998).

These kinds of data, along with artifacts from the towns and mound centers associated with the Mississippians, have been sufficient to convince archaeologists that these societies were chiefdoms (Figure 11.27). The precise nature of

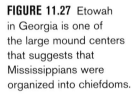

FIGURE 11.27 Etowah in Georgia is one of the large mound centers that suggests that Mississippians were organized into chiefdoms.

the chiefdoms is not known, and many aspects deserve exploration. For example, the extent to which elite status was hereditary as opposed to achieved during an individual's lifetime is not understood. Some archaeologists believe that long-standing Eastern Woodlands ideologies associated with membership in communities and lineages were replaced during Mississippian times with ideologies that elevated key individuals to positions of power. This would have meant a change from rituals honoring ancestors and establishing membership in a community to rituals reinforcing the power of chiefs who controlled agricultural surplus.

The Non-Mississippian Late Prehistoric

As Figure 11.20 indicated, Mississippian societies did not develop in all parts of the Southeast. In southern and eastern Florida as well as in parts of North Carolina, social groups generally have been considered Late Woodland rather than Mississippian. The primary basis for this categorization is the observation that there was less emphasis on corn, beans, and squash agriculture and less involvement in the ceremonial aspects of Mississippian lifestyles. However, some of these non-Mississippians were organized into chiefdoms, and many of them interacted with Mississippian societies.

Two examples of non-Mississippian Southeastern societies that flourished after 1000 BP are the **Colington phase** (Algonquian) and the **Cashie phase** (Iroquoian) societies of North Carolina's Coastal Plain. Colington phase societies on the outer Coastal Plain sometimes developed chiefdoms, while the Cashie phase people of the inner Coastal Plain were tribally organized. All these people grew some maize, beans, and squash (Phelps 1983; Herbert 2002).

St. Johns tradition cultures of east and central Florida, which left large shell middens and mounds, are another example. Contact with Mississippians is suggested by the presence of Southeastern Ceremonial complex items in some mounds. Bottle and other gourd use is well documented, but the extent of reliance on maize agriculture as opposed to wild resources is unclear (Milanich 1994).

Finally the **Glades** and **Caloosahatchee** societies of South Florida, which exploited wetland and coastal environments were different than Mississippian societies. At the site of Key Marco, Frank Hamilton Cushing's 1896 excavations recovered remarkable wooden and fiber artifacts in the shell platform mounds. The people did not practice agriculture, but they did develop complex socio-political institutions during the Late Woodland, and they left a remarkable series of shell middens and mounds (Milanich 1994, 1995; Widmer 2002).

PROTOHISTORIC AND HISTORIC TIMES

The chiefdoms of the Mississippian period sometimes persisted into early Historic times in the Southeast. Thus, there are protohistoric and sometimes historic components at sites of importance to Mississippian archaeology. For example, Moundville and its associated sites may correspond to the **Apafalaya chiefdom** of the de Soto chronicles (Knight and Steponaitis 1998). These connections make the Protohistoric and early Contact periods particularly fascinating to archaeologists.

When the first Europeans arrived, the Native peoples of the Southeast, despite their many cultural similarities, spoke languages representative of five different language families: Algonquian, Iroquoian, Siouian, Muskogean, and

Caddoan. Non-Mississippian groups in present-day Florida included the Calusa of the Fort Myers area and the Tequesta of the Miami area (Milanich 1995). In addition, a number of small Algonquian-speaking groups, such as the Croatoans and Pamlico, inhabited the Atlantic Coastal Plain in North Carolina, where the Late Prehistoric archaeological record suggests a series of small chiefdoms. Among the Iroquoian speakers, the Tuscaroras of the interior Coastal Plain of North Carolina, who moved north to New York State in the early 1700s, may have been descendants of people represented by the Late Prehistoric Cashie phase of the interior Coastal Plain.

The rest of the tribes of the Southeast at the initiation of contact with Europeans generally can be related to Mississippian groups. The other southern Iroquoian speakers were the Cherokee of the southern Appalachians in north-west Georgia, southeastern Tennessee, and western South Carolina. Several groups of Cherokee towns can be recognized, and this tribe figures importantly in the later history of this part of the Southeast. Initially the Cherokee lived in nucleated towns with plazas, some of which have been excavated. The bulk of Southeastern tribes were Muskogean-speaking groups, such as the Alabama, Apalachee, Muskogee, Timucua, Chickasaw, Choctaw, and Creek, whose original territories were in Georgia, Alabama, Mississippi, Louisiana, northern Florida, and adjacent areas. The Natchez of the Mississippi River valley and the Tunica of Louisiana spoke languages that some have considered linguistic isolates. The Seminoles, a major Southeastern tribe today, are a more recent amalgamation of Indians in Florida who speak a Muskogean language. Siouian-speaking tribes were found in the lower Mississippi River valley and include the Ofos, the Biloxi, and the Quapaw, as well as tribes located to the north and west. The Catawba of the Carolinas and the Yuchi of Tennessee sometimes are considered linguistic isolates, although their languages are related to Siouan languages. Caddoan speakers were found only on the western margins of the Southeast, where the Caddo tribes of Arkansas and Louisiana were its main representative. The Mississippian Spiro chiefdom is the best-known Caddo antecedent (Hudson 1976).

Spanish, French, and British Colonialism

The story of the Spanish exploration and settlement in the Southeast is not widely known. You may think of the Southwest and California as the part of North America colonized by the Spanish. However, the Spanish were the earliest colonizers in the Southeast and Spain controlled much of Florida into the early nineteenth century. The Spanish period technically began in 1513, when Ponce de Léon of "Fountain of Youth" fame made his first voyage to Florida. Other explorations and efforts at establishing colonies followed. The most important expedition was led by Hernando de Soto, who landed at Tampa Bay in late May 1539. The de Soto expedition proceeded through the Southeast for more than four years. Many men lost their lives, including de Soto himself, who died in Arkansas near the Mississippi River in 1542. About half the party made it back to New Spain in September 1543, having finally built boats and sailed down the Mississippi into the Gulf of Mexico (Hudson et al. 1989). The route of the de Soto expedition has been carefully researched and correlated with archaeological evidence. It is shown in Figure 11.28, along with the Florida expedition of Ponce de Léon. Besides the Moundville example already given, other associated sites have been identified. The Little Egypt site on the Coosawattee River in northwest

FIGURE 11.28 The routes taken by Ponce de Léon in 1513 and by Hernando de Soto between 1539 and 1543 have been carefully researched.

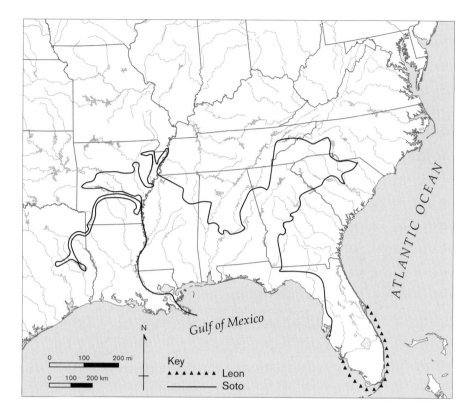

Georgia is believed to be the main town of the Coosa chiefdom (Marvin T. Smith 2000), and the expedition's winter camp in 1539–1540 among the Apalachee is believed to be the Martin site near modern Tallahassee, Florida (Ewen 1989).

In September 1565, the Spanish under Pedro Menendez destroyed Fort Caroline, a French colony established in 1564 at the mouth of the St. Johns River on the Atlantic coast, and established St. Augustine. Other outposts such as Santa Elena on Parris Island also were established. The Spanish Jesuits and Franciscans built a mission system both northward along the Atlantic coast and inland (Milanich 1999). Spanish holdings in La Florida were lost to the English in 1763 after the Seven Years War in Europe, but Spain retook Florida through a military campaign in 1781. The communities, however, remained multiethnic. Spain also acquired Louisiana from France in 1763 and held it as a colony until 1802 when King Charles IV secretly returned the territory to France. The archaeology of St. Augustine, which remains the oldest continuously occupied non-Native community in the United States, has been studied intensively (Deagan 1983), as have other aspects of the Spanish colonialism in the Southeast (Thomas 1990).

Although the French did not successfully settle along the Atlantic coast, they were a force in the Mississippi River valley during the seventeenth and eighteenth centuries. The Mississippi was partially explored by Marquette and Joliet in 1673. In 1682 La Salle made it to the Gulf, establishing a small settlement, the Arkansas Post, at the mouth of the Arkansas. His disastrous later expedition via the Gulf of Mexico missed the mouth of the Mississippi. It ended when he lost all his ships, and his men murdered him as he tried to go overland to find the Mississippi. Centuries later, La Salle's ship *Belle* was found and excavated; it had sunk in Matagorda Bay, off the coast of Texas (Bruseth and Turner 2005; Roberts 1997). Eventually the French established the Louisiana colony in the lower Mississippi valley, creating a network of settlements and military posts along the Gulf Coast and along the rivers. For a time French trade with Native peoples was extensive. As noted earlier, France ceded Louisiana to Spain in 1763 but reacquired it in time to negotiate the Louisiana Purchase of 1803 with the Americans. French forts have been investigated archaeologically, as have French settlements, particularly at places like Mobile on the Gulf Coast.

Historic Indian sites from the French period also have been investigated archaeologically. The most important of these may be the long-standing investigations into Natchez sites such as the Fatherland site or Grand Village of the Natchez near Natchez, Mississippi (e.g., Ian W. Brown 1990). This was the site of the Natchez capital, where the French Jesuit missionary du Pratz lived in the early eighteenth century. It was du Pratz who provided the detailed accounts of Natchez life that have been used by archaeologists to model the Mississippian chiefdoms preceding the Historic period.

Of course, the British also colonized the Southeast, establishing the Carolina Colony at Charles Town (Charleston, South Carolina) in 1670. Along the Atlantic coast the British established a plantation system that produced crops and other commodities for export. This system depended on slave labor, a need initially met by trading guns and ammunition for Indian captives. After rapidly depleting Native populations along the coast, the British removed thousands of Indian slaves from the interior. From 1700 onward African slaves began to be used. Archaeological studies of the material culture of pre–Revolutionary War African slave communities are exploring the development of the African American identity in the context of American slavery (Singleton 1995). The British also established trade for deerskins with many Native groups throughout the Southeast. Natives variously allied with the French or the British. Archaeologists have investigated plantations, trading posts, forts, and Indian towns associated with British colonialism.

The American Period

Control of the Southeast by "Americans" began with the revolution of 1775–1783. Of course control of Louisiana, which included massive portions of the Great Plains, did not come until 1803 when Jefferson purchased this territory from France. The United States did not gain control of Florida until even later. There was a long period of border disputes between the Spanish in Florida and Americans from approximately 1785 to 1821, when the United States gained control of Florida in return for relinquishment of U.S. claims to Texas.

Archaeological investigations can make many contributions to understanding the American period in the Southeast, but studies in three areas are particularly significant. First, one of the most important historical topics for this period is that of Indian removals from the Southeast. Some Native American tribes of the Southeast had been able to survive the colonial period, but by the turn of the nineteenth century a tide of Euro-American settlers flooded into their lands, causing a series of conflicts like the Creek War of 1813–1814. The Cherokee were the most acculturated to Euro-American ways, having established a democratic government and devised a written version of their traditional language. The Creeks, Choctaws, Chickasaws, and Seminoles also were farmers holding coveted land.

After the passage of the Indian Removal Act in 1830, most of the Indians of the Southeast were resettled west of the Mississippi. One forced relocation march, known as the **Trail of Tears** began when federal troops routed thousands of Georgia Cherokee from their homes in 1838; nearly one quarter of those who set out died en route. A number of Indians did escape removal, including about a thousand Cherokees, who remained in North Carolina where the Eastern Cherokee live today. The Seminole resistance is famous, but only about 300 Seminoles managed, by hiding in the Everglades, to escape removal. The archaeology of Cherokee towns before removal, of Seminole resistance sites, and of American forts built during the second Seminole War has provided important insights into the Southeastern historical past (Bense 1994).

Second, the stories of African Americans after the colonial period also have been profitably investigated by archaeologists. The lives of slaves are very poorly documented in the written record. This lack of documentation is particularly scandalous because in many parts of the South black slaves actually outnumbered other inhabitants. Archaeologists have been developing a rich body of data about the lives of African Americans (e.g., Ferguson 1992; see also Singleton 1995).

Third, though extensively documented by historical records, the American Civil War also can be studied through archaeology. This chapter's opening sketch provides one example of what archaeology may be able to tell us about the Civil War, but many other aspects of this conflict can be explored through archaeology, as well. Studies of battles or military campaigns are obvious topics. For example, the defensive structures erected in 1864 at Atlanta have been archaeologically investigated (Fryman 2000), as has the retreat of Federal troops at the battle of Chickamauga in the Chattanooga area (Cornelison 2000). A wide variety of other archaeological studies of Civil War era sites are being done as well (see Geier and Potter 2000; Geier and Winter 1994). Much of this work is being performed as a result of CRM requirements.

CHAPTER SUMMARY

This chapter's introduction to what archaeologists have learned about the past in the Southeast culture area supplies a context for exploring Southeastern archaeology more fully. The specific points made in the chapter can be summarized as follows:

- The two main physiographic units of the Southeast are the Appalachian Mountain system and the Coastal Plain, which can be divided into Atlantic and Gulf sections, although portions of the Interior Low Plateau and the Mississippi River valley also are included in this area. Most of this area is part of the temperate deciduous forest biome, while more tropical forests characterize southern Florida.

- Even though it was not glaciated, the environment of the Southeast during the Pleistocene contrasted significantly with modern ones owing to cooler temperatures, the suppression of seasonality, and the lowering of sea level.

Both warmer climatic episodes after 9000 BP and human modification of the landscape by farmers also significantly altered Southeastern landscapes.

- Important possible Pre-Clovis sites do exist in the Southeast, but Clovis era and later Paleoindian occupation of the area is much better documented, and Southeastern Paleoindians apparently were generalized rather than specialized foragers.

- Generalized foraging continued to characterize the Archaic adaptations of the Southeast from about 10,000 BP, although lithic assemblage attributes such as the appearance of notched projectile points can be used to distinguish the Archaic from the Paleoindian.

- Key changes in subsistence during the Middle and Late Archaic include heavier reliance on shellfishing, as the rivers and coasts reached their modern configurations, and the cultivation and domestication of several types of plants in the interior Southeast. These changes are associated with a greater degree of sedentism as well as with the container revolution, which involved the manufacture of stone bowls and introduction of fiber-tempered pottery.

- Mound building and associated ceremonialism is first evident in Middle Archaic shell mounds and rings, as well as in mounds located in the lower Mississippi River valley. By the Late Archaic, one can recognize the Poverty Point complex, centered at the large earthwork site of Poverty Point in northeast Louisiana and characterized by interregional exchange and fine stoneworking.

- The Woodland period in the Southeast, which can be dated from 3000 BP until approximately 950 BP, was a time of widely varying cultural developments. Many Early and Middle Woodland mound-building complexes sprang from local roots, but especially the Middle Woodland ones suggest participation in interactions with the Hopewell of the Midwest.

- The Southeastern Late Woodland has a reputation for being a period of decline, but actually was highly variable and marked by the widespread adoption of the bow and arrow, higher population levels, settlement pattern change, and intensification of agricultural production in at least some cases.

- Mississippians were maize-bean-squash agriculturalists who built towns oriented around plazas with platform mounds and public buildings. The people were organized into chiefdoms of varying size and complexity, and they produced and exchanged raw materials and prestige items displaying sophisticated craftsmanship. Mississippian ceremonialism, exchange, and iconography all were expression of complex and changing political interactions in Mississippian times. However, in southern and eastern Florida, North Carolina, and some other coastal areas of the Southeast, Mississippian cultures did not develop.

- Many Native tribes are known to have existed in the Southeast at the initiation of contact with Europeans, and these tribes were variously affected by Spanish, French, and British colonization. Besides the archaeology of contact, Southeastern historical archaeology contributes to understanding of the removal of Southeastern Indians west of the Mississippi, documentation of the Southeast's African American heritage, and the interpretation of the events and consequences of the American Civil War.

SUGGESTIONS FOR FURTHER READING

For a thorough summary of the Southeastern past:

Bense, Judith A. 1994. *Archaeology of the Southeastern United States: Paleoindian to World War I.* San Diego: Academic Press.

For more information on the foragers of the Southeast:

Anderson, David G., and Kenneth E. Sassaman, eds. 1996. *The Paleoindian and Early Archaic Southeast.* Tuscaloosa: University of Alabama Press.

Sassaman, Kenneth E., and David G. Anderson, eds. 1996. *Archaeology of the Mid-Holocene Southeast.* Gainesville: University Press of Florida.

For more on the Woodland peoples of the Southeast:

Anderson, David G., and Robert C. Mainfort, Jr., eds. 2002. *The Woodland Southeast.* Tuscaloosa: University of Alabama Press.

For archaeological reviews of important Southeastern sites:

Gibson, Jon L. 2000. *The Ancient Mounds of Poverty Point: Place of Rings.* Gainesville: University Press of Florida.

King, Adam. 2003. *Etowah: The Political History of a Chiefdom Capital.* Tuscaloosa: University of Alabama Press.

Knight, Vernon James, and Vincas P. Steponaitis, eds. 1998. *Archaeology of the Moundville Chiefdom.* Washington, DC: Smithsonian Institution Press.

For a readable account of one of the chiefdoms encountered by de Soto:

Smith, Marvin T. 2000. *Coosa: The Rise and Fall of a Mississippian Chiefdom.* Gainesville: University Press of Florida.

OTHER RESOURCES

Sections H and I of the Student CD give web links, places to visit, additional discussion questions, and other study aids. The Student CD also contains a variety of additional resources, including the complete references as cited in this chapter and the case study that follows. Most relevant to Southeastern archaeology is the case study in Section D.5 of the Student CD: "The Dust Cave Archaeological Project: Investigating Paleoindian and Archaic Lifeways in Southeastern North America," by Walker et al.

CASE STUDY

Museum collections can be just as significant resources for archaeological research as new excavations. People often envision museum collections in terms of pots, stone tools, carved figurines, and other artifacts. Of course, these are important parts of archaeological collections, but this case study shows that documents, including maps, field notes, and drawings, can be equally important. In fact, if artifact collections lack written information about context, much less can be learned from the objects themselves. In this case study, maps and other records concerning excavations done by the Works Progress Administration (WPA) during the 1930s provide a basis to explore information about Late Mississippian communities and households and also allow the investigation of some aspects of mortuary behavior. Because the sites in question are now underwater, archaeologists interested in understanding this time period in southeastern Tennessee must rely on museum collections. Fortunately, the collections in this case are well documented, and the physical evidence can be combined fruitfully with existing ethnohistorical information on Southeastern Indians. This research also shows why mapping and spatial documentation are so critical to archaeological interpretation. As you read this case study, notice the various kinds of archaeological information that are used and think about what would have been lost if the WPA excavations had been less well documented.

MOUSE CREEK PHASE HOUSEHOLDS AND COMMUNITIES

Mississippian Period Towns in Southeastern Tennessee

Lynne P. Sullivan

Imagine that you could walk into an ancient town and step into the houses and public buildings. Without even speaking to the townspeople, you would learn a lot about how they live just from looking at the kinds of things they use, and the context and arrangements of these things within and around the houses and buildings. An archaeological site that is the remains of an entire town or village contains similar information; much less of the town or village is intact, of course, and the archaeologist must make inferences. Nevertheless, the kinds of information these sites produce are invaluable for learning about many aspects of the lives of ancient peoples.

Excavating a town or village site is a daunting task because these sites typically cover several acres and contain very complex deposits. Archaeological investigations of large sites require large staffs, considerable funding, and a lot of time. But, a scholar does not necessarily have to spend years in the field to study a village site. Without ever wielding a shovel, an individual researcher can reap the benefits of large excavation projects by studying existing collections. Museums curate vast numbers of professionally excavated archaeological collections, some of them the result of many years of excavation, or excavations by very large crews, at large sites. In some cases, only preliminary studies have been made of the materials. In nearly all cases, there is much more to be learned from the curated collections.

WPA ARCHAEOLOGY

The collections made by **Works Progress Administration** (WPA) crews before flooding of reservoirs by the **Tennessee Valley Authority** (TVA) offer a good example of museum collections from large village sites. The circumstances under which these collections were made also provide a glimpse into the history of archaeology in the United States. Both the WPA and TVA were part of Franklin D. Roosevelt's New Deal programs to give jobs to people who had become unemployed and to improve the quality of life during the Great Depression. WPA crews provided the labor for extensive archaeological excavations that were supervised by professional archaeologists. The large WPA excavations in the southeastern United States also helped build an infrastructure for archaeological research, as universities hired archaeologists and set up departments to administer the projects.

The Chickamauga Basin Project, on the Tennessee River near Chattanooga, was one of several WPA/TVA archaeological projects that excavated large town sites dating to the Mississippian period. Archaeological work for the Chickamauga reservoir began in early 1936 and continued through 1939. An earlier survey of the basin, conducted under the direction of William Webb of the University of Kentucky, had located some 70 sites. Thomas M. N. Lewis, who had worked with the well-known archaeologist W. C. McKern at the Milwaukee Public Museum, was hired by the University of Tennessee to run the excavation and analysis portion of the project. Lewis was the university's first archaeologist, and he worked in the newly established Division of Anthropology, a section of the Department of History. He hired young archaeologists as field supervisors, including several of Fay-Cooper Cole's University of Chicago students. Cole ran one of the first field training programs for student archaeologists in the United States. Jesse D. Jennings, one of Cole's students and later a well-known archaeologist in the Great Basin, was the main field supervisor for the Chickamauga project. Lewis also hired Madeline Kneberg, another Chicago student, to be the director of the laboratory (Sullivan 1999). At the lab in Knoxville, she oversaw materials preparation, restoration, and cataloging, as well as analysis.

Thirteen of the 70 sites located by the survey, including portions of nine prehistoric town sites, were chosen for excavation. The large WPA crews (sometimes as many as 100 workers) made it possible to excavate huge areas of these sites, and as Lewis notes in the project's manual of field and laboratory procedures, the field supervisors had to expend "much shoe leather" to keep up with the excavations. Artifacts were cleaned in the field and shipped to the Knoxville laboratory, where they were cataloged and analyzed with the assistance of several specialists from other institutions. For the Chickamauga Project alone, the lab classified over 360,000 pottery sherds and some 100,000 stone, bone, shell, and copper artifacts; workers identified almost 7000 animal bones to species, reconstructed several hundred pottery vessels, and examined all of the nearly 2000 recovered human skeletons to determine age, sex, and pathologies.

When the United States entered World War II in 1941, the New Deal archaeological projects were shut down and many of the staff were drafted for the war effort. Nevertheless, the information and materials collected by this project comprise the only systematic documentation of major archaeological sites that now are inundated or destroyed. The collections are especially precious because the opportunity for continued excavation no longer exists at most of the sites. However, the work that was completed laid so much of the groundwork for subsequent research in the upper Tennessee valley that the archaeological phases in the region are named for sites in the Chickamauga Basin.

Data available from the large town sites in the Chickamauga Basin include documentation of large portions of the town plans, showing spatial relationships between structures and other features; plan drawings of many structures; large and detailed data sets for studies of mortuary practices and human biology; and large numbers of intact artifacts for technological and stylistic comparative studies. These collections, which have enormous potential for continuing research, exemplify the need to care for and preserve such archaeological materials so that future scholars can use them. The Chickamauga Basin collections are suitable for a wide range of research precisely because of the systematic and standardized collecting and recording techniques used by the WPA-era archaeologists, and the preservation of within-site provenience information and large samples of various materials. The meticulous records kept by the field and laboratory archaeologists contain this informa-

tion and are what make these collections valuable for continuing research.

In 1946, Tom Lewis and Madeline Kneberg published a report on the Hiwassee Island site, one of the large, excavated town sites in the Chickamauga Basin (Lewis and Kneberg 1946). They chose this site because it contained examples of several of the archaeological cultures they wished to define for this region. Earlier they had drafted, with other project supervisors, a report for the entire Chickamauga Basin Project, but the report remained an incomplete draft for over a half century. The curated project records and collections made it possible to complete and publish this important document in 1995 (Sullivan 1995). While the report contains descriptive information about the excavated sites, and the kinds of artifacts and features found in the Chickamauga Basin, it gives little interpretation of the sites and, of course, does not include the types of analyses and interpretations possible with an additional 60-plus years of knowledge and research.

A CONTEMPORARY ANALYSIS OF TWO CHICKAMAUGA BASIN SITES

In the late 1980s, as part of my doctoral dissertation project, I analyzed several excavated village or town sites in the Chickamauga Basin. This work exemplifies the process archaeologists use to study such collections, and the kinds of questions that can be asked and addressed about ancient life in pre-Columbian towns of the Southeast. The archaeologists of the WPA era defined an archaeological complex known as the **Mouse Creek phase** based on their investigations of three large sites. We now know that the Mouse Creek phase is a Late Mississippian (500–400 BP/AD 1450–1550) complex, located mainly along the lower Hiwassee River, a tributary of the Tennessee River in southeastern Tennessee (Figure 11.29). I will examine two of the Mouse Creek phase sites, Mouse Creeks and Ledford Island, in some detail.

The archaeologists of the 1930s did not have the advantage of absolute dating techniques, such as radiocarbon dating, to help assign sites to different archaeological complexes, so they classified sites and complexes solely on the basis of the kinds of things they found and the stratigraphic relationships (if any). The WPA archaeologists segregated the Mouse Creek

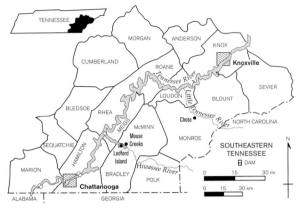

FIGURE 11.29 Location of the Mouse Creek phase sites discussed in the case study.

sites from other Mississippian sites based on differences in the remains of buildings, in the pottery, and in mortuary practices. They interpreted these differences as indicating that the Mouse Creek phase represented the remains of an ethnic group or culture different from other Mississippian period sites in the region. Such interpretations were commonplace during the years before radiocarbon dating (first used for archaeological purposes in the early 1950s) because the antiquity of the archaeological record in the Americas was not known, and differences in archaeological assemblages often were attributed to migrations and/or changes in people or ethnic groups within a region, rather than to temporal differences. We now know that the Mouse Creek phase sites postdate most of the other Mississippian period sites in the

Chickamauga Basin (Table 11.4). The ethnic and biological relationships of the earlier and later Mississippian groups in the basin remain an unresolved question.

One of the first steps in studying the collections representing the Mouse Creek towns was to assemble maps of the excavations. The field workers created detailed maps of the excavated archaeological features (e.g., structure patterns, palisade lines, refuse pits), but the excavated areas were so large that many maps had to be made. To be able to look at entire excavated areas, these maps had to be assembled—similar to putting together a puzzle—so that the layouts or plans of the towns could be discerned. Maps of two of the sites, Ledford Island (Figure 11.30) and a portion of the Mouse Creeks Site (Figure 11.31), are particularly instructive for analysis of the plans of Mouse Creek phase communities.

The compiled maps provide spatial contexts for the recovered artifacts, as well as information on the arrangements of buildings and other elements of these ancient communities. To supplement this information, ground surface elevations, recorded with a surveying instrument by a WPA surveyor, were used to create topographic maps for each site. These maps show how the various features of the towns (e.g., rises, depressions, level areas) were situated on the landscape. Other maps of distributions of artifacts and certain kinds of archaeological features add more information that can be used to help interpret the town plans.

The various maps of the Ledford Island site in particular reveal rudimentary information about the overall plan and the uses of certain areas of this ancient community. The map of the excavated

TABLE 11.4 Comparison of the WPA-Era and Current Chronological Sequences for Late Prehistory in the Chickamauga Basin

WPA-Era Sequence	Dates	Cultural Period	Dates	Current Sequence
Cherokee	AD 1650	Historic	300 BP (AD 1650)	Cherokee
			500 BP (AD 1450)	Mouse Creek
			650 BP (AD 1300)	Dallas
Dallas/Mouse Creek			750 BP (AD 1200)	Hixon
Hiwassee Island			850 BP (AD 1100)	Hiwassee Island
	AD 1400	Mississippian	1050 BP (AD 900)	Martin Farm
Hamilton	?	Late Woodland	1250 BP (AD 700)	Hamilton[1]

[1] Hamilton is now understood as a mortuary tradition that spans the Late Woodland and Early Mississippian periods. This tradition begins at 1250 BP, while the end date for use of Hamilton mounds is approximately 750 BP.

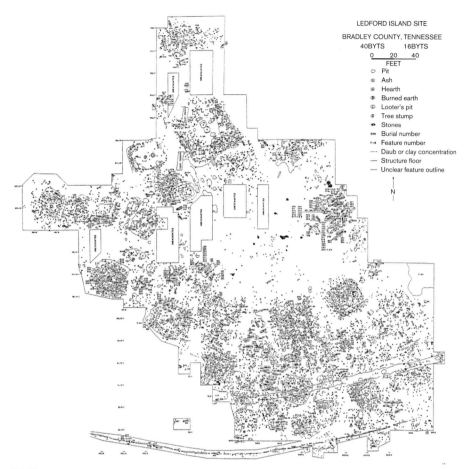

FIGURE 11.30 Excavation map of the Ledford Island site showing the archaeological features.

archaeological features shows a large area that is devoid of features (Figure 11.30). This "empty" area represents the town square or plaza. To its north is the pattern of a very large building, while the super-imposed patterns of many smaller buildings, which were rebuilt and/or repaired several times in the same locations—surround the rest of the plaza. Near the plaza's northeastern corner is a cemetery in which were interred mostly adult males. Diagonally across the plaza is another smaller cemetery, but these skeletons were in so poor a state of preservation that for most of the individuals age and sex could not be determined. Other graves are in scattered groups throughout the town, and a line of postmolds along the southern periphery of the excavated area indicates that a wooden palisade surrounded the community.

The topographic map of the Ledford Island site especially is interesting because it shows a large depressed area in the center of the site that corresponds with the plaza. Figure 11.32 shows the topographic map superimposed on a map of artifact distributions. Artifact distributions are based on numbers of artifacts found in the upper level of soil at the site, the **plow zone**, which was disturbed by modern farmers who plowed the soil for agricultural crops. Artifact counts for each unit in the excavation grid used by the WPA workers reflect the general pattern of artifact densities across the site. A statistical procedure called **trend surface analysis** was used to smooth the resulting contours. The artifact distributions show that the center of the site was devoid of artifacts. This clear area again coincides with the plaza,

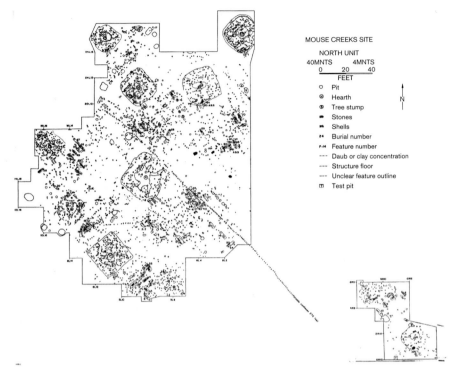

FIGURE 11.31 Excavation of the Mouse Creeks site (north unit) showing the archaeological features.

the depressed area that also is generally devoid of archaeological features. The lack of artifacts suggests that the townspeople kept this public area of their community very clean. In fact, it is possible that the area became depressed from repeated sweepings over a long period of time.

Another of the Mouse Creek phase sites, Mouse Creeks, provides more detail on the households of the townspeople. A portion of this site was not occupied as long as was the Ledford Island site, as evidenced by fewer episodes of rebuilding and repair of structures. A relatively short occupation span is of benefit to archaeologists because there is less confusion in the town plan due to overlapping and noncontemporary features. Examination of the assembled map of this site shows a line of postmolds, representing a wooden palisade that must have been an early feature of the town because it is superimposed by other features (Figure 11.31). Perhaps the town expanded beyond the extent of this early wall, but this is difficult to determine because there is less information about the overall town plan of this site than

Ledford Island. The Mouse Creeks site map does show a pattern of house basins (large square-shaped areas filled with dark-colored soil that are the remains of semisubterranean house floors), with adjacent concentrations of postmolds that are surrounded by graves. A map illustrating counts of postmolds by an excavation unit (excluding the house basins) shows that the postmold concentrations are to the southeast of each house basin (Figure 11.33). The house basins also include central hearths made of clay, surrounded by a floor area of hardened, likely trampled, clay. Short trenches, typically in the southeastern corner of each basin, are the remains of doorways. Graves of infants and young children also are found in the house basins, while those of older children and adults are placed near the postmold concentrations.

The repetition of this combination of house basins, postmold concentrations, and graves at Mouse Creeks likely reflects the remains of numerous household facilities that were the residences of the families who once occupied the town. The presence of repeated, similar architectural patterns and similar

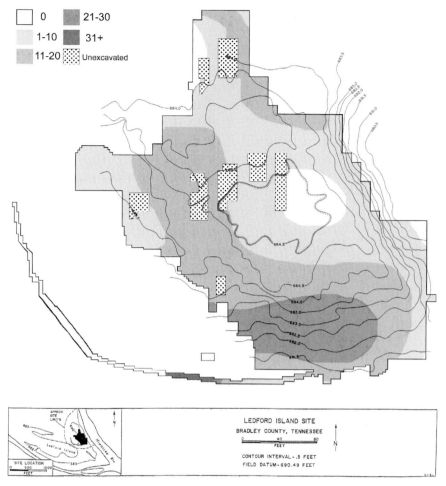

FIGURE 11.32 Topographic map of the Ledford Island site superimposed on a sixth-order trend surface analysis of the numbers of artifacts in the plow zone in each 10 by 10 foot (3 × 3 m) excavation unit.

arrangements of features also indicates a cultural preference or tradition for the organization of household facilities. Each household had a large dwelling made with log support posts, and the floor was dug into the ground. The lowered floors would have provided some additional insulation for winter months (although southeastern Tennessee has a moderate climate, winter temperatures quite often drop below freezing). The small sheltered doorways and central hearths in these buildings would have offered further protections from the elements. In contrast, the postmold concentrations adjacent to these buildings likely represent less substantial structures, possibly

to provide shade from the summer sun and shelter from the region's typical, drenching rainstorms. The graves associated with these buildings likely represent "family cemeteries."

Ethnographic information from accounts written by early European explorers, traders, and settlers in the region provides clues for interpreting these archaeologically observed patterns. These accounts often mention the "summer" and "winter" houses of many native, southeastern groups. The Cherokee, who first were encountered in the eastern Tennessee region in the 1700s, had such household buildings. The Cherokee winter house was a circular structure

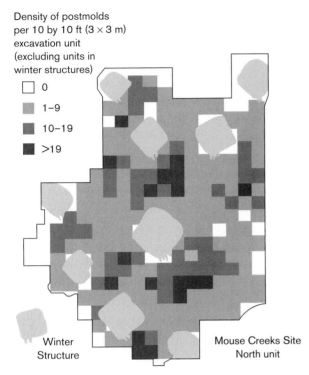

Density of postmolds
per 10 by 10 ft (3 × 3 m)
excavation unit
(excluding units in
winter structures)

☐ 0

■ 1–9

■ 10–19

■ >19

Winter   Mouse Creeks Site
Structure   North unit

FIGURE 11.33 Postmold concentrations suggesting
summer houses at Mouse Creeks.

with a central hearth. It was paired with a rectangular, less substantially built summer house, where the
family gathered in good weather to cook, eat, work
on various projects, store some items, and visit, or do
other typical day-to-day activities. Patterns of such
Cherokee households have been found archaeologically at the eighteenth-century Cherokee town of
Chota in the valley of the Little Tennessee River (see
Figures 11.1 and 11.29). Graves were associated with
the Cherokee summer houses (Schroedl 1986).

The plans of the Cherokee and Mouse Creek
households are not identical (e.g., the Cherokee
winter house is circular, while the Mouse Creek one
is square), but there are similarities in the design
of archaeologically observed and ethnographically
recorded eighteenth-century Cherokee household
facilities with the archaeologically observed household facilities, dating at least two centuries earlier,
at Mouse Creeks. These similarities do not necessarily mean that the residents of Mouse Creeks
were Cherokee, but the historic case does provide an

ethnographic analogy to help interpret the observed
archaeological patterns. Archaeologists often use such
analogies as a basis for generating ideas to test with
archaeological data, and the best analogies typically
derive from historically known Native groups living
in the region of the prehistoric sites. We will return to
this subject later.

The information about the household plans
derived from the Mouse Creeks excavations also can
be used to help interpret the community plan at the
Ledford Island site. The apparently longer occupation span there created more complex archaeological
deposits, but the understanding of the "template" of
household plans, as observed at the less-complicated
Mouse Creeks site, can be used to make sense of the
morass of features at Ledford Island. Enough elements of household plans can be seen in the map of
archaeological features at Ledford Island, including
clusters of burials and postmold concentrations
grouped near house basins, to allow us to infer that
household facilities similar to those at Mouse Creeks
also once surrounded the plaza at Ledford Island.

Thus the overall community plan at Ledford
Island can be envisioned as having numerous
households—each composed of winter and summer
houses and a small cemetery—surrounding a large,
central plaza with a very large building, architectur-
ally similar to the smaller winter houses, and larger
cemeteries flanking the plaza. A wooden palisade
enclosed the community.

This interpretation of the fundamental arrangement of a Mouse Creek phase community, based on
compilation and visual inspection of maps and
ethnographic analogies of several kinds, provides a
setting for examining other aspects of the organization of this pre-Columbian society. When graves are
located in residential sites, such as the Mouse Creek
phase towns, mortuary practices are yet another way
to learn about the social life of the community.
Mortuary practices are a data set that archaeologists
have found particularly useful for understanding the
composition of social groups and the variety of social
roles that individuals filled in ancient societies.

Studies of the social dimensions of mortuary practices rely on the principle that, in general, the treatment of an individual in death reflects the esteem he
or she was accorded in life. This principle, which generally is applicable to most cultures, can be observed
in many funeral rites and cemeteries of today. For
example, wealthy persons often have elaborate tombs

or grave markers; soldiers often are buried in special cemeteries (e.g., Arlington); and high-ranking politicians typically have specialized burial plots often associated with architecture (e.g., a presidential library). Such correlations are not perfect (consider the modern cemeteries in which all graves have identical bronze markers), and one must remember that mortuary treatments primarily reflect how the living choose to honor or commemorate the deceased, not necessarily the actual circumstances of the deceased's social position. Even given these caveats, mortuary treatments provide useful insights to ancient cultures. The spatial arrangements and locations of graves, as well as funerary objects interred with the deceased, along with biological information such as sex and age, can be used to assess possible differences in status, and gender and age-related roles. We note parenthetically that archaeologists who study social dimensions of mortuary practices typically work with biological anthropologists, who study the physical aspects of human skeletal remains. Under the federal Native American Grave Protection and Repatriation Act, studies of human remains may require consent of affiliated descendant groups.

Cemeteries are elements of the town plan at the Ledford Island site; they are associated both with households and with the town square or plaza. This spatial distinction in itself is interesting because the households can be considered "private" residences, while the plaza clearly is a public space. Age and sex distributions of burials, as mapped at the Ledford Island site, show noteworthy patterns. As noted earlier, the cemetery on the plaza's eastern edge contained the remains mainly of adult males. In contrast, the cemeteries around the households include individuals of both sexes and all ages, except that those who died in infancy or as very young children typically were buried in the floors of the winter houses. Also, more females than males are interred near the households, in comparison to the plaza cemeteries. Other distinctions can be seen in the kinds of artifact interred with the dead. Some are associated with individuals of a particular age or sex (e.g., pots with females, pipes with males), but others also are specific to location. Several kinds of items associated with the plaza burials (e.g., large ceremonial celts or axes, large chipped stone blades made of imported chert, clusters of finely made projectile points) are not found with graves in other parts of the town. Such items can be inferred to have special meaning

because they were costly to make in terms of time, craftsmanship, and/or materials. For example, the ceremonial celts are too thin actually to use for woodworking, suggesting that these items were specifically made to honor the deceased person with whom they were interred, or to reflect the honored position the person had held in society.

To interpret how these patterns may reflect principles of the organization of a single ancient society, archaeologists again turn to ethnographic analogy and studies of mortuary practices worldwide. The worldwide studies, as noted, provide general insights, while analogies from Native societies of the Southeast give clues to specific cultural practices. An understanding of the typical, ethnographically recorded kinship and residence practices of Southeastern Indians especially is relevant and necessary to interpret and understand such mortuary practices, as may be applied to the pre-Columbian Mouse Creek phase communities.

Most Southeastern groups were (and some still are) matrilineal and matrilocal (Hudson 1976). By "matrilineal," anthropologists mean that kinship was reckoned though the mother's line. A child belonged to his mother's larger kin group or clan, and although the biological father did have a relationship with and influence on his children, the most important male figure in a Southeastern Indian child's life was a maternal uncle. Most Southeastern Indians lived in **extended family** (multigenerational) households that were **matrilocal**—that is, a married couple lived in the house of the woman's family. Houses and property also passed through the female line. A married man thus lived with his in-laws; his family of origin and the children he was most responsible for educating and helping to care for (those of his sister) lived in a different house. These social constructs, based on kinship and residence, are important to keep in mind when considering the organization of Mississippian period peoples. The social dynamics accompanying these kinship and residence traditions are quite different from those of most modern-day residents of the United States.

Ethnographic information about how many of the Southeastern groups chose leaders also is relevant for considering the patterning observed at the Ledford Island site because leaders quite often were afforded distinctive mortuary treatments. Mortuary practices also can provide insights into the degree to which heredity was the means for determining leaders. Burial of children in the same manner as adult leaders suggests that heredity was a more important factor for determining leadership than personal ability, since a child would not have had the opportunity to develop leadership qualities. In the Southeast, some leadership positions tended to be inherited through certain kinship groups, such as lineages or clans. A chiefly title (some groups had a variety of chiefs) thus would be filled through a particular kin group, but the stringency of the inheritance rules for determining the holders of these positions varied considerably among groups. Some groups, such as the Natchez of current-day Mississippi, had a strictly determined, hereditary chiefly lineage. In other groups, such as the Cherokee, the senior women or clan mothers would decide which of several potentially eligible men would ascend to a chiefly office, based on each candidate's ability to lead.

The mortuary practices of the historically and archaeologically documented, eighteenth-century Cherokee are congruent with the latter scenario, and again offer particularly relevant analogies for the Mouse Creek phase. As previously mentioned, graves were associated with households of the eighteenth-century Cherokee town of Chota. Several graves also were located near the large townhouse, or public meetinghouse adjacent to the town square. These were graves of adult males, and one was known to be the resting place of Chief Oconostota. These plaza graves likely reflect acknowledgment of the interred individuals' participation in community leadership. The absence of the remains of children suggests that leadership ability, rather than inheritance, was an important factor of the status these men had acquired (see also Sullivan 2001).

The large building adjacent to the plaza and near the large plaza cemetery at the Ledford Island site appears to be analogous to the Cherokee townhouse. If the spatial patterning of the graves at Ledford Island is analogous to that at Chota, the adult males buried in the plaza cemetery can be supposed to have held positions important to the community, such as leaders or chiefs, and to have ascended to these positions largely through their ability, rather than strictly by inheritance. This interpretation is reinforced by the different kinds of objects interred with the men in the plaza and near the dwelling houses. Such objects may well represent the special status of the principal men in the community.

Another relevant aspect of eighteenth-century Cherokee society is that the townhouse, the public meetinghouse on the plaza, also served as a gathering place for the men of the community; men could go there to be away from the world of women. The households and kin groups were the realms of women, especially because the married men lived with their wives' families, the men did not own the houses, and kinship was determined through female lines. Cherokee women essentially were in charge of the households and families, including agricultural production, and they derived considerable political power and influence from these functions. In contrast, male leaders served as representatives of the entire community and were in charge of intercommunity relationships such as trading and alliances.

Until recently, many archaeologists would have suggested that the men in the Ledford Island plaza cemeteries were the sole political leaders and the "movers and shakers" in this ancient community. But, such interpretations ignore the social dynamics of matrilineages and matrilocality. Given differing political roles based on gender as in the Cherokee case, interpretations of men as the sole leaders in many Mississippian societies may well misrepresent the political power and influence of women in these communities, and undermine the significance of household cemeteries. Gerald Schroedl, the University of Tennessee archaeologist who supervised the excavations of the Chota site, argues that graves associated with households reflect a public acknowledgment of the ancestors linked to certain household groups (Schroedl 1986). That is, the household cemeteries honor the kin groups, in contrast to the plaza cemeteries, which honor the community. One is connected to the female realm of kin, the other with the male realm of community.

THE VALUE OF MUSEUM COLLECTIONS

Did the influential men interred in the Ledford Island plaza cemetery once sit in the large public building, sharing hunting stories, talking of great warriors, and contemplating ways in which to gain influence and obtain exotic goods at distant towns? Meanwhile, did the women, who are interred in cemeteries near their houses, speak of their dissatisfaction with the amount of deer meat in their larders and decide which man they would support (by supplying food and verbal influence) to lead a hunting party? Did they discuss, now that one of the elder chiefs had passed on, who should take his place? Did they help keep peace between communities by refusing to supply potential war parties with food? Many more questions can be asked about the patterning of architecture, artifacts, and graves at this site.

Archaeologists can only speculate about what life really was like in these ancient communities, but as we have seen, household and community plans can provide a wealth of data to shape insightful interpretations. More data sets and dimensions of analysis could be explored to answer questions about other aspects of the Mouse Creek phase communities. Archaeologists are becoming more and more aware of cultural variation and diversity across the Mississippian period Southeast. While the Mouse Creek phase communities provide examples of Mississippian period towns, they are not necessarily representative of other archaeologically known communities at other places and other times in the Southeast. Museum collections representing large communities will continue to provide data for studying and learning more about this diversity as new ideas and new analytical techniques are developed.

Study of these collections is as close as we will get to stepping into the vanished towns.

DISCUSSION QUESTIONS

1. What were Mouse Creek phase communities like? What were Mouse Creek households like? Summarize what you have learned about these topics.

2. Think about the assumption that the treatment of an individual in death reflects his or her position during life. Does this make sense to you? Think of examples in addition to those given in the case study that support or contradict this assumption.

3. Consider the kinds of analogy that can be drawn to known Cherokee and other Southeastern Indian communities and households. How appropriate is it for archaeologists to turn to such information? Explain your answer.

4. Construct an argument for the value of recording and mapping during excavation and for the curation of documented archaeological collections. Use your argument to point out how uncontrolled excavation and looting can destroy opportunities to learn about the past.

CHAPTER 12

Foragers and Farmers of the Midwest and the Upper Great Lakes

In 1988 a heavy-equipment operator was borrowing dirt for a road construction project in southern Indiana when he encountered some spectacular artifacts. He collected the artifacts and took them home to Illinois. Next he contacted a well-known artifact collector from Indiana, sold the artifacts he had found for $6000, and showed the collector the site without obtaining permission from the landowner, the General Electric Company. Over the course of that summer, the artifact collector recruited helpers and proceeded to dig into what turned out to be a large, previously unrecognized Middle Woodland mound. Large quantities of artifacts were recovered, and some were later sold at an Indian relic show in Kentucky. Other collectors also removed artifacts from this site. Looting stopped only when security guards encountered looters on the property and required them to leave (Munson et al. 1995).

As word leaked out, it became clear that an important cultural resource had been harmed. Archaeologists did their own investigation and concluded that the mound had not been recognized during the course of a preconstruction survey because it was so large that it looked like a natural ridge. Probable dimensions of 400 by 175 feet (120 × 50 m) by 15 to 20 feet (4.6 × 6.1 m) in height make this mound one of the five largest known Middle Woodland mounds. Efforts to recover as many artifacts as possible began. Eventually over 3000 artifacts from nine collections were returned. Among these artifacts were copper celts and panpipes, pearl and shell beads, finely made stone and bone tools, mica cutouts, and leather wrappings. Many of these items were truly rare and valuable. Archaeologists used these artifacts and their exploration of the mound itself to identify the site as Hopewell, dating it between 1850 BP and 1950 BP. They also concluded that those who constructed the mound participated in interregional exchange and ceremonialism with people as far away as southern Ohio (Seeman 1995). Yet, the internal structure of the mound, the actual positioning of artifacts, and the number of individuals that might have been buried in the mound cannot be determined. The recovered artifacts also no longer can be studied because they were ceremonially reburied.

Unfortunately, clandestine looting and sale of Indian artifacts for profit isn't unusual (see the opening of Chapter 6). Illegal pot hunting goes on all over the United States, destroying cultural resources and the information they could have provided. Sometimes the sites damaged are highly significant, as was the case with the mound in Indiana, now called the GE Mound. What was different about the GE Mound case is that eventually five people were convicted under the Archaeological Resources Protection Act (ARPA) of 1979 (see Table 1.1), setting an important precedent for enforcement of this act's prohibition on interstate trafficking in artifacts.

The GE Mound was on property that was privately owned, and this was a critical issue in the court case. Whereas in some countries all known cultural resources are the property of the state, in the United States federal protections are not provided for cultural resources on private property unless federal funds or permits are involved. Under ARPA, however, it is illegal to sell, exchange, transport, or receive across state lines any artifacts that were obtained in violation of state or local law. State and local laws may or may not protect sites on private property. In Indiana, a state law requiring an approved plan for all excavation into archaeological sites was not passed until 1989, after the looting of the GE Mound had come to light (Munson et al. 1995). This means that excavation into the GE Mound would not have been illegal per se if permitted by the landowner. Some collectors maintain that General Electric at first gave tacit approval to their activities because the company did not immediately stop the digging and collecting, and it has even been alleged that GE was intentionally borrowing the mound in the first place (Gifford 1994). The looters of GE Mound admitted their actions, but they argued that ARPA was unconstitutionally vague and did not apply to the Indiana artifacts. The federal court did not find merit in the defendants' arguments, and the Supreme Court declined to review the decision.

The story of the GE Mound is instructive insofar as it reveals what different stakeholders in the past think about collecting and looting. Many archaeologists were outraged and strongly supported the prosecution of the looters. To an archaeologist, the looting of sites is fundamentally destructive to knowledge, while the sale of artifacts only encourages more looting. However, artifact collectors and some amateurs questioned the ARPA prosecution and thought the defendants were being made scapegoats for professional and landowner negligence. Prominent among their arguments were the claims that what happened at the GE Mound was not a serious offense and that collecting and trafficking in antiquities is not truly harmful to anyone. Moreover, ignoring the contention that the GE Mound artifacts at issue were stolen property, the collectors argued that their rights to private property (i.e., to have artifact collections) were being threatened. Native Americans were outraged primarily over the desecration of a burial site of their ancestors. Some Native Americans also were interested in what could be learned from the artifacts and mound. For others, however, the issue of respect for the ancestors outweighed any interest in obtaining knowledge about the past; these Native Americans successfully insisted on reburial of the artifacts. The final stakeholder in the proceedings was the local public, which truly had its consciousness raised concerning the nature and value of local antiquities. There was tremendous growth in public concern for the local heritage. Contained in these varying positions are the main elements in today's disagreements over the North American past and what should be done to protect this heritage.

The GE Mound story reminds us that the archaeological record of the areas covered here includes the remains of some of the most spectacular pre-Columbian societies that existed in North America. Archaeologists are deeply interested in these past societies and their cultures, but so are many others, for different reasons. These interests can be destructive as well as benign. Deciding how to resolve competing perspectives fairly is important. Much is at stake. Will we find ways to preserve resources and gain knowledge while respecting Native people, or will inadequate inventory of cultural resources, human greed, and a lack of legal protections result in the sweeping away of most of the record of the traces of the past?

DEFINITION OF THE AREA

The second Eastern Woodlands culture area is the Northeast culture area. This chapter is about the western part of this area as traditionally defined (Figure 12.1). The Northeast culture area stretches between the southern border of the boreal forest in Canada and the Ohio River and its tributaries in Kentucky and West Virginia. Eastern Missouri and Iowa are its western limits, and the Atlantic Ocean, extending southward to northern North Carolina, is its eastern margin. In this chapter we discuss only the Midwest and the Upper Great Lakes, encompassing northern Ontario around Lake Superior as well as eastern Wisconsin, all of Michigan including the Upper Peninsula, all of Illinois, Indiana, and Ohio, small portions of eastern Missouri and Iowa, the northern portion of Kentucky, and the western half of West Virginia. The rest of Northeast culture area is discussed in Chapter 13. As you read this chapter you should be alert for the many similarities with the Southeast culture area as well as some with the Plains culture area to the west. Table 12.1 shows that the general chronology of the Midwest and Upper Great Lakes closely resembles the chronology for the Southeast.

THE ENVIRONMENTS OF THE MIDWEST AND UPPER GREAT LAKES

The Midwest and Upper Great Lakes have a generally humid climate controlled by the interaction of Gulf, Pacific, and polar air masses; precipitation levels are reasonably constant throughout the year. Temperature is seasonally variable throughout these regions. Summers generally are warm and winters cold, but summer temperatures are higher and winters are milder in the southern margins of this area.

Most of the area covered in this chapter is part of Central Lowland physiographic province, although parts of Appalachian Plateau, the Interior Low Plateau, and the Laurentian Upland provinces also are included (Fenneman 1938). The primary agent that has shaped this area's topography is glaciation. The Till Plains stretch south from the basins of the Great Lakes and include areas now covered by rock and sediments left as the glaciers melted. The **Driftless area** in the upper Mississippi valley was never glaciated area but sometimes was enclosed by ice lobes. Of course, the southern margins of the Midwest also were never glaciated, and older, eroded landforms are visible there as well. As was the case on the Great Plains, many of the landforms in this chapter's area are covered with a mantle of Late Wisconsin loess, with the deepest deposits having accumulated on the margins of the Mississippi River trench (Ruhe 1983).

FIGURE 12.1 The Midwest and Great Lakes areas within the Northeast culture area, showing the location of sites mentioned in Chapter 12.

Most of the Midwest and Upper Great Lakes areas naturally were forested areas, although farming resulted in the clearing of many areas historically. The boreal coniferous forest biome occurs only in a small area north of Lake Superior, while the temperate deciduous forest biome naturally covers the southern half of the Midwest and Upper Great Lakes areas. Between this forest and the boreal

TABLE 12.1 Introduction to Midwest and Upper Great Lakes Culture History

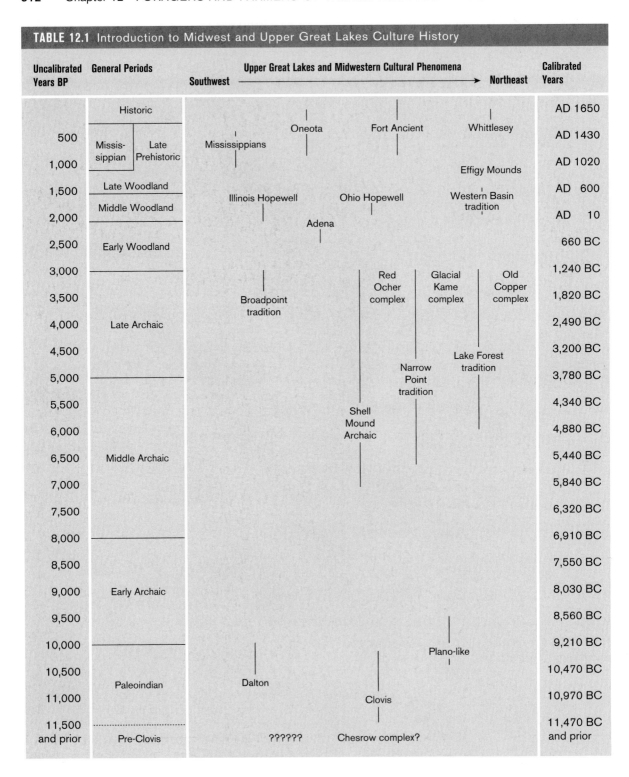

Uncalibrated Years BP	General Periods	Southwest	Upper Great Lakes and Midwestern Cultural Phenomena → Northeast	Calibrated Years
	Historic			AD 1650
500	Missis-sippian / Late Prehistoric	Mississippians	Oneota · Fort Ancient · Whittlesey	AD 1430
1,000				AD 1020
			Effigy Mounds	
1,500	Late Woodland	Illinois Hopewell	Ohio Hopewell · Western Basin tradition	AD 600
	Middle Woodland			
2,000			Adena	AD 10
2,500	Early Woodland			660 BC
3,000			Red Ocher complex · Glacial Kame complex · Old Copper complex	1,240 BC
3,500		Broadpoint tradition		1,820 BC
4,000	Late Archaic			2,490 BC
4,500			Lake Forest tradition	3,200 BC
5,000			Narrow Point tradition	3,780 BC
5,500				4,340 BC
6,000			Shell Mound Archaic	4,880 BC
6,500	Middle Archaic			5,440 BC
7,000				5,840 BC
7,500				6,320 BC
8,000				6,910 BC
8,500				7,550 BC
9,000	Early Archaic			8,030 BC
9,500				8,560 BC
10,000			Plano-like	9,210 BC
10,500	Paleoindian	Dalton		10,470 BC
11,000			Clovis	10,970 BC
11,500 and prior	Pre-Clovis	??????	Chesrow complex?	11,470 BC and prior

coniferous forest, lies a broad belt of transitional forest, containing a mix of coniferous and deciduous species. Tree species characteristic of these areas include northern conifers like spruce and fir as well as other coniferous species such as pine and hemlock and many deciduous species, including birch, beech, elm, basswood, and sugar maple (Cleland 1966; Mason 1981).

A fourth ecological area, the Illinoian biotic province, or the Prairie Peninsula, also is important. Prairie vegetation naturally extends into the areas discussed in this chapter in a broad wedge across southern Wisconsin, northern Illinois, and northern Indiana, as well as in patches into southern Michigan and western Ohio. Here various tall-grass species dominate, but patches of oak-hickory forest may occur in the uplands, and the river valleys support a diverse deciduous forest. Prairie species as well as forest species are found in this area, which is a broad ecotone.

Resources are also structured by the two massive drainage systems, each with its own fish fauna, which drain the areas considered in this chapter. These are St. Lawrence River system, which includes the Great Lakes, and the Mississippi River system, which includes the Ohio River. In addition to the Great Lakes, many smaller lakes that often are remnants of glacial activities can be found. Aquatic resources are significant throughout the region, and migratory waterfowl pass through the Midwest and the Upper Great Lakes seasonally, tracking along a major flyway.

Climatic Change

Obviously, the most important climatic changes to archaeologists working in the Midwest and Upper Great Lakes are those associated with the Wisconsin glaciation and its waning. In Illinois, Indiana, and western Ohio, the Wisconsin ice sheet extended south to the approximate latitude of 37° north (see Figure 2.12). The tremendously complex story of the ice sheet's retreat, which is beyond the scope of this text, is partially written on the landscape. However, deglaciation had begun by at least 14,000 BP, and after 10,000 BP ice was gone from all but the most northern areas.

The Great Lakes are glacial features carved out in the valleys of preglacial rivers by repeated movements of glaciers. When massive glaciers covered this area, the earth's crust also was depressed under the weight of the ice, and as glaciers retreated, the earth rebounded, complicating the formation of lakes and drainage patterns as the ice melted. For each of the Great Lakes, a series of predecessor lakes has been named and correlated with glacial advances and retreats by geologists. Similarly the **moraines** and glacial lake beaches visible in the midwestern states have been named and dated. The earliest Great Lakes were essentially proglacial lakes made up of waters trapped between the retreating ice front to the north and the moraines or ice dams to the south. Because these various lakes could not drain northeastward through the St. Lawrence River until the glacier had retreated a considerable distance to the north, other drainage patterns through the Mississippi and Ohio valleys were established. Both drainage patterns and the Great Lakes themselves were dynamic well into the Holocene. The rivers of the area were cold, fast-flowing, often braided streams that were carrying large volumes of water. River regimes took millennia to stabilize (Baker 1983).

Vegetation patterns also changed dramatically as the glaciers melted. At the glacial maximum a narrow band of tundra covered the land south and west of the ice, but pollen studies have shown that a mosaic of habitats was established south of the ice, so that we should not envision simply a southward shifting, during the Pleistocene, of the zonal communities of recent times. These data also indicate that this mosaic rapidly characterized newly deglaciated areas as temperatures warmed (e.g., Brown and Cleland 1968). Reconstruction is difficult because there is no modern analogue for these conditions. Pollen isopoll maps (e.g., Bernabo and Webb 1977) indicate that as the glacier was shrinking, spruce forests did not become extensive. Rather, they were rapidly replaced by pine-dominated forests, which became established in a broad band stretching across the Great Lakes into New England, only to be replaced over time by the transition forest with which we are familiar. Further south, oak-dominated deciduous forests quickly developed (Bernabo and Webb 1977).

Also during deglaciation the Prairie Peninsula ecotone was established, and it grew during the Hypsithermal interval after 9000 BP. The position of the prairie–forest border continued to shift eastward in the Midwest until about 7000 BP, when prairie stretched across Indiana into Ohio and was more extensive in Illinois and southern Wisconsin. After this date, the dry conditions waned and prairie vegetation retreated westward (King 1981; King and Allen 1977).

Following the mid-Holocene after approximately 5000 years ago, essentially modern conditions prevailed throughout the Midwest and the Upper Great Lakes. However, this does not mean that more minor oscillations in climate were not occurring. Nor does it mean that humans did not have to adjust to these. In addition, humans themselves began to alter the landscape, managing or clearing the forest to promote prey species or for farming. These more subtle changes are harder to reconstruct, but they were significant locally in both pre-Columbian and Historic times.

HUNTERS AND FORAGERS OF THE DISTANT PAST

First Occupation: The Paleoindians

The first inhabitants of the Midwest and Upper Great Lakes were hunter-gatherers who arrived at the end of the Wisconsin glaciation. Precisely when these Paleoindians arrived is not yet clear. The Sheguiandah site on Manitoulin Island in Lake Huron originally was proposed to predate the Wisconsin maximum in age (Lee 1956), but this early Pre-Clovis claim has been rejected. Still, there are hints of possible Pre-Clovis settlement before 11,500 BP. For example, in Chapter 3 we mentioned two sites in southeastern Wisconsin, the Schaefer and Hebior sites, where mammoth bones exhibiting possible human butchering have been found in association with bifaces, flakes, and stone choppers. Dates in the thirteenth millennium BP have been obtained by accelerator mass spectrometry for collagen in the mammoth bones (Overstreet and Stafford 1997). Other nearby mammoth sites have yielded only bones that exhibit possible cut marks. Overstreet has proposed a possible Pre-Clovis lithic complex called **Chesrow**, which includes lanceolate bifaces. Most early sites, even those with remains of extinct fauna, either date no earlier than the Clovis time period or contain fluted points. Of course, some of this chapter's area was still covered with glaciers or glacial lakes until at least 11,500 BP.

Evidence for Paleoindians from the twelfth millennium BP onward is widespread throughout the Midwest and the Upper Great Lakes. Surface finds of fluted points are very common from these regions, as they are in Southeast culture area (Anderson and Faught 1998). However, particularly high densities of fluted points have been found in the Ohio River drainage and portions of Ohio. Archaeological sites with excavated fluted point components are less common, but present throughout the Midwest and Upper Great Lakes.

Radiocarbon-dated Paleoindian sites from these regions are rare. At the Paleo Crossing site in Ohio, dates in the neighborhood of 10,980 BP are consistent with Clovis dates; but another cluster of dates from this site (ca. 12,150 BP) is more problematical (Brose 1994a). Other Ohio dates from Sheriden Cave, where stone tools but no fluted points were recovered in association with extinct fauna, are 11,200 BP to 10,600 BP. Still other dated sites contain only extinct fauna that may have been butchered. For example, a date of 10,395 ±100 BP was obtained for the Pleasant Lake mastodon in Michigan (Fisher 1984), and dating for the Burning Tree mastodon site in Ohio is between 11,660 BP and 11,450 BP (Fisher et al. 1994). A thermoluminesence (TL) date (12,360 ±1224 calendar years—not radiocarbon years) has been obtained for the Gainey site in Michigan (Simons et al. 1984), as well. It also is possible to use geological data such as the otherwise established dating of glacial lakes to gain chronological perspective on sites (e.g., Storck 1984). Considered together with technological similarities in artifacts, information of these kinds leads to the conclusion that the fluted point era in the Midwest and Great Lakes began in the Ohio Valley before 11,000 BP and ended before 10,000 BP (Ellis and Dellar 1990; Lepper 1999).

The classic fluted point is the Clovis point, but just as in other areas, more types of fluted points, including some not found further west, have been recognized by archaeologists (Figure 12.2). A temporal sequence from Gainey to Barnes to Crowfield points may exist in Ontario and Michigan (Shott and Wright 1999). This sequence of points is much less clear south and west of Michigan and southern Ontario. Folsom points are common in Illinois, Wisconsin, and northwestern Indiana, especially in what is today the Prairie Peninsula (Munson 1990). Barnes, Cumberland, and Crowfield points all are sometimes found in Ohio (Vickery and Lifton 1994).

Several unfluted points are believed to mark the end of the Paleoindian period (Late Paleoindian) in the Midwest and Upper Great Lakes. Lanceolate forms with lateral basal grinding reminiscent of Plano point types on the Great Plains are known from southern Ontario. Both stemmed and unstemmed varieties, a little like Hell Gap points in the West, are believed to date between 10,400 BP and 9500 BP. Other smaller forms have concave bases, and may be called Hi-Lo or Unfluted Holcombe points. The Dalton point appears in the southern parts of this chapter's areas beginning as early as 10,500 BP, and other Late Paleoindian forms such as Quad and Beaver Lake points (see Figure 11.3) also occur. These various Late Paleoindian forms may be found together with notched Early Archaic forms.

Besides projectile points, Paleoindian assemblages from the Midwest and Upper Great Lakes include a variety of other stone tools such as gravers, scrapers, and knives, as well as bifaces that served as blanks from which other tools were made. Archaeologists have been able to develop a fairly complete picture of how these blanks generally were reduced to points and other tools (e.g., Wright and Roosa 1966). There also are a few Paleoindian artifact caches known from the Great Lakes and Midwest. For example, a cache of 80 gravers was found at the Kouba site in southern Wisconsin (Lepper 1999). As with other cache sites found further west, the function of these caches is unclear.

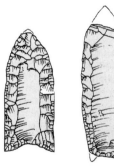

Gainey   Barnes

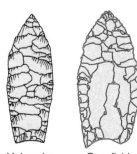

Holcombe   Crowfield

FIGURE 12.2 Paleoindian projectile point styles from the Midwest and Upper Great Lakes.

In keeping with Paleoindian finds elsewhere, Paleoindian sites in the Midwest and the Great Lakes indicate a preference for high-quality stone. For example, at the Gainey site in Michigan at least five distinct types of lithic raw material were noted (Simons et al. 1984). These raw materials were present in various quantities, came from various distances, and had diverse properties, indicating that the site's inhabitants were selective in their usage of stone and probably carried raw materials over great distances. Sometimes chert was worked into biface preforms at workshops near quarries. For example, at the Lincoln Hills site near Grafton, Illinois, archaeologists found a quarry workshop with 150 preforms from the locally available high-quality Burlington chert (Koldehoff 1983).

Very little data on Paleoindian subsistence in the Midwest and Upper Great Lakes has been acquired. There is reason to believe that Paleoindians utilized mammoths and mastodons. The Kimmswick site, located in Jefferson County, Missouri, provides the best evidence of the interaction of Clovis hunters with megafauna (Graham et al. 1981). Here buried pond deposits, lying beneath Archaic materials were found with Clovis lithics. One Clovis point was found lying among the foot bones of a mastodon. Even though radiocarbon dates cannot be obtained at this site, Clovis–mastodon interaction is clearly indicated. In fact, a number of sites without lithics have produced apparently modified bones of mammoths and mastodons. Besides those associated with the possibly Pre-Clovis Chesrow complex, other sites show suggestive patterns of skeletal disarticulation and cut marks. One important question is whether these sites represent intentional hunting of megafaunal species or simply the scavenging of bones from animals that died of natural causes. Comparisons between butchered and unbutchered mastodons suggest to some that humans were preferentially selecting male mastodons as prey during the winter (Fisher 1987). If the sites we find are the remains of winter meat caches rather than kill sites, this might explain the lack of utilized waste flakes and other tools that should be at butchery sites.

Whether or not Paleoindians in the Midwest and Upper Great Lakes exploited megafauna for food, other species probably were used. Additional species represented in the Clovis levels at the Kimmswick site include white-tailed deer, long-nosed peccary, ground sloth, coyote or wolf, mink, cottontail rabbit, woodchuck, tree and ground squirrel, muskrat, vole, and shrew, as well as birds, turtles, and fish (Graham and Kay 1988). While some of these faunal remains may have been incorporated naturally, the spatial distributions of much of this bone in concentrations of stone tools as well as various studies of how the deposits were formed indicate human activity. Unfortunately the preservation of bone in sites situated in glacially derived gravels has often been poor, while ethnobotanical analysis for such early sites has also been lacking.

Just as in other culture areas, the accumulation of Paleoindian data, as incomplete as it is, interests archaeologists because of what it may contribute to continent-wide patterns for Paleoindians. It has long been thought that the extensive distribution and usually small size of known sites in the Midwest and the Upper Great Lakes supported the idea that Paleoindian populations were highly mobile foragers. However, more variability in site type and structure is now being recognized, leading us to consider new ideas about Paleoindian settlement and lifestyle.

Meltzer's model (Meltzer 1988; Meltzer and Smith 1986), introduced in discussing Southeastern Paleoindians (see Table 11.2), can be applied. Several large sites in the Great Lakes area are believed to represent communal base camps from which the hunting of caribou herds took place (Storck 1984). This interpretation is based on the positioning of these large sites in places with excellent views, their internal structuring into discrete artifact clusters, and their similarity to sites in the Northeast with caribou bone. For example, at the Fisher site, located in the Georgian Bay area of Ontario, 19 artifact concentrations were found over approximately 55 acres. Located adjacent to glacial Lake Algonquin, the site probably afforded an excellent view of the surrounding spruce parkland.

However, some large sites further south have been understood as quarry-related base camps or workshops. It is assumed that these lithic workshop sites appear large compared with hunting camps because of repeated use of the quarry rather than because many people used them at once (Lepper and Meltzer 1991). Nevertheless, examination of the lithics from the Nobles Pond site in Ohio suggested that large Paleoindian sites with several discrete artifact clusters were aggregated camps rather than the result of repeated short-term visits by small groups. Seeman (1994) used the similarity in raw materials and refits of flakes across clusters at Nobles Pond to make this argument.

Because it is believed that large sites of this nature had disappeared by Late Paleoindian times, a reorientation in subsistence and settlement may have occurred. Some have argued that Paleoindian strategies in the Midwest and Upper Great Lakes changed as Paleoindians settled into the East and as the post-Pleistocene environment became more modern. For example, Tankersley (1988) suggests that the data confirm the view of Clovis as a colonizing population from the west with a distinctive technology.

Just as in the Southeast, archaeologists will need more data to sort out these various ideas. There is no question that Paleoindians were hunter-gatherers who moved frequently, but several possibilities can be suggested to explain what structured their settlements and movements. Excavations that provide floral and faunal information are particularly needed.

What Happened in the Archaic?

As in the Southeast, archaeologists working in the Midwest and the Upper Great Lakes usually discard the concept of an Archaic stage and simply assign the 7000 years following the Paleoindian period to an Archaic period. Three subperiods are recognized: the Early Archaic (10,000–8000 BP), the Middle Archaic (8000–5000 BP), and the Late Archaic (5000–3000 BP). Note that the dates used for the Middle and Late Archaic are a little different from those used most often in the Southeast. Although the Archaic was long held to be the least exciting part of Eastern Woodlands prehistory, Midwestern archaeological work over the last 30 years has been changing this impression (Jefferies 1995). Both interdisciplinary investigations at deeply stratified sites with good preservation (see the case study by Michael D. Wiant and Sarah W. Neusius, "It Takes a Team: Interdisciplinary Research at the Koster Site," in Chapter 2) and major CRM projects documenting settlement distribution have added to archaeological understanding in significant ways. Not only is there evidence in the Late Archaic for exchange networks, plant cultivation, population aggregation, some degree of sedentism, mortuary ceremonialism, and social differentiation, but these attributes are apparent in some locales beginning in the Middle rather than the Late Archaic.

The same traits in lithic technology used in the Southeast can distinguish the Early Archaic from the Paleoindian in the Midwest and Upper Great Lakes;

FIGURE 12.3 Archaic period projectile point styles from the Midwest and Upper Great Lakes.

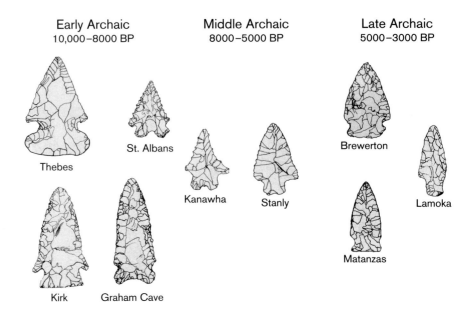

Early Archaic
10,000–8000 BP

Middle Archaic
8000–5000 BP

Late Archaic
5000–3000 BP

Thebes

St. Albans

Kanawha

Stanly

Brewerton

Lamoka

Matanzas

Kirk

Graham Cave

the appearance of notched projectile forms is possibly the most diagnostic. Review Table 11.3, which lists traits in morphology, raw material, and manufacture for the Eastern Woodlands. In addition, many bone tools were associated with the Archaic, and in some parts of the areas covered in this chapter copper implements from the Middle to Late Archaic have been found as well. These copper implements mark the beginning of a long-standing technology shared among the inhabitants of Eastern North America. Mining and working of native copper included the manufacture of ornaments as well as tools by many Eastern groups and continued for many millennia into the Historic period (Levine 1999; Susan R. Martin 1999).

Some of the projectile point types Midwestern and Great Lakes archaeologists recognize for the Archaic are introduced in Figure 12.3. Side notched and corner notched projectile points are often found in conjunction with Late Paleoindian Dalton points (Figure 11.3), marking the Paleoindian–Early Archaic transition. Some authorities (e.g., Shott 1999) would designate a Plano horizon at the very beginning of the Early Archaic because of the wide distribution throughout the Upper Great Lakes at about 10,000 BP of projectile points resembling Plano points from the Great Plains. Early Archaic forms include Graham Cave Side Notched, Kessel, or simply Large Side Notched (e.g., Stothers et al. 2001), and Thebes, Hardin Barbed, and Kirk Corner Notched points. Some archaeologists (e.g., Ellis et al. 1990) argue that side-notched forms represent a horizon that precedes corner-notched forms. Marking the latter part of the Early Archaic, between approximately 9000 BP and 8000 BP, are a variety of bifurcate forms such as St. Albans, Kanawha, and LeCroy. The Middle Archaic, in turn, is indicated by stemmed forms of several types, notably the Stanly Stemmed, Morrow Mountain, Otter Creek, Raddatz Side Notched, and weak stemmed points. Variable Late Archaic projectile point forms have been identified, including Brewerton Corner Notched, Brewerton Eared Notched, Matanzas, Merom

Expanding Stem, Trimble Side Notched, and Lamoka. Similar to the pattern in the Southeast, as the Archaic proceeds an emphasis on side- and corner-notched forms diminishes, and points with bifurcated bases become more prevalent, followed still later by points with stems.

There also are archaeological traditions based on projectile points and other attributes that have been suggested for the Middle to Late Archaic in the Northeast as a whole (Tuck 1978). One of these is the **Lake Forest Archaic**, associated with sites in the transitional forest of the Great Lakes and southern Canada, which are characterized by broad-bladed, side-notched points. Also apparently associated with deciduous forest sites further south, with many narrow-bladed and stemmed projectile points, is the **Narrow Point tradition**. Finally, beginning around 4000 BP, a variety of broad-bladed stemmed points were made, which archaeologists associate with the Broadpoint tradition, also mentioned in Chapter 11. Whether these groupings are truly meaningful in terms of lifestyle is unclear.

Another parallel with the Southeastern record is found in the area of subsistence: considerable amounts of high-quality data on Archaic subsistence, especially from the river valleys of the Midwest, clearly indicate complex patterns of plant and animal usage. Early Archaic foragers were not focused on a few large game resources; rather, they utilized a variety of animal resources. For example, at the Koster site in the Illinois River valley (see the case study in Chapter 2), Early Archaic faunal assemblages suggest resource diversity, with shellfish, fish, birds, and mammals all being present. Small mammals like tree squirrels are surprisingly important as well. Later in the Middle Archaic, deer, shellfish, and fish predominate, suggesting more focal rather than diffuse strategies as time went on (Neusius 1986b). Similarly, the Koster plant materials indicate that a variety of nuts and other plant foods were utilized from the beginning of the sequence, while hickory nuts became highly important during the Middle Archaic (Asch et al. 1972). These plant and animal assemblages may be attributable to changes in human settlement strategies combined with the advent of the Hypsithermal interval and the maturation of the river valley (Brown and Vierra 1983). However, Koster is just one example, and we should expect the archaeological record to show subsistence and settlement diversity as Archaic foragers adapted to local resource distributions as well as to small-scale environmental changes.

One important subsistence change evident in the Archaic record is an increase in the use of freshwater mussels beginning as early as 7000 BP in some areas (e.g., Bonnie W. Styles 1986). After 5000 BP, during the Late Archaic, mussels certainly were significant resources. Large shell midden sites dating to this period are known from the Midwest as well as from further south. Important examples of Late Archaic shell midden sites include Carlston Annis, Indian Knoll, and other sites assigned to the Shell Mound Archaic of the Green River in northern Kentucky (Marquardt and Watson 1983) as well as Riverton, Robeson Hills, and Swan Island sites assigned to the **Riverton culture** of the Wabash River valley (Winters 1969). The best explanation for heavier use of mussels at this time is not that Archaic foragers had just discovered their edibility—some mussels have been found in earlier Archaic components. Instead, as rivers matured from fast-flowing, down-cutting streams to the more stable, slow-moving, and meandering rivers we know today, habitats for large mussel beds became more frequent, and this resource increased in abundance and ease of exploitation. Of course, other aquatic fauna such as fish also were affected by these changes in the rivers, and their remains are abundant in Archaic sites where flotation has been done.

The river valleys of the Midwest were just as important as those of the interior Southeast in the development of early plant cultivation and domestication (Smith 1992). During the Middle Archaic, as the floodplains of these rivers matured, the floodplain habitat became more important to Archaic people. Repeated reuse of this habitat year after year may have created the kind of anthropogenic habitat that favors weedy seed plants that can rapidly colonize disturbed areas. In turn, these are precisely the plants that were eventually cultivated and domesticated. Squash or gourds dated to at least 7000 BP have been found at the Koster site and at the Napoleon Hollow site in the lower Illinois River valley, and specimens dating to more than 5700 BP have come from the Carlston Annis site on the Green River in Kentucky. These earliest squash remains can be interpreted as evidence of domestication because they are outside the currently known distribution of native gourds. However, another possible explanation is that the distribution of these native gourds used to be much greater than it is today (Decker-Walters 1993), in which case these finds would not represent domesticated species.

By 5000 BP to 3000 BP (3050–1050 BC), Late Archaic groups in the major river valleys had domesticated several subspecies of gourd and a number of weedy seed plants like marsh elder and goosefoot that naturally colonize disturbed environments. Maygrass, little barley, and erect knotweed probably also were cultivated, but perhaps not truly domesticated during the Late Archaic. These plants added significant starches and oils to the diet, but they did not replace the use of wild plants and the hunting of game. Further north in the Upper Great Lakes, there is little evidence for experimentation with plant cultivation among Late Archaic hunter-gatherers. Even in the resource-rich parts of the Midwest, true food-producing economies did not develop for another millennium (Fritz 1990; Smith 1992).

Midwestern ethnobotanists and archaeologists are still piecing together the details of what seems to have been a long and variable process of developing food production. With modern techniques like flotation and AMS dating, we can gain a much better understanding of plant use than was possible just a few decades ago (Chapman and Watson 1993). As a result, this is an exciting area of current research.

Subsistence change was closely related to population growth, settlement organization, and mobility strategies, other topics of great interest to Midwestern and Great Lakes archaeologists. Simple counting of known site components suggests fairly stable population levels during the Early and Middle Archaic, with considerable population growth during the Late Archaic. Although this is a problematic way to measure population growth because it doesn't consider variation in site recording due to differential burial of old land surfaces or differences in site size, most archaeologists accept that human population levels were much larger at the end of the Archaic than at its beginning. Moreover, diverse data suggest that, at least in the major river valleys of the Midwest, people were becoming more sedentary in the Middle Archaic.

Early Archaic hunter-gatherers are believed to have lived in fairly small residential groups that moved frequently, camping in both upland and river valley locations. However, in the Middle Archaic in some Midwestern river valleys and in the Late Archaic throughout the areas covered in this chapter, people shifted from a residential to a logistical pattern of settlement (Binford 1980). Base camps from which collecting parties were dispatched to obtain resources were established. Among other things, the establishment of larger and more permanent settlements was the beginning of significant human modification of habitats. However, living in larger more permanent groups meant changes in the social environment as well. Some archaeologists argue that the roots of the complex social systems of the Woodland period can be found in these first steps toward group integration during the Middle and Late Archaic (e.g., Brown 1985).

Midwest and Great Lakes archaeologists have been developing very interesting data about the establishment of exchange networks during the Archaic. Archaeologists have long known that exchange was taking place over great distances during the Late Archaic. For example, recovery of copper, exotic stone, and marine shell from Shell Mound Archaic burials at the Indian Knoll site in Kentucky has led to several analyses of exchange (e.g., Rothschild 1979; Winters 1968). However, more recently archaeologists have realized that there also are examples of long-distance movement of commodities during the Middle Archaic and even the Early Archaic. Notably, marine shell beads from the common Atlantic *Marginella* snail have been reported from Early Archaic levels dating between 7000 BP and 8000 BP at the Modoc Rock Shelter in Illinois (Ahler 1991).

A number of Middle to Late Archaic base camps, including **Helton phase** components at the Koster site (Cook 1976a) and Middle Archaic zones at the Black Earth site in southern Illinois (Jefferies and Lynch 1983), also provide strong evidence for exchange. First, nonlocal raw materials, notably copper and galena, are found. Second, carved bone pins (Figure 12.4) in various shapes have been decorated far beyond functional necessity. These pins are so similar among sites that their use as symbols within a broad intergroup social network seems probable. It may be that less mobility during the Middle Archaic required Archaic groups to establish some means of intergroup cooperation, and that trade and exchange provided that means (Brown 1985).

Several Late Archaic burial complexes provide strong evidence for exchange and social integration across the Midwest and Upper Great Lakes as well. The **Old Copper culture** may be the most colorful of these. This complex represents the first time Native peoples extensively used copper to make implements and ornaments. Most of these artifacts have been found in burials or in caches rather than in habitation sites, perhaps indicating that copper was traded in fairly small quantities at this time. Extensive copper deposits are found along Lake Superior

FIGURE 12.4 Carved bone pins from the Black Earth site in southern Illinois.

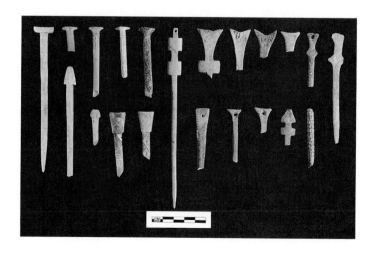

FIGURE 12.5 Examples of turkey-tailed points found in Red Ocher burials.

at the northwestern margins of the areas covered in this chapter, although smaller sources are more widely distributed (Levine 1999). Old Copper artifacts were made by cold hammering and **annealing**, or heating the copper to work it. Then projectile points, knives, celts, awls, fishhooks, bracelets, beads, and other items were made. The Old Copper Osceola site in Wisconsin has a radiocarbon date of approximately 3450 BP, while the Riverside Cemetery site in Menominee, Michigan, has a date of about 3040 BP (Robertson et al. 1999).

The **Glacial Kame mortuary complex** derives its name from the practice of placing the dead in the gravel ridges or kames left by glaciation. Glacial Kame cemeteries are found in the northern Midwest and Upper Great Lakes, including portions of southern Ontario. They usually contain the tightly flexed remains of bodies that were covered with red ocher and buried in circular pits, along with drilled **sandal-sole gorgets** of marine shell, copper and shell beads, bone pins and awls, and **birdstones**. A similar, perhaps related, complex is simply called the **Red Ocher mortuary complex** because of the use of this crumbly iron oxide in the burials. Red Ocher burials and cremations are found in Illinois and western Indiana, Ohio, and Michigan. Bodies were placed in low artificial mounds along with large amounts of red ocher, cache blades, and distinctive turkey-tailed points (Figure 12.5). Turkey-tail blades or points often were made out of a high-quality bluish chert, called Harrison County chert, found in southern Indiana. Red Ocher burials also seem to continue into the Early Woodland period, given the presence of pottery in some mounds (Esarey 1986).

The study of skeletal populations is a final area of exciting research concerning Middle and Late Archaic groups of the Midwest and Upper Great Lakes. While it can be argued on the basis of the low incidence of anemia and **dental caries** that Archaic populations were reasonably healthy, there also is unmistakable evidence for intergroup violence in some instances. For example, in the Green River Archaic there is evidence for decapitation, scalping, and limb dismemberment, as well as examples of stone or antler projectile points embedded in bone (Mensforth 2001). It is not clear whether the higher population levels and perhaps greater degree of group aggregation in the Late Archaic were factors in the apparent onset of intergroup violence.

Second, a significant change in mortuary behavior begins to occur during the Middle and Late Archaic. This is the appearance of cemeteries. Prior to the Middle Archaic, individuals often were buried within sites. After this, in the lower Illinois River valley, most people are buried in bluff top or floodplain cemeteries (Charles 1995). Late Archaic cemeteries are common elsewhere in the Midwest as well. These cemeteries imply that human populations were territorial and may have been organized into clans. Members of these groups are believed to have used the symbols of burial to mark group membership and the cemeteries themselves to mark social boundaries (Charles and Buikstra 1983).

It is clear that profound changes took place during the 7000 years of the Archaic period. Besides this, a growing body of archaeological data documents cultural variability during these millennia, causing archaeologists to explore new models and explanations for this long-lasting period. Many of the known cultural changes first happened in resource-rich Midwestern river valleys. In these locales the Middle Archaic may be the period of change, while developments in subsistence and settlement, exchange, and social differentiation were widespread throughout the Midwest and Upper Great Lakes by the Late Archaic. These changes foreshadow the development of more complex social systems in the Woodland period that followed (Brown 1985).

WOODLAND FARMERS AND MOUND BUILDERS

The less mobile lifestyle, the domestication of native seed plants, and the elaborate mortuary behavior now known from the Middle and Late Archaic in the river valleys of the midcontinent all belie abrupt change at the Archaic–Woodland boundary at approximately 3000 BP (1050 BC). The phenomena that have long been considered Woodland actually appear in a time-transgressive manner. For example, although ceramic technology generally was not developed before the Woodland in the Midwest and Great Lakes, dates of 3450 BP in southern Ohio and 3325 BP in northern West Virginia (Applegate and Mainfort 2005) indicate that it was being made before 3000 BP on the eastern margins of the Midwest. We have chosen to treat the Woodland as a period and to begin it at the traditional point of 3000 BP, while recognizing the difficulty in distinguishing this boundary.

The distinction between the Early and Middle Woodland also is difficult to make in a uniform manner. Hopewell ceremonialism, the classic delineator of the Middle Woodland, does not appear simultaneously or evenly throughout the Midwest and Upper Great Lakes. Adena ceremonialism begins in the Early Woodland but may overlap with Hopewell. Our use of 2150 BP (200 BC) as the boundary between the Early and the Middle Woodland is conventional and takes into account **Illinois Hopewell** developments. Local sequences may vary, however, and in many areas Middle Woodland would not be considered evident until after 2000 BP. Certainly **Ohio Hopewell** can be understood as starting closer to this point. The end of the Middle Woodland can be dated at 1500 BP (AD 450), but the collapse of the Hopewell system certainly preceded this in some areas.

As is the case for some parts of the Southeast, Late Woodland phenomena are recognized from about 1500 BP until European contact in much of the Upper Great Lakes and northern Midwest. However, Mississippian variants follow the Late Woodland in many other areas covered in this chapter and were especially

FIGURE 12.6 These fragments of Middle Woodland Crab Orchard tradition vessels found in Southern Illinois show the characteristic flat bottoms.

significant in the southern Midwest. The beginning of the Mississippian tradition is thought by some archaeologists to be apparent along the Mississippi and lower Ohio rivers as early as 1150 BP.

Diagnostic Early and Middle Woodland Material Culture

A few technological attributes can be useful in recognizing the Early and Middle Woodland in the Midwest and Upper Great Lakes. First, thick-walled, grit- or limestone-tempered pottery often is associated with the Early Woodland. This pottery most often has **cordmarking** on both the exterior and interior of the vessel or is fabric impressed. Even when ceramic artifacts are deeply conoidal or cone-shaped overall, flat vessel bottoms are common (Figure 12.6). Archaeologists have constructed a number of pottery sequences spanning the Early and the Middle Woodland.

The first pottery in the Midwest and Upper Great Lakes appears in the Upper Ohio drainage in West Virginia, Ohio, and Kentucky between 3500 BP and 3000 BP. Pottery making was adopted over the next millennium, moving westward and northward. Another route of entry of ceramic technology into the Midwest probably was down the Tennessee Valley into northern Kentucky and southern Illinois. The fabric-impressed pottery of these latter areas represents a distinct tradition, called the **Crab Orchard tradition**, which extends into the Middle Woodland (Butler and Jefferies 1986). A broad area of the Midwest from about the latitude of St. Louis northward has varieties of Marion thick ware during the Early Woodland (Emerson 1986). This pottery may have developed into distinctive wares of the Middle Woodland period. In the northern Midwest several Early Woodland pottery types, like Black Sand ware, were tempered with both sand and grit and decorated with rectilinear incising over plain or cordmarked surfaces. This pottery has been interpreted in various ways but seems to be found north and west of St. Louis in Illinois, Missouri, Iowa, Wisconsin, and Minnesota, extending into areas not covered in this chapter (Munson 1986).

Second, although Early Woodland pottery associated with the Adena mortuary complex discussed shortly, already was thin walled, vessel walls generally became thinner as the ceramic technology developed. In addition, the temper became finer over time. Procedures for sand and grog tempering were introduced, and vessel shapes became more variable. Most notably, a wide variety of decorative treatments were introduced including incising, punctating, dentate and other stamping, and various zoned motifs. Archaeologists who study ceramic assemblages also note variations in lip shape and treatment. One classic Middle Woodland pottery type is Havana ware, while the various Hopewell wares were very finely made and decorated ceramics found in sites associated with Hopewell exchange and ceremonialism during the Middle Woodland (Figure 12.7).

Third, lithic attributes also can be used to recognize the Early and Middle Woodland. During the Early Woodland several types of contracting stemmed points as well as the square-stemmed Kramer point have been considered diagnostic. Figure 12.8 indicates how similar such points are in various parts of the Midwest and Upper Great Lakes. One point type that is diagnostic of the Middle Woodland over a broad area of the Midwest and Upper Great Lakes is the Snyders point, which is a very broad-bladed, corner-notched point. Affinis Snyders is a related but smaller point found in many Midwestern Middle Woodland components.

FIGURE 12.7 Hopewell pot from west central Illinois; note bird design.

FIGURE 12.8 Early and Middle Woodland projectile point forms from the Midwest and Upper Great Lakes.

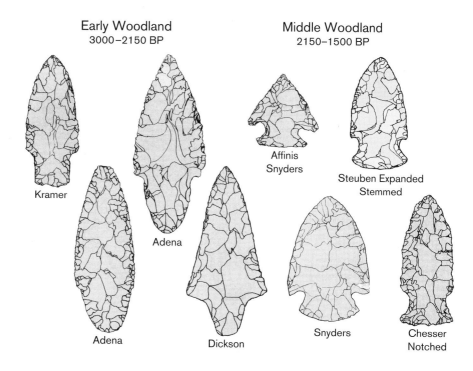

Early Woodland
3000–2150 BP

Kramer

Adena

Adena

Dickson

Middle Woodland
2150–1500 BP

Affinis
Snyders

Steuben Expanded
Stemmed

Snyders

Chesser
Notched

Besides projectile points, Middle Woodland lithics are notable because of the presence of blades, and their cores. Studies have shown that these blades were used for a variety of domestic and ceremonial purposes (Odell 1994). Perhaps even more interesting is the wide variety of raw materials found in Middle Woodland lithic assemblages. Some of these materials have come great distances. For example, obsidian from Yellowstone was brought to Ohio in large amounts during Middle Woodland times, although it has been argued that the entire stock was transported in a single journey (de Boer 2004; Griffin et al. 1969). Cherts were often **heat treated** to improve their flaking properties, as well. It appears that lithic manufacturing was very important to Middle Woodland people.

Mound Building and Mortuary Ceremonialism

Although mortuary ceremonialism and mound building began during the Archaic of the Midwest and Upper Great Lakes, truly spectacular constructions distinguish the Early and Middle Woodland. They remain enigmatic even today, fueling both archaeological and other interest as illustrated by the story of the GE Mound.

Between approximately 2500 BP and 2000 BP, the central and upper Ohio River valley was at the center of Adena mound building. Adena mounds are usually conical mounds of earth or stone, but their size varies, and they may or may not be surrounded by a ditch and embankment. The largest known Adena mound is the Grave Creek Mound located at Moundsville, West Virginia (Figure 12.9), which when first measured was nearly 70 feet (21 m) in height with a diameter of 295 feet (90 m) (Woodward and McDonald 2002). Beneath many Adena mounds archaeologists have found circular patterns of postmolds, indicating that one or more structures once stood there. Some of these structures,

FIGURE 12.9 The Grave Creek Mound in Moundsville, West Virginia.

which are most likely mortuary facilities, may not have been roofed. Inside Adena mounds, the remains of large numbers of individuals sometimes were accumulated in repeated episodes of burial. The people used a variety of burial forms: **extended burial** in bark-lined pits and log tombs and cremations, performed soon after death, as well as bundle burials, in which decomposed remains were gathered together for secondary burial. Adena mounds also contain a diagnostic inventory of artifacts including Adena stemmed points, finely made cache blades, and Adena Plain pottery, which is grit or limestone-tempered and relatively thin walled, plain surfaced, and undecorated. Perhaps more notable are a variety of eye-catching objects including ground stone axes and celts, pieces of hematite and barite, copper beads, bracelets, rings, and gorgets, as well as other gorgets and pendants and tubular stone and ceramic pipes. Elaborately carved stone tablets also are considered diagnostic of Adena (Figure 12.10). It is not clear whether Adena should be thought of as a separate culture or simply as a ceremonial complex and exchange system that transcended cultural boundaries.

As the third millennium BP waned, new ceremonial complexes are first apparent in Illinois and later in Ohio, where they are called Illinois and Ohio Hopewell after the Hopewell site located near Chillicothe, Ohio. It also is unclear

FIGURE 12.10 Carved stone tablets with elaborate designs such as these are considered diagnostic of Adena.

how Adena relates to Ohio Hopewell. The use of some Adena mounds seems to overlap in date with Hopewell phenomena (Cochran 1996).

The influence of the Hopewell is evident over a much wider area. We mentioned linkages with Hopewell at sites like Marksville in Louisiana and Pinson in Tennessee in Chapter 11's discussion of Middle Woodland in the Southeast. Hopewell artifacts also are found throughout all but the most northern parts of the Midwest and Upper Great Lakes, as well as further east. Struever (e.g., 1964) has called this broad archaeological phenomenon the **Hopewell Interaction Sphere**, and this term has been widely used to explain evidence suggesting that many regional Middle Woodland traditions participated to some degree in exchange of Hopewell material culture. Artifacts and ecofacts commonly associated with Hopewell exchange include shark and alligator teeth, copper and pottery earspools, copper gorgets, panpipes and celts, obsidian artifacts, marine shell beads, cut sheets of mica, worked bear canines, plain and effigy **platform pipes**, pottery effigies, and Hopewell series pottery (Figure 12.11). These items often are

FIGURE 12.11 the Hopewell made ornaments of mica and copper in a variety of shapes as well as earspools of stone (left center). (After Jennings 1989.)

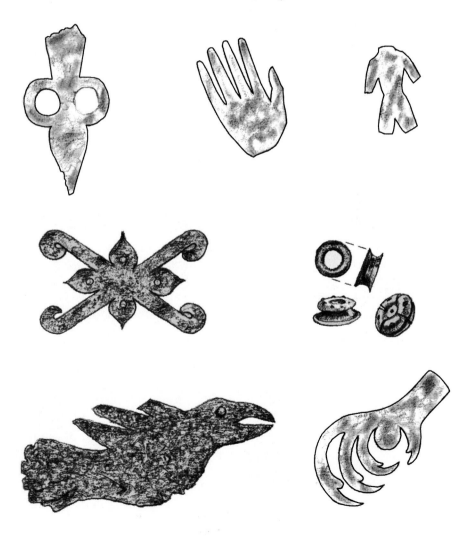

found in burial contexts and in association with earthworks and mounds, suggesting common ideology and leading some archaeologists to argue that Hopewell was a religious cult. Exhibit 12.1 discusses one common type of Hopewell artifact.

CLUES TO THE PAST

EXHIBIT 12.1

Stone Platform Pipes

One diagnostic Hopewell artifact is the stone platform pipe. These pipe forms have a central bowl placed on top of a curved platform that extends to either side of the bowl. Several varieties of these pipes have been found, including ones in which the bowl is an effigy of an animal such as a bird, a bear, or a frog (Figure 12.12). These effigy pipes may be elaborately carved and finely polished; sometimes bits of copper or freshwater pearls have been set in the eyes of the effigy figures. Effigies usually faced the smoker. Other forms are spool-shaped bowls, rounded bowls or V-shaped bases. Although these types are simpler, they also can be finely made (Figure 12.13). The platform itself contained a narrow hole for a stem although platform pipes may have been smoked by placing the stone platform directly in the mouth rather than by adding a stem. Study of the distribution of these various types of platform pipe has

FIGURE 12.12 Effigy platform pipes depicting various animals.

FIGURE 12.13 Plain bowl effigy pipes also tend to be finely made.

suggested temporal variation in form within Hopewell (Seeman 1977). Platform pipes differ from the tubular pipes found in Adena contexts as well as from other earlier tubular and later elbow pipe forms. There also are later examples of platform pipes, but these usually differ from those found in Hopewell contexts by having flatter platforms and ridges on the platform (Gehlbach 1998).

Platform pipes were made of a variety of raw materials, but the most common material is appropriately known as Ohio pipestone. This stone is a soft buff, olive gray, or dark red limestone containing a good deal of iron. Pipestone outcrops in Ohio near the Scioto River, where many Ohio Hopewell sites are found. When originally mined, this stone is easy to work, but it hardens through exposure to air and through heating. Other raw materials were also used for pipes including sandstone, other limestone, slate, steatite, and quartzite.

The first step in making a stone pipe was to rough out the form through pecking with a hammerstone and abrading with sandstone. Partially shaped pipe blanks have been found by archaeologists, and some pipe specimens show striations from sandstone abrasion. The bowls and the smoke holes of these pipes were made with flint drills or reamers or with reeds or bone and a grinding agent like fine sand. Effigy pipes were carved with flint tools as well. This process was laborious and time-consuming. Pipes probably also were polished with the aid of animal oils and leather or fabric cloths.

Although these pipes are intriguing, they are reasonably rare in Hopewell sites, and more have been found in Ohio than in Illinois. They are nearly always found in burial as opposed to domestic contexts. Effigy platform pipes are even rarer, with only a few examples having been found outside of Ohio (Otto 1992). The largest numbers of known effigy platform pipes came from large caches of both effigy and plain platform pipes found below mounds at Mound City in Chillicothe, Ohio, and at the Tremper Mound in Scioto County, Ohio. These caches seem to have been adjacent to crematory features. Many of the pipes have been intentionally broken, a ritual practice akin to "killing" a pottery vessel by putting a hole in it.

The rarity of platform pipes and their association with burial mounds makes it clear that they were ceremonially significant items. The fact that many have been intentionally broken before burial suggests they were thought to have great power. Among Native Americans, what has been called the **smoking complex** is an important feature of ritual and ideology (Rafferty and Mann 2004; von Gernet 1992). Hopewell platform pipes certainly are linked to this complex, and the appearance of tobacco in archaeological contexts dating to the Middle Woodland is significant. Whatever else these pipes mean, they minimally indicate that smoking was a ritually important act in eastern North America nearly 2000 years ago.

Many interesting questions arise about how such ritual items might have been produced in Hopewell societies, which are presumed to have been tribal in organization. In such societies full-time specialists are rare. Yet it seems obvious that even though there is variation in the quality of pipe fabrication, making these items took some artistic skill. Could anyone who was so inclined learn to make platform pipes, or were they considered so ritually powerful that only shamans or clan leaders could make or commission them? Were specialists partially supported by the lineages, or were they independent artists? Did individuals commission the making of platform pipes, perhaps to mark the status of an individual after death, or were they produced for lineages or other groups of people to use in corporate or group ritual? Finding pipes in individual burial contexts might suggest the former, while caches of pipes next to crematory features would support the latter interpretation. Archaeological investigations of the contexts of production need to be done to explore these questions (Spielmann 1998). Archaeologists also need to learn about the relationships between platform pipes and other Hopewell ritual items. These beautiful pipes, made by highly skilled artisans who took great care both technically and spiritually in their manufacture, are of great interest to Hopewell researchers.

The two main regional centers for Hopewell from the Midwest, Illinois and Ohio Hopewell, are both alike and different. Illinois Hopewell is known primarily from the Illinois River valley, where many burial mounds have been found on the bluffs and in the floodplain. The Gibson–Klunk mounds, located along the western bluff line of the Illinois River valley at Kampsville, Illinois, have been particularly well studied (e.g., Braun 1979; Buikstra 1976). These mounds had central features, many of which the builders lined with logs, and grave goods including distinctive Hopewell artifacts were recovered in abundance. Although cremations were not common in these mounds, both primary burials and secondary burials of remains that had originally been buried elsewhere occurred in all parts of the mounds as well as beneath the mounds themselves. There is some status differentiation evident in the burials, but sex and age rather than heredity seem to be the primary determinants of burial treatment. Earthwork sites are rare in Illinois, but one is known from Golden Eagle, near where the Illinois River enters the Mississippi.

Ohio Hopewell sites often include both mounds and earthworks. Many Ohio mounds cover the remains of structures and contain massive quantities of artifacts. In fact, the largest quantities of Interaction Sphere objects are known from Ohio Hopewell sites. For example, a feature within one building beneath Mound 13 at Mound City, near Chillicothe, Ohio, was lined with sheets of mica and contained the cremated remains of several individuals. Besides burials and grave goods, drilled human crania and mandibles from some mounds have been interpreted as trophy skulls (Seeman 1988) or possibly relics of revered ancestors. The Ohio mounds vary in size and shape. Some mounds are loaf shaped, as the GE Mound apparently was; these may cover more than one structure and represent a conjoining of two smaller mounds. At Marietta, along the Ohio River in southeastern Ohio, low platform mounds were constructed. Platform mounds in the Midwest rarely represent the Middle Woodland; in the Southeast, however, they can be Middle Woodland as well as later in origin.

The massive geometric earthworks of the Ohio Hopewell are particularly famous structures. These earthworks are circular, square, or irregular in shape. Some encircle hilltops, many are associated with mounds, and some seem to border pathways or roads. Lepper (1996) believes that a long road once connected Chillicothe and Newark in Ohio, a distance of over 60 miles (90 km). The earthworks at Newark (Figure 12.14) are the largest known, but there are many other impressive constructions, like the Hopeton works, which is the focus of Mark Lynott's case study for this chapter, "The Hopeton Earthworks Project: Using New Technologies to Answer Old Questions." Hopewell people built these mounds with great precision and care, and we marvel at their skill. The snake effigy earthwork known as the Serpent Mound may be the best-known Ohio earthwork, but recent radiocarbon dating beneath the earthwork suggests that it wasn't built until long after Hopewell times.

Mounds are also known from many other areas of the Midwest and Upper Great Lakes. Mound groups from southwestern Wisconsin within the Driftless area have produced Hopewell Interaction Sphere objects. The same can be said for Woodland mounds in southwestern Michigan and in the Saginaw Basin. The **Mann focus** represented by the GE Mound was a large Hopewell manifestation centered in southern Indiana.

FIGURE 12.14 A portion of the Newark earthworks is part of a golf course today.

Subsistence, Settlement, and the Eastern Agricultural Complex

Part of the debate about when the Early Woodland begins has to do with variability in subsistence and settlement change. In some parts of the Midwest and Upper Great Lakes, the archaeological record suggests that Late Archaic adaptive strategies continued with the addition of pottery. In others, there is clear change. This variability results in part because the more aggregated and sedentary settlements of the Late Archaic were mainly restricted to major river valleys of the Midwest. Elsewhere Late Archaic sites are fairly small encampments. A similar pattern of high residential mobility and small sites seems to characterize the Early Woodland throughout most of the areas covered in this chapter. This looks like change where large Archaic base camps were found formerly, but not where people had remained more residentially mobile.

Although it has been proposed that early pottery was used to process nuts for oil (Ozker 1982), pottery also may have been important in processing the seeds of domesticated and cultivated weedy plants. The amounts of domesticated and cultivated weedy seed plants in archaeological floral assemblages increase dramatically in the Early and Middle Woodland, though the precise timing seems to vary locally. At Salts Cave in Kentucky, an estimated 74 percent of the diet is attributable to cultivated and domesticated native plants during the Early Woodland (Yarnell 1974). Elsewhere high percentages of native seeds seem to characterize the Middle but not the Early Woodland (Fritz 1993). Noting this, Bruce Smith (1992, 1994) has argued that pre-maize food-producing economies based on multiple cropping of native domesticates emerged at the onset of the Middle Woodland throughout the Eastern Woodlands. Because of regional variation, archaeologists do not agree about the actual dependence on food crops of Middle Woodland people (e.g., Wymer 1996); but a trend toward heavier use of native crops is well documented. Although maize was present by Middle Woodland times, it was only a minor food resource or a ceremonially important plant. The oldest directly dated maize from the Eastern Woodlands, at 2077 ±70 BP, is from the Holding site in Illinois (Riley et al. 1994).

The character of settlement associated with the post-2500 BP Adena and Hopewell is much debated. The traditional assumption is that Woodland trade, mound building, and production of ritual items must have been associated with human populations aggregated into large, sedentary villages. Minimally, such aggregated settlements would have provided the labor needed for construction projects and could have been organized to accomplish the variety of economic, craft, and ritual activities suggested by the archaeological record. However, evidence to support these assumptions has been lacking. Even though an emphasis on mound and earthwork sites has long been bemoaned, identifying the habitations that go with these more spectacular remains has proved difficult.

Recently, archaeologists working with Ohio Hopewell materials have been reconsidering a model known as the **vacant center model** (Prufer 1964), which considers mounds and earthworks as centers of seasonal or occasional ceremonial activities conducted by communities of dispersed farmers. Archaeologists have found a preponderance of small hamlets and extractive camps rather than large, aggregated communities. Some domestic refuse has been found at large earthwork centers, but much of this seems to be related to craft production or to suggest only short-term occupancy (Dancey and Pacheco 1997). Although this model is being explored primarily for Ohio Hopewell groups, it could also apply more generally to what happened in the Early and Middle Woodland (Smith 1992). As populations came to focus more on the cultivation of floodplain plants and on other floodplain resources, they may have most often dispersed into family groups, living in small agricultural hamlets. However, the evidence on Illinois Hopewell settlement is ambiguous, suggesting a fairly substantial population and sites of several types in the Illinois Valley. For example, the large Napoleon Hollow site (Wiant and McGimsey 1986) associated with the Elizabeth Mound group apparently was a **mortuary encampment** rather than a village, while the Apple Creek site (e.g., Struever 1968c) had a domestic orientation.

Middle Woodland Outside Core Hopewell Areas

Our brief review has focused on some of the more spectacular developments, but it is important to avoid equating this period of time with Hopewell alone. In the Upper Great Lakes, many Middle Woodland groups participated much less in the Hopewell Interaction Sphere. For example, the **Western Basin tradition** of northern Ohio, southeastern Michigan, and southwestern Ontario dating from 1950 BP to 1450 BP was apparently non-Hopewellian (Kingsley 1999). In northern Wisconsin, pottery called Nokomis and North Bay was not made until Middle Woodland times after about 1950 BP (AD 0). The people who made it are thought to have been hunter-gatherer-fishers who relied on water travel. Still further north, archaeologists define the Laurel culture mentioned briefly in Chapter 4 across a broad area of Ontario. Although campsites from Laurel sites are small, and mobility is presumed to have been high, Laurel people made pottery, notched projectile points, stone platform pipes, net sinkers, and adzes, as well as small copper tools. Laurel burial mounds have been found in Minnesota and elsewhere.

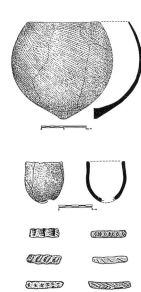

FIGURE 12.15 These vessels from the American Bottom in Illinois are typical of the plainer, cord-marked ceramics associated with the Late Woodland in the Midwest and Upper Great Lakes; drawings at bottom show variations in superior lip decorations.

The various northern archaeological phases may be grouped as the **Lake Forest Middle Woodland** (Fitting 1970), while Mason (1981) grouped the non-Hopewell groups of the Upper Great Lakes into the **Middle Tier Middle Woodland**.

The Good Gray Cultures of the Late Woodland

The Late Woodland of the Midwest and Upper Great Lakes begins at approximately 1500 BP, when the production and exchange of Hopewell artifacts ceases and large earthwork complexes are no longer being made. In many parts of this area, the Late Woodland ends at approximately 1100 BP, when the Mississippian tradition becomes evident. However, in the north, Late Woodland phenomena persist until European contact. It is probably unfair to call this period drab or gray, however, even though it has long been considered a time of decline because its beginning corresponds with the end of Hopewell phenomena. In fact, owing to their variability, Late Woodland societies may be important indicators of how and why the cultural developments of Late pre-Columbian times took place (Emerson et al. 2000).

There were changes in material culture during the early Late Woodland. Ceramics were plainer than those made during the Middle Woodland; a common surface treatment was cord marking (Figure 12.15). Nevertheless, continuing earlier trends, vessel walls were thinner and temper particle size was smaller. These changes are consistent with the reduction of thermal shock, a necessary design concern if pots were being used to boil seeds (Braun 1983, 1986). The Late Woodland stone tool industry also is characterized by the disappearance of various exotic stone types as well as a reliance on utilized or minimally worked flakes rather than more formal tools for many tasks.

A widespread adoption of the bow and arrow after 1350 BP (AD 600) is marked by the predominance of small notched and un-notched triangular projectile points. These points often were made from flakes instead of directly from cores of stone. Several examples of Late Woodland and Mississippian point types are shown in Figure 12.16. Interestingly, the Eastern Woodlands archaeological record indicates that the bow and arrow was present in some locations before it was widely adopted and that the timing of adoption varies (Nassaney and Pyle 1999). There has been an argument that the bow and arrow was present during Middle Woodland times (Justice 1987), but arrows may also have been made as early as the Late Archaic. Regardless, a predominance of small arrow points in lithic tool assemblages across the region is not found until after 1350 BP. It is possible that this trend is associated with significant increases in population or with more nucleation of villages.

Although less productive adaptive systems might be expected if the early Late Woodland were a period of decline, subsistence data indicate, instead, variability based in part on a localization of resource use. Within the major Midwestern river valleys, archaeologists (e.g., Simon 2000; Styles 2000) have documented intensification of the plant cultivation as evidenced by the widespread presence and large quantities of native seeds. People also used some corn and tobacco, as well as many aquatic resources, such as fish species that spawn in river backwaters. However, proportionately lower use of seed plants and greater reliance on white-tailed deer are evident in upland sites and in less productive habitats to the north.

Settlement pattern data also show change and variation during the early Late Woodland. In the Ohio Valley above the Falls of the Ohio, archaeologists

FIGURE 12.16 Several varieties of Late Woodland and Mississippian period points found in the Midwest and Upper Great Lakes.

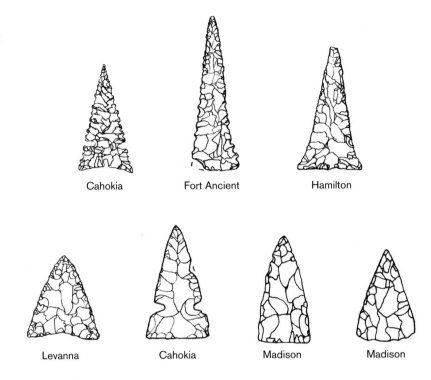

Cahokia   Fort Ancient   Hamilton

Levanna   Cahokia   Madison   Madison

have found strong evidence for the nucleation of settlements. Elsewhere, particularly in the lower Ohio, the Illinois and the Mississippi drainage settlements may decrease in size as the Late Woodland begins. Site locations indicate the use of a variety of habitats at this time. Complexes of stone walls and mounds often called "stone forts" first were made in southern Illinois and Kentucky at this time. These constructions, as well as the nucleated settlements in Ohio, which have moats and fortifications, may indicate defensive concerns.

Late Woodland people continued to make and use mounds throughout the areas covered in this chapter. The **Intrusive Mound culture** of Ohio refers to people who often buried their dead in mounds constructed by earlier groups. Other groups still were building new mounds as needed. Some of the most colorful of these Late Woodland mounds are the **Effigy Mounds** of the upper Mississippi valley in Wisconsin and adjacent portions of Illinois, Iowa, and Minnesota. Dated between approximately 1250 BP and 900 BP (AD 700–1050) these mounds were low, seldom over 5 feet (1.5 m) in height, but made in a variety of animal shapes such as panther, bear, turtle, bird, and lizard (Figure 12.17). Effigy mounds are found in clusters along with linear, conical, and oval mounds. Construction of these mounds often began with creation of a depression or an **intaglio** in the shape of the mound and continued with layering of differently colored soils. Mounds may contain flexed and bundle burials as well as cremations, but grave goods are relatively uncommon. Fireplace altars are common within the mounds, as is extensive burning. Evidence from associated small, probably seasonal, habitation sites indicates that the builders of these mounds were primarily mobile hunter-gatherers who ate only small quantities of cultivated plants like sunflower and maize (Stoltman and Christiansen 2000). Exactly what these mounds signify

FIGURE 12.17 Historic drawing of an effigy mound group from southern Wisconsin.

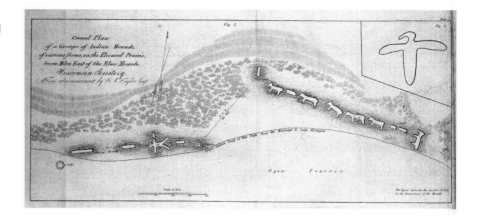

remains unclear, though various ideas have been suggested, including the possibility that they represent clan totems.

Further south, the end of the Late Woodland is marked by the widespread shift to maize agriculture during the eleventh century BP. This shift is evident both in the greater amount of maize found in sites and in changes in $^{12}C/^{13}C$ **ratio** found in human bone. Corn was present before this, but only in small amounts. What happened to make it so important in human subsistence? Apparently at some time between 1050 BP and 950 BP (AD 900–1000), perhaps in Ohio, a new variety of corn known as **Eastern Eight Row** or **Northern Flint corn** was developed. This maize variety apparently was hardier and more cold tolerant than earlier types of corn, which had 10 or more rows of kernels per cob. While this type of corn successfully spread across the Great Lakes into Wisconsin during the tenth century BP, archaeobotanical studies also show that it was never important in the American Bottom (Fritz 1992; Simon 2000), where maize agriculture first was adopted. Thus, the new variety of corn cannot be considered the cause of the shift to maize agriculture. Instead, the causes of this change must be sought in sociopolitical developments at the end of the Late Woodland.

It is these sociopolitical developments that most clearly mark the end of the Late Woodland and the beginning of a new period between 1150 BP and 950 BP (AD 800–1000) in the southern parts of the Midwest. Of course, further north and east, where Mississippian societies did not develop at all, the Late Woodland continues after 950 BP (AD 1000) and is often called simply the Late Prehistoric.

THE MISSISSIPPIANS AND OTHER LATE PREHISTORIC PEOPLES

Mississippian tradition societies were significant in the Midwest by at least 950 BP. The Mississippian society centered at Cahokia and located in the American Bottom of Illinois is the largest known polity, although Mississippian towns and other settlements elsewhere in the Midwest also were notable (see Box 12.1).

Commonly recognized temporal subdivisions are as follows: Emergent Mississippian, 1150 BP to 950 BP (AD 800–1000); Early Mississippian, 950 BP to 800 BP (AD 1000–1150); Middle Mississippian, 800 BP to 650 BP (AD 1150–1300);

Late Mississippian, 650 BP to 450 BP (AD 1300–1500); and Protohistoric, 450 BP to 350 BP (AD 1500–1600). Many areas of the Midwest appear to have been abandoned by Mississippians during Late Mississippian times, although populations may have simply dispersed into the uplands, returning to older lifeways. Actual depopulation may have characterized the lower Ohio valley and adjacent areas of southern Illinois and northern Kentucky after approximately 500 BP (AD 1450) (Cobb and Butler 2002). This area has been called the **Vacant Quarter** (Williams 1980, 1990).

ISSUES AND DEBATES

BOX 12.1

How Big and Powerful Was Cahokia After All?

Cahokia is an impressive place (Figure 12.18). Located east of the present city of St. Louis in the broad floodplain of the Mississippi known as the American Bottom, this ancient community still can be glimpsed amid the urban sprawl of Collinsville, Illinois. Even diminished by 200 years of American farming, road building, and occupation, this Mississippian mound center stands out among archaeological sites in North America. At the center of Cahokia is Monks Mound (Figure 1.4), North America's largest known mound, that rises about 100 feet (30 m) above the floodplain in four different terraces and covers more than 13 acres at its base. Monks Mound is so large that you might mistake it for a hill if it weren't in the middle of the floodplain. All you have to do is climb it to gain real respect for its builders. Yet Monks Mound is only the beginning of the human constructions at Cahokia. About 100 mounds, not to mention the debris of

FIGURE 12.18 Artist's conception of the central plaza at Cahokia; Monks Mound is in the distance.

centuries of Mississippian occupation, have been found within an area of 10 square kilometers (3.9 mi^2). Many of these mounds are platform mounds; others are lineal or conical mounds containing elaborate burials. Cahokia also contains plazas that have been scraped off and then leveled with new fill, the remains of a long wooden palisade that probably once enclosed the central area, large numbers of domestic as well as other structures, and several **woodhenges**, circular wooden structures resembling Stonehenge, that may track astronomical events. Today, the central part of Cahokia is preserved in a state park that is classified as a World Heritage Site by UNESCO. A wonderful museum with state-of-the-art presentations tells the story of Cahokia. The visitor cannot help but come away impressed with this one-of-a-kind site.

Everyone agrees Cahokia is a special place, and yet, archaeologists don't agree about its peak size or about the level of political and economic organization it represents. The conventional wisdom about Cahokia has been that it was a great and powerful political entity, the apical community at the top of a four-tiered hierarchy of communities controlled by Cahokia and its elites. With Cahokia as the premier mound center, slightly smaller centers, in turn, would have controlled still smaller communities with only one mound, which were themselves centers for surrounding agricultural hamlets. This complex polity could have been an incipient North American state, and with a population of 20,000 to 40,000 people, Cahokia would have been a city by ancient standards.

In this model, functionally differentiated communities within the hierarchy and separate precincts inside Cahokia produced the prestige goods and other commodities that moved around the society. The production and movement of these goods as well as labor for construction projects were controlled by the elite, whose position was validated by religious belief and symbolism. Large markets and extensive trade also characterized Cahokia, and its influence was felt far and wide—perhaps even among proto-Iroquoians in what today is New York State (Dincauze and Hasenstab 1989). Perhaps Cahokia served as a gateway between the northern frontier and the Mississippian heartland of

the Southeast, and derived much of its power from controlling trade on the Mississippi and other nearby rivers (John Kelly 1991). This is a compelling model, which certainly accounts for the unique features of Cahokia.

The question, however, is whether the evidence supports these characterizations. Thanks to major CRM projects in the American Bottom during the last 30 years, we now have much very detailed information about Mississippian communities in the American Bottom. Recently, in consideration of the picture these data present, it has been argued that simpler models may account more closely for the actual evidence (Milner 1990). Rather than being a state, Cahokia can be viewed as only a very large example of a paramount chiefdom that in many respects resembled other known Mississippian polities. In this view, the regional system was fairly decentralized and consisted of a series of potentially autonomous smaller centers headed by their own chiefs and linked by unstable political alliances (Figure 12.19). Rather than having fixed positions in an unchanging hierarchical system of settlements, different mound centers are thought to have occupied different levels of importance, in which they exerted varying levels of power over the nearly 400 years of Mississippian developments in the American Bottom.

Moreover, careful assessment of the probable numbers of structures per acre in various time periods throughout the American Bottom suggest that Cahokia's population was much lower than some archaeologists have argued. Population actually peaked in Early Mississippian times and began to decline several centuries before the end of the Mississippian sequence in the American Bottom (Milner 1998). Cahokia itself probably had no more than 8000 inhabitants at its peak, while the population in the American Bottom as a whole might have been as large as 50,000 at one time. Although a kin-based social hierarchy is also central in this alternative model, high status is seen as based primarily on wealth and symbols of prestige amassed by individuals rather than on direct elite control of the prestige good production. Finally, although trading was an important activity, the amount of exotic goods indicated by

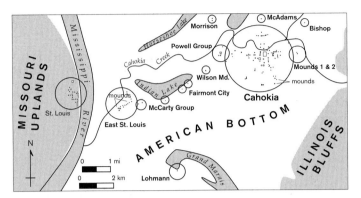

FIGURE 12.19 Mississippian mound centers in or adjacent to the American Bottom of Illinois; note that Cahokia is one of several such centers.

archaeological data was simply too small for Cahokia to have been controlling vast exchange networks.

Other archaeologists studying Mississippians are wrestling with debates similar to those posed by the alternative models of Cahokia (Muller 1997; Pauketat and Emerson 1997). There is some convergence of views toward downsizing population estimates and the scale of trade, and positing lack of a rigid hierarchy of mound centers. Differences of opinion remain, however, on the degree and means of domination by

Cahokia and other paramount Mississippian centers. The result is that although we probably can reject older characterizations of Cahokia as a state, its uniqueness remains important and poorly understood by all. The fact is, archaeologists have much more to learn about the nature of Mississippian polities (Pauketat 2005). On a positive note, these debates focus us on the central archaeological problem of how to interpret the material record. What data would you collect to help resolve the questions raised by these alternative models?

Cultural Remains

Although also found in a few Middle Woodland sites, the classic physical diagnostic for Mississippian sites is the presence of one or more platform mounds. These mounds are essentially flat-topped pyramidal structures of earth that were the substructures for wooden buildings. Such buildings may have been ceremonial structures, chiefs' houses, sweat lodges, or council houses. Excavations into platform mounds often show that a series of buildings were used, burned, and covered in succession with layers of dirt chosen for color and composition (Figure 12.20).

As mentioned in Chapter 11, platform mounds frequently were arranged around plazas and are found with conical and linear mounds, which were used for burial. Plaza surfaces were constructed by removing, importing, and leveling sediments. At Cahokia, for example, geophysical testing and coring indicates that overlying clay deposits were stripped from the northern part of the great plaza south of Monks Mound, and then this area was reclaimed by deposits of midden mixed with clay (Dalan 1997). One interesting Mississippian structure is the woodhenge, mentioned in Box 12.1. Several of these circles of large

FIGURE 12.20

Reconstruction of a Mississippian structure standing inside a modern building that protects exposed surfaces of Mound B at Wickliffe Mounds in Kentucky. Note the posthole depressions on the surface of the mound, the walls of the modern building have been painted to show the mound's multiple layers.

posts with possible solar alignments have been found at Cahokia. Mississippian houses usually were rectangular or square. Wall-trench houses were constructed by digging a trench into which the posts of the wall were set. Houses with individually set posts also appear, especially at early sites. Commonly, wattle-and-daub walls were then made by weaving cane between posts and plastering mud over it. Chunks of daub that were fired when houses burned are common on Mississippian sites.

Some Mississippian sites in the Midwest, like Kincaid along the lower Ohio River in southern Illinois, seem to be nucleated settlements, but many others have a more dispersed settlement pattern. This is true for Cahokia itself, where scattered hamlets and mound groups were strung out along the ridges in the American Bottom in a nonnucleated pattern (Milner 1998). The most common Mississippian settlement in the river valleys of the Midwest may be an agricultural hamlet rather than a large town or mound center. Identifying households and their component features within habitation sites is an important task (e.g., Mehrer 1995; Rogers and Smith 1995).

Archaeologists have identified many ceramic and lithic types in the various Mississippian sequences, but a few generalizations can be made. As noted in Chapter 11, pottery most often was tempered with shell. A variety of vessel forms, including jars, bowls, and plates, have been identified, as have wares with finer and coarser, presumably utilitarian, paste. Finer ware types were more likely to have been decorated. Slipping and painting, as well as incising and the creation of human and animal effigies (Figure 12.21), were common forms of decoration. Projectile points typically were small isosceles triangles that clearly were arrow points. Large, carefully made hoes, often of high-quality Mill Creek chert (Cobb 2000), also were used. Some examples of these hoes have been highly polished

FIGURE 12.21

Head pots similar to this one have been found in Mississippian sites from the Midwest.

by use. Many Mississippian lithic tools were simple flakes used expediently, though drills, long knife blades, and celts also were made. Ceremonially significant items, including marine shell beads and gorgets, stone palettes and figurines, copper plates, and ground stone ceremonial axes, were placed in Mississippian mound and burial contexts. **Discoidals** also were made. In the Historic period, these disk-shaped stones were used in a game called **chunkey**: the stones were rolled along the ground, and players threw spears at them.

Mississippians Sociopolitical and Economic Systems

Mississippians are thought to have lived in socially ranked societies headed by chiefs and divided into elite and commoner strata. The larger the mound center and its apparent sphere of influence, the greater the degree of hierarchy and chiefly power envisioned (Cobb 2003). Whether such ideas about Mississippians are essentially correct is debated, as indicated in Box 12.1. In fact, there probably was a good deal of variability within the Midwest, not to mention the Southeast, in the size and complexity of Mississippian polities. Different Mississippian polities have been categorized in the literature as simple or as complex/paramount chiefdoms. The Midwestern examples of paramount chiefdoms were Cahokia, and perhaps Kincaid in southern Illinois and Angel near Evansville, Indiana.

Archaeologists find evidence for hierarchy in aspects of the Mississippian record not limited to variability in size. For example, in Mississippian cemeteries, some individuals had greater quantities of imported materials and finely crafted objects (e.g., Goldstein 1980; Rothschild 1979) indicating probable status differences. Often cited in this respect is Cahokia's Mound 72, where several burial groups contained the remains of up to 53 individuals. The remains of four males whose hands and heads had been cut off indicate sacrificial practices. Also found in this mound were two skeletons covered with thousands of shell beads. Other caches of projectile points, ground stone gaming disks, and mica were also buried in Mound 72 (Fowler et al. 1999). Headless skeletons, some with pots at the top of the neck, also were found at Dickson Mounds in central Illinois mentioned in Chapter 14 (see Box 14.2).

It has long been argued that Mississippian populations were adapted to a specific meander belt habitat in the major river valleys of the Midwest and Southeast, although both temporal and spatial variation in this adaptation has also been noted (Smith 1978). There is good evidence that maize was an important source of food for Mississippians. Squashes and gourds also were cultivated, as were the suite of native seed plants so important earlier. Beans are a second tropical food plant that was very important in Native agriculture by the Historic period but apparently introduced only in the Late Mississippian period. Whether we call food production patterns at this time horticulture or agriculture, it is important not to forget that Mississippians also utilized a wide variety of wild plants and animals. White-tailed deer were very important, but so were raccoons, various species of fish, waterfowl, turkeys, several types of nuts (processed both for their meat and for their oil), wild seed plants, greens, fruits, and berries. Mississippian systems of production also involved the acquisition of raw materials to make houses, baskets, pottery, stone tools, and other implements. In addition, specialized items were produced for trade, exchange, and ritual.

Archaeologists interested in Mississippians are asking a wide variety of questions about economic production within Mississippian societies. If we accept that social ranking and some form of chiefly control characterized these societies, the production and distribution of goods can be seen as important aspects of Mississippian systems. One commodity extracted was salt, which is known to have existed in natural deposits like the Great Salt Spring in southern Illinois (Muller 1986). Current evidence is that salt production occurred as a domestic activity rather than as specialist production (Muller 1997, 308–332). In fact, most staple items, whether for food or raw materials, seem to have been produced in the Mississippian household by nonspecialists. Prestige goods may have been manufactured by specialists, but even at Cahokia, evidence for full-time craft specialists has been lacking (e.g., Yerkes 1983).

A final topic of great interest to archaeologists studying Mississippian polities has been whether dietary differences can be ascertained between elites and commoners. For example, there is some evidence in faunal assemblages that elites residing in the central part of Cahokia were provisioned with deer from elsewhere. There also is some evidence that deer meat was redistributed along class lines once it had been brought to the site (e.g., Kelly 1997). It is possible that Mississippian elite used feasting to bolster their prestige, as part of a tribute system that redistributed food and products (Lucretia S. Kelly 2001).

The Fort Ancient and Oneota Traditions

While we can consider many Midwestern populations after 950 BP (AD 1000) Mississippian, other important cultural manifestations occurred at this time, and Late Woodland cultural patterns continued in some areas. Two cultural traditions (Figure 12.22), **Fort Ancient** and Oneota, which was mentioned in

FIGURE 12.22 Locations of Oneota tradition and Fort Ancient tradition sites.

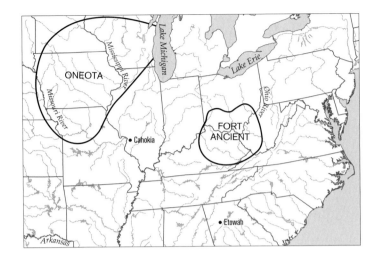

FIGURE 12.23 Visitors to Sunwatch Village, a reconstruction of the Incinerator site near Dayton, Ohio, walk toward the large post at the center of the village's plaza; the original post at this spot may have provided a means to track the movements of the sun.

Chapter 10, sometimes have been considered regional variants of Mississippian despite certain obvious distinctions.

Fort Ancient developed in the central Ohio River drainage after approximately 950 BP (AD 1000) and continued in some areas for about 700 years (Drooker and Cowan 2001). The people made shell-tempered ceramics that have some Mississippian stylistic elements. Fort Ancient subsistence was centered on maize and native cultigens but also included wild plants and animals. Fort Ancient settlements are primarily found in the floodplains, and villages were nucleated by 850 BP (AD 1100), but social hierarchy is less evident in this tradition than among Mississippians. Early Fort Ancient houses were small, semisubterranean rectangles associated with large storage pits, but the houses increased in size over time. Central plazas and large, possibly communal structures, have been noted after 750 BP at Fort Ancient sites, as have stockades. At the Incinerator site (Sunwatch Village) near Dayton, a large central post was erected in the plaza, possibly as a means to track the sun (Figure 12.23).

In Late Fort Ancient times, settlements of the Madisonville horizon (500–260 BP) sometimes were quite large. **Stone box graves**, in which individuals were interred in coffinlike boxes of stone, are found, as well as burial mounds. The stone box graves often are located within villages, near plazas, but temporal change in this pattern also has been observed. Studies of grave goods suggest that there was little ascribed ranking among Fort Ancient populations, and the people may have been organized into a tribal confederacy rather than a hierarchical chiefdom (Drooker and Cowan 2001). On the basis of highly similar ceramics, greater interaction among Fort Ancient populations seems probable after 500 BP (AD 1450), but breakdown of the tradition occurred after approximately 350 BP. The Shawnee may be the descendants of Fort Ancient.

Oneota, which has been called **Upper Mississippian**, was mentioned in Chapter 10 because it is found at the margins of the Midwest and Great Plains. Oneota was once thought to have developed only as Mississippians first expanded into northern Illinois and southern Wisconsin. However, better radiocarbon information now indicates that Oneota is a separate cultural tradition that emerged

FIGURE 12.24 A Van Meter Trailed pot is one example of Oneota ceramics.

about 950 BP (AD 1000), at the beginning of the Late Prehistoric, and continued until after 350 BP (AD 1600), the approximate beginning of the Protohistoric period (Brown and Sasso 2001). Oneota people made shell-tempered ceramics sometimes with distinctive decoration called trailing (Figure 12.24). Oneota lived in large villages and buried their dead in cemeteries rather than mounds. A mixed and variable subsistence base has been documented including hunting of bison and other animals, wild plant gathering, fishing, and some cultivation of maize and native crops. Although Oneota may have depended less on maize agriculture than Middle Mississippians, **ridged field systems** have been discovered in some Oneota sites like the Sand Lake site in western Wisconsin (Gallagher et al. 1985). There has been much debate about how intensive Oneota production was, about how large Oneota populations were, and about how climatic changes may have affected these northern agriculturalists.

Relationships between Oneota and Middle Mississippian are poorly understood, especially where these societies overlap in time and space. For example Aztalan, a mound and village complex centered on a plaza and surrounded by a palisade, is located in southern Wisconsin. Its main occupation was between 850 BP and 650 BP (AD 1100–1300). Archaeologists found ceramics that remind them of Middle Mississippian pottery from the American Bottom at Aztalan. Some have seen Aztalan as a Mississippian intrusion into the north, although grit-tempered, cord-marked, or cord-impressed ceramics typical of the local Late Woodland also are common there. This site suggests interactions between Mississippian, Oneota, and Late Woodland people, but these interactions remain poorly understood (Goldstein and Richards 1991). The complexity of such interactions is also suggested by findings of Oneota materials in the American Bottom (550–350 BP; AD 1400–1600) and elsewhere to the south after the Mississippian decline (e.g., Milner et al. 1984).

Other Late Prehistoric Peoples of the Midwest and Upper Great Lakes

Elsewhere in the Midwest and Upper Great Lakes, Late Woodland cultural patterns persisted into Protohistoric times. Archaeologists have assigned a series of phase names to these cultural phenomena. This does not mean that Late Prehistoric adaptations were unchanged from earlier Late Woodland ones. Each had its own history that played out without much influence from the Mississippians or even from Fort Ancient or Oneota societies. In fact, developments to the east (see Chapter 13) may have influenced these societies more than those to the south and west.

Although these Late Prehistoric groups certainly were less hierarchically organized than Mississippians, many groups adopted agriculture and settled into more or less permanent communities. For example, Parker (1996) has shown that the occupants of site 20SA1034, a site found in the Saginaw Basin of Michigan, used a full complement of cultigens, including maize, during Late Woodland times. In the **Whittlesey tradition** of northeastern Ohio, particularly after 500 BP (AD 1450), people congregated in villages surrounded by palisaded embankments and buried their dead in associated cemeteries. The South Park Village site (Brose 1994b) is one Whittlesey site at which archaeologists have documented mixed economies based on maize, bean, and squash agriculture, hunting, fishing, and gathering.

Even where hunting, fishing, and gathering remained the primary means of subsistence, Late Prehistoric people sometimes developed mortuary rituals that linked them in clan and tribal groups. A shift from burying people individually in cemeteries to the use of group ossuaries marks the Late Prehistoric in many areas of the Upper Great Lakes. This latter pattern involves the secondary processing of human remains after death and then placing them in a patterned way into a group burial (O'Shea 1988).

THE PROTOHISTORIC AND HISTORIC PERIODS

Europeans, notably French trappers, traders, and missionaries, pushed into the Upper Great Lakes and down the Mississippi valley in the seventeenth century AD. On the other hand, the Ohio country was not much explored until the eighteenth century. The Protohistoric begins even before this, when European goods such as glass beads, brass wares, and iron implements were traded into the Midwest and Upper Great Lakes along Native networks. In the Middle Ohio valley, the Protohistoric began as early as the middle of the sixteenth century. In the Chicago area trade beads are first evident in sites dated between AD 1620 and 1630. This period before major disruption of Native lifestyles by Europeans is truly fascinating for archaeologists. It is important to note, however, that the first Europeans entered a social context that was rapidly changing (Brose et al. 2001).

One factor was the demand for furs among Native groups to the east. Iroquois efforts to control the fur trade resulted in the forced dispersal of many groups in Ohio and adjacent areas during the second half of the seventeenth century (Tanner 1986). In general this meant that Algonquian-speaking people began to arrive in the vicinity of Siouan tribes in Illinois and Wisconsin. A period of general abandonment in the middle Ohio River valley during the seventeenth century is usually accepted, although the archaeological evidence concerning the end of Fort Ancient is more ambiguous (Drooker and Cowan 2001).

Newly arrived Europeans encountered a variety of cultural groups speaking Algonquian languages and a few Siouan-speaking tribes as well. A basic distinction among the Native groups of the area was between foraging groups living at the northern margins, such as the Ottawa and Chippewa-Ojibwa, and those to the south, who practiced some agriculture. More agriculturally based tribes included the Shawnee of Ohio, the Mascouten of southern Michigan, the Miami of Indiana, and the Menominee and Ho-Chunk (Winnebago) of Wisconsin and the Illinois, whose territory extended southward along the Mississippi River. Some of the Potowatomi of Michigan appear to have been hunter-gatherers, and some seem to have adopted agricultural lifestyles during the Protohistoric (Callender 1978). A number of agricultural tribes were displaced during the Protohistoric, notably the Fox (Mesquakie), the Sauk, the Kickapoo, all of whom originally were located in Michigan or northern Ohio but were first contacted by the French in Wisconsin. Of these tribes, only the Ho-Chunk spoke a Siouan as opposed to Algonquian language, but some of the poorly understood peoples of the Ohio Valley probably also were Siouan speakers. Archaeological research, particularly on material culture, can help scholars better understand the complex ethnic situation in the Midwest and Upper Great Lakes during the Protohistoric. However, direct linkage of sites to historically known tribes is not always possible.

The movements of people at this time were not just responses to European arrival or to the fur trade. Just as often they resulted from Native interaction, alliance formation, and stress on local resources. In fact, removals and relocations were multidirectional, and possibly a continuation of patterns in the Late Prehistoric. For instance, Shawnee Indians, who are presumed to have been related to Fort Ancient people, moved in various directions in the seventeenth century. Some went to South Carolina and then Alabama because of an alliance with the Upper Creek Indians. Others gathered near the newly established city of Philadelphia and then returned westward during the eighteenth century. Shawnee also are reported at Fort St. Louis on the Illinois River at Starved Rock in 1682. Such records suggest that the Shawnee not only were dispersed by the depradations of the Iroquois but also moved to take advantage of trade and alliance opportunities (Drooker and Cowan 2001).

French and British Colonialism

The French began to explore the Midwest and Upper Great Lakes with Samuel de Champlain's visit to Huronia in 1615. After Nicolet's visit to the Green Bay area in 1634, important expeditions were led by Marquette and Joliet in 1673 and by La Salle between 1679 and 1683. Archaeological sites can document some aspects of what the world explored by the French was like. For example, it is known that La Salle stopped at Rock Island at the tip of the Door Peninsula in Wisconsin to trade with Potowatomi. The probable village visited is represented by the Rock Island II site, where Huron, Petun, and Ottawa refugees earlier had built a fortified village. Excavations at this site have produced trade goods like glass beads, gunflints, clay pipes, brass kettle scraps, and French clasp knives (Mason 1981).

Missionaries also began to come among the Native people throughout the Upper Great Lakes and the Illinois country at the end of the seventeenth century. The Zimmerman site, which was excavated in 1947 (Figure 12.25) (Orr

FIGURE 12.25 Excavations at the Zimmerman site in 1947.

and Brown 1974), most likely represents the Grand Village of the Kaskaskia, where many Indian groups congregated at this time to be near French traders and missionaries. However, it was not until the early eighteenth century that French settlement began in earnest as a means of impeding English expansion. Many forts were established to control the trade. One important fort was Fort Ponchartrain, established at Detroit in 1701, to which a number of Indian communities relocated. Beginning in 1718 settlers were brought to Illinois via the Mississippi River. A group of French colonial settlements along the Mississippi were located in an area roughly between modern St. Louis, Missouri, and Chester, Illinois. St. Phillippe (established in 1723), Prairie du Rocher (established in 1723), Fort de Chartres (established around 1721), and St. Geneviève (established about 1750) joined older mission settlements at Cahokia and Kaskaskia. Settlers traded with Native peoples, grew crops, and shipped agricultural products, salt, and lead downriver to New Orleans. Archaeological investigations at the remains of these settlements have produced insights into French colonialism in the Illinois country (Walthall 1991).

Conflicts between various Native groups continued throughout the French period. Between approximately 1712 and 1740 a series of conflicts involving the Fox (Mesquakie) pitted this tribe and their allies among the Sauk, Mascouten, Kickapoo, and Dakota, a Plains tribe, against the Illinois, who were closely allied with the French. Conflicts also developed during the eighteenth century between the Ojibwa and the Dakota in the area of Lake Superior (Tanner 1986).

The French tried to control trade in the Ohio country from their base at Detroit and from other forts and trading posts established in various parts of Ohio. Here they had much more direct competition from British colonists from Pennsylvania and Virginia, who traded and eventually settled in Ohio River valley. The first European to visit the Ohio River valley probably was Gabriel Arthur, an English trader, captured by Indians in 1674. By the middle of the eighteenth century a large multiethnic trading community existed at Shawneetown, located at the confluence of the Scioto and Ohio rivers. Various Indian tribes moved back into this country during the eighteenth century, among them Shawnee and Delaware bands from Pennsylvania, Huron from the north, and various Iroquois bands, often called Mingo, from New York and Pennsylvania.

This situation as well as broader conflicts between France and Great Britain in Europe eventually led to the French and Indian War. This is the name Americans use for the Seven Years' War (1754–1763) or "War of the Conquest" between Great Britain and France. Although actual battles during this series of campaigns between two of the major colonial powers happened east of the areas covered in this chapter, the defeat of the French did cause their withdrawal from the Great Lakes and adjacent areas. Particularly the tribes that had been allied with the French suffered from this withdrawal. In Pontiac's War (1763–1764), many tribes joined the Ottawa chief in an attempt to

remove the British from the Ohio country. Section D.6 of the Student CD, "Ethnicity and Class in Colonial Foodways," explores the ethnic situation at Fort Michilimackinac (see Figure 12.1) after the arrival of the British in 1761. Although the Treaty of 1763 established a Proclamation Line at the crest of the Appalachians, separating Indian lands to the west from British colonies to the east, colonial traders and settlers did not honor this boundary. Hostilities between Indians and the British and later the Americans continued in the Ohio country for many years.

American and Canadian Control

The history of American and eventually Canadian control in the Midwest and Upper Great Lakes is much better documented and known than that of the colonial period, although a great deal can still be learned from archaeology. Fortunately the CRM mandate has required archaeologists to explore these aspects of the historic past. Five specific topics are especially significant.

First, the record of the American Revolution and of the War of 1812 can be investigated archaeologically. We often forget that the Midwest and Great Lakes witnessed a number of important battles in these conflicts. George Rogers Clark's taking of towns in the Illinois country in 1778 is one example. The dismantling of Fort Michilimackinac in 1780–1781 is another event that has been documented archaeologically (Pilling and Anderson 1999).

Second, the daily lives of Native Americans, European settlers, and later inhabitants of the Midwest and Upper Great Lakes can be explored through archaeology. The story of this area's transformation from a frontier region to an agricultural heartland can be told archaeologically through the excavation of farmsteads, mills, and early mercantile operations.

Third, gradual urbanization and industrialization in this part of the country also can be documented through archaeology. Excavation within urban areas leads to an interesting perspective on the growth of the major cities of the areas covered here (e.g., Pilling 1982). Archaeological work also has documented much about early technology as well as about daily life (McBride and McBride 1996). Besides excavations, archaeological survey is responsible for identifying the early industrial sites so widely scattered through the Midwest and Upper Great Lakes.

Fourth, the American Civil War is a topic of archaeological interest. Although most events and battles took place to the south, a few sites provide some information about this era. For example, archaeology has been done at a Civil War prison camp that was located on Johnson's Island, in Lake Erie off Ohio (Bush 1999).

Fifth, shipping and commerce through the Great Lakes is an important part of the story of the past. Both terrestrial and underwater archaeology can explore these topics (Figure 12.26). Tremendous resources for the elaboration of maritime history lie submerged in the Great Lakes (Pott 1999).

FIGURE 12.26 Lithographic depiction of the first steamer on the Upper Great Lakes at Detroit in 1820.

CHAPTER SUMMARY

This chapter has provided an introduction to what archaeologists have learned about the past in the Midwest and the Upper Great Lakes. Although there are many obvious similarities to the archaeological past in the Southeast, there also are differences that should be kept in mind if you explore this archaeological area further. The main points made in this chapter are as follows:

- The topography of the areas covered in this chapter has been shaped by the repeated glaciations that also formed the basins of the Great Lakes and the river drainages. Most of the area is part of the temperate deciduous forest biome, but the Prairie Peninsula, a lobe of tall-grass prairie, stretches from the Plains into this area primarily in Wisconsin, Illinois, and Indiana. The extent of this Illinoian biotic province has varied over time, expanding during periods of warmth and drought and shrinking when cool and moist conditions have prevailed.

- A possible Pre-Clovis complex called Chesrow complex has been proposed for southern Wisconsin on the basis of butchered mammoth bones and associated stone tools, but most Paleoindian sites in the Midwest and Upper Great Lakes contain fluted points and are no older than the twelfth millennium BP. Large aggregated base camps supporting caribou hunting or in association with quarries suggest a highly mobile, specialized Paleoindian adaptation, although in the southern Midwest and later in Paleoindian times, generalized foraging may have been characteristic.

- As is the case throughout the Eastern Woodlands, Archaic projectile points may first have been side or corner notched, then bifurcated and, in the Late Archaic, stemmed. The adaptive significance of these trends is unclear, however.

- Archaic subsistence and settlement suggest a trend from generalized, broad-based foraging to more focused logistical collecting associated with seasonal sedentism. This trend, which also is linked with small-scale cultivation and domestication of gourds and weedy seed plants, begins in the Middle Archaic in the major river valleys and is more widespread during the Late Archaic.

- Long-distance exchange of copper, galena, carved bone pins, and other items, as well as mound building and mortuary ceremonialism begins in the Middle and Late Archaic. Mortuary complexes like Old Copper, Glacial Kame, and Red Ocher, as well as the first appearance of cemeteries, suggest that at least by the Late Archaic people identified with kin or other groups and recognized group territories. These developments may be linked to population growth.

- The Early Woodland is associated with Adena mound building, mortuary ceremonialism, and interaction centered in the upper Ohio River valley, while the Middle Woodland is associated with Hopewell. Hopewell had both Illinois and Ohio centers, but Hopewell interaction, mound and earthwork construction, and elaborate ceremonialism are widespread throughout the Eastern Woodlands at this time. Hopewell people cultivated the plants of the Eastern Agricultural complex as well as a little maize, but they may not have been aggregated into large communities, and they seem to have had relatively little social ranking.

- As in other parts of the East, the Late Woodland was a time of great cultural variability marked by the adoption of the bow and arrow. In the major river valleys of the Midwest, first intensification of native plant cultivation and then a shift to maize agriculture during the eleventh century BP foreshadowed the appearance of Mississippian. Elsewhere, the Late Woodland can be seen as continuing until European contact.

- Mississippian developments were significant in many parts of the Midwest, as exemplified by the largest known Mississippian site, Cahokia. Midwestern Mississippians built platform mounds and towns with central plazas, although mound groups were sometimes dispersed rather than nucleated. They made shell-tempered pottery, triangular projectile points, hoes, and a wide variety of prestige items. Archaeologists believe they were organized into chiefdoms of varying size and complexity.

- The Fort Ancient tradition of the central Ohio drainage and the Oneota of the northern and western margins of this chapter's areas are two Late Prehistoric cultural traditions that were influenced by Mississippians. Other Late Prehistoric peoples in the Great Lakes and Eastern Midwest were less influenced by the Mississippians and more closely tied to Late Prehistoric developments to the East.

- The complex movements and disruptions of Protohistoric and colonial times in the Midwest and Upper Great Lakes are not easy to trace, though archaeology can contribute to an understanding of this dynamic period. Archaeology can also contribute to knowledge of later Historic period events and trends.

SUGGESTIONS FOR FURTHER READING

For a review of the prehistory of eastern North America with emphasis on the mound-building cultures:

Milner, George R. 2004. *The Moundbuilders: Ancient Peoples of Eastern North America.* London: Thames and Hudson.

For an account of investigations of Archaic sites in southern Illinois:

Jefferies, Richard W. 1987. *The Archaeology of Carrier Mills: 10,000 Years in the Saline Valley of Illinois.* Carbondale: Southern Illinois University Press.

For recent perspectives on Ohio Hopewell:

Pacheco, Paul J., ed. 1996. *A View from the Core: A Synthesis of Ohio Hopewell Archaeology.* Columbus: Ohio Archaeological Council.

For recent perspectives on the Late Woodland in the Midwest:

Emerson, Thomas E., Dale L. McElrath, and Andrew C. Fortier. 2000. *Late Woodland Societies: Tradition and Transformation Across the Midcontinent.* Lincoln: University of Nebraska Press.

For a thorough review of the evidence from Cahokia:

Milner, George R. 1998. *The Cahokia Chiefdom: The Archaeology of a Mississippian Society.* Washington, DC: Smithsonian Institution Press.

For a review of Michigan's past and insight into the archaeology of the entire Upper Great Lakes area:
Halsey, John R., ed. 1999. *Retrieving Michigan's Buried Past: The Archaeology of the Great Lakes State.* Bloomfield Hills, MI: Cranbrook Institute of Science.

For information on the underwater archaeology of the Great Lakes as well as the rest of the Americas:
Bass, George F., ed. 1996. *Ships and Shipwrecks of the Americas.* London: Thames and Hudson.

OTHER RESOURCES

Sections H and I of the Student CD provide web links, places to visit, additional discussion questions, and other study aids. The Student CD also contains a variety of additional resources including the complete references as cited in this chapter and an appropriate case study: see Section D.6, where Elizabeth Scott's "Ethnicity and Class in Colonial Foodways" provides a fascinating look at ethnicity at Fort Michilimackinac in Michigan during the British period.

CASE STUDY

The mound and earthwork complexes of Ohio have excited American imaginations for nearly two centuries (see Section A of the Student CD). But although archaeologists have put to rest the most fanciful myths about who built these large topographic features, we still know surprising little about how they were constructed. The large size of these sites makes it difficult to excavate significant portions of a mound complex, posing a problem both for scholars and for managers who must preserve and interpret earthworks in a responsible manner. This case study shows how archaeologists from the National Park Service are using modern geophysical techniques to explore earthwork sites and then ground-truthing their findings with informed testing. The Hopeton Earthworks Project has shown that far from casual accumulations of earth, these constructions represent placement of different, carefully selected sediments. The color and perhaps the texture of the earth seem to have mattered to the designers and builders of the earthworks. The project also has shown that the dating of these earthworks can be more variable than archaeologists have thought. The possible Late Woodland modification or construction of part of Hopeton raises many questions. As you read this case study, ask yourself how its findings might alter understanding of Middle and Late Woodland cultures in Ohio. What new perspectives do you gain from reading about this project?

THE HOPETON EARTHWORKS PROJECT
Using New Technologies to Answer Old Questions

Mark Lynott

When European colonists entered the Ohio River valley, they discovered a large number and variety of earthen mounds and geometric earthworks. Small conical mounds were present throughout eastern North America, but in the Ohio River valley the early settlers encountered giant enclosures with walls 10 feet (3 m) tall and higher. The earthen enclosures were built in geometric shapes: circles, squares, and rectangles. Some of them included several of these geometric forms, as well as pairs of long, linear parallel walls. The accumulation of the vast amount of soil needed to build the long and tall earthen walls seemed to represent considerable organized effort. Many of the colonists viewed the Native people of the Ohio River valley as savages, incapable of constructing such impressive monuments.

In the first half of the nineteenth century, a few scientific reports (e.g., Atwater 1820; Brackenridge 1814) fueled considerable speculation about the origin and nature of the earthen monuments in the eastern United States. This led to the development of theories about a lost race of mound builders that were variously identified as migrating Polynesians, Egyptians, Greeks, Romans, Israelites, Vikings, Welsh, Scots, and Chinese (Silverberg 1968).

The first scientific studies of the earthworks began to appear in the mid-nineteenth century. *Ancient Monuments of the Mississippi Valley* by E. G. Squier and E. H. Davis was published by the newly created Smithsonian Institution in 1848. This massive study provided detailed drawings of earthworks throughout eastern North America, but the focus of the authors' effort was southern Ohio in the area near Chillicothe.

The question of who built the earthen mounds and geometric enclosures in eastern North America continued to be debated among the growing scientific community in the United States throughout the nineteenth century. The answer to the question was finally addressed when Cyrus Thomas directed investigators conducting surveys and mound excavations throughout eastern North America. His published report of their research (Thomas 1894) demonstrated the continuity between the Historic Native residents of North America and the pre-Columbian people who built the mounds.

Once the fledgling discipline of archaeology had demonstrated that the great earthen monuments had been built by the Indians, archaeologists turned their attention to exploring the mounds and studying their contents. In their landmark study, Squier and Davis explored more than 100 mounds in southern Ohio. Their excavations revealed the presence of human burials with associated mortuary objects. In many cases the mounds were built as a series of events, which were exposed as discrete strata in the mounds. Excavation of the mounds also revealed evidence of complex mortuary rituals that included cremation of the deceased, and deposition of the remains, along with a range of wonderful objects and ornaments on platforms or altars. Most noteworthy was the discovery of more than 200 beautifully carved stone animal effigy pipes in one of the small mounds at Mound City group near Chillicothe.

The spectacular mortuary objects and ornaments incorporated into many of these burial mounds served to focus early archaeological research on the excavation of burial mounds. Warren K. Moorehead con- ducted excavations at a large mound group in 1891 and 1892 for the purpose of recovering materials to display at the **World's Columbian Exposition** in Chicago. His excavations revealed numerous burials and elaborately prepared altars. He collected a massive number of artifacts, including carved stone pipes depicting animal and human figures, necklaces of pearls and perforated bear canine teeth, and sheets of mica cut into a variety of elaborate shapes. In one mound he found a cache of 7000 chipped flint disks, and throughout the excavations he found a vast number and variety of copper objects. These included panpipes, breastplates, axes, adzes, earspools, and sheets of copper cut into birds, fish, serpents, and geometric shapes. One of the most impressive copper ornaments he collected was a deer antler headdress that must have been used by a shaman. At the time of Moorehead's excavations, the site was owned by Captain M. C. Hopewell, a former military officer, and archaeologists later named the culture that built the mounds after this site.

When the early colonists began settling the Ohio River valley, there were literally thousands of mounds and hundreds of geometric earthworks in this region. However, as towns developed and grew, and farmers cleared forests and cultivated the rich valley bottoms, the earthen monuments began to diminish in size and number. Even nineteenth-century scholars lamented the destruction of the archaeological record and noted the damage resulting from annual cultivation. Today, mounds and earthworks are still present in southern Ohio, but mainly in cemeteries or parks where they have been intentionally preserved. Only a handful of mounds, and even fewer earthwork sites, have been preserved in a manner that allows us to appreciate their original size and grandeur. In most cases, those that remain are but a shadow of their original size and form. Fortunately, new technologies and new archaeological methods are making it possible to extract valuable information from sites that have been nearly destroyed by years of cultivation.

HOPETON EARTHWORKS

The Hopeton Earthworks are located a few miles north of downtown Chillicothe, Ohio. The site is located on a Pleistocene terrace in a horseshoe bend of the Scioto River. Known since early in the nineteenth century, the earthworks were mapped and described by Squier and Davis in *Ancient Monuments of the*

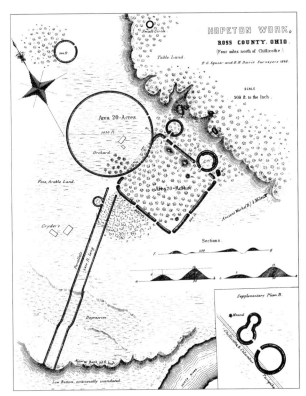

FIGURE 12.27 Squier and Davis's map of the Hopeton earthworks, Ross County, Ohio.

Mississippi Valley (Figure 12.27). The earthworks consisted of "a rectangle, with an attached circle, the latter extending into the former, instead of being connected with it in the usual manner" (1848, 51). The authors also described two smaller circles that were integrated into the north side of the rectangle and a pair of parallel walls that extend from the northwest corner of the rectangle 2400 feet (730 m) to the southwest. The walls of the two larger geometric enclosures were formed by a series of wall segments. The walls of the great circle had three segments and three gateways. The rectangle had 11 segments and 12 gateways. The large circle was reported to be 1050 feet (320 m) in diameter, and the rectangle was measured at 900 by 950 feet (275 × 290 m). Each was estimated to enclose 20 acres.

Like most of the great Ohio earthen enclosures, the Hopeton Earthworks were of monumental size. Here is the report of Squier and Davis:

[The] walls of the rectangular work are composed of a clayey loam, twelve feet high by fifty feet base, and are destitute of a ditch on either site. They resemble the heavy grading of a railway, and are broad enough, on the top, to admit the passage of a coach. The wall of the great circle was never as high as that of the rectangle; yet, although it has been much reduced of late years by the plough, it is still about five feet in average height. It is also destitute of a ditch. It is built of clay, which differs strikingly in respect of color from the surrounding soil. (1848, 51)

As with most of the other great earthen enclosures in southern Ohio, the vast size of the site served as a deterrent to systematic archaeological investigations. Most of these great sites have been subjected to only one or two summers of archaeological research, so investigators have tended to focus their efforts on mounds associated with the enclosures, rather than the enclosure walls. Consequently, after more than 150 years of study, archaeologists are still unable to state definitively when the walls were built. Also, how were they built? And why were they built?

These are not new questions. Questions about the origin and antiquity of the earthworks of southern Ohio are present in the earliest descriptions of the sites. Many of the early writers also speculated about the function of these giant geometric enclosures. Some thought the enclosures were for defense; sacred or religious purposes were suggested by others. In their description of the Hopeton Earthworks, Squier and Davis observed that since there were no ditches and only a few relatively small "dug holes" in association with the large earthen walls of the enclosure, vast amounts of soil had had to be carried from another location. Although they did not elaborate on this issue, they clearly raised the question of how the walls were built.

GEOPHYSICAL INVESTIGATIONS

Archaeologists have been using geophysical instruments to prospect for subsurface archaeological features for many decades. Most of the early instruments were slow and cumbersome to use, and data had to be first recorded by hand and then manually entered into a computer program for analysis. In the last decade, digital technology, improved sensors, and microcomputers have combined to increase the efficiency and effectiveness of these instruments manyfold.

A survey that required 2.5 hours a quarter-century ago can be accomplished today in under 20 minutes. In addition to the increased speed in recording data, the new instruments are many times more sensitive, and data can be directly downloaded to a computer. This makes it possible for archaeologists to begin conducting large-scale geophysical surveys and looking at large sites comprehensively, rather than in small pieces.

The National Park Service initiated the geophysical survey at the Hopeton Earthworks in 1997. Initially, it was hoped that the geophysical survey could be useful in identifying subsurface features associated with Hopewell habitation sites and possibly locating vestiges of earthen walls that are no longer visible. However, the efficiency and effectiveness of this approach soon convinced us that it would be possible to survey the entire site, and for the first time, take a comprehensive look at a large Ohio Hopewell earthwork site.

Under the leadership of internationally recognized geophysicist John Weymouth, we started work on the southwest edge of the rectangular enclosure at Hopeton. The area to be studied was laid out in a grid measuring 20 by 20 meters (65 × 65 ft). Each 20-by-20-meter block was individually surveyed by means of instrument readings along linear transects spaced one meter (3.28 ft) apart. Thus each survey block consists of 21 linear transects of instrument readings. To analyze data across a large area, a computer may be used to combine individual survey blocks.

The initial geophysical study at Hopeton incorporated three geophysical instruments: an RM-15 resistance meter, which measures resistance to an electrical current, and, to measure magnetic fluctuations, an FM-36 fluxgate gradiometer and a G-858 cesium gradiometer. After survey of an area measuring 80 by 140 meters (265 × 460 ft), and careful consideration of the resultant data, archaeological testing was conducted to evaluate the utility and accuracy of the instrument data. Overall, the archaeological testing showed that the geophysical survey was highly effective in identifying the location of larger subsurface pits and other features. However, the instruments were ineffective in identifying small features, like postholes. Although we thought it might be possible to increase the number of transects surveyed within a 20-by-20-meter block to identify smaller features, this diminished so greatly the number of blocks that could be surveyed in the time available that survey coverage of the entire site would have been nearly

impossible. The balance between the intensity of the survey coverage, the size of the site, and the time and funding available for a project must be considered on a site-by-site basis. The initial study at Hopeton also suggested that the cesium gradiometer provided the best combination of speed and sensitivity for survey work at this site.

The Geometrics G-858 cesium gradiometer has two magnetic sensors attached to a staff. For this project, we used the staff and sensors in a vertical configuration, with the lower sensor 30 centimeters (12 in.) above the surface and the upper sensor 100 centimeters (40 in.) above the lower sensor. The upper sensor records the total magnetic field at the same time that the lower sensor is recording the magnetic field of the soil below the sensor. The survey was conducted in walking mode, using a 0.2-second cycle with traverses spaced at intervals of 1.0 meter and readings spaced at 14 cm (5.5 in.) along transects (Figure 12.28).

After the initial geophysical survey and testing project demonstrated that this combination of methods was an effective way to study large and diffuse archaeological sites, plans to study the entire site were developed. While we were confident that our geophysical survey would be effective on the large flat areas that surround the earthworks, we were uncertain as to how effective the geophysical survey would be over the earthen walls that form the earthwork. With assistance from John Weymouth, Bruce Bevan, Rinita Dalan and a number of other archaeologists and geophysicists, we began geophysical survey on the south wall segments of the large rectangle

FIGURE 12.28 Geophysical survey at the Hopeton earthworks in progress.

in 2001. Once again we tried several different instruments to evaluate their relative effectiveness for this project. While each of the instruments produced valuable data in particular circumstances, we once again decided that the cesium gradiometer was most effective for overall survey coverage.

Agricultural activities have reduced the height and widened the width of the walls of the rectangular enclosure considerably. Walls that were twelve feet high in 1848 are no more than three feet high in most cases today, and in some places are only barely visible. The most important accomplishment of the geophysical survey was the discovery that the wall segments of the rectangular enclosure are distinctly visible in the magnetic survey data (Figure 12.29). The sharp boundaries on the interior and exterior of the wall segments are in marked contrast to the topography of these features, which is very gradual due to years of annual cultivation. The sharp magnetic contrast between the core of the wall and the surrounding soils of the landform suggested that the interior of the wall must have been constructed from soils that differ markedly from the naturally occurring soils of the alluvial terrace.

Careful examination of the magnetic data shows that the interior and exterior of the wall segments are separated by approximately 15 meters (50 ft), which is consistent with the nineteenth-century descriptions

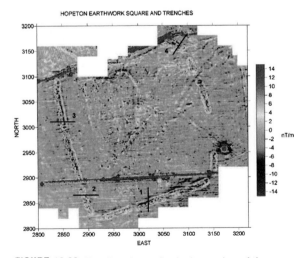

FIGURE 12.29 Results of geophysical mapping of the rectangular enclosure at Hopeton, indicating numbered trenches (1–4); magnetic readings shown in nanoteslas per meter (nT/m).

of the earthwork. The magnetic data also depicts the earthen wall in segments with gateways, just as the site was mapped in the mid-1800s. In an effort to determine how much of the original wall was preserved at Hopeton, we used the geophysical survey data to select four locations around the rectangular enclosure for test excavations.

EXCAVATION OF THE RECTANGULAR ENCLOSURE

In the summer of 1996, Bret J. Ruby of the National Park Service directed the excavation of a trench one meter wide across a segment of earthen wall at the northwest corner of the rectangular enclosure at Hopeton. Aerial photographs indicate that this section of wall had been preserved in a fence row since at least 1938 and is currently 20 meters long and 1.5 meters high. The 1996 test trench revealed that there were three different soil deposits in the core of the wall, each representing a different stage of construction. Using the information gained from this initial testing project, we developed a plan for testing other less well preserved wall segments to determine whether we might be able to learn how and when they were constructed.

We used the geophysical survey data to evaluate the potential preservation of the core of the wall segments to select a location in the central segment of the south wall of the rectangle for testing in 2001 (Lynott and Weymouth 2002). We aligned the trench location to cross-section the wall, and laid it out with stakes and string. It was 1.5 meters (5 ft) wide and 48 meters (160 ft) long. The length of the trench was selected to ensure the exposure of the core of the original wall and most of the soil that had been pulled down off the wall by annual cultivation. We excavated the trench by backhoe, with the operator carefully removing small amounts of soil along the trench alignment. Several archaeologists watched closely as the soil was removed, and backhoe work was frequently halted as the archaeologists examined an exposed soil change or the appearance of charcoal. In several places where potential features were exposed, the backhoe operator left large amounts of soil in situ for later excavation by hand. Although very few artifacts were observed during the excavation of Trench 1, three prehistoric features were exposed, recorded, and excavated. When that work was completed, one wall of the trench was carefully scraped, cleaned, and examined to better understand how the wall had been constructed.

Examination of the trench wall permitted us to record the construction sequence for this segment of the south wall (see Figure 12.30). Construction began by removing all the dark topsoil that was present at this location and exposing the compact yellow silt–loam subsoil. On top of the exposed subsoil, archaeologists found a large burned oak log. Since none of the adjacent soil had been oxidized or hardened by fire, it appeared that the log had been burned elsewhere. The visible portion of the log was 80 centimeters (31.5 in.) long and extended into the east wall of the trench. The exposed section of the log was nearly 20 centimeters (8 in.) in diameter, too large for the piece to have been accidentally deposited at this location as part of a basket of soil. It is more likely that the log was part of a ritual associated with construction of the wall segment. In excavations of other wall segments at Hopeton we have revealed more features indicating that rituals involving fire were a common part of wall building at this site.

We were able to reconstruct part of the procedure for creating the south wall as follows. After the burned log was laid on top of the subsoil, large amounts of additional yellow silt–loam sediments were piled up in a row to form the base of the wall segment. Next, red sandy–loam sediments were piled on the top and south (outer) side of the yellow silt loam. A gray-brown loam was then added to cover the top and both sides of the wall. These soils were slightly more than a meter deep and represent only the basal third of the original wall. These layers can be discerned in the portion of Figure 12.30 labeled "North Wall, Trench #1, 33RO26." Agricultural activities had truncated the wall above this level, so it is impossible to determine whether other types of soil were used in building the upper two-thirds of the wall segment. Trench 1 exposed gray organic layers that sloped upward from the margins of the wall toward the center of the wall. Although these have been truncated by cultivation and buried by slope wash from the top of the wall, they appear to be the original interior and exterior wall surfaces, organic soil layers that formed on the base and sides of the wall after it was constructed.

Three other trenches have been excavated across the rectangular enclosure at Hopeton using the same methods described for Trench 1 (Figure 12.30).

Trenches 2 and 3 were excavated across segments forming the west wall of the enclosure. Trench 4 was excavated across the curved segment that forms the northeast corner of this enclosure. Although there was general similarity in the manner in which these wall segments were constructed, there was also significant variability between the segments.

The west wall of the enclosure is composed of three wall segments and the associated gateways. Trench 2 was excavated in an east–west direction to cross-section the segment at the south end of the wall. Trench 2 was 43 meters long (140 ft) and 1.5 meters (5 ft) wide. Trench 3 was oriented east–west across the northernmost wall segment in the west wall. This trench was 50 meters long and 1.5 meters wide. Excavation of both trenches revealed that construction of the wall segments also had been initiated by removing the topsoil from the area and exposing the yellow-brown silt–loam subsoil. Construction of the wall segments began with large amounts of gray-brown silt–loam being piled on top of the exposed subsoil. The next step in the construction of these wall segments was to pile large amounts of yellow-brown silt–loam on the eastern half of the dark gray-brown silt–loam layer. A red-brown sandy loam was then piled on the top and west side of the developing wall segment. The amount, configuration, and color of these soils differed quite markedly between the two wall segments, but both were built with three different types of soil that had been deposited in large homogeneous strata. Compare the parts of Figure 12.30 showing trenches 2 and 3. The outer and inner surfaces of both original walls were visible, but they were truncated near the center of the wall and covered by wall fill that has been pulled down and outward by years of cultivation.

During the construction of these wall segments, the wall builders built small fires on the top of the various soil materials prior to covering one soil with a soil of a different type. These burning episodes were preserved as small features, usually covering less than 0.25 square meter (2.7 ft^2). The features mainly comprised small charred wood fragments and red and oxidized soil, indicating that burning had occurred at this location. Sometimes a small number of fire-cracked rocks, burned bones, chipped stone objects, or tiny fragments of mica were found in the features.

Trench 4, excavated in the summer of 2003, was oriented southwest to northeast across the curving wall segment that forms the northeast corner of the

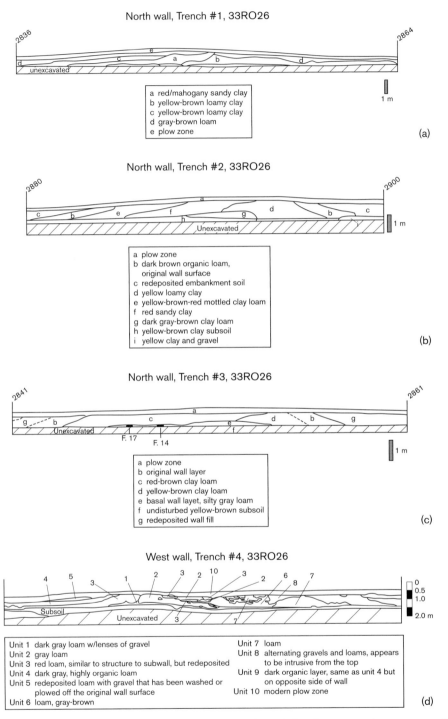

North wall, Trench #1, 33RO26

a red/mahogany sandy clay
b yellow-brown loamy clay
c yellow-brown loamy clay
d gray-brown loam
e plow zone

(a)

North wall, Trench #2, 33RO26

a plow zone
b dark brown organic loam,
   original wall surface
c redeposited embankment soil
d yellow loamy clay
e yellow-brown-red mottled clay loam
f red sandy clay
g dark gray-brown clay loam
h yellow-brown clay subsoil
i yellow clay and gravel

(b)

North wall, Trench #3, 33RO26

a plow zone
b original wall layer
c red-brown clay loam
d yellow-brown clay loam
e basal wall layet, silty gray loam
f undisturbed yellow-brown subsoil
g redeposited wall fill

(c)

West wall, Trench #4, 33RO26

Unit 1 dark gray loam w/lenses of gravel
Unit 2 gray loam
Unit 3 red loam, similar to structure to subwall, but redeposited
Unit 4 dark gray, highly organic loam
Unit 5 redeposited loam with gravel that has been washed or
   plowed off the original wall surface
Unit 6 loam, gray-brown

Unit 7 loam
Unit 8 alternating gravels and loams, appears
   to be intrusive from the top
Unit 9 dark organic layer, same as unit 4 but
   on opposite side of wall
Unit 10 modern plow zone

(d)

FIGURE 12.30 Of the four trenches across the Hopeton earthworks, Trench #4, dug across the western wall of the enclosure, showed distinctive sediments and structure.

rectangular enclosure. The trench was 1.5 meters wide and 41 meters (135 ft) long. The relationship of this wall segment to the Great Circle at Hopeton (see 20-acre round enclosure in Figure 12.27) suggests that this was either the first or the last segment of the rectangular enclosure to be constructed. This is the only curved segment of wall associated with the rectangular enclosure.

Just as in the first three trenches, construction of this wall segment was initiated by removal of topsoil from the area where the wall segment was placed. However, in this case, the topsoil was not removed from the area to the north of where the wall was constructed. The subsoil is reddish in this area of the site, which is in strong contrast to the yellow-brown subsoil that was exposed under the other wall segments. The different colored subsoil is a reflection of different naturally occurring soil types that are present on this landform. Once the topsoil was removed, a dark gray loam with lenses of fine gravel was laid down, covering the red subsoil under the wall segment and merging with the dark gray topsoil that was not removed from the north side of the wall segment.

The core of this wall segment comprises three large fairly homogeneous soil deposits and dozens of smaller ones (see Trench 4 in Figure 12.30). A thick layer of gray loam was placed on top of the dark gray loam and gravel, and this material forms the central core of the wall segment. A red sandy-loam was deposited immediately south of the gray loam. The red material partly overlies the gray sediments and extends about 10 meters (33 ft) to the south. The contact between the red and gray sediments is sharp and clear, just as we observed in other wall segments. On the north side of the gray loam core, the situation is different. The gray loam deposit thins on its north edge, and a gray-brown loam was piled on top of this and extends to the north about 5 meters (16 ft). The contact between the gray and the gray-brown loam is marked by numerous lenses of gray loam, gray-brown loam, red sandy-loam, and gravel. Many of these lenses appear to have resulted from the dumping of basketloads. This is unique among the wall segments that have been examined at Hopeton; that is, this segment has a different construction history than the others we explored. As noted in the other wall trenches, a dark gray organic soil zone that dipped down and outward from the top of the wall segment was present on both the interior and exterior of this wall segment.

Several features were exposed by the excavation of Trench 4. Two unusual linear features comprising burned wood and a white **calcined** material were found resting on top of the dark loam that forms the base of this wall segment. It is unclear what these features represent, but obviously they were placed at this location as part of the initial wall construction. Within the fill of the wall, there were three different small features consisting of burned wood and burned soil. These were similar in size and form to the features described earlier from the other wall segments. Another small area of burned soil and charred wood was found about 7 meters (23 ft) north of the exterior of the wall. With the exception of the last feature, all the features described from Trench 4 are associated with stages of wall segment construction.

Because the contacts between all the soil layers exposed in all the wall segments were generally very sharp and distinct, we believe that very little time elapsed between depositions of the different materials. To test the validity of this observation, we collected soil samples from each of the trenches for micromorphological study, the analysis of thin sections of intact sediment columns. Microscopic analysis of the sediment grains may provide evidence of how they were deposited and whether they exhibit evidence of weathering or other alteration after deposition. Thus far, analysis of sediments from Trench 1 indicates no evidence of weathering or soil formation at the contact between the soil materials used to build the wall (Mandel et al. 2003). This means that the construction of the wall segment must have occurred in a few years or less.

One of our goals has been to determine when the walls of the rectangular enclosure were built. Although the micromorphological study of the soils used to build the wall segments indicates rapid construction of each segment, we are unable to determine from the soils alone whether the wall segments were built about the same time or sequentially, over a number of years. Fortunately, the people who built the wall segments seem to have conducted rituals that included burning wood and other materials in association with the various stages of wall construction. Wood charcoal collected from these feature was used for radiocarbon dating. Four radiocarbon dates from features in Trenches 1, 2, and 3, plus two other radiocarbon dates, were obtained from features in a 1996 trench (Ruby 1997). Although radiocarbon dating can at best produce results that can be confidently assigned to a century, our results suggest these wall segments were likely built between 1800 BP and 1700 BP (AD 150 and 250).

As already discussed, we noted that the construction of the wall segment exposed by Trench 4 was significantly different from the other trenches at the rectangular enclosure (Lynott 2004). Features associated with construction of this wall segment produced two radiocarbon dates, and both are at least 800 years more recent than the dates obtained from the other trenches. Since one of the samples was taken from a feature at the very base of the wall segment, it isn't likely that the younger dates represent intrusive episodes that postdate actual construction of the wall segment. When these later dates are considered in association with the unusual construction methods recorded in Trench 4, it seems likely that this wall segment either was built many centuries after the other wall segments or, more likely, was modified or repaired at this later time.

WHAT DOES IT ALL MEAN?

You may be wondering why this detailed description of the layering and construction history of the Hopeton earthwork segments is important. Systematic recording and study of the great Hopewell earthworks of southern Ohio began in the mid-nineteenth century. Efforts to understand when and how the giant earthen walls that formed these enclosures were built have been ongoing for more than 150 years. Archaeologists have excavated single trenches across earthen walls at several large earthworks and extrapolated the data obtained to the entire site. However, the work on the rectangular enclosure at Hopeton demonstrates that variation in wall construction methods, and even in the age of wall construction, may be significant within individual earthworks. This is a new and significant finding.

Understanding the methods and materials used to build these walls also is important, because the amount of time and energy invested in construction is a reflection of the values and social organization of the people who built the enclosure. Study of the materials used to construct the walls at Hopeton indicates that all the soil and gravel selected for this purpose was available on the landform where the site is located, or in the adjacent streambed. The massive amounts of soil used to build the walls were being

quarried with hand tools and carried in baskets, and it is apparent that vast amounts of soil were being moved all across the site. This substantial earthmoving resulted in the creation of a cultural landscape that reflected the worldview of the people who built it.

Rather than simply scooping up soil and piling it into an earthen wall, people built the wall segments at Hopeton with carefully selected soils. The entire process began by removing all topsoil from the area in which a wall segment was to be built. The action of exposing the yellow or red subsoil certainly provided a very stable foundation for the wall segment, but it also probably was related to the Hopewell people's efforts to manage the spirit world. In the wall segments that have been examined on the south and west sides of the Hopeton rectangular enclosure, the wall builders always placed red or reddish-brown soil on the side of the wall that would be viewed from the outside of the enclosure. Yellow soils were always placed on the side of the wall that would be viewed from the inside of the shelter. The contacts between the different soils used to build these wall segments are sharp and clear, and it is obvious that both the selection of soil and its placement in the wall were carefully engineered. These wall segments were all built about 1750 BP (AD 200).

The curving wall segment that forms the northeast corner of this enclosure is quite different. In this area, the topsoil was removed to expose red subsoil. This wall segment is constructed primarily of red sandy-loam and two different shades of gray loam. There are large homogeneous deposits of these materials, but the contacts between the different soil materials are frequently marked by mixing of the types, with basket-loading sometimes apparent. In this instance, the red soil was placed to be visible from the inside of the rectangular enclosure, and the gray loam would have been visible from the outside. Of course, as time went by, and soil formed on the earthen walls, the wall colors would have become less noticeable. The variation we have noted in the color placement and construction methods between these wall segments may be related to some intended differences in function. However, the radiocarbon dates from the curved wall segment suggest that this wall segment was constructed about 800 years after completion of the other wall segments. This discovery is very important and makes us want to know whether earthen wall construction, or at least repair or modification of earthen walls, continued into the Late Woodland period at other large geometric enclosure sites in southern Ohio.

As archaeologists and geophysicists continue to study the relationship between geophysical data and the archaeological record, it is apparent that these data will provide a more accurate depiction of the original placement and size of the wall segments than can be obtained from either current topographic maps or even the historic maps of nineteenth-century archaeologists. Recent interpretations suggest that gateways at Hopeton and other Hopewell enclosures were specifically situated to view solar and lunar events. Evaluation of these hypotheses can be accurately conducted through large-scale geophysical mapping of these sites. Geophysical survey also provides an efficient and effective way to develop a holistic view of the archaeological record of these giant earthen monuments. This can be a particularly effective way to view large sites, especially when done in concert with systematic surface collections and strategic testing efforts.

The timing of the introduction of these new technologies to the study of Ohio Hopewell is critical. Earthworks and mounds were once plentiful across all of southern Ohio. Urban growth, agriculture, and other development activities have damaged or destroyed nearly every single earthen monument in this region. The forces that are impacting the archaeological record continue to escalate as population grows, cities expand, and agriculture continues.

A number of important sites have been purchased and preserved. Unfortunately, now that methods and technologies that permit effective study of these large sites are becoming available, the vast majority of large Ohio Hopewell sites are being erased from the cultural landscape. Increased efforts to preserve sites for future study are certainly needed, but more large-scale archaeological studies of these great places are also needed before the resources are lost forever.

DISCUSSION QUESTIONS

1. What sequence of construction seems to be typical at the Hopeton earthworks? How does the earthwork section exposed in Trench 4 differ? Why might this be?

2. Compare the geophysical investigations with those conducted at the Double Ditch Village site described in Chapter 10's case study. What arguments would you make for the incorporation of these techniques in archaeological projects in general?

3. What alternative explanations can you think of for the disparate dates obtained by this project? How would you test these alternatives?

4. Explain why the accelerating pace of mound and earthwork destruction is such a concern. Structure your explanation as if you were addressing the general public rather than the archaeological community.

CHAPTER 13

Fishing, Foraging, and Farming in the Northeast and Mid-Atlantic

St. Patrick's Day, 1936, was a bad day for western Pennsylvania. On this day, spring meltwater, ice jams, and heavy rain combined to cause serious flooding in Pittsburgh, Johnstown, and many other towns. Seventy people lost their lives, and property damage was estimated to be in the hundreds of millions of dollars. Not surprisingly, in the aftermath of the flooding there were calls for more effective flood control measures. In response, the U.S. Army Corps of Engineers began an ambitious construction program along the rivers and streams that form the headwaters of the Ohio River above Pittsburgh. This construction transformed the landscape and, in some cases, the lives of people upriver.

In Smicksburg, a small agricultural center some 65 miles (105 km) northeast of Pittsburgh, the Corps took possession of about two-thirds of the town because it was in the floodplain of the Little Mahoning Creek. With just under 400 residents, Smicksburg was a small unimportant place. The town itself had been laid out in 1827, and over the years it had provided most of the services that the farmers of the area needed—a blacksmith, a wagon maker, a doctor, a dairy (Spence 1996). It even had its very own important son, Joseph McCormick, who invented an early turbine engine. For the people who lived there, Smicksburg was home and having to move because their property was becoming part of Mahoning Creek Lake was difficult, no matter what the settlement with the government. Longtime residents say that some folks never got over it. In any case, over several years people made property settlements and moved uphill or away. The graves in the cemetery down by the creek were dug up and moved to the top of the hill; the houses were dismantled.

Other towns with more services became more important to people living in the area. In the 1960s and 1970s many of the small farms around Smicksburg were bought by Amish people. This settlement gave the area a picturesque character. The Amish began to sell quilts and other crafts. A weaving school and a pottery were established in Smicksburg, while a cheese factory and a winery were set up just outside the town. By the 1990s Smicksburg had become a destination for an afternoon outing in the country, and a stop on local tourist bureau bus tours.

It was in this context that a few longtime residents and the pastor of the Lutheran church began to think about **heritage tourism**. From the pastor's perspective, the townspeople needed a boost in spirit. From others' perspective, maybe the town could use its heritage to economic advantage. Like so many small communities across the country, Smicksburg had a story to tell. Not only that, but it had a virtual ghost town in its abandoned section, which far from being underwater most of the year was a pretty and interesting place to take a walk. Only occasionally would Mahoning Creek Lake be backed up far enough to flood Old Smicksburg. The streets, even those paved with brick, were still intact, as were the foundations of the houses and businesses. Thus, the Smicksburg Heritage Association was born with the goal of creating a museum, a park, and a walking tour of Old Smicksburg with signage about the community's history.

Those involved had enthusiasm and some knowledge of the workings of historic preservation in Pennsylvania, but certainly very little money. The major hitch in this idea was that Smicksburg's ghost town now belonged to the U.S. Army Corps of Engineers. While a lease agreement with the Corps might be possible, because this was federal land, such a lease required a heritage plan and careful assessment of the cultural resources that might be impacted. To those dreaming of what might be, these requirements were a little daunting. This was where experts in planning, historic preservation, and archaeology from the Indiana County Planning Commission and Indiana University of Pennsylvania (IUP) came in. Over the next few years, the Smicksburg Heritage Association was able to make its goals realities because these experts donated their services. IUP even conducted parts of three archaeological field schools in Smicksburg. While explaining their work to tourists who wandered by, student archaeologists mapped structure foundations and features and conducted test excavations in advance of a picnic shelter and parking lot. Students taking a class in museum methods also prepared small exhibits about Smicksburg archaeology. Archaeological work revealed the presence of older structures that had been abandoned or burned down long before condemnation of the property in the 1940s, and this information added to the town's story in several ways.

Today if you take an afternoon trip to Smicksburg, you can visit craft shops, eat some very good food, visit the museum, and walk through Old Smicksburg. In the fall there is a festival during which interpreters dressed in period costume will take you on a hayride, telling historical ghost stories. Smicksburg isn't much larger in population than it was before 1990, but it clearly is more prosperous.

Although there are many other places in the Northeast and Mid-Atlantic with more historical and archaeological significance, Smicksburg's story illustrates how many archaeologists today become involved with local communities. As small farms have failed and as industry has moved elsewhere, heritage tourism has begun to be one viable means of economic survival in the Northeast and Mid-Atlantic. Americans are interested in the past, and their pursuit of history can be profitable for communities with cultural resources. Archaeology has an important role to play in documenting specific resources and also in enriching understanding of the past. Today being ready to work with local people, historians, and planners in places like Smicksburg is part of being an archaeologist.

DEFINITION OF THE AREA

Smicksburg is just one small town in an area rich in both prehistory and history—the Northeast. As indicated in Chapter 12, the Northeast culture area as usually defined includes the entire area from the southern border of the boreal forest in Canada south to the Ohio River and its tributaries in Kentucky and West Virginia, and from the western edge of the Eastern Woodlands to the Atlantic coast. Along the coast, this culture area is considered to extend south into North Carolina, the Historic home of a number of Iroquoian and Algonquian language speakers. In this chapter we treat the parts of the Northeast culture area not covered in Chapter 12: the Atlantic coast from the Canadian Maritime Provinces south to North Carolina and inland New England, New York, and Pennsylvania, including the Upper Ohio watershed, the Lake Ontario Basin, and portions of the eastern Lake Erie Basin, southern Quebec, and Ontario (Figure 13.1). We call these subareas the Northeast and the Mid-Atlantic. Not only do some similarities exist between these areas and the Midwest and Great Lakes regions covered in the last chapter, but you will notice likenesses between the Mid-Atlantic and the Southeast, as well as the Northeast and the Subarctic. The cultural developments of the Northeast and Mid-Atlantic can be placed in the chronological framework shown in Table 13.1; note that a Mississippian period is absent from the Northeast and Mid-Atlantic, just as it was in the Upper Great Lakes.

THE ENVIRONMENTS OF THE NORTHEAST AND THE MID-ATLANTIC

Today the Northeast and the Mid-Atlantic have a moist climate during all seasons, but the summers are either hot or warm and the winters are cold. In the extreme southern part of the Mid-Atlantic the summers are hot and long and the winter is fairly mild.

Physiographically, the dominant feature in these areas is the Appalachian Mountain system that runs from the southwestern edge of the Northeast in a northeasterly direction, ending in eastern Canada. The mountain system includes a variety of distinct physiographic provinces, among which are the Ridge and Valley province encompassing the deeply folded Appalachian mountains, the Appalachian Plateau province with both glaciated and unglaciated sections, the Adirondack province of northern New York State, and the Piedmont province. The Piedmont is an eroded **peneplain** on the eastern margins of the Appalachian Mountains, extending from the northeast into the western Mid-Atlantic. North and west of this mountain system are the St. Lawrence and Great Lakes lowlands and southern portions of the Canadian Shield. The New England physiographic province also can be subdivided into a mountain section, the Connecticut Valley lowland, and the New England coastal shore itself. Further south, there is the wide Mid-Atlantic Coastal Plain (Fenneman 1938).

Like most of the areas discussed in the last two chapters, the Northeast and the Mid-Atlantic are forested regions. Two of the biomes introduced in Chapter 2, the boreal coniferous forest biome and the temperate deciduous forest biome, have been represented in the Northeast and the Mid-Atlantic through much of the Holocene. As is true further west, there is a broad ecotone of mixed coniferous

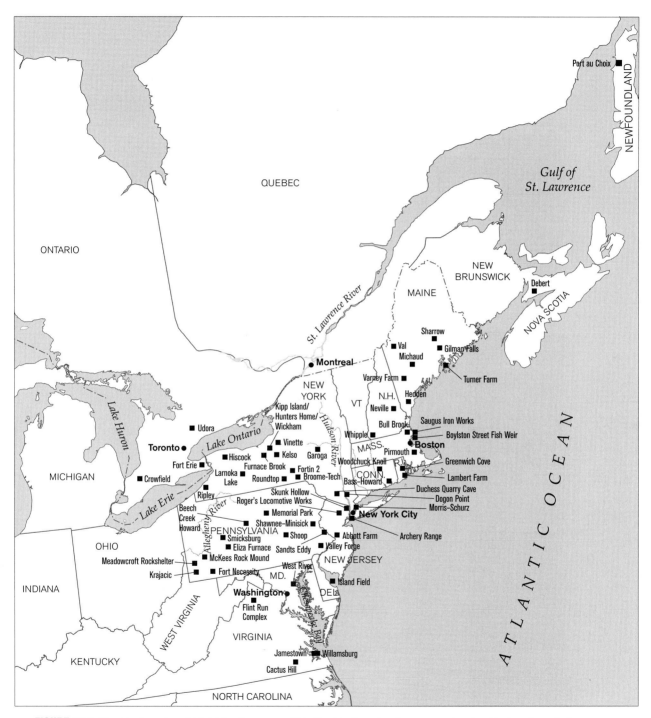

FIGURE 13.1 The Northeast and Mid-Atlantic areas within the Northeast culture area, showing the location of sites mentioned in Chapter 13.

TABLE 13.1 Introduction to Northeast and Mid-Atlantic Culture History

Uncalibrated Years BP	General Periods	Mid-Atlantic and Northeastern Cultural Phenomena South → North	Calibrated Years
	Historic		AD 1650
500		Northern Iroquoians	AD 1430
	Late Woodland	Monongahela	
1,000		Clemson Island	AD 1020
1,500	Middle Woodland	Abbott Farm Squawkie Hill	AD 600
2,000		Middlesex Meadowood	AD 10
2,500	Early Woodland	complex complex	660 BC
3,000	Terminal Archaic	Susquehanna tradition	1,240 BC
3,500			1,820 BC
4,000			2,490 BC
4,500	Late Archaic	Lake Forest Archaic	3,200 BC
5,000		Mast Forest Maritime Archaic Archaic	3,780 BC
5,500			4,340 BC
6,000			4,880 BC
6,500	Middle Archaic		5,440 BC
7,000			5,840 BC
7,500		Gulf of Maine Archaic	6,320 BC
8,000			6,910 BC
8,500			7,550 BC
9,000	Early Archaic		8,030 BC
9,500		Varney Farm	8,560 BC
10,000		Dalton/Hardaway	9,210 BC
10,500	Paleoindian		10,470 BC
11,000			10,970 BC
11,500 and prior	Pre-Clovis?	????????????	11,470 BC and prior

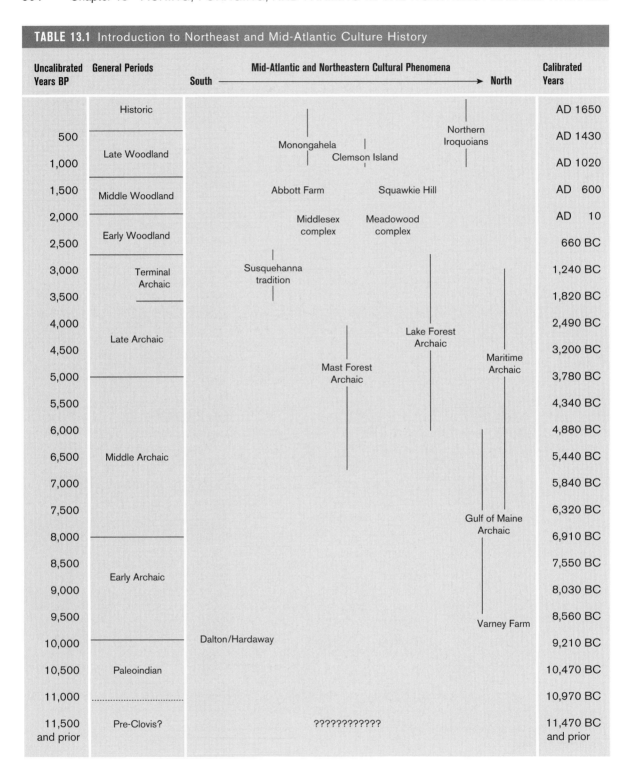

and deciduous forest between these biomes that often is called the transition forest. These biomes can be subdivided into a wide variety of habitats and communities. Truly boreal forest types that are dominated by spruce and fir are confined to portions of Quebec and the Maritime Provinces. Deciduous oak hickory forest is important in southern New England and portions of Pennsylvania and the Mid-Atlantic states. In the Great Lakes lowlands an elm–ash–cottonwood forest type also is found, while sugar maple and beech mix with oak and hickory in southern Ontario. However, transition forest types are particularly common in the Northeast, with various proportions of maple, beech, and birch mixed with hemlock, pine, and spruce dominating the forests. In the Mid-Atlantic, mixed forests dominated by pine occur along the coast and in some inland areas (Gaudreau 1988).

Climatic Change

The history of environmental change in the Northeast and Mid-Atlantic is of considerable archaeological interest, especially the record of glacial retreat after about 16,000 years ago. The Laurentian glacier had several lobes that variously retreated across the landscape, following the existing topography (Mickelson et al. 1983). This complex history is partially preserved in the surface deposits and landforms of the Northeast. During the greatest extent of the glaciers in the Late Wisconsin (Figure 2.12), the southern margin of the ice sheet in New York and Pennsylvania was uneven. Familiar features such as the Chesapeake and Delaware bays, Long Island, and Cape Cod either were not present or were buried under ice, while unfamiliar landforms such as the exposed Georges and Browns banks in the vicinity of the Gulf of Maine defined the coastline. Rivers like the Hudson, the Susquehanna, and the Delaware were much longer, extending out across a much broader coastal plain as well.

The northward retreat of the Laurentian glacier out of the Northeast took several millennia. By 12,000 to 11,500 years ago, the ice front had retreated further, to a position cutting across southern Ontario and Quebec north of the St. Lawrence lowlands, while the ice caps of the Maritimes receded into areas of higher ground. At approximately 10,000 years ago the glaciers had shrunk out of the Northeast altogether.

Sea-level changes, isostatic rebound of the earth's crust as it was freed of the weight of glaciers, the drainage of glacial meltwaters, and the colonization of exposed land areas by plant and animal species also made the millennia of glacial retreat a period of extreme environmental change in both the Northeast and Mid-Atlantic. The Chesapeake Bay, a large **estuary** in the coastal plain where the mouth of the Susquehanna has been drowned as the river flows into the Atlantic, provides one example of these complex interactions. A series of Chesapeake Bays existed during the glacial advances of the Wisconsin and disappeared during interglacials as the level of the ocean varied, and this estuary did not reach its full extent until about 3000 years ago (Dent 1995). Another area in which there were complex interactions between postglacial sea-level rise and isostatic rebound is the area of the Gulf of Maine, once buried by the Laurentian ice sheet. As the ice sheet shrank, the ocean covered the depressed land that had been beneath the glacier, drowning what we know as the coast of Maine. Then the land began to rapidly rebound and the ocean receded, but it was not until the outer banks off the New England coast were submerged some time after 7000 BP that the modern intertidal ecosystems supporting shellfish began to be established (Kellogg 1988).

In the interior, the processes of glacial retreat and isostatic rebound proceeded sequentially inland so that the coastal areas rose before interior areas more recently covered with ice. At the same time, the runoff from melting glaciers flowed in huge amounts into river drainage channels. The meltwaters from the glacial lobes retreating northward were unable to drain into the ocean, either because of coastal rebound or because of moraines left as the glacier paused in its retreat, and the result was the formation of long linear lakes.

Lake Erie, Lake Ontario, and the St. Lawrence River valley also have a fascinating history of Pleistocene and Holocene changes. Both Lake Erie and Lake Ontario were preceded by several lakes as the ice front retreated even further north. In addition, the upper part of the St. Lawrence Valley was depressed by more than 655 feet (200 m) below its modern elevation after 12,800 BP. Sea level was rising at this time, and the result was the invasion of the St. Lawrence lowlands by the waters of the Atlantic, creating an inland sea called the **Champlain Sea** (Figure 13.2), which did not disappear until approximately 10,000 BP (Kirkland and Coates 1977).

Paleoecological reconstruction of biotic variables associated with these changes in glacial extent, landforms, and drainage obviously is a difficult but relevant task for archaeologists and other scholars. Although locally variable, biotic colonization of land exposed by the retreating glacier occurred in a reasonably steady manner. At the glacial maximum, only a narrow band of tundra was present south of the ice sheet. South of this band an open parkland existed in some areas, and boreal forests intermixed with patches of transitional and deciduous forest were found elsewhere. Initially forest may have existed mostly in the river valleys. During the Holocene, oak gradually came to dominate the forest in the south, while a transition forest with birch, maple, beech, and hemlock as dominants developed between the boreal and deciduous forests. Pine remained an important tree species along the coast, however. Quite detailed mapping of the changing vegetational patterns has been attempted (Bernabo and Webb 1977;

FIGURE 13.2 One of the many features of the glacial retreat in the Northeast was the Champlain Sea, which formed in the depressed St. Lawrence lowlands and persisted until approximately 10,000 BP.

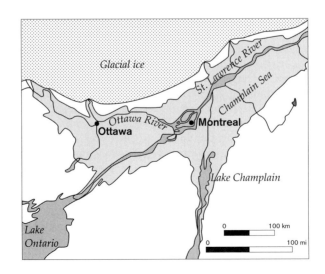

Gaudreau 1988), although the most meaningful reconstructions probably are on a local scale.

Three other climatic periods have been of most interest to archaeologists working in the Northeast and the Mid-Atlantic. The first period is the Hypsithermal, the mid-Holocene warming and drying period mentioned in many of this text's chapters. Most researchers believe that climate continued to warm during the early and mid-Holocene, reaching a peak in warmth and at first dryness in the East that began after 9000 BP and continued until 2500 BP. By 5000 BP, hemlock was declining in frequency within forests, while pine was becoming more dominant on the Mid-Atlantic coastal plain (Joyce 1988). There also is some evidence that the Medieval Warm period between approximately 1150 BP and 750 BP may have been significant because it expanded the land area suitable for farming. A third climatic episode that may have affected Northeastern peoples is the Little Ice Age (650–100 BP). This cooler period affected growing season length in ways that may have been significant to horticultural groups living in the Northeast. However, precisely how these periods might have affected humans can be debated.

HUNTERS AND FORAGERS OF THE DISTANT PAST

Paleoindians in the Northeast and Mid-Atlantic

Initial settlement of the Northeast and Mid-Atlantic may have occurred during Pre-Clovis times, perhaps as early as the seventeenth millennium BP. Two sites mentioned in Chapter 3, Meadowcroft Rockshelter in southwestern Pennsylvania and Cactus Hill along the Nottoway River in Virginia, have provided potential evidence of this initial human occupation. Based on its lithic assemblage, the Krajacic site, in the Cross Creek drainage near Meadowcroft, may be a contemporaneous Pre-Clovis site. The principal archaeological evidence from these sites consists of stone tools (e.g., unfluted bifaces, small blades, cores) and lithic debitage. Deer, smaller game, hickory nuts, walnuts, and hackberries may have been used by the foragers living at Meadowcroft Rockshelter. Carr and Adovasio (2002b) suggest these first settlers were generalized foragers rather than hunters focused on large game.

The amount and quality of archaeological data for Paleoindians in the Northeast and Mid-Atlantic improves significantly after 12,000 to 11,000 years ago, just as it does in most areas of the continent. Surface finds of fluted projectile points and data from site excavations have contributed to archaeological understanding of Paleoindians in these areas.

A number of excavations of sites with fluted points have provided archaeological information and radiocarbon dates. Radiocarbon dates from the Debert site suggest that Paleoindians were using areas as far north as Nova Scotia more than 10,500 years BP, with the dates from the Vail site in Maine, the Shawnee–Minisink site in Pennsylvania's Delaware valley being comparable or a little older. As more radiocarbon dates have been obtained from the region, the eleventh millennium BP has been established as the time frame for settlement by fluted point makers. In the southern part of this area, Paleoindian settlement may have been earlier—even Pre-Clovis in timing. Nevertheless, the fluted point levels at Cactus Hill have yielded a date of 10,920 ±250 BP (McAvoy and McAvoy 1997),

FIGURE 13.3 The Debert point, an example of early fluted point forms in the Northeast; note deeply indented base.

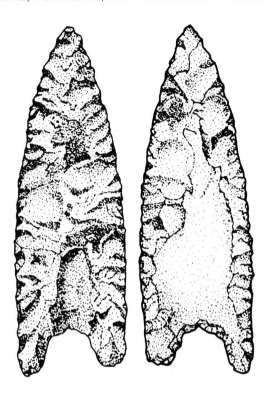

which is consistent with the time frame indicated at the Debert site. Interpreting the Paleoindian radiocarbon dates is a complex and important matter (e.g., Levine 1990), but beyond the scope of this text.

Of course the best-known attribute of Northeastern and Middle Atlantic Paleoindians is the fluted point itself. Points like those from the Bull Brook site in Ipswich, Massachusetts, and those from the Debert site near Debert, Nova Scotia (Figure 13.3), are commonly cited as indicative of Northeastern Paleoindians. These points typically have deeply concave bases. They are large and parallel sided like classic Clovis points and can be considered Clovis variants. However, many fluted points from the Northeast and Middle Atlantic have other size and shape characteristics. Archaeologists understand this variation largely in terms of temporal change, just as they do in other parts of the Eastern Woodlands. There may be some difference in forms from north to south and from east to west as well (Gardner and Verrey 1979; Ellis and Deller 1997; Spiess et al. 1998). The earliest fluted forms tend to be large and thick with relatively short flutes and often with deeply concave bases. Over time, fluted points become thinner, while the fluting first lengthens and then disappears in favor of basal thinning. The width of the point may also narrow, and distinct basal ears may be present. Resharpening of points also can produce pentagonal forms. Both actual radiocarbon dates and geoarchaeological information have been used to estimate fluted point sequence dating. Most of these changes seem to have taken place between 11,000 BP and about 10,000 BP. Very Late Paleoindian unfluted forms, such as those from the Varney Farm site in Maine (Petersen et al. 2002), are younger still, dating to approximately 9400 BP (Figure 13.4). These northern unfluted forms

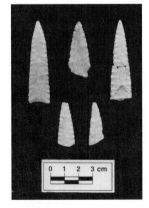

FIGURE 13.4 Late Paleoindian projectile points from the Varney Farm site in Maine.

are reminiscent of the Plano points on the Great Plains, while to the south Dalton and Hardaway points characterize the transition from Late Paleoindian to Early Archaic.

It is important to remember that projectile points are only one small part of the tools and other items Paleoindians must have made. Relatively few Paleoindian manufactures have been preserved in the temperate climate of the Northeast and Mid-Atlantic. However, Paleoindian chipped stone toolkits contain a number of other tools, including various bifaces, drills, end and side scrapers, gravers, flake shavers, and wedges. Each of these tool types can tell archaeologists about the makers, and tool type proportions in sites suggest various aspects of site usage. Bone artifacts also have been recovered from a few sites, including the Hiscock site in western New York State (Laub 2002). Here, in conjunction with Gainey-type fluted points, 13 bone and ivory tools were found. For example, a mastodon rib fragment had been shaped into a point at one end and perhaps used to scrape animal hide.

One other aspect of Paleoindian technology, the selective use of high-quality lithic materials such as flint, jasper, and chalcedony, has been mentioned in other chapters. Even though Paleoindians did use local as well as exotic stone, there was an obvious preference for high-quality stone and a consistent use of material that outcrops only many miles distant from the sites where it is now found. As we have discussed in other chapters, this attribute of lithic use generally underscores Paleoindian flintknapping knowledge and skill as well as the great importance of stone hunting implements in their survival. It also raises questions about how Paleoindians acquired stone for making tools—indirectly through exchanges between members of different Paleoindian bands or directly through band movement. Although these alternatives are difficult to distinguish archaeologically, many archaeologists have assumed direct acquisition and have used these data to explore group mobility and settlement strategies among Paleoindians (Curran 1999).

Questions also remain about Paleoindian subsistence, another topic of continental significance. Finds of extinct faunal species in direct association with Paleoindian artifacts are not known from the Northeast and Mid-Atlantic. However, several cases of more indirect association can be cited (e.g., Laub et al. 1988). Worked mastodon remains, such as the rib fragment from the Hiscock site just mentioned, could have resulted from bone scavenging of long-dead mastodons as well as from direct predation.

In New England, the Maritime Provinces, and southern Ontario, use of caribou is better documented, although faunal assemblages are largely confined to calcined fragments of bone. Caribou bones have been recovered from the Whipple site in New Hampshire, the Bull Brook site in Massachusetts, the Michaud site in Maine, the Udora site in Ontario, and elsewhere. Split caribou bone has also been found at the Dutchess Quarry Cave in New York State (Funk et al. 1970). Arctic fox, beaver, and hare also have been found in faunal assemblages from Northeastern Paleoindian sites. Floral remains are almost nonexistent, though a charred berry seed was recovered from the Michaud site and blackberry, grape, wild sarsaparilla, and bunchberry seeds have been identified at the Hedden site (Spiess et al. 1998).

These data may support the northern pattern suggested in Meltzer's model (see Table 11.2). Here subsistence possibly was centered on caribou hunting and collection of other small mammals, with some use of berries and other plants in season. However, the subsistence data are very scant. The positioning of sites like the Vail site in western Maine, at a valley that narrows through which caribou herds presumably would have migrated, also reinforces archaeologists' ideas that Northeastern Paleoindians were caribou hunters. A possible Paleoindian preference for the shores of proglacial lakes has been interpreted as evidence for following migrating waterfowl northward as well (Dincauze and Jacobson 2001).

Further south, the stratified Shawnee–Minisink site in the Delaware valley provides a picture of more generalized use of resources. Notably fish remains and carbonized seeds including blackberry, hawthorn plum, hackberry, wild grape, and chenopodium have been recovered from a hearth feature. These data, though based on only a small number of identifications, are usually considered to support arguments for a more generalized foraging economy among Mid-Atlantic and southern Paleoindians (e.g., Meltzer and Smith 1986).

Archaeologists have proposed a number of other models for Paleoindian subsistence and settlement strategies. William M. Gardner's (1977, 1983) site types and settlement models based on the Flint Run complex in Virginia have received a great deal of attention in the Mid-Atlantic. His argument that movements and site locations were conditioned by the distribution of lithic raw materials has been particularly influential. Understanding the earliest Paleoindians in the Northeast as colonizers may also be fruitful. The lithic assemblages of large Northeastern Paleoindian sites like Bull Brook I, Debert, Shoop, and Vail have a predominance of exotic stone as well as the earliest types of fluted points. Dincauze (1993) suggests that these sites may represent discrete pioneering settlement events in the Northeast. The precision in dating that might help us sort out such diversity in site function has not been achieved, and this is one of the many aspects of Paleoindian lifestyles in the Northeast and Mid-Atlantic that remain elusive.

Finally, there are hints of the ritual practices for Paleoindians. For example, at the Crowfield site in southwestern Ontario a Paleoindian feature contained many burned or heat-fractured stone tools. This feature has been interpreted as a cremation, although preservation was so poor that no human bone was recovered. These artifacts do not appear to have been specially made for burial, but instead they may approximate the typical Paleoindian toolkit (Deller and Ellis 1984).

What Happened in the Early and Middle Archaic?

The Eastern Archaic was originally defined as a preceramic stage on the basis of materials from the Lamoka Lake site in New York State (Ritchie 1932). Thus, the Archaic Stage has long been an important concept in the Northeast. Nevertheless, today most archaeologists here as in other parts of the Eastern Woodlands treat the Archaic as a period of time rather than a stage. The first 5000 years of the Archaic typically are subdivided into the Early Archaic, from 10,000 BP to 8000 BP, and the Middle Archaic, from 8000 BP to 5000 BP. The treatment of the end of the Archaic by Northeastern and Mid-Atlantic archaeologists is distinctive enough from that of archaeologists working elsewhere in the Eastern Woodlands to warrant its own subsection in this chapter. First, we discuss the Early and Middle Archaic.

Changes in lithic technology occur at the juncture between the Paleoindian period and the Archaic period in the Northeast and Mid-Atlantic just as they do in other parts of the Eastern Woodlands. The appearance of notched points, and later stemmed points, may be the most obvious diagnostic marker, but differences in raw material usage and manufacture as listed in Table 11.3 for the Southeast also can be recognized. However, some archaeologists understand the Early Archaic as merely an extension of the Late Paleoindian period. They argue that Early Archaic foragers were not using the landscape and its resources in ways profoundly different from those of the generalized foragers of the Paleoindian period; thus it makes little sense to designate a new cultural period. The timing of the Hypsithermal interval is sometimes invoked as an explanation for the onset of new adaptive strategies in the Middle Archaic. For example, Dincauze (1990) labels both Paleoindian and Early Archaic people Pioneers, making a distinction between them and more populous and aggregated Settler groups beginning about 8000 BP in what we call the Middle Archaic.

The chronology of Archaic projectile point forms used in the areas covered in this chapter is mostly based upon sequences established in stratified sites in the Southeast and Midwest (see Figures 11.5 and 12.3). Side- and corner-notched projectile points, including varieties of the Hardaway, Palmer, and Kirk points, are considered diagnostic of the beginning of the Early Archaic during the tenth millennium BP. The end of this period is recognized by the presence of bifurcate points such as the LeCroy, St. Albans, and Kanawha points, which appear between 9000 BP and 8000 BP, here as well as further west. Archaeologists who do not distinguish the Early Archaic from the Paleoindian often consider bifurcates as the marker for the beginning of the Middle Archaic (e.g., Custer 1990), but they do not dispute the order of appearance. Elsewhere the Middle Archaic is indicated by various stemmed point forms that follow the bifurcate forms. Middle Archaic varieties like Stanly and Morrow Mountain are found, but in New England similar points called Neville, Stark, and Merrimack, after points found at the Neville site in New Hampshire, are recognized (Figure 13.5) (Dincauze 1976). Note the similarities between these points and Southeastern types.

Based on projectile point sequences, sites from the Early and Middle Archaic altogether are relatively scarce in these regions. In fact, "Where are the Early and Middle Archaic sites?" has been one of the classic conundrums of Northeastern archaeology. The Paleoindian presence throughout the Northeast is clear. Does the small number of Early and Middle Archaic sites mean that the Northeast was depopulated as tundra and spruce parkland habitats retreated northward during the Holocene? Archaeologists no longer think so.

In the first place, a number of Early and Middle Archaic sites now have been found, and the high volume of CRM archaeology is producing additional sites at a constant rate. For example, at Sandts Eddy, a site in the Delaware Valley, deposits spanning the Early and Middle Archaic from 9420 ±90 BP to 7080 ±70 BP have been excavated (Bergman et al. 1998). In the second place, dramatic changes in sea level, riverine drainage regimes, and landforms have meant that many early Holocene landforms have been drowned, deeply buried, or destroyed. This certainly could explain the relative lack of Early and Middle Archaic sites on the surface. Of course, sites from the Paleoindian period have been similarly affected, but differing land-use patterns in the various periods may have led to the comparatively higher frequency of Paleoindian surface finds throughout the region. Finally, the density of Early and Middle Archaic sites may appear to be low simply because highly diagnostic artifacts are rarer than during Paleoindian times and assemblages harder to identify with respect to period.

FIGURE 13.5 Stemmed points are diagnostic of the Middle Archaic in New England.

In Maine and the Maritime Provinces, as the number of radiocarbon-dated contexts older than 5000 BP has grown, archaeologists have rejected the idea that human populations were small during these periods. A **Gulf of Maine Archaic tradition** (9500–6000 BP) characterized by the use of metamorphic rock in the creation of rods, gouges, and other ground and chipped stone artifacts has now been recognized. For example, the Gilman Falls site (Sanger 1996), a quarry site on the Stillwater River north of Orono, Maine, has a Middle Archaic zone dated to 7300 BP to 6300 BP. In this zone minimally flaked pieces of phyllite, a low-grade metamorphic rock, are common, while stemmed bifaces like the Neville and Stark points of southern New England are absent. Other tools include ground stone gouges that have full-length grooves, celts, unifacial quartz scrapers, battered cobbles, and especially rods of varying lengths.

Heavy use of ground stone technology, of course, is a diagnostic feature of the Archaic in general. This technology is evident in Early as well as Middle Archaic sites throughout the regions discussed in this chapter (Figure 13.6). Many tool forms such as adzes, celts, and gouges probably are associated with woodworking. Especially in the Early Archaic, these forms sometimes are flaked and then ground on the surface (e.g., Dent 1995, 170). Pestles and various abraders also are commonly found. Ground stone knives, plummets, and ground slate *ulus* or semilunar knives are found in sites in New England as well. Perhaps the classic Middle Archaic ground stone implement is the spear-thrower weight, or bannerstone (see Figure 11.6).

FIGURE 13.6 These ground stone implements recovered from the Beech Creek Howard site in the Bald Eagle Valley in central Pennsylvania are typical of the Archaic; the two items at the upper left are fragments of a bannerstone and a birdstone, both of which probably served as spear-thrower weights when complete.

Traditional ideas that the subsistence base was broader in Archaic than in Paleoindian times are as problematic in the Northeast and Mid-Atlantic as they are elsewhere. Unfortunately, the acidic soils of these eastern regions have obliterated much evidence concerning subsistence practices, although the scarcity of data is partially explained by the lack of routine flotation sampling. Archaeologists have continued to rely on functional analyses of tools, environmental data, and information from sites outside the region to infer how plants and animals were used. Despite the lack of systematic data, there is good reason to believe that Early and Middle Archaic people throughout this region used a variety of fruits and berries, nuts of several kinds, and many other species of plants for food, medicine, and various perishable artifacts (see Asch-Sidell 1999; Dent and Kauffman 1985). Faunal remains recovered from sites in the region indicate that Early and Middle Archaic foragers used many species of mammals, including white-tailed deer, raccoon, beaver, woodchuck, and cottontail rabbit, as well as birds such as the wild turkey and the now-extinct passenger pigeon. They also collected many species of fish and turtles (see Whyte 1990).

It is not clear when Archaic foragers began to exploit shellfish intensively. In the Northeast and Mid-Atlantic, riverine and coastal shellfishing may not have been important until the Late Archaic. In these areas a critical factor may have been the appearance of coastal estuaries, whose saline waters are important to populations of oysters and other shellfish. On the other hand, because sea levels had not stabilized until about 5000 years ago, early sites along the coast and in major river valleys may have been destroyed, with the result that we have an incomplete picture of the extent to which Early and Middle Archaic foragers utilized these areas. Sites like the Dogan Point site, a shell midden site in the lower Hudson River valley, indicate that at least some Middle Archaic foragers used shellfish as a resource (Claassen 1995). Here oyster shell has been dated to the sixth millennium BP (i.e., during the Middle Archaic). There are other indications that Middle Archaic peoples may have used marine and riverine resources heavily in some areas even when the landscape was quite different from what we know today (e.g., Dunford 1999). A related question of when and how pre-Columbian peoples began to exploit East Coast anadromous fish such as shad and alewife also is of interest (Carlson 1988). Many sites in the Northeast and Mid-Atlantic contain riverine, marine, and anadromous fish, while fish weirs such as the Boylston Street fish weir in Boston also have been discovered.

In addition, while there are hints of early cultigens during the Middle Archaic, elsewhere in the Eastern Woodlands lack of ethnobotanical data has limited understanding of agriculture's possible development in the Northeast and Mid-Atlantic. Two recent finds of gourd rind have raised the possibility that limited cultivation began in these areas at roughly the same time as it did further west. The first find was at the Sharrow site in central Maine (Peterson and Asch-Sidell 1996), where gourd rind was AMS-dated to 5695 ±100 BP. This gourd could not have been growing wild in Maine, but it may have been traded into the region or intentionally cultivated. Other gourd rind fragments have been found at the Memorial Park site in north central Pennsylvania, where they were also dated to the sixth millennium BP (Hart and Asch-Sidell 1997).

Transitions in the Late Archaic

Archaeologists generally believe that major changes in human adaptation in the Northeast and Mid-Atlantic occurred at the end of the Archaic. Because sites attributed to the Late Archaic, between approximately 5000 BP and 2700 BP, also are much more common than earlier sites, more attention traditionally has been paid to this subperiod than to earlier ones.

Four broad Middle–Late Archaic cultural traditions commonly have been recognized (Tuck 1978). In the Maritime Provinces, Maine, and Labrador, the Maritime Archaic, mentioned in Chapter 4, was apparently focused on the ocean and its resources (Figure 13.7). Originally largely defined on the basis of a cemetery at the Port au Choix site in Newfoundland (Tuck 1971, many of the sites of this tradition have been burial sites. The Lake Forest Archaic, first appearing late in the Middle Archaic and continuing through the Late Archaic, is found throughout the northern parts of the areas considered in this chapter as well as in the Upper Great Lakes and the northern Midwest. The term "Lake Forest" has been applied based on the idea that this tradition represents an adaptation to the transitional forests of the Eastern Woodlands. The Narrow Point/**Mast Forest Archaic** has been recognized from coastal New England southward through the Mid-Atlantic and into the Southeast, as well as across the Hudson and Delaware valleys into western New York and Pennsylvania and possibly beyond. This is the Late Archaic manifestation of Dincauze's proposed Atlantic Slope Macro tradition. It has been proposed that this tradition represents an adaptation to the deciduous forests dominated by oak, chestnut, hickory, and beech (nut- or mast-producing forests) that characterize the coast and the piedmont (Snow 1980).

The Lamoka Lake site, mentioned earlier as the type site for Ritchie's Archaic stage (Ritchie 1932), is an example of a Mast Forest Archaic site located in western New York State. The people who inhabited this large site apparently hunted,

FIGURE 13.7 Martime Archaic chipped and ground stone artifacts.

fished, and gathered for food and other resources. They produced large quantities of bone tools, net sinkers, projectile points, woodworking tools, and other implements, and they constructed rectangular houses that were rebuilt often during the site's long period of habitation. They buried their dead in the village rather than in a special cemetery, and the remains of at least two individuals who had been intentionally mutilated (decapitated; hands amputated) were found in the refuse (Ritchie 1980).

Finally, at the end of the Late Archaic, many areas show evidence of the Broadpoint tradition known in the Mid-Atlantic as the **Susquehanna tradition**, after the Susquehanna broadpoint. Because the Susquehanna tradition originally was conceptualized as transitional between the Archaic and Woodland stages, a separate period called the **Transitional** or the **Terminal Archaic** may be recognized. Following Snow (1980), the Terminal Archaic can be dated between about 3700 BP and 2700 BP. However, a separate period seldom is designated on the western edges of the Northeast and the Mid-Atlantic. Still other researchers working in the Mid-Atlantic (e.g., Custer 1984, 76) have argued that it makes most sense to group the Terminal Archaic with the beginning of the Woodland period. For southern New England, Dincauze (1990) believes Terminal Archaic, Early Woodland, and Middle Woodland people would be better placed under the common heading of Late Settlers.

FIGURE 13.8 Variability in characteristic projectile point forms between the Mast Forest tradition, Lake Forest tradition, and the Terminal Archaic in the Northeast and Mid-Atlantic.

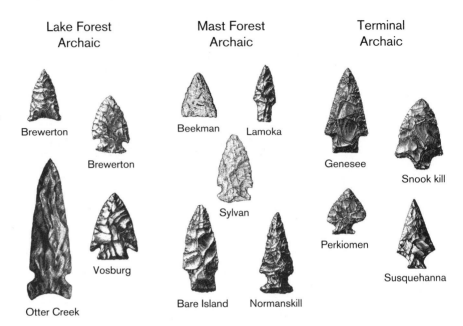

Lake Forest Archaic

Brewerton

Brewerton

Vosburg

Otter Creek

Mast Forest Archaic

Beekman

Lamoka

Sylvan

Bare Island

Normanskill

Terminal Archaic

Genesee

Snook kill

Perkiomen

Susquehanna

The variation in projectile point forms among the latter three traditions is suggested in Figure 13.8. Of course other tools were also used. The relationships between these traditions are poorly delineated, and it isn't clear that they correspond to different ancient ethnicities. One debate is over whether the Lake Forest tradition predates the Narrow Point/Mast Forest tradition or coexists with it. The archaeological record at some sites tends to support the idea of a temporal relationship, although elsewhere the distinction seems to be geographic, with Lake Forest having an interior orientation and Narrow Point/Mast Forest having a more coastal and southerly one.

Another point of discussion has to do with the relation of the three traditions just named to the **Moorehead burial complex**. This complex, which is reminiscent of the Late Archaic burial complexes mentioned in Chapter 12, is known from northern New England beginning about 8500 BP. Burials containing gouges, adzes, celts, rods, plummets, and ground slate points have often been found (Robinson 1996). The substantial amounts of red ocher in these burials led early researchers to call the people of this tradition the "Red Paint People." This complex has long been thought of as associated with the Maritime Archaic, though some researchers have argued that it is a distinct cultural phase that developed out of the Lake Forest Archaic. Using the sequence of occupations at the Turner Farm site in Maine, Bourque (1995) considers Moorehead to be distinct from these traditions, exhibiting trading ties both to Maritime Archaic groups to the north and to people associated with Narrow Point/Mast Forest tradition in southern New England.

Archaeological debate concerning the appearance of the Broadpoint tradition has centered on whether the appearance of broad points and associated elements of this tradition represent an actual migration of people into the Mid-Atlantic and Northeast from the Southeast (Cook 1976b; Turnbaugh 1975). The alternative

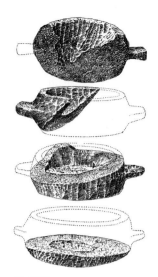

FIGURE 13.9 Steatite vessel fragments; note lug handles.

viewpoint is that the appearance of new artifacts represents diffusions of new technology and subsistence practices.

One fascinating aspect of the Terminal Archaic is the appearance in assemblages of steatite bowls and the first ceramics. Vessels made of steatite tend to be shallow, thick walled, and round to oblong, with lug handles (Figure 13.9). Both steatite and ceramic technologies were thought to have originated in the Southeast, with stone bowls preceding ceramic vessels. Recent evaluation, however, suggests that steatite and pottery vessels may have appeared together in the Mid-Atlantic, while in the Northeast the use of steatite may precede pottery by only a century (Sassaman 1999). Distribution patterns indicate that steatite was exchanged among Transitional groups. As mentioned in preceding chapters, this "container revolution" may be associated with growing emphasis on the processing of native seeds. However, the inclusion of steatite vessels in burial settings in southern New England around 2700 BP may indicate ritual or ethnic significance as well.

In the Mid-Atlantic, a variety of ceramic types made during the Terminal Archaic have been considered "experimental wares" under the assumption that people were experimenting with ceramic technology at this time. One example of this early pottery is the steatite-tempered variety called Marcey Creek ware, which occurs as far north as New Jersey. Vessels were made from clay slabs, and their flat-bottomed forms were similar to those of steatite bowls. In New York State and southern New England, the oldest pottery generally is the Vinette I type, which has been dated as early as 3200 BP. Vinette I pottery is grit tempered, made by coiling, cord marked inside and out, and characterized by conoidal bases (Figure 13.10).

Environmental factors such as the end of the Hypsithermal interval or the stabilization of the coastline may have been important stimulants for cultural experimentation during the Terminal Archaic, but this is not yet fully understood. Some archaeologists think that the greater use of coastal and riverine resources might have allowed a degree of sedentism as well as the beginnings of social complexity. For example, Dent (1995) has defined an "intensification era" from approximately 4200 to 3000 years ago in the Chesapeake Bay area. He suggests that at this time people exploited anadromous fish runs and various estuarine

FIGURE 13.10 Vinette I vessels from New England are examples of the early pottery made in the Northeast and Mid-Atlantic.

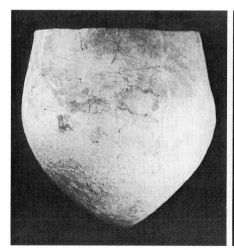
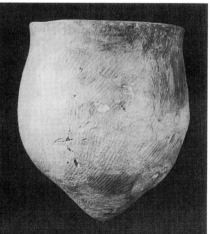

resources, including shellfish, exchanged lithic raw materials, and were more restricted in their settlement mobility. Less mobile lifestyles can be associated with a collector strategy as opposed to a foraging strategy (see also Binford 1980). Further north, intensive use of coastal resources became important as well. Ritchie's (1980) **Orient phase** on Long Island and in the lower Hudson River valley provides an example of intensive use of shellfish.

There also is evidence for use of the plants important in the Eastern Agricultural complex at a variety of Late Archaic sites in the Northeast and Mid-Atlantic. For example, Terminal Archaic components at the Bliss–Howard and Woodchuck Knoll sites in the Connecticut River valley indicate that chenopodium was a significant subsistence item and that it was stored by people living in semi-permanent villages, but it is not yet clear whether the plant had been domesticated (George and Dewar 1999). The Broome-Tech site in the Chenango River valley of southern New York State also produced a seed assemblage including plants like chenopodium, marsh elder, and false buckwheat that are part of the complex. Moreover, this seed assemblage and the wood charcoal composition, as well as high amounts of nutshell, suggest that there might have been intentional burning of the climax forest to promote both nut production and pioneer species with edible seeds (Asch-Sidell 2002). Such manipulation of the environment through fire has also been proposed for this period in the Mid-Atlantic (Stevens 1991). Only further study will establish whether the use of these plants involved the exploitation of wild stands or cultivation.

FARMING, FISHING, AND SEDENTISM IN THE EARLY AND MIDDLE WOODLAND

The Woodland, which is often called the Ceramic period in Maine and the Maritime Provinces, is the period in which the various developments of the Late and Terminal Archaic came to fruition. This doesn't mean that cultural sequences and events mirrored those of other parts of the Eastern Woodlands. In fact, neither the Early nor the Middle Woodland period included as much mound building or as much movement of high-status items through exchange as is evidenced in the other parts of the Eastern Woodlands. Although sedentary horticultural societies with at least some degree of ranking developed in some parts of these areas, this did not happen until the end of the Woodland Period after about 1000 BP. Regardless, the Early and Middle Woodland periods between about 2700 BP and 1300 BP are important to the story of the past in the Middle Atlantic and the Northeast.

The period between about 2700 BP and 1300 BP has been referred to as Woodland I (Custer 1984). Snow (1980) called this the **Early Horticultural period**, arguing that during this period some social groups first began to cultivate crops. However, Dincauze (1990) groups Middle Archaic through Middle Woodland people under the heading of Settlers and does not consider farming important in southern New England until after 1000 BP. Although we refer to both the Early and the Middle Woodland, there is much less reason to make a distinction than in areas where Hopewell phenomena are pronounced. In Table 13.1, we have used 1950 BP (AD 0) as the boundary between Early and Middle Woodland in recognition that it is generally after this juncture that any hints of Hopewell influence appear in the Northeast and Mid-Atlantic. In addition, we have chosen to start the Early Woodland at 2700 BP because the Terminal Archaic is recognized throughout so much of the area covered in this chapter. Finally Mid-Atlantic and Northeastern archaeologists also usually extend the Middle Woodland beyond what would be Hopewell times in the Midwest and Southeast to between 1300 BP and 1000 BP. We think using the earlier of these dates makes the point that developments during the first few centuries after 1300 BP are more closely related to those after 1000 BP than to Middle Woodland phenomena. Archaeologists have defined a number of phases and complexes for the Early and Middle Woodland in the Northeast and Mid-Atlantic based on both ceramics and chipped stone artifacts. Some of these cultural historical entities, like the Early Woodland **Meadowood complex**, are broadly diagnostic over much of the area covered in this chapter. Others are much more localized in their importance.

The array of projectile point types used in Early and Middle Woodland sequences is somewhat bewildering. Various stemmed, notched, and even triangular forms have been noted, not to mention the many indistinct forms that are encountered in sites from this time range. Some of the better-known forms are named and illustrated in Figure 13.11. Compare these projectile points with those described for this period in Chapters 11 and 12. Another interesting trend in stone tool assemblages at this time, particularly in northern New England, is a decrease in the frequency of ground stone tools like gouges, adzes, and celts.

FIGURE 13.11 Some of the various projectile point forms assigned to the Early and Middle Woodland in the Northeast and Mid-Atlantic.

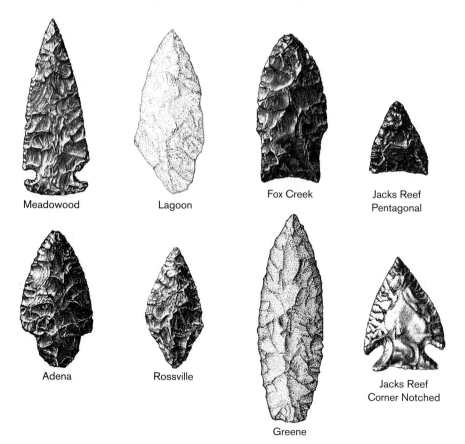

Meadowood

Lagoon

Fox Creek

Jacks Reef Pentagonal

Adena

Rossville

Greene

Jacks Reef Corner Notched

Snow (1980, 298) suggests that this change may be linked with a switch from dugout to birchbark canoe technology.

In thinking about the many ceramic types one will encounter in a detailed study of the pre-Columbian past of the Northeast and Middle Atlantic, it is important to recognize that Early and Middle Woodland ceramics from these areas most often are tempered with various types of crushed rock, and in some instances with shell. Early Woodland potters made pots by coiling, and vessel forms were often conoidal. In contrast to the smooth surfaces of the earliest wares, Early Woodland ceramics usually were cord marked on both exterior and interior surfaces, reflecting use of a cord-wrapped paddle and anvil to meld and thin the coils. The earlier forms of pottery, including Vinette I and other Early Woodland varieties, tend to be thick walled, while by the end of the Middle Woodland, thin-walled ceramics were being made. The size of the temper particles also was reduced in some cases. Various forms of decoration, including net impressions, incising and stamping, dentates, and punctates, distinguish different Middle Woodland types of pottery within the regions we discuss here. There is reason to believe that here, as well as elsewhere in the Eastern Woodlands, a synergy could have developed between improvements in ceramic technology, the processing of seeds and other plant foods, and population growth.

Unfortunately, the archaeological record of horticultural developments is much spottier than it is from the Midwest and Southeast. Nevertheless, archaeological understanding of ecological and sociocultural developments during the Early and Middle Woodland has been increasing. Archaeologists once thought that at least the Middle Woodland peoples of the Mid-Atlantic and Northeast cultivated maize, beans, and squash (Ritchie and Funk 1973), but a growing body of data generated through CRM and research projects has begun to challenge this assumption, and direct dating of plant remains using AMS techniques also has been significant in this respect. This chapter's case study by John P. Hart, "A New History of Maize-Bean-Squash Agriculture in the Northeast," exemplifies the kind of study that is changing our perceptions. There is evidence that farming appeared later than it did further west and south and that maize, bean, and squash agriculture was not established until quite late in the Mid-Atlantic and Northeast. What is much less clear is whether pre-maize farming based on native plants was a significant aspect of Early and Middle Woodland subsistence in these areas. Studies of seed size and morphology are still needed to establish when intentional cultivation began.

It is possible that intensive use of coastal and riverine resources inhibited the development of farming in many parts of the Northeast and Middle Atlantic between 3000 and 1300 years ago. The attractiveness of estuarine and other coastal habitats that developed along the Atlantic coast after sea level and isostatic rebound stabilized should not be underestimated. Fish and shellfish are just part of the high biomass in such areas, which provide habitat for many reptiles and amphibians, nesting sites and food for a wide variety of birds, and prey for many species of mammals, as well as plants that could be used for food and to manufacture baskets and mats. River floodplains were also areas in which a number of resources could be found in close proximity. The intensive use of such areas began, as we have said, in the Late Archaic and continued to increase during the Early and Middle Woodland periods. One example of this process comes from Narragansett Bay in Rhode Island, where excavations at Greenwich Cove and other sites led Bernstein (1993) to argue for increasing sedentism over time without the adoption of agriculture. Other models suggest a seasonal alternation between the coast and interior river valleys during this time. Throughout the Northeast and Mid-Atlantic, at least some larger and more permanent sites have been dated to the Early and Middle Woodland periods, but human groups may have remained mobile throughout most of the pre-Columbian era in southern New England (Chilton 2002).

Data on both exchange and mortuary ceremonialism can also be found in the Early and Middle Woodland. Adena mounds and burial sites per se do not occur further east than southwestern Pennsylvania, where the McKees Rock mound complex near Pittsburgh was probably the most significant example (Dragoo 1963). The pattern with respect to Hopewell seems to be similar. In extreme southwestern Pennsylvania, the **Fairchance phase** (1900–1550 BP) represents participation in the Hopewell Interaction Sphere, but the center of this phase is to the west of the areas covered in this chapter.

Nevertheless, Adena artifacts are not lacking from sites in the Middle Atlantic and Northeast, and numerous burials contain artifacts suggestive of Adena. For example, the West River site located near Annapolis, Maryland, may have had remains of a charnel house, as suggested by postmolds surrounded by a large pit containing five smaller cremation pits and three fire pits. Artifacts recovered here include blades made from nonlocal cherts, tubular pipes, gorgets, a paint cup, a grooved piece of hematite, and copper beads found with red ocher (T. Latimer Ford 1976). Some archaeologists identify a **Middlesex complex** or phase that encompasses materials of these kinds in the Mid-Atlantic and the Northeast (Ritchie 1980). Evidence of Hopewell influence also can be found. Elaborate Middle Woodland burials are known from the Island Field site in Delaware (Thomas 1987). Artifacts such as platform pipes, copper ear ornaments, axes, mica sheets, and projectile points made of Ohio chert, as well as mounds with central stone tombs, also have been found in burials associated with the **Squawkie Hill phase** in New York and northwestern Pennsylvania.

Although burial mounds are not common in the Middle Atlantic, the Abbott Farm site located near Trenton, New Jersey, produced hints of Hopewell influence. The pottery from the Middle Woodland component includes shell-tempered vessels with complex zoned-incised, dentate, and stamped designs (Figure 13.12). This Abbott Farm series pottery is also found with exotic items, including possible earspools, mica sheets, caches of large argillite and jasper bifaces, conch shell fragments, and platform pipes. Other sites, like the Morris–Schurz site located along the East River in the Bronx, which contained a cache of 150 sheets of mica as well as Abbott Farm pottery and artifacts made of argillite from the Delaware Valley, indicate that exchange was taking place between the area of New York City and the Delaware Valley (Cantwell and Wall 2001). Although these data don't indicate migration out of the Midwest or Southeast, or perhaps even true connections with the Hopewell, they do indicate that Middle Woodland exchange networks existed in the Northeast and Mid-Atlantic as well as further west (Kraft 2001).

Despite some farming, possible greater sedentism, exchange, and burial ceremonialism, Early and Middle Woodland people of the Northeast and Middle Atlantic were most likely egalitarian in their social structure. There is little indication of marked status differentiation in burials or in site plans, and not much distinction between males and females. It is probable that individuals attained higher status based upon their life achievements and that levels of ritual

FIGURE 13.12 Abbott Farm series pot; note zoned-incised designs similar to Hopewell ceramics found in the Midwest (e.g., Figure 12.7).

participation also varied, but there is little evidence for ranked social systems in the materials from these time periods.

LATE WOODLAND AND LATE PREHISTORIC PEOPLES

Beginning about 1300 years ago, the Woodland peoples of the Northeast made cultural changes that archaeologists commonly see as the culmination of the trends we have followed from the Late Archaic. These reflect heavier emphasis on maize agriculture, settling into permanent, year-round villages, and the development of tribal confederacies. This period continues until approximately the sixteenth century AD, when European exploration and settlement began to be a factor for the Native peoples of the Northeast and Mid-Atlantic. Dincauze labels the period the Farmers' period, but archaeologists call it either the Late Woodland or the Late Prehistoric. We use the latter terms interchangeably.

Questions of ethnic identification and population movement have been particularly important issues in studying the Late Prehistoric in the Northeast and Mid-Atlantic. In part this is because of temporal proximity, but it also is because of the extensive ethnographic and ethnohistorical records for these areas, which has made possible linkages between historically known villages and archaeological sites. For example, Late Woodland peoples of much of New Jersey can be linked rather directly with Delaware or Lenape groups known from the Contact period (Kraft 1986). Detailed village movement sequences have been constructed for Iroquois tribes, such as the Seneca and the Mohawk. In this approach the known village sites of a historic community are related to an earlier site believed to be the ancestral location of the same community. A wide variety of cultural, demographic, and ecological research questions can be addressed with this approach, although even when village movements cannot be determined, the rich literature on the area provides important insights.

Small, triangular projectile points have long been viewed as one diagnostic artifact for the Late Woodland period in the Northeast and the Middle Atlantic. Triangular forms do appear in assemblages from earlier times, but around 1150 BP they become more common. Some archaeologists recognize several types of triangular form based on overall size and shape (Figure 13.13). For example, among Iroquoians early forms, usually called Levanna points, are large and more equilateral in shape, while later forms, usually called Madison points, are smaller, resembling more an isosceles triangle (Ritchie 1980, 278). All these small projectile points are believed to be arrow points as opposed to spear or dart points. Just as is the case elsewhere in the Eastern Woodlands, it is only during the Late Woodland that this technology became widespread. This development may be linked to increases in warfare as much as to changes in hunting strategies (Nassaney and Pyle 1999).

It is also traditional to understand the Late Woodland in the Mid-Atlantic and the Northeast as characterized by the manufacture of pottery with complex

FIGURE 13.13 Small triangular projectile point forms characteristic of Late Woodland sites in the Northeast and Mid-Atlantic.

FIGURE 13.14 Pot from the Ripley site in southwestern New York State (see case study in Section D.1 of the Student CD).

incised designs as well as cord-wrapped stick impressions, punctates, and handles of various types. Many pottery types were tempered with shell or limestone, and vessel forms varied considerably. Vessels from this time period commonly have **collars** and **castellations** (Figure 13.14). One distinction between Iroquoian pottery and that of other Late Woodland groups appears to be in the method of pot construction, with modeling rather than coiling being the Iroquoian technique. In modeling, vessels are built from a lump of clay that is shaped into a pot by means of a paddle and anvil rather than by coiling of ropelike lengths of clay. Pottery developments in the Late Woodland of the Northeast and the Mid-Atlantic reflect technological trends of the same sorts observed further west by Braun (1983) (see Chapter 12).

The subsistence and settlement changes associated with the Late Woodland begin about 1250 BP in a variety of local areas, though there is much less change in northern New England and along the coast. Where change occurred, people began to make a greater commitment to farming, and in doing so, they settled more permanently into hamlets and villages. Concurrent changes in social organization, exchange, and intergroup alliances also accompanied such developments.

Clemson Island sites, dated between 1150 BP and 650 BP in north central Pennsylvania, provide an example of this transition (Stewart 1994). Clemson Island pottery is tempered mainly with various types of crushed rock, and vessels have cord or fabric impressions, but usually no incised decoration. Instead, a distinctive row of punctations or raised bosses was placed on the rim of vessels, which also are coil constructed and conoidal. Subsistence evidence from the Memorial Park site (Hart and Asch-Sidell 1996) indicates the cultivation of maize, chenopodium, little barley, and sunflower, and the botanical assemblage as a whole suggests the presence of cleared and fallow agricultural fields in the site's vicinity. However, hunting of mammals and birds, fishing for catfish and suckers, and gathering of nuts, fruits, and berries, as well as other plant foods, also were important economic activities. It is probable that this agricultural hamlet was occupied from the late spring through the fall, with large storage pits possibly indicating storage of agricultural products while the site was abandoned in the winter. In fact this pattern may characterize many Clemson Island hamlets, which sometimes seem to have been associated with burial mounds that were slowly built up through repeated interments. It has been suggested that several hamlets shared burial mounds and that this sort of confederation of hamlets is indicative of a tribal level of organization, with extended families or parts of lineages inhabiting hamlets and cooperating in mortuary ritual. Since only some individuals seem to have been buried in the mounds, there may have been status distinctions among Clemson Island people (Stewart 1990).

A wide variety of Late Woodland archaeological complexes have been defined for the Northeast and Mid-Atlantic. These include the foraging groups of the northern Northeast, interior settled agriculturalists like the **Monongahela** of southwestern Pennsylvania, who often lived in stockaded villages, and the coastal groups of southern New England and the Mid-Atlantic, who grew maize, beans, and squash but also relied on marine and riverine resources. There has been a good deal of debate among archaeologists about the degree of sedentism and the reliance on agriculture of these coastal groups (Bendremer 1999; Ceci 1990; Chilton 1999), and it has been argued that large agricultural settlements in interior New England might be buried in the active floodplains of this area (Hasenstab 1999).

One fascinating aspect of the Late Woodland is the practice of secondary burial in ossuaries. Cemeteries and ossuaries probably indicate some sense of collective identity, and they occur in many parts of the Northeast and Mid-Atlantic, but are well preserved in the coastal shell middens of this period. In the Archery Range **ossuary** site located in Pelham Bay Park in the Bronx, for example, nine individual bundle burials were found, arranged in a rough circle with a white boulder in the middle (Kaeser 1970). Two dog burials were found in association with these human burials. Dog burials also were made in apparent ceremonial context at the Lambert Farm site, a multicomponent shell midden at Narragansett Bay, Rhode Island (Kerber 1997). These sites remind us that Late Woodland societies had important, ideological aspects that archaeologists have only begun to understand.

Some of the best-known archaeological cultures of the Late Woodland are the **Northern Iroquoian tradition** groups located in New York State, southern Ontario, and portions of Quebec. Because we can link the archaeological evidence with later ethnohistorically described villages and tribes, Iroquoian archaeology can lead to richer reconstructions of the past than is possible elsewhere. There are Northern Iroquoians, however, about whom we still know relatively little and for whom lineal descendants are hard to identify. The Erie mentioned in the case study in Section D.1 of the Student CD, and the Susquehannock, who lived along the Susquehanna River in Pennsylvania (Kent 1984), are two examples of Northern Iroquoians known primarily from archaeology.

The Iroquoian cultural tradition has been thought to begin with the **Owasco** sites (ca. 1000–600 BP) of the upper Susquehanna River drainage in Pennsylvania and New York, although recent evaluation has suggested that the Owasco designation is problematic (Hart and Brumbach 2003). In southern Ontario the Early Iroquoian period is characterized by **Glen Meyer** and **Pickering phases** between 1050 BP and 650 BP. As discussed in Box 13.1, there is controversy about how these cultures developed, and it is doubtful that this complex problem can be explored by simply identifying cultural historical units. Nevertheless, early Iroquoian sites are generally hamlets or villages containing multifamily houses, perhaps representing matrilineages, and with large bell-shaped storage pits inside. The Roundtop site that figures prominently in this chapter's case study has been considered to be Owasco.

As the Little Ice Age began around 650 BP, the climate cooled, arable land shrank in extent, and cultural changes took place that archaeologists associate with the beginnings of Middle Iroquoian period. Apparently villages congregated at this time in areas that were most viable for agriculture. Population may also have been growing, as there are more and larger villages such as the palisaded Kelso and Furnace Brook sites near Syracuse, New York, which are estimated to have had 330 and 500 residents, respectively, during the late sixth century BP (Snow 1994, 35). These trends continue after 550 BP in what has been called the Late Iroquoian period, and clusters of villages begin to be recognizable in areas that historically were the homeland of different Iroquois tribes. By 400 BP Iroquoian villages were larger still and often located in what seem like defensive positions. In addition, houses within villages grew larger or longer and were packed more densely than before. For example, Snow estimates that at the Garoga site, a Mohawk site in Fulton County, New York, 820 people lived in nine longhouses within an area of 9876 square meters (25 acres) (Snow 1994, 50).

ISSUES AND DEBATES

BOX 13.1

Iroquoian Origins

The distribution of Algonquian and Iroquoian language groups in the Northeast at the time of European contact raises some interesting questions. Notably, Iroquoian-speaking tribal groups occupying the interior were more or less surrounded by Algonquian-speaking groups (Figure 13.15). Moreover, differences among these tribes went beyond language. Iroquoian groups had matrilineal social structures as well as matrilocal residence patterns and lived in multifamily longhouses within compact, often fortified settlements. Their subsistence also was based on maize-bean-squash agriculture. In contrast, Algonquian groups usually were patrilineal, had **patrilocal residence**, lacked the longhouse, and often had more dispersed settlement patterns. Many Algonquians were not dependent on farming, maintaining mixed economies even when they lived in larger settlements or relying solely on hunting, fishing, and gathering. From Figure 13.15, it is easy to imagine that Iroquoians migrated northward into the Northeast, forming a wedge between the western and eastern Algonquians. Is this what happened? If so, when did it happen? What exactly were the origins of Northern Iroquoians?

This is a long-standing problem, but one that has recently generated new discussion and investigation. Early in the twentieth century, archaeologists generally assumed that Northern Iroquoians had arrived in the interior Northeast shortly before European contact. Arthur Parker (1916) situated their origins in Mississippian developments around the mouth of the Ohio River and reconstructed a multipronged migration into the current territory, using folklore and assumptions about migration common at the

time. He didn't develop archaeological data in support of his migration schemes, however. As regional archaeological sequences were constructed, it became obvious that there was an Iroquoian tradition stretching back in time for at least a millennium. By the middle of the twentieth century, archaeologists were questioning the uncritical use of the concept of migration to explain culture change. The Iroquoian ceramic sequence (MacNeish 1952) established that there was considerable cultural continuity in the interior Northeast and that Iroquoians could not be understood as transplanted Mississippians. On this basis, MacNeish proposed that Iroquoians had developed culturally within the Northeast, or *in situ*.

Buttressed by the **neoevolutionism** of processual archaeology, this "*in situ* hypothesis" became the established explanation for Iroquoian origins. MacNeish had seen ceramic continuity between the Iroquoian ceramics beginning with Owasco about 1000 BP and the ceramics of the preceding **Point Peninsula tradition**. Linguistic glottochronological analyses estimated the date of separation of Northern Iroquoians from the Cherokee, whose Southern Iroquoian language is distinct, at somewhere between 3500 and 4000 years ago (Lounsbury 1978). On this basis it sometimes was argued that ancestral Northern Iroquoians pushed northward around the time of the Terminal Archaic (3700–2700 BP), not becoming the Iroquois until much later. In this view, the appearance of the Broadpoint tradition would represent such a migration into the Northeast. A gradual transition to agriculture and a gradual process of sedentarization attended by the development of matrilineality and matrilocality were envisioned.

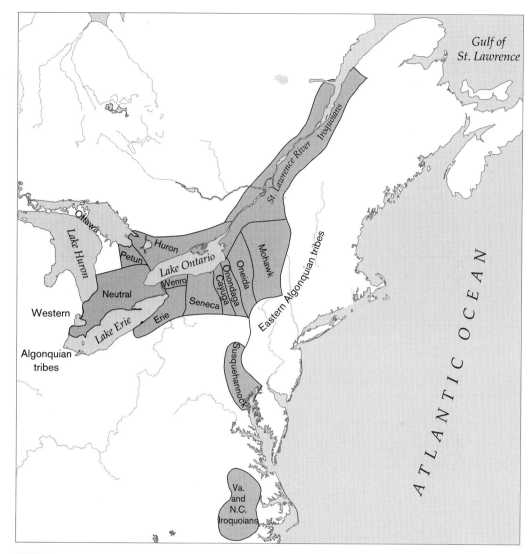

FIGURE 13.15 During early Historic times, Iroquoian language speakers (shaded tribes) were located in the interior and surrounded by Algonquian-speaking tribes.

Unfortunately, the "*in situ* hypothesis" was not necessarily evaluated any more critically than earlier migration scenarios had been. Because migration as an explanation was out of vogue within archaeology altogether, possibly anomalous data were largely ignored. In the 1990s, Snow (e.g., 1995) began arguing that existing contradictory data sufficed to warrant serious reconsideration of migration as opposed to *in situ* Iroquoian origins. First, Snow questioned

the validity of the **Hunters Home phase** at the end of the pre-Iroquoian Point Peninsula tradition, mentioned earlier. He argued that instead of demonstrating continuity between Point Peninsula and Owasco, this phase was an amalgamation of some distinct assemblages that spanned a discontinuity between Point Peninsula and Owasco. Originally, he found a similar discontinuity between Princess Point and Glen Meyer ceramics in Ontario. An important aspect of this discontinuity is the shift among Iroquoians from ceramics made by coiling to ceramics made by molding. Snow also argued that the Point Peninsula and Princess Point groups were seasonally mobile hunter-gatherers who only supplemented their diet through horticulture, while Iroquoians were committed to growing maize. Finally, Snow argued that there is not enough linguistic diversity within Northern Iroquoian languages to argue for more than a thousand years of development from the proto-Iroquoian stage (see also Fiedel 1987).

Given these data, Snow originally proposed that the Clemson Island culture of north central Pennsylvania was ancestral to the Iroquoians. Supposedly, Clemson Island people moved northward, colonizing the areas that had become appropriate for maize agriculture by the beginning of the Medieval Warm period. In this view the Iroquoian complex, including longhouses, molded rather than coiled ceramics, maize agriculture, matrilineality, and matrilocal residence, arrived in New York State and Ontario already

developed. New data on Princess Point from southern Ontario now indicate that maize was cultivated much earlier than previously thought. Other data also suggest more continuity between Princess Point and Iroquoian Glen Meyer phase ceramics, as well as more sedentary Princess Point communities (Crawford and Smith 1996). This could mean that the Iroquoian tradition developed in situ, but it also may mean only that migration took place earlier than originally envisioned by Snow (1996).

As with other issues we have raised in this book, present data are insufficient to resolve the debate about Iroquoian origins. This debate should be understood less as a search for the correct ancestral archaeological taxon than as a chance to explore significant issues in the development of sociocultural traditions. It brings into focus questions about the relationships between agriculture, settlement pattern, social organization, and ethnic identity, and it requires archaeologists to reconsider assumptions about migration and cultural development.

Several features of the Northern Iroquoian tradition are particularly worthy of attention. First, the Iroquois are famous for their large multifamily longhouses, which reached their classic form by 550 BP (Figure 13.16). These bark-covered houses were up to 400 feet (120 m) in length and more than 20 feet (6 m) in width, often with storage compartments and doors at either end and roofs shaped like an arbor. Located down the center of the structure were a row of hearths while the structure was divided into a series of compartments, occupied two to a hearth, by the families of related women. The historically known Iroquois were matrilineal tribes, and it was customary for a married man to live in the longhouse associated with his wife's lineage.

Second, clay elbow pipes were an important item of Iroquois material culture (Figure 13.17). Archaeologists believe that these pipes were made by men, had their own complex series of attributes that changed over time, and can be used to mark Iroquoian culture history. In later times there were highly uniform styles of Iroquois pipes. More significantly, pipes were widely traded, and their presence as early as the sixth century BP far from where they had been made may indicate that the historic pattern of high male mobility and gift exchange has great time depth among the Iroquois. Moreover, these pipes are evidence of Iroquoians smoking, most likely as part of shamanistic activities. Native tobacco (*Nicotiana rustica*), which is stronger than modern commercial tobacco, was probably the main substance, but Native Americans are known to have smoked a wide variety of plant mixtures (von Gernet 1992).

FIGURE 13.16 The long linear, bark-covered structures in this artist's conception are Iroquoian longhouses, which were inhabited by multiple families.

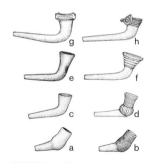

FIGURE 13.17 Onondaga pipe forms changed over time; in this sequence, the oldest forms are shown on the bottom, with each successive layer showing more recent pipes.

Finally, trade and gift exchange certainly were not the only type of interaction among Iroquois villages and nations. Warfare, in the sense of raiding and a cycle of feuds and revenge killing, unquestionably occurred among these people and was the cause of some of what archaeologists find in the material record. For example, the defensive positioning, aggregation, and fortification of later Iroquoian settlements provides strong evidence for conflict between groups and communities. Englebrecht (2003, 112–114) argues that alliance formation between communities was perpetuated through intermarriage. He believes it is indicated by the clustering of communities noted from the fifth century BP onward. This process eventually led to the tribal or nation entities such as Mohawk or Seneca among the Iroquois. On the other hand, such alliances would not have resolved wider conflicts in the Iroquois world, including competition for resources (e.g., Gramly 1977). It is in this context that the five Iroquois nations, Seneca, Cayuga, Onondaga, Oneida, and Mohawk, formed the famous **League of the Haudenosaunee** (People of the Longhouse). The league, which archaeologists believe was in place by about 425 BP, was both an alliance against other tribal groups and a means of reducing the warfare then pervasive. As such, it serves as a model of other Northeastern tribal confederacies that developed in the Late Prehistoric.

THE PROTOHISTORIC AND HISTORIC PERIODS

The Norse or Vikings explored the northeastern edges of the Northeast around 900 BP, briefly establishing a settlement in Newfoundland at L'Anse aux Meadows, but their impact on Native lifeways is barely discernible, especially to the south (see Box 4.1 in Chapter 4). The Historic period in the Northeast and Mid-Atlantic begins at the onset of the sixteenth century AD. Cabot's voyage to the vicinity of Newfoundland in AD 1497 was the actual beginning of exploration, and a series of other Europeans followed him in exploring the eastern American coast during the early 1500s. These explorers often were searching for the presumed Northwest Passage, but they charted the coastline and noted the land's resources. Although they encountered Native peoples, the explorers had relatively little impact on North American societies.

More influential were European fishermen, who began to arrive in coastal waters each summer shortly after the explorers' voyages became known. Attracted by the cod fishery and the whaling prospects off North America's coast, Portuguese, French, Basque, and a little later other European fishermen brought their ships, fishing methods, and navigational skills to the area. They also established seasonal encampments in prime fishing spots along the Strait of Belle Isle. As they did so, they not only explored the northern coast and its resources, but first brought its people into the web of European mercantile capitalism. As American cod and furs made their way to Europe, iron, cloth, and arms began to appear in Native societies. Far from being passive recipients, from the beginning some Native societies altered their own lives to participate in trade with Europeans. St. Lawrence Iroquoians as well as Thule people from the North made summer trading and raiding trips to the area. This pattern was repeated again and again along the coast.

At the beginning of European settlement, the Northeast and Mid-Atlantic were home to many Native American tribal groups. An important cultural distinction among them was between those who spoke Iroquoian languages and those who spoke Algonquian languages. Generally, Algonquians lived along the coast and in the immediate interior, including the Maritime Provinces of Canada, much of New England, the Delaware River drainage, New Jersey, the Delmarva Peninsula, and the Chesapeake Bay area. The Algonquin and the Nipissing of southern Ontario and Quebec also spoke Algonquian languages. As discussed in Box 13.1, Iroquoians lived inland, in Ontario, the St. Lawrence drainage, New York, Pennsylvania, Virginia, and North Carolina as well. Northern Iroquoians include the tribes of the League of the Iroquois and also many of the enemies of these people located in southern Ontario, extreme western New York State, and the Susquehanna River drainage in Pennsylvania. Southern Iroquoians include several groups that originally inhabited portions of the Piedmont and the Coastal Plain. One of these groups, the Tuscaroras, moved north to New York State beginning in the early eighteenth century, after the Tuscarora Wars in North Carolina. Around 1723 they were adopted formally into the League of the Iroquois (Landy 1978).

Archaeologists have much to tell about the interaction between these people and Europeans that adds to the familiar story of European colonization and nation building in these areas. For example, archaeological research conducted in conjunction with the Mashantucket Pequot tribe of eastern Connecticut (e.g., McBride 1990) is providing new insights about the Pequot War in southern New England. Archaeology also can contribute to other stories of agriculture and mercantilism, of war and social upheaval, and of the industrialization of the United States and Canada. Cultural resources from the Historic period are many and diverse throughout the Mid-Atlantic and the Northeast. Thus, much of the archaeological work done by CRM firms and research archaeologists is now focused on this period. Before ending this chapter, we comment briefly on a few areas in which Northeastern and Mid-Atlantic archaeologists have been contributing particularly important insights.

Transformations During the Protohistoric and Early Contact Periods

In most of the areas covered in this chapter, indirect and direct European contact began at approximately AD 1500 and continued until colonization in the seventeenth or even the eighteenth century. Written records were not produced until Europeans were on the scene directly, but because of prior participation in trade networks and gift exchange, the Native peoples of the Northeast acquired European goods and were caught up in the fur trade ahead of actual contact. There are a number of other ways in which Native peoples probably obtained European goods during this period. These include the scavenging of shipwrecks, the looting of abandoned settlements, and the taking of European clothing and belongings after hostile encounters (Pendergast 1994). Of course, once contacts became more common, existing Native systems of trade and exchange were rapidly co-opted into the burgeoning global economic system. This had disastrous consequences for some Native nations, while others profited, at least for a time, as intertribal conflicts developed over the trade. For example, the Iroquois Wars between 1641 and 1701 were a series of conflicts between the Iroquois and other tribes that developed after the local beaver population had been exhausted. These conflicts resulted in the dispersal of a number of tribes (e.g., the Erie, the Huron, the Neutral) and extended westward into the Upper Great Lakes. Ultimately the French and western enemies of the Iroquois forced the Native Americans to make peace.

The most important point underscored by the archaeology of the Protohistoric is that the sociocultural systems into which Europeans were beginning to interject themselves were dynamic systems in their own right. Like people everywhere, the Late Woodland and Protohistoric inhabitants of the Northeast and Mid-Atlantic were enmeshed in complex economic, social, and political interactions. Confronted with Europeans, they were not really the passive recipients of change portrayed in popular stereotypes. As a result, both Natives and Europeans shaped what happened in the colonial encounter (Axtell 2001).

For example, in Virginia's coastal plain, the Powhatan chiefdom amalgamated a number of Algonquian tribes. The rise of chiefs in this area was a Protohistoric phenomenon rather than having much time depth. This was not a direct response to Europeans as we might imagine (Rountree and Turner 2002). Instead, aggregation took place in response to incursions by other Native groups from the Piedmont onto the Virginia's inner coastal plain. Just as intergroup conflict increased among Iroquoian people in the Late Woodland, it seems to have affected people in the Chesapeake area. Military consolidation, stronger alliances, and the establishment of a hierarchy of chiefs are suggested to archaeologists by the appearance of palisaded towns, by trends in the ceramics, by the presence of high-status goods such as copper, freshwater pearls, and shell beads and gorgets, and by the appearance of large, sturdy house structures assumed to be chief's residences.

Of course, this was the context into which the fabled Jamestown settlement was inserted by the English in 1607, after about 50 years of intermittent Spanish and English presence in the Virginia area. Initially, the interaction between the Powhatans and the English was characterized by both sides' attempts to make productive alliances. The English wanted to exploit the land for commodities that could be sold at home, while the Powhatans wanted allies against their enemies, including other tribes and the Spanish with whom they had had previous dealings. Neither party to these early contacts fully understood the other's intentions or behaviors, but each continued to play out its stratagems according to its own cultural rules.

Another topic archaeologists have helped scholars explore consists of the consequences of European contact for Native American health and population size. Although ethnologists once understood this number to be as low as 2 million and fairly constant over time, the work of historical demographers such as Sherburne F. Cook (1976) has suggested much higher numbers of people (e.g., 18,000,000 people). Specifically, it has now been widely accepted that Europeans spread diseases to which Native Americans had no immunity, leading to large-scale depopulations among Native populations early in the Historic period. In central New York State one important question is whether depopulation occurred during the Protohistoric or only as a result of historically documented epidemics such as the smallpox epidemics of 1633–1635. Answering this question is complicated because population movements and amalgamations were also taking place during the sixteenth and seventeenth centuries. If population decline began among the Iroquois people of central New York State during the sixteenth century, it precedes sustained European presence in the area (Dobyns 1983; Ramenofsky 1987). Overcrowding in palisaded villages that can be attributed to Native militarism and politics might also have caused epidemic disease (Lorraine P. Saunders 1992).

Colonial Archaeology

Perhaps as intriguing as the Protohistoric and early Contact periods is the colonial period, during which men and women from France, Holland, and England actually settled in the Northeast and Mid-Atlantic. Archaeologists working with colonial remains can still address questions related to the transformation of Native societies during this period, but usually the term "colonial archaeology" is applied to the study of European colonists and encompasses a wide variety of research questions. Archaeological work at places like Williamsburg in Virginia or the Plimouth Plantation in Massachusetts has long provided information for the reconstruction of colonial lifestyles. However, the archaeology of this period contributes much more than details for reconstructions. Important anthropological and historical questions also can be addressed.

Two examples will have to suffice. First, consider what the archaeology of Dutch colonial sites has to contribute to understanding of the development of the global economy during the seventeenth century. The Dutch established their colony, New Netherland, to participate in the fur trade; their goal was profit. New Amsterdam, now New York City, became a significant port, and archaeological finds from this period often contribute insight into the colony as a center of commerce. In addition, they supply information about lifestyles not contained in historical records. For example, the excavation of early privy pits in New York City has yielded a tremendous amount of information about the material culture of this colony (Cantwell and Wall 2001).

Second, think about the archaeology of the colonial period exploration and settlement west of the Appalachian mountains. Western Pennsylvania was one setting for a contest between the rival colonial powers of France and England that culminated in the French and Indian War (Seven Years' War) between 1756 and 1763. Archaeological excavations at the various forts established in this region by France and by England provide interesting information about construction and provisioning. They document events, recorded in early accounts such as young George Washington's defeat at Fort Necessity. In both cases, by adding important information to what can be gleaned from documentary sources, archaeological excavations can guide historical reconstructions.

Other Topics in Historic Archaeology

Besides the French and Indian War, much of the action in the Revolutionary War, the War of 1812, and the Civil War took place in the Northeast and the Mid-Atlantic. As a result, the study of these conflicts has been a key topic for historical archaeology in these areas. Although there is no shortage of traditional history about these wars, battlefield archaeology and archaeological research at forts, cemeteries, hospitals, farms, and the towns associated with them contribute greatly to increasing the accuracy of historical knowledge. For example, a military graveyard from the War of 1812 was found in Fort Erie, Ontario, in 1987. Excavations uncovered the remains of soldiers who had died during the American occupation of this fort, providing a detailed profile of these men and their lives (Litt et al. 1993). Archaeologists also can provide insight into more mundane aspects of life, such as what people ate, how they farmed, and what kind of structures they lived in. Such data proved particularly instructive when archaeologists working at Valley Forge in Pennsylvania, documented details about how troops were quartered there and what they ate (Figure 13.18). At other times archaeological study opens a window on people left out of the story as usually told. For example, archaeological excavation of the remains of a boardinghouse operated during the various occupations of Harper's Ferry during the Civil War has taught us much about the diet and lifestyle of noncombatants trying to survive under wartime conditions (Shackel 2000).

African Americans are another group whose story has not been well told in historical records. Archaeology has much to contribute to this narrative in the Northeast and Mid-Atlantic, where early African populations have been particularly invisible. In Chapter 1's discussion of New York City's African Burial Ground (Box 1.2), we provided some insight into this topic. Another example is the story revealed by archaeology done at Skunk Hollow in New Jersey, a nineteenth-century free black community that persisted until the turn of the twentieth century (Geismar 1982).

Early American industry developed largely in the Northeast and the Middle Atlantic, leaving a fascinating material record that archaeologists have begun to investigate. These areas were the site of early extractive industries such as mining, oil drilling, and lumbering, and they also were the location of early manufacturing enterprises. Beginning in the eighteenth and continuing into the nineteenth century, paper mills, textile factories, pottery factories, glass factories, and ironworks were started throughout the area. Archaeology can document the actual processes and organization of production. For example, excavations in Paterson, New Jersey, provided new insights into the development of this early center of

FIGURE 13.18
Archaeologists from the Pennsylvania Archaeological Council touring the excavations of the officers' quarters at Valley Forge.

manufacturing in the United States by exploring the evolution of the Rogers Locomotive Works during the nineteenth century (Ingle 1982). In addition, the transportation industry left an early mark on these regions in the form of the canals and railroads that once crisscrossed the landscape. When excavations produce domestic refuse, archaeology also can reveal much about the lifestyles of both the owners and the laborers in these industrial enterprises. Exhibit 13.1 presents an example of the kinds of cultural resource that might be studied by archaeologists doing **industrial archaeology**.

Finally, as this chapter's opening about Smicksburg may suggest, historical archaeology contributes significantly to investigations concerning the development of agricultural centers and rural farmsteads. Much of the Northeast and Mid-Atlantic was agricultural, and there is much about past rural societies that archaeology can reveal. For example, archaeological excavations have provided important perspectives on tenant farmers in rural Delaware (De Cunzo 2004).

CLUES TO THE PAST

EXHIBIT 13.1

Iron Furnaces

Ruins like the one shown in Figure 13.19 still can be found throughout the Northeast and Mid-Atlantic regions. These flat-topped, almost pyramidal, cut stone structures are the remains of iron furnaces. Iron making is one of the most important examples of early industrial development in the United States. The abundance of iron ore from which iron could be obtained, coupled with the availability of limestone used in the extraction process and wood for fuel, as well as

FIGURE 13.19 The Eliza Furnace in Vintondale, Pennsylvania, was once at the center of an extensive iron-making operation; it is unusual because of the intact heat exchanger at its top.

the presence of many fast-flowing streams for power, made the Northeast and the Mid-Atlantic ideal for iron production. In the eighteenth and nineteenth centuries, iron-making complexes centered on **blast furnaces** such as the Eliza Furnace proliferated. Though the ruins of the furnace stack itself may be all that remains visible aboveground, there is a great deal to be learned about these early endeavors through archaeology.

Two processes of iron extraction were brought to the Americas by European colonists. The older extraction process was to heat the ore in a charcoal fire until it was reduced to a spongy mass, or **bloom**; water-driven bellows increased the temperature of the flames. The impurities in the ore were removed through repeated heating and hammering. Bloomery forges that undertook this process were common in colonial America, but they were not as productive as blast furnaces, which by then had been developed in Europe. In a blast furnace a **flux**, usually limestone, was added with the ore to the fire to promote the separation of iron. Blast furnace technology was introduced to the Americas in the middle of the seventeenth century. An attack by Indians had ruined an earlier attempt to build a blast furnace in Virginia in 1622 (Bining 1973). In 1640 a successful ironworks was established in Saugus, Massachusetts (Gordon 1996). By the time of the American Revolution, ironworks including blast furnaces were very common throughout the Northeast and Mid-Atlantic, and these enterprises continued to be common until late in the nineteenth century.

The Eliza Furnace shown in Figure 13.19 was a charcoal blast furnace. Its construction and interior was similar to that shown in Figure 13.20. Thick outer walls of unmortared stone formed a hollow furnace stack 25 to 35 feet (7.6–10.7 m)

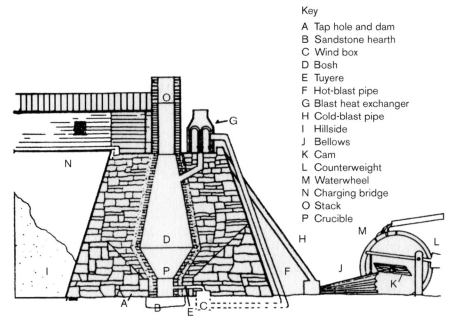

Key

A Tap hole and dam
B Sandstone hearth
C Wind box
D Bosh
E Tuyere
F Hot-blast pipe
G Blast heat exchanger
H Cold-blast pipe
I Hillside
J Bellows
K Cam
L Counterweight
M Waterwheel
N Charging bridge
O Stack
P Crucible

FIGURE 13.20 Section of a hot-blast charcoal-fired iron furnace like Eliza Furnace.

high. The interior chamber, lined with sandstone or firebrick, was narrowest at the top, widening to about 7 feet (2.1 m) at the **bosh** and then narrowing again to a small bottom chamber called the **crucible**. Furnace stacks usually were built next to a hill, to permit access to the top of the furnace by means of a wooden charging bridge. Furnaces also were flanked with waterwheels that propelled leather bellows or, later, **blowing tubs**. These bellows or blowing tubs provided the air blast needed to keep the fire burning at temperatures high enough for smelting (ca. 2600–3000°F). The air was conducted to the fire through a copper **tuyere**. Many furnaces used blasts of cold air, but hot-blast furnaces, like the Eliza Furnace, were introduced after the 1830s. In the latter type of furnace the air blast was forced through pipes that were heated over a fire or by the furnace gases themselves. The coiled pipes of the heat exchanger can still be seen at the top of the Eliza Furnace stack (see Figure 13.19). In front of the furnace was the **cast arch**, where the molten iron was tapped for use.

In operation, the furnace was filled with charcoal that was fired from the bottom and allowed to burn for several days before being charged or filled with alternate layers of charcoal, iron ore, and limestone. As the ore descended to the bosh, it became molten, and excess oxygen was removed as gas while other impurities interacted with the melting limestone. Fluid iron and **slag** collected on the furnace hearth at the bottom, but the slag was lighter and was drawn off at the **cinder notch**. The heavier iron was tapped through a hole in the dam stone normally plugged with clay. This molten iron ran into prepared molds in the sand floor of the casting shed, constructed of wood over the casting arch. The cooled bars of iron were called **pigs**. Pig iron had to be further refined at a refinery forge to burn away the carbon, which made pig iron brittle. After several reheatings and hammerings, bars of this refined or wrought iron were sent directly to blacksmiths for shaping or, eventually, to rolling and slitting mills for further cutting into nails and sheets of iron. **Blister steel**, an alloy of iron and carbon, could also be produced by keeping bars of wrought iron at red heat for up to two weeks in a pot packed with charcoal (U.S. National Park Service 1983).

Although not all these processes were necessarily accomplished at the iron furnace itself, iron furnaces were at the center of extensive iron plantations staffed by numerous people. Besides the ironmaster, who usually lived with his family in a spacious home near the furnace, there were many workers. Founders kept the furnace operating while a company clerk kept the books and managed the company store, and molders produced the pigs. Fillers charged the stack; colliers made the charcoal, and wood-cutters cut the logs for charcoal. Miners mined the iron ore, usually from surface pits; teamsters transported materials, and farmers grew food to feed the workers. If forges and rolling mills were included in the operation, even more types of workers were included in the community. A hierarchy of individuals existed, with the iron-master and his family at the apex. The impact of this hierarchy can be glimpsed through excava-tions at ancillary and domestic structures. When we excavate at iron furnace complexes, we can learn about the social context of this early indus-try as well as the technology.

A variety of improvements were introduced into the process of iron making during the eighteenth and nineteenth centuries. One impor-tant innovation was the introduction of **coke**, a purified form of coal, as fuel. Although American furnaces did not adopt this innovation until well into the nineteenth century because of the abundant wood available, coke allowed for hot-ter and more rapid melting of the ore. Together with such other improvements as the replace-ment of bellows with blowing tubs and the conversion to hot-blast furnaces, noted above, these improvements led to a great increase in production at the middle of the nineteenth cen-tury that was only matched by an increase in demand as manufacturing and railroads grew. Ultimately, to meet high demand, the iron and steel industry became more centralized in urban centers such as Pittsburgh, and the small blast furnace became obsolete. Though pilfered for usable wood and metal, many furnace stacks still dot the rural landscape of the Northeast and Mid-Atlantic. These clues to the past truly remind us of other times and allow archaeolo-gists to explore the technology and lives of ear-lier Americans.

CHAPTER SUMMARY

This chapter has introduced the archaeological past in the Northeast and the Mid-Atlantic. Although not an exhaustive treatment, the material should make further study of archaeology in these areas understandable. The main points made in this chapter are as follows:

- As in the Southeast, the main physiographic division in the Northeast and Mid-Atlantic is between the coastal plains and the Appalachian or other mountain systems. These areas were forested with a transition forest of mixed coniferous and deciduous trees separating the boreal coniferous forest biome on the north from the temperate deciduous forest biome on the south.

- Postglacial environmental change was significant as isostatic rebound from the glacial retreat, the drowning of the coast, the drainage of glacial meltwaters, and the biotic colonization of newly exposed areas combined in complex ways after the Pleistocene. However, other climatic changes such as the Hypsithermal, the Medieval Warm period, and the Little Ice Age may have been important as well.

- Pre-Clovis settlement of the Northeast and Mid-Atlantic may be documented at Meadowcroft Rockshelter in Pennsylvania and at Cactus Hill in Virginia. Evidence from fluted points is extensive, especially during the eleventh millennium BP. These early people appear to have been generalized foragers to the south and more specialized caribou hunters in the north.

- Early and Middle Archaic sites in the Northeast and Mid-Atlantic once were considered rare, but with the help of CRM archaeology, their presence is now more widely documented. In Maine and in the Maritime Provinces, the Gulf of Maine Archaic tradition, characterized by the use of metamorphic rock to make ground stone tools such as rods and gouges, is evident beginning in the Middle Archaic.

- The Late Archaic in the Northeast and Mid-Atlantic was a time of possible population growth and cultural change. Shellfishing and use of anadromous fish and other fish, some cultivation of native plants, exchange and burial ceremonialism, experimentation with the manufacture of new containers from steatite and ceramics, and longer-term settlements have all been proposed for various Late Archaic groups. Archaeologists working in these areas often identify a Terminal Archaic period from 3700 BP to 2700 BP, in which changes of these kinds foreshadow the Woodland period.

- The Early and Middle Woodland of the Northeast and Mid-Atlantic from about 2700 BP to 1300 BP suggest mostly marginal involvement with the Adena and Hopewell phenomena to the west, although a few sites have yielded diagnostic Adena and Hopewell artifacts. Horticultural and other developments found elsewhere in the Eastern Woodlands may have been inhibited by the intensive use of coastal and riverine resources through these periods.

- Beginning around 1300 BP, cultural changes related to heavier reliance on agriculture, settling into permanent villages, and the development of tribal confederacies begin to take place. However, the Mississippian tradition did not develop in the Northeast and Mid-Atlantic, and archaeologists recognize only a Late Woodland or Late Prehistoric. Maize-bean-squash agriculture was not fully established at first, and cultural changes were not uniform.

- Late Prehistoric Northern Iroquoian societies, which are relatively well known historically, provide one model for the tribal confederacies that variously developed in this chapter's areas during the Late Prehistoric. However many other societies at this time, including coastal and northern ones, differed in significant ways from those of the Iroquois.

- Although the Vikings briefly settled in Newfoundland in approximately 900 BP, it was not until the sixteenth century AD (beginning at 450 BP) that Europeans seriously began to affect the Native cultures of the Northeast through trade, alliance, and the spread of disease. The population movements, conflicts, and disruptions of this period can be studied archaeologically as well as through written documents.

- The colonial period in the Northeast and Mid-Atlantic involves colonization efforts by the French, the British, and the Dutch, and archaeology adds much to the picture of the development of global capitalism as well as to understanding of colonists' lifestyles. A wide variety of more recent historic topics also can be investigated through archaeology, some associated with war and nation building in the United States and Canada, and others relating to early industrialization, early agricultural lifestyles, and early African American communities.

SUGGESTIONS FOR FURTHER READING

For a compendium of recent studies of interest to students of Northeastern archaeology:

Levine, Mary Ann, Kenneth E. Sassaman, and Michael Nassaney. 1999. *The Archaeological Northeast.* Westport, CT: Bergin and Garvey.

For an introduction to aspects of Mid-Atlantic archaeology:

Custer, Jay F. 1996. *Prehistoric Cultures of Eastern Pennsylvania.* Anthropological Series 7. Pennsylvania Historical and Museum Commission, Harrisburg.

Dent, Richard J., Jr. 1995. *Chesapeake Prehistory: Old Traditions, New Directions.* New York: Plenum Press.

For studies of past coastal adaptations:

Bernstein, David. 1993. *Prehistoric Subsistence on the Southern New England Coast: The Record from Narragansett Bay.* San Diego: Academic Press.

Bourque, Bruce J. 1995. *Diversity and Complexity in Prehistoric Maritime Societies: A Gulf of Maine Perspective.* New York: Plenum Press.

For a fascinating account of what lies beneath New York City:

Cantwell, Anne-Marie, and Diana di Zerega Wall. 2001. *Unearthing Gotham: The Archaeology of New York City.* New Haven, CT: Yale University Press.

For treatment of the Iroquoian people's lifestyle using both ethnohistory and archaeology:

Engelbrecht, William. 2003. *Iroquoia: The Development of a Native World.* Syracuse, NY: Syracuse University Press.

For an interdisciplinary look at how Virginia Algonquin life was transformed in early Contact times:

Rountree, Helen C., and E. Randolph Turner III. 2002. *Before and After Jamestown: Virginia's Powhatans and Their Predecessors.* Gainesville: University Press of Florida.

OTHER RESOURCES

Sections H and I of the Student CD give web links, places to visit, additional discussion questions, and other study aids. The Student CD contains a variety of additional resources including the complete list of references as cited in this chapter and the following case study. The case study in Section D.1 of the Student CD, discusses archaeological work at a Northern Iroquoian site in New York State.

CASE STUDY

School-children often learn that the Indians taught the Pilgrim settlers at Plymouth, Massachusetts, how to grow corn, beans, and squash by planting them together in hills to ensure sufficient food for the New England winter. This colorful story may have some basis in reality. It is clear that at European contact the Indians of southern New England did grow these crops together, and they could have taught the Pilgrims to do the same. Moreover, these plants complement each other, both as crops and as sources of food. How important was this agricultural complex to the stability and complexity of Native societies? When was maize-bean-squash agriculture introduced in the Northeast? These are questions that contemporary archaeologists are exploring. The perspective that this agricultural complex was a late development in the Northeast has been gained recently from applying new techniques to ethnobotanical and artifactual evidence preserved in archaeological collections. This case study, which tells the story of that reanalysis, indicates the potential importance of collecting and preserving plant remains. It also indicates how new techniques, applied to old evidence, may change our understanding of the past. Finally, it provides an example of how experiments may be integrated with other archaeological research. As you read, pay attention to how a variety of approaches have been used to generate new information. Did you ever think that museum collections might provide new data?

A NEW HISTORY OF MAIZE-BEAN-SQUASH AGRICULTURE IN THE NORTHEAST

John P. Hart

Most of the case studies presented in this book relate the thrill of discovery, addressing important research questions and solving seemingly intractable problems through archaeological fieldwork and analyses of materials obtained through fieldwork. The general public, students, and professional archaeologists are drawn to the process of unearthing remains of our species' history and evolution. Newspapers, magazines, television news programs, and other media often relate exciting stories on archaeological field studies that challenge our notions of the past and what it means to be human.

Every one of the archaeological field projects that you read about and participate in produces collections of artifacts and other debris of past human activities. This is the stuff of archaeology—what sets the discipline of archaeology apart from other social and behavioral sciences. The analysis of these artifact collections and their contextual documentation, such as field notes, site plans, and photographs, allows archaeologists to gain new insights into how people in the past lived, and how people's lives changed through the generations.

What happens to these collections as documents of the past once the project archaeologists complete their analyses and publish their reports gets much less public attention than the unearthing process. All these collections should, and many do, eventually make their way into museums. It is the primary job of museums to care for collections that document research, like the materials generated by archaeological excavations. Many, hopefully all, of the collections generated by the case studies you have read in this book now sit in cabinet drawers or in boxes on shelves in museums throughout North America.

But why? Once the analyses and publications for an archaeological project are complete, what use are the collections? Surely the most attractive pieces ought to be put on display, but what value can all those pottery sherds and chipped stone flakes have? They've already been analyzed, and the data are published in site reports.

There are a number of possible answers to these questions. To my mind, two are critical. First, archaeological theories, methods, and techniques are constantly changing. What represents the state of the art today may be very dated in just a few short years. Curation of collections allows archaeologists to discover new information about the past when new analytical techniques and methods, especially when combined with new theoretical approaches, can be applied to such stored materials. Often it makes more sense to reanalyze existing collections than to excavate new ones. Second, curation of collections gives archaeologists the ability to observe, examine, and compare the three-dimensional objects that are depicted as two-dimensional photographs or summarily described in the tables and charts. Nothing can substitute for the examination of actual objects to generate new ideas and draw new conclusions that otherwise might never arise.

Not all important discoveries about the past, then, come about through new excavations [see, e.g., the collected papers in *Museum Anthropology* 19(3) 1995]. Analyses of existing collections, often made many decades ago, contribute important advances in our knowledge of the distant past. In this case study I relate how our knowledge of maize-bean-squash agriculture in the Northeast generally, and New York specifically, has been radically altered recently as a result of the application of new techniques and methods to museum collections.

CHANGING THE HISTORY OF MAIZE, BEAN, AND SQUASH AGRICULTURE

Maize, beans, and squash were the primary American Indian crops during the Late Prehistoric and Early Historic periods (Hurt 1987). Frequently these crops were found in what is known as a **polyculture**, an agricultural system in which plants from different species are grown together, much like a natural community of plants (Woolley and Davis 1991). Each plant in the polyculture contributes some benefit to the others, ideally resulting in higher yields per unit of land than if the crops were grown separately. This is the source of the Northern Iroquoian name for the maize-bean-squash system, the **Three Sisters**, with each sister (crop) taking care of the others (Engelbrecht 2003). The maize stalk provides a climbing pole for the bean plant; the bean plant fixes nitrogen in the soil that may be available to the maize and squash plants; the squash plant, growing low to the ground with its large leaves, acts as a mulch to discourage weed growth and maintain soil moisture (Perkl 1998).

In addition to the agronomic benefits of growing the three crops together, consuming the crops together provides nutritional benefits. Maize kernels are high in starch and calories; bean seeds provide high levels of protein, and consuming maize kernels and beans seeds together provides a complete set of amino acids (Kaplan 1963); squash seeds are high in fats and oils, and squash flesh is high in calories and various vitamins and minerals (Robinson and Decker-Walters 1996).

The agronomic and nutritional benefits of the maize-bean-squash complex, as well as its widespread use not only in northeastern North America, but in many ecological settings throughout the Western Hemisphere, make it seem like a natural system—a system that would have been adopted by American Indian groups wherever it was introduced. For many years the crops of this polyculture were thought to have been established in what is now New York, the home of the historic Northern Iroquoian nations, by approximately 950 BP (Ritchie 1980; Snow 1995). The crops were thought to have been adopted either in quick succession or as a unit. The establishment of the

polyculture was thought to have triggered the evolution of other cultural traits that became recognizable as Northern Iroquoian soon thereafter (Hart 2001).

Intensive reliance on maize-bean-squash agriculture is one of the defining traits of the historic Northern Iroquoian groups of New York, surrounded as they were by speakers of Algonquian languages, many of whom relied much less heavily on agricultural produce in their subsistence systems. It had long been assumed that either the adoption of the three crops or the migration into New York (and southern Ontario) of agriculturists who grew the three crops was the catalyst for the evolution of other nonlinguistic cultural traits that came to define the Northern Iroquoians and set them apart from their Algonquian neighbors (Ritchie 1980; Snow 1995).

THE ROUNDTOP SITE

It was a major find, therefore, when in 1964 a crew from the New York State Museum, under the direction of State Archaeologist William Ritchie, found maize kernels and squash and bean seeds together in a large pit feature (Feature 35) at the Roundtop site in the Susquehanna River valley west of Binghamton, New York (Ritchie and Funk 1973). The recovery of crop remains at archaeological sites prior to the development and employment of systematic flotation processing techniques in the 1970s and 1980s was a matter of happenstance. To recover the remains of all three crops together in a single context was quite exciting. In his publications on the site, Ritchie connected the crops to a radiocarbon date of approximately 900 BP from a different context (Feature 30), which made the remains the earliest evidence of maize-bean-squash agriculture not only in New York, but in all of eastern North America. While remains of maize had been found in earlier contexts elsewhere in the East, no site had yielded beans as well as squash at such an early date, and thus not the three crops together. Over the next few decades, Roundtop was frequently cited as the earliest evidence for beans in the East (Ford 1985; Riley et al. 1990; Yarnell 1976).

At the time of the Roundtop excavations, radiocarbon dating was still a relatively new technique. Obtaining a radiocarbon date required several grams of charcoal. The charcoal that Ritchie chose for radiocarbon dating was from Feature 30, a large pit feature presumably used for storing foodstuffs, as was

Feature 35, the pit in which the maize, bean, and squash remains were found. By the early 1980s archaeologists were able to use the new radiocarbon dating technique called accelerator mass spectrometry dating, which can yield a date from very small amounts of charcoal. Currently as little as 2 or 3 milligrams of charcoal will suffice to obtain an AMS date. To get an idea of how little material this is, think about a typical aspirin tablet weighing 500 milligrams. Now think about one one-hundredth of that aspirin tablet: 5 milligrams is in some cases twice the amount of charred plant material needed to obtain an AMS date. This means that critical early crop remains can be dated directly. Thus AMS is a very important tool for archaeologists interested in the chronology of crops.

The collections from the Roundtop site excavations by Ritchie's crew and later excavations by Binghamton University's field school are housed in the New York State Museum. When I joined the museum's staff in 1994, I wanted to work with a collection that would introduce me to the Late Prehistoric period of the state, especially a collection from a site with information about agriculture. Roundtop fit the bill. My initial goal was to obtain direct AMS dates on the famous crop remains to substantiate their age. After some searching in the museum's collections, I was able to find maize kernels, bean seeds, and squash seeds from Feature 35 in the context Ritchie attributed to the occupation of approximately 900 BP. After confirmation of the identifications by C. Margaret Scarry, a paleoethnobotanist at the University of North Carolina at Chapel Hill, I sent maize kernels, a bean cotyledon, and part of a twig from the same context for AMS dating. To my surprise at the time, the dates came back at calibrated 650 BP (Hart 1999a). While direct dates on maize kernels from other contexts at the site were consistent with Ritchie's earlier date, beans from other contexts yielded even younger dates than those from Feature 35.

A subsequent analysis of the pottery assemblages from Features 30 and 35 revealed that the pottery from Feature 35 was dominated by sherds from pots of a type that is consistent with the 650 BP date. The pottery from Feature 30 came mostly from one large pot of a type consistent with Ritchie's date from that feature. Additional radiocarbon dates from Roundtop and analysis of pottery assemblages from other features indicated that there had been at least three temporally distinct occupations of the site. Roundtop was not the predominantly single-component site that

Ritchie believed, and the maize, bean, and squash remains from Feature 35 were 250 years younger than he believed (Hart 1999a, 2000).

The presence of beans on the Roundtop site and Ritchie's belief that they dated to 900 BP or thereabouts led many archaeologists to expect that beans and maize-bean-squash agriculture would be found elsewhere in contexts in the Northeast dating to that time, and they were; but in only one other case had the bean remains been directly dated (ca. 550 BP) (Heckenberger et al. 1991). The results of the Roundtop dating project led me to question the whole history of the crops of the polyculture and to start a long-term research program, drawing primarily on museum collections, that has rewritten the history of the three crops. While my research has been directed toward the goal of a better understanding of the history of the polyculture, it has investigated each of the specific crops individually. As a result, the following summary of the research is organized by individual crops.

MAIZE (*Zea mays* ssp. *mays*)

The earliest maize remains are found in Mexico and date to approximately 6000 years ago (Piperno and Flannery 2001). These remains came from a small cob with relatively few kernels. From this inauspicious beginning, maize has spread worldwide and is one of the world's most important grain crops. The earliest macrobotanical remains found thus far in eastern North America date to approximately 2100 years ago, based on a direct AMS date (Riley et al. 1994). These remains were recovered from the Holding site in the Illinois River valley near its confluence with the Mississippi (see Figure 12.1). While maize pollen has been identified in earlier contexts in the Southeast, the Holding macrobotanical remains are the earliest accepted dates for maize in eastern North America. Other early direct AMS dates have been obtained on maize macrobotanical remains in Tennessee, Ohio, and southern Ontario (Crawford et al. 1997). Maize macrobotanical remains associated with wood charcoal dates of around 2300 BP at the Meadowcroft Rockshelter in Pennsylvania (Adovasio and Johnson 1981) are intriguing but remain controversial pending direct AMS dating of the remains themselves. The earliest direct date on maize macrobotanical remains in New York, in the southeastern part of the state, has been 1000 years old (Cassedy and Webb 1999).

FIGURE 13.21 Early maize dates (BP) for northeastern North America.

As shown in Figure 13.21, the distribution of dates on and associated with macrobotanical remains across northeastern North America suggests a gradual southwest-to-northeast spread across the region. However, it was likely that this apparent trend was more a result of recovery bias than a reflection of the true history of maize across the region. For example, the Holding site produced 19 fragments of maize, but only after over 5000 liters (175 ft³) of soil from feature and midden contexts had been processed through water flotation, followed by intensive identification efforts by paleoethnobotanists. No other site of Holding's age to the east has been subjected to so great a level of sampling. Thus any history of the crop inferred from the distribution of early dates is suspect.

Excavating an archaeological site is a very expensive and time-consuming endeavor, especially if one is interested in finding the earliest evidence for maize in a region. The level of sampling and flotation processing done at Holding is staggering and is unlikely to be repeated at another site any time soon. In any event, there is no guarantee that maize macrobotanical remains would be found by another such investigation even if maize had been used at the site (Hart 1999b). The challenge, then was to find another

means of determining whether maize was present in New York earlier than 1000 BP. It turned out that museum collections held the key to radically changing our understanding of the history of this crop in New York.

The New York State Museum's archaeological collections contain more than 2 million objects. Tens of thousands of these objects are prehistoric pottery sherds. When surveying the collections, on occasion one will come across a sherd that has a layer of charred material on its inner surface. This material is referred to as cooking residue. My colleague Robert Thompson (University of Minnesota) has developed a process for extracting the microscopic silica bodies that plants produce as they take up water and nutrients from the soil from cooking residues (Hart et al. 2003). These tiny units are called opal phytoliths, and the chaffs of grasses produce a particular phytolith form called rondels. Rondels in turn have many forms, for which Thompson has created a taxonomy. By using this taxonomy to classify 100 rondels from a cooking residue, Thompson is able to determine, through statistical comparison with modern samples from grass chaffs, what species of grass was cooked in a pot. In fact, he can even determine the genetic lineage of rondel assemblages identified as maize. Coupled with direct AMS dating of the same residues, this form of analysis provides a powerful, and relatively inexpensive, means of expanding knowledge about the history of maize (and other crops).

Working with my colleague Hetty Jo Brumbach (State University of New York, Albany), I initially selected six residue samples for Thompson to analyze. These were from three sites in the northern Finger Lakes region of New York: Hunters Home, Kipp Island, and Wickham. Collections from these sites had been in the museum for five to six decades. Based on pottery types and wood charcoal radiocarbon dates obtained by the original excavators, Brumbach and I thought that the samples would date several centuries earlier than 1000 BP. Thompson was able to extract ample rondel phytolith assemblages from all the samples for statistical analysis. That analysis indicated that maize had been cooked in all the pots, along with wild rice (*Zizania aquatica*), a grass species that occurs naturally in much of eastern North America. Thompson also identified squash (*Cucurbita* sp.) and sedge (*Cyperus* sp.) phytoliths in the residues. The AMS dates on the residues from Kipp Island and Wickham were as early as the first half of the fourteenth century BP. In analyzing just six residue samples, we were able to demonstrate that maize was present in New York some 350 to 400 years earlier than the macrobotanical record suggested (Hart et al. 2003).

More recently Brumbach and I submitted to Thompson samples for analysis from two sites that we believed would date even earlier. One of these, Vinette, is located near the sites in the original analysis. The second, Fortin 2, is from the upper Susquehanna River valley to the east. Here again, the sherds with residues had been in the museum's collections for decades. We submitted three samples from each site to Thompson. He and his colleague Robert Lusteck were able to extract ample rondel phytolith assemblages from two samples from each site for classification and statistical analysis. The statistical analysis identified each of the four phytolith assemblages as having originated from maize. The AMS dates on the residues from Vinette went back to the twentieth century BP, while those from Fortin 2 dated to the sixteenth century BP. The results indicate that maize was being cooked, and presumably grown, in New York a full 900 to 1000 years earlier than the macrobotanical record suggests (Thompson et al. 2004).

THE COMMON BEAN (*Phaseolus vulgaris*)

Like maize, the common bean originated in Mexico, but unlike maize, there is genetic evidence to suggest that populations in Andean South America were also brought under cultivation by ancient Native Americans (Kami et al. 1995). The earliest dates on cultivated bean in Mexico are about 2500 BP, while from South America we have 4400 BP (Kaplan and Lynch 1999). As related earlier, it has been accepted that the common bean was adopted by 1000 BP in northeastern North America. Even though bean remains were reported from 1000 BP contexts and earlier across the Northeast following Ritchie's publications of Roundtop, until the direct dating of beans from Roundtop, beans from only one other site in the Northeast had been subjected to direct dating, and the result was approximately 600 BP. After the Roundtop results, I set out with my colleague C. Margaret Scarry to directly date other beans from early contexts in the Northeast. We were able to obtain bean samples from six additional sites in Vermont, New York, and Pennsylvania from contexts reported to be as early as 1200 BP. These samples were obtained from museums and from other collection repositories. The samples from one of the Pennsylvania sites were determined by Scarry to contain no bean remains, although the others were confirmed as beans. All the bean samples yielded AMS dates at right around calibrated 650 BP, consistent with the results from Roundtop (Hart and Scarry 1999). These results, then, strongly suggest that the common bean was not a regular part of Native American cropping systems until well over a millennium after the appearance of maize.

While we had resolved the issue on the timing of bean's appearance in the archaeological record of the far Northeast, there remained an issue of its timing across the greater Northeast, specifically in Ohio, Kentucky, Indiana, Illinois, and southern Ontario, where it was reported in numerous contexts earlier than 650 BP. My colleagues David Asch (then of the Illinois State Museum), Scarry, Gary Crawford (University of Toronto), and I assembled bean samples, in some cases with maize samples from the same contexts, from 20 more sites as far west as the lower Illinois River valley. In all cases the beans were obtained from museums or other artifact repositories. The direct AMS dates on these samples, combined with those from original samples in the Northeast,

FIGURE 13.22 Early bean dates (BP) for northeastern North America.

meant that there were now 51 dates from 26 sites stretching from Illinois to Vermont. None of the dates was earlier than approximately calibrated 700 BP (Hart et al. 2002). That is, the earliest date in Illinois is statistically no older than the earliest date in Vermont (Figure 13.22). Based on the macrobotanical record, then, it appears that after the common bean had been introduced to the northern portions of eastern North America, it spread rapidly east and north, becoming an important component of agricultural systems and diets by 700 BP to 650 BP. Interestingly, beans become evident on sites from the Central Plains region a few centuries earlier than in the Northeast (Adair 2003). This suggests, but by no means conclusively proves, that beans entered the Northeast from the Plains.

SQUASH (*Cucurbita pepo*)

The third crop, squash, has a much longer history in the Northeast than maize and beans. There are two subspecies of the primary squash species present in the East prior to the crop distribution changes induced by Euro-American contact (Robinson and Decker-Walters 1996). *Cucurbita pepo* ssp. *pepo* originated in Mexico. This subspecies is represented today by many autumn squash cultivars and some ornamental gourds. The second subspecies, *Cucurbita pepo* ssp. *ovifera*, originated in the Ozarks of southern Missouri and northern Arkansas and perhaps the greater Gulf Coastal Plain. Present-day cultivars include many of our summer squashes, acorn squashes, and ornamental gourds. The *ovifera* subspecies is the most likely to account for most of the squashes under cultivation by Late Prehistoric and early Historic Indian agriculturists in the Northeast.

One thing that makes the evolution of this species so interesting is its presence on archaeological sites across the greater Northeast during the mid-Holocene, as early as calibrated 7900 BP in Illinois (Asch and Asch 1985) and calibrated 6500 BP in Maine (Petersen and Asch Sidell 1996) (Figure 13.23). Based on seed size and rind thickness, it is thought that the remains represent *C. pepo* gourds. Native stands of *C. pepo* gourds produce a chemical called cucurbitacin that makes their flesh and seed coats extremely bitter (Robinson and Decker-Walters 1996). If the mid-Holocene *C. pepo* gourds shared this trait, and there is presently no reason to believe they did not, why would Indians have made use of the gourds? Why

FIGURE 13.23 Early squash dates (BP) for northeastern North America.

would they apparently have facilitated their spread from the Gulf Coastal Plain to the far Northeast? These questions have caused considerable debate in the archaeological literature.

The gourds are very small, about the size of a small adult human's fist. Each gourd contains over 100 seeds about a third to half the size of a seed from a large pumpkin. Two hypotheses for their mid-Holocene use have generated the most interest: (1) dried gourds served utilitarian purposes such as fishnet floats or containers and (2) the bitterness was removed from the seed coats and the highly nutritious seeds were eaten (Hart et al. 2004). Of course these hypotheses are not mutually exclusive, although at times they have been so treated in the archaeological literature.

There is scant evidence in the ethnohistoric record for Indians using gourds as fishnet floats in the East. While there is archaeological evidence from Florida to suggest that they were used for this purpose (Gilliland 1975), no archaeologist had ever reported on any experiments to determine how well the gourds would have functioned as floats. My museum colleagues Robert Daniels, an ichthyologist, and Charles Sheviak, a botanist, and I decided to test the fishnet float hypothesis (Hart et al. 2004). We first obtained two dried *C. pepo* ssp. *ovifera* gourds from southern Missouri. We extracted the seeds from one of the gourds and successfully germinated six of them. The six seedlings were raised under artificial light until each had four leaves. When there was no danger of frost, they were planted in four locations in the

FIGURE 13.24 Using experimental gourd floats to seine for fish.

Albany, New York, region. Two lived long enough to produce 50 or more gourds. These were allowed to dry. Then we tested the ability of the gourds to float in water while supporting weight. We found that the gourds could support as much weight without submerging as a modern Styrofoam fishnet float of similar size.

We then attached gourds to two kinds of nets, gill nets and a seine, to determine whether they would work well as net floats (Figure 13.24). The gill nets were placed in two different ponds and left for 12 or more hours each. There was no loss in buoyancy during the trials, and the gourds suffered no obvious damage from being in the water for such long periods of time. The seine net was dragged through both calm and turbulent water in a nearby stream. The gourds kept the net open, allowing the capture of large numbers of fish of varying size. Our tests determined that *C. pepo* gourds work very well as fishnet floats—as well as modern Styrofoam floats. These results certainly added key support for the net-float hypothesis, but did not in any way disprove the seed consumption hypothesis.

Bruce Smith and C. Wesley Cowan, paleoethnobotanists who did extensive fieldwork on the natural history of *C. pepo* ssp. *ovifera* populations in the 1980s, related that they had been able to make the gourd seeds edible by boiling them for 5 to 10 minutes (Cowan and Smith 1993). David Asch (1995) subsequently reported that he had been unable to duplicate those results. I boiled the seeds for 10 minutes and also failed to remove the seed coat bitterness (Hart et al. 2004). I subsequently undertook a series of other experiments to determine whether the seeds could be made edible (Hart 2004). Indians used wood ash dissolved in water to process a number of food items, including bitter acorns, to make them palatable. I was able to remove the bitterness from gourd seeds by boiling them in water with wood ash for one hour. I was able to speed this to 20 minutes by slightly crushing the seed coats before boiling. The bitterness was also removed by soaking slightly crushed seeds in water with wood ash for 48 hours. Soaking whole seeds in water with wood ash for a week failed to remove all of the bitterness.

The fishnet float and wood ash processing experiments have clearly demonstrated that *C. pepo* ssp. *ovifera* gourds could have been used by mid-Holocene Indians for various purposes. But they were gourds, not the fruits with edible flesh that we commonly call squash and so clearly associate with American Indian agriculture. When did these edible fruits enter Indian agricultural systems? Based on the presence of larger seeds and thicker rind fragments at archaeological sites in the Midwest, squashes were being grown by calibrated 4900 BP (Frances B. King 1985). The earliest evidence in the Northeast for squash is calibrated 2750 BP (Hart and Asch-Sidell 1997) in the Susquehanna Basin of Pennsylvania. The earliest evidence in New York had been the 650 BP squash seeds at Roundtop. However, as noted earlier, squash phytoliths, presumably produced by *C. pepo* ssp. *ovifera*, from cooking residues, were dated as early as calibrated 1400 BP in New York (Hart et al. 2003, 2004).

ON THE IMPORTANCE OF MUSEUM COLLECTIONS IN MODERN ARCHAEOLOGICAL RESEARCH

The ongoing museum-collections-based research program on the history of maize-bean-squash has revised our knowledge of that history considerably. No longer can we envision a process in New York, or the greater Northeast, whereby the three crops were adopted late, relative to the Midwest, as a unit or in quick succession around 1000 years ago. Rather, it is now apparent that maize and squash had much longer histories, and were, in fact, being cooked together by at least 1550 years ago. Beans, on the other hand, are not evident until much later, approximately 700 to 650 years ago. Thus, the polyculture system that characterized Late Prehistoric and early Historic American Indian agriculture in the Northeast was not in place until only a few centuries before it was first observed by European explorers (Biggar 1924).

Just a few short years ago, none of these major changes in the crop histories were envisioned. The sudden occurrence of maize-bean-squash agriculture in New York about 1000 years ago was the foundation of interpretations on the "origins" of the Northern Iroquoians in New York (Hart 2001). That traditionally assumed association has now completely broken down (Hart and Brumbach 2003). Our understanding of the crops' histories now encompasses a much longer period of time, opening up new possibilities for restructuring our conceptions of how agriculture did, or did not, influence the development of various socioeconomic traits that have been used to characterize Late Prehistoric and early Historic American Indians in the Northeast (Hart 2001). Much exciting research lies ahead as a result of these new understandings of the crops' histories.

I opened this case study with a discussion of the importance of archaeological collections. I hope that you are now convinced of the importance of preserving these collections for future research. That little of the research reviewed here could have been accomplished in such a relatively short period of time without the museum collections should amply demonstrate the importance of professionally curated collections in modern archaeological research. The collections used in this research were made decades ago, well before the development of modern recovery methods. The advent of new recovery techniques over the past several decades, which ensure the recovery of a wider spectrum of the human behavioral evidence, potentially make collections made today even more valuable to future archaeologists. Having these collections curated and made available for research will ensure continued excitement of discovery about the history of our species.

DISCUSSION QUESTIONS

1. What has been the traditional perspective on when maize-bean-squash agriculture spread into the Northeast? Why does it matter that the crops in the maize-bean-squash agricultural complex now seem to have different histories?

2. How has cooking residue on pottery sherds been used to date the presence and use of maize? Does this suggest anything to you about how archaeologists should treat pottery sherds that they find in future excavations?

3. Do you think it more likely that *Cucurbita pepo ovifera* seeds were used for food, that the gourds were used as fish floats, or both? How conclusive is the experimental evidence concerning possible use? Can you think of other ways to evaluate the problem?

4. What do you think of Hart's argument that museum collections are important to future archaeological research? How does this relate to the issues discussed in "The Curation Crisis," Section F.2 of the Student CD?

Part 3

THE FUTURE OF NORTH AMERICAN ARCHAEOLOGY

CHAPTER 14

North American Archaeology for the Twenty-first Century

ach year school-children across Pennsylvania are invited to participate in an essay contest about archaeology. Their essays must address the following question: Why is it important to protect archaeological sites? Students may enter individually, or a teacher can enter a group of essays from an entire class. Entries for the essay contest are solicited during Pennsylvania Archaeology Month, which is usually October. Members of the Pennsylvania Archaeological Council, which sponsors the contest, read the students' essays and score them based on understanding of archaeological ethics concerning site preservation as well as on expressive merit. Essays from fourth through sixth graders are considered separately from essays written by seventh to ninth graders. Those essays that most readers score high win prizes, including subscriptions to *Archaeology* magazine, posters, plaques, and certificates. An awards ceremony often is held at the Pennsylvania State Museum beneath the imposing statue of William Penn that stands in the vestibule, reminding everyone of Pennsylvania's important past.

It's a small contest, but the professional archaeologists who volunteer to read essays and organize the awards ceremony put many hours into the work. The contest also uses some of the limited budget of the Pennsylvania Archaeological Council, an organization of no more than 70 or 80 archaeologists employed in universities, CRM firms, and state agencies. Why bother? What makes this annual exercise worthwhile? Of course the answer is simple. The children involved, as well as their parents and their teachers, are the future of archaeology in Pennsylvania. It is not enough for professionals in the field to know why sites should be saved, or even for students who take a course in North American archaeology to adopt the archaeological ethic of site preservation. The public at large must realize that sites of importance exist in Pennsylvania, and people must view these sites as resources worth saving.

There was a time when archaeologists were less concerned with public perceptions and less mindful of any responsibility to report their findings in a publicly accessible manner. However, one result of the growth of CRM archaeology has been to heighten the explicit awareness that what we do must be justifiable to more than

FIGURE 14.1 Archaeologist showing students how to chip stone to make a stone tool during an educational program.

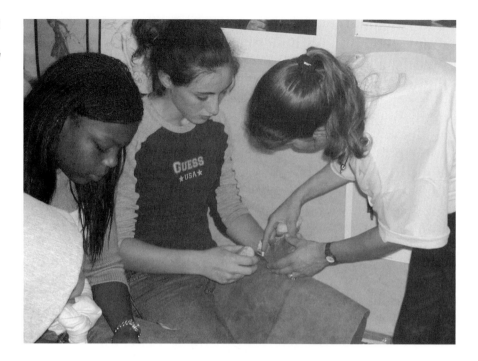

a small community of scholars. Part of this involves making archaeology intelligible to the public at large. Thus, Pennsylvania's essay contest is just one of many activities in the United States and Canada that seek to educate the public about North American archaeology (Figure 14.1). Public education promotes a preservation ethic that ultimately will both help lower the incidence of looting, and ensure that the public supports enlightened management of cultural resources. A few minutes of browsing on the Internet should turn up a wealth of information about archaeology months, weeks, or days and about public lectures, archaeology exhibits, and digs you may visit in your state or province. You may find the website for local archaeological associations as well. We have included resources of this type in Section H of the Student CD.

As we conclude our consideration of North American archaeology, it is important to consider aspects of contemporary practice such as the new emphasis on public education. This chapter takes stock of what is known about the North American past and highlights changing aspects of the field of North American archaeology.

A PERSPECTIVE ON NORTH AMERICA'S PAST

In Chapter 1 we indicated that it would not be possible to provide a complete discussion of the North American past. Even though we have covered a great deal of material in this text, there is much more that you can find out by pursuing other sources. We encourage you to investigate aspects of North American archaeology that have interested you as you've read this book. Archaeologists in many places throughout the continent can help you discover our past more deeply. Nevertheless, we hope that this book has provided a basic understanding of what is known and an idea of what archaeologists may yet find out, for we believe Confucius was right when he said, "Study the past if you would divine the future." Now that you can recognize some sites and cultures from pre-Columbian and Historic North America, you should have a new perspective on the North American past that will remain useful in present and future circumstances.

Beyond the obvious point that there is much to know about North America's past, we hope this new perspective includes the rejection of common stereotypes about Native North Americans and their history. Most important among these inaccurate stereotypes is the conception that North American Natives were all alike. Clearly this is grossly untrue. All Native Americans were not war-bonneted, teepee-dwelling, equestrian hunters of bison. Neither were they uniformly the peace-loving tribal environmentalists envisioned in popular culture (Krech 1999). There was both great diversity in Native adaptations and great change among them over time. The cultural distance between Archaic hunters on the Great Plains and Mississippians living at Cahokia at AD 1100 was nearly as profound as that between English colonists in New England and the Algonquians they encountered. Hundreds of different ethnicities once existed, and these peoples did not have uniform customs or beliefs. Similarly, change among societies since European colonization has not been uniform. That we only partially know the story of North America's past should not be an excuse for thinking all Native people were or are alike.

A second stereotype that Native Americans were primitive or simple also should seem ridiculous. Exactly what is meant by the term isn't always clear, but generally "primitive" seems to refer to people living in small-scale, egalitarian, and foraging societies. Regardless of whether these characteristics in fact make people backward, which we would dispute, variability may be the most important attribute of past cultures in North America. The archaeological record also makes it clear that among the Native societies of pre-Columbian North America there were a number of chiefdoms characterized by agricultural production or the intensive use of marine resources, dense populations, long-distance trade and exchange, sophisticated art or craft items, social ranking, and complex ideologies. Some Native American constructions, like the earthworks of the Hopewell, still are marvels for their geometric precision and size. While these North American societies did not rival Mesoamerican civilizations, calling them primitive is inappropriate for many reasons. Popular ideas about how to categorize human cultures have encouraged many inaccurate stereotypes, and Native American societies provide examples that can help revise classifications based more on ignorance and prejudice than on facts.

Finally, we hope this book has dispelled the common misperception that there is nothing of archaeological importance to preserve in North America. Archaeological knowledge can be obtained in so many ways that even the smallest and most unexciting sites may contribute important information. Besides, some exciting sites are evident in ruins, and others are not highly visible on the surface. You've seen this throughout the text in case studies and other references to sites and artifacts. It is true that the archaeological record of North America's past will always be incomplete because not everything preserves, but it is also

FIGURE 14.2
Archaeological site being graded during construction near Oceanside, California. The stone mortar fragment and pestle in the foreground were noted by an archaeological monitor and collected. The white specks are fragments of shell from the Pacific Ocean.

true that the thoughtless destruction and mistreatment of important cultural resources have made the record more incomplete than it would have been as a result of natural processes. Unfortunately North American archaeological sites are routinely threatened, as discussed in Box 14.1. Not only do unscrupulous people loot and destroy sites, but new roads, shopping centers, and housing projects bulldoze them away (Figure 14.2). Legislative protections have been greatly increased in the last 30 to 40 years, but the question of how to sensitively and responsibly manage North America's cultural resources continues to need discussion. We believe that the policy issues involved are not perceived because North America's past is not widely known. Knowledgeable citizens represent a first defense against the loss of North America's archaeological resources. We hope that the readers of this book can be counted among those who are prepared to participate in public debate about the management of cultural resources.

RECONSIDERING THE NORTH AMERICAN ARCHAEOLOGICAL STORY

As you have learned in this text, archaeologists know much about North America's past before and after Columbus. We have learned much in recent decades as CRM archaeology has required more uniform documentation of the traces of the past. We have often pointed out here that older, simpler explanations for archaeological phenomena have proved inadequate as more data have been gathered. Yet, there is much more archaeologists would like to know. New discoveries and new techniques promise that we will find out. Of course, it is a truism in science that the more you learn, the more you realize what you don't

ISSUES AND DEBATES

BOX 14.1

How Can We Stop Looting of Archaeological Sites?

A central value among archaeologists is that since archaeological sites, artifacts, and features are irreplaceable resources for understanding past cultures, their preservation is highly desirable. Promoting the stewardship of such resources is an ethical obligation for archaeologists. Steward-ship involves managing sites responsibly and taking care of collections as well as deterring looting. The problem of looting, however, is longstanding, and no more resolved now than it was a hundred years ago when the Antiquities Act of 1906 banned the removal of artifacts from federal lands. If anything, the problem of destruction of sites through looting may have become worse in recent years (Hollowell-Zimmer 2003). Looting is an international prob-lem closely related to art theft and trafficking in stolen art. However, the GE Mound case described in Chapter 12 reminds us that illegal acquisition and sale of antiquities is a concern in North America as well.

Encounters with collectors such as de-scribed in the opening to Chapter 7 also remind us that archaeological values are not neces-sarily shared universally. The issues involved are not straightforward. Some collectors argue that they preserve items that otherwise would be lost or destroyed. Archaeologists counter that out-of-context artifacts may be attractive, but they tell us much less than carefully documented items in site collections.

Who is a looter or **pothunter** anyway? Generally, "looting" refers to the illegal removal of artifacts and other property from Historic or Prehistoric sites or museums. It is clear that the people who removed antiquities from the Baghdad Museum immediately after the fall of Iraq to American forces in 2003 can be called

looters. Can we apply the term to someone who collects arrowheads from the surface of a plowed field without the landowner's permis-sion? Should we confine the use of "pothunting" to digging into a site illegally? Is the intent to sell an object essential to defining the person who removed the artifact from its site as a looter? In reality, there is a wide range of activities that cause destruction of sites and information and might fall under the heading of looting or pothunt-ing. Some of these activities result in major site destruction; thefts on a smaller scale are called "low-end looting" (Hollowell-Zimmer 2003).

Our difficulty with defining "looting" and "pothunting" precisely results from the absence of widespread agreement about what actions are appropriate, or at least acceptable, at archaeo-logical sites and with respect to artifacts. It is diffi-cult to stop activities that are not widely regarded as undesirable, and it is even more difficult to deter behavior we don't understand. Several recent examinations have provided insights into the culture of pothunting. For example, Early (1989) found that in Arkansas, three groups of people participate in a subculture involved in the trafficking of antiquities. These are diggers, who actually dig into sites and remove artifacts (Figure 14.3), dealers who buy and sell the arti-facts obtained by diggers, and financiers, the wealthy collectors who want antiquities for their own collections. Many people involved in activ-ities of these kinds are interested in Indian arti-facts, but they do not think of undocumented and careless digging as destructive. Participants in the subculture of looting are entrepreneurial; they seek a monetary profit from their activities. Diggers may see pothunting as a possible means of getting rich akin to hitting a lottery

FIGURE 14.3 A particularly destructive aspect of pothunting is the focus on finding complete artifacts, which can be sold or displayed; the result is the disturbance and destruction of a great deal of material that might have provided insight into the past.

jackpot; dealers see themselves as engaged in a business undertaking; financiers often are seeking investments and may donate unwanted materials to museums as tax write-offs.

Understanding these aspects of trafficking is important to devising strategies for curbing site destruction due to looting. Various approaches might be possible. In the United States, legislation like the Archaeological Resources Protection Act (ARPA) has been designed to deter looting. This act makes it illegal to excavate or sell any archaeological resource located on federal or Indian land without a permit. Violation of ARPA can lead to a fine of $10,000 to $20,000 and/or five years in jail. Since ARPA does not apply to private land, laws against interstate

trafficking in stolen property can be invoked in situations like the GE Mound case. We can work for strict implementation of laws like ARPA. However, laws, even if they are consistently enforced, may not be the whole answer. Except perhaps for the most casual diggers, illegality may add intrigue to pothunting.

What else might we do to protect sites? Museums, universities, and art galleries can insist on careful documentation of ownership and **provenance** for any antiquities or collections offered them. However, most reputable institutions already do this; it's collectors who often fail to obtain such information before purchasing artifacts. Currently, antiquities offered on the Internet can be obtained without the kinds of documentation that museums routinely ask for. Thus people without any understanding of the issues involved are at risk of buying stolen property. Perhaps educational efforts by archaeologists can reduce looting and antiquities trafficking.

However, educating the public must involve more than stirring up popular interest in North America's past. Pothunters often are interested in an area's past, and many times quite knowledgeable about it. They may even have read some of the professional archaeological literature to find out where sites are and how they are structured. It appears that the destruction caused by pothunting and the antiquities market is fueled by conditions beyond simple ignorance or even simple greed. Interest in the past and fascination with its traces also are involved. The challenge is finding ways to promote a conservation ethic while still allowing the public to enjoy the traces of the past (Figure 14.4). This is a challenge for the twenty-first century.

FIGURE 14.4 This sign at Pinson Mounds in Tennessee is a reminder to visitors that cultural and natural resources should be conserved for the future; of course as heritage tourism increases in sites with very high rates of visitation, even the footprints of thousands of visitors might erode surfaces and damage structures.

know. This is certainly the case in archaeology, where once one question has been settled, a host of new questions often develops. As we finish this introduction to North American archaeology, it makes sense to take account of some of the things archaeologists have found out about this continent's past as well as to comment on what research areas may be important in the immediate future.

First, there is growing evidence related to the initial human migration across the globe, which is the first of the broad anthropological themes mentioned in Chapter 2. North American data contribute significantly to worldwide understanding of human migration at the end of the Ice Age. As we discussed in Chapter 3, the consensus about when and how the Americas were settled by humans is changing; the Clovis-First scenario is no longer an adequate explanation, either with respect to timing or with respect to what these first settlers were like. It is probable that humans did enter this continent before Clovis times, though claims of human entry before approximately 16,000 BP remain suspect, and the evidence is very limited. However, the Monte Verde site and others in South America, as well as other evidence that Upper Paleolithic people made watercraft, help support the scant data from North America itself.

This opens up the possibility of significant research on possible Pre-Clovis settlement, on various routes of entry, on similarities with early Siberian and other technologies, and on the nature of the first settlers' adaptations. In addition, as the biological characteristics of early skeletons have come to light, the possibility of biologically distinct populations and multiple migrations has been raised. Osteological, dental, and genetic analyses can now be profitably undertaken. Surely, we will be learning much more about all these topics during the next few decades.

Second, humans obviously adapted to the diverse environments of North America in a variety of ways. Simplistic notions about Native American subsistence, economics, and settlement certainly need to be discarded. The people of the North American past sometimes got most of their foods from the sea, and they used many wild plants and animals from terrestrial habitats as well. They also were not just hunter-gatherers; many were farmers, especially in the Southwest, on the Great Plains, and in the East. Even when they were hunter-gatherers, North Americans organized themselves in varied ways, such as the complex hunter-gatherer societies of the West Coast. Whether they were mobile or sedentary themselves, throughout the continent people traded raw materials and finished products over long distances. Some of the items traded were very finely made and represent sophisticated craftsmanship. Thinking about the large quantity of archaeological information that has been introduced in this text should convince you that North America is hardly a backwater; rather, it can be viewed as a laboratory for investigating the many ways humans have survived over time.

Third, North America is the location for a very important part of the record of early food production. This has been appreciated only in recent decades, after flotation and ethnobotanical analysis have become more routine in archaeological research projects. As a result, archaeologists are just beginning to understand the cultivation and domestication of native plants in the Eastern Woodlands as part of the Eastern Agricultural complex. The societal implications of this early type of food production can now be explored. Certainly it is important that food production was invented independently here, just as it was in other primary centers of domestication like Southwest Asia or Mesoamerica.

The timing and nature of the adoption of tropical cultigens in the Southwest, on the Great Plains, and throughout the Eastern Woodlands also is being profitably investigated by archaeologists. As indicated in Chapter 13's case study, "A New History of Maize-Bean-Squash Agriculture in the Northeast," one surprise has been that the maize-bean-squash triumvirate was not adopted as a package by easterners. Rather, each plant has its own history of acceptance.

As these aspects of North America's past are rewritten by today's archaeologists, contributions to anthropology and human history in general are being made. The puzzle of why humans became food producers is of great scholarly interest. Recent discoveries make it clear that many parts of North America represent a laboratory for testing ideas about the adoption of agriculture. We predict much more archaeological and ethnobotanical study as this is widely realized.

Fourth, discussions in many of our chapters have made clear that native North Americans developed fascinating systems of social ranking and sociopolitical integration. As indicated in Chapter 2 this is a recurring theme of interest to archaeologists. North American complex hunter-gatherers along the West Coast, in Alaska, and in southern Florida represent particularly interesting examples of social complexity among maritime foragers. In fact, North America affords some of the best examples of this sort of adaptation in the world, and its past should convince scholars that societies can be socioculturally complex without being agricultural. Important questions regarding the emergence of complexity may be addressed by archaeologists working in these areas. For example, see the case study in Chapter 4.

However, the topic of complexity is also important in studying agricultural polities in the Southwest and the Eastern Woodlands. Here the degree and nature of elite power, the production and exchange of prestige items, and the significance of mortuary and other ritual behavior will continue to be of great interest to archaeologists. Notably, developments like those among the Hopewell or in Plains Village societies that appear to have been tribal seem important to understanding how humans shifted from largely egalitarian lifeways to ranked societies. The North American archaeological record suggests that anthropological ideas about sociopolitical complexity have been too narrowly defined. There probably are several ways that complexity, defined as social inequality and integration, can develop in human societies. For example, heterarchies, in which different communities share power and communal mobilization of labor, may have been important among North American societies. Once again, North America provides a field for testing many ideas developed elsewhere in the world, and we think important anthropological contributions will be made by North American archaeologists in the years to come.

A fifth theme, also introduced in Chapter 2 was the problem of tracing ethnic identities in the past. We hope you have a better sense of how archaeologists use material culture to identify ethnic groups from reading this text. Because so many unknown ethnic groups existed over the millennia of the North American past, the archaeological record is potentially useful for studying the history of Native groups. This is true even though we cannot always identify historically known ethnic identities from the data we have, and it is very important when material culture can be linked to ethnic identity. Several topics of growing interest archaeologically are related to efforts to trace the history of past ethnic groups.

On the one hand, archaeologists have a renewed interest in identifying human migrations based on biological and artifactual evidence. During the second half of the twentieth century, North American archaeologists tended to reject explanations based on human migration in favor of in situ evolution. Overly simplistic attributions of social change to the arrival of new groups certainly should be rejected, but the wholesale rejection of past group movements also is inappropriate. Recent discussion of possible key migrations in various areas of North America such as the Great Basin, the Southwest, the Great Plains and the

Northeast (see Box 13.1 in Chapter 13), are healthy signs of a more sophisticated interest in this topic. Advances in genetic techniques provide new tools with which to address such problems.

A related question calls for an examination of the various ways human populations can influence each other and how such influence is recognized archaeologically. Thus, the old question of Mesoamerican influence in both the Southwest and the Southeast is being explored. We can expect archaeologists to profitably investigate issues of these kinds more intensively in decades to come.

In addition, contemporary archaeologists understand the nature and range of pre-Columbian warfare and violence only partially. Older models based on generally peaceful tribal societies may not always encompass the conflicts between ethnic groups that did exist, particularly as population levels increased over time. This is most obvious in the Southwest, where recent claims of can- nibalism among the Ancestral Puebloan populations have been getting attention (see Section F.4, "Was There Cannibalism in the Prehistoric Southwest?" of the Student CD). In many areas, the most conflict may have developed during the Late Prehistoric, as indicated by widespread aggregation and fortification. How- ever, intersocietal violence also has a long, though variable, record in other parts of North America (Milner 1999), and archaeologists are just beginning to explore its significance. While this does not mean that even older views of Native Americans as violent savages should be resurrected, it is clear that conflict occurred among the pre-Columbian ethnic groups of North America. New research will allow us to discard stereotypical ideas about tribal people and to adopt a more realistic understanding of the dynamic nature of past societies and their interactions.

The sixth theme noted in Chapter 2, culture contact as Europeans arrived in North America, might be understood as a special case of concern with ethnic groups and their interactions. We hope this text has made clear that for the Protohistoric and Contact periods, there is fruitful research to be done through- out North America. The complexity of Native–European interaction is very poorly known, but the story of these times is certainly not simply one of conquest by Europeans. Natives sometimes prevailed in early hostile encounters, as with the Pueblo Revolt in 1680. Regardless of ultimate outcomes, Native peoples always had their own stratagems, particularly with respect to trade and political alliances. Unfortunately, standard histories poorly document the Native side of the story. Studies that combine archaeology and ethnohistory seem to be growing in num- ber (e.g., LaVere 1998; Marvin T. Smith 2002). Both scholars and Native Americans interested in tribal heritage find these studies important. Contemporary native perspectives also can add significant insight as shown in the case study for Chapter 7, "Cultures in Contact at Colony Ross." We expect that research on colonial cultural interactions will grow in importance during the next few decades.

The seventh and last thematic question listed in Chapter 2 is the historical development of the United States and Canada. We have provided examples of projects in historical archaeology throughout this text. Archaeology isn't less rele- vant to investigations of this part of the past just because documentary evidence exists, perhaps abundantly. CRM archaeology gathers evidence from historic as well as prehistoric times, and many significant insights have been gained since its inception. We believe two topics in historical archaeology are most likely to receive increased attention in the immediate future.

First, archaeology can provide insights about the history of African Americans. Written accounts are seriously lacking in the details of lifestyles and circumstances for both slaves and free blacks during the eighteenth and nineteenth centuries. This is true in both the North and the South (see Box 1.2; Harrington 1996). Besides cemeteries, plantation slave quarters can be profitably excavated. In several states, there also is great interest at present in documenting Underground Railroad contexts (e.g., Delle and Levine 2004). Because there is intense interest in better documentation of this history, we can expect many more archaeological contributions during the next few decades. Perhaps more African Americans will choose archaeological careers as a result.

A final area in which research seems to us to have just begun is the archaeological investigation of our industrial history. As we have said in several chapters, this is an area of growing interest fueled in part by CRM laws requiring investigation of all cultural resources. Technology is, of course, a traditional area of archaeological research, so documenting the nature of early industrial production (see Exhibit 13.1) is right up an archaeologist's alley. The impact of mass production on society is a related topic that can be documented through archaeological studies of material culture. Finally, the story of life in early company towns has been poorly told in written history, but the archaeological remains of these places can still be explored, adding to the quality of our social history. Thus, many aspects of industrial archaeology are likely to catch the imagination of both archaeologists and the public, and we anticipate much more industrial archaeology in decades to come.

The body of knowledge generated by North American archaeology is large and potentially important in several ways, but we do not know everything. We have tried to point out the value of this body of knowledge to understanding humans in general and to suggest possible areas for future research. Other archaeologists undoubtedly would add to our list, and probably significant topics of study will arise that no one can anticipate today. Theoretical perspectives will also change and affect the questions archaeologists ask as this century continues. For example, research in the areas of gender and individual agency may grow in importance as postprocessual arguments continue to influence North American archaeologists. Perhaps you will help define additional research topics if you pursue North American archaeology. We are still learning about North America's past, and there is no shortage of interesting research to be done by those who pursue this field (Figure 14.5). On the other hand, you should stay tuned even if you don't formally pursue archaeology because North America contains important clues in the search for helpful answers about the human past.

THE CHANGING DISCIPLINE

As we think ahead about North American archaeology in the twenty-first century, besides new research directions, we can anticipate that the field itself will continue to change in a variety of interesting ways. New methods will be adopted, and preservation laws will change. Moreover, ethical concerns will need to be addressed as the social context of archaeology itself changes. It makes sense to note current trends of this type in our final chapter.

New Methods in Archaeology

Although both muscle and brain power remain important to archaeologists, contemporary archaeology relies heavily on modern technologies from global

FIGURE 14.5 Excavations underway at the Leetsdale site in southwestern Pennsylvania for the U.S. Army Corps of Engineers: there is a great deal still to be learned about North America's past, and archaeological studies done in the context of CRM are making important contributions to our knowledge each year.

FIGURE 14.6 Within the last decade, the use of handheld GPS units has become standard in archaeology; additional technological advances are likely to impact the field in the future.

positioning units (Figure 14.6) and ground-penetrating radar to the use of scanning electron microscopes and all sorts of computer-assisted mapping hardware and software. We have mentioned some of these techniques in the text and case studies, and they are reviewed as well in Sections B and C of the Student CD. It is clear that this "high tech" trend will continue during the next few decades. Three specific areas seem most likely to impact the field in the twenty-first century.

First, geophysical survey is of increasing importance in archaeology. Techniques today include electrical resistivity measurements, use of ground-penetrating radar, and use of seismic or acoustic methods that pass various kinds of energy below the surface of the ground or water, recording the response as a means of detecting subsurface characteristics. Geophysical survey also includes more passive techniques such as magnetic survey methods that measure slight distortions in magnetic fields and metal detectors that locate objects containing metal. Such techniques allow archaeologists to learn about site structure without destroying it and to target hand excavations accordingly. The usefulness of geophysical approaches can be seen clearly in several of the case studies in this book. At this point we cannot use these techniques to locate and understand small-scale features as successfully as we can apply them to the assessment of large structural components like earthworks. However, such techniques have proliferated and improved rapidly over the last decade. We expect that they will become more effective, cheaper, and even more commonly used in the years to come.

A second tool that already is transforming the way archaeological analyses are done is GIS (Geographical Information System). This tool provides for map-based database management that is particularly useful in the analysis of the many types of spatial data archaeologists generate. Site data can be analyzed in conjunction with environmental data in these applications, making this software useful in developing site location models. Today, many state and federal agencies use GIS software to manage site file information. With GIS, these databases become powerful tools for both management and research. Similarly, archaeologists increasingly use GIS to develop the data from archaeological excavations and surveys, linking various maps with images and descriptions of artifacts and features. The next generation of archaeologists is likely to use GIS even more. Students should develop familiarity with this kind of software as part of their college experience.

Several types of chemical and molecular analysis also are now being used in archaeology. We have mentioned research topics that benefit from the current ease with which genetic studies of mtDNA can be conducted. Genetic studies are likely to become most important in archaeological research about colonization or interrelationships among populations. Traces of blood on stone tools also can be examined to determine what species of animal left the blood. Because blood residues can survive for tens of thousands of years, the potential of this type of analysis is great. Other techniques, including a wide array of **isotopic analyses,** which measure chemical signatures, also can contribute to archaeological questions about diet and population history as well as dating. These are studies that can be done on bone as well as directly on many artifacts, and applications are proliferating. Of course, study of soil chemistry is another tool for understanding site use. For example, concentrations of phosphate at sites with acidic soils may confirm heavy use of animals by area residents. The possibilities for contributions by archaeological chemists are just now beginning to be understood.

Finally, as indicated in several places in this text including the case study in Chapter 13, "A New History for Maize-Bean-Squash Agriculture in the Northeast," AMS dating techniques are providing a second radiocarbon revolution within archaeology. We can now directly date small organic objects like beans, and even tiny portions of one-of-a-kind specimens, without destroying them. We can also get dates from residues cooked onto pots or burned into pipes, and we can date contexts with the smallest traces of organic materials. Archaeologists stand to learn a tremendous amount from the application of this technique over the next few decades; we can only imagine how forthcoming results will change our understanding of North America's past.

We expect that there are many other advances in techniques that will be used by future generations of archaeologists, and we can be confident that new techniques and new applications will be found as the twenty-first century proceeds. North American archaeologists, like our colleagues working elsewhere in the world, are bound to benefit from these developments.

Managing and Protecting North America's Heritage

One of the most important issues archaeologists will face during the twenty-first century is the need to manage and protect the record of North America's past. How well we will succeed is not just a matter for CRM archaeologists to contemplate; all research will be limited by the nature of the record that is preserved. We discussed the importance of preserving sites in Box 14.1, but several other current issues help indicate the complexities being faced in this area.

First, as mentioned in Chapter 1, there is a real crisis in archaeological curation. Not only is there a need to preserve sites, the collections generated by archaeological research must be preserved, as well (Sullivan and Childs 2003). The facilities and personnel to adequately care for the archaeological collections we now have too often are lacking and more collections are being generated all the time. Curation is not just a matter of boxing up excavated artifacts (see Section F.2 of the Student CD). Materials must be stored so that they will remain intact, and collections must be accessible to researchers. As shown by several case studies in this volume, museum collections can be tremendously important in archaeological research. On the other hand, should we be saving everything encountered, or should most items in some categories, such as fire-cracked rock or brick, be counted, weighed, and discarded? Curation is a major issue for North American archaeologists. Although we expect that a variety of creative solutions will be found over the next few decades, the archaeological community is just waking up to the crisis at hand.

A second issue that is likely to be of great importance, particularly within CRM archaeology, is the impact of government regulation on private property rights. The Fifth Amendment to the U.S. Constitution states that no one can be deprived of property without due process or have private property taken without just compensation. On this basis today, some argue that certain environmental laws and regulations, including those that pertain to archaeological sites and historic preservation, are government "takings" for which property owners should be compensated. Of course, it is not at all clear that laws requiring the identification and assessment of cultural resources prior to development significantly limit the rights of property owners, nor are private property rights in the United States unlimited per se. Nevertheless, proponents of property rights are vocal, and key court decisions undoubtedly will affect legal interpretations with respect to environmental and cultural protection in the future. This is one of the areas in which developing public policy might be of great importance to archaeology.

Another area in which public policy is likely to continue developing has to do with the treatment of human skeletal remains and the interaction with descendant populations like Native Americans. You have learned in this text that some interactions between archaeologists and Native Americans have been quite positive (e.g., Chapter 5's case study, "Archaeological/Anthropological–Native American Coordination: An Example of Sharing the Research on the Northwest Coast of North America"). Yet as seen in the Kennewick case (Box 3.1), these interactions can be contentious, as well. The development of better policies for dealing with such cases is in order, and we can expect this to happen over the next few years. We anticipate additional changes in laws, regulation, and practice related to CRM archaeology to develop during the twenty-first century as well.

Finally, changes in CRM practice may also result from developments in the way laws and regulations are applied. For example, one question now being actively debated within the professional community is whether the significance of a site is affected by the state of archaeological knowledge about an area or a site type. We pointed out in Chapter 2 that only sites shown to be **significant cultural resources** receive full attention within the framework of CRM. Some people have suggested that after we have fully investigated a number of sites of a particular type—for example, small lithic scatters—another site of the same type is not really as significant. At least theoretically, once we fully understand the variability that exists, gathering redundant information at the public's expense is not warranted. The debatable question is whether such a point can be reached and if so, when that might be. A related idea under discussion is whether in some CRM projects **off-site mitigation** might be more justifiable than data recovery of redundant information. In such cases, although resources within a project right-of-way might be destroyed, information about more significant and somehow related resources might be obtained. In this manner a context for cultural resources within a project area can be established. It will be interesting to see how these debates about how to comply most responsibly with laws and regulations are resolved.

Archaeological Ethics in the Twenty-first Century

A recent discussion of the way archaeological ethics have changed over the last 30 or more years notes that archaeologists used to see ethics primarily in terms of the sites and artifacts they studied, but today they must accommodate concerns of living people as well (McGuire 2003). This provides a useful way to think about the ethics of doing archaeology today and in the future. More information about archaeological ethics can be found at the websites of the Society for American Archaeology (www.saa.org) and the Canadian Archaeological Association (www.canadianarchaeology.com).

It is still true that the archaeologists view the archaeological record as priceless and irreplaceable, and ethical practice centers on keeping this in mind. This aspect of archaeological ethics is basic and will remain so. This is why archaeologists are concerned with saving sites and preventing the Internet sale of illegally obtained artifacts. This is why curation is an issue we must address as a profession. This also is why the results of archaeological research must be published, or at least accessible, both professionally and publicly. The issue of sharing archaeological knowledge, discussed only briefly in this text, is one of the important ethical dilemmas archaeologists must address in the twenty-first century (Zimmerman 2003). It has often been hard for academic researchers to produce timely reports of their research, but it also is true that CRM reports, which usually must be produced rapidly for contractual reasons, seldom reach a wide audience and often languish in what has been called the "gray literature," known to only a few. Beyond all this is the issue we raised in the opening section of this chapter, sharing knowledge with the public. Practically, archaeologists need to share archaeological knowledge through public education so that people know that it is important to fund North American archaeology through research grants or in CRM. However, what we learn about the past doesn't really belong to archaeologists in the first place, and ethical practice dictates that we make our knowledge widely available.

This is the juncture at which new understandings of the archaeological ethics surrounding living people begin to come into play. Of course, we have ethical obligations to the professional community and to our students. However, most archaeologists today also understand that our professional skills and knowledge do not necessarily give us privileged access to the archaeological record. Descendant populations are important stakeholders with respect to the past, and their concerns cannot be ignored. Lay people with an interest in the past, such as collectors (La Belle 2003), must be considered as well. A definition of ethical conduct with respect to these other interested parties remains contested, but archaeologists will have to address this issue over the next few decades. The ethics of being an archaeologist are much more complicated than one might first think, as illustrated in Box 14.2. If you pursue archaeology, you will have to respectfully negotiate a web of obligations, so it will be helpful to begin thinking about them while still a student.

ISSUES AND DEBATES

BOX 14.2

Displaying the Past at Dickson Mounds

Many valuable places for learning about the past are sites at which parks and museums have been constructed to commemorate the peoples of the Native past. One such place is Dickson Mounds, located in west central Illinois (see Figure 12.1). Although today this part of Illinois is rural, from the Middle Woodland through the Mississippian periods it was an area of major population concentrations. Six large centers of Illinois Hopewell people, including the Ogden–Fettie site on the museum grounds, are in the vicinity of the museum. A large Late Woodland village, known as the Myer–Dickson site, also was once located on the museum grounds, as was a Mississippian center known as the Eveland Village, and a cluster of low mounds and cemeteries from the Mississippian period. It is because of these last sites that Dickson Mounds is a museum. The story of the development of Dickson Mounds as a museum reminds us that how we interpret the past is a public as well as a scholarly concern.

Local relic hunters considered the mounds on the Dickson farm a great spot to dig for artifacts from at least the end of the nineteenth century. They disturbed the mounds just as landowners did as they farmed and built homes without attempting to preserve what lay within the earthworks. Then, in 1927 Dr. Don Dickson, a chiropractor whose family had owned the land since the 1860s, decided to excavate into one area to study the human skeletons found there. According to all accounts, Dickson was mainly curious, but his experience transformed him into one of the best-known amateur archaeologists in the Midwest. Dickson's main innovation was to leave the skeletons in place, carefully excavating around them with small tools and brushes. This preserved the position of the remains of

individuals in the mound, opening up a whole series of questions about burial practices and culture. Dickson's method of excavation incorporated a standing invitation for family, friends, and neighbors to come by and view the work as it progressed. The onlookers asked so many questions that Dickson saw an opportunity to tell even more people about his new interest. He opened his excavations to the public, charging a small fee of 50¢ to adults to help with cost. Eventually he erected a permanent tile-block building over his excavation, which became the first Dickson Mounds exhibit hall.

To our modern sensibilities, exposed human burials may seem ghoulish, but it was never Dr. Dickson's intent to titillate morbid fancies. He wanted people to learn about the Indian past, which fascinated him. Obviously it fascinated the local public as well. Over 40,000 people came to the excavation at Dickson Mounds during the first year it was open (Harn 1995). Out of these beginnings grew a great deal of local interest in archaeology and pride in the Indian heritage of this part of Illinois. Dickson also attracted professionals, most notably Dr. Fay-Cooper Cole of the University of Chicago, who in the early 1930s ran one of the first archaeological field schools in North America near the site. So began the archaeological tradition of investigating the mounds and other sites of the area.

Despite public interest, it was not possible for Dickson to maintain the museum privately forever. Over the years, Dickson Mounds went through various administrative transfers, first becoming a state park, which Dickson and his family maintained. After Dickson's death in 1964, Dickson Mounds became part of the Illinois State Museum. The museum's exhibits, collections, and research facilities were enlarged and updated, but through it all two things stayed the same: the original burial area in which over 200 human skeletons were displayed remained open for viewing, and members of the general public kept coming to what they saw as an educational resource. Then, beginning in the late 1980s and early 1990s, Dickson Mounds was swept into the national debate over the treatment of human skeletal material, and major change came to the facility.

At this time Native Americans across the nation were saying that the remains of their ancestors should be repatriated and reburied, not studied by anyone, and certainly not displayed. Human burials were a focal point as Native Americans found their voice and insisted on their rights. These were the years in which NAGPRA was being crafted; these were the years when archaeology and museology woke up to Native concerns and issues. The Illinois museum staff, aware of national debate, recommended that the burial exhibit be closed. Initially the governor agreed, but then the public in Fulton County learned of the plan. Local residents were outraged. How could the state close "their museum"? Why should it have to listen to Indians, few of whom resided in Illinois any longer? People were unwilling for outsiders to have a say about what happened to Dickson Mounds. In an election year, the governor capitulated and reversed the decision to close the museum. At this point Native American protests began in earnest; Dickson Mounds was at the center of a nationally publicized controversy. Native activists saw Dickson's educational display as an outrage. At one protest Indian demonstrators even jumped the railing of the burial exhibit and covered skeletons with blankets.

Fortunately, the story of Dickson Mounds doesn't end in animosity and stalemate; a compromise was found. In 1991 a new governor decided that the burial exhibit would be closed but approved a $4 million renovation initiative for Dickson Mounds Museum. Among other improvements, completely new exhibits that better told the Native story would be undertaken. The museum closed for a year, and the skeletons were given a final examination before their reburial. When the museum reopened, not only had the cemetery been sealed over once again,

FIGURE 14.7 New exhibits at Dickson Mounds seek to use state-of-the-art technology and interpretive techniques to tell the story of the mounds from both a scientific and a Native perspective.

but in its place was a mix of exhibits telling the story of Dickson Mounds from both scientific and Native perspectives (Figure 14.7).

Today's visitor to Dickson Mounds learns about the succession of cultures in the area's prehistoric past from the viewpoint of archaeological science, but the experience culminates in a dramatic, multimedia presentation called "Reflections on Three Worlds." As visitors walk down a ramp around the cemetery site, they encounter symbols, music, and voices of Native peoples introducing the Mississippian worldview. Emerging from this experience, visitors enter a photographic gallery of contemporary Native Americans that makes the point that the Indian is still very much with us today.

Many people have been happy with the compromise reached at Dickson Mounds; others complain that nonscientific perspectives are portrayed by the museum. Still others may be critical of the scientific and historical focus of most of the exhibits. Many local people are probably just glad to have "their museum" back. Nevertheless, if you know the story of Dickson Mounds, and especially if you had visited the burial exhibit when it was open, you can't go there now without asking two questions. First, how should the past be publicly interpreted? Second, who should have a say about how we interpret it? These are questions that all of us who study the past must constantly consider.

CONCLUDING THOUGHTS

We end our introduction to North American archaeology with the hope that finishing this text is more a beginning than the end of your interest in North American archaeology. There are so many fascinating things to learn about North America's past, and a number of lessons for our increasingly multicultural society. In addition, this is a dynamic field in which there are many opportunities for meaningful work. We hope you stay interested in archaeology and keep tabs on what archaeologists are learning, even if you are not inclined to pursue the field yourself. Of course you can continue to read about North American archaeology in popularly oriented publications such as *Archaeology* and *American Archaeology*, but you also can explore the field more directly.

First, there is much North American archaeology to see and visit (Figure 14.8) with information about the continent's past accessible in a wide variety of museums throughout the United States and Canada. However, archaeological sites also often have been interpreted for the public on federal, state, and private properties. These range from elaborate reconstructions with costumed interpreters

FIGURE 14.8 Students and professors view a display in the museum at Angel Mounds State Historic Site in southern Indiana, one of many museums, parks, and sites that the public can visit in order to learn about North America's past.

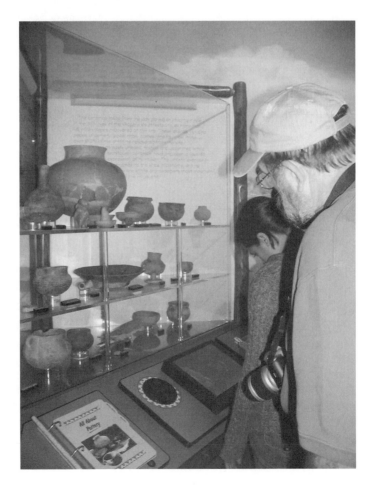

FIGURE 14.9 An archaeologist from the State Museum of Pennsylvania provides a public tour of excavations and displays on City Island, located in the Susquehanna River near Harrisburg.

such as can be found at Fort Michilimackinac (see Section D.6 of the Student CD) to sites with small visitor centers, or even just a little signage. Guides to places you can visit have been listed in several of our Suggestions for Further Reading sections, including the one for this chapter. Section H of the Student CD lists places to visit as well.

Second, there are many volunteer and avocational opportunities to learn about local archaeology and even to participate in archaeological projects. These range from lectures to workshops to lab tours, many of them organized by museums and universities with archaeologists on staff (Figure 14.9). Your state or province also probably has an amateur society you might wish to join. The address of some amateur societies can be found under the Council of Affiliated Societies on the website of the Society for American Archaeology. Many amateur societies have their own websites, which you can find directly. Centers like the Crow Canyon Archaeological Center in Colorado and the Center for American Archaeology in Illinois have program offerings for adults and children. A list of archaeological fieldwork opportunities worldwide is available online from the Archaeological Institute of the Americas, and you might find a North American project that will accept volunteers from this source. Organizations like Earthwatch sometimes provide opportunities for volunteer participation in fieldwork in North America. The U.S. Department of Agriculture Forest Service has a program called Passports in Time, through which you may participate in archaeology on a volunteer basis. Websites for such opportunities are listed in Section H of the Student CD.

Third, if you are a teacher, you will be able to find a variety of resources for working with students. You can begin by looking at the Society for American Archaeology website, where the Public Education Committee posts lesson plans

FIGURE 14.10 Field training is essential for prospective archaeologists: these students are enrolled in a field school associated with Indiana University of Pennsylvania.

FIGURE 14.11 Indiana University of Pennsylvania students taking a quiz as part of their laboratory training. Undergraduate students of archaeology typically obtain training in identifying artifacts by this and other means.

and other resources for teachers. A great deal of effort has gone into creating materials for teachers at the middle school and junior high level, but these materials may be adaptable for other grade levels. The U.S. Department of the Interior Bureau of Land Management also makes available "Intrigue of the Past," a teacher's activity guide for students in the fourth through seventh grades (Smith et al. n.d.). Often these resources can be supplemented with materials produced by archaeologists in your own state or province (e.g., Wolynec n.d.). Teachers' workshops on archaeology may be found by searching for public programs at museums and universities.

Finally, if you have become interested enough to pursue additional course-work in archaeology and to contemplate archaeology as a career, you will prob-ably find that the Department of Anthropology at your local university offers basic courses. Students who are considering North American archaeology as a career ideally should acquire a background in all the fields of anthropology as well as specific courses in archaeological fieldwork (Figure 14.10) and laboratory techniques (Figure 14.11) at the undergraduate level. Sometimes you can gain experience by assisting a professor with a project rather than by taking a specific course. There is currently a great deal of debate among archaeologists about how to educate the next generation of archaeologists (e.g., Bender and Smith 2000). This issue is discussed in Box 14.3. If you have a choice of programs, it is advis-able to select one that will provide some exposure to the topics indicated by the curricular principles listed in Table 14.1.

Graduate training in archaeology also can be obtained at a variety of institu-tions, but individuals will want to select a program based on specific interests and on the presence of congenial professors rather than program location. You will have a better sense of such matters after taking a number of undergraduate courses in archaeology.

TABLE 14.1 Principles of Curricular Reform for the Twenty-first Century

1. **Stewardship**. Archaeological resources are nonrenewable and must be fully documented.
2. **Diverse interests**. Various publics as well as archaeologists have a stake in the past, although members of these groups may approach it differently.
3. **Social relevance**. Knowledge of the past is useful in thinking critically about effective social policy for areas as diverse as the environment, social inequality, multiculturalism, and human health.
4. **Ethics and values**. Ethical considerations are central to the practice of archaeology.
5. **Written and oral communication**. Archaeologists must think logically and be able to communicate effectively both in writing and orally because archaeology depends on the support of the public.
6. **Fundamental archaeological skills**. Archaeologists must have mastered skills in excavation, analysis, report writing, and the long-term curation of artifacts.
7. **Real-world problem solving**. Analysis of case studies and internship experiences can contextualize and enhance the training of student archaeologists.

Adapted from Bender (2002, 32–33).

ISSUES AND DEBATES

BOX 14.3

Can Academia Train Archaeologists for the Twenty-first Century?

As the twentieth century closed, archaeologists throughout North America began to realize how much the discipline had changed since the 1970s as a result of legislation designed to better protect and preserve cultural resources. Besides increased resource protection and increased knowledge about the past, these laws have led to the growth of CRM archaeology. As one archaeologist has pointed out, this growth really represents success—both success in creating new jobs in the field and success in influencing public policy concerning archaeological sites (Snow 2002). In addition, of course, techniques have changed as new ways of gathering information have been developed.

A sometimes forgotten result of our success is that archaeologists need different skills now than they did 40 years ago. Today, the market for professional archaeologists is largely outside academia, and the M.A. rather than the Ph.D. is the degree required for entry into the profession. In addition, many people with bachelor's degrees find work as archaeological technicians in the field and laboratory phases of CRM projects. Despite frequent lack of mutual respect noted in Section F.1 of the Student CD, most of today's archaeology students are likely to work in the CRM industry, either temporarily or permanently. Are academic departments reflecting this situation, or are the curricula offered still focused on producing members of the professoriat? Many North American archaeologists agree that traditional curricula do not provide sufficient training, but there is active debate about what specific changes ought to be made, and curricular reform is just beginning (Krass 2002).

On the one hand, many academics continue to express concern about adopting a strictly vocational focus in archaeological curricula. They argue that archaeology students pursuing CRM careers still need to develop background knowledge about diverse cultures and to understand the theoretical debates taking place within the discipline. Otherwise the CRM work they do will add little to our understanding of the past. On the other hand, the disparaging view of CRM archaeology held by some of the professoriat is clearly flawed (Schuldenrein 1998a, 1998b). Public archaeology is not a second-rate form of archaeology practiced only by the least capable of archaeologists. Instead, increasingly, it is the main context for doing archaeology in North America (McGimsey and Davis 2002). Archaeologists' concerns about the overall quality of CRM work cannot be addressed by ignoring the field when training student archaeologists.

While debate continues, attempts to address curricular reform have begun. In 1998, the Society for American Archaeology held a workshop at Wakulla Springs in Florida, bringing together archaeologists who taught undergraduate and graduate students and archaeologists who worked for government agencies and CRM firms to discuss how curricula should be changed. These discussions resulted in the development of the principles for curricular reform shown in Table 14.1, as well as an invitation to the professional and student archaeological communities to comment on these via the SAA website. The SAA also published a discussion of the key issues involved in how archaeology should be taught in the twenty-first century (Bender and Smith 2002). The grant-funded project called M.A.T.R.I.X. (Making Archaeology Teaching Relevant in the XXI Century), which is intended to provide aids to develop undergraduate and graduate courses in archaeology, is another outgrowth of these SAA initiatives. Individual departments also have begun to respond by developing new curricula. Today, resources for developing appropriate courses are available on the web (http://www.indiana.edu/~arch/saa/matrix).

Discussion among archaeologists about what these principles mean for the development of archaeology curriculum is ongoing, and it will be interesting to see how changes are incorporated over the first few decades of the twenty-first century. Because of the way course and curricular revision must proceed at a university, one cannot realistically envision a complete revamping of curricula overnight. Instead, a few new courses can be added, internship experiences can be offered, and the content of existing courses can be modified to include materials not presented in the past. If you are reading this text as part of a course on North American archaeology, you may very well have an example of how an existing course might be updated effectively in how your instructor has handled the course. Certainly, we have tried to write this text to allow an instructor to introduce topics such as those indicated in the principles of curricular reform. If you pursue archaeology, you can also make sure to select courses and experiences that combine to give the broad training and perspective you will need if you work in North America. The future of archaeology in North America is bright, but its practitioners must be prepared for the complexities of twenty-first century practice.

CHAPTER SUMMARY

With this chapter we complete our archaeological introduction to the North American past. The following final points have been made:

- Study of North American archaeology provides a different perspective on what happened in North America's past and helps us discard stereotypical notions that all Native Americans were alike or that they were primitive people. It also indicates why it is important to preserve the traces of this continent's past.

- The archaeological story of North America's past has contributed important insights about human migration into the Americas, about the diverse patterns of survival humans have created, about the origins of food production, about sociopolitical complexity and its origins, about ethnic groups and their history, about the encounter between Native Americans and Europeans, and about the history of the United States and Canada. Significant future research is likely in each of these thematic areas.

- A variety of methods, including the application of geophysical methods, the incorporation of GIS software, the development of various chemical analyses, and the application of AMS dating, promise to transform the discipline of North American archaeology during the twenty-first century.

- The management of archaeological resources entails complex issues such as determining how to curate the large volume of archaeological material produced by CRM and other archaeology, how to protect cultural resources on private property, and when sites can be written off or off-site mitigation can be used to manage the resources more effectively.

- That the archaeological record is irreplaceable and that diverse constituencies have a claim to the past will present ethical challenges to contemporary archaeologists. Increased cooperation with Native American and other descendant populations will be critical.

- There are many ways to get involved with North American archaeology, from casual visits to sites or websites to participation in excavations to acquiring degrees in the field. Materials that help readers explore these possibilities further are included in the Student CD.

SUGGESTIONS FOR FURTHER READING

For a collection of essays with new perspectives on North American archaeology:

Pauketat, Timothy R., and Diana Di Paolo Loren. 2005. *North American Archaeology.* Malden, MA: Blackwell.

For essays on archaeological interpretation and public education:

Jameson, John H., Jr. ed. 1997. *Presenting Archaeology to the Public: Digging for Truths.* Walnut Creek, CA: AltaMira Press.

For essays on archaeologists working with local communities:

Derry, Linda, and Maureen Malloy, eds. 2003. *Archaeologists and Local Communities: Partners in Exploring the Past.* Washington, DC: Society for American Archaeology.

For published guides to the archaeological sites and museums you can visit:

Morse-Kahn, Deborah. 2003. *Archaeology Parks of the Upper Midwest.* Lanham, MD: Roberts Rinehart.

Thomas, David Hurst. 1999. *Exploring Ancient Native America: An Archaeological Guide.* New York: Routledge.

Woodward, Susan L., and Jerry N. McDonald. 2002. *Indian Mounds of the Middle Ohio Valley: A Guide to Mounds and Earthworks of the Adena, Hopewell, Cole and Fort Ancient People.* Blacksburg, VA: McDonald and Woodward.

For a series of essays about the complex ethics of doing archaeology today:

Zimmerman, Larry J., Karen D. Vitelli, and Julie Hollowell-Zimmer, eds. 2003. *Ethical Issues in Archaeology.* Walnut Creek, CA: AltaMira Press.

For perspectives on the relationship between Native Americans and North American archaeology:

Dongoske, Kurt E., Mark Aldenderfer, and Karen Doehner, eds. 2000. *Working Together: Native Americans and Archaeologists.* Washington, DC: Society for American Archaeology.

Watkins, Joe E. 2000. *Indigenous Archaeology: American Values and Scientific Practice.* Walnut Creek, CA: AltaMira Press.

OTHER RESOURCES

Sections H and I of the Student CD supply web links, places to visit, additional discussion questions, and other study aids. The Student CD contains a variety of additional resources, including the complete list of references as cited in this chapter and two sections that address issues raised in this chapter (see Sections F.2 and F.3).

GLOSSARY

Note: The Glossary contains terms found in the text and on the Student CD.

absolute dating   The determination of chronological age based on a specific time scale or calendar; compare **relative dating**.

accelerator mass spectrometry (AMS) dating   A method of obtaining radiocarbon dates that measures carbon isotopes directly, by means of a particle accelerator and a mass spectrometer and thus, can date a sample containing very little carbon.

achieved status   A position within a society and the associated rights and responsibilities that result from an individual's actions, talents, and accomplishments; compare **ascribed status**.

Adena   An Early Woodland mound-building culture or ceremonial complex centered in the central and upper Ohio River valley (ca. 2500–1900 BP); Adena mounds are conical burial mounds often surrounded by ditches and covering postholes.

Advisory Council on Historic Preservation (ACHP)   The independent federal agency that promotes historic preservation in the United States, advises the president on preservation policy, and administers the **Section 106** process.

adze   A woodworking tool that, unlike an axe, has its working edge at a right angle to the long axis of the tool's handle.

akchin   A term that refers to the mouth of an arroyo, where Hohokam and other Southwestern farmers often planted their crops to take advantage of runoff and floodwaters.

Alaska Native Claims Act (ANCSA)   U.S. law that gave Native Alaskans title to vast tracts of ancestral lands around the state through the establishment of regional native corporations; passed in 1971 and paved the way for the Alaska oil pipeline.

Aleutian tradition   A marine-based hunting and gathering cultural tradition that developed in the area of the Aleutian Islands and western Alaska beginning about 5000 BP and had a chipped stone rather than ground slate tool industry.

alluvial fan   A fanlike or cone-shaped deposit of sediment and loose rock left by a stream as it enters a valley; changes the terrain from a steep to more level slope.

Alta California   "Upper California" formed in 1804 by the Spanish north of Baja (Lower) California; the line between these colonies separated the area of the Franciscan missions in the north from the Dominican missions in the south.

altimeter   An instrument for measuring altitude with respect to sea level or another fixed level, generally by using pressure gradients.

Altithermal   The second period of Antevs's tripartite scheme for postglacial climate during which climate was warmer, and drier than it is at present (7000–4500 BP); this term generally isn't used in the East where archaeologists are more likely to reference the longer **Hypsithermal Interval**.

AMS   See **accelerator mass spectrometry dating**.

anadromous fish   Fish species (e.g., various species of salmon) that have the ocean as their habitat but spawn and hatch in freshwater rivers.

Anasazi tradition   The archaeological tradition of the northern Southwest that was ancestral to contemporary Puebloan people; this name is disliked by many Native Americans today because of its Navajo meaning: enemy ancestor (see **Ancestral Pueblo**).

Anathermal   The first period in Antevs's tripartite scheme for postglacial climate in the North American West, when the climate was cooler and moister than at present (9000–7000 BP).

Ancestral Pueblo   An alternative name for the archaeologically known Puebloan people of the northern Southwest. Some people argue that this term is preferable to **Anasazi** because it is not offensive to the descendants of these people.

annealing   The process of heating and cooling glass or metal to make it less brittle and more workable; used to work copper in North America.

Antelope Creek phase   A Late Prehistoric archaeological culture of the **Southern Plains Village tradition** in the Texas panhandle known for its stone slab, multiroom house structures, which may suggest influence from the Southwest.

anthropogenic sediments   Sediments introduced or created as a result of human activities as opposed to natural processes.

anthropology   The study of humans including the physical, cultural, and social aspects in the past and present. In North America, this field traditionally is divided into biological, cultural, archaeological, and linguistic subdisciplines.

Apafalaya chiefdom   A chiefdom encountered by the De Soto Expedition in AD 1540; may correspond to the archaeologically known chiefdom centered at Moundville in Alabama.

arborglyphs   A carving also known as aspen art on the aspen trees of the Sierra Nevadas and the Rocky Mountains; apparently made by Basque sheepherders in the late nineteenth and early twentieth centuries.

archaeological deposits   A term that refers to the cumulative nature of human-derived sediments in an archaeological landscape; more general than **archaeological site** because it recognizes continuous variation in the intensity of the **archaeological record**.

archaeological record   The artifacts and other physical remains of past human activities that document the past and are interpreted by archaeologists.

Archaeological Resources Protection Act of 1979 (ARPA)   A U.S. law designed to prevent destruction of archaeological resources; its enforcement component imposes penalties, and its permitting component may allow recovery of cultural resources.

archaeological site   Any location at which there are material remains, including artifacts, features, or ecofacts, proving evidence of the human past.

archaeological site survey   The systematic process archaeologists use to locate, identify, and record the distribution and nature of archaeological sites on the landscape.

archaeology   The study of past human behavior and culture through the analysis of material remains.

Archaic period   A period from approximately 10,000 BP to 3000 BP that is recognized in most North American culture areas except those of the West Coast and the Arctic; the Archaic is not a general developmental stage, as originally thought.

Arctic culture area   The most northerly of the North American culture areas, defined largely by the tree line on the south; from Alaska's Yakutat Bay to the Aleutians and the Bering Sea as well as the Arctic coast east to Greenland and northern Labrador.

Arctic Small Tool tradition   A microlithic stone tool tradition associated with the first foragers to utilize North America's Arctic coast; originally called the **Denbigh Flint complex** and found in both Siberia and the North American Arctic after about 4000 BP.

artifact   Any portable object used, manufactured, or modified by humans that includes stone, ceramic, metal, wood, bone, or objects of other materials. See **ecofacts**.

artifact use life   The trajectory an artifact takes from manufacture to discard. Events in the use life of an artifact (e.g., breakage, repair) can alter the form of the artifact.

ascribed status   A position within a society and the associated rights and responsibilities, determined without individual initiative or choice (e.g., by being born into a particular family or being female); compare **achieved status**.

aspartic acid racemization (amino acid racemization)   A dating method based on changes in the structure of amino acids after death; results can be difficult to translate into absolute dates, but the technique is applicable to bones up to 100,000 years old.

aspect   In the **Midwestern taxonomic system**, this unit grouped one **focus** with others that were similar based on formal characteristics in material culture; in turn, aspects were grouped into **phases**, but time and space were not incorporated; rarely used today.

asphaltum   Natural asphalt such as found in seeps like the La Brea Tar Pits near Los Angeles. This natural petroleum product was used as a mastic and to caulk the plank canoes of southern California.

assemblage   A collection of artifacts and/or ecofacts from the same archaeological context (e.g., a feature, a house, a site component). Term may refer to all the materials or simply to one material class. See **subassemblage**.

atlatl   A spear-thrower or throwing board that increases the thrust of a spear by increasing the length of the lever arm; made by many groups in North America and all over the world.

Augustine pattern   A cultural pattern evident in Late Prehistory in central California; intensive fishing and hunting and gathering, dense populations, burial ceremonialism, possibly associated with movement of Wintuan people into the area.

avocational archaeologists   People who lack formal education in anthropology and archaeology and are not paid for work that they do in the field.

Avonlea phase   A Late Woodland Plains bison hunting culture (1500–950 BP) that used the bow and arrow; found in southern Alberta, southern Saskatchewan, southwestern Manitoba, North Dakota, Montana, South Dakota, and northern Wyoming.

baidarka   A term derived from Russian that refers to a hunting boat made from skins and propelled by one to three paddlers using single- or double-bladed paddles; type of a kayak.

ball court   A structure with flat courts and walls reminiscent of Mesoamerican ball courts but built by the Hohokam (oval with sloping walls) and Casas Grandes people (I-shaped with straight walls) in the Southwest; integrative and ritual in nature.

band   A small mobile group of related people, usually hunter-gatherers, among whom there is relatively little social differentiation; leadership is by consensus and group membership is fluid.

bannerstone   A polished stone piece with a central drilled hole and bilateral symmetry that is presumed to have been an **atlatl** weight but is often found in Archaic burial contexts, especially in the East.

Basketmaker   In the **Pecos classification** of the Southwest, this term denoted the pithouse portion of the sequence before people built aboveground, multiroom pueblos (Basketmaker I–III); the specific definition has been modified and is used only in the Ancestral Pueblo area today.

Baytown period   The early Late Woodland period (1650–1250 BP) in the central Mississippi River valley; Baytown ceramics are clay tempered and cord marked, and the people used small notched and stemmed arrow points.

bedrock milling feature   A feature for grinding of seeds, acorns, and other plant foods located within an outcrop of bedrock; mortar cups, bedrock metates, and other features related to food grinding or crushing may occur in clusters.

behavioral archaeologist   An archaeologist who has adopted an approach to archaeology formulated in the mid-1970s by Michael Schiffer and focusing on the behaviors involved in the production, manipulation, and disposal of material culture.

Beringia   The land area of northwestern North America and northeastern Asia that was exposed when the sea level dropped during the Pleistocene.

Berkeley pattern   A cultural pattern that follows the **Windmiller pattern** in central California (4000–500 BP); intensive use of coastal resources and acorn processing.

Besant phase   Bison hunting culture of the northern Great Plains beginning about 1850 BP; associated with pottery and burial mounds and in the Dakotas with the **Sonota burial complex**; considered Archaic by some archaeologists and Woodland by others.

biface   A chipped stone tool that has been worked extensively on both surfaces or faces rather than merely being retouched at the edges; bifaces can be tools themselves, serve as cores for flake production, or be **preforms** for specific tools such as **projectile points**.

big men Individuals in some tribal societies who enjoy higher status and power owing to personal entrepreneurship and skillful use of social obligation rather than to inheritance of wealth.

bioarchaeological analysis The analysis and interpretation of human biological remains such as skeletons found in archaeological contexts.

biological anthropology The study of the biological aspects of humans, including human biological evolution and past and present human biological diversity.

biome A macrolevel biological community of interacting plants and animals, as exemplified by tundra or coniferous forest.

bipolar technology A technique of percussion flaking in which a stone core is placed on an anvil and struck from above; practical for breaking up small pebbles.

birdstone A stylized bird effigy in polished stone commonly found in Late Archaic and Early Woodland contexts in the Midwest, Great Lakes, and Northeast; commonly interpreted as an atlatl weight.

Birnirk culture The archaeological culture that immediately preceded the **Thule culture** itself (northern Alaska, 2200–1250 BP) with a sophisticated maritime hunting technology including a distinctive flat toggling harpoon head.

Black Rock period An eastern Great Basin period from 6000 BP to 1500 BP in which the uplands, sparsely used before, began to be utilized; Elko and Gypsum Cave points mark the beginning, while Rose Springs and Eastgate points were introduced near the end.

Blackduck culture An archaeological culture and ceramic style beginning about 1450 BP and continuing until European contact in the boreal forests of northern Ontario, northern Minnesota, and southern Manitoba; ancestral to Historic Ojibwa.

blade A flake at least twice as long as it is wide and more than 1.2 centimeters (0.5 in.) long, with bladelets or **microblades** being shorter; several North American archaeological cultures, including **Clovis**, developed blade industries.

blast furnace A furnace in which iron is extracted from its ore by means of blasts of hot air in the presence of a **flux**, like limestone; more productive than a bloomery forge; common in North America between the late seventeenth and nineteenth centuries.

blister steel An alloy of iron and carbon produced by early iron makers by keeping wrought iron packed with charcoal red hot for up to two weeks; surface texture is blistered, hence the name.

blood residue analysis The study of traces of blood adhering to tools; differences in the hemoglobin in blood among animal species provide a means of identifying the source of a specimen, which may retain its signature characteristic for thousands of years.

bloom The product of a bloomery forge; ore heated to a spongy state so that impurities can be hammered out of it.

blowing tubs In iron making, a pair of tubs with water-powered pistons used to pump air into the **tuyere** of the furnace; this innovation replaced bellows as iron-making techniques developed.

Bonneville period This period (11,000–9500 BP) in the eastern Great Basin is seen at only a few sites; stemmed points suggest a possible affiliation with the **Western Pluvial Lakes tradition**.

Borax Lake tradition   A Middle to Late Archaic tradition of the North Coast Range in California; Borax Lake points, millingstones, and manos indicating generalized foraging.

borrow pit   An excavated area, the material from which has been used as fill in another place.

bosh   The widest part in the interior of an iron furnace through which molten iron and slag descended to the **crucible**.

BP   A date designation that means "before present" or more precisely before AD 1950, the date from which calculations in radiocarbon years are made by archaeological convention.

Broadpoint tradition   A Late Archaic tradition in the Eastern Woodlands that is marked by the appearance of broad-bladed and stemmed points (e.g., Susquehanna point) after about 4000 BP; associated with the adaptive changes of the Transitional Archaic along the Atlantic Coast.

Buffalo Soldiers   Name given to two regiments of African American cavalry established by the U.S. Congress in 1866 and posted throughout the West to help protect the frontier.

bullboat   A boat made of skins by Plains Indians; shallow and saucer-shaped.

bundle burial   The gathering up, or bundling, of disarticulated, defleshed remains into a **secondary burial** context; the deceased were sometimes exposed to the elements until the soft tissue had decayed, and the bony remains reburied later.

burin   A small tool created when a blow is struck transversely to one of the edges rather than into the interior of the tool, creating a sturdy chisel-like tip, useful for working antler, ivory, and bone.

burin spall   The flake that results from making a **burin**; sometimes used as graver tips in the Arctic.

^{12}C/^{13}C   The ratio between two stable isotopes, carbon-12 and carbon-13, which are retained after death in bone collagen; since various food categories have different isotopic signatures, values of this ratio can indicate dietary composition.

calcined   Describing bone that has been so thoroughly burned or highly heated that all moisture and grease have been removed and the bone has been reduced to a white or blue chalky or crumbly state.

California culture area   The culture area that includes most of the modern state of California and the northern portion of Baja California, where a diverse group of Native cultures including complex coastal hunter-gatherers once existed.

California Environmental Quality Act (CEQA)   A state law enacted in 1970 for the purpose of monitoring land development in California by requiring review and permitting of proposed projects.

California Native American Burial Act   A state law enacted in 1984 requiring notification of the California Native American Heritage Commission when Native American skeletal material is encountered; the most likely descendant consults on the disposition of the remains.

Caloosahatchee culture   A non-Mississippian culture of the west coast of Florida that focused its subsistence on the sea rather than agriculture; characterized by shell platform mounds and shell middens.

Campbell tradition   A cultural tradition of the Santa Barbara region in coastal California at the onset of the Pacific period; intensive use of marine and shoreline resources and various artifacts suggest that these are the ancestors of the Chumash.

Canaliño   The Late Prehistoric occupants of the Santa Barbara region and California's Channel Islands. Canaliño sites show a focus on marine resources, and the culture is thought to be similar to that of the ethnographic Chumash.

Carabelli's cusp   A small tubercle located on the lingual surface, or tongue side, of some people's upper molars, most often the right first molar; occurs in higher frequencies in European populations than in other populations.

carrying capacity   The number of organisms (human or other) that an area can support; estimated on the basis of characteristics of the natural environment and, in the case of humans, the available technology.

Cascade phase   An archaeological culture recognized in assemblages from the Snake River in Washington State and adjacent areas; leaf-shaped Cascade points date from 9000 BP to 7800 BP, after the **Windust phase**.

Cashie Phase   A Late Woodland culture of North Carolina, found inland from the coast, that extends to the Historic period and has affinities with the Iroquoian societies further north; the people made quartz-tempered, stamped, incised, and plain ceramics.

cast arch   The arch at the bottom of an iron furnace, where the molten iron was tapped.

castellation   A projecting or raised section on the rim of a pot that gives the vessel a squared opening.

cataloging   The systematic recording of artifacts and other items that includes information about the items' **provenience** and a basic description; this step precedes analysis but is essential for future retrieval and research.

celt   A kind of axe or chopping implement hafted to a bone or wooden handle; sometimes celts are so finely made that ceremonial uses are suspected.

cenote   A sinkhole formed when underground water erodes away limestone, the cavern ceiling collapses, and access to the water is gained; common in regions of karstic topography; term is the Mayan word for such sinkholes that had ritual importance.

Central Plains tradition   A subdivision of **Plains Village**, grouping sites from the central Plains in Kansas, Nebraska, and western Iowa (1000–500 BP).

Central Subarctic Woodland culture   Ceramic-using archaeological cultures of northern Ontario and Manitoba dating after about 2200 BP; best known is the **Laurel culture**.

Ceramic period   An alternative term for **Woodland period** used by some Plains archaeologists and also used in Maine and the Maritime provinces of Canada.

Cerbat   A regional branch of the **Patayan tradition**, which encompasses northwestern Arizona between the Coconino Plateau and the Colorado River (ca. 1250–750 BP).

Chaco Branch Anasazi   A regional branch of Ancestral Pueblo archaeological cultures centered at Chaco Canyon in northwestern New Mexico.

Chaco phenomenon   A term used by archaeologists to refer to the unique developments associated with the regional system associated with Chaco Canyon in northwestern New Mexico; characteristics include greathouses, roads, and exchange items (900–650 BP).

Champlain Sea   An inland sea created in the lowlands of the St. Lawrence River as the glacier retreated; sea level rose before the valley, having been depressed by the weight of the glacier, could rebound; as a result, parts of Quebec, Ontario, New York, and Vermont were flooded.

chaparral biome   Biome consisting of the various communities of arid-adapted plants and animals found in southern California, Baja California, and portions of southern Oregon.

charmstone   A ground stone artifact in various shapes and sometimes with a drilled hole found in central California after 4000 BP; often associated with burials and believed to have been a ritual item.

check dam   A small rock feature constructed to retain water from rainfall runoff; useful in arid areas of the Southwest that receive rainfall in sudden cloudbursts but often lack permanent streams that can be diverted by more permanent irrigation features.

Chesrow complex   An early, possibly Pre-Clovis archaeological complex represented by sites in southeastern Wisconsin; modified bone and lithics dated before 11,500 BP.

chiefdom   A kin-based, ranked society in which access to resources and political power, as well as social status, are determined by hereditary proximity to the chief, who often controls the redistribution of goods and is wealthy as well as powerful.

Chihuahua tradition   A poorly understood Archaic tradition of the southeastern portions of the Southwest (ca. 7950–1700 BP).

Choris culture   The first part of the Norton tradition sequence found in northern Alaska north of the Bering Strait (3000–2500 BP); people made **feather-tempered pottery** that was cord marked, stamped, or incised and is related to pottery from northeast Asia.

Chumash   A Native American tribe that inhabited the southern coastal regions of California including several of the Northern Channel Islands; known as maritime complex hunter-gatherers both archaeologically and ethnographically.

chunkey   A game played by Southeastern Indians who rolled a stone disk with concave sides at which opposing players threw poles; the object was to hit the disk or to come close to it where it stopped.

cinder notch   A notch above the hearth of an iron furnace through which **slag** could be drawn off.

Civil Works Administration (CWA)   A federal program established as part of Franklin Roosevelt's New Deal during the Great Depression to create jobs for thousands of people who had become unemployed; some of these jobs were in archaeology.

clan   A social grouping defined by a kin connection in which descent is traced unilineally rather than through both parents; important feature of social organization in tribes.

Classic Period Hohokam   The culmination of the **Hohokam tradition** sequence in the southern Arizona desert (800–550 BP); compounds, multistory pueblos, and platform mounds were characteristic.

clay cooking balls   Fired balls of clay that could be heated in a fire and placed in earth ovens for indirect cooking of food; used in places where stone was scarce, such as the coastal plains of the Southeast.

Clemson Island culture   An early Late Prehistoric designation for sites of the Susquehanna River drainage; people used cord- or fabric-impressed grit-tempered vessels, practiced maize and native plant cultivation, and constructed burial mounds.

Clovis culture   This Paleoindian culture (11,500–10,800 BP) is associated with the distinctive fluted Clovis point and the hunting of mammoths, although a wider range of resources probably was used, particularly outside the Great Plains.

Clovis-First   The idea that the Clovis fluted point makers were the first humans in the Americas, having followed large game through an **ice-free corridor** as the Ice Age waned; no longer the archaeological consensus, this scenario is still accepted by some archaeologists.

Coalescent tradition   A third **Plains Village tradition** subdivision first evident around 650 BP but continuing into the Historic period; fusion of **Central Plains Village** and **Middle Missouri traditions**.

Cochise tradition   The Archaic tradition in the southwestern Southwest (ca. 7950–1700 BP) that includes the Sulphur Springs, Chiricahua, and San Pedro phases; these people were foragers who added maize and other cultigens at the end of the sequence.

Cody complex   A Late Paleoindian archaeological complex known for finely made, unfluted, lanceolate points and the shouldered asymmetrical Cody knife; Great Plains and Southwest distribution.

Cohonina   A regional branch of the **Patayan tradition**, which developed in the area around Flagstaff, Arizona, between about 1250 BP and 750 BP.

coil-and-scrape technique   A pottery-making technique in which vessels are built up by coiling rolled lengths of clay, and then the interior and exterior surfaces are scraped and smoothed with a piece of gourd, a pottery sherd, or other expedient tool.

coiling   A method of basket making in which a bundle of strands or rods is stitched into a spiraling oval or round form; compare **twining** and **plaiting**.

coke   A purified form of coal that replaced charcoal as the fuel for iron furnaces after the mid-nineteenth century in America; hotter fires allowed for more efficient melting of iron ore.

cold-air drainage   The flow downslope of cold, dense air that tends to occur as the ground surface cools on calm nights in steep-sided mountain valleys; a layer of warmer air is found higher up the side of the valley, inhibiting the formation of frost.

cold desert biome   The desert biome of the Great Basin in the western United States, which is very arid but experiences cold winters.

Colington phase   A Late Woodland culture of coastal North Carolina that extends to the Historic period and apparently has affinities with the Algonquian societies further north; characterized by shell-tempered ceramics, ossuary burials, and Algonquian longhouses.

collar   In pottery, a raised and extended vessel mouth that begins above the neck and does not reduce the opening relative to the body diameter.

collectors   Individuals who buy, sell, and collect artifacts and art for personal enjoyment or financial gain rather than to learn about the past; such collecting only fuels the illegal acquisition of antiquities and contributes to the destruction of sites. Also used by archaeologists to refer to hunter-gatherers who establish long-term, larger base camps from which foraging parties are sent out; compare **foragers**.

colluvial fan   A fan-shaped deposit of loose sediment that accumulates at the base of a hill owing to erosion and slopewash.

Colonial period Hohokam   The second period in the **Hohokam tradition** sequence of the southern Arizona deserts (1175–975 BP), characterized by pithouse villages and ball courts.

Comancheros Multiethnic traders of the Southern Plains who traded in buffalo robes, meat, guns, ammunition, horses, Indian captives, and other commodities from the eighteenth to the nineteenth centuries.

community In ecology, a group of interacting plants and animals within a habitat; usually named for the most conspicuous species.

complex hunter-gatherers Human groups who depend on wild resources for their subsistence but have economic surplus, prestige goods, social hierarchies, hereditary leadership structures, settled villages, and other aspects of sociocultural complexity.

compliance archaeology Archaeological investigation done in response to various **CRM** laws and regulations; this kind of archaeology does not originate with a research question but often contributes important archaeological information.

component An archaeological unit that includes a culturally homogeneous stratigraphic or spatial unit within a site and is thought to represent a single occupation of the site; components are grouped into **phases**.

composite fishhook A three-piece fishhook with two pieces of wood lashed together in a V shape and a bone barb attached to one leg of the V; made by Northwest Coast groups.

conical core A type of flaked rock nodule from which **blades** have been removed from the circumference; usually with a single core platform, which may or may not be prepared, and an end opposite the platform that tapers so that the core is cone-shaped.

coniferous forest biome Dominated by coniferous trees such as pine, spruce, fir, and hemlock, this large biome stretches across Canada south of the tundra and in the U.S. Rocky Mountains; coniferous forest also occurs in the mountains of northern Mexico.

conjunctive approach A methodological approach suggested by Taylor in the 1940s as a critique of culture history; argues for the exploration of a full range of cultural variables rather than chronology and spatial and temporal distributions alone.

conservation archaeology An approach that stresses the conservation of archaeological sites because they are irreplaceable, discouraging excavation except as part of the management of resources for the greatest scientific, historical, and public benefit.

container revolution The profound changes associated with the introduction of stone and ceramic bowls at the Late Archaic–Woodland boundary in the East; possibly associated with boiling new foods like seeds to make them more palatable.

context Refers to where an object or a feature is found as well as to what it is associated with; objects found out of context are less useful to archaeologists than objects found in place.

Copena Mortuary complex A Middle Woodland burial complex of the Tennessee Valley in northwest Alabama that often is considered Hopewell because of the log and bark burial containers and the many Hopewell Interaction Sphere artifacts they contain.

coprolite Human or animal feces preserved by desiccation, fossilization, or being waterlogged; provides evidence of diet.

cordmarked Describing a surface texture created by pressing a cord-wrapped paddle into the wet surface of a clay pot before firing; this technique was used widely throughout North America.

Cordilleran ice sheet   The ice cap that expanded over the northern Rocky Mountains of Canada and the United States during the Pleistocene.

core tablet   A flake removed from the top of a core to form or rejuvenate the platform; also called a core rejuvenation flake.

cortex   The weathered outside surface of an unmodified rock; often a different color from surfaces that have been broken.

Crab Orchard tradition   The Early and Middle Woodland ceramic tradition of southern Illinois and adjacent areas characterized by cord-marked and fabric-impressed conoidal, flat-bottomed vessels; also used to denote a Middle Woodland culture in the area.

crested blade (*lame à crêtes*)   A blade bearing bidirectional flake scars on the dorsal surface as a result of a flintknapper's preparation of a ridge to guide the blade.

CRM   See **cultural resource management**.

crucible   The narrow chamber at the bottom of an iron furnace below the **bosh**; air was conducted into the crucible via the **tuyere**.

cultural anthropology   The study of the cultural aspects of humans, especially recent and contemporary social, technological, and ideological behaviors observed among living people.

cultural ecology   A school of anthropological thought that influenced North American archaeology in the late twentieth century; associated with the anthropologist Julian Steward, this approach focuses on the interactions between human societies and their environment.

cultural process/culture process   The mechanisms inherent in a culture that cause stability, change, or both; beginning in the 1960s, archaeologists argued that exploring these processes was their primary goal.

cultural resource management (CRM)   An applied form of archaeology under-taken in response to various laws that require archaeological investigations as part of governmental programs.

cultural resources   Sites, buildings, artifacts, and other remains that compose the nonrenewable and irreplaceable material traces of the past, including archaeological remains and historical records.

culturally modified tree (CMT)   A tree that has been used in bark stripping or other activity that scarred the surface; there is debate over how many of these trees, which are common in the forests of the West, should be preserved.

culture area   A geographical region within which there is general similarity of culture; originally developed to group ethnographically known cultures, but often extended into the archaeological past of indigenous peoples.

culture history   An archaeological approach that emphasizes the ordering of artifacts into a sequence in time and space; most important in North American archaeology in the early to mid-twentieth century, but a baseline for further study of culture.

culture stage   An archaeological construct that refers to a general level of development based on formal attributes presumed to reflect cultural evolu-tion; the Lithic, Archaic, and Formative stages usually are not used by North American archaeologists today.

curated   A term referring to stone tools, that have been maintained by resharpening or reworked into another tool form, possibly indicating concern with the availability or quality of stone; may also refer to the care of collections, as in **curation**.

curation   The professional care of archaeological remains with the goal of best preserving specimens for future research and public education. A crisis exists with respect to the curation of archaeological collections.

Custer phase   An archaeological culture of the **Southern Plains Village tradition** found in western Oklahoma between 1150 BP and 700 BP; characterized by maize horticulture and wild plant gathering as well as bison hunting and wattle-and-daub houses.

Cuyamaca complex   The Late Prehistoric occupation of mountains of the San Diego region, thought to represent the ancestors of the Yuman-speaking Kumeyaay; cremation, small triangular projectile points, and ceramics are characteristics of this complex.

Darwinian archaeologist   An archaeologist who approaches archaeology by trying to explicitly apply the principles of selection and evolutionary theory to the study of archaeological phenomena.

data recovery program   In CRM archaeology, any excavation program designed to recover information about cultural resources that are likely to be destroyed by construction or other development.

datum point   The base point used as the main reference station in setting out a grid at a site or in recording site locations; controls vertical as well as horizontal information.

Death Valley I   An early Holocene complex found in and around Death Valley; generally considered to be part of the Lake Mohave complex and also included in Bedwell's Western Pluvial Lakes tradition.

debitage   The material, including chips, flakes, and other debris, produced when stone is flaked to make tools.

Denali complex   An early archaeological culture of Alaska and the western Yukon (11,000–9000 BP) with clear affinities to the **Dyuktai tradition** of Siberia; core and blade technology including microblades and wedge-shaped cores.

Denbigh Flint complex   The original complex of the **Arctic Small Tool tradition** based on materials from the bottom of the Iyatayet Creek site at Cape Denbigh but eventually found over a much wider area of the High Arctic.

dendrochronology   A dating method that compares the rings in wood to a master sequence of rings for a region; trees add rings annually, but the width of the rings depends on the climate, thus creating a sequence for comparison with archaeological specimens.

dental caries   The disease associated with tooth decay or cavities; evidence of dental caries can be used to draw conclusions regarding the health of a population.

dentalium shell   A tubular, tusk-shaped shell from the Pacific Coast, but traded into the interior of North America; used for ornamentation.

Deptford tradition   An Early and Middle Woodland cultural tradition of South Carolina, Georgia, and northern Florida defined by distinctive checked and simple stamped vessels and possibly associated with the somewhat later **Swift Creek tradition**.

Desert Archaic   A term applied to the hunting and gathering adaptations of the Great Basin and adjacent arid areas that are now known to have been variable over time and space.

Desert culture   The name for the hunting and gathering adaptations in the Great Basin and adjacent arid areas assumed to have been basically uniform for 11,000 years into the Historic period; this idea has been abandoned as variability over time and space has become clearer.

dew claw A vestigial or nonfunctional toe in a deer, antelope, or other animal reflecting the reduction in the number of functional toes from the five per foot of the earliest mammalian species.

diagnostic artifact An artifact that allows archaeologists to identify a particular archaeological culture or time period; in effect it allows one to "diagnose" who made and left the item where it was found.

Dinétah phase An archaeological phase of the upper San Juan River drainage that some archaeologists have argued represents pre–Pueblo Revolt (AD 1680) Navajo presence in the northern Southwest; other archaeologists reject assertions that the Navajo can be associated with this phase.

discoidals A round stone with slightly concave or flat sides, apparently used in the game of **chunkey** played by Southeastern Indians.

Dismal River phase A Protohistoric archaeological culture from southern Nebraska, central and western Kansas, and southeastern Colorado thought by many to represent proto-Apache Indians; characterized by garden plots, hunting and gathering, and large villages.

distolateral scraper A scraper that has a steep working edge on the sides and on the ends.

domestication The selective breeding of plants and animals to render them more beneficial to humans; domesticated species have been altered by human control of reproduction for generations.

dorsal surface This term, used in lithic analysis, refers to the outer surface of a flake that prior to detachment was the face of the core.

Dorset tradition A cultural tradition of the Eastern Arctic between 2500 BP and 800 BP that was displaced by the Thule; sea mammals, especially seals, were important for subsistence, and the people used closed-socket harpoon heads, had substantial sod winter houses, and created highly developed portable art.

Driftless area An area in southwestern Wisconsin and northeastern Iowa that was never glaciated, though glaciers advanced around it at various points in the Ice Age; the topography here is more highly dissected than in surrounding areas.

Dyuktai tradition A Paleolithic tradition of western Beringia dating from approximately 35,000 BP to 10,500 BP; associated with a bifacial technology generally similar to that of early sites in Alaska.

Early Agricultural period A term for the Late Archaic in the Southwest that defines the period from the introduction of maize cultivation at approximately 3500 BP to the beginnings of the regional sequences such as Hohokam, determined on the basis of ceramics.

Early Horticultural period The term sometimes used in New England for the Early and Middle Woodland because there is less distinction between these Woodland subperiods than elsewhere in the Eastern Woodlands; people made limited use of horticulture.

Early period In the Plateau culture area, this refers to the archaeological period at the Pleistocene–Holocene boundary between approximately 11,000 BP and 6000 BP; Clovis and Old Cordilleran assemblages date to this period; sometimes used in the Chumash area of California (ca. 6800–2500 BP).

earspool An ornamental earplug, usually a flat and round copper or pottery piece worn in the earlobe, sometimes big enough to stretch the earlobe greatly; common among the **Hopewell** and also the **Mississippians** of the Eastern Woodlands.

earthlodge   A common house structure on the Great Plains, considered a **Plains Village tradition** trait and still built by Historic period tribes; square or circular earth-covered dwelling with post supports and covered entrance passage.

Eastern Agricultural complex   A group of plant cultigens and domesticates of the East first cultivated in the Middle and Late Archaic; included are species of native gourds, marsh elder, chenopodium, sunflower, maygrass, little barley, and erect knotweed.

Eastern Eight-Row corn (see **Northern Flint corn**)   A variety of corn developed between 1050 BP and 950 BP; this variety was more cold tolerant than earlier varieties and possibly is responsible for the spread of maize agriculture across the Great Lakes and Northeast.

ecofact   An unmodified natural item, such as part of a plant or animal, that is recovered from an archaeological site and provides information about human interaction with past environments. See **artifact**.

ecotone   A community of plants and animals found at the transition between biomes or other large biotic units; characterized by a mixture of species that may attract predators, including humans.

Effigy mounds   Burial mounds whose outline resembles that of an animal or, rarely, a human; these features were most common between 1250 BP and 900 BP in the upper Mississippi River valley and nearby areas; usually found in groups with linear and conical mounds.

egalitarian society   A society without marked differences in wealth, power, and prestige; status differences are largely based on age, gender, or an individual's achievements.

electrical resistivity survey   A geophysical technique that measures differences in the way soils transmit an electric current, which may indicate varying retention of water and compactness between subsurface feature and nonfeature areas.

Emergent Mississippian   A term used, particularly in the Midwest, for the period from approximately 1150 BP to 950 BP when the first hints of the **Mississippian tradition** begin to be archaeologically apparent; other scholars include this time in the Late Woodland.

end scraper   A tool with a steep working edge on one end, usually made by unifacial retouch or flaking of part or all of the edge of a flake or core; perhaps most often used to scrape hides.

Environmental Impact Statement (EIS)   A document produced as a result of required assessment of the environmental effects or impacts of a proposed federal project; the impact on cultural as well as natural resources must be assessed.

estuary   A part of a river such as its mouth, a bay, a salt marsh, or a lagoon where the river meets the sea and fresh water is mixed with the salt waters of the ocean tides.

ethnicity   Membership in an ethnic group based in part on the circumstances of one's birth and in part on one's own identification with that group's cultural traits, in contrast to those of other perceived ethnic groups.

ethnoarchaeology   The ethnographic study of living people to learn how material items are used and discarded as the archaeological record is created.

ethnobotanist   A person who investigates how plants are used in various cultures; often ethnobotany is an interdisciplinary subfield within archaeology that identifies and interprets plant remains recovered from archaeological sites.

ethnohistory   A multidisciplinary field allied with archaeology that reconstructs the past history of human groups, especially nonliterate ones, based upon a combination of indigenous or foreign written sources, oral traditions, and linguistic and archaeological data.

evolutionary ecologist   An adherent of the school of thought within the evolutionary sciences that explicitly focuses on the current and historical interactions among species; some archaeologists have adopted this ecological perspective in studying the human past.

experimental archaeology   The controlled reproduction of human activities (e.g., toolmaking, structure building, pottery firing) to understand how archaeological remains were produced and used.

extended burial   A burial in which the deceased has been placed with legs extended and arms to the side; variation in placement of deceased may be culturally significant.

extended family   A family group in which at least three generations are represented in a single household or in closely situated households.

fabric-impressed ceramics   A type of pottery in which fabric has been pressed into the wet clay surface during finishing, either to help meld the coils or to roughen the surface.

Fairchance phase   A Middle Woodland phase of southwestern Pennsylvania between 1900 BP and 1550 BP that participated in the Hopewell Interaction Sphere.

fall line   The boundary between the Piedmont section of the Appalachian Mountain system and the Coastal Plain in the Southeast, often marked by waterfalls as rivers flow toward the ocean.

feather-tempered pottery   Pottery made from clay mixed with feathers; found in **Choris culture** sites in the Alaskan Arctic.

Federal Emergency Relief Administration (FERA)   The first step in the economic relief programs of Franklin Roosevelt established in 1933; its programs included the **Civil Works Administration** programs under which archaeology was done.

fiber-tempered pottery   Pottery made from clay mixed with various plant fibers; the first pottery on the Great Plains and in the Eastern Woodlands often was fiber tempered.

fire-cracked rock (FCR)   Cobbles and other pieces of rock that have been heated to the point of fracturing; common by-products of cooking in open fires and found at many sites.

flexed burial   A burial in which the deceased has been placed on its side with the legs drawn up to the chest and the arms bent; in a fetal position.

flotation   A process by which small **ecofacts** and **artifacts** are collected by suspending or floating the lighter materials in agitated water and collecting the heavier items that fall to the bottom; may be done in a handheld tub or with a machine.

flux   A substance used in the processing of metals; limestone was a common flux that helped remove impurities from iron ore.

focus   In the **Midwestern taxonomic system** as originally proposed, components could be grouped together into a "focus" based on formal similarities; this term is less commonly used today.

foragers   Often treated as a synonym for hunter-gatherer, this term should refer only to hunter-gatherers who live in bands that move as residential units to utilize seasonally and spatially restricted resources; compare **collectors**.

Fort Ancient tradition   A Late Prehistoric cultural tradition of the central Ohio River valley (950–250 BP); these people were settled agricultural, tribal villagers who made shell-tempered pottery with some Mississippian stylistic elements and may have been ancestral Shawnee.

Fort Walton Mississippian   A Mississippian tradition regional development or chiefdom of the Florida panhandle and adjacent areas; **Southeastern Ceremonial complex** involvement and elaborate mound building in the Middle Mississippi period.

Fremont culture   An archaeological tradition with several regional variants of the eastern Great Basin (1600–700 BP) associated with maize agriculture and baskets made through coiling, as well as pithouses and surface architecture.

Fremont dent corn   A drought- and cold-tolerant variety of corn whose kernels become indented at maturity.

frequency seriation   A form of **seriation** and relative dating that orders assemblages by the percentages or frequencies of different artifacts within them based on the idea that artifact styles first will be rare, then more important, and finally will decline in popularity.

functionalism   A school of thought that sees social phenomena in terms of their function either in integrating society or in meeting the needs of the individuals that make up the society; influenced North American archaeologists in the mid-twentieth century.

Gadsden Purchase   Land purchased by the United States from Mexico in 1854 to assure U.S. possession of practicable railroad routes west; negotiated six years after the end of the Mexican War, this acquisition gave the United States much territory in the Southwest.

galena   A soft blue-gray mineral that was widely traded prehistorically; when galena is crushed, a silver glitter is produced, and the powder can provide a white pigment when oxidized; smelted into lead for shot by Mississippi Valley tribes in the Historic period.

garden hunting   The practice of trapping or otherwise procuring the animals attracted to gardens and fields; for farmers this practice allows the acquisition of meat with relatively little energy expenditure while reducing competition for planted crops.

general theory   The broadest level of archaeological theory that contributes to anthropology; theoretical frameworks that describe and attempt to explain cultural behaviors and processes that operated in the past, as opposed to **middle-range theory**.

geoarchaeologist   An archaeologist also trained in geology who evaluates sediments and stratigraphy to reconstruct the depositional history of a site or other geological questions about a site and its contents; one of the interdisciplinary methods that helps archaeologists reconstruct past environments.

Geographical Information System (GIS) A computer program designed to retrieve, store, and manipulate geographic information; used to manage and analyze site locations, environmental attributes acquired from maps and images, and distributions within sites.

geophysical prospecting/survey The use of geophysical techniques to investigate subsurface features without excavation; the most common instruments employed are **ground-penetrating radar (GPR), magnetometers** and **electrical resistivity survey**.

glacial The cold part of the warm-and-cold alternation within a major period of glaciation during which ice expands (see **interglacials**).

glacial kame A mound or ridge that formed when glacial meltwater deposited poorly sorted gravels and sands; often associated with kettle holes.

Glacial Kame mortuary complex Late Archaic complex found in the Midwest and Upper Great Lakes and characterized by red ocher burials placed in glacial deposits; also recovered are copper and marine shell artifacts, bone pins and awls, and **birdstones**.

Glades culture Coastal South Florida societies that were not Mississippian although they coexisted with this tradition in time; subsistence was based mostly on marine resources including whales, sharks, crabs, rays, sailfish, and marlin.

Glen Meyer phase An early Iroquoian phase designation for southwestern Ontario dating from about 1050 BP to 650 BP; compare **Pickering phase**.

glottochronology A method of linguistic analysis that compares two languages and estimates the time of probable divergence from a common language; somewhat controversial within linguistics but sometimes yields useful additions to archaeological data.

good gray cultures A label for the Late Woodland of the East that characterizes these cultures as drab in comparison to Middle Woodland and Mississippian; misses the importance of the variable cultural reconfigurations and changes that occurred during this period.

gorget A large ornament of shell, copper, wood, or stone worn suspended on a cord from the neck.

GPS (Global Positioning System) A system of satellites that allows one's position to be calculated with great accuracy by the use of an electronic receiver; used widely by contemporary archaeologists to acquire precise locational information.

graver A chisel-like tool, often a flake with an edge worked into a sharp point, that can be used to score incisions and grooves in relatively soft material; characteristic of Paleoindian assemblages.

gray literature Unpublished archaeological reports, most often produced as part of a **CRM** project and submitted in compliance with CRM laws and regulations; these reports often contain important information but are not readily available and the data they contain can't be utilized easily.

Great Basin culture area The large internally drained area between the Sierra Nevada of eastern California and the Rocky Mountains in which hunter-gatherer lifeways persisted for millennia, ending only after ranching began in the late nineteenth century.

great house A term used by Southwestern archaeologists for large, multi-room, or multistoried, aboveground structures that are bigger than average in size or in numbers of the individual rooms and kivas; interpreted as having had integrative purposes.

great kiva   An oversized pit structure or kiva in the northern Southwest that archaeologists understand to have had ritual integrative functions at the community level.

Great Salt Lake Fremont   A regional variant of the Fremont culture found around Great Salt Lake and in southern Idaho; lacking in masonry architecture that made heavier use of wild resources than other Fremont variants.

grog-tempered ceramics   Ceramics that have crushed, prefired ceramic pieces mixed with the clay before firing; usually crushed sherds from broken vessels in North America but in some parts of the world such tempering materials are specially fired and crushed.

ground-penetrating radar   A geophysical technique that transmits waves of electromagnetic radiation into the ground and records the attributes of the reflected energy, which can reveal subsurface evidence for structures and other features.

Gulf Coastal tradition   A Southeastern Woodland period pottery tradition found in the Mississippi River valley and the Gulf Coastal Plain; vessels sometimes had pod-shaped supports at the base, and their surfaces were incised, pinched, brushed, and stamped.

Gulf Formational stage   A proposed cultural stage spanning the Late Archaic–Early Woodland boundary in the Southeast's Gulf Coastal Plain; not recognized by most authorities, but makes note of cultural changes that contrast with early forager lifestyles.

Gulf of Maine Archaic tradition   An Archaic tradition of Maine and the Maritime provinces in which ground stone rods, gouges, and adzes predominate; spans 9500 BP to 6000 BP, and its variations are not yet well understood.

Gypsum period   The name for the Middle Archaic in the southwestern Great Basin and Mojave Desert; millingstones as well as projectile points suggest diverse subsistence.

habitat   An area of land with physical characteristics such as minerals, soils, rainfall, and temperature that affect which plants and animals live there; habitats are modified as the plants and animals develop, use resources, deposit waste material, and eventually die.

Hakataya   A term that is essentially synonymous with **Patayan tradition** and refers to the archaeological tradition of the western Southwest after the Archaic.

haplogroup   A related group of alleles or lineage found in **mtDNA** analysis that tends to be inherited as a package; useful for tracing ancestry and relatedness.

haplogroup X   A particular **mtDNA** lineage that is found in roughly 3 percent of modern Native American populations as well as in 4 percent of European populations, raising the hypothesis that some Native Americans have a connection to Caucasian lineages.

harpoon valve   A part of a composite harpoon head; two valves form a complete head, often with the addition of a stone or metal point or end blade.

heat treating   The practice of heating chert or flint to temperatures that allow the stone to be more effectively flaked; color changes, sharper edges, increased brittleness, and faster wear may all be results of heat treating.

Helton phase   A Middle–Late Archaic phase found at sites in Illinois and Missouri; characterized by side-notched and stemmed points, carved bone pins, and channel basin metates; there is evidence for exchange of copper, galena, and other artifacts.

heritage tourism   The industry that supports the public presentation of the past through reconstructions of sites, buildings, and events; this kind of tourism is a growing part of the economy in some areas of North America.

heterarchy   A network system in which all the elements share roughly equal positions; contrasts with hierarchies in which positions are unequal and ranked.

Historic period   An archaeological period that begins when written records about the past are available; in North America this is associated with contact with Europeans.

historical archaeology   A branch of archaeology that uses a mixture of archaeological and historical methods to study literate people who made written records; generally exclusive of the archaeology of ancient civilizations such as Roman or Maya.

historical particularism   An anthropological school of thought that saw cultures as unique products of specific historical developments; this approach had a strong influence on archaeologists early in the twentieth century, causing them to focus on **culture history**.

Hohokam tradition   A cultural tradition, based on irrigation farming, that developed in the southern Arizona desert area after approximately 1750 BP and persisted through several phases until at least 500 BP.

Holocene   The geologic epoch beginning at the end of the Pleistocene, or roughly the last 10,000 years; this period of relative warmth may simply be an interglacial, but it is the period of most of the human past in North America.

Hopewell   A Middle Woodland mound-building culture with two main centers, in Ohio and in Illinois; exchange of artifacts and exotic raw materials throughout the East; large earthwork and mound complexes, but few large habitation sites.

Hopewell Interaction Sphere   The intercultural exchange of raw materials, ritual items, and shared symbolism among Middle Woodland people of the Eastern Woodlands; participation at some level is evident from Florida to Ontario, Kansas to North Carolina.

hopper mortar   A shallow mortar on which a conical basket without a bottom is affixed to contain the ground material.

horizon   As defined by Willey and Phillips (1958), an archaeological unit that links phases based on traits of material culture that appear to have spread widely during a relatively short period of time; compare **tradition**.

hot desert biome   The desert biome of southern California, Arizona, New Mexico, and many parts of northern Mexico, which is very dry and very hot in the summer and dominated by creosote bush.

households   The smallest social units that live together and cooperate economically as a family; inferred by archaeologists from structures, features, and artifacts.

hydration rim (obsidian)   A thin layer of hydrated rock, visible under polarized light that builds up on the surface of obsidian after flaking; if environmental factors and type of obsidian are held constant, the thickness of this layer can be a measure of relative age.

Hypsithermal Interval   A Holocene warm climatic episode from about 9000 BP to 2500 BP; may be treated as the eastern equivalent of the Altithermal but more properly the name of a longer warm climatic regime with variable precipitation.

Hunters Home phase   Supposedly the last Middle Woodland Phase in New York, dating between 1150 BP and 950 BP; the validity of this designation is questioned along with **In situ hypothesis**.

Hunting phase   The archaeological unit defined as following Oak Grove in the Santa Barbara area; mortars and pestles are a part of the inventory, as are projectile points, suggesting a greater emphasis on hunting than in the **Oak Grove phase**.

ice creeper   A flat piece of bone or ivory or, in modern times, other material, with pointed projections carved into one side; when strapped to boots, these devices provide traction on ice and snow; made by Dorset and Inuit people of the Arctic.

ice-free corridor   A strip of land east of the Rocky Mountains in Alberta where the Cordilleran and Laurentian ice sheets parted during warmer parts of the Ice Age; thought to have been a possible route for early hunters and game to enter the continental interior.

Illinois Hopewell   The variant of Hopewell culture found in the Illinois River valley; also called Havana Hopewell.

Independence phase   An early variant of the Arctic Small Tool tradition found in northern Greenland (4000–3700 BP); the first documented human occupation this far north.

index fossil   The fossil remains of an organism believed to have existed over a wide area for a relatively short period of time; can be used to correlate strata in terms of their relative age.

Indian Removal Act of 1830   The law by which Congress ordered the removal of Native people east of the Mississippi River to Indian Territory in Oklahoma; rich farmlands were confiscated for Euro-American use despite some Native resistance. See **Trail of Tears**.

indigenous archaeology   Archaeology controlled by indigenous people and consistent with native values and goals.

industrial archaeology   An archaeological subfield that is focused on investigating the nature and development of industry, especially that of the early part of the Industrial Revolution.

in situ   Unmoved from the original position; describing artifacts that are the best candidates for archaeological study because context and association are known.

In situ hypothesis   The proposal that Northern Iroquoian culture originated in the Northeast from earlier cultural traditions; now being questioned based on data that could suggest in-migration into the Northeast.

intaglio   A design or pattern cut into a surface, as when effigy mound builders began by outlining the shape of the mound on the ground surface.

integrity   The condition of particular remains such as structures and features; the extent to which they have been disturbed/modified, which lowers integrity; this term is used widely in the field of historic preservation to help assess the relative importance of remains.

interglacial   The warm phase in the warm-and-cold alternation within a major period of glaciation, during which glaciers shrink in size and thickness. (See **glacials**.)

Intrusive Mound culture   A Late Woodland archaeological culture of Ohio that postdated the mound-building Hopewell but used the Hopewell mounds to bury their own dead.

Ipiutak culture   Part of the Norton tradition that begins after 2000 BP in north Alaska; lacks pottery but is known for its elaborate art style, which shows some similarities to Siberian art styles.

isolated artifact   A single artifact, unassociated with other artifacts or features, usually recovered from the surface during archaeological survey; usually not considered by itself sufficient evidence of an archaeological site.

isostatic   A term that refers to the pressure equilibrium for layers of the earth's crust that results from gravity, layer thickness, and density; during the Pleistocene the weight of the ice sheets depressed the crust, and following it the crust began rebounding.

isotopic analysis   Analysis of the isotopic ratios preserved in human and animal bone; these chemical signatures left by different foods are an important source of information on the reconstruction of prehistoric diets; see **^{12}C/^{13}C ratio**.

Issaquena phase   A Late Middle Woodland phase that dated between 1750 BP and 1450 BP in the lower Mississippi River valley; this phase shows less evidence of Hopewell influence than the preceding Marksville phase.

jacal   A wall construction technique using wooden stakes plastered with mud; can also refer to a building constructed in this manner and roofed with straw.

Jesuit Relations   A collection of texts about New France and its inhabitants written by various Jesuit missionaries in the seventeenth and eighteenth centuries.

Jornada Mogollon   A regional branch of the **Mogollon tradition** found in south central New Mexico, far west Texas, and northern Chihuahua, Mexico (ca. 1750–550 BP).

Kachemak stage   The second part of the **Kodiak tradition** (3500–1000 BP) of Pacific Alaska; maritime hunter-gatherers who made both chipped stone and ground slate tools including the *ulu*; some archaeologists consider this a separate tradition, rather than a stage of Kodiak.

Kansas City Hopewell   A Woodland cultural complex that developed in the Missouri River valley north of Kansas City after 2000 BP; pottery similar to Illinois Hopewell pottery in the Midwest; these people built mounds and practiced horticulture.

Katchina cult   A set of Pueblo spiritual beliefs and ritual practices revolving around katchinas, who mediate with the gods; possibly established 500 years ago as Mogollon and Anasazi peoples integrated in the region of the Little Colorado River.

Kayenta Branch Anasazi   A regional branch of Ancestral Pueblo archaeological cultures in northeastern Arizona (ca. 1400–650 BP).

kazigi   A large structure that served both as a ceremonial house and as a men's house among the Eskimo; apparent prehistoric examples come from some Norton tradition sites in the Bering Strait area.

Keith complex   A Late Woodland complex dating between 1350 BP and 1050 BP evident in western Kansas and Nebraska between the Platte and

Arkansas rivers; characterized by Scallorn points and cord-roughened, calcite-tempered pottery.

Kennewick skeleton A 9000-year-old skeleton recovered from the Columbia River near Kennewick, Washington, in 1996 that became the center of a major legal controversy over how **NAGPRA** should be implemented in cases of very old skeletal material.

Kensington stone A roughly rectangular slab of stone covered in runes found in Kensington, Minnesota, in 1898; originally cited as proof that Viking explorers were in the interior of North America, this object is now considered a fraud of unknown origin.

kettle hole A depression in the ground formed by the melting of a buried block of ice within deposits left as glaciers retreated; in formerly glaciated areas, these holes often have filled with water and become lakes.

kiva A room used for ritual purposes by both pre-Columbian and modern Puebloan peoples in the Southwest; generally round and subterranean prehistorically, but modern examples are built aboveground and often are square.

knapping The process of working stone by flaking it, as opposed to grinding or polishing.

Kodiak tradition A cultural tradition of Kodiak Island and adjacent areas of Pacific Alaska beginning about 3500 BP; **Takli** and **Kachemak stages**.

Koniag culture The archaeological culture of the late Prehistoric period on Kodiak Island and in adjacent areas that is clearly ancestral to Historic Alutiiq culture; the people were complex maritime hunters of the last thousand years.

La Jolla complex An archaeological culture of southern California and Baja California that is part of the Millingstone horizon and is found at coastal shell midden sites.

labret An ornament inserted into an incision in the lower lip or cheek; worn by several different peoples of the Americas.

ladrillo A flat, fired tile, used for floors and other construction in Spanish colonial settlements.

Lake Agassiz A proglacial lake formed by the meltwater of the Wisconsin ice sheet in the center of North America; at one time this lake was bigger than all the present-day Great Lakes combined.

Lake Creek focus A Middle Woodland archaeological complex of the Southern Plains in the Texas and Oklahoma panhandles; shows some contact with Southwestern groups, as evidenced by the presence of Jornada Mogollon brownware.

Lake Forest Archaic A Middle-to-Late Archaic archaeological tradition in the Midwest, Upper Great Lakes, and Northeast thought to be associated with adaptations to the Transitional or mixed coniferous/deciduous forest; characterized by broad-bladed, side-notched points.

Lake Forest Middle Woodland One name given to the group of non-Hopewellian Middle Woodland cultures of the northern part of the Upper Great Lakes (e.g., **Laurel**).

Lake Mohave complex An archaeological complex that includes lozenge-shaped, stemmed points found in the Mojave and Colorado deserts of southeastern California (11,000–9000 BP); an example of the Western Pluvial Lakes tradition.

Late period   The end of the pre-Columbian sequence in the Plateau culture area from 4000 BP to AD 1720; at this time the ethnographic pattern of settlement in large pithouse villages and heavy reliance on salmon developed; sometimes used in the Chumash area of California for the time after about 1000 BP.

Late Prehistoric period   A period sometimes used by archaeologists working in the Great Plains or the Eastern Woodlands to designate cultural groups that appear archaeologically between about 900 or 1000 years ago and the Historic period.

Laurel culture   A Middle Woodland culture of the central Subarctic associated with distinctive coarsely tempered conoidal pots and burial mounds; Hopewell ceramics have been recovered from the mounds.

Laurentian ice sheet   The massive glacier that expanded over much of Canada east of the Rocky Mountains during the Pleistocene; this ice sheet met the Cordilleran during the coldest periods.

law of association   Items found together in the same stratigraphic unit are associated temporally and culturally; although exceptions are possible, this assumption is a useful working hypothesis in archaeology.

law of superposition   Layers of sediment or rock are older than layers above them and younger than those below them unless they have been disturbed by some natural or human process.

League of the Haudenosaunee   The confederacy of the five Iroquois nations in New York, the "people of the longhouse"; apparently established by about 425 BP.

level   A term archaeologists use for the vertical sections of sediment removed in excavation; a level may correspond to a natural or cultural stratum or be an arbitrary thickness.

linguistic anthropology   The study of the structure, history, and diversity of human languages as well as of the relationship between language and other aspects of culture.

Little Ice Age   A period of cold climate that began around 650 BP (AD 1300) and did not end until the middle of the nineteenth century; may be associated with cultural shifts in various parts of North America.

Little Pluvial   A period of increased effective rainfall from about 4000 BP that filled some lakes in the Great Basin.

Llano complex   An alternative name for the **Clovis culture**.

Lochnore phase   An archaeological culture of the Northern Plateau in Canada representing the beginning of the **Plateau Pithouse tradition**; these foragers utilized anadromous fish, lived in pithouses, and may have been the area's first Salishan speakers.

loess   Unconsolidated, wind-deposited sediment composed largely of silt-sized particles apparently derived from reworked glacial outwash deposits; occurs widely in the central part of the North American continent.

longhouse   A long, narrow house often inhabited by multiple families; such structures were made in various ways by different Native American groups, with the wood and bark Iroquoian longhouse of the Northeast being the most famous.

macroband   A group of related hunter-gatherer families who come together seasonally in large camps but disperse into small family bands at other times of the year.

magnetometer survey   The geophysical technique of measuring the earth's magnetic field to identify patterns in intensity and direction that may have resulted from human activities; subsurface features may be detectable in this fashion.

malacologist   A scientist who studies mollusks including snails, which can be particularly sensitive indicators of past environments.

Manifest Destiny   The opinion common during the nineteenth century that the United States was destined and obligated to expand its territory to the western coast. Displacement of Native populations, often considered inferior, was justified as an inevitable consequence.

Mann focus   A Hopewell culture represented by nearly 100 sites located in southwestern Indiana; named after the large habitation site, the Mann site, and known for high-quality **Hopewell Interaction Sphere** artifacts; the GE Mound is representative.

mano   A handheld grinding stone used with a **metate** to process seeds, nuts, maize, and other items.

Marginella bead   A bead made from the shell of a marine snail belonging to the genus *Marginella*; the presence of these beads in inland sites indicates long-distance exchange from coastal regions.

Maritime Archaic tradition   A maritime tradition of the east coast of the Subarctic (7500–3000 BP); elaborate burials are characteristic; the people used ground slate, bone, antler, and ivory tools; Southern Branch extends into the **Northeast culture area** and Northern Branch along the Labrador coast.

Marksville phase   A Hopewell tradition phase dating from approximately 2150 BP to 1750 BP in the lower Mississippi River valley; named after the Marksville earthworks in Louisiana, where ceramics with Hopewell iconography and other Hopewell artifacts were found.

Mast Forest Archaic   Another name for the Middle–Late Archaic **Narrow Point tradition**, which emphasizes the presumed coincidence between this tradition and the oak–hickory deciduous forest of the East; "mast" refers to the nuts produced in this forest.

matrilocal residence   Describing a social norm in which married couples reside with the wife's family; this arrangement is common in societies in which descent is through the female line, or matrilineal.

Meadowood complex   An Early Woodland cultural complex of New York, southern Quebec, and southern Ontario; characterized by Vinette I pottery, Meadowood points, and cremations and other burials in hilltop locations.

meat weight estimate   An estimate of how much usable meat is represented by the bone fragments from each animal taxon in a faunal assemblage; potentially useful in determining relative dietary importance of food items.

medicine wheel   A round surface, stone feature, usually with a central stone cairn and spokes emanating from the center; these features, made on the northern Plains from the Archaic to the Late Prehistoric, apparently had ceremonial significance.

Medio period   The period in the Casas Grandes (Paquimé) sequence in which Casas Grandes reached its height (ca. 750–500 BP).

Medithermal   The third period of Antevs's tripartite scheme for postglacial climate in the West (after 4500 BP) during which climate has been essentially modern in character.

megafauna   The big-game animals that existed during and shortly after the Pleistocene (e.g., the mammoth and the mastodon); there is some debate concerning the role humans played in the extinction of the megafauna.

memorandum of understanding (MOU)   In CRM archaeology, a formal document between government agencies and/or other parties providing a description of each party's responsibilities in managing cultural resources.

Menlo phase   An archaeological culture in the Surprise Valley of northeastern California from approximately 6500 BP to 4500 BP; semisubterranean, multifamily houses suggesting base camps, in contrast to other more mobile Archaic adaptations in the Great Basin.

Mesa Verde Branch Anasazi   A regional branch of Ancestral Pueblo archaeological cultures from the Four Corners area; named after the cluster of famous sites at Mesa Verde in southern Colorado.

mestizo   A term of Spanish origin for people of mixed Native American and European descent.

metate   A flat or shallowly concave stone that serves as the base on which seeds, nuts, maize, and other items are ground with a **mano**.

Métis   An ethnic category for the descendants of aboriginal women and fur traders in Canada; rebelled unsuccessfully against Canadian sovereignty when **Rupert's Land** was annexed in 1870.

microblade   A small, narrow **blade** that is less than 1.2 centimeters (0.5 in.) long, made from **wedge-shaped cores** by means of pressure flaking; diagnostic of early archaeological cultures found in Alaska, western Canada, and northwestern United States, as well as Siberia.

midden   Rubbish or debris resulting from human activities; many permanent sites have specific areas where trash was disposed, and these can be archaeological gold mines because of the **artifacts** and **ecofacts** they contain.

midden ring   A ring of rubbish or occupation debris surrounding structures or other living areas in a site.

Middle Eastern tradition   A Southeastern Woodland period pottery tradition found in the interior Southeast as well as further north; vessel surfaces were treated with fabric-wrapped dowels, paddles, or stamps.

Middle Missouri tradition   A second **Plains Village tradition** subdivision centered along the Missouri River in the Dakotas; characterized by earthlodges, mixed horticulture, and bison hunting and exchange networks.

Middle period   In the Plateau culture area, this is the period from approximately 8000 BP to 4000 BP for which various hunting and gathering cultures are known, including some who built pithouses, lived in semisedentary villages and ate large amounts of salmon; sometimes used in the Chumash area of California (ca. 2500–1000 BP).

middle-range theory   Theoretical statements about how specific human behaviors correlate with observed empirical patterns such as in the archaeological record; contrasts with **general theory** about broad cultural processes to which archaeology also contributes.

Middle Tier Middle Woodland   A name sometimes given to non-Hopewellian Middle Woodland groups of the Upper Great Lakes area.

Middlesex complex   A phase designation sometimes used for Early Woodland components with Adena ceremonial objects in the Mid-Atlantic and the Northeast.

midpassage   An area enclosed by parallel rock slab walls in houses otherwise defined by elliptical rings of rock; midpassages apparently served as storage areas for **Independence**, **Pre-Dorset**, and **Dorset** people.

Midwestern taxonomic system   A method of cultural historical classification based on formal similarities and differences in material culture without reference to time and space; developed in the 1930s. (See **component**, **focus**, **aspect**, **phase**, and **pattern**.)

Millingstone horizon   Coastal southern California sites of Archaic hunter-gatherers contain many millingstones and manos and are interpreted as indicating the addition of seed processing to older foraging lifeways.

Mimbres culture   A Mogollon variant from southwestern New Mexico and southeastern Arizona (950–820 BP); Classic Mimbres is known for exceptionally well-made and beautiful pottery with geometric and animal designs.

minimum number of individuals (MNI)   The lowest number of animals that will account for the collection of bones from an animal taxon; some faunal analysts believe that this statistic provides a better estimate of dietary importance than **NISP**.

Mississippian tradition   The broad archaeological pattern that characterizes much of the Midwest and the Southeast in Late Prehistoric times; variable in nature but associated with platform mounds, agriculture, shell-tempered pottery, and chiefdoms.

mitigation   Measures taken to reduce negative impacts on the natural or cultural environment; in CRM archaeology this can include avoidance but may mean full-scale excavation of a site that otherwise would be destroyed by a construction project. (See also **off-site mitigation**.)

Modern period   A term used by archaeologists to refer to the Protohistoric and Historic periods along the Northwest Coast.

Mogollon tradition   An archaeological tradition of the mountainous Southwest in eastern Arizona, southern New Mexico, and the Mexican states of Sonora and Chihuahua after the Archaic; not easily linked with historically known tribes.

moist temperate forest biome   The forest biome of the northern Pacific coast of North America, which receives very high rainfall and is dominated by conifers like hemlock and red cedar.

monolithic axe   An axe made from a single large piece of stone and usually not intended for actual use; associated with the **Southeast Ceremonial complex** in the Eastern Woodlands.

Monongahela culture   A Late Prehistoric archaeological culture of southwestern Pennsylvania; characterized by maize-bean-squash agriculture, shell-tempered pottery, and stockaded villages.

Moorehead burial complex   A Late Archaic mortuary complex of northern New England once associated with "Red Paint People" because of the use of red ocher in the burials; artifacts and other remains suggest affinities to the Maritime Archaic and the Terminal Archaic.

moraines   The rocks and soil or till carried and deposited by glaciers into mounds or ridges as the ice melts; end or terminal moraines mark the furthest extent of a glacier.

Moresby tradition   An early cultural tradition on the Queen Charlotte Islands in British Columbia (7500–5000 BP); characterized by microblade technology.

mortuary encampment   A special-purpose camp occupied only while rituals associated with cremating, burying, or otherwise processing the dead are conducted.

mound   An artificial pile of dirt or stone that is not the result of natural deposition processes; in pre-Columbian North America, complex mounds of various sizes and shapes were used to bury the dead, to elevate important structures, and to mark territory and ritual spaces.

Mount Mazama   A volcano in the Oregon part of the Cascade Range that erupted between 7000 BP and 6700 BP, leaving a distinctive ash layer in many areas of the West; today Crater Lake is in the collapsed caldera of this volcano.

Mouse Creek phase   A Late Mississippian phase dating from 500 BP to 400 BP (AD 1450–1550) along the Hiwassee River of eastern Tennessee; the Mouse Creeks and Ledford Island sites are representative.

mtDNA   Mitochondrial DNA, found in the mitochondria of a cell; this part of a person's genetic inheritance is an important tool in tracing lineage because it is passed on only through the maternal line.

NAGPRA   Native American Graves Protection and Repatriation Act of 1990; a federal law that requires all public institutions in the United States to inventory and possibly return human remains and culturally sensitive items to the Native American descendants.

Narrow Point tradition   A Middle to Late Archaic archaeological tradition possibly representing adaptation to deciduous forests south of the transition forests of the East (see **Mast Forest Archaic**); characterized by narrow-bladed and stemmed projectile points.

National Historic Preservation Act (NHPA)   The U.S. act at the center of federal historic preservation policy; set up the **National Register of Historic Places**, and its **Sections 106** and **110** mandate the protection and inventory of cultural resources.

National Register of Historic Places   A list of significant sites, buildings, and historic districts maintained by the secretary of the interior as required by the **National Historic Preservation Act**; these properties are eligible for grants and may be protected from development.

Neanderthal   Describing a hominim that lived during the late Pleistocene in Europe and Southwest Asia; considered by some to be an Archaic form of *Homo sapiens* and by others to be a species separate from modern humans.

Nebo Hill phase   A Late Archaic phase known from the Missouri River valley at the Kansas–Missouri border (4500–2600 BP); characterized by lanceolate points, hilltop sites, fiber-tempered pottery, and some burial mounds suggesting Eastern affinities.

Nenana complex   A blade and biface industry found in the earliest components from sites in central Alaska (12,000–11,000 BP); Chindadn points and other chipped stone tools with general affinities to Paleoindian complexes are found, but no fluted points.

Neoevolutionism   An anthropological school of thought based on the idea that human behavior and cultural change are characterized by distinct patterns and mechanisms that can be explained by evolutionary processes; developed by Leslie White.

nephrite   A hard, fibrous semiprecious stone that varies in color from green to white and is a form of jade also called greenstone; used to make adzes and other tools.

Nesikep tradition   An archaeological tradition of the Northern Plateau in British Columbia during the Middle period; the people were foragers to whom hunting of deer and elk apparently was important.

New Deal archaeology   Archaeological work done as part of President Franklin Roosevelt's plan to bring economic relief, recovery, and reform to the country during the Great Depression; several major excavations generated large archaeological collections.

NISP   See **number of identified specimens**.

Northeast culture area   The culture area encompassing the northern part of the Eastern Woodlands; divided in this text into the Midwest and the Great Lakes on the one hand and the Northeast proper and the Mid-Atlantic on the other.

Northern Archaic tradition   A cultural tradition that groups together a number of artifact complexes that include side-notched points, large bifaces, various scrapers, notched pebbles found in the boreal forests of northwestern North America dating from about 6500 BP.

Northern Cordilleran complex   A term used to group materials lacking microblades but containing leaf-shaped points and blades in the western Subarctic between 10,000 BP and 7000 BP (see **Nenana complex** and **Old Cordilleran tradition**).

Northern Flint corn   Another name for **Eastern Eight-Row corn**; probably developed in the Northeast and perhaps was responsible for the spread of maize agriculture in Late Prehistoric times.

Northern Iroquoian tradition   The cultural tradition associated with Iroquoian language speakers in the interior Northeast; includes the Iroquois tribes of New York and a number of other ethnic groups, which may be best known archaeologically.

Northern Pottery tradition   A Southeastern Woodland Period pottery tradition found in parts of the northern and eastern Southeast and reminiscent of Woodland pottery found to the north; vessel surfaces were marked by paddles or stamps wrapped with cord.

Northwest Coast culture area   The narrow culture area that stretches along the coast of the Pacific from northern California to southern Alaska; relatively complex native cultures developed here, with economies based on spawning fish and marine resources.

Northwest Microblade tradition   A term used for early assemblages from the western Subarctic and the Northwest Coast that include microblades; other archaeologists subsume these materials under the **Paleoarctic** or the **Northern Archaic** when notched points are present.

Norton culture   A culture of the western Arctic that developed out of the **Choris culture** and was found from the Alaska Peninsula southward beginning about 2500 BP; check-stamped pottery, stone lamps, caribou hunting, and sealing were characteristic.

Norton tradition   A cultural tradition of the western Arctic from 3000 BP to 1200 BP, including the **Choris**, **Norton**, and **Ipiutak** cultures; stone tools similar to Arctic Small Tool tradition tools, but with ceramics and the oil lamp.

number of identified specimens (NISP)   The count of bone and shell fragments present in a faunal assemblage; comparison of these counts among taxa may be used to determine the nature of past subsistence; compare **minimum number of individuals**.

Numic speakers   People who speak a Numic language such as Shoshone, Paiute, or Ute; historically, Numic speakers occupied nearly the entire Great Basin.

Numic spread   The migration of Numic speakers across the Great Basin; the timing of this migration is much debated, as is the archaeological signature of Numic speakers.

Nunavut   A new Canadian territory created in 1999 in the eastern Arctic as a result of the Nunavut Land Claims Agreement in 1993; Inuit make up 85 percent of the population.

Oak Grove phase   An Archaic group in the Santa Barbara area that emphasized millingstones; followed by the **Hunting phase**.

obsidian   A naturally occurring black volcanic glass that produces some of the sharpest edges known on stone tools; traded over long distances in North America.

Ocean Bay tradition   The earliest maritime tradition along the northern Pacific coast of Alaska (ca. 7000–4500 BP); originally dominated by chipped stone implements, but ground slate tools became common in later traditions.

off-site mitigation   The mitigation of deleterious effects on cultural or other resources involving compensation for resource loss by investigating or protecting resources similar to or more important than those actually being damaged.

Ohio Hopewell   The variant of **Hopewell** found in the southern Ohio center of Hopewell.

Okvik culture   A culture associated with the earliest part of the **Thule tradition**, known for its elaborate art style that emphasizes zoned geometric patterns more than the related **Old Bering Sea culture**; developed on St. Lawrence Island of western Alaska and the Chukchi Peninsula.

Olcott   A term used to group heavily patinated material, generally from surface contexts, found in western Washington State (9000–5000 BP); characterized by leaf-shaped points (Cascade points) and pebble tools; part of the Old Cordilleran tradition.

Old Bering Sea culture   A culture associated with the earliest part of the **Thule tradition**, known for its elaborate art style that is more curvilinear than the related **Okvik** style; found on St. Lawrence Island and adjacent areas, including the Asian coast.

Old Copper culture   A Late Archaic complex of the Midwest and Upper Great Lakes characterized by burials or caches with copper artifacts that were cold-hammered or annealed before working; copper apparently came mostly from deposits along Lake Superior.

Old Cordilleran tradition   An archaeological complex including leaf-shaped points, pebble tools, and blades but lacking microblades found in sites in the Pacific Northwest; sometimes called the **Pebble Tool tradition**; see also **Northern Cordilleran**.

Old Women's phase   A Late Prehistoric/Protohistoric archaeological culture found in southern Alberta and Montana; characterized by bison hunting, Plains Side Notched points, and sometimes pottery.

Olivella   A genus of small marine snails from the Pacific Coast; its shells, made into ornaments, were traded into the interior prehistorically; and treated as a medium of exchange.

olla   A wide-mouthed vessel with tapered sides used as cooking pot or jar.

Oneota tradition   A Late Prehistoric culture of southern Wisconsin, northern Illinois, Minnesota, and Iowa, with a mixture of Mississippian and Plains

Village traits including horticulture and seasonal bison hunting, shell-tempered pottery, and mounds.

one-rod-and-bundle coiling   A type of basket construction in which a single rod is combined with a fibrous bundle (see Figure 8.15). The sewing elements pass through the bundle and wrap around the rod.

opal phytolith   A hard silica body within a plant cell that may remain within sediments after the plant has decayed; distinctive shapes allow identification of the plants that once grew in a locality, contributing to environmental reconstructions.

optically stimulated luminescence (OSL)   A method of measuring age based on time elapsed since the exposure of sediments to sunlight; sediments accumulate ionizing radiation, and optical stimulation causes them to luminesce (i.e., to produce light).

Orient phase   A phase defined for Long Island and the lower Hudson River valley in New York in which Terminal Archaic people heavily used shellfish; Orient Fishtail points are characteristic, as well as cemetery burial with red ocher and grave goods.

Oshara tradition   The Archaic tradition (ca. 7450–1550 BP) of the northern Southwest including the Jay, Bajada, San Jose, Armijo, and En Medio phases; the people were foragers who added maize horticulture during the last two phases.

ossuary   A mass human burial in which the bones of many individuals are placed together in a pit or vault; generally cremation has not occurred.

overshot flaking   A difficult technique used extensively in the manufacture of Clovis points that "thins" a biface by removing a flake that travels across the face beyond the midpoint to the opposite edge.

Owasco   The name archaeologists have given to the archaeological sites that apparently precede the development of the Iroquois in New York; the validity of Owasco as a cohesive archaeological taxon has been questioned.

Pacific period   A term for the period after the Archaic on the West Coast, this designation is meant to emphasize the development of complex hunter-gatherers dependent on marine resources.

Packard complex   A Late Paleoindian or very Early Archaic complex on the Plains–Woodland border and including Agate Basin–like Plano points.

packrat midden   An accumulation of food remains and debris left by packrats (*Neotoma* spp.) that may be useful in reconstructing past environments.

paddle-and-anvil technique   A technique of pottery construction in which vessel walls are smoothed and finished by holding a stone or other anvil on the inside and paddling the outer surface into shape.

Paleoamerican   An alternate term for Paleoindian proposed by some researchers to emphasize that the biological continuity long assumed between the first settlers of the Americas and modern Indians may not have existed.

Paleoarctic tradition   A term used for early American traditions in Alaska and some adjacent areas that include microblades, wedge-shaped cores, burins, and bifaces.

Paleocoastal people   An alternative term for the early inhabitants of coastal areas; sometimes used to distinguish such people who depended on ocean and shoreline resources from the big-game hunters evoked by "Paleoindian."

Paleoeskimos A term used for pre–**Thule tradition** people considered the ancestors of the Inuit in the eastern Arctic; some archaeologists apply the term to the **Arctic Small Tool** and **Dorset traditions**.

Paleoindian period The beginning of the North American cultural record, which lasts from first settlement to about 10,000 years ago; no longer viewed as a formal Lithic stage, but treated as a period of time within which there was significant cultural variation.

paleolith The term given to stone tools dated to the Paleolithic period by early North American antiquarians; these objects resembling European Lower Paleolithic tools that probably were later tool **preforms** somehow mixed into deposits of glacial age.

Paleolithic "The Old Stone Age"; this term is used worldwide to designate the period of cultural evolution from the first stone tools (ca. 2.5 million years ago) to the end of the Pleistocene, approximately 10,000 years ago.

Pallisades complex The earlier of two archaeological complexes of the Northern Archaic as recognized at the Onion Portage site in Alaska; characterized by side-notched points with convex bases and, eventually, notched pebbles (6000–4500 BP).

palynology The field of study that identifies fossil pollen and uses this information to reconstruct past environments; often an interdisciplinary specialization of importance in archaeology.

Parowan Fremont A regional variant of the **Fremont culture** found in southwestern Utah and influenced by the **Kayenta Anasazi**; Parowan people lived in settlements with pithouses and surface structures, left distinctive bone artifacts, and practiced maize agriculture.

passenger pigeon This North American migratory pigeon, killed in great numbers because it was prized by restaurants, had become extinct by the end of the nineteenth century; passenger pigeons once traveled in huge flocks and the species may have had a population as high as 5 billion birds.

Patayan tradition The archaeological tradition of the western Southwest after the Archaic; a number of regional cultures (e.g., **Prescott**, **Cerbat**, **Cohonina**) have been suggested.

patrilocal residence A social norm in which married couples reside with the husband's family after marriage; common in societies in which descent is through the male line, or patrilineal.

pattern In the **Midwestern taxonomic system**, phases were grouped into patterns based on formal attributes in material culture; the term is not used extensively today.

Pauma complex A term applied to Archaic sites in extreme southern California; sites lack shell middens but have millingstones and a variety of flaked stone items.

Pebble Tool tradition An alternative name for the **Old Cordilleran tradition** of the Pacific Northwest.

Pecos classification A cultural sequence encompassing Basketmaker and Anasazi material from the Southwest, devised by Kidder in 1927 at the first Pecos Conference; still used, with modification, today in the northern Southwest.

peneplain A gently rolling land surface that results from the advanced erosion of mountains; the Piedmont on the eastern side of the Appalachian Mountain system is such a surface.

permafrost   Permanently frozen ground underlying a surface layer that thaws and freezes seasonally; found in the Arctic tundra regions of North America.

phase   An archaeological unit consisting of several components at a number of sites defined by similar artifacts and other characteristics and found in a unique geographical area and time period; phases are thought to loosely represent cultures.

Pickering phase   An early Iroquoian phase designation for southern Ontario dating from about 1050 BP to 650 BP; compare **Glen Meyer phase**, located to the southwest.

piece plotting   An excavation technique in which the three-dimensional positions of all artifacts and ecofacts are plotted; time-consuming but produces detailed information about context.

pig   (iron making), the name given to the bars of cooled iron (thought to resemble little pigs nursing from their mother's belly) formed in the sand floor in front of the **cast arch**; pig iron contains impurities such as carbon and needs further refinement.

Pinto period   The name given to the Early Archaic period in the southwestern Great Basin; comes from the triangular-bladed Pinto point form and is related to the Pinto tradition in the Southwest.

Pinto tradition   The Archaic tradition of the western Southwest from approximately 8000 BP to 1450 BP; the people were broad-based foragers who made Pinto points, various millingstones, and other tools.

Pioneer period Hohokam   The beginning of the **Hohokam tradition** sequence (1750–1175 BP) in the southern Arizona desert; characterized by wattle and daub houses in shallow pits.

pithouse   A semisubterranean structure built by various areas of North America, the lower walls were earthen or lined with rock while a wooden superstructure supported the upper walls and roof.

Pithouse-to-Pueblo transition   The change in the northern and mountainous Southwest from settlements consisting of pithouses and surface storage rooms to multiroom surface structures; occurs between 1250 BP and 950 BP as people settled into villages.

Plains culture area   The vast culture area encompassing the grasslands of North America's midcontinent that stretch from southern Canada to central Texas; bison hunting was important in this area, although many later groups also farmed in the river valleys.

Plains Village tradition   Plains cultures from about 1150 BP to Historic times in which bison hunting and horticulture were combined by people living in **earthlodge** villages in river valleys; subdivisions are Central, Middle Missouri, and Southern Plains.

Plains Woodland   The term used for cultures that began to develop on the eastern margins and in the river valleys of the Great Plains after 2500 BP as pottery was adopted and, in some cases, horticulture, and burial mounds began to be constructed.

plaiting   A method of weaving in which two or more elements are interwoven; compare **twining** and **coiling**.

Plano complex   A general term for Late Paleoindian on the Great Plains; subsumes a number of phases such as Hell Gap and Agate Basin in which unfluted lanceolate projectile points were made; points of these types sometimes are found further east.

Plateau culture area The interior culture area that lies between the Rocky Mountains and the mountain ranges along the Northwest Coast; native hunter-gatherers of this area relied both on salmon in the rivers and on land resources.

Plateau Pithouse tradition A cultural tradition in the Fraser and Thomas river drainages of the Canadian Plateau that first appeared between 5500 BP and 5000 BP; believed to be associated with the northward migration of Salishan-speaking people who fished for salmon.

platform The surface that receives the blow in flaking a piece of stone; a platform surface may be prepared or naturally occurring.

platform mounds A mound that is flat on the top and more or less resembles a truncated pyramid; the **Hohokam** built this type of mound of rubble and refuse, but the platform type of mound is best known from the East, especially among **Mississippians**.

platform pipe A smoking pipe with the bowl centered on top of a curved or flat platform; may be made in the form of an animal effigy and is diagnostic of the **Hopewell Interaction Sphere** in the Eastern Woodlands (see Figures 12.12 and 12.13).

Pleistocene The geologic epoch known as the Ice Age lasting from 1.8 million years ago to 10,000 years ago; the earlier part of the Quaternary period during which glaciers alternately expanded and retreated across northern North America and Eurasia.

plow zone The uppermost soil level composed of soil that has been disturbed by plowing; artifacts found within the plow zone also have been disturbed, making them potentially less significant than items found in undisturbed contexts.

Plum Bayou period The terminal Late Woodland in the central Mississippi River valley (1250–950 BP); grog-tempered and some shell-tempered ceramics were made, and large towns with mounds were built, suggesting the emergence of Mississippian.

pluvial lakes Pleistocene lakes that formed in closed basins of the West as a result of locally wetter conditions combined with colder climate worldwide.

pochteca Long-distance traders of Mexico; sometimes claimed to have traded with North American societies.

Point Peninsula tradition The Middle Woodland cultural tradition of New York and southern Ontario dating from 2200 BP to 1300 BP; distinct from the Hopewell tradition and possibly ancestral to the development of Iroquoian cultural phenomena in the Northeast.

polyculture A term that refers to the practice of growing multiple crops together in one plot or field, as in maize-bean-squash agriculture.

Portage complex The second of two Northern Archaic complexes recognized at the Onion Portage site in Alaska (4500–4400 BP).

positivism A school of philosophy according to which objective reality can be known through empirical testing of hypotheses; influenced much of modern science, including archaeological **processualism**, but is questioned in the postmodern era.

postmodernist A person whose philosophical position opposes the emphasis in modern thought on scientific method, stresses that reality is a social construction, and deconstructs totalizing systems of knowledge.

postmolds A hole that at one point held an upright post and now gives a negative impression of it; often the sediments filling the hole can be differentiated from those surrounding it, allowing one to plot the pattern of posts that once existed.

Post pattern An archaeological complex of California's North Coast Ranges in the vicinity of Borax Lake (12,000–11,000 BP); characterized by Clovis points with single-shouldered points and crescents as well as evidence of generalized foraging.

postprocessualism A series of theoretical approaches critical of **processualism**, especially its materialist and positivist aspects; stresses the social aspects of interaction in society, especially human agency, and often incorporates Marxist and feminist ideas.

pothunter A term archaeologists use for individuals who disturb archaeological sites to gain access to artifacts without concern for investigating the culture that produced these artifacts; see **relic hunter**.

Poverty Point complex Various Late Archaic sites including the Poverty Point site itself that were located in the lower Mississippi River valley between 3700 BP and 2500 BP spanning the Woodland transition; characterized by extensive trade, earthworks, and stoneworking.

Pre-Clovis Early North American material that is dated prior to the well-documented Clovis culture (11,500–10,800 BP) that is associated with the earliest fluted points; some archaeologists do not accept the identification of any materials as Pre-Clovis.

Pre-Dorset An eastern Arctic expression of the **Arctic Small Tool Tradition** that apparently postdates **Independence** and may be represented by the **Sarqaq culture** in Greenland.

preform An unhafted **biface** that is roughly shaped but unfinished and unused; suitable for further working or refining into a finished tool.

Prescott A regional branch of the **Patayan tradition** found in west central Arizona (1100–950 BP).

presidio A Spanish period military post or garrison.

primary burial The original interment of an individual; may be only the first step in a complicated burial program; compare **secondary burial**.

prismatic blade A specialized **blade**, often triangular or trapezoidal in cross section and having several facets or flake scars on the **dorsal surface**; common in Paleoindian lithic assemblages.

probability survey An archaeological survey in which sample portions of the area of interest are selected based on environmental or other characteristics and surveyed systematically so that the results can be used to estimate overall site distributions.

processualism An approach to archaeology developed in the 1960s and 1970s that stressed application of the scientific method, took an ecological and systems approach to culture, and sought to explain **culture process**; criticized by the postprocessualists.

projectile point A bifacial tool that has a haft area and may take a variety of forms; often called an arrowhead although all projectile points are not used on arrows.

provenance The region of origin of a raw material such as chert type or shell; also used in collections management in museums to refer to the history of ownership of an artifact or piece of art; compare **provenience**.

provenience The exact location at which an object is found in an archaeological site; an artifact's location relative to the site's grid system; compare **provenance**.

pueblo   Spanish for town; in the **Pecos classification** Pueblo I–V encompassed the periods in which Southwesterners lived in aboveground, multiroom buildings rather than in pithouses.

quid   A mass of chewed fibers or tobacco; chewed yucca quids have been found in dry caves in the West.

radiocarbon dating   A dating technique that uses the ratio of carbon-14 to the stable carbon isotope carbon-12 as a measure of the amount of time since the death of the organism; must be calibrated to obtain calendar years.

rain shadow   A dry region that is downwind from a mountain barrier; there is little precipitation in this region because moist air masses drop their precipitation on the windward side of the mountain barrier.

rancherias   Dispersed settlements found among Native people in several areas of the Southwest and California during Historic times; contrasts with pre-Columbian nucleated pueblos.

ranked society   A society in which status, power, and access to goods and services is based on an internal system of ranking; rank is often based on the genealogical relationship of an individual or a family to a chief.

reciprocity   Exchange among persons relatively equal in social rank that establishes or reinforces social obligations between the parties.

reconnaissance   A basic form of archaeological survey designed to locate archaeological deposits (or sites) where they were previously unknown may precede more systematic or intensive **archaeological site survey**.

red ocher   A red pigment made by grinding iron-rich rocks like hematite; used around the world by hunter-gatherers and others, often mixed with oil or fat to create paint for decorating the body and numerous inanimate objects.

Red Ocher mortuary complex   A Late Archaic and Early Woodland complex of the Midwest in which individuals were buried with large amounts of red ocher; characterized by distinctive cache blades and **turkey-tailed points**.

Register of Professional Archaeologists (RPA)   An organization of archaeologists who have agreed to certain standards of research performance and ethical conduct. The RPA designation also indicates certain training and experience in archaeology.

relative dating   Determining the chronological age of a specimen based on its relative position in a stratigraphic or typological sequence, without reference to a specific time scale; compare **absolute dating**.

relic hunter   A term sometimes used for individuals who search for artifacts without regard for investigating the culture that produced these artifacts (see **pothunter**).

remote sensing   A general term encompassing a variety of techniques used by archaeologists to locate subsurface features; includes **geophysical survey** techniques and aerial photography.

repatriation   The return of cultural materials and human remains to the country of origin or descendant population; for example, materials from Native American burials now are routinely returned to tribal descendants, who often rebury them.

research design   The plan of an archaeological project, including a statement of the research problem, background information, methods, and timetable; having a research design is good practice in any archaeological research and is required by granting and contracting agencies.

ridged field system   A labor-intensive technique known to have been used by Oneota and Mississippian groups in the East in which fields were raised by mounding the earth into ridges, possibly to reclaim wetlands, prevent frost damage, or control erosion.

Rio Grande Branch Anasazi   A regional branch of Ancestral Pueblo archaeological cultures in the northern Rio Grande valley of New Mexico; population aggregation took place here after the abandonment of much of the northern Southwest around 650 BP.

Riverton culture   A Late Archaic archaeological culture from the valley of the Wabash River, which flows between Illinois and Indiana; characterized by seasonal movements between base and extractive camps and by the use of freshwater mussels, microperforators, and bone and other tools.

ruderal plant   A plant that grows in disturbed land, rubbish, or waste; may be associated with gardens or fields.

Rupert's Land   A Canadian territory from 1670 to 1869 originally owned by the Hudson's Bay Company and named after Prince Rupert, the first governor of the company.

S-twist   A method of making cordage in which the fibers are twisted up to the left producing an **S** shape in the finished product; if visible on cord-marked pottery or in actual cordage, may be interpretable in terms of ethnicity.

Salado   An enigmatic Late Prehistoric (after 600 BP) phenomenon associated with Gila polychrome pottery; some believe it represents the migration of new groups into the Hohokam area; others interpret it as indicative of the development of a religious cult.

salvage approach   An approach to archaeology that concentrates on recovery of information from a site that is about to be destroyed; this precursor to **cultural resource management** did not attempt to research questions or to long-term manage cultural resources.

San Dieguito complex   An early archaeological culture of Southern California (ca. 10,000–8500 BP); because of the lack of millingstones and the presence of large leaf-shaped points and knives, San Dieguito is assumed to represent a population of hunters of large game.

San Luis Rey complex   A Late Prehistoric complex found in southern California north of the **Cuyamaca complex** with different kinds and proportions of ceramics; seen as ancestral to the Shoshonean speakers of the area; the people practiced cremation and used small triangular points.

San Rafael Fremont   A regional variant of the **Fremont culture** that developed in southeastern Utah, influenced by the **Kayenta Anasazi**; there are surface storage structures along with pithouses and maize agriculture.

sandal-sole gorget   A gorget that archaeologists think was shaped to resemble the sole of a foot or sandal; made from marine shell often found in Late Archaic burials in the Upper Great Lakes and Midwest; these artifacts are associated with the **Glacial Kame mortuary complex**.

Santarosae   The large island that connected the Northern Channel Islands off Santa Barbara, California, during the Pleistocene, when the sea level was lowered.

Saratoga Springs period   A time (1500–800 BP) in the southwestern Great Basin when projectile points became smaller, suggesting the introduction of the bow and arrow; as in the preceding Gypsum period, millingstones continued in use.

Sarqaq (Saqqaq) culture   A Greenlandic culture of the later **Arctic Small Tool tradition**; the people were terrestrial and marine hunters who used ground burins and burinlike tools, as well as open-socketed harpoon heads.

scientific method   The systematic investigation of phenomena by identifying a problem, developing hypotheses and test implications, making empirical observations, and reconsidering the original idea in the light of the results obtained.

scientism   The belief that there is only one method of science and that legitimate scientific conclusions can be reached only by using this method.

secondary burial   A human interment that has been moved and buried again (see **bundle burial**); can be part of a continuing program of mortuary activity and preceded by **primary burial**.

Section 106   The section of the **National Historic Preservation Act** that requires federal agencies to determine if their undertakings might have any adverse effects on properties eligible for the **National Register of Historic Places**; effects must be mitigated if they are likely to occur.

Section 110   A section first added to the **National Historic Preservation Act** in 1980s amendments, requiring federal agencies to integrate historic preservation into their activities and responsibly manage the historic properties under their jurisdiction.

Sedentary Period Hohokam   A subperiod in the **Hohokam tradition** sequence of the southern Arizona desert (975–800 BP); multiroom pueblos were surrounded by compound walls.

Selkirk culture   An archaeological culture of Ontario, Manitoba, and Saskatchewan from about 1050 BP to the Historic period; the people were boreal hunters and fishers, apparently ancestral to the Cree.

selvage   The narrow edge of a woven fabric that runs parallel to the **warp**.

seriation   A method for the relative dating of artifacts based on variations in style and decoration within **assemblages**; uses the theory that artifacts will most closely resemble items that are closest to them in time. (See **frequency seriation**.)

Sevier Fremont   A regional variant of **Fremont culture** found in west central Utah and adjacent Nevada; characterized by small sites with pithouses and adobe surface rooms, Sevier gray pottery, and use of marshes with less use of maize than found among other Fremont variants.

Shaft wrench   A bone tool thought to have been used to straighten arrow or spear shafts; an example is illustrated in Figure 3.16.

Shaman's teeth   A Dorset artifact consisting of a bone mouth with teeth that apparently was clasped in the shaman's mouth during ritual activities.

Shasta aspect   An expression of the Augustine pattern on California's northwest coast; this is a period of semi-sedentary lowland villages and seasonal upland camps. Artifacts include Gunther Barbed points, **hopper mortars**, **manos** and **metates**, bifaces of chert, **charmstones** and spire-lopped *Olivelia* beads.

shell midden   A type of archaeological site formed when people discard large quantities of oyster, clam, mussel, and other bivalve shells as food refuse, along with other trash.

Shell Mound Archaic A Middle-to-Late Archaic series of shell middens that have accumulated into mound sites, located in the river valleys of the interior Southeast and the Midwest.

shell-tempered ceramics Ceramics in which the paste contains crushed shell inclusions; often considered a marker of **Mississippian** and other **Late Prehistoric** peoples in the Eastern Woodlands.

sherd A broken piece of a pottery vessel; equivalent terms are potsherd and shard.

Shield Archaic tradition A hunting and gathering tradition that developed in the boreal woodlands of the eastern Canadian Subarctic after Plano or Late Paleoindian people migrated into the area; persisted into Historic times.

Shoshonean period Dated to after 800 BP, this period is marked by the presence of Desert Side Notched points and ceramics in the southwestern Great Basin.

shovel-shaped incisor An incisor in which the lateral borders have a thickening or extension toward the tongue so that in cross section the tooth resembles a shovel; more common among people of Asian descent, including most Native Americans, than among other populations.

shovel test pit (STP) A small pit excavation into areas in which the surface is obscured by vegetation or when cultural materials are believed to lie buried in sediments; used to find sites or establish the extent of buried deposits.

Sicco-type harpoon head An open-socket harpoon head with a conspicuous central constriction that is associated with the spread of the Thule people in the Arctic.

side scraper A tool with a steep working edge on one side, usually made by unifacial retouch or flaking of part or all of the edge of a flake or core.

significant cultural resources Cultural resources that meet the criteria for being added to the National Register of Historic Places; a site or structure can be deemed significant even it is not actually listed.

Silvernale phase An Oneota tradition phase (850–650 BP) from the margins of the Mississippi River at the Wisconsin–Minnesota border; possible Mississippian-derived traits include platform mounds, village fortification, and pottery designs.

Sinagua A regional farming tradition of the southwest found between Flagstaff and Phoenix, Arizona (ca. 1250–550 BP); this tradition has been variously grouped under other regional traditions but is now best treated separately.

sinkhole A circular depression in the ground surface that forms when underlying rock such as limestone is dissolved by water and collapses; sinkholes may contain artifacts and other evidence of human activities.

sinodont A dental pattern including shovel-shaped incisors, three rooted first lower molars, and other dental traits believed to be characteristic of North Asian populations and Native Americans. See **sundadont**.

sipapu A small hole or indentation in the floor of kivas used by the Ancestral Puebloans as well as modern-day Puebloans, symbolizing the portal through which the ancient ancestors first emerged into the present world; may be unaltered or plastered.

Skraelings The name Vikings used for the Native people of North America; considered derogatory.

skeletal mass allometry   A method of making **meat weight estimates** that uses a formula for converting bone weight to meat weight; the weight of all bones assigned to a taxon is plugged into the formula, and total meat weight for the taxon is estimated.

skreblo   Large Siberian side scrapers often made from cortical flakes; some possible early artifacts from southern California superficially resemble these tools.

slag   A by-product of smelting iron; the impurities that can be drawn off at the cinder notch above the hearth itself, which when cool have a glassy blue-black appearance.

slip   A mixture of clay and water applied to a pottery vessel to obtain a smooth finish.

smoking complex   The group of artifacts, behaviors, and beliefs associated with ritual smoking of tobacco and other substances by the Native peoples of North America; both archaeologically and ethnographically evident.

Solutrean connection   The idea that there was a direct cultural connection between the Solutrean culture and Paleoindians of North America resulting from migration across the North Atlantic; based on similarities in lithic technology.

Solutrean culture   An Upper **Paleolithic** culture of western Europe dating between 22,000 and 18,000 years ago; famous for finely made leaf-shaped bifaces.

Sonota burial complex   A Plains Middle Woodland burial pattern found along the Missouri River in northern South Dakota and southern North Dakota between 1950 and 1500 BP; possibly associated with the **Besant phase**.

South Appalachian tradition   A Southeastern Woodland period pottery tradition found in southeastern Alabama, large parts of Georgia, and some of northern Florida; vessel surfaces were stamped with various curvilinear or checked designs.

Southeast culture area   The culture area that encompasses the southern part of the Eastern Woodlands stretching from East Texas to the Atlantic. Some of the most complex Native American chiefdoms developed among the farmers of this area.

Southeastern Ceremonial complex (SECC)   A widespread Mississippian complex between 800 BP and 600 BP, also called the **Southern cult**; recognized by motifs such as the hand and eye and the sun circle, and by finely made artifacts of stone, shell, and copper.

Southern cult   Another name for the Southeastern Ceremonial complex (SECC).

Southern Plains tradition   A subdivision of the **Plains Village tradition** referring to village people of the Southern Plains in Late Prehistoric times; characterized by horticulture and bison hunting, arrow points, cord-marked pottery, and bone tools.

Southwest culture area   The culture area of the arid West encompassing most of Arizona and New Mexico as well as portions of southern Utah, Colorado, and northern Mexico; farming peoples developed relatively complex polities in this area.

Southwest Regional cult   The idea that the distinctive designs of Gila polychrome pottery that was made in the southern Southwest after 600 BP represent the spread of a pan-ethnic religious ideology associated with fertility and water control.

split-twig figurine   A figurine constructed by splitting willow twigs and wrapping the two half stems around each other to construct an animal; the figure might be pierced with another piece, suggesting use in hunting magic; found in caves in the arid West.

Squawkie Hill phase   A Middle Woodland phase in New York and western Pennsylvania associated with mounds containing central stone tombs and Hopewell Interaction Sphere objects.

St. Johns tradition   A Late Prehistoric culture of Florida's Atlantic coast with large mounds and shell middens; some interaction with Mississippians is indicated, but subsistence focused on coastal and marine resources rather than agriculture.

state   A politically autonomous form of society with a strong centralized government, a large population, substantial settlements, a stratified class system, and a market economy; states did not develop in pre-Columbian North America.

State Historic Preservation Officer (SHPO)   The government official who has the responsibility for a U.S. state's historic preservation program; usually appointed by the governor.

steatite   A soft stone also called soapstone that can be carved into figurines, beads, and vessels or used in **stone boiling**; widely used by North America's pre-Columbian inhabitants.

Steed–Kisker phase   A **Central Plains Village tradition** phase from the Kansas City area in which people made shell-tempered, incised ceramics resembling those of the **Mississippians** further East; probably a result of contact rather than actual migration.

stone boiling   Heating or cooking by dropping rocks, preheated in a fire, into a pit or basket containing liquid or food to be cooked.

stone box grave   A burial pit lined with stone slabs to form a coffinlike box; occurs in the Late Prehistoric and Mississippian societies of the Eastern Woodlands.

stratification   Soil or rock layers laid down in sequence; useful in associating artifacts and establishing **relative dating**.

stratified society   A society in which there are sharp class-based distinctions in wealth, access to resources, prestige, and power; often associated with the state.

stratigraphy   The description and study of stratigraphic layers; may be used to determine **relative dating** among artifacts and features in a site.

stratum   A layer of sediment or rock whose characteristics distinguish it from layers above or below it; generally the bottom strata are older than overlying ones.

Subarctic culture area   The North American culture area that stretches from the tree line southward across the continent; includes most of the Canadian coniferous forests that were inhabited by different groups of Native hunter-gatherers at European contact.

subassemblage   A collection of associated artifacts thought to represent a particular set of activities by a particular group of people; a subset of an **assemblage**.

sundadont   A dental pattern believed to characterize South Asians but generally lacking among North Asians and Native Americans; shovel-shaped incisors, for example, are rare among sundadonts (see **sinodont**).

Susquehanna tradition   A Terminal Archaic cultural group of the coastal regions of Northeast and Mid-Atlantic; characterized by soapstone vessels, the broad-bladed Susquehanna point, and possible focus on coastal and riverine resources (see **Broadpoint tradition**).

Swift Creek tradition   A Middle-to-Late Woodland cultural tradition of northern Florida, southeastern Alabama, and the Georgia Coastal Plain and Piedmont; defined primarily on the basis of complicated stamped pottery from shell middens and mounds.

Takli stage   The first of two stages of the **Kodiak tradition** in Pacific Alaska, characterized by slate points, the oil lamp, and chipped stone tools.

Taltheilei tradition   The archaeological tradition of northwestern Canada after 2600 BP; the people were caribou hunters apparently ancestral to the Historic Dené of the area.

Tchula phase   An Early Woodland phase in the central and lower Mississippi River valley, which dates to the third millennium BP; characterized by temperless pottery, sand and **grog-tempered ceramics**, and small, conical burial mounds.

temperate deciduous forest biome   The forest biome of the eastern North America, which stretches south from the coniferous forest to central Florida and contains a variety of communities in which deciduous trees dominate or are mixed with some conifers.

temperate grassland biome   The large area of grassland that spans the midsection of the North American continent from southern Canada to Texas and northeastern Mexico; also includes areas of bunchgrass between the Rocky Mountains and the West Coast.

temporal type   A class of artifacts, like index fossils in paleontology, that are defined by the consistent presence of key attributes and assumed to have been made and used only for a specific period of time.

Tennessee Valley Authority (TVA)   Established as a U.S. government corporation in 1933 to control flooding and create electric power in the Southeast; many archaeological excavations have been associated with resultant instances of site destruction and site management.

tephra   Volcanic ash and other materials that were expelled into the air during the eruption of a volcano and cooled as they were deposited.

tephrochronology   The dating and stratigraphy of volcanic ash layers (e.g., the Mount Mazama ash in the North American West).

Terminal Archaic   The period between approximately 3700 BP and 2700 BP in the Northeast and Mid-Atlantic; characterized by intensive use of riverine and coastal resources, a greater degree of sedentism, steatite bowls, and pottery (see **Transitional period**).

Tertiary   The geologic period that extends from approximately 65 million to 1.8 million years ago when the Quaternary, consisting of the Pleistocene and Holocene epochs, begins.

Three Sisters   In Iroquoian tradition maize, bean, and squash, which are grown together assisting each other; the beans climb the maize stalk while they return nitrogen to the soil and the squash prevents weeds and helps the soil retain moisture.

Thule culture The Arctic archaeological culture (pre-Inuit) that developed in northwestern Alaska, spread rapidly across the Arctic all the way to Greenland after 1050 BP, and persisted to Historic times.

Thule tradition The archaeological manifestation of ancestral Inuit cultures in the Arctic, including the **Thule culture** itself; the people were sophisticated sea mammal hunters with an elaborate material inventory.

toggling harpoon A type of harpoon having a head that detaches from the shaft and turns sideways, or toggles, in the prey animal; used for large sea mammals by the maritime hunters of the North.

tomol The plank canoe of the **Chumash** of coastal southern California; made from split redwood planks sewn together and caulked to achieve water-tightness, these canoes could travel on the rough ocean waters.

tradition As defined by Willey and Phillips (1958), the archaeological unit that links phases and sites based on general attributes of material culture that persist over a long period; compare **horizon**.

traditional cultural property (TCP) Place that has special meaning to members of an ethnic group or a community; TCPs may be eligible for the National Register of Historic Places.

Trail of Tears A name given to the forced relocation of Southeastern Indians as a result of the Indian Removal Act of 1830; specifically the 1838 removal of the Cherokees which resulted in the deaths of many people.

Transitional period An alternative term for the **Terminal Archaic** (ca. 3700–2700 BP) in the Northeast and Mid-Atlantic, may mark a shift toward more sedentary societies and intensive use of key resources; steatite bowls and pottery are characteristic.

tree line The edge of the habitat at which trees are capable of growing either in the North or in the high mountains; actually a broad zone in which trees first become sparser and dwarfed and eventually give way to tundra.

trend surface analysis The statistical procedure that takes the components of a spatially distributed variable and develops a function to highlight the main features of the distribution, making trends and patterns apparent.

Tribal Historic Preservation Officer (THPO) A designated tribal official with responsibilities for cultural resources on tribal lands parallel to those of a **State Historic Preservation Officer (SHPO)**.

tribe A social grouping larger than a band that has a steady subsistence base from farming, herding, or a mixed economy but is still largely egalitarian, with social institutions based on kinship and age.

tribelet A term applied to autonomous cultural groups with hereditary leaders in California; emphasizes the small size of many of the indigenous groups; although independent, tribelets sometimes confederated.

trincheras Terraces or walls constructed of local stone on a hillside to retain soil and moisture; found in the desert Southwest of the United States and in Mexico.

tumpline A strap worn across the forehead or the chest to support a load carried on the back; apparently used with large burden baskets.

tundra biome The treeless Arctic biome that stretches across North America above latitude 57° north.

turkey-tail point   A thin, leaf-shaped point with side notches that results in a small triangular base; points like this are found both in the **Red Ocher mortuary complex** in the Midwest and in the **Western Idaho burial complex**.

tuyere   The pipe, often made of copper, that conducted air into the interior of an iron furnace stack so that the fire remained hot.

twining   A method of basketmaking in which two or more elements are twisted around a base element (**warp**) as they are interwoven; compare **plaiting** and **coiling**.

type site   A site that is the first or the best example of a particular cultural taxon (e.g., a phase or tradition); reference to the characteristics of the type site helps define the cultural historical unit.

type specimen   A particular artifact that is the first described or the best example of an artifact type; the formal attributes of the type are based on this artifact's characteristics.

typology   A classification of material objects that systematically sorts items according to morphological, technological, functional, or other attributes; typologies may be used to construct chronologies for a region or site.

Uinta Fremont   A regional variant of the **Fremont culture** that developed in the northeastern part of Utah; characterized by small sites, lack of Utah metates, hunting, gathering, and not a great deal of maize use.

ulu   A semicircular or half-moon shaped knife made and used by various peoples in the North; known archaeologically as early as 6000 years ago in the Maritime Archaic and often made of ground slate; woman's knife among the Inuit of recent times.

umiak   An open boat, with a wooden frame covered by bearded seal or walrus hide; made by Thule and Historic Inuit people.

underwater archaeology   The investigation and study of archaeological deposits, especially shipwrecks, that are located beneath the surface of various bodies of water.

uniface   A chipped stone tool that has been worked on only one face or surface.

Upper Mississippian   A term for Late Prehistoric horticultural societies on the northern margins of the Mississippian area (e.g., Oneota) that once were thought to be Mississippian regional variants.

Upper Republican phase   A **Central Plains Village tradition** phase from western Kansas and Nebraska; characterized by square houses, bell-shaped storage pits, horticulture, and bison hunting.

Utah metate   A distinctive type of metate with a troughlike grinding surface and a shelf at one end. This type of metate is associated with the Fremont occupations of the Great Basin.

vacant center model   The proposal that Hopewell mound and earthwork centers were primarily seasonal ceremonial centers that served to cement social relations between dispersed farming hamlets rather than large habitations; the evidence is mixed.

Vacant Quarter   An area in southern Illinois, southern Indiana, northern Kentucky, and central Tennessee centered on the central Mississippi and lower Ohio River valleys, which apparently was depopulated late in prehistory, after 500 BP.

Ventana complex   The artifact assemblage from Ventana Cave in Arizona that seems to have both San Dieguito and Folsom affinities in manufacturing technique; from the Pleistocene–Holocene boundary.

ventilator   The ventilation system of a **pithouse** or **kiva**; ventilator shafts are connected to the main structure by a tunnel that lets in fresh air.

Virgin Branch Anasazi   The branch of the **Ancestral Puebloan tradition** that is located furthest west, found in northern Arizona, southern Utah, and southern Nevada (1450–650 BP).

Wakulla culture   A Late **Weeden Island tradition** manifestation of northwest Florida for which increasing reliance on agriculture can be documented; precedes **Fort Walton Mississippian**.

warp   In basketry and weaving, the elements running lengthwise; compare **weft**.

wedge-shaped core   A type of core or rock nodule commonly flaked in the making of microblades in early North American industries.

Weeden Island tradition   A Late Woodland tradition (1750/1650–950 BP) of southeast Alabama, northern Florida, and southern Georgia; characterized by complicated stamped and check-stamped ceramics, marine adaptations, mounds, and mortuary ceremonialism.

weft   In basketry and weaving, the horizontal elements perpendicular to and interlaced with the **warp**.

Wendover period   The period from 9500 BP to 6000 BP following the Bonneville period in the eastern Great Basin; sites of this period occur in a number of environmental settings and suggest a mobile way of life; milling-stones are part of the assemblage.

Western Basin tradition   A Middle Woodland cultural tradition of Northern Ohio, southeastern Michigan and southwestern Ontario apparently not linked to Hopewell.

Western Clovis   A term sometimes used to refer to fluted points found in the Far West; these points have not been found in kill sites for megafauna, as on the Plains, but have been associated with lake margin sites.

Western Idaho burial complex   An enigmatic set of burials from western Idaho with unusual artifacts including **turkey-tail points**; large, thin bifaces, and trade items; dated between 6000 BP and 4000 BP.

Western Pluvial Lakes tradition   A tradition suggested by Bedwell for early adaptations around the pluvial lakes of California and the Great Basin at the Pleistocene–Holocene boundary; characterized by stemmed points and crescents; see **Western Stemmed Point tradition**.

Western Stemmed Point tradition   A pre-Archaic, nonfluted point tradition (11,000–7000 BP) in the Great Basin and surrounding areas; characterized by large stemmed points, crescents, and other tools (see **Western Pluvial Lakes tradition**).

wet site   A waterlogged archaeological site; wet sites often contain unusually well-preserved organic materials, such as wood and bone artifacts, as well as food remains.

White method   A method for calculating **meat weight estimates** in which the **MNI** for a taxon is multiplied by an average weight estimate; fails to take into account variability in body size or the possibility that entire carcasses were not utilized.

Whittlesey tradition   A Late Prehistoric cultural tradition of northeastern Ohio (950–300 BP); large, hilltop villages were surrounded by embankments, where the people practiced mixed horticulture and hunting and gathering.

Windmiller pattern   An archaeological culture found in central California, especially the Sacramento Delta, that marks the transition from the Archaic period to the Pacific; characterized by elaborate burials and exploitation of riverine and marsh resources.

Windust phase   An early period archaeological culture from the Snake River area on the Columbia Plateau in Washington State, north central Idaho, and parts of northern Oregon; the people were generalized foragers who made stemmed projectile points and other artifacts.

wing wall   A low wall that often partitions the main chamber of Ancestral Pueblo pithouses; often found in two, nonmeeting segments abutting either side of the main chamber walls.

Wisconsin glaciation   The last major episode of glacial advance in the Pleistocene of North America; from about 100,000 BP to 10,000 BP.

Wood henge   A circular arrangement of posts that may have been used for astronomical observations or for aligning buildings and mounds; more than one of these constructions apparently was built at Cahokia.

Woodland period   A cultural period recognized in areas south of the Subarctic and east of the Rockies in which agriculture, settled villages, pottery, and burial mounds usually were found; usually follows the **Archaic period** and begins 3000 to 2000 years ago.

Works Progress Administration (WPA)   A work program established in 1935 to help ease the Great Depression; the United States government employed American workers and commissioned large-scale archaeological excavations that generated important data. In 1939 the name was changed to **Works Projects Administration**.

World Heritage Site   A site designated by UNESCO as part of the cultural or natural heritage of all people worldwide; UNESCO maintains a list designed to promote conservation; only eight U.S. and five Canadian properties are listed.

World's Columbian Exposition   The World's Fair held in Chicago in 1893; the exhibits included large archaeological and ethnological collections; millions of Americans visited this fair, stimulating museums to develop collections in these areas.

Yent Ceremonial complex   A Deptford burial mound complex named after the Yent site in northwest Florida; mounds and burials included Middle Woodland exchange or ceremonial items like plummets, copper panpipes, earspools, and shell gorgets.

Z-twist   A method of making cordage in which the fibers are twisted up to the right, producing a Z-shape in the finished product; if visible on cord-marked pottery or actual cordage may be interpretable in terms of ethnicity.

zooarchaeologist   An archaeologist who identifies animal remains from archaeological sites and then investigates their physiology and ecology in relation to cultural activities; this interdisciplinary specialty also is referred to as archaeozoology.

INDEX

Abbott Farm site, 581
Accelerator mass spectrometry. *See* AMS dating
Acoma Pueblo, 385
Adena, 473, 478, 523, 532, 581
African American, 340, 495, 593, 620–621; burial ground, New York City, 22, 593
Agate Basin point, 153, 414
Agate Basin site, 129
Agriculture. *See* Food production
Ahtena tribe, 177
Alabama tribe, 492
Alaskan Native, 183, 303, 305, 307
Alaskan Native Claims Settlement Act, 183
Alberta point, 414
Aleut, 174
Aleutian tradition, 152, 156–157
Algonquian, 174, 177–178, 491, 492, 544, 586, 590, 601; as descendents of the Shield Archaic, 153–155
Alibates quarries, 432
Allen site, 416
Altithermal. *See* Hypsithermal
Alutiiq, 186
American Civil War, 452, 495, 547, 593
American Revolution, 494, 547, 593
American Paleolithic, 100, 274
Amino acid racemiztion dating. *See* Aspartic acid racemiztion dating
AMS dating, 106, 514, 520, 623; and cultigens, 580, 602, 604–605
Anasazi, 45, 370, 371–375, 376–378; Chaco Branch, 371; Kayenta Branch, 333–334, 371, 375, 389; Mesa Verde Branch, 371, 375, 389; Rio Grande Branch, 371, 375; Virgin Branch, 324–325, 371, 389. *See also* Ancestral Pueblo

Anathermal, 316
Ancestral Pueblo, 45, 325, 371, 393. *See also* Anasazi
ANCSA. *See* Alaskan Native Claims Settlement Act
Angel site, 540
Antelope Creek phase, 432–433
Antiquities Act of 1906, 16, 615
Anzick cache, 130–131, 415
Apache tribe, 177, 392, 394, 434, 437
Apafalaya chiefdom, 491
Apalachee tribe, 492, 493
Apple Creek site, 532
Arapaho, 436
Archaeological Resources Protection Act, 305, 509, 618
Archaic stage, 71, 74, 87, 367, 368. *See also specific culture areas*
Archery Range ossuary, 585
Arctic culture area, 46, 144–191, 195; Archaic, 152–153, 155–157; Historic period, 174–178
Arctic Small Tool tradition, 158–163
Arikara tribe, 436, 438, 442, 450
Arkansas Post, 493
Arlington Springs site, 136, 137, 276
Armijo phase, 366
ARPA. *See* Archaeological Resources Protection Act
Arzberger site, 431
Aspartic acid racemiztion dating, 274–275
Assiniboin tribe, 436, 443
Athapaskan, 174–177, 219, 253, 254; and the Avonlea phase, 425; as possible descendents of the Northern Archaic, 153
Atlantic Slope Macro tradition, 574
Atlatl, 209, 328, 417

Augustine pattern, 286–288
Avonlea phase, 425
Awotovi site, 393
Aztalan site, 543

Backhoe Village site, 332, 334
Baghdad Museum, looting of, 615
Bajada phase, 366
Baker site, 248
Ball Court, 33, 380–381, 399, 402, 403
Bannerstones, 464, 572
Bannock tribe, 338
Basin and Range province, 237, 314–315, 359
Basketmaker II, 371
Basketry: and ethnicity, 229–230; at Qwu?gwes, 228–231; techniques, 212
Basque, 199, 590
Bat Cave, 368
Bateman Island site, 234
Batoche site, 439
Baytown period, 480–481
Bean, 79, 368, 370, 380, 431, 541, 584, 604–605; earliest dates, 604, 605; origins, 604
Bear Cove site, 202
Bear River sites, 334
Beaver First Nation group, 177
Bella Bella tribe, 219
Bella Coola tribe, 219
Berelekh site, 113
Berkeley pattern, 286
Beringia, 66, 107, 114–115, 135, 149; archaeological record, 112–118; eastern, sites in, 116–118; earliest dates, 112–113
Bering land bridge. *See* Beringia
Besant phase, 424

Betatakin site, 375
Biederbost site, 230
Biesterfeldt site, 436, 437f
Biloxi tribe, 492
Birnik culture, 171–172
Bison: extinct, 317–318, 363, 418, 460; hunting, 408, 415–416, 418, 445; as Paleoindian prey, 127
Blackduck culture, 173–174, 434
Black Earth site, 521
Blackfeet tribe, 436
Black Rock period, 327, 328–330
Blackwater Draw, 103, 128, 150, 413
Blodget site, 287
Blood residue analysis, 149–150, 623
Blood tribe, 434
Bluefish Caves, 111, 118, 149, 150
Blue Jacket's Creek site, 205
Boardwalk site, 208
Bonfire Shelter, 129
Bonneville period, 327
Borax Lake tradition, 278–279
Boston Saloon, 340
Bottle collectors. *See* Relic hunter
Boylston Street fish weir, 574
Broadpoint tradition, 462, 519, 575, 576–577, 586
Broken Mammoth site, 116, 150
Broome-Tech site, 578
Browns Bank, 565
Buena Vista Lake sites, 276, 278
Buffalo Soldiers, 394
Bull Brook site, 568, 569, 570
Bunchgrass prairie, 56–57
Burial groups, 38
Burial mounds, 216, 427, 482, 530, 581
Burials: Adena, 526; African American, 23–34; California, 278, 285, 286, 287; Hohokam, 36–41; Midwest and Upper Great Lakes, 521, 523; Mississippian, 538; Northeast and Mid-Atlantic, 575, 585; Northwest Coast, 205, 215–217; Paquimé, 400; Plateau, 252, 254; primary, 423; secondary, 423; and sedentism, 327; Southeast, 466; Woodland period, 477, 478–479
Burnham site, 413
Burning Tree mastodon site, 515
Button Point site, 166–167
Bylot Island, 166–167

Cache, food. *See* Storage
Cactus Hill site, 111, 567–568
Caddoan language family, 492
Caddo tribe, 492
Cahokia, 429, 535, 536–538
Cahuilla tribe, 293
Caldwell Village, 332

Calico site, 105–106, 274
California culture area, 46, 195, 237, 268–309, 311; Anglo-American period, 297–299; Archaic pattern, 277–280; Central California Archaic, 278, 288; Central Valley Pacific period, 285–286; Clovis, 275; Exploration period, 292–294; Hispanic period, 294–296; Historic period. 290–299; Hohokam artifacts in, 285; Mexican period, 296; Pacific period, 270, 280–291, 287–288; Pre-Clovis, 274–275
California Environmental Quality Act, 17, 305
California Native American Burial Act, 292
Calispell Valley, 253
Caloosahatchee culture, 491
Calusa tribe, 492
Camas, 245, 249, 251, 253
Campbell tradition, 280–281
Camp Peace, 340
Canadian Archaeological Association, 625
Canadian Shield, 148, 153, 562
Canaliño tribe, 281–282
Cannibalism, 339, 391, 620
Cannonball River, 430, 443
Caribou, 51, 517, 569
Carlton Annis site, 519, 520
Carrier tribe, 177
Carson-Conn-Short site, 461
Carson Mound site, 484
Casa Grande, 34, 369, 381, 389
Casas Grandes. *See* Paquimé
Casa Rinconada, 377
Cascade phase, 244
Cascade Range, 195, 238
Cashie phase, 491, 492
Casper site, 414
Catawba tribe, 492
Cathlapotle site, 220
Cayuga, 589
Cayuse tribe, 254, 255
Cazador phase,
Central Plains tradition, 427, 430
Central Subarctic Woodland culture, 173
CEQA. *See* California Environmental Quality Act
Ceramic Period. *See* Plains Woodland; Woodland Period
Chaco Canyon, 14–15, 18, 369, 376
Chaco Phenomenon. *See* Chaco regional system
Chaco regional system, 19, 355, 375, 376–378, 382
Channel Islands, California, 120, 136, 280, 292
Charles Town, 494
Charmstones, 279, 285, 287

Chaw'se Indian Grinding Rock State Historic Park, 290
Cherokee Sewer site, 414, 418, 586
Cherokee tribe, 492, 494, 503–504, 506
Chesrow complex, 514, 516
Cheyenne tribe, 436
Chickasaw tribe, 492, 495
Chiefdom, 76; Chaco, 377; Chumash, 283; Mississippian, 482, 488, 490; Southeast, 455, 491
Chihuahua tradition, 367
China Lake, 317
Chinookan language, 254
Chinook tribe, 219, 220, 253
Chipewyan, 177
Chippewa tribe, 544
Chirachua phase, 367
Choctaw tribe, 492, 495
Choris complex, 167–168
Chota site, 503, 506
Chuck Lake site, 201
Chumash tribe, 80, 137, 282–282, 292
Chutkotka, 113
Clallam, 219
Classic stage, 71
Clemson Island culture, 584, 588
Climate, 61–67
Cloudsplitter Rockshelter, 467
Clovis, 105, 107–108, 128, 130–131, 414–415
Clovis-first scenario, 103–112, 120, 618
Clovis point, 103, 104, 241, 363, 459
Clovis sites, 200, 275, 363; dates, 103
Coalescent tradition, 430–431
Coastal migration route, 119–120
Coastal occupations, early, 135, 181–182
Coastanoan tribe, 292
Cocanour locality, 322
Cochise tradition, 319, 366–367
Cochiti Pueblo, 394
Cocopa tribe, 393
Cody complex, 363, 414
Coeur d'Alene tribe, 254
Coffey site, 419
Colby site, 129
Colington phase, 491
Collectors, artifact, 24–25, 615, 616
Colony Ross, 301–309. *See also* Fort Ross
Colville tribe, 124, 244, 254
Comancheros, 438
Comanche tribe, 436, 438
Complex hunter-gatherers, 74, 181–182, 282, 618, 619
Confederated Tribes of the Collville Reservation, 244
Conway site, 229, 230
Cooking balls, clay, 285, 464, 468, 473. *See also* Poverty Point Objects

Cooperton site, 413
Coosa chiefdom, 493
Copena Mortuary complex, 478
Coppermine River Valley, 167
Corn. *See* Maize
Coronado expedition, 393, 436, 437
Coso Range, 323
Cotton, 368, 370, 380
Cowboy Cave, 323
Crab Orchard tradition, 524
Craig Mound, 490
Crater Lake, 239, 349
Cree, 178, 436
Creek tribe, 492, 494, 545
Creek War, 494
Crescentic, 141, 320–321
CRM. *See* Cultural resource management
Croatoan tribe, 492
Cross Creek site, California, 277
Crow Creek site, 431
Crowfield site, 570
Crow tribe, 436
Crystal River site, 478
Cultivated plants: Great Plains, 423, 426;
    Hohokam, 380; Middle Missouri
    tradition, 430; Midwest and Upper Great
    Lakes, 520; Mississippian, 489, 541;
    Mogollon, 385; Oneota tradition, 433;
    Southeast, 466, 467; Southwest, 367–369,
    370; Woodland period, 476, 531, 534
Cultural resource legislation, 16
Cultural resource management, 15, 32, 614,
    624–625; and academic training, 631;
    projects, characteristics of, 26
Culture area, 5, 44–49
Culture stage, 70
Cumberland point, 460, 515
Cumberland River, 459, 461, 483
Cupeño tribe, 293
Curation, 28, 355, 498; and cultural heritage,
    623–624; importance of, 351, 600
Custer Battlefield site, 439
Custer phase, 431–432
Cuyamaca complex, 284–285

Daisy Cave, 120, 135–143, 276–277
Dakota tribe, 436, 546
Dalles, The, 203, 254, 253. *See also*
    Roadcut site
Dalton period, 460–461
Danger Cave, 311, 318–319, 326, 327, 328
Dating, 81–83. *See also specific types of dating*
Deadwood Chinatown, 439
Debert site, 129, 567–568, 570
Delaware River, 565, 581, 590
Delaware tribe, 546, 583
Del Mar burial, 275
Deluge Shelter, 327

Denali complex, 117, 201
Denbigh Flint complex, 158–161
Dené, 45, 174
Dental characteristics, 126, 618
Dentalium shells, 251
Dent site, 128, 413
Deptford mounds, 478
Deptford tradition, 477, 478
Descendant population, 21–24, 625
Desert Archaic, 319–320
Desert Culture, 318–320
De Soto expedition, 491, 492
Dickson Mounds, 541, 626–627
Dinétah phase, 392
Dismal River phase, 434
DNA, Mitochondrial. *See* Mitochondrial
    DNA
DNA studies, 453
Dogan Point site, 573
Dogrib tribe, 177
Donner party, 339–340
Dorset tradition, 163–167
Double Ditch site, 431, 434, 442–451
Drake cache, 415
Dry Creek site, 116–117, 150
Drynoch Slide site, 243
Dust Cave, 461
Dutchess Quarry Cave, 569
Dutton site, 413
Dyuktai tradition, 113–115, 116f, 150

Early Agricultural period, 365
Early Horticultural period, 578–579
Earthlodge, 430, 431, 488
Eastern Agricultural Complex, 466–468,
    578, 618
Eastern Woodlands, 78, 453, 455, 619. *See also*
    Woodlands
East Wenatchee Clovis cache. *See* Richey-
    Roberts Clovis cache
Eel Point site, 276–277
Elites, 188; Chaco, 378; Hohokam, 381–382;
    households of, 252; Mississippian, 484,
    489, 489, 541; Paquimé, 400, 404
Elizabeth Mound group, 532
Eliza Furnace site, 595–596
Emergent Mississippian, 474, 480, 482
English: California, 294; Great Plains, 438;
    Midwest and Upper Great Lakes,
    545–546; Northeast and Mid-Atlantic,
    591–592, 593; Southeast, 492–494
En Medio phase, 366
Epidemic disease, 254, 293, 438, 443, 592
Erie tribe, 585, 591
Eskimo, 45, 146, 168, 174
Esselen, 292
Ethnicity, 80, 434–435, 464, 465, 619
Etowah site, 484, 485

Evans Mound, 332, 334
Eva site, 468
Exchange: Adena, 532; Cahokia, 537;
    California, 290; Chaco regional system,
    377; Great Basin, 325; Great Plains, 425,
    429, 437–438; Hopewell, 508, 532;
    Midwest and Upper Great Lakes, 521;
    Mississippian, 482, 489, 541; Northeast
    and Mid-Atlantic, 581, 589; Paquimé,
    398; Plateau, 250, 251, 254; Poverty Point,
    468–473; Southeast, 465, 473; Woodland,
    478, 479, 481, 482
Eveland Village site, 626

Fairchance phase, 581
Fall River skeleton, 175
Fant site, 476
Fatherland site, 494
Ferndale site, 203
Ferry Hall, 256
First Nation, 45, 146
First Native Americans, 97, 98–132,
Fisher site, 517
Fishing: California, 280, 282, 287; Hohokam,
    380; Midwest and Upper Great Lakes,
    519; Mississippian, 482, 489; Northeast
    and Mid-Atlantic, 580; Northwest Coast,
    205, 214; Plateau, 238, 243, 245, 249, 266;
    Woodland, 476, 480, 482
Fishtown site, 229, 230
Fish trap. *See* Fish weir
Fish weir, 207, 227–228, 574
Five-Mile Rapids, 203, 242. *See also*
    Roadcut site
Flenniken-Thomas debate, 326
Flint Run complex, 570
Flotation analysis, 41, 90, 353, 520, 601
Fluted points, 104–105; Alaska, 105, 118;
    Alberta, 105; Arctic, 149; California, 275;
    Eastern North America, 105; Great Basin,
    338; Midwest and Upper Great Lakes,
    514–515; Northeast and Mid-Atlantic,
    567, 568; Southeast, 459. *See also specific
    point types*
Fluted Point tradition, 276, 277
Folsom culture, 128, 363, 415
Folsom point, 102, 275, 317, 413
Folsom site, New Mexico, 101–102, 103, 413
Food production, 78, 618; Anasazi, 371–373;
    Great Plains, 416, 425; Mogollon, 382;
    Northeast and Mid-Atlantic, 578, 580,
    584, 585; Paquimé, 400; Southeast, 455,
    458, 462, 473; Woodland period, 480
Formative stage, 71, 74
Fort Ancient, 541–543, 544, 545
Fort Caroline, 493
Fort du Chartres, 546
Fort Erie, 593

Fortin site, 604
Fort Langley, 220
Fort Michilimackinac, 546, 547, 629
Fort Necessity, 593
Fort Ponchartrain, 546
Fort Rock Cave, 240, 320
Fort Rock Valley, 320, 324
Fort Ross, 294–296. *See also* Colony Ross
Fort St. Louis, 545
Fort Union, 439
Fort Vancouver, 220
Fort Walton culture, 482, 489
Fox tribe, 544, 546
Fremont culture, 312, 327, 330–335; Great
    Salt Lake variant, 332, 334; Parowan
    variant, 332, 334; San Rafael variant, 332,
    333–334; Sevier variant, 332, 334; Uinta
    variant, 332, 333
Fremont moccasins, 330–331, 335
French, 438, 492–494, 544–546, 590–593
French and Indian War, 546, 593
Furnace Brook site, 585
Fur trade, 178, 219, 338, 438, 544–545,
    590–591

Gainey site, 515, 516
Gargoa site, 585
Gatecliff Shelter, 72, 320, 326, 343–354
Gault site, 132f, 415
GE Mound, 508–510, 525, 615
Georges Bank, 565
Gibson-Klunk mounds, 530
Gifford Pinchot National Forest, 198
Gila River, 33, 360, 378
Gilman Falls site, 572
Givens Springs site, 247
Glacial Kame mortuary complex, 522
Glades culture, 491
Glen Meyer phase, 585, 587–588
Glenrose Cannery site, 202, 205
Glottochronology, 435, 586
Golden Eagle earthworks, 530
Gore Creek burial, 243
Gore Pit site, 417
Gourd, 368, 380, 458, 480, 520, 541, 574;
    bottle, 465, 480; experimental
    archaeology and, 606–607.
    See also Squash
Grand Village of the Natchez, 494
Grave Creek Mound, 9, 525–526
Grayson site, 278
Great Basin culture area, 48, 72, 237, 270, 275,
    310–354; American period, 338, 339;
    Archaic, 312, 318–330; Early Archaic,
    322; Fluted Point Tradition in, 320;
    Historic Period, 337–340; Late Archaic,
    324, 335; Mexican period, 338; Middle
    Archaic, 322; Pre-Archaic, 317–318;

Protohistoric Period, 337–339; Spanish
    period, 338
Great house: Chaco regional system, 378,
    381; Hohokam, 33, 35, 40, 357–377
Great Plains culture area, 48, 234, 311, 363,
    406–451, 510, 569; American period,
    439–440; Canadian period, 439–440;
    Clovis, 413–415; Folsom, 413–416;
    Historic period, 430, 435, 442; Late
    Prehistoric, 433–434; Paleoindian,
    412–416; Pre-Clovis, 412–413;
    Protohistoric period, 435, 442;
    Terminal Paleoindian, 414
Great Salt Spring, 541
Green River Archaic, 522
Greenwich Cove site, 581
Gros Ventre tribe, 434, 436
Ground Hog Bay, 120, 200, 201
Ground Penetrating Radar, 26, 622
Guest site, 460
Gulf Coast tradition, 474
Gulf Formational stage, 462–463
Gulf of Maine Archaic, 572
Gypsum Cave, 317
Gypsum Cave point, 322, 330
Gypsum period, 322

Haida tribe, 202, 219
Hakataya, 325. *See also* Patayan
Halloran Springs, 325
Hanat Kotyiti, 394
Hanging Rock Cave, 322
Harper's Ferry, 593
Harris site, C.W., 275
Haskett locality, 320
Hatwai site, 247
Havasupai tribe, 393
Hawken site, 418
Hayes site, 466
Head-Smashed-In site, 425
Hebior site, 111, 514
Heiltsuk tribe, 219
Hell Gap complex, 415
Hell Gap point, 414, 515
Helton phase, 521
Heritage Conservation Act, 198
Heterarchy, 80, 391, 619
Hidatsa tribe, 431, 343, 436, 442, 443, 450
Hidden Cave, 322
Hidden Falls site, 200, 201
Higgs site, 467
Hill site, 435
Hiscock site, 569
Historical archaeology, 8, 13, 81
Hiwassee Island site, 499
Ho-Chunk tribe, 544
Holding site, 532, 602, 603
Hogup Cave, 319, 326, 327, 328, 334, 335

Hohokam, 32–41, 45, 74, 371, 375–382;
    Civano phase, 40; Classic period, 32,
    36–41, 379, 381; Colonial period, 378;
    Pioneer period, 378, 381; Polvorón phase,
    40; Sedentary period, 379; Soho phase, 40
Hokan language stock, 292, 338, 393
Hoko River site, 193, 209, 210–213, 218, 224
Holding site, 602
Holocene, 63, 65, 91, 458
Hopeton Earthworks, 530, 550–559
Hopewell, 473; Interaction Sphere, 527, 530,
    532, 581
Hopewell site, 526
Hopi, 385
Horr's Island shell mound, 466
Horses, 48, 254–255, 338, 436–437;
    as food, 338
Horticulture. *See* Food production
Huff site, 430
Human remains. *See* Burials
Hunters Home phase, 587
Hunters Home site, 604
Hunting phase, 278
Huron tribe, 545, 546, 591
Hypsithermal, 67, 86; Great Basin, 316; Great
    Plains, 412, 419; Midwest and Upper
    Great Lakes, 90, 91, 514; Northeast and
    Mid-Atlantic, 571, 577; Southeast, 458;
    Southwest, 364

Ice-free corridor, 65, 107, 118, 411–412
Ikhine, 2, 113
Illinois Hopewell, 523
Incinerator site, 542
Independence phase, 161–163
Indian. *See* Native Americans
Indian Knoll site, 519, 521
Indian Removal Act, 49, 495
Ingalik, 177
Intensification, 207, 214, 533, 577–578
Intrusive Mound culture, 534
Inuit, 45, 146, 174, 178
Ipiutak, 167, 168
Iowa tribe, 436
Iroquoian, 75, 491, 492, 537, 585, 586–588,
    590, 601
Iroquois tribe, 545, 583, 589
Iroquois Wars, 591
Island Field site, 581
Isostatic change, 66, 199, 458, 513, 565
Isotopic analysis and diet, 205, 243, 248, 249,
    332, 535, 623
Issaquena phase, 479

Jaguar Cave, 318
Jamestown, 591–592
Jay phase, 366
Johnson Creek site, 247

Johnson site, 459
Jomon culture, 126
Jones-Miller site, 415
Judd Cave, 201
Jukebox Cave, 310–311, 318

Kachemak stage, 156, 186, 189–190
Kalispel tribe, 254
Kallapuya tribe, 219
Kamchatka, 113
Kampsville, 87–87
Kanosh site, 334
Kansas City Hopewell, 423, 425, 426
Kansas Monument site, 435
Kaplan-Hoover site, 406–408, 413, 418
Karluk wet site, 183, 186
Kaskaskia, Grant Village of, 546
Kato tribe, 293
Katz site, 208
Kawaiisu tribe, 338
Keatley Creek, 253
Keewatin District, 153
Kelso site, 585
Kennewick skeleton, 69, 121–125, 259
Kensington stone, 175, 176f
Keresen language family, 393
Kettle Falls, 244, 251, 254
Kickapoo tribe, 544, 546
Kieth complex, 425
Kiet Siel site, 375
Kimmswick site, 131, 516
Kincaid site, 539, 540
Kiowa-Tanoan language family, 393
Kiowa tribe, 436
Kipp Island site, 604
Kitwnga Fort, 220
Klamath tribe, 237, 254
Klatskanie tribe, 219
Klo-kut site, 174
Knife River flint, 450, 476
Knife River Indian Villages National Historic
   Site, 434, 445
Knoll site, 334
Kodiak Island, 155, 178, 181–191, 303
Kodiak tradition, 152, 155–156
Kolomoki site, 479
Kootenai tribe, 254
Koniag tradition, 156, 186, 190
Koster site, 86–93, 519, 520, 521
Kouba site graver cache, 515
Krajacic site, 109, 567
Kruse site, 422
Kumeyaay tribe, 292
Kutchin tribe, 174, 177

Lachane site, 210
La Jolla complex, 277–278
Lake Bonneville, 314, 318–319

Lake Cahuilla, 316
Lake Creek focus, 424
Lake Forest Archaic, 519, 574, 576
Lake Forest Middle Woodland, 533
Lake Lahonton, 314, 320
Lake Mohave complex, 320
Lake Mohave point, 275, 320, 321, 327
Lakota tribe, 436
L'Anse Amour, 158
L'Anse aux Meadows, 176–177, 589
Lambert Farms site, 585
Lamb Spring site, 413
Lamoka Lake site, 570, 574–575
Lanaak set site, 227
La Purisima Concepción Mission, 294
La Sena site, 413
Laser Cave, 201
Lashley Vore site, 421, 422
La Tinaja site, 403, 404
Laurel culture, 173, 532
Laws. *See* Cultural resource legislation
Ledford Island site, 499–507
Lehman phase, 245
Lehner Ranch site, 129, 363
Lenape tribe, 583
Levee site, 334
Lewis and Clark expedition, 46, 220, 234,
   254, 255, 434, 436, 439; and the Double
   Ditch site, 443, 444
Lewisville site, 415
Lillooet people, 254
Lime Hills, Cave, 151
Lincoln Hills site, 516
Lind Coulee site, 243
Lindenmeier site, 129, 416
Little Egypt site, 492
Little Ice Age, 67, 149, 567, 585
Little Pluvial, 322
Little Salt Spring, 112, 459, 460
Locknore phase, 245, 253
Looting, 509, 615–617
Los Angeles, Pueblo of, 294
Lost City, 325
Louisiana Purchase, 439, 494
Lovelock Cave, 318, 322, 330
Lower Mississippi valley mound sites, 479
Lowry Ruin, 15
Lubbock Lake site, 132, 415, 416
Luiseño tribe, 293
Lummi tribe, 219
Lushootseed, 219, 225, 229
Lysine, 370

Madisonville horizon, 542
Maidu tribe, 292
Maize, 41, 79; Armijo phase, 366; Cochise
   tradition, 367; earliest, 602; Midwest and
   Upper Great Lakes, 532, 533, 541, 542;

Northeast and Mid-Atlantic 582, 584,
   602–604; Plains Village tradition, 428,
   431, 432, 442; Plains Woodland, 423, 426;
   Southeast, 476, 480, 481, 483; Southwest,
   368, 370, 380; spread of, 603
Maize-beans-squash complex, 427, 466, 482,
   489, 491, 543, 580, 586, 599; amino acids
   and, 601; new research into, 600–608;
   nutritional benefits of, 601
Makah Cultural and Research Center,
   192–193
Makah tribe, 192–193, 214, 219, 224
Mammoth, 103, 111, 113, 115, 127; at Clovis
   sites, 128, 363; Great Plains, 413, 415;
   pygmy, 120, 136; Southeast, 460
Mandan tribe, 431, 434, 436, 438, 442
Mandeville site, 479
Manis site, 112, 199
Mann focus, 530
Marial site, 203
Maricopa tribe, 393
Marietta site, 530
Maritime Archaic, 157–158, 576
Marksville phase, 474, 476, 479
Marksville site, 479, 527
Marmes Rockshelter, 243, 244
Martin site, 493
Mascouten tribe, 544, 546
Mashantucket, Pequot tribe, 590
Mast Forest Archaic, 574–575, 576
Mastodon, 112, 131, 199, 460, 516, 569
McEuen Cave, 368
McKees Rock mound complex, 581
MCRC. *See* Makah Cultural and
   Research Center
Meadowcroft Rockshelter, 109–110,
   567, 602
Meadowood complex, 579
Medicine House site, 418
Medieval climatic anomaly. *See* Medieval
   warm period
Medieval warm period, 67, 149, 283, 567, 588
Meier site, 214–215
Memorial Park site, 574, 584
Menlo phase, 320
Menominee tribe, 544
Mesa site, 118, 149
Mesa Verde, 369
Mesoamerica, 5, 399; agriculture, spread of,
   367, 370, 618; North American cultures,
   influences on, 620; Paquimé, origins of,
   390; Southeastern Ceremonial Complex
   design elements, 486–487; Southwest,
   404, 620
Mesquakie. *See* Fox tribe
Metini village, 206
Métis, 178, 438, 439
Mexican War, 394

Miami tribe, 544

Michaud site, 569

Microblade tradition, 200–202

Middle Eastern tradition, 475

Middle Missouri tradition, 429–430; Terminal Variant of, 430

Middle Tier Middle Woodland, 533

Midwest and Upper Great Lakes subarea, 49, 508–559, 562; American period, 547; Archaic, 517–523; Canadian period, 547; Clovis points, 515; Early Archaic, 517; fortified villages, 545; Historic period, 541, 544, 545–547; Late Archaic, 517; Late Prehistoric, 535–545; Late Woodland, 533–535; Middle Archaic, 517; Paleoindian, 514–517; Pre-Clovis, 514; Protohistoric period, 544–545

Mill Branch site, 468

Miller complex, 109

Miller site, 259–267

Milliken site, 202

Millingstone horizon. *See* Millingstone tradition

Millingstone tradition, 137, 277, 279

Mimbres, 382–384, 420

Mingo tribe, 546

Missions, 294, 295f, 296, 303, 393

Mississippian, 75, 480, 482–491, 498, 523–524, 627

Missouri River, 429, 430–431, 439, 442, 443

Missouri tribe, 436

Mitochondrial DNA, 126–127, 623

Miwok tribe, 287, 292, 302, 307

Modoc Rock Shelter, 89, 521

Modoc tribe, 237, 254

Mogollon, 45, 371, 382–386; Anasazi influences, 385; Georgetown phase, 385; Jornada, 382, 424–425; Pine Lawn phase, 385; San Francisco phase, 385; Three-Circle phase, 386

Mohave tribe, 387, 393

Mohawk tribe, 583, 585, 589

Molala tribe, 254

Monks Mound, 8, 536, 538

Monongahela tribe, 584

Mono tribe, 338

Montagnais, 178

Monte Verde, 110, 618

Montezuma's Castle, 388

Monticello, 69

Moorehead burial complex, 576

Moresby tradition, 201

Morris-Schurz site, 581

Mortuary ceremonialism: Adena, 524; Midwest and Upper Great Lakes, 544; Mississippian, 484, 490, 541; Northeast and Mid-Atlantic, 584; Southeast, 462, 473; Woodland, 525

Mound Builders, 9, 8–10, 98, 551

Mound building: Great Plains, 425; Northeast and Mid-Atlantic, 578; Southeast, 455, 462, 468, 473; Woodland, 477–480, 523–535

Mound City, 530, 551

Mounds, 8, 550; Adena, 478, 525, 532; burial (*see* Burial mounds); destruction of, 551, 554, 559; Great Plains, 429; Hohokam 380–381; Hopewell, 532; Mississippian, 487, 489, 538; Northeast and Mid-Atlantic, 584; Southeast, 468; Woodland, 477, 478, 481

Moundville, 9, 485, 489, 490, 491, 492

Mount Mazama, 239, 240, 349–351, 354

Mouse Creek Phase, 498–507

Mouse Creeks site, 499–507

Mowry Bluff site, 428

MtDNA. *See* Mitochondrial DNA

Multnomah tribe, 219

Mummy Cave, 351, 417

Murray Springs site, 129, 150, 363

Musequeam site, 230f

Museum collections, 497, 600, 607–608

Muskogean language family, 491, 492

Muskogee tribe, 492

Mustang Springs site, 419

Myer-Dickson site, 626

Naco site, 128f, 129, 363

Na Dene, 153

Na Dene language stock, 293

NAGPRA. *See* Native American Graves Protection and Repatriation Act

Namu, 201, 205

Napoleon Hollow site, 91, 93, 520, 532

Narrow Point tradition, 519, 574, 576

Naskapi tribe, 178

Natchez tribe, 494, 506

National Historic Preservation Act, 21, 124–125, 262

Native Alaskan. *See* Alaskan Native

Native American, use of the term, 44–45

Native American Graves Protection and Repatriation Act, 21, 80, 292, 305, 505, 627; and the Kennewick skeleton, 123–125

Native Americans, 21–24; Asian origins, 97; cultural resource management programs, 21, 223, 224, 305; perspectives, 620; stereotypes about, 9–10, 613

Native Americans and Archaeologists, 11, 224, 231; collaboration, 21, 223, 224–232, 305

Native plants, domestication of, 368, 426, 466, 523

Navajo tribe, 45, 127, 177, 391–392

Nawthis Village, 334

Nebo Hill phase, 420–421

Nenana complex, 117, 150

Nephi site, 334

Nesikep tradition, 245

Neville site, 571

Newark, Ohio, earthworks, 8–9

Newberry Cave, 322

Newport Tower, 175

Newt Cash Rockshelter, 467

New Orleans, 546

New World culture regions, 6

Nez Perce tribe, 124, 254

Nipissing, 590

Nipomo Dunes, 297

Nobles Pond site, 517

Nootka tribe, 219

Norse, 174, 175–177, 589

Northeast and Mid-Atlantic subarea, 49, 510, 560–608; Archaic, 570–574; Historic period, 589–597; Late Archaic, 574–578; Late Prehistoric, 582–589; Late Woodland, 582–589; Paleoindians, 567–570; Pre-Clovis, 567; Protohistoric period, 589–592; Terminal Archaic, 575, 578, 586; Transitional Archaic, 575, 577; Woodland, 575, 578–582

Northeast culture area, 49

Northern Archaic tradition, 150–153, 160

Northern Cordilleran complex, 150

Northern Iroquoian tradition, 585, 588

Northern Pottery tradition, 474

North Piegan tribe, 434

Northwest Coast culture area, 46, 192–272, 234, 237, 270; Archaic, 200–204; art style, 205, 209, 217–218; Early Pacific period, 205–207; Late Pacific period, 214–219; Middle Pacific period, 207–214, 270; Modern period, 219–221; Pacific period, 204–219; Northwest Microblade tradition, 150–152

Northwest Microblade tradition, 150–152

Northwest Passage, 174, 178, 590

Norton complex, 167, 168

Norton tradition, 167–168

Numic language, 213, 319, 325, 338

Numic speakers, 335–337

Nursery site, 279

Nuu-Chah-Nulth tribe, 127, 219

Nuxalk tribe, 219

Oak Grove phase, 278

Ocean Bay tradition, 152, 154f, 155, 186, 188–189, 190

Ocmulgee site, 489

Ofo tribe, 492

Ogden-Fettie site, 626

Ohio Hopewell, 523, 526–527

Ojibwa tribe, 127, 436, 544, 546

Okanagan tribe, 254

Okvik culture. *See* Old Bering Sea and Okvik
   cultures
Olcott complex, 202–203
Old Bering Sea and Okvik cultures, 170–171
Old Copper culture, 521
Old Cordilleran tradition, 202–203, 242
Old Crow Flats, 106, 149
Old Women's phase, 434
Olsen-Chubbock site, 416
Omaha tribe, 436
Oneida tribe, 589
Oneota tradition, 430, 433, 541–543
Onion Portage site, 152, 160, 198
Onondaga tribe, 589
Oregon Trail, 255, 256, 339
Orient phase, 578
Osage tribe, 436, 454
Osceola site, 522
Oshara tradition, 366
Ossuaries, 426–427, 544, 585
Osteological analysis, 618
Ottawa tribe, 544, 545, 546
Owasco, 585, 587
Owl Cave, 317–318
Ozette site, 192–193, 214, 218, 224

Packard complex, 414
Packard site, 414
Page-Ladson site, 459
Paipai tribe, 393
Paiute tribe, 330, 335, 338
Paleoamericans. *See* Paleoindian period
Paleoarctic tradition, 150
Paleocoastal tradition, 135, 141–143
Paleoeskimo, 158
Paleoindian period, 71, 100–132
Paleoindian to Archaic transition, 463
Paleolithic, 100, 618. *See also* American
   Paleolithic
Pallisades complex, 152
Pamlico tribe, 492
Papago tribe, 45
Paquimé, 378, 390, 397–405; Medio period,
   399, 401, 402; Mogollon, affinities
   with, 390
Paragonah site, 334
Paramount chiefdom, 537, 540
Patayan, 45, 371, 386–388, 393; Cerbat, 387;
   Cohonina, 387; Prescott, 387. *See also*
   Hakataya
Paulina Lake, 244
Paul Mason site, 201, 207
Pauma complex, 278
Pawnee tribe, 435, 436
Pebble Tool tradition. *See* Old Cordilleran
   tradition
Pechanga Band, 292
Pecos classification, 371

Pecos Pueblo, 394
Pedra Furada, 111
Pender Canal site, 205
Pendejo Cave, 362
Penutian language stock, 219, 292
Pequot War, 590
Perishables, preservation of: Arctic, 173; dry
   caves and, 212, 311, 343, 386; wet sites
   and, 212, 226
Petaluma adobe, 296
Petun tribe, 545
Pharo site, 334
Pickering phase, 585
Pictographs. *See* Rock art
Piedmont, 455, 463, 468, 472, 476, 590
Pima tribe, 379, 392–393
Pine Springs historic site, 394
Pine Springs Paleoindian site, 73
Pinson Mounds site, 479, 527
Pinto period or tradition, 321, 366
Pinto points, 321, 322, 326, 328, 366
Pithouse, 204, 215, 245, 246–248, 249,
   264–265; Anasazi, 373; California, 278;
   Fremont, 331, 332, 333, 334; Great Basin,
   320; Great Plains, 417; Mogollon, 382,
   385; Plains Archaic, 417; Southeast, 468;
   Southwest, 368–369, 380
Pithouse-to-Pueblo transition, 374
Pithouse village, 248
Plains Archaic, 406, 416–423
Plains Cree tribe, 436
Plains Ojibwa tribe, 436
Plains Village tradition, 75, 427–433, 619
Plains Woodland, 417, 409, 423–427; Eastern
   Woodlands contact, 425; Southwest
   influences, 425
Plano complex, 104–105, 128, 129, 318, 518
Plateau culture area, 46, 194–195, 201,
   233–267, 240, 270, 311; Early Late
   subperiod, 249–250; Early Middle
   subperiod, 245; Late Late subperiod,
   252–253; Late Middle subperiod,
   246–249; Late period, 249–253; Middle
   Late period, 250–252; Middle period,
   245–249; Modern period, 253–256; Old
   Cordilleran tradition, 202; Plains
   influences, 255; Pre-Clovis, 239
Plateau Pithouse tradition, 248
Platform mound, 33; Hohokam, 381;
   Mississippian, 482, 487, 489, 538;
   Paquimé, 399, 402
Platform pipe, 527, 528–529, 581
Pleasant Lake mastodon, 515
Pleistocene, 63–66, 73, 112, 317
Plimouth Plantation, 592
Plum Bayou period, 481–482
Pluvial lakes, 314, 316
Point Peninsula tradition, 586, 587

Pomo tribe, 292; Kashaya, 301–309
Pontiac's War, 546
Population movements, 375, 390, 436,
   454–455, 545, 582, 620; abandonment,
   389; migration, 375, 389, 618–619
Portage complex, 152
Port aux Choix site, 158, 574
Post-Classic stage, 71
Post pattern, 275
Pothunter. *See* Relic hunter
Potlatch, 186
Potowatomi tribe, 544, 545
Poverty Point, 468–473; Complex, 462–463,
   468–473, 474
Poverty Point Objects, 473
Powhatan chiefdom, 591–592
Prairie du Rocher, 546
Pre-Clovis, 105–112, 120, 618
Pre-Dorset, 161–163
Pre-maize farming, 467–468, 477, 531, 580
Presidio, 294, 295f, 393
Prince Rupert Harbor, 208, 209, 210
Processualism, 304–305, 586
Proglacial lakes, 66, 131
Projectile points: basal grinding, 515; as
   temporal indicators, 326, 351–352;
   transformation of types, 326–327
Promontory caves, 334
Public archaeology, 407, 632
Pueblo (Spanish), 294, 295f
Pueblo III, 372
Pueblo Alto, 377
Pueblo Bonito, 376
Pueblo Grande, 32, 35
Pueblo people, 372, 389, 393, 438
Pueblo Revolt, 392, 393, 437, 620
Puzzle House, 15
Pygmy mammoth, 277

Quapaw tribe, 492
Quechan tribe, 45, 387, 393
Qwu?gwes site, 224–232

Radiocarbon dating, 81, 515, 601;
   calibration, 82, 83t; reporting results, 82
Rancho, 296, 394
Raven Cave, 318
Red ocher, 186, 245, 522
Red Ocher mortuary complex, 522
Red Paint People, 576
Remote sensing, 445–448
Relic hunter, 15, 20–21, 233–234, 508, 615;
   excavations contrasted with
   archaeologist, 269. *See also* Looting
Report, archaeological 28, 39, 356, 625
Richardson site, 219–220
Richey-Roberts Clovis cache, 200,
   239–241, 242f

Richfield site, 334
Rio Grande Pueblos, 436
Riverside Cemetery site, 522
Riverside Chinatown, 297
Riverton culture, 519
Riverton site, 519
Roadcut site, 203, 242
Robeson Hills site, 519
Rock art, 323, 331, 345
Rock Island II, 545
Rock middens, 417
Rogers Locomotive Works site, 594
Round house, 302
Roundtop site, 585, 601–602, 604
Rupert's Land, 438, 439
Russell Cave, 466, 467–468
Russia, 178, 183, 219, 294–296, 301–309
Russian Orthodox Church, 178, 183
Ryan site, 415

Sadmat site, 320
Sahaptin language, 254
Sakha Republic, early sites, 113
Salado, 389–390
Salinan tribe, 292
Salish tribes, 219, 225, 253, 254
Salts Cave, 531
Salton Trough, 316
Saltville Valley sites, 458–459
Samish tribe, 219
San Antonio de Padua Mission, 294
San Bernardo de Aguatubi Mission, 393
San Clemente Island, 276–277
Sandia Cave, 362
San Diego Chinatown, 297
San Dieguito complex, 275–276, 319, 320, 363, 366
Sand Lake site, 543
Sandts Eddy site, 571
Sandy Hammock site, 477
San Francisco Presidio, 294
San Jose, Pueblo of, 294
San Luis Rey complex, 284
San Miguel Island, 135–143, 276–277, 292
San Pedro phase, 367
Sanpoil-Nespelem, 254
Santa Barbara Channel, 136–137, 288, 290
Santa Cruz Island, 136, 290
Santa Elena, 493
Santarosae, 136, 273
Santa Rosa Island, 136, 276–277
Santiago Pueblo, 393
Saqqaq culture. *See* Sarqaq culture
Saratoga Springs period, 324
Sarqaq culture, 163
Saturated archaeological sites. *See* Wet sites
Sauk tribe, 544, 546
Scoggin site, 418

Sea level, 65, 136, 143; rise, 199, 273, 457, 459, 565
SECC. *See* Southeastern Ceremonial Complex
Selkirk culture, 174
Seminoe Beach site, 414
Seminole tribe, 492, 495
Seminole War, 495
Seneca tribe, 583, 589
Sepulveda adobe, 296
Serpent Mound, 9, 530
Seven Years War, 493, 546, 593
Shaefer site, 111, 514
Shaffert site, 413
Sharrow site, 574
Shasta aspect, 287–288
Shasta tribe, 292
Shawnee Minisink site, 131, 567, 570
Shawnee tribe, 542, 544, 545, 546
Shellfish: California, 279; Hohokam, 380;
    Midwest and Upper Great, 519;
    Mississippian, 489; Northeast and
    Mid-Atlantic, 573, 580; Paleoindian, 136;
    Plateau, 238, 245, 249; Southeast, 461;
    Woodland, 476, 480, 482
Shell midden, 69; Northeast and Mid-
    Atlantic, 573, 585; Northwest Coast,
    205, 225–226; Midwest and Upper
    Great Lakes, 519; Southeast, 491;
    Woodland, 477
Shell Mound Archaic, 466, 519, 521
Shenguindah site, 514
Sheriden Cave, 515
Shermer site, 430
Shield Archaic, 153–155
Shoop site, 129, 570
Shoshonean period, 324, 325, 327, 335–337
Shoshone tribe, 335, 338
SHPO. *See* State Historic Preservation Officer
Shuswap, 254
Siberia, 112–115, 618
Siberian-American Paleoarctic tradition, 150
Sierra Nevada, 270, 280, 289, 311
Silcott, Washington, 256
Silverhole site, 202
Silvernale phase, 433
Sinagua, 371, 388
Sinodont dental pattern, 126
Siouian language family, 491, 492, 544
Sioux tribe, 127, 436, 443, 450, 451
Sipapu, 373
Site SV-2, 458–459
Skagit Atlatl, 209
Skraelings, 174, 177
Skunk Hollow, 593
Skyrocket site, 278, 280
Slaves: Arctic, 186, 188, 189; Great Basin, 338;
    Northwest Coast, 205, 219; Plateau, 494;
    Southeast, 494, 495

Slavey tribe, 177
Slocan Valley region, 253
Smicksberg, Pennsylvania, 560–561, 594
Snake River plain, 132
Social status: achieved, 206, 582; ascribed,
    206, 282, 542; differentiation, 427;
    inherited, 282, 491, 530
Society for American Archaeology, 18, 69, 73;
    code of ethics, 305, 307, 625; Principles of
    Curricular Reform, 631, 632; Public
    Education Committee, 629
Sociopolitical systems, complex, 79, 182, 280,
    618, 619
Solutrean, 121
Sonota Burial complex, 424
South America, 6, 110–111
South Appalachian tradition, 474
Southeast culture area, 48, 452–507, 510;
    American period, 494–495; Archaic,
    462–473; Clovis, 459; Early Paleoindian,
    459; Early Woodland, 473; Historic
    period, 491–492; Late Paleoindian, 459;
    Late Woodland, 473, 480–482; Middle
    Paleoindian, 459–460; Middle
    Woodland, 473; Mid-Holocene, 458;
    Non-Mississippian Late Prehistoric, 491;
    Paleoindian, 458–462; Pre-Clovis,
    458–459; Protohistoric period, 491–492;
    Terminal Late Woodland, 481–482;
    Woodland, 473–482
Southeastern Ceremonial Complex,
    485–487, 491
Southern Cult. *See* Southeastern Ceremonial
    Complex
Southern Plains tradition, 431
South Park Village site, 543
Southwest culture area, 48, 311, 355–405;
    Archaic, 364–369; Historic period,
    393–394; Mexican period, 394;
    Paleoindian, 362–363; Plains, historic
    interactions with, 394; Spanish
    settlement, 393
Southwest Regional Cult, 391
Spain, 294, 303, 219, 438, 492–494
Spein Mountain site, 118
Spiro, 485, 490, 492
Spring Creek site, 419
Squash, 79, 368, 370, 380, 605–607; Midwest
    and Upper Great Lakes, 520, 541;
    Northeast and Mid-Atlantic, 584; Ozarks,
    605; Plains Village tradition, 431;
    Southeast, 458, 480; Woodland, 423, 426
Squamish tribe, 219
Squawkie Hill phase, 581
Squaxin Island Tribe, 224–232
Stahl site, 321, 366
Stakeholders in the past, 5, 24–25, 509, 625
Stalker site, 121

Stanton Cave, 323
State Historic Preservation Officer, 19, 28, 226
St. Augustine, 493
St. Catherine's Island, 72, 478
Steatite, 281, 290, 429, 472; bowls, 464, 577
Steed-Kisker phase, 429
St. Geneviève, 546
St. Johns tradition, 491
St. Phillippe, 546
Stockaded villages, 584
Storage, 188, 205, 214, 290; baskets, 214; boxes, 207, 214; caves, 252, 328; in ceramic vessels, 290; in clay lined pits, 189; seed caches, 476; of surplus meat, 418, 516; pits, 220, 542, 584, 601; pits at Fremont sites, 331, 333; pits in the Great Plains, 419, 428, 449; pits in the Plateau, 248, 249; pits in the Southwest, 366, 367; rooms, 333, 334
Subarctic culture area, 46, 144–178, 195
Sudden Shelter, 327
Sulphur Springs phase, 367
Sundadont dental pattern, 126
Sunset Crater, 240, 388
Sunwatch village. *See* Incinerator site
Susquehanna tradition, 575
Susquehannock tribe, 585
Sutter's Fort, 297
Swallow Shelter, 334
Swan Island site, 519
Swan Point site, 116, 150
Swift Creek tradition, 479, 482

Taber child, 121
Tahkenitch Landing site, 203
Takli stage, 155
Taltheilei tradition, 174
Tanana tribe, 177
Tchula phase, 478
Technology, archaeology of, 621
Tequesta tribe, 492
Texas Street site, 274
Theosophical Society site, 297–299, 299f
Thompson tribe, 254
Thorne River site, 200
THPO. *See* Tribal Historic Preservation Officer
Thule tradition, 168–173, 590
Timucua tribe, 492
Tlingit tribe, 202, 219
Tobacco, 430, 431, 480, 533, 588
Tohono O'odham, 45, 378, 392–393
Tolowa tribe, 219
Toltec Mounds site, 481

Tongva tribe, 293
Topper site, 111, 458
Tornillo Rockshelter, 368
Trenton gravels, 100
Tribal Historic Preservation Officer, 229
Trincheras, 403
Trowbridge site, 425, 426
Tsimshian tribe, 219
Tubac presidio, 393
Tulare Lake, 275
Tularosa Cave, 368, 385
Tule Springs, 106, 317
Tunica tribe, 492
Turkey-tail points, 245, 246f, 522
Turner Farm site, 576
Turquoise, 325, 339, 377, 400
Tuscarora tribe, 492, 590
Tuscarora Wars, 590
Tutchone tribe, 177

Udora site, 569
Umatilla tribe, 124, 254
Umpqua tribe, 219
Unakleet site, 168
Upper Republican phase, 427–429
Ural Mountians, microblade sites, 151
Ushki 1, 113
Ust-Mil 2, 113
Ute tribe, 335, 338, 392
Uto-Aztecan language family, 393
Utopian communities, 297

Valley Forge, 593
Vail site, 567, 570
Varney Farm site, 568
Varsity Estates site, 118
Verkhne-Troitskaya, 113
Ventana Cave, 363, 367
Ventana complex, 363, 364f
Verde Valley sites, 388
Vikings. *See* Norse
Vinette site, 604
Virginia City, 340

Waiilatpu, 255
Wailaki tribe, 293
Wakashan language family, 219
Wakemap mound, 251
Wakulla culture, 482
Walapai, 393
Walker Road site, 150
Walnut Canyon National Monument, 388
Walpi, 393
Wanapum tribe, 124
Wappo tribe, 293

War of 1812, 547, 593
Wasco tribe, 254
Washo tribe, 329, 338
Water Hazard site, 230
Watson Brake site, 468
Weeden Island phase, 482
Wendover period, 327–328
West Berkeley site, 286
West River site, 581
Western Basin tradition, 532
Western Idaho Burial complex, 245
Western Pluvial Lakes tradition, 276, 277, 320–321
Western Stemmed Point tradition, 105, 132
Wet sites, 182, 183, 202, 210, 223–232, 464
Whipple site, 569
White Hall culture, 88
Whitman Mission, 255
Whittlesey tradition, 543
Wichita tribe, 436
Wickham site, 604
Wickliffe Mounds, 69
Williamsburg, 592
Windmiller pattern, 285
Windover site, 464, 465
Windust phase, 132, 244
Winnebago tribe. *See* Ho-Chunk tribe
Wintuan peoples, 287
Wintu tribe, 292
Wishram tribe, 254
Woodchuck Knoll site, 578
Woodhenge, 537, 538–539
Woodland period, 74–75, 523–535, 578–582; Hopewell influence, 478, 479
Woolen Mills Chinatown, 297
Wupatki National Monument, 388

Yahi, 292
Yakima tribe, 124, 127, 254
Yana tribe, 292
Yaquina Head site, 205
Yaquina tribe, 219
Yavapai tribe, 393
Yent Ceremonial complex, 478
Yokut tribe, 292
Young's River site, 203
Yuchi tribe, 492
Yukian languages, 293
Yuki tribe, 293
Yuman languages, 393
Yuman tribes, 45, 387
Yup'ik, 45

Zimmerman site, 545–546
Zuni Pueblo, 385, 393